REDEFINING CAPITALISM IN GLOBAL ECONOMIC DEVELOPMENT

T0363915

REDEFINING CAPITALISM IN GLOBAL ECONOMIC DEVELOPMENT

KUI-WAI LI

The Kui-Wai Consultancy for Economic Development, Inc., Toronto, Canada

ACADEMIC PRESS

An imprint of Elsevier

Academic Press is an imprint of Elsevier
125 London Wall, London EC2Y 5AS, United Kingdom
525 B Street, Suite 1800, San Diego, CA 92101-4495, United States
50 Hampshire Street, 5th Floor, Cambridge, MA 02139, United States
The Boulevard, Langford Lane, Kidlington, Oxford OX5 1GB, United Kingdom

Copyright © 2017 Elsevier Inc. All rights reserved.

No part of this publication may be reproduced or transmitted in any form or by any means, electronic or
mechanical, including photocopying, recording, or any information storage and retrieval system, without
permission in writing from the publisher. Details on how to seek permission, further information about the
Publisher's permissions policies and our arrangements with organizations such as the Copyright Clearance
Center and the Copyright Licensing Agency, can be found at our website: www.elsevier.com/permissions.

This book and the individual contributions contained in it are protected under copyright by the Publisher
(other than as may be noted herein).

Notices
Knowledge and best practice in this field are constantly changing. As new research and experience broaden our
understanding, changes in research methods, professional practices, or medical treatment may become necessary.

Practitioners and researchers must always rely on their own experience and knowledge in evaluating and using
any information, methods, compounds, or experiments described herein. In using such information or methods
they should be mindful of their own safety and the safety of others, including parties for whom they have a
professional responsibility.

To the fullest extent of the law, neither the Publisher nor the authors, contributors, or editors, assume any liability
for any injury and/or damage to persons or property as a matter of products liability, negligence or otherwise, or
from any use or operation of any methods, products, instructions, or ideas contained in the material herein.

British Library Cataloguing-in-Publication Data
A catalogue record for this book is available from the British Library

Library of Congress Cataloging-in-Publication Data
A catalog record for this book is available from the Library of Congress

ISBN: 978-0-12-804181-9

For Information on all Academic Press publications
visit our website at https://www.elsevier.com/books-and-journals

Working together
to grow libraries in
developing countries

www.elsevier.com • www.bookaid.org

Publisher: Nikki Levy
Acquisition Editor: Scott Bentley
Editorial Project Manager: Susan Ikeda
Production Project Manager: Jason Mitchell
Cover Designer: Mark Rogers

Typeset by MPS Limited, Chennai, India

Contents

III

CAPITALIST DEVELOPMENT: ASIA LESSONS

IV

THE FRONTIER OF CAPITALISM: CHINA VERSUS HONG KONG

V

WHY HAS CAPITALISM SUCCEEDED?

List of Figures

List of Tables

Preface

Since the turn of the 21st century, there have been a number of accumulated international issues that challenge world peace, stability and economic development. While the world community is consuming oil exports from mainly Middle East OPEC members, much of the oil revenues have not been used productively and may have been deployed to fund terrorist and religious extremist activities. Ironically, the world community buys oil from the oil exporting Middle East countries which have been faced with multilevels of conflict, and instead of looking for solutions within the region, some of these conflicts in turn spread and came to haunt the rest of the peaceful world. The unpreparedness to look for solutions would spill over to other international issues.

Since the end of the Second World War, economic growth in many western economies has also led to expansion in technology and industrial outputs, but the adoption of "demand-side" economic policies by prowelfare political regimes that aimed at redistribution using such fiscal instruments as tax and welfare spending generated unfavorable long-term results. While business cycles fluctuated, welfare spending and high taxation regimes tended to stay, resulting in continuous fiscal deficits and accumulated national debts. Indeed, the redistribution policies were often politically-oriented, but the unfavorable consequences were exhibited in the economics. Typically, those that were visible were the level of inequality and the size of poverty, but the invisibles would include the departure of capital resources as investors looked for business-friendly destinations, and the rising cost of production together with higher tax rates and large welfare provisions eroding the economy's competitiveness in terms of fall in output, employment and exports. The fall in economic competitiveness in the home economy as capital departed would mean a rise in competitiveness in the host country. A worse result was that the home economy would have to import back from the host economy the industrial products that otherwise would have been produced at home, thereby increasing pressure on the home currency.

The Cold War lasted for decades, but it was the ingenuity of the Reagan−Thatcher diplomacy that eventually brought it to an end, with the subsequent collapse of the former Soviet Union which gave independence to other Eastern European and West Asian states along the southern border of the former Soviet Union. Unfortunately, different Russian leaders have taken different attitudes towards the west, and due to the lack of resources and economic progress, there was every possibility that Russia could slip back to the former ideology and became confrontational to the west. The "Nixon−Kissinger initiative" that attempted to lure China to the side of the United States in the Cold War in the early 1970s led to mixed results. Politically, China was invited to the United Nations to replace Taiwan, thereby lifting communist China from a closed-door economy into the international arena. The economic phase that began in 1978 led to large inflows of capital into communist China, taking advantage of China's low costs of production. These two sequences of events, however, did not alter China's ideology. China and Russia have become the two dominant socialist countries.

One can keep listing various international issues that would produce unfavorable results in the global economy, such as the prolonged use of low interest rates that were supposedly to promote investment, but could have led to speculation that distorted both the financial sector and the real economy, and the lack of economic progress among the "fragile" states that would only survive on international assistance but could not even maintain basic stability. Many of these "fragile" states were former colonies, which exploited the history of imperialism as the cause of their underdevelopment, but they gained political independence after the end of the Second World War.

Beginning in the mid-19th century, various inadequacies that appeared in the early stage of capitalism led to the emergence of communist thoughts and ideology, with the argument that communism could provide a better form of societal organization. In much of the 20th century, however, socialism and communism were "practiced" through either revolutionary movements, in the case of the Soviet Union and the People's Republic of China, or by the election of prosocialist governments that adopted prosocialist economic policies in the name of "equality" and "redistribution" through high tax rates and large government spending, but ended up with a loss of economic competitiveness and accumulation of huge national debts that effectively limited the development of future generations.

After the exercise of different degrees of socialist and leftist practices and policies over the entire 20th century, it is time to make an assessment to see if there has been an excessive application of socialism. Indeed, the tables could have been turned, and the situation in the 19th century when advocates were looking for an alternative to capitalism would be the inverse of the situation in the 21st century when extensive application of socialist policies had done harm and should be reversed, and capitalist economic policies would be needed to rejuvenate the world economy to a new phase of development. The various socialist policies have impeded parts of the world economy from growing, and at the same time slow growth has been faced challenges from terrorist activities, instabilities in different world regions, and the ideological challenge from socialist countries.

By "redefining" capitalism, this book makes a bold attempt to point out that the century-long practice of socialist policies has caused the freer part of the world economy to face unprecedented and unfavorable challenges and problems, and that a revision and revival of capitalist economic policies is required. Socialist policies have been implemented in the domestic and external policies of industrialized countries. Domestic issues include redistribution, accumulation of deficits and debts, and the prolonged use of low interest rates that expanded only the financial sector, while external policies include economically aiding ideologically unfriendly countries, absorption of debts from neighboring countries, and extending open arms to refugees that would pose burden to tax payers.

It would be a "back-to-basics" kind of intuition that the various challenges facing the free world would mean the need for economic revival, regaining competitiveness, increasing output, and growing industrially. Capitalist and "supply-side" policies would have to be adopted in order to enable industrialized countries to achieve recovery, revitalization, and rejuvenation through further application of technology, appropriate pricing of industrial goods, and expansion of the domestic economy by giving priority to internal growth and employment rather than exporting capital to other parts of the world economy, especially those who would turn ideologically to challenge the freer countries in the global economy.

The various discussions, hypotheses, intuitions, and conjectures in this book are divided into five related sections. Section I is basically conceptual and intuitive, as the six chapters are intended to address six related issues in the "redefinition" of capitalism in the contemporary world. Beginning with a discussion of the individual in an economy, the analysis considers the fundamental elements of capitalism and is extended to the distinction between "private cost" and "social cost," the relationship between economics and politics, and between economics and welfare provision, and understanding the difference between income inequality and poverty. There is a need to clarify the different impacts and consequences of "demand-side" and "supply-side" economic policies. Of course, no economy can avoid the role of the government, even though there have been debates on the size of the government. Given that governments have to exist, the concern is the relevant role the government can take in policy and development terms. Section I ends by outlining the practical differences between capitalism and socialism.

Section II contains four chapters that begin by using world data to examine which have been the "top ten" countries since the 1980s using a total of nine economic variables. While numerous technical empirical analyses on globalization examine the global economy in different aspects, the data used in Chapter 7, The Top 10 World Economies, show the performance of the strongest and weakest countries in the world economy. The data reviews some obvious situations, but also shows some surprising results. Nonetheless, these are real data that provide a true picture of the world economy. The performance of some countries could be strong in some macroeconomics, but the same countries could show weak performance in other variables. The data do show the changing trends in the global economy.

The analysis on the "top ten" would be useful in reclassifying the global economy into five contemporary groups that reflect more of the similarities between countries within the groups. Such a grouping of countries should be pioneering when compared to the general usage, contrasting between "developed" and "developing" countries. There are indeed vast differences between "developed" countries and "developing" countries. While the discussion focuses on the economic features in each country group, analyses concentrate on outlining both the strengths and weaknesses in each of these groups. Strengths include their potential, while the weaknesses reflect the possible problems that could have externality effects.

Having further analyzed the global political economy, Chapter 9, Cases of Economic Vulnerabilities, uses three cases of vulnerability that the capitalist world is facing. These three cases actually reflect the problems of adopting prolonged interest rates in the monetary economy, and the drawback of heavy debt accumulation. The third case relates to the lack of ideological improvement in China, given its continuous economic progress. Discussions in Chapter 10, Reviving Capitalism, attempt to provide the "solution," by pointing out the various possibilities of economic reorientation. Indeed, the need for both domestic improvement and international coop-eration is stressed. By using the Canadian economy as a "sample" economy, and with discussion of the potential of the countries in Eastern Europe as the next "new comers" on the global economic development ladder, the intention is to lend support to the importance of "supply-side" economics.

The successful economic development in East Asia forms the focus of discussion and analysis in Section III. Each of the three chapters has a clear purpose. Beginning with Chapter 11, The Japanese Economy: Successes and Challenges, an account of the successful economic performance of Japan is shown as the "benchmark" in Asian development. The post-Second World War development in Japan has shown both successes and recessions, but the economic rise of Japan has turned out to be a blessing to the world economy, especially its foreign direct investment as all foreign countries welcomed investment from Japan. The East Asian economies have followed Japan's footsteps in their economic growth, though "supply-side" factors have equally made a major contribu-tion. In addition to a large number of analyses that explain the economic success of East Asia, Chapter 12, East Asia: Flying Geese Against Wind Currents, stresses on some of the major causes. The three East Asian economies of Singapore, South Korea, and Taiwan have their share of success and drawbacks, depending on how these economies steer their "supply-side" economic policies. Of course, there are new factors contributing to their next phase of development, typically China, who holds a completely different ideology and geopolitical reality which could be destabilizing. Chapter 13, The Latecomers: Opportunities, Challenges, and Comparisons, examines the Asian region interregionally, by making comparison with countries in Western Europe, and intraregionally, by looking at the performance of different countries in the region. Southeast Asian economies are shown to have potential as the next "new comer" in global development, but the China factor could make a difference in the region, as China's involvement in the Asian region will not be confined only to economics, but will touch on geo-political, ideological, and military considerations.

The "battle" between capitalism and communism can best be seen in the China—Hong Kong relationship in the 50 years of 1997—2047. Section IV contains five chapters that discuss extensively the "ideological battle" between China, the richest communist country, and Hong Kong, the freest capitalist economy. As a British colony for over a century since 1842, the sovereignty of Hong Kong was returned to communist China in 1997 in the "one country, two systems" framework when China promised autonomy, self-rule, and the capitalist way of life in Hong Kong for 50 years. Chapter 14, China's 1911 Revolution and Sun's Legacy, begins by looking at China's 1911 revolution, the ideology of the Nationalist government and the missed opportunities. Given the rich resources China has geographically, had and the entrepreneurial attitude of the Chinese people, business devel-opment should have been the more appropriate mode of economic production than collectivism. Chapter 15, China's Economic Reform Path, deals extensively with China's reform after 1978, outlining the key issues in China's "market socialism."

A discussion of the Sino—British Negotiation over post-1997 Hong Kong is given in Chapter 16, Frontier of Capitalism: The Sino — British Negotiation. Other than the different schools of thought in the negotiation, the issue of the change of sovereignty could cause legitimate concern, as post-1949 China was not a signatory in the treaties and lease concluded by the Qing government, and post-1949 China was not a continuation of the Qing government. Indeed, post-1949 China has lost no territory to any foreign government through colonialism. This chapter also touches on the strategies between Britain and China, and the way that "one country, two systems" can be interpreted, or misinterpreted. The last two chapters in this section showcase the economics and post-1997 political situations in Hong Kong.

The two chapters in Section V serve as the concluding section. Chapter 19, Why Has Socialism Failed?, outlines the drawbacks and inadequacies of socialism and communism. Power concentration in communism and the large burden of "social cost" in socialism are the consolidated criticisms. The chapter also raises the Brexit case by making the hypothesis that the British economy could be better off leaving the European Union, as that should reduce the social cost burden from the influx of refugees, and the ability to chart its own path of development. Brexit should be seen more as an arrangement than a change or reduction in fundamentals. Chapter 20, How Capitalism Works, starts by discussing how various world economies can be improved by choosing "supply-side" economic policies, and how economic revival is highly feasible. While the global economy is still influenced and directed mainly by the industrialized countries, the comparison between the two ideologies clearly shows that capitalism is the lesser evil, as freedom, flexibility of individuals, market forces, and functions of civic insti-tutions produce ample room for individuals to progress, businesses to prosper, governments to develop, and economies to grow. It is only through a reduction in socialist economic policies and in turn, the adoption of capi-talist economic policies, that the industrialized countries can be revitalized, reenergized and rejuvenated to lead the global economy.

Although this book primarily touches on the economics of the global economy, the political economic framework has been used extensively. The entire structure is first to concentrate on the conceptual aspects, followed by the way the world economy could be considered and interpreted, before using the Asian development experience as a 'showcase'. The two ideologies are highlighted in the discussion of the relationship between China and Hong Kong, as their relationship is ongoing, and the outcome can definitely be historic.

The ultimate message is that the excessive application of various socialist policies in the last century have generated numerous world problems that can only get worse, and there does not seem to be a light at the end of the tunnel. As such, the use of capitalist policies should be the better alternative. By putting back more vigor to individuals and business achievements, by pursuing "supply-side" policies and trimming the size of governmental institutions, by lowering the desire to redistribute and instead encouraging more "able" individuals, by focusing more on domestic economic strength through the reallocation of resources from the financial sector to the real economic sector, and by adopting the use of appropriate technology and pricing strategies, the world economy would turn around as these policies would definitely revitalize the economic strength and competitiveness of the industrialized countries, which in turn could foster development in friendly emerging countries.

This book is ambitious, as it touches on a multiple number of economic and ideological issues, countries, and regions, but the discussions are timely, contemporary, and should provide "foresights" to the next stage of global development. It can serve as a "manifesto" of capitalism in the 21st century, or it can be criticized as discussions just shot in all directions in general. Nonetheless, it is hoped that this book provides "food for thought" to the advocates of capitalism, or a stimulus to critics to have a second thought about ideological choices. As this book covers a wide range of the global political economy, it is possible that similar arguments are used on more than one occasion in the book. The arguments are not meant to be repetitive, but are used appropriately in the context of different chapters. Readers should find and relate the arguments in the context addressed in each chapter.

In writing this book, I have received assistance from a number of institutions and individuals. The institution to which I was formerly affiliated, the City University of Hong Kong, has facilitated me with time in the writing and related research work. During my sabbatical in the Fall of 2015−16, I visited George Mason University in Fairfax Virginia, US, and benefitted from discussions with many prominent scholars including Peter J. Boettke. During my stay in Washington, D.C., I also visited the Federal Reserve and the Institute of Humane Studies, and met with prominent scholars. My sabbatical visits also took me to Hosei University and Aoyama−Gakuin University in Japan. In the course of writing this book, I have been data-assisted by a number of research assistants, teaching assistants, and postgraduate students, including Coleman H. M. Cheung, Yuen-Hoi Lau, Gobin Rana, Tianyu Wang, Penne P. Y. Wong, Angela J. Yao, and Jimmy Siyang Ye.

There are two groups of people to whom I would like to convey my gratitude. The first group is people who I would like to thank from my heart, and that go beyond the choice of words. The second group of people contains my colleagues whom probably were in my age group having spent much of their time and life career in restricting me from making progress. I thank them for their harshness, as their expectation of me was higher than my own expectation. Instead of feeling dispirited, demoralized, and frustrated, their treatment eventually turned out to provide me with strength, motivation, stamina, and persistence in my writing. In academic writing, it is one's intellectuality that counts, not how high on the academic administrative ladder one reaches.

Scholars, professions, officials, students and readers are most welcome to communicate with me, and comments and feedback will be most appreciated.

Kui-Wai Li
January 2017
Toronto
Economic relativity is preferable to political absolutism.
Upholding one's private cost lessens the social cost burden.

CHALLENGES TO CAPITALISM: THE ANALYTICAL STRUCTURE

There have been numerous political—economic world events since the turn of the 21st century that have important and challenging economic implications and consequences, and the global economy must locate new directions for the next phase of development or which ideological path would be most suitable to follow. For decades, the world economy has relied on the petroleum supply mainly from the Oil and Petroleum Exporting Countries (OPEC), and the world economy has experienced numerous "oil crises" as the trade traffic was mainly unidirectional. The huge trade surplus that OPEC countries amassed in turn did not contribute much back to development. The situation was worsened when funds from some oil exporting Middle East countries were used in noncivic, war-like, and terrorist activities that were mixed with religious, political, racial, territorial, military, ideological, and historical conflicts and differences, whereas the application of economic development as an alternative peaceful solution has been missing.

Second, the ideological debate between capitalism and communism in much of the 20th century has resulted in a few industrialized countries following a pro-welfare or socialist-oriented doctrine in pursuit of "equity." Policies on economic redistribution conducted by pro-welfare or socialist-oriented governments were geared to attract votes for their political platform but such policies were unsustainable and not growth-oriented. While economic growth went according to the boom and bust of business cycles, committed welfare expenditures had to be made even in times of economic downturn. Over the decades, prolonged reliance on welfare support has not only reduced the economy's competitiveness, it also drained the government's fiscal ability. Economic debts have increasingly accumulated and the burden of the welfare the current generation have enjoyed will have to be paid by the future generation. Even though we have institutions that protect children, animals, and environment, there exists no institution that speaks on the danger, damage, and drawback of a "debt-prone" economy that would constrain its future economic possibility. A few key countries since the turn of the 21st century have come to the brink of economic collapse when the huge cumulated national debt could not be rescued. Prolonged welfare economic policies cannot be sustained, and it would be utterly unfair for the overspending behavior of the current generation to pass on their debt burden to the future generation. Rewinding socialism and welfare policies must take place by instituting a more productivity-oriented policy.

Third, the emergence of the two socialist countries of Russia and China has opened up a new global phase. Due to the prolonged economic weakness under communism in competing with the Western world, the collapse of Soviet Union in 1991 ended the "Cold War." However, Russia has since built up its foreign reserve through the export of oil and gas and its regional interference in Ukraine in 2014 has shown a revival of the Russian ambition in territorial annexation. China since its economic reform in 1978 has built up a much stronger economy than Russia, claiming to be the largest socialist economy by the first decade of the 21st century. Being one of the poorest countries before the 1980s, China has over the years attracted much international aid, official assistance, foreign direct investment, and repatriation of investment funds by overseas Chinese. Assisted by the massive supply of workers, China has turned itself into a production house, generating massive exports and attaining the largest foreign reserve in the world. With its economic strength, China is building up alternative international relationships with countries from different continents, and a few Asian countries are worried as its military build-up could raise territorial and military uncertainties. While one is the political leader and the other is the economic leader in the socialist world, one concern is whether Russia and China would cooperate or compete in their different leading positions? Would Russia tolerate the economic power of China, or would China's economic power overtake Russia's political dominance? Their bilateral relationship would generate further dissemination to other issues in the world economy.

In the Western world, the decades-long ultralow interest rate in the United States and much of the developed world has boosted the world financial market, but it becomes increasingly difficult to distinguish between investment and speculation. In theory, a low cost of borrowing would mean erosion in the store of value function of money. Equally, the prolonged period of low-interest rates is meant to stimulate productive investment, but unfortunately, it could have stimulated speculation and contributed to the 2008 financial crisis and subsequent world economic recession.

These various world events have led to a number of scholarly, intellectual, and political debates, including: (1) whether the ideology of capitalism is out of date, and new economic paradigms are needed to explain and solve contemporary world problems; (2) whether the prolonged period of low-interest rates could revive the world economy and whether the huge financial support in the form of quantitative easing in much of the developed world has led to "overfinancing," and countries are "trapped" in a "low-interest rate, low growth" scenario; (3) whether trade surplus countries can rechannel their resources to help the weaker world economies or generate new hegemonies; (4) whether there are new economic alternatives that can balance the unfavorable impacts from activities conducted by political and religious extremists; and (5) whether China's economic success in the new century would repeat the path of Japan's success in the 1970s, or whether China's successes and difficulties would spill over to other world economies.

There are recent publications that have attempted to bring new explanations to contemporary events, especially development in much of the developing world. For example, recent studies (Acemoglu and Robinson, 2012; Kruger, 2012) have provided an explanation on failures in the establishment of institutions, especially in the developing world. The discussion touched on some of the truth on the problems in developing countries, but the other aspect of the truth is that some weaker developed countries, such as Greece, also faced severe economic recessions. Since the 2008 global financial crisis, there has been a series of debates on capitalism, with various scholars asking more questions than providing answers (Przeworski, 1985; Thurow, 1996; Parijs, 1997; De Soto, 2000; Rogoff, 2011; Becker, 2012; Piketty, 2014). By reading these pioneering articles, one concludes that there is a need to "redefine" capitalism and new insights are needed to reinvigorate the virtues of capitalism in the context of the contemporary world. While many economic activities in the new century probably have challenged the functions and mechanics of capitalism, unsophisticated opinions have equally become popular. On the contrary, one can argue that capitalism that bases itself on the success of individual activity can be adjusted and reformed and can remain as an evergreen and sustainable ideology. Proper and sophisticated interpretations are needed to explain contemporary world problems. Parallel to the discussion on capitalism are the numerous publications that explain differences in growth. For example, the debates on endogenous growth and regional difference have been considered in economic development. Socioeconomic variables have been examined in studying the economics of globalization (Sen, 1992; Aghion and Howitt, 1998; Barro, 2000; Bhagwati, 2004; Milanovic, 2005; Li and Zhou, 2010; Zhou and Li, 2011).

In many ways, there is no single answer to all these challenging world problems. What is more important is to see how many of the superficial events can be explained by more in-depth intuition, conceptual understanding, and theoretical frameworks. It is against such global events that a "redefinition" of capitalism is needed to reinterpret the capitalism ideology in the modern context, highlighting the virtues of classical economics and how it can be used to solve contemporary global problems. One can argue that recent world events are not due to the growing irrelevance of capitalism, but rather are due to a lack of renewed understanding and the need to reorientate the various elements and texture of capitalism in light of the global events. Indeed, many economic activities in much of the modern world have deviated from the origins of capitalist economic principles.

This book attempts to use capitalist concepts to explain contemporary world events. There are five sections in this book. The first section is theoretical and conceptual, explaining the fundamentals of capitalism, elaborating the conceptual strengths and how human economic activities can still be best conducted within the framework of capitalism. In many ways, this section is intended to "redefine" capitalism using contemporary language and concepts, and set the scene for the analysis. Section I relates to the individual, interpretation on inequality, the role of modern government, the relationship between economics and politics and welfare needs, the contrast between capitalism and socialism, and finally discusses the "relative" nature of economics in capitalism.

Section II examines the global economy, data on the world's GDP, and debts, and how fiscal deficits and trade deficits and reserve are used to compare the economic performance of different world economies over the last few decades. Instead of referring the global economy to advanced countries and developing countries, this section dissects the world economy into five categories of capitalist countries, socialist countries, religion-dominant and oil exporting countries, newly emerging countries, and the remaining fragile states. A total of three contemporary global events will be discussed within the concepts of capitalism. This section concludes by raising some issues and identifying economies that can help to revive world capitalism.

Section III concentrates on the economic development experience of Asian countries, and how it can be used as lessons for other developing countries. The growth and development experience of Japan since the 1950s shall be used as a showcase of success. The discussion is then extended to the other "flying geese" in East Asia and various development issues will be elaborated. This section will end by examining the growth and development of the "late comers," namely the countries in the Southeast Asian region and China, contrasting their development and the growing China economy.

Discussion on the China economy is extended in Section IV by considering the two economies of China and Hong Kong, as Hong Kong's sovereignty reversion in 1997 produced an interesting and living case where the largest socialist country took over the most free capitalist economy. Both the China economy and the Hong Kong economy will be studied appropriately in order to reflect on their essential ideological differences, systemic divergence, and economic strength. While sovereignty reversion took place in 1997, Hong Kong has been promised "self-rule" in the form of a "one country, two systems" framework over the 50 years from 1997–2047. The "systemic" issue has become political since 1997 as trust in the central government has not been built up. The cumulative political crashes over the years led to the "Umbrella Movement" in 2014. Divergent political views have been sharpened, including a discussion on the "legitimacy" issue as Hong Kong was ceded to Great Britain in 1842 during the Qing Dynasty which was overthrown by the Nationalist Government, while the People's Republic of China was established only in the 1949 revolution that removed the Nationalist Government. The "China – Hong Kong" relationship can be considered as the "battle front" between the two ideologies of socialism and capitalism.

The various conclusions in Section V serve a number of purposes. The first intention is to argue and conclude that communism and socialism have failed to bring growth, peace, and advancement to the world economy. On the contrary, it is appropriate to understand how capitalism serves as an *ex ante* condition in the next phase of development in the contemporary world. Indeed, many industrialized countries need to adopt a "self-strengthening" strategy so as to reinvigorate their economies to ensure growth, productivity, and trade. Having cleared the discussion on the two ideologies, the purpose is to identify the possible growth regions in the world. The prediction is that the next growth regions shall consist of medium-sized countries which are prepared to adopt capitalist market ideologies, as the promotion of medium-sized promising economies shall bring stability and inter- and intraregional competition.

The five sections together pose the message that capitalism is the viable solution to many worldly issues, and the emergence of "right wing" governments in the industrialized countries will bring transformation to revive the world economy. Indeed, countries in the industrialized world shall be better off by redirecting its resource usage, especially in reducing dependence on oil consumption, by shedding the redistributive and pro-socialist policies that have eroded their competitiveness and productivity, by effectively cutting their government spending and reducing the growing debts, by rejuvenating their own industrial growth and development, by re-engineering domestic production, especially focusing investment in the real sector to create jobs and mobility, and by promoting other medium-sized emerging countries which have taken up market instruments in the next phrase of their development path.

CHAPTER

1

The Individual

I INTRODUCTION

Societies are composed of individuals, as economic decisions are mostly conducted by individuals. Although modern economics owes much to the monumental works of Adam Smith (1776) and Paul Samuelson (1947), some economic philosophers argued that the earliest teaching of Confucius (551–479 BC) had already established the relevance and importance of individuals looking after their own welfare achievements (Hofstede and Bond, 1988; Zhang, 1999, 2000). Had the Confucian doctrines been elaborated more scientifically and extensively, then the Confucian idea of individuals pursuing their own gains could have been the foundation of modern capitalism. Unfortunately, the discipline of economics as an academic subject was absent at the time of Confucius. On the contrary, it was Adam Smith's (1776) metaphor of the "invisible hand" that had piercingly symbolized the advantages of individuals' achievements, the capitalist mode of production, and the minimum role of the government in conducting economic activities (Butler, 2007). When all individuals utilize their own endowments to achieve their utmost, society is said to have reached its maximum level of growth, development, and output capacity (Sowell, 1974).

However, individuals perform differently, with some being more successful than others, with some having more individual endowments than others, and with some exposed to more economic opportunities than others. In economics, the capability of an individual is indicated by that individual's productivity. It is true that through education and training, society produces individuals who would take up different professions and jobs that yield different productivity, and are therefore rewarded differently. Unfortunately, not all individuals show the same level of productivity. In the productivity hierarchy, there are always more "low-productivity" or "low-endowment" individuals than "high-productivity" or "high-endowment" individuals. At the extreme, "low-productivity" individuals could face a survival problem if their pecuniary earnings are not sufficient to pay for their survival cost. Hence, the discussion on capitalism would extend to the role of government, and the need for redistribution, while the contrary argument would be the extent of disincentive on the part of "high-productivity" individuals (Wade, 1990; Tanzi and Schuknecht, 1997).

The debate on economic redistribution leads many to a discussion on income inequality, which has received academic and policy attention, though for decades the magnitude of global income inequality has remained.

© 2017 Elsevier Inc. All rights reserved.

Growth versus inequality has been debated in a large number of studies, and the relevant question would be whether a high degree of income inequality would result in a higher rate of economic growth, and whether income inequality has inevitably led studies to examine poverty reduction (Kuznet, 1955; Sen, 1973; Atkinson, 1983; Mosley, 2015; Ravallion, 2016; Summer, 2016). Ultimately, the inequality debate is mixed with politics, involving discussions on ownership of resources, coordination of workers, and economic sustainability (Schumpeter, 1942; Friedman, 1962, 1981).

As an introduction, this chapter clarifies some fundamental concepts in capitalism, leaving the bigger and more controversial issues to the following chapters. Depending on their personal endowment, each adult individual will have to participate in the production process. Differences in endowments would mean difference in productivity, contribution, and returns. Similarly, not all individuals' production would contribute positively, and externality would emerge when some "economically bad" outcomes are produced. A distinction between competition and competitiveness is needed to understand capitalism, as that can explain how and why capitalism is a sustainable ideology. It is equally important to understand the relationship between "private cost" and "social cost." This chapter also discusses the relevance of "supply-side" economics, as it is the more suitable strategy when compared to "demand-side" economics in promoting long lasting growth.

II BEGINNING WITH THE INDIVIDUAL

Each individual possesses some personal endowment, such as skills, experience, qualifications, knowledge, information, and wealth, which can be turned into a stream of earnings through either working for employment or establishing a business. In a free and dynamic market economy, individuals can gather information on the marketability of their own endowment. While an employed individual can progress by switching to jobs with higher wages when the individual's endowment has become more marketable, the individual could pick up new skills or learn a new profession if the existing endowment is losing its marketability or competitiveness. If an individual prefers to establish a business, the market should provide sufficient information on the marketability of the individual's business skills and other environmental factors, such as the rate of profit tax, rental cost, and market demand. Similarly, a business person would switch between businesses when there is a more profitable alternative. Either the individual works as an employee or starts a business, and the market economy should provide sufficient room for all individuals to maximize the return on their endowments. Given the choice in the market and the possibility of changing jobs, the worker—employer relationship should be seen more as complementary, or of mutual assistance where both are needed for the success of the business rather than as conflicting opponents, where workers and employers are seen as opposites in pursuing their economic interests. Workers who receive wages are given certainty of their pecuniary rewards, while employers who may get a bigger profit are faced with market risk.

The idea behind Adam Smith's "invisible hand" is that through the available information, choices, and opportunities, individuals in the market should on the one hand find their best possibilities, and on the other hand maximize their individual welfare with minimum assistance from the government. The market serves and directs individuals and allocates resources to their most productive outcomes, meaning that individuals could not obtain any higher pecuniary return in the market, and resources are allocated to their greatest possible usage. In economics jargon, output is maximized when it is produced at the lowest possible marginal cost. By maximizing individuals' welfare and minimizing producers' cost of production, the economy is said to have reached its maximum output at any point in time.

Given the limited resources in an economy, individuals will have to compete in the market for resources and opportunities. In theory, the analysis in the Pareto-efficiency argues that resources are efficiently allocated "when no person can be made better off without some other person being worse off" (Debreu, 1954). The idea is that when there is an idle resource, individuals will utilize the resources to further their economic gains. This will occur until all the available resources are exhausted, and no further gain can be made unless it occurs at the expense of another unit of resource. The Pareto-efficiency assumes a situation of open competition, and that the economic activities of individuals would utilize all available resources. An economic optimum is said to have been reached when individuals and businesses have decided on what to produce and how to produce it through the market mechanism. In economic theory, the market equilibrium is reached when the market price of a good or service equals the marginal cost of producing it.

As the market situation changes owing to the ups and downs in business cycles, and at the same time the individual may improve their endowment through increase in experience, skill, or education, the individual would always look to the market for a better possibility of jobs and employment. Indeed, the market could even provide information to individuals if they should remain in employment or switch to start their own business. In the upturn of the business cycle, one would expect a rise in economic activities and jobs would be forthcoming. On the contrary, unemployment rises in an economic recession and businesses run down. Basic microeconomic theory of supply and demand tells us that business cycles will swing up and down due to dynamic changes in aggregate supply and demand. Changes in aggregate supply and demand do generate economic forces, variations, and volatility unpredictably. It is true to say that individuals make use of the market information, but the activities of individuals in the market also generate economic changes. The market forces work both ways so that individuals observe and react to market information, but at the same time information enters into the market for others to observe. The "invisible hand" does the allocation through market operations, but one individual may not know what another individual does. Thus, the effect is twofold.

At the macroeconomic level, when all individuals are in charge of their own economic activities, economic progress would produce positive spillover effects. One advantage is full employment, and improvement in personal experience would result in rise in wages and earnings, which in turn would lead to improved economic welfare or even upward social mobility for the individuals. If the individual engages in business, the rising demand and business prosperity would equally result in higher profit earnings. The first principle in economics is Say's law, which states that "supply creates its own demand" (Sowell, 1972). The implication is that economic growth would spread through the multiplier effect to other businesses and create additional demand for other goods and services.

Another advantage is that the more able and capable individuals are, the greater their chance of securing jobs with handsome pecuniary returns and, subsequently, decrease the need to seek welfare subsidy. With the growth in jobs and employment, the advantages to the government are twofold: the government would have a higher ability to collect both salary tax and profit tax revenues, and with a fall in unemployment, the number of individuals relying on government welfare subsidy would fall. Eventually, the government needs to spend less on welfare. Putting these two effects together, the outcome is that the government will likely have a fiscal surplus that can be used to expand and enrich future economic capacity, such as building a stronger infrastructure, nurturing better human capital through education, and engaging in research and development that would enrich the capability of industries. With the economic path being drafted for future generations, the individuals in turn have more to do for the future. Economic growth will eventually exhibit a "virtuous circle" of growth and individual welfare expansion.

The economic advantage could even be cross-generational, as the welfare generated by individuals will pass on to their children, who will then have a better personal endowment through family support when they grow up. Ultimately, there will be a fall in the overall poverty level. With ample job opportunities, individuals with different levels of endowment can have their desired jobs and employment, and the rise in their economic welfare ensures a reduction in poverty. With a "virtuous circle," the increase in earnings will result in upward social mobility, and a reduction in the need for redistribution permits the government to accumulate a fiscal surplus that can be used for economic capacity enlargement.

The ultimate advantage of capitalism is its ability to regenerate and rejuvenate economic activities despite the emergence of business cycles that result in economic volatility, as it is the individuals who know best their marketability given the different and changing economic conditions. In economic cycles, some businesses make profits while others experience losses, but market dynamism would always permit new businesses to emerge and prosper. Capitalism allows automatic market replenishment through the voluntary activities of individuals.

III EXTERNALITY AND ETHICS

The economics of externality, commonly known as "market failure," argue that while people are maximizing their economic welfare, it is possible that their activities infringe on other people and resources, either positively or negatively (Buchanan and Stubblebine, 1962; Trenery Dolbear, 1967; Dahlman, 1979). However, there can be complications, such as the availability of required information and the number of individuals involved. The cost of bringing the case to justice through legal action can be high and time consuming. A clear definition of property rights is crucial in the analysis of externality (Demsetz, 1967). When both private cost and private benefit arising from the externality are quantifiable, mutual or legal settlements can eventually be formulated. Illegal activities are cases of negative externalities, when individuals or firms infringe on the legal rights of other persons and firms. Complications arise when social cost and social benefit are involved, or they differ from private cost and private benefit. In the first place, social cost and social benefit may not be quantifiable. Second, the ownership right may not be clearly defined. Executing and monitoring the resulting damage from externality cases can be problematic, and it is common for the government to get involved.

The situation is less controversial in the case of positive externality, especially if the benefits last for generations. The construction of new infrastructure can bring long-term economic benefits to the community. In most cases, the problem arises in negative externality, especially when the private benefit so derived occurred at the expense of social cost. In short, some private individuals gained from the externality, but society has to bear the cost. This often relates to social or common goods that private individuals can have access to, and it becomes difficult to monitor the action of private individuals. The ultimate question is the lack of property rights in a number of common goods, such as forests, natural resources, rare animal species, clean and fresh air, as well as a number of "common bad," such as carbon emission, natural disasters, garbage disposal, drug abuse, and so on. In all these cases, the lack of property right implies that individuals and firms are interested in obtaining the private benefits, but are not interested in bearing the social cost.

Ignoring the social cost can be the result of a lack of law enforcement and monitoring. The role of government as a law maker and monitor is important in ensuring that private benefits will not spill over to social cost. Strong ethics at all levels are vital in letting individuals and firms be aware that private benefits should not impose a burden on social cost (Sen, 1987; Hausman and McPherson, 1993). The "Pareto optimality" at the individual level and endowment usage can then be extended to include social cost. The "Pareto social optimality" can be achieved "when no private benefit can be increased without increase in social cost." In short, private benefit cannot take place at the expense of social cost.

Externality is often considered as "market failure" because it is believed that these are areas that go beyond normal market practices. This is true, but is not the whole truth. At the individual or firm level, a sound, equitable, and transparent legal system can minimize externality as compensation, or lawful restrictions can be imposed on negative externalities. The high cost of legal action, however, may deter the affected minority parties unless there are independent bodies that can serve as mediators in the externality dispute. Individual and business ethics can be a good instrument in minimizing externality, but to build up a strong ethic requires time and education on the treatment and usage of "common goods." Education and media are good vehicles through which high ethical standards can be promoted. Indeed, ethical behavior is the best policing instrument in safeguarding "common goods," as ethics directs the individual mindset in preserving the "common goods" where policing is difficult to execute.

Technological development can be an answer to externality and preservation of "common goods," as it can either help to develop more resources or reduce the consumption of resources. In other words, while it is the human race that utilizes the world's resources and pollutes the environment as a result, it is also the human race that could institute a rescue mechanism through which the world's natural resources could be saved and replenished. Ultimately, human development through economic growth is probably the more effective means of improving people's welfare in the world economy. Similar to an input—output analysis, the sequence of priority is such that because of the need to improve economic development in all corners of the world economy, growth will have to come before conservation, but it is also through growth that more resources could be devoted to natural conservation.

It was perhaps inappropriate to use the term "market failure" to explain externality. A free market and capitalism do not operate in a vacuum, but require strong institutions, well-established legal frameworks, and a mature civic environment so that the market concept can gradually be extended to new areas. Externality can be considered as an example in which the institution of markets will dynamically be extended to uncharted areas. A free market is not a one-time affair, but develops dynamically and continuously along with other aspects of development. The "invisible hand" in the allocation of resources is a dynamic concept where resource availability and utilization change as new development occurs. This is the true spirit of the "invisible hand," and the function of the free market mechanism.

IV COMPETITION VERSUS COMPETITIVENESS

Few would have bothered to explain the difference between competition and competitiveness. Competition relates to individuals when they come to seek employment in the job market and firms when they enter and engage in production. Competitiveness is an economy-wide concept and reflects the overall performance of one economy when compared to another. Measures of competitiveness can cover various indicators, such as economic growth, industrial capability, development potentiality, technological sustainability, social fabric, and ethical standards.

Microeconomic theories tell us that classical economics begins with the virtue of perfect competition with four assumptions of a homogenous product, perfect market information, freedom of exit and entry of firms, and the presence of a large number of firms. In perfect competition, firms cannot influence each other and are price-takers, as consumers are aware of the supply and demand conditions through the available market information. By varying the assumptions of perfect competition, a few theoretical versions of imperfect competition have been developed, including monopoly, duology, and oligopoly that involve, respectively, only one, two, and few firms in the market, and monopolistic competition and contestable markets that lie between perfect competition and monopoly (Robinson, 1933; Baumol, 1982).

The concept of competition, however, is fluid, in that there are other observations and considerations. First, it is natural for firms to get away from competition, as lower competition will mean a greater chance of making a bigger profit and taking a larger market share. Second, competition is a process and firms in different markets are faced with different degrees of competition, with firms in one market experiencing an early stage of competition, while firms in another market are faced with a more mature stage of competition. Hence, competition differs in different markets. Most world economies have instituted competition or antitrust laws to avoid unfair market control and anticompetition practices by firms (Li, 2012a). It is most important in capitalism that there is freedom to market entry, but whether there are new entrants will depend on the decision of firms based on the cost of production, market size, and other economic conditions. The drive to reduce competition gives rise to a number of activities. On the product front, activities firms can undertake include advertising, brand-name creation, consumer loyalty development, and product differentiation. At the firm level, it is possible for larger, successful, and financially strong firms to engage in mergers and acquisitions or takeover bids. Firms can change their ownership patterns from entrepreneurial, family business, and small- and medium-sized enterprises to share-holding corporations. While the owners are the shareholders who do not look into the routine activities of the corporation, it is often the salaried managers who run the corporation on behalf of the shareholders. There are numerous studies that discuss the relationship arising from differences in interest between the shareholders and management of corporations. These include principal–agent, rent seeking, and asymmetric information theories (Akerlof, 1970; Ross, 1973; Krueger, 1974; Murphy et al., 1993). The essence of these theories concerns how bona fide decisions are made by the corporate managers. How truly and faithfully are decisions made by the management beneficial to the shareholders? Would managers have vested interests in the corporation? A typical example is that shareholders would prefer to have a greater return on assets, while the management would prefer to use the profit for market expansion.

Monopoly appears when the market is supplied by only one firm. In product markets, this is possible but unlikely, as laws can be instituted against the single supplier, and there are always distant substitutes in the market for consumers. The more likely case of a single supplier appears in infrastructure or "common goods" that require either a large capital investment, or where the market can only allow one supplier to survive. This is referred to as "natural monopoly." Typically, public utilities, such as bridges, trains, fire service, police, and military involving either huge investments or national security would usually be supplied by a single supplier. In a geographically large country, it may be true that even infrastructure can be made competitive in different states or regions. Other experiences of "natural monopoly" cases are that the government or the state will be responsible for the building of key infrastructure, either wholly or jointly with the private sector, in order to minimize the price charged by the monopolistic supplier. In public utilities, such as schools and hospitals, there can be dual supply in the market, and both the public sector and the private investors can compete to provide educational and health services. The dual supply model allows service users a choice between public or private schools and hospitals, and can serve as a check and balance between different suppliers in terms of price, quality, and service to ensure high professional and ethical standards. On the contrary, countries thinking that social equality would be achieved by state-owned institutions, e.g., in hospital and health services, can end up with low quality supply and excess demand due to the imposition of a ceiling price.

The various dimensions of competition among firms tend to show that competition is a process, and that competition can take different forms at different times, and competition can differ between products and markets. Given that the market is open for new entrants, firms cannot stop competition. As such, what could stop competition is really the market itself, namely whether new entrants see the potential in the market, either due to the large capital needed and the risk involved, the market is saturated and profit may not be forthcoming, the business environment is not favorable for new firms to enter because of economic recession and low demand, there is a lack of creativity on the part of the investors in exploring the market potential, or that the policy is not market-friendly. In short, market competition goes beyond simply supply and demand, but includes the market and policy environment and conditions in which firms operate.

Market friendliness is crucial in an economy's competitiveness. There is a distinction between "market" and "friendliness." A "market" can be large or small, but whether the business is viable will be judged by the investors or suppliers, who probably would make the best out of the market. In short, the market is a natural entity, and the market can grow over time as the level of demand changes. "Friendliness" is often determined by policies and political factors. A low profit tax or tariff rate, a flexible, disciplined and efficient work force, and the presence of civic stability with sound and reliable institutions, are regarded as the key factors in business friendliness (Singh, 1994). There are numerous studies, measures, and annual indicators, such as the *Index of Economic Freedom* conducted by the Heritage Foundation, the *Economic Freedom of the World Index* conducted by the Fraser Institute, and the *Global Competitiveness Report* conducted by the World Economic Forum, that point to the importance of economic openness, market friendliness, and economic freedom in the overall competitiveness of an economy (Friedman, 1962; Gwartney and Lawson, 2003; Li, 2012a). Once instituted, many of these policies will become permanent and form the business infrastructure of the economy.

Economic competitiveness works in two ways. A high profit tax or high cost of production may deter private investment, and the drop in domestic investment would lower production and employment. On the other hand, investors will seek other investment channels overseas where production activities would be more market-friendly. Hence, investment disappears from the home economy but appears in the host economy, and employment and production go to the host economy. Competitiveness means that the home economy's loss of production, investment, and ultimately competitiveness would be to the benefit of the host economy.

One has to understand that different production factors can have different mobility potentials. A "mobility filter" can be constructed for the production factors. Out of the three production factors of land, labor, and capital, the least mobile is land as it is unlikely land would be "exported" to other economies. However, natural resources and raw materials can be made mobile through exports, if the land category includes natural resources and raw materials. Labor can be made mobile through change of jobs, immigration, and training. Typically, a high percentage of the labor force remains immobile. The most mobile factor is capital, as financial resources can be exported easily through legal channels. Once transferred overseas, the financial capital will be used as investment to promote growth and development in the host economy overseas. The home economy will suffer in the two aspects of loss in competitiveness: loss in financial capital and competitiveness at home, and a rise in production and competitiveness emerge in host economy. The long-term effect is that the fall in the competitiveness of the "outward-investment" economy will improve the economic competitiveness of the "inward-investment" economy. Hence, there appears to be a "competitiveness transfer" between the two economies.

V COMPLEMENTARY OR DICHOTOMOUS?

In mature capitalist market economies where a high degree of economic discipline has been instituted, the freedom to start a business and freedom to change employment are allowed. It would be ethical for both the employer and worker to understand how the business is organized in terms of cost of production and sources of finance, profitability, and market potentials, and the extent of competition that firms face. There is certainly some degree of confidentiality on the part of the employer in disclosing the amount of business information to the workers. It is mostly the employer who bears the business risk of making a loss or profit. Workers are secured with a fixed salary, but could be laid off when the business is not profitable. The fundamental question is whether the relationship between employers and workers is always dichotomous, or can they complement each other.

The success of each ideological paradigm has its own learning process, and capitalism is no exception (Epstein, 1968; Perelman, 2000; Kocka, 2016). One simplified way to look historically at the "primitive" stage of capitalism is to examine the key characteristics that had probably been observed in the past two centuries. It would generally be fair to argue that capitalism succeeded from feudalism with distinct social classes of landowners and peasants. The emergence of capitalism gave rise to a new class of producers who utilized resource inputs for their production, and the result was an increase in output and trade. Early capitalism relied much on individual entrepreneurship in organizing productive activities, and businesses flourished as outputs were consumed and traded. Production required resource inputs, including labor input. Similarly, workers needed jobs and supplied their labor time. The capitalist mode of production requires investors who engaged in production, and workers who were hired to work in the production process. Both the employers and workers need to survive economically, and it would be logical for employers to minimize their wage payments, while workers would seek the highest possible market wage. Such an economic difference has shallowly been seen as an opposition between employers and workers.

Capitalism cannot function in a vacuum, but requires a number of socioeconomic complements. Indeed, the employer—worker relationship in the "primitive" stage of capitalism was worsened by noneconomic inadequacies, including a lack of social security provision, unavailability of civic protection, and deficiency in institutional support. There could be a number of unfavorable considerations and imbalances in the early stage of capitalism. Given the profit motive and imbalance in social status, many factory workers were faced with poor working conditions and long working hours. Social equity between the employer and worker was missing, and given that many industrial jobs were routine and mechanical, training for higher skills was inadequately provided. The industrial workers did not experience social upward mobility, especially workers in large-scale mechanized factories or geographical regions that were dominated by one or two industries. Social security in the form of government welfare assistance provided to those with survival difficulties was not instituted, and public provision of medical services was far from adequate. In many ways, the "dark" side of primitive capitalism related much to the "industrial revolution" that began in the mid-1800s in Great Britain before the same production mode spread to other European countries (Von Tunzelmann, 1978; Lindert and Williamson, 1983; Crafts, 1985).

Although the industrial revolution in Great Britain and other European countries led to much economic growth in the form of industrial expansion, export, and technological advances, the various drawbacks in the primitive stage of capitalism produced diverging ideological, social, and institutional consequences. First, the Marxian ideology of communism believed in a class society divided into the capitalists and the workers (Marx, 1867; Parkin, 1981; Read, 2002; Eagleton, 2006). In the Marxian ideology, employers and workers are situated at the two opposing ends in the economic arena, with the gain of one leading to the loss of another. The outcome of the employer—worker relationship was seen as a "zero-sum game" (Thurow, 1980). The Marxian ideology basically politicized the different but inevitable economic outcomes. Economics is about productivity, and since each individual has a different endowment, it is clear that the outcome of an individual's productivity will differ. Politicizing the differences in economic outcomes is against the natural law of economics, as no one can equalize economic outcomes due to differences in factor inputs. It is true that political opportunists can capitalize on differences in economic outcomes.

The Marxists imposed a political criterion on economic outcomes. In a planned Marxian economy, individuals are controlled by the state and economic outcomes are "equal" when they are given similar materials allocations from the state. But in actuality, the extent of inequality has shifted from one of economic inequality to political inequality, in that power is concentrated in the hands of state officials. To ensure "equality" in economic outcomes, the state in communism controlled all factor inputs. It turned out that the "life-long" nature of political inequality could be more detrimental than income inequality, and the chances for making individual progress would disappear for those not affiliated to the political party in a communist state.

Second, in "post-primitive" capitalist economies, laborers are often represented in decisions concerning wages, working conditions, and government policies in a more civic and organized manner (Barling et al., 1992; Western, 1997). Employers' associations have also flourished in order to seek better business opportunities or influence government's policies. Indeed, with the institutionalization of the "employer—employee" relationship in the form of labor organizations and business associations, discussions can be made more open and transparent, and negotiations can be made according to the state of the economy. Democratically elected pro-welfare governments tend to expand welfare provision. Fiscal welfare expenditures could provide a more equitable economy, and economically-weak individuals can be sheltered from the government's redistributive policies. There is definitely a need to provide shelters to households with difficulty in economic survival. In addition to the government's welfare provision, there are other established civic institutions that would assist and promote workers' welfare (Pattanaik and Suzumura, 1994).

The Russian revolution in 1917 highlighted Marxian ideology as a ruling ideology (Wade, 2005; Trotsky, 2008). History has shown that the battle between the two ideologies lasted for decades, and culminated in the "Cold War" between the Soviet Union and the West after the two World Wars (Gaddis, 1992). There are studies that discussed the economics of Marxism and the influence of the socialist doctrine (Jenkins, 1970; Wilczynski, 1970; Fine, 1975; Howard and King, 1976). While economic growth and prosperity occurred in many capitalist economies, socialist economies practiced economic planning and remained weak, as the restrictions on the input end of the economic equation discouraged incentives to produce and innovate.

Some world economies have taken up the Marxian ideology, labor unions have grown through increase in union members and collection of union fees, and pro-welfare governments have introduced strong welfare policies in other economies. These developments, however, have not replaced capitalism in the global economy. Socialist economies are faced with different degrees of difficulty in a number of areas, such as political succession, economic sustainability, territorial disputes, corruptive practices, internal conflicts, and international acceptability. Equally, some European economies with either strong and militant labor unions or high government welfare provisions are faced with loss of competitiveness, with high unemployment and economic crises.

On the contrary, economic events in the past decades have shown that a mature capitalist economy is more sustainable, effective, and embracing, because the development of other complementary ingredients helped to sustain capitalist development, making it an "evergreen" ideology. First, the protection of individuals comes with property rights of ownership and transfer. Each individual would probably have two types of endowments. Education, training, and skills will increase an individual's ability and productivity, which should be reflected in their salaries. The other aspect of individual endowment relates to physical and pecuniary assets. The assets could be savings, investment earnings, and inheritances. These two forms of endowments are considered as the "wealth" of an individual. With personal enrichment, the individual will not need to rely on the government for assistance. In turn, the individual would look after his or her own economic welfare, including raising a family and accumulating for retirement. The individual could start a business and create jobs and employment, thereby enhancing the welfare of another individual, and the individual would contribute to tax payments and the fiscal revenue of the government.

Economic freedom is another crucial ingredient in capitalism. Numerous studies have concluded that economic freedom promotes growth, development, and prosperity, because individuals are given the freedom to do their best unhindered. Individual satisfaction in their job performance would also mean a new frontier in their own profession and talent, thereby generating more economic activities that would accumulate, spread, or trickle down to other economic aspects. Ultimately, it is the contribution by individual activities at the microeconomic level that push the macro-economy to grow, expand, and prosper.

It is true that there are economic fluctuations in capitalist market economies, with the appearance of different stages of business cycles, and periods of economic recessions and booms, and different individuals may face different outcomes as a result. However, the fact is that given the strength of the system and practices, capitalism is a "renewable" ideology that allows new things to emerge while economic failures do occur. Capitalism has been "tested" as a sustainable ideology, and the question is not whether the ideology can survive, but how capitalism can work better to serve the future world economy.

VI MAXIMIZING PRIVATE COST, MINIMIZING SOCIAL COST

Conceptually, the desire for individuals to maximize their own economic welfare relates to the understanding of the private cost. Since the individuals know their own endowment best, and through efficient operation of the market, individuals are free to maximize their welfare through different channels of earnings. When all individuals are able to shoulder their private cost of economic survival, there will be no need to receive rescue from society. The simple equation is that the totality of the individual's ability is greater than, or at least equal to, their private cost of economic survival. Thus, there is no need to pass any of their unfulfilled private cost to the society, thereby increasing the level of social cost. On the contrary, "ability-lacking" individuals may face survival problems, the individual's ability is lower than the private cost of economic survival, and the remaining private cost would have to be paid for by the society, which effectively increases social cost. When individuals cannot shoulder their own private cost, some portions of their private cost will have to be shouldered by the society through welfare assistance, thereby passing the private cost to social cost.

Capitalism encourages and allows individuals to do their best, so that they can take care of their private cost, leaving a minimum of endowment-low individuals that cannot meet their economic survival and whose needs will have to be passed on to the society. Hence, the more economically able individuals there are, the less the need to pass on their private cost to society, and the less the need for social welfare, the lower the social cost would become. The incentive for individuals to take care of their private cost and the minimization of social cost is another ingredient of capitalism, because this can allow economies to grow to their fullest extent, and at the same time provide a minimum economic net or security for endowment-low individuals. More importantly, individuals can improve their personal endowment to make economic progress over time.

Minimizing the social cost naturally implies a lower fiscal burden. It follows that the less the need for the government to shoulder the social cost, the less the need for a high government revenue, or that government revenue can be used to promote other aspects of the economy. While government intervention in the economy is disincentive-imposing and unwise (Hayek, 1944), one productive role the government can exercise is to use the revenue to improve and enrich the future capability of the economy. On the contrary, it increases the public burden unnecessarily if the government is actively shouldering the social cost of individuals. The large and increasing public burden usually forms the root of fiscal deficit and public debt.

VII WHY SUPPLY-SIDE ECONOMICS IS PREFERRED

Individuals and firms in a capitalist economy will exercise their endowment to the best possible extent. There is a multiplying effect, as one aspect of growth leads to other aspects of growth, and the individual's growth at the microeconomic level would aggregate to form overall growth at the macroeconomic level. With income and profit earnings made, individuals would consume in order to improve their welfare, utility, and satisfaction. Since the ability to consume would depend on the ability to earn, it follows that production must come before consumption. Although an individual can dis-save by borrowing, the amount of loans borrowed also depend on the future earning ability of the individual. The spirit of Say's Law that "supply creates its own demand" implies that individuals have to supply their endowment in order to gain the market returns, from which consumption can be made.

In contemporary economics, Say's Law is discussed within the context of "supply-side" economics (Canto et al., 1983; Feldstein, 1986; Helliwell, 1986; Marshall and Arestis, 1989; Lucas, 1990). By using simple supply and demand curves, David Harper has given a simple explanation of "supply-side" economics in the website of *Investopedia*. The simple argument is that situations of "over" or "under" production cannot last long as variation in inventory and prices will eventually remove any excesses or shortages. Supply-side economics argues that demand is irrelevant, as consumers will respond to the price set by the suppliers. The three pillars that formed the backbone of supply-side economics include: (1) a low marginal tax rate that does not impose unnecessary disincentives to businesses and workers; (2) a small government with least intervention that allows maximum economic freedom; and (3) a prudent monetary policy that would not create excessive liquidity and inflation.

As summarized in *Wikipedia*, there have been heated debates on the effectiveness of supply-side economics, especially in the context of "Reaganomics" and that the tax rate cut had not been growth generating in the United States under the leadership of two Republican Presidents, Ronald Reagan and George Bush (Krugman, 1994). However, there can be a number of economic instruments under the framework of supply-side economics, and tax reduction is just one of the instruments. Other concerns included the stage of the business cycle in which tax reduction was instituted, and promotion in research and development. Indeed, supply-side economics shall be regarded more as a long-term policy direction which both individuals and government institutions should adopt, rather than as a short-term instrument in alleviating economic hardship.

The importance of supply-side economics can crucially be discussed in two situations. One relates to the situation of a growing economy, and the other relates to the situation of a crisis economy, though the mechanisms could be similar in both situations. Beginning from an early phase of a growing economy, income is expected to remain low, but the relevant question is how to utilize resources for production-oriented activities. Individual endowments will become the first and primary consideration; namely how individuals can produce some output from their own endowment, which can be a combination of skill, capital, knowledge, and information. Such usage of individual endowment in producing output shall be the first action in the "supply chain." One production activity will lead to another activity, either horizontally or vertically, as the production process requires other inputs. This shall generate a "supply-side multiplier" where the supply of one good will lead to the supply of another good.

In an economic or financial crisis where the economy is faced with sudden shocks due to a financial collapse that has ruined numerous economic activities, the sharp economic downfall would lead to economic shrinkages. Low economic expectation and pessimism would delay economic revival. Aggregate demand will fall, inventory starts to build up, and business will find it harder to survive. However, economic slowdown creates excess capacity, and producers could face a lower cost of production. Business cycles come and go, and expectation that changes over time can be nurtured or nourished. Economic scenes are always dynamic. A low expectation today can be changed through productive activities and become more favorable tomorrow. The low expectation and low demand can be temporary and revive when sufficient individuals make use of their endowment productively in improving their personal wellbeing.

The solution to a financial crisis is to rebuild economic confidence and expectation. By making use of the falling cost of production, creative, innovative, and adventurous individual producers would hire workers for new production and create new supply. The low demand could be temporary as more workers are hired, and sooner or later the increase in individual spending would lead to an increase in aggregate demand. Indeed, it is possible that the faster the increase in supply, the quicker it would lead to demand revival.

Supply-side economics is preferred, because supply is first in a chain of economic activities. Once supplied, the goods and services would then be demanded in the market. Market forces will eliminate unsuccessful and uncompetitive supply when there is insufficient demand. In the process of supply, jobs are generated due to the need for production inputs, and employment gives rise to wage payments. Workers would then use the wage for consumption, thereby giving rise to demand. On the contrary, "demand-side" economics is important only when individuals have sufficient earnings to consume. The ability to consume depends on the ability to earn, the possibility to earn depends on employment opportunities and job security, employment depends on productive activities, and production ultimately relates to the ability to supply.

Supply is a more fundamental economic element than demand, as supply is related to production, through which demand takes place as a result of more goods and services being made available in the market, and as a result of more employment that increases workers' purchasing power. Many have argued that the root of "demand-side" economics can be found in the Keynesian school of thought (Keynes, 1926, 1937). After the end of the Second World War when the United Kingdom and other European countries were in economic recession, Keynes advocated for a fiscal solution by increasing government intervention through public expenditure as a main instrument in reviving the recessed postwar economy. It has some truth in it as some government expenditure is better than no expenditure in times of economic depression. The public sector is often thought to serve as a cushion against economic recession, because unlike workers in the private sector who may suffer a reduction in wage as the economy recesses, employees in the public sector tend to have a stable wage. The two arguments against Keynes were that government expenditure can have a "crowding-out" effect, in that the more government spent, especially in investment, the less the private sector would invest, thereby limiting the economic potential in the private sector. Second, a considerable amount of government expenditure could have ended up in welfare provision that had boosted demand, but since there was no parallel increase in output, the rise in demand resulting from welfare expenditure would either boost inflation that lowered the purchasing power, hurting those who are not receiving welfare assistance, or resulting in higher imports and a trade imbalance.

Demand-side economics can best be regarded as a short-term strategy. Immediately after a major crisis, the "ultra-low" economic expectation would need stimulus in order to avoid further hardship. The government can then exercise its fiscal ability by making short-term spending. Once the imminence of the economic crisis was over, demand-led economic strategy should give way to supply-led economic strategies. It is true that supply-led strategies tend to take time to materialize, as business decisions and productive activities would take time to execute, but ultimately it is the rise in physical output that can see more goods available in the market. The increase in goods' supply would help to lower inflation and promote purchasing power. In short, supply-side economics produces a "virtuous circle" of economic activities.

The difference between "demand-side" economics and "supply-side" economics is whether a quick short-term impulse is needed to deal with an economic shock or the desire to build up a long lasting capacity enlargement that can lead to economic revival and expansion in the long run. Short-term impulse policies are usually immediate expenditure that does alleviate some economic hardship, but it can also generate inequity to nonrecipients of welfare if the short-term expenditure produces inflationary pressures. By building up long-term economic capacity, the benefits will be available and open to all. The supply-side economic strategy turns out to be the superior choice, especially when a supply-multiplier can be generated.

Cutting tax is a popular instrument used in supply-side economics. A lower tax would stimulate businesses, the increase in subsequent investment would be productive, and the increase in output and employment would eventually promote growth and lift the economy from recession and crisis. However, the positive impact of cutting tax could depend on a number of factors. With a lower tax, investment would take time to materialize, and supply would take time to produce. The delay could differ among businesses and industries. Second, it also depends on what kind of investment a lower tax would stimulate, as some investments may not be output-oriented, or even speculative in nature. Third, the sustainability of the tax cut can be another factor. Investment, which often involves long-term activity, may not consider a tax cut favorable if the expectation was that the cuts were meant to be short-lived and would be revived in due course. In short, the short-term impact of a tax cut might not be obvious, as it is the consistency of a low tax regime, not the fluctuation of tax rate, that counts. A low tax rate should be seen more as a fiscal infrastructure that constantly promotes investment than as an instrument that influences business cycles.

VIII CONCLUSION

This chapter began with the discussion of an individual as a crucial player in market economies, and all individuals are different from each other. While most individuals produce "goods," some "bad" production could generate externality. Other individuals may have survival problems, and the economy would have to shoulder their private cost in the form of welfare assistance. Economic survival is discussed within the context of competition among individuals and competitiveness among economies.

The conceptual discussion elaborates on the advantage of capitalism as an ideological framework that allows economic changes and variations through time. Business cycles may produce economic booms and recessions, but the economic drive of individuals eventually brings vigor and revival to the economy. Other advantages of capitalism include the willingness of individuals to take up their private cost, and will not pass their economic survival problems to increase the social burden. The preference of "supply-side" economics over "demand-side" economics in capitalist economies is discussed, especially in the initial situations in economic growth and in a crisis situation.

The conceptual elaboration of capitalism serves only as a starting point, as the more important elaborations and in-depth analyses will be discussed in the following chapters. For example, different individual endowment leads to inequality, which is more of a political concept than an economic concept, as economic outcomes are always "unequal." When an individual's ability falls short of their private cost, the role of government in shouldering social cost is a key component in contemporary capitalism. Welfare provision will lead to discussion on fiscal policy, while democratic elections in capitalist economies will bring a discussion between economics and politics. In other words, to "redefine" capitalism will not only be focused narrowly on the conventional values of private ownership, minimum government intervention, profit maximization of business corporates, but will relate and widen the discussion to the intellectual relationship among the three disciplines of economics, welfare studies, and politics. In addition, the political economy of capitalism will lead to contemporary interpretations within the framework of "economic relativity." Economic activities are mostly "relative," with positive-sum outcomes, and the capitalist ideology provides the most effective and sustainable vehicle, as it can incorporate changes and variations which can bring revitalization, replenishment, restructuring, and reform in economic advancement.

CHAPTER

2

Inequality, Poverty, and Opportunity

I INTRODUCTION

Where can one find perfect equality in this world? Inequality is as old as humanity, and perfect equality can never be achieved. It is the human race that exerts one kind of inequality or another on each other. History has shown that there are numerous kinds of inequality: sex, race, religion, geographical and regional, language, ethnic and tribal, aristocracy and social class, political and ideological. It would be worse if more than one aspect of inequality appeared at the same time. A typical example would be a combination of sex, religious, ethnic, and class inequalities. A major problem with these types of human inequality is that they can be permanent and last for a life time, and there is no chance that such inequality and discrimination could be eradicated. Many inequalities are "human-made" and can still be found in different parts of the contemporary world.

Seen in this light, one can argue that income inequality probably will be the "best" form of inequality, because income inequality need not be permanent and can be improved in one's life time, provided that a progressive economic environment is generated. The methods of income inequality measurement can also vary and produce different implications. There is a dilemma in understanding inequality in many contemporary economies. Individuals will receive different training based on their talents, innate ability, academic performance, and family background. Hence, different types of professionals are trained, nurtured, and produced, and the earnings are different among professionals, jobs, and employment opportunities. The dilemma is that the economy spends resources to train highly skilled professionals, but at the same time complains about the inequality in wage earnings among different jobs.

One way to understand such a dilemma is that the term "income inequality" comes from two separate disciplines. Income is an economic term and it reflects the productivity level of individual workers. Someone with a highly skilled job would have higher productivity and a higher degree of marketability, and therefore the skilled individual should earn a handsome reward. On the contrary, a low-skilled worker would have lower productivity and marketability, and could only earn a lower reward. The difference represents the market outcome of individuals with different skills. On the contrary, the term "inequality" is more of a political and social term. In a civilized and humane world, people simply prefer to see a greater degree of equality. The dilemma arises as a result of binding together an economic outcome and a political or moral desire. As such, it would be desirable to seek "income equality," even though the law of economics is that outcomes are often "unequal."

© 2017 Elsevier Inc. All rights reserved.

The problem in the income inequality dilemma is conceptual, not theoretical, as it is mixed with two academic areas. Income difference is an economic outcome as resources are rewarded differently, while equality reflects a political or social criterion that there should be equality in humanity. The term "income inequality" is based on an economic outcome, but is dressed up using a noneconomic criterion, or using a noneconomic criterion to judge an economic outcome. Such a lack of clarity in concept has given rise to a large number of studies on income inequality, and yet in reality and after so many decades it is not possible to eradicate income inequality. While many studies advocate for ways to reduce income inequality, others compare inequality performances over time. But, in reality, income inequality still exists and could even be rising (Bourguignon, 1979; Myrdal, 1989; Deininger and Squire, 1996, 1997; Gottschalk and Smeeding, 1997; Li et al., 1998; Sala-i-Martin, 2002; Chen, 2003; Hoeller et al., 2014).

In capitalist market economies, wage payments are based on the productivity of workers. Highly trained professionals are expected to exhibit higher productivity than those doing low-skilled jobs. In business, some firms enjoy higher profits than others, reflecting such differences as management, marketing, and product differentiations. Differences in economic outcomes among individuals and businesses are unavoidable. In many ways, economic differences and diversity do bring advantages, including the possibility of high tax revenue, upward mobility, and wealth accumulation. In pro-equality economies, the wage gap between highly trained professionals and low-skilled job holders is narrower, because wage payments are based on noneconomic considerations and criteria. A politically oriented redistributive policy usually imposes high and progressive taxes on high income earners and subsidized low income earners. Nonetheless, these policies cannot eradicate income inequality.

In short, the inequality issue has long been debated, and yet the extent of income inequality in the global economy has not been much improved. Perhaps the alternative is to examine and understand the concept of inequality itself, and separate the intellectual discussion between the economics arena and social arena. In economics, income inequality arises from the fact that individuals' endowments are rewarded differently. Poverty is the more popular term used to describe "endowment-low" individuals. The society should not penalize "endowment-high" individuals as they are productive, but should look for means to aid the poor to avoid unnecessary economic hardship. Hence, the discussion would be extended to examine the issues in poverty.

Similar to inequality, poverty itself is another well-developed area of study. Beginning from the three volumes of *Asian Drama* (Myrdal, 1968), analyses on poverty have focused on a number of areas, including discussions on the measurement of absolute poverty in developing countries (Ahluwalia, 1976; Sen, 1976; Foster et al., 1984; Atkinson, 1987; Ravallion, 1997). Many poverty measurements quantify poverty statically, but poverty should be looked at from a dynamic context; namely a poor person today may not be poor tomorrow, and equally there will be new poor tomorrow. Hence, poverty should not be looked at merely by using a "stock" concept, but a "flow" concept. Policies should not just consider the amount of funding needed to take care of the stock (the poverty pool), but policies should include how to prevent new poor entering the poverty pool, and how to remove the poor from the poverty pool.

This leads to the concept of economic opportunity (Li, 2012a, 2014b), which could be another aspect of economic scarcity. The discussion on economic opportunity relates to the width and depth in the deployment of resources or endowments. The width concerns the quantifiable amount of resources, while the depth concerns how resources are being used in conjunction with numerous possibilities and noneconomic complementarities. Indeed, it is probable that economic outcomes are different given a similarity in factor endowment between two individuals or two economies, but the economic opportunity available to the two individuals or economies would differ, and that would lead to divergence in economic outcomes.

The 2014 Nobel Peace prize was awarded to two individuals, Malala Yousafzai and Kailash Satyarthi, for their efforts on the right for all children to receive education and the right against child oppression. In particular, at the age of only 17 years, Malala Yousafzai has become the youngest winner of the prize. Being citizens from India and Pakistan respectively, these awardees symbolize the need to eradicate and fight against various forms of human inequality, deprivation, discrimination, alienation, exploitation, and unfairness that would have a lifetime impact on children, either because of their sex, religion, or the region which they come from. Indeed, much of the origins of these human inequalities are related to the culture, customs, and religion of the particular region or country.

Fighting human inequality can be a generation-long battle, but income inequality is an economic issue that can be changed over time. This chapter focuses on the relationship between income inequality, poverty, and opportunity. It is argued that income inequality may not be detrimental if there are other complementary conditions that would allow individuals to have "second chances" in their economic life. It would be a conflicting goal if societies on the one hand devoted resources to train able and productive individuals, but on the other hand lamented the difference in the rewards received by trained individuals. Due to the presence of endowment-low individuals, there are always cases of "poverty." Therefore, attention should be devoted to eradicate poverty rather than focus on income inequality.

II INCOME INEQUALITY: BASIS OF COMPARISON

The Lorenz curve (Lorenz, 1905) has become the most common graphical presentation to show the extent of income inequality. Fig. 2.1 shows the typical Lorenz curve with the cumulative share of income earned on the vertical axis and the cumulative share of population on the horizontal axis. The cumulative share in both cases range from 0% to 100%. The diagonal 45 degrees line is the line of perfect equality. One usual interpretation is to see how the poorest 20% of the population performed on the income scale, namely the percentage of income earned by the poorest 20% of households. One can then look at the income performance of the next poorest 20%, and so on. The "curve" indicates a deviation from the line of perfect equality and, normally, the poorest 20% of households would receive a much smaller percentage of earned income. On the contrary, the richest 20% of households would receive much more than 20% of earned income.

The Lorenz curve indicates the extent of income inequality. The further away the Lorenz curve is situated from the line of equality, the more unequally is income distributed, and vice versa. Income inequality can intuitively be measured by the ratio between area (A), namely the area between the line of equality and the Lorenz curve, and area (A + B), namely the entire triangular region underneath the line of equality. Income inequality indicated by the Lorenz curve can be shown by the ratio A/(A + B). An alternative measurement has popularly been calculated using the Gini Coefficient, or Gini Ratio (Gini, 1912). For individual world economies, periodic or annual data on the cumulative percentage of households and income earned are fed into a standardized formula to estimate the Gini Coefficient. *Wikipedia* has reported that the Gini Coefficient can be estimated from a number of mathematical formulae (Bronfenbrenner, 1971; Johnson, 1973; Sen, 1997; Aghion et al., 1999; Silber, 1999; Cowell, 2000).

The Gini Coefficient estimate normally ranges from 0 to 1. The closer it is to 0, the more equally is income distributed. Income inequality rises as the Gini Coefficient approaches 1. Typically, economies reaching a Gini Coefficient of 0.6 or above are said to be approaching extreme inequality. Low-income or developing countries tend to have a higher Gini Coefficient than advanced or industrialized countries (Zhou and Li, 2011; Li and Zhou, 2013). Inequality measurements have been extended to numerous empirical studies in individual economies and over different economic issues. Salverda et al. (2011) extended income inequality to individual advanced countries, while other studies concentrated on inequality performance in different Asian countries (Birdsall et al., 1995; Haggard, 2016).

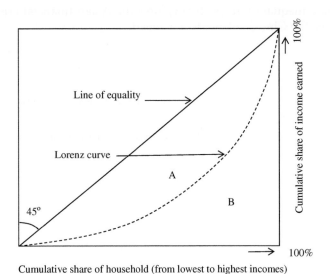

FIGURE 2.1   The Lorenz curve.

While income inequality measurement has been used extensively, there are numerous studies pointing to the inadequacies of the Gini Coefficient measurement. Some studies queried the simplicity of the income inequality measure and suggested the inclusion of other economic variables to make judgments on economic inequality, including considerations of welfare policy, tax policy and social opportunity, morality and justice (Rawls, 1971; Meade, 1976; Blackcorby and Donaldson, 1978; Dworkin, 1981; Frankfurt, 1987; Arneson, 1989; Young, 1994; Bénabou, 1996). Sen (1991, 1993) developed a normative theory based on the "capability and functioning" of individuals and argued that "the capability of a person reflects the alternative combinations of functioning the person can achieve." Sen (1997) proposed five types of parametric variations: personal heterogeneities, environmental diversities, variations in social climate, differences in relational perspectives, and distribution within the family. Other studies supported the importance of "equality in opportunity" (Frankel, 1983; Coleman, 1983). The validity of equality as a social ideal has been raised by Letwin (1983) and Lucas (1983). The ultimate explanation is that income inequality discussion is a mixture of an economic outcome within the social and political context.

There can be a number of other considerations in income inequality measurement. One is the difference between an "inter-personal" comparison and an "intra-personal" comparison. An inter-personal comparison in income inequality is a comparison between any two or more persons at a particular point in time, as indicated by the Gini Coefficient that shows a "snapshot" of income differences among different persons. By looking at two or more persons, it is true that one person will be "richer" than another person. This is the essence of the Gini Coefficient when you put all individuals into one single scale at a particular point in time. Such a simplistic approach faces many problems. One is the age of the population, as usually young workers tend to have a lower income earning capacity than more experienced middle-aged workers. Different stages of the business cycles could show different income distributions. After a major financial or economic crisis where people's income tends to fall, the Gini Coefficient would naturally show deterioration, as there would be fewer high-income earners and more low-income earners (as income fell resulting from the crisis).

Consider the situations shown in Fig. 2.2 and assume the triangle "abc" as the original pattern of income inequality, with a rather low Gini Coefficient of, say, 0.35. A financial crisis emerged and the negative economic shock led to a fall in income, the number of high-income earners shrunk, and the number of low-income earners expanded, resulting in a situation indicated by the triangle "def." By comparison, triangle "def" produced a more unequal economy than triangle "abc," and the Gini Coefficient would have deteriorated, say to 0.38. Hence, business cycles and unfavorable financial shocks that led to economic downfall literally produced a more unequal economy. The fall in the number of high-income earners is indicated by the vertical downward arrows, while the expansion in the number of low-income earners would be indicated by the horizontal arrows pointing out from triangle "abc" to triangle "def." Since the low-income population indicated by the horizontal distance "ef" is bigger than the distance "bc" after the crisis, it follows that the extreme between the high-income point "a" and the low-income earners of "bc" is more severe than the extreme between high-income point "d" and the low-income distance "ef." Income inequality has deteriorated. This will become a general phenomenon when economies are faced with sudden crisis. For example, both the Hong Kong economy and the US economy suffered deterioration in income inequality, respectively, after the Asian financial crisis in 1998 and the financial crisis in 2008. In both situations, the Gini Coefficients worsened.

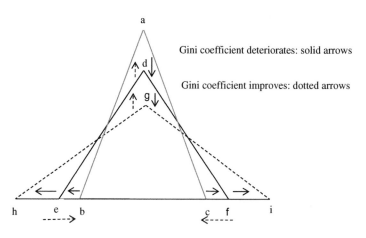

FIGURE 2.2 The income inequality triangle.

Immigration can be another factor in determining the Gini Coefficient. In some countries rules and standards would be imposed to screen the new immigrants so that newly arrived immigrants would not fall into the welfare net and immediately impose a burden on the fiscal purse. Hence, the increase in population will not mean an increase in the number of poor seeking welfare assistance. In Hong Kong, the deterioration of the Gini Coefficient after 1998 was worsened by the number of unqualified immigrants from mainland China for the purpose of "family reunions" at a daily quota of 150 households, who would likely be unskilled and would seek welfare assistance upon arrival. Such an inflow of unqualified migrants would lead to a rise in the low-income population that further pull the inequality triangle down to "ghi," and the extreme between high-income point "g" and the low-income population indicated by the horizontal distance "hi" shows a further deterioration in income inequality. The Gini Coefficient would have further deteriorated, say to 0.44.

The solution to the deterioration in income inequality should be a rise in income that permits and encourages upward mobility. In other words, the Gini Coefficient will improve over time if income rises and movement in the triangle is reversed in Fig. 2.2. As income rises, there would be fewer low-income earners and more high-income earners, and the shape of the inequality triangle should move from triangle "ghi" upwards to "def," and eventually upwards to "abc." As such, the Gini Coefficient would improve, for example, from 0.45 down to 0.38, and would be lowered further to 0.35 eventually. Hence, the rise in income and a rise in employment possibilities should naturally improve income inequality, but would not eliminate inequality. The idea is that with rising income and job possibilities, individuals' economic welfare will be improved, and how unequal one individual is when compared to another individual may not be crucial or detrimental. In short, "intra-personal" inequality comparison is more important than "inter-personal" comparison. What is needed is how one individual could move up the income ladder, though there would still be a difference in income earned when compared to another individual, which cannot be eradicated due to differences in individual's endowment.

Hence, it would be more appropriate to engage in policies that promote jobs and possible rise in income, as this would narrow income inequality over time. Indeed, economic development among key Asian economies since the 1950s has shown that, as income increased between the 1960s and 1970s, income inequality had been narrowed and the Gini Coefficient improved in much of the 1980s. However, economic downfall as a result of the Asian financial crisis and the subsequent economic recession at the turn of the 21st century led to rapid deterioration in income equality, and this would result in deterioration in the Gini Coefficient.

It follows that improvements in income inequality might not be permanent, and the Gini Coefficient of any economy would move up and down depending on economic cycles. To reverse the trend of deterioration in income inequality, economic policies should be employment-enhancing. Indeed, one can argue that it would take a longer time to improve income inequality than for income inequality to deteriorate. A major and sudden crisis that resulted in recession would immediately result in deterioration in income inequality. But for income inequality to improve, the rise in income and employment would require time, as it would require other complementary activities, such as productive investments that are job-enhancing.

There can be numerous faults in the "inter-personal" comparison of income inequality, as the Gini Coefficient is just a "snap shot" that shows a static picture of where individuals stand on the income scale. Time, age, sex, business cycles, immigration policy, geographical differences, and economic capability are not reflected in the Gini Coefficient measure. On the contrary, the "intra-personal" comparison would look into the income of an individual over time. Typically, a young person's income is lower, but there is an income ladder in most professions and jobs. When a young person is equipped with experience, the person will rise up the income ladder. The difference between inter-personal and intra-personal comparisons of income can be seen in Fig. 2.3 (Li, 2002, p. 8). The inner circle shows the original level of income and, for simplicity, there are two individuals, with individual A being the rich individual and individual B the poor individual. Income distribution or inequality is indicated by the areas A and B, respectively. Comparing areas A and B in the inner circle gives the inter-personal comparison.

With the rise in income and economic growth, the economy has expanded to the outer circle. However, even if the degree of inequality remained, the rich individual will now get A + A', while the poor individual will obtain B + B'. The intra-personal comparison for the rich individual A is between area A in the original level of income and area A + A' in the new level of income, while for the poor individual B the level is between area B and area B + B'. Thus, although it is true that income inequality remains (inter-personal comparison), the increase in the economic pie would benefit both (intra-personal comparison). Intra-personal comparison would mean that the rise in income and expansion of the economic pie is equally, if not more, important than simply focusing on the difference in the inter-personal comparison. Given that income inequality cannot be eradicated, it would be more pragmatic to consider "intra-personal" comparison that looked at the income ladder of an individual over

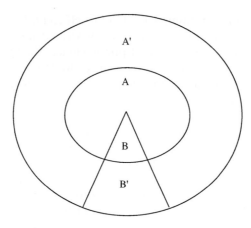

FIGURE 2.3   Inter-personal versus intra-personal comparison.

time, rather than the "inter-personal" comparison that defies the economic law of difference in productivity among individuals.

III POVERTY: STOCK VERSUS FLOW

It is worth having some discussion on "individual endowment." One assumes that "individual endowment" would become effective when an individual starts working full time. An individual's childhood and youth-hood life can make a huge difference to an individual's prework endowment. The individual's family background and circles, health, innate intelligence, educational achievement, and social and cultural environment can all be the determining factors in an individual's "starting point" when the individual enters the society to work. To begin with, different individuals will become employed at different ages, and that can determine the endowment "path" of the individual.

The basic endowment an individual has is the 24 hours of time per day. How an individual makes use of the daily hours can contribute to the "value-added" amount of an individual's endowment. The provision of one's physical labor is the lowest level of endowment an individual possesses. The "value-added" process can appear through various possibilities. Working with one's physical labor will normally give a lower value-added amount in the individual's endowment. An individual's endowment will increase if the individual's "value-added" figure includes skills and expertise, knowledge and information, creativity and innovation, entrepreneurship and talents, branding, and marketing. There is thus an endowment "ladder" among individuals, with some endowments having higher "value-added" and market returns than others.

Although "endowment inequality" forms the basis of income inequality, individuals can improve their endowment through various enhancement channels, such as taking up part-time education to enrich one's knowledge, vocational training to learn a skill, additional employment when the market conditions allow, or starting a small business. In other words, the advantage of a capitalist market economy is the availability and possibility of additional chances for individuals to improve their endowment over time. Nonetheless, there are at any particular point in time some endowment-low "poor" individuals. It is a social, civic, and ethical standard that the society should help "poor" individuals, though the policies differ considerably, producing different degrees of effectiveness.

One should start by examining the approach in solving the poverty issue. At any particular point in time, and whichever measure one uses, there is always a group of poor people who are faced with difficulty in economic survival. Consider the two approaches shown in Fig. 2.4. When quantified, a certain stock of poor individuals will be included in the "poverty pool." Welfare assistance will likely be confined to some sort of redistributive pecuniary assistance, which will expand the consumption and purchasing power of the people in the poverty pool. The policy recommendations will likely be "demand-driven," and the provision of cash as a transfer payment will ease the economic hardship of the poor people. This is a static approach to the poverty issue, and assumes that the same stock will remain. There is no long-term solution and the policy assumes these people will permanently need assistance.

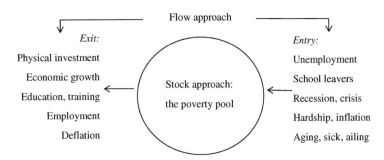

FIGURE 2.4 Stock versus flow approach to poverty reduction.

Fig. 2.4 suggests the "flow" approach as an alternative. The numbers in the poverty pool should not be considered as a static quantity, but are fluid as the poor could "flow" in and out of the pool. In other words, there will be new poor joining the pool, but there will also be people leaving the poverty pool. The ideal would be to minimize the number of entries and maximize the number of exits. As such, the success of a poverty reduction policy would be to shrink the poverty pool to its smallest possible size.

There are a number of factors that would lead to a rise in the size of the poverty pool, including a rise in unemployment, young school leavers, economic recessions, and crises that lead to a fall in investment and various kinds of social hardships; the aging population, the sick and ailing will all contribute to the enlargement of the poverty pool. These are the various kinds of endowment-low individuals that would fall into the poverty pool. Other possibilities include inflation and unqualified immigration that could possibly contribute to the size of the poverty pool. The dynamics of the "flow" approach assume that people would depart from the poverty pool and regain their endowment ability. Situations that facilitate people exiting from the poverty pool include an increase in physical investment so that employment and jobs are forthcoming. A rise in educational achievement and vocational training would enrich a person's employability. Economic growth and revival from crises and shocks would bring back jobs, especially in the upturn stage of the business cycle. A deflationary policy would increase purchasing power and people could afford to consume more, thereby improving their standard of living.

The flow approach considers the dynamics of the poverty issue, and instead of looking at the quantity of poor alone, it considers the possibilities of "entry prevention" and "exit promotion." There should be different policies that address these two possibilities. Namely, there should be policies that prevent people from entering the poverty pool, and policies that help people to exit from the poverty pool. However, given the inter-connected nature of economic policies, it is possible that some policies can serve both functions. Expansion in physical investment will lead to economic growth and employment, and the rise in job opportunities will lower unemployment. The reduction in unemployment should help people to exit the poverty pool, and at the same time prevent people from entering the poverty pool. Aging can lead to a rise in the poverty pool, but delaying the retirement age, for example, should provide more jobs for near-retiring workers. Additional provision of vocational training will enable school leavers to gain more vocational skills and at the same time, a greater chance of gaining jobs will in turn enable more school leavers to exit the poverty pool.

When compared to the stock approach that considers the mainly "demand-driven" policy of welfare provisions, the flow approach will need to institute "supply-driven" policies that enlarge the physical capability of the economy. It is true that "supply-driven" policies are more sustainable than "demand-driven" policies in solving the poverty problem, because "supply-driven" policies ensure that they have their own ability to stay in the job market. The difference, as the metaphor suggests, is whether you are "giving a fish to the person" or "teaching the person how to fish."

The overall consequences would be similar to the discussion of "supply-side" economics, where investment enhancement would promote employment, the rise in employment would result in a rise in the standard of living, and the rise in earnings would in turn provide a greater tax potential to the government. The rise in tax revenue on the one hand, and the reduction in welfare spending on the other hand, will enable the government to have more fiscal resources to spend on productivity enhancing items. Hence, the problem of poverty is not so much the existence of poverty, but the policy adopted by governments to reduce poverty could be the more crucial and determining factor. If the stock approach is adopted in dealing with the level of poverty, a pro-welfare, short-sighted government regime would obviously choose to opt for larger government expenditure to rescue the poor, with no regard to the fiscal ability of the economy. In some ways, welfare policy can be "self-fulfilling," as more welfare assistance is given, and since welfare assistance is mainly "demand-driven," enabling the recipients to spend and not to work, it is likely that more recipients would opt for the "free lunch" nature of welfare assistance. Hence, more welfare is needed in the next round of assistance, and such a "welfare-breeds-welfare" scenario could easily be built up.

On the contrary, if the flow approach was adopted, a multidimensional policy will be needed to prevent entry on the one hand and facilitate exit on the other. A multidimensional policy will relate improvements in human capital development, and a business-friendly environment would attract more investment. Over time, the "supply-driven" policy should reduce the size of the poverty pool as additional jobs are forthcoming and upward mobility should improve the inequality indicator. As compared to the stock approach, where the increase in welfare assistance is expected, the multidimensional policy in the flow approach would form part of the overall process of economic growth.

Which approach is adopted will depend on both the resource factor and the human factor. Resource-wise, the government has to ensure that there is sufficient fiscal resource without having to pile up a large fiscal debt. On the contrary, the human factor will involve three related issues: the political insight of the governing regime, the nature of the funding body especially if it has to come from foreign institutions, and the ideology of the officials directly involved. Bearing in mind that there are always some individuals having difficulty with economic survival, the question is how to minimize the number of needy individuals at all times.

The flow approach in dealing with the poverty issue shows that poverty is not a "one-time" problem, but continuous efforts are needed. Indeed, the poverty issue differs between countries. In development studies, poverty has been associated with low levels of development, or regions lacking modernization, such as in sanitation, clean water supply in remote areas, health and prevention of disease, infrastructure like transportation, and sustainable living conditions are the various factors that contribute to poverty. While different national governments will have their own poverty-reduction agenda, it has been a constant issue among world organizations. In September 2000, for example, the United Nations (2000) launched the Millennium Development Goals (MDGs) that aimed to reduce global poverty, promote prosperity, and sustain development. A total of eight goals ranging from reducing poverty by half, provision of universal primary education, and halting the spread of HIV/AIDS were specified, with a target date of 2015. By 2014, the United Nations reported that the MDGs have shown great impact on millions of lives, but much remains to be done. There will be another "development agenda beyond 2015" that will continuously address issues related to inequalities and sustainable development in the form of climate change and disaster risk reduction.

The World Bank (2013) also made a similar call for poverty reduction and reported that more than 1 billion people still live in destitution; the goal is to end extreme poverty in one generation and to reduce inequality in developing countries. Additional measurements and indicators in the form of a "Shared Prosperity Indicator" will be used to check the income growth of the poorest 40% in each developing country. Similarly, the Asian Development Bank (2014) has focused its attention on poverty in Asia, and reported that "more than 700 million people in Asia and the Pacific live below the global poverty rate of $1.25 per day." The 2014 study "redefined" poverty in Asia and the Pacific to include "the cost of living in the region, the impact of spikes in food prices and the poor's rising vulnerability to calamities, crises and other shocks." The continuous efforts by international organizations on poverty reduction confirm that poverty is more of a flow problem than a stock problem. Indeed, it is not the quantity that is in question, but the continuous emergence of new poor as a result of changing human conditions. For example, the outbreak of the Ebola epidemic in the West African states will not only rewind development backwards, but will create a new round of poverty for residents in that part of the world.

However, one can recognize that the poverty issue in many underdeveloped countries concerned absolute poverty, whereby the conditions for economic progress are missing or not instituted. Typically, modern economic progress cannot be made if the society's development is still in its primitive and tribal stage. Weak governance in many fragile states imposed much hardship and uncertainty on their own citizens, resulting in large flow of illegal immigrants to neighboring countries. In these extreme cases, it would be inappropriate to exercise the concept of "poverty" into these underdeveloped societies where economic gains and welfare cannot constitute nor improve their daily living standards. As such, one is dealing with underdevelopment, rather than poverty. It would be useless to impose a poverty line if money was rarely used as the medium of exchange, work was not paid by wages, and food supply was made through hunting or people were living off their farming life in precivilized societies. What should be needed in these societies is not to eradicate poverty, but to help them to take up modern life in preparation for possible economic progress.

IV INEQUALITY AND DEVELOPMENT

The relationship between income inequality and economic development has popularly been characterized by the Kuznets' inverted-U curve (Kuznets, 1955), which argued that income inequality tends to increase at an initial stage of development and then decrease as the economy develops, implying that income inequality will fall as income continues to rise in developing countries. However, when income has kept rising and reached a high level, income inequality increases again. The intuition of the inverted-U curve is that when an economy's income is at a low level, there are only a few rich individuals, and the Gini Coefficient will be quite extreme. As the overall income increases, it is accompanied by a rise in employment and job opportunities. This will result in upward mobility on the income ladder, and a middle class of income earners will emerge, thereby improving the Gini Coefficient. This is the prediction of the Kuznets' relationship that inequality improves as income expands. However, when an economy's income level keeps rising to a high level, there are more people who could achieve high incomes. Portfolio investment and windfall gains from speculation in stocks and property, for example, can result in the rise of super-rich individuals (Piketty, 2014). And while the majority of the population is engaged in paid jobs, income inequality will deteriorate as a result. The inverted-U curve actually describes income at different stages of economic development (Chen, 2003).

The empirical studies on Kuznets' inverted-U relationship have been diverse. For example, whether the relationship can be considered as a law and improved through appropriate economic policies has been studied. Depending on the use of econometric modeling, Kuznets' inverted-U relationship could face misspecification when parametric quadratic models are used, and nonparametric models using cross-sectional data have been used. Similarly, the use of control variables could be added in the regression model. Technically, some empirical studies have followed the original Kuznets' inverted-U relationship and examined its total effect, instead of its direct effect, of development on inequality by using unconditional models. Such an econometrics specification considered the inequality–development relationship as a law, and minimized the impact of economic policy. Other studies considered the determinants of inequality and examined the impact of policy in affecting inequality. As such, the regressors in the regression model include other policy variables and/or economic indicators (Kanbur, 2000; Bulíř, 2001; Mushinski, 2001; Wan, 2002; Huang, 2004; Iradian, 2005; Lin et al., 2006).

The two empirical studies by Zhou and Li (2011) and Li and Zhou (2013) presented both the nonparametric (without control variables) and semiparametric (with control variables) investigations on the inequality–development relationship by using unbalanced panel data from 30 developed countries in the OECD and 45 non-OECD developing countries for the period 1962–2003. In both studies, the Gini Coefficient is used as the inequality proxy, while real GDP per capita is the proxy for economic development. In addition, to study the total relationship between inequality and development, the two studies examined the effect of development on inequality by controlling the effects of some variables on inequality, using such control variables as openness, urbanization, investment, growth, and inflation.

The first observation from the data is that non-OECD countries on average have larger inequality (Gini Coefficient of 0.445) and a larger variation than OECD countries (Gini Coefficient of 0.343), while OECD countries have higher levels of development with greater variations than non-OECD countries. Poorer countries are more unequal than rich countries, and the difference is quite large. There can be various reasons for the difference. Lack of institutional support would provide less economic security for individuals in non-OECD countries. Aspects of discrimination and inequality in poorer countries would restrict social mobility. Other possible reasons include the lack of infrastructure that made employment for the poor inaccessible. In premodern tribal societies, jobs done often were not paid in pecuniary terms.

The empirical results provided fresh lessons on the inequality–development relationship in the OECD and non-OECD countries. For example, the empirical results for both OECD and non-OECD countries showed the presence of turning points at both low and high levels of income, similar to other studies on the Kuznets relationship (Barro, 1991; Ram, 1991; Anand, 1993). For the OECD countries, inequality generally decreased with development, with the exception of an upturn at a higher income level. The control variables helped to reduce income inequality at lower income levels, but they tended to increase inequality when development exceeded a threshold level. For the non-OECD countries, the inequality–development relationship appeared to be in a "roller coaster" mode with two turning points, and one upturn appeared at a very high income level. When compared to the performance in OECD countries, the effect of development on inequality via the control variables was always negative in non-OECD countries, except after an upturn at a high income level. Non-OECD countries faced serious inequality at the middle or high income level.

One can conclude that the lack of economic development could be the reason for the higher level of income inequality among developing countries. Very often, the modern form of employment could not increase and mobility could not occur if the level of economic development was below a certain threshold level. For example, economic openness has been considered as an important element in economic development (Li and Zhou, 2010). A certain level of industrialization and infrastructure achievement are needed before employment can occur and income can increase, which in turn could have multiplying impact on upward mobility. Indeed, it is the reduction of poverty that is more crucial than the lessening of income inequality. Ultimately, it is economic growth that will reduce poverty, though in the process of poverty reduction there is the possibility of creating income inequality. The rise in income should permit mobility, but while it can generate inequality in the process, the more important principle is the equality in opportunity.

V GROWTH AND ECONOMIC OPPORTUNITY

New concepts are needed to understand poverty reduction, upward mobility, and income inequality. The first lesson in economics is that "supply creates its own demand," the second lesson in economics is that there are three factors of production: land, capital, and labor. Given the same amount of production factors, evidence shows that some countries are doing better than others. Indeed, it is possible to find that high-income countries have less natural resources than low-income countries, and resource-poor countries are performing stronger than resource-rich countries. There is thus an intellectual missing link in explaining such differences in the performance of countries with similar resource-endowments, or countries' economic performance and resource-endowment are inversely related. There are numerous theoretical and empirical studies discussing economic growth using data from world economies, as well as evidence from individual countries. Solow (1957) opened the theoretical discussion on exogenous growth, meaning that growth would be affected by factors that are outside the control or influence of the economy. The typical significant Solow exogenous growth factors include investment, population growth, and initial income level. Other examples of exogenous factors include foreign investment and trade, and such geographical factors as island economies or landlocked countries (Gallup et al., 1999; Sachs and Warner, 2001). Similarly, empirical studies have been conducted on growth variations among world economies (Romer, 1986; Levine and Renelt, 1992).

However, studies soon realized that many growth factors were affected by domestic conditions, and have come up with the endogenous theory of growth (Aghion and Howitt, 1998). Typical endogenous growth factors include education and human capital, health and mortality rate, and such other noneconomic factors as economic freedom, corruption, and independent judiciary. These are "endogenous" in the sense that these factors can be controlled within the economy itself. The domestic performance on education can influence the extent of human capital, but education spending is determined by the domestic government. Nonetheless, empirical studies have used large numbers of exogenous and endogenous factors to explain growth (Durlauf and Quah, 1999; Sala-i-Martin et al., 2004; Durlauf et al., 2005). Empirical growth studies have extended to discussion on growth and income convergence across world economies, with the intention of analyzing how low income countries could catch up with high income countries (Quah, 1996; Li et al., 2016).

One explanation on the lack of uniformity among growth studies is the possibility of a missing conceptual link. The fact that studies used many quantifiable variables in their explanation may have reflected only the "extensity" of the available variables. Namely, studies have taken into account only the "width" of the existing variables. Variations in the impact on growth, however, could exist in relation to how these existing variables were used. The condition in which the variables had been exercised and how the variables were used in combination with other variables might not be able to be distinguished or separately captured in the growth empirical studies. In other words, there exists an "intensity" dimension that shows the "depth" through which variables were used. The "intensity" factors could be the complementarity from available infrastructure, or how resources can be extended when new investment appeared. Other noneconomic factors, such as the independence of the judiciary, or the level of corruption can impact on such quantifiable variables as foreign direct investment and trade.

This intellectual gap has brought Li (2014b) to come up with an analysis on "economic opportunity" by arguing that where countries differed in their economic performance would be due to differences in the availability of economic opportunity. It is true that both the quantity and quality of production factors and resource endowments are crucial; what is equally important is whether the production factors can be put into effective use. The chance of a production factor being used comes under the availability of economic opportunity. Of course, the effective use of the production factor can relate to the discussion on efficiency, but the more important decision is whether the production factor was being used in the first place.

The term "economic opportunity" has not been analyzed as a topic on its own. Following the use of an "idea" gap in Romer (1993), Li (2014b) regarded economic opportunity as an "internality" that impacted growth and development potentials as a result of certain economic activities. Conceptually, economic opportunity possesses the following features: intuitive, invisible, intangible, nonquantifiable, and immeasurable, but it is cumulative and multiplicative. Instead of the traditional input—output analysis, Li (2014b) argues that economic opportunity can be seen in a process that indicates the degree of effectiveness between an *ex ante* situation, where there are production factors, and an *ex post* situation where economic outcomes are generated. Hence, economic opportunity serves as "a channel through which possibilities and chances are created from extensive and intensive application of production factors" (Li, 2014b).

As economic opportunity is conceptual and cannot be measured, it can empirically be treated as a latent variable predicted by other observable variables (Joreskog and Goldberger, 1975; Loehlin, 1998). Conceptually, economic opportunity can be studied through other variables that can either expand the amount of available resources or increase economic activities, given the available production factors. The two channels used to study economic opportunity empirically are the "extensity" channel relating to the "width" of available resources and the "intensity" channel indicating the "depth" through which economic opportunities are generated from available resources. The "intensity" channel includes other socioeconomic, political and environmental variables in the measurement. Li (2014b) identified a sample of 184 economies for a period of 11 years from 2000 to 2010. Economic opportunity can be indicated by its *ex post* outcomes, such as outputs in industry, services and exports, employment, and communication. The six proxies for the "extensity" channel are the physical resources available either from domestic origin, such as domestic investment, market capitalization and bank credits, or from foreign sources, such as portfolio inflow, foreign direct investment, and official foreign aid. The "intensity" channel poses a challenging decision in the choice of variables, as they can come from different qualitative categories, such as education, health, political factors, environmental, and business factors. After making appropriate tests on the variables, the nine "intensity" proxies can be classified into measures of the quality of life, health and education, and human rights.

After standardizing the data, Li (2014b) first applied principle component analysis (PCA) to construct the three indices for economic opportunity, extensity, and intensity for the whole sample period. The advantage of PCA is that it selects the weights by the data itself. The empirical study began by calculating the weights, mean, and median values of the whole sample and the two subsamples of OECD and non-OECD economies. For the three indices, the mean and median values of OECD economies are higher than non-OECD economies. Among the various weights, there are a couple of observations worth mentioning. For example, in the proxies for economic opportunity, export and communication have higher weights, implying the importance of economic openness. Among the intensity proxy variables, the weight for human rights is higher than the weight for education, implying that political maturity can have a positive impact on economic opportunity.

In the empirical study, the economic opportunity index becomes the dependent variable, while both the extensity index and intensity index are the independent variables in the regression analysis. The empirical study uses both parametric and nonparametric equations. The empirical results of the parametric analysis for the whole sample for individual years showed that the extensity channel is more important than the intensity channel. For the non-OECD countries, the intensity variables are not as useful as the extensity variables in the creation of economic opportunity, due probably to their lower level in various intensity variables. However, the nonparametric results provided more interesting results, as they provide the contingent relationship between the marginal effects of the two indices on the growth of economic opportunity. The two observations from the whole sample suggested that the extensity index is more relevant than the intensity index to economic opportunity. First, at low level of extensity, the increase in extensity can promote economic opportunity, but the impact is constrained by the intensity index. Second, an improvement in the intensity index does produce a positive marginal effect of extensity on economic opportunity.

The nonparametric regression estimates for the OECD countries show that the marginal effects of both intensity and extensity indices on growth of economic opportunity are positive when the extensity index is high. Similarly, the marginal effect of extensity on economic opportunity is positive when the intensity index is high. For the non-OECD countries, the nonparametric estimates show that at low levels of the extensity index, the marginal effects of extensity on economic opportunity are positive and significant. This is an important finding, that the availability of more capital resources would help non-OECD countries to generate more economic opportunity when they experienced a low extensity index. But then, the marginal effect falls when the extensity index reaches a higher level. This suggested that the effect of extensity on economic opportunity needs to have strong support from the intensity index. Thus, for non-OECD countries, an increase in the intensity index would produce a positive marginal effect of extensity on economic opportunity. The conclusion is simply that improvement in the intensity variables could increase the impact of extensity on economic opportunity in non-OECD countries.

Economic opportunity will become an innovative concept in market capitalism, as it reflects both the width and depth in the deployment of individual and societal resources and endowment, and provides an alternative to understand why countries can differ in their economic performance, given a similarity in resources and endowments. It is equally true that economic opportunity may not be quantifiable, but its conceptual implications are strong, powerful, and useful. The ultimate answer is that it is opportunity that counts in reducing poverty and promoting growth, and while inequality is inevitable it is wise to have effective policies that can narrow the inequality gap over time.

There are several messages provided by the analysis on economic opportunity. In addition to the scarcity in production factors, it is often not the availability of production factors that governed growth, but how the productions factors are used, along with other supporting factors, such as infrastructure provision, business-friendly government, reliable institutions, macroeconomic stability, and so on. The production factors merely show the "width" in economic opportunity analysis, but they cannot explain why growth differed among countries with similar backgrounds in the provision of production factors. Collectively, economic opportunity reflects the "depth" at which production factors are being used in the process of growth.

VI CONCLUSION

One major feature of capitalism is that individuals are responsible for their own wellbeing through their own ability and possession of endowments. Yet, individuals are given their chances in gaining and improving their endowment through education, training, property rights protection, and markets. The society consists of individuals, and no two individuals are the same in their economic behavior. As such, it would be natural to have different outcomes among individuals in any economy, and it may not be appropriate to assume or impose income equality on economic behavior with different outcomes among individuals. It has been shown that static, "snap shot" inter-personal comparisons can provide an indicator of income inequality, but it has various disadvantages as it simply compares individuals without taking into account such factors as age, experience, business cycles, migration, and extent of social mobility. Intra-personal comparison examines the same individual over time, as a young person will most likely earn less than a more experienced person in their life-long income path.

In economics, income is a term for the return on an individual's productivity. Equality is more of a political criterion and social desire than an economic outcome. Given that individuals are different, it would also be true that income inequality arises as individuals maximize the return on their endowment. The society should not penalize able individuals that drive the economy forward. Rather, there are always endowment-low individuals who have economic survival problems. More attention should actually be given to the poverty issue. Similarly, poverty is not only a quantity problem, as there are "new" poor every day. While policies are needed to reduce the "stock," the more challenging aspect is the "flow" of poverty that examines dynamically the in-coming and out-going of poor individuals.

Poverty reduction requires "supply-side" economic policies. Increases in investment and business prosperity are the answers to poverty reduction. This in turn permits the creation of economic opportunities that can benefit the economic welfare of individuals. Higher economic welfare raises the possibility of upward mobility, while an increase in purchasing power gives rise to consumption and new economic opportunities in other areas. The economic opportunity multiplier will give rise to an economic virtuous cycle of growth, development, prosperity, and stability. Eventually, the expansion in economic opportunity will promote stability as individuals are engaged in their own activities, and stability comes with peace and progress.

Indeed, while the society encourages the able individuals to do better, the society will also have a strong ethical standard of assisting needy individuals so that the less-able individuals will be given a second chance. Indeed, it is true that education resources are given to the academically and intellectual able students, but individual abilities can emerge at different stages of life. A mature and diversified society will embrace and accept differences in economic performances. At the same time, there should be appropriate and sufficient institutions that will alleviate the difficulties some individuals face. It is the individual's innate ability, talent, educational qualifications and training that society will make use of. As such, opportunities should be given equitably to individuals, so that they can express and perform to their economic best. It is necessary to make a distinction between income inequality and human inequality. Provided there are institutions that help to eliminate extreme forms of income inequality, it is the various forms of human inequality that are more detrimental to individuals than income inequality in modern societies.

CHAPTER

3

Role of Government

OUTLINE

I INTRODUCTION

The discussion on the role of government does fall into the three academic disciplines of politics, economics, and sociology. In the politics discipline, the state includes all sovereign institutions, while the government represents the administrative ruling body. Hence, depending on popularity and political sentiments, the elected government comes and goes depending on the term of office specified in the country's constitution. The government forms the administration that is composed of numerous bureaux and departments that execute and implement policies (Niskanen, 2007; Self, 2010). In a laissez-faire economy, economic freedom is promoted and guaranteed in the hands of individuals who conduct businesses, engage in professions, or serve as workers, the government merely takes a back seat to facilitate the functioning of the private sector as much as possible, though a minimal level of assistance provided to needy individuals will be expected. The economic role of the government was highlighted after the Second World War, when postwar development was needed. It was Keynes (1926, 1937) who advocated the role of government in solving economic problems in times of economic recession when the government could adopt a "demand-driven" strategy that could spend its way out to reduce unemployment, and rescue private consumption.

There are a large number of studies debating the role of government as to whether the fiscal instrument the government uses would be growth-promoting. Tanzi and Schuknecht (1997, p. 168) concluded that "pressures for more spending are now clearly recognized as coming from *vested* interests rather than from the *public* interest," and that "many now realize that higher public spending is not necessarily the cure to many societal problems and does not necessarily contribute to higher wellbeing." Such a conclusion echoed the remark by Friedman (1993) that when making a contrast between a failed business enterprise and an inefficient government department, a loss-making business enterprise would close down, while a financially weak government department would even be expanded and more public resources could be committed to it. Other debates on the economic role of the government concerned the size of the government in relation to growth, policy effectiveness, and macroeconomic stability, and distortions in the development process (Ihori, 1978; Kruger, 1990a; Blanchard, 1984;

© 2017 Elsevier Inc. All rights reserved.

Tanzi 1995; Alesina and Wacziarg, 1998; Stiglitz, 1998; Fatás and Mihov, 2001; Garen and Trask, 2005; Andrès et al., 2008).

The role of government in the process of industrialization in developing countries has been a concern, as the debate has been divided on whether the government should form an industrial policy that involved the commitment of resources to R&D (Amsden, 1989; Smallbone and Welter, 2001). In promoting businesses, the tripartite relationship among "government – business – academics" has been successfully conducted in Japan's industrial strategy (Johnson, 1982; Leydesdorff and Etzkowitz, 1996; Leydesdorff, 2000; Etzkowitz, 2003). The advantage of the tripartite relationship is that while the academics did the innovative research work, business conducted the investment, and the government carried out appropriate policies for industrial development and export.

From the development experience of the four East Asian economies of Hong Kong, Singapore, South Korea, and Taiwan, Li (2002) suggested the metaphors of "fertilizer, pillar, and carpet" to symbolize the indirect nature of government. The use of economic "fertilizer" could bring a better harvest. The idea is that the government will institute some market instruments that could be used by businesses and employers in order to enhance their output. Economic "fertilizer" can be in the form of a reliable low tax system, or the establishment of market-friendly institutions that can be used by the business sector. The economic "pillar" means that the government will help to promote a few industries or businesses that would promote comparative advantage. While the economy is enjoying the success of some economic pillars, the government may have to explore new areas of comparative advantage so that there will be new economic pillars for future development. The metaphor of "carpet" deals with the need to provide welfare assistance to individuals, and that no endowment-low individuals will fall below the "carpet." This redistributive role of the government will be discussed in the "demand-led" approach. Equally, the government should welcome individuals who can rise above the carpet as much as possible, as suggested by the "supply-led" approach that the more able individuals are, the less the need for government assistance, and the more resources the government has in promoting, enhancing, or enlarging the capacity and capability of the economy.

A brief literature review on the role of the government can show that the discussion could expand into more than one discipline, and more than one area within the same discipline. Nonetheless, the role the government plays is ideological and is typically torn between the two extremes of least interventionist and heavily interventionist. Economies that adhere to capitalism and free markets tend to practice a lower degree of government intervention and leave the economy more to the private sector in conducting economic activities. Typically, government tends to be more interventionist, at least in the short-term when economies are faced with recessions. There are two broad types of economic intervention in a capitalist economy where private ownership is cherished. One type of government intervention can largely be grouped under infrastructure provision. One major feature of the infrastructural provisions is that they are meant to facilitate the "supply-side" of the economy, allowing businesses and individuals to have an easier way of going about their daily activities. The other type of government intervention can be regarded as redistribution.

It is possible that a government can experience a conflict between the two types of economic intervention. While infrastructure provision could enhance economic potential and nurture favorable conditions for growth and development, politics is often involved in redistributive policies, such as to what extent redistribution can be regarded as optimal. The extent of economics in the political debate is whether welfare assistance is sustainable in terms of fiscal capability, and the disincentive effect so generated from welfare provisions. One crucial consideration in the calculation is that once provided, welfare expenditure is "sticky" and cannot be reduced easily, but the government's fiscal capability can vary depending on the resulting disincentive to business and changes in the business cycle. In short, there is no guarantee whether the government will have the long-term fiscal ability to provide when a permanent welfare spending commitment is made.

In a socialist economy where state ownership is common, it would be the state that runs the economy. Individual incentives would be eliminated, as everyone would follow directives and instructions, while the state would be the sole decision-making body through various bureaux and departments. As such, the economy would be faced with an extreme form of intervention, as individuals' welfare would be "looked after" by the government, while private businesses could not exist due to the absence of property rights. Such kinds of intervention look "equal," as all individuals would receive the same economic treatment, but surely inequality would have shifted from economic to political inequality that could be more detrimental, irrevocable, and life-long.

It has been a common misconception that the government is powerful in that it has the authority to tax and the power to spend without knowing that the government, like any other individual, is equally faced with constraints on the ability to tax and the spending limit. Such a misconception could arise from a number of wrong assumptions that the government is powerful, has all the knowledge, and is equipped with able officials. There is some truth in the fact that some government activities would contribute positively to the economy, but government is composed of officials who could also make mistakes, pursue wrong policies, and show inaccurate calculations. Very often, governments are faced with political pressures that require short-term results that might have long run negative distortions and corrections which could be costly.

The reality is that the government itself can be a problem, but no economy can get rid of the government. It would thus be appropriate to see how best the government can do in order to make its existence useful and meaningful. A reliable government should have developed a system such that the most talented individuals are recruited, and avoid unwanted cronyism in the choice of selection and promotion of government officials. The truth is that the government normally monitors the various aspects of the economy, but there should be sufficient channels and avenues so that the activities of the government could also be monitored effectively.

The three economic roles of government are: developmental, monitorial, and redistributional. Each of these three roles contains a number of related activities that serve different functions. The more controversial and challenging role is the redistributional role. Two opposing approaches are discussed and compared. The "demand-led" approach considers the use of welfare as an instrument of redistribution, and on the contrary, the "supply-led approach" is used to compare whether the government can indirectly help individuals' economic survival. Before concluding, this chapter discusses the minimum wage legislation, which in effect turns out to be the "maximum wage." The difference in the goal of business leaders and political leaders helps to show how political and government leaders should manage the economy.

II THE DEVELOPMENTAL ROLE

The "developmental" role covers a discussion of three types of economic provisions: infrastructure, common goods, and public utilities. Infrastructural development can be both physical and nonphysical (Picot et al., 2015). Physical infrastructure consists of such basic physical provisions as sewage clearance, street lighting, and road networks. Physical infrastructure developments are costly and require periodic improvements and extensions. But, once constructed, the infrastructure could usually last for forever.

The government role in the building of infrastructure is that it provides positive and lasting social benefits to the public. These social benefits can roughly be quantified through a compounding exercise that estimates from all future gains discounted in today's price using the internal rate of return. One should not underestimate the positive economic multiplier effect of infrastructure, as individuals and businesses could utilize the infrastructure for economic activities. Hence, the economy gains in two aspects. One is that the same construction work will definitely cost more due to inflation the longer it waits. Second, there are multiplier economic benefits that arise from the new construction. One advantage of government involvement is to maximize the social benefits so that all individuals and businesses are free to utilize the infrastructure for their own purposes. The government will in turn benefit through the subsequent higher economic growth that eventually can provide more salary and corporate tax revenue to the government.

Infrastructure provisions can also be developed by private enterprise or some kind of joint venture or consortium, as private involvement can be more efficient and can provide the needed financial input. The public concern is whether private involvement in infrastructure leads to a high price in the future. The other alternative is for the government to fund the construction of infrastructure by issuing government bonds. The economic argument is that since the constructed infrastructure will benefit the future generations, it would be right to use future resources through the issuing of government bonds to pay for the construction, and it will have to be the responsibility of the future generation to pay back the cost of construction when the duration of the government bonds mature. For developing countries, another alternative is to seek international assistance. The impact of infrastructure provision in developing countries tends to be cumulative and multiplicative, in that each additional piece of infrastructure provision can have an exponential contribution to growth and development. Basic life-survival infrastructure construction, such as the provision of clean water for irrigation, road construction to avoid seasonal flooding and facilitate the delivery of merchandise can help tremendously.

Infrastructure can be nonphysical in nature. This includes the establishment of sound institutions and systems. An effective government administration, for example, can serve as a showcase to other economic sectors and societal groups. A reliable rule of law provides confidence to businesses, while an anti-corruption body can equally demonstrate a high degree of fairness and transparency. Professional and social institutions serve as another piece of infrastructure that have a positive impact on the economy. Having more professional and nongovernmental institutions does not necessarily mean a bigger government, because institutions can have their own professional code of conduct and protocol to follow. Indeed, since professional institutions are normally independent agents, they can serve as an intermediary between the people and the government. Individuals and businesses can turn and seek help from professional institutions and organizations, and that in turn lessens the need to seek government assistance.

Both physical and nonphysical infrastructure provisions usually help to enhance the economy's future capacity and capability. Infrastructure development can extend to the provision of common goods, such as provision of public parks and museum. Common goods tend to provide more social benefits than economic benefits. The more controversial common good provision by the government is the funding of research and development (R&D) activities. On the one hand, R&D activities tend to be costly, as the outcomes might not have an immediate economic impact. The government's role in R&D development is often incorporated in an industrial policy. On the other hand, government involvement can be extensive and interventionist, resulting in large subsidy provisions and fiscal deficits. The argument is that R&D activities can also be considered as a private good, and that the property right of the R&D innovation will be enjoyed by private enterprise.

In a capitalist market economy, the developmental role of the government can generate a number of advantages. Through the development of infrastructure, the government does open up a number of "doors" that nurture growth and development. By absorbing the cost of infrastructure provision, the government can generate numerous social benefits. Expansion in economic activities will bring more government revenue in the form of tax, and the rise in opportunities will require less government assistance in terms of welfare. It follows that economic stability can be achieved as opportunities allow mobility. The development role is continuous, as additional infrastructure will be needed when the economy improves and grows. Different stages of economic development will require different types of infrastructure construction. While the provision of clean water can be the kind of infrastructure needed for a developing country, the provision of laws against cybercrime will be the kind of infrastructure needed in a high-technology economy.

Improvement in economic competitiveness is a well-known advantage. The provision of infrastructure, and the abundance of common good supply and advancement in R&D will definitely add to the attractiveness of the economy. Individuals can seek employment easily, businesses are encouraged as the social fabrics are reliable, and foreign investors can see the chance of economic and market progress. Research and development in science and technology can promote new technology for human consumption. Other institutional development can enhance the civic aspect of the economy. In a capitalist economy, innovation and creativity through either technological advancement or individual talents should have no boundaries.

III THE MONITORIAL ROLE

The monitorial role deals with various economic externalities rather than restricting activities. The institutional aspects of the monitorial role include the proper establishment of a legal system and structure, such that the rule of law is not only effective, but is seen to be fair, equitable, and can serve as a "level playing field" to all businesses and citizens. The establishment of civic institutions and professional bodies ensure that professional activities are guarded by code of conduct and practices, away from government pressures and political influence. By allowing the establishment of civic and professional establishments, the government can perform two related monitorial roles. On the one hand, these institutions assist the government to "monitor" the various professional and civic affairs, ensuring the achievement of a high standard. On the other hand, citizens can rely on or seek assistance from these institutions in various professional and civic activities, without having to deal with government departments and bureaucracies.

Depending on the stage of development, the government can raise the quality of life through the initiation of ethical standards and practices. Regulations that promote individuals' behavior can be instituted, such as anti-smoking campaigns and environmental conservation. Many countries have competition laws to prevent unfair trade and market manipulations. The intention is that all economic markets should be open and entry should not be restricted, though due to differences in capital requirements at the entry points, different markets may contain different patterns of corporate ownerships, with some markets having large corporations while other markets are composed of small- and medium-sized enterprises.

The implementation of different monitorial roles rests on a number of government bodies and departments. The military monitors the country's borders and security, the police force protects life and flight crimes, while the custom office ensures legality in trade flow, and the immigration department is the legal authority that checks the flow of people. To avoid abuses by government officials, there should be channels through which the monitorial role of the government can also be "monitored" by independent bodies. The monitorial role should be considered as a continuous task, since the need, pace, and dimension of the monitorial task can change with time. A typical example is the use of the internet which has facilitated communications tremendously, but the existence of cybercrime has become a new security and safety problem as it is invisible, noncontractual, and cross-border.

The monitorial role of the government in eliminating externalities should be preventive, so that externalities can in the first instance be avoided, but it should also serve as a cure so that rescue provisions and solutions to externalities can be made available. The monitorial role of the government can vary according to the size, custom compositions, and culture of the country. For example, whether the country is a religious state, or whether armory possession is a civic right, the monitorial role will vary in terms of service provisions and cost involved. The monitorial role of the government should be small in a well-functioning capitalist market economy, because since much of the economic activity is conducted in the private sector, the monitorial role simply functions like a "fire fighter" to ensure various legalities and nurture a sound market-friendly system that permits and encourages opportunities to grow.

The government's monitoring role should also be "forward looking," in that the establishment of rules, laws, and policies is best instituted in advance. This is particularly so when the economy is not experiencing a crisis situation. There are two possibilities in the "forward looking" behavior; it can either be "demand-following" or "supply-leading." A "demand-following" role is *ex post*, and relates to a situation in which the monitorial duty takes place after an event has happened. This is a kind of "learning from mistakes" attitude. Unexpected events can happen and will lead to destruction and loss of property and lives, but the government can then act to prevent the same problem occurring again. Preventive work is needed to ensure similar problems will not be repeated. The government in a "supply-leading" role is *ex ante*, and will plan ahead in anticipation of an unexpected event that can lead to loss of life and property.

Provision of education and improvement in social conduct and ethical behavior are the long-term effective means through which the government can help to promote openness, transparency, and equality. This is the long-term role and requires cooperation from various civic bodies. It is even more fundamental for the government itself to show good conduct and ethical behavior. When the government officials engage in corruption, cronyism, and serve their own vested interests, it will be difficult, or even impossible, for the government to execute the monitorial role effectively and productively. Therefore, good governance is the first necessary condition in the monitorial role of the government.

IV THE REDISTRIBUTIONAL ROLE: DEMAND-LED APPROACH

The discipline of economics concerns productivity, and return is "distributed" according to individuals' endowments. Under capitalism, resources will be allocated according to market forces. Redistribution is an artificial political move that suggests, despite differences in endowment among individuals, a more equal outcome in terms of earnings received by different individuals. In other words, despite the *ex ante* endowment gap among individuals, economic redistribution through the "visible hand" of the government would artificially narrow the *ex post* earning gap.

The "demand-led" approach deals mainly with the provision of welfare assistance, though schemes may have to be instituted to avoid abuse. Usually the criteria include a low level of earnings below which an individual family unit will be entitled to welfare assistance. The simple argument is that endowment-low individuals have survival problems economically, and the welfare provision will enable the person to stay at or above the economic survival "carpet." Welfare provisions financed through the use of high tax rates have become the most common form of redistribution. The "demand-led" nature of all welfare is that the welfare assistance will most likely be spent within a short time, and the recipients will not be expected to make any savings. While welfare assistance serves as a transfer payment in national accounting, the cash assistance will probably be consumed within a short time, thereby raising the level of aggregate demand in the economy. The first economic impact is that if the economy is near full employment, welfare spending would add to inflation, as the increased spending raises demand within a short period of time and suppliers would be reluctant to lower prices.

The second feature in the "demand-led" approach is that the welfare spending will not make any improvement in the endowment of the recipients. The recipient stays the same in terms of skill, knowledge, experience, and marketability. In other words, the welfare assistance helps the recipient to survive, but will not enable the individual to make progress. It is "giving the person a fish," rather than "helping the person to fish." The economic "pain" of the person can be eased with welfare support, but if the person makes no improvement, the person will become dependent on welfare assistance. The ethical issue is whether it is fair for an individual to rely on welfare assistance for a prolonged period of time, as the individual may become unmarketable in terms of employment.

A welfare assistance system usually works in such a way that once given, it will be impossible to withdraw. Hence, welfare spending in the fiscal framework can only increase, as it would politically be impossible to reduce the amount of welfare assistance. Furthermore, welfare assistance tends to increase in economic good times when the government could accumulate large fiscal resources. However, the dynamics of welfare assistance are that when the economy is faced with difficulty, the government may not have enough fiscal resources to support the welfare assistance. Indeed, in economic recessions, it is likely that the amount of welfare provision would even increase, while the fiscal ability is weakened by the fall in tax revenue. Welfare assistance spending can remain high even though the economy suffers from recession.

When the fiscal equation does not match, the government will face a fiscal deficit as welfare spending keeps rising, while the economic recession cannot provide the government with sufficient fiscal revenue. Another way of putting the point of a fiscal deficit is that the current generation has over-spent. To deal with the deficit, there is a need to cut other spending, which means that other fiscal expenditure items will face a reduction. If not, one other alternative is to issue treasury bonds. Bonds are basically long-term borrowings to be spent today, but the repayment would have to be made by the future generation. If the bonds are raised to pay for a fiscal deficit, the consequence will be an increase in national debt, especially if the bonds so raised are used for the consumption spending of the current generation. A "debt-breeds-debt" scenario can easily emerge if the raised bonds are used to pay for current debts. Then, it would require the government to issue more bonds in order to cover the deficits, and debts will further increase. Many pro-welfare economies end up accumulating an amount of national debts larger than the size of the GDP.

Conceptually, bonds issued today will have to be repaid in the future. Thus, one is spending the money of the future generation today, because the future generation will have to pay back the bonds issued today. Thus, when the future generation comes to realize that the large debt was passed on from the past generation, the welfare of the future generation would be negatively affected, as they would have to shoulder the debt burden accumulated by their former generation. Thus, national debts can become cross-generational. The economy simply left the debt level to deteriorate, until one day the country opts for default and cannot repay even the interest on the debts. The country would suffer, as the weak economy fails to recover, the large debt would weaken the currency, and the government would be faced with more deficits. There comes a time when bonds could not be issued, as investors have lost confidence. The country could have to go bankrupt unless there is foreign assistance, which could equally be difficult to come by. Studies have confirmed that large national debts will weaken economies, and the use of bonds and debts can be abused, as there could be vested interests involved (Dornbusch, 1987; Claessens, 1990; Cavanaugh, 1996; Velasco, 2000).

A high-welfare economy naturally requires the imposition of high tax rates. There has been the belief that a high tax rate can bring an increase in tax revenue. The debate in the Laffer curve has shown that a higher tax rate does not necessarily mean a high tax revenue. Indeed, there exists an "optimal" tax rate, below which a rise in tax rates can bring in more revenue, but above which a rise in tax rates effectively reduces tax revenue (Hemming and Kay, 1980; Buchanan and Lee, 1982; Bender, 1984; Malcomson, 1986; Agell and Persson, 2001; Laffer, 2004).

Fig. 3.1 reproduces the graphical presentation of the Laffer curve. When the tax rate rises, as indicated on the vertical axis, tax revenue indicated on the horizontal axis increases. The rise in revenue, however, will reach a maximum level, beyond which a further rise in tax rate will have a negative effect on tax revenue. The dotted line shows the optimal tax rate that gives a reverse movement in revenue as the tax rate keeps rising. A tax structure will include the four components of tax rate, tax items, tax efficiency, and tax population (Li, 2006, 2012a). The tax rate is simply the percentage of tax levied. The tax items show the number of items to be taxed. Tax efficiency reflects how effectively the tax policy has been executed. The tax population shows the number of persons and business corporations that are subject to tax. The government has the authority and power to decide the first three components, but cannot control the tax population. This is the power of the Laffer curve. While tax payers will feel obliged to pay tax as good citizens, the rise in tax rate would have a growing disincentive effect. Individuals have the freedom of working less, or professionals can migrate to a foreign low-tax country. Businesses can also invest in foreign tax-friendly countries. In other words, the tax rate and tax population

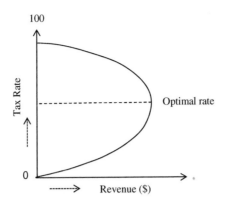

FIGURE 3.1 The Laffer curve.

should show an inverse relationship after a certain tax rate threshold. Hence, a fall in the tax population can produce lower tax revenues when the tax rate is too high.

Tax is always a disincentive, as it reduces individuals' earning power and businesses' return. Though it is agreed that the government has to commit to various fiscal expenditures, there is a level of "tax tolerance" beyond which the tax population would be discouraged. While excessive taxation will generate disincentive to the tax payers, excessive welfare provisions could discourage work, and could lead to abuse of the welfare system. The worst fiscal combination would be a falling tax population but a rising welfare commitment, as the government would end up with a fiscal deficit over time. In the long run, the economy would become uncompetitive, while domestic resources would migrate to business-friendly countries. The "demand-led" approach to redistribution that pledged short-term gains could end up with long-term losses.

Once resources have migrated to more business-friendly markets, they are unlikely to return. Hence, the loss of the home country's resources becomes the gain of the host country. Subsequently, there would be loss of employment and competitiveness. It could be worse if the country has to import back the goods, as that would lead to a loss of foreign earnings and a trade deficit. Second, once the resources have departed, the country is in turn becoming unattractive to foreign investment. Hence, there may not be any replenishment if the tax rates remain high and welfare expenditures remain large and the government is faced with increased debt. One could argue that the country's economic weakness as a result of the "demand-led" approach to redistribution is "homemade": it makes the domestic economy weak and uncompetitive, and unattractive to foreign investment. The economy can end up with a vicious circle of high tax, high welfare, low investment, low employment, low output, large fiscal deficit, and national debt, which in turn may require more welfare as unemployment rises. Poor economic performances would soon spill over to competitiveness, and poor performance in the external economy, such as trade deficits and pressure on currency depreciation.

In short, a "demand-led" approach to redistribution is an unsustainable policy that may have short-term alleviation, but the long-term damage is huge. The problem would be made worse when poor economic performance leads to unwanted and unintended political consequences that can have further destructive effects on the economy.

V THE REDISTRIBUTIONAL ROLE: SUPPLY-LED APPROACH

Given that any market economy cannot avoid the role of government, the more appropriate question is what the government can do in order to effectively and productively promote the economy so that economic competitiveness can be maintained, and economic capacity and capability can be enlarged. The intuition of the "supply-led" approach is that spending by the government will give rise to other productive activities so as to expand the output multiplier. The essence in the "supply-led" approach is that the government will indirectly assist to strengthen the individual in three different aspects. One aspect is to enhance the individual's market potential through establishing a market-friendly policy. Another aspect is to enhance the individuals' ability through the provision of adequate training and education, so that the individual can have stronger endowment. The third aspect is the provision of public goods and utilities so as to reduce the survival cost of individuals, and in turn maximize the purchasing power of individuals in ensuring a higher level of living standard.

There are typically three public goods of housing, education, and health that most individuals would find costly. However, one is not arguing for government intervention in these public goods, but some government provision could reduce the difficulties facing individuals. In some economically free and open economies, these goods are provided by the government as well as by the private sector. The "dual" supply enables individuals to have a choice between private or public medical care, and between private and public schools. Housing assistance can be provided to low-income earners, while high-income recipients can have the financial ability to purchase in the private market. A reduction in the individual's expenses on these public goods can allow them to have greater purchasing power for other private goods, and wages may not need to increase rapidly as their basic necessities are taken care of. Housing typically occupies the largest share of an individual's savings. The question is whether housing is considered as a necessity or a luxury good. Health expenditure can be high, depending on the physical health of the individual. Education expenses for children can be costly, and parents with low earnings may not have sufficient funds to educate their offspring well, thereby resulting in a possible situation of cross-generational poverty.

Controlling the portion of income that goes to pay for the individual's housing needs can have multiple economic advantages. The private sector should involve the purchase and transaction of luxury properties, and the market should be free for both developers and buyers to enter. Another market should consider housing as a necessity good, with the policy that all individuals should be housed as much as possible. The role of the government will be in the provision of housing to those in need, either the low-income earners or "sandwich class." One form of assistance is for the government to build public housing estates and rent to low-income earners at below-market price. The advantage of public housing provision is that the rental is affordable to low-income earners. The disadvantage is that the low-income earners will not have the chance to own a property, as the rental payment will not be capitalized. If their incomes remain low, these individuals will have to rely on public housing permanently.

One better possibility is for the government to exercise a "forced saving" option on the part of the low-income earners. Instead of public housing provision, the government can build and sell housing units at an affordable price, but instead of charging rent, the government can provide a "mortgage" to the occupants. Hence, instead of paying rent, the owner is actually buying the unit by paying a subsidized mortgage to the government. It may take a longer time for the mortgage to mature, but the housing units ultimately will be owned by the occupants. The amount paid by the occupant could be similar to the rent payments, but the difference is that the rental payments would be capitalized to form the future wealth or assets of the occupant. The "forced saving" principle is that the government is actually aiding low-income earners to save. Should one day the occupant have the ability to purchase in the private market, the occupant can sell the unit back to the government so as to have the financial capital for the new purchase in the property market. Such government "intervention" can be justified if the occupants would have their own property in the long run, as this is how individuals can become better off and enjoy their economic prosperity.

Furthermore, when the unit is sold back to the government, the government can in turn sell the unit to another needy individual. Such a principle, of course, will have to depend on a number of considerations, including: (1) the size of the population that needs help; (2) the cost involved and land provisions; (3) the administrative machinery involved in managing and monitoring the housing units; and (4) the price to be charged, whether it should be an average price, a cost-based price, or proportional to the market price. These considerations need to be addressed, but should not restrict the advantage arising from the "forced saving" principle.

Property purchase is considered as a "terminal" good, meaning that the individual would have to spend a lot on property, and these capital resources cannot be used for other activities. The "terminal" nature of property acquisition is that the financial resources cannot generate any productive activities. At most, new properties can boost sales in the furniture market, household appliances, and so on. On the contrary, if the resources are used to purchase and invest in machinery, the committed resources would subsequently lead to more productive output. Hence, it follows that when property acquisition becomes popular and large amounts of financial resources are committed to property purchase and development, other investment activities would be reduced, as there would be less funding involved in other forms of productive investment. Consequently, a "property-dominant" economy will become less competitive over time, as less investment is geared to industrial production.

In ethically-strong economies where housing is considered to be more of a necessity than an instrument of speculation, government policy should ensure that individual households will have the ability to acquire their own living space, but speculation will be restricted or discouraged. There are a number of economic instruments that can tackle property speculation. A free-tax on the individual's first home ownership could encourage property acquisition, but a high-tax on the second or subsequent property ownership would discourage speculation.

Other policies include the way land is supplied or sold, the behavior of property developers, and the extent of competition among developers.

Another major aspect of government assistance in the "supply-led" approach is education provision, as it involves the high cost and prolonged expenditure a parent or an individual has to commit. Education is a private good when every child has the chance to receive it, but it becomes a public good when there is a larger educated workforce. A larger educated workforce can have several economic advantages. One is the possibility of upward mobility as earnings should be higher when individuals receive higher education. High earnings would in turn provide more tax revenue to the government. Development in R&D and technology can be promoted with a skillful workforce. The government expenditure on education could be seen as a fiscal loop, because the spending on education today would produce a more qualified workforce with a higher ability to pay salary tax tomorrow.

While illiteracy has mostly been eradicated in modern economies, it is the level of education and the depth of knowledge that counts in terms of economic competitiveness, job security, and technological advancement. While education is a way to promote long-term economic development through the "supply-led" channel, it distinguishes the ability of different individuals. The education received by every young individual will open up an infinite number of opportunities and possibilities, so increasing the social benefit of an educated workforce. A common policy on education would be a compulsory number of years of schooling provided to a young individual, as that would ensure a minimum level of economic survival.

However, in order to avoid excessive government interference and a large fiscal burden, the government should also allow private provision of education at all levels, though the standards and professional practices have to be monitored and checked regularly to ensure quality. Private provision of education has several advantages. Effective business principles can be introduced in private education institutions. Since, in theory, private enterprises tend to be more efficient and cost-effective, their presence can serve as competitors and references to government educational institutions. It has been argued that private educational institutions serve the "privileged" class of rich parents, but it depends how the private education institutions are being regulated and monitored. Other than academic institutions that provide formal education, numerous vocational and skill-oriented training institutions can serve as educational supplements to absorb individuals who are weak academically. Indeed, there are numerous employment possibilities that require talents, skills, and creativity rather than academic qualifications. The ultimate intention of education is to ensure employment possibilities and diversity in jobs and work. A successful education policy is the prerequisite to individuals' future employment.

In short, education is a public good, as it helps the young individuals in their job and career opportunities. A more qualified individual should have a high ability to earn, and it follows that the person's "permanent income" will be higher, and that in turn can enable the person to accumulate more funds for retirement. A larger saving accumulated for postretirement expenses will require less government assistance. Hence, the virtuous economic cycle is that a better educated or qualified individual would have greater employment opportunities, better chance to seek senior positions, and the high earnings should allow the individual to save sufficiently for retirement.

Medical care is a private good because it basically benefits the affected individual only. However, the high expenses could deter people from gaining adequate medical care. Hence, health is a public good when considering the overall economic performance, in that a healthier workforce will be more productive and efficient. Medical provision is also an expensive item, and misuse or even abuse can be easy. Hence, even though there is a need for government assistance, medical provision has to be carefully instituted. One possibility is to work on the prevention side of medical needs. For example, the government provides the very basic treatment, but efforts will concentrate on R&D in medical advances. Another possibility is to introduce private insurance policies, so that individuals can seek medical insurance from their own income. The third possibility is to have private provision of medical care. Again, a "dual" supply of medical services can direct some demand to the private sector, leaving only needy individuals to use public medical care. At the input end, there is also the need to train medical personnel and expertise so that the entire medical profession can be adequately served.

The bottom line is that the government should not intervene excessively and unnecessarily, assistance should be provided only minimally, and since each form of assistance will have its advantages and disadvantages, the best outcome is to institute a workable and effective system that can involve a number of supply channels through the public sector and the private sector, and to the individual through medical insurance, charitable and voluntary organizations, and so on. Government assistance will then be seen as infrastructural provision.

One intuitive argument is that in capitalist market economies where individuals are given the greatest possibilities for achieving economic gains, the able and successful individual will automatically take care of their own economic welfare, including their housing and medical needs. Able individuals will take over their private cost

TABLE 3.1 The Various Roles of the Government

Developmental Role	Monitorial Role	Redistributional Role	
		Demand-led Approach	**Supply-led Approach**
Nature: Indirect	*Nature*: Indirect	*Nature*: Direct	*Nature*: Indirect
Forms:	*Forms*:	*Forms*:	*Forms*:
a. Infrastructure:	a. Reduce externalities	Welfare provision	Public utilities
– Physical	b. Raise ethical standards	– Items	– Housing
– Institutional	c. Execute corrective and	– Amount	– Education
b. Common goods	inventive behavior	– Duration	– Medical care
c. R&D	*Effects*:	*Effects*:	*Effects*:
Effects:	Social equality, stability,	Fiscal burden, debt	Private and public provisions, minimize survival
Capacity building	security, safety	accumulation, disincentives	cost, ability enhancing

in the provision of education, housing, and health. As such, the role of the government should be the promotion of more able individuals that can shoulder their own private cost.

The three roles of government are summarized in Table 3.1 under the three headings of nature, forms, and effects. The developmental role concerns the building of infrastructure and provision of common goods. The monitorial role is merely the need to police the economy with focus on removing externalities. There are two opposing aspects in the redistributional role. The "demand-led" approach advocates government assistance through welfare assistance that provides short-term cash relief to recipients. The "supply-led" approach focuses more on sustainability and expansion in economic capability through the education, health, and housing policies. The intention is to ensure that individuals will have the ability to shoulder their own private cost.

One feature shown in Table 3.1 is the difference between direct and indirect assistance among the three government roles. Other than the "demand-led" approach in the redistributional role, all the other three aspects are involved with indirect support by the government. The indirect nature of assistance is to avoid dependence so that individuals can keep the incentive to conduct their own affairs. In addition to the incentive issue and the need to avoid a fiscal burden, the economic theory of "information asymmetry" is useful to explain the preference for indirect assistance (Balakrishnan and Koza, 1993; Mishra et al., 1998). Information on the need for welfare assistance between the government and the recipient is not perfect. It is probable that the recipients may not disclose full information on their eligibilities. The government can cross-check the information, but it could be administratively costly to do so.

The argument that a smaller government is better than a large government is to ensure that the private sector will take the lead in economic activities that maximize output and growth. The more prosperous the private sector is, the less the need for government assistance in terms of social welfare. Government resources can then be used to develop and build up long-term economic capability and capacity through developmental and supply-led activities. However, at all times there are always some endowment-low individuals that suffer from lack of ability to survive economically. Hence, the government will need to exercise a minimum but effective redistributional role, so that the immediate needs of the some endowment-low individuals can be catered for. Economic resources in the hands of the private sector are much better than in the hands of government officials.

VI MINIMUM WAGE OR MAXIMUM WAGE

One of the first lessons in supply and demand analysis is that for minimum wage legislation to be effective, the minimum wage has to be set above the equilibrium wage, implying that there would be an excess supply of workers as the high wage attracts more workers to enter the market, but at the same time employers would be reluctant to hire too many workers at the above-equilibrium wage. The excess supply of workers would mean that some workers would not be employed, while those who remain in employment would enjoy a higher wage. It follows that the minimum wage cannot be effective if the unemployed workers undercut the minimum wage and offer to work at the equilibrium wage. Hence, in the end, the equilibrium wage would prevail.

There are a number of arguments for and against the use of minimum wage legislation (Stigler, 1946; Card and Krueger, 1995; Cahuc and Michel, 1996; Freeman, 1996). In a time of economic expansion and rapid growth when jobs can easily be found, the minimum wage would become redundant as employers have to offer a higher wage in order to obtain suitable workers. Equally, a minimum wage is applicable mainly to those workers based on hourly wage payments. Most jobs based on hourly payments are unskilled or low-skilled jobs, and these jobs may face an excess supply of workers when the economy is in recession. Hence, the employer is likely to be interested to pay the worker the minimum wage, but not any promotion potential, and to take no account of the years of experience of the workers. The minimum wage would become the amount paid year after year to the same worker.

Since the years of experience will not be counted, the worker will not see that the job can have a career future or skill enhancement. The unskilled worker cannot ask for more payment, as the employer would likely just follow the minimum legislation requirement. Since the employer is unlikely to pay higher than the minimum wage, and the worker is unlikely to look elsewhere for the same job since the pay is the same, the unintended consequence of the minimum wage in practice is that it effectively becomes the "maximum" wage. Hence, it is true to argue that the minimum wage does protect the worker's wage, but it equally does restrict the wage to increase, because experience, contribution, and skill enhancement would not be honored.

A more business-like solution to enhance workers' welfare is to institute a "starting wage" in different low-skilled or manual jobs (Li, 2012a). The "starting wage" can be decided either by negotiation, by practice within the profession, or by using the equilibrium wage. Through the use of an effective formula, each job can come up with its "starting wage," meaning that this will be the wage a young or newly recruited worker will get. Once started, the worker can accumulate experience that can be used as an attribute. The employer can also monitor the performance of the worker. With experience accumulated, the worker can seek higher pay than the starting wage. In other words, even though the hourly paid jobs do not have much skill requirement, the worker can still feel dignified when experience is counted and rewarded, as that would serve as an incentive to a better performance. Similarly, employers would show a more positive attitude to the contribution by the workers, and may need to reward the worker with better pay. Hence there can be a "career" path, even for low-skilled jobs.

Another advantage is that the starting wage can differ between jobs. Hence, a young worker can choose what job to take given the market information. The worker can switch between jobs once there is a wage difference. Effectively, this allows workers to make improvements in their pay, jobs, and living standards. The institution of a starting wage could open up a number of advantages to employers and workers. All an economy needs to do is to come up with a reasonable starting wage for various low-skilled and semi-skilled jobs, and the market information would soon help to allocate the labor resource efficiently.

VII BUSINESS LEADERS VERSUS GOVERNMENT LEADERS

The government has to attend to current economic issues so as to minimize economic difficulties, and attend to future potential so that economic capability and capacity can be maximized. The government has to address the "poor," so that they are able to survive economically, but has to provide market friendliness to investors. While the needy are individuals seeking welfare assistance, it is the investors who are the true economic drivers. The government has to balance the interests between the two groups, the former being the dependent group of individuals, while the latter is the independent group of individuals in the economy. The dependent group concerns the "spending" side of the government, while the independent group forms the "contributing" side in the government's revenue.

The government requires a great deal of ingenuity in resource generation, deployment, and management. It is definitely the "contributing" side that counts more to the government. Like any other individual, the government has to "earn" before it "spends." In policy terms, this could be translated into a situation where the government has to institute more economic instruments and channels, such that the government could maintain its ability to "earn" without upsetting the contributors. At the same time, the government has to spend, but the spending behavior should not lead to economic distortions and erode incentives.

In the balance between short-term needs and build up of long-term capability and capacity, the fiscal resources will have to be appropriately structured, typically giving more emphasis on long-term capacity building, but providing sufficient attention to short-term requests. The government is always under pressure to meet different needs and satisfy different demands. In advocating the advantage of a small government, US President, Ronald Reagan (1980–88) remarked that "Government is not the solution to our problems. Government *is* the problem" (Reagan and Sanzone, 1981). To do an appropriate job, every government is fighting an uphill battle in that it often is swayed by short-term issues, and the more attention the government is given to address short-term issues, the less resources and attention can be allotted to promote long-term capacity.

The ethics standard is paramount in the behavior of government leaders and civil servants. Their impartial judgment and the avoidance of vested interests, cronyism, and favoritism form the basis of good governance. There is a saying that the background of a government leader or top civil servant should be "a paper whiter than white," meaning that their ethical standards and cleanliness have to remain high, and they should have a selfless and noble character such that their prime and only target is to serve the public. Vested interests, cronyism, and favoritism will appear once leaders and public civil servants are influenced by greediness. A high standard in the training of civic service is a must, and a transparent and crystal clear monitoring process and system will have to be instituted to ensure against abuse and wrong-doing of government leaders and public servants. In many advanced countries where the civil service system is well developed, one practice is that the pay to civil servants is generally high, and various benefits are amply provided so as to eliminate greed. Once mistakes are found, such as corruption, abuse, and embezzlement of public funds, the public servant will receive severe capital punishment. Such severity is meant to deter potential abuse and wrong-doings by government leaders and civil servants. In short, a reliable civic service system would reduce a large chunk of the problems in the government.

There is a clear conceptual, theoretical, and intuitional difference between the roles of business leaders and government leaders. Provided their activities are legal, business leaders explore and maximize economic and business opportunities that will provide them with a bigger market, sales, revenues, and profit. Through profit attainment and with their "power" in the market, business leaders can make huge earnings, but at the same time have to face market risk and losses in unsuccessful businesses. On the contrary, political leaders are supposed to perform their best to serve the public, and their service is rewarded with high earnings and reputation. Political leaders have "power" in the government administration to serve, not to corrupt in order to amass huge sums through abuses and exploitation. This is the difference between political leaders in a mature country versus political leaders in a developing country, especially in those "fragile" states that cannot even provide a decent level of stability. Political leaders in many underdeveloped countries consider the authority in the government as a source of profiteering. It is true that there can be a lack of systems and institutions, but the behavior of political leaders is such that they abuse their authority and exploit the immature situation to satisfy their vested interests by embezzling funds from the public purse. Indeed, these corrupt leaders in many fragile states are the very obstacles to development.

VIII CONCLUSION

Perhaps it is somewhat unfortunate, as often it is political orientation that drives economic decisions at government level. While the debate on the size of the government is important, it may not come to much fruitful conclusion as one cannot avoid the work of the government. Hence, a useful judgment on the government is to see how effective and positive the government can be in promoting growth and development in the economy, both in the short-term and long-term perspectives. The ultimate economic question is the ability of the government to balance public sector spending with revenues. Recent studies have shown that reforms are needed in economies with large public spending resulting from growing government intervention (Wyplosz, 2015; Philippopoulos, 2016).

Thus, it will be appropriate to discuss how a government can facilitate economic development and growth so that there can be an increase in output, employment, export, upward mobility, ability to survive economically, and living standards, and ultimately serve as a reference to future generations and other world economies. While political results tend to be more short-term oriented, nurturing economic development and growth takes a long period of time. Hence, it is likely that due to political pressure, the government will need to attend to short-term issues, but resources and attention are needed to promote and nurture long-term competitiveness and comparative advantages in the process of constructing and implementing economic policies. In fiscal policy, while short-term welfare is needed to aid the poor, it is more important to bring out the message that welfare-dependence could lead to debt accumulation and loss of economic competitiveness. Worse is that the loss of competitiveness in the home country will mean a gain of competitiveness in the host economy. The loss of economic competitiveness can be permanent, and it will take more effort to enrich and recover economic competitiveness at a later stage. The government needs to ensure that economic progress will be given a higher priority than political goals.

By comparing the various economic roles of the government, the "sure win" strategy should be the deployment of a "supply-led" strategy that can enhance the economy's future competitiveness, capability, and capacity.

Ultimately, it is the private sector that drives the economy in terms of investment, employment, technological development, and living standards. The "back-seat" role of the government will be more suitable to serve as a monitor, provider of infrastructure and supplier of common goods, so that individuals can make use of these government facilities for growth. With the practice of market-friendly policies, the government in turn will be ensured of a steady fiscal return. In short, the government can benefit only through indirect means and measures, because it will only be the prosperity of the private sector that can eventually bring a stable revenue return to the government.

The discussion on the metaphors of "fertilizer, pillar, and carpet" points to the need to maintain market-friendliness in a "supply-led" strategy. Similarly, minimum wage legislation that may look good in argument can generate unfavorable unintended consequences. Thus, instead of protecting the workers, it turns out to restrict the potential of the workers. Popular political demands need to be studied in the context of resource allocation when deciding on welfare policies. Economic gains are visible, and can be shared and produce multiplier effects. Obstacles that obstruct opportunities in producing economic gains should be eradicated. Once the economic gains are produced and shared through an effective, fair, and transparent system, individuals should adhere more to their economic goals. The role of the government is to ensure a greater economic gain, so that more individuals can benefit and there is more to share. Income inequality may still exist, but social and economic equality shall be the ultimate goal. In other words, the facilitation the government provides should be that all individuals will have their own chance, opportunity, and way to build up their career, work, and life. At best, the government facilitates, but at worst, it can corrupt, disrupt, distort, and destruct.

While economic policies have to address the short-term ills, and despite the emergence of crises and shocks, it is the attention and resources devotion to long-term potentials that should, would, and could expand the economic capacity and capability of the future generation. The other "arm" in policy decision and implementation is the desire and level of ethical standards of public servants in their selfless, noble, and impartial acts and judgments. To eradicate, eliminate, and minimize favoritism, cronyism, corruption, and abuse of public funds, a strong, transparent, and reliable system would have to be instituted. A high level of civic training on the rule of law, public security, and equity will be a plus in promoting government efficiency and effectiveness.

4

Conceptual Differences Between Economics, Welfare, and Politics

I INTRODUCTION

Although the three dominant academic disciplines of economics, social welfare, and politics are separated from each other, they are closely interconnected. In some aspects, their interaction can complement and reinforce each other, but very often are in conflict with each other, leading to dilemmas and suboptimal choices being made. When translated into policy terms, the differences could lead to opposing and unintended outcomes and dichotomies. Hence, a trade-off has to be made between economic, social, and political goals. The choice of one policy goal could unfavorably affect another policy goal. Similarly, the decision on which policy to pursue could unintentionally have favored one group of individuals at the expense of another group. Indeed, the worst scenario would be that often the wrong choices were made, producing new problems. There is a popular saying that "the solution of one problem leads to the rise of another problem." Like the issues of poverty and inequality, there are always new problems that emerge, but it would be acceptable if the new problem turns out to be smaller or easier to handle.

There have been numerous studies in the two debates between economics and social welfare on the one hand, and economics and politics on the other hand. In the relationship between economics and social welfare, there are primarily two debates. One debate concentrates on how economics functions in social organizations, their intellectual boundary and/or integration, including the implication of the Pareto optimal and the function of the market in sociological discussions (Swedberg, 1990; Boettke, 1998; Aspers, 2001; Piore, 2002; Dalziel and Higgins, 2006). The other debate relates to welfare economics that concern mainly utility theory. The earliest advocates and critics of welfare economics were followed by studies on social choice, ethics, and the welfare state (Pigou, 1920; Hicks, 1939; Lange, 1942; Graaff, 1957; Buchanan, 1959; Sen, 1979; Feldman, 1989).

While consumer utility theory has been taught in standard economics textbooks, the discussion on a "welfare state" is related to how fiscal resources have been distributed for welfare provision. The political ideology of socialism has often been assumed in the redistribution of resources and belief in social equality. However, as there can be a mismatch in the increase in welfare spending and economic growth performance, the resulting

© 2017 Elsevier Inc. All rights reserved.

fiscal unsustainability soon leads to debt, which has become the related discussion along with welfare economics (Modigliani, 1961; Diamond, 1965; Barro, 1979; Josten, 2002). The relationship between economics and politics is equally complicated. One area of the debate is whether economics and politics are complementary or at odds with each other. Numerous empirical studies have shown that a positive political scenario can aid economic development (Barro, 1999; Gwartney et al., 1999; Cunningham, 2002; de Haan and Sturm, 2003; Stroup, 2007; Sharansky, 2009). Another area of the debate concerns the political economy of growth and democratization. These studies basically incorporated the impact of political ideas and implications on economic outcomes (Gough, 1979; Weingast et al., 1981; Keohane, 1984; Haggard and Kaufman, 1995; Wintrobe, 1998).

It would be useful to make a distinction in conceptual understanding between economics and social welfare, and between economics and politics. The discipline of economics concerns the allocation of resources and the maximization of outcomes. Economics involves an "input and output" analysis, and the question is what and how much input is used, and how much output is generated from the combined use of inputs. Economic benefits arising from the output are usually shown as ex post outcomes, while the economic inputs are usefully shown on an ex ante basis. Because of the difference in ex ante inputs and ex post outputs, economics by its very nature should show differences in outcomes.

The discipline of sociology is concerned with numerous societal issues, but one common feature is that many social issues involve the spending side of the economic equation. Social services can have indirect economic benefits, but expenditures have to be made at the forefront, and welfare has to be committed before anything can be done. Social welfare spending contains a number of economic features. It is often committed when the economy is strong, but is unlikely to be reduced when the economic situation is weakened. The economy faces cycles, but welfare commitments are inflexible in most cases. Hence, social services involve unilateral movement of government resources.

The discipline of politics involves mainly absolute outcomes. In a political election, the voting is conducted on an ex ante basis, as voters do not know how well the candidate they voted for will perform. How well the political candidate could perform would be an ex post outcome. Politics often involves short-term results, while economic development involves long-term trends. Economic issues are often used as political instruments, resulting in various distortions.

By comparing the essence of the three disciplines, one can have a better conceptual understanding as to which issue is economic but mixed with social matters, and which economic issue has been used in political decisions. People with unsophisticated minds often think that there is no distinction between economics and politics, or that social equality can be achieved using economic instruments. Between the two comparisons, the discussion between economics and social welfare is that the former concentrates on the input side while the latter concentrates on the spending side of the fiscal equation. The discussion between economics and politics is more complicated, as it has often been argued that economics and politics are inseparable. This is not entirely true, because economic issues are often used as instruments in political activities. The "tangible" result of political outcomes has often been dressed up in economic terms.

This chapter elaborates on the conceptual differences among the three social science disciplines. The next two sections concentrate separately on the comparison between economics and welfare, and between economics and politics. Section IV uses US economic and election data to show the possibility of political business cycles, lending further support to show how economic issues have been incorporated into political activities. Before the conclusion, another major area of discussion is the role of democracy in politics. While economics produces relative income inequalities, political power and authority produces absolute inequality, which could be more undesirable than income inequality in economics.

II ECONOMICS VERSUS SOCIAL WELFARE: THE SPENDING SIDE

The discipline of sociology relates to numerous areas of studies in social science, ranging from the family as a social unit, adolescence, criminology, race and ethnics, women and minority studies, aging and elderly, urbanization, social class, work ethics, and social enterprise. Many of these sociological studies are related to economics. In economics, one considers productivity and investment returns. In social welfare, one talks about spending to help the needy. Social welfare relates to the "spending" side of the fiscal equation. All forms of welfare expenses involve some sort of unilateral government payment. The relationship is unilateral in that the transfer payment made by the government is always at the "giving" end, while welfare recipients are always at the "receiving" end. In other words, while the government may need to balance its inputs and outputs, the welfare recipients always "take," and may not aware of the difficulty the government faces in balancing the fiscal budget.

Welfare spending belongs to the "demand-side" approach, and such spending will only add to consumption. It is true that the rise in consumption due to welfare spending will provide a certain level of rescue and safety-net to the recipients, but there will not be any "output equivalent" to this welfare spending. One immediate consequence would be a rise in inflation, because as the level of aggregate demand rises, and given that the level of aggregate supply is fixed, prices will have to rise. Second, when the sellers realize that the welfare recipients have more to spend, the sellers may even increase the price, thereby counteracting the rise in purchase power of the welfare recipients. Either way, the economy will not gain from welfare spending. The effect of the "demand-led" approach to welfare spending is limited.

Consider the hypothetical but probable situation illustrated in Fig. 4.1, where the vertical axis shows the quantity in dollar terms, while the horizontal axis shows the time line. Of course, the absolute values of Gross Domestic Product (GDP) would be much higher than the welfare expenditure, the two curves may not give the absolute performance, but the intuitive idea is that the amount of welfare rises in proportion to the movement of GDP. The E curve shows the economic trend, while the W curve indicates the welfare payment line. Welfare payment and government assistance tend to increase during economically good times. This is so because a strong economy can afford to pay more welfare assistance. However, what one does not understand is that economic vibrancy could change over time, but welfare expenditure, once committed, would be unlikely to be reduced. Hence, when the economic trend is downward, welfare expenditure would remain high or even expand, thereby quickly exhausting the healthy fiscal budget.

Hence, in Fig. 4.1, the welfare assistance indicated by the W line keeps rising when the economy remains good, but stays high when the economic trend falls. On the horizontal axis, t_1 is the turning point before which economic vibrancy could afford the rising welfare bill, but after which the economy may not be strong enough to support the welfare spending, hence the economy would face fiscal deficits if the welfare spending remains high, as shown by the gap between the W and E curves after the turning point. One can see that the two gaps in Fig. 4.1 are indicated by the area S and area D. Area S conceptually indicates fiscal surplus as the economic trend lies above the welfare trend, but area D represents fiscal deficit when the welfare trend exceeds the economic trend.

The intuition in Fig. 4.1 is that welfare commitment may not be sustainable when the economy suffers a downturn. Indeed, a responsible fiscal policy will be to reduce welfare expenditure when the economy is rising, as there should be job opportunities and workers with different endowments and abilities should be able to access the job market. As such, government involvement should withdraw and instead let employment work through in the job market. Thus, government saving should rise in economic good times. And it is theoretically wrong to seek more government welfare during economic booms. On the contrary, the government should practice fiscal expansion in the downside of the business cycle, so that government spending can provide relief to the economy.

FIGURE 4.1   Economic and welfare trends.

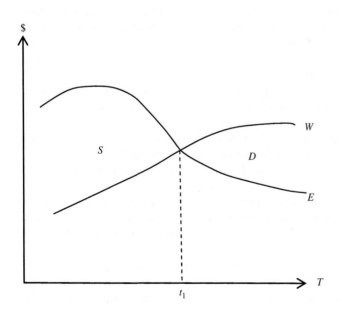

In other words, the fiscal policy on welfare expenditure should run in contrast to the economic trend, falling when the economy rises, and rising when the economy falls. The problem is that there can be no ceiling on welfare spending, and to the welfare recipients, it is always better to have more welfare. In an economic downturn, the unilateral nature of welfare payments can constrain, weaken, or delay economic recovery if decisions were made entirely based on political consideration.

Welfare can be a broad concept, as it can go beyond simply assistance to the poor, but can cover other expenditures in a wider sense, such as large entitlements to retired civil servants, and payment of nonwage benefits. Furthermore, all welfare spending is given to benefit the current generation. Hence, if there is fiscal deficit when faced with an economic downturn, it would mean that the current generation is "overspending," as the economy as a whole is spending more than it can earn. The government would have to borrow either from other governments, international organizations, or the future generation. The rising national debt simply means that this generation has overspent, and the future generation would have to pay for the spending made by this generation. Conceptually, then, when the next generation comes to life, they could already be in a debt situation, and would be left with the burden to pay back the debt. It is true that this generation could pass the burden of the debt to the next generation, since there are no institutions that represent the welfare of the future generation. There are civic institutions that protect animals, children, minorities, and the environment, but there are hardly any "antidebt accumulation" institutions that advocate the reduction of debt.

The issue of national debt could provide some resources to deal with current problems, but if the use of debts is to pay off previous debts, there can be negative consequences arising from a large national debt. If the borrowing is provided by other countries or international institutions, it would be at the mercy of the foreign loan suppliers to remove the debt. The other alternative is for the government to bail out the debt, but then the debt would simply be passed on to someone else. If all these channels are exhausted, the economy ultimately has to face the debt repayment. In the first place, a debt-prone economy tends to be weak and unfavorable to foreign investment. The international reserves of the economy may be low, making its trade vulnerable to exchange rate fluctuations. Eventually, the economy has to shrink, thereby imposing severe economic hardships. For example, welfare recipients may have to face the consequences of less welfare, or the economy will have to impose higher taxes, or the government will have to cut spending in order to balance the fiscal equation.

It would be more appropriate to look for the answer to welfare and support of the needy from within the economy. The "supply-led" approach is the more sustainable, long-lasting, and renewable solution. Just compare the economic consequences if the same amount of welfare spending the government committed every year were used to employ people. It would have the same effect on consumption, as the employed workers would receive wages instead of welfare assistance, but the difference is that the recipient has a job and is contributing to productivity. The rise in employment in turn could provide higher tax revenue to the government which would help to ease the fiscal burden. In short, the "supply-led" approach is generating a "virtuous economic cycle," and it can be contrasted with the "vicious economic cycle" that debt could be accumulated from adopting the "demand-led" approach. Debt is not only an economic "bad," it can drag the economy down, or could even be cross-generational, and the economy would lose its competitiveness. Furthermore, such a loss in competitiveness can be permanent, as the investment that fled to other economies will improve the competitiveness of the host economy. Debt accumulation is surely a "negative-sum" game, and the departure of economic resources would not only limit financial investment, but could also result in a "brain drain" that included professionals and other highly trained human resources (Bhagwati and Hamada, 1974; Beine et al., 2001).

Armed with this conceptual understanding between economics and welfare spending, one could understand that there has to be a limit to welfare spending, and indulgence in social welfare would result in unfavorable economic consequences, and the cost of a failed welfare strategy could be fatal to future generations. Hence, there needs to be a strong social ethic that national debts should be minimized so as not to burden the economic capacity of the next generation. To overspend in this generation by accumulation of debt will probably take away the opportunity of the next generation, weakening their resource capability. One solution would be to avoid debt accumulation, or the economy would have to face severe and sudden hardship when the debt got out of control.

The positive causality relationship between economics and welfare is one in which growth takes place and the rise in income allows the government to collect sufficient revenue to spend on welfare. To have the fiscal ability to shoulder welfare spending, the economy has to expand sufficiently to ensure inflow of fiscal revenue. A "vicious fiscal circle" will emerge if, in order to fund the fiscal deficit, a higher tax is imposed that discourages incentives and slows down economic activity, or investors are so discouraged that they may decide to leave the economy with their capital. If the fiscal deficit is to be financed by debt, the burden will then be passed to the future generation. Should debt-burdened countries decide to choose to default, the debt burden would then spill over to the lenders, and financial and currency crises could ensue, leading to economic instability and downfall, or in the extreme, the economy could collapse and disintegrate.

III ECONOMICS VERSUS POLITICS: WHO SERVES WHO?

The discipline of economics is about the allocation of resources for productive purposes so that people's living standards and the economy's overall performance can improve. Often, economic results require time to materialize as the entire process of production takes time, infrastructure requires time to build, and economic gains are meant to have a long-term impact. Physical investments also require time to mature. On the contrary, it is speculation that produces quick and windfall results. On its own, economics is apolitical, as the deployment of resources by either individuals or corporations produces output and returns; namely, people are engaged in an "input—output" process in the use of their own endowments and resources. The economic environment that could affect a person's deployment of resources depends on the stage of the business cycle, macroeconomic stability, and market opportunities. Hence, as a result of these conditions, economic outcomes can never be the same for different individuals at the same time, or to the same person at different times. Economic outcomes are always relative to one another, because the economic process will produce different returns, with some gaining more than others either with the same or different amounts of resources.

Politics is about the allocation of power and authority. Contrary to economics outcomes that often produce "positive-sum" games, the outcomes of politics are often absolute and produce a "zero-sum" game. Between the ruler and the ruled, between the winner and loser in a game, and between the winning party and losing party in a political election the results are all absolute outcomes, where the success of one would mean the failure of the other. While the unequal economics outcomes are relative in terms of differences in earnings and incomes, political inequality measured in terms of authority and power is definitely absolute. Political inequality in many ways is worse than economic inequality, because political inequality is absolute and total. The concepts of absolute political inequality, power, and political institutions have been written and elaborated extensively by Dahl (1957, 1992, 1996, 2006a,b).

While the terminology of "externality" in economics suggests negative side-effects, there could also be political externality in the form of abuse of power and exploitation of authority in political activities. Unlike economics, where things can mostly be quantified and visible, political opportunists could have their own private and undisclosed agenda and conduct "under the table" agreements. The potential lack of visibility and transparency, and the intention to serve vested interests, are the externalities that would equally produce negative side-effects in politics. The "absolute" nature of politics can produce more suicidal and detrimental impacts than the "relative" nature of economics. It would definitely be more difficult to remove political externalities than economic externalities.

The absolute nature of political outcomes is very different from the relative outcomes in economics. Furthermore, while economic outcomes have a physical form as they often are visible, tangible, and quantifiable, political outcomes often appear in the number of votes, and do not have other physical forms. In a democratic country, political popularity can mainly be seen from the number of votes. There are political instruments, such as mass rallying, lobbying, speeches, fund raising, and advertising that are often reported in the media. But how can political supporters gain in physical form depends a lot on what economic instruments are included and used in the political process. Whether a regime is supporting businesses so as to promote investment and employment, or favoring the masses with large redistributions so that large welfare payments are given out are all political issues dressed up in economic terms. For example, fighting against income inequality has often been politicized, but economic instruments, such as tax, welfare, or subsidies are often used to fulfill the political goal. Income redistribution has been considered as an instrument with political ends. The economy's tax regime has political implications. The employer—labor relationship in the production process has been dichotomized into a political conflict between the different social classes, or between the "have" and "do not have," even though there is no market restriction for any worker to become an employer.

Many unsophisticated analysts think that economics and politics are two sides of the same coin. The holder of such a view fails to see that economics has been continuously used as an instrument in political decisions, as economic outcomes are things that can be seen and have a physical form. The rise of unemployment, inflation, and investment are economics that can easily be interpreted politically. Typically, politics requires short-term results, and the needed economic outcomes include a reduction in unemployment or a rise in exports. But short-term economic consequences may lead to long-term distortions. The typical example is the prolonged use of low interest rates in the United States, Japan, and many countries with the intention of promoting and attracting investment, but the low interest rates can also stimulate speculation as the cost of borrowing becomes cheap. Hence, either economic issues are being used in achieving political goals, or political issues need to use economic instruments in order to show political results.

Having become aware of the differences between the two disciplines, it would be difficult to avoid using economic instruments for political goals. The difference, then, is whether the economic instruments used for political ends also benefit the economy, especially in building up long-term economic capability and capacity. The piling up of national debt would limit the future capability considerably, thereby making the economy uncompetitive and unattractive. Hence, the political difference rests with the choice of economic instruments used for the political goal. The ultimate question is who is serving who? If economics is used to serve political goals, the economic outcome may be politically biased. Many economically distorted situations end up with the need for more political involvement, as politicians would exploit economic outcomes for political ends. For example, most economic activities will generate differences in outcomes, but inequality may not be detrimental if there are sufficient investment and job opportunities. If politics was not involved, a favorable, long-term and sustainable policy would help to promote a suitable investment environment in order to promote jobs. On the contrary, if economics was used for political goals, the politicians will "rent-seek" the fiscal purse and advocate for a short-term policy on redistribution so as to provide more welfare to the low-income group without ensuring the country's fiscal ability, or the disincentive that it creates. The accumulated economic problems would eventually lead to crises and recessions because of wrong political decisions. Thus, it is preferable to deliver policies that consider economic results as the priority. Politics should be used to serve economic goals, and not vice versa.

IV POLITICAL BUSINESS CYCLES

Most industrialized countries are controlled by the election of political parties. Both the United States and the United Kingdom have a two-party political system, though smaller parties also exist. In the two-party system, one party normally tends to lean more to the business sector and believe in private economic activities, while the other party tends to favor the workers and supports the greater use of welfare and income redistribution. Political elections take place at regular intervals of 4 or 5 years, as stated in their constitutions. As a political election is an absolute "zero-sum" game, the winning party will govern the country while the losing party will have to wait for the next election.

In addition to using economic issues as political instruments, the studies on "political business cycles" argue that there is every possibility economic activities would be influenced by political elections (Nordhaus, 1975; McCallum, 1978; Golden and Poterba, 1980; Drazen, 2001; Blomberg and Hess, 2003). In an election year, the economy tends to improve, partly because of the large amount of spending on political campaigning, it is also time to show the "political report card" when the sitting political leader and the party has to show its achievements in the last 4 or 5 years. The best "political report card" will be whether economic growth has remained strong, or whether the ruling party has succeeded in bringing growth or reviving the economy from recession. Hence, given the timing and the need to show a "political report card," it would be reasonable to assume that the economy would improve and perform better in the year prior to or during the election year.

However, once a party has succeeded in an election, the ruling party has a 4- or 5-year time period. To make the "political report card" look good, one possible strategy would be to pull the economy down a bit for the first 2 years, but introduce policies so that economic growth reappeared after 2 years, or in time for the next election. The "perfect" political business cycle hypothesis would be a fall in the economy in the first 2 years after the election so as to paint a gloomy economic picture, but revive the economy thereafter so as to achieve a more rosy economy with low unemployment and low inflation. Hence, the political business cycle would be one in which the economy would perform weaker in the first 1 or 2 years after the election, but efforts would be made to ensure a revival and strong economic performance 1 or 2 years prior to the election.

One way to examine the presence of the political business cycle is to use the example of the United States, which has a presidential election every 4 years, and the election battle has mostly been fought between the Republican Party and the Democratic Party. The Republican Party is by and large probusiness and pursues free market capitalism, while the Democratic Party tends to lean more to welfare provisions in the domestic policy, though both parties share similar values of freedom and democracy. The choice of the US economy is easier as it has an election every 4 years. Other democratically elected countries may not have a fixed time period between elections, and the time period of one political regime may differ from another, resulting in one regime lasting longer or shorter than another.

The season-adjusted annual GDP data for the US economy for the period 1950−2013 can be found in the *International Financial Statistics* (IFS). The real annual GDP growth rates of the US economy, calculated using 2009 as the base year, are shown on Table 4.1, while Fig. 4.2 shows the graphical presentation, with the rate of real GDP growth shown on the vertical axis. Table 4.2 summarizes the dates, names, and party affiliation of the presidents in the United States from the early 1950s to 2013. Table 4.3 shows the matching of election years and the growth rates in the election year, the 2 years prior to the election year and the 2 years after the election year. The political business cycle hypothesizes that GDP growth rates tend to be higher near to the election year, due partly to the large amount of election-related expenditure, and partly because the sitting president and the ruling party have to show results on economic success.

Hence, the political business cycle hypothesis is that economic growth rate will be highest in the election year, but lower in the first year after the election, and economic performance could be even lowest in the middle period between the two elections. Such a hypothesis can be seen from the US data shown in Table 4.3, with the highest average growth of 3.66% in the election year, but an average lower rate in the year prior to an election (3.57%) and the year after the election (3.17%), while the lowest rate is in the middle year between the two

TABLE 4.1 The Real Annual GDP Growth Rates of the United States

Year	%	Year	%	Year	%	Year	%	Year	%	Year	%	Year	%
1951	8.06	1961	2.55	1971	3.29	1981	2.59	1991	−0.07	2001	0.98	2011	1.60
1952	4.07	1962	6.12	1972	5.25	1982	−1.91	1992	3.56	2002	1.79	2012	2.32
1953	4.69	1963	4.36	1973	5.64	1983	4.63	1993	2.75	2003	2.81	2013	2.22
1954	−0.56	1964	5.77	1974	−0.52	1984	7.26	1994	4.04	2004	3.79		
1955	7.12	1965	6.50	1975	−0.20	1985	4.24	1995	2.72	2005	3.35		
1956	2.13	1966	6.60	1976	5.39	1986	3.51	1996	3.80	2006	2.67		
1957	2.10	1967	2.74	1977	4.61	1987	3.46	1997	4.49	2007	1.78		
1958	−0.74	1968	4.91	1978	5.56	1988	4.20	1998	4.45	2008	−0.29		
1959	6.90	1969	3.13	1979	3.18	1989	3.68	1999	4.69	2009	−2.78		
1960	2.57	1970	0.21	1980	−0.24	1990	2.03	2000	4.09	2010	2.53		

International Financial Statistics (IFS).

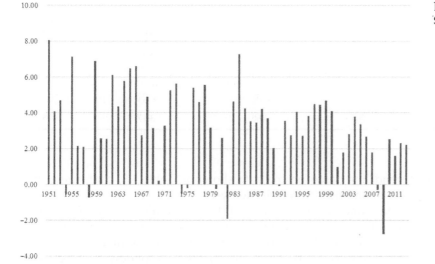

FIGURE 4.2 Growth of real GDP in the United States.

TABLE 4.2   Presidents of the United States

Years of office	Name of President	Political party
1945–53	Harry S. Truman	Democrat
1953–61	Dwight D. Eisenhower	Republican
1961–63	John F. Kennedy	Democrat
1963–69	Lyndon B. Johnson	Democrat
1969–74	Richard M. Nixon	Republican
1974–77	Gerald R. Ford	Republican
1977–81	James E. Carter, Jr.	Democrat
1981–89	Ronald W. Reagan	Republican
1989–93	George H. W. Bush	Republican
1993–2001	William J. Clinton	Democrat
2001–09	George W. Bush	Republican
2009–17	Barack H. Obama	Democrat

Wikipedia.

TABLE 4.3   Real GDP Growth Rates and Election Cycles (%)

Year and President	−2 Years	−1 Year	Election year	+1 Year	+2 Years
1950–54, Truman/Eisenhower	*	8.06	4.07	4.69	−0.56
1954–58, Eisenhower/Eisenhower	−0.56	7.12	2.13	2.10	−0.74
1958–62, Eisenhower/Kennedy	−0.74	6.90	2.57	2.55	6.12
1962–66, Kennedy/Johnson	6.12	4.36	5.77	6.50	6.60
1966–70, Johnson/Nixon	6.60	2.74	4.91	3.12	0.21
1970–74, Nixon/Nixon	0.21	3.29	5.25	5.64	−0.52
1974–78, Nixon, Ford/Carter	−0.52	−0.20	5.39	4.61	5.56
1978–82, Carter/Reagan	5.56	3.18	−0.24	2.59	−1.91
1982–86, Reagan/Reagan	−1.91	4.63	7.26	4.24	3.51
1986–90, Reagan/Bush	3.51	3.46	4.20	3.68	2.03
1990–94, Bush/Clinton	2.03	−0.07	3.56	2.75	4.04
1994–98, Clinton/Clinton	4.04	2.72	3.80	4.49	4.45
1998–2002, Clinton/G. Bush	4.45	4.69	4.09	0.98	1.79
2002–06, G. Bush/G. Bush	1.79	2.81	3.79	3.35	2.67
2006–10, G. Bush/Obama	2.67	1.78	−0.29	−2.78	2.53
2010–14, Obama/Obama	2.53	1.60	2.32	2.22	*
Average	2.38	3.57	3.66	3.17	2.38

*, Annual data covered period 1950–2013.

elections (2.38%). Fig. 4.3 shows the smoothed trend line based on the data shown in Table 4.3, confirming that on average economic growth tended to be stronger at and near to the election year.

The data can also be used to examine the average economic performance of the two political parties. Of course, business cycles can be the product of numerous other factors, and the political factor can only be one of the many factors. One can consider the economic growth rate of each president in the 4 years of his term from the year of taking office (year 1) until the end of his term (year 4). Table 4.4 separates the performance between

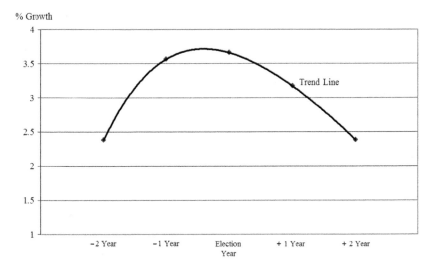

FIGURE 4.3 Political business cycle.

TABLE 4.4 Economic Growth Rates Performance Between the Two Parties in the United States (%)

	Year 1 take office	Year 2	Year 3	Year 4 end of term
DEMOCRATIC PARTY				
Truman			8.06	4.07
Kennedy	2.55	6.12	4.36	5.77
Johnson	6.5	6.6	2.74	4.91
Carter	4.61	5.56	3.18	−0.24
Clinton	2.75	4.04	2.72	3.8
Clinton	4.49	4.45	4.59	4.09
Obama	−2.78	2.53	1.6	2.32
Average	3.02	4.88	3.91	3.53
REPUBLICAN PARTY				
Eisenhower	4.69	−0.56	7.12	2.13
Eisenhower	2.1	−0.74	6.9	2.57
Nixon	3.13	0.21	3.29	5.25
Nixon	5.64	−0.52	−0.2	5.39
Reagan	2.59	−1.91	4.63	7.26
Reagan	4.24	3.51	3.46	4.2
Bush	3.68	2.03	−0.07	3.56
G. Bush	0.98	1.79	2.81	3.79
G. Bush	3.35	2.67	1.78	−0.29
Average	3.38	0.72	3.3	3.76

the two political parties and shows that, on average, the Democratic Party presidents showed higher GDP growth rates in the 2 years after taking office, while that growth performance of the Republican Party presidents were weaker in the 2 years after taking office. Fig. 4.4 shows the growth performance trend lines of the two parties in the United States. On average, the Democratic Party tended to show a rather high growth rate after the election, but the high growth rate tended not to be sustainable after the second year, and economic growth performed weaker toward the end of the term. On the contrary, the trend line of the Republican Party fitted the hypothesis

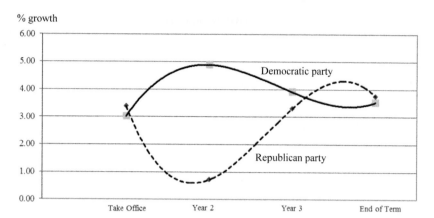

% growth

FIGURE 4.4 The economic growth trend lines between the two parties in the United States.

of the political business cycle, as economic performance was weaker at the beginning of the political term, and efforts were then made to rescue the economy toward the end of the term. Hence, economic growth tended to pick up considerably after the second year in office.

The study on political business cycles comes to the conclusion that economic activities have often been used as means and instruments in political goals. While it is inevitable, economic activities in the political business cycle could be "compartmentalized" into various short-term economic policies in order to achieve political goals. Obviously, given the ideological difference between the two parties in the United States, one would expect different economic performances under different political regimes and leaders. There can be other explanations about the political business cycle, and there can be other reasons for the movement of the growth trend in the US economy. Nonetheless, the use of economic instruments for political goals can generate a pattern of economic growth that moves along with the political scene. Although no one can chart what could otherwise have happened, the economic outcome of the political business cycles may not be the best or most appropriate for long-term growth and development. The appropriate strategy would be to deploy resources such that some would cater for short-term activities, while whenever possible, resources should be devoted to long-term economic development. Ultimately, political regimes are political in essence, but economic growth and development can enhance the long-term capability of the economy.

V THE ROLE OF DEMOCRACY

Another key difference between economics and politics is that economic outcomes are based on ex post performances. The growth trend, size of investment, and level of employment reflect the ex post situation. Similarly, at the microeconomic level, consumers can examine the product before they buy, and that activity is ex post, as consumers do not know what ex ante factors were used in the production process. In political elections, voters are making ex ante judgements as to the performance of the politician they are voting for. Candidates in an election will produce a manifesto that outlines the candidate's goals, ambitions, and desires on an ex ante basis.

However, the voters will not know how good the candidate can be until the candidate is finally in office. Thus, the performance of how good the elected candidate is could only be seen on an ex post basis. There is a high degree of uncertainty or margin of error, in that voters' ex ante decisions could turn out differently ex post, because there can be wide divergence between what the candidate said in the preelection time and what the elected candidate did after taking up office. Hence, there has to be a process whereby elected candidates that did not perform to the satisfaction of the voters can be removed from office. In other words, despite the ex ante nature of political elections, the ex post nature can be corrected if the voters are institutionally given a chance to remove the poorly performing candidate after the term of office comes to an end. In theory, democracy can help to soften the absolute ex ante nature of political elections should the successful candidate lose popularity after being elected. While freedom is the broadest concept that covers all aspects of human movements and contacts, democracy is political freedom that allows voters a choice in their selection of leaders. In democracy, the "absolute" nature of politics can be made "relative," in that voters have the right and are given the chance to remove an unpopular leader.

Dahl (2000) wrote that "democracy provides opportunities for participation, voting, control, inclusion and understanding, but full political equality is impossible to achieve." Studies on democracy argued that there is a distinction between "control by leaders" and "control of leaders" (Dahl, 1991; Vanhanen, 2000). Once elected, the absolute nature of politics is that the elected leader will exercise control. But the receptivity of the leader will be "tested" in the next election, as that is where the voters can control the leader. In other words, democracy gives an opportunity for "the ruled to rule the ruler."

Instead of the discussion between democracy and market capitalism, it is more appropriate to consider if the democratic system is well structured, sustainable, and mature. In advanced industrialized countries, the democratic system has been instituted for a long time, and the system is protected and supported by the constitution and civic institutions. Hence, the democratic system is mature, in that the elected leader would remain as the leader until the end of the term. The system is transparent, and people respect the rules of the game. Democracy is a collective behavior governed by some form of institutional establishment, and does not have a physical form.

However, the same may not be true in developing countries, as experience shows in a number of developing countries that their democratic system can be unstable. A country with an immature democratic system can ruin the very institution of democracy if the lost party, the nonelected leaders, and the political opponents rebelled, especially if it was supported by the military to form a *coup d'état* and seized power from the elected leader. In other words, political opponents did not wait until the next democratic election, but rebelled to form a so-called interim government so as to gain power by force. In a mature democratic system, the outcome of genuine elections have to be respected, and voters would have another chance to vote at the end of the specified term of office. Removing a democratically elected leader in the middle of the term of office by force is itself an undemocratic act, and would endanger the very democratic system and process that a democratic regime should uphold.

In many developing countries, the kind of democracy instituted could be fragmented, as voters are visibly biased towards the ethnic, regional, linguistic, tribal, and religious origin of the candidate, rather than making a judgment on the ability of the candidate. Rules on democratic elections have to be clearly specified, understood, and kept through reports in the media and various educational channels to avoid possible cases of political laundering, corruption, manipulation, and favoritism. Universal suffrage means a system of "one person, one vote," but the establishment of such a reliable and sustainable democratic institution can be an expensive political infrastructure for many developing countries. There are other considerations before a democratic system becomes mature. In socialist countries, e.g., the "democratic" election system could be that the candidates are prescreened before they are allowed to enter the race. This ensures the kind of candidate the state or ruling party wants, but it cannot be considered as a free election. Another example is that voters have to register before they can vote. Thus, not all citizens can vote if they do not register, thereby violating the "one person, one vote" principle, as the choice of voting can become a privilege rather than a right.

Perhaps there are prerequisites in instituting a mature system of democracy. An educated, well-versed public should be a major precondition for the establishment and implementation of a democratic system. In poor developing countries when the standard of public education is low, democratic elections could turn out to be nondemocratic or even violent. In other incidents, the democratic system and elections have been poorly executed, resulting in political disputes, faults, and social fragmentations that divide and antagonize the society.

While the advanced economies treasure the democratic system, some developing countries are keen to remain undemocratic, as that could preserve the power of the leaders. An election is an activity that gives an absolute outcome and there is no guarantee of winning, though opinion polls and the media do provide preelection opinions. The introduction of a democratic system could be a challenge to existing leaders, as it could mean replacement of power and authority away from the sitting leaders. By not instituting a fully fledged democratic system, the power would remain in the hands of the sitting leaders. In other words, it could be a deliberate effort of some undemocratic leaders not to introduce democratic institutions and systems in order to remain in power. The leaders' selfishness and fear of losing power in a game with an absolute outcome could be the reason not to indulge in introducing a democratic system. Their system is, therefore, "no system," and the absolute nature of a politically undemocratic regime would mean it remains in power.

The role democracy plays is to introduce an element of "relativity" in a game with otherwise an absolute outcome. Democracy is a civilized political act. In an election, the winning party will rule, and the losing side will have to work harder in the next election. The losers in the election will return to their normal life, and should not fear personal victimization, injury, or loss. In a mature democracy, election is not a "life or death" game, but is rather a civic behavior and another election will take place at another time. Instead of lamenting the loss in a political election, what is more important and useful is to monitor the activities of the elected leaders. Democracy is political freedom, and "one person, one vote" should be the most open form of democracy. In a mature democratic regime, elections become a personal choice, and individuals should not be coerced to vote for a particular candidate. However, the "dirty politics" spirit would mean the presence of influence by people with vested interests, or the use of cash in influencing voters' choice, thereby breaking the fairness and transparency of a clean election. To institute an effective democratic system, there is a need to introduce a comprehensive and clean process leading to true democratic elections, thereby turning an election into an exercise with a certain aspect of "relativity" in the outcome.

VI CONCLUSION

Economics occupies the production side of the equation, as resources are mobilized to ensure production that can be made available for consumption. Hence, consumption cannot take place before outputs are produced. However, differences in individual endowments often end up in inequalities, with some having made more economic gains and benefits than others. In the extreme, there are some individuals whose endowment is so low that they have difficulty surviving. It has been a mistaken thought that instead of providing or creating more job opportunities, a straightforward redistribution through the use of social welfare by the government is the solution.

By its very nature, social welfare deals with the spending side of the government, because by definition welfare assistance will never contribute back to the fiscal purse of the government. The "one way traffic" nature of welfare needs to have better economic understanding, as prolonged and excessive welfare assistance will weaken the overall economy in terms of competitiveness and capability potentials. One economic characteristic of welfare is that it is easy to give, but difficult to withdraw. Once given, it is more likely to increase than to decrease. Hence, a generous welfare policy can eventually impose an increasing burden on the financial ability of the economy. Experiences show that countries with prolonged fiscal deficits also face a prolonged period of national debt, as the government may need to borrow to pay for previous debts. Ultimately, the economy would collapse, either because no one comes to the rescue when the debt has become excessively huge, or the economic capability is so low that output cannot be sustained, and a vicious circle emerges as the debt has to pass on to the next generation.

Between economics and politics, it is a naivety when unsophisticated analysts argue that economics and politics are not separable and form two sides of the same coin. Economics is an independent discipline and its function is to allocate resources, but differences or inequality arises from both the input end and the output end of the production equation. Unfortunately, the focus has been on economic differences, rather than the extent of economic opportunities that arise to produce positive impacts on the economy. However, political intention or purpose has infiltrated into otherwise normal economic activities. In the political process, the normal functioning of various economic variables and instruments could have been twisted, ending with the worst outcomes of economic failures and crises. The analysis of the political business cycle demonstrates that, while there are political regimes that conduct economic activities to satisfy political goals, it is preferable to direct resources for long-term development and capability enhancement. Short-term shocks are inevitable, and economic resources will often be needed to address short-term ills. Long-term development and capability enhancement should be useful to the economy, regardless of which political regimes are in power. Indeed, while political elections come and go, it is economic development that provides the best outcome to any political regimes.

Combining the analyses on economics, welfare, and politics, one can conclude that economics is the most useful discipline. When compared with welfare assistance, economics talks not only about the spending side of the equation, but concerns resource deployment and the ability to produce, generate, and enhance economic capability for development. Welfare spending is an easy subject, but the ability to earn is always more difficult. This is true and can be applied to individual persons, individual enterprises or businesses, individual industries, and individual countries. The ability to earn is what an economy needs to generate. Indeed, once individuals have the ability to earn, the spending decision will just follow.

Political activities often infiltrate into the economics arena. Probably due to the fact that politics does not have a physical form, and political outcomes often are intangible, the tangible economic outcomes are therefore used in order to gain support. Political outcomes carry an "absolute" nature, and decisions based on ex ante scenarios could differ extensively from ex post situations. The "absolute" nature of politics can lead to extreme results and generate inequality. In mature democratic countries, absolute political inequalities are checked by periodic political elections, because what the political candidates have said or promised in an ex ante scenario could differ from what the candidates have enacted and done in an ex post situation. The institution of a democratic political system allows the citizens to have a say in the otherwise absolute nature of political inequality.

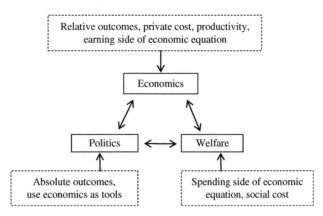

FIGURE 4.5 Relationships among economics, politics, and welfare.

While countries in the contemporary world cannot escape from politics, economic instruments are used for political ends, and there is a need to address short-term shocks and crises, there should be sufficient deployment of economic resources that can be geared to the long-term enrichment of economic capability so as to ensure economic sustainability, survival, and competitiveness. The greater the ability to generate future potential, the stronger the future economy will become. It is unfortunate that the "relative" nature of many economic outcomes has been misunderstood or politicized. Economic activities generate inequalities, but rewards are based on individual endowments. As such, there should be little restriction for individuals to enhance or enrich their endowments. Hence, given the market opportunity, individuals are free to conduct their own economic activities. In the final analysis, it is the extent of opportunity that is the more restrictive element than the "relative" degree of economic inequality.

While democracy is an instrument that can ameliorate the "absolute" nature of politics, there are also other aspects of human life that produce "absolute" outcomes: religion, marriage, sports, beauty contests, and so on. In civilized countries, many of these activities with "absolute" outcomes have been "personalized" through individual choice and freedom. Individuals are free to choose their religious faith, free to support certain teams in sports, and so on. There is no cohesion in individual choices. Thus, individual freedom can solve many conflicts in activities that produce "absolute" outcomes, including war and peace. Economic "relativity" will really be the solution to conflicts as choices are personalized into individual preferences.

Fig. 4.5 conveniently summarizes the triangular relationship between the disciplines of economics, politics, and welfare. Economics concerns productivity from existing endowments of individuals, and gives relative outcomes as individuals have different endowments and productivity yields on the earning side of the economic equation. Politics produces absolute outcomes, and the form of politics has to be exhibited through economic tools, including welfare, which relates purely to the spending side of the economic equation and accumulates social cost. Having understood the conceptual differences among the three social science disciplines, it will be appropriate to extend the discussion to a more conventional analysis on the crucial differences in the two ideologies of capitalism and socialism/communism.

5

Capitalism and Socialism: Sustainability Versus Popularity

I INTRODUCTION

Human activities are full of "opposites" and "dichotomies," but it is more relevant and important to look for "compromises" and "harmonies." In classical Chinese philosophy, there is the "yin and yang" that represents the extremes of "darkness and brightness" that pledges for the connectivity and complementarity of contrary forces in numerous aspects in the natural world, such as man and women, fire and water, day and night, black and white, love and hate, cold and heat, and so on. In introductory microeconomics theory, teachings on perfect competition and monopoly are considered as the two extreme forms of firm structure in the market, with complete freedom of entry to the market at one end, and control by a single firm at the other. There are numerous other examples of "opposites." In political economy, the dichotomy between capitalism and communism has been discussed and debated, yet more analyses are needed using a cross-disciplinary approach in the contemporary context.

The typical features of capitalism embedded in classical economics include private ownership and freedom to sell properties and assets, and it cherishes individualism. Individual economic activities are conducted through the "invisible hand" in the market. In business, individuals are welcome to become entrepreneurs and build up their own business. It is through the market that individuals can pursue their own interests and be rewarded according to their ability and capability (Friedman, 1981; Williamson, 1985). According to *capitalism.org*, "capitalism is a social system based on the principle of individual rights. Politically, it is the system of *laissez-faire* (freedom). Legally it is a system of objective laws (rule of law as opposed to rule of man). Economically, when such freedom is applied to the sphere of production its result is the free market."

Neoclassical economics refines the spirit of capitalism by including the need for infrastructure provision, establishment of civic institutions, and minimal and effective role of government in the provision of public services and utilities, ensuring equity and transparency through the rule of law without constraining individual incentives. For example, the excessive role of government in the economy has been considered as a concern, because it can have all the power in deploying national resources, which could be intended to serve the interest of a

© 2017 Elsevier Inc. All rights reserved.

minority. Effective institutional checks and balances are needed to ensure that government power is dispersed (Hayek, 1944; Friedman, 1993).

Economic freedom forms a major component in capitalism, as it reflects individual capabilities. Societies are composed of individuals, and it is the progress of individuals that leads to societal progress, because the freedom of individuals can ensure that individuals are given the chance to perform their best. Innovation and creativity of various kinds can be fostered in capitalism, as the best performance of individuals provides the highest possible output in the economy. As such, conventional economic literature argues that economic growth is said to have maximized. Recent studies go further to argue that it is the growth and maximization of economic opportunities that should be more important.

On the contrary, the ideology of socialism or communism arises from the Marxian school that the state would have the ultimate power and ownership of resources (Young, 1978; Larrain, 1983; Torrance, 1995). All individuals would devote themselves to the state, and would not be given the incentives to establish their business as it is considered as "exploitation." Economic activities are conducted through central planning. Individual wealth accumulation would not be allowed, as individuals would be assigned to work in a state enterprise or organization. The state takes over the input side of the economic equation. Every aspect of life is dictated or controlled by the state. Daily life and other living materials would be rationed to individuals by the state officials. The state takes over distribution in the output side of the economic equation. Various state organs would unilaterally decide on what, how, where, and when to produce output. State power would become supreme, while the lack of freedom deprives individuals of choices. In the name of the communist party, economic equality is said to have "achieved", but choice and freedom have been taken away from all individuals. Political inequality exists as those holding political power have control over those without power. Political inequality could become extreme, unfair, hidden, and life-long as individuals would not be provided with alternatives. By comparison, income inequality in capitalist economies could be changed through the use of appropriate policies, while political inequality in communism would be life-long and improvement would be impossible. The "laws" would be written to protect the state and its ideology. It would be naive to assume that there is equality in socialist countries, as political inequality could be more detrimental and irrevocable than income inequality. Because of ideological dominance in communist countries, individual activities and behavior will be closely watched and monitored.

One can simply use an analogy of a "bird freely flying in open space" versus a "bird captivated in a cage." Capitalism probably symbolizes a "bird freely flying in open space," free to go places, free to choose its residence, and free to hunt for food. Such a bird can venture into different areas and territories, but there is always competition for food. Creativity and ingenuity will be needed for survival. However, "inequality" will exist as one bird could obtain more food than another bird. On the contrary, the "bird captivated in a cage" will be safe, as food would be provided, but the cage is all the space the bird can have. There is no freedom to fly and venture out into the open space. The bird will probably be watched and its life is monitored.

One can conceptually show a scale in which capitalism is characterized by freedom and ownership rights on the one hand, and communism with absolute state control and central planning of economic production on the other. Indeed, most global economies are not situated in the two extremes of capitalism or communism, but capitalist economies could contain some aspects of socialist policies, while socialist countries have also introduced some elements of the market in their economies. The original or pure form of capitalism is the principle of *laissez-faire*, where economic freedom is complete. Deviating from *laissez-faire* will be some form of free market, but mixed with some welfare orientations. The government will play a more significant role in allocating resources, or will engage in redistribution. An economic structure that deviates further from economic welfare can be termed as "state capitalism," representing an economy in which the state plays a major role in the market. This happens often when the private sector is weak or controlled, and the state owns the bulk of economic resources by setting up national corporations that manage businesses (Kurlantzick, 2016).

At the other extreme, the few communist countries exercise a high degree of state control in running the country, and economic planning in resource allocation and deployment are practiced. All kinds of individual freedom are forbidden, and the state is responsible for all decisions. One feature among the few communist countries is that they are dynastic, with the power passing from one generation to another in the same bloodline. By pursuing a communist ideology in the country, the dynastic leaders can preserve power in their own hands. A slight deviation from communism is socialism, in which central planning is still dominant, but is controlled by one political party, though there is some form of elections within the single party system. A socialist market economy is one in which there is one leading political party, but resources are owned by state-owned and state-controlled enterprises. The People's Republic of China, since its economic reform in 1978, is said to pursue a socialist market economy, but due to the importance of forming and establishing "relationships" among party members, party elites, and top-ranking officials, a more recent debate termed China's market socialism as "relational capitalism" (Chu, 2010; Wang, 2013).

This chapter gives a summary discussion on the differences between the two ideologies of capitalism and socialism. The conceptual discussions shall show the usefulness, relevance, and appropriateness of the two ideologies, contrasting their merits and drawbacks. The complexity of these two ideologies cannot be explained by a single discipline, and it is important to make intellectual connectivity among the various disciplines. A cross-disciplinary approach is used to discuss different intellectual spheres, including economic, political, social, philosophical, historical, and psychological disciplines.

II COMPARING THE ESSENCE OF THE TWO IDEOLOGIES

The capitalist ideology has gone far and has survived amid different periodical crises and challenges. A discussion of the stages of development of capitalism is a convenient method to see that capitalism has progressed, improved, and matured. Nonetheless, it is useful to contrast the essence of capitalism in its classical form with the other extreme of communism.

Capitalism

The fundamental basis of capitalism comes from *laissez-faire* principles that advocate the importance of individual drive in economic activities and progress (Gerrard, 1989). Adam Smith's (1776) "invisible hand" means that given the market information that serves as indicators, individuals are free to engage in the market either by entering the market with the individual's skill, knowledge, experience, capital, and other endowments, or switch to another market where there is more room for expansion, less competition, or a higher return.

Since it is the individual people and firms who have full knowledge of their own endowments, it therefore would be most appropriate that the market conditions are made free and open so that individual people and firms can enter the market when they think fit. It probably is true that in the early days of capitalism, e.g., the era of industrialization in Europe from the mid-1700s to the mid-1800s, comprehensive education was not as common as in modern civilized countries today, apprenticeships and learning-by-doing then were the more popular form of enriching an individual's skill and other forms of endowment. The structure of social stratification was primitive, in that individual progress was restricted by social class. It probably was true, e.g., that the aristocrats in Victorian England in the early era of the industrial revolution in Great Britain possessed most of the wealth and capital resources, and it would turn out that they would naturally become the investors and employers.

The early stage of capitalism did expose a number of inadequacies, such as a lack of workers' protection and welfare support in difficult times, the lack of public education did not allow for different kinds of professional training, while low quality urbanization failed to provide support in transportation and other forms of social facilities, such as medical services. Radical economists and leftists would relate the economic relationship in the early stage of capitalism as "economic exploitation," as wages were paid at a low level, while profits were considered as surplus. There was a natural conflict between the employers and employees in the "class society."

However, one can also argue it was exactly because of the various economic and social inadequacies in the early stage of capitalism and subsequent economic growth and progress that forced changes and improvements in various social and economic spheres, thereby nurturing a more civilized and mature capitalist society. With the rise in modern education, individuals from different social strata were also given opportunities to enrich and improve their individual endowment in the market (Epstein, 1968). It is true that employment usually begins with a low wage, but at least the workers are given the chance as economic progress and accumulation of experience are then permitted. In addition to the changing supply and demand conditions in the market, the employees can enjoy economic progress and reach a higher level of economic gains, given time. Hence, the unfavorable situation in "early capitalism" was improved and perfected through endowment-enriching channels.

As employers need employees and vice versa in all mature market economies, one should then consider the "employer – employee" relationship as one of complementarity, rather than dichotomous. Employers need workers, while the workers need jobs. In the tradition of a *laissez-faire* free market situation, there is no restriction on entry to any business. Investors normally engage their capital resources, and there is always risk involved in conducting business. There are various kinds of risk that a business person faces, including the business strategy of competitors, lack of support for government policies, business cycles in which businesses operate, ease in the supply of suitable workers, changing conditions in the labor market, and exchange rate and interest rate risk.

There is no guarantee that businesses can prosper, and failed businesses are usually not reported. Hence, the choice to start a business is always available. Obviously, any entrepreneurs will have to make good business judgments before establishing new businesses. Given all these risk possibilities and considerations, it is certain that the economic return to businesses will differ from the wage gained as an employee.

All economies are developing and improving, hoping that the future is better than the past. Economic activities produce societal dynamism, but that cannot be risk-free. Most people will choose to minimize risk, but some prefer to engage in risky businesses. Similarly, not all businesses can be profit-making, but it will be the employers who bear and face the business risk, while the employees receive in most cases a wage payment, regardless of the business situation and conditions. Of course, the employees will become unemployed when the business closes down. Thus, the level of risk differs between employers and employees. The "surplus value" in the Marxian context is actually the reward for risk-taking by the business owners. Because there is no standard return on risk, the level of "surplus value" in the form of profit differs with different levels of risk. Hence, employers may gain more than employees, because employers are responsible for the business risk.

With an open market, some businesses will enter the market earlier than others, and some businesses will conduct a wider range of business activities than others. Both large and small firms exist, and all businesses are open to competition. Hence, employers are facing a different level of market competition than employees. The argument in the early stage of capitalism that there was "exploitation" and the resulting "class society" from the dichotomy between employers and employees could equally be found in the contemporary globalization debate. For example, while proglobalization advocates the thought that trade and investment in less developed countries would enhance their growth as more people could be employed at an appropriate wage comparable to their local conditions, antiglobalization advocates took a protectionist approach and held the leftist view of "exploitation" and argued that workers in the developing countries were "exploited" because they were paid much lower wages than workers in the advanced countries, but it was exactly the difference in the wage cost that attracted foreign investment to those developing countries. The employment arising from foreign direct investment should at least provide some job opportunities to the workers in developing countries, and in turn there could be output, exports, and growth. Instead, the antiglobalization advocates should concentrate on the working conditions and job security in developing countries (Lindert and Williamson, 2001; Stiglitz, 2002; Fischer, 2003; Bhagwati, 2004; Hallak and Levinsohn, 2004; Wallach and Woodall, 2004; Aisbett, 2005; Li and Zhou, 2010).

As the early stage of capitalism matures with the establishment of modern and professional institutions that serve to provide and protect the civic rights of individuals, the choice for the individual to start a business or serve as an employee will be seen more as the availability of economic opportunity and diversity than the dichotomy between the two opposing social classes as elaborated by the Marxian advocates. In other words, there is a "learning curve" in capitalist economies. As the capitalist economy enlarges and production increases, the economic pool will require more resources. Although the positions and roles of the employers and employees remain, the growing and expanding capitalist economy will produce new job opportunities that will benefit the employees. It would come to a point when employers have to find ways to retain good employees when a labor shortage appears. However, as individual drive differs among individuals, it follows that returns, rewards, and gains differ among individuals. This may lead to the debate on "inequality," but it is largely the differences in individual drive and effort that lead consequently to differences in outcome.

The conditions for market competition would be changing, as corporate activities could result in mergers and acquisitions, and the emergence of large firms and the survival of small firms would add to the composition of firms in the industry. Professional institutions would exercise their civic and ethical standards when new products are invented, such as pharmaceutical products using medical innovations. The emergence of "economic bad," such as cybercrime, drug trafficking, and numerous other illegal acts, would require vigorous, timely, and appropriate laws to protect the public.

There are new demands as society becomes more civilized. New institutions, such as nongovernment organizations, and new businesses, such as green businesses and social enterprises, would expand, thereby enlarging economic possibilities. This comes with a rising degree of social, environmental, and human awareness, but ultimately, individuals would benefit with the increase in expanded job and new business opportunities. Hence, it is true to say that different individual endowment mean individuals would enter the market at different levels, progress at a different pace, and receive different rewards. In modern civilized economies, there are more channels through which progress is possible for individuals, and it is expected that there will be differences in outcomes.

The essence of capitalism is that there is a high degree of freedom, and the basis of an economy rests on the ability, initiative, incentive, and drive of individuals in their economic activities, either in the form of business engagement, seeking to become professionals, or offering to work as employees. Economic activities among individuals are often complementary in nature as activities are interconnected or linked, so that the rise of one activity leads to another activity. In a modern civilized society where economic diversity works through the market, the function of price mechanisms, and the need for ethical standards and transparency indeed provide opportunities for individuals with different interests to pursue their goals and targets, thereby bringing the society to new heights of development and advancement. There is vibrancy and dynamism in the society as the rise in one aspect of living standards and quality of life would lead to improvement in another.

There are other complications, as economic debates can be divisive. For example, while businesses would like to see innovation and growth, protectionists would prefer to see slower growth to ensure a protected environment. Similarly, welfare advocates would prefer to see more redistribution, while investors prefer to face lower tax rates. The economic outcome is whether the economy should ensure jobs and employment, and that economic growth along with environmental protection should be better, or environmental protection should take place at all cost and the delay in development will mean less employment opportunities. Economic debates can be very political, and their outcomes depend on the political ideology of the leaders, the public sentiment, and issues at the time. Economic oscillation in a politicized society can cause delay and distortion, especially when resources are geared more to redistribution and protectionist policies, and do not allow sufficient growth and progress to propel the economy to new heights.

Economic growth and development, as well as environmental protection, require a long-term approach, but political decisions tend to look for short-term solutions. Repeated short-term policies could create economic distortions in the capitalist market economy, making the long-term goals more difficult to achieve. In the end, it could be one episode of short-term policy followed by another episode of short-term policy. Hence, the long-term would actually be composed of various short-term policies and the true long-term goal and development might have to be sacrificed.

In the contemporary world where economic competition is severe across countries, domestic resources should best be used productively so that the economy will not experience a drop in competitiveness. Indeed, given the high degree of globalization and openness, and the freedom and ease of capital movement, troubles that began in the home economy could invite capital to depart to the host economy. Macroeconomic stability is not only a prerequisite to growth, but can be "magnetic" in attracting capital as the economy improves its competitiveness. Hence, progress in the domestic economy often serves as a means to maintain its competitive edge in the global economy. Improvement in global competitiveness can be the result of progress in technology and other advances, or can be due to the weaker performance in other economies.

Communism and Socialism

The early stage of capitalism was faced with numerous inadequacies and led to economic and social criticisms, such as profiteering, discrimination, and inequality between bourgeois and proletariats in social classes, and imperialism at the international level as the powerful countries colonialized weaker countries. Marx (1867) pioneered the ideology of communism, and according to *Wikipedia*, believed that "the motivating force of capitalism is in the exploitation of labor, whose unpaid work is the ultimate source of surplus value.... The employer is able to claim the right to profits because he or she owns the productive capital assets (means of production), which are legally protected by the capitalist state through property rights." However, in a free market, workers are free to start their own business and own their productive capital assets. The protection of property rights was not a privilege to the capitalists, but is a right every legal individual can have.

Based on the inadequacies of early capitalism, Marx built and extended his ideology to include social and political issues. Numerous scholars have projected the economic arguments in the Marxian framework (Dobb, 1969; Morishima, 1973; Desai, 1974; Walker, 1978; Harvey, 1982). For example, the theory of value touched on the economics of production and reproduction, the profit received by the employer was considered as "surplus value," and since such surplus was not shared between the employer and employee, Marx pledged that as "exploitation" by capitalists of workers. Such economic inequality naturally led to social class struggles, as it was always the employers with capital resources who directed the work of the laborers. Accordingly, class struggles would be a continuous process, and there would be no end to it so long as there was exploitation and conflict between employers and employees. Socially, workers would be "alienated" from society, as they worked long hours and were not given chances to progress or move up the social ladder. There are various related debates in Marxian economics, including the discussion on prices and values, the circuits of capital, and the falling rate of profit.

Communism was Marx's answer to the inadequacies in the early stage of development in capitalist economies. In communism, there would be no individual or intellectual property rights as the state became the ultimate owner of resources. As such, the state was the only employer and there would be no exploitation, as everyone worked for the state. Income inequality should disappear as everyone was paid almost equally, and the state would look after the welfare of all individuals. There would be full employment as the state provided and assigned jobs to all able individuals. The surplus value disappeared as the state controlled the production process. Economic activities were conducted through central planning, where state officials and party members dominated, and all productive decisions were conducted centrally. Individuals would not be given the chance to show their incentive, initiative, or innovative behavior. The working life of all individuals was tightly scheduled and directed. Individuals could not have a character of their own, but to serve the state. The degree of political and economic centralization was extreme and total, as production and consumption were all decided for individuals. In short, the state took over both the supply-side and demand-side of the economic equation.

The first naive impression about communism was that all individuals were treated equitably as income inequality disappeared. Individuals would not need to worry about jobs, as employment was guaranteed. There would not be any economic recession as consumer demand was controlled, and individuals would be provided with their living consumption quota and welfare support. The "iron rice bowl" was the term used in Chinese communism, suggesting that economic support was provided for life and the "rice bowl" (meaning a person's economic life) would not be smashed since it was made of "iron" (meaning life-time support from the state). Since economic planning was implemented, there would be no economic recession or inflation as prices were dictated by the state, and money would not be considered as a "store of value," but could only be used for transaction purposes. Wages would simply be a token, since the state provided individuals with jobs, accommodation, retirement protection, and daily products and supplies. Other than production and consumption, other services, such as entertainment and sport, would also be directed and controlled by the state. The picture painted by communism is one in which people were living in a "Utopian" world.

The communist ideology has raised an equal amount, if not more, economic problems, as it is based on numerous short run, static, unrealistic assumptions. First, communism assumes a risk-free world in which all productive activities are risk-free, there will not be any mismatch between supply and demand, and there will be no distinction between cost and profit. It assumes a perfect allocation of resources, and that what is produced will be consumed, as choice will not be given to producers and consumers. State-owned enterprises are asked to fulfill the production quota, while consumables are allocated and distributed to households through the state system. No consideration was given to the possibility of economic shortages. If there were shortages in agricultural, industrial, and other household consumables, the answer was a fall in allocations to households. Hence, households had to be prepared to face the possibility of famine, and a fall in the standard of living as shortages appeared. The risk was the lack of choices and alternatives in economic activities.

It would be simplistic to think that central planning could produce a risk-free economy. There are numerous simple questions on the validity and functionality of a centrally planned economy. Could the state have information and knowledge about the entire economy? Could the officials make appropriate decisions for the public and there be no vested interests? How could the officials know about the people's needs? Who would be responsible for the economic problems resulting from distortions? Why would individuals not be given the freedom to make their own decisions? Why would all individuals have to be treated equally by state officials? Would state officials "rent-seek" activities, and create "moral hazards" that would be detrimental to the economy? Given there is asymmetric information between the people and the officials, how could the work of state officials be monitored? Would a more diversified economy be preferable to a centrally dictated economy? A communist economy would not be a risk-free economy; it is just that risks were suppressed because communism took away freedom from individuals. Decisions were made by a minority of state officials, probably with undisclosed intentions. In communist and socialist economies, there would be the risk of being controlled by government and party officials. Since economic management would be top-down, there was no way to check or monitor government decisions. While good economic results would be credited to the state, people would have less to consume when the economy suffered from, e.g., poor harvest or a drop in exports. Such economic risks would be suppressed as individuals might not even be informed.

As economic decisions are made collectively, the economy becomes static. Individuals are not given choices, and innovation and creativity would not be entertained. Economic and technological progress, if any, could only be made at the collective level. Indeed, a static economy would be the outcome, as the decision-makers did not need to handle new development and challenges. Typically, advanced communication channels, such as the internet, would not be made common, as the availability of information itself would bring unwanted challenges in communist countries. The risk under communism is the loss of individual freedom, as central planning could not be relied upon, and decision-making was centralized.

Second, a centrally planned economy would provide "security" to all individuals as jobs were guaranteed and wages were similar among workers with skill differences. Would this mean that income inequality was eliminated? When the same amount of wages was paid across different jobs, where would be the incentive for individuals to perform their best? On the contrary, there would be incentive to shed responsibility, as there would be little difference in the pay between skilled and unskilled jobs. Inequality appeared differently under communism, as party members were recruited as government officials, and the recruitment process would be selective. Indeed, the communist party behaved like a "private club," whereby members were selected and chosen. Typically, university students would be asked to join the communist party.

Inequality in communism appeared in the form of political inequality. The government that was composed of party members were the decision-makers. Nonparty members had little chance to be placed in a high ranking positon. Once a person became a communist member, the party member would have a "life-time" advantage over nonparty members, especially in the political hierarchy. Political inequality thus existed between party and nonparty members. And since the number of party members was only a fraction of the entire population, inequality emerged with a minority of party members controlling the majority of nonparty members. Since party membership was life-time, nonparty members would then be excluded from leadership, and there would not be any opportunity for social mobility. Such political inequality, hence, becomes extreme and life-long.

It would be worse if political inequality also led to economic inequality if party members exercised their power to "rent-seek" and obtain gains from people and activities. Equality under communism is a myth, as it ends up with two kinds of inequalities: political inequality resulting from the advantage of being a party member and an official, and economic inequality when party members and officials abuse their political power for economic gains. Since such economic gains were attached to political privilege, economic inequality became a permanent or life-long phenomenon. Eventually, political and economic power would further be consolidated and reinforced. Thus, a nonparty member and a nonofficial individual in a communist economy would involuntarily be faced with both political inequality and economic inequality.

Numerous literature on politics and sociology has touched on the political theory of the state, and that the state is the major decision organ in communism (Carnoy, 1984; Held, 1989). In economics, the work of Hayek (1944) warned that the excessive power of the government would remove freedom from individuals. The ideology of communism is driven largely by politics, and economics has turned into a political instrument. As such, all benefits and outcomes deriving from economic and societal activities are measured in political terms. Since society is being dominated by politics, and the communist ideology ensures that authority and power are vested in the hands of party members, the monopolistic nature of political activities would mean that deviations from the ideology would not be entertained. Consequently, various kinds of freedom would have to be sacrificed, and individuals would not be given chances and opportunities other than to follow the "party-line."

The two ideologies of capitalism and communism show large contrasts in individual freedom and opportunities in making individual, and subsequently societal, progress. It is exactly the removal of individual liberty in noncapitalist states that makes noncapitalist countries less prosperous, less developed, and less advanced in all aspects of human life, because individuals are not given the chance to show their best, to perform their utmost, and to pursue their own interests. The situation can even be "self-fulfilling," the lack of one aspect of individual liberty reinforces itself, and other aspects of human liberty would gradually be contained and eroded. In turn, the power of the ideology and the state composed of party officials would become more concentrated. Eventually, it would be the party that controls all aspects of human life: economic, political, social, and cultural.

III WHY IS SOCIALISM POPULAR?

One convenient point to begin the discussion on the ideology of capitalism would be the era of industrial revolution (1760–1870) that began with the invention of the steam engine in Great Britain, but industrial development and growth subsequently spread to other major European countries, the United States, and Japan. A summary look at the history of early industrialization suggests that with the invention of the locomotive, transportation of industrial goods could be facilitated. Industrial production in the textile industry spread to machine tools, iron and steel, and motor vehicles (Ashton, 1948; Kindleberger, 1993; Daunton, 1995; More, 2000; Lucas, 2004; Griffin, 2010). However, the Marxian ideology was developed from the criticisms and drawbacks of capitalism, and peaked in the Bolshevik revolution led by Lenin in 1917 that overthrew the Russia monarchy and established the communist state to become the Soviet Union (Lenin, 1976; Cohen, 1980; Carr, 1985).

The capitalistic mode of market economy developed almost naturally and instantaneously as inventions were created by individuals, while entrepreneurs and firms gathered sufficient capital and engaged in production. Businesses were given the freedom to produce at their own pace and risk, and profits were made. In the early stage of capitalism, it was probably true that entrepreneurs with capital came from wealthy families and aristocrats. This led to the "social class" debate on the polarization between "bourgeois and proletariat" in Marxian literature. Such a polarization of social class was obviously politically driven. However, the expansion of professional jobs promoted social mobility and opportunity, which has over the decades blurred the social class debate, as individuals from different social backgrounds could achieve new and higher qualifications through individual drive and formal education. Indeed, the "middle class" has become the more dominant and vocal social class. As capitalism matures, economic expansion does allow for the ability to ensure a higher degree of social security through various channels. Supply-side channels include education and health provision, infrastructure development, and research and scientific innovations, while demand-side channels include the provision of welfare through redistributive policies. Over the years, these changes and improvements have effectively enabled individuals to improve their quality of life without being classified into a particular "social class."

Modern economies have, over the decades, instituted various channels and avenues through which individuals can make progress despite their social background. Freedom and social transparency have enabled many individuals to make improvements in their standard of living. However, at any point in time in all societies, there are always more "less-able" individuals than "more-able" individuals. Here, "able" would include not only financial capital or formal education, but connections, experiences, knowledge, skills, creativity, business sense, economic environment, and personality. Similarly, there are always more "employees" than "employers." The interaction in economics between such divisions of individuals is that people with capital will invest and employ, while individuals without capital will have to offer their labor as workers. Workers need investors and employers, while employers cannot produce output without the help of workers. Hence, the "more-able" and "less-able" or the "employer" and "employee" relationship is not one of a substitute, but a complement, as they need each other to conduct economic activities. Similarly, such a complementary relationship produces a "positive-sum" game, where both parties would gain, and not a "zero-sum," where one-party gains at the expense of the other party.

It is true that income inequality exists, as the employer may receive more than the employee in return, but the employer has to bear the investment risk, and different workers are paid differently. Without investment, the chance of being employed will not exist, and the employee may lose out entirely. Hence, it is true that inequality exists, but both parties have gained. Also, the relationship can change. Once they have acquired sufficient capital and skill, employees could turn to be investors and become employers. This role switching is possible provided there are new opportunities arising from the growing capitalist economy. The inequality situation can hence be improved through the work of individuals, level of investment, and opportunities arising from investment activities.

As investment activities expand, the demand for labor rises as more jobs are made available, and the demand for labor will result in a rise in wages accordingly. Similarly, the expansion in the economy would allow more opportunities for various businesses, and employees who acquired sufficient skill and experience could also start their own business. The creative and entrepreneurial mindset of individuals could help in business promotion. The establishment of new businesses would in turn offer more job opportunities for others. Hence, in the economics arena, the "employer – employee" relationship is not one of "opposites," but is interconnected as their roles are fluid and can change given suitable opportunities, market conditions, and personal drive. Economic freedom and a strong ethical civic society help in improving the opportunities, so that income inequalities would not be seen as detrimental in restricting growth and development. Income inequality arises due to variations in economic activities, but it is more important to ensure that there are channels through which equality can be improved.

A problem arises when the economic relationship between employers and employees has been politically dichotomized into different conflicting social classes with opposing interests, orientations, and goals. One can generalize the discussion into the division between "rich" and "poor," or "more-able" and "less-able." Money, income, and wealth would obviously be used as a criterion in the distinction between "rich" and "poor," but other attributes could be included, such as ability, knowledge, skill, education, talent, connections, and experience. Given these classifications, one would agree that statistically there are bound to be more "poor," "less-able" or "ability-low" individuals than "rich," "more-able" or "ability-high" individuals in all economies.

Unfortunately, the division between "rich" and "poor" has often been used as a political instrument. Since political elections are often decided by the "majority," and by the very fact that there are more "ability-low" individuals than "ability-high" individuals, it is likely that political opportunists would lean to the side of the "majority," as they would then have a greater chance of winning an election and acquiring power subsequently. Thus, statistically it is politically popular to seek support from "ability-low" individuals, as they form the larger group of electors. It follows that welfare-prone, socialist-oriented ideas and suggestions would turn out to be more popular by offering economic promises so that "ability-low" voters could see "gains" from their votes. Elections are "political markets" through which exchanges take place between the politicians aiming to win an election and the benefits the voters get in return.

Political maturity among politicians and voters can have independent effects on the election. The choice is often between: (1) whether there are politicians and voters who prefer short-term policies that produce and earn some immediate gains without much regard to long-term implications or (2) both politicians and voters use a political election as a rallying mechanism aimed at producing a more productive, capacity enhancing, long-term perspective for the economy as a whole. The former choice would mean the use of resources for current needs so that the current generation can enjoy them, probably at the expense of future generations if there was a lack of fiscal resources to cover all expenditures. The latter choice would prefer a "defer gratification" attitude so that current resources would be geared more to promote economic capacity for the future generation than to spend on current consumption.

The choice of using a political solution in dealing with the "rich" and "poor" division was shown by the adoption of Marxism by Lenin in the 1917 Bolshevik revolution in Russia. The Bolshevik revolution overthrew the "ruling" class composed of landlords and capitalists. One problem in the rise of the proletariat was the absence of employers who served as organizers of resource utilization and production. The Marxian answer was to institute a state system where economic activities would be conducted at the central level. As the state became the owner of all resources, economic planning was executed by state officials, based on Marxian principles. The proletariat class did manage to dispose of the employers, but in turn, the state had become the "employer" and jobs were assigned. Consequently, economic activities became politicized, as production, employment, consumption, investment, inflation, price, and other economic variables were then decided based on political principles and ideologies, and not economic probabilities.

The first outcome in a communist revolution was that investors and business employers were removed, but in their place, the proletariat were subordinate to a new set of "employers," namely the state officials who would make decisions on their behalf. The authority and power exercised by state officials were absolute, and individuals were not given choice in any aspect of their economic life. Income was reduced and narrowed as the gains by capitalists and employers disappeared, but whether state control would improve the economic life of individuals in a socialist economy was debatable. Politically, it was a situation in which the minority of political party officials controlled the majority of the population, dictating the deployment of resources and calculating the economic needs of all individuals. The society had become totally sensitive to political decisions, and political power was absolute under communism. The first consequence of political revolution was the change of power, and the form of inequality changed from one of economic to political inequality.

With the state in control of all resources, central planning would mean individual needs would not be attended to, and central allocation ensured that all households would receive the same amount of economic supplies. This is the "bird in the cage" argument, where all individuals were given an "equal" amount of economic materials. It is possible that "endowment-low" individuals would prefer to see that food, shelter, and other life inputs were given and handed down by the state. Socialism could appeal to those individuals who prefer to be provided with some kind of life support, rather than face uncertainty in a competitive market. Hence, promises of welfare provisions could become popular in gaining political votes. But the resources needed for welfare expenses come from the taxpayers and the public purse, not from the elected politicians. As such, preaching socialist ideology and the promise of welfare provision in a political election is "costless" to the politician. Such redistribution would become a political act, but the consequences could have long lasting and unfavorable economic implications. Effectively, socialist politicians may just "rent-seek" the fiscal purse.

Socialism appears to be "popular" as it is used by politicians to please and win the votes and support from the larger number of "ability-low" individuals or the section of the population who have a weaker endowment. These "endowment-low" voters probably need some sort of economic support, and thus would prefer to have some kind of welfare protection as that could ease their economic hardship. The political election has become a business, as voters expect to have some gain in return for their support. Through socialism, endowment-low individuals would pass some of their "private costs" to be absorbed by society.

The socialist myth is that welfare support would reduce or restrict the economic power of employers, and that the removal of employers would psychologically produce a new political status that the workers have risen to rule the country. But in actual fact, the economic power has switched to another authority, namely the political authority concentrated in the hands of the state officials. Would the magnitude of political power between the ruler and the ruled in a communist state be more severe than the magnitude of economic power between employers and employees in a capitalist state? Would political inequality be worse than income inequality? On the contrary, given a free capitalist economy, individuals do have the freedom to improve their endowment, and absolute income can be increased, though a relative income difference can still remain. By comparison, which type of inequality is the worst of the two evils?

Because material allocations are rationed by the communist state, such allocations would not be directly related to the economic productivity of individuals. What an individual gets from state allocation may not match the individual's desires and wants. As such, economic outputs might not have any relationship to the amount of labor and material inputs, resulting in possible disproportions in productivity. With the removal of an individual's incentive and creativity, one should expect low output productivity in state-owned organizations. When political decisions are included in the economic input – output relationship, one probable outcome would be economic shortages. Economic shortages can appear in various forms. When there was a poor harvest, further food rationing was needed. In the case of the Soviet Union, economic resources were geared more to heavy industrial production, resulting in shortages in light manufacture and household consumables. As enterprises were state-owned, a host of economic behaviors that promoted productivity and efficiency were absent, including innovation, creativity, individual talents, and personal drive. Thus, a socialist economy looked "equal" as income received by households was controlled, and in the end showed a narrower gap between the high earning and low earning recipients. During the "Cold War" (1947–85) (McMahon, 2003; Gaddis, 2005) between the Soviet Union and the West, resources in the Soviet Union were geared mainly to war preparations, international and regional conflicts, and ideological battles, and given that the country was not rich in natural and agricultural resources, resources devoted to war-related industries would mean a severe shortage in consumables, and prolonged shortages of consumables would hurt the economic livelihood of households. Hence, material allocations that were decided at the central level would have to take into account a number of political realities and considerations, and shortages that occurred would mean a reduction in the allocation. In simple words, income was "equal" because people were made "equally poor" due to a lack of material provision and a low standard of living.

In a nutshell, communism and socialism implies an ideology that used political tools in making economic decisions, or that economics was used as an instrument for political ends. As a result, economic distortions in one aspect of the economy would lead to more distortions in other economic aspects. As private and individual economic decisions were not allowed, individuals in turn would not take up economic responsibilities, and the state would have to bear all the economic burden of ownership, allocation, production, and planning. In other words, households would no longer take up their "private costs," but these would all be absorbed by the state in the form of "social costs." As individuals do not need to shoulder their "private costs," they lost their freedom and choice. As the state had taken over all "social costs," the state would have the entire authority and power in resource deployment. Individuals lost their freedom at both the input end and the output end in the economic equation.

Looking at the long-term consequences of such an unsustainable communist or socialist style of economic organization, it is definitely true that individuals are faced with a bigger loss. Individuals lose in both economic and political freedom, as the absolute power in the one-party political system means a lack of freedom in economic decisions and a lack of choice in political decisions. Political inequality becomes absolute and spills over to economics through administrative means, political propaganda, and bureaucratic channels. The popular myth projected by communist advocates in the form of equality, rule by proletariats, state provisions of economic materials, and sharing in economic benefit end up with a rise in political absolutism, "tyranny of the minority," and economic poverty. The country became stagnant as progress could only be made on a collective basis, defying the advantages deriving from individual talent, creativity, and entrepreneurship. In the final analysis, communism produces an "economic trap" in which people are deprived of various sorts of freedom and personal choices, and have to follow orders from political organizations.

Unsophisticated analyses often mixed up economics with politics and argue that these two disciplines are closely linked or inseparable. This definitely is not the entire truth. There was of course the political dimension in the Bolshevik revolution in 1917, but it showed how economic issues were being manipulated in enhancing political ideological goals. In market economies, economic growth and expansion require time, and different market players perform differently in their economic roles. The simpler short-term and politically popular solution embedded in a policy of forced redistribution ensured the "haves" would have less and the "don't haves" would have more in an instant time. The result satisfied the political ambition, but this effectively could lead to other long-term unfavorable economic ills, such as a loss in competitiveness and distortion in the usage of resources, which in turn restricts economic progress elsewhere, thereby choking the economy to undesirable conditions.

The real danger of communism, or for economies adopting socialist policies, is that when people are not given freedom and chances, the resulting static nature of the economy makes the poor dependent on government or state support, and that would give the state and government officials power to keep a large government. Indeed, the preservation of the poor will preserve the need for more government actions, and ultimately a larger government. As such, redistribution was not meant to help the poor, but used the poor as the yardstick for promoting a larger government.

IV WHY IS CAPITALISM SUSTAINABLE?

One should not look for a perfect ideology, but identify a preferable and appropriate ideology that provides fairness, functionality, applicability, and sustainability. An ideology is preferable if it allows free movement of resources, freedom of expression and creation of ideas, individual drive and progress, and expansion of opportunities. Economic problems should be solved economically, while applying political solutions to economic problems could end up with distortions and vicious cycles. The rise of one economic aspect will multiply and lead to a rise in another economic activity. Similarly, using political tools to twist economic problems could weaken economic potentials, leading eventually to more economic problems and inviting further political interference.

Economics, in essence, is a process that connects material inputs to produce material outputs. Because societies and individuals possess different material inputs, it naturally will generate differences in material outputs. The society needs to have as much material output as possible in order to promote the standard and quality of life such that everyone will benefit from the rise in economic returns. Thus, capitalism becomes the appropriate political ideology through which the economic maximization of individuals can produce economic maximization of the entre society. In addition to a number of such attributes as economic freedom, intellectual property rights, private ownership and transfer, and a high degree of civility that includes improvement in ethical standards and the rule of law, capitalism permits flexibility and incorporates diversity in economic affairs. Although economic differences are expected, economic flexibility is important because the power to make economic decisions is dispersed among individuals and institutions at a different time, pace, and in a different environment. Diversity functions to allow individuals and organizations to go different ways, exploring their greatest potential. Together, they capture new developments and permit progress and technological innovation to take place. This is why creativity, whether it is in advancing technology, environmental protection, making movies, or drawing cartoons, can show its strength in capitalist economies.

Another feature in sustainability is the ability to rejuvenate as a new generation of capitalists emerges to invest and bring further innovation and promotion to the economy. A capitalist market economy is full of dynamism and changes occur periodically, resulting in economic ups and downs over time. Since the economy is comprised of individuals who act and behave according to their best interest, their collective behavior generates economic waves through expectation and changes in market supply and demand. Economic growth occurs when aggregate output is rising and job opportunities are created and expanded to permit a rise in income and mobility. On the contrary, the economy can pass through different stages of business cycles which, in extreme cases, can result in crises when numerous unfavorable conditions and expectations collapse at the same time. Given time and a reliable market system, economic recessions and crises come and go, and a new round of economic development emerges, exactly because flexibility and changes in market conditions can rejuvenate another round of investors and market players, and another round of economic activity.

The multiplicative nature of economic activities can generate both positive and negative results, and the solutions to externalities require the need to engage in other activities. Tourism expands output and employment, but the large number of visitors generates a huge volume of material waste and garbage that would be unfriendly to the environment. One firm taking over another firm can improve productive efficiency, but may lead to monopolistic practices when the firm gains a large market share. One can provide a number of economic examples whereby economic activities can have both positive and negative outcomes. Indeed, all human activities require the use of resources, and some resources can be replenished, but others cannot.

In capitalist market economies, economic variations do call for other required actions. For example, large corporations do make profits, but they also research in technological advances that could save and rescue other limited resources. Typically, most human economic activities are resource-depleting, but through technology, resources can either be saved, or new resources created, so that the process of resource depletion can be slowed down or new substitutes found. The capitalist mode of development enables individuals and firms to look for legal solutions and technical improvement when new problems arise. In environmental protection, pollution and environmental decay can be dealt with through technical improvements and greater human awareness and participation.

The economic theory of "Pareto optimality" suggests that even in an economically optimal situation, not all market players can be satisfied. Economic resources that are consumed in one activity would need to be replenished through other activities. The dynamic forces of supply and demand in the market ensure that new products and markets could be spotted and developed, and that new opportunities are created and exploited in the process. Through the signals and information available in the market, some interested investors would engage resources to gain the "first mover" advantage. The degree of firm competition depends on the development of the market, as some markets are more competitive than others. Competition is an ongoing process, and firms face more competition at the early stage of development, but would consolidate when the market becomes more mature. Nonetheless, freedom of market entry is most important in maintaining competition, though entry requirements differ between markets at different stages of competition. Business cycles are often caused by forces of supply and demand, business and investment expectations and behavior, and the extent of government involvement. While the private sector is the driver in capitalist economies, the pursuit of a stable and reasonable set of government policies can stabilize business cycles. The drawbacks that result from inappropriate government economic policies are distortions and disincentives.

In the early stage of capitalism, it is true that a number of development issues were not instituted, and opponents politicized the inadequacies of the capitalist system to form the ideology of communism that imposed political concepts on economic issues. In modern mature capitalist economies, many of these former inadequacies have been attended to, if not solved. For example, an individual's survival cost has been addressed and promoted through spending on education, support for infrastructure, and welfare provision as the last resort. Laws on equality and nondiscrimination are applied to respect human rights. Apolitical civic and professional establishments are constructed to ensure openness, transparency, and equity. Civic maturity helps to promote ethical standards in social behavior, business activities, and individual interactions.

In mature capitalist economies, the few endogenous economic problems that arise within the sphere of economic development itself include inequality, externality, competition, and business cycles. Inequality is the result of differences in individual endowments, and the solution to inequality is to adopt economic policies that can enrich individuals' endowments. Income inequality cannot be eradicated, but the best alternative is to ensure that individuals have the ability to take care of their own welfare. Economic externalities arise as a result of the spillover of one activity on another, and there can be various solutions, including the rule of law, change of locations, compensation, and mutual agreement on settlement. In the case of environmental protection, the solution rests on technological advances and education. One has to be aware that growth should precede protection, as growth allows the creation of wealth, and more resources in turn could be used to protect the environment. This is because many environmental protection activities involve the spending side of the fiscal equation. To ensure that there is no shortage in the revenue side of the fiscal equation means that economic growth has to proceed.

The success of capitalism can be narrowed down to the modern provision of three public goods: housing, health, and education. Unlike welfare provision that involves purely spending and is "demand-oriented," housing, education, and health provisions are considered as infrastructural investment. When housing is considered as an essential good, provision of public or low cost housing will reduce the survival cost of households, and simultaneously maximize their purchasing power. Education is a public investment and serves as a channel through which individual endowments can be enriched. Similarly, medical services can be costly, and some assistance will help to reduce the survival cost of low income earners. In short, a modern market economy will not only adopt capitalist principles, but focus also on "supply-side" economic areas. Securing these supply-side economic areas will produce in the long run a more reliable and sustainable economic environment for individuals to attain upward mobility and for businesses to make progress. The remaining issue is how these three supply-side areas should be organized. Housing provisions should first be regarded as a necessity, but the private market will dominate when housing is regarded as an investment. Both public and private schools could coexist, so that parents can have a choice in sending their children for the appropriate level of educational achievement. Medical services can be costly, but private hospitals should equally be allowed to operate so that consumers can have a choice in their treatment. Furthermore, private provisions can compete with public provisions, so that checks and balances exist to ensure standards.

Among different ideologies, capitalism is the most sustainable ideology because of its power in economic rejuvenation. It may not be a perfect system, but alternative solutions can often be found within the economic and market mechanisms. In other words, the capitalism engine runs on its own. Capitalism is a system that cherishes individual incentives and hard work, and channels and opportunities are provided for individuals to make progress. Of course, there are both successful and failed cases. Ethically, the capitalism ideology enables the economy to produce more able individuals, and those who succeed should be encouraged and not be penalized, while chances should be provided to the unfortunate ones. A minimum level of welfare assistance can be given to those who are in desperate need. But those successful individuals should look for ways to help others through increases in employment, charity, and donations. Similarly, the market system allows new products to emerge. The ability to rejuvenate or regenerate economic activities through the emergence of new investors and other market players is the most important ingredient in capitalism as this provides renewal, continuity, and sustainability. If not being politicized, economic problems can ultimately be solved using economic instruments.

The ideology of capitalism in the 21st century is definitely different from that in the 19th century. In capitalism, which historically began during the Industrial Revolution in the 18th century when owners of capital were dominant, investments were mostly conducted by the aristocrats, and farmers migrated to urban areas to serve as industrial workers. The ideological challenge to capitalism began as Marxism gained ground in the Soviet Union, and many European political parties and governments leaned toward socialist economic policies in the form of redistribution by taxing the rich and subsidizing the poor. However, capitalism has been modernized as the challenges from the other ideologies have led to various changes and improvements. One is the rise of the "middle class," as its development has blurred the conflicts between the various social classes and groups, while education has provided a new channel for social upward mobility that was restricted previously to capital holders only. Over the years, scientific progress has aided the quality of life as the market expanded. Increasing openness and civic rights have led to development in new industries and businesses, though there is contemporaneous development of large corporations and multinational enterprises. Small businesses coexisted with large corporations. In addition, the emergence of labor unions and chambers of commerce permitted civilized forms of communication to take place, though negotiations at times can be very political and militant. Indeed, one can argue that it is because of capitalism that diversity in all directions was permitted. Hence, what surrounds capitalism is a number of related institutions that provide a high degree of civility between the state and the people. Individuals can then seek assistance, advice, protection, and comfort in these civic organizations, without the need for any political affiliation.

Capitalist principles and practices have gradually become the infrastructural fabric on which economic activities rely. Individuals and businesses have come to accept capitalism, though disagreements may arise over the use of capitalist instruments. In other words, capitalism has over the years nurtured a number of complementary principles and practices that have added quality to human life. By the turn of the 21st century, capitalist principles and practices have become rooted in all market economies, variations can only exist in form but not in functionality. Democratic elections may bring in governments that pursue different policies, and economies are faced with business cycles, crises, and opportunities, but capitalism has become the core or fundamental framework in all successful market economies. One can keep comparing capitalism with other aspects of human performance, and there is definitely no end to such global differences as inequality, extent of liberalism, institutional development, and so on (Sklair, 2002; Robinson, 2004). Ultimately, the changes have to be accessed in economic terms.

V CONCLUSION

This chapter primarily aims to provide some guiding concepts in the understanding of capitalism, and communism and socialism is used to give an ideological contrast. In many ways, the failed ideology of communism has actually served two functions in making capitalism the more successful ideology. The various malpractices in communism might have brought out more vividly the virtues of capitalism. Practices in capitalist market economies have been improved through the drawbacks found in communist countries. Hence, communism arises because of inadequacies or drawbacks of capitalism, but in turn, the communist ideology provides room for capitalist advocates, policy makers, and government officials to introduce changes and improvements within the capitalist ideology, making capitalism the more sustainable, durable, and preferable ideology practiced in all successful economies. Capitalism has shown itself to be an "evergreen" ideology.

The three ideologies of capitalism, welfare provisions, and communism can conveniently be shown in Fig. 5.1. The upper portion indicates the functioning of capitalism where the government (G) is relatively small, while the bulk of activities are conducted by businesses (B) and individuals (P). The middle portion shows a situation

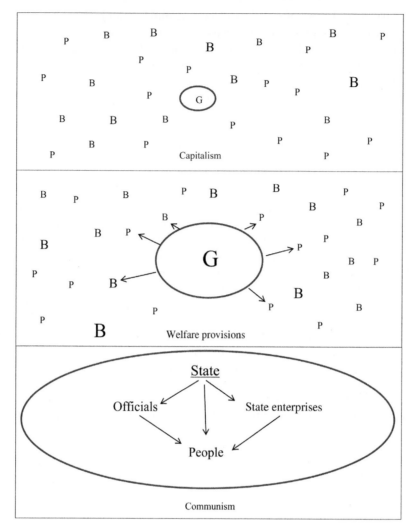

FIGURE 5.1   The three ideologies.

where welfare and subsidies are given by the government to people and businesses. Communism, illustrated in the lower portion, shows that the state is supreme, supported by officials and state enterprises, while the people come under the control of the state, officials, and state enterprises.

Of course, regardless of their size, countries in the world are faced with new problems every day. Economic challenges include the emergence of financial crises, imbalance in trade performances, inequality and poverty, distortions resulting from inappropriate policies, lack of instruments in distortion correction, and so on. Noneconomic challenges can be more deadly as they include conflicts of various sorts: political, ideological, territorial, religious, ethnic, military, regional, racial, and cultural. However, many of these challenges and conflicts are man-made. Differences in the level of civilization in the world economy has often added to mutual misunderstanding that ends up with unilateral actions that upset the balance of regional harmony.

Nonetheless, conflicts in one world region would mean economic activities are badly needed in other world regions to avoid recessions in the peaceful part of the world. After centuries of practices and the challenges from communism, a mature and modern form of capitalism has become the dominant ideology in most successful countries. The ability to recreate itself is the very basic essence of capitalism, coupled with a list of complements. Behavior-wise, the complements to capitalism include individual freedom, democratic principles, openness, and dynamism. The ability to take care of one's private costs is the foundation of capitalism. In the area of fiscal discipline, the higher the ability of individuals through enrichment in endowments will provide more handsome fiscal revenue, so that there are more fiscal resources available for needy individuals. In the business area, there is market freedom of entry and exit, and large corporations coexist with small enterprises. Market freedom is protected by relevant laws to avoid manipulation and distortion. On the question of equality, the more relevant and important aspect is the promotion of opportunities. A high degree of market-friendliness is considered as a prerequisite to business expansion and promotion of opportunities.

Capitalism does offer the more sustainable ideological infrastructure that permits all individuals to utilize their highest potential, and subsequently, allows the society to progress to the highest possible extent. It is true that there are always economic and noneconomic problems emerging on a daily basis, and solutions require different scales of operation. Capitalism may not provide all solutions, but it serves as a framework upon which solutions can be based. Capitalism works like a conduit through which a better result can come forward, one improvement leads to another improvement, and one opportunity gives rise to another opportunity.

is relevant laws to avoid manipulation and distortion. On the question of equality, the more relevant and important aspect is the promotion of opportunities. A high degree of market-friendliness is considered as a prerequisite
to business expansion and promotion of opportunities.

Capitalism does offer the more sustainable ideology of infrastructure that permit all individuals to utilize their
highest potential, and subsequently allows the society to progress to the highest possible extent. It is true that
there are always economic and macroeconomic problems emerging on a daily basis, and solutions require different
scales of operation. Capitalism may not provide all solutions, but it serves as a framework upon which solutions
can be based. Capitalism works like a conduit through which a better result can come forward, one improvement
leads to another improvement, and other opportunity gives rise to another opportunity.

6

Economic Relativity and Capitalism

I INTRODUCTION

The theory of relativity developed by Albert Einstein argues that "measurements of various quantities are relative to the velocities of observers" (*Wikipedia*). Although the theory of relativity has become a cornerstone in physics, its concepts and implications can intuitively be used in economics. In economics, the two most likely outcomes in game theory are either "zero-sum" or "positive-sum." A "zero-sum" game is one in which one person gains at the expense of another person. In a "positive-sum" game, both persons gain, though it is possible that one person gains more than the other person. In the economics theory of "Pareto optimality," an acceptable economic situation is where one person gains, but no other person faces any loss. These economic theories can have wide implications in such situations as inequality and whether economic outcomes are being affected by noneconomic activities. For example, income inequality suggests that economic outcomes are "relative" to each other, depending on how it is measured and who is affected. Depending on time, space, and conditions, the "velocity" of earning differs among individuals.

Activities are full of "relativities." The fluid and dynamic nature of the market provides continuous waves of change in activities. The price yesterday may not be the same today. Lacking response in market "relativity" may result in a loss, as supply and demand conditions may have changed. Similarly, changes in political elections and the emergence of different political leaders will result in policy changes that can impact on other economic relationships. A high tax resulting from a redistributive policy can create new relativities, as welfare recipients may receive more subsidies, while investors may look to investment opportunities elsewhere. Thus, "observers" can show different variations or "velocities" in the "measurement."

In economic transactions, there are always participants or "observers" from two or more parties, and numerous kinds of human activities or "measurements" that involve people and resources. How fast and extensive human economic activities are being conducted provides the speed or "velocities" through which outcomes are obtained. There can be numerous examples. In economics, there are the sellers and buyers, different kinds of goods for sale in the market, and different paces at which the market is cleared. In politics, there are voters and candidates, different levels of elections, and differences in the periodic setting over which elections take place.

© 2017 Elsevier Inc. All rights reserved.

In social work, there are government officials, social workers, and nongovernment organizations that are involved in different kinds of social assistance, and the time involved differs from case to case in social work.

This chapter uses the concept of "relativity" to make a difference between noneconomic and economic activities. By comparison, activities with "absolute" outcomes can be problematic, because the loser may not be happy with the victor, or may contend with the outcome. The following sections use economic concepts to elaborate how the difference between "absolute" and "relative" outcomes can be accommodated, and how capitalism is the most suitable ideological vehicle through which relative outcomes can be achieved.

II ABSOLUTE OUTCOMES: SYSTEMATIZED AND PERSONALIZED

One commonality among noneconomic activities is that the outcomes tend to be "absolute" or "zero-sum," and that the gain of one party would be at the expense or loss of another party. Numerous examples of activities with "absolute" outcomes can be found. In a political election, a winning candidate means all other competing candidates have lost. Indeed, affiliating to one political party means the same politician cannot show loyalty to another political party. In the pursuit of religious faith, the religion chosen by an individual means that the same individual is restricted to choose another religion. In conventional wars and battles, there is clearly a victor and loser. In sport, there is only one winner or winning team, and other competitors become the losers. In a beauty contest, the winning beauty queen means all others are losers. Many personal decisions, such as choice of spouse and whether to have a child and raise a family are activities with "absolute" outcomes.

Another feature among all the activities with "absolute" outcomes is that a "second chance" would not readily be available. A losing candidate in a political election may not be able to gain sufficient support in the next election. A loser in a game will have to wait for the next round of competition. A loser in a beauty contest is unlikely to be selected in the next contest. A victor in a war will remain historic, and it is unlikely for the loser to fight another war. In other words, these outcomes become historic and cannot be changed as soon as the activity is over. In politics, unfortunately, instability can arise if the losing party does not feel content with the outcome. Religious conflicts arise as followers of one religion take to the extreme and impose their religious beliefs on others with different religions. History has shown numerous wars and battles were fought on religious grounds.

In other words, a number of human conflicts arise from activities with "absolute" outcomes. The question is how to reduce human conflicts, given that "absolute" outcomes are unavoidable. The battle between political candidates in an election is fought based on rules and regulations. Religious freedom and openness should allow individuals to choose their own religious faith, and one religious faith cannot overrule another religious faith. Perhaps it is true to say that modern "wars" are fought on sports grounds, where individuals and teams compete with each other based on rules, and referees are used to ensure fairness.

One improvement is the introduction of a civic system that can monitor the different parties in activities with "absolute" outcomes. Armed with a system that consists of appropriate rules and regulations that are known in advance to all parties in the activity, transparency in the outcome of the activity can be seen and readily accepted. In other words, standing between the various parties is a highly civilized system that governs the behavior of the engaging parties and the outcome of the activity so as to avoid faulty transactions or wrong-doing in the process. Thus, there are laws that protect the different parties in a legal case. There are civic institutions and nongovernment organizations that eradicate abuse of authority by government officials. The Olympics and other international sport associations have instituted rules and checks on competitors to ensure fair play.

The institution of a sound, effective, and appropriate system will reduce or provide a solution to a large number of human conflicts. The idea is that once the rules of the game are stated, all affected parties in the activity know about the nature of the activity or game, so that the "absolute" nature of the outcome will be willingly accepted and respected. Modern and civilized countries have continuously aimed to improve the various systems that ensure human safety, discrimination, and equality, while at the same time activities with "absolute" outcomes can be conducted peacefully and effectively. In other words, it is the system and its diversity that stands between different individuals, between individuals and the government, and between different organizations and institutions. Individuals are protected not only by the security force and police, but are civilly and institutionally protected by various rules, regulations, practices, and standards instituted by professional organizations. A well-established civic system can eventually eliminate numerous human conflicts.

The provision of individual freedom and choices can reduce conflicts arising from activities with "absolute" outcomes. Sports generate "absolute" outcomes, but individuals have the freedom to select their choice of sport and personality in the game. In modern countries where religious pluralism is permitted, it would be up to individuals to choose their religious faith. Indeed, faith is very much a personal matter, and freedom must be exercised so that the selected religion is respected. Religious plurality and individual freedom should lead to mutual respect among individuals of different faiths and religious pursuits. Provided that activities are being conducted legally, the provision of individual freedom and liberty would allow individuals to make their choice and see the alternatives in conducting activities with "absolute" outcomes.

Personalization and the availability of choices is the answer to activities with "absolute" outcomes. With individuals exercising their choices freely, the "absolute" nature of the outcome would be softened and become more moderate. As such, variation in outcomes will provide a higher degree of personal utility or satisfaction, and together with mutual respect in their decisions and choice, society is better off as conflicts are reduced and harmony is achieved. Democratic political elections can be used as an example. Political elections are activities with "absolute" outcomes, as there would only be one winner in the political race among the competitors. Since political elections involve ex ante decisions that voters are committing prior to the candidate being elected, voters have the freedom to vote for their preferred candidate. Such personalized choices soften the risk of political instability and uncertainty. If the elected candidate failed to perform as expected after taking office, voters could, on an ex post basis, change their mind on the choice of candidate and make another choice in the next election.

Activities with "absolute" outcomes are biased, in the sense that the winning party will have a "winner takes all" gain, while the loser may be dispirited and could take revenge and introduce activities that destabilize other societal situations and affairs. In other words, there is a need to have a "referee" so that the parties in the two sides come to agree, even though the outcomes only favored one party. The institution of a sound and reliable system serves as a "referee" that stands between the various opposing parties. As rules and regulations are clearly stated and practiced, all parties would observe and have to agree to the outcome. A civic system could provide civic protection to all individuals when engaged in activities with "absolute" outcomes. Since individuals are given the choice, it must be true that individuals would make their best decision and adhere entirely to the outcome of the activity.

III THE RELATIVE NATURE OF ECONOMICS

One key difference between economics and other social disciplines is that economic activities tend to produce "relatives" with "more or less" outcomes. Differences in individual endowments and ownership rights produce differences in one's economic ability, and exercising this economic ability would bring varied results and outcomes among individuals. Typically, two university graduates with a similar educational background would end up doing different jobs and getting different salaries. Two similar investment projects would earn different rewards. Two similar real estate properties in the market would fetch different prices. Hence, economic activities are full of "relative" outcomes.

Another feature is the complementary nature of economic activities, depending on the role each individual plays. In business, the two roles of employer and employee are complementary to each other. Employers cannot survive without employees, since much of the production is done by employees. Likewise, employees cannot survive without employers providing them with jobs. The relationship between buyers and sellers is also complementary, and one cannot survive without the other. The first classical economic lesson that "supply creates its own demand" conveys the very basic message of economic complementarity, and that outcomes have a "relative" nature.

Economic outcomes are "relative" to one another in that one outcome, one player, or one activity is always relative to another in space, time, amount, and kind. Economic relativity also means the existence of variation, diversity, rejuvenation, and recreation. There is indeed no "end" to any economic activity, as the engagement in one activity would naturally bring out the need to have another economic activity. In a nutshell, economic activities are nondiscrete, continuous, and "chained" to each other. Economic activities are interconnected like a globe that is "knitted" together with no end points. One aspect of production requires numerous economic acts with material inputs, while wholesale and retail activities are involved with the output end of the production. The production process also involves a number of supplementary activities, such as financing, transportation, administrative work, insurance, and so on. Similarly, the act of consumption involves not only buying or purchasing, but packaging, advertising, delivery, shop rental and property transactions, inspection, and sampling. One government decision on an economic policy would generate ripple effects. The decision to build infrastructure would need to mobilize materials, labor, and finance for a projected period of time. In turn, each of these ripple effects would multiply outward to generate other activities.

All these interconnected activities would have different prices for various material inputs, and the gains to different parties would differ. The relativity is the "linked" or "chained" nature of economic activities, but the outcomes differ depending on market conditions, the level of value added, and the noneconomic environment in which the activities are being conducted. Normally, one would expect "positive relativity," in that economic activities generate a "positive-sum" outcome to participants, though the gains by different participants may differ. There is the possibility of "negative relativity" when one person's gain becomes another's loss. This occurs when there are "negative-sum" outcomes. Very often, "negative relativity" occurs when noneconomic factors interfere in economic activities.

Consider the activity of wars that generate "absolute" outcomes but will have other economic consequences, for example, in the trading of military products and/or the need for finance. When countries are engaged in a war, materials, human, and financial resources are geared to war preparation and production. Wars could last for a long time, and other than employment in the military sector, shrinkage in other nonmilitary activities would mean economic activities are sacrificed. There will be less production of durable and other service goods, and provision and construction of infrastructure would be absent. Very often, a war economy is reduced to production of the bare essentials only. Wars are activities with "absolute" outcomes, but would the victor in the war feel safe, or would the loser take revenge in a follow-up war? The deteriorating situation may generate a "war breeds war" phenomenon.

Activities with "absolute" outcomes could be transformed into or replaced by economic activities with "relative" outcomes, so that all participants would gain. In some religious states, for example, the practice of a certain religion is not only a matter of individual faith, but is an instrument of control, and inequality is practiced to the extent that some individuals are permanently discriminated against, or would not receive equal treatment in certain aspects of human development. For example, women in some religions are regarded as subordinates to men, and an unequal social position is accorded to the female population. Because of the treatment of subordination, women become less educated and do not have any role to play in an economy. This not only deprives the women's human rights, it leads to wastage of human resources. This calls for a more open attitude to religious faith, or a more contemporary interpretation of religious teaching is needed so as to reflect the basic principles of equality and nondiscrimination. One can easily find other examples of inequality, discrimination, and control in a religious state.

Similar arguments can be made in other forms of social and cultural practices that produce discrimination and permanent inequality, such as superstition, ethnic, and dialect differences. In the past, an aristocratic state benefitted a minority of individuals, and opportunities for the common people were restricted. Similarly, a caste system in India that artificially classified individuals into different social groups is humanly unnatural. It only works as a means to divide individuals through social endowment rather than economic endowment, so that the upper hierarchy in the caste system can enjoy privilege and material wealth at the expense of those in the lower hierarchy. And probably, there are more individuals in the lower hierarchy than individuals in the upper hierarchy in the caste system. It is nothing more than a social instrument through which inequality is generated and adhered to, permanently. Indeed, the caste system can end up with severe distortion in human resources, as individuals in the upper hierarchy may not be talented, while individuals in the lower hierarchy are not given the opportunity to show their potential that could contribute to the economy and even benefit individuals in the upper hierarchy. Activities with "absolute" outcomes can sometimes have "negative relativity" spillover to economic activities.

Intuitively and conceptually, one can argue that economics embraces a "diverse and interconnected pattern of relativities" where participants engaged in different relativity exercises attempt to show their best, so as to achieve the best possible outcome. In fact, because of its "relative" nature, economics can be the solution to a large number of human problems, because economic activities provide motivation and incentive to participants who perform continuously, hoping to have a higher return or a lower cost in the next round of economic activities. Individuals behave differently in any one market and in different markets. Personal preference and expectation enters the individual's production function, thereby determining the kind of economic activities one engages in, and the expected return one gains. Economic relativity permits and reflects market diversity and choice in individual decisions. As such, it would not be possible to produce equality in the outcome of economic activities. Rather, the never-ending chain of economic activities will generate possibilities for others in a new cycle of activities. Positive relativities are generated as a result of individuals searching for opportunities, and in turn the availability of opportunities produces a new round of relative outcomes.

In a nutshell, economic relativity occurs when individuals utilize their resources in exchange for their economic survival. The process of exchange is conducted through the market mechanism, where transactions are not restricted and economic information can openly be used. The economic engine produces nondiscrete and continuous movements where one activity is linked and interconnected with another in a chain-like relationship.

Globe-like, diverse and varied economic activities, together with the freedom to choose and the availability of alternatives, produce multiple dimensions of activities with outcomes "relative" to each other.

IV FROM ABSOLUTE TO RELATIVE OUTCOME: PEACE AGREEMENTS

It is not intended to provide a comprehensive study on war and peace, but the conceptual ideas about war and peace can be used as an example in which political activity with an "absolute" outcome (war) can be transformed into economic activities with a "relative" outcome (peace). War is fought due probably to political, ideological, racial, territorial, and religious conflicts between two or more nations. One can consider the use of economic activities with "relative" outcomes as a solution to wars and regional conflicts. Rather than a conflict intuition of "2 + 2 = 3," the economic intuition of "2 + 2 = 5" suggests that warring nations could turn the "battle" into a "more or less" game, where the act of fighting could be turned into an act of competition using economic instruments. Wars are usually economically damaging, as resources in the form of material inputs and human labor are drained away from normal production activities. Iron and steel would be used for building military equipment rather than machinery for production. Workers would be trained as soldiers rather than engaging in physical production. It follows that economic growth and development in war-prone countries would be kept to a minimal level, or even be frozen at a certain level. At best, production could barely be sufficient, imports of consumer goods may be high while exports would be low, if they exist at all. War is conducted by a small group of politicians and radicals, but is torturing to the majority of ordinary families and households who prefer to have a normal life.

While war is said to have started when shootings and casualties are reported, peace is said to have begun if guns were laid down. While wars are detrimental and should be avoided at all costs, peace can only be long-lasting provided peace is accompanied by postwar reconstruction and development. There are different causes of war, but long-lasting peace requires the use of economics (Luttwak, 2003; Alesina and Spolaore, 2005; de Mesquita, 2006; Paris and Sisk, 2009). Conceptually, peace agreements should mean that the nature of the activity would be changed from one of "absolute" outcome to activities that produced "relative" outcomes. When war is stopped and peace is restored, jobs and employment would have to increase as an alternative in order to absorb material and human resources. Otherwise, the end of war would mean the rise of unemployment and redundant resources, especially human resources. The lack of job provision could easily drag the country back to war.

In other words, for peace to be long-lasting, there must be alternative channels through which war-geared resources would be redirected, reoccupied, and productively used in another capacity, namely in economic growth and reconstruction. Ending a war definitely requires boldness from courageous and broad-minded leaders, but maintaining peace requires the appropriate use of economic alternatives. By absorbing resources into economic activities in a postwar situation, one ensures that economic growth would be the focus of the country, and the unpleasantness from wars would gradually be dissolved into activities with "relative" outcomes. Political and war conflicts would be replaced by economic competition in the market. Human resources would turn to become workers or business-persons. With individuals eager to attain growth and development, a high level of living standard could emerge, followed by prosperity and stability. Eventually, economic activities would overshadow the original conflicts. Peace will then be maintained through a redirected use of resources to postwar economic reconstruction that provides economic opportunities for progress in business, production, and trade.

Economic reconstruction under the Marshall Plan in much of Europe after the Second World War had successfully revived a number of European countries (Smolny, 2000; Hamre and Sullivan, 2002; Ginty and Richmond, 2007; Jacoby, 2007; del Castillo, 2008; Vonyó, 2008). At the domestic level, an injection of investment promoted employment and output, while the establishment of various international institutions after 1945 added stability to the world economy. The economic intuition was that with the injection of needed capital, war-torn economies could have a fresh and quick start in engaging resources for productive purposes, and the resulting employment that absorbed human resources would draw the attention of the workers away from the war experience, and their energy could focus on economic activities.

The postwar reconstruction in East Asia in the 1950s has been a success in laying the economic foundation for the economies of Japan, South Korea, Taiwan, Hong Kong, and Singapore. Li (2002) has documented that the United States had provided economic aid to postwar Japan, South Korea, and Taiwan, with emphasis on infrastructure construction. On the other hand, Great Britain and European countries have invested handsomely in the two small economies of Hong Kong and Singapore. The intention was to make use of the low labor costs, and the export mainly of textiles and other consumables supplied required goods to the growing postwar market in much of Europe. These foreign injections of capital through aid or investment provided the needed initial capital for their economic development.

The East Asian experience does provide useful lessons to other countries for postwar construction. A similarity in political ideology was one criterion in the provision of capital for postwar reconstruction. Even though Japan fought the United States in the Second World War, Japan shares the same political ideology with the United States, who came back to help Japan in reconstruction. Due probably to differences in ideology, the kind of capital injection that the East Asian economies enjoyed in the 1950s did not come forward in the case of the Vietnam War, and the socialist Vietnam economy remained weak until the call for economic reform in 1986 under the "Doi Moi" policy reestablished markets, followed by the initial inflow of foreign capital from European countries (Tan, 1985; Gibbons, 1995; Irvin, 1994; Freeman, 1996; Kokko, 1998; Nghiep and Quy, 2000; Turner and Nguyen, 2005; Beresford, 2008).

At the other extreme, where peace negotiations and agreements were not followed by economic reconstruction, the results not only showed a lack of economic progress, but the probability of renewed conflicts in the region arose. Consequently, wars were repeated, prolonged, and even extended and spread as other conflicts escalated to involve more neighboring countries. Short of going into the details, one observes that the numerous wars in the Middle East since the end of the Second World War have extended from one area of conflict, for example, territorial conflict, to another area of conflict, religious and ethnic conflicts. Even though there have been peace negotiations and agreements, they did not last long and conflicts were renewed (Said, 1996; Awartani and Kleiman, 1997; Wallensteen, 1997; Ross, 2004; Harbom et al., 2006).

On the contrary, if the available resources were geared specifically for postwar reconstruction after peace agreements in the Middle East, the replacement of economic activities would soften the old wounds. The rise of economic progress would overshadow the need and desire for reiterating the old conflicts. Typically, postwar reconstruction will involve massive infrastructural development, and the growing business community should turn its attention to exchange, trade, and market competition. The economics of supply and demand for goods and services will create opportunities. The rise and growth in economic activities will soon spread to provisions of other services and related activities. One can imagine the extent of economic gains for those involved if the amount of redundant land that once was battlefields were turned into land and property development. Land can provide strategic positions in a war and has no value when it used as battlefields, but there could be high value added when the same piece of land is turned into development for residential, industrial, and commercial purposes.

Successful peace agreements mean a game-switch from one with "absolute" outcome to one with "relative" outcome, so that different advantages can be realized by all participants. One prerequisite for peace negotiations is that the agreement must be completed so that all parties would have to stop fighting in order to give peace a chance. Also, peace agreement would have to accompany adequate economic and financial resources, so that new activities would be generated and resources taken away from war-related activities. In other words, there is a need to look for activity substitution, or else the same activity would reappear. Indeed, generations and generations of individuals who were born and live in war-torn, conflict-prone countries for all their life might not be aware of the necessity for peace, and the alternatives that peace could bring. On the contrary, one could imagine the economic advantages of a peaceful Middle East where the large population could be turned into consumers, and businesses could engage in productive activities. The rise in export and import trade in goods and services would have added advantages to the rest of the world economy, and peace in Middle East would provide greater global security.

Experiences of postwar or postconflict peace settlements can bring a completely different picture to the global economy. The successful stories in East Asia since the 1950s could be contrasted with the continuous war conflicts for the Middle East countries, when peace was not accompanied by reconstruction in economic activities. One significant factor for peace to become long-lasting is to have a regime change, probably from one in which resources are geared to military purposes to one in which resources are redirected to economic reconstruction, and that economic competition replaces military competition.

V CAPITALISM AS THE SUITABLE VEHICLE

Economics is not a religion, or a doctrine, but it is a methodology that provides a body of analyses through which human contracts and transactions can be conducted on a mutually inclusive basis. The essence of economic relativity argues that human transactions can best be conducted using economic means and instruments, as that will generate "more or less" outcomes. As such, whoever participates in an economic activity would have some gains, but the gain may be different to different participants.

As discussed earlier, there are numerous kinds of inequalities in the human world, many of which unfortunately are life-long and affect the equality of individuals permanently. Over the decades and centuries, history has told us that with the rise of human rights, a number of human inequalities have been dismantled. Studies have shown that freedom and civility have permitted more opportunities for human development, thereby removing or minimizing inequalities. A mechanism is needed in order to reduce and remove the different kinds of inequalities, or at least eradicate the life-long nature of inequalities. When other life-long inequalities are removed, what remains would be economic inequality, which may not be permanent and can be "adjusted" through individual drive and appropriate policies. In other words, income inequality may not be detrimental and can be rescued if there are economic opportunities for individuals to achieve economic and social mobility through employment, training, and business ventures.

The system that complements economic relativity most suitably is capitalism, as it permits a high degree of individualism, freedom, and civility. An economy is composed of individuals, who form themselves into organizations and associations. Individuals may choose to affiliate with organizations through work, habit, and behavior. Decisions that are taken by organizations are basically decisions by individuals. Hence, having individuals taking care of their own personal economic welfare should be the most equitable and effective form of economic behavior. The other features of capitalism, such as freedom and private ownership rights, are important complements to capitalism as these attributes can bring out the virtues of capitalism more vividly.

To a large extent, the adoption of a capitalist ideology would include the provision of freedom of ownership, transaction, and participation. This would mean that other aspects of inequalities, such as racial inequality, ethnic and religious inequality, and status and political inequality could be dismantled, as individuals become free from discrimination and are treated equally in social and political activities. Such a reduction and eradication of inequalities can promote human civilization to a higher level, where mutual respect occurs. Systematization and individualization turn games with "absolute" outcomes into personal choices, and freedom allows individuals to pursue their private alternatives.

Income inequality is inevitable in a situation when individuals have different endowments from each other, but income inequality could be the "best" form of inequality, as it is not permanent, is alterable, and can be self-correcting. Given the fluidity and dynamism that a market possesses, individual drive and creativity can make a difference in narrowing the income inequality gap. The social question is whether all individuals can have access to endowment-promoting instruments, such as education and training that can improve their overall personal endowment and marketability. A higher probability of employment and job promotion should be the best form of reduction in income inequality, as social mobility is open to all individuals. It is not the able-individuals that the society should penalize through higher tax, but it is the effort to promote more able-individuals that the society should concentrate on. When the pool of able-individuals is enlarged, the government's fiscal revenue will naturally increase. In other words, it is not the size of the cart that one has to worry about, but the health and strength of the horse.

The capitalist ideology is a useful "inequality reducing" vehicle, in that it helps to reduce and remove other life-long inequalities and narrow them down only to income inequality, which can be improved through economic channels and policies. The basis of capitalism adopts a "supply-side" approach such that individuals are given the chance and opportunity to do their best, and the market allows legal exchanges and transactions. Human competition would be exhibited in economic terms, rather than noneconomic terms.

VI CONCLUSION

This chapter serves to provide a wrapping on the usefulness and relevance of the capitalist ideology at the conceptual and analytical level, contrasting the economics of capitalism with other social disciplines of welfare provision and politics. All societies begin with work by individuals, and the nature of economics is related to productivity that differs among individuals due to differences in endowments. By using the relativity concept, this chapter argues that although there are variations in economic outcomes, the variation can be improved and adjusted through the appropriate use of a supply-driven policy of investment, employment, and opportunity creation. Economic inequality therefore may not be suicidal when compared to other life-long and irrevocable forms of inequality and discrimination.

The pursuit of economic activities and transactions allows all individuals to join a "race" that would have different outcomes controlled by the individuals themselves. Furthermore, economic activities that produce "relative" outcomes would gradually replace and substitute other activities that produce "absolute" outcomes. The various features of capitalism that adhere to openness, freedom, equal participation, and ownership would provide a suitable environment through which more economic activities could be nurtured and promoted. The amount of gains that each individual obtains through economic activities should outweigh the drawbacks of differences in gains that each individual obtains. When the sum of gains is larger than the sum of losses, some gains can be used to replenish those who suffer loss through a well-structured system.

No economic system can satisfy the needs of all individuals. Societies should treasure success, but provide more chances to those less fortunate. The capitalist system provides a high degree of flexibility and variety so that new and existing avenues and channels can be used and explored. In short, capitalism is the least of all evils when compared to other economic and noneconomic systems and ideologies that limit the activities of individuals or institute features that promote and preserve the power of control by a minority. The high degree of economic freedom in capitalism in itself is an "evergreen" infrastructure that provides sufficient dynamism and competition for individuals to choose and follow.

THE GLOBAL ECONOMY: PERFORMANCE, CLASSIFICATION, AND CHALLENGES

The World Divided

The global world has always been diverse, but the forms of diversity might have changed considerably. History has told us that there are always some stronger states that have either conquered, ruled, policed, assisted, or bullied others. A number of recent publications have discussed a number of contemporary global issues (Hunt, 2015; Razin, 2015; Van de Berg, 2016). The two World Wars were thought to have settled the dust from various prewar conflicts, such as imperialism and the Great Depression, and a new world order was thought to have begun. For example, the former imperial powers were weakened and many colonies were subsequently given independence, and these newly formed countries could start a new chapter in their development. Having developed extensively since independence in 1776, the United States at the end of the Second World War emerged to become the new world power and assist postwar economic reconstruction in Europe under the 1948 Marshall Plan, and in Japan and other Asian economies. The establishment of such international organizations as the United Nations, the International Monetary Fund, and the World Bank aimed to pursue and maintain global peace and development to ensure growth among the newly formed countries.

The Soviet Union after the Second World War had extended its ideological control or annihilated many Eastern European and Northwest Asian countries. Due obviously to ideological differences, the subsequent Cold War divided the world between the United States and Eastern Europe. In Asia, after its adoption of communism in 1949, China pursued a closed-door policy and was encircled by a number of capitalist market economies in East Asia. The spread of communism to North Korea drew the United States into the Korean War in the early 1950s. The ideological conflict between north and south Vietnam led to the prolonged Vietnam War, while neighboring southeast Asian countries formed the Association of Southeast Asian Nations (ASEAN) to combat the spread of communism to Southeast Asia.

Despite their status as newly independent states after the 1950s, most of these young nations unfortunately remained underdeveloped and constrained by instability, such as rampant corruption, militarism, and ethnic conflicts. While some countries in East Asia have advanced economically through the adoption of reliable systems, it is clear that some underdeveloped countries preferred not to introduce a reliable and civic system so that their leaders could "rent-seek" activities, and maintain and extend their vested interests. Hence, the pre-Second World War leftist argument of imperialism and economic exploitation of the colonies could no longer hold, as these countries experienced economic stagnation even after decades of independence. The situation was worsened by the fact that many of these young countries were resource-rich, but economic progress was absent.

The world also divided along the resource dimension. Many of the oil exporting countries are situated in the Middle East, which has experienced multiple conflicts: ethnic, territorial, and religious. Stability was absent among many Middle East oil exporting countries. Nonetheless, the decades-long massive injections of oil money made them rich, with excess liquidity. Other than a handful of oil exporting countries that used their earned wealth to enhance mega-development projects, many conflict-prone oil exporting countries did not use their oil wealth productively. Instead, much of the oil wealth has unfortunately been used for military purposes to fuel the conflicts in the Middle East region. By the turn of the 21st century, regional conflicts spread to civilized parts of the world in the form of terrorist attacks, using differences in religious faith as the reason.

In East Asia, despite its defeat by the United States at the end of the Second World War, the economy of Japan received postwar reconstruction aid from the United States in the 1950s. The Japanese economy expanded, and by the 1960s and 1970s it had become the world's supplier of consumer products and household appliances, competing successfully with many American and European brand names. However, unlike the oil exporting countries that amassed huge trade surpluses, and by investing extensively in other Asian countries, in North America, and in Europe, Japan contributed to the world economy, Japanese investments showed a "horizontal" pattern, especially in motor vehicles and appliances, in that the production lines of the same Japanese products have been invested in and exported abroad. Hence, the United States and European consumers can buy Japanese brands made in the United States and Europe.

The Soviet Union maintained its leadership of the communist world, especially in the pursuit of military power during the Cold War, but economically its limited resources cannot match those of the advanced world, and supply shortages have severely constrained economic welfare. The "Star Wars" strategy deployed by the United States under President Ronald Reagan in the 1980s eventually drained away and dried up much of the economic resources in the Soviet Union, leading eventually to its collapse and the end of the Cold War in 1989, symbolized by the fall of the Berlin Wall. The Soviet Union was dismantled, and since the 1990s, Eastern European and West Asian countries regained their independence and nationhood. However, with the export of oil the Russian economy grew, but the market economy was not well developed as state intervention continued. It was unfortunate that Russian leaders chose to follow the old ways and Cold War mentality, and in 2014 occupied territories in the Ukraine and the Crimean Peninsula.

While Russia still thinks it can claim to be the big brother in communism, communist China is richer in economic resources. One would wonder why mainland China has taken up the communist ideology when it is resource-abundant and its people are filled with entrepreneurial spirits. After 1949, communist China adopted a "self-sufficiency" policy that literally closed its doors to the outside world, except for short-term assistance from the Soviet Union in the 1950s. At the peak of the Cold War, under the geo-politic strategy of "détente" between the United States and Soviet Union, US President Richard Nixon lured mainland China to the side of the United States. Mainland China saw that as advantageous, and following the historical visit by President Nixon in 1971, mainland China replaced Taiwan and became a member of the Security Council of the United Nations. That started the process of opening up the mainland Chinese economy to the outside world, especially after its economic reform in 1978, because the low costs of production attracted foreign investment. However, President Nixon did not impose any conditions on political modernization in China's ideology. After nearly 40 years of economic reform, China is still a statist economy with the Communist Party controlling key activities. By the 2010s, while externally China aimed to boost its large foreign reserves by promoting its currency to be another internationally accepted currency, the domestic economy was slowing down and the exploitation of various economic inadequacies could easily explode into crises, including the possibility of regional conflicts with China's neighbors.

The financial crisis in 2008 had nominally weakened both the United States and Western Europe, but in effect it served as a "wake-up" call on a number of issues. "Welfare-prone" countries in Western Europe were suffering from huge debts and "beyond their ability" welfare commitments. These countries would face a painful process of economic revival, and there are only few viable alternatives: shed the large welfare expenditure, reduce the size of national debt, or face prolonged economic decline. For these European countries to regain economic strength and competitiveness, they have to redirect their economic policies to the "supply-side," with focus more on productivity than on welfare expenditure.

In the case of the US economy, the 2008 financial crisis should have rung a bell about the prolonged near-zero interest rate policy since the 1980s. The interest rate is theoretically the value of money. With a prolonged low interest rate, money loses its "store of value" function. With high inflation, the value of money would further be "eroded," and the emergence of a "negative real interest rate" would surely lead to more speculation as money had become "cheap." It has also been debated that the various postcrisis "quantitative easing" policies were used more to rescue the banks and the financial sector than to rescue the economy. For sustainable growth, the monetarists recipe is to revive the near-zero rate so that business and economic cycles will revolve around a stable and positive interest rate.

Has the world become more diverse or more difficult to govern? Has the world order become ineffective and out of date? Has human civilization moved too far or backwards? Will militarism or civic preaching be the answer to world conflicts? What could blend the world together that would allow peaceful coexistence, mutual respect, and provide opportunities for economic advancement? How could human energy be redirected from conflict to progress? There is no easy answer, nor is there one single answer. What the world economy could best accomplish is to locate a pathway or identify an approach that can work towards a more encompassing economic goal. In short, the world economy should engage more in "positive-sum" games that produce "relative" outcomes, rather than "zero-sum" games that generate "absolute" outcomes.

To have a better understanding and comprehensively analyze the divided world, the chapters in this section examine the performance of key economic variables across the world economy, understanding how different countries have changed their position over the decades. These statistical studies set the scene on how the divided world can be studied. Since the 1960s, the world has been classified into the first, second, and third world. Such a division is no longer relevant. In its place is the clear division of "five worlds," beginning with the advanced group of countries known as the Organization for Economic Cooperation and Development (OECD), the two socialist economies of Russia and China, the oil exporting countries and the Islamic countries, the emerging countries, and the fragile states.

The OECD countries are mainly the advanced market economies, but they are faced with periodic recessions. Russia and China are undergoing reform, but they are not entirely integrating to the world economy as they are still clinging to their socialist ideology. The oil exporting countries occupy a monopolistic position in oil supply, but much of the oil revenue has been channeled to terrorist activities, and their religion seems to have clashed with other forms of civilization. The emerging countries compose a large group of countries that are stable and want to move ahead, but somehow lack of resources, and have insufficient infrastructure, and investment has not been forthcoming. Their continued improvement will provide good alternatives as destinations for foreign investment. The fragile states are those weak, war-torn, and unstable countries that are plagued with civil unrest, due either to political, military, ethnic, racial, territorial, or religious conflicts, exposing the economy to a sequence of vicious cycles. Without an end to unrest, the chance of any economic development and steady growth in these fragile states is slim.

The world is full of inequalities: natural, institutional, and economic. Natural inequalities are due to geographical and geological differences. Countries are endowed with different natural resources and geographical exposure, but through exploration, countries can benefit from their natural endowments. Institutional inequalities are more constraining and unacceptable, as they often are man-made and life-long. Man-made and institutional inequalities exist due largely to cultural, political, social, and religious practices that provide advantage and power to some sectors of the population at the expense of other sectors. Freedom and capitalism allow individuals to have alternatives, choices, and seek opportunities. The functioning of economic instruments do create income inequalities, but it can remove and reduce other forms of inequality. Consequently, a capitalist civilized economy is faced with only one form of inequality, which is income inequality, that can be improved. The expansion of opportunity is a hidden virtue of capitalism, as it dispels all forms of human inequality, while the remaining income inequality can be dispersed through various means and channels.

This section examines the world economy using macroeconomic data on the "top 10" world economies. By looking at the data for two or more decades, one can see how the world has changed, and which economies have gained strength over the decades. Through the data analysis, one can "X-ray" the world economy in a dynamic setting, examining and making both intercomparisons across economies and intracomparisons within one economy as to how it has performed over the years. Examining both domestic and external economic variables can show the strengths of an economy in the context of civic stability and progress in capitalist development.

7

The Top 10 World Economies

I INTRODUCTION

The world is always changing. Like business cycles at different time periods, some economies rise, stay strong, but face crises and then decline. History tells us that empires and dynasties came and went, often because the over-concentration of political and economic power resulted in abuse, malpractice, and ultimately decline. In the modern world, an economy's natural and resource endowment, production capability, adopted policies, and ideological path are the factors that determine the economy's sustainability. In the contemporary world, however, one sure thing is that an economically freer and politically more democratic country tends to last and remain sustainable, though there can still exist business cycles and periodic crises, resulting from changes of expectations in supply and demand trends.

To see how the world has performed in the last few decades, one can examine the trends in economic variables among the world economies. By examining the data that shows the ex post situation, economic implications of the policies decided on an ex ante basis can be discussed. The data analysis that begins with output performance will extend to consider the economies' external strengths and internal abilities. The two sets of chosen data that can reflect the domestic economic performance are the budget, which shows the political orientation of government policy, and the size of the national debt which reflects the welfare commitment the economy has accumulated. The inability to fund the fiscal deficit is often referred to as the "fiscal crisis" (O'Connor, 1973; Block, 1981; Poterba, 1993; Toye, 2000; Auerbach and Gale, 2009).

As economic openness has been regarded as an instrument of economic success (Li and Zhou, 2013), the various data used to reflect external strengths of an economy include trade, foreign aid, foreign direct investment (FDI), and foreign reserves. These external variables can reflect the global acceptability and viability of an economy. While trade simply shows economic openness and the state of industrial ability, FDI reflects the economy's attractiveness and competitiveness. Foreign aid shows not only the economic health of the weaker recipient countries, but their development progress and potential. If recipient countries remain unstable, foreign aid could equally remain unproductive. Foreign reserves are the ultimate strength a country can have, as they summarize

© 2017 Elsevier Inc. All rights reserved.

various economic performances. The statistics also cover data on military expenditure. However, since military expenditures may not be used in parent countries, it would be appropriate to look at the picture among the different world regions. The discussion will include the issue of peace and stability in the world economy.

All economic data collected are available from public sources. Data on real Gross Domestic Product (GDP), per capita GDP, and international reserves originate from the World Bank. Data on fiscal balance and public debt are obtained from the International Monetary Fund (IMF). Trade and FDI data can be found in the United Nations Conference on Trade and Development (UNCTAD). Data on total foreign aid receipts and total flows by donors are obtained from the Organization for Economic Cooperation and Development (OECD). Both foreign aid receipts and flows by donors include the data on Official Development Assistance (ODA), Other Official Flows (OOF), and private sources. Data on military expenditure can be found in the SIPRI Military Expenditure Database that included 172 countries for the period 1988–2015. Where appropriate, the sources of other data will be specified.

II GDP TRENDS

A country's GDP is the direct measure of the ex post end of economic output. The use of GDP as a measurement has been criticized, as many activities are not included in the measure, while some inclusions in the GDP are unwanted products. The economic contribution of housewives and activities in the informal economy are not included in the GDP measure. Similarly, parallel trade and activities in the informal sector involve output that would not be counted in the GDP measure. Nonetheless, short of a perfect measure, GDP is still used as a convenient and aggregate measure of economic activities.

How the output performance of the world economy has changed over the last two to three decades can be seen from the statistical data on the top 10 best and worst performers available from the World Development Indicators by the World Bank. In general, one would expect a high GDP performance in the industrialized and advanced countries, while the worst performers are the countries that are constantly faced with instability and conflict. A summary picture can be seen from the growth rates of GDP. Table 7.1 shows the best and worst 10 performers in the average GDP growth rate for the period 1980–2015. The data are based on countries with the full data set.

Among the top 10 countries with the highest average real GDP growth rates shown in Table 7.1, many are Asian countries, with the largest being China. Many of these high growth rate countries are experiencing a low level of initial GDP. Hence, statistically, a low level GDP would give a small denominator, and GDP increases producing a large numerator will show a high percentage change. Countries with a low level of GDP initially tend to show a higher GDP growth rate, because the economic base (the denominator) is small, while countries which have achieved a high level of GDP (the denominator) tend to have a low growth rate. Most of the countries with high average growth rates tend to have a low GDP. Nonetheless, these are the better performers. China obviously has received much FDI and trade which has contributed to its high growth rate. Singapore is probably the best performer, given that its GDP is high already (Perry, 2016). South Korea has recovered quickly after the

TABLE 7.1   The Top 10 Best and Worst Average Annual Real GDP Growth Rates: 1980–2015

Highest		Lowest	
China	9.74	Brunei Darussalam	0.37
Iraq	7.01	Georgia	0.48
Singapore	6.63	Central African Republic	0.49
Botswana	6.55	Greece	0.87
India	6.29	Kiribati	1.09
Korea, Republic of	6.14	Liberia	1.14
Malaysia	5.92	Congo, Democratic Republic	1.17
Chad	5.80	Italy	1.22
Mali	5.52	Jamaica	1.39
Indonesia	5.47	Suriname	1.60

1997 Asian financial crisis, and its economic strength comes mainly from strong exports of technological products. India, Malaysia, Indonesia, and Thailand will, with stability, be the "next-tier" of countries that move up the growth ladder (Lim, 2009). There are two African countries (Botswana and Chad) which have achieved high growth rates, due probably to their low level of GDP in the first place, but stability has earned them credit. Despite its instability, and war for a number of years after 2002, Iraq's high growth was due to its oil production.

In the case of the 10 worst performers in average GDP growth, many were weak and small economies that did not provide growth potential. Greece and Italy are the two European countries that were faced with not only low growth rates, but national debts and trade deficits. Brunei Darussalam is a small oil producing country, but it is religious and keeps the monarchy. A major problem with the small countries is the lack of attractiveness, especially if domestic policies are not promarket, but are religiously sensitive and faced with instability.

The absolute level of GDP shows a country's economic ability. Table 7.2 summarizes the number of years when the countries scored in the top 10 highest GDPs in the world economy, measured at constant 2005 price for the period 1980−2014. The first observation is that the top 10 countries are concentrated in 14 world economies, suggesting that there is not much change in the position of the largest countries. The six countries that have scored in the 35 years of the top 10 are the United States, Canada, Japan, Germany, the United Kingdom, France, and Italy. Spain performed strongly. China has caught up quickly and performed better than Russia. South Korea is another Asia country that scored in the top 10 in some years. The two largest Latin American economies are Brazil and Mexico. On the contrary, the 18 countries with the smallest real GDP are all tiny or island states, and most of them obtained independence after the Second World War. The smallest four economies are Kiribati, the Marshall Islands, Tonga, and Dominica. These countries probably face a lack of resources, and depend largely on one or two industries, typically fishery and tourism. Some of these island economies are remote from major world economies, making them difficult to connect to key markets.

Table 7.3 gives details of the top 10 largest GDP countries. One observation is that the rankings remained constant in much of the 1980s. The Russian Federation entered the top 10 only in the 4 years of 1989−92, due probably to the high oil price in those years. South Korea joined the top 10th ranking, beginning from 2002 for 5 years

TABLE 7.2 The Number of Years of Top 10 Largest and Smallest Real GDP Countries (Constant 2005 Price): 1980−2014

Largest		Smallest	
United States	35	Kiribati	35
Japan	35	Marshall Islands	34
Germany	35	Tonga	34
United Kingdom	35	Dominica	30
France	35	Micronesia, Federated States	29
Italy	35	Comoros	26
Canada	35	Tuvalu	25
Spain	33	Palau	24
China	23	Vanuatu	21
Brazil	17	Equatorial Guinea	16
Mexico	13	Sao Tome and Principe	16
India	8	Cape Verde	13
Korea, Republic of	7	Samoa	14
Russia	4	St. Kitts and Nevis	10
		Liberia	7
		St. Vincent and the Grenadines	6
		Solomon Islands	3
		Grenada	1

TABLE 7.3　Top 10 Largest Real GDP Countries (Constant 2005 Price)

	1980	US$ bil	1981	US$ bil	1982	US$ bil	1983	US$ bil	1984	US$ bil	1985	US$ bil
1	United States	5920	United States	6070	United States	5960	United States	6237	United States	6689	United States	6973
2	Japan	2448	Japan	2550	Japan	2636	Japan	2717	Japan	2838	Japan	3018
3	Germany	1816	Germany	1825	Germany	1818	Germany	1847	Germany	1899	Germany	1943
4	France	1291	France	1305	France	1337	France	1354	France	1375	France	1397
5	United Kingdom	1241	United Kingdom	1231	United Kingdom	1256	United Kingdom	1309	United Kingdom	1338	United Kingdom	1386
6	Italy	1185	Italy	1195	Italy	1200	Italy	1214	Italy	1253	Italy	1288
7	Canada	596	Canada	617	Canada	599	Canada	614	Canada	648	Canada	679
8	Spain	557	Spain	556	Spain	563	Spain	573	Spain	584	Spain	597
9	Brazil	513	Mexico	511	Mexico	508	Mexico	486	Mexico	504	Brazil	542
10	Mexico	470	Brazil	491	Brazil	494	Brazil	477	Brazil	502	Mexico	517

	1986	US$ bil	1987	US$ bil	1988	US$ bil	1989	US$ bil	1990	US$ bil	1991	US$ bil
1	United States	7217	United States	7475	United States	7788	United States	8075	United States	8229	United States	8224
2	Japan	3104	Japan	3231	Japan	3462	Japan	3648	Japan	3851	Japan	3979
3	Germany	1988	Germany	2015	Germany	2090	Germany	2172	Germany	2286	Germany	2403
4	France	1430	United Kingdom	1509	United Kingdom	1599	United Kingdom	1639	France	1650	France	1667
5	United Kingdom	1430	France	1467	France	1536	France	1603	United Kingdom	1648	United Kingdom	1627
6	Italy	1325	Italy	1367	Italy	1424	Italy	1472	Italy	1502	Italy	1525
7	Canada	693	Canada	721	Canada	756	Russia	869	Russia	843	Russia	800
8	Spain	617	Spain	651	Spain	684	Canada	774	Canada	775	Spain	763
9	Brazil	585	Brazil	606	Brazil	606	Spain	717	Spain	744	Canada	758
10	Mexico	498	Mexico	507	Mexico	513	Brazil	625	Brazil	599	Brazil	608

	1992	US$ bil	1993	US$ bil	1994	US$ bil	1995	US$ bil	1996	US$ bil	1997	US$ bil
1	United States	8516	United States	8750	United States	9103	United States	9351	United States	9706	United States	10,141
2	Japan	4012	Japan	4019	Japan	4053	Japan	4132	Japan	4240	Japan	4308
3	Germany	2449	Germany	2425	Germany	2485	Germany	2527	Germany	2547	Germany	2593
4	France	1694	France	1683	United Kingdom	1745	United Kingdom	1789	United Kingdom	1837	United Kingdom	1884
5	United Kingdom	1635	United Kingdom	1678	France	1723	France	1759	France	1783	France	1825
6	Italy	1538	Italy	1524	Italy	1557	Italy	1602	Italy	1623	Italy	1653
7	Spain	770	Canada	785	China	844	China	937	China	1030	China	1126
8	Canada	765	Spain	762	Canada	820	Canada	843	Canada	857	Canada	893
9	Russia	684	China	747	Spain	780	Spain	802	Spain	823	Spain	854
10	China	655	Brazil	633	Brazil	667	Brazil	696	Brazil	711	Brazil	735

(Continued)

TABLE 7.3 (*Continued*)

	1998	US$ bil	1999	US$ bil	2000	US$ bil	2001	US$ bil	2002	US$ bil	2003	US$ bil
1	United States	10,592	United States	11,099	United States	11,553	United States	11,666	United States	11,874	United States	12,207
2	Japan	4221	Japan	4213	Japan	4308	Japan	4323	Japan	4336	Japan	4409
3	Germany	2644	Germany	2697	Germany	2777	Germany	2824	Germany	2825	Germany	2804
4	United Kingdom	1950	United Kingdom	2012	United Kingdom	2087	United Kingdom	2143	United Kingdom	2196	United Kingdom	2290
5	France	1890	France	1954	France	2030	France	2070	France	2093	France	2110
6	Italy	1679	Italy	1706	Italy	1769	Italy	1800	Italy	1805	China	1842
7	China	1214	China	1307	China	1417	China	1535	China	1674	Italy	1807
8	Canada	930	Canada	977	Canada	1027	Canada	1044	Canada	1073	Canada	1094
9	Spain	890	Spain	930	Spain	980	Spain	1019	Spain	1048	Spain	1081
10	Mexico	739	Mexico	759	Mexico	799	Mexico	794	Korea,Rep.	800	Korea,Rep.	824

	2004	US$ bil	2005	US$ bil	2006	US$ bil	2007	US$ bil	2008	US$ bil	2009	US$ bil
1	United States	12,670	United States	13,094	United States	13,443	United States	13,681	United States	13,646	United States	13,263
2	Japan	4513	Japan	4572	Japan	4649	Japan	4751	Japan	4702	Japan	4442
3	Germany	2838	Germany	2858	Germany	2964	Germany	3060	China	3183	China	3476
4	United Kingdom	2346	United Kingdom	2412	China	2543	China	2903	Germany	3093	Germany	2918
5	France	2169	China	2257	United Kingdom	2485	United Kingdom	2549	United Kingdom	2541	United Kingdom	2431
6	China	2028	France	2204	France	2256	France	2309	France	2314	France	2246
7	Italy	1836	Italy	1853	Italy	1891	Italy	1919	Italy	1898	Italy	1794
8	Canada	1128	Canada	1164	Spain	1206	Spain	1251	Spain	1265	Spain	1220
9	Spain	1116	Spain	1157	Canada	1195	Canada	1219	Canada	1233	Canada	1200
10	Korea,Rep	864	Korea, Rep.	898	Korea, Rep.	945	India	1001	India	1040	India	1128

	2010	US$ bil	2011	US$ bil	2012	US$ bil	2013	US$ bil	2014	US$ bil
1	United States	13,598	United States	13,816	United States	14,136	United States	14,450	United States	14,797
2	Japan	4648	Japan	4627	Japan	4709	China	4864	China	5270
3	China	3839	China	4196	China	4517	Japan	4785	Japan	4780
4	Germany	3038	Germany	3147	Germany	3159	Germany	3162	Germany	3227
5	United Kingdom	2478	United Kingdom	2518	United Kingdom	2535	United Kingdom	2579	United Kingdom	2677
6	France	2290	France	2337	France	2345	France	2352	France	2361
7	Italy	1825	Italy	1836	Italy	1794	Italy	1760	Italy	1745
8	India	1244	India	1326	India	1394	India	1490	India	1598
9	Canada	1240	Canada	1271	Canada	1293	Canada	1319	Canada	1360
10	Spain	1220	Spain	1212	Spain	1187	Korea, Rep.	1200	Korea, Rep.	1239

TABLE 7.4 Top 10 Lowest Real GDP Countries (Constant 2005 Price)

	1980	US$ bil	1981	US$ bil	1982	US$ bil	1983	US$ bil	1984	US$ bil	1985	US$ bil
1	Kiribati	0.06	Kiribati	0.06	Kiribati	0.06	Kiribati	0.07	Kiribati	0.07	Kiribati	0.06
2	Equ. Guinea	0.11	Marshall Is.	0.06	Marshall Is.	0.07	Marshall Is.	0.08	Marshall Is.	0.08	Marshall Is.	0.08
3	Bhutan	0.13	Equ. Guinea	0.12	Equ. Guinea	0.12	Equ. Guinea	0.13	Equ. Guinea	0.13	Equ. Guinea	0.15
4	Cape Verde	0.15	Tonga	0.15	Tonga	0.16	Tonga	0.16	Tonga	0.16	Tonga	0.17
5	Dominica	0.17	Bhutan	0.15	Bhutan	0.16	Bhutan	0.18	Bhutan	0.18	Bhutan	0.19
6	Vanuatu	0.17	Cape Verde	0.16	Cape Verde	0.17	St. Kitts&Nevis	0.18	Cape Verde	0.19	Cape Verde	0.21
7	St.Kitts &Nevi	0.18	Vanuatu	0.18	St. Kitts&Nevis	0.18	Cape Verde	0.18	St. Kitts&Nevis	0.20	St. Kitts&Nevi	0.21
8	StVincent &Gr	0.19	St. Kitts&Nevis	0.18	Dominica	0.20	Dominica	0.20	Dominica	0.21	Dominica	0.22
9	Comoros	0.21	Dominica	0.19	Vanuatu	0.20	St. Vincent&Gr	0.22	St. Vincent&Gr	0.23	St. Vincent&G	0.24
10	Grenada	0.24	St. Vincent&Gr	0.20	St. Vincent&Gr	0.21	Vanuatu	0.23	Vanuatu	0.25	Vanuatu	0.25

	1986	US$ bil	1987	US$ bil	1988	US$ bil	1989	US$ bil	1990	US$ bil	1991	US$ bil
1	Kiribati	0.06	Kiribati	0.06	Kiribati	0.07	Kiribati	0.07	Tuvalu	0.02	Tuvalu	0.02
2	Marshall Is.	0.09	Marshall Is.	0.10	Marshall Is.	0.11	Marshall Is.	0.11	Kiribati	0.07	Kiribati	0.06
3	Equ. Guinea	0.14	Equ. Guinea	0.15	Equ. Guinea	0.15	Equ. Guinea	0.15	Marshall Is.	0.11	Marshall Is.	0.11
4	Micronesia	0.17	Micronesia	0.17	Micronesia	0.18	Tonga	0.18	Equ. Guinea	0.15	Equ. Guinea	0.15
5	Tonga	0.18	Tonga	0.18	Tonga	0.18	Micronesia	0.18	Tonga	0.18	Palau	0.16
6	Cape Verde	0.21	Cape Verde	0.22	Cape Verde	0.23	Vanuatu	0.24	Micronesia	0.19	Tonga	0.19
7	Bhutan	0.21	Vanuatu	0.24	Vanuatu	0.24	Cape Verde	0.25	Cape Verde	0.25	Micronesia	0.20
8	Dominica	0.23	Dominica	0.25	Dominica	0.27	Comoros	0.26	Vanuatu	0.27	Cape Verde	0.25
9	St.Kitts&Gr	0.23	St. Kitts&Nevi	0.25	Comoros	0.27	Dominica	0.27	Comoros	0.28	Comoros	0.26
10	Vanuatu	0.25	Comoros	0.27	St. Kitts&Nevis	0.28	St. Kitts&Nevis	0.30	Dominica	0.28	Vanuatu	0.28

	1992	US$ bil	1993	US$ bil	1994	US$ bil	1995	US$ bil	1996	US$ bil	1997	US$ bil
1	Tuvalu	0.02	Tuvalu	0.02	Tuvalu	0.02	Tuvalu	0.02	Tuvalu	0.02	Tuvalu	0.02
2	Kiribati	0.07	Kiribati	0.07	Kiribati	0.07	Kiribati	0.07	Kiribati	0.08	Kiribati	0.08
3	Marshall Is.	0.12	Marshall Is.	0.13	Liberia	0.11	Liberia	0.10	Liberia	0.12	Marshall Is.	0.12
4	Palau	0.15	Palau	0.13	Marshall Is.	0.14	Marshall Is.	0.15	Marshall Is.	0.13	Palau	0.18
5	Tonga	0.19	Liberia	0.14	Palau	0.14	Palau	0.16	Palau	0.18	Tonga	0.21
6	Equ. Guinea	0.20	Tonga	0.20	Tonga	0.20	Tonga	0.21	Tonga	0.21	Micronesia	0.22
7	Liberia	0.21	Equ. Guinea	0.22	Micronesia	0.23	Micronesia	0.24	Micronesia	0.24	Liberia	0.24
8	Micronesia	0.21	Micronesia	0.23	Equ. Guinea	0.25	Comoros	0.29	Comoros	0.29	Comoros	0.30

(Continued)

TABLE 7.4 (*Continued*)

	1992	US$ bil	1993	US$ bil	1994	US$ bil	1995	US$ bil	1996	US$ bil	1997	US$ bil
9	Samoa	0.28	Vanuatu	0.29	Comoros	0.28	Equ. Guinea	0.30	Dominica	0.31	Dominica	0.32
10	Cape Verde	0.28	Samoa	0.29	Samoa	0.28	Samoa	0.30	Samoa	0.32	Samoa	0.33

	1998	US$ bil	1999	US$ bil	2000	US$ bil	2001	US$ bil	2002	US$ bil	2003	US$ bil
1	Tuvalu	0.02	Tuvalu	0.02	Tuvalu	0.02	Tuvalu	0.02	Tuvalu	0.02	Tuvalu	0.02
2	Kiribati	0.09	Kiribati	0.09	Kiribati	0.10	Kiribati	0.10	Kiribati	0.10	Kiribati	0.10
3	Marshall Is.	0.12	Marshall Is.	0.12	SaoTome &Pr	0.10	SaoTome &Pri	0.11	SaoTome &Pri	0.11	SaoTome &Pri	0.12
4	Palau	0.18	Palau	0.17	Marshall Is.	0.12	Marshall Is.	0.13	Marshall Is.	0.13	Marshall Is.	0.13
5	Tonga	0.22	Tonga	0.23	Palau	0.18	Palau	0.18	Palau	0.19	Palau	0.19
6	Micronesia	0.23	Micronesia	0.23	Tonga	0.23	Tonga	0.24	Micronesia	0.25	Micronesia	0.25
7	Comoros	0.30	Comoros	0.31	Micronesia	0.24	Micronesia	0.25	Tonga	0.25	Tonga	0.26
8	Liberia	0.31	Dominica	0.34	Comoros	0.31	Dominica	0.34	Dominica	0.33	Dominica	0.36
9	Samoa	0.33	Samoa	0.34	Dominica	0.34	Comoros	0.35	Vanuatu	0.35	Vanuatu	0.36
10	Dominica	0.33	Vanuatu	0.36	Samoa	0.36	Solomon Is.	0.36	Solomon Is.	0.35	Comoros	0.36

	2004	US$ bil	2005	US$ bil	2006	US$ bil	2007	US$ bil	2008	US$ bil	2009	US$ bil
1	Tuvalu	0.02	Tuvalu	0.02	Tuvalu	0.02	Tuvalu	0.02	Tuvalu	0.03	Tuvalu	0.02
2	Kiribati	0.11	Kiribati	0.11	Kiribati	0.10	Kiribati	0.11	Kiribati	0.11	Kiribati	0.11
3	SaoTome &Pr	0.12	SaoTome &Pr	0.12	SaoTome&Pr	0.14	SaoTome &Pri	0.14	Marshall Is.	0.14	Marshall Is.	0.14
4	Marshall Is.	0.13	Marshall Is.	0.14	Marshall Is.	0.14	Marshall Is.	0.15	SaoTome &Prin	0.15	SaoTome &Pri	0.16
5	Palau	0.20	Palau	0.21	Palau	0.20	Palau	0.21	Palau	0.20	Palau	0.17
6	Micronesia	0.24	Micronesia	0.25	Micronesia	0.25	Micronesia	0.24	Micronesia	0.24	Micronesia	0.24
7	Tonga	0.26	Tonga	0.26	Tonga	0.26	Tonga	0.25	Tonga	0.25	Tonga	0.26
8	Comoros	0.37	Dominica	0.37	Dominica	0.39	Comoros	0.39	Comoros	0.40	Comoros	0.40
9	Dominica	0.37	Comoros	0.38	Comoros	0.39	Dominica	0.41	Dominica	0.44	Dominica	0.44
10	Vanuatu	0.38	Vanuatu	0.39	Vanuatu	0.43	Vanuatu	0.45	Vanuatu	0.48	Samoa	0.48

	2010	US$ bil	2011	US$ bil	2012	US$ bil	2013	US$ bil	2014	US$ bil
1	Tuvalu	0.02	Tuvalu	0.03	Tuvalu	0.03	Tuvalu	0.03	Tuvalu	0.03
2	Kiribati	0.11	Kiribati	0.11	Kiribati	0.12	Kiribati	0.12	Kiribati	0.12
3	Marshall Is.	0.15	Marshall Is.	0.15	Marshall Is.	0.16	Marshall Is.	0.16	Marshall Is.	0.15
4	SaoTome&Pr	0.17	SaoTome&Pr	0.18	SaoTome&Pr	0.18	SaoTome&Pri	0.19	SaoTome&Prin	0.20
5	Palau	0.18	Palau	0.19	Palau	0.20	Palau	0.20	Palau	0.20
6	Micronesia	0.25	Micronesia	0.25	Micronesia	0.25	Micronesia	0.24	Micronesia	0.24
7	Tonga	0.27	Tonga	0.28	Tonga	0.28	Tonga	0.28	Tonga	0.27
8	Comoros	0.41	Comoros	0.42	Comoros	0.44	Dominica	0.43	Dominica	0.45
9	Dominica	0.44	Dominica	0.44	Dominica	0.44	Comoros	0.45	Comoros	0.46
10	Samoa	0.48	Samoa	0.51	Samoa	0.52	Samoa	0.51	Samoa	0.51

till 2006, though it returned to top 10th in 2013. India joined the top ranking in 2007. The United States, Japan, and Germany have been the largest economies over the period. However, China joined the ranking as the 10th in 1992, climbed to the sixth position in 2004, and to third position, overtaking Germany in 2008, eventually overtaking Japan as the second largest country in 2013. In value terms, the United States is still the highest country, and the US's GDP is much larger than all others. By 2014, even though China ranked second, China's real GDP was about one third of the GDP of the United States. The GDP showed a wide range among the top 10 countries. In all years, the GDP of the United States has been 10-fold larger than the top 10th country.

The tiny nature of the smallest world economies are shown in Table 7.4. One observation is that the GDP of these countries are no more than US$0.51 billion. Samoa is the only economy whose GDP has reached US$0.5 billion since 2011. The GDP movement in this group of economies has been slow, indicating that there has been little change in their economic activity in the sample period. The GDP of Kiribati in 1980 was US$0.06 billion, which doubled to US$0.12 billion in 2012 at constant 2005 prices. The GDP of Tuvalu, which was the lowest with US$0.02 billion in 1990, remained also the lowest in 2014, with a GDP of US$0.03 billion.

A slightly different measurement is to consider the highest and lowest GDP per capita, as this takes into account the size of population in the economy. GDP per capita is gross domestic product divided by mid-year population expressed at constant 2005 price. The per capita GDP is an average figure, as there can be varying degrees of income inequality. Table 7.5 summarizes the number of years in the top 10 of the largest and lowest

TABLE 7.5 The Number of Years in the Top 10 of the Largest and Lowest Per Capita GDP Countries (Constant 2005 Price): 1980—2014

Largest		Lowest	
Switzerland	35	Burundi	35
Norway	35	Malawi	35
Luxembourg	35	Ethiopia	34
Iceland	34	Rwanda	28
Bermuda	33	Liberia	25
Liechtenstein	30	Mozambique	22
Monaco	29	Eritrea	21
Denmark	28	Congo, Dem. Rep.	18
United Arab Emirates	19	Uganda	17
Qatar	19	Niger	17
Ireland	14	Nepal	15
Channel Islands	9	Madagascar	13
United States	9	Bangladesh	12
Sweden	7	Lao PDR	9
Brunei Darussalam	6	Guinea	9
Macao SAR, China	4	Afghanistan	8
San Marino	2	Burkina Faso	7
Netherlands	1	Tajikistan	7
		China	4
		Vietnam	4
		Cambodia	3
		India	2
		Sierra Leone	2
		Chad	2
		Central African Republic	2

per capita GDP countries. There are a total of 18 countries which have experienced the largest per capita GDP, while the number of countries with the lowest per capita GDP is concentrated on the 24 poorest countries. The countries with the highest per capita GDP are mainly the smaller European countries, with Switzerland, Norway, and Luxembourg remaining in the top 10 over the entire period of 35 years (1980–2014), while Bermuda, Macao SAR, Brunei Darussalam, and San Marino are tiny economies. Two oil producing countries are the United Arab Emirates and Qatar. The list of lowest per capita GDP countries consisted mainly of poor African and West Asian countries. There is no Latin American country in the list of lowest per capita GDP. China experienced 4 years from 1980 to 83, while India appeared twice in 1980 and 1981.

Table 7.6 produces detailed rankings of the top 10 countries with the largest per capita GDP. Several observations can be made. Monaco is the largest per capita GDP country for the period 1980 – 2008, and its per capita GDP has been higher than the second largest by a large margin. Other than the top two or three countries with the highest per capita GDP, the gap among the other top 10 countries tends to be quite narrow in most years. Other than the United States, which appeared as the top 9th or 10th in 9 years (1988 – 93, 2010, and 2014), the other high per capita GDP countries are mostly the smaller north and central European countries that have achieved high living standards and a high quality of life. The United Arab Emirates tended to stay strong and ranked second in much of the 1980s, but others have caught up and its ranking declined to 10th in 1998, and out of the top 10 after 1998. On the contrary, Qatar has appeared in the top 10 since 1997.

TABLE 7.6 Top 10 Largest Per Capita GDP Countries (Constant 2005 Price)

	1980	US$	1981	US$	1982	US$	1983	US$	1984	US$	1985	US$
1	Monaco	95,231	Monaco	94,627	Monaco	95,301	Monaco	94,830	Monaco	94,834	Monaco	95,377
2	UAEmirates	81,947	UAEmirates	79,802	UAEmirates	70,247	UAEmirates	63,631	UAEmirates	62,978	UAEmirates	57,563
3	Bermuda	52,903	Liechtenstein	54,007	Liechtenstein	52,561	Liechtenstein	52,342	Liechtenstein	54,099	Liechtenstein	57,366
4	Liechtenstein	52,227	Bermuda	53,788	Bermuda	50,579	Bermuda	51,151	Bermuda	50,948	Bermuda	49,511
5	BruneiDarus	42,876	Switzerland	43,104	Switzerland	42,292	Switzerland	42,380	Switzerland	43,498	Switzerland	44,898
6	Switzerland	42,657	Norway	36,621	Iceland	36,752	Norway	37,819	Norway	39,936	Norway	41,948
7	Norway	36,187	Iceland	36,461	Norway	36,532	Iceland	35,489	Iceland	36,563	Iceland	37,471
8	Iceland	35,371	BruneiDarus	33,326	BruneiDarus	33,643	Luxembourg	33,988	Luxembourg	36,054	Luxembourg	36,989
9	Luxembourg	32,946	Luxembourg	32,668	Luxembourg	33,010	BruneiDarus	32,871	Denmark	33,274	Denmark	34,599
10	Denmark	30,205	Denmark	29,946	Denmark	31,081	Denmark	31,927	Brunei Darus	32,159	Brunei Darus	30,801

	1986	US$	1987	US$	1988	US$	1989	US$	1990	US$	1991	US$
1	Monaco	97,003	Monaco	99,001	Monaco	103,309	Monaco	107,335	Monaco	109,705	Monaco	110,115
2	Liechtenstein	59,088	Liechtenstein	63,906	Liechtenstein	66,805	Liechtenstei	69,031	Liechtenstei	69,749	Liechtenstein	70,105
3	Bermuda	52,366	Bermuda	53,891	Bermuda	55,599	Bermuda	55,376	Bermuda	54,934	Luxembourg	54,604
4	UAEmirates	46,219	Switzerland	45,927	Switzerland	47,085	Luxembourg	48,974	Luxembourg	50,938	Bermuda	53,267
5	Switzerland	45,495	UAEmirates	45,010	Luxembourg	45,040	Switzerland	48,728	Switzerland	50,003	Switzerland	48,929
6	Norway	43,486	Norway	44,054	Norway	43,742	Norway	43,996	UAEmirates	48,855	UAEmirates	46,654
7	Luxembourg	40,499	Iceland	42,440	Iceland	41,743	UAEmirates	43,693	Norway	44,690	Norway	45,858
8	Iceland	39,530	Luxembourg	41,828	UAEmirates	41,261	Iceland	41,336	Iceland	41,495	Iceland	40,925
9	Denmark	36,263	Denmark	36,322	Denmark	36,253	Denmark	36,438	Denmark	36,964	Denmark	37,348
10	Sweden	30,153	Sweden	31,060	United States	31,854	United States	32,717	United States	32,966	United States	32,508

	1992	US$	1993	US$	1994	US$	1995	US$	1996	US$	1997	US$
1	Monaco	110,731	Monaco	108,721	Monaco	110,089	Monaco	111,405	Monaco	111,657	Monaco	113,165
2	Liechtenstei	71,655	Liechtenstei	73,706	Liechtenstein	77,628	Liechtenstei	80,987	Liechtenstei	85,298	Liechtenstein	90,104
3	Luxembourg	54,864	Luxembourg	56,407	Luxembourg	57,770	Luxembourg	57,780	Bermuda	58,001	Luxembourg	60,534

(Continued)

TABLE 7.6   *(Continued)*

	1992	US$	1993	US$	1994	US$	1995	US$	1996	US$	1997	US$
4	Bermuda	53,622	Bermuda	54,940	Bermuda	54,887	Bermuda	56,893	Luxembourg	57,862	Bermuda	60,300
5	Switzerland	48,372	Norway	48,228	Norway	50,377	Norway	52,214	Norway	54,599	Norway	57,232
6	Norway	47,201	Switzerland	47,873	Switzerland	48,096	Switzerland	48,005	Switzerland	48,081	Switzerland	49,074
7	UAEmirates	45,700	UAEmirates	43,917	UAEmirates	44,611	UAEmirates	45,279	UAEmirates	45,490	UAEmirates	46,609
8	Iceland	39,051	Iceland	39,164	Iceland	40,227	Denmark	40,759	Iceland	41,746	Qatar	45,347
9	Denmark	37,960	Denmark	37,800	Denmark	39,754	Iceland	40,056	Denmark	41,705	Iceland	43,440
10	United States	33,200	United States	33,663	Qatar	34,901	San Marino	35,345	San Marino	36,728	Denmark	42,886

	1998	US$	1999	US$	2000	US$	2001	US$	2002	US$	2003	US$
1	Monaco	116,108	Monaco	118,891	Monaco	122,439	Monaco	124,015	Monaco	124,187	Monaco	124,338
2	Liechtenstein	95,684	Liechtenstein	104,194	Liechtenstei	106,194	Liechtenstei	104,213	Liechtenstein	102,121	Liechtenstei	99,204
3	Luxembourg	63,667	Luxembourg	68,102	Luxembourg	72,865	Bermuda	73,482	Luxembourg	75,058	Luxembourg	75,034
4	Bermuda	62,193	Bermuda	63,938	Bermuda	69,276	Luxembourg	73,443	Bermuda	71,926	Bermuda	73,894
5	Norway	58,419	Channel Is.	59,278	Channel Is.	62,292	Norway	61,622	Norway	62,211	Norway	62,454
6	Channel Is.	57,518	Norway	59,196	Norway	60,726	Channel Is.	60,909	Channel Is.	59,475	Channel Is.	57,142
7	Switzerland	50,370	Switzerland	50,954	Switzerland	52,668	Switzerland	53,092	Qatar	53,200	Qatar	52,630
8	Qatar	48,521	Qatar	48,673	Qatar	50,673	Qatar	51,090	Switzerland	52,768	Switzerland	52,404
9	Iceland	45,744	Iceland	47,076	Iceland	48,637	Iceland	49,801	Iceland	49,582	Iceland	50,575
10	UAEmirates	44,292	Denmark	44,818	Denmark	46,342	Denmark	46,556	Ireland	47,020	Ireland	47,628

	2004	US$	2005	US$	2006	US$	2007	US$	2008	US$	2009	US$
1	Monaco	125,966	Monaco	126,599	Monaco	130,821	Monaco	147,140	Monaco	158,802	Liechtenstei	115,262
2	Liechtenstei	101,317	Liechtenstein	105,307	Liechtenstei	113,470	Liechtenstei	116,314	Liechtenstei	117,494	Luxembourg	79,003
3	Luxembourg	77,620	Luxembourg	79,594	Luxembourg	82,158	Luxembourg	86,127	Luxembourg	85,014	Bermuda	77,419
4	Bermuda	75,117	Bermuda	75,882	Bermuda	79,631	Bermuda	81,436	Bermuda	82,193	Norway	65,088
5	Norway	64,545	Norway	65,767	Norway	66,739	Norway	67,805	Norway	67,010	Iceland	57,873
6	Qatar	57,506	Channel Is.	57,209	Channel Is.	59,575	Channel Is.	62,649	Iceland	61,222	Switzerland	57,063
7	Channel Is.	56,846,	Iceland	56,611	Qatar	58,066	Iceland	61,663	Switzerland	59,038	Qatar	55,831
8	Iceland	54,258	Switzerland	54,799	Iceland	57,639	Switzerland	58,461	Qatar	57,389	Denmark	47,237
9	Switzerland	53,525	Qatar	54,229	Switzerland	56,641	Qatar	57,520	Ireland	50,502	Ireland	46,807
10	Ireland	48,907	Ireland	50,568	Ireland	51,915	Ireland	52,924	Denmark	50,036	Netherlands	43,435

	2010	US$	2011	US$	2012	US$	2013	US$	2014	US$
1	Luxembourg	81,565	Luxembourg	81,853	Luxembourg	79,780	Luxembourg	79,509	Luxembourg	82,924
2	Bermuda	76,394	Bermuda	74,483	Bermuda	70,601	Norway	65,240	Norway	67,223
3	Norway	64,590	Norway	64,613	Norway	65,617	Qatar	59,894	Qatar	62,169
4	Qatar	58,258	Qatar	60,290	Qatar	59,579	Iceland	59,061	Iceland	59,431
5	Switzerland	58,140	Switzerland	58,534	Switzerland	58,559	Switzerland	59,009	Switzerland	59,310
6	Iceland	56,255	Iceland	57,280	Iceland	57,629	Macao	54,092	Macao	52,256
7	Denmark	47,792	Denmark	48,144	Macao	49,177	Ireland	47,257	Ireland	52,219
8	Ireland	46,424	Ireland	47,538	Denmark	47,649	Denmark	47,220	Denmark	47,534
9	Sweden	44,878	Macao	45,925	Ireland	47,285	United States	45,710	United States	46,405
10	United States	43,961	Sweden	45,727	Sweden	45,260	Sweden	45,551	Sweden	46,036

Data for Monaco and Liechtenstein are unavailable since 2009 and 2010, respectively.

Table 7.7 shows the details of the top 10 lowest per capita GDP countries. These are poor African countries, as the per capita GDP among the 10 lowest ranged mostly between US$150 to US$400 over the sample period. The bulk of the poorest countries in the world are concentrated in Africa, and this group of countries showed no potential for economic development, and no single factor could explain their weakness. In addition to China and India, the other Asian countries that appeared in Table 7.7 include Vietnam, Laos, and Cambodia. Vietnam has performed better, but with the pursuit of economic stability and openness, the other two countries should gradually improve. Economic improvement can be instituted in the two West Asian countries of Tajikistan and Afghanistan if stability and market-friendly policies are pursued. In conclusion, the GDP data will set the scene for further examination of other economic data before a more complete picture on the world economy can be discussed in the following chapters.

TABLE 7.7 Top 10 Lowest Per Capita GDP Countries (Constant 2005 Price)

	1980	US$	1981	US$	1982	US$	1983	US$	1984	US$	1985	US$
1	Nepal	185.1	Ethiopia	158.3	Ethiopia	155.4	Mozambique	158.5	Mozambique	145.8	Ethiopia	132.1
2	Burundi	191.8	Nepal	196.0	Mozambique	191.9	Ethiopia	163.1	Ethiopia	153.5	Mozambique	145.8
3	Mozambique	205.8	Burundi	209.4	Nepal	198.8	Nepal	188.4	Burundi	197.3	Uganda	184.7
4	China	220.5	Mozambique	210.9	Uganda	199.5	Burundi	203.0	Uganda	197.5	Nepal	209.5
5	Malawi	230.4	Malawi	212.5	Burundi	201.5	Uganda	204.6	Nepal	202.0	Burundi	213.6
6	Bangladesh	243.5	China	229.1	Malawi	212.7	Malawi	215.0	Malawi	219.1	Malawi	219.4
7	Burkina Faso	247.9	Bangladesh	246.0	Bangladesh	245.2	Bangladesh	248.4	Lao PDR	239.3	Lao PDR	244.5
8	Rwanda	276.3	Burkina Faso	252.5	China	246.2	Burkina Faso	264.1	Burkina Faso	252.9	Bangladesh	255.7
9	India	291.8	Rwanda	281.8	Burkina Faso	269.9	China	269.0	Bangladesh	254.4	Rwanda	264.3
10	Chad	324.5	India	302.4	Rwanda	277.9	Rwanda	285.1	Vietnam	263.0	Burkina Faso	267.4
	1986	**US$**	**1987**	**US$**	**1988**	**US$**	**1989**	**US$**	**1990**	**US$**	**1991**	**US$**
1	Ethiopia	140.3	Ethiopia	154.7	Ethiopia	150.5	Ethiopia	145.0	Ethiopia	144.0	Ethiopia	129.2
2	Mozambique	141.8	Mozambique	162.9	Mozambique	176.6	Malawi	185.7	Liberia	177.1	Liberia	154.6
3	Uganda	179.1	Uganda	179.6	Uganda	187.5	Mozambique	187.4	Mozambique	186.9	Mozambique	191.5
4	Malawi	207.5	Malawi	198.4	Malawi	192.7	Uganda	192.3	Malawi	189.1	Malawi	201.2
5	Burundi	213.4	Nepal	213.0	Burundi	221.0	Burundi	217.0	Uganda	197.6	Uganda	201.5
6	Nepal	214.2	Burundi	217.6	Nepal	224.2	Nepal	228.6	Burundi	218.3	Burundi	223.5
7	Lao PDR	249.4	Lao PDR	238.9	Lao PDR	227.5	Rwanda	246.3	Nepal	233.5	Nepal	242.2
8	Bangladesh	259.5	Rwanda	252.7	Rwanda	252.6	Lao PDR	252.4	Rwanda	240.7	Rwanda	242.8
9	Rwanda	265.9	Bangladesh	262.1	Bangladesh	260.8	Bangladesh	260.8	Lao PDR	261.5	Lao PDR	265.0
10	Vietnam	268.7	Vietnam	271.5	Vietnam	278.7	Burkina Faso	280.4	Bangladesh	269.6	Bangladesh	272.2
	1992	**US$**	**1993**	**US$**	**1994**	**US$**	**1995**	**US$**	**1996**	**US$**	**1997**	**US$**
1	Liberia	102.2	Liberia	69.3	Liberia	53.9	Liberia	50.0	Liberia	53.1	Liberia	101.8
2	Ethiopia	113.9	Ethiopia	124.4	Ethiopia	124.1	Ethiopia	127.5	Ethiopia	139.0	Ethiopia	139.1
3	Mozambique	175.9	Mozambique	184.2	Rwanda	143.0	Burundi	173.6	Burundi	157.5	Burundi	153.2
4	Eritrea	176.7	Eritrea	199.7	Malawi	179.9	Mozambique	188.2	Mozambique	196.2	Tajikistan	206.5
5	Malawi	184.5	Malawi	201.5	Mozambique	189.5	Rwanda	195.6	Tajikistan	205.6	Mozambique	210.5
6	Uganda	201.4	Burundi	202.7	Burundi	191.5	Malawi	207.6	Rwanda	210.7	Rwanda	219.8

(Continued)

TABLE 7.7 (*Continued*)

	1992	US$	1993	US$	1994	US$	1995	US$	1996	US$	1997	US$
7	Burundi	220.7	Uganda	210.9	Uganda	217.2	Uganda	234.5	Malawi	218.7	Malawi	221.5
8	Nepal	245.8	Cambodia	241.8	Eritrea	240.5	Eritrea	244.4	Uganda	247.8	Uganda	252.4
9	Guinea	270.8	Nepal	248.7	Cambodia	254.9	Tajikistan	250.2	Eritrea	262.0	Congo, D. R.	256.9
10	Lao PDR	271.7	Niger	266.9	Nepal	262.3	Cambodia	262.7	Niger	265.2	Niger	262.8

	1998	US$	1999	US$	2000	US$	2001	US$	2002	US$	2003	US$
1	Liberia	122.1	Ethiopia	133.4	Ethiopia	137.5	Ethiopia	144.7	Ethiopia	142.7	Ethiopia	135.6
2	Ethiopia	130.5	Liberia	140.0	Burundi	150.3	Burundi	149.7	Burundi	151.9	Burundi	145.4
3	Burundi	158.5	Burundi	155.0	Liberia	166.8	Liberia	196.4	Congo, D. R.	202.0	Liberia	167.0
4	Tajikistan	214.7	Rwanda	212.1	Congo, D. R.	211.4	Congo, D. R.	201.7	Malawi	203.1	Congo, D. R.	207.2
5	Rwanda	215.9	Tajikistan	219.6	Rwanda	214.9	Malawi	204.9	Afghanistan	232.0	Malawi	208.8
6	Malawi	223.8	Malawi	224.0	Malawi	221.3	Rwanda	223.8	Rwanda	247.6	Eritrea	236.0
7	Mozambique	227.3	Congo, D. R.	232.4	Tajikistan	234.3	Sierra Leone	247.1	Madagascar	249.1	Afghanistan	241.6
8	Congo, D. R.	247.7	Mozambique	239.6	Mozambique	235.9	Tajikistan	254.0	Liberia	253.0	Rwanda	247.4
9	Uganda	256.7	Eritrea	263.3	Eritrea	245.7	Eritrea	256.7	Eritrea	253.3	Madagascar	265.4
10	Eritrea	272.4	Sierra Leone	265.9	Niger	255.0	Mozambique	256.8	Niger	261.6	Niger	265.7

	2004	US$	2005	US$	2006	US$	2007	US$	2008	US$	2009	US$
1	Burundi	147.4	Burundi	143.8	Burundi	146.4	Burundi	148.1	Burundi	150.3	Burundi	150.2
2	Ethiopia	149.7	Ethiopia	162.8	Ethiopia	175.6	Ethiopia	190.4	Eritrea	184.9	Eritrea	186.0
3	Liberia	155.5	Liberia	165.8	Liberia	175.8	Liberia	195.4	Ethiopia	205.4	Ethiopia	217.7
4	Malawi	213.1	Malawi	213.2	Malawi	211.3	Eritrea	211.8	Liberia	207.2	Liberia	226.5
5	Congo, D. R.	214.8	Congo, D. R.	221.5	Eritrea	216.0	Malawi	224.5	Malawi	235.9	Congo, D. R.	241.9
6	Eritrea	229.5	Eritrea	226.3	Congo, D. R.	226.7	Congo, D. R.	234.1	Congo, D. R.	241.8	Malawi	249.6
7	Afghanistan	235.0	Afghanistan	252.4	Afghanistan	258.4	Niger	261.7	Niger	276.3	Niger	264.2
8	Niger	256.4	Niger	258.3	Niger	263.4	Afghanistan	285.9	Afghanistan	288.8	Madagascar	282.1
9	Rwanda	260.9	Rwanda	273.8	Madagascar	281.1	Madagascar	290.3	Madagascar	302.3	Guinea	302.6
10	Madagascar	271.2	Madagascar	275.5	Rwanda	291.9	Guinea	304.9	Guinea	311.7	Rwanda	340.4

	2010	US$	2011	US$	2012	US$	2013	US$	2014	US$
1	Burundi	150.7	Burundi	152.0	Burundi	153.1	Burundi	155.3	Burundi	152.7
2	Eritrea	184.1	Eritrea	193.6	Eritrea	200.5	Eritrea	196.6	C.AfricanRe	226.4
3	Ethiopia	238.6	Liberia	256.9	Malawi	259.0	Malawi	264.3	Liberia	226.7
4	Liberia	242.6	Ethiopia	258.5	Madagascar	271.8	Madagascar	270.7	Madagascar	271.6
5	Congo, D. R.	252.0	Malawi	261.5	Congo, D. R.	272.9	C.AfricanRe	282.6	Malawi	274.3
6	Malawi	258.1	Congo, D. R.	262.0	Ethiopia	273.7	Congo, D. R.	288.2	Congo, D. R.	283.5
7	Madagascar	275.0	Madagascar	271.3	Liberia	275.7	Niger	290.6	Niger	293.2
8	Niger	275.7	Niger	271.5	Niger	290.1	Ethiopia	294.8	Guinea	295.3
9	Guinea	300.4	Guinea	304.2	Guinea	308.2	Liberia	299.5	Ethiopia	315.8
10	Rwanda	355.0	Rwanda	372.3	Rwanda	393.9	Guinea	307.4	Afghanistan	406.2

2014 data for Eritrea is not available.

III FISCAL PERFORMANCE

The fiscal performance gives a strong indicator of the domestic economy. It is an instrument that primarily reflects the ideological and political orientation of the government, and the ability to fulfill economic goals. A large, interventionist, and prowelfare government may engage in politically popular but economically unsustainable policies. Of course, there can be periods of difficulty, such as natural disasters and crises, when government assistance is needed to rescue the country from decline, or heavy military engagement imposes limits on economic progress. In normal times, it is unwise for governments to resort to large expenditure without ensuring fiscal sustainability. According to the IMF, general government revenues consist of "taxes, social contributions, grants receivable, and other revenue," while general government total expenditure consists of "total expenses and the net acquisition of nonfinancial assets."

Countries with the "twin" debts (fiscal deficit and public debt) tended to end up with vicious economic circles, and could be trapped in a "debt-breeds-debt" situation, making the economy extremely uncompetitive and unattractive to foreign investment, and thereby restricting growth. One would normally think that between the "twin" debts, it probably started with the accumulation of fiscal deficit. It is true that on some occasions, especially during crises and other forms of economic shock, the role of fiscal policy would be to rescue the economy from declining drastically. However, in normal times, the government's effort should try to achieve a "zero-deficit" as much as possible, so as not to impose an extra burden on the fiscal revenue. A healthy budget is a useful signal to a number of economic indicators, including investment and other growth-enhancing opportunities.

Other than the economic tools of revenue and expenditure in the fiscal framework, there are two other microeconomic theories that are also relevant in understanding fiscal policy. One is the "agency" theory (Ross, 1973; Noreen, 1988; Shapiro, 2005) which argues that the agent may not be acting on a *bona fide* basis for the principal. The "principal – agent" theory has mostly been applied to business and management studies. For example, it is the shareholders that are the owners of a business corporation, but the management who are employees in the corporation make all the business decisions. In fiscal policy, the government officials make fiscal decisions, but the expenditures are public money. Thus, would the fiscal decisions reflect the "best interests" of the public? Or is there politically popular but economically undesirable interference in fiscal decisions? Once fiscal instruments are being used for political goals, it is difficult to identify the "best interests," as there are different orientations. Hence, there exists a possible problem when it is the government officials (agent) whose decisions have implications for public resources. In turn, the tax payers (principals) may not have much influence, especially when there is a lack of "check and balance" mechanisms on fiscal expenditures made by the government (agent).

Another microeconomics theory which has been applied to finance is "asymmetric information" which argues that the information held by one party in a business deal may not be shared with the other party (Miller and Rock, 1985; De Meza and Webb, 1987; Mishkin, 1990). In the discussion on fiscal policy and debt accumulation, there could be situations of "asymmetric information." While committing to fiscal expenditure, the ideological orientation of the political leaders and the government's information on the severity and depth of the deficit and public debt may not be fully communicated to the public. Although it may be empirically difficult to identify the extent of the "principal – agent" problem and the damage done by "asymmetric information," these two theories do provide an explanation for the possible gap between what the government did in fiscal policy and how informed the public was.

Table 7.8 summarizes the number of years the top 10 world economies have experienced either fiscal surplus or deficit for the two periods of 1990 – 2000 and 2001 – 15. As far as the fiscal surplus countries are concerned, the picture between the two periods does review some changes. In 1990 – 2000, the economies with 5 or more years of fiscal surplus are mainly Asian economies (Singapore, Hong Kong, and South Korea). In 2001 – 15, however, the key fiscal surplus economies are mainly the oil exporting countries (Kuwait, Saudi Arabia, Russia, United Arab Emirates (UAE), Libya, and Iran). This reflects the high oil price in the years after the turn of the new century. In the deficit countries, the countries are quite consistent in the two periods of 1990 – 2000 and 2001 – 15, as they are mainly European and North American countries (France, Italy, Germany, the United Kingdom, United States, Spain, and Canada). France is the worst hit country, while India and China experienced prolonged fiscal deficits. Japan also performed weakly. Table 7.8 also shows that some economies experienced both large surpluses and large deficits within the sample period. For example, Canada, Russia, and Thailand appeared in both categories of top fiscal surplus and top fiscal deficit countries.

Tables 7.9 and 7.10, respectively, show the top 10 economies with a large fiscal surplus for 1990 – 2015 in terms of value and as a percentage of GDP. One can see from Table 7.9 that in the 1990s, the countries with

TABLE 7.8 Number of Years of Top 10 Fiscal Surplus and Deficit Economies: 1990—2015

Number of years in top 10 fiscal surplus				Number of years in top 10 fiscal deficit			
1990—2000		2001—15		1990—2000		2001—15	
Singapore	11	Norway	15	India	11	Japan	15
UAE	10	Kuwait	15	France	9	United States	15
Norway	7	UAE	12	Germany	9	India	15
Hong Kong	6	Singapore	12	United Kingdom	8	France	15
Chile	6	Korea, Rep.	10	United States	8	Italy	14
Korea, Rep.	6	Russia	9	Japan	8	United Kingdom	14
Kuwait	5	Saudi Arabia	9	Canada	7	China	11
Malaysia	4	Qatar	8	Mexico	7	Myanmar	11
Algeria	4	Macao	6	Sweden	5	Brazil	9
Libya	4	Libya	6	Brazil	5	Germany	8
Venezuela	3	Canada	5	Australia	4	Spain	8
Japan	3	Iran	5	Iran	4	Turkey	4
Sweden	3	Algeria	4	Saudi Arabia	4	Venezuela	4
Australia	3	Hong Kong	4	Myanmar	4	Greece	3
United States	3	Finland	3	China	4	Mexico	1
Canada	3	Nigeria	3	Kuwait	3	Canada	1
Mexico	2	Spain	3	Netherlands	2	Australia	1
Bangladesh	2	Kazakhstan	3	Argentina	2	Saudi Arabia	1
Jamaica	2	Germany	3	Italy	2		
Paraguay	2	Thailand	2	Sudan	1		
New Zealand	2	Australia	2	Russia Denmark	1		
Thailand	2	Denmark	2	Turkey	1		
Indonesia	2	Congo, Rep.	2		1		
Ireland	2	United Kingdom	1				
United Kingdom	2	New Zealand	1				
Finland	1	Switzerland	1				
Romania	1	Gabon	1				
Switzerland	1	China	1				
Iran,	1	Azerbaijan	1				
Colombia	1	Luxembourg	1				
Jordan,	1						
Philippines	1						
Germany	1						
Senegal	1						
Croatia	1						
Trin.&Tobago	1						

TABLE 7.9 Top 10 Largest Fiscal Surplus Economies: Ranked by Value (US$ Million)

	1990	US$ mil	% GDP	1991	US$ mil	% GDP	1992	US$ mil	% GDP	1993	US$ mil	% GDP
1	Japan	51,112	1.7	Japan	63,990	1.7	Japan	21,277	0.5	Singapore	9925	15.7
2	Sweden	10,038	3.8	UAE	7745	15.5	Singapore	6891	12.8	Hong Kong	2485	2.0
3	Singapore	4664	11.2	Singapore	4596	9.3	UAE	5503	10.5	UAE	1977	3.7
4	Norway	2510	2.0	Libya	3077	8.7	Hong Kong	2837	2.6	Malaysia	985	1.4
5	Venezuela	1726	3.8	Hong Kong	2893	3.1	Chile	925	2.1	Mexico	754	0.1
6	Finland	1660	6.6	Algeria	1532	3.8	Mexico	495	0.1	Chile	659	1.4
7	Algeria	1449	3.2	Sweden	990	0.3	Algeria	354	0.8	Philippines	382	0.6
8	Libya	1115	3.5	Chile	547	1.6	Bangladesh	149	0.4	Bangladesh	183	0.5
9	Australia	912	0.3	Romania	370	3.1	Jamaica	143	2.0	Paraguay	147	2.2
10	Switzerland	685	0.2	Colombia	180	0.3	Jordan	98	1.9	Jamaica	111	2.4

	1994	US$ mil	% GDP	1995	US$ mil	% GDP	1996	US$ mil	% GDP	1997	US$ mil	% GDP
1	Singapore	11,243	14.9	Korea, Rep.	12,607	2.3	Korea, Rep.	13,826	2.4	UAE	12,673	16.7
2	UAE	4439	7.7	Singapore	10,634	11.7	Norway	9935	6.1	Norway	11,585	7.4
3	Malaysia	2947	3.6	UAE	9237	14.5	Singapore	8352	8.5	Hong Kong	11,214	6.3
4	Hong Kong	1396	1.0	Thailand	4954	3.1	UAE	7437	10.5	Singapore	8431	9.4
5	Chile	858	1.5	Norway	4563	3.0	Venezuela	4905	7.9	Korea, Rep.	7655	2.4
6	New Zealand	703	1.2	Chile	2235	3.1	Thailand	4842	2.7	Kuwait	5185	17.2
7	Senegal	291	7.2	New Zealand	1723	2.8	Kuwait	3648	11.6	Malaysia	2878	3.7
8	Paraguay	282	3.6	Indonesia	1525	0.6	Libya	3420	11.7	Venezuela	2144	2.6
9	Croatia	243	1.3	Malaysia	1446	1.5	Hong Kong	3349	2.0	Chile	1667	2.1
10	Trin.&Tobago	150	3.2	Libya	1038	3.9	Indonesia	2599	1.0	Algeria	1395	2.9

	1998	US$ mil	% GDP	1999	US$ mil	% GDP	2000	US$ mil	% GDP	2001	US$ mil	% GDP
1	United States	33,700	0.6	United States	71,800	0.7	United States	152,800	1.5	Norway	23,154	13.3
2	UAE	8280	11.3	United Kingdom	11,958	0.8	Norway	25,909	15.2	Korea, Rep.	13,499	2.6
3	Korea, Rep.	5044	1.2	Canada	11,562	1.7	UAE	21,137	20.3	Kuwait	9962	28.7
4	Norway	4745	3.1	Norway	9094	5.8	Korea, Rep.	20,869	4.2	Russia	9510	3.0
5	Ireland	2402	2.0	UAE	9071	10.9	Canada	19,462	2.6	UAE	7282	7.0
6	Sweden	2254	0.9	Korea, Rep.	6170	1.2	Germany	19,300	1.0	United Kingdom	6311	0.4
7	Kuwait	1804	6.9	Australia	5338	1.3	Iran	18,821	6.8	Finland	6234	4.9
8	Singapore	1353	1.6	Singapore	4973	5.5	United Kingdom	17,884	1.2	Iran	4369	1.0
9	Australia	1268	0.3	Kuwait	4570	15.2	Kuwait	11,977	31.6	Canada	3805	0.5
10	Canada	877	0.1	Ireland	2231	2.4	Singapore	8678	8.9	Singapore	3475	4.0

	2002	US$ mil	% GDP	2003	US$ mil	% GDP	2004	US$ mil	% GDP	2005	US$ mil	% GDP
1	Korea, Rep.	22,136	3.4	Norway	17,401	7.2	Norway	32,141	10.9	Russia	61,113	7.6
2	Norway	20,227	9.0	Korea, Rep.	10,981	1.6	Russia	30,078	4.6	Saudi Arabia	59,113	18.0

(Continued)

TABLE 7.9 (*Continued*)

	2002	US$ mil	% GDP	2003	US$ mil	% GDP	2004	US$ mil	% GDP	2005	US$ mil	% GDP
3	Kuwait	7481	19.3	Kuwait	8375	17.3	Saudi Arabia	25,144	9.7	Norway	43,665	14.9
4	Finland	6187	4.0	Russia	6487	1.4	Kuwait	13,203	22.2	UAE	36,573	20.2
5	Singapore	4218	4.4	Singapore	6101	6.0	UAE	12,916	8.7	Kuwait	34,990	43.3
6	Russia	2456	0.7	Australia	5905	1.0	Australia	9218	1.3	Canada	18,960	1.6
7	UAE	1871	1.7	UAE	5162	4.2	Canada	8519	0.8	Libya	14,363	31.4
8	Libya	1552	7.2	Finland	4484	2.3	Nigeria	7183	5.7	Algeria	14,045	13.6
9	Qatar	1526	7.9	Algeria	3527	4.9	Singapore	7137	5.9	Spain	13,247	1.2
10	New Zealand	1275	1.8	Thailand	3082	2.0	Iran	6268	3.5	Denmark	12,247	5.0

	2006	US$ mil	% GDP	2007	US$ mil	% GDP	2008	US$ mil	% GDP	2009	US$ mil	% GDP
1	Russia	85,472	7.8	Russia	81,059	5.6	Saudi Arabia	154,909	29.8	Norway	43,403	10.3
2	Saudi Arabia	78,481	20.8	Norway	73,774	17.0	Norway	68,700	18.5	Kuwait	28,923	27.2
3	Norway	63,815	18.0	UAE	56,228	21.8	Russia	68,483	4.6	Qatar	14,622	15.0
4	UAE	56,184	25.3	Saudi Arabia	48,983	11.8	UAE	63,347	20.1	Macao	4308	20.1
5	Kuwait	32,506	31.9	Kuwait	44,648	37.4	Kuwait	28,951	20.2	Hong Kong	3793	1.7
6	Spain	29,164	2.2	Spain	31,827	2.0	Libya	23,405	27.5	Switzerland	3451	0.6
7	Canada	23,472	1.8	Canada	29,054	1.8	Nigeria	16,846	5.8	Azerbaijan	3295	7.4
8	Nigeria	19,429	8.9	Korea, Rep.	24,154	2.2	Algeria	14,048	9.1	Iran	3261	0.8
9	Libya	17,878	31.8	Iran	22,737	6.7	Korea, Rep.	13,354	1.5	Gabon	853	6.8
10	Algeria	16,661	13.9	Singapore	22,694	11.8	Singapore	11,989	6.4	Congo, Rep.	478	4.8

	2010	US$ mil	% GDP	2011	US$ mil	% GDP	2012	US$ mil	% GDP	2013	US$ mil	% GDP
1	Norway	48,216	10.9	Saudi Arabia	74,745	11.2	Saudi Arabia	88,078	12.0	Kuwait	60,110	34.0
2	China	38,069	0.6	Norway	61,487	13.2	Norway	72,101	13.5	Norway	53,042	10.5
3	Kuwait	30,595	26.0	Kuwait	50,454	33.1	Kuwait	57,640	33.3	Saudi Arabia	43,101	5.8
4	Saudi Arabia	18,835	3.6	Russia	26,734	1.4	UAE	40,610	10.9	UAE	40,395	10.4
5	Korea, Rep.	17,096	1.5	Singapore	22,906	8.5	Singapore	23,337	7.8	Qatar	33,782	16.7
6	Singapore	16,875	6.6	UAE	22,028	6.3	Libya	22,855	27.8	Singapore	16,713	5.6
7	Iran	12,761	2.8	Korea, Rep.	19,563	1.7	Qatar	20,870	11.0	Macao	15,596	30.2
8	Hong Kong	9663	4.1	Qatar	12,319	7.3	Korea, Rep.	20,043	1.6	Kazakhstan	11,557	5.0
9	Libya	8728	11.6	Kazakhstan	11,059	6.0	Macao	11,396	26.5	Korea, Rep.	8802	0.6
10	Qatar	8396	6.7	Macao	9667	26.3	Kazakhstan	9117	4.5	Germany	5755	0.1

	2014	US$ mil	% GDP	2015	US$ mil	% GDP
1	Kuwait	44,419	26.6	Germany	21,109	0.6
2	Qatar	38,003	18.1	Norway	19,394	5.4
3	Norway	35,851	8.4	Qatar	19,036	10.3
4	UAE	19,907	5.0	Macao	5872	12.7

(*Continued*)

TABLE 7.9 (*Continued*)

	2014	US$ mil	% GDP	2015	US$ mil	% GDP
5	Macao	11,863	21.4	Hong Kong	4553	1.5
6	Germany	10,843	0.3	Singapore	3259	1.1
7	Hong Kong	10,636	3.6	Kuwait	1473	1.2
8	Singapore	9765	3.3	Thailand	942	0.3
9	Korea, Rep.	5646	0.4	Congo Dem. Rep.	741	1.9
10	Denmark	4655	1.5	Luxembourg	568	1.0

TABLE 7.10 Top 10 Largest Fiscal Surplus Economies: Ranked by Percentage of GDP

	1990	% GDP	US$ mil	1991	% GDP	US$ mil	1992	% GDP	US$ mil	1993	% GDP	US$ mil
1	Seychelles	11.9	46	UAE	15.5	7745	Singapore	12.8	6891	Singapore	15.7	9925
2	Singapore	11.2	4664	Lesotho	11.3	75	UAE	10.5	5503	Lesotho	8.7	64
3	Lesotho	10.3	60	Singapore	9.3	4596	Solomon Is.	6.8	17	Solomon Is.	5	14
4	Burundi	9.5	111	Libya	8.7	3077	Seychelles	6.5	27	Bhutan	4.5	10
5	Finland	6.6	1660	Burundi	4.8	53	Lesotho	5.5	39	UAE	3.7	1977
6	Paraguay	6.6	317	Algeria	3.8	1532	Eritrea	5.3	23	Eritrea	3.3	17
7	Swaziland	6	68	Swaziland	3.6	43	Jamaica	2.9	143	Jamaica	2.4	111
8	Oman	5.7	640	Jamaica	3.2	96	Hong Kong	2.6	2837	Paraguay	2.2	147
9	Venezuela	3.8	1726	Seychelles	3.1	12	Chile	2.1	925	Hong Kong	2	2485
10	Sweden	3.8	10,038	Hong Kong	3.1	2893	Jordan	1.9	98	Comoros	2	5

	1994	% GDP	US$ mil	1995	% GDP	US$ mil	1996	% GDP	US$ mil	1997	% GDP	US$ mil
1	Singapore	14.9	11,243	UAE	14.5	9237	Libya	11.7	3420	Kuwait	17.2	5185
2	UAE	7.7	4439	Singapore	11.7	10,634	Kuwait	11.6	3648	UAE	16.6	12,673
3	Senegal	7.2	291	Lesotho	5.9	53	UAE	10.5	7437	Singapore	9.4	8431
4	Solomon Is.	7.2	26	Solomon Is.	5.5	23	Congo, Rep.	10.3	255	Norway	7.4	11,585
5	Eritrea	6.7	39	Guinea-Bissa	4.1	28	Singapore	8.5	8352	Hong Kong	6.3	11,214
6	Lesotho	6.6	53	Libya	3.9	1038	Venezuela	7.9	4905	Oman	5.7	866
7	Paraguay	3.6	282	Chile	3.1	2235	Angola	7.3	302	Congo, Rep.	4.1	92
8	Malaysia	3.6	2947	Thailand	3.1	4954	Norway	6.1	9935	Solomon Is.	3.8	15
9	Trin. &Tobago	3.2	150	Norway	3.0	4563	Solomon Is.	5.9	28	Luxembourg	3.7	17
10	Jamaica	2.5	144	Senegal	3.0	148	Guinea-Bissau	5.9	24	Kiribati	3.7	3

	1998	% GDP	US$ mil	1999	% GDP	US$ mil	2000	% GDP	US$ mil	2001	% GDP	US$ mil
1	Kiribati	11.7	9	Kuwait	15.2	4570	São Tomé&P.	51.5	37	Kuwait	28.7	9962
2	UAE	11.3	8280	UAE	10.9	9071	Kuwait	31.6	11,977	Equ. Guinea	14.4	246

(Continued)

TABLE 7.10 (*Continued*)

	1998	% GDP	US$ mil	1999	% GDP	US$ mil	2000	% GDP	US$ mil	2001	% GDP	US$ mil
3	Kuwait	6.9	1804	Solomon Is.	6.8	29	UAE	20.3	21,137	Norway	13.3	23,154
4	Paraguay	4.1	358	Libya	5.9	2121	Norway	15.2	25,909	Oman	8.9	1678
5	Fiji	3.7	62	Norway	5.8	9094	Oman	14.3	2707	UAE	7.0	7282
6	Luxembourg	3.5	18	Singapore	5.5	4973	Libya	14.1	5108	Congo, Rep.	6.4	175
7	Solomon Is.	3.1	13	Ukraine	5.0	1281	Gabon	11.1	607	Luxembourg	6.0	1234
8	Norway	3.1	4745	Bhutan	3.7	15	Algeria	9.7	5310	Finland	4.9	6234
9	St. Lucia	2.6	20	Luxembourg	3.6	721	Singapore	8.9	8678	Qatar	4.5	784
10	Benin	2.5	65	Morocco	3.5	1404	Botswana	8.6	482	Gabon	4.1	201

	2002	% GDP	US$ mil	2003	% GDP	US$ mil	2004	% GDP	US$ mil	2005	% GDP	US$ mil
1	Kuwait	19.3	7481	Kuwait	17.3	8375	Kuwait	22.2	13,203	Kuwait	43.3	34,990
2	Equ. Guinea	16.9	404	Equ. Guinea	12.6	417	Qatar	17.8	5646	Libya	31.4	14,363
3	Norway	9.0	20,227	Brunei Daru.	8.1	600	Libya	11.7	4040	São Tomé&P.	25.8	30
4	Qatar	7.9	1526	Gabon	7.8	564	Norway	10.9	32,141	UAE	20.2	36,573
5	Libya	7.2	1552	Norway	7.2	17,401	Equ. Guinea	10.4	599	Equ. Guinea	18.5	1440
6	Micronesia	7.1	17	Oman	7.0	1464	Saudi Arabia	9.7	25,144	Saudi Arabia	18.0	59,113
7	Oman	6.3	1225	Qatar	6.8	1591	UAE	8.7	12,916	Brunei Daru.	16.2	1716
8	Singapore	4.4	4218	Libya	6.4	1645	Brunei Daru.	8.6	773	Norway	14.9	43,665
9	Finland	4.0	6187	Solomon Is.	6.1	19	Lesotho	7.5	109	Congo, Rep.	14.6	845
10	Gabon	3.7	220	Singapore	6.0	6101	Macao	7.3	769	Algeria	13.6	14,045

	2006	% GDP	US$ mil	2007	% GDP	US$ mil	2008	% GDP	US$ mil	2009	% GDP	US$ mil
1	Niger	40.3	1544	São Tomé&P.	122.2	171	Brunei Daru.	36.0	5669	Kuwait	27.2	28,923
2	Cameroon	32.8	6188	Kuwait	37.4	44,648	Saudi Arabia	29.8	154,909	Macao	20.1	4308
3	Kuwait	31.9	32,506	Libya	28.6	19,924	Libya	27.5	23,405	Qatar	15.0	14,622
4	Libya	31.8	17,878	UAE	21.8	56,228	Congo, Rep.	23.4	2634	Norway	10.3	43,403
5	Mali	27.8	2013	Equ. Guinea	20.8	2413	Azerbaijan	20.6	9773	Azerbaijan	7.4	3295
6	UAE	25.3	56,184	Macao	20.6	3779	Kuwait	20.2	28,951	Gabon	6.8	853
7	Equ. Guinea	24.0	2308	Sierra Leone	20.1	435	UAE	20.1	63,347	Seychelles	4.8	50
8	Saudi Arabia	20.8	78,481	Norway	17.0	73,774	Macao	19.0	3986	Congo, Rep.	4.8	478
9	Brunei Daru.	19.9	2628	Oman	12.4	5066	Norway	18.5	68,700	Tonga	4.4	16
10	Norway	18.0	63,815	Singapore	11.8	22,694	Equ. Guinea	18.0	2742	Guinea-Bissau	4.1	35

	2010	% GDP	US$ mil	2011	% GDP	US$ mil	2012	% GDP	US$ mil	2013	% GDP	US$ mil
1	Kuwait	26.0	30,595	Kuwait	33.1	20,454	Kuwait	33.3	57,640	Kuwait	34.0	60,110
2	Macao	22.3	6249	Macao	26.3	9667	Libya	27.8	22,855	Macao	30.2	15,596

(*Continued*)

TABLE 7.10 *(Continued)*

2010		% GDP	US$ mil	2011	% GDP	US$ mil	2012	% GDP	US$ mil	2013	% GDP	US$ mil
3	Congo, Rep.	16.1	1948	Brunei Daru.	25.3	4534	Macao	26.5	11,396	Comoros	17.8	122
4	Azerbaijan	14.3	7629	Congo, Rep.	16.5	2208	Brunei Daru.	15.0	2919	Qatar	16.7	33,782
5	Libya	11.6	8728	Norway	13.2	61,487	Norway	13.5	72,101	Brunei Daru.	12.5	2235
6	Norway	10.9	48,216	Azerbaijan	11.6	7514	Saudi Arabia	12.0	88,078	St. Kitts&Navis	12.1	96
7	Brunei Daru.	7.6	1098	Saudi Arabia	11.2	74,745	Qatar	11.0	20,870	Norway	10.5	53,042
8	Comoros	7.0	38	Oman	9.4	6385	UAE	10.9	40,610	UAE	10.4	40,395
9	Qatar	6.7	8396	Solomon Is.	8.9	82	Singapore	7.8	23,337	Kiribati	9.3	16
10	Singapore	6.6	16,875	Angola	8.7	8907	Congo, Rep.	6.4	905	Saudi Arabia	5.8	43,101

	2014	% GDP	US$ mil	2015	% GDP	US$ mil
1	Kuwait	26.6	44,419	Macao	12.7	5872
2	Macao	21.4	11,863	Qatar	10.3	19,036
3	Kiribati	20.4	34	St.Kitts&Nevis	5.6	50
4	Qatar	18.1	38,003	Norway	5.4	19,394
5	Micronesia	11.3	36	Comoros	4.6	26
6	St.Kitts&Nevis	9.5	81	Micronesia	3.1	10
7	Norway	8.4	35,851	Seychelles	2.0	27
8	UAE	5.0	19,907	Congo Dem. Rep.	1.9	741
9	Seychelles	3.7	45	Hong Kong	1.5	4553
10	Hong Kong	3.6	10,636	Kuwait	1.2	1473

largest fiscal surpluses are East Asian economies (Japan, Singapore, Hong Kong, and South Korea), followed by the United States and Norway in the late 1990s. By the turn of the century, the top ranking countries are mainly oil exporting countries in the Middle East and Russia. The difference is that the fiscal surplus in East Asian countries relied mainly on exports and a small government size, while the oil exporting countries relied on the export of petroleum. When the top fiscal surpluses are presented in terms of the GDP as shown in Table 7.10, the data show that the top 10 countries are either small world economies or oil exporting countries. The small world economies, such as the Seychelles, have a much lower GDP, and their fiscal surplus is not large in value terms. The performance of fiscal surplus in oil exporting countries was largely due to the high petroleum price in the entire decade of the 2010s.

In the top fiscal deficit countries shown in Table 7.11, the United States and Japan are the two top fiscal deficit countries since 1993, and their deficits have been rising over the years. The United States experienced a big jump in fiscal deficit in 2002 after the September 11, 2001, terrorist attack, and in 2009 after the 2008 financial crisis. Other large deficit countries are the key European countries. When the top fiscal deficit countries expressed in GDP terms are as shown in Table 7.12, the smaller countries with low GDP tend to rank high in their fiscal deficits.

One can conclude that oil exporting countries amassed large fiscal surpluses. The other strong fiscal surplus performers are the developed economies in East Asia, which are less likely to have excessive government intervention in and subsidies to their economies. It is interesting and important to see how the best performers have changed over the decades. Countries with severe fiscal deficits expressed in value terms are mostly European and North American countries. Small economies tended to have severe fiscal deficits expressed as a percentage of GDP. Governments should restore a healthy fiscal picture and avoid prolonged deficits, as fiscal deficits erode economic competitiveness and impose burdens on the financing of the deficits. Fiscal deficits have spillover effects, including inflation, as a result of more welfare spending, and weakness in exchange rates if more imports occur.

Table 7.13 reports that out of a sample of 173 countries from the World Bank data for the period 2005 – 15, the number of fiscal deficit countries has ranged from the lowest at 53.2% in 2007, to the highest at 87.9% in 2009,

TABLE 7.11   Top 10 Largest Fiscal Deficit Economies: Ranked by Value (US$ Million)

	1990	US$ mil	% GDP	1991	US$ mil	% GDP	1992	US$ mil	% GDP	1993	US$ mil	% GDP
1	United States	−235,300	−3.9	United States	−287,700	−2.9	United States	−360,600	−5.5	United States	−326,200	−4.7
2	Canada	−35,434	−5.9	Canada	−50,765	−2.8	United Kingdom	−60,332	−5.9	Japan	−111,330	−2.5
3	India	−21,079	−6.5	United Kingdom	−34,995	−2.2	Canada	−51,994	−9.2	United Kingdom	−76,060	−7.2
4	United Kingdom	−17,950	−1.5	Germany	−33,001	−6.3	Germany	−27,249	−2.6	Canada	−50,412	−9.0
5	Iran	−12,515	−2.2	Iran	−17,185	−151.3	Sweden	−19,652	−8.5	Germany	−31,231	−3.1
6	Mexico	−8285	−2.9	Kuwait	−16,664	−2.1	India	−19,078	−6.5	Sweden	−21,454	−10.9
7				Netherlands	−7670	−5.0	India	−16,310	−3.2	Australia	−12,414	−4.2
	India	−20,031	−7.1									
8	Kuwait	−5994	−32.0	Australia	−7052	−2.9	Iran	−11,575	−1.1	Australia	−12,769	−4.1
9	France	−4958	−2.4	France	−5987	−8.4	Saudi Arabia	−11,118	−8.1	Saudi Arabia	−12,385	−9.3
10	Sudan	−3555	−14.5	Denmark	−4413	−4.7	Kuwait	−9544	−49.6	France	−12,270	−6.3

	1994	US$ mil	% GDP	1995	US$ mil	% GDP	1996	US$ mil	% GDP	1997	US$ mil	% GDP
1	United States	−253,800	−3.5	United States	−236,600	−3.1	Japan	−216,466	−4.9	Japan	−152,442	−3.8
2	Japan	−192,487	−3.9	Japan	−231,453	−4.7	United States	−171,800	−2.1	United States	−66,500	−0.8
3	United Kingdom	−72,694	−6.2	Germany	−123,634	−9.3	United Kingdom	−54,642	−3.8	Brazil	−47,791	−5.6
4	Canada	−39,158	−7.0	United Kingdom	−65,554	−5.4	Brazil	−43,965	−5.3	Germany	−31,024	−2.8
5	Germany	−29,611	−2.5	Canada	−33,441	−5.5	Germany	−41,943	−3.4	United Kingdom	−30,253	−2.1
6	India	−22,684	−6.8	India	−20,175	−5.8	India	−21,933	−5.6	India	−28,404	−7.1
7	Sweden	−20,518	−8.8	Sweden	−19,804	−7.0	Mexico	−19,833	−5.2	Mexico	−26,082	−5.5
8	Australia	−12,086	−3.2	Netherlands	−17,406	−8.6	Canada	−19,164	−0.03	Myanmar	−9138	−4.5
9	France	−11,915	−5.4	France	−12,811	−5.1	France	−9375	−3.9	France	−7870	−3.6
10	Saudi Arabia	−11,220	−8.3	Mexico	−11,739	−4.1	Sweden	−8680	−3.1	China	−7034	−0.7

	1998	US$ mil	% GDP	1999	US$ mil	% GDP	2000	US$ mil	% GDP	2001	US$ mil	% GDP
1	Japan	−214,260	−4.8	Japan	−352,920	−7.1	Japan	−346,719	−7.8	Japan	−231,647	−6.0
2	Brazil	−59,879	−7.2	India	−34,604	−7.4	China	−34,314	−2.8	United States	−61,616	−0.6
3	India	−36,438	−8.6	Mexico	−31,990	−5.5	India	−33,952	−7.3	Germany	−58,633	−3.1
4	Germany	−29,205	−2.4	Germany	−31,894	−1.5	Myanmar	−32,429	−7.3	India	−47,998	−9.8
5	Mexico	−26,178	−5.6	Brazil	−31,475	−5.2	Brazil	−20,365	−3.3	Italy	−38,842	−3.4
6	Myanmar	−15,247	−5.0	China	−25,274	−2.3	Mexico	−20,297	−3.0	China	−34,621	−2.6
7	Saudi Arabia	−13,027	−8.9	France	−22,328	−1.6	Turkey	−19,669	−7.9	Myanmar	−29,930	−5.0
8	Iran	−12,612	−6.2	Italy	−21,244	−1.8	France	−18,222	−1.3	Mexico	−22,719	−3.1

(Continued)

TABLE 7.11 (*Continued*)

	1998	US$ mil	% GDP	1999	US$ mil	% GDP	2000	US$ mil	% GDP	2001	US$ mil	% GDP
9	China	−11,140	−1.1	Myanmar	−15,636	−3.9	Italy	−15,264	−1.3	Turkey	−20,809	−12.6
10	Russia	−10,129	−7.5	Argentina	−11,728	−3.5	Argentina	−10,266	−3.0	France	−19,555	−1.4

	2002	US$ mil	% GDP	2003	US$ mil	% GDP	2004	US$ mil	% GDP	2005	US$ mil	% GDP
1	United States	−416,368	−3.8	United States	−545,653	−4.7	United States	−524,622	−4.3	United States	−409,814	−3.1
2	Japan	−320,807	−7.7	Japan	−362,724	−7.8	Japan	−287,690	−5.9	Japan	−205,629	−4.8
3	Germany	−89,949	−3.9	Germany	−114,034	−4.1	Germany	−113,214	−3.7	Germany	−88,422	−3.3
4	France	−51,623	−3.1	France	−79,815	−3.9	United Kingdom	−86,948	−3.6	United Kingdom	−80,869	−3.5
5	India	−51,481	−9.7	United Kingdom	−71,902	−3.4	France	−81,301	−3.5	Italy	−73,344	−4.2
6	Italy	−43,372	−3.1	Myanmar	−70,802	−4.6	Myanmar	−73,444	−3.9	France	−66,168	−3.2
7	China	−42,266	−2.9	India	−64,338	−10.3	Italy	−70,369	−3.6	Myanmar	−63,506	−2.7
8	United Kingdom	−37,037	−2.1	Italy	−59,958	−3.4	India	−61,573	−8.3	India	−58,782	−7.2
9	Myanmar	−31,523	−3.1	China	−39,674	−2.4	China	−29,474	−1.5	Brazil	−32,825	−3.5
10	Turkey	−30,700	−14.4	Turkey	−33,846	−10.4	Greece	−23,293	−8.8	China	−32,589	−1.4

	2006	US$ mil	% GDP	2007	US$ mil	% GDP	2008	US$ mil	% GDP	2009	US$ mil	% GDP
1	United States	−283,199	−2.0	United States	−414,029	−2.9	United States	−983,323	−6.7	United States	−1,896,010	−13.1
2	Japan	−155,490	−3.7	Myanmar	−153,029	−3.1	Japan	−227,002	−4.1	Japan	−531,879	−10.4
3	Myanmar	−121,004	−3.6	Japan	−93,946	−2.1	Myanmar	−127,800	−2.2	Myanmar	−272,886	−4.3
4	United Kingdom	−80,340	−2.9	United Kingdom	−88,943	−3.0	India	−115,743	−10.0	United Kingdom	−257,865	−10.7
5	Italy	−73,158	−3.6	France	−72,857	−2.5	United Kingdom	−111,328	−5.0	France	−200,068	−7.2
6	India	−59,859	−6.2	India	−55,761	−4.4	France	−88,417	−3.2	Spain	−170,332	−11.0
7	France	−57,158	−2.3	Brazil	−42,056	−2.7	Spain	−68,729	−4.4	India	−135,318	−9.8
8	Germany	−48,754	−1.5	Italy	−36,171	−1.5	Italy	−61,146	−2.7	Italy	−119,398	−5.3
9	Brazil	−40,244	−3.6	Greece	−22,975	−6.7	Greece	−34,244	−10.2	Germany	−107,354	−3.0
10	China	−32,163	−1.1	Turkey	−14,322	−2.0	Brazil	−20,411	−1.5	China	−90,622	−1.8

	2010	US$ mil	% GDP	2011	US$ mil	% GDP	2012	US$ mil	% GDP	2013	US$ mil	% GDP
1	United States	−1,634,858	−10.9	United States	−1,488,002	−9.6	United States	−1,273,536	−7.9	United States	−732,764	−4.4
2	Japan	−550,955	−9.3	Japan	−595,507	−9.8	Japan	−480,910	−8.8	Japan	−387,409	−8.5
3	Myanmar	−293,941	−4.1	Myanmar	−253,626	−3.1	United Kingdom	−203,261	−7.7	United Kingdom	−160,772	−5.6
4	United Kingdom	−234,853	−9.6	United Kingdom	−191,786	−7.7	Spain	−143,687	−10.4	India	−139,964	−7.7
5	France	−181,449	−6.8	France	−135,809	−5.1	India	−135,614	−7.5	France	−119,150	−4.1
6	India	−145,952	−8.4	India	−134,678	−8.2	France	−132,531	−4.8	Spain	−98,248	−6.9
7	Germany	−140,059	−4.1	Spain	−131,027	−9.5	Venezuela	−62,847	−16.5	China	−81,376	−0.8
8	Spain	−135,551	−9.4	Italy	−73,693	−3.5	Italy	−62,624	−2.9	Brazil	−66,931	−3.0

(*Continued*)

TABLE 7.11   (*Continued*)

	2010	US$ mil	% GDP	2011	US$ mil	% GDP	2012	US$ mil	% GDP	2013	US$ mil	% GDP
9	Italy	−91,023	−4.2	Australia	−66,098	−4.5	Brazil	−59,227	−2.5	Italy	−64,541	−2.9
10	Canada	−78,859	−4.7	Brazil	−58,083	−2.5	China	−57,656	−0.7	Venezuela	−50,418	−14.5

	2014	US$ mil	% GDP	2015	US$ mil	% GDP
1	United States	−718,903	−4.1	United States	−667,320	−3.7
2	Japan	−248,498	−6.2	China	−289,086	−2.7
3	United Kingdom	−159,518	−5.6	Japan	−216,944	−5.2
4	India	−138,559	−7.0	Venezuela	−168,263	−18.7
5	Brazil	−129,477	−6.0	Brazil	−155,786	−10.3
6	France	−102,139	−3.9	India	−147,436	−7.2
7	China	−96,008	−0.9	United Kingdom	−122,261	−4.4
8	Venezuela	−84,946	−15.2	Saudi Arabia	−106,295	−16.3
9	Spain	−74,447	−5.9	France	−86,650	−3.6
10	Italy	−59,226	−3.0	Spain	−53,535	−4.5

TABLE 7.12   Top 10 Largest Fiscal Deficit Economies: Ranked by Percentage of GDP

	1990	% GDP	US$ mil	1991	% GDP	US$ mil	1992	% GDP	US$ mil	1993	% GDP	US$ mil
1	Equ. Guinea	−160.2	−227	Equ. Guinea	−236	−339	Equ. Guinea	−557.5	−858	Equ. Guinea	−217.9	−338
2	Kuwait	−32.0	−5994	Kuwait	−151.3	−16,664	Kuwait	−49.6	−9544	Kuwait	−15.7	−3813
3	Lebanon	−29.8	−697	Sudan	−24.4	−3135	Lebanon	−23.7	−1223	Brunei Daru.	−15.7	−717
4	Greece	−14.7	−43	Lebanon	−19.2	−904	Sudan	−22.5	−548	Maldives	−13.9	−47
5	Sudan	−14.5	−3555	Suriname	−16.7	−560	Congo, Rep.	−14.2	−400	Samoa	−13.2	−26
6	Maldives	−12.7	−29	Congo, Rep.	−12.5	−370	Maldives	−12.6	−39	Togo	−13.1	−178
7	Italy	−11.1	−71	Italy	−11.0	−76	Greece	−11.8	−36	Djibouti	−13.0	−61
8	Yemen	−10.3	−1266	Greece	−10.7	−34	Djibouti	−11.4	−55	Yemen	−12.8	−2781
9	Mongolia	−9.7	−266	Maldives	−10.2	−27	Kenya	−11.2	−1127	Greece	−12.7	−37
10	Kiribati	−8.3	−3	Jordan	−10.2	−447	Yemen	−10.9	−1958	Congo, Rep.	−12.7	−326

	1994	% GDP	US$ mil	1995	% GDP	US$ mil	1996	% GDP	US$ mil	1997	% GDP	US$ mil
1	Equ.Guinea	−487.3	−606	Equ. Guinea	−123.4	−242	Lebanon	−25.3	−3335	Lebanon	−24.2	−3845
2	Brunei Daru	−29.9	−1416	Brunei Daru.	−27.0	−1418	Kiribati	−21.9	−18	Brunei Daru.	−14.4	−736
3	Lebanon	−28.7	−2669	Eritrea	−17.8	−111	Eritrea	−14.2	−105	Cabo Verde	−11.5	−60
4	Yemen	−14.0	−3930	Kyrgyz Rep.	−13.5	−195	Cabo Verde	−12.4	−66	Albania	−11.4	−264
5	CaboVerde	−12.8	−58	Lebanon	−13.5	−1520	Brunei Daru.	−11.1	−632	Ghana	−9.3	−942
6	Congo,Rep	−12.4	−228	Czech Rep.	−12.4	−7382	Burundi	−10.0	−82	Kyrgyz Rep.	−9.3	−164
7	Rwanda	−11.4	−138	Cabo Verde	−11.8	−63	Slovak Rep.	−9.7	−67	Qatar	−8.3	−938
8	Venezuela	−11.2	−5706	Greece	−10.9	−43	Seychelles	−9.7	−48	Moldova	−7.8	−150

(*Continued*)

TABLE 7.12 (*Continued*)

	1994	% GDP	US$ mil	1995	% GDP	US$ mil	1996	% GDP	US$ mil	1997	% GDP	US$ mil
9	Djibouti	−11.1	−55	Germany	−9.3	−123,634	Greece	−9.1	−38	India	−7.1	−28,404
10	Qatar	−9.5	−702	Hungary	−8.6	−3600	Kyrgyz Rep.	−9.1	−127	Mongolia	−6.9	−93

	1998	% GDP	US$ mil	1999	% GDP	US$ mil	2000	% GDP	US$ mil	2001	% GDP	US$ mil
1	Eritrea	−31.2	−245	Eritrea	−46.2	−312	Eritrea	−28.2	−188	Eritrea	−30.4	−188
2	BruneiDaru	−28.6	−1295	BruneiDaru.	−20.7	−1037	Lebanon	−23.6	−4075	Lebanon	−20.7	−3650
3	Lebanon	−17.0	−2962	Lesotho	−17.7	−144	Cabo Verde	−17.8	−106	Anti.&Barbu.	−14.3	−110
4	Seychelles	−16.7	−98	Lebanon	−16.5	−2872	Seychelles	−14.7	−83	São Tomé&P.	−13.7	−10
5	Lesotho	−13.6	−108	Kyrgyz Rep.	−13.5	−145	Anti.&Barbu.	−13.7	−107	Bhutan	−13.2	−58
6	Gabon	−13.1	−657	Angola	−13.0	−401	Slovak Rep.	−12.0	−80	Kiribati	−13.1	−8
7	KyrgyzRep	−12.0	−139	Seychelles	−11.5	−70	St. Kitts&Nevi	−11.9	−50	Turkey	−12.6	−20,809
8	Mongolia	−10.6	−129	Cabo Verde	−10.3	−64	Kyrgyz Rep.	−10.7	−145	Sri Lanka	−10.1	−1575
9	Suriname	−9.6	−142	St.Kitts&Ne	−10.1	−39	Sri Lanka	−9.2	−1446	St. Kitts&Nevi	−9.8	−45
10	GuineaBiss	−9.4	−37	Dominica	−9.1	−30	Belize	−9.0	−76	India	−9.8	−47,998

	2002	% GDP	US$ mil	2003	% GDP	US$ mil	2004	% GDP	US$ mil	2005	% GDP	US$ mil
1	Eritrea	−26.3	−187	Anti.&Barb	−19.9	−167	São Tomé&P.	−24.3	−26	Eritrea	−22.2	−244
2	Anti.&Barbu.	−19.3	−155	Eritrea	−17.2	−151	Kiribati	−23.0	−25	Anti.&Barbu.	−15.2	−151
3	Seychelles	−16.3	−123	SãoTomé&P	−15.5	−15	Eritrea	−16.6	−184	Kiribati	−15.0	−16
4	Lebanon	−16.0	−3049	Lebanon	−13.8	−2722	Micronesia	−15.5	−37	Lebanon	−8.7	−1843
5	St. Kitts&Nav	−14.5	−70	Kiribati	−12.2	−13	Anti.&Barbu.	−12.3	−110	Guyana	−8.5	−112
6	Grenada	−14.5	−78	Bhutan	−10.5	−63	Lebanon	−9.9	−2080	Maldives	−8.1	−91
7	Turkey	−14.4	−30,700	Turkey	−10.4	−33,846	Belize	−8.9	−95	Egypt	−8.0	−7897
8	São Tomé&P.	−11.1	−9	India	−10.3	−64,338	Greece	−8.8	−23,293	Hungary	−7.8	−8222
9	Egypt	−10.8	−9554	Malta	−9.1	−1270	India	−8.3	−61,573	Bhutan	−7.2	−54
10	India	−9.7	−51,481	Egypt	−8.6	−6123	Egypt	−7.8	−6533	India	−7.2	−58,782

	2006	% GDP	US$ mil	2007	% GDP	US$ mil	2008	% GDP	US$ mil	2009	% GDP	US$ mil
1	Kiribati	−15.3	−17	Kiribati	−16.0	−22	Eritrea	−21.1	−292	Maldives	−19.5	−419
2	Eritrea	−14.1	−170	Eritrea	−15.7	−206	Kiribati	−18.7	−21	Anti.&Barbu.	−18.2	−220
3	SãoTomé&P	−12.2	−16	Lebanon	−11.0	−2713	Iceland	−13.1	−1678	SãoTomé&P.	−18.1	−35
4	Lebanon	−10.7	−2328	Seychelles	−9.9	−86	Maldives	−10.7	−225	Greece	−15.2	−51,847
5	Hungary	−9.3	−11,754	Yemen	−7.2	−1551	Greece	−10.2	−34,244	Eritrea	−14.7	−273
6	Anti.&Barbu	−8.8	−100	Egypt	−7.2	−10,214	India	−10.0	−115,743	Ireland	−13.8	−33,648
7	Egypt	−8.7	−9943	Guinea-Biss	−6.9	−52	Lebanon	−10.0	−2870	Botswana	−13.3	−1568

(*Continued*)

II. THE GLOBAL ECONOMY: PERFORMANCE, CLASSIFICATION, AND CHALLENGES

TABLE 7.12   (*Continued*)

	2006	% GDP	US$ mil	2007	% GDP	US$ mil	2008	% GDP	US$ mil	2009	% GDP	US$ mil
8	Guyana	−8.0	−117	Sri Lanka	−6.9	−2263	Ghana	−8.4	−2099	United States	−13.1	a
9	Sri Lanka	−7.0	−1910	Greece	−6.7	−22,975	Egypt	−7.6	−13,022	Kiribati	−12.0	−18
10	India	-6.2	−59,859	Grenada	−6.3	−48	Botswana	−7.5	−744	Jamaica	−11.1	−1358

	2010	% GDP	US$ mil	2011	% GDP	US$ mil	2012	% GDP	US$ mil	2013	% GDP	US$ mil
1	Ireland	−32.2	−71,443	Kiribati	−22.1	−39	Venezuela	−16.5	−62,847	Eritrea	−15.1	−530
2	Eritrea	−16.0	−340	Eritrea	−16.2	−422	Eritrea	−15.3	−474	Venezuela	−14.5	−50,418
3	Maldives	−15.0	−348	Libya	−15.9	−5364	Ghana	−11.3	−4530	Slovenia	−13.9	−6879
4	Guinea	−14.0	−623	Ireland	−12.4	−27,933	SãoTomé&P	−10.9	−29	Egypt	−13.4	−35,561
5	Greece	−11.2	−33,850	Venezuela	−11.6	−36,686	Spain	−10.4	−143,687	Ghana	−12.5	−5295
6	Portugal	−11.2	−26,858	SãoTomé&P	−11.5	−27	Cabo Verde	−10.3	−185	Barbados	−11.7	−512
7	SãoTomé&P	−11.1	−23	Lesotho	−10.6	−239	Egypt	−10.0	−26,276	Cabo Verde	−8.9	−170
8	United States	−10.9	a	Greece	−10.2	−27,437	St. Lucia	−9.3	−122	Mongolia	−8.9	−1031
9	Cabo Verde	−10.7	−180	Japan	−9.8	−595,507	Mongolia	−9.1	−1090	Lebanon	−8.7	−4136
10	Venezuela	−10.4	−40,634	United States	−9.6	a	Equ. Guinea	−9.0	−1664	Japan	−8.5	−387,409

	2014	% GDP	US$ mil	2015	% GDP	US$ mil
1	Libya	−40.3	−17,081	Libya	−54.4	−21,574
2	Venezuela	−15.2	−84,946	Oman	−20.4	−11,927
3	Eritrea	−14.4	−582	Venezuela	−18.7	−168,263
4	Egypt	−12.9	−38,023	Djibouti	−16.6	−286
5	Ghana	−12.4	−4381	Saudi Arabia	−16.3	−106,295
6	Djibouti	−12.2	−193	Algeria	−15.3	−24,835
7	Mongolia	−11.1	−1303	Bahrain	−15.1	−4593
8	Mozambique	−10.7	−1691	Eritrea	−14.2	−663
9	Maldives	−9.4	−287	Congo, Rep.	−11.8	−1032
10	Niger	−8.0	−606	Egypt	−11.7	−36,417

For the US figures: 2009 = 1,896,010; 2010 = −1,634,858; and 2011 = −1,488,002.

TABLE 7.13   Number of Fiscal Deficit Countries

Year	2005	2006	2007	2008	2009	2010
No. of countries in deficit	108	95	92	107	152	136
% out of 173 countries	62.4	54.9	53.2	61.8	87.9	78.6
Year	2011	2012	2013	2014	2015	
No. of countries in deficit	136	134	140	141	151	
% out of 173 countries	78.6	77.5	80.9	81.5	87.3	

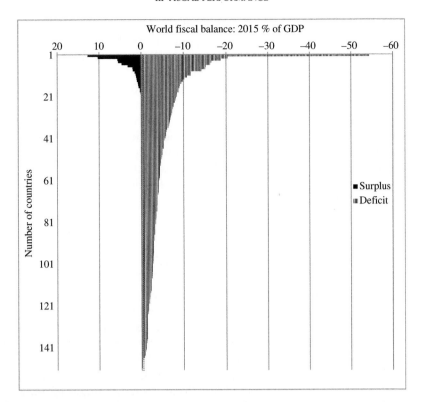

FIGURE 7.1 World performances in fiscal balance in 2015.

TABLE 7.14 Public Expenditure by Function for Selected Top Fiscal Deficit Countries in 2013

Countries	Fiscal deficit (US$ bil)	Expenses on education and health		Expenses on social protection	
		% of GDP	% of Budget	% of GDP	% of Budget
Japan	387	10.94	19.31	17.86	31.52
United Kingdom	161	13.07	28.69	16.94	37.20
France	119	13.57	23.80	24.48	42.93
Spain	98	9.90	22.85	17.57	40.18
China	81	4.79	16.37	7.59	25.93
Italy	65	11.27	21.95	20.98	41.19
Russia	26	7.63	20.61	12.94	30.69
Poland	22	9.82	23.11	17.39	40.91
Belgium	16	14.33	26.34	19.67	36.15
Portugal	11	13.58	26.82	19.15	37.83

giving an average of 73.1% of countries with fiscal deficits. To examine the magnitude of the fiscal deficit among world economies, Fig. 7.1 shows the world performance in 2015. Out of a total of 151 fiscal deficit countries in 2015, there are 12 countries whose fiscal deficit is greater than 10% of their GDP, while the rest of the 139 countries experienced a fiscal deficit of less than 10% of their GDP. Among the fiscal surplus countries, there are only a handful of countries whose fiscal surplus exceeded 10% of their GDP.

In fiscal policy, there are expenditures that are geared roughly to the "supply-side" of the economy, typically such items as education, health, and housing, while the key "demand-side" item is social welfare. In a welfare-prone country, it is likely that the percentage of fiscal budget used on welfare would be higher than the percentage of spending on "supply-side" factors. Table 7.14 shows a sample of top fiscal deficit countries in 2013, giving the value of their fiscal deficit, the percentage of spending in GDP, the total budget spending on the two "supply-side" items of education and health, and the "demand-side" item of welfare. In all the 10 large fiscal deficit countries shown in Table 7.14, the "demand-side" welfare spending exceeded the corresponding spending on "supply-side" factors. In some sample countries, such as France, Spain, and Italy, the difference in the percentage of GDP between the two types of spending is large, with nearly a 10% gap. The performance expressed in the percentage of total budget spending conveys a similar result as shown in Table 7.14.

Although one can argue that in such developed countries as France and Italy, the infrastructure on education and health should have been well established, new public expenditure on building new schools and hospitals may not be required, and thus their spending would be geared mostly to recurrent expenditure. This may not be true in developing countries, such as China, where physical infrastructure geared to education and health institutions would still be needed. In the case of China, the two types of spending shown as a percentage of GDP is far lower than other countries in Europe and Japan.

IV PUBLIC DEBT

Fiscal and public debt performances normally go hand in hand. A country with fiscal surplus often faces a low public debt. On the contrary, countries with fiscal deficits would require extra funding channels, and borrowing both at the national and international levels would seem to be an easy answer, but the consequence would be the accumulation of public debt. Thus, a large fiscal deficit and public debts are often positively correlated. Countries that have large fiscal deficits would also accumulate large public debt. Studies have shown a number of drawbacks an economy would have when faced with large debts and deficits (Barro, 1979; Eaton, 1987; Woodford, 1990; Cavanugh, 1996; Sutherland, 1997; Bohn, 1998; Ardagna et al., 2007; Kumar and Woo, 2010). According to the IMF, public debt is defined as the "gross general government debt," expressed as a percentage of GDP (IMF, 2012). Table 7.15 summarizes the number of years with the worst performance of public debt for the three decades from 1980 to 2012. There are a number of interesting observations regarding the rankings. In the decade 1980 − 90, basically all the worst public debt performers were the small countries with a weak economic base that were not competitive globally. The only exception could be Israel. The situation in 1990 − 2000 was similar, except that a few oil-exporting Middle East countries (Kuwait, Jordon, and Yemen) have joined the list. In 2000 − 12, however, there are a few weaker countries from the European Union (EU) included (typically, Greece, Italy, Portugal, and Ireland), while the largest global economies of the United States and Japan are also listed.

By looking at the three decades (1980−2012), the worst debt performers are still the weaker and smaller world economies in Africa and Central America. Although small countries tended to have less resource endowment, what would equally be relevant could be the policy orientation these countries adopted, including a weak performance in economic openness and freedom, ineffective political regimes and government, and uncompetitiveness to foreign investment due to unsustainable factors and a large informal economy. Growth would be restricted, and debt could easily be accumulated when these countries over-spent, and were faced with the inability to repay. Basically, these countries lived on debt. The higher their debt, the lower the ability to repay, and the more borrowing or global assistance would be needed. As borrowing was made to pay for the previous debt, a "debt-breeds-debt" vicious circle would emerge. If it was at all possible, it would take generations to repay these debts. The situation would turn for the worse if these governments decided to choose to default, as this would make the international community less likely to come to their aid.

Table 7.16 shows the detailed performance of the 10 largest public debt countries for the period 1980−2012. By 2012, such European countries as Greece and Italy are in the top 10 countries with largest public debt. In Asia, Japan and Singapore are the worst performers. However, unlike the weak European countries, both Japan and Singapore are Asian countries with a strong performance in international reserves. Many large public debts countries are small and weak developing countries, known as "fragile states." They are characterized by weak economic performance, due to instability and internal fragmentation. Many of these countries were former colonies, but have gained independence gradually after the Second World War. However, while these countries have claimed to be developing countries, their economic performance has been unsatisfactory and growth has remained insignificant. All along, some of these countries adopted the leftist ideology and complained about their colonial status. As colonies or "third world" countries, they were exploited as their resources were extracted by former imperial powers, leaving them to become "dependent or peripheral" states (Fanon, 1967; Lichtheim, 1971;

TABLE 7.15 Number of Years of Top 10 Largest Public Debt Economies

1980–90		1991–2000		2001–12		1980–2012	
Guyana	11	Guyana	10	Eritrea	10	Guinea-Bissau	24
Zambia	11	Nicaragua	10	Guinea-Bissau	9	Zambia	23
Nicaragua	11	Guinea-Bissau	10	Congo Demo.	9	Mauritania	23
Mauritania	11	Zambia	9	Japan	9	Guyana	21
Equ. Guinea	10	Sierra Leone	9	Lebanon	9	Nicaragua	21
Congo Rep.	8	Mauritania	7	Liberia	8	Congo Rep.	17
Israel	7	Sudan	6	St. Kitts & Nev.	7	Sierra Leone	14
Bolivia	6	São Tomé	6	Greece	6	São Tomé	12
Jamaica	6	Congo Rep.	5	São Tomé	6	Equ. Guinea	12
Guinea-Bissau	5	Myanmar	4	Mauritania	5	Congo Demo.	11
Egypt	4	Lao Peop. Rep.	3	Jamaica	5	Jamaica	11
Togo	3	Syria Arab Rep.	3	Congo Rep.	4	Lebanon	11
Madagascar	3	Equatorial	2	Sierra Leone	4	Eritrea	11
Haiti	3	Guinea	2	Singapore	3	Liberia	9
Syria Arab Rep.	2	Vietnam	2	Zambia	3	Japan	9
Chile	2	Bulgaria	2	Burundi	3	Israel	7
Lebanon	2	Nigeria	2	Italy	3	St. Kitts & Nev.	7
Lao People Rep.	2	Congo Demo.	1	Guinea	2	Bolivia	6
Costa Rica	1	Kuwait	1	Seychelles	2	Sudan	6
Jordon	1	Jordon	1	Ireland	2	Greece	6
Myanmar	1	Haiti,	1	Portugal	2	Syria Arab Rep.	5
Sierra Leone	1	Angola	1	Grenada	2	Myanmar	5
		Yemen	1	Gambia,	1	Lao People Rep.	5
		Liberia	1	Togo	1	Egypt	4
		Serbia	1	United States	1	Togo	4
		Eritrea	1			Haiti	4
						Madagascar	3
						Burundi	3
						Singapore	3
						Italy	3
						Chile	2
						Jordon	2
						Vietnam	2
						Bulgaria	2
						Nigeria	2
						Guinea	2
						Seychelles	2
						Ireland	2

(Continued)

TABLE 7.15   (*Continued*)

1980–90	1991–2000	2001–12	1980–2012	
			Grenada	2
			Portugal	2
			Costa Rica	1
			Kuwait	1
			Angola	1
			United States	1
			Yemen	1
			Serbia	1
			Gambia	1

TABLE 7.16   Top 10 Largest Public Debt Economies: Ranked by Percentage of GDP

	1980	% GDP	1981	% GDP	1982	% GDP	1983	% GDP	1984	% GDP	1985	% GDP
1	Guyana	318.9	Guyana	357.5	Guyana	509.3	Guyana	598.3	Guyana	610.2	Guyana	664.5
2	Israel	154.3	Equ. Guinea	223.3	Equ. Guinea	263.3	Equ. Guinea	261.9	Israel	284.0	Nicaragua	218.0
3	Nicaragua	152.1	Nicaragua	149.1	Nicaragua	159.1	Israel	260.5	Equ. Guinea	260.5	Bolivia	205.2
4	Equ. Guinea	147.7	Egypt	127.6	Bolivia	155.4	Nicaragua	211.6	Nicaragua	198.0	Israel	199.0
5	Egypt	121.7	Bolivia	121.7	Egypt	134.4	Bolivia	157.3	Bolivia	166.5	Congo, Rep.	195.0
6	Bolivia	100.0	Costa Rica	103.6	Congo, Rep.	126.6	Congo Rep.	146.4	Congo, Rep.	162.4	Equ. Guinea	185.6
7	Zambia	100.0	Mauritania	100.9	Lebanon	125.1	Mauritania	132.4	Jamaica	158.7	Jamaica	181.3
8	Mauritania	93.3	Jamaica	100.6	Mauritania	123.6	Lebanon	131.9	Mauritania	148.4	Mauritania	173.5
9	Togo	92.1	Togo	99.2	Zambia	115.1	Jamaica	127.9	Zambia	140.7	Chile	165.5
10	Jamaica	87.8	Zambia	97.4	Togo	108.4	Zambia	126.5	Egypt	123.1	Zambia	157.3

	1986	% GDP	1987	% GDP	1988	% GDP	1989	% GDP	1990	% GDP	1991	% GDP
1	Guyana	717.7	Guyana	615.2	Nicaragua	629.2	Guyana	602.5	Nicaragua	2092.9	Guyana	784.4
2	Zambia	238.7	Nicaragua	266.6	Guyana	603.1	Nicaragua	477.0	Guyana	678.1	Nicaragua	333.7
3	Mauritania	178.5	Guinea-Biss	231.8	Guinea-Biss	293.9	Guinea-Biss	258.6	Guinea-Biss	244.0	Guinea-Bissau	267.0
4	Congo Rep.	175.9	Madagascar	219.1	Madagascar	172.7	SyriaArab Re	206.8	Jordon	219.7	Myanmar	223.1
5	Jamaica	160.6	Zambia	181.7	Zambia	168.6	LaoPeop. Rep	201.8	LaoPeop.Re	202.6	Zambia	213.3
6	Chile	165.0	Congo Rep.	172.6	Congo Rep.	168.0	Equ. Guinea	188.9	Myanmar	192.1	Kuwait	203.4
7	Israel	162.5	Mauritania	168.0	Mauritania	167.2	Mauritania	167.8	SyriaArabRe	182.6	Jordon	200.6
8	Nicaragua	159.2	Equ. Guinea	157.9	Equ. Guinea	156.0	Haiti	166.7	Sierra Leone	178.5	Lao Peop. Rep.	180.9

(Continued)

TABLE 7.16 (*Continued*)

	1986	% GDP	1987	% GDP	1988	% GDP	1989	% GDP	1990	% GDP	1991	% GDP
9	Equ. Guinea	154.0	Haiti	147.0	Haiti	153.4	Zambia	161.1	Zambia	177.8	Equ. Guinea	171.2
10	Guinea-Bis	153.2	Israel	146.7	Israel	145.4	Madagascar	159.9	Congo Rep.	162.1	Syria ArabRep.	161.0

	1992	% GDP	1993	% GDP	1994	% GDP	1995	% GDP	1996	% GDP	1997	% GDP
1	Guyana	711.9	Guyana	624.6	Guyana	526.8	Guyana	447.7	Guinea-Biss	322.4	Guinea-Bissau	316.0
2	Sudan	454.9	Nicaragua	445.9	Nicaragua	446.6	Nicaragua	362.7	Guyana	310.3	Guyana	271.2
3	Nicaragua	448.6	Guinea-Bissau	306.3	Sudan	355.0	Guinea-Biss	318.4	Zambia	236.3	São Tomé	252.0
4	Guinea-Bissau	311.0	Bulgaria	289.6	Guinea-Biss	326.9	São Tomé	229.0	YemenRep.	231.0	Nicaragua	231.0
5	Vietnam	229.3	Sudan	262.6	Sierra Leone	241.4	Zambia	226.3	Nicaragua	222.4	Congo Rep.	220.0
6	Myanmar	214.4	Myanmar	196.1	Equ. Guinea	218.1	Angola	222.1	Congo Rep.	212.2	Zambia	190.4
7	Haiti	194.6	Nigeria	193.7	Zambia	208.3	Sudan	219.6	Sudan	208.1	Sierra Leone	178.1
8	Sierra Leone	180.7	Zambia	181.3	Nigeria	183.7	Sierra	185.4	São Tomé	176.0	Mauritania	158.2
9	Bulgaria	170.6	Sierra Leone	179.5	Myanmar	174.3	Leone	172.3	SierraLeone	161.2	Sudan	149.9
10	Syria Arab Rep.	165.7	Vietnam	174.6	Mauritania	174.3	Congo Rep.	160.0	Mauritania	160.4	Syria Arab Re.	146.1

	1998	% GDP	1999	% GDP	2000	% GDP	2001	% GDP	2002	% GDP	2003	% GDP
1	Guinea-Bissau	434.9	São Tomé	385.6	São Tomé	376.0	São Tomé	388.4	Liberia	367.7	Liberia	523.4
2	São Tomé	345.0	Guinea-Bissa	381.1	Liberia	360.5	Liberia	361.7	São Tomé	341.1	Guinea-Biss	314.8
3	Congo Rep.	264.4	Congo, Dem.	262.8	Guinea-Biss	344.4	Guinea-Biss	328.8	Guinea-Bissau	338.4	São Tomé	306.4
4	Congo, Dem.	257.9	Guyana	234.8	Serbia	241.7	Nicaragua	227.5	Nicaragua	235.7	Nicaragua	236.2
5	Guyana	249.3	Congo, Rep.	231.6	Guyana	233.0	Congo, Dem.	220.3	Congo, Dem.	214.2	Congo, Rep.	204.4
6	Zambia	244.5	Zambia	221.6	Zambia	226.2	Zambia	197.9	Zambia	204.2	Zambia	183.5
7	Nicaragua	225.9	Nicaragua	221.3	Sierra Leone	211.2	Congo,Rep.	195.8	Eritrea	190.5	Congo, Dem.	180.4
8	Sierra Leone	211.8	Sierra Leone	208.7	Nicaragua	204.9	Sierra Leone	186.1	Congo, Rep.	180.3	Sierra Leone	177.7
9	LaoPeop. Rep.	187.6	Mauritania	188.4	Mauritania	195.7	Mauritania	180.7	Mauritania	176.7	Burundi	172.0
10	Mauritania	177.3	LaoPeop. Rep.	169.8	Eritrea	185.7	Eritrea	167.1	Sierra Leone	174.6	Mauritania	169.7

	2004	% GDP	2005	% GDP	2006	% GDP	2007	% GDP	2008	% GDP	2009	% GDP
1	Liberia	487.4	Liberia	402.4	Liberia	357.7	Guinea-Biss	186.9	Liberia	315.1	Japan	210.2
2	São Tomé	328.2	São Tomé	300.9	São Tomé	265.9	Japan	183.0	Japan	191.8	Liberia	171.1

(*Continued*)

TABLE 7.16 (Continued)

	2004	% GDP	2005	% GDP	2006	% GDP	2007	% GDP	2008	% GDP	2009	% GDP
3	Guinea-Biss	284.4	Guinea-Biss	232.1	Guinea-Biss	213.8	Lebanon	167.7	Eritrea	174.9	Guinea-Biss	164.3
4	Congo, Rep.	198.7	Japan	186.4	Japan	186.0	Eritrea	156.7	Guinea-Bissau	157.7	St. Kitts&Nev	148.5
5	Congo,Dem.	196.0	Mauritania	182.1	Lebanon	178.0	St. Kitts&Nev	134.0	Lebanon	156.3	Lebanon	147.6
6	Burundi	181.0	Lebanon	176.0	Eritrea	151.6	Seychelles	130.2	Congo, Dem.	133.1	Eritrea	145.7
7	Japan	180.7	St.Kitts&Ne	159.9	Congo, Dem.	149.0	Burundi	128.5	StKitts& Nevis	131.0	Jamaica	142.8
8	Lebanon	164.6	Eritrea	156.2	St.Kitts& Ne	145.3	Congo, Dem.	126.1	Seychelles	130.7	Congo, Dem.	136.3
9	Nicaragua	160.5	Guinea	150.2	Gambia	142.3	Togo	107.8	Jamaica	127.3	Greece	129.0
10	Sierra Leone	160.5	Congo,Dem.	147.9	Guinea	137.1	Greece	107.4	Greece	112.6	Mauritania	124.4

	2010	% GDP	2011	% GDP	2012	% GDP
1	Japan	215.3	Japan	229.9	Japan	238.0
2	St.Kitts&Ne	163.9	Greece	165.4	Greece	156.9
3	Eritrea	144.8	St.Kitts&Ne	154.3	Jamaica	148.7
4	Greece	144.5	Jamaica	140.1	Lebanon	139.5
5	Jamaica	142.8	Lebanon	137.4	Italy	127.0
6	Lebanon	141.7	Eritrea	133.8	Eritrea	125.8
7	Italy	118.7	Italy	120.1	Portugal	123.8
8	Singapore	103.6	Singapore	108.3	Ireland	117.4
9	Grenada	102.4	Portugal	107.8	Singapore	111.4
10	United States	98.7	Ireland	106.5	Grenada	109.5

Brown, 1974; Amin, 1976). However, after decades of political independence, these countries are still unsettled, disorganized, and remain "infant," even though some of these countries are blessed with rich natural resources and have received aid and assistance from foreign countries and international institutions. Unfortunately, these countries never focus on the "supply-side" factors, and lack a "home-grown" ability.

The removal of public debt depends on the ability of the economy to repay. The emergence of debt probably means that this generation has over-spent at the expense of the future generation. The moral question is whether it is fair for this generation to over-spend, while future generations have to shoulder the economic burden. A better alternative is to see what actions could one take in order to boost an economy's resource endowments, so that more growth would take place, rather than over-spending, especially if the spending was made for welfare purposes. There is a need to check if the debt has been committed to "demand-driven" causes, or if there was a lack of "supply-driven" channels through which resource endowment could promote the capability of the economy. Equally, debt has been financed through international and foreign assistance. To help countries to reduce the size of their public debt, international agents providing assistance to debt-prone countries should see that borrowing was geared to enrich the country's economic capacity, and not use the new borrowing to pay for the previous debt.

Table 7.17 summarizes countries with the lowest public debts expressed as a percentage of the country's GDP for the three decades 1980—2012. One observation is that these countries are either oil exporting countries, such as United Arab Emirates, or well-behaved European countries, such as Finland and Luxemburg. In Asia, China is a young performer, while South Korea and Thailand are showing good performance. One also finds a number of African countries which have shown strong performance in ensuring the lowest possible level of public debt. These African countries included Ghana, Botswana, and Swaziland. Another notable fact from Table 7.17 is the good performance from a number of "emerging countries" which have gained their own statehood after the

TABLE 7.17 Number of Years in the Top 10 of Smallest Public Debt Economies

1980–90		1991–2000		2001–11		1980–2012	
UA Emirates	12	Luxembourg	10	Estonia	11	UA Emirates	28
Vanuatu	11	China	10	Chile	10	Luxembourg	26
Luxembourg	9	Korea, Rep.	10	Equ. Guinea	9	China	18
Bahrain	9	UA Emirates	10	Turkmenistan	9	Estonia	18
Bahamas	8	Latvia	7	Botswana	8	Korea, Rep.	15
Finland	8	Czech Republic	6	Libya	8	Botswana	15
Malta	7	Estonia	6	Brunei Darus.	7	Bahrain	13
China	7	Belarus	5	Luxembourg	7	Vanuatu	12
Oman	6	Botswana	5	UA Emirates	6	Oman	12
Bhutan	6	Thailand	5	Kazakhstan	6	Chile	11
Korea, Rep.	5	Romania	4	Belarus	5	Belarus	10
Ghana	4	Bahrain	4	Oman	5	Equ. Guinea	10
Kuwait	3	Swaziland	4	Lesotho	4	Libya	10
Trinidad &Tobago	3	Lithuania	4	Australia	3	Finland	9
Australia	3	Azerbaijan	3	Latvia	2	Latvia	9
Iran	2	Qatar	2	Algeria	2	Turkmenistan	9
Botswana	2	Vanuatu	1	Saudi Arabia	2	Bahamas	8
Solomon Is.	1	Finland	1	Uzbekistan	2	Brunei Darus.	8
Qatar	1	Slovak Republic	1	China	1	Malta	7
Libya	1	Namibia	1	Kuwait	1	Bhutan	6
Colombia	1	Chile	1	Azerbaijan	1	Australia	6
Romania	1			Cameron	1	Czech Republic	6
St. Lucia	1					Kazakhstan	6
						Romania	5
						Thailand	5
						Kuwait	5
						Ghana	4
						Swaziland	4
						Lithuania	4
						Azerbaijan	4
						Lesotho	4
						Trinidad &Tobago	3
						Qatar	3
						Iran	3
						Algeria	3
						Saudi Arabia	3
						Uzbekistan	3
						Solomon Is.	1
						Namibia	1
						Colombia	1
						St. Lucia	1
						Slovak Republic	1
						Cameron	1

collapse of the Soviet Union, including Latvia, Estonia, Kazakhstan, and others. These new emerging countries have built up a certain level of economic infrastructure and human capital, and are ready to grow should sufficient and relevant investment resources be available. These "emerging countries" can perform more strongly if they adopt "supply-side" economics to enrich their productive capability.

The 10 countries with lowest public debts are shown in Table 7.18. The Fiscal Affairs Department of the IMF has made available the Historical Public Debt Database. For example, the graphic description in Fig. 7.2 shows the debt performance of the world and the five regions since 1950. One can observe that the debt situation was more stable before 1980, but large deteriorations and fluctuations have appeared since the 1980s. Among the different regions, the African countries were the worst performers, while Asia−Pacific and countries in the Western Hemisphere performed stronger than the world average. European countries showed a closer performance to the world average. The Middle East and Central Asia group of countries have shown large fluctuations. However, all country groups showed rapid improvement since 2000.

TABLE 7.18　Top 10 Smallest Public Debt Economies: Ranked by Percentage of GDP

	1980	% GDP	1981	% GDP	1982	% GDP	1983	% GDP	1984	% GDP	1985	% GDP
1	Kuwait	0.6	Kuwait	2.5	Bhutan	1.7	Bhutan	3.5	China	1.0	China	3.3
2	UA Emirates	3.5	UA Emirates	3.2	UA Emirates	4.6	Vanuatu	4.5	Bhutan	3.1	Luxembourg	6.3
3	Luxembourg	6.4	Vanuatu	4.2	Ghana	5.0	UA Emirates	5.5	UA Emirates	5.7	Vanuatu	7.1
4	Oman	7.0	Ghana	5.7	Vanuatu	5.1	Ghana	7.1	Vanuatu	5.7	Iran	10.2
5	Bahamas	8.7	Luxembourg	6.7	Kuwait	5.1	Luxembourg	7.4	Luxembourg	7.7	UA Emirates	10.9
6	Bahrain	9.0	Oman	7.0	Luxembourg	6.9	Bahrain	8.6	Iran	9.2	Bahrain	11.7
7	Ghana	9.0	Bahrain	7.3	Trini&Tobag	8.0	Trini.&Tobag	11.0	Bahrain	13.3	Bhutan	12.1
8	Solomon Is.	10.7	Trini. &Tobago	9.0	Bahrain	8.6	Oman	14.0	Bahamas	14.2	Bahamas	12.1
9	Libya	10.7	Bahamas	11.4	Oman	10.1	Bahamas	14.6	Oman	15.0	Malta	14.2
10	Colombia	12.4	Finland	11.5	Malta	12.5	Malta	14.8	Finland	15.1	Finland	15.8

	1986	% GDP	1987	% GDP	1988	% GDP	1989	% GDP	1990	% GDP	1991	% GDP
1	China	3.2	China	3.6	China	4.5	Luxembourg	4.0	Romania	1.0	Romania	2.7
2	Luxembourg	7.9	Luxembourg	6.7	Luxembourg	5.1	China	6.5	UA Emirates	6.5	Luxembourg	4.0
3	Vanuatu	8.7	UA Emirates	8.6	UA Emirates	7.7	UA Emirates	7.1	China	6.9	China	7.4
4	UA Emirates	10.2	Bahamas	11.5	Bahrain	12.2	Korea, Rep.	10.4	Korea, Rep.	8.4	Korea, Rep.	7.8
5	Bahamas	11.7	Vanuatu	13.7	Bahamas	12.3	Bahrain	12.1	Qatar	10.7	Bahrain	7.9
6	Malta	11.9	Malta	15.4	Korea, Rep.	13.5	Finland	14.3	Finland	13.8	UA Emirates	8.2
7	Bhutan	15.2	Korea, Rep.	16.6	Vanuatu	14.0	Malta	17.6	Botswana	17.1	Qatar	17.9
8	Finland	16.4	Finland	17.6	Bhutan	14.4	Vanuatu	17.9	Vanuatu	21.4	Botswana	18.5
9	Bahrain	17.8	Australia	22.1	Finland	16.5	Botswana	21.7	Australia	21.6	Vanuatu	20.7
10	Korea Rep	19.0	St. Lucia	24.3	Malta	17.9	Australia	22.8	Oman	21.6	Finland	21.9

	1992	% GDP	1993	% GDP	1994	% GDP	1995	% GDP	1996	% GDP	1997	% GDP
1	Luxembourg	4.8	Luxembourg	6.0	Luxembourg	5.5	China	6.1	UA Emirates	5.9	UA Emirates	4.8
2	China	5.0	China	6.7	China	6.1	Korea Rep	7.1	China	6.8	Estonia	6.2
3	Bahrain	7.7	Bahrain	7.1	Bahrain	6.8	Luxembourg	7.4	Korea, Rep	6.8	China	6.6
4	Korea, Rep.	7.7	Korea, Rep.	7.5	Korea, Rep	7.7	UA Emirates	8.6	Estonia	7.4	Luxembourg	7.4

(Continued)

TABLE 7.18   (*Continued*)

	1992	% GDP	1993	% GDP	1994	% GDP	1995	% GDP	1996	% GDP	1997	% GDP
5	UA Emirates	9.1	UA Emirates	9.1	Lithuania	7.8	Lithuania	8.8	Luxembourg	7.4	Azerbaijan	8.6
6	Romania	11.1	Romania	11.7	UA Emirates	9.1	Estonia	9.0	Latvia	10.7	Latvia	10.3
7	Botswana	19.2	Thailand	18.1	Latvia	9.6	Latvia	11.8	Belarus	10.7	Belarus	10.4
8	Thailand	19.9	Swaziland	18.2	Thailand	14.3	Azerbaijan	11.8	Thailand	10.7	Korea, Rep.	10.7
9	Qatar	19.9	Czech Rep.	18.3	Romania	14.4	Thailand	12.2	Azerbaijan	11.1	Swaziland	13.0
10	Slovak Repub.	21.5	Namibia	18.3	Swaziland	16.2	Czech Rep.	14.6	Lithuania	11.8	Czech Rep.	13.1

	1998	% GDP	1999	% GDP	2000	% GDP	2001	% GDP	2002	% GDP	2003	% GDP
1	Estonia	5.5	UA Emirates	4.8	UA Emirates	3.1	UA Emirates	2.7	Brunei Darus.	2.0	Brunei Darus.	1.0
2	Luxembourg	7.1	Estonia	6.0	Estonia	5.1	Brunei Darus.	2.9	UA Emirates	3.6	UA Emirates	4.4
3	UA Emirates	7.1	Luxembourg	6.4	Luxembourg	6.2	Estonia	4.8	Estonia	5.7	Estonia	5.6
4	Latvia	10.0	Belarus	12.7	Botswana	10.8	Luxembourg	6.3	Luxembourg	6.3	Luxembourg	6.2
5	China	11.4	China	13.8	Belarus	11.9	Botswana	8.3	Botswana	7.0	Belarus	10.3
6	Czech Rep.	15.0	Botswana	15.2	Chile	13.3	Belarus	11.4	Belarus	10.9	Equ. Guinea	10.4
7	Korea, Rep	15.4	Latvia	15.9	Latvia	15.0	Chile	14.4	Australia	15.0	Botswana	11.2
8	Lithuania	15.4	Czech Rep.	16.4	China	16.4	Latvia	15.9	Chile	15.2	Chile	12.6
9	Botswana	16.1	Korea, Rep.	17.6	Korea, Rep.	18.0	Australia	17.0	Latvia	16.5	Australia	13.2
10	Belarus	16.2	Swaziland	19.9	Czech Rep.	18.5	China	17.7	Kazakhstan	17.6	Turkmenistan	13.3

	2004	% GDP	2005	% GDP	2006	% GDP	2007	% GDP	2008	% GDP	2009	% GDP
1	Brunei Darus.	0.4	BruneiDarus.	0.3	Libya	0.5	Libya	0.0	Libya	0.0	Libya	0.0
2	Libya	0.9	Libya	0.6	Brunei Darus.	1.0	Brunei Darus.	0.7	Equ. Guinea	0.7	Turkmenistan	2.4
3	Estonia	5.0	Equ. Guinea	3.0	Equ. Guinea	1.6	Equ. Guinea	1.1	Turkmenistan	2.8	Lesotho	3.5
4	UA Emirates	5.6	Estonia	4.6	Turkmenistan	3.3	Turkmenistan	2.4	Estonia	4.5	Equ. Guinea	5.1
5	Equ. Guinea	6.2	Turkmenistan	5.4	Estonia	4.4	Estonia	3.7	Oman	4.7	Chile	5.8
6	Luxembourg	6.3	Luxembourg	6.1	Chile	5.0	Chile	3.9	Chile	4.9	Oman	6.3
7	Belarus	7.3	UA Emirates	6.6	Botswana	5.6	Kazakhstan	5.9	Lesotho	5.1	Estonia	7.2
8	Turkmenistan	9.0	Belarus	6.9	Kazakhstan	6.7	Luxembourg	6.7	Botswana	6.2	Kazakhstan	10.2
9	Botswana	9.9	Chile	7.0	Luxembourg	6.7	Oman	6.9	Kazakhstan	6.7	Algeria	10.4
10	Chile	10.3	Botswana	7.4	UA Emirates	6.8	Botswana	7.5	Azerbaijan	7.3	Cameroon	10.6

	2010	% GDP	2011	% GDP	2012	% GDP
1	Libya	0.0	Libya	0.0	Libya	0.0
2	Lesotho	4.9	Oman	5.0	BruneiDarus.	2.4
3	Equ. Guinea	5.0	Lesotho	5.9	Saudi Arabia	3.7
4	Oman	5.3	Estonia	6.0	Oman	6.0
5	Estonia	6.7	Saudi Arabia	6.1	Kuwait	6.4

(*Continued*)

TABLE 7.18   *(Continued)*

	2010	% GDP	2011	% GDP	2012	% GDP
6	Chile	8.6	Equ. Guinea	6.8	Equ. Guinea	7.8
7	Saudi Arabia	9.8	Turkmenistan	7.3	Uzbekistan	8.6
8	Uzbekistan	10.0	Kuwait	8.1	Iran	9.5
9	Turkmenistan	10.6	Uzbekistan	9.1	Estonia	9.7
10	Kazakhstan	10.7	Algeria	9.5	Algeria	10.5

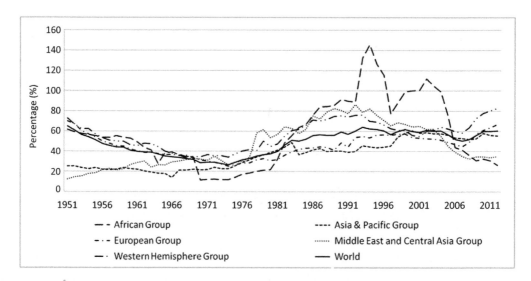

FIGURE 7.2   Debt as percentage of GDP: world regions. *Source: International Monetary Fund.*

As the worst performer in the debt ratio, the intention to improve among the Africa group of countries could take into account both internal and external factors. In their study to examine the different impact between external and internal factors on growth in developing countries, Li and Zhou (2010) and Zhou and Li (2011) have shown that, although improvement in the performance of external factors would promote growth, it was the improvement in internal factors and conditions that could improve the performance of external factors and growth. Hence, improvements in internal factors hold the key to growth and development. Typical internal factors include infrastructure, individual freedom, and a sound legal system.

Nonetheless, Fig. 7.2 conveys the point that the debt-to-GDP ratio showed rapid deterioration after the early 1980s, but has shown an equally rapid improvement since 2010. The world economy has passed through a debt crisis cycle over the three decades from 1980 to 2010. Indeed, the slope of the rise after 1980 and the fall after 2008 have been steep. There can be a number of reasons that explain the rise in the debt − GDP ratio since 1980; e.g., the rise in oil price and the fall in interest rates could be the probable reasons. By the early 2010s, the world debt − GDP ratio was around 60%, which is higher than the ratio before 1980.

V TRADE

The volume of trade in a country serves as a good indicator of economic openness and participation in the global economy. In a pure economic argument, a country's trade depends on the theory of comparative advantage, which argues that countries which specialize in the production and export of goods that can be produced with the lowest marginal cost compared to the same production in other countries have an advantage. When countries follow such a pattern of product specialization, and given free trade, the income of exporting countries should rise, as advocated by the convergence theory that income among world economies would narrow through trade liberalization (Dornbusch et al., 1977; Grossman and Helpman, 1990; Tamura, 1991; Ben-David, 1996; Slaughter, 2001; Li and Bender, 2007; Li et al., 2016).

However, the theory of comparative advantage in trade is only part of the truth. The other part of the truth depends on the kind of exports the country is trading in. In reality, a poor country tends to export low value-added agricultural and raw materials, while an industrialized country tends to export high value-added technological products. The terms of trade can simply be seen by the ratio between export price and import price in world trade data (Deardorff, 2006). Intuitively, the terms of trade show how much can be imported from a country's own exports. A country is said to have a good/poor terms of trade if the export price-to-import price ratio exceeds or is below unity The terms of trade are usually poor for developing countries, but are high for industrialized countries, because developing countries export low priced, low value-added products, and import expensive and high value-added products, but it is vice versa for industrialized countries. As such, differences in world income could not converge. For a developing country to improve the terms of trade, the long-term answer is to improve the content of its exports. A developing country has to industrialize, adopt a technological mode of production, and improve the value-added content of exports, or develop high value-added service exports.

Typically, it is the small and developing countries which would export to large developed countries. After the Second World War, the international body of the General Agreement of Trade and Tariff (GATT) was established in 1948 under the United Nations, to promote multilateral trade with the intention of reducing trade barriers and liberalizing trade. Trade negotiations were conducted in various "rounds" that covered from a few years to a decade. For example, the Kennedy Round lasted from 1962 to 1967, the Tokyo Round covered 1973 – 79, and eventually the Uruguay Round lasted from 1986 to 1994. However, while the export-oriented developing countries favored multilateral trade, it was the industrialized countries that often ended up with large trade deficits and the loss of jobs in their domestic economies. Multilateral trade meant that trade in developed countries would be open to all imports from developing countries. Hence, the developed and industrialized importers tended to favor bilateral trade negotiations. With bilateral "free" trade agreements (FTAs), the importing country would only open its import market to favored exporting countries (Urata, 2002; Brown et al., 2003; Shadlen, 2005; Saggi and Yildiz, 2010). Thus, bilateral trade agreements become more favored by the industrialized countries. Bilateral trade agreements are conducted along ideological lines. Usually, a developed country makes bilateral trade agreements with an exporting country under specific terms and conditions. FTAs are basically not "free," as the content and volume of trade is agreed. Thus, there is a political divide in the trade preferences between developing and industrialized countries. While exporting countries preferred openness in trade, industrialized countries adopted a more protectionist policy in the form of bilateral trade agreements.

The World Trade Organization that succeeded GATT in 1995 extended its coverage to include service trade, intellectual property rights, and trade dispute settlements (Jackson, 1997; Rose, 2004; Subramanian and Wei, 2007; Matsushita, 2015). WTO accession required bilateral negotiation, and the acceding member had to seek approval from all the major industrialized countries. Since 2000, a new round of WTO trade negotiations known as the Doha Round has taken place, though it has not been successful because of the different attitudes between developing and industrialized countries over a number of issues, including market access, agricultural subsidies, and the use of standardized rules (Ackerman, 2005; Charlton and Stiglitz, 2005; Hertel and Winters, 2006; Gallagher, 2007; Hoekman and Nicita, 2010). Trade negotiation has been used as a political instrument by the importing countries to help the developing countries selectively. While exporting countries preferred multilateral policies, as their intention was trade expansion, importing countries preferred "market equalization" so as to avoid prolonged and severe trade deficits (Tait and Li, 1997).

Table 7.19 summarizes the performance of trade surplus countries in the three decades from 1980 to 2013. One can see a definite pattern of change. Both the Netherlands and Japan were the best performers in the 1980s and 1990s, and the top 10 trade surplus countries spread wider among world economies. In the decade 2001 – 10, however, trade surplus countries have become more concentrated in Russia and China, the three successful European countries of the Netherlands, Germany, and Norway, and the oil exporting country of Saudi Arabia. These six countries scored 10 years in the top 10 performers. The top 10 trade surplus countries in the three decades also covered a number of successful Asian countries, such as Japan, Singapore, and Malaysia, and such oil exporting countries as the United Arab Emirates, Venezuela, and Kuwait. There are also a few other European countries, such as France, Switzerland, and Sweden. Canada is the North American country that has performed most successfully in trade.

Looking at the three decades, the strongest trade performers are the Netherlands, Japan, Germany, and China, followed by Norway, Saudi Arabia, Russia, Canada, Switzerland, Singapore, and France. Other than Saudi Arabia and Russia, there are a number of oil exporting countries in the top 10 trade surplus countries. The list includes Venezuela, Kuwait, Iran, Nigeria, the United Arab Emirates, and Algeria. This reflects that the world economy has depended excessively on petroleum, and trade imbalances tend to be unidirectional.

TABLE 7.19 Number of Years in the Top 10 of Trade Surplus Economies

1980–90		1991–2000		2001–13		1980–2013	
Japan	10	Japan	10	Russian Fed.	13	Netherlands	32
Germany	10	France	10	Germany	13	Japan	28
Netherlands	10	Netherlands	10	China	13	Germany	27
UAE	7	China	7	Saudi Arabia	13	China	22
Venezuela	7	Belgium	7	Norway	12	Norway	21
Taiwan	7	Italy	7	Netherlands	12	Saudi Arabia	17
Brazil	7	Switzerland	6	Singapore	10	Russian Fed.	17
South Africa	6	Sweden	5	Switzerland	9	Canada	15
Canada	6	Singapore	5	Japan	8	Switzerland	15
Norway	5	Norway	4	Kuwait	6	Singapore	15
Mexico	5	Denmark	4	Canada	5	France	13
Korea, Rep.	4	Russian Fed.	4	Qatar	4	Brazil	11
United Kingdom	3	Canada	4	Malaysia	3	UAE	11
Saudi Arabia	3	Germany	4	UAE	3	Taiwan	9
Kuwait	2	Brazil	3	France	2	Korea, Rep.	8
Nigeria	2	Korea Rep.	3	Taiwan	1	Kuwait	8
China	2	Malaysia	2	Korea, Rep.	1	Italy	8
Hong Kong	2	Taiwan	1	Brazil	1	Belgium	8
Argentina	2	UAE	1	Ireland	1	Venezuela	7
France	1	South Africa	1			South Africa	7
Italy	1	Thailand	1			Malaysia	6
Spain	1	Saudi Arabia	1			Denmark	5
Belgium	1					Mexico	5
Denmark	1					Sweden	5
Romania	1					Qatar	4
Libya	1					United Kingdom	3
Indonesia	1					Nigeria	2
Malaysia	1					Hong Kong	2
Iran	1					Argentina	2
						Spain, Ireland,	1
						Romania, Libya,	1
						Indonesia, Iran,	1
						Thailand	1

However, as shown in Table 7.20, quite a few of the top 10 trade surplus countries also appeared as top 10 trade deficit countries during the three decades. There are changes in the position of countries between the three decades. In the 1980s, many of the large trade deficit countries are European countries that are key importers from developing countries. In the 1990s, many of the top 10 trade deficit countries are developing and emerging countries. In the decade 2001–13, the largest trade deficit countries are more concentrated in the five countries of the United States, the United Kingdom, India, Greece, and Spain, together with a few other European countries.

TABLE 7.20 Number of Years in the Top 10 of Trade Deficit Economies

1980−90		1991−2000		2001−13		1980−2013	
United States	11	United States	10	United States	13	United States	34
India	11	Portugal	10	United Kingdom	13	India	31
Egypt	10	United Kingdom	9	India	13	United Kingdom	27
Pakistan	7	Greece	9	Greece	11	Greece	27
Saudi Arabia	7	Mexico	7	Spain	10	Portugal	25
Greece	7	India	7	Portugal	9	Spain	20
Australia	6	Brazil	6	Turkey	9	Mexico	17
Spain	6	Thailand	5	France	9	Egypt	14
Portugal	6	Korea, Rep.	4	Mexico	8	Australia	14
United Kingdom	5	Israel	4	Australia	6	Turkey	14
Italy	4	Poland	4	Canada	5	Pakistan	10
China	4	Spain	4	Philippines	4	Brazil	10
Turkey	3	Iran	3	Poland	4	France	10
Nigeria	3	Argentina	3	Pakistan	3	Saudi Arabia	9
Iran	3	Hong Kong	3	Brazil	3	Poland	8
Israel	3	Saudi Arabia	2	Romania	3	Thailand	7
Mexico	2	Germany	2	Japan	3	Israel	7
Thailand	2	Turkey	2	Italy	2	Iran	6
Syrian Arab R.	2	Australia	2	Egypt	2	Italy	6
Japan	1	Egypt	2			China	5
Brazil	1	Kuwait	1			Korea, Rep.	5
Germany	1	China	1			Canada	5
Korea, Rep.	1					Japan	4
France	1					Romania	4
Indonesia	1					Philippines	4
Venezuela	1					Nigeria	3
Romania	1					Argentina	3
						Hong Kong	3
						Germany	3
						Syrian Arab R.	2
						Kuwait	1
						Indonesia	1
						Venezuela	1

In the three decades, the top five trade deficit countries are the United States, India, the United Kingdom, Greece, and Portugal. Being the strongest country in the world, the United States is obviously the largest importing country, as most exporting countries would target the United States as their market. However, India and Greece are much weaker countries. Without a strong industrial base and relying only on tourism, the vulnerable Greek economy faces difficulty in shouldering trade deficits.

Table 7.21 shows the details of the top 10 trade surplus countries, while Table 7.22 presents the top 10 trade deficit countries for the period 1980−2013. Most top trade surplus performers are the oil producers, and a few

TABLE 7.21 Top 10 Largest Trade Surplus Economies: Ranked by Value (US$ Million)

	1980	US$ mil	% GDP	1981	US$ mil	% GDP	1982	US$ mil	% GDP	1983	US$ mil	% GDP
1	Saudi Arabia	50,972	31.0	Saudi Arabia	49,318	26.8	Germany	15,446	2.0	Japan	19,410	1.6
2	UAE	12,871	29.5	United Kingdom	14,664	2.7	Canada	11,505	3.7	Mexico	13,715	7.7
3	Kuwait	12,035	41.9	UAE	11,680	23.7	Saudi Arabia	9472	6.2	Germany	11,342	1.5
4	United Kingdom	11,872	2.1	Kuwait	7773	30.8	UAE	8560	18.4	Canada	10,381	3.1
5	Libya	9413	24.7	Japan	7200	0.6	United Kingdom	8475	1.7	Venezuela	6751	8.5
6	Nigeria	7058	3.5	Germany	5179	0.6	Japan	6630	0.6	UAE	6436	15.0
7	South Africa	6358	7.7	Netherlands	4899	3.0	Netherlands	5951	3.8	Netherlands	4955	3.3
8	Venezuela	4838	7.0	Norway	4505	7.0	Iran	5348	4.3	Taiwan	4314	8.0
9	Canada	4717	1.7	Venezuela	3835	4.9	Mexico	5117	2.5	Norway	4312	6.9
10	Norway	3516	5.4	Indonesia	2257	2.2	China	4737	1.6	Brazil	4062	2.4
	1984	US$ mil	% GDP	1985	US$ mil	% GDP	1986	US$ mil	% GDP	1987	US$ mil	% GDP
1	Japan	32,360	2.5	Japan	45,668	3.3	Japan	78,223	3.8	Japan	71,190	2.9
2	Germany	14,988	2.1	Germany	22,909	3.1	Germany	46,145	4.4	Germany	55,189	4.3
3	Mexico	12,790	6.1	Brazil	10,762	5.7	Taiwan	14,568	18.6	Taiwan	16,410	15.6
4	Canada	11,699	3.3	Taiwan	8277	13.0	France	8704	1.1	Korea, Rep.	10,678	7.1
5	Brazil	11,337	6.5	Canada	7782	2.1	Italy	8504	1.3	Mexico	8913	5.3
6	UAE	7426	17.8	Mexico	7683	3.5	Netherlands	6196	3.1	Brazil	8794	3.6
7	Venezuela	6885	11.9	UAE	7249	17.9	South Africa	5763	8.5	South Africa	8503	9.6
8	Taiwan	6407	10.5	Venezuela	5731	9.6	Brazil	5731	2.5	Netherlands	4912	2.0
9	Netherlands	6088	4.3	Netherlands	5553	3.9	Korea, Rep.	5529	4.6	Canada	4607	1.1
10	Norway	5002	8.0	South Africa	5034	8.5	Spain	4655	1.8	Malaysia	4461	13.1
	1988	US$ mil	% GDP	1989	US$ mil	% GDP	1990	US$ mil	% GDP	1991	US$ mil	% GDP
1	Japan	61,991	2.1	Germany	59,544	4.3	Germany	45,836	2.6	Japan	54,290	1.5
2	Germany	60,093	4.3	Japan	43,423	1.4	Japan	26,386	0.9	China	11,601	2.7
3	Brazil	16,145	5.8	Brazil	13,327	3.5	Netherlands	11,652	3.7	Netherlands	11,165	3.5
4	Korea, Rep.	13,927	6.9	Taiwan	9707	6.4	China	10,668	2.6	Norway	9326	7.6
5	Taiwan	8716	6.9	Netherlands	9156	3.6	Venezuela	9355	19.9	Denmark	8592	6.2
6	Netherlands	7884	3.1	Hong Kong	6149	8.9	UAE	8550	16.9	France	7540	0.6
7	South Africa	5977	6.3	Argentina	5109	5.6	Norway	8168	6.8	Taiwan	7252	3.9
8	Belgium	4851	3.0	South Africa	5083	5.1	Argentina	7954	4.7	UAE	6756	13.1
9	Romania	4120	6.5	Korea, Rep.	4748	1.9	Nigeria	7642	11.2	Brazil	6687	1.8
10	Hong Kong	3736	6.3	Venezuela	4712	11.4	Denmark	7487	5.4	Switzerland	5936	2.3
	1992	US$ mil	% GDP	1993	US$ mil	% GDP	1994	US$ mil	% GDP	1995	US$ mil	% GDP
1	Japan	80,801	2.1	Japan	96,333	2.2	Japan	96,131	2.0	Japan	74,434	1.4
2	France	22,364	1.6	Italy	32,235	3.0	Italy	37,010	3.4	Italy	40,379	3.4
3	Netherlands	12,131	3.4	France	25,451	1.9	France	25,096	1.8	France	28,923	1.8

(Continued)

TABLE 7.21   (*Continued*)

	1992	US$ mil	% GDP	1993	US$ mil	% GDP	1994	US$ mil	% GDP	1995	US$ mil	% GDP
4	Brazil	11,897	3.3	Netherlands	16,823	4.8	Netherlands	18,905	5.1	Netherlands	26,660	6.0
5	Switzerland	11,286	4.1	Switzerland	14,517	5.5	Switzerland	14,438	4.9	Canada	18,511	3.1
6	Denmark	10,405	6.8	Denmark	9816	6.9	Belgium	10,840	4.4	Germany	18,365	0.7
7	Norway	8736	6.7	Belgium	9151	4.1	Singapore	10,500	14.3	Belgium	16,022	5.5
8	Belgium	6359	2.7	Brazil	8739	2.2	Russian Fed.	9499	2.3	Switzerland	15,225	4.4
9	South Africa	5286	3.9	Norway	7653	6.3	Denmark	9035	5.8	Singapore	14,583	16.8
10	China	4998	1.0	Sweden	6782	3.2	Sweden	8542	3.8	Sweden	14,298	5.4

	1996	US$ mil	% GDP	1997	US$ mil	% GDP	1998	US$ mil	% GDP	1999	US$ mil	% GDP
1	Italy	56,203	4.3	Japan	47,673	1.1	Japan	72,800	1.9	Japan	69,048	1.6
2	France	31,223	1.9	France	45,205	3.1	France	45,068	3.0	France	36,728	2.4
3	Netherlands	27,121	6.1	China	42,824	4.3	Korea, Rep.	44,942	11.9	Russian Fed.	31,406	16.0
4	Germany	25,377	1.0	Italy	41,997	3.4	China	43,837	4.2	China	30,641	2.8
5	Canada	24,428	3.9	Germany	28,724	1.3	Italy	40,350	3.2	Korea, Rep.	27,735	5.7
6	Japan	21,304	0.5	Netherlands	25,562	6.2	Germany	29,983	1.3	Italy	24,662	2.0
7	China	17,551	2.0	Sweden	16,540	6.3	Netherlands	24,100	5.6	Canada	23,836	3.5
8	Sweden	16,938	5.9	Belgium	16,408	6.5	Singapore	18,452	21.7	Malaysia	19,828	23.2
9	Singapore	15,845	16.6	Singapore	14,676	14.8	Thailand	17,395	15.3	Netherlands	18,850	4.3
10	Russian Fed.	15,767	4.0	Switzerland	14,572	5.0	Belgium	16,529	6.4	Belgium	17,754	6.8

	2000	US$ mil	% GDP	2001	US$ mil	% GDP	2002	US$ mil	% GDP	2003	US$ mil	% GDP
1	Japan	68,945	1.5	Canada	40,678	5.6	Germany	83,298	4.0	Germany	95,107	3.8
2	Russian Fed.	53,083	20.4	Russian Fed.	38,990	12.7	Japan	51,592	1.3	Japan	72,070	1.7
3	Canada	41,158	5.6	Germany	34,194	1.8	China	37,384	2.6	Russian Fed.	48,966	11.4
4	Saudi Arabia	29,327	15.6	Norway	28,959	16.6	Russian Fed.	36,449	10.5	Saudi Arabia	44,232	20.6
5	China	28,874	2.4	China	28,084	2.1	Canada	31,910	4.2	Netherlands	37,011	6.5
6	Norway	28,635	16.7	Japan	26,430	0.6	Saudi Arabia	28,037	14.9	China	35,821	2.2
7	Malaysia	18,020	18.5	Saudi Arabia	25,093	13.7	Norway	25,807	13.2	Canada	32,070	3.6
8	Netherlands	17,642	4.3	France	21,360	1.5	France	24,589	1.6	Norway	29,257	12.8
9	Korea, Rep.	16,619	3.0	Netherlands	17,349	4.1	Taiwan	21,836	7.1	Singapore	26,761	27.9
10	France	16,503	1.2	Malaysia	16,182	16.8	Switzerland	21,355	7.0	Switzerland	24,673	6.9

	2004	US$ mil	% GDP	2005	US$ mil	% GDP	2006	US$ mil	% GDP	2007	US$ mil	% GDP
1	Germany	136,894	4.9	Germany	145,154	5.1	China	208,919	7.5	China	308,035	8.8
2	Japan	94,240	2	China	124,627	5.4	Germany	161,596	5.4	Germany	233,605	6.8
3	Russian Fed	73,132	12.4	Russian Fed.	104,589	13.7	Russian Fed.	125,655	12.7	Russian Fed.	112,027	8.6
4	Saudi Arabia	65,104	25.2	Saudi Arabia	104,406	31.8	Saudi Arabia	112,012	29.7	Saudi Arabia	104,027	25
5	China	51,175	2.6	Japan	69,798	1.5	Japan	63,165	1.4	Japan	83,439	1.9
6	Netherlands	46,660	7.2	Netherlands	56,286	8.4	Norway	60,396	17.5	Netherlands	70,688	8.5
7	Canada	42,013	4.1	Norway	48,796	15.8	Netherlands	59,822	8.3	Norway	58,894	14.7
8	Norway	36,509	13.8	Canada	41,816	3.6	Singapore	43,339	29.7	Singapore	57,113	32

(Continued)

TABLE 7.21   (*Continued*)

	2004	US$ mil	% GDP	2005	US$ mil	% GDP	2006	US$ mil	% GDP	2007	US$ mil	% GDP
9	Korea, Rep.	33,703	4.4	Singapore	36,830	29.4	UAE	39,503	17.8	Switzerland	45,700	9.5
10	Switzerland	29,808	7.5	Brazil	36,394	4.1	Kuwait	38,019	37.4	Kuwait	39,389	34.4

	2008	US$ mil	% GDP	2009	US$ mil	% GDP	2010	US$ mil	% GDP	2011	US$ mil	% GDP
1	China	348,836	7.7	China	216,620	4.2	China	218,844	3.7	Germany	189,236	5.0
2	Germany	226,185	6.0	Germany	159,144	4.7	Germany	185,940	5.4	China	178,355	2.4
3	Russian Fed.	155,453	9.4	Russian Fed.	97,957	8.0	Russian Fed.	123,851	8.1	Saudi Arabia	178,246	26.6
4	Saudi Arabia	146,163	28.1	Switzerland	57,318	10.5	Saudi Arabia	87,628	16.6	Russian Fed.	162,733	8.5
5	Norway	85,656	18.5	Norway	56,028	14.5	Japan	74,785	1.4	Qatar	77,601	45.7
6	Netherlands	74,747	8.0	Netherlands	53,234	6.2	Netherlands	64,703	7.7	Netherlands	76,691	8.6
7	Switzerland	60,318	10.8	Singapore	45,273	23.8	Singapore	62,459	26.8	Singapore	72,373	26.6
8	Kuwait	60,186	40.8	Malaysia	41,551	20.5	Switzerland	59,526	10.2	Kuwait	71,342	46.3
9	Malaysia	51,312	22.2	Saudi Arabia	39,987	9.3	Norway	54,887	12.8	Norway	66,484	13.3
10	Singapore	39,843	20.9	Ireland	35,516	15.2	Qatar	48,094	38.4	Switzerland	65,907	9.4

	2012	US$ mil	% GDP	2013	US$ mil	% GDP
1	China	230,227	2.8	China	233,512	2.5
2	Germany	197,587	5.6	Germany	217,971	5.8
3	Saudi Arabia	184,214	25.1	Saudi Arabia	159,433	21.3
4	Russian Fed.	146,766	7.3	Russian Fed.	123,551	5.9
5	Qatar	88,229	46.4	Qatar	89,221	44.1
6	UAE	83,904	22.5	Netherlands	87,703	10.3
7	Kuwait	83,141	47.8	UAE	83,389	20.7
8	Netherlands	69,663	8.5	Switzerland	75,076	10.9
9	Norway	66,619	13.1	Kuwait	74,237	42.2
10	Singapore	64,358	22.6	Singapore	68,568	23.2

European and East Asian countries. Japan was the largest trade surplus country for most of the 1980s and 1990s, followed by Germany. China appeared in the top 10 occasionally in the 1980s and early 1990s, but China's trade surplus position climbed to top five after 1997. Since 2006, China has mostly ranked first in the top 10. In terms of GDP, Japan's trade surplus remained around 2% of its GDP. China's trade surplus in terms of its GDP varied between 2 and 5%. In other top 10 trade surplus countries, their trade surpluses occupied a higher percentage in their GDP, especially the oil-producing countries in the Middle East, reflecting that oil export has been the dominant export item.

On trade deficits, the United States has been the worst hit country. Some trade surplus countries in Europe are also in the list of the top trade deficit countries. Other than Greece, such European countries as the United Kingdom, Turkey, Spain, and France are listed as the top trade deficit countries. Such emerging countries as India and Brazil showed poor performance in their trade, though their trade deficits occupied a low percentage of their GDP. As far as the industrialized countries are concerned, the change in their industrial structure, away from technology production to services, could explain their large deficits. Due to high labor costs and strong trade union pressures, there is a strong possibility that investments in industrial production plants have shifted to more market-friendly countries in Asia and other emerging countries, resulting in a loss of exports and a larger trade deficit if imports remained high. In the top trade deficit countries, and even though the United States has remained the largest trade deficit country, it has not exceeded more than 6% of GDP, reflecting the large size of the US economy. This is true also in the case of most key European countries, such as the United Kingdom and Spain. On the contrary, Greece's trade deficit in terms of GDP has been high, reflecting its economic

TABLE 7.22 Top 10 Largest Trade Deficit Economies: Ranked by Value (US$ Million)

	1980	US$ mil	% GDP	1981	US$ mil	% GDP	1982	US$ mil	% GDP	1983	US$ mil	% GDP
1	United States	−18,920	−0.7	United States	−15,653	−0.5	United States	−23,535	−0.7	United States	−57,142	−1.6
2	Italy	−12,967	−2.7	Italy	−9444	−2.2	France	−7644	−1.3	Saudi Arabia	−20,462	−15.8
3	Japan	−9990	−0.9	Mexico	−7383	−2.5	Italy	−5688	−1.3	India	−4513	−2.1
4	Brazil	−5957	−3.1	Portugal	−6640	−20.8	Nigeria	−5663	−3.1	Egypt	−4192	−22.1
5	Spain	−5864	−2.5	India	−6163	−3.1	India	−5359	−2.7	Israel	−3298	−10.3
6	India	−5654	−3.1	Australia	−5371	−2.7	Australia	−−5346	−2.8	Nigeria	−3062	−1.7
7	Mexico	−4979	−2.1	Nigeria	−5239	−2.9	Portugal	−4685	−15.3	Pakistan	−2945	−8.1
8	Germany	−4882	−0.5	Spain	−4496	−2.2	Spain	−3665	−1.8	Thailand	−2924	−7.1
9	Korea, Rep.	−4830	−7.1	Iran	−4066	−4.1	Egypt	−3642	−23.1	Greece	−2824	−5.7
10	Turkey	−4461	−4.8	Egypt	−3869	−28.7	Pakistan	−3567	−9.9	Indonesia	−2802	−3.0

	1984	US$ mil	% GDP	1985	US$ mil	% GDP	1986	US$ mil	% GDP	1987	US$ mil	% GDP
1	United States	−108,288	−2.7	United States	−121,110	−2.8	United States	−138,533	−3.0	United States	−151,681	−3.1
2	Saudi Arabia	−19,757	−16.5	Saudi Arabia	−15,146	−14.6	Saudi Arabia	−14,600	−16.8	Saudi Arabia	−11,384	−13.3
3	Egypt	−6323	−29.3	China	−12,592	−4.1	China	−7589	−2.5	United Kingdom	−8093	−1.1
4	Australia	−4434	−2.1	India	−6135	−2.7	India	−6156	−2.5	India	−7043	−2.6
5	India	−4434	−2.0	Egypt	−5381	−22.6	Iran	−5454	−7.5	Egypt	−4095	−14.9
6	Pakistan	−4069	−10.4	Australia	−4425	−2.4	United Kingdom	−4960	−0.8	Israel	−3298	−7.8
7	Greece	−2807	−5.8	Greece	−3814	−7.9	Australia	−4728	−2.5	Greece	−2829	−4.3
8	Israel	−2567	−8.6	Pakistan	−3581	−9.2	Egypt	−4192	−16.9	Pakistan	−2643	−6.1
9	SyrianArabR.	−2247	−11.6	SyrianArabR.	−2409	−24.0	Pakistan	−3164	−7.8	Portugal	−2505	−5.2
10	Turkey	−1924	−2.4	Italy	−1955	−0.4	Greece	−2736	−4.8	Iran	−2230	−2.5

	1988	US$ mil	% GDP	1989	US$ mil	% GDP	1990	US$ mil	% GDP	1991	US$ mil	% GDP
1	United States	−114,566	−2.2	United States	−93,142	−1.6	United States	−80,862	−1.3	United States	−31,134	−0.5
2	United Kingdom	−30,350	−3.4	United Kingdom	−34,628	−3.9	United Kingdom	−24,864	−2.3	Spain	−18,426	−3.1
3	India	−8112	−2.7	Spain	−12,772	−3.0	Spain	−17,275	−3.2	Saudi Arabia	−14,059	−10.7
4	Saudi Arabia	−8059	−9.1	Saudi Arabia	−8200	−8.6	Thailand	−6641	−7.5	Iran	−11,576	−12.1
5	Egypt	−5283	−17.7	India	−7844	−2.6	India	−6616	−2.0	United Kingdom	−10,890	−1.0
6	Spain	−4979	−1.3	Australia	−7670	−2.4	Greece	−6546	−6.7	Mexico	−9369	−2.7
7	Portugal	−4627	−8.2	China	−4927	−1.1	Portugal	−5592	−7.1	Korea, Rep.	−8104	−2.4
8	China	−4060	−1.0	Greece	−4914	−6.2	Turkey	−4482	−2.2	Kuwait	−8091	−73.5

(Continued)

II. THE GLOBAL ECONOMY: PERFORMANCE, CLASSIFICATION, AND CHALLENGES

TABLE 7.22   (*Continued*)

	1988	US$ mil	% GDP	1989	US$ mil	% GDP	1990	US$ mil	% GDP	1991	US$ mil	% GDP
9	Venezuela	−3891	−6.7	Egypt	−4802	−14.6	Egypt	−4196	−11.6	Portugal	−6877	−7.7
10	Pakistan	−3341	−6.8	Portugal	−3784	−6.2	Romania	−3521	−8.7	Germany	−6790	−0.4

	1992	US$ mil	% GDP	1993	US$ mil	% GDP	1994	US$ mil	% GDP	1995	US$ mil	% GDP
1	United States	−39,210	−0.6	United States	−70,313	−1.0	United States	−98,496	−1.3	United States	−96,385	−1.3
2	Mexico	−18,618	−4.6	Mexico	−16,010	−3.6	Mexico	−21,185	−4.5	Thailand	−11,955	−7.1
3	Spain	−17,813	−2.8	China	−11,497	−1.8	Argentina	−7918	−2.6	Brazil	−10,652	−1.4
4	United Kingdom	−13,628	−1.2	United Kingdom	−9578	−0.9	Thailand	−7456	−5.1	India	−10,212	−2.8
5	Saudi Arabia	−8765	−6.4	Turkey	−7340	−3.0	Portugal	−7052	−7.1	Hong Kong	−10,155	−7.0
6	Iran	−8630	−8.7	Portugal	−6685	−7.0	United Kingdom	−6981	−0.6	United Kingdom	−7841	−0.6
7	Portugal	−8621	−8.0	Israel	−6037	−7.9	Israel	−6497	−7.5	Israel	−7808	−7.8
8	Germany	−8474	−0.4	Greece	−5806	−5.3	India	−6312	−1.9	Portugal	−7300	−6.2
9	Greece	−6565	−5.6	Iran	−5723	−5.2	Greece	−5834	−5.0	Korea, Rep.	−6610	−1.2
10	Thailand	−5241	−4.5	Thailand	−5698	−4.4	Australia	−4324	−1.2	Greece	−5812	−4.2

	1996	US$ mil	% GDP	1997	US$ mil	% GDP	1998	US$ mil	% GDP	1999	US$ mil	% GDP
1	United States	−104,062	−1.3	United States	−108,268	−1.2	United States	−166,137	−1.8	United States	−263,753	−2.7
2	Korea, Rep.	−21,025	−3.5	Brazil	−15,961	−1.8	Brazil	−15,648	−1.9	United Kingdom	−24,747	−1.6
3	India	−13,984	−3.6	India	−13,360	−3.2	United Kingdom	−14,206	−0.9	Poland	−13,692	−8.1
4	Brazil	−13,512	−1.6	Hong Kong	−9732	−5.5	India	−13,601	−3.2	Portugal	−13,184	−10.3
5	Thailand	−12,066	−6.6	Portugal	−9206	−7.9	Portugal	−11,296	−9.1	Spain	−11,488	−1.8
6	Portugal	−8471	−6.9	Greece	−6716	−4.7	Greece	−9828	−6.8	India	−11,441	−2.5
7	Israel	−7916	−7.2	Poland	−6653	−4.2	Mexico	−9180	−2.0	Greece	−10,691	−7.1
8	Greece	−6609	−4.5	Argentina	−6508	−1.9	Poland	−8598	−5.0	Australia	−9639	−2.3
9	Hong Kong	−5986	−3.7	Korea, Rep	−6293	−1.1	Egypt	−8565	−9.8	Mexico	−8350	−1.6
10	United Kingdom	−5223	−0.4	Egypt	−6021	−7.4	Argentina	−7542	−2.1	Brazil	−8244	−1.4

	2000	US$ mil	% GDP	2001	US$ mil	% GDP	2002	US$ mil	% GDP	2003	US$ mil	% GDP
1	United States	−337,341	−3.6	United States	−362,340	−3.4	United States	−418,169	−3.8	United States	−490,550	−4.2
2	United Kingdom	−29,216	−1.9	United Kingdom	−39,614	−2.6	United Kingdom	−48,142	−2.9	United Kingdom	−48,067	−2.5
3	Spain	−17,689	−3.0	Mexico	−14,109	−2.0	Spain	−13,083	−1.9	Spain	−18,664	−2.1
4	India	−13,144	−2.8	Spain	−13,999	−2.2	Mexico	−12,553	−1.7	Australia	−13,532	−2.4
5	Portugal	−13,106	−11.1	Portugal	−12,307	−10.1	Greece	−11,248	−7.4	Greece	−12,582	−6.2
6	Greece	−12,158	−9.2	Greece	−11,469	−8.4	Portugal	−10,708	−8.0	Mexico	−11,304	−1.6
7	Mexico	−11,942	−1.8	India	−9181	−1.9	Philippines	−7532	−9.3	Portugal	−11066	−6.7

(*Continued*)

TABLE 7.22   (*Continued*)

	2000	US$ mil	% GDP	2001	US$ mil	% GDP	2002	US$ mil	% GDP	2003	US$ mil	% GDP
8	Turkey	−10,910	−4.1	Philippines	−8553	−11.2	Poland	−6447	−3.2	India	−8164	−1.4
9	Poland	−10,882	−6.3	Poland	−6859	−3.6	India	−5122	−1.0	Philippines	−7814	−9.3
10	Brazil	−7859	−1.2	Brazil	−5109	−0.9	Australia	−4309	−1.0	Poland	−5216	−2.4

	2004	US$ mil	% GDP	2005	US$ mil	% GDP	2006	US$ mil	% GDP	2007	US$ mil	% GDP
1	United States	−604,898	−4.9	United States	−707,914	−5.4	United States	−752,400	−5.4	United States	−699,061	−4.8
2	United Kingdom	−63,811	−2.8	United Kingdom	−79,984	−3.3	United Kingdom	−79,602	−3.1	Spain	−93,157	−6.3
3	Spain	−39,621	−3.7	Spain	−57,658	−5.0	Spain	−76,537	−6.1	United Kingdom	−91,812	−3.1
4	Australia	−17,522	−2.6	India	−27,275	−3.3	India	−31,770	−3.4	India	−38,703	−3.2
5	Portugal	−15,264	−8.1	Portugal	−17,799	−9.0	Turkey	−27,040	−5.1	France	−36,539	−1.4
6	India	−14,960	−2.1	Turkey	−17,260	−3.6	Greece	−25,024	−9.2	Greece	−34,055	−10.7
7	Mexico	−14,634	−1.9	Greece	−14,732	−5.9	France	−22,739	−1.0	Turkey	−32,772	−5.1
8	Greece	−12,381	−5.2	Mexico	−12,960	−1.5	Portugal	−16,794	−8.1	Romania	−23,822	−13.9
9	Turkey	−9727	−2.5	Australia	−12,830	−1.7	Romania	−14,815	−12.0	Portugal	−17,345	−7.2
10	Philippines	−7461	−8.2	France	−12,624	−0.6	Pakistan	−14,558	−10.7	Australia	−17,196	−1.7

	2008	US$ mil	% GDP	2009	US$ mil	% GDP	2010	US$ mil	% GDP	2011	US$ mil	% GDP
1	United States	−702,305	−4.7	United States	−383,658	−2.6	United States	−499,378	−3.3	United States	−556,839	−3.6
2	United Kingdom	−89,173	−3.2	India	−67,410	−5.0	India	−91,024	−5.3	India	−106,687	−5.5
3	Spain	−87,604	−5.4	United Kingdom	−40,391	−1.7	United Kingdom	−56,201	−2.3	Turkey	−68,808	−8.9
4	India	−74,360	−5.7	France	−34,251	−1.3	France	−42,555	−1.3	France	−62,733	−2.2
5	France	−62,888	−2.1	Greece	−25,172	−7.6	Italy	−39,910	−1.9	United Kingdom	−45,311	−1.7
6	Greece	−39,421	−11.1	Spain	−23,030	−1.5	Turkey	−39,910	−5.5	Japan	−42,328	−0.7
7	Turkey	−33,560	−4.6	Canada	−21,301	−1.6	Canada	−31,690	−2.0	Italy	−32,045	−1.4
8	Romania	−26,908	−12.9	Portugal	−16,404	−6.7	Spain	−26,665	−1.9	Canada	−23,913	−1.3
9	Poland	−25,393	−4.8	Mexico	−15,077	−1.7	Greece	−19,902	−6.6	Greece	−17,511	−6.1
10	Mexico	−24,736	−2.2	Pakistan	−12,838	−7.9	Portugal	−16,578	−7.0	Mexico	−15,623	−1.3

	2012	US$ mil	% GDP	2013	US$ mil	% GDP
1	United States	−534,657	−3.3	United States	−474,496	−2.8
2	India	−135,776	−7.2	Japan	−125,231	−2.6
3	Japan	−104,074	−1.8	India	−95,580	−4.9
4	United Kingdom	−61,390	−2.3	Turkey	−56,682	−6.9
5	France	−48,758	−1.8	United Kingdom	−52,225	−1.9
6	Turkey	−42,458	−5.4	Brazil	−45,216	−2.0
7	Canada	−38,131	−2.1	France	−34,574	−1.2
8	Australia	−23,826	−1.5	Canada	−32,921	−1.8
9	Brazil	−21,075	−0.9	Pakistan	−18,812	−8.3
10	Egypt	−20,200	−7.8	Egypt	−18,005	−7.1

II. THE GLOBAL ECONOMY: PERFORMANCE, CLASSIFICATION, AND CHALLENGES

weakness and the lack of instruments in addressing the trade deficits. Together with Greece's frequent occurrence in fiscal deficit in Table 7.12 and public debt in Table 7.16, the Greek economy was facing deficits on all three fronts: fiscal deficit, public debt, and trade deficit. It is only a matter of time before the Greek economy explodes.

Greece is a good example of a "debt-breeds-debt" economy. While the Greek economy can rely on assistance from the EU and the IMF, one wonders how much funds both the EU and IMF could inject into the Greek economy, knowing that there could be little chance for Greece to repay, given that Greece is a "mono-industry" economy that relies only on tourism. Hence, drastic economic reorientation would be needed if Greece is to make a sustainable recovery. This requires a "cut" in all three forms of deficits, though a proper strategy is needed in order to have a better sequence of reduction. In short, Greece's current generation are not only living at the expense of the future generation, the over-spending of this and previous generations hurt the economic potential of their future generation severely and unfairly. Externally, cuts involve a reduction in imports or an expansion of exports. Internally, cuts require reductions in welfare spending and the size of the government. There should be sufficient incentives for the private sector to grow and expand.

The trade performances of world economies can also be seen in terms of their GDPs. Tables 7.23 and 7.24, respectively, report the top 10 trade surplus and trade deficit economies expressed in terms of their GDPs. The observations from Table 7.23 show that most of the top 10 trade surplus countries are either oil exporters or small economies, and their trade surpluses occupy quite a substantial percentage of their GDP. In 1980, e.g., Kuwait's trade surplus occupied 41.9% of its GDP. In 1987, Botswana's trade surplus occupied 45.7% of its GDP. In 2013,

TABLE 7.23 Top 10 Largest Trade Surplus Economies: Ranked by Percentage of GDP

	1980	% GDP	US$ mil	1981	% GDP	US$ mil	1982	% GDP	US$ mil	1983	% GDP	US$ mil
1	Kuwait	41.9	12,035	Macao	41.0	425	Macao	24.7	271	Macao	24.9	270
2	Macao	35.7	350	Kuwait	30.8	7773	UAE	18.4	8560	UAE	15.0	6436
3	Saudi Arabia	31.0	50,972	Saudi Arabia	26.8	49,318	Netherlands A.	16.4	191	Oman	14.6	1222
4	UAE	29.5	12,871	Netherlands A.	23.9	260	Gabon	14.9	682	Gabon	10.3	444
5	Libya	24.7	9413	UAE	23.7	11,680	Oman	14.5	1151	Kuwait	8.8	1832
6	Netherlands A.	23.9	226	Oman	23.7	1788	Bahrain	8.2	365	Venezuela	8.5	6751
7	Oman	23.3	1459	Gabon	16.3	798	Saudi Arabia	6.2	9472	Taiwan	8.0	4314
8	Gabon	17.2	934	Trin. &Tobago	9.5	665	Norway	5.0	3181	Mexico	7.7	13,715
9	Bulgaria	12.1	1308	Bahrain	8.7	369	Bolivia	4.9	192	Norway	6.9	4312
10	Trin.&Tobago	11.3	705	Norway	7.0	4505	Taiwan	4.8	2376	Ecuador	5.0	751

	1984	% GDP	US$ mil	1985	% GDP	US$ mil	1986	% GDP	US$ mil	1987	% GDP	US$ mil
1	Macao	31.0	390	Macao	26.9	349	Macao	25.6	372	Botswana	45.7	704
2	UAE	17.8	7426	Botswana	21.4	180	Taiwan	18.6	14,568	Macao	31.7	598
3	Congo	15.5	340	UAE	17.9	7249	Botswana	16.9	189	Oman	18.4	1568
4	Kuwait	12.9	2790	Côte d'Ivoire	14.1	987	Liberia	14.5	126	Taiwan	15.6	16,410
5	Oman	12.1	1123	Liberia	13.7	121	Bahrain	12.6	472	Malaysia	13.1	4461
6	Venezuela	11.9	6885	Taiwan	13.0	8277	South Africa	8.5	5763	UAE	11.1	4031
7	Taiwan	10.5	6407	Oman	12.1	1245	Bahamas	8.1	205	Suriname	10.3	138

(Continued)

TABLE 7.23 (*Continued*)

	1984	% GDP	US$ mil	1985	% GDP	US$ mil	1986	% GDP	US$ mil	1987	% GDP	US$ mil
8	Côte d'Ivoire	10.0	684	Bahrain	11.7	524	Côte d'Ivoire	7.7	705	South Africa	9.6	8503
9	Gabon	9.0	404	Libya	9.7	2887	Hong Kong	6.8	2804	Angola	9.3	689
10	Norway	8.0	5002	Venezuela	9.6	5731	Mauritius	6.5	97	Maldives	8.9	16

	1988	% GDP	US$ mil	1989	% GDP	US$ mil	1990	% GDP	US$ mil	1991	% GDP	US$ mil
1	Macao	29.3	649	Suriname	35.8	270	Macao	31.7	1007	Macao	25.6	945
2	Botswana	19.8	354	Macao	29.6	780	Venezuela	19.9	9355	Gabon	13.5	809
3	Panama	12.6	701	Botswana	17.1	517	Syrian ArabR.	18.6	2075	UAE	13.1	6756
4	Bahrain	10.8	450	SyrianArabR.	12.6	1293	Trin.&Tobago	17.0	862	Singapore	10.2	4589
5	Malaysia	9.6	3600	Venezuela	11.4	4712	UAE	16.9	8550	Algeria	10.1	4698
6	Oman	8.7	726	UAE	9.9	4124	Gabon	15.2	919	Syrian ArabR.	9.2	1146
7	Zambia	7.8	271	Congo	9.5	230	Nigeria	11.2	7642	Trin.&Tobago	8.2	435
8	Suriname	7.3	117	Kuwait	9.1	2213	Libya	8.1	2508	Norway	7.6	9326
9	Taiwan	6.9	8716	Hong Kong	8.9	6149	Paraguay	7.4	345	Denmark	6.2	8592
10	Korea, Rep.	6.9	13,927	Trin.&Tobago	8.0	347	Congo	7.4	206	Venezuela	5.2	2698

	1992	% GDP	US$ mil	1993	% GDP	US$ mil	1994	% GDP	US$ mil	1995	% GDP	US$ mil
1	Macao	26.1	1266	Macao	24.5	1365	Macao	23.3	1446	Macao	28.4	1977
2	Gabon	12.8	796	Papua NewGu.	19.5	972	Gabon	21.0	981	Papua NewGu.	22.5	1087
3	Trin.&Tobago	10.8	587	Gabon	12.8	770	Papua NewGu.	17.9	954	Gabon	22.1	1222
4	Singapore	9.3	4842	Ireland	9.9	5185	Singapore	14.3	10,500	Singapore	16.8	14,583
5	UAE	9.0	4863	Trin.&Tobago	9.5	434	Trin.&Tobago	12.7	630	Trin.&Tobago	12.9	688
6	Oman	8.2	1009	Anti.&Barbu.	7.6	41	Côte d'Ivoire	9.5	786	Bahrain	9.9	675
7	Slovenia	7.4	971	Singapore	7.5	4552	Ireland	9.2	5233	Ireland	8.2	5663
8	Ireland	7.2	4015	Denmark	6.9	9816	Botswana	9.0	384	Botswana	7.8	371
9	Barbados	6.9	135	Norway	6.3	7653	Venezuela	7.9	4529	Finland	7.8	10,500
10	Denmark	6.8	10,405	Latvia	6.3	332	Oman	7.5	962	Suriname	7.8	66

	1996	% GDP	US$ mil	1997	% GDP	US$ mil	1998	% GDP	US$ mil	1999	% GDP	US$ mil
1	Macao	31.3	2215	Macao	30.4	2159	Macao	29.7	1954	Qatar	29.0	3588
2	Gabon	26.6	1689	Gabon	21.5	1282	Singapore	21.7	18,452	Macao	26.0	1638
3	Singapore	16.6	15,845	Congo	15.7	364	Malaysia	20.4	15,895	Malaysia	23.2	19,828
4	Venezuela	15.4	10,501	Singapore	14.8	14,676	Thailand	15.3	17,395	Gabon	19.4	1002

(*Continued*)

TABLE 7.23   (*Continued*)

#	1996	% GDP	US$ mil	1997	% GDP	US$ mil	1998	% GDP	US$ mil	1999	% GDP	US$ mil
5	Angola	13.8	899	Botswana	13.2	665	Korea, Rep.	11.9	44,942	Brunei Daru.	18.3	841
6	Oman	13.6	2051	Oman	11.0	1725	Indonesia	10.3	10,820	Singapore	17.2	14,637
7	Papua NewGu.	13.0	670	Kuwait	10.4	3165	Finland	8.1	10,798	Russian Fed.	16.0	31,406
8	Botswana	11.7	569	Algeria	9.6	4610	Ireland	7.1	6364	Bahrain	13.9	1053
9	Trin.&Tobago	10.9	626	Ireland	9.4	7775	Côte d'Ivoire	6.4	810	Congo	13.4	315
10	Kuwait	10.8	3417	Bahrain	8.3	607	Belgium	6.4	16,529	Ireland	12.4	12,233

#	2000	% GDP	US$ mil	2001	% GDP	US$ mil	2002	% GDP	US$ mil	2003	% GDP	US$ mil
1	Congo	44.6	1435	Qatar	36.8	6457	Equatorial Gu.	48.8	1018	Equatorial Gu.	49.3	1357
2	Qatar	41.6	7388	Brunei Daru.	35.5	1989	Macao	33.9	2374	Brunei Daru.	39.2	2569
3	Macao	33.8	2177	Macao	34.6	2251	Qatar	32.2	6238	Macao	35.0	2773
4	Gabon	32.5	1843	Congo	23.8	666	Brunei Daru.	30.4	1779	Qatar	33.2	7820
5	Oman	27.9	5418	Gabon	23.6	1225	Congo	27.7	836	Congo	32.2	1124
6	Angola	27.6	2449	Oman	23.0	4473	Luxembourg	25.8	6018	Singapore	27.9	26,761
7	Kuwait	26.3	9929	Aruba	22.4	430	Oman	21.2	4263	Luxembourg	23.9	6958
8	Bahrain	22.6	2044	Bahrain	20.2	1812	Gabon	17.5	948	Gabon	22.4	1468
9	Equatorial Gu.	20.9	246	Malaysia	16.8	16,182	Singapore	17.5	15,874	Saudi Arabia	20.6	44,232
10	Russian Fed.	20.4	53,083	Norway	16.6	28,959	Malaysia	15.8	16,565	Malaysia	19.0	21,756

#	2004	% GDP	US$ mil	2005	% GDP	US$ mil	2006	% GDP	US$ mil	2007	% GDP	US$ mil
1	Equatorial Gu.	60.6	2892	Equatorial Gu.	67.6	4869	Equatorial Gu.	63.2	5397	Equatorial Gu.	59.9	6486
2	Macao	40.7	4176	Brunei Daru.	45.5	4335	Brunei Daru.	48.6	5570	Luxembourg	45.6	22,453
3	Brunei Daru.	40.6	3200	Congo	36.9	2243	Trin.&Tobago	43.7	8026	Libya	42.6	26,712
4	Qatar	38.0	12,048	Qatar	35.4	15,774	Libya	40.3	22,179	Brunei Daru.	42.4	5196
5	Congo	35.4	1645	Libya	34.9	15,860	Luxembourg	39.6	16,534	Azerbaijan	39.6	13,093
6	Luxembourg	27.6	9443	Gabon	33.5	3210	Kuwait	37.4	38,019	Kuwait	34.4	39,389
7	Gabon	26.4	2073	Luxembourg	32.6	12,071	Saudi Arabia	29.7	112,012	Singapore	32.0	57,113
8	Singapore	25.7	28,944	Kuwait	32.6	26,309	Singapore	29.7	43,339	Angola	30.4	18,402
9	Saudi Arabia	25.2	65,104	Macao	32.4	3817	Macao	29.0	4229	Aruba	29.2	767
10	Kuwait	21.7	12,874	Saudi Arabia	31.8	104,406	Azerbaijan	27.7	5822	Trin.&Tobago	29.1	6075

#	2008	% GDP	US$ mil	2009	% GDP	US$ mil	2010	% GDP	US$ mil	2011	% GDP	US$ mil
1	Equatorial Gu.	62.8	10,277	Macao	45.0	9600	Macao	55.9	15,856	Macao	59.3	21,717
2	Brunei Daru.	50.8	7305	Brunei Daru.	40.7	4370	Brunei Daru.	48.5	6005	Brunei Daru.	51.0	8510

(*Continued*)

TABLE 7.23 (Continued)

	2008	% GDP	US$ mil	2009	% GDP	US$ mil	2010	% GDP	US$ mil	2011	% GDP	US$ mil
3	Azerbaijan	42.3	20,668	Luxembourg	39.5	19,819	Luxembourg	39.5	20,607	Kuwait	46.3	71,342
4	Luxembourg	41.0	22,533	Kuwait	31.8	33,722	Equatorial Gu.	39.3	5256	Qatar	45.7	77,601
5	Kuwait	40.8	60,186	Azerbaijan	29.3	12,972	Qatar	38.4	48,094	Equatorial Gu.	38.5	6924
6	Libya	37.9	36,155	Equatorial Gu.	24.8	2760	Kuwait	35.3	40,785	Luxembourg	37.1	21,866
7	Trin.&Tobago	37.3	9680	Singapore	23.8	45,273	Azerbaijan	34.0	17,998	Azerbaijan	32.3	21,331
8	Macao	33.5	6947	Qatar	22.1	21,638	Singapore	26.8	62,459	Bahrain	31.2	9062
9	Qatar	33.3	38,376	Malaysia	20.5	41,551	Trin. &Tobago	25.4	5223	Oman	29.7	20,676
10	Saudi Arabia	28.1	146,163	Bahrain	19.0	4351	Oman	24.4	14,334	Saudi Arabia	26.6	178,246

	2012	% GDP	US$ mil	2013	% GDP	US$ mil
1	Macao	59.4	25,551	Macao	61.0	31,582
2	Kuwait	47.8	83,141	Qatar	44.1	89,221
3	Qatar	46.4	88,229	Kuwait	42.2	74,237
4	Luxembourg	38.4	21,594	Aruba	40.4	1046
5	Equatorial Gu.	36.0	7048	Luxembourg	39.2	23,542
6	Libya	29.8	28,592	Bahrain	27.3	8974
7	Gabon	27.9	4448	Singapore	23.2	68,568
8	Azerbaijan	27.7	19,293	Oman	22.4	17,848
9	Oman	26.7	20,702	Azerbaijan	22.3	16,419
10	Bahrain	26.4	8134	Ireland	21.9	50,771

the trade surplus of Macao occupied 61% of its GDP. Since 1999, the trade surplus of all top 10 economies showed double-digit performance in their GDP, reflecting that exports occupied a central role in their economic openness. However, this "good news" could be constrained by world economic recessions. The important issue for these trade surplus countries is to widen and diversify their economic base, so that the trade surplus can be sustained and diversification can help to improve other comparative advantages.

Performances in the trade deficit countries are poor, as shown in Table 7.24. Firstly, most trade deficit countries expressed by their GDP percentages are weak and small world economies. Secondly, the extremes of the trade deficit countries can exceed 100% of their GDP. All top 10 worst performers have a trade deficit of more than 20% of their GDP. These weakest world economies would likely be faced with other economic problems, probably debt and fiscal deficits. Virtually all these heavy trade deficit countries lack industrialization, though some have rich natural resources. As such, there is a need for these economies to seek a more sustainable development path, especially with a strategy that would help them to industrialize and utilize their resources more productively. Beginning with the development of economic stability, construction of physical and social infrastructure should be the top priorities. Next should be the issue of business-friendliness in promoting investment. Small economies may not have too many resources, but they can be flexible in mobilizing their resources to cater to different market needs. It is also true that the informal sector in many small countries tends to be quite active. Although informal economic activities are not reported in their GDP, not all informal economic activities are "bad." For example, tourist spending on souvenirs in small shops would probably not be reported in the formal GDP calculation, but such spending does have multiplier effects. In other words, small world economies can have their own way of development, survival, and expansion.

TABLE 7.24 Top 10 Largest Trade Deficit Economies: Ranked by Percentage of GDP

	1980	% GDP	US$ mil	1981	% GDP	US$ mil	1982	% GDP	US$ mil	1983	% GDP	US$ mil
1	Yemen, Dem.	−163.6	−581	Yemen, Dem.	−159.4	−650	Yemen, Dem.	−153.4	−746	Yemen, Dem.	−145.4	−746
2	Yemen ArabR.	−127.6	−2066	Lesotho	−119.0	−424	Lesotho	−131.4	−430	Lesotho	−133.3	−474
3	Lesotho	−109.5	−384	Mongolia	−112.8	−797	Yemen ArabR.	−102.2	−2069	Mongolia	−88.7	−793
4	Kiribati	−65.9	−22	Yemen ArabR.	−106.2	−1891	Mongolia	−101.5	−825	Yemen ArabR.	−87.0	−1842
5	Dominica	−55.7	−39	Kiribati	−68.3	−27	Kiribati	−65.7	−26	Cape Verde	−50.8	−80
6	Cape Verde	−42.2	−68	Jordan	−53.9	−2308	Jordan	−52.5	−2392	Kiribati	−49.3	−18
7	Jordan	−41.2	−1652	Cape Verde	−50.1	−79	Cape Verde	−48.7	−78	Jordan	−45.3	−2155
8	Samoa	−41.1	−46	Samoa	−42.5	−45	Bhutan	−46.3	−70	Bhutan	−44.2	−76
9	St.Vincent&G	−35.0	−25	Botswana	−41.1	−400	Grenada	−38.8	−40	St. Kitts&Nevis	−34.7	−26
10	Swaziland	−32.2	−214	Bhutan	−37.7	−55	Benin	−36.7	−465	Grenada	−33.2	−36

	1984	% GDP	US$ mil	1985	% GDP	US$ mil	1986	% GDP	US$ mil	1987	% GDP	US$ mil
1	Yemen, Dem.	−146.4	−801	Lesotho	−128.8	−319	Lesotho	−117.7	−342	Lesotho	−118.7	−438
2	Lesotho	−140.4	−426	Yemen, Dem.	−128.5	−685	Yemen, Dem.	−107.8	−500	Yemen, Dem.	−101.8	−486
3	Mongolia	−71.5	−701	Mongolia	−71.9	−768	Mongolia	−88.7	−1059	Mongolia	−77.3	−979
4	Yemen ArabR.	−66.4	−1451	Kiribati	−57.7	−17	Kiribati	−64.0	−19	Kiribati	−71.4	−24
5	Comoros	−56.4	−61	Yemen ArabR.	−49.3	−1145	Bhutan	−43.3	−88	Yemen ArabR.	−50.0	−1284
6	Bhutan	−51.5	−87	Bhutan	−43.0	−74	Samoa	−34.9	−31	Samoa	−42.7	−43
7	Cape Verde	−41.5	−62	Cape Verde	−41.1	−64	Yemen ArabR.	−33.8	−825	Bhutan	−38.6	−95
8	Jordan	−39.5	−1920	Comoros	−38.6	−44	Tonga	−31.5	−25	Equatorial Gu.	−36.4	−44
9	Swaziland	−33.3	−184	Samoa	−36.7	−31	Cape Verde	−30.6	−66	Montserrat	−33.4	−14
10	Samoa	−31.7	−31	Jordan	−34.3	−1758	Montserrat	−30.6	−12	Comoros	−30.5	−60

	1988	% GDP	US$ mil	1989	% GDP	US$ mil	1990	% GDP	US$ mil	1991	% GDP	US$ mil
1	Yemen, Dem.	−137.7	−692	Lesotho	−125.0	−564	Lesotho	−120.1	−654	Lesotho	−128.0	−779
2	Lesotho	−123.9	−533	Yemen, Dem.	−111.4	−644	Kiribati	−88.1	−35	Kuwait	−73.5	−8091
3	Mongolia	−72.5	−999	Mongolia	−79.4	−1184	Montserrat	−52.9	−36	Samoa	−67.1	−75
4	Kiribati	−59.2	−26	Kiribati	−65.6	−27	Samoa	−45.0	−50	Kiribati	−58.2	−28
5	Equatorial Gu.	−42.6	−55	Montserrat	−46.9	−26	Mongolia	−40.0	−603	Equatorial Gu.	−49.7	−65
6	YemenArabR.	−38.4	−1038	Soloman Is.	−40.8	−68	Equatorial Gu.	−35.0	−47	Montserrat	−46.2	−26
7	Soloman Is.	−38.0	−67	Samoa	−38.4	−42	Soloman Is.	−29.1	−61	Yemen	−32.6	−1361
8	Samoa	−36.2	−43	Equatorial Gu.	−32.1	−36	Jordan	−26.3	−1058	Soloman Is.	−29.6	−65

(Continued)

TABLE 7.24   (*Continued*)

	1988	% GDP	US$ mil	1989	% GDP	US$ mil	1990	% GDP	US$ mil	1991	% GDP	US$ mil
9	Tonga	−33.3	−48	Yemen ArabR.	−30.6	−879	Cape Verde	−26.3	−92	Cape Verde	−27.7	−101
10	Montserrat	−30.8	−15	Cape Verde	−29.0	−88	St. Kitts&Nevi	−24.8	−50	Mozambique	−22.9	−736

	1992	% GDP	US$ mil	1993	% GDP	US$ mil	1994	% GDP	US$ mil	1995	% GDP	US$ mil
1	Lesotho	−120.0	−865	Lesotho	−106.4	−768	Lesotho	−91.8	−693	Lesotho	−98.6	−847
2	Kiribati	−77.5	−37	Samoa	−70.3	−83	Rwanda	−52.2	−630	Kiribati	−79.3	−44
3	Samoa	−77.1	−91	Kiribati	−63.1	−30	Kiribati	−37.9	−21	Palestine St.	−61.7	−2026
4	Yemen	−37.2	−1670	Yemen	−38.5	−1838	Mozambique	−36.6	−899	Equatorial Gu.	−61.3	−102
5	Montserrat	−36.1	−21	Mozambique	−34.3	−818	Cape Verde	−36.2	−169	Tonga	−39.7	−81
6	Cape Verde	−35.1	−143	Albania	−32.9	−574	Tonga	−32.8	−64	Cape Verde	−37.8	−211
7	Albania	−34.6	−539	Cape Verde	−32.2	−132	Congo	−32.8	−583	SaoTome& Prin.	−36.6	−36
8	SaoTome& Prin	−33.7	−30	Bhutan	−31.8	−70	Comoros	−27.4	−51	Armenia	−33.2	−427
9	Mozambique	−31.3	−712	Jordan	−29.8	−1672	Albania	−26.5	−513	Haiti	−26.1	−609
10	Jordan	−31.1	−1655	SaoTome& Prin	−26.6	−32	Samoa	−25.6	−50	Mozambique	−25.5	−644

	1996	% GDP	US$ mil	1997	% GDP	US$ mil	1998	% GDP	US$ mil	1999	% GDP	US$ mil
1	Equatorial Gu.	−108.3	−296	Lesotho	−94.1	−809	Lesotho	−83.7	−671	Lesotho	−76.5	−613
2	Lesotho	−101.1	−825	Palestine St.	−71.0	−2669	Bosnia& Herz.	−69.2	−2925	Kiribati	−70.0	−48
3	Palestine St.	−73.6	−2511	Kiribati	−69.4	−47	Montserrat	−68.9	−26	Bosnia& Herz.	−66.5	−3118
4	Kiribati	−72.5	−48	Montserrat	−46.3	−19	Kiribati	−60.6	−40	Palestine St.	−59.2	−2582
5	Armenia	−32.6	−520	Armenia	−38.0	−622	Equatorial Gu.	−58.2	−256	Montserrat	−51.5	−18
6	Azerbaijan	−31.0	−986	Tonga	−29.5	−63	Palestine St.	−57.8	−2350	Cape Verde	−33.0	−224
7	Cape Verde	−30.7	−176	Cape Verde	−27.2	−152	Armenia	−34.7	−656	Anguilla	−32.2	−47
8	Tonga	−25.5	−56	Albania	−25.4	−586	Tonga	−32.7	−62	Tonga	−30.7	−60
9	Jordan	−25.3	−1753	Samoa	−25.1	−60	Azerbaijan	−31.8	−1415	Armenia	−29.0	−536
10	SaoTome& Prin	−24.4	−31	Azerbaijan	−24.0	−951	Cape Verde	−31.8	−190	Kenya	−28.1	−4119

	2000	% GDP	US$ mil	2001	% GDP	US$ mil	2002	% GDP	US$ mil	2003	% GDP	US$ mil
1	Lesotho	−100.5	−775	Lesotho	−84.7	−598	Chad	−96.6	−1919	Lesotho	−79.6	−772
2	Montserrat	−65.9	−24	Kiribati	−68.7	−45	Lesotho	−77.7	−510	Kiribati	−74.6	−70
3	Kiribati	−61.8	−46	Montserrat	−63.6	−23	Kiribati	−73.7	−54	Montserrat	−68.4	−29
4	Palestine St.	−52.3	−2257	Palestine St.	−62.3	−2494	Montserrat	−55.0	−22	Palestine St.	−52.1	−2066
5	Bosnia&Herz.	−46.4	−2578	Bosnia& Herz.	−47.1	−2730	Palestine St.	−54.8	−1950	Bosnia& Herz.	−45.0	−3822

(*Continued*)

TABLE 7.24 (Continued)

	2000	% GDP	US$ mil	2001	% GDP	US$ mil	2002	% GDP	US$ mil	2003	% GDP	US$ mil
6	Anguilla	−36.5	−55	SaoTome& Prin	−39.6	−29	Bosnia& Herz.	−46.4	−3121	Tonga	−37.1	−77
7	SaoTome& Prin	−30.0	−22	Tonga	−39.0	−65	Tonga	−35.6	−65	Chad	−36.9	−1006
8	Cape Verde	−29.4	−180	Chad	−35.0	−598	SaoTome& Prin	−32.2	−26	Haiti	−36.6	−947
9	Tonga	−28.2	−53	Cape Verde	−28.7	−184	Cape Verde	−31.9	−226	Moldova	−33.7	−667
10	Armenia	−27.2	−519	Samoa	−28.4	−68	Haiti	−28.1	−829	SaoTome& Prin.	−32.6	−32

	2004	% GDP	US$ mil	2005	% GDP	US$ mil	2006	% GDP	US$ mil	2007	% GDP	US$ mil
1	Liberia	−140.7	−741	Liberia	−134.3	−816	Liberia	−174.4	−1225	Liberia	−147.5	−1205
2	Kiribati	−78.4	−80	Kiribati	−95.1	−107	Kiribati	−75.0	−81	Kiribati	−67.9	−89
3	Lesotho	−73.5	−907	Lesotho	−72.2	−988	Lesotho	−66.6	−951	Lesotho	−63.5	−1014
4	Montserrat	−67.8	−30	Montserrat	−71.1	−35	Palestine St.	−63.0	−3095	Palestine St.	−62.3	−3432
5	Palestine St.	−62.3	−2697	Palestine St.	−60.0	−2901	Anguilla	−53.8	−153	Tajikistan	−53.8	−2002
6	Bosnia&Herz.	−40.8	−4138	Mauritania	−50.5	−1102	Montserrat	−52.3	−27	Moldova	−52.7	−2320
7	Tonga	−39.6	−95	Jordan	−41.5	−5224	Moldova	−47.0	−1603	Anguilla	−50.1	−178
8	Mauritania	−38.5	−728	Moldova	−40.6	−1212	SaoTome& Prin	−44.3	−61	Montserrat	−50.1	−27
9	SaoTome& Prin	−36.4	−39	Bosnia& Herz.	−39.9	−4346	Tonga	−40.4	−119	SaoTome& Prin.	−46.5	−70
10	Cape Verde	−32.9	−346	Tonga	−39.3	−104	Grenada	−34.4	−240	Tonga	−45.3	−139

	2008	% GDP	US$ mil	2009	% GDP	US$ mil	2010	% GDP	US$ mil	2011	% GDP	US$ mil
1	Liberia	−150.1	−1381	Liberia	−122.1	−1250	Liberia	−130.2	−1398	Liberia	−133.9	−2061
2	Kiribati	−84.3	−118	Kiribati	−81.2	−106	Kiribati	−77.1	−118	Sierra Leone	−66.3	−1945
3	Montserrat	−67.2	−39	Lesotho	−72.4	−1238	Lesotho	−68.5	−1490	Lesotho	−56.6	−1407
4	Lesotho	−59.8	−976	Tonga	−60.0	−196	Haiti	−53.4	−3285	Montserrat	−53.3	−33
5	Anguilla	−55.5	−197	Palestine St.	−53.1	−3856	Montserrat	−52.7	−30	Tajikistan	−47.2	−3082
6	Montenegro	−54.4	−2460	Montserrat	−47.5	−29	Tonga	−45.0	−168	Haiti	−45.8	−3137
7	Palestine St.	−53.6	−3575	Afghanistan	−42.1	−5292	Palestine St.	−44.5	−3965	Palestine St.	−45.2	−4730
8	Moldova	−53.1	−3216	SaoTome& Prin	−38.3	−83	SaoTome& Prin	−44.4	−96	SaoTome& Prin.	−45.2	−118
9	Tonga	−49.6	−169	Tajikistan	−37.0	−1844	Tajikistan	−43.9	−2480	Tonga	−44.3	−199
10	SaoTome& Prin	−47.9	−96	Moldova	−36.6	−1989	Moldova	−39.3	−2283	Moldova	−40.9	−2872

	2012	% GDP	US$ mil	2013	% GDP	US$ mil
1	Liberia	−104.9	−1820	Montserrat	−60.7	−36
2	Lesotho	−71.3	−1661	Lesotho	−60.6	−1352
3	Montserrat	−59.5	−37	Liberia	−60.4	−1176
4	Kyrgyzstan	−50.7	−3348	Mozambique	−51.6	−8068

(Continued)

TABLE 7.24 (*Continued*)

	2012	% GDP	US$ mil	2013	% GDP	US$ mil
5	Mozambique	−47.6	−7113	Tajikistan	−48.1	−4090
6	Tajikistan	−47.5	−3629	Kyrgyzstan	−46.2	−3339
7	Palestine St.	−46.0	−5190	Palestine St.	−39.0	−4910
8	Comoros	−41.0	−235	Tonga	−37.8	−166
9	Moldova	−40.4	−2945	Haiti	−37.5	−2883
10	Haiti	−40.0	−2868	Moldova	−37.4	−2980

TABLE 7.25 Number of Years in the Top 10 of the Largest Reserve Economies: By Value

1980−89		1990−99		2000−14		1980−2014	
United States	10	United States	10	United States	15	United States	35
Japan	10	Japan	10	Japan	15	Japan	35
France	10	Germany	10	Korea, Rep.	15	Switzerland	28
Switzerland	10	Italy	10	Hong Kong	15	China	28
Italy	10	Switzerland	10	China	15	Germany	27
Germany	10	France	9	India	14	France	24
Netherlands	10	Singapore	9	Russia	12	Hong Kong	21
United Kingdom	9	China	8	Saudi Arabia	10	Italy	21
Saudi Arabia	7	Spain	7	Singapore	10	Singapore	19
China	5	Hong Kong	6	Switzerland	8	Saudi Arabia	17
Spain	5	United Kingdom	5	Brazil	8	Korea, Rep.	16
Belgium	4	Netherlands	3	Germany	7	United Kingdom	14
		Brazil	2	France	5	India	14
		Korea, Rep.	1	Italy	1	Netherlands	13
						Spain	12
						Russia	12
						Brazil	10
						Belgium	4

VI RESERVE

A major indicator of a country's economic health is the level of international reserves, as it shows the strength of the country's external trade and portfolio investment, as well as being a reflection of the country's currency. Table 7.25 summarizes the number of years the top 10 world economies with their reserves measured in terms of value, while Table 7.26 shows the reserve measured as a percentage of GDP for the three decades from 1980 to 2014. The first observation one can make from the top 10 economies with the largest reserves measured in value terms is that in the 1980s, the largest world reserve economies came mainly from the United States and European countries. The other three exceptions were Japan, China, and Saudi Arabia. In the 1990s, there were more Asian economies, including Singapore, Hong Kong, and South Korea. Brazil is the only Latin American country that made the top 10. However, by the turn of the 21st century, in the period 2000 − 14, the only four European countries that remained in the top 10 were Germany, France, Switzerland, and Italy. The newcomers were India and Russia. The United States and Japan showed consistent performance in the top 10 reserve countries. China's position has risen considerably in the three decades.

TABLE 7.26　Number of Years in the Top 10 of the Largest Reserve Economies: By Percentage of GDP

1980–89		1990–99		2000–14		1980–2014	
Bahrain	10	Bhutan	10	Botswana	15	Singapore	35
Malta	10	Botswana	10	Hong Kong	15	Botswana	33
Singapore	10	Hong Kong	10	Lebanon	15	Bhutan	29
Switzerland	10	Lebanon	10	Singapore	15	Lebanon	27
Cape Verde	9	Singapore	10	Bhutan	14	Hong Kong	25
Cyprus	8	Malta	10	Libya	14	Malta	24
Botswana	8	Guyana	8	Algeria	12	Macao	18
Tonga	6	Lesotho	7	Macao	12	Lesotho	14
Bhutan	5	Macao	6	Saudi Arabia	9	Libya	14
Portugal	5	Samoa	4	Lesotho	7	Bahrain	13
Samoa	3	Micronesia	4	Malta	4	Switzerland	13
Kuwait	3	Malaysia	4	Jordan	3	Algeria	12
Jordan	3	Bahrain	3	Switzerland	3	Guyana	10
Togo	3	Mauritius,	1	Malaysia	2	Cape Verde	9
Trinidad&Tobago	3	Kuwait	1	SyriaArabRepub.	2	Cyprus	9
Lebanon	2	Cyprus	1	Timor-Leste	2	Saudi Arabia	9
Vanuatu	1	Jordan	1	Guyana	2	Samoa	7
Suriname	1			Micronesia	2	Jordan	7
				Bolivia	1	Tonga	6
				Iceland	1	Malaysia	6
						Micronesia	6
						Portugal	5
						Kuwait	4
						Togo	3
						Trin&Tobago	3
						SyriaArabRep	2
						Timor-Leste	2
						Bolivia	1
						Mauritius	1
						Suriname	1
						Iceland	1

　　Table 7.26 summarizes the largest reserve countries ranked in terms of percentage of GDP for the three decades of 1980 − 2014. One observation is that many of these countries are small world economies that are scattered among various continents. A few oil exporting countries are included, such as Kuwait and Algeria. The more notable Asian economies include Singapore, Hong Kong, and Malaysia. Singapore is the best performer in the three decades. Unlike Table 7.25, where the top 10 largest reserve holders in the three decades included only 18 economies, Table 7.26 shows that when measured as a percentage of GDP, the top 10 included 31 world economies. Although many of the economies shown in Table 7.26 are small economies, the point is that smaller economies tended to perform stronger in reserves.

　　Table 7.27 shows the details of the rankings by value of reserves. In much of the 1980s, the top largest reserve countries are the United States, Germany, France, Switzerland, and Italy. By the late 1980s and early 1990s, the

TABLE 7.27 Top 10 Largest Reserve Economies: Ranked by Value (Percentage of GDP)

	1980	US$ mil (% GDP)	1981	US$ mil (% GDP)	1982	US$ mil (% GDP)	1983	US$ mil (% GDP)
1	United States	171,412 (6.2)	United States	123,907 (4.0)	United States	413,445 (4.4)	United States	123,110 (3.5)
2	Germany	104,702 (11.4)	Germany	81,553 (10.5)	Germany	88,250 (11.7)	Germany	78,986 (10.6)
3	France	75,582 (11.0)	France	54,798 (9.1)	France	53,929 (9.4)	France	51,078 (9.3)
4	Switzerland	64,748 (57.5)	Switzerland	47,082 (45.7)	Switzerland	53,510 (59.7)	Switzerland	46,804 (44.5)
5	Italy	62,428 (13.6)	Italy	46,635 (11.2)	Italy	44,553 (10.8)	Italy	45,549 (10.7)
6	Japan	38,919 (3.6)	Japan	37,839 (3.1)	Japan	34,404 (3.1)	Japan	33,845 (2.8)
7	Netherlands	37,549 (20.8)	Saudi Arabia	34,051 (18.5)	Saudi Arabia	31,649 (20.7)	Saudi Arabia	29,041 (22.5)
8	United Kingdom	31,755 (5.9)	Netherlands	26,806 (17.6)	Netherlands	30,209 (20.6)	Netherlands	26,934 (18.9)
9	Belgium	27,974 (22.3)	United Kingdom	22,802 (4.4)	United Kingdom	21,083 (4.3)	China	19,832 (8.7)
10	Saudi Arabia	26,129 (15.9)	Belgium	18,540 (17.9)	Belgium	19,545 (21.5)	United Kingdom	18,593 (4.0)

	1984	US$ mil (% GDP)	1985	US$ mil (% GDP)	1986	US$ mil (% GDP)	1987	US$ mil (% GDP)
1	United States	104,856 (2.7)	United States	117,982 (2.8)	United States	139,884 (3.1)	United States	161,738 (3.4)
2	Germany	69,486 (9.9)	Germany	75,504 (10.7)	Germany	88,941 (8.8)	Germany	124,834 (9.9)
3	France	46,175 (8.9)	France	53,354 (9.8)	France	63,450 (8.4)	Japan	92,702 (3.7)
4	Italy	41,349 (9.8)	Switzerland	45,248 (44.4)	Switzerland	54,339 (37.2)	France	72,674 (7.9)
5	Switzerland	40,970 (40.8)	Italy	37,397 (8.6)	Japan	51,727 (2.5)	Switzerland	67,791 (37.1)
6	Japan	33,899 (2.6)	Japan	34,641 (2.5)	Italy	46,049 (7.5)	Italy	62,489 (8.0)
7	Saudi Arabia	26,165 (21.9)	Saudi Arabia	26,507 (25.5)	Netherlands	28,368 (15.3)	United Kingdom	50,918 (7.3)
8	Netherlands	22,784 (17.1)	Netherlands	25,151 (18.0)	United Kingdom	25,853 (4.5)	Netherlands	37,275 (16.4)
9	China	21,281 (8.3)	United Kingdom	19,082 (4.1)	Spain	20,548 (8.4)	Spain	36,439 (11.8)
10	Spain	16,465 (9.9)	China	16,881 (5.5)	Saudi Arabia	20,120 (23.1)	Belgium	25,899 (17.5)

	1988	US$ mil (% GDP)	1989	US$ mil (% GDP)	1990	US$ mil (% GDP)	1991	US$ mil (% GDP)
1	United States	144,177 (2.8)	United States	168,583 (3.1)	United States	173,094 (3.0)	United States	159,273 (2.7)
2	Japan	106,668 (3.5)	Germany	98,877 (7.3)	Germany	104,547 (6.1)	Germany	96,647 (5.3)
3	Germany	97,576 (7.2)	Japan	93,673 (3.1)	Italy	88,595 (7.8)	Japan	80,626 (2.3)
4	Italy	62,067 (7.2)	Italy	73,455 (8.2)	Japan	87,828 (2.8)	Italy	72,254 (6.0)
5	France	58,944 (5.9)	Switzerland	58,670 (30.7)	France	68,291 (5.5)	Spain	71,345 (12.7)
6	Switzerland	58,367 (29.5)	France	57,434 (5.7)	Switzerland	61,284 (25.1)	France	60,227 (4.8)
7	United Kingdom	51,900 (6.1)	Spain	47,770 (11.9)	Spain	57,238 (11.0)	Switzerland	58,451 (23.7)
8	Spain	42,835 (11.7)	United Kingdom	42,382 (4.9)	United Kingdom	43,146 (4.2)	United Kingdom	48,572 (4.6)

(Continued)

TABLE 7.27   (*Continued*)

	1988	US$ mil (% GDP)	1989	US$ mil (% GDP)	1990	US$ mil (% GDP)	1991	US$ mil (% GDP)
9	Netherlands	34,102 (14.1)	Netherlands	34,129 (14.3)	China	34,476 (9.7)	China	48,165 (12.7)
10	China	23,752 (7.7)	China	23,053 (6.7)	Netherlands	34,401 (11.7)	Singapore	34,187 (79.4)

	1992	US$ mil (% GDP)	1993	US$ mil (% GDP)	1994	US$ mil (% GDP)	1995	US$ mil (% GDP)
1	United States	147,526 (2.4)	United States	164,620 (2.5)	United States	163,591 (2.3)	Japan	192,620 (3.6)
2	Germany	122,686 (5.9)	Germany	114,822 5(0.7)	Japan	135,146 (2.8)	United States	175,996 (2.4)
3	Japan	79,697 (2.1)	Japan	107,989 (2.4)	Germany	113,841 (5.3)	Germany	121,816 (4.8)
4	Switzerland	61,007 (23.7)	Switzerland	65,167 (26.1)	Switzerland	66,645 (24.1)	China	80,288 (11.0)
5	France	54,306 (4.0)	France	54,624 (4.2)	Singapore	58,296 (84.2)	Singapore	68,816 (85.2)
6	Spain	50,709 (8.3)	Italy	53,590 (5.2)	Italy	57,817 (5.5)	Switzerland	68,620 (21.2)
7	Italy	49,862 (3.9)	Singapore	48,416 (80.7)	China	57,781 (10.3)	Italy	60,690 (5.4)
8	United Kingdom	42,844 (3.9)	Spain	47,146 (9.2)	France	57,677 (4.2)	France	58,510 (3.7)
9	Singapore	39,941 (81.4)	Netherlands	45,036 (13.8)	Hong Kong	49,277 (36.3)	Hong Kong	55,424 (38.3)
10	Netherlands	36,581 (10.9)	United Kingdom	43,982 (4.4)	United Kingdom	48,079 (4.5)	Brazil	51,477 (6.7)

	1996	US$ mil (% GDP)	1997	US$ mil (% GDP)	1998	US$ mil (% GDP)	1999	US$ mil (% GDP)
1	Japan	225,594 (4.8)	Japan	226,679 (5.2)	Japan	222,443 (5.7)	Japan	293,948 (6.6)
2	United States	160,660 (2.1)	China	146,448 (15.4)	China	152,843 (15.0)	China	161,414 (14.9)
3	Germany	118,323 (4.9)	United States	134,836 (1.6)	United States	146,006 (1.7)	United States	136,450 (1.5)
4	China	111,729 (13.1)	Germany	105,208 (4.9)	Germany	108,265 (5.0)	Hong Kong	96,255 (58.1)
5	Singapore	76,964 (81.3)	Hong Kong	92,823 (52.3)	Hong Kong	89,669 (53.1)	Germany	93,407 (4.4)
6	Italy	70,566 (5.6)	Italy	75,086 (6.3)	Singapore	75,077 (78.3)	Singapore	77,047 (89.6)
7	Switzerland	69,183 (22.2)	Spain	72,935 (12.7)	France	73,773 (5.0)	Korea, Rep.	74,114 (16.6)
8	Hong Kong	63,833 (40.0)	Singapore	71,390 (68.3)	Switzerland	65,158 (23.4)	France	67,927 (4.7)
9	Spain	63,699 (10.2)	Switzerland	63,195 (23.2)	Spain	60,881 (10.1)	Switzerland	60,492 (22.1)
10	Brazil	59,685 (7.1)	France	54,693 (3.8)	Italy	53,880 (4.4)	Italy	45,302 (3.7)

	2000	US$ mil (% GDP)	2001	US$ mil (% GDP)	2002	US$ mil (% GDP)	2003	US$ mil (% GDP)
1	Japan	361,639 (7.6)	Japan	401,958 (9.7)	Japan	469,618 (11.8)	Japan	673,554 (15.7)
2	China	171,763 (14.3)	China	220,057 (16.6)	China	297,739 (20.5)	China	416,199 (25.4)
3	United States	128,400 (1.3)	United States	130,077 (1.3)	United States	157,763 (1.5)	United States	184,024 (1.7)
4	Hong Kong	107,560 (62.7)	Hong Kong	111,173 (65.6)	Korea, Rep.	121,498 (21.1)	Korea, Rep.	155,472 (24.2)
5	Korea, Rep.	96,251 (18.0)	Korea, Rep.	102,875 (20.4)	Hong Kong	111,919 (67.3)	Hong Kong	118,388 (73.4)
6	Germany	87,497 (4.6)	Germany	82,132 (4.4)	Germany	89,142 (4.4)	India	103,737 (16.8)
7	Singapore	81,085 (84.5)	Singapore	76,600 (84.0)	Singapore	83,413 (92.1)	Singapore	97,743 (104.7)
8	France	63,728 (4.8)	France	58,637 (4.4)	India	71,608 (13.7)	Germany	96,835 (4.0)

(Continued)

TABLE 7.27 (*Continued*)

	2000	US$ mil (% GDP)	2001	US$ mil (% GDP)	2002	US$ mil (% GDP)	2003	US$ mil (% GDP)
9	Switzerland	53,621 (20.9)	Switzerland	51,550 (19.6)	France	61,697 (4.2)	Russia	78,409 (18.2)
10	Italy	47,201 (4.3)	India	49,051 (10.0)	Switzerland	61,276 (21.4)	France	70,762 (3.9)

	2004	US$ mil (% GDP)	2005	US$ mil (% GDP)	2006	US$ mil (% GDP)	2007	US$ mil (% GDP)
1	Japan	844,667 (18.1)	Japan	846,896 (18.5)	China	1,080,756 (39.8)	China	1,546,365 (44.3)
2	China	622,949 (32.2)	China	831,410 (36.8)	Japan	895,321 (20.6)	Japan	973,297 (22.3)
3	Korea, Rep.	199,195 (27.6)	Korea, Rep.	210,552 (24.9)	Russia	303,773 (30.7)	Russia	478,833 (36.8)
4	United States	190,465 (1.6)	United States	188,259 (1.5)	Korea, Rep	239,148 (25.1)	Saudi Arabia	309,287 (74.4)
5	India	131,163 (18.2)	Russia	182,272 (23.9)	Saudi Arabia	228,957 (60.7)	United States	277,549 (2.0)
6	Russia	126,258 (21.4)	Saudi Arabia	151,387 (47.9)	United States	221,089 (1.7)	India	276,578 (22.3)
7	Hong Kong	123,569 (73.1)	India	131,825 (16.5)	India	178,050 (18.8)	Korea, Rep	262,533 (25.0)
8	Singapore	114,162 (104.4)	Hong Kong	124,278 (68.4)	Singapore	138,653 (99.7)	Brazil	180,334 (13.2)
9	Germany	97,179 (3.6)	Singapore	118,061 (95.6)	Hong Kong	133,211 (68.8)	Singapore	166,161 (98.5)
10	France	77,353 (3.8)	Germany	101,676 (3.7)	Germany	111,637 (3.8)	Hong Kong	152,693 (72.2)

	2008	US$ mil (% GDP)	2009	US$ mil (% GDP)	2010	US$ mil (% GDP)	2011	US$ mil (% GDP)
1	China	1,855,037 (43.5)	China	2,452,899 (49.1)	China	2,813,712 (49.0)	China	3,254,674 (43.4)
2	Japan	1,030,763 (21.3)	Japan	1,048,991 (20.8)	Japan	1,096,069 (19.9)	Japan	1,295,838 (21.9)
3	Saudi Arabia	451,279 (86.8)	Russia	439,341 (35.9)	United States	488,928 (3.4)	Saudi Arabia	556,571 (83.1)
4	Russia	426,279 (25.7)	Saudi Arabia	420,984 (98.1)	Russia	479,222 (31.4)	United States	537,267 (3.5)
5	United States	294,046 (2.1)	United States	404,099 (2.9)	Saudi Arabia	459,313 (87.2)	Russia	497,410 (26.1)
6	India	257,423 (21.0)	India	284,683 (20.9)	India	300,480 (17.6)	Brazil	352,010 (13.5)
7	Korea, Rep.	201,545 (21.6)	Korea, Rep.	270,437 (32.4)	Korea, Rep.	292,143 (28.8)	Switzerland	330,586 (47.5)
8	Brazil	183,783 (11.7)	Hong Kong	255,841 (119.5)	Brazil	288,575 (13.5)	Korea, Rep.	306,935 (25.5)
9	Hong Kong	182,527 (83.2)	Brazil	238,539 (14.7)	Switzerland	279,480 (49.0)	India	298,739 (16.3)
10	Singapore	177,543 (99.2)	Singapore	192,046 (98.9)	Hong Kong	268,743 (117.5)	Hong Kong	285,399 (114.8)

	2012	US$ mil (% GDP)	2013	US$ mil (% GDP)	2014	US$ mil (% GDP)
1	China	3,387,513 (40.0)	China	3,880,368 (40.9)	China	3,900,039 (37.7)
2	Japan	1,268,086 (21.3)	Japan	1,266,851 (25.8)	Japan	1,260,680 (27.4)
3	Saudi Arabia	673,739 (91.8)	Saudi Arabia	737,797 (99.1)	Saudi Arabia	744,441 (98.8)
4	United States	574,268 (3.6)	Switzerland	536,235 (78.3)	Switzerland	545,787 (77.9)
5	Russia	537,816 (26.7)	Russia	509,692 (24.5)	United States	434,416 (2.5)
6	Switzerland	531,302 (79.8)	United States	448,509 (2.7)	Russia	386,216 (20.8)
7	Brazil	373,161 (15.2)	Brazil	358,816 (14.6)	Brazil	363,570 (15.0)
8	Korea, Rep.	327,724 (26.8)	Korea, Rep.	345,694 (26.5)	Korea, Rep.	362,835 (25.7)
9	Hong Kong	317,362 (120.8)	Hong Kong	311,210 (112.9)	Hong Kong	328,517 (112.9)
10	India	300,425 (16.4)	India	298,092 (16.0)	India	325,081 (15.9)

top three are the United States, Japan, and Germany. From 1995 to 2005, Japan stayed as the largest reserve country. However, China moved up rapidly. Appearing as the 9th largest in 1983, China has topped the list since 2006 as the largest reserve country in the world. The size of China's reserve is massive, as it is much larger than Japan and the United States, the second and third largest reserve countries, respectively. By 2009, China's reserve was more than twice as large as Japan's, and was equivalent to 49% of China's GDP. Russia first appeared as 9th largest in 2003, and climbed to become the 4th largest in 2010, after China, Japan, and the United States. Among the oil exporting countries, Saudi Arabia is the only other oil exporter in the top 10.

Germany, who appeared as the second largest in much of the 1980s, has fallen outside the top 10 after 2007. Since 2007, the top 10 largest reserve countries have all been non-European countries. Switzerland was the only European country in the top 10 in 2010. The four economies with the top 10 largest reserves in 2014 include China, Japan, Saudi Arabia, and Switzerland. Brazil is the only Latin American country in the top 10. Despite the large amount of oil exports from various Middle East countries, Saudi Arabia is the only oil exporting country listed in the top 10 in 2014. For the United States, the size of its reserve is equivalent to a small percentage of GDP. In 2014, e.g., the reserves of the United States are equal to only 2.5% of its GDP. Most European countries show a similar small percentage, while other emerging economies, such as China, Russia, and India, show a two-digit percentage.

In terms of the value of reserves expressed in percentages as shown in Table 7.28, the best performers are again the smaller economies. In some cases, the percentage shares exceed 100% of the country's GDP, though the

TABLE 7.28 Top 10 Largest Reserve Economies: Ranked by Percentage of GDP

	1980	% GDP (US$ mil)	1981	% GDP (US$ mil)	1982	% GDP (US$ mil)	1983	% GDP (US$ mil)
1	Malta	99.7 (1246)	Malta	100.9 (1255)	Malta	104.9 (1295)	Malta	110.0 (1292)
2	Switzerland	57.5 (64,748)	Singapore	53.4 (7549)	Singapore	52.9 (8480)	Singapore	52.3 (9264)
3	Singapore	55.4 (6567)	Trini.&Tobago	49.2 (2269)	Switzerland	50.7 (53,510)	Switzerland	44.7 (46,804)
4	Trini.&Tobago	45.1 (2812)	Bahrain	46.2 (1604)	Bahrain	44.0 (1603)	Bahrain	39.7 (14,836)
5	Jordan	44.0 (1744)	Switzerland	45.7 (47,082)	Trini.&Tobago	38.9 (3105)	Tonga	34.4 (21)
6	Portugal	42.7 (13,863)	Jordan	34.0 (1511)	Portugal	35.0 (10,541)	Cape Verde	33.1 (46)
7	Bahrain	33.9 (1042)	Portugal	29.6 (9334)	Cyprus	33.9 (733)	Cyprus	32.1 (694)
8	Botswana	31.5 (334)	Cyprus	29.2 (609)	Kuwait	32.8 (7073)	Botswana	32.1 (376)
9	Cape Verde	29.8 (42)	Cape Verde	27.1 (38)	Cape Verde	30.5 (43)	Portugal	30.4 (8181)
10	Cyprus	29.7 (639)	Iraq	26.6 (8655)	Jordan	28.5 (1378)	Kuwait	29.5 (6161)
	1984	% GDP (US$ mil)	1985	% GDP (US$ mil)	1986	% GDP (US$ mil)	1987	% GDP (US$ mil)
1	Malta	102.9 (1134)	Malta	101.9 (1139)	Malta	92.5 (1328)	Botswana	192.4 (2103)
2	Singapore	53.1 (10,416)	Botswana	68.0 (758)	Botswana	83.4 (1161)	Malta	83.7 (1640)
3	Switzerland	40.8 (40,970)	Singapore	67.5 (12,847)	Singapore	69.8 (12,939)	Singapore	73.1 (15,227)
4	Tonga	40.5 (26)	Bahrain	46.8 (1709)	Bahrain	50.7 (1548)	Samoa	37.4 (37)
5	Botswana	35.5 (454)	Tonga	45.8 (28)	Switzerland	37.3 (54,339)	Switzerland	37.1 (67,790)
6	Bahrain	34.5 (1349)	Switzerland	44.4 (45,248)	Kuwait	36.3 (6493)	Bahrain	36.0 (1221)
7	Cape Verde	31.0 (41)	Cape Verde	40.2 (55)	Tonga	33.0 (22)	Tonga	35.4 (29)
8	Cyprus	29.9 (682)	Togo	39.4 (301)	Togo	32.7 (347)	Bhutan	34.3 (87)
9	Togo	28.8 (207)	Bhutan	31.0 (53)	Bhutan	30.3 (61)	Cape Verde	34.3 (81)
10	Portugal	27.2 (6774)	Cyprus	30.7 (745)	Cyprus	30.2 (932)	Vanuatu	30.7 (40)
	1988	% GDP (US$ mil)	1989	% GDP (US$ mil)	1990	% GDP (US$ mil)	1991	% GDP (US$ mil)
1	Lebanon	143.7 (4761)	Lebanon	170.6 (4636)	Lebanon	148.7 (4210)	Lebanon	101.9 (4536)
2	Botswana	83.8 (2217)	Botswana	90.5 (2791)	Botswana	87.9 (3331)	Botswana	94.3 (3719)

(Continued)

TABLE 7.28 (*Continued*)

	1988	% GDP (US$ mil)	1989	% GDP (US$ mil)	1990	% GDP (US$ mil)	1991	% GDP (US$ mil)
3	Malta	77.0 (1556)	Malta	68.2 (1446)	Singapore	77.0 (27,790)	Singapore	79.4 (34,187)
4	Singapore	67.5 (17,073)	Singapore	66.9 (20,371)	Samoa	61.6 (69)	Samoa	60.6 (68)
5	Samoa	41.5 (49)	Samoa	50.3 (55)	Malta	58.6 (1492)	Malta	50.0 (1375)
6	Bahrain	35.5 (1313)	Bhutan	43.6 (90)	Hong Kong	32.1 (24,656)	Bhutan	40.5 (101)
7	Bhutan	33.7 (96)	Switzerland	30.7 (58,670)	Bahrain	30.6 (1293)	Kuwait	39.2 (4307)
8	Cape Verde	30.8 (81)	Bahrain	28.7 (1110)	Cyprus	30.1 (1684)	Guyana	37.0 (124)
9	Switzerland	29.5 (58,367)	Cyprus	28.7 (1308)	Bhutan	29.6 (89)	Bahrain	34.0 (1568)
10	Tonga	28.6 (31)	Cape Verde	27.9 (75)	Mauritius	28.7 (761)	Hong Kong	32.5 (28,889)

	1992	% GDP (US$ mil)	1993	% GDP (US$ mil)	1994	% GDP (US$ mil)	1995	% GDP (US$ mil)
1	Botswana	91.5 (3799)	Botswana	98.5 (4097)	Botswana	103.3 (4401)	Botswana	99.3 (4695)
2	Lebanon	82.4 (4570)	Singapore	79.8 (48,416)	Singapore	79.0 (58,296)	Singapore	78.3 (68,816)
3	Singapore	76.6 (39,941)	Lebanon	77.8 (5863)	Lebanon	77.3 (7419)	Lebanon	69.1 (8100)
4	Guyana	51.1 (188)	Guyana	55.9 (247)	Malta	63.0 (1890)	Lesotho	53.2 (457)
5	Samoa	43.6 (58)	Malta	51.7 (1402)	Lesotho	49.4 (373)	Malta	45.0 (1620)
6	Malta	43.3 (1308)	Malaysia	42.1 (28,183)	Guyana	45.7 (247)	Guyana	43.3 (269)
7	Bhutan	33.9 (85)	Bhutan	41.6 (98)	Bhutan	44.8 (121)	Bhutan	43.0 (130)
8	Hong Kong	33.8 (35,250)	Samoa	38.1 (51)	Hong Kong	36.3 (49,277)	Hong Kong	38.3 (55,424)
9	Bahrain	30.5 (1448)	Hong Kong	35.7 (43,013)	Malaysia	35.4 (26,339)	Macao	34.4 (2257)
10	Malaysia	30.5 (18,024)	Lesotho	35.0 (253)	Macao	33.5 (1966)	Jordan	33.9 (2279)

	1996	% GDP (US$ mil)	1997	% GDP (US$ mil)	1998	% GDP (US$ mil)	1999	% GDP (US$ mil)
1	Botswana	103.7 (5028)	Botswana	113.0 (5675)	Botswana	124.0 (5941)	Botswana	113.6 (6229)
2	Singapore	79.8 (76,964)	Singapore	71.3 (71,390)	Singapore	87.6 (75,077)	Singapore	89.3 (77,047)
3	Lebanon	68.2 (9337)	Lesotho	66.5 (572)	Lesotho	70.2 (575)	Bhutan	69.8 (292)
4	Bhutan	60.1 (190)	Lebanon	54.9 (8653)	Bhutan	68.1 (257)	Lesotho	62.3 (500)
5	Lesotho	56.4 (461)	Hong Kong	52.3 (92,823)	Lebanon	53.4 (9210)	Lebanon	60.1 (10,452)
6	Guyana	46.7 (330)	Bhutan	51.6 (189)	Hong Kong	53.1 (89,669)	Hong Kong	58.1 (96,255)
7	Malta	44.6 (1636)	Guyana	42.1 (316)	Micronesia	46.3 (102)	Macao	48.3 (2857)
8	Micronesia	40.9 (90)	Micronesia	41.5 (86)	Malta	43.7 (1664)	Malta	45.8 (1790)
9	Hong Kong	40.0 (63,833)	Malta	41.0 (1491)	Macao	39.8 (2463)	Micronesia	42.0 (93)
10	Macao	36.5 (2422)	Macao	37.9 (2533)	Guyana	38.5 (277)	Malaysia	39.1 (30,931)

	2000	% GDP (US$ mil)	2001	% GDP (US$ mil)	2002	% GDP (US$ mil)	2003	% GDP (US$ mil)
1	Botswana	109.2 (6318)	Botswana	107.4 (5897)	Botswana	100.6 (5474)	Singapore	100.8 (97,743)
2	Singapore	84.6 (81,085)	Singapore	85.5 (76,600)	Singapore	90.7 (83,413)	Libya	81.9 (21,513)
3	Bhutan	72.3 (318)	Bhutan	67.9 (323)	Libya	77.6 (15,892)	Lebanon	81.5 (16,367)
4	Hong Kong	62.7 (107,560)	Hong Kong	65.6 (111,174)	Hong Kong	67.3 (111,919)	Hong Kong	73.4 (118,388)
5	Macao	54.5 (3323)	Lesotho	54.7 (386)	Bhutan	66.1 (355)	Botswana	71.1 (5340)

(Continued)

TABLE 7.28 *(Continued)*

	2000	% GDP (US$ mil)	2001	% GDP (US$ mil)	2002	% GDP (US$ mil)	2003	% GDP (US$ mil)
6	Lesotho	54.2 (418)	Macao	53.9 (3508)	Lesotho	61.9 (406)	Bhutan	58.9 (367)
7	Lebanon	49.1 (8475)	Libya	47.1 (16,079)	Lebanon	54.3 (10,405)	Macao	54.8 (4343)
8	Micronesia	48.5 (113)	Lebanon	42.9 (7564)	Macao	54.2 (3800)	Malta	53.3 (2730)
9	Guyana	42.8 (305)	Malta	42.6 (1668)	Malta	51.5 (2211)	Jordan	52.6 (5366)
10	Jordan	40.7 (3441)	Guyana	41.3 (287)	Micronesia	48.6 (117)	Algeria	52.2 (35,455)

	2004	% GDP (US$ mil)	2005	% GDP (US$ mil)	2006	% GDP (US$ mil)	2007	% GDP (US$ mil)
1	Singapore	100.0 (114,161)	Singapore	92.7 (118,061)	Libya	113.2 (62,229)	Libya	123.3 (83,260)
2	Libya	83.7 (27,714)	Libya	88.5 (41,880)	Singapore	93.8 (138,653)	Singapore	92.3 (166,161)
3	Lebanon	75.3 (15,774)	Lebanon	78.1 (16,618)	Lebanon	88.3 (19,239)	Botswana	89.5 (9790)
4	Hong Kong	73.1 (123,569)	Hong Kong	68.4 (124,278)	Botswana	78.9 (7992)	Algeria	85.2 (114,972)
5	Botswana	63.2 (5661)	Botswana	63.5 (6309)	Algeria	69.6 (81, 463)	Lebanon	83.8 (20,599)
6	Bhutan	56.7 (399)	SyriaArab Rep.	61.6 (17,774)	Hong Kong	68.8 (133,211)	Saudi Arabia	74.4 (309,287)
7	Algeria	53.6 (45,692)	Algeria	57.3 (59,167)	Macao	62.7 (9132)	Macao	73.3 (13,230)
8	Malaysia	53.2 (66,394)	Bhutan	57.1 (467)	Saudi Arabia	60.7 (228,957)	Hong Kong	72.2 (152,693)
9	Macao	53.0 (5436)	Macao	56.7 (6689)	Bhutan	60.7 (545)	Lesotho	62.8 (1003)
10	Malta	48.4 (2734)	Malaysia	49.1 (70,458)	SyriaArab Rep	51.0 (16,997)	Bhutan	58.4 (699)

	2008	% GDP (US$ mil)	2009	% GDP (US$ mil)	2010	% GDP (US$ mil)	2011	% GDP (US$ mil)
1	Libya	110.6 (96,335)	Libya	164.6 (103,754)	Libya	142.0 (106,144)	Libya	318.6 (110,539)
2	Lebanon	98.0 (28,265)	Hong Kong	119.5 (255,841)	Hong Kong	117.5 (268,743)	Lebanon	119.4 (47,859)
3	Singapore	92.4 (177,543)	Algeria	113.0 (155,112)	Lebanon	117.0 (44,476)	Hong Kong	114.8 (285,399)
4	Saudi Arabia	86.8 (451,279)	Lebanon	111.4 (39,132)	Algeria	105.7 (170,461)	Algeria	95.7 (191,369)
5	Algeria	86.6 (148,999)	Singapore	99.8 (192,046)	Singapore	97.8 (231,260)	Macao	92.9 (34,026)
6	Botswana	83.3 (9119)	Saudi Arabia	98.1 (420,984)	Saudi Arabia	87.2 (459,313)	Singapore	88.5 (243,798)
7	Hong Kong	83.2 (182,527)	Macao	86.1 (18,350)	Macao	83,7 (23,726)	Saudi Arabia	83.1 (556,571)
8	Macao	76.8 (15,930)	Botswana	84.8 (8704)	Bhutan	63.2 (1002)	Iceland	58.3 (8548)
9	Bhutan	60.8 (765)	Bhutan	70.4 (891)	Botswana	61.7 (7885)	Botswana	51.5 (8082)
10	Lesotho	59.6 (972)	Lesotho	68.9 (1180)	Jordan	51,6 (13,633)	Bolivia	50.1 (11,995)

	2012	% GDP (US$ mil)	2013	% GDP (US$ mil)	2014	% GDP (US$ mil)
1	Libya	152.2 (124,648)	Libya	182.7 (119,714)	Libya	227.5 (93,615)
2	Lebanon	121.6 (52,531)	Hong Kong	112.9 (311,210)	Hong Kong	112.9 (328,517)
3	Hong Kong	120.8 (317,362)	Lebanon	107.9 (47,856)	Lebanon	110.8 (50,699)
4	Algeria	96.0 (200,587)	Saudi Arabia	99.1 (737,797)	Saudi Arabia	98.8 (744,441)

(Continued)

TABLE 7.28   (*Continued*)

	2012	% GDP (US$ mil)	2013	% GDP (US$ mil)	2014	% GDP (US$ mil)
5	Saudi Arabia	91.8 (673,740)	Algeria	96.1 (201,437)	Algeria	87.3 (186,351)
6	Singapore	91.7 (265,910)	Singapore	91.9 (277,798)	Singapore	85.0 (261,583)
7	Switzerland	79.8 (531,302)	Switzerland	78.3 (536,235)	Switzerland	77.9 (545,787)
8	Timor-Leste	68.2 (884)	Bhutan	55.1 (991)	Bhutan	63.6 (1245)
9	Bhutan	52.3 (955)	Timor-Leste	52.1 (687)	Botswana	52.6 (8323)
10	Botswana	51.6 (7628)	Botswana	51.6 (7726)	Lesotho	49.1 (1071)

size of the percentage may vary considerably with the value. Bhutan, e.g., shows a large percentage, but the value is extremely small. For a number of years, Libya has ranked first in the top 10 largest reserve economies ranked by percentage of GDP, with 113.2% in 2006, rising to 227.5% in 2014.

VII FOREIGN AID AND DONORS

In the OECD statistical data, total receipts of foreign aid by country or region includes official development assistance (ODA), other official flows (OOF), and private sources. ODA comprises official bilateral transactions that are not concessional, while OOF are assets related to trade facilitation. Private sources are bilateral long-term assets in the private sector related to guaranteed export credits, private direct investment, portfolio investment, loans by private banks, and flows from the multilateral sector not classified as concessional. Usually, it is the poor developing countries that have received foreign aid from developed countries for development assistance (Boone, 1996; Alesina and Dollar, 2000; Svensson, 2000; Easterly, 2003a; Dalgaard et al., 2004). However, questions remain as to the effectiveness of foreign aid in promoting growth, as the concern is whether foreign aid is used to satisfy short-term, welfare-oriented demands, or is used to promote economic capability.

Table 7.29 summarizes the number of years the top 10 recipients of foreign aid in the three decades 1980–2014. Again, there are changes between the three decades. While the largest recipients in the 1980s and the 1990s were the poor countries and a few smaller oil exporting countries, China had been one of the top recipients. China has become the second most frequent recipient since the 1990s. The top five recipients in the number of years are Mexico, China, Indonesia, Brazil, and Turkey. While Mexico, China, Brazil, and Turkey are geographically large countries, others are small and developing countries, with the exception of Israel, Singapore, and Hong Kong. However, the aid to Hong Kong might have been redirected to China. The list also included a few oil exporting countries, such as Saudi Arabia.

Table 7.30 shows the details of the top 10 aid recipients. While Brazil and Mexico topped the list in the early half of the 1980s, China first emerged in the top 10 in 1985, and climbed to top in 1989. The list of the top recipients in the 1980s and 1990s are quite similar. After the turn of the century, the two countries competing for the top are Brazil and China. India has ranked mostly in the top five recipients since 2006. Another observation is that many of these recipients are geographically large countries, such as China, Brazil, and India, so the foreign aid they received often comprised a small percentage of their GDP. There are, of course, a few exceptions where foreign aid occupied over 100% of the country's GDP, and these usually are small island countries, such as the British Virgin Islands and Bermuda. In regional terms, Asian countries tended to be favorable recipients. In 2014, e.g., a total of six top 10 recipients were Asian countries, four of which (Thailand, Indonesia, Vietnam, and Malaysia) are Southeast Asian countries.

Total flows by donor countries also include ODA, OOF, and private source donations. The aggregate data from the OECD covered flows from all bilateral and multilateral donors, including nongovernmental organizations (NGOs). Table 7.31 summarizes the list of donor countries for the three decades. It is clear that the major donors are exclusively from countries in North America and Europe, and Japan and Australia. The consistent large donors in the three decades are the United States, the United Kingdom, Germany, France, the Netherlands, Sweden, and Japan. As seen from previous tables, many of these countries, typically the United States and Japan, are also countries with the largest reserves and trade deficits.

TABLE 7.29 Number of Years in the Top 10 of Recipients of Foreign Aid

1980—89		1990—99		2000—14		1980—2014	
Egypt	10	Indonesia	10	Mexico	14	Mexico	28
Indonesia	9	China	9	China	12	China	27
Israel	9	Thailand	9	India	12	Indonesia	26
Brazil	7	Korea, Rep.	9	Brazil	11	Brazil	25
Mexico	6	Mexico	8	Turkey	11	Turkey	20
China	6	Brazil	7	Malaysia	10	India	19
India	6	Israel	6	Chile	9	Egypt	17
Argentina	5	Hong Kong	6	South Africa	8	Thailand	17
Panama	5	Singapore	5	Indonesia	7	Malaysia	15
Singapore	4	Turkey	5	Thailand	7	Israel	15
Turkey	4	Argentina	5	Egypt	6	Chile	13
Venezuela	4	Bermuda	4	Vietnam	6	Argentina	12
Nigeria	4	Philippines	3	Iran	4	Panama	11
Hong Kong	4	Malaysia	3	Panama	4	Korea, Rep.	11
Colombia	2	Panama	2	Philippines	3	Hong Kong	10
Chile	2	Chile	2	Venezuela	3	South Africa	9
Malaysia	2	South Africa	1	Iraq	3	Singapore	9
Iraq	2	Netherlands Ant.	1	Ukraine	3	Venezuela	7
Korea, Rep.	2	India	1	Argentina	2	Philippines	7
Bermuda	2	Egypt	1	Bahrain	2	Vietnam	6
Algeria	1	Cayman Is.	1	Nigeria	2	Nigeria	6
Philippines	1	Iran	1	Mauritius	2	Bermuda	6
Cayman Is.	1	British Virgin Is.	1	Kazakhstan	1	Iran	5
Netherlands Ant.	1			Congo,Dem.Rep.	1	Iraq	5
Thailand	1			Liberia	1	Ukraine	3
				Slovenia	1	Netherlands Ant.	2
				Serbia	1	Colombia	2
				Croatia	1	Bahrain	2
				Saudi Arabia	1	Mauritius	2
				Afghanistan	1	Cayman Is.	2
				Korea, DPR.	1	Kazakhstan	1
						Dem.Rep.Congo	1
						Liberia	1
						Slovenia	1
						Serbia	1
						Croatia	1
						Saudi Arabia	1
						Afghanistan	1
						Korea, DPR.	1
						Algeria	1
						British Virgin Is.	1

TABLE 7.30 Top 10 Largest Recipients of Foreign Aid: Ranked by Value (US$ Million)

	1980	US$ mil	% GDP	1981	US$ mil	% GDP	1982	US$ mil	% GDP	1983	US$ mil	% GDP
1	Brazil	3841.1	2.0	Brazil	7060.8	3.1	Brazil	6836.2	2.9	Brazil	4912.1	2.9
2	Mexico	3806.4	1.6	Mexico	6190.0	2.1	Mexico	4301.3	2.1	Mexico	3601.6	2.0
3	Argentina	2728.5	3.0	Indonesia	4028.2	3.7	Egypt	2974.5	19.4	Egypt	2895.3	15.4
4	Egypt	1991.4	9.9	Argentina	2449.5	2.6	Indonesia	2086.5	1.9	Indonesia	2441.0	2.4
5	Algeria	1465.3	3.5	Egypt	2071.9	16.3	Nigeria	1859.4	1.0	Israel	2187.3	7.0
6	Turkey	1344.3	1.5	Hong Kong	1758.4	5.7	Venezuela	1833.2	2.3	Nigeria	1917.6	1.1
7	Venezuela	1329.3	1.9	Nigeria	1587.8	0.9	Panama	1603.8	33.2	Malaysia	1608.2	4.9
8	Indonesia	1325.3	1.6	China	1468.7	0.5	Israel	1580.6	5.7	Hong Kong	1094.6	3.7
9	Israel	1278.3	5.3	Chile	1420.6	3.9	Argentina	1390.9	1.4	Colombia	964.6	1.8
10	Nigeria	1136.8	0.6	Singapore	1387.1	9.7	Colombia	1258.3	2.3	India	887.0	0.4

	1984	US$ mil	% GDP	1985	US$ mil	% GDP	1986	US$ mil	% GDP	1987	US$ mil	% GDP
1	Mexico	13,021.2	6.2	Egypt	2667.9	11.2	Argentina	4436.4	3.5	Hong Kong	4202.1	8.3
2	Brazil	6547.4	3.7	Israel	2568.9	9.3	Venezuela	2799.2	4.8	Bermuda	3589.0	206.8
3	Egypt	2764.1	12.8	Argentina	1899.3	1.8	China	2683.9	0.9	China	3562.6	1.1
4	Indonesia	2674.6	2.6	Panama	1583.4	27.7	India	2327.2	1.0	Panama	2274.7	36.5
5	Israel	1992.7	6.8	China	1573.7	0.5	Israel	2289.3	6.7	Egypt	2273.8	8.2
6	Iraq	1933.9	16.5	Korea, Rep.	1432.9	1.4	Egypt	2254.8	9.0	Israel	2108.3	5.1
7	Chile	1748.7	8.2	India	1245.0	0.6	Panama	1680.4	27.8	Venezuela	2094.9	4.5
8	Korea, Rep.	1510.0	1.6	Iraq	926.9	7.7	Turkey	1141.9	1.1	India	1928.8	0.7
9	Malaysia	1326.3	3.6	Cayman Is.	833.8	200.4	Bermuda	1015.2	64.0	Indonesia	1873.0	2.1
10	Singapore	1322.7	6.8	Indonesia	832.6	0.8	Philippines	929.6	2.8	Turkey	1687.5	1.4

	1988	US$ mil	% GDP	1989	US$ mil	% GDP	1990	US$ mil	% GDP	1991	US$ mil	% GDP
1	Israel	6289.5	12.5	China	4442.7	1.0	China	3808.0	1.0	Mexico	6096.6	1.7
2	Turkey	4263.2	3.5	Brazil	3727.0	1.0	HongKong	3494.8	4.5	Indonesia	4523.4	3.0
3	China	3951.6	1.0	Indonesia	3344.3	2.8	Singapore	3409.6	8.8	Thailand	3762.3	3.7
4	Egypt	3462.9	11.6	India	3210.6	1.1	Thailand	2849.4	3.2	China	3694.3	0.9
5	Brazil	3221.6	1.2	Mexico	3030.2	1.2	Indonesia	2319.7	1.7	Egypt	3434.8	8.8
6	Hong Kong	2601.9	4.4	Singapore	2980.6	9.5	India	2281.7	0.7	Israel	3136.1	4.6
7	Netherlands Ant.	1699.2	101.6	Panama	2623.5	46.9	Cayman Is.	1742.9	187.4	Korea, Rep.	2991.7	0.9
8	Singapore	1680.8	6.3	Thailand	2409.2	3.2	Malaysia	1543.7	3.2	Hong Kong	2513.4	2.8
9	India	1660.6	0.6	Israel	2025.4	4.0	Korea,Rep.	1464.3	0.5	Bermuda	2265.3	107.1
10	Indonesia	1449.0	1.4	Egypt	1921.8	5.9	Israel	1443.4	2.4	Turkey	2129.5	1.0

	1992	US$ mil	% GDP	1993	US$ mil	% GDP	1994	US$ mil	% GDP	1995	US$ mil	% GDP
1	Mexico	6777.9	1.7	Mexico	15,553.7	3.5	China	11,321.0	2.0	China	10,891.6	1.5
2	Indonesia	5026.6	3.1	China	7070.5	1.1	Argentina	8093.1	2.6	Brazil	9399.5	1.2
3	China	4612.9	0.9	Turkey	5670.5	2.3	Thailand	7507.0	5.1	Korea, Rep.	7597.8	1.4
4	Thailand	4104.6	3.6	Malaysia	5120.6	7.1	Hong Kong	7315.0	5.4	Thailand	7590.5	4.5
5	Bermuda	4041.0	187.9	Israel	4394.8	5.8	Mexico	6614.4	1.4	Indonesia	7429.6	3.1

(Continued)

TABLE 7.30 (*Continued*)

	1992	US$ mil	% GDP	1993	US$ mil	% GDP	1994	US$ mil	% GDP	1995	US$ mil	% GDP
6	Turkey	3353.9	1.6	Brazil	4341.4	1.1	Singapore	5741.6	7.8	Argentina	6270.9	2.0
7	Singapore	3288.7	6.3	Hong Kong	3998.2	3.3	Iran	5632.0	4.9	Malaysia	4242.4	4.4
8	Israel	3219.1	4.2	Singapore	3615.0	6.0	Indonesia	5584.7	2.7	Singapore	4238.4	4.8
9	Brazil	2419.4	0.7	Bermuda	3008.6	131.4	Korea, Rep.	4539.8	1.0	Hong Kong	3754.5	2.6
10	Korea, Rep.	2414.9	0.7	Indonesia	2960.5	1.6	Israel	4095.5	4.7	Panama	3432.9	38.0

	1996	US$ mil	% GDP	1997	US$ mil	% GDP	1998	US$ mil	% GDP	1999	US$ mil	% GDP
1	Brazil	10,155.7	1.2	Brazil	18,205.1	2.1	Brazil	21,535.0	2.5	Argentina	23,428.6	6.9
2	China	9288.0	1.1	Argentina	12,484.3	3.6	Korea, Rep.	10,336.0	2.8	Brazil	20,154.5	3.4
3	Korea, Rep.	9220.9	1.5	Korea, Rep.	10,000.7	1.8	Argentina	9727.0	2.7	Mexico	12,592.4	2.3
4	Indonesia	9201.5	3.5	China	9875.1	1.0	Mexico	7739.1	1.6	Korea, Rep.	7802.5	1.6
5	Hong Kong	7876.8	4.9	Mexico	8200.8	1.8	Thailand	7436.1	6.6	Panama	7202.7	62.9
6	Mexico	7772.6	2.1	Indonesia	8009.3	3.2	Indonesia	5382.6	4.8	Indonesia	7145.0	4.4
7	Thailand	7571.3	4.1	Thailand	6193.4	4.1	China	5200.1	0.5	Philippines	6772.1	8.2
8	Israel	5700.3	5.2	Philippines	5443.0	6.0	Chile	4766.6	5.8	Thailand	6450.8	5.1
9	Netherlands Ant.	5353.4	198.9	South Africa	4992.9	3.3	Philippines	4009.1	5.6	Chile	6344.0	8.4
10	Bermuda	5302.8	195.4	Turkey	4879.4	1.9	Turkey	3912.9	1.5	British VirginIs.	4342.8	645.3

	2000	US$ mil	% GDP	2001	US$ mil	% GDP	2002	US$ mil	% GDP	2003	US$ mil	% GDP
1	Brazil	17,694.3	2.7	Brazil	12,579.6	2.2	Mexico	5850.6	0.8	Mexico	8935.2	1.3
2	Turkey	7733.1	2.9	Mexico	5896.3	0.8	Nigeria	4883.1	5.1	China	6868.6	0.4
3	Argentina	6767.6	2.0	Chile	3700.4	5.2	Malaysia	3594.2	3.4	South Africa	5116.2	2.9
4	Panama	3242.6	27.9	Egypt	3045.4	3.4	Iran	3127.9	2.1	Indonesia	4622.5	1.8
5	Egypt	3215.6	3.4	Venezuela	2646.5	2.2	South Africa	2718.4	2.4	Liberia	4486.1	1036.0
6	Venezuela	2539.1	2.2	Bahrain	2585.1	28.8	Serbia	2503.4	12.4	Congo.Dem. Rep	4287.2	48.0
7	India	1824.1	0.4	Philippines	2108.0	2.8	Philippines	2375.7	2.9	Iran	4243.2	2.8
8	Philippines	1533.0	1.9	Thailand	2025.2	1.7	Panama	2352.2	19.2	Chile	3247.5	4.3
9	Indonesia	1532.9	0.9	Kazakhstan	1704.4	7.7	Slovenia	1956.0	8.3	India	3091.9	0.5
10	Bahrain	1432.1	15.8	Iran	1620.1	1.4	Egypt	1888.3	2.2	Turkey	2465.4	0.8

	2004	US$ mil	% GDP	2005	US$ mil	% GDP	2006	US$ mil	% GDP	2007	US$ mil	% GDP
1	China	17,175.7	0.9	China	21,992.8	1.0	Brazil	27,588.9	2.5	Brazil	46,677.1	3.3
2	Mexico	10,061.4	1.3	Brazil	21,208.2	2.4	Turkey	15,245.9	2.9	Turkey	26,602.9	4.1
3	South Africa	9956.9	4.4	Iraq	20,519.3	56.6	China	14,178.5	0.5	India	25,201.7	2.1
4	Iraq	4587.2	17.5	Mexico	17,216.9	2.0	India	11,428.1	1.2	Mexico	21,016.4	2.0
5	Iran	4275.0	2.3	South Africa	14,413.6	5.6	Saudi Arabia	10,352.6	2.7	China	20,813.3	0.6
6	India	3714.1	0.5	Thailand	12,852.6	6.8	Mexico	10,081.0	1.0	South Africa	13,213.9	4.4
7	Egypt	3558.1	4.5	Turkey	11,338.4	2.3	South Africa	8224.8	3.0	Mauritius	12,505.0	160.5
8	Mauritius	2868.4	43.6	Ukraine	9929.9	11.1	Malaysia	7692.7	4.7	Ukraine	11,479.2	7.7

(*Continued*)

TABLE 7.30 (*Continued*)

	2004	US$ mil	% GDP	2005	US$ mil	% GDP	2006	US$ mil	% GDP	2007	US$ mil	% GDP
9	Thailand	2622.5	1.5	Indonesia	8028.8	2.6	Venezuela	7642.2	4.2	Malaysia	10,580.1	5.5
10	Malaysia	2037.0	1.6	Nigeria	7365.3	4.1	Iraq	6884.2	12.6	Croatia	9042.5	15.1

	2008	US$ mil	% GDP	2009	US$ mil	% GDP	2010	US$ mil	% GDP	2011	US$ mil	% GDP
1	China	31,068.6	0.7	Brazil	18,384.4	1.1	China	48,570.5	0.8	China	49,909.8	0.7
2	India	18,345.8	1.4	India	16,076.5	1.2	Brazil	35,222.2	1.6	Brazil	42,382.5	1.6
3	Egypt	16,243.2	9.9	Mexico	14,698.6	1.6	India	23,574.9	1.4	Turkey	22,968.6	3.0
4	Mexico	16,047.5	1.5	China	14,337.2	0.3	Mexico	23,258.4	2.2	India	17,196.2	0.9
5	Turkey	11,174.0	1.5	Panama	8430.8	31.7	Turkey	7357.4	1.0	Mexico	11,543.1	1.0
6	Ukraine	9386.0	5.0	Malaysia	5687.3	2.8	Malaysia	6731.3	2.7	Indonesia	10,437.7	1.2
7	Chile	7406.4	4.1	Afghanistan	5182.7	41.2	Thailand	6252.9	1.8	Thailand	10,278.4	2.8
8	South Africa	6132.3	2.1	Chile	4752.8	2.8	Chile	6119.3	2.8	Chile	8341.3	3.3
9	Vietnam	5523.9	5.6	Egypt	4586.8	2.4	Panama	5974.4	20.7	Malaysia	7424.4	2.6
10	Argentina	5282.5	1.3	Vietnam	4278.8	4.0	Vietnam	5615.6	4.8	South Africa	6541.4	1.6

	2012	US$ mil	% GDP	2013	US$ mil	% GDP	2014	US$ mil	% GDP
1	Brazil	33,616.3	1.4	China	54,103.1	0.6	Brazil	60,907.1	2.6
2	Mexico	19,134.9	1.6	Brazil	34,977.8	1.5	China	56,258.5	0.5
3	China	18,802.0	0.2	Mexico	22,735.9	1.8	Mexico	20,657.6	1.6
4	India	18,183.2	1.0	Turkey	14,168.7	1.7	India	14,624.1	0.7
5	Turkey	12,983.6	1.6	Vietnam	11,616.1	6.8	Turkey	11,565.5	1.4
6	Chile	11,937.5	4.5	India	10,039.1	0.5	Thailand	9,669.3	2.4
7	Malaysia	10,230.9	3.4	Malaysia	9556.8	3.1	Indonesia	8827.2	1.0
8	Korea, DPR.	8905.2	56.0	Thailand	7127.1	1.7	Vietnam	7487.5	4.0
9	Vietnam	7592.9	4.9	Indonesia	7079.2	0.8	Malaysia	6802.4	2.1
10	Indonesia	7433.1	0.8	Chile	6730.1	2.4	Chile	6309.9	2.4

TABLE 7.31 Number of Years in the Top 10 of Donors of Foreign Aid

1980−89		1990−99		2000−14		1980−2014	
Canada	10	Canada	10	France	15	United States	35
France	10	France	10	Germany	15	United Kingdom	35
Germany	10	Germany	10	Japan	15	Germany	35
Italy	10	Japan	10	Netherlands	15	France	35
Japan	10	Netherlands	10	Sweden	15	Netherlands	35
Netherlands	10	Sweden	10	United Kingdom	15	Sweden	35
Sweden	10	United Kingdom	10	United States	15	Japan	35
United Kingdom	10	United States	10	Canada	14	Canada	34
United States	10	Italy	9	Italy	9	Italy	28
Australia	8	Denmark	7	Spain	9	Australia	12
Norway	2	Norway	2	Norway	7	Spain	11
		Spain	2	Australia	4	Norway	11
				Denmark	2	Denmark	9

Table 7.32 provides the detailed figures of the top 10 aid donors. One can observe that the amount these top aid donors provided occupied only a very small percentage of their GDP. In most cases, the percentages were less than 1%. Despite the rise in the value of aid donations over the years, the United States had not spent more than 0.3% of its GDP in foreign aid. The three north European countries of Denmark, Sweden, and Norway have committed regularly 1% of their GDP. Such consistency in the low levels of GDP commitment should have

TABLE 7.32 Top 10 Largest Donors of Foreign Aid: Ranked by Value (US$ Million)

	1980	US$ mil	% GDP	1981	US$ mil	% GDP	1982	US$ mil	% GDP	1983	US$ mil	% GDP
1	United States	7138.0	0.3	United States	5782.0	0.2	United States	8202.0	0.3	US	8081.0	0.2
2	Germany	3566.5	0.4	Germany	3181.2	0.4	Germany	3151.6	0.4	Japan	3761.0	0.3
3	Japan	3353.0	0.3	Japan	3170.9	0.3	France	3049.8	0.5	Germany	3176.4	0.4
4	France	2889.0	0.4	France	2963.6	0.5	Japan	3023.3	0.3	France	2908.7	0.5
5	United Kingdom	1854.2	0.3	United Kingdom	2191.6	0.4	United Kingdom	1800.2	0.4	United Kingdom	1610.2	0.4
6	Netherlands	1630.4	0.9	Netherlands	1510.0	1.0	Netherlands	1471.8	1.0	Canada	1429.4	0.4
7	Canada	1075.1	0.4	Canada	1188.6	0.4	Canada	1196.7	0.4	Netherlands	1195.3	0.8
8	Sweden	962.3	0.7	Sweden	919.5	0.8	Sweden	987.0	0.9	Italy	833.7	0.2
9	Italy	683.3	0.2	Italy	665.5	0.2	Australia	882.4	0.5	Sweden	753.8	0.8
10	Australia	667.4	0.5	Australia	649.5	0.4	Italy	810.8	0.2	Australia	753.4	0.4

	1984	US$ mil	% GDP	1985	US$ mil	% GDP	1986	US$ mil	% GDP	1987	US$ mil	% GDP
1	United States	8711.0	0.2	United States	9403.0	0.2	United States	9564.0	0.2	United States	9115.0	0.2
2	Japan	4318.7	0.3	Japan	3796.8	0.3	Japan	5634.4	0.3	Japan	7341.6	0.3
3	France	3026.0	0.6	France	3133.5	0.6	France	4042.1	0.5	France	5249.6	0.6
4	Germany	2782.0	0.4	Germany	2942.0	0.4	Germany	3831.6	0.4	Germany	4390.5	0.4
5	Canada	1624.9	0.5	Canada	1631.1	0.5	Italy	2403.5	0.4	Italy	2615.3	0.3
6	United Kingdom	1429.6	0.3	United Kingdom	1529.8	0.3	Netherlands	1740.4	0.9	Netherlands	2094.3	0.9
7	Netherlands	1267.8	1.0	Netherlands	1135.9	0.9	United Kingdom	1737.1	0.3	Canada	1885.3	0.5
8	Italy	1132.8	0.3	Italy	1098.0	0.3	Canada	1695.2	0.4	United Kingdom	1871.1	0.3
9	Australia	776.8	0.4	Sweden	839.8	0.8	Sweden	1089.8	0.8	Sweden	1375.0	0.8
10	Sweden	741.2	0.7	Australia	748.7	0.4	Norway	798.0	1.0	Norway	890.3	1.0

	1988	US$ mil	% GDP	1989	US$ mil	% GDP	1990	US$ mil	% GDP	1991	US$ mil	% GDP
1	United States	10,141.0	0.2	Japan	8964.9	0.3	United States	11,394.0	0.2	United States	11,262.0	0.2
2	Japan	9133.7	0.3	United States	7677.0	0.1	Japan	9068.8	0.3	Japan	10,952.24	0.3
3	France	5463.2	0.6	France	5801.8	0.6	France	7163.5	0.6	France	7385.52	0.6
4	Germany	4730.9	0.4	Germany	4948.1	0.4	Germany	6319.7	0.4	Germany	6889.73	0.4
5	Italy	3192.8	0.4	Italy	3613.3	0.4	Italy	3394.0	0.3	Italy	3347.24	0.3
6	United Kingdom	2644.9	0.3	United Kingdom	2586.8	0.3	United Kingdom	2638.1	0.4	United Kingdom	3200.85	0.3

(Continued)

TABLE 7.32 *(Continued)*

	1988	US$ mil	% GDP	1989	US$ mil	% GDP	1990	US$ mil	% GDP	1991	US$ mil	% GDP
7	Canada	2346.7	0.5	Canada	2320.4	0.4	Netherlands	2538.1	0.9	Canada	2603.86	0.4
8	Netherlands	2231.1	0.9	Netherlands	2093.6	0.9	Canada	2469.9	0.4	Netherlands	2516.71	0.8
9	Sweden	1533.6	0.8	Sweden	1799.3	0.9	Sweden	2007.0	0.8	Sweden	2116.43	0.8
10	Australia	1101.0	0.5	Australia	1019.6	0.3	Norway	1204.8	1.0	Spain	1261.69	0.3

	1992	US$ mil	% GDP	1993	US$ mil	% GDP	1994	US$ mil	% GDP	1995	US$ mil	% GDP
1	United States	11,709.0	0.2	Japan	11,259.0	0.3	Japan	13,238.5	0.3	Japan	14,489.3	0.3
2	Japan	11,151.0	0.3	United States	10,123.0	0.2	United States	9927.0	0.1	France	8443.4	0.5
3	France	8260.0	0.6	France	7915.1	0.6	France	8466.0	0.6	Germany	7523.6	0.3
4	Germany	7583.1	0.4	Germany	6954.0	0.4	Germany	6818.0	0.3	United States	7367.0	0.1
5	Italy	4121.9	0.3	Italy	3043.4	0.3	United Kingdom	3197.0	0.3	Netherlands	3226.1	0.8
6	United Kingdom	3243.1	0.3	United Kingdom	2920.2	0.3	Italy	2704.6	0.3	United Kingdom	3202.2	0.3
7	Netherlands	2752.8	0.8	Netherlands	2525.4	0.8	Netherlands	2516.7	0.7	Canada	2066.7	0.4
8	Canada	2515.2	0.4	Canada	2399.6	0.4	Canada	2249.6	0.4	Sweden	1704.0	0.7
9	Sweden	2459.5	0.9	Sweden	1768.5	0.9	Sweden	1819.2	0.8	Denmark	1622.7	0.9
10	Spain	1518.2	0.3	Denmark	1339.9	1.0	Denmark	1446.0	0.9	Italy	1622.7	0.1

	1996	US$ mil	% GDP	1997	US$ mil	% GDP	1998	US$ mil	% GDP	1999	US$ mil	% GDP
1	United States	9439.3	0.2	Japan	9358.0	0.2	Japan	10,640.1	0.3	Japan	12,162.6	0.3
2	Japan	9377.0	0.1	United States	6878.0	0.1	United States	8786.0	0.1	United States	9145.3	0.1
3	France	7600.9	0.3	France	6306.6	0.4	France	5741.6	0.4	France	5639.3	0.4
4	Germany	7451.3	0.5	Germany	5856.8	0.3	Germany	5580.7	0.3	Germany	5515.3	0.3
5	Italy	3246.3	0.8	United Kingdom	3433.1	0.3	United Kingdom	3863.5	0.3	United Kingdom	3426.3	0.2
6	Netherlands	3198.7	0.3	Netherlands	2946.7	0.8	Netherlands	3041.6	0.8	Netherlands	3134.0	0.8
7	United Kingdom	2415.5	0.2	Canada	2044.6	0.3	Italy	2278.3	0.2	Italy	1805.7	0.2
8	Canada	1999.0	0.7	Sweden	1730.6	0.7	Canada	1706.6	0.3	Denmark	1733.3	1.0
9	Sweden	1795.5	0.3	Denmark	1636.6	1.0	Denmark	1704.3	1.0	Canada	1706.3	0.3
10	Norway	1772.4	1.0	Norway	1306.1	0.8	Sweden	1572.7	0.6	Sweden	1629.9	0.6

	2000	US$ mil	% GDP	2001	US$ mil	% GDP	2002	US$ mil	% GDP	2003	US$ mil	% GDP
1	Japan	13,508.0	0.3	United States	11,429.4	0.1	United States	13,290.1	0.1	United States	16,319.5	0.2
2	United States	9954.9	0.1	Japan	9846.8	0.2	Japan	9283.0	0.2	Japan	8879.7	0.2
3	Germany	5030.0	0.3	Germany	4989.5	0.3	France	5486.2	0.4	France	7253.1	0.4
4	United Kingdom	4501.3	0.3	United Kingdom	4566.2	0.3	Germany	5324.4	9.3	Germany	6784.2	0.3
5	France	4104.7	0.3	France	4198.0	0.3	United Kingdom	4929.0	0.3	United Kingdom	6261.8	0.3

(Continued)

TABLE 7.32 (*Continued*)

	2000	US$ mil	% GDP	2001	US$ mil	% GDP	2002	US$ mil	% GDP	2003	US$ mil	% GDP
6	Netherlands	3134.8	0.8	Netherlands	3172.5	0.8	Netherlands	3338.0	0.8	Netherlands	3972.2	0.7
7	Sweden	1799.0	0.7	Spain	1737.0	0.3	Italy	2332.1	0.2	Italy	2432.9	0.2
8	Canada	1743.6	0.2	Sweden	1665.6	0.7	Sweden	2011.6	0.8	Sweden	2400.1	0.8
9	Denmark	1664.2	1.0	Denmark	1634.4	1.0	Canada	2004.2	0.3	Norway	2043.9	0.9
10	Italy	1376.3	0.1	Italy	1627.0	0.1	Spain	1712.2	0.3	Canada	2030.6	0.2

	2004	US$ mil	% GDP	2005	US$ mil	% GDP	2006	US$ mil	% GDP	2007	US$ mil	% GDP
1	United States	19,704.9	0.2	United States	27,934.7	0.2	United States	23,532.1	0.2	United States	21,786.9	0.2
2	Japan	8922.5	0.2	Japan	13,125.6	0.3	United Kingdom	12,459.0	0.5	Germany	12,290.7	0.4
3	France	8472.6	0.4	United Kingdom	10,771.7	0.5	Japan	11,135.7	0.3	France	9883.6	0.4
4	United Kingdom	7904.7	0.4	Germany	10,082.2	0.4	France	10,600.6	0.5	United Kingdom	9848.5	0.4
5	Germany	7534.2	0.3	France	10,026.2	0.4	Germany	10,434.8	0.4	Japan	7697.1	0.2
6	Netherlands	4203.8	0.7	Netherlands	5114.7	0.8	Netherlands	5451.7	0.8	Netherlands	6224.3	0.8
7	Sweden	2722.0	0.8	Italy	5090.9	0.3	Sweden	3955.0	1.0	Spain	5139.8	0.4
8	Canada	2599.1	0.3	Canada	3756.3	0.3	Spain	3813.7	0.3	Sweden	4338.9	0.9
9	Italy	2461.5	0.1	Sweden	3361.7	0.9	Canada	3683.2	0.3	Canada	4079.7	0.3
10	Spain	2437.0	0.2	Spain	3018.3	0.3	Italy	3641.1	0.2	Italy	3970.6	0.2

	2008	US$ mil	% GDP	2009	US$ mil	% GDP	2010	US$ mil	% GDP	2011	US$ mil	% GDP
1	United States	26,436.8	0.2	United States	28,831.3	0.2	United States	30,353.2	0.2	United States	30,919.6	0.2
2	Germany	13,980.9	0.4	France	12,601.6	0.5	United Kingdom	13,053.0	0.6	Germany	14,092.9	0.4
3	United Kingdom	11,499.9	0.4	Germany	12,079.2	0.4	Germany	12,985.4	0.4	United Kingdom	13,832.4	0.6
4	France	10,907.6	0.4	United Kingdom	11,282.6	0.5	France	12,915.1	0.5	France	12,997.2	0.5
5	Japan	9600.7	0.2	Japan	9466.6	0.2	Japan	11,057.7	0.2	Japan	10,831.4	0.2
6	Netherlands	6992.6	0.8	Spain	6584.1	0.5	Netherlands	6357.3	0.8	Netherlands	6344.0	0.8
7	Spain	6866.8	0.4	Netherlands	6426.1	0.8	Spain	5949.5	0.4	Sweden	5603.1	1.1
8	Italy	4860.6	0.2	Sweden	4548.2	1.1	Canada	5214.1	0.3	Canada	5458.6	0.3
9	Canada	4794.7	0.3	Norway	4081.2	1.1	Sweden	4533.5	1.0	Australia	4982.9	0.3
10	Sweden	4731.8	1.0	Canada	4000.1	0.3	Norway	4371.6	1.0	Norway	4755.6	1.0

	2012	US$ mil	% GDP	2013	US$ mil	% GDP	2014	US$ mil	% GDP
1	United States	30,687.0	0.2	United States	31,266.7	0.2	United States	33,095.5	0.2
2	United Kingdom	13,891.4	0.8	United Kingdom	17,871.4	0.7	United Kingdom	19,305.7	0.6
3	Germany	12,939.5	0.4	Germany	14,228.3	0.4	Germany	16,566.2	0.4
4	France	12,028.3	0.4	Japan	11,581.6	0.2	France	10,620.3	0.4

(Continued)

TABLE 7.32 (*Continued*)

	2012	US$ mil	% GDP	2013	US$ mil	% GDP	2014	US$ mil	% GDP
5	Japan	10,604.5	0.2	France	11,338.9	0.4	Japan	9266.3	0.2
6	Canada	5650.3	0.3	Sweden	5827.3	1.0	Sweden	6232.7	1.1
7	Netherlands	5522.8	0.7	Norway	5581.4	1.1	Netherlands	5573.0	0.6
8	Australia	5402.7	0.4	Netherlands	5435.5	0.6	Norway	5085.9	1.0
9	Sweden	5239.8	1,0	Canada	4947.2	0.3	Australia	4382.4	0.3
10	Norway	4753.0	1.0	Australia	4845.6	0.3	Canada	4240.0	0.2

become the norm among the aid donors. The size of the donation varies a lot among the top 10 donors. In 2014, the amount of aid donated by the United States, the top donor, was more than eight times that of Canada, the top 10th donor. The four largest donors are still the traditional advanced countries of the United States, the United Kingdom, Germany, and France. In 2014, the top 10 donors gave a total of US$114,368 million. However, the top 10 aid recipients in 2014, received a total of US$203,109.1 million. The difference must have come from the donors outside the top 10.

VIII FOREIGN DIRECT INVESTMENT

The data on FDI are available from the Division on Investment and Enterprise within the UNCTAD. FDI is defined as "an investment involving a long-term relationship and reflecting a lasting interest in and control by a resident entity in one economy (foreign direct investor or parent enterprise) of an enterprise resident in a different economy (FDI enterprise or affiliate enterprise or foreign affiliate)." The level of FDI indicates an economy's openness, and world acceptability in the global economy. In general, FDI is always welcome, as it provides additional productive resources to the receiving country. According to the theory of comparative advantage, investment should flow to economies with lower costs of production. On the contrary, advocates of protectionism focus more on job losses when investments move abroad. To balance this debate, one has to ask whether the foreign host country is attractive and competitive, or whether the domestic home economy is becoming unattractive and losing competitiveness. There are thus two sides to the argument. The "pull" argument suggests that foreign economies are more attractive due to low costs of production. The "push" argument believes that it is the high cost of domestic production that makes domestic investment unattractive, and investors naturally choose to leave and invest overseas where conditions are more market-friendly. Hence, is the reason for the loss of investment due to the low cost abroad, or due to the high cost at home?

Many successful Asian economies have been attractive to FDI, partly because they adopted market-friendly policies. However, one also has to understand that many uncompetitive economic features, such as high taxes, high labor wages, and high welfare provisions, were "home-grown." Once market-unfriendly policies are adopted, it would become a matter of time before capital migrates outward. Outward investment is due not so much to attractive conditions overseas, but to unattractive policies adopted at home. Once capital, which is always the most mobile economic resource, departs, it is not easy for the investment to return. Hence, it would be better for these decision-makers to be aware of the subsequent economic consequences (Borensztein et al., 1998; Smarzynska Javorcik, 2004; Moran, 2012).

Table 7.33 summarizes the number of years in the top 10 of the largest inward and outward FDI countries for the period 1980−2014. One observation is that both the largest inward and outward foreign investment countries are mainly the developed industrialized countries from North America and Europe, suggesting cross-country investment among these countries. Depending on the actual content of the investment, their performance shows that these countries are both the investors overseas, as well as the recipients of inward FDIs. In short, the industrialized countries are still the main targets for foreign investment flows. Unlike the Asian countries whose comparative advantages are market-friendly policies, the comparative advantages of industrialized countries would probably be their technology and natural resources.

TABLE 7.33 Number of Years in the Top 10 of Foreign Direct Investment Countries

1980–89		1990–99		2000–14		1980–2014	
INWARD FOREIGN DIRECT INVESTMENT							
United States	10	United States	10	United States	15	United States	35
France	10	United Kingdom	10	China	15	United Kingdom	32
Spain	10	France	10	Hong Kong	14	China	27
United Kingdom	9	Belgium	10	United Kingdom	13	Canada	24
Australia	9	Netherlands	8	Belgium	9	France	23
Canada	8	China	8	Germany	9	Belgium	23
Mexico	8	Canada	7	Canada	9	Spain	23
Brazil	6	Singapore	6	Spain	8	Netherlands	21
Netherlands	5	Spain	5	Netherlands	7	Hong Kong	21
Belgium	4	Germany	5	British Virgin Is.	7	Australia	17
Saudi Arabia	4	Brazil	4	Russia	7	Germany	17
China	4	Hong Kong	4	Singapore	6	Brazil	16
Singapore	3	Sweden	4	Brazil	6	Mexico	15
Hong Kong	3	Australia	3	Australia	5	Singapore	15
Germany	3	Mexico	3	Mexico	4	British Virgin Is.	7
Italy	3	Malaysia	2	France	3	Italy	7
Netherlands	1	Italy	1	Italy	3	Russia	7
				India	3	Saudi Arabia	5
				Ireland	2	Sweden	4
				Saudi Arabia	1	India	3
				Switzerland	1	Malaysia	2
				Denmark	1	Ireland	2
				Luxembourg	1	Switzerland	1
						Denmark	1
						Luxembourg	1
OUTWARD FOREIGN DIRECT INVESTMENT							
United States	10	United States	10	United States	14	United States	34
United Kingdom	10	United Kingdom	10	Japan	14	Japan	34
Germany	10	Germany	10	Canada	13	France	32
Netherlands	10	Netherlands	10	France	12	Germany	32
France	10	France	10	Germany	12	Netherlands	31
Japan	10	Japan	10	Netherlands	11	United Kingdom	30
Sweden	10	Switzerland	9	United Kingdom	10	Canada	28
Canada	9	Hong Kong	7	Spain	9	Switzerland	19
Australia	7	Canada	6	Hong Kong	9	Hong Kong	17
Italy	6	Belgium	6	Belgium	7	Sweden	16
Switzerland	3	Italy	4	British Virgin Is.	7	Belgium	15

(Continued)

TABLE 7.33   *(Continued)*

1980—89		1990—99		2000—14		1980—2014	
Belgium	2	Sweden	4	Switzerland	7	Italy	15
South Africa	1	Spain	3	China	7	Spain	12
Hong Kong	1	Singapore	1	Russia	6	Australia	7
Taiwan	1			Italy	5	British Virgin Is.	7
				Luxembourg	3	China	7
				Sweden	2	Russia	6
				Singapore	1	Luxembourg	3
				Ireland	1	Singapore	2
						Taiwan	1
						Ireland,	1
						South Africa	1

The top Asian countries included China, Hong Kong, Singapore, Malaysia, and India. China has performed much more strongly in inward FDI, with 4, 8, and 15 years in the top 10 in the 1980s, 1990s, and 2000—14, respectively. On the contrary, China's outward FDI has become strong only since the turn of the century, with 7 years in the top 10 from 2000 to 2014. Both Hong Kong and Singapore showed strong performances in inward FDI. Hong Kong is much stronger than Singapore when it comes to outward FDI, implying that Hong Kong's inward investment would have been meant for China, since Hong Kong has been serving as a mediator for China (Sung, 1991). Other than China, Russia has also come into the top 10 since the turn of the century, with 7 and 6 years, respectively, in the inward and outward FDI in the period 2000—14. Mexico and Brazil are the only two countries from Latin America, while South Africa is the only African country, with 1 year in the top 10 in the outward category. The British Virgin Islands are probably more of an offshore investment center than a destination for FDI. Lastly, Saudi Arabia is the only Middle East country that scored 5 years in the top 10 in inward foreign investment. Surprisingly, the oil exporting countries are not large foreign investors.

Table 7.34 shows the top 10 recipients of inward FDI in the period 1980 — 2014 expressed in value terms. The United States has remained the largest recipient of inward FDI, and the amount has been increasing over the years. However, the large inward investment has occupied only a small percentage of GDP in the United States, with 2.1% as the highest in 2008. This pattern of a low percentage of GDP is similar in most other European countries and China. It is only the smaller economies, typically Singapore and Hong Kong, where their inward FDI occupied a two-digit GDP percentage in most cases. The only exception is the British Virgin Islands, whose inward FDI is 1000 times higher than its GDP, reflecting its nature as an off-shore investment center.

Table 7.35 shows the largest inward FDI recipients measured by percentage of GDP. These recipients are mainly small world economies, with Singapore and Hong Kong being the stronger economies in the group. While in the 1980s, the largest recipients experienced a two-digit percentage of GDP in most cases, there are also cases of countries that showed a three-digit GDP percentage in their inward FDI. Table 7.35 also shows that this group of economies is quite diverse, and although many have an FDI which is a large percentage of GDP, the actual amount of inward FDI is very small. Nonetheless, the sample period shows that many island economies in the 1980s were replaced by African countries, small oil exporting countries, and in some years, European countries were included. The economic lesson is that these small economies should make good use of the inward FDI for growth and development, especially if the inward investment occupies a large percentage of their GDP. The high inward investments also reflect the correct decision to adopt market-friendly policies. Remaining competitive and adopting attractive market-friendly policies ensures inward FDI that promotes growth and development in small economies.

The data on outward investment are shown in Tables 7.36 and 7.37, respectively, in value terms and in percentage of GDP. The most important observation is that most outward foreign investors are mainly the conventional strong industrialized countries of the United States, the United Kingdom, Germany, France, and other European countries. In Asia, Japan has shown a strong performance, while both China and Russia have been

TABLE 7.34　Top 10 Largest Inward Foreign Direct Investment: Ranked by Value (US$ Million)

	1980	US$ mil	% GDP	1981	US$ mil	% GDP	1982	US$ mil	% GDP	1983	US$ mil	% GDP
1	United States	16,918.0	0.6	United States	25,195.0	0.8	United States	13,810.0	0.4	United States	11,518.0	0.3
2	United Kingdom	10,122.8	1.8	Saudi Arab.	6498.1	3.5	Saudi Arab.	11,128.4	7.3	United Kingdom	5178.8	1.1
3	Canada	5807.3	2.1	United Kingdom	5879.4	1.1	United Kingdom	5413.3	1.1	Saudi Arab.	4943.9	3.8
4	France	3328.2	0.5	Mexico	3075.9	1.0	Brazil	3115.2	1.3	Australia	2991.0	1.6
5	Netherlands	2518.7	1.3	Brazil	2521.9	1.1	Australia	2286.3	1.2	Mexico	2191.6	1.2
6	Mexico	2099.3	0.9	France	2426.1	0.4	Mexico	1900.3	0.9	Canada	2001.8	0.6
7	Brazil	1910.2	1.0	Australia	2346.5	1.2	Spain	1782.7	0.9	Germany	1711.1	0.2
8	Australia	1866.2	1.1	Hong Kong	2062.8	6.6	Singapore	1601.9	10.1	France	1631.0	0.3
9	Belgium	1544.8	1.2	Netherlands	1883.4	1.2	France	1559.0	0.3	Spain	1622.4	1.0
10	Spain	1492.7	0.6	Spain	1706.8	0.8	Belgium	1472.2	1.6	Brazil	1326.1	0.8

	1984	US$ mil	% GDP	1985	US$ mil	% GDP	1986	US$ mil	% GDP	1987	US$ mil	% GDP
1	United States	25,567.0	0.6	United States	20,490.0	0.5	United States	36,145.0	0.8	United States	59,581.0	1.2
2	Saudi Arab.	4849.9	4.1	United Kingdom	5668.3	1.2	United Kingdom	8274.7	1.5	United Kingdom	14,684.8	2.0
3	Canada	4753.4	1.3	France	2207.8	0.4	Australia	5369.8	2.8	Canada	8114.7	1.9
4	France	2196.5	0.4	Australia	2098.6	1.2	Spain	3450.6	1.4	Hong Kong	6249.8	12.3
5	Spain	1771.8	1.0	Mexico	1983.6	0.9	Netherlands	3355.6	1.7	Australia	5190.5	2.3
6	Mexico	1541.0	0.7	Spain	1967.8	1.1	France	2861.5	0.4	France	4899.2	0.5
7	Brazil	1501.2	0.9	China	1956.0	0.6	Canada	2852.8	0.8	Spain	4570.7	1.4
8	China	1419.0	0.5	Netherlands	1615.7	1.1	Mexico	2400.7	1.6	Italy	4174.6	0.5
9	Italy	1320.6	0.3	Brazil	1418.4	0.8	Germany	2319.2	0.2	Singapore	2836.2	13.2
10	Singapore	1301.9	6.7	Canada	1372.4	0.4	China	2243.7	0.7	Mexico	2634.6	1.6

	1988	US$ mil	% GDP	1989	US$ mil	% GDP	1990	US$ mil	% GDP	1991	US$ mil	% GDP
1	United States	58,571.0	1.1	United States	69,010.0	1.2	United States	48,422.0	0.8	United States	22,799.0	0.4
2	United Kingdom	20,566.7	2.3	United Kingdom	28,478.0	3.1	United Kingdom	30,461.1	2.8	France	16,186.5	1.3
3	Australia	8476.4	2.9	France	13,074.4	1.3	France	16,520.2	1.3	United Kingdom	14,846.2	1.3
4	France	7196.7	0.7	Spain	8428.4	2.0	Netherlands	11,063.3	3.5	Spain	9633.0	1.7
5	Spain	7020.6	1.9	Australia	7936.1	2.5	Spain	10,797.2	2.0	Belgium	9362.6	4.4
6	Italy	6801.4	0.8	Netherlands	7836.9	3.1	Belgium	8046.7	3.9	Sweden	6353.2	2.3
7	Canada	6124.9	1.2	Belgium	7020.3	4.3	Australia	7904.4	2.4	Netherlands	6074.6	1.9
8	Belgium	5212.5	3.2	Germany	6927.8	0.5	Canada	7582.3	1.3	Singapore	4887.1	10.7
9	Hong Kong	4978.9	8.3	Canada	6010.2	1.1	Italy	6344.9	0.5	Mexico	4761.5	1.4
10	Netherlands	4752.2	1.8	China	3392.6	0.7	Singapore	5574.7	14.3	Germany	4727.2	0.3

	1992	US$ mil	% GDP	1993	US$ mil	% GDP	1994	US$ mil	% GDP	1995	US$ mil	% GDP
1	United States	19,222.0	0.3	United States	50,663.0	0.7	United States	45,095.0	0.6	United States	58,772.0	0.8
2	France	18,750.7	1.3	China	27,515.0	4.4	China	33,766.5	6.0	China	37,520.5	5.1

(Continued)

TABLE 7.34 *(Continued)*

	1992	US$ mil	% GDP	1993	US$ mil	% GDP	1994	US$ mil	% GDP	1995	US$ mil	% GDP
3	United Kingdom	15,472.8	1.3	France	16,628.3	1.2	France	15,680.6	1.1	France	23,562.5	1.5
4	Belgium	11,285.8	4.8	United Kingdom	14,804.5	1.4	Mexico	10,972.5	2.3	United Kingdom	19,969.4	1.6
5	China	11,007.5	2.2	Belgium	10,750.0	4.8	United Kingdom	9252.8	0.8	Sweden	14,448.3	5.5
6	Spain	10,665.7	1.7	Spain	8571.5	1.6	Spain	8883.5	1.7	Germany	12,024.5	0.5
7	Netherlands	6392.1	1.8	Hong Kong	6929.6	5.8	Singapore	8550.2	11.6	Singapore	11,942.8	13.6
8	Australia	5479.4	1.7	Netherlands	6359.1	1.8	Belgium	8513.6	3.5	Netherlands	11,723.7	2.6
9	Malaysia	5138.0	8.0	Malaysia	5741.0	7.9	Canada	8204.1	1.4	Australia	11,678.8	0.3
10	Canada	4723.7	0.8	Canada	4731.6	0.8	Hong Kong	7827.9	5.8	Belgium	10,688.7	3.7

	1996	US$ mil	% GDP	1997	US$ mil	% GDP	1998	US$ mil	% GDP	1999	US$ mil	% GDP
1	United States	84,455.0	1.0	United States	103,398.0	1.2	United States	174,434.0	1.9	United States	283,376.0	2.9
2	China	41,725.5	4.8	China	45,257.0	4.7	United Kingdom	74,321.3	4.8	Belgium	119,692.9	46.0
3	United Kingdom	24,435.3	1.9	United Kingdom	33,226.6	2.3	China	45,462.8	4.4	United Kingdom	87,978.9	5.6
4	France	21,746.7	1.3	France	23,382.6	1.6	Netherland	37,277.3	8.6	Sweden	61,135.0	22.6
5	Netherlands	16,186.8	3.6	Brazil	18,992.9	2.2	France	31,239.8	2.1	Germany	56,075.7	2.5
6	Belgium	14,063.9	5.0	Singapore	15,701.7	15.7	Brazil	28,855.6	3.4	France	46,546.0	3.1
7	Singapore	11,432.4	11.9	Mexico	12,829.6	2.9	Germany	24,593.2	1.1	Netherlands	41,203.2	9.3
8	Brazil	10,791.7	1.3	Germany	12,244.6	0.6	Canada	22,803.4	3.6	China	40,318.7	3.7
9	Hong Kong	10,460.2	6.5	Belgium	11,998.3	4.7	Belgium	22,690.5	8.7	Brazil	28,578.4	4.8
10	Canada	9633.8	1.5	Canada	11,525.2	1.8	Sweden	19,918.9	7.5	Hong Kong	25,355.3	15.3

	2000	US$ mil	% GDP	2001	US$ mil	% GDP	2002	US$ mil	% GDP	2003	US$ mil	% GDP
1	United States	314,007.0	3.0	United States	159,461.0	1.5	United States	74,457.0	0.7	China	53,504.7	3.2
2	Germany	198,276.5	10.2	Netherland	51,927.5	12.2	Germany	53,523.0	2.6	United States	53,146.0	0.5
3	United Kingdom	121,897.7	7.8	China	46,877.6	3.5	China	52,742.9	3.6	Belgium	33,476.1	10.5
4	Belgium	88,738.7	37.3	United Kingdom	36,934.9	2.4	Spain	39,222.6	5.6	Netherlands	32,819.6	5.7
5	Canada	66,795.1	9.0	Mexico	30,032.0	4.3	Ireland	29,323.8	22.9	Germany	32,376.9	1.3
6	Netherlands	63,855.0	15.5	Hong Kong	29,060.7	17.2	Netherland	25,038.3	5.4	Spain	25,819.3	2.8
7	Hong Kong	54,581.9	31.8	Spain	28,408.1	4.5	Mexico	24,036.0	3.3	Ireland	22,781.3	13.8
8	China	40,714.8	3.4	Canada	27,663.4	3.8	Canada	22,155.5	2.9	Italy	19,424.4	1.2
9	Spain	39,575.1	6.6	Germany	26,402.4	1.4	France	21,514.6	1.4	Mexico	18,890.6	2.6
10	Denmark	33,823.5	20.6	Brazil	22,457.4	4.0	United Kingdom	21,138.4	1.3	Hong Kong	17,830.8	11.0

	2004	US$ mil	% GDP	2005	US$ mil	% GDP	2006	US$ mil	% GDP	2007	US$ mil	% GDP
1	United States	135,826.0	1.1	United Kingdom	183,822.5	7.6	United States	237,136.0	1.7	United States	215,952.0	1.5
2	United Kingdom	61,679.3	2.7	United States	104,773.0	0.8	United Kingdom	148,739.5	5.7	United Kingdom	181,660.8	6.1

(Continued)

II. THE GLOBAL ECONOMY: PERFORMANCE, CLASSIFICATION, AND CHALLENGES

TABLE 7.34   *(Continued)*

	2004	US$ mil	% GDP	2005	US$ mil	% GDP	2006	US$ mil	% GDP	2007	US$ mil	% GDP
3	China	60,630.0	3.1	China	72,406.0	3.2	China	72,715.0	2.6	Netherlands	119,635.9	14.3
4	Belgium	43,557.9	11.7	Germany	47,449.4	1.7	Canada	60,293.9	4.6	Canada	116,820.6	8.0
5	Australia	39,611.7	5.8	Netherlands	39,047.2	5.8	Belgium	58,893.0	14.4	Belgium	93,429.3	19.8
6	Hong Kong	29,153.8	17.2	Belgium	34,370.5	8.9	Germany	55,653.9	1.9	China	83,521.0	2.4
7	Mexico	25,130.0	3.3	Hong Kong	34,057.8	18.8	Switzerland	43,717.9	10.1	Germany	80,212.1	2.3
8	Spain	24,760.7	2.3	France	33,233.7	1.5	Italy	42,580.9	2.2	Spain	64,264.4	4.3
9	Singapore	24,390.3	21.4	Canada	25,691.6	2.2	Hong Kong	41,810.6	21.6	France	63,499.6	2.4
10	Italy	20,125.9	1.1	Spain	25,020.2	2.2	Russia	37,594.8	3.8	Hong Kong	58,403.5	27.6

	2008	US$ mil	% GDP	2009	US$ mil	% GDP	2010	US$ mil	% GDP	2011	US$ mil	% GDP
1	United States	306,366.0	2.1	United States	143,604.0	1.0	United States	198,049.0	1.3	United States	229,862.0	1.5
2	China	108,312.0	2.4	China	95,000.0	1.9	China	114,734.0	1.9	China	123,985.0	1.7
3	United Kingdom	93,364.3	3.3	United Kingdom	90,590.9	3.9	Hong Kong	70,540.7	30.9	Hong Kong	96,580.8	38.9
4	Spain	76,992.5	4.7	Belgium	75,169.2	15.5	Germany	65,642.4	1.9	Belgium	78,257.6	14.8
5	Russia	74,782.9	4.5	Hong Kong	55,535.2	25.9	Belgium	60,634.8	12.5	Germany	67,514.6	1.8
6	Canada	61,552.5	4.0	BritVirgin Is	46,503.3	a	United Kingdom	58,954.3	2.5	Brazil	66,660.1	2.5
7	Hong Kong	58,315.4	26.6	Netherland	38,752.1	4.5	Singapore	55,075.8	23.3	BriVirginIs	57,695.2	a
8	BritVirgin Is	51,722.4	a	Russia	36,583.1	3.0	BritVirgin Is	50,645.5	a	Australia	57,050.1	3.7
9	India	47,102.4	3.7	Saudi Arab	36,457.8	8.5	Brazil	48,506.5	2.2	Russia	55,083.6	2.9
10	Australia	46,896.4	4.4	India	35,633.9	2.7	Russia	43,167.8	2.8	Singapore	48,001.7	17.4

	2012	US$ mil	% GDP	2013	US$ mil	% GDP	2014	US$ mil	% GDP
1	United States	169,680.0	1.0	United States	23,0768.0	1.4	China	128,500.0	1.2
2	China	121,080.0	1.4	China	123,911.0	1.3	Hong Kong	103,254.2	35.5
3	Luxembourg	79,645.0	142.3	BriVirginIs.	92,300.0	a	United States	92,397.0	0.5
4	Hong Kong	70,179.8	26.7	Hong Kong	74,294.2	26.9	United Kingdom	72,241.0	2.4
5	BriVirginIs	67,973.0	a	Canada	70,565.2	3.8	Singapore	67,523.0	21.9
6	Brazil	65,271.9	2.7	Russia	69,218.9	3.3	Brazil	62,494.8	2.7
7	United Kingdom	59,374.7	2.3	Singapore	64,793.2	21.4	BritVirgin Is	56,540.8	a
8	Singapore	56,659.2	19.5	Brazil	63,995.9	2.7	Canada	53,864.0	3.0
9	Australia	55,802.4	3.5	Australia	54,239.1	3.5	Australia	51,854.2	3.5
10	Russia	50,587.6	2.5	United Kingdom	47,675.3	1.8	India	34,416.8	1.7

[a]*The % GDP figures for British Virgin Islands are: 2008 = 5214.0%; 2009 = 5308.6%; 2010 = 5665.0%; 2011 = 6298.6%; 2012 = 7474.9%; 2013 = 10,080.8%; 2014 = 6265.7%.*

included in the list since 2009. Canada has also performed strongly in a number of years. The high performance by Hong Kong and the British Virgin Islands, e.g., probably reflected their open status in investment transactions as off-shore investment centers. In 2014, Hong Kong ranked second highest for the first time.

In value terms, the outward investment from the United States has been much larger than other countries, though in some years, the highest ranking has been taken over by others, typically by Japan, the United Kingdom, and other European countries. The outward investment by the United States and key European countries occupied only a small percentage of their GDP. It is only the smaller European countries, such as the Netherlands, Switzerland, and Belgium that showed a two-digit GDP percentage in their outward FDI.

TABLE 7.35 Top 10 Largest Inward FDI Recipients: Ranked by Percentage of GDP

	1980	% GDP	US$ mil	1981	% GDP	US$ mil	1982	% GDP	US$ mil	1983	% GDP	US$ mil
1	Saint Lucia	22.8	30.9	Cayman Is.	47.2	97.1	Liberia	34.3	312.9	BritVirgin Is	22.3	17.5
2	Antigua& Bar.	14.6	19.6	Liberia	32.7	288.0	Saint Lucia	14.1	26.5	StKitts& Nevis	15.9	13.5
3	Botswana	13.1	111.6	Saint Lucia	22.0	38.2	Antigua& Bar.	13.6	23.0	Suriname	6.7	81.5
4	Cayman Is.	11.3	19.6	Antigua& Bar.	14.7	22.4	Singapore	10.1	1601.9	Singapore	6.3	1133.9
5	Singapore	10.2	1235.8	Singapore	11.6	1660.0	Cayman Is.	8.1	19.9	Liberia	5.4	49.1
6	Yemen, Dem	9.5	33.9	Yemen, Dem	9.8	40.0	Panama	7.6	366.6	PapuaNew Gui	5.3	138.9
7	Liberia	9.4	71.9	Botswana	9.1	88.4	Saudi Arabia	7.3	11,128.4	Seychelles	5.2	9.1
8	Panama	5.4	218.5	Hong Kong	6.6	2062.8	Vanuatu	6.5	6.9	Cayman Is.	5.1	17.5
9	Seychelles	5.2	9.5	Panama	6.6	303.2	Yemen, Dem	6.2	30.0	Vanuatu	5.1	5.9
10	Togo	3.8	42.7	Vanuatu	6.6	7.1	Seychelles	5.5	10.0	Saint Lucia	4.9	10.0

	1984	% GDP	US$ mil	1985	% GDP	US$ mil	1986	% GDP	US$ mil	1987	% GDP	US$ mil
1	Cayman Is.	173.8	668.2	Cayman Is.	109.1	454.0	Montserrat	10.2	4.7	Montserrat	22.4	11.2
2	Singapore	6.7	1301.9	BritVirgin Is	18.3	16.4	Singapore	9.1	1710.3	Cayman Is.	19.6	104.7
3	Botswana	6.4	62.2	StKitts&Nevis	7.5	8.0	Antigua&Bar.	7.8	22.6	Singapore	13.1	2836.2
4	StKitts&Nevi	6.3	6.0	Saint Lucia	6.8	17.0	Neth.Antilles	7.5	115.8	Hong Kong	12.3	6249.8
5	Saint Lucia	5.4	12.0	Botswana	6.4	53.6	StKitts&Nevis	7.3	9.2	StKitts&Nevis	11.8	16.7
6	Seychelles	5.3	9.8	Antigua&Bar	6.4	15.6	Botswana	6.3	70.4	Antigua&Bar	11.4	38.6
7	Vanuatu	5.3	7.4	Seychelles	5.7	11.7	Equ. Guinea	5.6	5.6	Vanuatu	9.4	12.9
8	PapuaNewGu	4.5	115.7	Singapore	5.6	1046.8	Seychelles	5.6	14.2	Dominica	9.1	13.5
9	Saudi Arabia	4.1	4849.9	Chad	5.4	53.7	Swaziland	5.5	34.2	Grenada	8.3	14.7
10	Liberia	4.1	36.2	Egypt	4.9	1177.6	StVincent&G	4.9	7.4	Botswana	7.4	113.6

	1988	% GDP	US$ mil	1989	% GDP	US$ mil	1990	% GDP	US$ mil	1991	% GDP	US$ mil
1	Liberia	30.0	290.2	Liberia	65.8	656.0	Liberia	46.2	225.2	Equ. Guinea	31.4	41.3
2	Montserrat	16.8	9.5	BritVirgin Is.	45.4	71.0	StKitts&Nevis	23.4	48.8	Aruba	21.2	184.7
3	Singapore	13.8	3655.0	StKitts&Nevis	22.0	40.8	Aruba	17.1	130.5	Montserrat	12.5	8.0
4	Hong Kong	8.3	4978.9	Cayman Is.	10.6	79.5	Singapore	14.3	5574.7	Vanuatu	12.5	25.5
5	Antigua&Bar.	8.3	33.0	Antigua&Bar.	9.8	43.1	Anguilla	14.3	10.8	Bahrain	11.9	619.5
6	StKitts&Nevis	7.9	13.1	Dominica	9.3	17.2	Antigua&Bar.	12.8	58.8	Saint Lucia	11.9	59.4
7	Grenada	7.6	15.0	Singapore	9.2	2886.7	Montserrat	12.7	9.6	Antigua&Bar.	11.4	54.8
8	Dominica	6.9	11.9	Montserrat	7.7	4.9	BritVirgin Is.	12.5	18.4	Singapore	10.7	4887.1
9	Seychelles	6.8	23.2	Swaziland	7.1	72.5	Saint Lucia	9.9	45.9	StKitts&Nevis	10.2	21.4
10	Vanuatu	6.7	10.8	Solomon Is.	6.9	11.6	Equa. Guinea	8.3	11.1	Anguilla	7.9	6.1

	1992	% GDP	US$ mil	1993	% GDP	US$ mil	1994	% GDP	US$ mil	1995	% GDP	US$ mil
1	Guyana	24.6	146.6	BritVirgin Is	286.2	676.0	BritVirgin Is	220.8	677.5	Equ. Guinea	38.1	63.3
2	Anguilla	18.3	15.4	Cayman Is.	41.6	459.8	Cayman Is.	38.9	467.1	Dominica	20.8	54.1

(Continued)

TABLE 7.35 (*Continued*)

	1992	% GDP	US$ mil	1993	% GDP	US$ mil	1994	% GDP	US$ mil	1995	% GDP	US$ mil
3	Yemen	16.0	718.0	Yemen	18.9	903.0	StVincent&GE	16.5	47.3	Anguilla	16.9	17.6
4	Bahrain	16.0	868.6	Equ. Guinea	13.8	22.3	qu. Guinea	14.2	17.0	Singapore	13.6	11,942.8
5	Vanuatu	12.4	26.5	Vanuatu	11.8	26.0	Vanuatu	12.4	29.8	Slovakia	13.0	2587.1
6	Dominica	9.0	20.4	StVincet&G	11.1	31.4	Guyana	12.3	106.7	Vanuatu	11.4	31.0
7	Grenada	8.9	22.6	Congo	10.6	286.1	Viet Nam	11.9	1944.5	Brunei Darus	11.1	582.8
8	Malaysia	8.0	5138.0	Zambia	9.6	314.4	Singapore	11.6	8550.2	Hungary	11.0	5103.5
9	Saint Lucia	7.4	40.9	Guyana	9.3	69.5	Anguilla	10.8	11.1	Turkmenistan	10.6	233.0
10	Montserrat	6.9	4.6	Solomon Is.	8.3	23.4	Trini&Tobag	10.5	521.0	StVincent&G	9.8	30.6

	1996	% GDP	US$ mil	1997	% GDP	US$ mil	1998	% GDP	US$ mil	1999	% GDP	US$ mil
1	BritVirgin Is	247.1	1109.6	BritVirgin Is	696.7	3636.7	BritVirgin Is	1460.5	8777.5	BritVirgin Is	1176.1	7915.4
2	Equ. Guinea	90.5	247.6	Cayman Is.	205.7	3150.9	Cayman Is.	216.6	4354.1	Cayman Is.	297.2	6475.8
3	Cayman Is.	87.6	1231.7	Liberia	62.4	213.8	Equ. Guinea	62.3	274.8	Liberia	50.8	256.3
4	Anguilla	30.3	33.2	StVincet&G	26.6	92.5	Liberia	45.5	190.3	Belgium	46.0	119,692.9
5	Bahrain	29.0	2048.2	Azerbaijan	26.5	1051.0	Madagascar	44.2	1652.3	Angola	30.0	2471.4
6	Azerbaijan	18.6	591.0	Trini&Tobag	17.4	999.6	StVincent&G.	23.7	89.0	Aruba	27.1	467.5
7	StVincent&G.	13.0	42.6	Anguilla	17.3	21.2	Azerbaijan	23.0	1023.0	Anguilla	25.8	38.0
8	Singapore	11.9	11,432.4	Singapore	15.8	15,701.7	Anguilla	20.2	28.1	Sweden	22.6	61,135.0
9	Vanuatu	11.6	32.7	Panama	12.9	1299.2	Eritrea	18.4	148.5	Montserrat	22.2	8.2
10	Brunei Daru.	11.5	653.6	Aruba	12.8	195.9	Bahamas	15.4	847.0	Congo	22.1	520.6

	2000	% GDP	US$ mil	2001	% GDP	US$ mil	2002	% GDP	US$ mil	2003	% GDP	US$ mil
1	BritVirgin Is	1315.9	9877.3	BritVirgin Is	430.0	3483.2	BritVirgin Is	187.3	1472.0	BritVirgin Is	437.1	3110.5
2	Cayman Is.	334.9	7626.9	Cayman Is.	167.9	3922.8	Chad	40.9	924.1	Liberia	86.0	372.2
3	Cook Is.	64.5	59.1	Equ. Guinea	55.5	940.7	Anguilla	24.2	38.2	Brunei Darus	45.4	3298.1
4	Belgium	37.3	88,738.7	Chad	23.6	459.9	Slovakia	23.7	5864.9	Azerbaijan	45.1	3285.0
5	Hong Kong	31.8	54,581.9	Anguilla	22.4	34.7	Ireland	22.9	29,323.8	Equ. Guinea	25.1	689.8
6	Anguilla	28.7	43.0	StKitts&Ne	19.6	90.3	Azerbaijan	22.3	1392.4	Chad	23.0	712.7
7	Ireland	25.8	25,779.4	Singapore	19.0	17,006.9	Luxembourg	18.2	4243.2	Antigua&Bar	21.4	179.4
8	StKitts&Nev	23.6	99.0	Angola	19.4	2145.5	Aruba	17.1	332.1	Anguilla	20.2	34.4
9	Denmark	20.6	33,823.5	Hong Kong	17.2	29,060.7	StKitts&Nevis	16.9	81.1	Angola	20.1	3504.7
10	Singapore	16.2	15,515.3	Antigua&Ba	14.5	111.9	Brunei Daru.	16.0	1035.5	Myanmar	18.7	1855.2

	2004	% GDP	US$ mil	2005	% GDP	US$ mil	2006	% GDP	US$ mil	2007	% GDP	US$ mil
1	BritVirgin Is	a	17,605.5	Cayman Is.	336.0	10,221.2	BritVirgin Is	800.5	7548.9	BritVirgin Is	a	31,763.7
2	Cayman Is.	363.3	9669.1	Anguilla	51.8	118.6	Cayman Is.	466.6	14,962.8	Cayman Is.	660.4	23,218.4
3	Anguilla	45.6	91.8	Marshall Is.	39.2	54.7	Luxembourg	76.9	32,219.5	Anguilla	33.8	120.1
4	Azerbaijan	41.0	3556.1	Mauritania	37.2	811.9	Anguilla	50.4	143.2	Iceland	32.0	6824.4
5	Mauritania	21.4	404.1	Antigua&B.	23.8	237.5	Antigua&Bar.	31.8	361.0	Bulgaria	27.7	12,388.9
6	Singapore	21.4	24,390.3	Estonia	20.0	2799.2	SaoTome&Pr	28.3	38.0	Hong Kong	27.6	58,403.5
7	Bermuda	18.5	831.6	StKitts&Ne	19.2	104.3	Malta	27.2	1843.6	Singapore	26.5	47,733.3

(Continued)

TABLE 7.35 *(Continued)*

	2004	% GDP	US$ mil	2005	% GDP	US$ mil	2006	% GDP	US$ mil	2007	% GDP	US$ mil
8	Hong Kong	17.2	29,153.8	Hong Kong	18.8	34,057.8	Singapore	25.0	36,924.0	Antigua&Ba	26.4	340.5
9	Tonga	15.8	37.5	Iceland	18.4	3080.7	Jordan	23.5	3544.0	Marshall Is.	26.1	40.7
10	Luxembourg	15.1	5179.6	Jordan	15.8	1984.5	Bulgaria	22.8	7804.9	SaoTome&P	24.7	36.0

	2008	% GDP	US$ mil	2009	% GDP	US$ mil	2010	% GDP	US$ mil	2011	% GDP	US$ mil
1	BritVirgin Is	a	51,722.4	BritVirgin Is	a	46,503.3	BritVirgin Is	a	50,645.5	BritVirgin Is	a	57,695.2
2	Cayman Is.	553.4	19,634.2	Cayman Is.	612.1	20,425.8	Cayman Is.	265.3	8666.5	Cayman Is.	451.4	15,116.4
3	SaoTome&P	41.7	79.1	Luxembourg	54.2	27,313.3	Luxembourg	73.7	38,587.5	Malta	161.9	15,510.3
4	Liberia	30.8	283.8	Montenegro	36.9	1527.3	Liberia	41.9	450.0	Liberia	51.0	785.3
5	Anguilla	28.5	100.8	Hong Kong	25.9	55,535.2	Solomon Is.	33.1	237.9	Mongolia	45.3	4714.6
6	Hong Kong	26.6	58,315.4	Turkmenista	22.5	4553.0	Hong Kong	30.9	70,540.7	Hong Kong	38.9	96,580.8
7	StKitts&Nev	25.0	183.9	Liberia	21.3	217.8	SaoTomeP.	25.9	50.6	Sierra Leone	32.4	950.5
8	Marshall Is.	24.4	40.5	Seychelles	20.2	171.4	Mongolia	23.5	1691.4	Mozambique	27.1	3558.5
9	Djibouti	23.5	228.9	StKitts&Nev	19.2	136.0	Singapore	23.3	55,075.8	Seychelles	19.4	207.3
10	StVincet&G	22.9	159.3	Solomon Is.	18.8	119.8	Seychelles	21.7	210.9	Bahamas	19.4	1533.3

	2012	% GDP	US$ mil	2013	% GDP	US$ mil	2014	% GDP	US$ mil
1	BritVirgin Is	a	67,973.0	BritVirgin Is	a	92,300.0	BritVirgin Is	a	56,540.8
2	Cayman Is.	215.6	7366.8	Cayman Is.	362.9	12,636.6	Cayman Is.	533.2	18,553.5
3	Luxembourg	142.3	79,645.0	Malta	95.7	9575.2	Malta	88.1	9278.9
4	Malta	130.3	12,061.2	Liberia	54.5	1061.3	Congo	39.1	5502.3
5	Liberia	56.8	984.6	Mozambique	38.5	6175.1	Hong Kong	35.5	103,254.2
6	Mozambique	36.9	5629.4	Luxembourg	37.6	23,248.5	Mozambique	28.7	4901.8
7	Mongolia	36.2	4451.8	Hong Kong	26.9	74,294.2	N.Caledonia	22.4	2287.7
8	N.Caledonia	30.7	2887.2	N.Caledonia	22.9	2260.9	Singapore	21.9	67,523.0
9	Mauritania	28.7	1388.6	Mauritania	22.3	1125.7	StVincent&G	19.0	138.6
10	Hong Kong	26.7	70,179.8	StVincet&G	22.2	159.9	Bahamas	18.8	1595.9

*The % GDP figures for British Virgin Islands are: 2004 = 2360.0%; 2007 = 3161.8%; 2008 = 5214.7%; 2009 = 5305.8%; 2010 = 5665.0% 2011 = 6298.6%; 2012 = 7474.9% 2013 = 10,080.8%; 2014 = 6265.7%.

Table 7.37 demonstrates the message that countries whose outward FDI is measured in GDP percentages are small economies, though the top 10 also included in some years such European countries as the United Kingdom, Sweden, Luxembourg, Ireland, and Belgium, and such Asian economies as Hong Kong and Singapore. In recent years in the sample period (1998–2014), a number of economies have emerged, including the emerging Eastern European countries of Estonia and Hungary. Other newcomers included Kuwait, the State of Palestine, Togo, and Cyprus.

The few economies whose outward investment occupied a three or larger digit GDP percentage are mainly island economies. Indeed, these island economies serve as offshore investment centers, and the large inward and outward investments could just be transfers rather than physical investments. Among the cases of two-digit GDP percentages, only a few exceeded 50% of their GDP, while mostly are in the low two-digit range, with a few with single-digits only. One can also note that although their GDP percentages are large, the equivalent amount in value terms is small, except those European and Asian countries. A typical example is the Marshall Islands, which in 2014 had only US$23.9 million in outward investment, yet that represented 11.7% of its GDP.

TABLE 7.36 Top 10 Largest Outward Investors: Ranked by Value (US$ Million)

1980	US$ mil	% GDP	1981	US$ mil	% GDP	1982	US$ mil	% GDP	1983	US$ mil	% GDP
1	United States	19,230.0	0.7	United States	13,227.0	0.4	Japan	4540.0	0.4	United States	9525.0	0.3
2	United Kingdom	7880.6	1.4	United Kingdom	9386.3	1.7	United Kingdom	3706.9	0.8	United Kingdom	5302.2	1.1
3	Netherlands	4832.8	2.5	Canada	5548.4	1.8	Netherlands	3065.0	2.0	Germany	3680.2	0.5
4	Germany	4699.3	0.5	Japan	4894.0	0.4	France	3063.1	0.5	Japan	3612.0	0.3
5	Canada	4098.5	1.5	France	4614.4	0.7	Germany	3020.2	0.4	Canada	2632.2	0.8
6	France	3137.3	0.4	Germany	4482.1	0.6	Canada	2401.7	0.8	Netherlands	2613.3	1.7
7	Japan	2385.0	0.2	Netherlands	4415.5	2.7	Sweden	1360.1	1.2	Italy	2022.4	0.5
8	South Africa	755.0	0.9	Italy	1391.8	0.3	United States	1078.0	0.0	France	1841.0	0.3
9	Italy	740.0	0.2	Sweden	825.4	0.6	Italy	969.0	0.2	Sweden	1522.6	1.5
10	Sweden	624.6	0.5	Australia	733.2	0.4	Australia	692.8	0.4	Hong Kong	566.0	1.9

1984	US$ mil	% GDP	1985	US$ mil	% GDP	1986	US$ mil	% GDP	1987	US$ mil	% GDP
1	United States	13,045.0	0.3	United States	13,388.0	0.3	United States	19,641.0	0.4	United Kingdom	31,309.3	4.2
2	United Kingdom	7733.4	1.7	United Kingdom	11,068.4	2.3	United Kingdom	17,294.1	2.9	United States	30,154.0	0.6
3	Japan	5965.0	0.5	Japan	6440.1	0.5	Japan	14,402.4	0.7	Japan	20,100.7	0.8
4	Germany	4737.2	0.7	Germany	5654.6	0.8	Germany	10,064.2	1.0	Germany	8726.5	0.7
5	Canada	3684.7	1.0	Switzerland	4572.8	4.2	France	5230.7	0.7	France	8701.0	0.9
6	Netherlands	2748.0	1.9	Canada	3862.4	1.1	Netherlands	4428.3	2.2	Netherlands	8535.9	3.5
7	France	2126.5	0.4	Netherlands	3088.2	2.2	Sweden	3947.7	2.7	Canada	7120.0	1.7
8	Italy	1881.6	0.4	France	2225.9	0.4	Canada	3500.5	0.9	Australia	5099.5	2.2
9	Sweden	1558.5	1.4	Australia	1886.3	1.0	Australia	3418.5	1.8	Sweden	4789.8	2.7
10	Australia	1403.2	0.7	Sweden	1827.2	1.6	Italy	2455.8	0.4	Belgium	2782.2	1.9

1988	US$ mil	% GDP	1989	US$ mil	% GDP	1990	US$ mil	% GDP	1991	US$ mil	% GDP
1	United Kingdom	37,205.8	4.1	Japan	46,251.2	1.5	Japan	50,774.9	1.6	United States	32,696.0	0.5
2	Japan	35,436.0	1.2	United States	37,604.0	0.7	France	38,302.2	3.0	Japan	31,638.3	0.9
3	United States	18,599.0	0.4	United Kingdom	35,163.5	3.8	United States	30,982.0	0.5	France	25,786.9	2.1
4	Germany	14,545.0	1.0	France	20,703.3	2.0	Germany	24,234.8	1.4	Germany	22,937.2	1.2
5	France	12,753.7	1.2	Germany	15,093.9	1.1	United Kingdom	17,948.2	1.6	United Kingdom	16,408.7	1.4
6	Switzerland	8694.7	4.1	Netherlands	14,543.1	5.7	Sweden	14,746.2	5.7	Netherlands	13,484.5	4.2
7	Sweden	7470.9	3.7	Sweden	10,286.5	4.8	Netherlands	14,371.9	4.6	Italy	7326.1	0.6
8	Netherlands	7233.2	2.8	Switzerland	7923.4	3.9	Italy	7613.5	0.6	Sweden	7054.7	2.6

(Continued)

TABLE 7.36 (*Continued*)

	1988	US$ mil	% GDP	1989	US$ mil	% GDP	1990	US$ mil	% GDP	1991	US$ mil	% GDP
9	Australia	6845.8	2.4	Taiwan	6951.0	4.6	Switzerland	7175.6	2.8	Switzerland	6541.2	2.5
10	Canada	6224.9	1.2	Belgium	6486.2	3.9	Belgium	6314.4	3.1	Belgium	6270.9	3.0

	1992	US$ mil	% GDP	1993	US$ mil	% GDP	1994	US$ mil	% GDP	1995	US$ mil	% GDP
1	United States	42,647.0	0.6	United States	77,247.0	1.1	United States	73,252.0	1.0	United States	92,074.0	1.2
2	France	31,854.1	2.3	United Kingdom	26,033.4	2.5	United Kingdom	32,199.5	2.8	United Kingdom	43,562.2	3.5
3	Germany	18,599.5	0.9	France	19,716.1	1.5	France	24,538.6	1.7	Germany	39,048.6	1.5
4	United Kingdom	17,738.6	1.5	Hong Kong	17,713.0	14.7	Hong Kong	21,437.0	15.8	Hong Kong	25,000.0	17.3
5	Japan	17,304.2	0.4	Germany	17,196.2	0.8	Germany	18,859.4	0.9	Japan	22,630.3	0.4
6	Netherlands	13,153.8	3.7	Japan	13,913.0	0.3	Japan	18,120.9	0.4	Netherlands	19,223.0	4.3
7	Belgium	11,407.0	4.8	Netherlands	9930.1	2.8	Netherlands	17,242.6	4.6	France	15,681.7	1.0
8	Hong Kong	8254.0	7.9	Switzerland	8764.1	3.3	Switzerland	10,793.4	3.7	Switzerland	12,210.0	3.5
9	Switzerland	6056.7	2.2	Italy	7221.3	0.7	Canada	9293.5	1.6	Belgium	11,603.0	4.0
10	Italy	5946.7	0.5	Canada	5702.0	1.0	Sweden	6701.1	3.0	Canada	11,461.6	1.9

	1996	US$ mil	% GDP	1997	US$ mil	% GDP	1998	US$ mil	% GDP	1999	US$ mil	% GDP
1	United States	84,426.0	1.0	United States	95,769.0	1.1	United States	131,004.0	1.4	United States	209,391.0	2.2
2	Germany	50,804.7	2.0	United Kingdom	61,586.1	4.3	United Kingdom	122,815.6	8.0	United Kingdom	201,450.7	12.9
3	United Kingdom	34,047.5	2.6	Germany	41,798.1	1.9	Germany	88,824.9	4.0	France	126,854.4	8.4
4	Netherlands	31,182.0	7.0	France	35,906.0	2.5	France	49,016.3	3.2	Belgium	122,304.2	47.0
5	France	30,123.5	1.9	Japan	25,993.1	0.6	Netherlands	36,822.5	8.5	Germany	108,688.4	4.9
6	Hong Kong	26,530.9	16.6	Netherlands	24,618.1	6.0	Canada	34,350.1	5.4	Netherlands	57,610.2	13.0
7	Japan	23,427.8	0.5	Hong Kong	24,406.8	13.8	Belgium	28,845.3	11.1	Spain	44,382.3	7.0
8	Switzerland	16,152.0	4.9	Canada	23,065.5	3.5	Sweden	24,478.6	9.2	Switzerland	33,276.2	11.4
9	Canada	13,096.2	2.1	Switzerland	17,731.9	6.1	Japan	24,152.1	0.6	Japan	22,743.0	0.5
10	Singapore	9196.4	9.5	Spain	14,396.6	2.4	Spain	20,375.9	3.3	Hong Kong	22,191.2	13.4

	2000	US$ mil	% GDP	2001	US$ mil	% GDP	2002	US$ mil	% GDP	2003	US$ mil	% GDP
1	United Kingdom	235,398.2	15.1	United States	124,873.0	1.2	United States	134,946.0	1.2	United States	129,352.0	1.1
2	France	161,947.7	11.8	United Kingdom	57,857.5	3.8	United Kingdom	50,699.7	3.0	United Kingdom	67,433.3	3.5
3	United States	142,626.0	1.4	France	52,823.7	3.8	Spain	32,714.7	4.6	Netherlands	55,812.8	9.8
4	Belgium	86,361.7	36.3	Netherlands	50,593.0	11.9	Japan	32,280.8	0.8	Belgium	38,322.5	12.0

(Continued)

TABLE 7.36　(*Continued*)

	2000	US$ mil	% GDP	2001	US$ mil	% GDP	2002	US$ mil	% GDP	2003	US$ mil	% GDP
5	Netherlands	75,634.4	18.3	Germany	39,889.6	2.0	Netherlands	32,017.6	6.9	Japan	28,800.5	0.7
6	Spain	58,213.3	9.8	Japan	38,332.9	0.9	Canada	26,772.7	3.6	Spain	28,717.5	3.2
7	Germany	56,557.0	2.9	Canada	36,028.8	4.9	France	23,299.6	1.5	Canada	22,924.2	2.6
8	Hong Kong	54,078.8	31.5	Spain	33,106.4	5.3	Germany	18,942.2	0.9	Sweden	21,112.4	6.4
9	Canada	44,678.2	6.0	BritVirginI.	23,714.6	a	Hong Kong	13,163.0	7.9	France	18,440.6	1.0
10	Switzerland	44,673.0	16.3	Singapore	20,027.0	22.4	Belgium	12,277.1	4.7	Switzerland	15,441.7	4.3

	2004	US$ mil	% GDP	2005	US$ mil	% GDP	2006	US$ mil	% GDP	2007	US$ mil	% GDP
1	United States	294,905.0	2.4	Netherlands	106,008.8	15.6	United States	224,220.0	1.6	United States	393,518.0	2.7
2	United Kingdom	100,141.0	4.4	United Kingdom	78,376.6	3.2	Germany	116,679.5	3.9	United Kingdom	319,329.6	10.8
3	Spain	60,531.9	5.7	Germany	74,542.4	2.6	Spain	104,248.0	8.2	Germany	169,320.5	4.9
4	Hong Kong	43,636.9	25.8	France	68,057.0	3.1	France	76,766.8	3.3	Spain	137,051.7	9.3
5	Canada	43,346.8	4.3	Switzerland	51,117.5	12.4	United Kingdom	75,852.8	2.9	France	110,643.0	4.1
6	Netherlands	37,018.2	5.7	Japan	45,781.2	1.0	Switzerland	75,823.7	17.5	Italy	96,231.0	4.4
7	Belgium	34,018.1	9.2	Spain	41,829.5	3.6	Netherlands	75,582.8	10.0	Belgium	80,127.2	17.0
8	Japan	30,951.4	0.7	Italy	39,362.3	2.1	Belgium	50,684.9	12.4	Japan	73,548.8	1.7
9	Switzerland	26,269.4	6.6	Belgium	32,658.1	8.4	Japan	50,265.9	1.2	Luxembourg	71,293.7	141.7
10	France	22,964.7	1.1	Sweden	27,712.3	7.1	Canada	46,213.7	3.5	Canada	64,627.1	4.4

	2008	US$ mil	% GDP	2009	US$ mil	% GDP	2010	US$ mil	% GDP	2011	US$ mil	% GDP
1	United States	308,296.0	2.1	United States	287,901.0	2.0	United States	277,779.0	1.8	United States	396,569.0	2.5
2	United Kingdom	189,044.9	6.8	France	100,865.0	3.7	Germany	125,450.8	3.7	United Kingdom	107,801.0	4.2
3	Japan	128,019.5	2.6	Japan	74,698.7	1.5	Hong Kong	86,247.2	37.7	Japan	107,599.1	1.8
4	France	103,281.9	3.5	Germany	68,541.3	2.0	Switzerland	85,700.7	14.6	Hong Kong	96,340.8	38.8
5	Canada	79,277.3	5.1	Hong Kong	59,201.6	27.7	China	68,811.0	1.1	Germany	77,929.5	2.1
6	Spain	74,717.2	4.6	China	56,530.0	1.1	Netherlands	68,358.0	8.2	China	74,654.0	1.0
7	Germany	71,506.9	1.9	Russia	43,280.5	3.5	Japan	56,263.4	1.0	Russia	66,850.8	3.5
8	Netherlands	68,491.6	7.3	Canada	39,601.1	2.9	BritVirginI.	54,162.0	a	BritVirgin I.	59,944.0	a
9	Italy	66,999.7	2.8	BritVirginI.	35,143.0	a	Russia	52,616.3	3.5	Italy	53,628.6	2.4
10	China	55,910.0	1.2	Ireland	26,615.5	11.3	France	48,156.1	1.8	Canada	52,147.9	2.9

	2012	US$ mil	% GDP	2013	US$ mil	% GDP	2014	US$ mil	% GDP
1	United States	311,347.0	1.9	United States	328,343.0	2.0	United States	336,943.0	1.9
2	Japan	122,548.7	2.1	Japan	135,748.8	2.8	Hong Kong	142,700.5	49.1
3	China	87,804.0	1.0	China	101,000.0	1.1	China	116,000.0	1.1
4	Hong Kong	83,410.5	31.8	Russia	86,506.5	4.2	Japan	113,628.8	2.5
5	Luxembourg	68,428.2	122.2	BritVirginI.	81,520.0	a	Germany	112,227.0	2.9

(Continued)

TABLE 7.36 (*Continued*)

	2012	US$ mil	% GDP	2013	US$ mil	% GDP	2014	US$ mil	% GDP
6	Germany	66,089.4	1.9	Hong Kong	80,773.1	29.3	Russia	56,438.0	3.1
7	BritVirginI	54,078.0	a	Netherlands	56,925.9	6.6	BritVirginI.	54,287.0	a
8	Canada	53,937.8	2.9	Canada	50,536.0	2.7	Canada	52,620.0	2.9
9	Russia	48,822.4	2.4	Luxembourg	34,555.0	55.9	France	42,869.1	1.5
10	Switzerland	43,321.2	6.5	Italy	30,759.3	1.4	Netherlands	40,808.7	4.6

aThe % GDP figures for British Virgin Islands are: 2001 = 2927.7%; 2009 = 4011.8%; 2010 = 6068.4%; 2011 = 6544.1%; 2012 = 5946.9%; 2013 = 8903.4%; 2014 = 6015.9%.

TABLE 7.37 Top 10 Largest Outward Investors: Ranked by Percentage of GDP

	1980	% GDP	US$ mil	1981	% GDP	US$ mil	1982	% GDP	US$ mil	1983	% GDP	US$ mil
1	Liberia	30.9	236.1	Nauru	22.5	10.1	Cayman Is.	22.9	56.1	Liberia	6.7	61.0
2	Bahamas	7.3	115.0	Liberia	4.8	41.9	Liberia	17.7	161.2	Hong Kong	1.9	566.0
3	Cayman Is.	2.9	5.1	Seychelles	3.9	7.2	Seychelles	2.8	4.9	Seychelles	1.8	3.2
4	Netherlands	2.5	4832.8	Netherlands	2.7	4415.5	Netherlands	2.0	3065.0	Netherlands	1.7	2613.3
5	Seychelles	2.1	3.8	Canada	1.8	5548.4	Singapore	1.9	304.2	New Zealand	1.6	403.5
6	Canada	1.5	4098.5	United Kingdom	1.7	9386.3	Sweden	1.2	1360.1	Sweden	1.5	1522.6
7	Kuwait	1.4	407.0	Malaysia	1.1	293.0	Malaysia	0.9	260.1	Cayman Is.	1.4	4.7
8	United Kingdom	1.4	7880.6	South Africa	0.8	643.9	Canada	0.8	2401.7	Kuwait	1.2	240.2
9	Swaziland	1.2	9.0	France	0.7	4614.4	Yemen	0.7	3.5	United Kingdom	1.1	5302.2
10	South Africa	0.9	755.0	Israel	0.7	171.0	United Kingdom	0.7	3706.9	Canada	0.8	2632.2

	1984	% GDP	US$ mil	1985	% GDP	US$ mil	1986	% GDP	US$ mil	1987	% GDP	US$ mil
1	Liberia	6.7	59.5	Liberia	28.9	255.0	Bahamas	5.1	129.3	Nauru	8.1	3.0
2	Belize	3.3	6.9	Cayman Is.	11.0	45.8	Hong Kong	3.3	1372.0	Liberia	6.7	60.7
3	Hong Kong	3.2	1076.0	Seychelles	5.2	10.6	United Kingdom	2.9	17,294.1	Cayman Is.	5.8	31.1
4	Nauru	2.5	1.0	Switzerland	4.2	4572.8	Sweden	2.7	3947.7	Hong Kong	4.6	2318.0
5	Seychelles	2.1	3.9	Nauru	3.0	1.0	Seychelles	2.3	5.8	United Kingdom	4.2	31,309.3
6	Netherlands	1.9	2748.0	Hong Kong	2.7	961.0	Netherlands	2.2	4428.3	Netherlands	3.5	8535.9
7	United Kingdom	1.7	7733.4	United Kingdom	2.3	11,068.4	Norway	2.0	1604.2	Kuwait	3.5	755.1
8	Sweden	1.4	1558.5	Netherlands	2.2	3088.2	Australia	1.8	3418.5	Sweden	2.7	4789.8
9	Switzerland	1.1	1139.3	Belize	1.9	4.0	Belize	1.6	3.8	Australia	2.2	5099.5
10	Canada	1.0	3684.7	Norway	1.9	1227.7	Niger	1.5	29.4	Belgium	1.9	2782.2

	1988	% GDP	US$ mil	1989	% GDP	US$ mil	1990	% GDP	US$ mil	1991	% GDP	US$ mil
1	BritVirgin Is.	120.2	157.6	BritVirginI.	a	3237.0	Aruba	63.7	486.9	BritVirgin Is.	a	1524.3
2	Liberia	20.9	202.2	Cayman Is.	7.2	54.1	Cayman Is.	30.3	281.6	Liberia	83.1	366.4
3	Cayman Is.	19.1	124.4	Liberia	6.5	64.6	Nauru	8.1	4.0	Aruba	20.3	177.1

(*Continued*)

TABLE 7.37   (*Continued*)

	1988	% GDP	US$ mil	1989	% GDP	US$ mil	1990	% GDP	US$ mil	1991	% GDP	US$ mil
4	Nauru	9.3	4.0	Netherlands	5.7	14543.1	Sweden	5.7	14746.2	Cayman Is.	7.3	71.3
5	Hong Kong	4.2	2533.0	Sweden	4.8	10286.5	Singapore	5.2	2033.8	Nauru	6.6	3.0
6	Switzerland	4.1	8694.7	Taiwan	4.6	6951.0	New Zealand	5.2	2363.1	Netherlands	4.2	13,484.5
7	United Kingdom	4.1	37,205.8	Kuwait	4.1	993.9	Netherlands	4.6	14,371.9	New Zealand	3.4	1468.7
8	Sweden	3.7	7470.9	Hong Kong	4.0	2740.0	Hong Kong	3.2	2448.0	Hong Kong	3.2	2825.0
9	Taiwan	3.3	4121.0	Belgium	3.9	6486.2	Taiwan	3.1	5243.0	Belgium	3.0	6270.9
10	Netherlands	2.8	7233.2	Switzerland	3.9	7923.4	Belgium	3.1	6314.4	Sweden	2.6	7054.7
	1992	**% GDP**	**US$ mil**	**1993**	**% GDP**	**US$ mil**	**1994**	**% GDP**	**US$ mil**	**1995**	**% GDP**	**US$ mil**
1	BritVirgin Is.	24.1	42.4	BritVirgin Is.	a	4906.3	BritVirgin Is.	595.9	1828.8	BritVirgin Is.	830.6	3297.6
2	Liberia	20.7	58.5	Cayman Is.	30.1	332.7	Liberia	54.5	91.3	Cayman Is.	20.5	266.0
3	Hong Kong	7.9	8254.0	Liberia	25.1	50.9	Hong Kong	15.8	21,437.0	Hong Kong	17.3	25,000.0
4	Cayman Is.	5.2	53.3	Hong Kong	14.7	17,713.0	Singapore	6.2	4577.1	Singapore	8.3	7282.9
5	Belgium	4.8	11,407.0	Singapore	3.5	2151.9	Netherlands	4.6	17,242.6	Netherlands	4.3	19,223.0
6	Papua NewGu.	4.2	182.4	Switzerland	3.3	8764.1	Finland	4.3	4490.8	Sweden	4.2	11,215.4
7	Nauru	3.9	1.7	Netherlands	2.8	9930.1	New Zealand	3.8	2008.9	Belgium	4.0	11,603.0
8	Netherlands	3.7	13,153.8	Kuwait	2.7	652.7	Switzerland	3.7	10,793.4	Palestine St.	3.9	129.0
9	Singapore	2.5	1317.0	United Kingdom	2.5	26,033.5	Swaziland	3.5	58.3	Cook Islands	3.7	3.9
10	France	2.3	31,854.1	Belgium	2.2	4903.6	Bahrain	3.1	198.7	Switzerland	3.5	12,210.0
	1996	**% GDP**	**US$ mil**	**1997**	**% GDP**	**US$ mil**	**1998**	**% GDP**	**US$ mil**	**1999**	**% GDP**	**US$ mil**
1	BritVirgin Is.	570.1	2559.6	BritVirgin Is.	799.4	4173.0	BritVirgin Is.	479.9	2884.2	BritVirgin Is.	a	10,582.0
2	Cayman Is.	60.5	850.6	Cayman Is.	248.6	3807.9	Cayman Is.	161.3	3241.6	Cayman Is.	176.9	3854.8
3	Hong Kong	16.6	26,530.9	Liberia	144.5	495.1	Finland	14.0	18,788.4	Liberia	61.6	310.6
4	Singapore	9.5	9196.4	Hong Kong	13.8	24,406.8	Belgium	11.1	28,845.3	Belgium	47.0	122,304.2
5	Cook Islands	7.8	8.3	Singapore	12.2	12,252.0	Hong Kong	9.8	16,625.6	Hong Kong	13.4	22,191.2
6	Netherlands	7.0	31,182.0	Switzerland	6.1	17,731.9	Sweden	9.2	24,478.6	Netherlands	13.0	57,610.4
7	Kuwait	5.5	1740.1	Netherlands	6.0	24,618.1	Netherlands	8.5	36,822.5	United Kingdom	12.9	201,450.7
8	Switzerland	4.9	16,152.0	Sweden	4.8	12,647.7	United Kingdom	8.0	122,815.6	Switzerland	11.4	33,276.2
9	Bahrain	4.3	304.8	United Kingdom	4.3	61,586.1	Switzerland	6.3	18,767.4	Denmark	9.6	17,014.9
10	Palestine St.	4.2	142.0	Palestine St.	4.2	156.1	Canada	5.4	34,350.1	Singapore	9.4	8111.0
	2000	**% GDP**	**US$ mil**	**2001**	**% GDP**	**US$ mil**	**2002**	**% GDP**	**US$ mil**	**2003**	**% GDP**	**US$ mil**
1	BritVirginI.	a	34,459.0	BritVirginI.	a	23,714.6	BritVirgin Is.	a	10,576.5	BritVirgin Is.	853.0	6073.6
2	Cayman Is.	335.9	7649.3	Cayman Is.	318.2	7435.2	Liberia	71.7	402.9	Cayman Is.	212.4	5366.2

(*Continued*)

TABLE 7.37 (*Continued*)

	2000	% GDP	US$ mil	2001	% GDP	US$ mil	2002	% GDP	US$ mil	2003	% GDP	US$ mil
3	Liberia	147.8	779.9	Singapore	22.4	20,027.0	Luxembourg	43.8	10,217.5	Liberia	39.9	173.0
4	Belgium	36.3	86,361.7	Netherlands	11.9	50,593.0	Palestine St.	9.7	346.2	Azerbaijan	12.8	933.3
5	Hong Kong	31.5	54,078.8	Hong Kong	10.7	18,055.3	Ireland	8.6	11,025.4	Belgium	12.0	38,322.5
6	Finland	19.1	24,030.3	Palestine St.	9.1	363.7	Hong Kong	7.9	13,163.0	Malta	10.1	544.8
7	Netherlands	18.3	75,634.4	Denmark	8.1	13,360.9	Netherlands	6.9	32,017.6	Netherlands	9.8	55,812.8
8	Switzerland	16.3	44,673.0	Botswana	6.9	379.7	Finland	5.3	7371.2	Hong Kong	7.5	12,057.1
9	Denmark	16.2	26,549.1	Switzerland	6.5	18,319.5	Azerbaijan	5.2	325.6	Bahrain	6.7	741.4
10	Sweden	15.7	40,906.9	Finland	6.5	8370.4	Belgium	4.7	12,277.1	Sweden	6.4	21,112.4

	2004	% GDP	US$ mil	2005	% GDP	US$ mil	2006	% GDP	US$ mil	2007	% GDP	US$ mil
1	BritVirgin Is.	653.9	4877.8	BritVirgin Is.	a	17,754.8	BritVirgin Is.	a	27,185.2	BritVirgin Is.	a	43,667.8
2	Cayman Is.	145.1	3862.2	Cayman Is.	201.3	6122.0	Cayman Is.	249.8	8012.7	Cayman Is.	264.6	9302.6
3	Liberia	57.8	304.5	Cook Islands	162.0	295.8	Cook Islands	61.7	115.9	Luxembourg	141.7	71,293.7
4	Hong Kong	25.8	43,636.9	Liberia	71.8	436.8	Liberia	49.3	246.4	Iceland	47.8	10,185.5
5	Luxembourg	19.7	6773.2	Iceland	42.3	7090.1	Iceland	32.5	5533.1	Cook Islands	45.0	102.5
6	Iceland	18.8	2581.1	Marshall Is.	36.9	51.4	Luxembourg	23.9	10,035.0	Liberia	44.4	362.6
7	Azerbaijan	13.9	1204.8	Luxembourg	22.2	8211.0	Hong Kong	23.0	44,475.2	Hong Kong	30.3	64,165.8
8	Singapore	9.6	10,960.0	Netherlands	15.6	106,008.8	Switzerland	17.5	75,823.7	Marshall Is.	21.6	33.7
9	Ireland	9.3	18,068.8	Hong Kong	14.9	27,003.1	Singapore	12.6	18,638.0	Singapore	20.5	36,897.2
10	Belgium	9.2	34,018.1	Switzerland	12.4	51,117.5	Belgium	12.4	50,684.9	Belgium	17.0	80,127.2

	2008	% GDP	US$ mil	2009	% GDP	US$ mil	2010	% GDP	US$ mil	2011	% GDP	US$ mil
1	BritVirgin Is.	a	44,118.4	BritVirgin Is.	a	35,143.0	BritVirgin Is.	a	54,162.0	BritVirgin Is.	a	59,944.0
2	Cook Islands	412.6	963.1	Cayman Is.	189.1	6310.9	Cayman Is.	406.0	13,263.0	Cook Islands	284.2	813.5
3	Cayman Is.	377.1	13,376.6	Liberia	35.5	363.6	Cook Islands	211.7	540.3	Cayman Is.	283.0	9479.0
4	Malta	151.9	13,634.4	Hong Kong	27.7	59,201.6	Luxembourg	44.4	23,243.2	Hong Kong	38.8	96,340.8
5	Liberia	41.5	381.9	Iceland	17.8	2291.9	Hong Kong	37.7	86,247.2	Togo	28.7	1059.8
6	Hong Kong	22.1	48,379.3	Luxembourg	16.3	8200.7	Liberia	34.4	369.4	Liberia	24.1	371.7
7	Marshall Is.	21.0	34.8	Singapore	13.6	26,239.0	Malta	22.0	1920.5	Luxembourg	18.3	10,736.6
8	Luxembourg	20.8	11,485.7	Ireland	11.3	26,615.5	Switzerland	14.6	85,700.7	Marshall Is.	15.6	29.4
9	Cyprus	9.9	2717.3	Kuwait	8.1	8581.8	Singapore	14.1	33,377.4	Malta	9.6	921.8
10	Switzerland	8.1	45,333.4	Estonia	7.0	1375.0	Ireland	10.2	22,348.3	Singapore	8.9	24,489.8

	2012	% GDP	US$ mil	2013	% GDP	US$ mil	2014	% GDP	US$ mil
1	BritVirgin Is.	a	54,078.0	BritVirgin Is.	a	81,520.0	BritVirgin Is.	a	54,287.0
2	Cook Islands	425.3	1307.3	Cayman Is.	417.4	14,533.0	Cayman Is.	390.4	13,584.0

(*Continued*)

TABLE 7.37 (*Continued*)

	2012	% GDP	US$ mil	2013	% GDP	US$ mil	2014	% GDP	US$ mil
3	Cayman Is.	323.2	11,042.0	Cook Islands	300.5	887.0	Hong Kong	49.1	142,700.5
4	Luxembourg	122.2	68,428.2	Luxembourg	55.9	24,555.0	Malta	22.2	2335.3
5	Liberia	78.1	1345.1	Liberia	35.9	698.4	Singapore	13.2	40,659.9
6	Hong Kong	31.8	83,410.5	Hong Kong	29.3	80,773.1	Ireland	12.7	31,795.2
7	Malta	27.8	2573.9	Malta	26.0	2603.0	Marshall Is.	11.5	23.9
8	Marshall Is.	11.9	23.8	Cyprus	14.5	3472.5	Togo	10.1	464.1
9	Togo	10.8	420.3	Ireland	10.1	23,875.0	Cyprus	9.4	2175.6
10	Hungary	9.2	11,678.1	Kuwait	9.6	16,648.0	Kuwait	8.0	13,108.4

[a]*The % GDP figures for British Virgin Islands are: 1989 = 2072.4%; 1991 = 1111.2%; 1993 = 2077.5%; 1999 = 1572.4%; 2000 = 4588.4%; 2001 = 2927.7%; 2002 = 1345.6%; 2005 = 2040.8%; 2006 = 2882.8%; 2007 = 4319.3%; 2008 = 4447.4%; 2009 = 4011.8%; 2010 = 6058.4%; 2011 = 6544.1%; 2012 = 5946.9%; 2013 = 8903.4%; 2014 = 6015.9%.*

IX MILITARY EXPENDITURE

War begins when shots are fired; peace emerges when guns are laid down. Although war and peace relates more to politics than economics, there is an increasing focus on the economics of war and peace, especially on the funding of war (e.g., DeGarmo and Wrobbel, 2015). A statistical analysis of the amount of military expenditure by each country may not be entirely accurate, as one country's military expenditure could be consumed by its allies elsewhere. Equally, a warring country may receive military aid from allies elsewhere. War is a game that requires an "absolute outcome." On the contrary, peace agreements cannot be just a document signed by different parties. For peace to last, it is more important to redirect productive resources and human energy away from war-related activities. There has to be a genuine process of postwar reconstruction that buries the conflict which existed during wartime, and in its place permits the market to regulate activities.

Modern wars have been fought on the grounds of ideological, religious, ethnic, and racial issues. In many ways, while there are parts of the world that have achieved a high level of civilization, there are still wars in various other parts of the world that look to human differences and exploit conflicts for vested interests more than they treasure mutual acceptance, peaceful coexistence, and respect. Very often, wars are fought between different neighboring regimes that are dominated by mistrust, discrimination, and the intention to annihilate. In some cases, one wonders if maintaining, prolonging, and extending war could be in the best interest of some regimes rather than the people of neighboring countries.

Subsequent to the end of the Second World War, wars have been fought on ideological grounds, such as the Korean War and the Vietnam War. The Cold War between the two powers of the United States and Soviet Union lasted for decades, but there was no physical fighting. On the contrary, the conflicts and wars in the Middle East have become much more complicated. They started with the territorial and racial conflicts between Israel and Palestine, but with the rise of Islamic regimes, conflicts in the Middle East extended to neighboring countries. Probably funded by the inflow of oil revenue, religious extremism has involved other industrialized countries, as well as other Islamic factions in developing countries. The terrorist attack on the World Trade Center in New York and the Pentagon in Washington, DC, on September 11, 2001, was a turning point, as it effectively started the "third world war" that highlighted the conflict between industrialized countries in the West and a number of Islamic countries in the Middle East. Terrorism conducted by religious extremists in the outside world has killed large numbers of innocent citizens in the United States, the United Kingdom, France, Germany, and other countries. With the continuous inflow of oil revenues, one really was left to wonder why the oil resources were not deployed productively to benefit everyone in the region. Are there really no broad-minded leaders in the Middle East states that would bring a stop to all activities with "absolute" outcomes, and instead introduce activities with "relative" outcomes? With the degree, extent, complications, and deep-rooted conflicts in the Middle East states, one was left to conclude that there was a lack of ability, preparedness, and will to introduce solutions from all affected parties.

From the SIPRI Military Expenditure Database, Table 7.38 shows the military expenditure in various world regions for the period 1988 – 2015. One has to understand military expenditure committed by one region might

TABLE 7.38 Military Expenditure by Region (US$ Billion, Constant 2014 Price and Exchange Rates)

Year	World total	Africa	Americas	Asia & Oceania	Europe	Middle East
1988	1595	15.6	649	138	717	75.8
1989	1572	15.7	645	145	695	70.7
1990	1503	15.5	611	152	629	95.7
1991	–	13.9	539	155	–	106.0
1992	1222	13.0	564	163	395	86.8
1993	1180	15.6	543	167	370	84.1
1994	1144	14.8	518	168	363	81.2
1995	1092	13.4	492	173	336	77.7
1996	1070	12.8	467	177	334	79.1
1997	1083	13.9	463	183	336	86.2
1998	1069	13.6	456	183	324	91.5
1999	1093	20.6	458	194	331	90.3
2000	1132	17.2	476	198	342	98.4
2001	1158	18.1	484	211	345	101.0
2002	1230	20.2	534	222	354	101.0
2003	1308	19.4	594	231	361	102.0
2004	1384	20.0	646	245	366	107.0
2005	1443	21.3	679	258	370	114.0
2006	1491	23.3	694	274	376	124.0
2007	1548	24.0	714	293	387	130.0
2008	1634	27.9	768	311	397	130.0
2009	1745	29.1	826	349	404	136.0
2010	1774	31.3	847	357	397	142.0
2011	1779	34.7	838	372	390	145.0
2012	1774	35.6	800	387	394	158.0
2013	1746	39.0	747	404	387	169.0
2014	1746	41.3	706	427	390	181.0
2015	1760	39.1	689	450	397	–

−, data unavailable. Figures may not add up to total due to rounding.

be used in another region. It is expected that countries in North America and Europe are the largest military spenders. However, the data trend shows that although the Americas region remained the largest spender, Europe has fallen and has been caught up by the Asia and Oceania region since 2013. Indeed, the three regions of Africa, Asia and Oceania, and the Middle East are committing to a steady increase in military expenditure, while the military expenditure of the Americas region has been falling since 2010.

Table 7.39 shows the number of years in the top 10 of the largest military spenders in value terms, and in percentage of GDP, for the 28 years period of 1988 − 2015. The top 10 largest military spenders measured in value terms comprise exclusively the two military giants of the United States and USSR/Russia, followed by the four conventional European countries (France, Germany, the United Kingdom, and Italy) and Japan. The other two Asian countries include China and India. Saudi Arabia and Kuwait are the two oil exporting countries in the Middle East, while Brazil is the only country from Latin America. Table 7.39 also shows the largest military spending countries measured in percentage of GDP. Although the number of countries is much more

TABLE 7.39   Number of Years in the Top 10 of Largest Military Expenditure: By Value and Percentage of GDP (1988–2015)

By value				By percentage of GDP			
United States	28	Oman	28	United States	8	Vietnam	3
France	28	Saudi Arabia	28	South Sudan	8	Bahrain	2
Germany	28	Israel	28	Croatia	7	Zimbabwe	2
United Kingdom	28	Jordan	25	Singapore	7	Armenia	2
Japan	28	Kuwait	19	Pakistan	7	Sri Lanka	1
Saudi Arabia	27	Syria	18	Ethiopia	6	Macedonia	1
China	27	Yemen	17	Chad	6	Russia/USSR	1
Russia/USSR	26	UA Emirates	15	Azerbaijan	5	Sudan	1
Italy	25	Lebanon	15	Algeria	5	Libya	1
India	19	Angola	13	Laos	4	Iraq	1
Korea, Rep.	9	Burundi	10	Cyprus	4	Namibia	1
Spain	4	Brunei	8	Georgia	4		
Brazil, Canada,	1						
Kuwait	1						

diverse, the list contains mainly countries engaged in wars in Africa, the Middle East, Latin America, and West Asia. Many countries in this list are oil producers. The United States and Singapore are probably the only exceptions in the list.

However, when one looks at the top 10 largest military spenders in value shown in Table 7.38, one observes that the military spending by the United States has remained the largest, and these values are much higher than the second largest. Russia has been the second largest in military expenditure in the late 1980s, but its ranking has dropped considerably in the 1990s. However, Russia returns to be the third largest after 2008. On the contrary, China was first ranked ninth in 1989, but has steadily climbed and stayed the second largest since 2003. All four European countries and Japan tended to show a steady expenditure throughout the year, ranging between US$40 and US$60 thousand million. India is a newcomer and entered the top 10 in 1998. Saudi Arabia is the only Middle East country in the top 10, South Korea has appeared as the top 10th since 2013.

Table 7.39 shows the top 10 countries with the largest military expenditure ranked by share of GDP. Due to the possibilities of more than one country with a similar share in GDP, there are more than 10 countries in some years. Other than Singapore and the United States, most of the top 10 countries are either oil exporting countries, countries in the Middle East, or countries facing severe instability and conflicts. The data shows that it is only in a minority of cases that the share of military expenditure exceeded 10% of GDP. The only exception is Kuwait in the period 1990–92, where it topped the list with large percentage of their GDP spent on the military. Oman has stayed at the top for a number of years, with its military spending exceeding 10% of GDP. By the way, the positions of the top 10 countries varied over the sample period. This variation is reflected in the long list of countries.

Tables 7.40 and 7.41, respectively, show the top 10 countries with largest military expenditure measured in value terms and in percentage of GDP. Table 7.42 shows the top 15 countries with the largest average growth rates in military expenditure. The top three countries (Georgia, Azerbaijan, and Kazakhstan) are the border states of Russia. The notable country in Table 7.42 is China, whose average growth rate is 11.37%. The others mainly comprise African countries and Latin American countries. Indonesia is the only other Asian country, with an average of 9.9%. When the percentage increase between 1990 and 2015 is considered, as shown in Table 7.43, China has the largest percentage increase of 873.83%, followed by Saudi Arabia with 214.65%, while the United States shows an increase of only 7.34%. Russia has shown the largest decrease of 66.21%, followed by the traditional powers in Western European (the United Kingdom, Germany, and France).

TABLE 7.40 Top 10 Countries With Largest Military Expenditure: Ranked by Value (US$ Million Constant 2014 Price and Exchange Rates)

	1988	US$ mil	1989	US$ mil	1990	US$ mil	1991	US$ mil	1992	US$ mil
1	United States	586,731	United States	580,705	United States	554,742	United States	487,221	United States	514,822
2	Russia/USSR	343,617	Russia/USSR	318,616	Russia/USSR	269,545	France	69,991	France	67,789
3	Germany	69,498	France	69,847	Germany	73,042	Germany	67,596	Germany	64,288
4	France	69,001	Germany	69,308	France	69,538	United Kingdom	65,413	United Kingdom	61,097
5	United Kingdom	64,010	United Kingdom	64,574	United Kingdom	64,666	Japan	43,875	Russia/USSR	57,641
6	Japan	39,104	Japan	40,797	Japan	42,794	Italy	37,313	Japan	44,535
7	Italy	37,955	Italy	38,254	Italy	36,794	Saudi Arabia	25,870	Italy	36,240
8	Saudi Arabia	22,844	Saudi Arabia	21,586	Saudi Arabia	27,127	Kuwait	24,304	China	28,426
9	Spain	19,444	China	20,212	China	22,025	China	23,398	Saudi Arabia	24,314
10	Canada	19,352	Brazil	19,777	Spain	19,618	Spain	18,854	Spain	18,392

	1993	US$ mil	1994	US$ mil	1995	US$ mil	1996	US$ mil	1997	US$ mil
1	United States	487,764	United States	460,072	United States	433,220	United States	409,656	United States	407,537
2	France	67,038	France	67,382	France	64,047	France	62,510	France	62,725
3	United Kingdom	58,306	United Kingdom	56,702	United Kingdom	53,183	United Kingdom	52,865	United Kingdom	51,200
4	Germany	57,793	Germany	53,898	Germany	53,011	Germany	51,977	Germany	50,087
5	Russia/USSR	50,389	Russia/USSR	47,635	Japan	45,074	Japan	45,896	Japan	46,279
6	Japan	44,355	Japan	44,340	Italy	32,452	Italy	35,770	Italy	37,506
7	Italy	36,434	Italy	35,533	Russia/USSR	31,342	Russia/USSR	29,596	Russia/USSR	32,355
8	China	26,222	China	25,256	China	26,213	China	27,837	China	29,858
9	Saudi Arabia	25,769	Saudi Arabia	22,242	Korea, Rep.	21,347	Korea, Rep.	21,648	Saudi Arabia	26,583
10	Korea, Rep.	18,979	Korea, Rep.	19,528	Saudi Arabia	19,606	India	19,687	Korea, Rep.	22,179

	1998	US$ mil	1999	US$ mil	2000	US$ mil	2001	US$ mil	2002	US$ mil
1	United States	398,332	United States	399,314	United States	414,768	United States	418,135	United States	469,486
2	France	61,091	France	61,607	France	60,897	France	60,711	France	61,963
3	United Kingdom	51,485	United Kingdom	51,421	United Kingdom	52,766	United Kingdom	54,901	China	60,642
4	Germany	50,248	Germany	51,272	Germany	50,448	China	52,179	United Kingdom	58,458
5	Japan	46,331	Japan	46,084	Japan	46,315	Germany	49,619	Germany	49,753
6	Italy	38,744	Italy	40,263	China	43,230	Japan	47,156	Japan	47,576
7	China	32,715	China	39,800	Italy	42,956	Italy	42,250	Italy	43,406
8	Saudi Arabia	30,704	Saudi Arabia	27,331	Saudi Arabia	30,123	Saudi Arabia	32,083	Russia/USSR	34,530

(Continued)

TABLE 7.40 (*Continued*)

	1998	US$ mil	1999	US$ mil	2000	US$ mil	2001	US$ mil	2002	US$ mil
9	India	22,737	India	26,424	Russia/USSR	28,838	Russia/USSR	31,171	Saudi Arabia	28,166
10	Korea, Rep.	21,404	Russia/USSR	21,370	India	27,266	India	28,215	India	28,128

	2003	US$ mil	2004	US$ mil	2005	US$ mil	2006	US$ mil	2007	US$ mil
1	United States	534,351	United States	582,400	United States	610,176	United States	619,653	United States	635,921
2	China	65,496	China	72,415	China	79,809	China	92,586	China	103,716
3	France	63,826	France	65,573	France	64,235	France	64,525	United Kingdom	66,370
4	United Kingdom	62,661	United Kingdom	63,392	United Kingdom	63,922	United Kingdom	64,334	France	64,773
5	Germany	49,073	Germany	47,570	Japan	47,155	Russia/USSR	47,601	Russia/USSR	51,814
6	Japan	47,435	Japan	47,245	Germany	46,830	Japan	46,558	Saudi Arabia	49,872
7	Italy	43,758	Italy	43,897	Russia/USSR	43,010	Germany	45,749	Japan	45,954
8	Russia/USSR	36,200	Russia/USSR	37,847	Italy	42,227	Saudi Arabia	43,297	Germany	45,789
9	India	28,756	India	33,403	Saudi Arabia	38,008	Italy	40,867	Italy	39,600
10	Saudi Arabia	28,374	Saudi Arabia	31,543	India	35,548	India	35,718	India	36,151

	2008	US$ mil	2009	US$ mil	2010	US$ mil	2011	US$ mil	2012	US$ mil
1	United States	682,967	United States	737,747	United States	757,992	United States	748,646	United States	706,082
2	China	113,527	China	137,401	China	144,383	China	155,898	China	169,321
3	United Kingdom	69,332	United Kingdom	70,679	United Kingdom	69,192	United Kingdom	66,271	Russia/USSR	75,364
4	France	64,124	France	68,451	France	65,322	Russia/USSR	65,040	United Kingdom	63,446
5	Russia/USSR	56,933	Russia/USSR	59,730	Russia/USSR	60,940	France	63,725	France	62,844
6	Saudi Arabia	48,949	Saudi Arabia	50,299	Saudi Arabia	52,350	Saudi Arabia	53,062	Saudi Arabia	60,041
7	Germany	47,104	Germany	48,885	Germany	49,418	India	48,940	Germany	49,149
8	Japan	45,515	India	48,277	India	48,470	Germany	48,004	India	48,766
9	Italy	41,049	Japan	46,364	Japan	46,527	Japan	47,161	Japan	46,584
10	India	41,003	Italy	39,897	Italy	38,772	Italy	38,047	Italy	35,342

	2013	US$ mil	2014	US$ mil	2015	US$ mil
1	United States	650,081	United States	609,914	United States	595,472
2	China	182,930	China	199,651	China	214,485
3	Russia/USSR	79,030	Russia/USSR	84,697	Russia/USSR	91,081
4	Saudi Arabia	68,810	Saudi Arabia	80,762	Saudi Arabia	85,354
5	France	62,686	France	63,614	France	60,747
6	United Kingdom	60,766	United Kingdom	59,183	United Kingdom	59,730
7	India	48,406	India	50,914	India	51,116
8	Japan	46,380	Germany	46,103	Germany	47,046
9	Germany	46,312	Japan	45,867	Japan	46,346
10	Korea, Rep.	36,175	Korea, Rep.	37,286	Korea, Rep.	38,640

TABLE 7.41 Top 10 Countries With Largest Military Expenditure: Ranking by Percentage of GDP

	1988	% GDP	1989	% GDP	1990	% GDP	1991	% GDP	1992	% GDP
1	Angola	22.0	Angola	19.4	Kuwait	48.5	Kuwait	117.3	Kuwait	31.8
2	Oman	18.3	Oman	16.7	Angola	17.5	Israel	17.5	Oman	16.2
3	Israel	17.1	Israel	13.6	Oman	16.5	Oman	14.8	Israel	12.3
4	Saudi Arabia	15.2	Saudi Arabia	13.4	Saudi Arabia	14.0	Saudi Arabia	12.5	Saudi Arabia	11.3
5	Jordan	9.4	Ethiopia	9.9	Israel	13.7	Syria	10.4	Cyprus	9.1
6	Ethiopia	8.3	Jordan	9.1	Ethiopia	9.0	Jordan	10.0	Syria	9.0
7	Kuwait	8.2	Kuwait	8.5	Vietnam	7.9	Cyprus	7.3	Laos	8.7
8	Syria	7.9	Syria	8.0	Jordan	7.8	Angola	7.1	Lebanon	8.0
9	Vietnam	7.1	Vietnam	7.3	Lebanon	7.6	Yemen, Pakistan	6.6	Croatia	7.6
10	Pakistan	6.8	Pakistan	6.5	Cyprus	7.4	Brunei Daru.	6.4	Jordan	6.9

	1993	% GDP	1994	% GDP	1995	% GDP	1996	% GDP	1997	% GDP
1	Angola	17.5	Oman	15.7	Oman	14.6	Oman	12.5	Oman	12.5
2	Oman	15.4	Kuwait	13.3	Kuwait	13.6	Kuwait	10.3	Saudi Arabia	11.0
3	Israel	13.0	Israel	11.3	Croatia, Saudi Arabia	9.3	Israel	8.7	Croatia	8.9
4	Saudi Arabia	12.5	Croatia	11.1	Israel	8.9	Saudi Arabia	8.5	Israel	8.5
5	Kuwait	12.4	Saudi Arabia	10.6	Syria	6.9	Croatia	8.3	Kuwait	8.1
6	Croatia	10.7	Yemen	7.9	Lebanon	6.7	Brunei Daru.	6.2	Brunei Daru.	7.2
7	Laos	8.1	Laos	7.5	Yemen	6.0	Syria, Jordan	6.0	UAE	6.8
8	Syria	7.2	Syria	7.4	Sri Lanka	5.9	Burundi	5.9	Burundi	6.4
9	Jordan	7.0	Lebanon	7.0	Laos, Pakistan	5.8	Lebanon	5.7	Jordan	6.1
10	Yemen	6.6	Jordan	6.5	Brunei Daru.	5.5	Pakistan	5.6	Cyprus	6.0

	1998	% GDP	1999	% GDP	2000	% GDP	2001	% GDP	2002	% GDP
1	Saudi Arabia	14.3	Angola	17.3	Oman	10.8	Oman	12.5	Oman	12.4
2	Oman	12.6	Oman	11.5	Saudi Arabia	10.6	Saudi Arabia	11.5	Zimbabwe	10.7
3	Kuwait	8.8	Saudi Arabia	11.4	UAE	8.3	Burundi	8.0	Saudi Arabia	9.8
4	UAE	8.6	Ethiopia	8.9	Ethiopia	7.5	Kuwait	7.7	Israel	8.3
5	Israel	7.9	UAE	7.7	Kuwait	7.2	Israel	7.4	Kuwait	7.4
6	Brunei Daru.	7.5	Kuwait	7.6	Israel	7.1	Macedonia	6.6	Burundi	7.2
7	Croatia, Burundi	6.6	Israel	7.4	Angola	6.4	Jordan	5.9	Yemen	6.0
8	Ethiopia, Jordan	6.3	Jordan, Burundi	6.3	Jordan	6.3	UAE	5.6	Jordan, Syria	5.4
9	Syria	5.8	Brunei Daru.	6.1	Burundi	6.0	Syria	5.5	Brunei	5.3
10	Yemen	5.7	Syria	5.8	Brunei Daru.	5.7	Lebanon	5.4	Singapore, UAE	4.9

	2003	% GDP	2004	% GDP	2005	% GDP	2006	% GDP	2007	% GDP
1	Oman	12.2	Oman	12.1	Oman	11.8	Oman	10.8	Oman	10.3
2	Saudi Arabia	8.7	Israel	8.2	Saudi Arabia, Israel	7.7	Saudi Arabia	7.8	Georgia	9.2

(Continued)

II. THE GLOBAL ECONOMY: PERFORMANCE, CLASSIFICATION, AND CHALLENGES

TABLE 7.41   (*Continued*)

	2003	% GDP	2004	% GDP	2005	% GDP	2006	% GDP	2007	% GDP
3	Israel	8.5	Saudi Arabia	8.1	Syria	5.0	Israel	7.5	Saudi Arabia	8.5
4	Burundi	7.3	Burundi	6.6	Jordan	4.8	Georgia	5.2	Israel	6.8
5	Kuwait	6.5	Kuwait	5.8	Lebanon, Angola	4.5	Jordan	4.7	Jordan	6.0
6	Syria	6.2	Syria	5.5	Burundi	4.4	Lebanon	4.6	Lebanon	4.7
7	Jordan, Yemen	6.0	Jordan	5.1	Kuwait, Yem., Sing.	4.3	Syria, Angola	4.4	Chad	4.5
8	Singapore	4.9	Yemen, Sudan	4.7	Pakistan	3.9	Singapore	3.9	Syria, Yemen	4.1
9	Angola	4.8	UAE, Lebanon	4.6	USA	3.8	USA	3.8	USA	3.8
10	UAE, Leb., Bah.	4.7	Singapore, Zimb.	4.4	UAE	3.7	Pakistan	3.7	Kuwait, Sing.	3.6

	2008	% GDP	2009	% GDP	2010	% GDP	2011	% GDP	2012	% GDP
1	Georgia	8.5	Saudi Arabia	9.6	Saudi Arabia	8.6	Oman	9.8	Oman	16.2
2	Oman	7.6	Oman	9.3	Oman	8.3	Saudi Arabia	7.2	South Sudan	9.5
3	Saudi Arabia	7.4	Chad	8.0	Israel	6.3	Israel, South Sudan	5.9	Saudi Arabia	7.7
4	Israel	6.6	Israel	6.8	UAE	6.1	Jordan, UAE	5.5	Israel	5.7
5	Jordan	6.2	Jordan	6.6	Chad	5.8	Yemen	5.2	UAE	5.1
6	Chad	5.9	Georgia	5.6	Jordan	5.7	Chad	5.0	Yemen	5.0
7	South Sudan	5.8	UAE	5.5	Yemen, USA	4.7	Azerbaijan	4.7	Jordan	4.8
8	USA	4.2	South Sudan, Yem.	5.0	Armenia	4.3	USA	4.6	Azerbaijan	4.7
9	Lebanon	4.1	USA	4.6	Angola, Lebanon	4.2	Algeria	4.3	Algeria	4.5
10	Yemen, Sing.	3.9	Angola	4.3	South Sudan, Syria	4.1	Lebanon	4.1	USA	4.2

	2013	% GDP	2014	% GDP	2015	% GDP
1	Oman	15.0	Oman	13.9	Oman	16.2
2	Saudi Arabia	9.0	South Sudan	11.8	South Sudan	13.8
3	South Sudan	8.3	Saudi Arabia	10.7	Saudi Arabia	13.7
4	UAE	6.1	Libya	7.3	Iraq	9.1
5	Israel	5.8	Israel	6.0	Algeria	6.2
6	Chad	5.6	UAE	5.7	Israel, Russia/USSR	5.4
7	Algeria	5.0	Algeria	5.6	Azerbaijan, Bahrain	4.6
8	Angola	4.9	Angola	5.2	Armenia	4.5
9	Yemen	4.7	Yemen, Azerbaijan	4.6	Namibia	4.4
10	Azerbaijan	4.5	Lebanon	4.5	Jordan	4.2

UAE, United Arab Emirates; Leb., Lebanon; Bah., Bahrain; Zimb., Zimbabwe; Yem.,Yemen; Sing., Singapore.

TABLE 7.42 Top 15 Highest Average Military Expenditure Growth Rates: 2001–15

Georgia	24.73	Algeria	10.36
Azerbaijan	21.27	Ecuador	10.21
Kazakhstan	14.54	Belarus	9.98
Malawi	13.21	Indonesia	9.90
Ghana	11.58	Seychelles	9.80
China	11.37	Oman	9.80
Mali	10.92	Honduras	9.36
Namibia	10.76	Argentina	8.63

TABLE 7.43 Military Expenditure Performance in Selected World Economies

Country	1990	2015	Percentage change
United States	554,742	595,472	7.34
Canada	19,236	17,210	(10.53)
China	22,025	214,485	873.83
Japan	42,794	46,346	8.30
Australia	14,296	27,793	94.41
France	69,538	60,747	(12.64)
Germany	73,042	47,046	(35.59)
United Kingdom	64,666	59,730	(7.63)
Russia	269,545	91,081	(66.21)
Israel	13,451	17,512	30.19
Saudi Arabia	27,127	85,354	214.65

Figures are in US$ million at constant 2014 prices and exchange rates; (.) = percentage decrease.

X CONCLUSION

However, by examining the trend in various variables, one can have a contemporary and comprehensive understanding of the world economy, especially when considering the movement among individual world economies over the last three decades. There should be sufficient materials for one to draw useful conclusions on the global economy, and examine how the world economy could be studied, dissected, grouped, and predicted for the next development path in the 21st century.

There are several global development trends one can draw from the world economic data. The United States and other key European countries are still the strongest economies, as they are the key investors and donors of development assistance to other developing countries. However, the industrialized countries are also faced with economic saturation at least in the short-term, as seen from their growth rates. The Asian economies tend to be the next best performers in the global economy. In particular, China has caught up considerably in the last three decades, and has scored top 10 places in some indicators. On the contrary, the weaker world economies can be seen from their poor performance in such indicators as fiscal deficits, trade deficits, and debt. The unfavorable impact would be worse in the smaller nonindustrialized countries, as their economic capability may not be able to lift their economies up to service the debts. There are a large number of developing and weak economies that require much assistance, but the economic impact of foreign assistance and investment has remained weak.

One can begin to group the world economy based on a number of observations. There are two groups of countries that are absorbing world resources. The largest group of countries are the oil exporting countries that have been absorbing global oil revenues from their monopolistic position as oil exporters. Yet, the huge revenues that this group of oil exporting has amassed have not been plowed back to the rest of the world productively. While some rich oil exporting Middle East countries are building up mega-cities and individual consumption of luxury goods, much of the oil revenues have been used to finance unstable countries, some of them engaged in terrorist attacks in various parts of the world.

The other group of countries consists of trade surplus countries, typically China, who has been enriched by large trade surpluses and reserves. While some trade surplus countries, such as Japan, continue to invest, China's ideological differences have not been making much contribution to the world economy. China's large potential domestic market has been the envy of the world, and many developed countries have aimed at capturing a share, but the lack of openness and extensive protectionist attitude in China's domestic market have served as an alarm bell to the foreign investors as to the degree of ease in undertaking trade and investment with China.

The developing countries have largely remained unchanged over the decades, despite prolonged periods of international and foreign assistance and funding that have been poured into these countries. Many of these weak states are former colonies which have achieved political independence, but progress has been minimal or even detrimental, and development has been plagued by instabilities in the form of corruption, conflicts with different origins, poor terms of trade, and lack of industrialization and infrastructure construction.

Despite the continued dominance of the industrialized countries, there are signs of economic fatigue as the high oil price, trade deficits, and budget and national debts have impoverished and weakened the industrialized countries, with periodic crises and the rise in terrorist activities further draining their resources. There are many complaints about the global economy in one form or another. Are there shortages of resources in the world economy, or have resources been inappropriately deployed? Have economic resources been used in the conduct of politics, or can economics only be conducted through politics? Are there insufficient economic policy choices, or have too few right choices been made? Are there too many economic theories, is there still a lack of effective economic theory, or are the theories not keeping pace with global problems?

Ultimately, economic development is shaped by an economy's ideology, which can be considered and judged by the four key aspects of resources, policy, leadership, and systems. An economy's resources are one major aspect in the deployment of ideology as it governs the economic life of the country. Resources go beyond natural resources of land and raw materials, and include availability and quality of human resources, conditions to attract inflow of resources, ability to increase the "value-added" content of resources, and technological capability that enhances the value and effectiveness of other resources. The second aspect in the component of an economy's ideology is the policies that are adopted to deploy the resources to produce results. Due to contrasting ends, no one policy could cater for all needs, and there has to be a combination of policies that work through different aspects to minimize problems and maximize results. Policies on infrastructure development, medical support, and the promotion of education, e.g., have to be complemented with policies that enhance business development, technological advancement, and development in peace and civilization.

Leadership is another crucial element in an economy's ideology. An economy's leaders need to show great understanding of resources deployment and policy orientations. Political leaders have to be different from business leaders, as the former maximize societal results and outcomes, while the latter maximize individual wealth and business assets. Political leaders are meant to serve, and are not supposed to take advantage of their position for vested interests. As it could be easy to rip the benefit from the leadership position, the integrity of the leader should be the paramount consideration in ensuring maximum utilization of resources and appropriate deployment of policies. One should not forget that it often will be the people around the leader, who are not accountable, that make policy proposals to the leaders. The establishment of a reliable and dynamic civic system will serve as a monitor over the leaders, so that no one will be above the law, and every wrongdoing will be brought to justice.

These components of an economy's ideology will reflect the fact that there are always human errors. As such, there cannot be a perfect ideology, but it is important to identify a functioning and effective ideology that adheres to freedom, allows activities to be organized more by individuals, and allows individuals to be in charge of their own welfare. When compared to other political ideologies and civic systems, capitalism proves to be the appropriate channel through which economic activities will be in the hands of individuals, will produce a minimal but effective government, and will promote business-friendliness to maximize economic opportunities, then economic rejuvenation and revitalization will emerge through the decisions of individuals after the outbreak of economic crises. An examination of the key data of the global economy will allow new interpretation of the global economy, and that insightful analysis will bring new foresight to the next stage in the capitalist development of the global economy.

8

The Five Groups of World Economies

I INTRODUCTION

Based on the difference in income, the World Bank has classified the world into four income groups: low, lower-middle, upper-middle, and high. Such a classification is based solely on income figures, and countries with changes in income can move up over time. However, there are various inadequacies in such a classification. For example, payment to work in some countries may not be made in monetary terms, or income arising from informal economic activities may not be recorded statistically. Income is an ex post variable, and shows the end product of an economic activity. On the contrary, the ex ante situation could include the various means through which income is generated across countries.

Another common usage is to refer to the industrialized countries as "developed" countries, while the nonindustrialized countries are the "developing" or "less developed" countries. This distinction is based on the industrial or "value-added" content in the country's output, since industrial outputs carry a higher "value-added" compared to agricultural output. Hence, most industrialized countries are considered as developed countries, while countries relying largely on agriculture and raw materials are considered as less developed countries. There are, however, exceptions to such a classification. Due to the rising price of raw materials, such as oil, many raw material-based countries have achieved a high level of income. On the contrary, some stagnant industrialized countries have been marginalized and become peripheral.

The theoretical base of the "developed" versus "less developed" distinction comes from the concept of "stages of growth" that describes how a low income country catches up with industrialized countries with economic development and improvements. The concept of "stages of growth" has been used extensively (Lewis, 1954; Rostow, 1960; Baran and Hobsbawm, 1961). For example, Rostow's (1960) five stages of growth are sequentially known as: Traditional Society, Preconditions for Take-off, Take-off, Drive to Maturity, and Age of High Mass Consumption. The Take-off stage is considered as the turning point from a less developed to a developed country status. The five stages of growth can also be translated into the dominance of either one of the three economic sectors of agriculture, industry, and service. The Traditional Society would probably be dominated by agriculture, followed by services, while industries would be minimal. Here, one is referring to the traditional services

© 2017 Elsevier Inc. All rights reserved.

that surrounded domestic work and basic personal services. Similarly, industries were mainly agriculture-related, family-related, and primitive.

With the Preconditions for Take-off, the second stage would see a rise in agricultural surplus, more industries developed as a result of surplus in agricultural products, and markets begin to develop. Examples included development of the food preservation industry. Hence, agriculture would still be the dominant sector, while industry had become the second most important sector, and services that remained primitive had fallen to the weakest sector. However, in the third, Take-off stage, industries would become dominant, followed by agriculture and services. Modern industries would be developed, and technologies emerge. Family businesses would be gradually replaced by large corporations, product specialization would emerge, and mass production would reduce the cost of production. However, as economic modernization took place, industries would have caught up with agriculture. As industries developed, there would be a rise in modern services, such as banking and travel. Hence, in the fourth stage of the Drive to Maturity, the large industry sector requires modern services. Services become the second most important economic sector, while agriculture falls to the smallest economic sector.

Expansion in industries and services give rise to consumption and improvements in living standards. The final stage arrives with the Age of Mass Consumption, where modern services would be the dominant economic sector, supported by industries as the second largest economic sector, while agriculture remains as the smallest economic sector. Using A, I, and S to represent agriculture, industry, and services, respectively, the movements of the three economic sectors in the five stages of economic development are: ASI, AIS, IAS, ISA, and SIA. In the first stage, the dominance of agriculture is followed by service as the second most important sector, while industry is the weakest sector. Hence, between the five stages, agriculture that dominated at the beginning drops to become the least important sector. Industries were least important in the beginning, and flourished in the later stage, but were overtaken by services. Services have been transformed from the primitive activities to the modern form of services. In the process, service climbed to become the dominant economic sector after transformation.

The "developed" and "less developed" division does allow economies to advance when the economy's output is composed of industries and modern services, and has advanced to a higher stage of development. For example, the four East Asian economies of Singapore, Hong Kong, South Korea, and Taiwan were considered by the OECD in the early 1970s as "newly industrializing economies" (NIEs) (Balassa, 1981; Haggard, 1990). Other than their growth in international trade, these four economies have gone through an industrialization cycle, and instead of being recipients of foreign direct investment, these four economies have in turn served as investment headquarters in the Asian region (Li, 2002). By 1979, these four economies had graduated from the Generalized System of Preference that provided an umbrella of multilateral free trade. Since then, the four NIEs were treated as "developed" countries in their exports (Kwok and Li, 1992; United Nations, 1992).

A politics-oriented line of classification in the world economy is the "three world" hypothesis. During the decades-long Cold War between the United States and Western European countries under the command of the North Atlantic Treaty Organization (NATO), and the Communist Bloc led by the Soviet Union, China, and probably Cuba, the group of poorer "nonaligned" countries were considered as "Third World" countries. Hence, the NATO countries were regarded as the "first world," while the Communist bloc countries were considered as the "second world."

The world has changed in the last three decades. Firstly, industrialized countries are faced with such economic challenges as financial crises. The 2008 world financial crisis reflected in an ex post manner a chain of "vicious" economic relationships, possibly due to the prolonged policy of a near-zero interest rate that could have stimulated speculation and risky financial investment rather than investment that promoted physical output and employment. The financial collapse in much of the industrialized world could not be rescued by the shrinking industrial sector in key industrialized countries. In addition, the large national debt in a number of industrialized countries suggested the unsustainability of a lengthy period of fiscal deficit resulting from huge government expenditure. Secondly, there are also noneconomic challenges, such as regional and religious conflicts. Many developing countries, especially those who gained political independence after the Second World War, have turned from bad to worse economically. With decades of independence and continued aid support from foreign countries and international institutions, these countries are still faced with waves of conflicts and instability of one sort or another. When it comes to genuine economic development, one still cannot see light at the end of the tunnel for these countries.

Thirdly, two groups of countries have amassed large trade and export surpluses that had taxed the world economy considerably, as many countries suffered from high petroleum prices and trade deficits. The first group included many of the petroleum exporting countries that have kept the price of petroleum high for decades.

While many of these petroleum exporting countries did not engage themselves with the world economy, others were channeled to religious extremists that threatened world peace. The second group of countries included China, which has for decades absorbed much of the world foreign direct investment, and its exports led to continued trade surpluses. China has become the country with the largest reserves in the world, but it is using the resources for its own interest. For example, studies show that much of China's outward investments have been tied to secure energy imports and other raw materials that are in shortage in China (Cheung and Qian, 2009; Dong et al., 2011; Wang and Yu, 2014; Yao and Wang, 2014).

In a nutshell, there are numerous complexities in relation to how the world has been classified, but the world economy is getting more confused in terms of crises, regional and religious conflicts, excessive pursuit of "demand-driven" policies that ended up with more fiscal debts, and incompetent governments and regimes that did not do a proper job in promoting stability and growth. The data and statistics in the discussion of the "top ten" world economies suggested that there are five groups of world economies. Each of the five groups has their own distinctive features. This chapter will analyze the world economy within this framework to see how the world can better and appropriately be understood and analyzed.

II FRAGILE STATES

One can start to dissect the world economy by examining the weakest group, known in general as the "failed states." According to *Wikipedia*, a failed state is "a state perceived as having failed at some of the basic conditions and responsibilities of a sovereign government." The nonprofit institution known as the Fund for Peace (FFP) in Washington, DC, suggested four related features commonly found in a "failed state": loss of control of its territory, erosion of legitimate authority to make collective decisions, inability to provide public services, and inability to interact with other states as a full member of the international community. Since 2005, the FFP publishes the "Fragile States Index" (formerly known as the "Failed States Index") (FSI) that shows the list of weakest countries in the world, pointing out their sources of weakness and making suggestions for possible improvements.

In the 2014, e.g., FFP (Fund for Peace, 2015) surveyed a total of 178 countries in the FSI. Different categories are used in the FSI, with the top five worst performers considered as Very High Alert, followed by 11 next-tier of poor performers known as High Alert. The next category is Alert (18 countries), followed by Very High Warning (32 countries), High Warning (43 countries), and Warning (17 countries). The better performers are termed Less Stable (12 countries), Stable (15 countries), and Very Stable (12 countries). The remaining 13 countries are considered as the best performers under Sustainable and Very Sustainable. All the worst performers are African countries. The five Very High Alert countries in the 2014 FSI are South Sudan, Somalia, the Central African Republic, the Democratic Republic of Congo, and Sudan. On the contrary, the best performers in the Sustainable categories are all Western European countries, together with Canada, Australia, and New Zealand.

The focus is obviously on the weak performers in the six "Alert and Warning" categories. Studies using geographical reasons to explain the poverty in the fragile states include discussion on the tropic zone and the warm climatic weather that could have contributed to low levels of development. Others point to the landlocked nature of some fragile states (Gallup et al., 1999). The discussion on "the curse of natural resources" (Sachs and Warner, 2001) focused on the fact that countries with rich natural resources tended to be poor, while many rich industrialized countries are poor in natural resources. The "natural resource curse" thesis can probably be counter-explained by the "value-added" content of output in the Prebisch − Singer hypothesis, which argued that the price of primary goods declined relative to the price of industrial manufacturing, and over time, the terms of trade of countries that export primary goods would deteriorate (Hausmann et al., 2005; UNCTAD, 2005; Harvey et al., 2010).

There are two schools of thought in the political economy of development. On the one hand, the radical Marxian school considered the external factors in economic development, and focused on the political view that colonialism and resource exploitation by foreign imperialists were the cause of underdevelopment. Colonialism has left many colonies in a nonrepairable state. The territorial borders of many African countries were drafted by foreign imperialists, and raw materials were extracted at a low price, but in turn the materials were processed into high-end industrial products and exported back to the colonies at a high price. The Marxian thesis of "unequal exchange" believed that trade between the imperial countries and the colonies can never be equal, while the "dependency" thesis argued that colonies have to rely on the imperial countries for exports and imports (Baran, 1952; Fanon, 1967; Amin, 1976; Frank, 1981).

However, these Marxist analyses and arguments are becoming outdated as the events and development in the postindependence era unfolded. Although one could still argue that the situation left behind by the imperialists was unfavorable, many fragile states have indeed been independent for decades, and their political autonomy should enable them to make corrections and readdress distortions. After decades of self-rule, can the Marxian arguments on imperialism still stand? Or are the Marxian theses still used as a "scapegoat" to turn attention away from the lack of development and progress in these fragile states in Africa? For example, a call for the unification of the African states was suggested in the 1960s by the president of Ghana, Kwame Nkrumah (Nkrumah, 1963; Thompson, 1969), but there was no consensus to integrate to become a single African continent for large-scale development. Indeed, many fragile African states are still faced with multiple levels of intertwined domestic problems that have ethical, religious, territorial, racial, and cultural origins. As such, continued and prolonged instability would not allow any development, let alone whether there was sufficient funding or aid available from foreign governments and institutions. In short, the underdevelopment in fragile states today is due probably more to the inability of the domestic government to manage economic development than to the historical colonial influence of foreign governments.

On the other hand, the neoclassical school tends to focus more on internal factors, and believes that improvements in internal or domestic factors would contribute positively to economic development. The neoclassical school of thought will focus more on the importance of domestic and internal development (Gillis et al., 1983; Nafziger, 1997; Agénor and Montiel, 1999; Thirlwall, 2006). Development must start from the home economy and improve domestic factors, including development in education and human capital, infrastructure provisions, reliable institutions, effective markets and businesses, eradication of corruption and administrative bureaucracy, and fiscal effectiveness. Such cultural factors as religion or ethnic fragmentations could also be determining factors (Lucas, 1988; Easterly and Levine, 1997; Alesina et al., 2003; Li and Zhou, 2010; Durlauf et al., 2012).

The neoclassical school argued that if a developing country does its "homework," the cumulative effect would eventually multiply to produce promising scenarios of economic growth and development. It is true that the presence of ethically strong and market-friendly policies could nurture and foster economic improvements. Once a fragile state has started to make domestic improvements, it would be a matter of time for investments to increase. An economy's attractiveness and competitiveness would need to be cultivated so as to produce a "virtuous cycle" of economic activities. The theory of capital accumulation has been used to promote growth (Swan, 1956; Cass, 1965; Barro and Sala-i-Martin, 1995; Howitt and Aghion, 1998). Capital accumulation requires a succession of economic activities involving increases in income and wealth, quantity and productivity of capital, and technological progress. Capital accumulation would begin with an increase in real savings, which is then channeled to investors through the banking and financial sector. The savings would eventually be transformed into productive investment with an increase in physical output.

A multidimensional approach is needed in understanding how the problems in fragile states have been so entangled that there is no single factor that can explain everything, and equally, there is no single solution to deal with all the problems. Both "soft" and "hard" politics could have negatively affected economic development in the fragile states. The "soft" politics relate to the internal politics of the ruling regimes. For example, the same "power-hungry" leaders have been in power for decades in some African states, and these leaders formed a hardcore group of cronies in the government that ensured and prolonged their power and authority. Some of these states were even considered as "democratic," as elections had been instituted, but they were often manipulated to the advantage of the same ruling regime. Power and authority could have been perpetuated through the "invisible hand of coercion." In situations of "primitive democracy," the political debates would unfortunately involve such primitive and irrelevant issues as the village from which the candidate came, ethnic background, territorial and geographical preferences, and religious attachment. Many of these fragile states were not short of natural resources, but the lack of reliable civic institutions and incompetent governmental organizations ensured that the ownership and use of natural resources would end up in the wrong hands (see, e.g., Acemoglu, 2005). The governments in many fragile states worked like a "private club," whereby members were either "invited or selected" to maintain the dominant position of the private club. A situation of a totalitarian state could emerge as leaders in fragile states could deploy the military to maintain "stability" and, in addition, the closed media restricted many sensitive reports.

A related question is why these fragile states would not change and improve. Many international institutions and foreign governments have provided funds to help these fragile states through development aid and humanitarian assistance. Yet, after decades of foreign assistance and millions of dollars of foreign aid injected into these fragile states, the end result is that they remained as fragile states. The simple answer is why should the leaders introduce change and promote development if underdevelopment and lack of progress served their interests and worked to their advantage in grabbing both political power and economic benefits. Many of these leaders and their associates lived like emperors, amassing as much resources and power to themselves as possible. A dynastic political arrangement would even suit these ruling regimes best, as that would prolong and pass their rule to their next generation or close family members and associates. Indeed, these regimes would prefer to see their countries remain underdeveloped, as they could "rent-seek" the economy and gain by capitalizing instability and underdevelopment.

There is the dimension on "hard" politics. Many of these former colonies gained their political independence after the Second World War, when the conflicting ideologies of capitalism and socialism were dominant. Popularized by the revolutions in the Soviet Union in 1917, China in 1949, and Cuba in 1965, socialism or communism was considered by many newly independent infant states as the more "appropriate" ideology, as socialism was meant to generate equality, a classless society, and eradicate exploitation. Initially, these infant states might have received aid and subsidies from the Soviet Union and become friendly to China, but the analysis should go farther. Indeed, during the Cold War years, the then Soviet Union, though itself experiencing economic shortages especially in consumables, provided assistance to ideologically friendly countries.

Firstly, many of these former colonies have never experienced capitalism as the industrialized countries had. There could be the existence of landlords and village chiefs, but certainly not a class of capitalists that engaged in manufacturing production. By adopting socialist-oriented policies, these economies passed from a rural mode to a socialist mode of production that resulted in government interventions, economic plans, and subsidy provisions. In other words, "demand-side" policies were adopted from the very beginning. The first question is how effective and reliable were the economic plans, and the first obstacle would be the unavailability of government resources to fund the welfare interventions. In other words, these economies jumped from a primitive stage of development with limited industrial production to severe provision of subsidies or welfare by the government. With limited production and output, there certainly would have been a funding problem.

The adoption of welfare-oriented policies had created a mismatch in supply and demand. With intervention and subsidy provision, people learned the "free-ride" attitude of "take, obtain, and receive." But there is a lack of emphasis on such "supply-side" activities as investment and production. The lack of entrepreneurship failed to generate a strong productive force. Hence, people demanded modern consumables, but there was a lack of industrial development and the economy could only produce raw materials and agricultural products that contained a low "value-added" content. Output and exports remained low, but subsidy provision generated spending and consumption, leading to a rise in imports and a weak currency as trade deficits mounted, a low level of international reserves, and ultimately a rise in national debt. The mismatch rested in the adoption of "spend-oriented" policies, without corresponding emphasis on "production-oriented" policies.

The path of development was worsened when there was a shortage of funds and consumables, and through economic planning and government intervention, resources could only be allotted to "priority" activities. The government bureaucracy, the military, and the police were certainly the "priority" activities, as government departments have to "exist" while law and order have to be "kept." Material shortages would become apparent, though the rural sector would have hidden the material shortages by keeping the standard of living to its lowest possible level. The lack of employment opportunities in the modern sector could be seen from the "surplus labor" in the rural economy (Ranis and Fei, 1961; Ranis, 2004). A primitive economy could have a sustainable life of its own. There would not be modern forms of employment, but assistance would be sought within the family or village, and a lack of communication could have hidden all the unpleasantness of these remote and underdeveloped communities. The local village chief could even be a more vocal and influential leader than the government officials.

In situations where there was a lack of reliable institutions, the easiest mean to overcome shortage would be the use of an informal instrument—corruption, which can be in pecuniary and other relational and invisible forms. Corruption has traditionally been studied within social science disciplines, and there are economic causes of corruption (Rose-Ackerman, 1975, 1999; Lambsdorff, 2007). Corruption involves two parties: the offering party that wants to get things done quickly and the corrupted amount worked like an "efficiency tax," though one major residual is the unfairness that generated, and the accepting party that took the bribe but abused the authority and misused the power.

Through corruption, the power and authority held by government officials had now become a privilege they exercised for their own benefit and vested interests. The situation would worsen if officials maintained a low level of professional ethics and there was a lack of an effective monitoring system, resulting in low official accountability. The emergence of such a "privileged" class could "rent-seek" and eventually lead to exploitation and abuse. To preserve their "legitimacy," undemocratic leaders could promote strong bondage and alliance between the bureaucracy, military, and business corporates, as that would enforce their power and coercion and protect their vested interests (Reno, 1997; Haque, 1998). The so-called "socialist pursuit" ended up with the emergence of a privileged class and control through the abuse of accountability. Indeed, this would certainly not produce an equitable and classless society, but a structured and systematic way of enforcing inequality, discrimination, and exploitation.

Such a political misalignment between the socialist ideological framework and economic reality has resulted in unfavorable consequences. For example, the customary outcome would be the "free-ride" attitude in many fragile states. Given that many people may not be economically productive, creative, and scientific, the Marxian colonialism argument could have made them feel that they were entitled to have compensation from former colonizers. Also, the socialist ideology would provide them with an additional desire to wait for subsidy. In addition, people in former colonial African states were not customarily strong in establishing businesses, and that would encourage them to become more dependent, rather than self-reliant and enterprising. Hence, the more subsidies that were given and the more foreign assistance that was provided, the prolonged "free-ride" attitude only told them to "take" from all possibilities. Making an effort to "earn" their entitlement may not have been a popular consideration.

Such a "take" attitude in many fragile states can contrast sharply with successful development experience from East Asian countries, where Confucian thoughts and customs promote a self-reliant, hard-working, look-after-oneself and enterprising entrepreneurial attitude. Some successful Asian countries have also been colonialized, but many have learned and picked up good practices and lessons from their colonial experiences, and built up their economic strength. Thus, rather than lamenting on the colonial past and accusing the colonialists, the colonial history of East Asia economies turned out to be an asset, e.g., in business practices and the rule of law, so as to gain foreign acceptance and confidence in trade and investment. One conjecture could make the point. Though situated on different continents, Singapore and Cuba have similar geographical and locational advantages. Had Cuba pursued a capitalist market economy, Cuba could probably be the financial center of the Caribbean today, like that of Singapore acting as the financial center in Southeast Asia.

Many fragile states face the worst of "three worlds." The leadership in the government was not prepared to promote development, and capitalizing on underdevelopment would seem a way out to keep their vested interests. The fragmented domestic economy was not able to initiate any sustainable development, as the rural economy remained primitive and, equally, there were insufficient changes in the urban economy to advance in any direction, and the economy was unattractive to investment as the business environment remained not market-friendly. Many fragile states continued to receive foreign aid and assistance, but one wondered how effective this economic assistance could be. The internal economic weaknesses of many fragile states have been worsened by the operations of international terrorists who took advantage of the religious, ethnic, and racial fragmentation, and conducted uncivilized terrorist activities. There is no easy answer to introduce effective development in these fragile states. Changes and regime switches have to come from within. Leaders have to understand that effective governance will be the better way to maintain their leadership. When providing foreign assistance by foreign governments and institutions, the assistance has to be conditional to ensure that certain aspects of improvement and directions of development can be achieved.

Economic development in the fragile states provides a clear understanding between the concept of "absolute advantage" and "comparative advantage." Many of these fragile states are small and are faced with "absolute disadvantage" over the advanced industrialized countries. But they could start to examine their "comparative advantage," and concentrate on a few aspects of production they can do well. For example, value-added industrialization can be promoted through various possibilities, not solely and necessarily by technology, but by design, marketing gimmicks, and advertising. Enlarging an economy's "comparative advantage" would be an economic answer if the fragile states could maintain stability in the first place. Indeed, there are small, island, and tiny economies that have done well by focusing on some selected areas of "comparative advantage." For example, by obtaining the status of an offshore financial center, some small economies facilitated the business of their foreign clients and international banks. Although they may look "peripheral" in the world economy, the international business attachments provide them with stability, development, and growth. Similarly, by adopting a capitalist market structure and serving as tourism centers, many island economies have participated in the global economy as they allowed foreign investment in the hospitality business, and act as a research post for marine science.

The neoclassical theories are more appropriate, as development must first come from the domestic economy and start with what resources the country possesses. A capitalist market economy allows flexibility and creativity, and business pioneers can venture to new horizons and open new opportunities. Capitalism opens up new revenues for those who create, and at the same time makes use of the opportunities arising from development.

Economic opportunity could be another scarcity in contemporary economic development. For the fragile states to improve, their governments must remain effective in assisting development. Ultimately, the answer lies in the promotion of "supply-side" activities, including infrastructure, human capital, and industrial enhancement.

III EMERGING STATES

Different definitions and classifications, analyses, and studies have been used in *Wikipedia* to illustrate the term "emerging markets." Kvint (2010) defined an emerging market country as "a society transitioning from a dictatorship to a free-market-oriented-economy, with increasing economic freedom, gradual integration with the global market, ... an expanding middle class, improving standards of living, social stability and tolerance, as well as an increase in cooperation with multilateral institutions." Vercueil (2012) specified three characteristics in the definition, including the income range of the emerging country, evidence of "catch-up growth" in the decade, and "institution transformations and economic opening." The term "emerging" conveys dynamism and fluidity, and changes in domestic conditions should qualify a country's "emerging" status. Emerging countries should include those countries that are constantly making positive improvements to promote their economies. This condition can be translated into a number of related characteristics:

1. Stability: exhibit a high degree of stability, or seen to be actively ensuring stability;
2. Domestic strength: improving domestic conditions through infrastructure and institutional developments;
3. Global connectivity: engage and connect with the global economy in attracting inward economic activities; and
4. Drive to modernization: modernization drive in various dimensions to ensure a higher degree of civic achievement.

Stability has to be the first condition to qualify to become an emerging country. Stability should be a continuous process over the years, extend to political and social exhibits, and produce peaceful civic engagement and improvement in the reliability and effectiveness of the democratic system should problems and disagreements arise. One example of disruption would be the military taking over the country, despite a democratic political system. Improvement in the domestic economy is a crucial criterion, as it relates to how economic results and outcomes are being delivered through the appropriate use of policies in deepening the economy. Typical examples include a healthy fiscal performance and use of economic instruments in promoting businesses and investment to widen economic capability. The adopted policies would be tested through promoting sufficient upward mobility and opportunity. In other words, the economy must dynamically be seen to move in the direction of enhancing growth and development.

The emerging country should engage positively in the global community, adhering to and promoting civic values. Although it may not be strong enough to contribute to international affairs, such as peace keeping, the emerging country would at least participate in economic openness, accepting various international standards, requirements, and practices. At the same time, the emerging country is expected to engage in various forms of modernization and civic upgrading. For example, a religion that practices discrimination would have to be modernized, and social and customary norms would be given contemporary interpretations scientifically.

Given that the term "emerging" implies a certain degree of change and progress, it is more important to consider the country's overall direction and intention, while it would take time for policies to come to preferred fruition. In any case, the combined results from these characteristics would be an adherence to the functioning of a market economy, with a clear trend in the increase in output and economic opportunities. Using the stages of growth in Rostow (1960), the "emerging countries" are probably countries in the second stage with "preconditions to take-off." Namely, these countries are getting ready and making preparations to reach a higher stage of growth. The "preconditions" would include a mixture of appropriate policies, progressive attitude, a proper modern mindset, and useful connections that bring changes and produce a stronger performance.

The BRIC countries (Brazil, Russia, India, and China) are an recent group of emerging countries indicating "a similar stage of newly-advanced economic development" (O'Neill, 2001; Cooper, 2016). The first BRIC summit was held in 2009, but South Africa joined and it became BRICS in 2010. The BRICS leaders have various ambitious and global agenda, including, e.g., the creation of the Chinese yuan as a reserve currency, in addition to the conventional improvements in economic interaction among themselves. However, despite the similarities in economic performances and indicators of the BRICS countries, questions are raised as to how these five countries from different continents with diverse cultures, races, and languages could piece things together without involving other countries and world regions. Russia and China are very different from the other three countries. Firstly, both Russia and China can influence global affairs, as they are the permanent members of the United Nations Security Council along with France, the United Kingdom, and the United States. Since its economic reform and opening in 1978, China has grown rapidly to become the second largest economy of the world. China is using its economic strength to build up its own global influence. Hence, Russia has been the "political" leader in the socialist ideology, while the strength of the economy makes China the "economic" leader in the socialist world.

Another difference between Russia and China and the other three BRICS countries is that Russia and China are interacting with the global economy in a "two-way traffic" through both inward and outward activities. These activities go beyond simply trading, but quite a few prosocialist countries do look to Russia and China for economic, military and political support and assistance. On the contrary, Brazil, India, and South Africa are less influential in international affairs, and engage mainly in a "one-way traffic" with inward activities only. However, the potential of these three countries is huge. Although they are still keen to attract inward investment, it is possible that these three countries can serve as regional headquarters in their own region. For example, India would serve the entire Indian subcontinent, while Brazil serves the neighboring countries in Latin America, and South Africa could be the more advanced country in sub-Saharan Africa.

Two groups of global economies could be qualified as "emerging countries." One group includes those medium-sized countries that are stable and prepared to move ahead. The major obstacles of these prospective countries could relate more to their internal inadequacies than to their external environment. Typical examples of internal inadequacies include weakness in domestic institutions, such as lacking standards and bias in civic judgment. Corruption is seen to be undesirable, but the ruling regime has not been able to eradicate corruption through institutional means. The lack of reliable and sustainable infrastructure and business-friendly policies would deter development in the private sector. The presence of a large informal economy could have restricted employment. Poverty has not been solved through job creation, while welfare subsidy has imposed an undesirable fiscal burden. There could be such local monopolies and informalities as drug trafficking, parallel trade, or family corporates in key industries that would have restricted fair development in other areas. As such, the prerequisite condition would be an open and transparent domestic economy. These emerging states needed a domestic "push" so as to set the scene for hyper-growth. Steering the economy in the right direction could already produce a cumulative but promising environment. Once their domestic issues could be "fixed," foreign investment could follow, as they would always respond to improvement in business-friendliness.

The other potential emerging states are those countries occupied by the former Soviet Union. After being freed and regaining their independence and autonomy since the collapse of the Soviet Union, many of these states are keen to integrate with the global economy through trade and investment. The advantages of these former Soviet states included stability, a fairly high level of human capital, and eagerness to catch up with the rest of the modern world. Their disadvantages, however, included a lack of entrepreneurial attitude, and the residual influence and presence of the Soviet-style institutions with its mentality of socialism and reliance on subsidy. Although some of these countries are rich in natural resources, they must be seen to be making efforts to turn and become a more market-driven economy. As such, the prerequisites would depend on improvements in the domestic economy.

These former "Soviet-annihilated" states could offer several economic advantages to foreign investors, including the low cost of production and a potential market. In some ways, the conditions in these countries are not different or even better than those in India or China. Indeed, some Eastern European countries have joined the European Union, and investment could have the advantage of geographic proximity. There is definitely huge potential for these East European countries to become strong emerging states. The political consideration, however, is whether the governments of these countries are sufficiently strong to build a market economy, or prefer to drift back to the Soviet-style path of stagnation and isolation. It is likely that the faster the emerging states are developed, the less likely they will drift back to their former socialist past.

Development in the emerging states will have various impacts on the world economy. On the one hand, international investors will have more investment destinations and diversity when the economic environments in the emerging states become competitive. Foreign investment will diversify away from the other destinations, such as China, to these emerging states. As income in the emerging states rises, they in turn provide new markets for consumables, leading to an enlarged world trade in industrial output. Collectively, these emerging states do form a formidable share of the world market, and their integration with the global economy can produce an alternative to many investors and producers. The economic rise and success of the key emerging states could become the new "latecomers" that compete with the Chinese economy in the supply of industrial output to the world market. In turn, there is also competition among the emerging states for the world market, as one better prepared and performing emerging state would compete successfully with another.

IV OPEC AND THE MIDDLE EAST

The list of countries that are holding the world economy to ransom are the Organization of the Petroleum Exporting Countries (OPEC), because they have a monopoly in the supply of oil, though there are unexplored oil resources in various parts of the world. OPEC was established as a permanent, intergovernmental organization at the Baghdad Conference in September 1960 by five Founding Members (Iran, Iraq, Kuwait, Saudi Arabia, and Venezuela). The other nine members joined later: Qatar (1961), Indonesia (1962, membership suspended since January 2009), Libya (1962), the United Arab Emirates (1967), Algeria (1969), Nigeria (1971), Ecuador (1973, membership suspended from December 1992 to October 2007), Angola (2007), and Gabon (1975–1994). In 1965, the headquarters of OPEC moved to Vienna in Austria. As stated in the official OPEC website, the objective of OPEC is to "coordinate and unify petroleum policies among Member Countries, in order to secure fair and stable prices for petroleum producers; an efficient, economic and regular supply of petroleum to consuming nations; and a fair return on capital to those investing in the industry."

There are other oil producing but non-OPEC countries, such as Malaysia and Brunei in Asia. As a cartel, OPEC tends to set its monopolistic price and members have to follow. Hence, the smaller oil producers could be restricted in their exports. The economic interest between the large and small oil producing countries could differ. The larger producers chose an "inelastic" demand strategy and wanted to prolong its "product life-cycle" by imposing a high price, so that demand is lower and revenue is higher. However, the economics of the smaller non-OPEC oil producers chose an "elastic" demand strategy, and undercut the OPEC price in order to sell more so as to increase their exports and reserves.

There are a few economic characteristics about this group of OPEC countries. None of them is considered as an industrialized or advanced country. Most of them are from the Middle East, with the remainder from Africa and Latin America. Many of these countries adopted the Islamic culture and religion, and have remained unstable and are faced with various degrees of religious, ethnic, racial, military, and territorial conflicts. The large oil export revenue has been referred to as "black gold" (Mahmoud and Jeffe, 2010). Some OPEC countries have built up tremendous wealth for themselves, while others are still faced with unreliable and unstable regimes, resulting in a stagnant economy with no development, and extreme poverty with refugees fleeing the country. There is a great contrast between the OPEC countries (Al Faris and Soto, 2016; Devlin, 2016).

There can be a number of hypotheses one can pose about the development of the OPEC countries. Have the oil resources brought them wealth but not growth and development, or have the rich resources not matched their low stage of development, or have the resources not been properly used for genuine development, or there are so many problems in these less-developing countries that the oil resources came at the wrong time? The simple truth is that these OPEC countries have been receiving oil revenues for decades, but are still underdeveloped and conflict-prone. This is an unfortunate outcome for the world economy, and there are more signs of deterioration and conflict than signs for improvement (see, e.g., Wärneryd, 2014).

Indeed, as oil is one of the key resources with its supply coming from the largest cartel, volatility in the oil price would attract a large volume of studies on the movement of the price, how oil price has affected other economies, speculation in financial markets, and the politics of the energy crisis (Abeysinghe, 2001; Zivot and Andrews, 2002; Kilian, 2006; Alquist and Kilian, 2010; Kim, 2012; Juvenal and Petrella, 2015). Some data analysis can bring out the various issues. Both the price and demand for oil have increased tremendously, especially after the turn of the 21st century, as shown in Fig. 8.1 (OPEC, 2014; Energy Information Administration, 2015) (The export trend did not include data from Iran. For the price trend, OPEC generated the weighted average price, and after 2005, the price of one oil field from Iran was included.). One observes that price and export trends tended to move together. Between 1975 and 2013, the three periods of oil price increase that started in 1978 – 79, 1988 – 90, and 1998 – 2000 were lower than that since 2002 – 03, when the price of oil increased vertically, and increased even higher after the 2008 – 09 financial crisis.

Table 8.1 shows some economic indicators among the OPEC members in 2012. There is a vast difference among the OPEC members, with Indonesia having the largest GDP, followed by Saudi Arabia, but the weakest members of Ecuador and Libya had only 10% of Indonesia's GDP. Most OPEC members have achieved a relatively high literacy rate, with the lowest around 51% in Nigeria. The data on public expenditure measured as a percentage of GDP shows that Venezuela had the highest percentage (6.87%), followed by Saudi Arabia (5.14%), others have lower percentages, though there are countries with missing data. While the debt data for key Middle East OPEC members are not available, the data shows that the four non-Middle East OPEC members were faced with an external debt close to 20% of their GDP (Indonesia, Venezuela, Angola, and Ecuador). A better performance can be found in the level of investment, shown as Gross Capital Formation, as many OPEC countries had

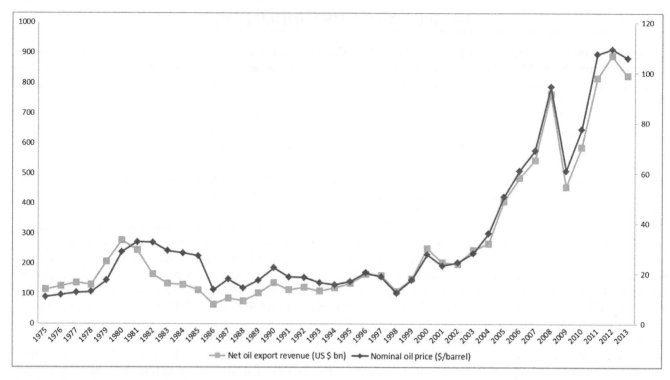

FIGURE 8.1   Oil: price and export trends.

achieved higher than 20% of their GDP, with the weaker ones being Nigeria, Iraq, Angola, and Libya. Despite their high oil revenue, OPEC countries received different levels of development assistance and grants from foreign governments and institutions. The two largest recipients were Nigeria and Iraq, due probably to the high degree of instability in these two countries in 2012.

It is clear that those OPEC members that had the largest crude oil reserves, production, and export are all Middle East countries, with the exception of Venezuela. The performance of oil rent was steady among all OPEC countries between 2012 and the average of the decade (2003 − 12), as the two percentages are similar for all countries. Those countries that had high petroleum exports would have high oil rent as well. Examples include Libya, Angola, Kuwait, Saudi Arabia, and Iraq. The high degree of military expenditure could reflect instability in these OPEC countries. Countries that spent more than 3% of their GDP on the military included Saudi Arabia, the United Arab Emirates, Algeria, Kuwait, and Angola. How much oil income was spent on the military can be seen from the military expenditure to oil rent ratio. The six countries whose military spending to oil rent ratio was greater than 10% in 2012 were Indonesia, Saudi Arabia, the United Arab Emirates, Algeria, Qatar, and Ecuador. Obviously, the dominance of the Middle East countries is alarming, as they hold the key to the supply of oil in the world market. With the exception of Indonesia, other non-Middle East suppliers are weak in their economic development. Two worrying aspects include the large wealth they possess, and the high degree of instability and conflict-proneness. A few strong oil exporters tried to stay away from instability, used the resources to build mega-cities, and live luxuriously.

There is definitely a severe mismatch between the availability of resources and the level of civic development, including reliable institutions and ethical behavior. Despite the large oil revenues, these countries are "mono-industry" economies, namely oil production is probably the only major industry, and there is a lack of economic diversity. Economic shallowness has important implications on employment opportunities, job creation, and investment. The lack of a reliable and sustainable economic, political, and business system and structure could not generate any positive development. Consequently, the rich resources in most oil producing countries could not be used effectively to enrich the "real economy" in the form of manufacturing.

The troubling element in the Middle East is religious extremism. The causality analysis between oil production and the Islamic religion is whether oil exporting enabled these countries to have resources to acquire military equipment and become involved with religious conflicts. Or do they prefer to engage in conflicts and wars in order to control oil resources? An understanding of the origin of the religious divide would show the depth of

TABLE 8.1 Economic Performance of OPEC Countries in 2012

	GDP (US$ mil)	Literacy Rate	Public Exp. on Education (% GDP)	External Debt (% GDP)	Gross Capital Formation (% GDP)	Development Assistance (US$ mil)	Grants (US$ mil)
Indonesia	876,719	92.8	3.35	29.07	34.74	67.81	735.98
Saudi Arabia	733,956	94.4	5.14	–	24.85	0.00	0.00
Iran	502,729	84.3	3.61	2.28	–	148.89	59.12
Nigeria	459,616	51.1	–	2.19	12.85	1915.82	1089.56
UA Emirates	383,799	90.0	–	–	22.66	0.00	0.00
Venezuela	381,286	95.5	6.87	18.91	26.60	48.13	28.09
Iraq	215,838	79.0	–	–	18.00	1300.79	788.52
Algeria	204,331	72.6	4.33	2.76	37.48	144.50	79.81
Qatar	189,945	96.7	2.45	–	28.75	0.00	0.00
Kuwait	183,219	95.5	3.76	–	–	0.00	0.00
Angola	115,332	70.6	3.48	19.22	11.58	242.35	175.09
Ecuador	84,040	93.3	4.36	20.15	29.48	149.43	135.57
Libya	81,874	89.9	–	–	15.10	87.09	95.51

	Crude Oil (MN barrels)		Petroleum Exports (% GDP)	Oil Rent		Military Spending (% GDP)	Military Spending to Oil Rent Ratio
	Reserves	Production		(% GDP)	2003–12 Average (% GDP)		
Indonesia	4030	763	–	2.61	3.95	0.63	24.2
Saudi Arabia	265,850	9763	46.2	45.77	46.89	7.35	16.1
Iran	157,300	3740	18.5	21.96	30.07	2.14	9.7
Nigeria	37,139	1954	36.8	15.31	26.45	0.78	5.1
UA Emirates	97,800	2653	30.8	21.9	20.59	3.67	16.7
Venezuela	297,735	2804	24.5	26.73	29.69	1.37	5.1
Iraq	140,300	2942	42.8	45.49	53.67	2.18	4.8
Algeria	12,200	1200	24.5	17.07	18.90	3.02	17.7
Qatar	25,244	734	60.4	12.06	20.64	2.01	16.7
Kuwait	101,500	2978	65.1	53.79	52.47	3.01	5.6
Angola	9055	1704	60.6	42.14	53.60	3.75	8.9
Ecuador	8235	504	19.2	19.13	19.86	2.67	13.9
Libya	48,472	1450	73.5	52.35	52.94	1.18	2.3

–, not available. Development Assistance consists of disbursements of loans made on concessional terms by the OECD and multilateral institutions. Grants are defined as legally binding commitments. Oil rent is the difference between the value of crude oil production at world prices and total costs of production. Data are in current US dollars.
The World Bank.

the contemporary conflict in the Middle East. Indeed, the conflicts in the Middle East have multiple causes, and it would be difficult to distinguish between the causes and consequences, as the conflicts range across religion, resources, territory, military, political, and historical to international security and relations (Cleveland, 1994; Lapidus, 1997; Enderlin, 2002; Gopin, 2002; Karatnycky, 2002; Norris and Inglehart, 2002; Sheikh, 2003; Ismail, 2006; Momani, 2007; Salt, 2008; Fawcett, 2013).

According to *Wikipedia*, the adherents of Islam are known as Muslims and are divided into two major denominations. The majority, with over 70%, are the Sunni, while Shia are the remainder. The division was historically due to the choice of the successor to the Islamic prophet. Sunni supported the choice of the followers as the successor, while Shia insisted that the leadership should stay within the family members of the prophet. Over the centuries, the conflict between the two denominations has increasingly evolved into battles over power and politics in the form of oppressive governments, terrorist organizations, and military engagements. The term "jihad" in the Islamic Quran, meaning "striving in the way to God," has been debatable. *Wikipedia* documented the two meanings of "jihad" as "an inner spiritual struggle and an outer physical struggle against the enemies of Islam." The focus has been on the second meaning that may take a violent form, as it has a military attachment to the meaning. The Islamic preaching of the "Holy War" has been considered as armed struggle against "wrong doers." However, this interpretation could be abused, with disastrous consequences, in the hands of unscrupulous authority holders (BBC News, June 20, 2014; and Factank, *News in the Numbers*, PEW Research Center, June 7, 2013).

Closely associated with the Middle East is the conflict between Palestinian Arabs and Israeli Jews that dates back to the end of the 19th century, though religious difference was not the root cause. It has been a conflict over the occupation of land. The area internationally known as Palestine, which was part of the Ottoman Empire in the 19th century, was claimed by both. During the First World War, the British promised to establish an independent Arab state in an exchange of letters known as the Hussein − McMahon correspondence if the Arab would revolt against the Ottomans. However, around the same time, the British also expressed official support for the international Jewish community in Palestine, in a document known as the Balfour Declaration. The British motivation was twofold—sympathy for the Zionist cause and a desire to rally the Jews to the side of the Allies. Thus, both Arabs and Jews thought they had the right to rule over the region. The Arabs fought against the Turks and organized themselves into various national entities of Iran, Iraq, and Palestine. The Jews migrated into the region and set up their community, economy, and governance. In 1937, the British and United Nations settled the disputed by partitioning the West Bank and Gaza Strip to be under Palestinian rule, and the rest being Israel under Jewish jurisdiction. However, there were populations residing within each other's border, and the conflict continued. Over the decades, the conflicts developed into wars, and the various peace settlements did not seem to provide a lasting solution.

There is a clear lack of modernity in the interpretation of Islam in contemporary terms. The trouble in the Arab world is deep-rooted. From the start, there was a lack of development in the independent political institutions as the Islamic faith's claim to combine both earthly and spiritual authorities did not provide strong segregation between the authorities of the state and religion. As a result of the strong religious influence and interference, the state has never had a strong fabric to function independently from the religion. Even after the First World War and the fall of the Ottoman Empire, the Arab countries were controlled by the colonial power until the 1960s. The Arab countries do not have a long history of nation building, and lacked experience in democratic institutions and civic development, such as protection of minorities, free press, sex equality, and independent rule of law. During the Cold War from the 1960s to the 1980s, the Arab countries leaned more to the Soviet Union, and economic development was absent. Thus, the Arab regimes tended to be socialist, characterized by government intervention, cronyism, and rent-seeking.

The conflict actually deteriorated. With the strong and continuous financial support from oil revenue in military and terrorist activities, the "third world war" basically started on September 11, 2001, when the World Trade Center in New York and the Pentagon in Washington, DC, were attacked by the Islamic extremist group al-Qaeda. Since 2001, conflicts between Islamic extremists and the rest of the civilized world have intensified in the Middle East region, as well as in other countries, culminating in the establishment of the Islamic State by the militant jihadist group. The "third world war" differs from previous world wars, as there is no fixed battle ground and enemies are hidden and not concentrated. Instead of solely concentrating on high technology military hardware, intelligence and security have occupied a central position.

Combining the economic impact of the key oil producers and the conflicts in the Middle East suggests the probability of "oil imperialism." On the one hand, the large oil producers are enjoying monopolistic power and the OPEC cartel holds the world economy to ransom. On the other hand, the large oil revenues that the Middle East accumulated are not used productively and effectively to enhance economic growth and development in their own region and across the global economy. Instead, the multiple levels of conflict these countries indulge in are games with "absolute" outcomes. The extent of regional instability, religious extremism, and weak governance is also holding the world to ransom on peace, stability, and civic development. "Oil imperialism" is characterized by sucking the resources of the world economy through their oil exports, but releasing back to the world various elements of instability and uncivilized extremism.

There are too many problems entangled in the Middle East conflicts. Attempts to solve these conflicts concentrated mainly in the political and military arena, which produced only "absolute" outcomes that could not satisfy the desires of all parties. Unfortunately, economic solutions have not been applied to solve conflicts in the Middle East. Economic activities involve "relative" outcomes and "positive-sum" games that can benefit all parties. Instead of using a war to deal with the division of land, different parties can use the market to solve the land problem through ownership arrangements. One can thus imagine the use of markets and business instruments to develop the land. Typically, manufacturing activities can be conducted to provide employment. Ex-soldiers would be using computer programs to figure out the extent of the economic capability and capacity in their countries. Stability should invite investment for productive purposes.

While militarism could still be the short-term solution to the conflicts in the Middle East, the long-term solution may rest with the use of civic and economic instruments in providing alternatives for the residents and citizens in all Middle East countries. One can think about both the "supply-side" and the "demand-side" of the equation. On the "supply-side," the world will need to depend less and less on oil consumption, and the long-term fall in oil revenue to the oil exporters would provide a sense of scarcity of export revenue in future. This effectively would make the oil producers value the oil revenue they possess. At the international level, there should be either a reduction of oil consumption or availability of alternative energy.

The "supply-side" solution is to seek a reform and modernization drive within OPEC itself. Armed with the large cushion of oil reserves and revenue, OPEC members should simply change from a "take" to a "give" mentality and attitude in various dimensions in their contact with the global community. The OPEC Fund for International Development (OFID), e.g., declared a total mobilizable resource of US$6885 million in January 2014, but the assistance was extended only to member states and non-OPEC developing countries (Official website of OFID). The OFID can mobilize funds more effectively for promoting the global economy. In the technology arena, e.g., OFID can fund the development of new energy and technology. For example, new technology on avoiding further deterioration in deserts or a revival in afforestation in the Middle East region would definitely be useful. There should be more activities that involve improvement in the establishment of civic institutions among OPEC member and nonmember developing countries. In addition, OFID can spend more resources in building up stable and conflict-free states in the region. This necessarily means the greater use of a market economy, and privatization to increase and promote economic opportunities.

On the "demand-side," the pursuit of peace and stability among the Middle East countries requires a multidimensional strategy. On the political front, there has to be a change of strategy from one of exclusion to one of coexistence and mutual respect. The deployment of military forces would solely be for security purposes, while peace agreements would have to be long-lasting and ensure sustainability. On governance, there should be a clearer division and separation between religion and the state. A process of modernization would have to bring culture and faith more in line with the ethical standards of the contemporary world. Between the state and religion, there should be the establishment of reliable institutions that provide civic protection to citizens. In the final analysis, there should be more activities with "relative" outcomes, and greater use of economic instruments would allow more business and civic opportunities. A market-friendly policy will gradually bring stability to the region as people will engage their energy in production, manufacturing, and business activities. Differences and competition would then be seen in the market rather than on the battlefield.

Changes in the conflict-prone countries in the Middle East would require work on both the "supply-side" and "demand-side" of the development equation. In other words, there should be both exogenous and endogenous actions. Activities from outside the region can help by changing the level of oil consumption and replacing militarism with civic activities over time. Activities from within the region can foster an attitude of mutual acceptance and coexistence, a process of cultural and religious modernization, and a reorientation of resources from military activities to economic development and business promotions. In short, there is a need for paradigm change as economic activities produce "relative" outcomes that encourage peaceful engagements.

V RUSSIA AND CHINA

Both the Russian Federation and the People's Republic of China belong to a class of their own. They are large countries, and their pursuit of socialism has influenced each other and the world economy at various times and to various degrees. History shows that they have been friends when they saw common interests with each other, especially in cases when support was needed to rally against the West. They were at odds with each other when each saw its own competitiveness had been challenged. As the former Soviet Union, Russia has been the political leader in the communist world; China once leaned toward the former Soviet Union and did not have the same world political status as that of Russia. However, the Chinese economy has grown since the 1980s, becoming the world's second largest economy, and has definitely outgrown the Russian economy. Would such a distinction of "political leadership versus economic leadership" lead to more acceptance or would conflicts arise when either one does not feel comfortable with the other?

The Marxian ideology adopted by the Soviet Union after the 1917 revolution introduced hardline communism. With the state and party members as the ruling class, the Soviets defied the "classless" society that communism preached. Economic collectivization meant that private ownership was eradicated and consumables were allocated. Instead of "capitalists and workers," central planning produced the dichotomy between "state and workers." Due to the drive for military supremacy, industrial production was concentrated on heavy industries. Economic hardship appeared frequently as trade was restricted, and the lack of resources led to further reduction in the provision of materials. The Soviet Union also bailed out pro-Soviet Union countries, but its economic weakness led eventually to collapse when President Ronald Reagan of the United States engaged in the "star wars" project of national defense that required massive resources and leaders in the Soviet Union found it difficult to compete. The collapse of the Berlin Wall in 1991 led to the downfall of the Soviet Union. Other formerly annihilated territories in Eastern Europe and West Asia regained their independence and autonomy (Nove, 1961; Schroeder, 1985; McAuley, 1991; Lebow and Stein, 1994; Fischer, 1997; Hartung, 1998; Gaddy and Ickes, 1998).

Like other socialist countries in the early 20th century, the 1917 Russia revolution was considered as a "showcase" in building up a socialist country that would preach better ideals than capitalism. Leaders in the communist movement in China thought that was an alternative to an equal and classless society. Having established the People's Republic of China in 1949, the communist party adopted socialist principles of centralization in the policy of the Great Leap Forward, with Mao's propaganda that aimed to "catch up with the UK economy in five years and the US economy in seven years," but the famine in 1958 led to severe shortages in agricultural production (Eckstein, 1975; Howe, 1978; Lardy, 1978). China after 1949 was isolated, as a trade embargo was imposed by the United States and other key European countries. China leaned toward the Soviet Union in the early 1950s, adopted central planning, and engaged in heavy industries, resulting in severe shortages in consumer goods. However, the initial "honeymoon" years between China's Mao and Soviet Union's Khrushchev were soon over when there were differences between the two leaders. Politically, there were differences in the viewpoints on the Far East and policy in the Cold War, nuclear disarmament, and the relationship with the Third World countries, leading finally to the withdrawal of all Soviet aid in 1958 (Floyd, 1964; Lowenthal, 1971; Zagoria, 1974; Pei, 1994; Westad, 1998; Shen, 2000; Luthi, 2008).

Literature overlooked the economics between China and the Soviet Union. The Soviet Union wanted to remain dominant in the socialist world, and the rise of China would pose a challenge. China has more human and agricultural resources. With the huge population in China, the pursuit of Soviet-style heavy industrial development might not be appropriate. The Soviet leaders would have realized that the capability of the Chinese economy could eventually exceed that of the Soviet Union. Thus, providing economic aid to China would later result in a situation where the Chinese economy could become stronger than the Soviet economy, which would be an unwanted outcome on the part of the Soviet leaders. The withdrawal of economic assistance would then be seen as delaying development in communist China (Dittmer, 1974; Chen, 2001).

Along with the Soviet withdrawal was the political divide in China between Mao Tse-tung (Mao Zedong), the hardliner, and Liu Shao-chi, the reformist, in the late 1950s and early 1960s, leading to a heated ideological battle that eventually resulted in Mao's Cultural Revolution in the mid-1960s that was a human atrocity and catastrophe, as the number killed by the "red guards" amounted to millions, in addition to the huge amount of cruelty and inhuman treatment inflicted on many victimized people who held different political views. Communist China complained about the Japanese invasion in the Second World War, such as the Nanjing massacre, but the killing was conducted by foreign invaders in a war time, while the millions killed in the Cultural Revolution was commissioned by Mao in order to uphold his political ideology and ambition (Chang, 1997; Chang and Halliday, 2005).

The turning point for China came at the peak of the Cold War between the Soviet Union and the United States in the late 1960s. In the United States President Nixon's "détente doctrine," the political intention was to pull and lure China to the side of the United States so as to alienate the Soviet Union (Garthoff, 1982; Litwak, 1984; Roy, 1998). President Nixon's "ping pong diplomacy" and the historic visit to Beijing in 1971 marked the new Sino − US relationship (A more detailed discussion on the "Nixon − Kissinger initiative" is given in Chapter 15, Section 15.3.). China began a new path of economic reform and openness in 1978, while Russia had to reorganize its economy after the disintegration of the Soviet Union in 1991. Although the two countries adopted market principles, there were fundamental economic differences between Russia and China from the very beginning.

The initial stage of reform in China was supported crucially by capital from overseas Chinese, especially from Hong Kong and Taiwan. China's history of socialism since 1949 was short, and those capitalists who fled mainland China were still alive and had their businesses in Hong Kong, Taiwan, and other Asian countries. When Deng Xiaoping declared economic reform in China in 1978, many overseas Chinese showed "goodwill" and considered that as a chance to help China. Such an inflow of "free capital" to China was similar to the post-Second World War development in the East Asian countries (Li, 2002). A considerable amount of the "free capital" was spent on public goods and infrastructure, while other Hong Kong capital moved to China and engaged mainly in light manufacturing industries. On the contrary, socialism in the Soviet Union lasted for almost a century, and few "overseas Russians" could have the ability to send money back. The absence of such an inflow of "free capital" in Russia could make a huge economic difference from the start.

Table 8.2 summarizes some economic indicators between Russia and China. China has a much larger population and labor force, while Russia has a higher enrollment in tertiary education. In land usage, China should produce a stronger agricultural sector than Russia. Russia surely has the advantage in the area of energy production, but China performed stronger in coal exports. China showed a much stronger performance than Russia in all

TABLE 8.2 Economic Comparisons Between China and Russia

Variables	Year	China	Russia
Population (million)	1970	838.3	130.4
	1980	981.2	139.0
	1990	1135.2	148.3
	2000	1262.6	146.6
	2010	1337.7	142.4
Population aged 15–64 (% of total)	1990	64.92	66.82
	2000	67.53	69.38
	2010	73.51	71.98
Rural population (% of total)	1990	73.56	26.61
	2000	64.12	26.65
	2010	50.77	26.35
Labor force (million)	1990	633.2	76.8
	2000	724.3	72.8
	2010	774.2	76.3
Life expectancy	1990	69.74	68.90
	2000	72.14	65.34
	2010	74.89	68.86
School enrollment, secondary (% gross)	1990	37.77	96.45
	2000	58.03	–
	2010	83.13	–
School enrollment, tertiary (% gross)	1990	3.10	54.72
	2000	7.76	72.59
	2010	23.32	–
Land area (1000 sq. km)	2000	9327.5	16,381.3
	2010	9327.5	16,376.9
Arable land (% of total)	2000	12.97	7.59

(Continued)

TABLE 8.2 *(Continued)*

Variables	Year	China	Russia
	2010	11.94	7.33
Forest area (% of total)	2000	18.98	49.40
	2010	22.18	49.40
Total export of refined petroleum products (1000 barrels per day)	2000	218.71	1067.0
	2010	623.41	2230.0
Export of dry natural gas (billion cubic feet)	2000	95.28	6590.5
	2010	141.97	7407.3
Total coal export (1000 short tons)	2000	77,450.6	43,981.1
	2010	27,180.8	148,912.3
Energy production (1000 kt of oil equivalent)	1990	880.8	1293.1
	2000	1064.5	978.0
	2010	2262.0	1293.0
GDP (current US$ million)	1990	359,937	516,814
	2000	1,198,475	259,708
	2010	5,930,529	1,524,917
Current account balance (% of GDP)	1990	2.99	0.22
	2000	2.41	20.03
	2010	3.92	8.08
Fiscal surplus/deficit (% of GDP)	2000	−3.27	3.33
	2010	−1.53	−3.42
Total reserve (% of GDP)	2000	14.33	10.65
	2010	48.97	31.43
Inward foreign direct investment (current price and exchange rate, US$ million)	2000	40,714.8	2714.2
	2010	114,734.0	43,168.0
Net official development assistance and official aid (current US$ million)	1990	2032.4	254.0
	2000	1711.8	1553.7
	2010	646.1	−
Public debt (% of GDP)	2000	16.44	59.86
	2010	33.54	11.04
Market capitalization of listed companies (current US$ million)	2000	580,991	38,922
	2010	4,742,837	1,004,525
Gross capital formation (% of GDP)	1990	36.14	30.13
	2000	35.12	18.69
	2010	48.22	22.62

Natural resources:

China: Coal, iron ore, petroleum, natural gas, mercury, tin, tungsten, antimony, manganese, molybdenum, vanadium, magnetite, aluminum, lead, zinc, rare earth elements, uranium, and hydropower potential.

Russia: Oil, natural gas, coal, rare earth elements, timber, and other strategic minerals.

−, data unavailable.
World Development Indicators, The World Bank.

other economic indicators, though China's public debt as a percentage of GDP is rising, and both countries suffered from fiscal deficit. In the financial and investment markets, China is way ahead of Russia. China also has a more diverse supply of natural resources.

Despite its effort in economic restructuring, the Russian economy tended to remain narrow, as its export base concentrated largely on energy. While the traditional capital-intensive and military-related heavy industries have largely remained, there is little expansion in the manufacturing sector to widen its industrial base (Shmelev and Popov, 1990; Dyker, 1992; Braguinsky and Yavlinsky, 2000; Gaider, 2014). The slow pace of economic growth and diversification, together with a lack of institutional changes and improvements since the Soviet era could push the Russian economy backwards. Having practiced communism for nearly a century, many would have got used to a "take" attitude, the business entrepreneurship attitude would probably need to be recultivated. Otherwise, many would have preferred life in the "old days" when their life was subsidized. This requires much effort in economic capability expansion and modernization of institutions. The Russian economy today can no longer support other trouble-prone world economies solely through socialist affiliation and military deployment. However, if leaders still hold such an outdated mentality, it could easily drain away Russia's economic resources. Indeed, the Russia economy needs to promote competitiveness through resource enhancement, rather than engaging in the uncompetitive socialist path of military engagement.

Labor abundance in China helped its development in light manufacturing industries for the export market. Studies have shown that capital input has been the key factor in China's total factor productivity in the postreform years (Li and Liu, 2001, 2004, 2006; Li, 2009). Due to China's richness in resources, and probably influenced by centuries of Confucianism, the spirit of entrepreneurship, hard work, and self-reliance are the "built-in" features in China. This is particularly strong in the coastal provinces, where economic openness to the external world had traditionally led businesses to flourish. China's socialism was considered to be "short-lived," and since 1978, the market economy has been reestablished. In the early years of reform, the Chinese economy made much use of funds and loans from international institutions and foreign governments. The foreign funds could supplement infrastructural development in the domestic economy, while domestic funds would be freed and deployed to politically preferred activities. China's growth benefitted from both the external sources of funds and domestic deployment of funds. Economic growth was accompanied by policy reforms, such as price and industry reform in the 1980s, banking and state-owned enterprises reform in the 1990s, and trade reform that resulted in accession to the World Trade Organization (WTO) in 2001 (Li, 1999, 2000, 2001; Li and Ma, 2004). Due to its rapid development and expansion in the manufacturing industry and exports, China claimed to be the "factory of the world," even though many foreign importers found that the quality of Chinese exports was often questionable. By 2010, China had boosted itself to be the second largest economy in the world after the United States (Overholt, 1993; Eichengreen and Tong, 2006; Perkins, 2015; Kroeber, 2016).

However, while many have optimism about China's growth, others think that China's economic "hardware" may not be supported by its "software," as the mounting growth has led to numerous domestic problems (Wedeman, 2004; Cheng and Ma, 2009; Wu, 2005; Wu, 2015; Wu and Ma, 2016) (A more detailed discussion is given in Chapter 15.). The annual growth rate projected by the Chinese prime minister at the National People's Congress held annually in March tended also to be the realized growth rate at the end of the year. The various reforms concentrated on results, but those hurt in the process might not be properly compensated. The dismantling of state-owned enterprises displaced many workers whose welfare provision had not adequately been compensated through public welfare and health. The production of toxic and unreliable food products ended up in expansion of parallel trade that effectively hid China's import figures. Anticorruption was used more as a political instrument and personality target than the institution of a system. Party members and officials who have acquired wealth rehabilitated their family overseas. In short, while the external economy has been polished for the foreigners, there exist in the domestic economy layers of economic inadequacies and distortions.

China was one of the poorest and most underdeveloped countries, its reform was seen by foreign countries and international institutions as a means to reduce poverty in China (World Bank, 1983). International funds that poured into China thought that developing China could serve two purposes: to reduce China's poverty, and development could be used as a showcase to other developing countries (World Bank, 1988a,b). However, there was insufficient pressure on China to make improvements on noneconomic fronts. Few would have surmised the impact on the world economy when China became developed. For example, the population of China amounted to 1.381 trillion in May 2016, equivalent to 18.72% of the total world population (http://www.worldometers.info/world-population/china-population/). The rise in China's demand for food and energy would lead to global inflation and added environmental pollution.

Many industrialized countries often single-mindedly "kowtowed" to the huge Chinese market, both in terms of its cheap labor and land for production, and the potential market for consumption and exports from the industrial world. After over three decades, China's Communist Party has become the richest institution as it holds the largest foreign reserves in the world. China can use its economic power to extend its political influence both at home and abroad (Bell, 2015; Ju, 2015). China needs a steady supply of oil from other oil producing countries, including Russia. China has taken various initiatives in making extensive trade and cooperative agreements with Russia (Voskressenski, 2003). Other unilateral activities China conducted included the establishment of the Shanghai Cooperation Organization (SCO) in 2001 that incorporated the former Soviet states in the Euroasian region. Although it began with the Shanghai Five in 1996, membership expanded in 2001 to include Kazakhstan, Kyrgyzstan, Tajikistan, Uzbekistan, and Russia. These former Soviet states are land-locked countries, but are rich in natural resources. With their departure from the Soviet Union, China took advantage of the "leadership vacuum" and seized the opportunity to incorporate these countries. In the meeting in July 2015, the SCO incorporated both India and Pakistan as full members (*China Daily*, July 11–12, 2015).

For some years, China intended to make the Chinese currency an international currency, along with the United States dollar in trade settlements (*South China Morning Post*, April 14, 2015). China has been cautious in declaring the full convertibility of the currency in the capital account, fearing the possibility of "capital flight" as the supply of the Chinese yuan may exceed demand. China's 2015 proposal of the "one belt, one road" that aimed to extend China through the land route all the way to Turkey and the Netherlands, and the sea route from southern China to the Indian subcontinent, passing East Africa, the Middle East, and eventually to Western Europe. This initiative led to the 2015 formation of the Asian Infrastructure Investment Bank (AIIB). A total of 57 countries including Britain, Germany, Israel, and others have joined the AIIB as the founding members, and China would provide "up to a 30% stake" in the AIIB (Kennedy and Parker, 2015; Larkin, 2015; Stokes, 2015) (*South China Morning Post*, April 2 and 15, and May 22, 2015; and *Global Trade Review*, July 1, 2015). The high degree of optimism seems to be that China faces no objections from other countries in the right to construct transportation infrastructure projects across the regions. Nonetheless, the "one belt, one road" will define China's global role westwards, encircling the entire southern and western Russia (Section 13.6 provides more discussion on "one belt, one road.").

There is also the "cyber war" between the United States and China, and at times Russia as well, as media reports showed that Chinese military hackers tried to steal information from US government websites, military maneuvers, and business companies. The issue has reached a state-level discussion in the United States as China did reveal its secrets in the cyber war. Analysts consider this "invisible and intangible" conflict between the United States, China, and probably Russia as the "New Cyber War" (*The Wire News from the Atlantic*, May 28, 2013; *The Fiscal Times*, March 21, 2014; *Fortune*, October 13, 2014; *The Daily Beast*, March 18, 2015; *ZD Net*, March 20, 2015; *Reuters*, June 21, 2015; *The Times of India*, June 23, 2015; *The Arizona Republic*, June 23, 2015; and *The Independent*, June 24, 2015). The cyber conflict can lead to security problems and terrorism, should the leaked information be passed to careless hands.

China has been labeled as the "new hegemony" in Africa, as Chinese companies have taken over "the proprietorship of African natural resources using Chinese labor and equipment without transferring skills and technology." Effectively, China extracts the natural resources at a low price, but sells manufactured goods to the Africa consumers at a higher price. The Human Rights Watch reported that "Chinese owners of copper mines in Zambia regularly violate the rights of their employees by not providing adequate protective gear and ensuring safe working conditions." Similar observations can be found in other African countries (De Morais, 2011; Okeowo, 2013; Dorsey, 2015).

Similarly, the soft side of the "new China" had been introduced to the foreign world through the establishment of Confucius Institutes, which is a chain of academic centers run by the agents of the Chinese government in a growing number of countries. By the end of 2013, it was reported that there are 440 Confucius Institute and 646 smaller Confucius Classrooms across 120 countries (*CNN Special*, October 21, 2014). However, underneath its official function, many argued that its main purpose was to conduct a worldwide ideological campaign and spread political propaganda. Indeed, communism and Confucian teaching should not go together, as the former preaches collectivization while the latter upholds individualism. Indeed, during the Cultural Revolution, Mao and his wife started the "Criticize Lin Biao, Criticize Confucius" political propaganda campaign that lasted from 1973 to 1976. The part on "Criticize Lin" was aimed at criticizing Lin Biao, and later Zhou Enlai and the political enemies of Mao ("Criticize Lin, criticize Confucius", *Wikipedia*). The part on "Criticize Confucius" was to glorify collectivism against individualism, and reinterpreted Mao's own revolutionary views on Chinese history.

History would judge as to whether the "Nixon – Kissinger initiative" was a wise move. China has grown in economy but remained socialist in politics, and it has even been thought that the new regime in 2014 under

President Xi Jinping had "slipped back to Mao era ideology" (*South China Morning Post*, April 15, 2015). Between the 1960s and 2010s, the table has turned, as now China is a more powerful socialist economy than Russia. Would the behavior of a strong China be acceptable to the rest of the world? Or is China gradually replacing Russia in global socialism? How would a "politically leading but uncompetitive Russia" versus an "economically strong China" react to each other? For Russia to gain economic strength, Russia may have to be more pragmatic, further shed its socialist attitudes, and adopt decentralization and greater market instruments by integrating more with the West (Blanchard and Shleifer, 2000). Steady economic progress can further be achieved if Russia works politically with the West through, e.g., accession to the European Union, and stands on the side of the West in key international issues.

China displays socialism differently from Russia, especially at the international level. China's large population forms an abundant resource of influence. The "locust" principle has been commonly referred to when China deployed massive numbers of its own people. The "locust" principle was used in the Korean War in the early 1950s, as it had demonstrated that people were China's instrument. After the opening up of China, large numbers of students were sent to study in the United States and other foreign countries. While many remained in foreign countries, others returned to China with knowledge and skill that helped China to modernize, especially in high-tech industries. After 2003 in Hong Kong, and around 2010 in Taiwan when China decided to "aid" these two economies, "visa free" travel permits were given to a large number of Chinese citizens, especially those along the coastal provinces, so that they could travel to "boost" the Hong Kong and Taiwan economies.

Compared to Mao, who followed the Soviet Union's style of showing military hardware, Deng in his 1978 economic reform gained world sympathy by declaring China as a poor developing country that needed a lot of foreign resources for development. Another strategy is the "bringing in" policy of absorbing foreign capital, knowledge, experience, and practices that strengthened the Chinese economy, while the local resources could be left tightly in the hands of the state. Once China has gained economic strength and political power, China would deploy its "going out" policy and declare its unilateral influence on other world economies in its own terms, with the eventual intention of establishing a communist world power compatible to Russia, the United States, and other industrialized countries.

VI THE ADVANCED COUNTRIES

A number of international institutions were established after the Second World War for economic construction. Prior to the Organization for Economic Cooperation and Development (OECD), the Organization for European Economic Cooperation (OEEC) was first established in 1948 as the international institution to execute the Marshall Plan for postwar reconstruction in Europe. The significant success of the OEEC led to discussion about a permanent body for economic cooperation. The US and Canada joined in, and the OECD was officially launched in 1961. Other countries joined or were invited in, including Japan in 1964. Today, the OECD has a total of 34 members. The mission of OECD is "to promote policies that will improve the economic and social wellbeing of people around the world." Among the OECD members some are world leading economies, such as the United States, the United Kingdom, Germany, and France, while others are young and emerging members, such as Estonia and Slovenia. Some are strong hi-technology exporters, such as Germany and Japan, while others are facing a debt crisis, such as Greece and Iceland. In principle, none of the OECD countries are socialist countries, but some OECD countries are governed by socialist-oriented political parties.

The primary objective of the EU is economic integration in the entire European region. Balassa (1962) used the European experience and theorized the five stages of economic integration. A Free Trade Area is the first stage, when there is the abolition of tariffs and quotas. The second stage is a Customs Union, where common tariffs and quotas were established among the members. The formation of the Common Market extended the goods and service markets to the factor price market, where there was integration in wages and the cost of other production inputs. The fourth stage is Economic Union, where economic policies are coordinated across members, including the establishment of common domestic laws. The final stage is Total Economic Integration, where supranational authorities are formed and supranational laws and policies adopted. Another theory of economic integration is the Optimum Currency Area (Mundell, 1961), which argued that the precondition for integration is the formation of a monetary union where members adopt a common currency and monetary policy. The successful convergence of key macroeconomic variables, such as interest rates, inflation rates, and income, is a prerequisite to economic integration.

Although many European countries are members of both the OECD and EU, the difference is that the OECD is a cohesive organization that promotes policies, while the EU aims at integration among the members. The EU consists of countries that have different economic backgrounds and strengths, and typically, some are much stronger than others economically. Hence, under the EU umbrella and the concept of "total economic integration," economically stronger countries are meant to lend support to weaker countries. This assumes there is income convergence within EU members (Fischer and Stirböck, 2004). However, experience seems to show that the weaker EU countries might likely have imposed economic burdens on other EU countries. Hence, instead of the economically stronger EU members helping and alleviating the weaker members, it is the poor performance in the weaker members that "rent-seek" and eventually pulled down the economic strength of the stronger member countries.

There are also other world groupings that have particular objectives. Founded in 1999, e.g., the Group of Twenty (G20) is an international forum for the governments and central bank governors from 20 major economies with "the aim of studying, reviewing, and promoting high-level discussion on policy issues pertaining to the promotion of international financial stability." The G20 is a platform through which discussions on key economic issues, such as financial crises and exchange rates, are made to ensure global stability. When there is a need to foster consensus on global issues, the G20 meeting can take place with only the eight key industrialized nations of France, Germany, Italy, the United Kingdom, Japan, the United States, Canada, and Russia. Similarly, with the exclusion of Russia, the G7 consists of the seven finance ministers and central bank governors of the seven advanced countries, though the EU is also represented. Hence, the G7 composes of the most powerful group of advanced countries in the world economy.

There is no doubt that the advanced countries are the strongest group of capitalist countries. Economically, they are the largest markets for exports from less developed countries (Berger, 2015; Smil, 2015). These countries hold the technological key in the world. Militarily, the G7 countries, especially the United States, are the police of the world. Their institutions, rule of law, code of conducts, systems, and professionalism are the reference points for the rest of the world. In other words, they are the pioneers in shaping world civilization. The most fundamental economic system that supports the structure of the G7 countries is the long pursuit of the capitalistic mode of production that allows private ownership, individual drive and entrepreneurship, freedom and openness, mutual respect and recognition, competition and the timely legislation of appropriate laws, regulations, and infrastructure provisions. However, one can only make progress, but can never reach a "perfect economy" or a Utopia. All capitalist market economies experience cycles in different periods.

As the world's leading economies, the G7 are taking a number of external responsibilities worldwide, while they are faced with internal problems that could have weakened their strength. External activities include the keeping of world peace, and minimizing global conflicts. Diplomacy has to be exercised in international relations, and military deployments have often been the last resort as they are politically controversial. Rescuing peripheral countries across the world has been another major responsibility of the G7 countries. For example, through international organizations, the G7 countries have provided both continuous and short-term *ad hoc* assistance to many developing and trouble-prone countries. The intention obviously is to ensure unnecessary human sufferings, tragedies, disasters, and loss are alleviated. Their "policing" role is a tough job, as there are always new problems emerging across the world economy.

The advanced countries are also faced with their own domestic problems. While there is a need to deepen and improve their institutions, economic performance in different business cycles and time periods would result in undesirable consequences. Typically, prowelfare political parties introduce welfare-related economic policies that have short-term advantages but may have undesirable economic consequences over time. Fiscal deficits and national debts are the "twin deficits" when prowelfare governments overspend on the current generation at the expense of the future generation. Governments might have used inappropriate policy instruments that generate undesirable economic outcomes. The prolonged use of a low interest rate policy was meant to keep investment costs low, but it also meant the cost of holding money is low. This could have numerous undesirable consequences.

There are other possibilities that could cause economic policies to backfire. A high minimum wage could turn out to be a rigid policy, while business cycles are fluid and change over time. Together with high income taxes, the economic policy that was meant to protect the domestic economy would backfire if investors found overseas investment was more attractive than investing at home. Hence, the intention of protecting the workers would end up inviting investment to leave the country for better investment opportunities elsewhere. In the end, unemployment would rise as the economy loses its competitiveness. In short, many so-called redistributive economic policies are politically oriented. These policies would satisfy the short-term political thirst, but the economy has to bear the long-term cost of a potential reduction in employment and loss in output and competitiveness. The choice simply is between higher pay that superficially increases the welfare of the employees, or a more competitive wage that would be attractive to investment, enhance employment opportunities, and probably promote social mobility. Few could have worked out the opportunity cost, social cost, or welfare loses of foregone alternatives when redistributive economic policies were adopted (Hoff, 1981).

Despite all the challenges, the G7 countries represent the backbone of the world economy, and they still serve as reference economies to other growing economies. While their success would hope to be transferred, the difficulties they have experienced would serve as lessons for others to avoid. There are a number of long-term possibilities that the G7 countries can initiate in order to promote a stronger world economy. One possibility will be for the G7 to diversify their investment to other newly emerging and market-promising countries. This can reduce cost of production, avoid concentration of trade surplus in a few world economies, and promote competition among foreign investment recipients. The G7 countries can strategically invite or incorporate other resource-rich, trade-surplus countries to participate. Another possibility is to have further innovation and commercialization of high-tech consumer products to reduce the consumption of oil or increase exploration into alternative forms of energy.

VII GLOBAL POLITICAL ECONOMY

The world in the 21st century is different from previous analyses on international economic relations in various ways (Brandt, 1980; Helleiner, 1980; Ostry, 1990; Williamson and Milner, 1991; Cutter et al., 2000; Spero and Hart, 2010). Discussions on the "Third World," "North — South" or "South — South" relationships and cooperation have been challenged by the distinction between fragile states and emerging countries because of a clear difference in their potentials. Although the United States and Europe are still the most attractive market for exports and international trade, many of these countries have been weakened for a number of reasons. Large redistributive and welfare policies have led to prolonged fiscal and national debt in some countries, thereby weakening the purchasing power of consumers. The prolonged low interest rate regime has led to the dominance of the financial economy over the real economy, as governments and investors worry more about stock market fluctuations than industrial output growth. The high cost of production in many industrialized countries has led to the outflow of investment searching for low cost production destinations in Asia, resulting in a loss of competitiveness and jobs in the home economies.

Although it was the 1944 Bretton Woods meeting that initiated the contemporary global monetary system and established both the International Monetary Fund and the World Bank as the two key international institutions in the pursuit of global economic development, these two worldly institutions have over the decades been criticized for not doing sufficient to rescue the world economy (Krueger, 1997; Mussa and Savantani, 2000; Woods, 2002, 2006; Easterly, 2003b; Dreher, 2004; Steil, 2014). Criticisms include the prescription of a similar recipe to countries facing different backgrounds. Policies have also been influenced by socialist ideologies. Indeed, it has been over 50 years since their operation, but the same global problems of poverty, inequality, and underdevelopment have occupied their attention. Given that these international institutions committed massive spending on developing countries, one wondered whether there was policy effectiveness. However, though it is natural to expect more from the performance of the two institutions, there is no doubt that the two institutions have, over the decades, done much to promote world development.

The relationships among the five groups of global economies can be seen in Fig. 8.2. Firstly, all the five groups of global economies are connected to each other. The advanced countries are the leading group of countries. However, the trade surplus countries are mainly the OPEC group and the socialist countries, especially China. The OPEC and Middle East group contains many of the conflict-prone Muslim countries. Thus, the advanced countries have to face challenges from two fronts: religious conflicts and trade deficits. On the contrary, the two groups of emerging countries and fragile states are not expected to contribute much to the world economy, as they are the recipients of various assistance, supported mainly from the advanced countries and occasionally from Russia and China. Indeed, the lack of stability and vulnerability in some fragile states has been exploited by cross-border terrorists to destabilize and spread conflicts to other world regions. The group of emerging countries cannot show a strong performance, due largely to domestic inconsistencies, such as weak governance and a large informal economy.

To start with, the world relies excessively on oil, and the OPEC countries hold a monopolistic position. This is made worse by the fact that the OPEC countries are mainly Middle Eastern countries, and some of them are

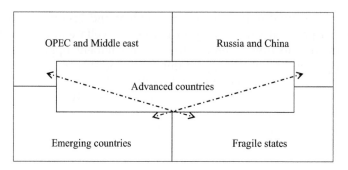

FIGURE 8.2   The five groups of global economies.

hostile to other world regions due to religious, racial, territorial, and historical reasons. The rich resources that oil exporters in the Middle East amassed are not put to effective use, and do not channel back to the rest of the world in a productive manner. Hence, on the one hand, the world buys oil from the oil exporting countries, but on the other hand the world has also been destabilized by the fact that some oil revenues were channeled to unscrupulous regimes that practiced terrorism.

Secondly, despite the establishment of civic institutions in the advanced countries, prosocialist governments have instituted prowelfare policies that imposed a high long-term social cost on their economies, resulting often in a decline in economic competitiveness. Typically, the high degree of redistribution through tax revenue, and the rising production costs and strong labor power effectively invited investment to depart from these economies, causing a reduction in the overall level of employment, especially in the production sectors. Similarly, large welfare provisions could have occurred during economically strong times, but while the instituted welfare policies tended to stay and become rigid eventually, and even if the prosocialism governments were voted out of office in the elections that followed, the cynical movements in business cycles could lead to economic downfall, resulting in fiscal deficits and accumulation of national debt. The combined result of high costs, prolonged welfare provisions, and large national debt would deter investment and the economy would then enter a "vicious cycle" of low growth.

The outward investment from advanced countries had been made easier when many advanced countries adopted a prolonged low interest rate regime. In the 1960s and 1970s, it was the East Asian countries that benefitted from the inflow of foreign investment. Since then, the East Asian countries have achieved prolonged growth, due also to the success of the capitalist market system. Investment since the 1990s had poured into China, thereby enriching socialist China. After three decades of growth, China has become the country with the largest international reserves that could be used more to enhance its own domestic and international agenda. The debate as to whether China will be a threat to the capitalist world or China would join hands with the rest of the world will depend on China's own political agenda.

In general, as the neoclassical school argues, the emerging countries are restricted more by their domestic constraints, typically in the development of more reliable institutions and the establishment of a transparent and equitable system. For the former Eastern European states, a speedier adoption of market-friendly policies should invite new investment. If not, the worry would be a reversion to the former socialist conduct of activities. For other emerging countries, a major domestic constraint rests often in their old-fashion customs, beliefs and superstitions, and culture. For example, it was reported in 2015 that two brilliant student brothers from a lower caste in India faced stone-pelting by people from their own village (*The Huffington Post*, July 17, 2015). Sheer discrimination in receiving education and job opportunities due to sex, caste, and geographical reasons cannot be tolerated in the modern civilized world. In some Latin American countries, there are powerful local monopolies, such as drug lords or arms traders that encouraged an underground economy and restricted the development of formal economic activities. There are also situations where a lack of transport infrastructure has restricted accessibility to remote regions in emerging countries.

In short, the problem in emerging countries may not entirely be due to resource constraint, but to the lack of reliable domestic institutions. Improvements can occur in two directions. The domestic solution would be for the government to promote reliable institutions and systems. A system-driven economy would become more transparent and equitable. It would equally be preferable for international institutions and foreign governments to work with local government to raise the overall civic standards through exchange of "good practices." In short, there are development potentials among the emerging countries, but improvements in domestic conditions are their prime responsibility.

The fragile states are probably the most dependent group of countries for foreign aid and assistance. Their lack of stability is detrimental. The maintenance of stability could at least allow daily life to function, such as provision of basic health and hygiene, housing, and other basic needs. The effective strategy for the fragile states is to concentrate more on economic development than on political fighting between social factions. Without a minimum level of stability among the fragile states, assistance will not be effective in bringing any results. In other words, there is a need to institute a process of the "virtuous cycle," so that the achievement of one activity would spill over and lead to another activity. One thus has to create positive and effective opportunities in these fragile states, provided stability can be instituted and sustained.

VIII CONCLUSION

There can be a cluster of conclusions and recommendations from the analysis when the world economy is partitioned into five groups of distinct economies. Firstly, the theory of comparative advantage and specialization of production is still strong, but its essence could have gone too far. The oil producing countries have the upper hand in energy supply, and the rest of the world is largely dependent on oil imports. This is the demand-side of the equation. On the supply side, car manufacturers, e.g., are slow in producing vehicles that use alternative forms of energy. Even if the technology exists, the price of the product may be too high for ordinary consumers. There is a need for further commercialization of alternative forms of energy in vehicles and other products that use oil.

While high technology businesses are mainly concentrated in the advanced countries, the bulk of manufacturing for consumables is no longer in the industrialized countries. The high cost and labor protection in industrialized countries have encouraged investment and production of light manufacturing has migrated to low cost countries. There are several economic outcomes. One is simply that advanced countries become mainly consumers and not producers, and the economy turns to become an importer and not an exporter. There will be a loss of jobs and employment opportunities as investment migrates. If the outward investment is technology-related, the industrialized country may even lose its comparative advantage in the progression of high technology, leading in the long run to a loss in economic competitiveness.

It is true that the service sector is dominant in industrialized countries, but many service jobs do not require much skill. Unskilled service jobs would normally have a low wage and a rather short employment-life. An aging saleslady, e.g., could easily be replaced. A lot of service-related business may engage in informal activities. A souvenir shop in a tourist town, e.g., may not report its true business for tax purpose. The extent of "value-added" is generally low among many service businesses. There can still be employment in service businesses, but their overall economic contribution tends to be low. As skill is not high, upward mobility of workers is restricted. For example, because the lines of production are mostly predetermined, jobs in many fast food restaurants do not pay highly, and the chance of obtaining a pay increase is low. There are far too many problematic countries that need help and funding assistance. Effectively, even in some oil exporting and Middle Eastern countries, most countries in the fragile states group and some emerging countries require assistance from the industrialized countries. Many problems in weak states are indigenous, and the assistance is often granted on humanitarian rather than economic grounds. There is a need to promote more responsible governments and citizenry in order to maintain stability and build up the economy.

"Supply-side" economics is still the more reliable and sustainable solution to economic development. One cannot keep demanding, asking, and taking, though this is easier to do, the economy cannot survive without production, accumulation, and supply. While demand is unavoidable, the economy has to devote more resources to the "supply-side" of the economic equation. Supply creates jobs, employment, output, and productivity. Demand requires one to spend, buy, shop, and use. The best combination would be to produce and consume one's product and output, so that job creation can be kept, and a rise in employment be provided by the purchasing power of the employed. The economy would engage in a virtuous cycle of production and job creation. The worst combination would be the inability to produce domestically, but assistance from foreign funds would allow one to consume. With the absence of local output, goods would have to be imported. The economy would face the need to repay the foreign assistance, and foot the import bill, while domestic employment would become low if the production sector remained weak.

Of course, these "best" and "worst" scenarios are conjectures, as economic openness could not restrict trade, and the process of globalization would encourage countries to engage more with the global economy.

Nonetheless, "supply-side" economics conveys the idea that for healthy and sustainable development, an economy cannot just rely on consumption and spending without some attainment in physical output and industrial production. There can be two implications of "supply-side" economics. One simpler idea is that economies cannot entirely rely on such nominal economic activities as tourism, because economic sustainability requires physical output that is skill-enhancing and provides a longer employment life. Secondly, conflict-prone countries should best restructure their priorities in order to engage the economy in production activities as so as ensure employment and absorption of labor and workers. A market economy should provide an "invisible hand" in resource deployment, so that at least some sections of the economy would begin with production activities, which could then multiply and enlarge the production sector. In short, the global economy will be different if all individuals and economies can stand on their own feet and be responsible for their own deeds.

I INTRODUCTION

The forces of supply and demand are often the causes that lead to economic fluctuations in a business cycle, though business cycles differ in time, length, magnitude, and severity (Lucas, 1977, 1981; King et al., 1988). The theory of rational expectation adds to the analysis that investors and consumers hold different expectation in their economic decisions. There is also the "political business cycle" in that businesses are affected by the timing of political elections (Muth, 1961; Sargent and Wallace, 1976; Gali, 2015). The ups and downs of businesses are expected, and there can be a number of economic spillovers in different stages of the business cycle. However, the forces of supply and demand can also "heal" the downside of the business cycles, as the changes in prices and costs of production would provide different market signals to investors and producers. The more important element in all stages of business cycles is the economic opportunities generated. Indeed, the more economic opportunities there are, the more solid the economy can become as it can successfully shoulder, defend, and absorb the negative impact of the business cycle.

Closely linked to the discussion of business cycles are economic crises, especially financial crises involving collapses in the stock market, banking difficulties, and foreign exchange volatility (Dore, 2000; Feldstein, 2002; Tirole, 2002; Reinhart and Rogoff, 2009; Kindleberger and Aliber, 2011). It is true that crises usually emerge unpredictably, but the aftermath of a financial crisis would always be a period of economic recession. Similarly, investors, businesses, and government would have different reactions to economic crises, but no two economic crises are the same, as they can be economy-specific, region-specific, and policy-specific. Different crises require different recipes and solutions.

There are numerous studies on the causes of economic crises. The Mexican crisis in 1994 – 95 was due to the government's inability to handle their debts, while the Asian financial crisis in 1997 – 98 involved Asian currencies and was explained by fundamental factors, contagion, and panic. There are other causes discussed in other financial crises, such as the crises in Russia and Brazil (Calvo and Mendoza, 1996; Cole and Kehoe, 1996; Kaminsky and Reinhart, 1998; Radelet and Sachs, 1998; Haggard, 2000; Sutela, 2000). The International Monetary Fund (IMF) has advised countries to institute a warning system in order to avoid the emergence of crises, but when they have occurred, the IMF has always been the first institution to provide prescriptions and recipes, and

© 2017 Elsevier Inc. All rights reserved.

the usual recommendation was to encourage the crisis-affected country to take up austerity measures and reduce the size of government spending to avoid severe deficits (Edison, 2003; Bussiere and Fratzscher, 2006).

Although the economy suffers in a downward business cycle, there can be difference between an economic downturn and a crisis. Normally, the domestic economy would have to heal itself through market forces and short-term measures, such as export promotion and currency depreciation. An economy in recession normally does not expect to receive assistance from foreign governments or international institutions. The case of a crisis is different. When a crisis breaks out, typically in an emerging country, it is possible to have multiple levels of assistance. In Asian countries, assistance mainly comes from the IMF, and often austerity conditions are set to ensure economic revival and improvement. In the case of South Korea during the Asian financial crisis in 1997, e.g., many of the brand name corporations sold to foreign buyers, while stringent austerity conditions were imposed by the IMF. The South Korea economy recovered after a few years. The experience of Indonesia was that the economy recovered following the recipe from the IMF. Both South Korea and Indonesia soon returned to trade surplus, and increase in their foreign reserves (Kartasasmita and Stern, 2015; Lee, 2016).

Greece's debt crisis in 2014 − 15 was prolonged and lengthy, and effective solutions were not forthcoming. The Greek crisis was assisted by the IMF, individual European countries, and the European Union (EU) as a collective body. Billions of dollars of bailouts were provided to the Greek economy sequentially. But, despite all these layers of assistance, the Greek economy remained dependent and weak. Although there were conditions attached to the rescue, and Greece was given time to handle its own domestic economic ills, the question is whether it is good for a crisis-economy to receive bailouts and rescue but leave the fundamental problems unsolved, or should the economy swallow a bitter pill so that the economy could make a fresh start and return to a more effective development path.

In economic recessions, the performance of different economic sectors could soon balance out each other. Typically, a recessed economy would turn round when cost and price have fallen sufficiently low to attract new opportunities. Hence, reversal in economic performance will promote physical output and employment. Given time, the economy can recover, based on both the "flow" and the "stock" sides of the economy. While the "flow" economy relates mainly to the nominal nature of the economy, such as money supply, stock market movements, and exchange rate changes, the "stock" economy relates more to real economic activities, measured in terms of industrial manufacturing, employment, and human capital advancement.

In financial crises, on the contrary, the trouble concentrates mainly on financial variables, such as currency depreciation, capital flight, and stock market collapse. All these financial variables are the "flow" side of the nominal economy, and their movements could be sudden and quick. The panic and contagion behavior of investors and speculators would lead to irrational market transactions and trends. Because financial crises are always sudden and severe, they require immediate attention and need quick solutions, which often could not be found easily without using fiscal and monetary austerity measures. There is thus a need to monitor the effectiveness of the fund assistance.

However, the outburst of any financial crisis by its very nature is an ex post event. One has to examine the ex ante factors, which can be difficult because there are probably multiple causes in a crisis. A scientific reason to examine the ex ante factors would be to look at some of the adopted economic policies, and whether economic distortions could have accumulated but were not addressed. This is particularly true in financial activities, because the performance of financial variables usually reacts to adopted policies. Investors react to the policy on interest rates, traders react to the policy on exchange rates, and banks react to the lending rate. Prolonged welfare provisions would drain fiscal resources. National debts are accumulated because of the inability to generate sufficient fiscal revenue. As such, one missing link in the study of a financial crisis is not so much about what can be done to rescue a crisis, but what policy prescriptions should be applied in order to avoid a crisis. Numerous studies on financial crises tended to concentrate on the ex post analysis, but in fact the more relevant analysis would be to tackle the potential situation of a financial crisis on an ex ante basis.

Very often, economic policies were made for political reasons, while economic distortions or deviations went unnoticed. Typically, high government spending was decided on for political reasons, but fiscal unsustainability would not be noticed, especially when the economy was on the upside of the business cycle. And when a fiscal deficit appeared, national debts would be accumulated. One way to handle national debt would be to borrow through the issue of treasury or government bonds, hoping that the debts would be repaid at a later stage. But if the economy remained weak, more borrowing would have to take place to cover the debts. The ex ante situation could be the political desire to commit more government spending, while the ex post situation would be the emergence and accumulation of national debt. Hence, together with other economic ills, the debt would spill over to other financial variables, such as pressure on the currency to devalue, exhausting foreign reserves, and borrowers defaulting. The unexpected list of ex post consequences would accumulate and explode into a financial crisis. Hence, was the crisis caused ex post by the size of the debt, or ex ante by the policy decision on high welfare spending?

The traditional stock market is for corporations to raise capital in the primary market through the initial public offering (IPO) process, and the issued shares can be bought and sold in the stock market, which is considered as the secondary market. However, the distinction between investment and speculation is becoming increasingly blurred, and there are numerous financial instruments in the market that cause investors to speculate. The provision in trading of margins, derivatives, and shadow banking are clear examples of financial instruments that serve speculative activities. One can question whether these financial instruments are really useful for the healthy development of the investment market, or whether their existence facilitates speculation. Hence, when the market is bullish and speculators gain, there is asset appreciation which contributes to a greater degree of income inequality (Dore, 2000; Piketty, 2014), but when the market bursts, these speculative financial instruments would lead to sharper depreciation and the downfall of the asset market, thereby resulting in a greater degree of market volatility.

Instead of concentrating on ex post analysis, this chapter provides an ex ante analysis to describe the trends and performance of some world economies. The prolonged low interest rate in the United States would have contagion effect on the rest of the world. Hence, the 2008 financial crisis that resulted in the closure of banks, financial institutions, and property companies in the United States and elsewhere were ex post analysis, while the decision on the low interest rate in the United States since the 1980s provided an ex ante analysis. The 2008 financial crisis exposed, on an ex ante basis, the problem of the excessive role the government played in the economy. The Greek crisis demonstrated vividly how a welfare-prone but growth-weak country would provide lessons to other European countries, with a similar extent of government intervention and involvement. The 2008 financial crisis also caught the Chinese economy unexpectedly, as the world recession forced China to restructure its exports and industries. In turn, there are more economies that needed help as a result of the 2008 crisis. International investors would also take the chance to look for attractive investment destinations other than China. Hence, China faced an uncertain situation between a "crossroad," where there were still alternatives, or a "turning point" where economic capability would have reached saturation (Li, 2014a).

The political economy of the 2008 financial crisis opened up many discussions, including the undesirable consequences of socialist policies, and conversely the strength and ability of market capitalism in providing economic sustainability. The 2008 crisis should serve as a "wake up" call to those welfare-prone economies, so that they could take time to end their interventionist policy before they headed into another crisis. The 2008 financial crisis brought out an important point on economic competitiveness. It is not only the desire to avoid a financial crisis, but it is the question of how an economy stays competitive and maintains reasonable growth.

II POLITICAL ECONOMY OF THE 2008 CRISIS

The September 2008 financial crisis had an entirely different dimension that could have a long-lasting and multiple impact on the world economy. It began in the United States, where the collapse of the subprime mortgage industry in early 2007 resulted in the closures of Lehman Brothers and Washington Mutual. Between February and March 2007, it was reported that the US subprime mortgage industry collapsed, with an estimated loss of US$1.3 trillion. By August, 2007, many hedge funds and banks were found to have heavily invested in subprime mortgage-backed securities. The US Federal Reserve injected US$100 billion into the banking system for banks to borrow at a low rate. By March 2008, one of the largest investment banks, Bear Stearns, was badly affected by the subprime mortgage crisis. The emergency loan provided by the US Federal Reserve to avoid collapse of the company was not helpful, and Bear Sterns was sold to JP Morgan Chase for about US$10 per share.

On September 7, 2008, the two largest mortgage-backed security companies, Fannie Mae and Freddie Mac, were taken over by the US Federal Reserve, followed by the closure of Lehman Brothers, while Merrill Lynch was sold to Bank of America on September 14, 2008. The other two events on September 17 and 25, 2008, respectively, were that a total of US$85 million loans were provided by the US Federal Reserve to the American International Group, which was a major American Insurance Corporation, and the seizure of Washington Mutual, which was the largest savings and loan association in United States, by the Federal Deposit Insurance Corporation and its banking assets were sold to JP Morgan Chase. The saga ended on October 3, 2008, when President George W. Bush announced that the US government would create a US$700 billion bailout program to purchase failing bank assets.

As the leading financial center of the world, the financial policies of the United States would lead to similar movements in other countries. Fig. 9.1 shows the downward interest rate movements of the G7 countries. The Federal Fund Rate (FFR) is used for the United States, while the end-of-month bank rate is used for Canada, the Bank of England base rate for the United Kingdom, the average cost of funds for the Bank of France, the discount

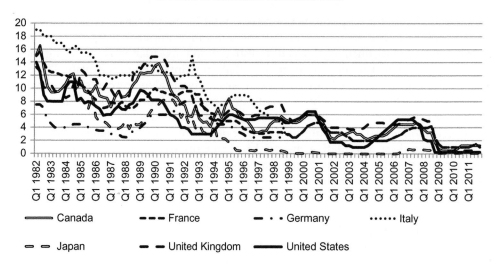

FIGURE 9.1 Interest rate movements of G7 countries.

rate for both Germany and Italy, and the uncollateralized overnight call money rate for Japan. The interest rate data for the G7 countries can be found from DataStream for the period 1982Q1–2011Q4. Some G7 countries experienced a period of high interest rates during the 1980s, but these remained low afterwards, with some having dropped to zero after the subprime mortgage crisis. The interest rate in Japan was obviously much lower than other countries, as it had been close to zero since 1995, and fluctuated widely between 1996 and 2008. On the contrary, the United Kingdom has kept a higher interest rate for most of the time in the sample period. Since 1999Q4, the interest rates of France, Germany, and Italy coincided with each other. After the 2008 financial crisis, the interest rate of all G7 countries remained at a near-zero rate.

Obviously, the G7 and a number of Asian countries suffered from the 2008 financial crisis, typically with a downfall in a number of financial markets, followed by economic recession in the world. The first wave of corrections concentrated mainly on the need to strengthen financial fundamentals, such as financial regulations, bank liquidity, role of the Chief Executive Officer (CEO), moral hazards, and corporate governance of financial institutions, including the debate on "too big to fail" among gigantic financial corporations (International Monetary Fund, 2009; Financial Services Authority, 2009; Samwick, 2009; French et al., 2010). In the case of moral hazards, discussion concentrated on whether the information about a bank client should be disclosed to other sections within the bank, typically from the bank deposit section to the investment section. The high rates of pay received by the CEOs in financial institutions were considered not in alignment with the performance of the bank.

While there were many postcrisis discussions on the rescue, the United States and other European countries conducted a series of "quantitative easing" (QE) policies that involved the purchase of a specified amount of financial assets from commercial banks in order to increase the monetary base when the interest rate could not be lowered any further. The QE strategy was meant to provide a short-term solution aimed at rescuing the banks and financial institutions by purchasing assets of longer maturity than short-term government bonds. As reported in *Wikipedia*, the US Federal Reserve has, between November 2008 and the end of 2012, provided three episodes of QE accumulating to an amount of US$2.054 trillion spent at different times on bank debts, mortgage-backed securities, and treasury notes (http://en.wikipedia.org/wiki/Quantitative_easing).

It would be useful to consider the situation in the world economy at the time of the 2008 financial crisis. Notably, the September 11, 2001, terrorist attack in New York and Washington, DC, was followed by wars in Iraq, conflicts in the Middle East, and terrorist attacks. Since the 1980s, the world economy, led by the United States, has engaged in a prolonged period of low and near-zero interest rates, which was supposed to stimulate investment, but the United States and the world economy did not seem to show a high growth rate, despite the low interest rate regime. In the case of the EU, growth has been restricted by the debt-prone countries that needed assistance and bailouts. Many of these debt-prone countries have adopted welfare policies that were not favorable to growth. Hence, a low growth regime that coexisted with high welfare spending could not last long. The EU consisted of both strong and weak economies. In reality, it seemed that the weaker members did not perform and their large national debt did hold the EU to ransom. On the one hand, the EU faced the dilemma of rescuing the weaker members to preserve integration, and on the other hand, was committed to spend large amounts in bailouts. The worst was that a lot of the bailouts were used to rescue banks so that banks could stay open for citizens to withdraw cash, but bailouts were not meant to promote growth.

The 2008 financial crisis also impacted the rising Chinese economy. Over the last three decades, the Chinese economy had been the major economy absorbing foreign direct investment and exports. There was obviously the substitution effect. Given that the world resources were fixed in the short run, the more investment that went to China, the less would be made available to other countries. Similarly, given that world trade was fixed in the short run, the more China exported would mean the less could be exported from other countries.

To the surprise of foreign investors, while the Chinese economy expanded, there have been few internal improvements. At the same time, production costs in China have become high enough for investors to make comparisons with other investment destinations. The large Chinese market has supposedly been an attractive factor for foreign investors, but setting up a market network across all of China could be costly, as protectionism, state intervention, and control remained severe. With the rising status of the Chinese currency, the Renminbi is becoming more acceptable and reliable. As of October 2016, the Renminbi has been included in the IMF's Special Drawing Rights (SDRs) basket of currencies (*South China Morning Post*, November 30, 2015). Foreign investors would now have a choice of either investing and producing in China, or producing elsewhere and exporting to China.

One can identify three aspects of the international political economy. One would be the urgency in reconsidering the effectiveness of the prolonged low interest rate regime adopted by the United States and other advanced countries. While it has been dressed up as an instrument in promoting investment, the prolonged low interest rate in the industrialized countries has unfavorable theoretical and conceptual implications. Firstly, it can be argued that the low interest rate has effectively been used as an additional welfare instrument in aiding investors and speculators in the financial market and in the property market, enabling them to have a "subsidized" source of funds. Such financial welfare works similarly to the use of a fiscal subsidy to low income earners. Secondly, it is also questionable if the low interest rate did stimulate investment, or if it encouraged speculation, in the financial market. If used in physical production, physical investment could be output promoting. On the contrary, speculations are nominal activities that lead to a greater amount of financial transactions, promote financial bubbles, and increase market volatility, but would have no equivalence to physical output. The low interest rate also has wider implications on the property market. As money is losing its value and interest rates (cost of money) are low, investors would not hold money, but instead would look for alternative assets, and the rise in the demand for property would push the price up. To hedge against the rising prices, buyers would buy even though the price is rising, leading to a situation of an "upward sloping" demand curve, where more is demanded as price goes up (Li, 2006).

The second aspect of the 2008 crisis is that it serves as a "wake up call" to those "large welfare, heavy debt" countries as to their sustainability. In the case of Greece, and while the world is trying to rescue Greece, the question is how much the world is prepared to bail out Greece, or should the resources be alternatively used to promote growth elsewhere. Should Greece and other similar countries that required financial bailouts start to reverse their economic policies that would depart from the large welfare commitment to adopting growth-oriented policies? In the final analysis, prowelfare countries and governments had to reconsider the choice between "demand-driven" policies that encourage spending and welfare provision, and "supply-driven" policies that focus on productivity, job possibilities, and growth.

The third aspect of the international political economy is the possible limit on further expansion of the Chinese economy. The 2008 financial crisis has led to economic recession across many world economies, meaning that the world may not have the same commitment to resources to the Chinese economy. With this change in international investment behavior, the Chinese economy would have to make readjustments, by not relying excessively on inward investment and exports. The slower growth of exports and inward foreign investment would imply that the Chinese economy, for the time being, has reached its full industrial and economic capacity. The emerging problems, if any, would force China to make changes in their economic policies. As China claimed to be the second largest country, China would in turn have to contribute back to the world. The question remained if China could restructure effectively to avoid economic slowdown and play a constructive role in the world economy. The direction for China is to conduct more economic openness externally and institute a better and stronger system domestically. Despite China's acquisition of various "hardware," there is certainly the need to improve the "software" in the Chinese economy. Given its "socialist market" structure, the world is yet to see if this will be easier said than done.

The commonality among these three aspects of a political economy is that strong productivity and output-oriented policies are needed for success in the next stage of the world economy. Both "financial socialism," through the use of low interest rates as a form of financial subsidy, and "fiscal welfare" through redistributive policies have often led to economic stagnation, low growth, loss in competitiveness, and accumulation of large debts. On the whole, the world economy needs a policy reversal and revival with the adoption and institution of proactive economic policies that encourage physical investment and production, not speculation in financial markets and bailouts of debts. Advocates of capitalism and a market economy suggested that strong welfare approaches through the use of subsidies and bailouts, and socialist-oriented policies through instituting high wages and costs, are shown not to generate much progress. This is because the disincentive effect so generated would "push" investors to look for more market-friendly investment destinations. The continuation of large subsidies and welfare-oriented policies drained away economic resources and reduced competitiveness. In short, there is a greater need to reinstate a capitalistic and entrepreneurial mentality and attitude in the industrialized world. Economic resources would have to be left more in private hands for physical investment, while economic policies would have to reverse to provide a growth-oriented environment and not an expenditure-oriented situation.

III FINANCIAL SOCIALISM AND THE "LOW INTEREST RATE TRAP"

In monetary economics, one of the functions of money is that it is a store of value. Money is a liquid asset and has value. The higher the rate of interest, the more costly it is to spend because of the higher value money possesses. Hence, the theory goes that at a higher rate of interest, people are more willing and prepared to save than to spend. On the contrary, when the interest rate is low, money becomes "cheap," and people are more prepared to get rid of money as its value is falling. The "substitution effect" argues that as the value of money falls, spending would either increase, or people will be prepared to hold alternative assets that will give them a higher value and return. Alternative assets could include shares in the stock market and other financial instruments, real estate, gold and commodities, foreign currencies, and antiques. Hence, when the interest rate is low, especially if it is kept for a prolonged period of time, the price of other assets would rise.

When people are more willing to save, the level of saving in banks and financial institutions would typically increase. On the contrary, the interest rate also serves as the cost of investment. Thus it follows that the higher the rate of interest, the higher the cost of borrowing, and vice versa. The policy of the monetary authority would be to set an interest rate such that it balances between investment and saving. In reality, however, the political orientation of governments may have different views on the use of the interest rate as an instrument in achieving growth and stability. Thus, the interest rate could be driven by economic policy targets, rather than through the market forces of supply and demand.

The traditional form of physical investment would relate to industrial production and manufacturing. This is normally considered as the "real economy," where physical output is shown in the form of industrial production and goods for export, and in turn the rise in physical output leads to increases in employment and income. However, there is also portfolio investment that relates largely to financial transactions. Corporations do raise capital through new issues of shares, known as the initial public offering (IPO), in the primary market. Traditionally, the trading price in the stock exchange, known as the secondary market, should reflect more on the performance of the corporation, which is seen from the dividends paid out annually. However, the financial market has grown far beyond simply the stock market. There is the bond market that allows governments to buy and sell treasury bills in order to control the money supply. Over the decades, however, there are new layers of financial instruments that are often based on the performance of other shares in the stock market. The various types of derivatives and margin trading are typical examples. A characteristic in many financial instruments is the high risk attached, but they are popular among "speculators" who are keen to make quick windfall gains in the short run. Thus, there is really a lack of distinction between the activities of investors and speculators in the financial market.

The movement of the interest rate has other economic implications. It is partially true that at a high interest rate, borrowing is discouraged as investors find it costly to borrow. This is true, but not the whole truth, because investors would also consider the rate of investment return. If the rate of return on the investment is high, or higher than the cost of borrowing, borrowing can still take place at a high interest rate. The level of the interest rate, therefore, would carry a different meaning between investors and policy decision-makers. It is indeed an economic myth that a lower interest rate would stimulate investment, because at a low interest rate, low return investments could also be stimulated. Similarly, speculators would find it cheaper to speculate, as the cost of borrowing reduces. It is equally true that at a lower interest rate, there will be a greater chance of borrowing, as both high-return and low-return investments (and speculations) could have the same market access to bank loans. Given that there is an equal chance to borrow when the interest rate is low, and that in any given period of time the amount of funds available for lending is limited, this means that funds that were lent to low-return investments would not be made available to high-return investments, if the low-return borrower came forward before the high-return borrower.

Hence, if a low interest rate and an equal access to borrowing is assumed, the level of high-return investment would probably be lower, or even discouraged. In other words, the low interest rate could drive away some high-return investment. In theory, then, the low interest rate could stimulate more investment, but some of the investment so stimulated would have a low-return or would be speculative in nature. Naturally, there are more investments that yield "low-return" than investments that yield "high-return." There is, thus, a difference between the quantity and the quality of investment. At a low interest rate, more "low-return" investment would probably be encouraged. On the contrary, at a high interest rate, "low-return" investment would be discouraged, and would not be able to secure borrowed funds. Hence, the role of the interest rate is that it serves as a "screening" device in the return on investments. This aspect of movement in the interest rate has rarely been discussed in monetary theory.

Furthermore, the implication of a low interest rate means that it becomes cheap to borrow, the value of money is low and, at the same time, the price of other assets rises. This naturally would invite speculators and financial risk-takers, as the low cost of borrowing would mean a reduction in risk. Thus, it is probable that speculation would emerge once the interest rate falls below a certain level. Most speculators tend to concentrate their speculation on financial instruments in the stock market and property market. Hence, at a low interest rate, it is more likely that speculative investments are encouraged. As speculation spreads, it would soon become more profitable to speculate in financial instruments than to invest in output production. Hedging activities could also become popular. Speculators would borrow to hedge against the rising asset price. Expectation could turn positive, and the rise in asset price could be self-fulfilling as more speculators joined in, as the rise of one asset price would spill over to the rise of another asset price. And one type of speculation would spread to another type of speculation, which could eventually dominate the "investment" market. The first consequence of a low interest rate would invite speculators, and the expansion in the nominal economy would lead to asset appreciation in the financial economy, but there might not be an equivalent increase in output in the real economy. The missing link in monetary economic theory is the lack of distinction between investment and speculation.

The rise in speculative activities would lead to the emergence of fragile investors. In the property market, e.g., the rise in property price would soon invite buyers trying to hedge against the rising price in anticipation of a higher property price. This would be made worse if at the same time there was a prowelfare fiscal policy intended to help individual households to buy property, regardless of their financial status and ability. Hence, some fragile property "investors" would take advantage of the favorable government policy in borrowing, even though they might not have the financial ability to repay. This welfare policy appeared in the form of "Ninja loans" in the United States when "no income, no asset" borrowers could secure a mortgage loan. The prowelfare policy makers in the government would think that "Ninja loans" would help the poor households, but this was just a financial subsidy that had unfavorable consequences.

Firstly, it is true that these fragile borrowers are faced with a low interest rate, but the property price was rising and high. The rising property price added to the risk of a financial bubble, and these "Ninja loan" borrowers would be in trouble should a burst in the property price bubble occur. Indeed, the policy makers could not foresee which of the following two situations would provide a higher utility to the borrower: (1) a lower borrowing rate but a higher property price, or (2) a higher borrowing rate but a lower property price. It seems that the magnitude of the interest rate variation is lower than the magnitude of the property price variation. Hence, a higher interest rate but a lower property price should provide a higher utility to the property buyer. But when speculation is rampant and buyers hedge against the price before it is increased, demand for property would remain high even when the property price was rising. This illustrates the abnormal "upward sloping" demand curve, that demand for property rises as the property price goes up. The demand for property is positively correlated to the price. It is even possible that the two prices reinforced each other, and the rapid rise in property price would lead to an equally rapid increase in demand.

In fiscal policy, a prowelfare government would institute a high tax and high welfare spending, so that wealth could be redistributed through different "demand-driven" policies. A situation of "financial socialism" arises when the government deliberately engages in a prolonged ultra-low interest rate policy, thinking that the low interest rate will help both investors and home buyers to lower their cost of borrowing. The low or submarket interest rate policy, unfortunately, serves as a welfare function in the financial sector that investors and home buyers are aided through a lower cost in their borrowing. However, what such a prowelfare policy failed to see was the various unintended consequences, such as the growth in fragile investors and speculators, and rising property prices. The answer is simply that the state can decide on the policy rate of interest, but the number of players and their behavior in both financial and property markets are not controlled by the state. Indeed, players in these two markets would react "rationally" to the government's low interest rate policy. The low or submarket interest rate policy might have its own political orientation, but it generated various unfavorable economic implications and distortions. Indeed, the low interest rate policy does have a redistributive effect, as it benefitted the speculators and financial institutions, but high-return investments would then be reduced and the rising property price in fact lowered the purchasing ability of the buyers. The situation would be worse should a financial crisis or a property bubble burst, as both investors and speculators would experience losses. Indeed, governments have to weigh up the political and economic cost of "financial socialism."

There can be more discussion between the rate of interest and the rate of inflation. In monetary theory, the rate of interest is considered as a long-term economic instrument in influencing investment, because physical investment does take time to mature. On the contrary, financial investments tend to be short-term, and take advantage of fluctuating asset prices. In economics, inflation is considered more as a short-term problem. The monetarist school would argue that inflation can be managed indirectly through the money supply (Friedman, 1991). However, it is true that the monetary authority can have ultimate power in controlling the money supply, but banks and financial institutions can also create money through the lending process. Hence, a low interest rate that stimulated speculation and investment would lead to an increase in money supply, which could be inflationary.

The traditional and more direct method of dealing with inflation is known as "demand management" and involves mainly the use of fiscal variables, such as taxation and government spending (Ljungqvist and Uhlig, 2000; Hemming et al., 2002; Arestis and Sawyer, 2003). Fiscal instruments are thought to be the short-term, direct, and effective variables in managing inflation, while the interest rate instrument relates more to the long-term and is indirect in dealing with inflation through changes in investment activities. Hence, it would be inappropriate, ineffective, and incorrect to use the interest rate, a long-term instrument, to deal with inflation, a short-term phenomenon. The economic situation could be even worse if the government's redistributive policy that subsidized low income through high taxes and high government spending was combined with a financial policy that subsidized investors or speculators and home buyers through an artificial and prolonged ultra-low interest rate. The government's prowelfare ideology is effectively extended from fiscal policy to monetary policy.

There are two diverging schools of thought relating to the 2008 crisis. The financial market school advocated for the correction of financial fundamentals (Greenspan, 2004; Bernanke, 2015; Shiller, 2008, 2015). The monetarist school argued for a need to reexamine the theoretical role of the interest rate (Gokhale and Van Doren, 2009; Meltzer, 2009; Schwartz, 2009). In particular, there are a number of monetary features that called for attention, especially when Mr. Alan Greenspan chaired the US Federal Reserve (Fed) from July 1989 to August 2005 (The FOMC Chairmen from 1970 to 2014 are: Arthur F. Burns, 1970–78; G. William Miller, 1978 – 79; Paul A. Volcker, 1979–87; Alan Greenspan, 1987 – 2006; and Ben S. Bernanke, 2006 – 14. Janet Yellen took over in 2014 as the new Chairperson of the FOMC.). Mr. Greenspan practiced an interest rate smoothing policy that involved a stepwise interest rate trend movement, and often made known the direction of the trend such that investors could have predicted the trend. For example, the Federal Open Market Committee (FOMC) changed the FFR 68 times from June 1989 to January 2006, 51 of those were of 25 basis points, while 16 of those were 50 basis points. The only exception was the 75 basis point increase on November 15, 1995. In terms of frequency, a total of 18 separate steps were taken in the monetary contraction exercise in 1988 – 89. Shortly afterwards, the FOMC took another 24 steps to lower the interest rate by 681 basis points. In 1999 – 2000, the FOMC took a total of 7 steps to raise interest rates by 175 basis points, and another 11 steps to lower interest rates by 425 basis points after the dotcom bubble in mid-2000. These data included only those steps when the pattern of the stepwise policy was conspicuous, and excluded the few changes in the middle of periods where there was no particular direction to the change in the FFR (e.g., an increase followed by a decrease of 0.25% within the period).

Studies have pointed to the advantages of interest rate smoothing, which included stability and certainty of the financial system (Doyle, 2006; Bullard and Mitra, 2006). Others argued that the smoothing policy could be anticipated in advance and the public could react to monetary changes, and that would lead the FOMC to respond too slowly to shocks. Consequently, inflation variability was greater than it otherwise would be, and the policy might actually introduce instability and volatility into the real economy (Caplin and Leahy, 1996; Cecchetti, 1996; Lowe and Ellis, 1997).

Secondly, Mr. Greenspan followed an inflation targeting principle and acknowledged publicly its implicit priority for low long run inflation (Bernanke and Mishkin, 1997; Judd and Rudebusch, 1998; Mankiw, 2002; Blinder and Reis, 2005; Goodfriend, 2005). Mr. Greenspan practiced discretion in setting monetary policy. Arguments against discretion are the uncertainty facing policy makers and the time-inconsistency problem when setting monetary policy (Kydland and Prescott, 1977; Barro and Gordon, 1983; Fischer, 1990). Others argued that a precommitted rule produced an optimal solution (McCallum, 1988). Mr. Greenspan also adopted the Taylor rule, though there were periods of deviation when the FOMC reacted to special macroeconomic developments (Taylor, 1992, 1993; Woodford, 2001; Yellen, 2004; Mehra and Minton, 2007). Mr. Greenspan's personalization of the monetary policy has led to discussion on the "Greenspan put" (Miller et al., 2002), which was an ill-advised belief by the investors that Mr. Greenspan would save them if stock markets went down. Such a belief acted as a "put" to investors, in that they felt insured against the downside risk by the FOMC, which often took swift action to prevent the market from falling, but not to stop it from rising. For example, during the market crash of 1987 and the liquidity crunch of 1998, Mr. Greenspan acted swiftly to lower interest rates and pumped in liquidity for the stock market.

The monetary performance of the US economy has been documented in Li (2012b, 2013, 2014c), who provided an empirical analysis on the US economy and conjectured the unfavorable consequences of a prolonged low interest rate regime, especially in proposing the hypothesis of a "low interest rate trap" (the "Greenspan trap?"). The analysis has been extended to other G7 countries and the empirical result of QE policy in the United States (Li, 2017). Fig. 9.2 hypothetically stylizes the steps in Mr. Greenspan's interest rate smoothing policy, the vertical axis, r, indicates the rate of interest, while the horizontal axis, t, represents the time period. When interest rates fell and investors could fully anticipate the next round of interest rate movement, it would be rational for investors to act when the interest rate had fallen to its lowest predictable level (Sargent and Wallace, 1975; Modigliani, 1977). Thus, the initial fall in the interest rate might not lead to much economic adjustment, and anticipated monetary policy changes could only add "monetary noise" to the real sector (Barro, 1976). The downward interest rate trend can be shown by the arrow "a." When investors fully anticipated that the pattern of interest rates would fall further, the initial fall in interest rates might not have generated the expected rise in investment. As such, policy makers would have thought that a further drop in the interest rate was needed in order to "stimulate" investment. Knowing this, investors would have a further incentive to wait for a further rate cut. It would only be when the interest rate had subsequently reached a very low level, say point "b," that investors would decide to borrow. The extremely low or submarket interest rate now encouraged investment, including unproductive, low-return, and speculative varieties.

With a loose loan policy, the rapid increase in loans provision could soon produce signs of overheating, and the subsequent rise in inflation would then call for a policy reversal, as indicated by the arrow "c." It was even possible that the initial period in the reversal of the interest rate generated a rise in investment, as indicated by the dotted circles, because investors anticipated the end of a low interest regime and a higher cost of borrowing was expected to come. As the movement of interest rates revised further upwards, a fall in investment would indeed lower economic activity. Furthermore, those fragile investors who borrowed at the lowest interest rate at "b" might now face a repayment problem. By the time the stepwise interest rate reached a high level at "d," e.g., economic slowdown emerged and the monetary authority would then have to revise the interest rate downward. As this happened, there would be a new round of stepwise downward movements in interest rates, and investors would similarly repeat their behavior, as shown by the arrows and sequence of points indicated by a', b', and c'.

When investors could fully anticipate interest rate movements, speculators and fragile investors could have waited until the interest rate reached the lowest possible level. For example, home ownership was encouraged during the second term of President Bill Clinton's administration in the United States, as the subsequent low interest rate that encouraged home ownership resulted in rises in property prices. It could have turned out that as property prices increased the demand for property also increased, as home buyers now feared that the property price would rise further. Some home buyers might not have full financial credibility, but were provided with "Ninja loans" and were prepared to take risks and hedge against the rising property price. Studies have shown that banks over-extended their credit in the housing bubble between 2000 and 2007 (Shiller, 2008). At a persistently low interest rate, the rise in demand for home ownership led to a rise in property prices, and more

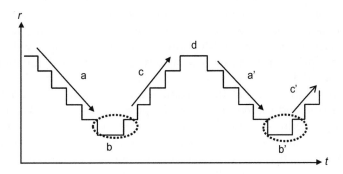

FIGURE 9.2 The "low interest rate trap."

home buyers entered the market before the property price went higher, thus generating a self-fulfilling prophecy of a rising property demand and price spiral.

Low productivity investments were encouraged at the lowest interest rate if their investments were largely speculative in nature, and these fragile investments would face repayment difficulty once the interest rate was revised upwards. The threat of economic recession at a higher rate of interest would discourage the monetary authority from keeping a high interest rate for too long, and instead they would prefer to maintain a prolonged period of low interest rates that eventually encouraged more speculation and promoted the financial economy. The economy was "trapped" at the lowest interest rate level at points b and b′ in Fig. 9.2, as on the one hand the investors got used to the low interest rate, and on the other hand the monetary authority found it difficult to reverse to a higher level of interest rate for long, say at point d. And at a low interest rate, speculation could not be discouraged and economic shallowness accumulated to form a financial bubble. The stepwise interest rate smoothing policy turned out to be an unsustainable form of monetary policy, as the persistent and prolonged low interest rate policy helped more to fuel financial instability than to build up sustainable economic capacity.

By using the simple Investment Saving—Liquidity Preference Money Supply (IS—LM) macroeconomic theoretical framework, Li (2014c, 2017) and Li and Hazari (2015) proposed that the investment demand function did not take into account the possible performance of speculators, who could emerge only when the interest rate had fallen to a certain low level. The demand for investment was mixed with the behavior of the speculators at low interest rates, but this was not distinguished in the IS—LM macroeconomic framework. Indeed, the demand for investment and the subsequent economic effect would be very different had speculation been incorporated in the IS—LM macroeconomic theory. For example, a substitution effect between investors and speculators could exist, as more loans borrowed for speculative purposes would mean fewer funds devoted to productive physical investments, given a fixed amount of loanable funds at a particular point in time. However, since speculative varieties were not output-oriented, the output effect would therefore show an inverse relationship between the level of speculation and physical output.

At the extreme, when the use of funds were dominated entirely by various speculative varieties, total physical output could even fall and that would have negative implications on the real economy, such as the level of physical production, exports, and employment. On the contrary, the increase in speculative activities could generate financial transactions and probably an increase in money supply in the nominal economy. With too much money chasing too little physical output, inflation and other unfavorable consequences emerge. And, instead of using fiscal instruments in demand management, a reversal in the interest rate in controlling inflation would produce another round of the investment – speculation relationship. The problem of the "low interest rate trap" in the "interest rate—speculation" relationship was that the FOMCs decisions were, in effect, reacting to changes in the "financial business cycle" through the prolonged low interest rate regime. This ran contrary to the theoretical role of the interest rate as an instrument in fine-tuning investment activities in a business cycle. In other words, rather than keeping a relatively high and constant interest rate so that investment and business activities would "evolve around" the interest rate for long-term sustainable growth, the FOMCs interest rate policy would instead simply respond to fluctuations in the business cycles. Instead of using the interest rate instrument to "lead" the business cycle, the interest rate was effectively "led" by the financial sector. Thus, activities in the financial economy are given a higher economic position than activities in the real economy. Such a policy bias does lead to economic distortions and sends out misleading market messages.

This was made worse by the fact that the low interest rate policy was used for political ends. A prowelfare government would think that such a "financial welfare" instrument could help home buyers. But investment in manufacturing would be discouraged as speculative varieties turned out to be more "profitable" than production in manufacturing. Financial institutions in turn saw the opportunity to create more financial instruments that would be popular with speculators. Banks would have to lend, as bank agents had to fulfill the loan quota. Speculators gained by taking advantage of the FOMCs interest rate trend. Property developers surely would supply more and raise the property price. Property owners would experience asset inflation, and would prefer to see rise in property price. "Ninja loan" holders thought they gained from the financial subsidy provided by the government, without being aware of the fact that they would be hurt severely should the property bubble burst. Fearing the possibility of recession and the political cost, the government would keep the interest rate low for as long as possible. This is a "trap," because no parties in such a scenario would like to see a reversal in the interest rate policy, and the financial economy expanded probably at the expense of the real economy. And, as such, the government would mistakenly think that the low interest rate should be kept longer, so as to "promote" investment and growth. The "low interest rate trap" becomes self-fulfilling. There is no economic instrument, other than a reversal of the policy itself, that would correct the various distortions.

Fig. 9.3 captures the argument of an "interest rate-led" business cycle. Assuming that the rate of interest was steadily kept at r^* on the vertical axis, the horizontal axis indicates the time involved. The arrows represent economic activities and cycles. With a rather high and stable interest rate at r^*, investors would not be misled by undesirable interest rate movements. Investment would thus take and shape its own path, and investment decisions would then be based largely on returns and productivity. The arrows show that economic activities would eventually evolve around the interest rate, which should also indicate the rate of return in investment.

There have been debates on whether the FOMC is really responding to the needs of the US economy (Conti-Brown, 2016; Jacobs and King, 2016). Nonetheless, the government's influence in setting the interest rate should be kept minimal, though there are adjustments in fine-tuning economic activities. Business cycles will take their own pace and path. Economic activities, as indicated by the various cyclical arrows in Fig. 9.3, would gradually evolve around the stable interest rate. If a stable and steady rate of interest is set at a relative high level, the analysis in the "low interest rate trap" would be reversed, as the high rate would encourage high-return investment, discourage speculation, provide a decent value to money, and check inflation. Of course, there could still be other economic forces, such as the fluctuation in the oil price, that would lead to economic fluctuations and cycles, but investors could no longer take advantage of the stepwise interest rate policy. Alternatively, as speculators were being warded off, investors would then go back to invest in the real economy.

The government would think that the low rate would be used to provide courteous economic conditions for growth and employment, but it turned out that the prolonged low policy rate trapped the economy in a "low rate—low growth" vicious cycle. The trap could also produce a political dilemma as, on the one hand, growth would stay low, and on the other hand, there was political pressure to bring the economy back to a growth-promoting scenario. Thus, by keeping a low rate of interest, the authorities would mistakenly think that this would stimulate investment further. The political cost would be high, especially if the government delayed the decision to revise the policy rate upwards. And the longer the delay, the longer the possibility of sustainable growth would further be delayed.

To provide an indication of the extent of speculation, Fig. 9.4 shows the performance of four financial variables in the US economy (Unless otherwise stated, the US data are obtained from the CEIC.). The Consumer Price Index of Urban Consumers obtained from the Bureau of Labor Statistics was used to deflate both the FFR and Gross Domestic Private Investment. While the real FFR shows the interest rate trend, the real investment trend is used as a proxy for investment in the real economy. The upper portion of Fig. 9.4 shows that while these two trends behaved similarly before 1980, real investment deviated from the low interest rate trend beginning from the late 1980s, with two dips in the September 11, 2001, terrorist attack, and the 2008 financial crisis. The large increase in real investment includes all kinds of investment: industrial, commercial, and real estate.

On the other hand, the lower portion of Fig. 9.4 provides possible evidence of speculation. The Standard and Poor 500 (S&P500) indicates the stock market trend, while the securities margin debt data obtained from the New York Stock Exchange (NYSE) can be used as a proxy for financial speculation. One can see that the two variables show a similar trend. The two trends accelerated sharply after the mid-1990s, fluctuated wildly in 2001 and 2008, and reached new heights in 2014 − 15. Although the value of investment was obviously much higher than the Securities Margin Debt , it does show that speculative activities moved along with investment activities at low interest rates. One can argue further that expansion in the financial sector might have outgrown expansion in the real economy, because expansion in financial instruments, such as derivatives, margin trading, and so on, could be transacted more easily and speedily than investment in physical production. Indeed, the government's low interest rate policy was more advantageous to the speculators in the financial market than investors in the real economy.

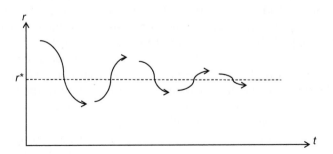

FIGURE 9.3 An "interest rate-led" business cycle.

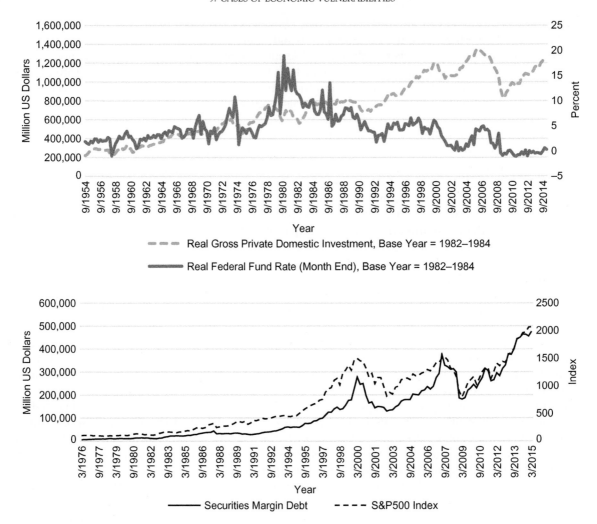

FIGURE 9.4 Financial performances in the US economy.

As Akerlof and Shiller (2015) pointed out the possibility of manipulation and deception in the economy, the solution to the "low interest rate trap" would have to be a policy reversal so that business and investment activities would evolve around a steady, constant, and positive interest rate. The FOMC has to make the interest rate a leading instrument that could proactively determine other economic activities. For a reversal in the interest rate, the first battle would be the political will, as the policy reversal would be expected to create short-term shocks, and even a potential economic downturn. Thus, the FOMC would have to identify a time when the political cost was lowest, either at a time before an election when the economy was usually favorable, or when the economy was in favorable shape.

The last quarter of 2015 could be considered as good timing for revising the interest rate in United States. By August, 2015, the oil price had dropped considerably, which eased the pressure on inflation and consumer purchasing power. The United States had a political election in 2016, which meant the economy would have expanded as a result of election spending. There have been constant rumors that the FOMC would revise its interest rate since the FOMC stopped the QE policy in 2014. Thus, even though the revision would introduce another shock, the impact would be marginal and temporary. In fact, the decision to revise the FFR rate should be seen more positively, because it cleared market uncertainty. Externally, the US dollar has remained strong for various reasons. The fall in the oil price and the weakness of the Euro due to the Greek debt crisis have favored the US currency. Other than Greece's debt incidence, the Chinese economy was faced with pressure on the devaluation of the Chinese currency after years of appreciation. A stronger US dollar may hurt US exports, but the weakened world economy would mean exports from China would not be as strong as previously (*Forbes*, August 31, 2015; *New York Times*, August 28, 2015; *Fortune*, August 19, 2015; *The Wall Street Journal*, June 17, 2015). In short, the interest rate revision shock would be absorbed along with other international and domestic economic events. Furthermore, the revision of interest rates should be seen as a means to lead the economy back to a sustainable growth path, and not as bargaining chips with participants in the financial market.

What level of interest rate could be considered as "high and stable?" One possibility was the average rate in the pre-1994 period shown in Fig. 9.1, when all G7 countries adopted a high interest rate. By distinguishing between the high and low interest rate period among the G7 countries, Li (2017) concluded an interest rate that ranged between 5% and 6% should be considered as stable. This range could be regarded as the r^* in Fig. 9.3. One is not advocating for a one-time increase, but a gradual increase over a period of time. It is most important that the high rate would be kept stable, so that the business cycles evolve around it.

Another related concept is the "public role" of banks, as banks are increasingly becoming a public entity. Even though banks charge for their services, people use banking facilities to conduct all sorts of financial transactions. In other words, banks are holding the financial key for individuals. As such, both the public and political cost is high should banks close, and the troubles banks faced would quickly radiate to other activities. However, banks could misbehave and involve losses due to poor governance, excessive risk-taking, asymmetric information issues, moral hazards, and management problems. The severity of banking mistakes would certainly spill over to the financial sector. The first institution that the government rushed to rescue in a financial crisis would be the banks, in order to contain the crisis and not let it deteriorate and cancer-spread to other sectors. There could certainly be a high political cost if the banks cannot deliver financial transactions, or have insufficient liquidity. The ability for banks to stay open and function normally has become a sign of public stability.

IV EMBRACING SOCIAL COST: GREECE

With the collapse of the Soviet Union, studies on the economics of socialism have subsided, as socialism has proved to be an unsustainable form of organization. Those socialist countries that were affiliated to the former Soviet Union have become weaker economically, while others are on the brink of collapse. Another more challenging aspect is not so much the few remaining socialist countries, but those countries which have adopted the prosocialist economic policies of large welfare spending and persistent redistribution of wealth and income. These policies cannot be sustained, because they concern only the "spending" side and lack emphasis on the "earning" side of the economic equation. These economies experience the worst of two worlds: (1) growing national debt with decreasing ability in repayment and difficulty in securing funds; and (2) prolonged use of prosocialist economic policies have reduced and restricted the economy's capability, and the shrinking economy is faced with difficulty in promoting growth. The end result is the emergence of an economy burdened by debts, which has remained uncompetitive, unattractive, and lacking growth potential.

There is a major conceptual difference in the basic economics between a capitalist economy and a socialist economy. In a capitalist economy, individuals have to look after their own economic welfare. In economic jargon, this means that individuals are taking care of their "private costs" of survival. By taking care of one's own economic cost of survival, the individual can master his or her own way of life, earning ability, and spending behavior, and need not to take orders from anyone, or wait for assistance. However, a society has to show its caring attitude to those in need, but social assistance should be temporary for individuals to pass over their difficult times. Such assistance is justified as it ensures only a decent level of economic survival. Lending a hand to help individuals experiencing economically difficult times should not carry any ideological implication. Once the assisted individual can recover from their difficulty in economic survival, the assistance can be withdrawn.

Economic assistance in the form of welfare spending is regarded as a "social cost," as it is the society that will ultimately have to shoulder the cost burden of all fiscal expenditures. The greater the welfare spending a government commits to, the higher the "social cost" burden the society is faced with. Thus, when an individual is faced with difficulty in economic survival and looks for welfare assistance, the individual is basically passing his or her "private cost" of economic survival to society's "social cost." Some examples can illustrate the worsening of the "social cost" burden. Illegal immigrants entering a host country would immediately require welfare support, as the immigrants are faced with difficulty in economic survival. In some advanced countries, immigration policies would ensure that immigrants are economically capable so that the new immigrants would not raise the "social cost."

A government policy that embraces a higher social cost will expand the power of the government. Higher fiscal spending would mean a bigger social cost pool, which in turn would mean a need for more fiscal revenue through tax income and other revenue. Economically, the larger the social cost burden the society faces, the greater the need for a bigger government. Politically, it could be popular to have greater welfare spending, as that would justify and reinforce the need for a bigger government. The political dimension can generate an interesting debate. On the one hand, there are always endowment-low individuals, who would be keen to receive welfare assistance. On the other hand, there is a group of political opportunists who would advocate for high welfare spending, as that could boost their political popularity, and could even enable them to gain power in an election. The question would be whether these elected politicians would really come to help the endowment-low individuals. Or would it be better to keep a large pool of endowment-low individuals, as this was their source of support and basis of power? In a worse scenario, would it be even better to produce a deteriorating situation, because a larger pool of endowment-low individuals would in turn need more welfare and a bigger government. It has been shown time and time again that economies that followed prowelfare policies tended to stay poorer than economies that followed "supply-side" policies of job creation and investment promotion. The conjecture is that socialism is not an ideology to become free, but an ideology to control. Capitalism is an ideology that promotes individual growth and achievement, and less reliance on government assistance.

The "private cost—social cost" concept can be extended to the understanding of political ideologies and provide an analysis on the economics of socialism. When one is taking care of his or her own private cost, the person is effectively in the "driver's seat" in directing his or her own economic affairs and welfare. On the contrary, when the person receives assistance or subsidies from the government, the rise in social cost would have various implications: (1) there would be more work for the officials, and more resources would have to be deployed; and (2) the recipient would have to come under the administrative sphere of government officials, and assistance would be provided according to rules and regulations. These two effects would mean that the size of the government will have to expand to cater for the larger pool of needy individuals.

Through the political desire to redistribute, it would be easy to expand the social cost by increasing the number of channels through which private costs could be passed and covered by the social cost. It is true that people with difficulty in economic survival should be aided, but to draw the line between assistance and redistribution can be vague. Since the politicians who decided to shoulder the private cost of individuals (and turn the private cost into social cost) are the agents, while the financier of the social cost would be the tax payers, there exists asymmetric information and moral hazard or agency problems (Hölmstrom, 1979). The officials who exercised the redistribution policy using welfare assistance would "rent-seek" and capitalize on the policy, but they would not be responsible for the welfare expenses. The burden of the large social cost rests with the tax payer. Also, the decision to raise or lower tax rates come under the same group of officials, but a high tax rate would mean the tax payers would have to pay more, not the officials.

Economic inequality is "bad," but it can be varied because given the market system and mechanism, individuals can make improvements. On the contrary, political inequality is fixed, as party officials would have all the say and individuals would not be given any opportunity to exercise their comparative advantages. Recruitment to the political party may not be entirely open and free, and may probably be selective. In the case of the People's Republic of China, e.g., new party members would typically be selected from university students (Crichton, 2006). Situations would be similar for those democratically elected governments which have adopted redistributive policies in the form of large welfare assistance to endowment-low individuals, high taxation on able individuals, and generous retirement benefits for the ageing population. The economic consequences and outcomes are equally undesirable, especially if the economy has reached its full productive capacity and there is no growth potential. The economy is likely to end up with a vicious circle that comprises a "large welfare, large debt, low competitiveness, and low growth" scenario.

Politically, redistributive policies are attractive to voters as there are more endowment-low than endowment-high individuals. Indeed, if what was spent by the current generation could not be covered by the available sources of funds, the deficit so produced would mean that the current generation has overspent, and the future generation has to shoulder the economic burden of the current generation. The national debt today is the overspending made by previous generations, but the repayment of debt would have to be paid by future generations. The passing of such a social burden would be unfair and unethical, as it generates "cross-generational" inequality. Hence, it would always be popular to adopt policies that help endowment-low individuals at the expense of endowment-high individuals. But when the policy is excessively generous and disregards the economy's ability to pay, sooner or later it generates disincentives to the endowment-high sector of the population. While the assistance given to endowment-low individuals is politically visible, the loss in economic competitiveness occurs invisibly. Policies that aim to enlarge the social cost usually take place when the economy is in good shape, namely income is growing and there is fiscal surplus. However, economic cycles can fluctuate severely, and when the economy experiences a low growth scenario, the previously committed welfare expenses cannot be reduced, and may even increase as income will have fallen in an economic recession. The appearance of fiscal deficit will be accumulated to become national debt. The larger the national debt, the greater the economic burden and social cost, and the less attractive the economy becomes. It is ultimately the adoption of "supply-side" policies that enable individuals to take up their own private costs. The higher ability individuals have in taking care of their private costs, the less the need for society to shoulder the social cost. Ultimately, the economy engages in a "virtuous economic circle" of low debt, improvement in competitiveness, and high growth potential.

It is within the analytical framework of the "private cost versus social cost" discussion that the Greek economic crisis in 2014−15 can be studied. The Greek nation was created in 1830, joined the EU in 1981, and the Eurozone in 2000 with the intention of having access to low cost finance (Ioannides and Pissarides, 2015). An OECD study (OECD, 2013) pointed to the unsustainable path of the public debt, though in 2012 the Greek Parliament's approval of the Medium Term Fiscal Strategy (MTFS) intended to reverse the fiscal budget from a deficit of 2.7% of GDP to a surplus of 4.5% of GDP between 2011 and 2016. Such a reversal was expected to introduce a negative economic shock, with rise in unemployment, fall in average wage (by 12.5% between 2009 and 2012), and a reduction in the minimum wage. The OECD study argued that social welfare expenditure was "relatively low in international comparison" (OECD, 2013, p. 17), but the difficulty would rest in the ability to widen the sources of fiscal reduction.

Dimoulas (2014) argued that the 2008 international financial crisis had exposed Greece's vulnerability in terms of welfare and debt accumulation, and discussed in detail the rising burden of the welfare state and the bias in employment policies between the "insiders" and "outsiders" in the clientele's structure of favoritism. In the "dual and unequal" welfare system, the pension system was particularly favorable in providing generous pensions to retired civil servants and some professionals, but the same payment to farmers and laborers was minimal. Greece's weak economic performance when compared to other European countries is provided in a comprehensive study by McKinsey & Company (2012), which bluntly pointed out the growing problem of the public sector debt, heavy reliance on official loan support, unattractiveness to foreign investment, and large payroll expenses that culminated into a crisis involving social, economic, and political factors. Having produced a consultancy study, McKinsey & Company (2012) proposed a growth path involving "five production sectors and eight 'rising star' sectors" that could generate within a decade over half a million jobs and a gross output value exceeding 50 billion euros.

By using a political economy approach, Phelps (2015) pointed to such historical factors as the "economic ills rooted in the values and beliefs of Greek society." In particular, "Greece's public sector is rife with clientelism (to gain votes) and cronyism (to gain favoritism)." Michas (2011) argued that "Greece has a system in which political support is provided in exchange for material benefits known as 'rousfeti' in Greek." The state has a strong influence both economically and politically, and as a result, rent-seeking in the form of influencing the political allocation of benefits by individuals and groups became widespread. The large pension for public employees has also been discussed as one of the causes of the crisis. Greece has a high civil servant-to-inhabitant ratio, and salaries in the civil service are much higher than the private sector (Tsoucalas, 1978).

Other studies on the Greek debt crisis identified different macroeconomic causes, such as fiscal and taxation, financial, borrowing, and employment difficulties. Galenianos (2014) discussed the fall in GDP and the irresponsibility and inability of the Greek government in reducing public deficits and debts, while Bitros (2012) considered the drawbacks of "hard core socialist provisions" introduced in the 1975 constitution that extended the power of the state and destroyed the international competitiveness of the Greek economy. Clause 1 of Article 106 in the 1975 Greek Constitution specified the economic role of the Greek State, stating that "... the State shall plan and coordinate economic activity in the Country, aiming at safeguarding the economic development of all sectors of the national economy...." Effectively, Greece has become a socialist country. Evidence showed that the large state sector cannot "safeguard the economic development of all sectors of the national economy."

Many questioned how the Greek debt problem has become a crisis without finding any solution on the part of the Greek government (Alogoskoufis, 2013; Petralias et al., 2013). Cruces and Trebesch (2012) and Nikiforce et al. (2015) discussed the need to have a "haircut" in Greek's unsustainable public debt. Other macroeconomic studies have concentrated on a revision in the taxation system, the need for economic restructuring, further market liberalization, reduction in bureaucracy, the use of interest rates as an economic stimulant, and an improvement in inequality (Apergis and Cooray, 2013; Gechert and Rannenberg, 2015; Giannitsis and Zografakis, 2015; Ostry et al., 2015).

However, analysis of the solution to the debt crisis has been largely pessimistic about Greece's ability to solve the debt problem and bring economic recovery. The few studies which hold more optimism about the Greek crisis argued that despite the popular unfavorable assessments, the bailouts would work if there were sufficient "exit-rules" to minimize political haggling and moral hazards, and if Greece's debt could be reduced should there be an improvement in the current account (Fahrholz and Wójcik, 2010; Monokroussos and Thomakos, 2012). Kaletsky (2015) optimistically commented on the bailout agreement between Greece and the EU that "... The agreement may be remembered as the culmination of a long series of political compromises that, by correcting some of the Euro's worst design flaws, created the conditions for a European economic recovery." Exadaktylos and Zahariadis (2012) simply argued that the lack of "political trust" in Greece's socialist government could undermine the government's implementation track record, resulting in failures and responsibility drift.

The IMF (2013) noted that although the Stand-By Arrangement (SBA) provided to Greece in May 2010 did bring some success, such as financial market stability and fiscal consolidation, market confidence could not be restored, and the banking system ended up with a loss of deposits, while the economy was faced with a "much-deeper-than-expected" recession with high unemployment. The public debt remained excessively high, and restructuring of debts was imminent. Weichenrieder (2015) argued that the deterioration of the debt crisis might have been halted by late 2014, but the political elections could result in "wrong priorities."

Cecchetti and Schenholtz (2015) commented that whatever the outcome of the choice chosen by the Greek government and people on the austerity plan and the preference to remain as a member of the EU, the Greek economy would already have suffered in the process. Liargovas (2015) analyzed that the 2010 Eurogroup and IMF loan of 110 billion euros was conditional on the implementation of austerity measures to restore the fiscal balance of privatization programs, but the causes that led to its failure included the ever changing conditions, renegotiations, and spillovers by other events. Liargovas (2015) concluded that Greece was led to an "austerity trap" that produced further economic deterioration and unsustainability. Joyce (2015) commented that the failure in Greece's austerity was due to a lack of improvements in other economic complements, such as increases in consumption spending, investment, and net exports. Ioannides and Pissarides (2015) argued that Greece would not have the ability to catch up with other European countries, even if Greece's debt was removed. The debt is just too high, and that left no room for any positive adjustment, either through fiscal or structural changes.

As shown in Table 7.1, Greece was one of the world's lowest real GDP growth rate countries in 1980–2015, with an average of 0.97%, the fourth lowest in the world. As such, Greece's weak economic performance should and could have been captured much earlier. The weakness of the Greek economy can be seen from the data in Table 9.1. To begin with, the country's reserve level has shown a stronger performance in the 1990s, but it has fallen since the turn of the new century. With a level of reserves of less than 3% of GDP, the country's reserve has literally dried up. The public debt level has been close to 100% of GDP, and has deteriorated since 2006, reaching a height of 165.4% of GDP in 2011. McKinsey & Company (2012, Exhibit 2) raised concerns about private debt as well. For example, the total country debt (sum of both public and private debts) in 2008 was 214% of GDP, suggesting that the private debt amounted to over 100% of GDP already.

The other two economic indicators in Table 9.1 on budget and current account balances are equally weak, as they are all negative. The weak fiscal performance can further be considered in Table 9.2, which shows that government expenditures have amounted to over 50% of GDP since 2008. Among the various expenditure items, expenditure on Social Protection has consistently occupied over 30% of total government expenditure. Economic intervention by the Greek government has been extensive. In 2013, the three largest "demand-side" items of General Public Services, Economic Affairs, and Social Protection amounted to 74.2% of total government expenditure. On the contrary, the three "supply-side" items of Housing, Health, and Education amounted to only 16.7% of total government expenditure, thus reflecting the imbalance in policy priorities the Greek economy experienced.

Other than the large "demand-side" items, businesses remained unattractive, as there were multiple layers of tax rates in Greece, as shown in Table 9.3. Capital gains tax, which is added to the regular income of a company, was 20% in 2014. The economic situation was worsened by the low productivity performance of workers in Greece. Table 9.4 shows a comparison in the GDP per hour worked between Greece and other EU and OECD countries. Measured in terms of constant value, Greece's performance was consistently lower than other countries, and there are more negative growth rates in Greece when compared to other countries. Greece has not been attractive to foreign investment, other than the popular tourism industry as reflected in its service export performance, and has not been a key player in manufacturing industry. Table 9.5 shows that both the outflow and inflow of foreign direct investment composed only about 1% of GDP in most years in the sample period. Market restriction in Greece has also been stronger than in other European countries.

TABLE 9.1 Performance of the Greece Economy (Percentage of GDP)

Year	Total Reserve	Public Debt	Budget Balance	Current Account Balance
1980	6.66		−2.40	−0.07
1981	5.12		−7.58	−0.05
1982	5.05		−5.75	−0.09
1983	5.05		−6.50	−0.10
1984	4.84		−7.63	−0.08
1985	4.86		−10.31	−0.09
1986	5.23		−9.24	−0.08
1987	6.87	52.5	−8.63	−0.07
1988	6.89	57.2	−10.39	−0.08
1989	6.07	60.0	−12.98	−0.10
1990	5.06	73.3	−14.51	−0.12
1991	6.38	74.8	−10.37	−0.12
1992	5.36	80.1	−11.50	−0.11
1993	8.80	100.5	−12.40	−0.10
1994	14.22	98.5	−9.02	−0.08
1995	12.35	99.2	−6.83	−0.10
1996	13.61	101.6	−6.64	−0.10
1997	10.14	98.7	−5.89	−0.10
1998	13.68	96.6	−3.82	−0.11
1999	14.53	102.5	−3.10	−0.11
2000	11.73	103.4	−3.73	−0.14
2001	4.81	103.7	−4.44	−0.14
2002	6.46	101.7	−4.84	−0.14
2003	3.01	97.4	−5.71	−0.13
2004	1.19	98.9	−7.42	−0.10
2005	0.95	101.2		−0.09
2006	1.09	107.3	−6.04	−0.11
2007	1.19	107.4	−6.79	−0.14
2008	1.02	112.6	−9.90	−0.14
2009	1.71	129.0	−15.60	−0.11
2010	2.17	144.5	−10.74	−0.09
2011	2.33	165.4	−9.44	−0.08
2012	2.91			−0.05
2013			−4.57	

Table 9.6 reports the Product Market Regulation Indicators constructed by the OECD. With a scale that ranges from the least restrictive with a score of 0 to the most restrictive with a score of 6, Greece's performance in all scores has been weaker than the three other countries of France, Germany, and the United Kingdom. However, one can note that between 1998 and 2013, Greece's performance has been improving, though the extent of

TABLE 9.2 Greece's General Government Expenditures by Function (Percentage of Total)

Functions/Year	2006	2007	2008	2009	2010	2011	2012	2013
General Public Services	23.7	24.1	22.2	22.1	23.4	23.9	19.9	16.3
Defense	5.8	5.9	5.9	6.4	4.9	4.4	4.4	3.6
Public order and safety	3.2	3.2	3.1	3.3	3.4	3.2	3.4	3.1
Economic affairs	9.1	9.6	11.1	9.9	8.3	7.5	12.4	25.5
Environmental Protection	1.7	1.7	1.8	1.6	1.3	1.3	1.3	1.4
Housing, Community Amenities	0.5	0.5	0.5	0.7	0.4	0.3	0.4	0.5
Health	13.2	12.8	12.7	12.6	13.1	11.9	10.6	8.6
Recreation, Culture, Religion	1.3	1.3	1.4	1.2	1.1	1.2	1.2	1.1
Education	7.7	7.3	7.3	7.5	7.6	8.2	8.2	7.6
Social Protection	33.9	33.7	33.9	34.7	36.4	38	38.1	32.4
Total (% of GDP)	44.8	46.9	50.5	54.0	52.1	53.7	53.8	59.2

Eurostat.

TABLE 9.3 Tax Rates in Greece

Year	Corporate Tax	Personal Income Tax[a]	Indirect Tax[b]	Commercial Tax	Highest Employee Social Security Rate[c]	Highest Employer Social Security Rate[c]
2003	35					
2004	35					
2005	32					
2006	29	40	19	49.5		
2007	25	40	19	48.9		
2008	25	40	19	46.7		
2009	25	40	19	46.7	16.0	28.06
2010	24	45	23	46.7	16.0	28.06
2011	20	45	23	45.9	16.0	28.06
2012	20	45	23	44.1	16.0	28.06
2013	26	42	23	44.0	16.5	27.46
2014	26	42	23		16.5	27.46
2015	26	42	23		15.5	24.56

[a]*Top marginal rate on personal income is 42,000 euros of taxable income.*
[b]*The standard VAT rate is 23% (but from March 15 to June 20, 2010, the standard VAT rate was 21%). There are cases where the standard VAT rates could be reduced to 13% and 6.5%. For the Aegean Islands, all VAT rates are deducted by 30% at 16%, 9%, and 5%, respectively, provided certain conditions are met. Such reduction may not apply to certain goods, and exemptions can apply.*
[c]*Rates vary as different social security funds cater to different sectors. In addition to the basic social security funds, employees must also be covered by a supplementary retirement fund, such as the Social Insurance Fund and the Employees' Supplementary Insurance Fund.*
http://www.theglobaleconomy.com/Greece/corporate_tax_rate; http://www.kpmg.com/Global/en/services/Tax/tax-tools-and-resources/Pages/tax-rates-online.aspx; and http://www. tradingeconomics.com/greece/corporate-tax-rate.

improvement differed between the indicators. For example, there has been a larger improvement in the Barrier to Trade and Investment than the other two indicators of State Control and Barrier to Entrepreneurship.

Table 9.7 reports Greece's tourism industry. Tourism is a tradable service, but there a lot of "informal" activities in the tourism business. For example, the sale of souvenirs and personal services would be under-reported in many cases. Nonetheless, Table 9.7 shows that the direct contribution to GDP has consistently been no higher than 7% of GDP. Similarly, the direct contribution to employment has remained less than 10% of total

TABLE 9.4   GDP per Hour Worked: Greece, EU, and OECD

	US$ Constant			Percentage Growth		
	Greece	European Union (28 Countries)	OECD Total	Greece	European Union (28 Countries)	OECD Total
2000	23.0	30.2	30.5			
2001	24.9	31.7	31.8	3.7	1.9	1.7
2002	26.5	33.2	33.0	1.1	1.6	1.7
2003	27.6	34.2	34.3	5.3	1.6	2.4
2004	29.0	35.7	36.0	2.9	1.6	2.2
2005	28.1	37.1	37.7	− 2.6	1.0	1.5
2006	31.0	39.8	39.8	4.5	1.9	1.6
2007	32.0	41.4	41.5	2.9	1.0	1.5
2008	33.8	43.0	42.7	− 1.5	− 0.3	− 0.1
2009	33.9	43.4	43.4	− 2.7	− 1.4	0.3
2010	34.0	44.9	44.7	0.1	2.7	1.8
2011	31.8	46.7	46.2	− 7.2	1.4	1.1
2012	34.0	47.9	47.1	5.0	1.0	0.3
2013	35.4	48.9	48.0	− 0.2	0.6	0.9
2014	36.2	50.0	49.0	0.9	0.2	0.5

OECD.

TABLE 9.5   Greece's Foreign Direct Investment

Year	Net Outflows (% of GDP)[a]	Net Inflows (% of GDP)[b]	Net (BoP, Current US$ Million)[c]	Net Inflows (BoP, Current US$ Million)[d]
2005	0.61	0.28	818.35	689.96
2006	1.55	1.98	− 1175.03	5409.24
2007	1.65	0.61	3303.10	1957.67
2008	0.90	1.62	− 2527.38	5733.41
2009	0.74	0.84	− 322.36	2762.59
2010	0.57	0.18	1163.64	533.53
2011	0.63	0.38	725.54	1091.98
2012	0.27	0.67	− 984.81	1663.33
2013	− 0.29	1.22	− 3643.18	2945.42

[a]*Net outflow of investment from the reporting economy to the rest of the world divided by GDP.*
[b]*Net inflows (new investment inflows less disinvestment) in the reporting economy from foreign investors divided by GDP.*
[c]*Total net FDI in the reporting economy from foreign sources less net FDI by the reporting economy to the rest of the world.*
[d]*Net inflows (new investment inflows less disinvestment) in the reporting economy from foreign investors.*
The World Bank.

employment. In 2014, the total contribution of tourism to the Greek economy amounted to 17.3% of GDP, while the total contribution to employment was 19.8% of total employment. The percentage was similar in the gross value-added that was composed of value-added from wholesale and retail trade, transport, accommodation, and food services. In 2014, the gross value-added amounted to about 23.1% of GDP. It is fair to conclude that tourism contributed less than 20% of GDP. Tourism is often regarded as a "derived" service, meaning that its business would flourish only when other economies do well, but could suffer instantly when other economies are faced

TABLE 9.6 Product Market Regulation Indicators

Indicators	1998	2003	2008	2013
OVERALL SCORE				
Greece	2.75	2.51	2.21	1.74
France	2.38	1.72	1.52	1.47
Germany	2.23	1.80	1.41	1.29
United Kingdom	1.32	1.10	1.21	1.08
STATE CONTROL				
Greece	4.24	3.81	3.33	2.82
France	3.41	2.83	2.41	2.37
Germany	2.57	2.15	1.99	1.86
United Kingdom	1.68	1.15	1.63	1.57
BARRIERS TO ENTREPRENEURSHIP				
Greece	3.06	2.89	2.53	1.91
France	3.18	2.09	1.74	1.68
Germany	2.95	2.41	1.90	1.66
United Kingdom	1.96	1.82	1.74	1.49
BARRIERS TO TRADE AND INVESTMENT				
Greece	0.96	0.82	0.79	0.49
France	0.54	0.40	0.40	0.35
Germany	1.16	0.84	0.34	0.36
United Kingdom	0.32	0.32	0.25	0.20

The Product Market Regulation Indicators are a comprehensive and internationally-comparable set of indicators that measure the degree to which policies promote or inhibit competition in areas of the product market where competition is viable. They measure the economy-wide regulatory and market environments in 34 OECD countries.
OECD.

with recession. In other words, economic activities can fluctuate considerably as business cycles could change within a short time.

These data suggest that Greece does not have a strong and competitive economy, as it relies on tourism and is subject to the volatility of business cycles in other parts of the world. Being a small economy geared mainly to service export, the Greek economy should maintain flexibility in its economic policy. Other than infrastructure or maintenance of public goods, indulging large commitments on government spending should be avoided, as its sustainability could be a problem should economic difficulties emerge. The policy makers would have to take into account the risk of committing long-term expenditure policies, because what could be affordable during an economically strong period may not be sustainable when the economy becomes weak. In short, while the Greek economy has become more open to trade and investment, there is much state intervention and a need for a more entrepreneurial attitude.

The IMF has been more cautious and demanding in aiding the Greek debt crisis. Firstly, all IMF assistance carries conditions, and the recipient country would have to carry out austerity measures to address and correct the roots of the debt problem. Committeri and Spadafora (2013) pointed out that the IMF rules that deal with sovereignty debt are based on two pillars: (1) the lending framework that prescribed appropriate policies and resources designed to support macroeconomic adjustments; and (2) the complementary pillar represented by the Collective Action Clauses (CAC) aimed to facilitate coordination so as to contain the possible costs of a debt default. The CAC was applied to the debt undertaken by Greece in 2012. In a Debt Sustainability Analysis (DSA) (IMF, 2015a), the IMF reckoned that Greece's public debt since November 2012 was being assessed positively, as by summer 2014 it appeared that no further debt relief would be needed, partly because of the lower interest rates. According to the

TABLE 9.7 Economic Contribution of the Tourism Industry in Greece

Year	Percentage of GDP		Percentage of Total Employment		Gross Value-Added (Percentage of GDP)
	Direct Contribution	Total Contribution	Direct Contribution	Total Contribution[a]	
1988	6.1	16.3	8.5		
1989	6.0	16.0	8.4		
1990	6.0	16.4	8.0		
1991	5.8	16.1	7.9		
1992	6.0	16.1	8.0	19.2	
1993	5.8	15.4	7.9	18.3	
1994	5.8	15.3	8.0	18.4	
1995	6.4	16.4	8.6	19.4	24.3
1996	6.1	15.8	8.2	18.8	25.0
1997	5.8	15.4	8.2	18.7	25.1
1998	5.3	14.4	8.3	19.1	24.4
1999	5.9	15.9	8.5	19.4	23.5
2000	6.1	16.6	8.5	19.3	24.3
2001	6.0	17.1	8.4	19.0	23.5
2002	5.7	16.6	8.2	18.7	22.6
2003	5.4	15.9	7.7	17.8	23.0
2004	5.6	16.3	7.6	17.9	22.9
2005	6.2	17.6	8.3	19.2	23.2
2006	6.3	17.9	8.3	19.6	21.9
2007	6.1	17.5	8.1	19.2	22.4
2008	6.0	16.9	7.9	18.5	22.9
2009	5.5	16.0	7.4	17.5	21.7
2010	5.9	16.1	7.8	17.9	21.4
2011	6.0	15.6	8.1	17.6	20.5
2012	6.0	15.3	8.2	17.4	20.9
2013	6.6	16.6	9.0	18.8	21.5
2014	7.0	17.3	9.4	19.8	23.1

[a]*Percentage share = Thousands of jobs/Total employment.*
The direct contribution reflects the country's "internal" spending, namely, total spending on travel and tourism by residents and nonresidents for business and leisure purposes, as well as spending by government directly linked to visitors. The direct contribution to GDP is calculated to be consistent with the output expressed in National Accounting, namely, tourism-characteristic sectors such as hotels, airlines, airports, travel agents, and leisure, and recreation services that deal directly with tourists. The direct contribution to GDP is calculated from total internal spending by "netting out" the purchases made by the different tourism sectors. This measure is consistent with the definition of Tourism GDP. Gross value-added includes wholesale and retail trade, transport, and accommodation and food service activities.
World Trade and Tourism Council.

DSA, Greek's debt/GDP ratio was projected to fall from 175% of GDP at end-2013 to about 128% of GDP in 2020, and further to 117% of GDP in 2022. The assumptions included medium-term primary surpluses of at least 4% of GDP, the timely implementation of structural and financial sector reform, and privatization projects that would promote growth. If these assumptions were achievable, Greece's medium-term debt profile would improve, producing a 13% increase in GDP and a drop in the debt-to-GDP ratio in line with expectation.

However, the situation has changed since early 2015. The DSA reported that the 2014 primary fiscal balance fell short of the target, implying that further financial needs of 13 billion euros would be required in 2015—18.

Also, the projected privatization proceeds were 23 billion euros over 2014—22, half of which would have to come from privatization in the banking sector. But the rising and high nonperforming loans could not produce the expected level of proceeds, thereby adding another 9 billion euros to financing needs during 2015—18. In addition, the Greek economy has not been able to deliver structural reforms, and the real long-term growth rate was downgraded to only 1.5%. The situation was worsened by the fact that the Greek government has been accumulating such arrears as unprocessed pension claims that amounted to over 7 billion euros. All these suggest that the weak reform effort, a lower primary surplus, and poor performance in growth and privatization rendered the "debt dynamics unsustainable." To ensure sustainability, "haircuts on debts" would be necessary, and policies would have to be on track.

The IMF Country Report (IMF, 2015b) confirmed the unsustainability in Greece's public debt, due to the "deterioration in the domestic macroeconomic and financial environment because of the closure of the banking system adding significantly to the adverse dynamics." The closure of banks was accompanied by an imposition of capital control. The financing need has been revived upwards to 85 billion euros, while the debt was expected to peak to about 200% GDP in the coming 2 years. It concluded that "Greece's debt can only be made sustainable through debt relief measures...." Another IMF report (IMF, 2015c) documented the financial assistance provided to Greece through an stand-by arrangement (SBA) in May 2010 and an extended arrangement in March 2012, with an amount of 30 billion euros and 28 billion euros, respectively. The two repayments, due in June 2015 and July 2015, which amounted to 1.5 billion euros and 456 million euros, respectively, were not made. By July, 2015, Greece's outstanding obligation to the IMF amounted to 21.2 billion euros. With its failure to repay, Greece could no longer receive financing from the IMF until it cleared the arrears.

The motto of the EU is "United in diversity." Over the decades, though the EU has enlarged to a total of 28 member states, covering numerous political, economic, and regional issues, it has attracted both supporters and critics (El-Agraa, 2011). In particular, the incorporation of weak countries means that these countries could utilize the EU market for economic improvement, so that mutual prosperity could be achieved to produce a stronger and more integrated EU. The Greek crisis seems to produce the reverse, namely that Greece passed its debt burden to the EU, effectively holding EU to ransom. Instead of gaining strength in an integrated EU, other EU members have to shoulder the Greek debt. Other alternatives include the removal of Greece from the EU, or Greece would have to leave the Eurozone and create its own currency. Unless either party would "bite the bullet," it would be a difficult decision economically and politically, as the choices of either shouldering the Greek debt or excluding Greece from the Eurozone would be risky.

The reality in the Greek debt crisis is that there is no chance Greece could ever repay the borrowed funds, though both the IMF and EU are keen to find an exit strategy. The IMF (IMF, 2015c) recommended a "two-leg" approach: Greece takes steps to reform its economy, and other EU members provide additional financing. In short, the IMF could no longer provide any relief to Greece until Greece honored its commitments. The EU tended to be more generous to Greece and was still keen to pump funds into Greece, though individual EU leaders may have held different views and were reluctant to provide further funds to Greece. After the conclusions from the IMF, and the political elections in Greece in summer 2015, the EU became very favorable to aid Greece. An EU plan to create jobs and growth in Greece was presented to the European Commission on July 15, 2015, that "for 2014—20, the EU is providing Greece with more than 35 million euros," and at the same time reckoned that the fund "will not solve the short-term liquidity problem that Greece is facing, but they can be decisive to set the basis for a crisis exit strategy" (Creu, 2015).

While the new agreement imposed conditions of economic restructuring, there were sideline supports that could provide Greece with extra funding. For example, in the name of border improvement, it was announced on July 28, 2015, that "a new EU supported program worth more than 54 million euros will help regions in Greece and all of Cyprus further develop their local economies with measures that will create jobs, improve infrastructures, and protect the environment" (European Commission, 2015). Echoing the IMF recommendation and after the resignation of the leftist Prime Minister Tsipras, a new agreement was reached among EU members that Greece will be kept within the Eurozone, on the condition that Greece will have to show "concrete and tangible evidence to reform its economy and public administration," and "only after that can negotiations start on a new program in the order of around 80 billion euros." On August 14, 2015, the Eurogroup endorsed a third stability support program for Greece. By giving Greece an opportunity to improve its economic fundamentals, the support program should bring stability, resilience, and growth to the Greek economy (Moscovici, 2015).

To aid or not to aid Greece involves political decisions and dilemmas. Excluding Greece from EU would set a poor precedent. Realistically, Greece is not alone, because there are also other EU members who are faced with large debts. Some stability would be restored should Greece be excluded from the Euro currency area, but the chance of Greece recovering would be even more remote. However, the advantage of some economically weak

EU countries would keep the exchange rate of the euro low, so that export-strong EU countries would benefit. Indeed, the euro currency could appreciate should Greece leave the EU. As such, a higher exchange rate for the euro would increase the export price of the exporting countries, typically Germany.

The approach to the Greek debt crisis by the IMF has put economic priorities before political considerations, as the IMF cannot tolerate Greece's inability to repay. The truth is that whether there are repeated elections in Greece in order to gather political support and to buy time, whether the elections would have a majority government, or whether elections bring back a socialist regime, political elections could not solve an economic problem. The question is whether the Greek people would be willing to deal with the debt problem, or just wait for rescue from EU. Effectively, Greece is passing the "social cost" of the debt problem to EU.

Table 9.8 shows a summary of events through the news on the Greek debt crisis from early 2010 to August 2015. Following the details of the events, one can conclude that Greece was quite prepared to work out the austerity plan, which was tough but the strategy was to have "a short pain, but a long gain." There were efforts to

TABLE 9.8 Chronology of the Greek Debt Crisis

Date/Source	Events
12/15/2009 DT	Greek promised spending cuts and admitted "lost credibility" in its debts
1/13/2010 FT	Greece's 2009 deficit 12.5% of GDP, revised 2008 deficit up to 7.7% from 5%
2/4/2010 IHT	Greece was warned to curb a deficit of 12.7% of GDP (more than four times the permitted ceiling in the EU), and was told to cut public sector wages and introduce pensions reform
2/17/2010 DT	Greece to strip off EU voting right, comply with austerity demands, or lose control over its own taxation and spending policies
3/4/2010 FT	Greece turned to the IMF for support after the EU failed to assist
3/27/2010 IHT	Europeans reached a rescue deal for Greece: combined bilateral loans from European nations that use the euro with cash from the IMF
4/9/2010 IHT	The European Central Bank said Greece would not be allowed to default
4/20/2010 IT	Greece cut public sector wages, froze pensions, and raised taxes to try to cut its budget deficit by a third to 8.7% of GDP
5/3/2010 FT	The Eurozone and IMF approved a 110 billion euro package of emergency loans. The Eurozone contributed 80 billion euros. Reduce budget deficit from 13.6% GDP to below 3% of GDP by 2014, stabilize the public debt at about 140% of GDP
6/3/2010 FT	Greece: a privatization program aimed to raise 3 billion euros by 2014 to reduce its public debt under the terms of the 110 billion euro bailout
8/13/2010 TG	Greece's recession deepened, Q2 GDP fell by 1.5%, 3.5% less than a year before
10/5/2010 IHT	Greece raised 5 billion euros from new tax measures, cut spending by 1.5 billion euros, cut deficit from 13.6% of GDP in 2009 to 7.8% in 2010, below the initial goal of 8.1%
11/16/2010 TG	Greece's budget deficit reached 15.4% of GDP in 2009, higher than estimates of 13.6%. Greece's debt projected to account for 126.8% of GDP in 2009
11/19/2010 IT	Greece raised VAT, froze pensions, and cut government waste further in 2011 to meet the EU/IMF terms. The deficit will shrink by 5.1 billion euros to 16.8 billion euros, or 7.4% of GDP, in line with the terms of the bailout deal
12/23, 2/11/2010 FT	Greece approved tough budget: 14 billion euros in spending cuts. Unemployment rose to 13.9%. Greece prepared a fresh austerity package amounting to an additional 12.5 billion euros in spending cuts and tax rises between 2012 and 2014
3/14/2011 TG	Projected public debt 158% of GDP, Greece denationalized loss-making public companies and sold off land holdings estimated by the IMF to be worth between 200 and 300 billion euros. Opposed by powerful unions
3/24/2011 FT	Greece selected international advisers for a 50 billion euro privatization program
4/5/2011 TI	Greek's debts amounted to 150% of GDP, high interest rates charged by the markets and IMF/EU loans, uncompetitive economy, spending cuts, and tax hikes
5/13/2011 FT	IMF: Greece has potential to use privatization to win back investor confidence
5/25/2011 FT	Opposition rejected Greek government's fiscal austerity measures, dashed hopes for political consensus, threatened negotiations with the EU over a revamped rescue package, since cross-party agreement is a key component
6/7/2011 IHT	Greece sold state assets to cut huge debt deficit totaling 330 billion euros

(Continued)

TABLE 9.8 (*Continued*)

Date/Source	Events
6/11/2011 IHT	Greece's 4-year austerity plan: cut public spending, new taxes, and 25% reduction in civil service. Aimed to raise 6.4 billion euros
7/2/2011 IHT	Europe ready to release 12 billion euros for Greece
7/23/2011 TD	Second Greek bailout (65 billion euros has been lent to Greece) in addition to the first 110 billion euro bailout in 2010. Eurozone/IMF bailouts amounted to 219 billion euros. Greece's annual output was 230 billion euros
8/3/2011 DT	The OECD warned Greece to implement a series of unpopular reforms and austerity measures aimed to cut budget overspending to 7.5% of GDP by end 2011
9/12/2011 TG	Greece announced a new tax to calm fears of default or even leave the Eurozone, or risk being denied 8 billion euro rescue loan from the EU and IMF
10/4/2011 IHT	Greece cut 30,000 civil service worker jobs, missed a deficit-reduction target of 7.6% of GDP due to delays and recession, economy expected to contract 5.5% in 2011
11/3, 11/4/2011 IT	EU and IMF ultimatum to Greece to pass a referendum on bailout or lose the 8 billion euro rescue loan. Greece opposition pledged to back its EU – IMF bailout if Premier left power and called an election
12/15/2011 DT	Tax evasion in Greece lost 13 billion euros in revenue every year, about 5% of GDP
12/17/2011 TG	Capital flight from Greece. Investors pulled 12.3 billion euros from domestic banks
1/4/2012 DT	Greece out of Eurozone unless it agrees to terms of a 130 billion euro international bailout
1/28/2012 IHT	IMF forecast a rise in debt ratio of 135% of GDP by 2020
2/13/2012 DT	Greece riots over the second bailout of 130 billion euro loan from the EU and IMF
2/22/2012 IHT	Greece accepted a new bailout of 130 billion euros under which private investors will take steeper losses
2/24/2012 FT	EU creditors demanded 38 specific changes in Greek tax, spending, and wage policies
3/15/2012 FT	Greece won approval for a new bailout of 174 billion euros, with a first release of 39.4 billion euros to be used for rapid recapitalization in banking sector
3/16/2012 DT	The IMF approved 28 billion euros for Greece, as part of a 130 billion euro package
3/31/2012 TG	Greece needed a third bailout weeks after it secured a second package of rescue funds. The EU and IMF committed a total of 240 billion euros
5/16/2012 IHT	Greek political leaders failed to find consensus to form a government, political instability and volatility in financial markets
6/18/2012 DT	Greek elections failed to produce a strong government with a mandate to deliver the country's austerity program
6/25/2012 IHT	Greece hoped to renegotiate: revoke certain taxes, suspend public sector layoffs. Germany told Greece to follow the agreed austerity program
7/6/2012 DT	Greece's bailout needed 31.5 billion euros to avoid running out of money
7/23/2012 IT	IMF pull-out would create a funding shortfall of 50 billion euros in Greece's program
7/30/2012 IHT	The troika of lenders (European Commission, European Central Bank, and IMF) extended Greece two loan deals worth 240 billion euros, but expressed frustration at the Greek's slow implementation of overhauls
8/15/2012 FT	Greece asked for a 2-year extension of austerity program. Struggled to find 11.5 billion euros of spending cuts (about 5% of GDP) to be implemented in 2013 and 2014
9/28/2012 FT	Greece's fractious coalition government agreed on the "basic outlines" of a new 13.5 billion euro package of spending cuts and tax increases
10/13/2012 IHT	Greece unlikely to achieve the IMF conditions for second bailout of getting its national debt down to 120% of GDP by 2020
11/9/2012 IT	Greece's third austerity package contained wage, pension, and welfare cuts worth 13.5 billion euros (4.5% of GDP), and additional 5 billion euro cutbacks for 2015–16
11/28/2012 IHT	The IMF and EU agreed to unlock aid worth $56.6 billion for Greece on the condition that Greece continued to fulfill its pledges under the bailout plan
2/4/2013 IT	Under the terms of a 172 billion euro bailout, 2.5 billion euros to be supplied by private investors. But difficult to attract private sector money

(Continued)

TABLE 9.8 *(Continued)*

Date/Source	Events
4/10/2013 FT	Wages fell as collective labor agreements were replaced with individual contracts under the terms of the 172 billion euro second bailout
4/30/2013 IHT	EU officials gave Greece an additional 2.8 billion euros in loans: but lawmakers had to approve thousands of public-sector job cuts
7/18/2013 FT	Greece reformed civil service and taxes in return for 6.8 billion euros in aid disbursement. Committed to sack 15,000 civil servants by 2014 under the bailout terms
8/13/2013 IT	Better-than-expected Q2 figures indicated gradual deceleration of economy. Greece's economy shrank by 4.6% on an annual basis
9/28/2013 TG	Greece faced high unemployment, social unrest, endemic corruption, and disillusionment with the political establishment. The European parliament reported that Greece was the most corrupt state in the 28-nation bloc, and voiced fears of extremism
11/21/2013 BBC	Greek's primary budget surplus expected to rise to 812 million euros in 2013, 0.4% of GDP and 2.9 billion euros, 1.6% of GDP in 2014
12/10/2013 NYT	Greece's 2012 population was 11.06 million, 3.8 million were employed, pensioners and unemployed totaled 4.1 million. Fewer people are shouldering the country's burden. A 25% drop in GDP since 2008
3/6/2014 WSJ	Greece's four big banks needed another 5.8 billion euros for their balance sheets
4/11, 5/22/2014 ANM	Greece raised 1.3 billion euros in 6-month treasury bills, boosted financial markets. Greek's new plan supported sectors of strategic advantages, such as shipping, agriculture, energy, transit trade, pharmaceuticals, metal industry, and services
10/13/2014 TG	Greece wanted early exit from IMF, can finance its debt from the bond markets
11/14/2014WSJ	Greek economy returned to growth. Q3 GDP rose 1.7%
12/9/2014 DT	Eurozone ministers agreed to give Greece a 2-month extension to its bailout
12/30/2014 WP	Greek government collapsed, new election in 4 weeks, public anger over the austerity but alternative could be worse
1/25, 1/30, 2/4. 2/ 17, 2/21, 2/26, 3/23/2015 WP	Greeks rejected austerity and elected a leftist party, which gave unconditional support to Russia. Rolled back the austerity measures imposed along with bailout package. Rejected bailout extension for 6 months. The Greek and European officials strike a deal giving Greece another round of bailouts. Party hard-liners felt the pledges given to European leaders differed from election manifestos. Greece entered into a financial war with Germany on war reparation, claimed that Germany owed Greece
5/16/2015 NYT	Greece not ready to accept further austerity measures like pension cuts
5/29/2015 DT	IMF: Greece could leave Eurozone. Failure to pay debt meant Greece falls to arrears
6/3, 6/6, 6/12, 6/20, 6/25, 7/1, 7/6, 7/9, 7/11, 7/14, 7/15, 7/17, 7/23/2015 NYT	Premier Tsipras not accepting the current package, talked on cooperation with Russia. The IMF recalled delegation, cannot lend when a debtor deemed to have a level of debt that it cannot service in the future. European central bank offered emergency funding to Greece for the second time in a week. Abrupt end to the Eurozone talks on Greece. Greece missed the debt payment to IMF, placed in "Arrears." Greece rejected the austerity measures decisively. Greeks cashed out and buy up value-retaining assets. Greek parliament proposal for 3 year 59 billion euro rescue package with austerity measures similar to the one that voters rejected in referendum. The agreement included a raise in VAT and cuts in pensions. The IMF withdrew support to Greece bailout unless European leaders agree to substantial debt relief. European officials agreed on new bailout plan totaling 85 billion euros, on condition that Greece adopts measures to overhaul its economy. Greek banks open for first time in 3 weeks
7/31/2015 NYT	Cash fled. Greeks has withdrawn 40 billion euros since December 2014
8/12/2015 NYT	Greece agreement on new bailout package worth 85 billion euros, offered no relief package on the current debt which exceeds 315 billion euros, almost 200% of its GDP
8/16/2015 NYT	The IMF backed out from the third bailout program, as Greece's debt has become unsustainable and cannot restore sustainability solely through action of its own
8/20/2015 CNN	Greek premier Tsipras resigned
8/25/2015 NYT	Called for new election. Antiausterity party formed a coalition government
8/28/2015 NYT	A court judge who supported antiausterity appointed as a caretaker premier

NYT, New York Times; WP, The Washington Post; WSJ, Wall Street Journal; DT, The Daily Telegraph; TG, The Guardian; ANM, Asia News Monitor; IT, Irish Times; IHT, International Herald Tribune; FT, Financial Times; TI, The Independent.

implement the austerity plan that did reduce growth in the short-term, but once sufficient corrections were made and the economy was restored back to a sound foundation, growth would proceed. Although it would be harsh for the current generation to suffer the downfalls from the debt burden, once the debt issue was "healed," the Greece economy would show a stronger performance.

However, the breaking point was political when the elected antiausterity leaders rejected the austerity path. Changes in the political scene brought several unintended outcomes. Firstly, what had been done previously on the austerity path would have been lost, and the debt issue would remain unsolved and could even deteriorate further. Indeed, those who faced the austerity pressures could prefer the political alternative as a choice to lessen their economic pain. Secondly, the antiausterity government leaned to Russia, hoping that Russia could provide some "free lunch." Such a move could have some political muscles, but the move was fruitless, as today's Russia is not that economically strong, and resource-wise, Russia might not repeat the policy practiced by former Soviet Union leaders. Failing to obtain support from Russia, Greece had to be economically realistic, and had to return to the negotiating table with the EU and IMF. Austerity conditions for bailout funds remained unchanged, and Greece had to accept many of the conditions that the antiausterity government rejected in previous bailout plans. In short, the political election could not be a short-cut as national debt is an economic issue, and the longer the delay in carrying out austerity, the longer it would take for economic recovery to occur.

Indeed, compared with countries in the Asian financial crisis in 1997, Greece was "fortunate" to have bailouts from several funding sources (Lee, 2015). But then, the multiple sources of funds from the EU and IMF could also pose a problem, as Greece would have depended on these bailouts without making its own domestic efforts. A major difference when compared to the situation in the 1997 Asian financial crisis was that it was mainly the IMF and private investors that assisted the troubled countries, such as South Korea and Indonesia. In Asian countries, including those hard-hit countries, the private market rebounded quickly within a short time. The lesson is that, between Asia countries and Greece, the private sector has been the more dominant economic sector.

The Greek economy had largely been absorbed by the state, and private businesses played only a secondary role. Such policies as high wages, strong unions, handsome pensions, and lack of industrial diversity would deter private investors. Worse is that a weaker private sector would mean the need for more state intervention, and in turn, the result was a "crowding out" effect as the more the state intervened, the less attractive to private investors the economy became. The fall in economic competitiveness would become "self-fulfilling," and could even produce a "vicious circle" of "state intervention—low growth—unattractiveness to investors—more state support—falling competitiveness—more welfare and state funds—rise in debt...." Greece's debt crisis has originated purely from its own domestic policies, and the solutions must have to come from changes within the Greek economy. Effectively, Greece has to shed many of its socialist policies in order to revise and regain its economic vitality. If not, the current generation can always pass their debt to the future generation.

Table 9.9 provides a picture of the Greece debt crisis. Greece's debt situation began to deteriorate after the 2008 financial crisis, when nominal GDP experienced a negative growth rate of 1.9% in 2009, resulting in an increase in both borrowing and the level of gross debt. Nominal GDP kept falling and by 2010, nominal GDP decreased by 8.2%. Between 2009 and 2015, Greece's nominal GDP accumulated a loss of 29.9%. However, the level of gross debt kept rising, and has exceeded 150% of GDP since 2011. The different phases of the bailouts could be seen from the change in gross debt, especially in 2010, 2011, and 2013. The economic harshness reflected the weakness of the Greek economy in terms of its capability, and the depth of the debt that showed the extent of overspending committed by previous generations.

There are two channels through which social cost can be increased and accumulated. One channel works through the individual, while another channel works though political decisions. When endowment-low individuals have difficulty with their economic survival, they look for "economic shelters" so that their economic difficulties can be alleviated. This necessarily means that part of their private cost will be taken up by the public. The passing of the individual private cost to the public means that the government has a greater social cost burden. This is the channel through which the individual passes private costs to the public. The other channel is that the government for political reasons is prepared to provide more economic assistance in the form of welfare provision and redistribution. The decision probably would be due to political popularity, and the political decision does not take into account the subsequent rise in the social cost burden in the economy. After all, it would ultimately be the tax payers, not the politicians, who have to foot the fiscal expense. The outcome of either channel will be the same, namely that the social cost burden would be increased. Welfare support is usually "one-way traffic," as it is irreversible in most situations.

TABLE 9.9 Greece General Government Gross Debt Ratios

Year	Nominal GDP Growth Rate (%)	Net Borrowing + Interest Payments (% of GDP)	Level of Gross Debt (End of Year) (% of GDP)	Change in Gross Debt (% of GDP)
2006	0.4	10.6	103.4	
2007	6.9	11.3	103.1	−0.3
2008	4.0	14.8	109.3	6.2
2009	−1.9	20.3	126.8	17.5
2010	−4.7	17.0	146	19.2
2011	−8.2	17.5	171.3	25.3
2012	−6.5	13.7	156.9	−14.4
2013	−6.1	16.3	175.0	18.0
2014	−1.8	7.4	177.1	2.1
2015	−0.7	6.3	180.2	3.1
2016	3.6	6.1	173.5	−6.7

Under the European System of Accounts, debt means total gross debt at nominal value outstanding at the end of the year and consolidated between and within the sectors of general government. General government debt consists of liabilities of general government in the categories of currency and deposits, debt securities, and loans.

General Government Data: General Government Revenue, Expenditure, Balances and Gross Debt, Part 1: Tables by Country, Economic, and Financial Affairs, European Commission. Spring 2015, Table 5D.

FIGURE 9.5   Passing the private cost.

The next question is the payment of the social cost. The payment problem does not arise when the economy is flourishing, as rising fiscal revenue can cover the spending. However, when the economy is not growing, debts can accumulate as the government is faced with fiscal deficit. By issuing debts, the government is effectively showing its inability to shoulder its social costs. The Greek crisis is a showcase of mounting social costs. An even larger problem is how the world economy should proceed with similar countries experiencing excessive and prolonged policies of high government expenditures. Realistically, the funds given to rescue Greece's debt will not be returned; it will better be considered as a default more than a loan, as the ability to repay is extremely remote. Even if a repayment formula that extends to future decades could be agreed and constructed, it would be decades before Greece could have the economic ability to repay. Fig. 9.5 captures the "one-way traffic" in the passing of individual private costs to society that increased the burden of social costs. The passing of private costs begins internally, but when the social cost (debt) becomes excessive, there is a need to seek external sources of rescue. Hence, when the economy is no longer able to shoulder the social cost the mounting national debt means the need to seek assistance from elsewhere, either regionally or internationally, arises.

The political choice facing the people in Greece is equally difficult. To Greece, leaving the EU would surely mean an economic downfall, and leaving the Eurozone currency would mean a new, but extremely weak, Greek currency. Staying in the EU would mean the country has to adopt austerity measures so as to reverse its excessive welfare spending. But that would mean the economy would suffer severely, especially those whose economic life depended on retirement funds. The political tactics of seeking elections and reelections would provide the government with a mandate, but the elections would equally shift the country into extreme situations, while in effect elections were more of a time-delaying tactic than a way out of the debt crisis. An austerity plan that reverses the policy would provide a long-term solution, but the economy will face short-term shock and pain. Alternatively, the problem could remain, as no one wants to take back their private costs from the mounting social costs, but the economy would stay weak in the long run as the social cost burden remained excessively high. In sum, the economic choices facing the Greek people are: (1) short-term pain, but long-term gain and recovery; or (2) stay put in the short-term, but the economy remains weak in the long-term. The simple but hard decision, therefore, is whether the Greek people keep overspending now, or rescue the debt situation and have a better future.

The debt crisis reflects an extreme situation of inequality imposed by the current generation on the future generation. The extent of inequality appears in two ways: (1) the policies on overspending are created by the current generation, there are no representatives from the future generation in all decisions; (2) the future generation has no choice but to swallow the debt left behind by the previous generation, and the weaker country would produce a poorer economy as a whole. When the next generation does not have the ability to repay, the debt would simply pass on to the third generation. This could be the worst form of human inequality brought about by the accumulation of large debts resulting from the adoption of socialist economic policies.

The fact is that the burden of social cost reflected in the size of the national debt is ultimately an economic issue. It is fruitless to use a political instrument, namely general elections, to solve the debt problem. Elections cannot produce funds that could be used to solve the debt issue, but can only weaken the economy further. At worst, political elections could lead to further deterioration, as the delay would also mean more resources would be required to satisfy the welfare needs. Put simply, the problem began with a wrong policy on fiscal spending on welfare which, over the years, weakened the economy. The solution must have to come from willingness and ability to reverse the prosocialist economic policy. Hence, to the Greek people and government, the first priority would be to avoid economic deterioration and further accumulation of debt. To do so, there are only two possibilities that can be executed, either individually or collectively as a nation.

One possibility would be to promote growth so that more output can be available to cover the debt. The other possibility would be to reduce spending and restructure the welfare system. Each of these possibilities would have favorable and unfavorable impacts on the economy. To promote growth may not be easy, given the weak and uncompetitive nature of the Greek economy. Greece's "country risk" is high in terms of its potential sources of instability, including the lack of a viable solution to its debt problem. Economic growth from within the country could be difficult, given its unfavorable labor relations. In short, given its lack of business-friendliness, economic growth in Greece is unlikely to stay high in the years to come.

The ultimate solution is a revision of the decades-long welfare and statist policy that has become outdated and unsustainable. The immediate effect of a policy reversal would be the loss suffered by the welfare recipients, who could naturally look for possible channels, such as political elections, to avoid the penalizing impacts of austerity measures. This demonstrates the point that committed welfare spending could not be reversed, because it would mean the passing of the social cost burden back to the individual's private costs. The irreversible feature of welfare spending would mean huge resistance, especially from the affected sector of the population. There is no quick fix in debt removal or reduction, other than an effective "resource switching" policy that, on the one hand, limits the rise of the debt in the short run, and on the other hand lowers its size in the long run (Dornbusch, 1987, 1993).

A reorientation of the socialist economic policy can be conducted. Typically, a break in such a policy could be introduced, firstly by separating the different groups of welfare recipients and minimizing those who are affected. Secondly, a revised policy of lower welfare payments would have to be introduced to all potential recipients. Those who are already in receipt of welfare would have to face cuts, and welfare to the newcomers would have to be reduced considerably. Thirdly, there need to be "growth-promoting" economic policies that can reorientate individuals to new skills and employment opportunities, because it is only through economic revival and recovery that the number of welfare recipients can be reduced. An effective debt-reduction strategy will involve a simultaneous reduction on the "demand-side," and a promotion on the "supply-side" of the economy. This would be a "two-leg" strategy, such that the reduction of welfare spending would be accompanied by an increase in investment and job opportunities, so that the rise in job availability would result in a reduced need for welfare. A redistribution of resource usage is needed, as the reduction in the resources used for the "demand-side" will be reorientated to promote "supply-side" activities.

V CHINA: AT THE CROSSROADS OR A TURNING POINT?

The contemporary Chinese economy dates back to Deng Xiaoping's 1978 economic reform. After visiting the United States and Japan, Deng realized that communist China was backward. Deng boldly remarked that "it does not matter whether the cat is black or white so long as it catches mice," "crossing the river by touching the stones," and "let some people get rich first." Deng's new ideological statements included "using market to serve socialism," and "Chinese-style market socialism," though these statements were often undefined. The pace of reform in the initial years was slow, due to the need to consolidate and define the strategy and the "wait and see" attitude as to whether Deng meant business. Known as the "four modernizations" in agriculture, science and technology, industry, and defense, the five features in China's economic reform were monetization, pragmatism, marketization, liberalization, and privatization (Baum, 1980; Bettleheim, 1988; Perkins, 1988; Li, 1997).

Overseas Chinese and foreign countries began their investment back in China. Capitalists who fled mainland China after 1949 saw that Deng's economic reform would reintroduce market mechanisms to the Chinese economy. Much of these funds injected to China were considered as a "pay back" to the motherland for infrastructure and construction. These free capital injections by overseas Chinese to aid China's development served as pioneers in the initial reform years. Foreign governments and international institutions equally welcomed Deng's reforms. Japan was one of the first countries that recognized and provided economic aid to China, and China's economic reform was seen as a reference to other developing countries (Blejer et al., 1991; Bell et al., 1993). However, few would have calculated how the world economy would be affected when China started consuming as incomes rose. The economic rise of a large populated country like that of China would generate such economic and material results as a rise in the number of vehicles on their roads, an impact on international oil prices, and a rise in the demand for agricultural and consumable products. The inflow of foreign capital eased the resource constraint of the communist government, and domestic resources could then be used for other state-led construction.

Analysts have overlooked the role of the state in China's economic reform. Early studies that used neoclassical economic frameworks to examine China's GDP were questionable, as they assumed that China's market economy was no different from other market economies (Chow, 1985). Indeed, every component in the GDP identity was infiltrated, manipulated, and controlled by the communist state. Consumption has long been manipulated by state organs through provision of subsidies, and inflation was controlled. Investment was definitely state-controlled through provision of bank loans. Exports in the early years were conducted by designated enterprises, due to the restricted use of foreign currencies. Government expenditures were definitely a state activity. It would be unrealistic to assume that China's economy could be analyzed using neoclassical economic theories.

One piece of evidence of state control has been the annual GDP growth rate. When the National People's Congress meets in every March, the Chinese Premier declares the real GDP growth rate for the coming year. In the 1990s, Premier Zhu Rongji committed around 9%, while Premier Wen Jiabao in the first decade of the new century declared around 8%. Since 2013, Premier Li Keqiang announced a real growth rate of 6–7%. At the end of each year, China's statistical office would declare a real growth rate that matched exactly what the Premier had announced in March. A simple statistical understanding would suffice to show the problem of such an announcement. When the denominator of a fraction gets larger, a similar increase in the percentage growth rate would require a much larger numerator. This shows that pursuing a similarly large percentage growth rate over a long period of time was unrealistic, as the denominator has grown a lot.

However, few had ever wondered if these growth rates had been dressed up by economic agents. Indeed, no market economies in the world and in history could make such perfect economic predictions. To fulfill the GDP growth could be easy, as banks would keep lending in order to boost investments to the required GDP level. Studies have questioned the accuracy of economic data in China (Rawski, 2001; Chow and Li, 2002). Domestic investment in China could have over-expanded to meet the growth target. An example was the "ghost cities" where real estate and residential properties were built but left empty (*Reuters*, April 22, 2015; *Forbes*, July 20, 2015; *The Washington Post*, August 24, 2015; and *CNBC*, September 4, 2015). Some aspects of growth in China were used to "window dress" the economy.

The extent of intervention in economic life could mean that economic recession in China would not be allowed, as political spillover and ideological challenge would not be tolerated. The state has the final say, and always comes to the rescue to ensure growth and stability. Similarly, economic sectors could always count on state support should they face difficulties and debts. In many ways, the nature of the Chinese communist state has not changed since economic reform. The state has an enormous ability to shoulder "social cost," given the wealth (shown by the size of foreign reserves) the Chinese communist state possessed. However, China faced a dilemma in making growth predictions. Since 2013, questions have been raised as to whether China could still maintain a high growth rate (*China Daily Hong Kong Edition*, March 6, 2013; *South China Morning* Post, January 19, 2015, and January 20, 2015). As economic activities in China are always political, the problem China faces is political spillover should the economy experience lower growth. There is a political "vested interest" in maintaining a high growth rate. The answer is to keep declaring a relatively high growth rate and deploy economic instruments so that the declared growth rate would be achieved. In short, China has not accepted a true market economy, where output is expected to move according to private activities.

Indeed, the role of the state in the entire economic reform era has remained strong in land usage and deployment of natural resources, regional development, and household subsidies. The establishment of Special

Economic Zones (SEZs) in the early 1980s along the southern coast was a state policy aiming to attract foreign capital for export of light manufacturing outputs. In the 1990s, Shanghai was designated to be the city for various developments, including the stock market, even though Shenzhen, the city adjacent to Hong Kong, started stock trading earlier than Shanghai after 1978 (Li and Wong, 1997). Large subsidies given to households and industry continued. After the 2008 financial crisis, when China suffered a decline in exports, Premier Wen Jiabao activated an economic rescue package amounting to Rmb 4 trillion (US$586 billion) (Haley and Haley, 2008, 2014; Naughton, 2009; Wong, 2011) (The 10 subsidy items in Premier Wen's rescue package: (1) housing provision and renovation in rural areas; (2) provision and improvement of infrastructure in rural areas; (3) speed up development in land transport; (4) speed up development in medical and health provision at all levels; (5) promote environmental protection at all dimensions; (6) support innovation and new technology in agriculture; (7) speed up post-earthquake redevelopment; (8) raise the price of agricultural products, increase subsidies to rural areas; (9) use tax incentives to aid industrial restructuring; and (10) relax restrictions on loans provided by commercial banks. See, e.g., *Reuters*, June 4, 2008; *Business Insider*, January 18, 2012; *Bloomberg*, November 9, 2008; *South China Morning Post*, November 10, 2008; and *Singtao Daily*, November 10, 2008 (in Chinese).)

One inaccurate concept is that China's economic reform has been "incremental" (Gelb et al., 1993; Gang, 1994; Goldstein, 1995; Young, 2000; Zhang and Tan, 2007) (A similar discussion on "incremental versus experimental" is given in Chapter 15: China's Economic Reform Path.). By "incremental," studies seemed to suggest that China's economic reform expanded gradually, as if there was a sequence or path that the Beijing government would follow. The "incremental" concept of development missed the "exit" possibility that adopted policies could be withdrawn should the results be undesirable, especially results that challenged the political authority of the state. It would be correct to argue that China's economic reform has been "experimental," in that changes and policies were introduced on a "testing the water" basis. Indeed, numerous aspects of economic reform introduced since 1978 were primarily experimental in nature. The introduction of the SEZ, the use of the foreign exchange certificates (FECs), the family responsibility system in the rural sector, and the establishment of the "A" and "B" shares in the two stock markets were all experimental in that these policies would be dropped should they generated unwanted results.

One other observation in China's economic reform is whether China would introduce changes by itself indigenously, or would changes be introduced exogenously from external forces, events, and requirements. In other words, could the forces of change originate within China itself, or would changes in economic development be conducted only in reaction to exogenous forces and conditions imposed from the outside world? At the time of economic reform in 1978, China just emerged from decades of closed-door policies. The western way of life and thinking, attitudes, ethics, practices and behavior, and personal integrity had been destroyed during the Cultural Revolution (CR), where social circles were organized into ideological lines. The leftist and Maoist attitude developed in the CR, conveniently known as the "Cultural Revolution mentality" (CRM), was that everything was seen as opposites antagonistically, and there could only be games with "absolute" outcomes of win and lose, rise and fall, and life and death.

Typical CRM behaviors include: (1) "capping" or "tagging" would be a way to separate friends and associates with similar ideas from enemies who hold different, not necessarily opposing, ideas: and "capped" enemies would strategically be isolated, victimized, and destroyed; (2) "shade hunting" shows that junior officials and individuals would be better off to get close and be associated with a high level official in the communist regime for protection, shelter, and security; (3) inconsistency or gaps exist between said and done, and in many cases did the opposite of what was said or not said; (4) "goal shifting" or use of double standards in judgments and statements to ensure that the regime is always on the winning side, regardless of the reasoning; and (5) political spillovers that weaken the state would not be accepted. While China absorbed large amounts of foreign direct investment and export to foreign markets, there were still instances where "foreign" values and reasoning were visibly warded off (See, e.g., *South China Morning Post*, November 3, 2014, January 30, 2015, and February 23, 2015.).

If left on its own, the antagonistic and uncompromising nature of the CRM was unlikely to bring domestic forces that would propel changes in China. Indeed, there existed a huge social (cultural and ethical), economic (market and state intervention), and political (free and nonfree) gap between post-CR China and the outside world. The decade-long antagonistic nature of the CRM had eradicated much of the cultural and ethical values originating from classical Confucian teachings. How could post-CR China catch up in time, in materials, in civic behavior, in business organizations, and in developing the social and economic fabric? In other words, there was a need to reintroduce a civic mentality and attitude, so that activities would be conducted in "relative" terms with coexistence, divergence, mutual recognition, and respect.

Mao's ambition was shown in his remark made in the mid-1950s that communist China would catch up with Great Britain in 7 years, and the United States in another 8—10 years (Huang, 1958) (*The Economist*, December 20, 2005). Such remarks reflected the ambition of Communist China to conquer the industrialized world. Deng's reform package had carried Mao's ambition in a hidden manner. When compared to Mao's aggressive approach, Deng took a humble attitude and concentrated on China's economic weakness, which included a low level of economic development, mass poverty, and a desire to improve and change. The two comparative advantages the Chinese economy had were the large pool of low cost labor, and the potential large domestic market. By exposing these attributes to the outside world, Deng's reform would save efforts by "bringing in," attracting, deploying, and using both the hardware and software from foreign countries. Hardware would include foreign capital and exports. Software would comprise management and skills.

The external world was keen to jump onto China's "reform wagon." Similarly, the economic successes of other Asian countries were lessons on market economy which could easily be absorbed. Hence, China secured the "best of both worlds": external capital provided the funding and exports, while political control over deployment of resources remained in the hands of the communist government. As such, the control by the communist state was strengthened rather than weakened. Li (2000, 2001) argued that the industry, prices, and fiscal reforms in the 1980s were meant to reintroduce economics back to China, while the banking and state-owned enterprises reform in the 1990s aimed to reinstate economic efficiency and productivity. In these reforms, numerous foreign experiences and standardized international practices were introduced and utilized in China, with the intention of ensuring firm control by the state.

To make contact with the external world would require China to introduce changes. The accession to the World Trade Organization (WTO) in 2001, the 2008 Olympics, and the 2010 Shanghai Expo were the events that meant to introduce foreign criteria into China, as China had to follow and adopt guidelines and practices which otherwise would not be introduced. China had to make changes domestically to satisfy the various conditions, and domestic improvements would then have to be made.

Armed with the successful experience of the SEZs since the early 1980s, and even though the Chinese economy had expanded tremendously, there are still other new "experimental" creations intended to lure more foreign capital for high technology development. For example, the State Council launched, in September 2013, the establishment of the Shanghai Free-Trade Zone (SFTZ) that covered over 120 square kilometers and integrated four existing bonded zones in the Pudong district. The intention was to allow favorable reform policies to foreign investors that did not exist elsewhere in China ("Shanghai Free-Trade Zone," *Wikipedia*; and *China Daily Hong Kong Edition*, September 27, 2013). The areas of development included finance and high-tech industries. Shanghai has been the envy of other Chinese metropolitan cities as it has been the designated city for growth and development since the early 1990s. While other cities in the inner regions needed development, the SFTZ led to new political questions as to why Shanghai had to be made more developed when it was already the number one city in the country. The first market reaction in Shanghai was that property prices rose by 20—30% (*Bloomberg Business*, September 26, 2013). The rising cost in China has also raised concerns about the attractiveness of inward investment to China.

The other example is the Qianhai Shenzhen — Hong Kong Modern Service Industry Cooperation Zone, officially approved by the State Council on August 26, 2010, where construction is expected to be complete by 2020. Qianhai covers an area of 15 square kilometers located across the border of Hong Kong and west of the Shekou Peninsula in Shenzhen that encircles the Shuanjie River, Moon Bay Avenue, Mawan Avenue, and Qianhai Bay. The objective is to "serve as an experimental business zone for better interaction between mainland China and Hong Kong in the financial, logistics, and IT service sectors." Major industries for development include financial and information services, logistics, technology, cultural and creative industries, and professional services. Various incentives were provided, with preferential tax reduction to 15% in both corporate and income taxes. By adopting and capitalizing policies similar to that in Hong Kong, it is clear that Qianhai would probably duplicate the development path of Hong Kong, hoping that it could compete with or even overtake Hong Kong eventually ("Qianhai," *Wikipedia*; *China Briefing*, September 25, 2014; and *South China Morning Post*, December 8, 2014).

China's accession to the WTO in 2001 was the obvious example where forces of domestic change were imposed exogenously. The WTO that succeeded the General Agreement on Trade and Tariff (GATT) in 1995, covered also services and intellectual property rights (IPR) issues. The Ministerial Conference has the ultimate authority, and the two powerful committees are the Trade Related Aspects of Intellectual Property Rights (TRIPs) and the Trade Policy Review Mechanism Committee (TPRM). Members can make appeals to the WTO for arbitration on the violation of free trade and IPR matters. Accession is governed by Article XII of the Marrakesh Agreement, stating that "any State or separate customs territory possessing full autonomy in the conduct of its external commercial relations may accede to the WTO on terms to be agreed between it and the Member States of the WTO."

The principles for China's accession were that "China's accession will set the stage for further expansion in trade and investment through the dismantling of tariff and other barriers and reach a common set of rules and standards through which solutions in trade can be made," and that it served as a "milestone towards eventual integration of the global economy." In China's accession, the Working Party that consisted of the "quad" members of the United States, the EU, Canada, and Japan considered five areas of concern: (1) quantitative restrictions; (2) national treatments; (3) industrial policy; (4) market access; and (5) other issues. The six conditions on China's accession included: (1) a grace period to eliminate quantitative restrictions; (2) adopt an open system by eliminating foreign trade rights; (3) apply similar regulations to both domestic and foreign products; (4) remove discrimination on inspection and certification; (5) adopt a multilateral trading spirit with free and open trade; and (6) IPR protection with more legal and administrative measures. China's status as either a developed country or as a developing country raised concerns, as the conditions on tariffs would differ between the two statuses. China claimed itself to be a developing country, but China's level of consumption measured by the Purchasing Power Parity method was equivalent to a developed country. Nonetheless, China was eventually granted developing country status in the WTO accession.

However, there were basically two schools of thought in the Working Party. The flexible school adopted an "accession first, change later" attitude, and China would be given a grace period to introduce changes. The hardline school adopted by the United States advocated for "change first, accession later," believing that China should compile with all conditions before accession. The United States argued that once admitted, China would be unlikely to make changes, and it would be better to ensure that China made all necessary improvements before accession.

Tait and Li (1997) argued that the theoretical difference is that the flexible approach considered the importance of the trade effect, namely that the expansion of trade would benefit China and the world. The hardline approach advocated for market equalization, namely that China's exports to the United States would have to match with China's imports from the United States, so that the United States could avoid a large trade deficit with China. Prior to the visit to the United States by Premier Zhu Rongji in April 1999, the US International Trade Commission had conducted a thorough study on the impact of China's accession to the WTO on the United States and world economy (US International Trade Commission, 1999). The estimates and predictions on bilateral trade and multilateral trade were considered as positive and favorable in the long run, in that the United States would not face a huge trade deficit provided China also increased its imports from the United States. On multilateral trade, it was estimated that the increase in the volume of world trade would benefit the world economy, though China's exports could temporarily replace some of the exports from nearby Asian countries.

The Sino—US trade agreement on China's accession to the WTO was finally concluded on November 15, 1999 (Holbig and Ash, 2003; Feng, 2006) (*Bilateral Agreement on China's Entry into WTO between China and the United States*, Ministry of Foreign Affairs of the People's Republic of China, April 10, 1999). Prior to WTO accession, China had already been making bilateral trade agreements with individual industrialized countries. The bilateral trade agreements benefitted both parties, especially foreigners with eyes on the huge Chinese market. For a while in the mid-1990s, China remarked that there was no rush to accede to the WTO, as the rules would restrict China's choice and preferences in selecting trade partners. Premier Zhu's final offer in the Sino − US bilateral trade agreement was seen to benefit the United States more than China (Borich, 1999). The offers proposed by Premier Zhu included: (1) import liberalization and reduction in tariffs, e.g., the tariff on imported cars would be reduced to 25%; (2) eliminate nontariff quotas within 5 years, especially on agricultural goods; (3) allow a maximum of 49% ownership of foreign investment in telecommunications; (4) foreign banks would be allowed to conduct Renminbi business for companies and for individuals in 2 years and in 5 years, respectively, and foreign banks would be unrestricted in opening up branches; and (5) no restriction on foreign investment in the internet. The only benefit China got was the concession on textile exports. The other concern was whether China's domestic agricultural products could compete with US imports. China's WTO accession would ensure economic openness; trade and the pace of reform could not be reversed, as trade would have to follow the WTO rules and guidelines. China would have to make references to standardized practices, guidelines, and rules used internationally. Such a "bringing in" policy served two purposes: save time and economic reform could not go backward in times of political rivalries. The WTO conditions and practices would become an economic fabric in China, as trade and economic openness could no longer be dismantled.

The two decades (1990—2010) were China's golden era, as its economic capability kept expanding. Other than China's large labor supply and the potential large domestic market that served as the "pull" effect, the various unfavorable economic conditions in foreign countries served as the "push" effect. Typically, the high labor costs and high tax rates in many advanced countries were accompanied by a period of prolonged low interest rate that lowered the cost of borrowing. Low cost loans obtained from industrialized countries could have been diverted to China. Foreign businesses should gain as the "double low" (with low borrowing cost in their home countries, and the low production costs in China) would provide them with a larger profit when the manufactured goods produced in China were then exported back to the investors' home countries.

In the early years, China's industrial capacity had mainly been geared to light manufacturing for exports. Through foreign direct investment, China also gained access to high technology, since "home grown" technology needed development time. Given its export orientation, the China economy reached its peak in 2008 when the country hosted the Olympics in August, 2008, followed by the organization of the Shanghai Expo in summer 2010. China has reached its "full capacity," given its existing economic attributes in terms of labor supply, cost of production, and such complements as infrastructure provisions and export market absorption. The rise in income and output has been supported by China's existing economic structure, and long-term expansion of economic capability is constrained by the slow changes in economic structure. Labor shortages began to emerge, and labor costs were predicted to rise. With the rise in income and the "one child" policy, parents were increasingly reluctant to see their children working in factories. Labor-intensive industries were increasingly facing competition from various fronts (After over 30 years of adoption, the "one child" policy was finally repealed in the Fifth Plenum meeting held in October 2015. The "one child" served as "head tax," as parents having a second child would have to pay "tax" to the local government. See, e.g., the case of the Chinese film director "Zhang Yimou," *Wikipedia*; and *China Daily Hong Kong Edition*, October 30, 2015.). The capacity constraint was exposed after the 2008 financial crisis, when many industrialized countries faced economic recession and exports from China and industrial output declined. The world economy became "poorer," and there was less inward foreign investment to China (See, e.g., *China Daily eClips*, March 16, 2012; *South China Morning Post*, November 10, 2014, April 13, and September 1, 2015; and *China Daily Hong Kong Edition*, November 13, 2014.).

With the rise in income and the claim to be the second largest country in the world, other countries would become hesitant in making further inward investment to China. Foreign investors began to realize that it was not that easy to penetrate the Chinese market, and could have second thoughts about investing in China. For example, a protectionist attitude was still strong at the local level, and in telecommunications. The building of a national business network would be subject to local restrictions, while protection of IPR could not be guaranteed despite the available legality at the official level. With the inclusion of the Renminbi in the IMF as a reserve currency in October 2016, foreign businesses have a choice between investing in and trading with China.

China has become an excess liquidity, or simply "cash rich," country in that there have been large increases in both domestic and international sources of finance (Section VI gives a detailed discussion on the "cash rich" issue.). The two sources of external funds of foreign direct investment and trade balance have shown rapid expansion, while loans and assistance from the World Bank remain steady. All these contributed to the rapid increase in reserves held by the central authority. Outward foreign investment from China has also increased since 2013. The Renminbi depreciated by 30% in 1994, but has experienced appreciation since 2005 due to the large trade surplus. Similarly, there are large increases in domestic investment in fixed assets, bank loans, and funds raised from the stock markets. China's excess liquidity would mean that the communist government has large amounts of resources at its disposal, and mainland Chinese would have high spending power. The large cash circulation would also imply a situation where money could be circulating outside the formal banking system, and that individuals hoarded cash. For example, it was reported that corrupt officials accumulated tons of cash in their homes, and that luxurious villas overseas were bought by Chinese officials (See, e.g., *South China Morning Post*, October 31, December 16, 2014, and March 18, 2015; and *China Daily*, November 1–2, 2014.). Both individuals and big businesses in mainland China are buying foreign corporations in Hong Kong and elsewhere. While the nominal implication was to acquire foreign assets, the truth could be a formal way to take the capital out.

One could assess China's performance after over more than three decades of economic reform through the three dimensions of economics, politics, and international relations. The economic reform has produced high economic performance, as shown by its GDP. There were improvements in economic complements, such as infrastructure, urbanization, and modernization. Industries have expanded beyond labor-intensive, light manufacturing production, though China remained keen to import high technology. Indeed, every aspect of the Chinese economy has been on the upside: the economy kept growing, trade kept expanding, foreign direct investment kept coming, industrial output kept rising, income kept increasing, consumption kept flourishing, and wealth entered an endless saga of expansion. There are large numbers of Chinese billionaires who should have been considered as capitalists (See, e.g., *Business, China Daily Hong Kong Edition*, November 27, 2015.).

Indeed, there been no single country that has received such generous attention and contribution from the world community than that of China since the 1980s. By 2010, China claimed to be the "number two" country in the world, only second to the United States. Echoing Mao's ambition, China could surpass the United States, though ideological differences could pose another challenge.

China faces a number of dualities or dichotomies. What foreigners reported about China from the outside was surely different from the situation seen from inside. For example, the rapid rise in income could be seen to match with growing inequality, and the rapid increase in industrial output has the price of growing environmental pollution. For example, while President Xi Jinping was speaking at the Paris climate summit in December 2015, Beijing was cloaked in smog 25 times higher than the safe level (*South China Morning Post*, December 1 and 2, 2015). The progress in such hardware as foreign direct investment, bank loans, and export and import of technology has not been complemented by development in such software as ethics, management, and governance. Like any other country whose development would soon face bottlenecks and constraints when the existing economic structure reached near full capacity, China has somewhat come to "saturation" point, unless economic restructuring takes place at a faster pace. After 2008, the Chinese leaders were slow to become aware that the world economy had changed and could no longer support the Chinese economy through trade and inward investment. However, with the "bringing in" approach, economic restructuring that requires indigenous improvements and innovations may not be forthcoming, and may take time to materialize.

After the 2008 crisis, Chinese leaders switched their policy to focus on promoting domestic consumption, assuming that the industrial capacity that served the export market could also serve the home market, and that what was not exported could be consumed at home. The duality was that many household consumables and food products were unreliable, as local food production and processing were fake, faulty, toxic, unhygienic, or dangerous health-wise. Dangerous and poor quality materials were used in industrial production, especially in consumables. Poor quality and fake production extended to such luxurious expensive products as a fake sports car, and such low cost commodities as fake eggs, toxic baby formulae, and toxic soya sauce (See, e.g., *The Guardian*, July 5, 2007; *International Herald Tribune*, July 5, 2007; and *South China Morning Post*, January 28, and April 16, 2015.). The monitoring of industrial production was probably affected by the presence of corrupt officials, as high ranking officials were sometimes involved.

The conclusion is that Chinese residents tended not to prefer locally made products, and either buying foreign brands locally or making shopping trips to Hong Kong and overseas became popular. In addition, the consumption tax in China has encouraged shopping trips to Hong Kong. There are several economic implications in the parallel trade activities. One will be the rise of an informal economy in the cities that border Hong Kong, as traders become agents making cross-border shopping trips. The amount of currency exchanged between the Renminbi and Hong Kong dollar would be large, thereby reinforcing the informal currency economy. Chinese imports would rise as locally produced consumables were unpopular, thereby adding pressure on the trade balance and the value of the Renminbi. The poor quality of some export products had somewhat destroyed the goodwill of exports, and foreign importers would start looking for substitutes elsewhere.

Politically, China made minimal advances toward open participation and freedom, and President Xi Jinping has been regarded more as a Maoist (See, e.g., *South China Morning Post*, September 29, 2014, February 25, April 15, and December 2, 2015.). There are numerous cases of underreporting and suppression of individuals and institutions holding unacceptable political views. In many cases, the incidents were first reported in Hong Kong or in foreign media, before attention was given inside China. The political duality has not changed much in the reform decades. There is still the "one party, two factions" dichotomy between the reformists and the hardliners. This could be seen in the appointment of presidents and premiers, as it probably had become a political formula that the president would be more of a hardliner dealing with political issues, while the premier could be more of a reformist who handled mainly economic issues. That basically reflected the political compromise reached between the two factions. Another aspect of political duality was the regional divide between the richer coastal region and the poorer inner regions. Regional imbalances definitely have political implications. The regional divide appeared also between the north, which looked more to the political sphere, and the south, which was keener on businesses (See, e.g., *South China Morning Post*, November 22, 2014, and April 22, 2015.).

Another controversial regional divide was the "Cantonese − Putonghua" debate, as Cantonese is the dialect used in Guangdong and other southern provinces, while Putonghua or Mandarin is mainly a northern dialect. With the growing influence and dominance of Beijing and the migration of workers from the northern provinces to southern coastal cities, it has been debated as to whether Cantonese should be scrapped in official activities, in education, and in media broadcasting. The debate turned political, as it touched on a number of economic, historical, and social values and practices. Political symbolism is important, as it would mean the total control of the north over the south of China. Although there is still much open support in the use and preservation of the Cantonese dialect, the political expectation is that, if unopposed, the role and importance of Cantonese would be reduced gradually in various dimensions (See, e.g., *Shenzhen Daily*, July 8, 2010, December 26, 2011, and August 20, 2013; *Shanghai Daily*, August 2, 2010; *Los Angeles Times*, August 30, 2010; *Global Times*, December 19, 2011, July 22, and July 24, 2014; *China Daily Hong Kong Edition*, September 28, 2012, March 14, and August 26, 2014.).

The third level of political duality was the corruption of officials, which has become structural. A Chinese survey based on 103 cases of corrupt officials for the three decades from 1981 to 2012 summarized various features of corrupt behavior among Chinese officials (Tian, 2015). The most popular causes of corruption included: (1) illegally helping others to acquire documents or qualifications; (2) practicing favoritism; (3) helping businesses to obtain various types of illegal loans and funds; (4) illegally helping others to run businesses in violation of laws and regulations; (5) illegally helping others to acquire land and real estate properties; (6) providing coverage for illegal behavior; (7) illegally helping others to gain promotion; (8) embezzlement and misappropriation of public funds; and (9) abusing authority including arranging "power and sex" deals. The survey also found that among the 103 cases, 63% of the corrupt officials were promoted despite having committed crimes; 80% of officials accepted bribes; 50% of the cases involved extramarital affairs; and 53% faced the death penalty, suspended death sentence, or imprisonment. The majority of cases involved officials aged 53 or above. In terms of education attainment, a total of 89 cases had obtained a minimum college qualification. In the 1980s, the maximum amount of money involved in each case was Rmb 20,000, rising to Rmb 550,000 in the 1990s, but escalating to approximately Rmb 200 million in 2000 − 10. Other observations included the fact that most corrupt officials come from the better-developed regions and cities, and most were operating in the financial sector and the rail network. There was an increasing trend that family members, relatives, and lovers of the corrupt officials were involved. While some officials would not accept the bribes themselves, their close relatives and family members served as the agent to collect the bribes.

The term "naked official" was used to refer to those officials who have secured their future by sending their children and families aboard. Through these foreign connections, their wealth could be sent abroad. There are reported cases where large sums of cash had been transferred to foreign accounts, despite the fact that the Renminbi was not a convertible currency. An underground cash economy must have been active in China in serving the high-ranking officials. The privilege received by the high ranked officials demonstrated simply the presence of extreme political inequality in communist countries (The most widely reported corruption cases included Bo Xilai and his wife, Gu Kailai, and Zhou Yongkang, but the highest case of graft disclosed was related to the family members of Premier Wen Jiabao. See, e.g., *Wall Street Journal*, September 22, 2013; *South China Morning Post*, November 5, 2012, November 15, 2013, May 27, and June 13, 2015; and *China Daily Hong Kong Edition*, July 30, and December 14, 2014.). Since 2014, President Xi Jinping has engaged in an anticorruption "beating both tigers and flies" program, thereby charging a number of high-ranked (tigers) as well as low-ranked (flies) corrupt officials with legal liabilities. Since the anticorruption campaign, a number of peculiarities emerged, including: (1) the blame on Western ideology and market economy; (2) presence of fake Chinese military officials; (3) working with the US government in extraditing corrupt officials; and (4) the need to strengthen inspection guidelines and reform the anticorruption bureau (See, e.g., *China Daily Hong Kong Edition*, November 15, 2013; and *South China Morning Post*, November 3, November 25, November 26, December 3, 2014, and March 3, March 10, and April 15, 2015.).

It was reported that the antigraft campaign produced contrasting results, as some officials became reluctant to do a good job for fear of being accused of abuse of power (*China Daily Hong Kong Edition*, August 14, 2015). It seemed that the anticorruption campaign targeted some selected officials, and was seen more as an instrument to combat opponents than the establishment of a long-lasting institution that systemically eradicates corruption. Thus, although the severity of corruption would subside in the meantime, anticorruption could only be considered as selective and temporarily. One unintended consequence of the anticorruption campaign would be the large outflow of people and capital. The 2014 Barclays Wealth Report showed that 47% of wealthy mainland Chinese planned to move abroad in the coming 5 years, and entrepreneurs were twice as likely to leave (*The Rise of the Global Citizen*, Barclays Wealth Report, Volume 18, 2014; and *South China Morning Post*, September 15, 2014).

On international economic relations, and with its growing economic might, China could flex its economic and political muscles in its "cheque book diplomacy" to both developed and developing countries through provisions of aid and trade. Large cash handouts had been common in building up international economic relations wherever President Xi went. Examples included: (1) a big oil deal with Russia; (2) pledged US$2 billion in aid to lift the world's poorest states; (3) make tracks for Europe; (4) built railroad in Mexico; (5) prepared to inject

US$10 billion of funds into the Balkans; (6) brought US$46 billion in deals to Britain; (7) numerous cases of large cash handouts to other developing countries, such as India; (8) boost of soft power by spending large amounts to build overseas cultural centers; and (9) US$60 billion of development funds to Africa (See, e.g., *China Daily*, October 23, 2013, May 27, December 18, 2014, and November 5, 2015; and *South China Morning Post*, November 7, December 16, 2014, and February 13, March 8, September 27, October 10, and December 4, 2015.).

China has been providing favorable outward investment, but much outward investments were aimed to serve China's economic inadequacies, typically in energy and other natural resources. Table 9.10 shows the distribution of China's outward investment to seven world regions for the period 2005—13. Energy and metal are the two largest forms of China's outward direct investment. In other words, the major function of China's outward investments was to ensure supply at home. China's outward investments were conducted mostly by state-owned or state-controlled enterprises which might not be profit-oriented. With little private sector involvement in outward investment, the long-term implication would likely be loss-making. For example, it was reported in 2006 by the Ministry of Commerce that 70% of overseas Chinese firms were "in the black." (*China Daily BizChina*, September 17, 2007) Furthermore, Chinese workers were sent to work on foreign projects, rather than recruiting workers from local sources. Unhappy incidents occurred between local workers and Chinese investors and workers residing in the host countries. Anti-Chinese demonstrations had occurred (*South China Morning Post*, July 6, 2015). Giese (2015) reported that Chinese entrepreneurs in Africa engaged more in cut-throat competition among each other than improving ethnic networks, cooperation, and community building.

A contrast can be made between China's current outward investment and Japan's outward investment in the 1970s and 1980s. Japan, from the 1960s to the 1980s, was faced with a similar situation to that of contemporary China, with a large trade surplus and the world's largest reserve. Countries also pressurized Japan to appreciate its currency in the 1970s. Similarly, Japan was reluctant to let its currency appreciate too much, as that would discourage exports. Instead, Japan had made outward investments to numerous world economies. There are two major differences in the characteristics of Japanese outward investment compared to China's outward direct investment. Japanese outward investments were conducted largely by private corporations. Japan's "horizontal" nature of outward investment aimed at investing and exporting the same production plan to foreign countries, so as to increase employment in the host countries. Typically, Japan's popular brand names of household consumables were invested and produced in such Asian countries as Malaysia and India. Industrial training was also conducted by Japanese companies in order to boost the skills of workers in the host country. Japanese outward investments in turn increased the industrial production and export of those Asian countries. In motor vehicles, the assembly and production plans were invested and shifted to the United States and other European countries. Hence, models of Japanese vehicles are now produced in the United States and Europe.

Japan did not invest overseas in order to secure its own internal supply, such as oil and energy, as its outward investments were employment- and skilled-centered in the host countries. Japanese outward investments had been well-received by host countries, though one long-term result was that Japan lost its own export market. The goodwill of Japanese investment in Asia, e.g., can be seen by the good rating from other Asian countries in a survey report by the US think tank Pew Research Center (2015) (See, e.g., *South China Morning Post*, September 3, 2015.). The survey report was based on interviews of more than 15,000 people in 10 Asia-Pacific countries and the United States from April 6 to May 27, 2015. Major findings show that 71% of respondents had a favorable

TABLE 9.10 China's Outward Direct Investment: 2005—13

Region US$ Billion	Percentage Share							
	Energy	**Metal**	**Finance**	**Real Estate**	**Agriculture**	**Transportation**	**Chemical**	**Other**
North America $91.24	48	8	22	6	6			10
Europe $80.24	45		11	9		9	6	20
Asia $66.64	41	28		14		8		9
Oceania $57.77	39	51		3	4			3
Africa $57.69	39	41	10	7				3
Latin America $54.85	55	29	2		6	3		5
Middle East $22	77	10			9			4

Heritage Foundation, reported in "ODI Set to Become More Diverse," China Daily Hong Kong Edition, October 16, 2013.

view of Japan, compared to 57% for China. The positive view of Japan outweighed the negative by more than five-to-one. Almost half of Japanese respondents were "very unfavorable" toward China, while 53% of Chinese respondents were "very unfavorable" toward Japan. Among the four Asian giants of Japan, China, India, and South Korea, respondents considered Japan most favorable with a score of 71, followed by China with a score of 57, India with a score of 51, and South Korea with a score of 47. On the contrary, respondents considered China most unfavorable with a score of 33, followed by India with a score of 31, South Korea with a score of 23, and Japan with a score of 13. Table 9.11 reproduces the ratings from the report by the Pew Research Center (2015). Out of the 10 Asia-Pacific economies, Japan has scored best with over 71% from five countries (Malaysia, Vietnam, the Philippines, Australia, and Indonesia). Only two countries (Malaysia and Pakistan) have given China a score higher than 70%, while Vietnam is the only country that gave South Korea a score over 70%. India has a much lower score.

Although China's "cheque book diplomacy" has gathered supporters, Asia's neighboring countries viewed China as a potential threat (For example, in the area of financial liberalization, the World Bank removed a critical section from the China report that urged China to accelerate reform of the state-dominated financial sector, *South China Morning Post*, July 6, 2015.). Within the Asia region, a number of countries, typically the Philippines, Vietnam, Indonesia, and Japan, have disputes over territorial claims with China in the South China Sea. The United States warned and opposed China's unilateral action, and urged for dialogue among the affected countries, as the Spratly Islands dispute has long-term strategic and military implications (See, e.g., *BBC Asia*, April 17, 2015; *East Asia Forum*, October 4, 2015; and *South China Morning Post*, November 22, December 7, and December 12, 2014, April 21, May 30, May 30, June 21, and October 27, 2015.). Other international economic issues included the rise of the Renminbi, which from October 2016 will be included in the IMF's SDR basket of currencies (See, e.g., *The Economist*, August 5, 2015; and *South China Morning Post*, November 40, 2015.). China has been using trade as an instrument to make the Renminbi a more visible currency by declaring that trade with China would have to be settled in Renminbi, though this met with resistance from many trading partners (See, e.g., *South China Morning Post*, November 26, 2014.).

Geopolitics has been a major concern in China's external and diplomatic relationships with its neighbors and other world regions, typically the United States. There are incidents when the two countries made agreements within the umbrella of the Asia − Pacific Economic Cooperation (APEC) (See, e.g., *China Daily Hong Kong Edition*, November 12, and November 13, 2014; and *South China Morning Post*, November 12, and 13, 2014.). The clear ideological difference between China and the United States, especially when China has not been making any progress on noneconomic fronts, and the battle to become the world's "number one" has turned their relationships antagonistically friendly (Ghosh, 2015; Guidetti, 2015; Overholt, 2015). Both the China and the United States have developed their own geopolitical strategy. In the case of China, President Xi in 2015 proposed the ambitious

TABLE 9.11 Percentage of Asians Expressing Favorable Views on Four Asian Countries

Views of	Japan	China	South Korea	India
Views in:				
Malaysia	84	78	61	45
Vietnam	82	19	82	66
Philippines	81	54	68	48
Australia	80	57	61	58
Indonesia	71	63	42	51
Pakistan	48	82	15	16
India	46	41	28	−
South Korea	25	61	−	64
China	12	−	47	24
Japan	−	9	21	63
Median	71	57	47	51

Pew Research Center. 2015. Poll Shows Asians View Japan More Favorably Than China. South China Morning Post, September 3, 2015.

plan commonly known as the "one belt, one road" (Economic Intelligence Unit, 2015). Similar to the establishment of "Confucius institutes" in a number of foreign universities, Confucian teachings and culture that contradicted communism were destroyed in the CR's "anti-Confucius" campaign. Indeed, some host countries see these cultural centers as propaganda institutes (See, e.g., "Criticisms of Confucius Institutes," *Wikipedia*.). China's proposal for the Asian Infrastructure Investment Bank (AIIB) is meant to serve the "one belt, one road" strategy (Chanda, 2015; Zhang, 2015). While China regarded the AIIB as a "going out" strategy in its "cheque book diplomacy," others think that it could be another "bringing in" policy, as China would learn from other AIIB members (See, e.g., *Global Trade Review*, January 7, 2015; and *South China Morning Post*, December 8, 2014, and March 24, April 1, April 2, April 14, April 15, May 22, and June 1, 2015.).

While individual countries would take advantage of China's "cash richness" through the funding of infrastructural construction, countries would have to weigh the economic gain in political and ideological terms. There are thus the political costs and benefits yet to be calculated (Chung, 2015; Godement, 2015; Price, 2015; Taylor, 2015). For example, the countries along the "one road" are situated south of Russia, and this effectively encircles Russia's entire east, south, and west borders. Russia would have to tolerate China's influence on its doorstep, and the political risk when Russia is encircled by China, especially when the Chinese economy is stronger than the Russian economy (Trenin, 2015).

Others have considered the Trans-Pacific Partnership (TPP) agreement as the political dimension of the US geopolitical strategy. The origin of the TPP was the Trans-Pacific Strategic Economic Partnership Agreement (TPSEP) signed by four APEC countries of Brunei, Chile, New Zealand, and Vietnam in 2005. The TPP agreement was reached on October 5, 2015, with a total of 12 Pacific Rim countries (Australia, Brunei, Canada, Chile, Japan, Malaysia, Mexico, New Zealand, Peru, Singapore, the United States, and Vietnam). The goal of the TPP is to "enhance trade and investment among the TPP partner countries, to promote innovation, economic growth and development, and to support the creation and retention of jobs." (Trans-Pacific Partnership," *Wikipedia*; "The Trans-Pacific Partnership: Leveling the Playing Field for American Workers and American Businesses," Office of the United States Trade Representative.)

The TPP is a multilateral trade agreement that provides low tariffs among members. While bilateral trade has become the dominant form of trade agreement under the WTO, multilateral trade will bring greater results in trade and development among partners. Hence, there would be greater trade leading to more cross-border investment, as partners would build up their own comparative advantage. The TPP will then set new rules and standards on world trade, and may even show a better trade performance than under the WTO system (Lee and Lee, 2015). The TPP agreement is theoretically open to all Pacific Rim countries, though application for accession will have to be conducted in line with upheld principles and values. The absence of China in the TPP so far has given rise to political debates that the TPP agreement is considered as a geopolitical strategy of the United States to encircle China by incorporating China's eastern and southern neighbors. In addition, the United States has also felt that China has not been performing as agreed under the terms of the WTO. Typical examples included the continued violation of intellectual property rights, and local restrictions that protected the Chinese market considerably. By comparison, the TPP agreement will be easier to operate, as it involves existing trade, and partner countries will redirect their resource usage to take advantage of trade in TPP markets. On the contrary, China's "belt, road, and bank" initiative is still in its infant stage.

Many foreign countries kowtowed to China's potential cash provision and dared not raise concerns about China's inadequacies and ideological and political differences. Internally, the CRM has reemerged, and "ways of doing things" are still not in alignment with the modern civilized world. For example, in 2010 when the Nobel Peace Prize was awarded to a mainland dissident, a group of official-backed scholars created the "Confucius Peace Prize." Since its establishment, recipients have included former Cuban leader Fidel Castro and Russia President Vladimir Putin, though none had claimed the prize in person. The 2015 prize was awarded to Zimbabwean President Robert Mugabe (*South China Morning Post*, October 22, 2015). The CRM does reflect ideological and political inconsistencies and divides among factions in China.

With its economics, China has caught up with the rest of the world, but whether there was also substantive improvement in the rise in GDP, or the rise in GDP was achieved through asset inflation and speculative activities is uncertain (*China Daily Hong Kong Edition*, July 14, 2015; and *South China Morning Post*, November 3, 2014). The extent of state control in China meant that policies could be executed, but were often *ad hoc* and changed according to situations (See, e.g., *South China Morning Post*, June 25, 2015.). In the absence of a sustainable system, policy variation would create more economic volatility. When it comes to state control, the difference between the prereform and postreform years is that China now is much richer and has plenty of resources at its disposal.

The Chinese economy is vulnerable in at least three major aspects. The "cash rich" nature of the Chinese economy comes from the huge reserves China has amassed. With the large amount of funds used to promote China's international status, the large reserve could be constrained and drained. In addition, with China's exports not rising as vigorously as previously, and the potential rise in imports as the domestic market expands to consume foreign goods, the long-term prospects in China's trade balance may be problematic. Furthermore, China's exchange rate may fluctuate, and the stability of the Renminbi could be challenged. The first challenge is the ability to maintain the huge reserves, and contrary signals will quickly be formed once the reserve falls.

Few would have noticed that China's rapid economic rise coincided with a period of low interest rates in the rest of the world. In socialist China, the interest rate has always been kept low, as it was meant more as an administrative instrument to minimize debts. Since the 1997 state-owned enterprise (SOE) reform that restructured large amounts of SOE debts through the use of asset management companies (AMCs), the local government debt has since grown and swelled. As both SOEs and local governments are state-controlled, the state would ultimately bail out local government debts (*The Wall Street Journal*, January 15, 2013). However, the challenge would emerge once the international interest rate revises upwards. With the gradual openness of the Chinese currency, the Chinese interest rate cannot deviate too much from the world interest rate. Otherwise, outward capital movements would pressurize the Chinese currency. On the other hand, the rise in interest rates would result in the accumulation of a larger debt in China. Although the authority has the ability to bail out debts, it would mean a fall in both GDP and reserves, and could even create a larger debt in the process. Although China's national debt-to-GDP ratio of 43% is regarded as low internationally by the IMF, local authorities have set up multiple "off-balance-sheet" channels to raise funds from banks and other lenders, thereby bypassing the rules that limited the selling of municipal bonds. Local government debts went mainly into infrastructural projects, such as highways, sewage works, and subways, but it was reported that declining revenue from land sales restricted their debt repayment ability (*The Business Times* (Singapore), May 15, 2015).

There is a third aspect of vulnerability in the Chinese economy. With massive and continued state control and support in economic activities, the Chinese economy strictly speaking would not experience recession, unless situations deteriorated into economic and financial crises. Adhering to the CRM, domestic citizens would naturally come to the expectation that the state would come to their rescue. China's "cheque book diplomacy" could have further implications in the domestic economy when domestic difficulties emerge; it would mean that the local people would expect the same degree and extent of assistance as was provided to foreign countries. The reasoning on the part of the indigenous citizens is simply that since the state has such an ability to assist foreign countries, the state should, could, and would use all possible options to bail out the domestic economy. The severe intervention and involvement by the state effectively meant the market in China was largely manipulated to ensure nothing could go wrong.

The best example occurred in July 2015, when the stock markets slumped and investors expressed their concern over their losses in stocks. It was reported that 80% of share investors were individual investors, and the stock market crisis could easily have political spillovers. Individual Chinese investors would simply argue that as an indigenous patriotic citizen buying shares issued by state enterprises in the domestic stock market, how come the share price could drop and the patriotic investor would make a loss. How can the state allow its own citizens to suffer losses in stock trading when it was making large cash provisions to foreign countries? By 2015, China's GDP growth turned soft as manufacturing and export indicators became less favorable. The Chinese stocks, however, experienced more than a twofold increase between November 2014 and May 2015, due largely to the rise in retail investors using borrowed money. The financial crisis appeared in summer 2015, when the Shanghai Composite Index suffered a cumulative fall of 30% between June 12 and July, 6, 2015, resulting in more than US$2.8 trillion evaporating from the two Chinese stock markets. The large increase in margin trading was considered as the last straw. The outstanding balance of margin trading increased to Rmb 2.2 trillion by mid-June, 2015, equivalent to a 116% increase from the end of 2014. Much of the selling of Chinese stocks was driven by "margin calls" that occurred when a brokerage, after extended credit to an investor to buy stocks, demanded cash or collateral back from the investor when the stock price had fallen (*Shanghai Daily*, July 6, 2015).

Before the crisis deteriorated further, the State Council intervened through a number of government institutions, including the China Securities Regulatory Commission, People's Bank of China, China Securities Finance Corporation, Ministry of Public Security, and Asset Supervision and Administration Commission. The list of state-interventions in rescuing the financial crisis included: (1) a total of the 21 largest brokerages set up a Rmb 120 billion (US$19.4 billion) fund to buy the exchange-traded funds of blue-chip shares and pledged to buy back shares of their own companies; (2) a total of 28 companies in the Shanghai Stock Exchange and the Shenzhen

Stock Exchange were told to suspend IPOs; (3) a 30% and 33% cut in stock transaction fees and transfer fees, respectively, became effective from August 1, 2015; (4) investors whose market assets fell below the Rmb 500,00 brokerage minimum were to continue trading, and brokerages were permitted to roll over margin trading contracts with clients; (5) short-selling was suspended and abnormal trading behavior of short-sellers was monitored; (6) the People's Bank of China rolled over Rmb 250 billion of medium-term loans to banks to ensure adequate liquidity; (7) a total of 25 Chinese mutual funds promised to buy stock funds and hold them for at least 1 year; (8) state-owned enterprises were forbidden to sell shares of their listed subsidiaries; and (9) more than 1300 of some 2800 companies listed in Shanghai and Shenzhen filed for a trading halt. This series of massive interventions stopped the price from falling, and trading in the Shanghai Stock Exchange and the Shenzhen Stock Exchange recovered by 5.76% and 4.25%, respectively, on July 9, 2015. However, once the two stock markets had been stabilized, the government returned to ease the monetary policy by lowering interest rates and minimum reserve requirements of commercial banks, thereby ensuring ample funds for stock investment (See, e.g., *China Daily Hong Kong Edition*, July 10, 2015; *Shenzhen Daily*, July 6, 2015; *Global Times*, July 9, July 14, and August 26, 2015; and *Shanghai Daily*, July 4, July 6, and July 10, 2015.).

In many ways, a comparison can be made between the China's "cash rich" economy and Greece's "debt-prone" economy. One similarity is that the state is prepared to absorb most, if not all, social costs. The difference is that the Greek government is financially weak, while the Chinese government is loaded with reserves. However, the Chinese economy was faced with more difficulties, as the ability to raise the growth rate was restricted, reflecting the capacity constraint (*Natixis Data Snap Economic Research*, November 11, 2015). With its large reserves, China has ample ability to shoulder social costs, which have been absorbed through state control and influence. However, whether the state would distribute resources appropriately could be another question. Without the need to shoulder much private cost by individuals and enterprises, the power of distribution would ultimately rest in the hands of officials.

Simply put, the international financial crisis in 2008 has led to unprecedented changes in China. The Chinese economy is faced with the "crossroad" because the economy is reaching full capacity and new economic paths have to be found. The 2008 crisis was also a "turning point" for the Chinese economy. Before 2008, the Chinese economy concentrated on how the economy could further expand. After 2008, the Chinese economy had to concentrate on how the economy could avoid possible contraction or decline.

VI CONCLUSION

The 2008 financial crisis brought a number of economic and financial difficulties, and many world economies suffered as a result, e.g., in financial collapse and economic recession, the need to rescue banks and financial institutions, the emergence of bankruptcies and fall in real estate assets, and the rise in unemployment and fall in investments. The 2008 crisis has also highlighted a few fundamental economic issues that policies and ideologies in some economies have either overlooked or adopted inappropriately. The 2008 crisis simply served as the "wake up call" that symbolized the need to reverse the policies and ideologies back to normal market disciplines so that growth can proceed. The cases of the "low interest rate trap" in the United States and other industrialized economies, the large Greek debt and China's economic vulnerabilities have one thing in common. That is the desire for the government to shoulder the social costs, which could and should have been dispersed into individualized private costs.

The three cases discussed in this chapter point squarely to the shortcomings of socialist economic policies, as their short-term "achievements" would have long-term repercussions on sustainable growth. Once the situation deteriorates, it would mean the social cost burden has expanded so much that it becomes impossible to sustain, and the economy would risk the outbreak of a financial crisis. In the end, the economic cost of the crisis could exceed the benefit, and it would even be more difficult to steer the economy back to a normal track of sustainable growth. The best combination involves the decisions of both the government and the individual. On the one hand, the government should adopt a policy that minimizes the size of the social cost, by sending more economic power, opportunity, and choice to the private sector. On the other hand, private individuals should maximize their economic power, and by taking up their private costs, individuals would in turn contain the intervention the government could exercise. A business-friendly and market-promoting government, together with the nurture of more endowment-high individuals and a capitalist economy in which individual economic freedom dominates, should be able to look after the endowment-low sector of the population through the adoption of economic policies that gear to promote the supply-side of the economy, thereby transforming more individuals into endowment-high individuals.

One is not saying that crises will not emerge in nonsocialist countries, but the difference is that nonsocialist economic policies tend to provide the troubled economy with the ability to reinvigorate and survive on its own, though the pace and time required for revitalization may differ among economies, and would depend on the severity of the crisis. The market signals from the forces of supply and demand, together with the voluntary participation of investors and the generated opportunities would work more productively, effectively, and efficiently than the "visible hand" of the government.

10

Reviving Capitalism

I INTRODUCTION

There are certainly no shortages of economic, political, and social theories, and empirical findings that explain and discuss capitalism. Similarly, there are no shortages of economic and political debates, and socioeconomic policies that governments thought they could have applied appropriately. There are also a great number of international institutions and "think tanks" that are so ready to provide recipes, suggestions, recommendations, and solutions to world economic affairs. And there are foreign governments that monitor the world through negotiations, diplomatic channels, and deployment of peace keeping forces, yet the world economy in the 21st century looks less secure and less promising as the emerging problems are ever more challenging. The world has experienced wars, conflicts, and terrorist attacks, and there are complex political, ideological, religious, regional, and historical accusations from one another across countries, borders, and peoples. There are "latecomers" prepared to challenge the dominance of the existing world powers. There are countries and people which are ready to "give" to save the world, equally there are countries and people which are ready to "take" from the rest of the world regardless. One wonders if the existing theories in social sciences, humanities, and business studies are rapidly becoming irrelevant, or if there exists a gap between theories and policies.

Given the world's limited resources, the technology that humans have created, and the different history and variation in civilization, it would be unacceptable if conflicts that emerged in the 21st century could push civilization backwards to issues that the civilized world would have thought to have passed. Yet, there are still human conflicts based on such outdated issues as ideology and religion. The worst is that many worldly conflicts are intangible and abstract, nonsubstantial, remote, and nonimmediate, and there are also feasible solutions, but conflicting parties are not prepared to consider or accept them. At one extreme, religious conflicts often argue over faith and spiritual issues, but alternative priorities could be given to human improvements in their current, living life. At another extreme, economies that have overspent would have to pass their debt to their neighbors, foreign governments,

© 2017 Elsevier Inc. All rights reserved.

and world institutions, thereby impoverishing their future generations when the need to repay arises. The existence of ideologies still serves more as a divisive than as an adhesive tool among nations and governments.

In many world conflicts, there is a lack of broadmindedness on the part of the leaders, and conflicting parties are ready to put the blame on others and pass the burden to someone else. Conceptually, this is similar to passing one's private cost burden to the broader society that eventually increases the social cost burden. Conflicting parties often look into the weakness of the opposing parties, rather than finding their own ways to prevent conflicts. There is the possibility of double standards, as one party or country often expects the most from their opponent, but only performs the least it can on its own. Indeed, there could also be vested interests for the conflict to continue, because some involved parties or persons would gain in the process.

The discussions have so far touched on the essence and ingredients of different ideologies, the performance in different world economies, how world economies differ from each other, and how the world changed after the 2008 crisis. The world economy is definitely getting more dichotomous than harmonious. Indeed, there is no perfection in economic development, but rather the deployment of economic activities and resources would allow advances in human civilization. The question of how to make a better world can itself arouse multiple suggestions and interpretations. Diversity allows choices, cooperation, and freedom to choose, but also freedom to antagonize and freedom to disagree. One could easily ask whether the world economy is faced with a shortage of solutions, or is not prepared to accept solutions.

There are four related sets of dichotomous concepts that have been identified in previous chapters. One set of concepts relates to activities that produce either "absolute" or "relative" outcomes. The second set concerns the adoption of either "demand-driven" or "supply-led" policies. The third set deals with the understanding of the "private cost" versus "social cost" burden in policy decisions. The last set of concepts is the economic dichotomy between "system-driven" and "personality-driven" governance. One can conjecture that many of the worldly problems and conflicts can be discussed and explained within these four sets of dichotomous concepts. Politics and ideology, wars, and territorial conflicts are definitely activities that produce "absolute" outcomes. Prowelfare economic policies tend to be more "demand-driven." Economic crises that result in more government intervention concern the redistribution between the "social cost" burden and "private cost" burden. In a politically mature economy where systems have been well-instituted, activities will adhere to the rules and practices governed by the system that can transparently be monitored. On the contrary, a politically unfree or immature economy tends to adhere more to "personality-driven" decisions that are often discrete and lack the support of transparent rules and standards.

An understanding of these four sets of dichotomous concepts will enable one to explain many worldly problems. Understanding the problems is always the first step to come up with solutions. Table 10.1 provides a simplified picture of the relationship between these four sets of dichotomous concepts. The northeast portion in Table 10.1 groups the relationship between "relative outcomes, supply-led policies, private cost, and system-driven" concepts, while the southwest portion groups the relationship between "absolute outcomes, demand-driven policies, social cost, and personality-driven" concepts.

In the northeast portion, activities with relative outcomes would probably be supported by supply-led policies, as that would provide more economic opportunities to be shared among individuals. For that to happen, it

TABLE 10.1   The Relationship Between the Four Sets of Dichotomous Concepts

	Absolute Outcomes	Relative Outcomes
Supply-led		Capitalist market economy Create economic opportunities Promote self-reliance, entrepreneurship Government constructs social capital Minimize the "social cost" burden Individuals take up "private cost" System-driven, high transparency
Demand-driven	Politics and ideology dichotomy Cultural and customary differences Welfare expenditure, redistribution Government controls resources State shoulders "social cost" Personality-led policies Strengthen check and balance	

would be more appropriate to institute minimal government intervention, so that activities in the private sector will be in the "driver-seat" and have a high degree of economic freedom to pursue businesses-related activities. A minimum level of government intervention necessarily means that the social cost burden would be minimized. On the contrary, the "back-seat" government will institute and promote social capital, such as infrastructure development, education, health, and public security. When economic and business power is dispersed among private individuals, it would mean the need for checks and balances through the establishment of a reliable, transparent, and equitable system so that market participants are aware of the required ethics, rules, practices, and standards. The reliable civic system stands between the individual and the government. An individual will be protected and secured more by a reliable system than by the policy or ideology of the government. The functioning of these four relationships reinforces each other to generate virtuous economic cycles.

The southwest portion of Table 10.1 shows an activity that generates absolute outcomes would produce an antagonizing, uncompromising, or even conflicting situation where the winning party would gain at the expense of the losing party. To commit to high government welfare spending, the government would need to amass a lot of economic resources and control. With higher welfare spending, the economy would increasingly have to rely on government expenditures and in turn, the government needs to control more resources in order to have sufficient resources to spend. The distribution of resources through the state would mean that individuals have to sacrifice their economic power, freedom, and choice, as the state would have to absorb more private costs and eventually shoulder the entire social cost. The state would become most powerful, as decisions could be influenced by the personality of the leaders, rather than relying on the functioning of a reliable system.

Table 10.1 shows the two hypothetically extreme scenarios. Capitalism allows the market to function and individuals to perform to their utmost. This necessarily means that even though the market economy fluctuates, there will be new participants entering at different stages of the economic cycle. Given that economics generates "relative" outcomes, there are always new investors, entrepreneurs, and risk-takers who would engage in new activities; such a reinvigorating feature of capitalism makes it an "evergreen" ideology and despite economic ups and downs, the "life of capitalism" would be self-generating and self-rejuvenating. The feature of "relative" outcome in market capitalism is that the economy can always be rejuvenated, recovered, and transformed by new participants that bring creative and innovative ideas and eventually produce new comparative advantages.

This chapter aims to discuss new economic possibilities that would promote economic growth across the world. The intended outcome is to minimize conflicts and "social cost" through improvements in economic competitiveness and/or the adoption of growth-promoting, business-friendly economic policies. By shifting activities that produce "absolute" outcomes to activities that produce "relative" outcomes would effectively mean greater use of economic tools. This can be done by switching economic policies so as to create more opportunities and growth possibilities. Given that inequality is inevitable, the goal is to ensure that all individuals can have some economic improvement, though there could still be differences in the amount of improvements received by different individuals. Economic relativity occurs in a situation where economics is the instrument used in handling human affairs, and differences in economic outcomes can be acceptable so long as all individuals are getting better off over time.

II REORIENTATING WORLD RESOURCES AND POLICIES

There are four aspects of the international economy that deserve attention and require resource reorientation, including the supply and demand for oil and peace in the Middle East, revision of prowelfare economic policies, rebalancing between the nominal sector and real sector, and further commercialization of technologies.

Oil and Peace

It is unfortunate that much of the oil revenues landed in unstable Middle East countries, and their conflicts have spilled over to the peaceful parts of the world, either due to their inability to handle the problems, or they blame other parts of the world that engaged in their problems. These countries engaged in games with "absolute" outcomes through multiple levels of conflict and antagonistic activities. In other words, the large oil revenue did not help the Middle East to switch from activities with "absolute" outcomes to activities with "relative" outcomes.

The "intraregional" dimension of the conflict in the Middle East region included "within-region" disputes among conflicting religious factions, territorial disputes, racial inequalities, historical controversies, and military engagements. In religion, one area of dispute related to the lack of modernization and mutual acceptability in the Islamic faith, and the other area of conflict is the two or more factional divisions within the religion. Unfortunately, these two conflicting aspects in the Islamic religion did not seem to have any signs of change, nor were they prepared to consider the possibility of mutual survival and respect. In territorial terms, there is a lack of compromise and agreement in the use and ownership of land, despite the fact that much of the land is still in its raw and undeveloped stage. There is real difficulty in identifying the causality effect in the "infraregional" conflicts in the Middle East. There are too many knots that needed to be untied in the Middle East.

The "interregional" dimension of the conflict involves the international community in military operations and prevention of terrorism through the infiltration of religious fanatics and radicalized extremists. However, given the "absolute" nature of militarism, one could never distinguish whether more military involvement would help to alleviate the situation, or whether it would deepen the severity of the conflict, as one military engagement could lead to another. Religious fanaticism has spread and infiltrated to western cities and other fragile states and regions. Terrorist activities carried out by radicalized religious extremists could cause trouble in any corner of the world, hurting innocent people and threatening other peaceful world regions.

These two "infraregional" and "interregional" dimensions reinforce each other, as the former would need financial, military, and material support from the external world. Similarly, the interregional dimension would draw foreign participants and states into the conflicting region. Eventually, it will develop into a "conflict-breeds-conflict" vicious-cycle, and the situation would lead also to other international controversies, such as the extent and funding of military engagement, the need for religious modernization, racial equality within religions, the extent of gathering intelligence, and the magnitude of security and acceptance of refugees from conflicting states. In the meantime, the high price of oil has weakened the world economy through a reduction in aggregate consumption and purchasing power. In short, the peaceful world experiences the "worse of two worlds": high oil prices, and exported instability and terrorist activities.

The Middle East crisis and global terrorism effectively constitute the "third world war." Given that most Islamic countries in the Middle East export only oil, but the militants and religious extremists are equipped with modern weapons, the oil revenue clearly provided funding in supporting the political, religious, territorial, and military conflicts. After the terrorist attack in Paris on Friday, November 13, 2015, other subsequent terrorist attacks in cities in the United States, Belgium, France, and Germany in 2016, and in addition extremist activities in various parts of Asia and Africa, it was clear that the religious extremists and terrorists were holding a "war-mentality," while leaders and citizens in much of the peaceful world, especially some European countries, were still holding a "fraternal-mentality" of acceptance and sympathy. Such a "mentality gap" among the leaders and citizens of many Western countries was exploited by the religious militants. For example, in dealing with the flood of Middle East refugees to European countries in October – November 2015, many European leaders held an accommodating attitude. Europe unconditionally accepted the "social cost" arising from such an attitude. There was evidence in the aftermath of the Paris terrorist attack in November 2015 that terrorists could have themselves posed as refugees.

As a short-term strategy, militarism could prevent deterioration, but itself could be an obstacle to long-term peace. The long-lasting solution has to look for ways and strategies that would switch from activities with "absolute" outcomes to activities with "relative" outcomes. Since the Middle East conflicts involved both "intraregional" and "interregional" dimensions, the solutions must also include strategies from both dimensions. One "intraregional" strategy is to create more economic activities that redirect the energy from war-like activities to activities that nourish businesses. The establishment of reliable institutions, the greater exercise of markets and extension of civic and social activities, the reorientation in the use of land and labor resources to nonmilitary activities, the increase of investment activities in the consumption market and industrial production, and the reorientation or commercialization of technology to civilian production are among numerous possibilities that a peaceful Middle East region could offer. One could imagine that instead of engaging in life-long conflicts, floods of refugee outflows, and human antagonism of one kind or another, citizens in Middle East countries would engage in business development, inward foreign investment and export of industrial or light manufacturing goods to other world markets, greening of deserts and scientific agrofarming, and reliable institutions that stood between different races and ethnicities, religions, and social strata.

There can be a number of possibilities in the "intraregional" dimension, but endogenous changes, improvements, and adjustments are required. Developing mutual respect and acceptance in land and religious diversity would probably be the first needed change. Modernization in civic life, attitude, thinking, and behavior is another needed change. Politically, rather than antagonism, broadmindedness in the leadership among religious states is desperately needed. This would require decisions that would take into account the more modern form of life and way of living, including equality, transparency, and system-driven policies. A broadminded, well-respected, modern, and knowledgeable leader would ensure that people would have a better life tomorrow, and that compromise is preferred to conflict, while selflessness is preferred to self-centeredness. What great leaders earn is respect and appreciation in history, and that goes beyond how much these leaders could make in pecuniary terms during their reign.

Similar to the discussion on the dichotomy of "private cost" and "social cost," it is advisable to let foreign countries become involved, as it is a sign of support. But this should not be taken as a way to pass the country's "social cost" of conflict to other countries. The country in conflict has to realize that both the "cost of conflict" and the "benefit of peace" can be "internalized," and that people should be given a chance to choose. Conflict should be regarded as a "negative externality," because it always creates unwanted hardship. At the "interregional" dimension, there are numerous exogenous strategies that foreign countries can exercise. A reduction in world oil consumption and a drop in oil revenue could impose a revenue constraint on oil exporters, though this is easier said than done because overall world oil consumption would increase as new demand from emerging countries rises. Nonetheless, oil exporting countries should utilize their revenue productively in promoting development and growth. Also, through investment in the financial markets, the oil revenue could expand into a larger pool of financial resources. In order to reduce oil consumption, cooperation from the business sector will be needed in the design of more fuel efficient vehicles.

There is no single solution to the multiple levels of conflict in Middle East states. In the first instance, there is a need for goodwill to emerge from all sides, followed by an effort to switch to activities with "relative" outcomes. There is room for capitalism to function in enhancing activities with "relative" outcomes, beginning with the dispersal of economic power to individuals so that their own ability, endowments, and productivity will govern their economic achievement and contribute to economic growth. Give market capitalism a chance in promoting development and change in those highly religious states. Once the private sector is promoted, the government can concentrate on promoting infrastructure development and reliable institutions.

Peace in the Middle East and among the Islamic states can only come with a paradigm shift. Conflicts will not disappear so long as these states are engaged in activities with "absolute" outcomes. What is needed is the restoration of peace, and conflict has to be replaced by competition in markets and businesses. It is only when peace is at hand that a new pattern of labor specialization and resource deployment could emerge. Economic development among these oil exporting states should not have funding constraints, as they are flooded with oil revenue, but the leaders in the conflicting states might have their own agenda and not be prepared to make a paradigm shift.

Given the multiple origins of the conflicts, it would be impossible to have one solution that solves all the conflicts. One can look for solutions initially at the local level and disaggregate the conflicts into compartments so that a "building block" approach could be applied to different levels of conflict. In other words, solutions or negotiations will have to take place together or separately in the dimensions of history, military, ideology, religion, diplomacy, economic, territorial, and so on. A process of "multitask, multilevel, and multilateral" negotiation is needed. This involves a breakdown of the conflict into various origins that allow the progress of peace negotiations to move forward one step or one dimension at a time. A "from absolute to relative" negotiation strategy could prioritize the different levels of conflict with the aim to "deescalate" the conflict gradually.

One can visualize the "from absolute to relative" strategy in the Middle East peace negotiations as follows. There will be at least three layers of discussions and negotiations, as shown in Fig. 10.1. The first layer in the peace negotiation would be regarded as the core, but it would be the most complicated as it involves a total of seven dimensions (historical, racial, territorial, religious, military, diplomatic, and ideological). All these seven dimensions involve absolute outcomes that need to be negotiated and discussed before progress could be made.

FIGURE 10.1 The three layers of peace negotiation in the Middle East.

Given their complexity, the difficult task should first be handled by an independent third party, such as the United Nations, as it would represent some degree of impartiality, unbiasedness, and scientific judgment. Although the seven dimensions are ultimately linked to each other, they should be discussed separately, as the negotiations may have to go all the way to the very origin of these problems. The advantage of making separate negotiations should help to breakdown and compartmentalize the complexity into manageable possibilities.

The second layer of peace negotiations should involve the regional aspects, typically with such institutions as the Oil and Petroleum Exporting Countries (OPEC), the European Union (EU), and Organization for Economic Cooperation and Development (OECD). With its massive oil exports, OPEC shall be one of the richest world institutions, and should lend a helping hand in reaching peace in the Middle East. Given that there is a lot of vested interests in the oil industry among the Middle East states and governments, OPEC should have the role in ensuring peace in the Middle East region, as benefits should reach all corners in the regions. Indeed, OPEC should be the first institution that benefits from a peaceful Middle East. As the EU is the nearest neighbor to the Middle East, and while the OECD represents the developed countries, both the EU and OECD should facilitate and support the various aspects in the peace negotiations. Those Middle East citizens who have migrated to EU and OECD countries could also play a role in promoting peace. The purpose of this layer in the negotiation is to introduce, activate, and establish peaceful institutions in the war-torn states.

The third layer of peace negotiation involves the participation of foreign governments and different international economic institutions. The main purpose is to introduce activities that produce "relative" outcomes. The World Bank typically would promote economic developments in the Middle East region, ranging from environmental protection to infrastructure and business development. The IMF should help in funding postconflict governments in the Middle East with the intention of beginning with a sound monetary, financial, and banking system. The World Trade Organization (WTO) could take the initiative in engaging the postconflict economies in the Middle East to have greater trade possibilities with other world economies. The intention of this third layer of negotiation is to ensure the rise of economic activities in the postconflict countries so that economic reconstruction and activities would gradually replace conflict-prone activities. Once these economic institutions are in place, the market economy should provide incentives to both local and foreign investment that eventually turn Middle East countries into true market economies.

Shortfall in Prowelfare Policies

While European leaders exhibited an accommodating attitude and capitalized on the influx of refugees from the Middle East countries, few considered the "social cost" burden that European tax payers would have to shoulder. As soon as the news that Europeans gave "open arms to the refugees" was radiated back to the home countries, more refugees were on their way. By the end of October 2015, e.g., the number of migrants entering Germany alone mounted to 800,000 (*Reuters*, April 17, 2015; *The Telegraph*, July 3, 2015; *Associated Press*, August 31, 2015; and *SBS*, September 1, 2015). Catering for the needs and demands from the influx would impose a huge and long-lasting economic burden on the residents and socioeconomic fabric in the host country. The rise in government spending should send signals to the tax payers. Although young refugees would provide a source of labor in the host countries, it was risky without prescreening as the level of skills they possess may not be suitable, and they may not integrate and contribute to the host economy. The social cost would probably be greater than the social gain, as it is uncertain.

The refugee case illustrated squarely the problems of prowelfare economic policies, even in countries where leaders were democratically elected. Using the concept of the agency theory, political decisions could have long-lasting adverse economic implications, as the leaders are the "agent," concerned more about their political image and acts than the fiscal ability to pay for the welfare expenses. Votes in political elections are ex ante decisions, and voters might not agree to what the elected leaders would do ex post after they took office. Periodic democratic elections, in principle, would minimize the agency problem.

When politicians need quick results, economic activities become their instruments, and economic policies committed by political leaders lead to results to be borne by the electorate later. The agency theory would argue that the policy decision-makers (politicians, welfare advocates) would not be the people responsible for the funding of welfare expenditure (tax payers). The economic conjecture is that extensive prowelfare economic policies usually result in long-term economic decline and falls in economic competitiveness. The weakening of the economy could even be self-fulfilling. Consider a hypothetical economy where there was fiscal surplus and the economy was experiencing decent growth. Instead of making improvements in infrastructure and expanding future economic capability, socialist-oriented policies provided large welfare to endowment-low individuals. Such a redistributive policy would eventually require an increase in tax once the fiscal surplus dried up. Hence, high fiscal spending would have to be coupled with a higher tax. This cannot be sustained when economic growth slackens, and the increase in deficit shall soon be followed by government borrowing to fund current spending and debt would begin to accumulate.

Next, there is the "push" effect as the rising tax would hurt businesses, and if investors were also faced with rising labor costs, the disincentives so generated would encourage businesses to invest abroad where the cost of production would be more accommodating. In turn, the rise in unemployment would mean more individuals would need to seek welfare assistance, leading eventually to higher welfare spending, fiscal deficits, and national debts. The investment that went abroad would return in the form of imports of manufactured goods. Even though the imports would be cheaper than local production, the rise in imports over time would weaken the currency, and currency depreciation would mean a higher import price leading to domestic inflation.

Such a hypothetical sequence of economic events would lead to a fall in domestic output, outflow of investment, a weaker business sector, loss of competitiveness, and eventually a rise in deficits and debts. On the contrary, those businesses that invested abroad would strengthen the host economy. By comparison, the home country would become weaker, as the loss of investment would mean a reduction in output and growth. And, as the economy of the host country expanded, economic growth and expansion would multiply and snowball into a much stronger economy, which in turn would, through exports, compete successfully with the home country. Eventually, the home country would become uncompetitive and face decline, especially if there was an absence of economic restructuring.

Economic development across countries also shows a "relative" outcome, meaning that countries can either rise together, or some rise faster than others, or some rise while others fall. It means that the country which experiences an economic rise today could fall in the future, and equally the weaker countries today could successfully improve their economic strength and compete with other countries tomorrow. The question is how one economy can ensure its own competitiveness by constantly enlarging its own economic capability.

It is true that there are always endowment-low individuals, but for the maintenance of economic competitiveness and expansion, it would be more preferable and proper to promote more endowment-high individuals, as they could then look after their own economic welfare. As endowment-high individuals take care of their own private cost, the social cost burden would then be lowered. Even at a time of fiscal surplus, the low social cost burden would mean the availability of more resources in promoting, enhancing, and strengthening the future capability of the economy. As the level of future economic capability expands, there is a greater chance for individuals to seek a better paid job, and the higher social mobility would mean a lesser need for welfare spending. In turn, the government can even reduce tax as an incentive to businesses and individuals to perform better. Because of differences in individual endowments, and while capitalism allows freedom, choice, and diversity, opportunities are generated and exploited, and individuals with different endowments can take advantage of the opportunities that increase exponentially. Inequality exists because of endowment differences, but is acceptable so long as everyone gets better off, however unevenly.

A number of criteria can be used in resource reorientation if the intention is to promote economic growth, achieve stronger economic health, expand economic capability, and gain competitiveness. Firstly, while politics is exercised in policy decisions, a higher priority and proper consideration should be given to the economic outcomes of the policy. At worst, the policy needs to ensure a balance between political and economic implications. At best, the policy should be in favor of positive economic implications and consequences. Secondly, policy makers would need to choose between whether the economic policy is demand-enhancing or supply-enriching. Namely, whether the economic policy simply promotes and satisfies short-term demand needs or enriches future potential and capabilities. Short-term gains would only be needed to address sudden shocks and crises. In noncrisis times, it would be preferable to reorient resource usage more to enhance the supply capability of the economy, as that is the only means to generate sustainable, progressive, and long-lasting growth.

Economic development can never be equal, and differences appear. The sequence is to ensure growth in the first instance, and when every person is making economic progress, the extent of "inequality" can then be addressed. The society should look into the "survivability," rather than the "equality," of needy individuals. And once survival is ensured, it would be proper to enhance the "marketability" of the individuals, so that they can stand on their own economic feet, contribute their energy and expertise to the economy, and ultimately generate their own assets and wealth. In a nutshell, prowelfare economic policies through government spending and various redistributive channels are often politically oriented, demand-driven, and resource-depleting. Although there is still a need for a certain amount of welfare provision, the proper role of economic policies should be resource-enhancing, sustainability-strengthening, capability-driven, and competitiveness-improving.

Rebalancing Financial and Real Sectors

There are two theoretical debates in rebalancing the financial and real economic sectors. The monetary approach typically employs such monetary instruments as the interest rate in promoting real physical investment. Unfortunately, it can be difficult to distinguish between investment and speculation. Due to differences in expectations, market economies do experience fluctuations in business cycles. Economic dynamism always generates movement and activities. Given the ability of capitalist economies to reinvigorate, recessions would end as the forces of supply and demand trigger and work in reverse to bring a new round of recovery. Hence, the analogy is that a stronger and sustainable economy armed with appropriate economic structures, systems, and policies should be able to weather all unexpected events and shocks.

There is little discussion on the balance between the financial sector and the real sector of the economy. Governments in advanced countries tend to have focused their concerns more on the financial sector. Before making policy adjustments, governments would sometimes inappropriately consider the impact of the financial sector first. There is some legitimacy in such behavior, as it would be the financial sector that could react immediately to policy changes. However, the question becomes whether the policy changes could also be made in favor of the real sector. There can be a missing link in the literature of monetary economics in distinguishing between investment and speculation. Although there are physical and portfolio investments, there is a lack of analysis as to when an investment is an investment, and when an investment becomes a speculation. Some so-called financial investments, such as margin trading, are speculative by definition. Other investment products can become speculative depending on the time and the stage of the business cycle. For example, a person purchases a property, which should be regarded as an investment, but when the asset price has increased, the owner of the property may decide to sell and obtain the windfall gain, which would become an act of speculation.

While investment is "good," speculation is "bad" and could lead to undesirable economic consequences. But speculation is unavoidable in contemporary financial markets, as there are numerous instruments that facilitate speculative investment. Activities in the financial market are merely financial transactions. Indeed, together with bank loans, financial market transactions could increase the money supply independently from the government's policy. Policy makers thus should not be overshadowed by immediate reactions from the financial sector, but have to strike a balance between the immediate impact in the financial economy and the longer-term impact in the real economy. Indeed, it would be more appropriate for the policy makers to spell out clearly the objectives that are meant to promote activities in the real sector of the economy, while speculative activities in the financial economy would have to take their own course according to the market conditions.

The second approach is known as the structural school, where the rebalancing between economic sectors requires: (1) the consideration of the entire financial sector in promoting economic development; and (2) the use of other relevant economic instruments that would positively influence the real sector, typically in the form of physical investment, employment creation, and industrial diversity (Van Wijnbergen, 1982; Taylor, 1983). Activities in the financial market are often short-term, and their reactions might not be appropriate when considering the long-term impact on the real economy. On the contrary, activities in the real economy tend to be slow, and require time to materialize. Thus, policy decisions should not be influenced too easily by movements in the financial sector, but have to ensure that activities in the financial sector can be geared to work for the real economy.

The structural approach proposes using fiscal and other instruments in promoting the real economy, including the avoidance of a high tax rate that creates disincentive effects. Business-friendliness is a prerequisite in ensuring growth in the real economy, and enhancing overall economic competitiveness is paramount in maintaining economic expansion. Economic competitiveness is a comprehensive concept, and the good use of one economic instrument spills over to performance of another economic instrument, thereby allowing a "virtuous circle" to develop. For example, a policy that favors redistribution would require a high tax rate, and strong unions would bargain for high wages that would "push" businesses and investments to other low cost production destinations. Together, the "deadweight" loss of redistribution and high wages will be a loss in economic competitiveness.

There is a "chicken and egg" problem in the argument. The fact is that the financial sector usually would not be affected by redistributive policies. For those economies that experience high tax rates and wage rates, investors (and speculators) would naturally be more willing to "invest" in the financial market as portfolio investment could avoid the disincentives arising from the business or market unfriendliness in the real economy. One should see that in portfolio investment (or speculation) gains can be realized within a short period of time, while investment in physical investment would require time and investment returns could be uncertain. It is true that the process of portfolio investment in the financial market is less complicated, and the investor (and speculator) could have a greater degree of control in the return on investment. As such, the rebalancing argument would require the need to change investment conditions in the real sector.

The economics is that it is easier for the financial sector to expand, or to contract, due to market shocks arising from various changes. Thus, the financial market by its very nature would be volatile. One can argue that the economy has been dominated by activities in the financial sector. Although many financial activities are really temporary and may not have much impact on the real economy, the media does report extensively on movements in the financial market. For example, there is full coverage of financial news, but in effect, only a small portion of the population are engaged in financial activities. Extensive coverage of financial activities naturally attracted much attention. But whether attention would require policy action could be another matter. Government officials, decision-makers, and analysts should see that financial activities are superficial, nominal, and short-term, while the real sector actually reflects the true economic capability. Thus, one has to distinguish between financial signals and economic signals. What is occurring in individual markets may have different implications on the aggregate economy. Between the two sectors, the real sector is ultimately the more important sector in the economy.

Commercialization of Technology

Commercialization refers to the situation where technology has been transformed into household products consumed by individuals. History has shown a number of successful cases of commercialization, including the production of wrist watches and conveyor belts. The classic example in the 1970s and the early 1980s was the "Walkman" developed by Japanese companies that commercialized existing tape recording technology and turned it into a personalized product that individuals could carry. Indeed, the successful development and commercialization of the "Walkman" pioneered a whole generation of personalized hi-fi products, laptop computers, and mobile phones. In the process, corporations from typically the United States and South Korea have joined the wagon of technological commercialization.

On the contrary, there is a classic case of failure. The supersonic jet, Concorde, developed in the 1970s by British and French aerospace companies, was considered as a masterpiece in technology, but the flight service after 1973 provided by the supersonic jet was uneconomical, as it only served a few routes across the Atlantic and the price was unaffordable to ordinary travelers. However, the commercial operation of Concorde ended after the tragic crash on a scheduled flight from Paris to New York, on July 25, 2000. The last Concorde flight was made on November 5, 2003, on its way to the Museum of Flight in Seattle. Since September 2015, however, it has been reported that the supersonic jet may fly again by 2019 ("Concorde", *Wikipedia*; *The Telegraph*, September 18, 2015; and *CNN Business Traveler*, September 21, 2015).

The two cases of Walkman and Concorde are interesting, as the former is based on an old technology that dated back to the First World War, while the latter is a masterpiece of technology that opened up futuristic possibilities. However, a major difference rests with the price and demand behavior. The Walkman aimed at mass consumers and assumed an elastic demand, such that more would be demanded at a lower price. On the contrary, Concorde aimed at the luxury market and assumed an inelastic demand, implying that total revenue can rise when the price is set at a high level.

The amount of fuel consumed by the supersonic jet should be a concern. Indeed, the high price of oil and energy, and the near-monopoly of oil supply have raised concerns because of the need to minimize the consumption of oil, environmental conservation, and development of alternative fuel. As motor vehicles consume oil continuously, the production of motor vehicles has concentrated on the development of electric and hybrid cars that provide a mixture of fuel and electricity, and hydrogen cars that depend entirely on an alternative energy. However, there is major difference in the production of electric cars between United States and Japanese producers. The Japanese manufacturers tend to produce lower priced hybrid and electric cars that aim at the user market. Japanese producers assumed an elastic demand, and a lower price will lead to larger sales. The US manufacturers produce only a few models and charge a high price comparable to other luxury brands. The assumption of the US manufacturer is one of inelastic demand, where sale revenues will rise only with a very high price and lower sales.

The consumer may still compare the price between two similar car models where one runs on petrol and the other runs on electricity. The high price charged on the electric vehicle could be seen as a capitalization on petrol consumption by the manufacturer. If the price of the electric vehicle is higher than the petrol vehicle, consumers would think it was a "prepayment" to petrol consumption. If it is the contrary, the demand for the electric vehicle should definitely increase, because consumers could save on the cost of petrol. The economics is that once developed, the cost of the electric car technology should become a "sunk cost." The business strategy could make a difference in the outcome, because commercialization can generate forward and backward, as well as vertical and horizontal, linkages in the production chains. The production of electric vehicles has a backward vertical linkage in reducing the demand for oil.

III INTERNATIONAL ECONOMIC ALLIANCES

The Trio

A "triangular" alignment among three capitalist countries is between the United Kingdom, Japan, and the United States. Although each of these three capitalist economies also exercises welfare policies at different degrees depending on the political affiliation of the ruling party, together they act as a monitor in their own respective continents, as well as on an international scale. Strictly speaking, all these three countries are "island" economies, and their currencies are internationally accepted. Traditionally, they are key investors in many parts of the world and their technological advancement has influenced other world economies. Although their experience on economic growth differed from each other in the post–Second World War decades, they often serve as the reference point to the development of other world economies.

However, each of these three countries can exercise their independent impact on the world. In the case of the United Kingdom, the long establishment and reliance on civic institutions, such as equality under the rule of law that dated back to the charter of Magna Carta instituted in 1215, has been the point of reference for a large number of contemporary English-speaking countries. Being in Europe, but geographically detached from the European continent, the United Kingdom can work with other European countries, but it can also choose to pursue more independent policies different from other European countries.

Since its economic rise in the 1970s, the "horizontal" nature of Japanese investment in the world has been welcomed, as it aided economic development and promoted employment and growth in the host economies. Japan's foreign investment showed that what was produced at home was invested abroad. One can hardly locate any literature that discussed the negative aspects of Japanese investment. For example, Japanese investment had rarely been accused of imperialism.

The United States remains the strongest country in the world. Through its role as an international "police," much resource from the US tax payers has been spent in ensuring international stability and security. As the largest capitalist country advocating democracy and freedom, the international policing role of the United States would surely uphold similar values. Nonetheless, the United States has been criticized, especially when it became involved in military deployment in other parts of the world, and with the emergence of destabilizing problems within its domestic economy, such as abuse in the use of guns, and poor race relationships. However, one thought could straighten out the issue. If each and every world economy had adhered to the values that all normal human beings long for, such as economic freedom, individual progress, respect of human rights, open elections, and democratic governments, there would not be any need for the presence of an uninvited monitor. Unfortunately, there are still a number of world economies that violate human freedom and threaten stability and peace. Nonetheless, these "trio" countries will be the defender in the international community, though often they have to be assisted and supported by their allies and institutions from the international community.

Among these three countries, the United States is probably the intermediator that handles Atlantic affairs with the United Kingdom, and Pacific affairs with Japan. In turn, both the United Kingdom and Japan have a number of similarities. Geopolitically, e.g., the United Kingdom served as the gateway to Europe, while Japan was the gateway to Asia. Their financial markets are the top three in the world, and their currencies are the strongest in the international community. Their combined economic and technological forces dominate and direct the global economy. Indeed, these three world powers will join forces to revive the world economy, bringing peace, prosperity, and growth in their own region, and in the international community.

With Brexit, e.g., the UK economy can have a more flexible and independent approach to global affairs (Li, 2016). The various incidences of religious terrorism have brought new attention in the United States to the need to maintain a strong domestic economy in the first instance. It could be historically the right timing for these three countries to act, in association with other allies in the region, more positively for the global community.

Europe and Russia

The world economy was faced with new challenges in 2015 as a result of three major world events: the Greece debt crisis in the summer, the flood of refugees from the Middle East in autumn, and the terrorist attack in Paris in November. The European countries would have to bear the greatest burden from the cases of the Greek debt and the inflow of refugees who might consist of potential terrorists. The case of refugees was dressed up in humanitarian grounds, there have been discussions as to how far these immigrants should be regarded as refugees (*The Independent*, October 4, 2015; and *The Guardian*, November 13, 2015). It was reported that the first thing refugees asked when arriving in camps was "where can they charge their mobile phone" (*Forbes*, October 15, 2015). It has been discussed that a "mentality gap" exists in the "holy war" between Middle East states and the West, as the former was already prepared to fight, while the latter was embracing the refugees. Could it be a part of the strategy that the influx of Middle East refugees was dressed up as an act of catastrophe, but aimed to weaken and confuse the "enemy"?

The November 2015 terrorist attack in Paris, and the various subsequent attacks, such as the attack in a Mali hotel in West Africa, had shown that the peaceful regions of the world could be vulnerable. The first lesson was that terrorists would have legally obtained resident or citizen status in Europe. The terrorists entered Europe posing as refugees, which enabled them to pass through check points. There are at least two competing terrorist factions in the Islamic states in the Middle East, and these two competing factions conducted terrorist activities in different parts of the world. The international community is now divided, not only on lines of ideological differences, but also along religious affiliations. France was attacked even though it has a socialist government. In another incident, terrorists placed a homemade bomb in a Russian Metrojet airliner that crashed over Egypt's Sinai desert in early November 2015 (*The Guardian*, November 5, and 19, 2015). To the peaceful regions of the world, the end result would be a need for greater security and alertness, which would involve a higher cost to maintain public security. Terrorist activities based on extreme religious ideology have effectively declared war on much of the developed world. The international community should not hold an accommodating attitude toward incidents of terrorism.

Given the new wave of terrorist activities and the emergence of the "third world war" that is fought more on religious ground than on ideological differences, there is a need to reassess economic and political realignment in the world community. One possible alignment is between the EU and Russia. Over the decades, the EU have been losing economic competitiveness, and have to absorb large amounts of social cost from three sources: (1) domestic strong welfare policies that produced disincentive on the part of investors, and government spending has been constrained; (2) providing financial support to debt-prone EU member countries, thereby absorbing the social cost of the weaker members; and (3) for humanitarian reasons EU members have absorbed huge social costs resulting from the flood of refugees.

With low industrial ability on the one hand, and the readiness to absorb the huge social cost burden from weaker countries within the EU and other trouble-prone countries in nearby regions on the other hand, the EU on the whole remained economically weak, though the EU still leads in technological development. Germany is probably the strongest EU economy in terms of industrial exports. The huge debt faced by a number of EU countries, the influx of refugees, and the threat of terrorism imposes a resource burden on EU countries.

The question is whether there is a need to change the existing accommodating attitude with a subsequent change in regional policy and strategy. It is crucial to ask if the assistance the EU provided to its members and nearby countries would just drain away the EU's own resources, or would the assistance have positive economic and political implications on the EU member countries in the long run. Instead of readily embracing the problems of other members and countries from the Middle East region, would it be more appropriate for the EU to pursue a "localization" or "indigenization" policy that requires the problematic countries to look for solutions indigenously and locally in the first instance? A "localization policy" could ensure in the first instance that problems arising from individual countries would have to be solved within the country, and would not be passed on to other countries. By not absorbing or taking up the problems of other countries, both inter- and infraregionally, the localization policy would restrict conflicts and problems to a local level. By doing so, the impact of the problems would be minimized, as the local problem might not escalate into a regional problem. For example, instead of receiving massive inflows of Syrian refugees, the localization policy would require the need to improve and change the situation in Syria. Receiving Syrian refugees does not mean the situation in Syria will improve. In fact, the instability in Syria has escalated into three problems: (1) instability continues to exist in Syria; (2) the outflow of refugees would give the unpopular Syrian leaders more resources for their own deployment; and (3) the large numbers of refugees that EU countries have to handle. Indeed, to the Syrian leaders, it could be a blessing, as the outflow of the refugees would reduce the burden on the already weak Syria economy. The EU countries may have to avoid internalizing the problems of other countries.

Russia also suffers from terrorist activities. The question, then, is whether it is appropriate for Russia to align and work more pragmatically with the EU, or should Russia still practice the "Cold War" mentality and consider the West as its enemy? Given the strong welfare policies that many EU countries have chosen over the decades, the so-called ideological divide between the EU and Russia is not that crystal-clear. Indeed, the only remaining strength Russia has is its military power, but it may not be sustainable because Russia's economic strength and capability has not been improved, other than in oil production. Russia is already losing its economic competitiveness to China. The iron-curtain nature of hardcore socialism in Russia has ended. In its place, a more market-friendly approach will be preferred if Russia wants to strengthen its economic competitiveness and investment attractiveness.

Aside from narrowing ideological differences, one can argue that some EU countries and Russia can economically complement each other in various directions and dimensions (Piazolo, 1996; Brenton et al., 1999; Baranovsky, 2000). When differences in politics are less clear and ideological divides are becoming less visible, the Russian economy could be transformed into a more contemporary economy through interacting more positively with EU members. Firstly, Russia could have a large EU market for its oil exports. In turn, EU countries could have greater chances to invest in Russia and other former East European countries. In short, pragmatic political reform in Russia can change to economic progress and a stronger Russian economy. One can think of the virtuous economic multiplier effects that can be generated in Russia and the former East European countries, such as Lithuania and Latvia, once there is a greater degree of political and ideological harmony between the EU and Russia. With Russia abandoning its outdated "iron-curtain" mentality, and instead picking up a market-friendly attitude, there is a great possibility that the EU and Russia will become more integrated or united, which would be followed by a reduction in military confrontation between Russia and the West. Indeed, the EU and Russia can politically, militarily, and diplomatically join hands in combating threats from the terrorist factions, and help to build up a stronger Europe and peace in the Middle East. Indeed, the "US – EU – Russia" relationship could become stronger in dealing with world conflicts and problems.

China, Africa, and Europe

The political relationship between China and some "third world" African countries has been friendly, even before China was admitted to the United Nations in the early 1970s. After nearly four decades of economic reform, China's "cash rich" or "excess liquidity" economy provides China with resources for its "cheque book diplomacy" that has handed out huge funds to every African country that China's President Xi visited. It is true that China's trade with developing countries has increased. For example, China is Africa's largest trade partner, amounting to some US$222 billion worth of goods and services traded in 2014. However, China's outward direct investment is concentrated considerably in energy and transport (*South China Morning Post*, December 5, 2015). The American Enterprise Institute reported that 41% (US$29.97 billion) of China's investment in Africa over the past decades had gone to energy products that supplemented shortages in China. Similarly, over the past decade, Chinese companies have won transport project contracts worth more than US$81.1 billion, equivalent to 49% of the total value of Chinese construction contracts in Africa. South Africa, e.g., is by far the largest recipient of Chinese investment in Africa with an amount of US$9.17 billion in the past decade. Other closely connected African countries include Nigeria and Algeria, where China has signed projects amounting to US$24.65 billion and US$18.69 billion, respectively, over the past decade. It was estimated that China's foreign aid to 51 African countries included a total of 2500 projects worth about US$94 billion. China's financial contribution and investment to African countries could be seen as necessary, as it probably has filled the resource gap. However, it has been criticized that China used imported labor in building government-financed projects like roads and hospitals, and China's interest has been on Africa's raw resources (*South China Morning Post*, November 25, 2015). Brautigam (2011, 2016) documented the political – economic relationship between China and Africa, providing an account on the myths and realities in their long-term motivations.

Many developing countries, especially those "fragile states," have been receiving economic aid and assistance from individual foreign countries and international institutions. One question is why these developing countries still remained weak after all these decades of assistance, trade, and inward investment. One would expect that China's economic assistance to developing countries would carry a political tag. Many African countries are "fragile states" and remained weak, and were the recipients of China's assistance. "Fragile states" are often faced with instability and extreme difficulties economically and politically. By providing free assistance to these poor countries, one wondered if these funds would end up in the hands of their ineffective leaders, who corrupted and provided poor leadership in their countries, or their economies are so stagnant that development potentials were very low. Whether these Chinese-assisted developing countries could play a significant political role internationally or provide political support to China would be unknown. It is more likely that they would "take" China's funding as another "free lunch." China's desire to drain the raw materials from these developing countries could face local resistance. The only positive economic impact would likely be that should these developing countries become stronger after receiving China's assistance, they probably would conduct more trade with the rest of the world, thereby indirectly benefitting other world exporting countries.

Despite China's international ambitions, the challenge may come from China's domestic economy, and whether the massive fund deployment overseas would cause displeasure at home. At the world level, many developed and developing countries would work favorably with China and intended to obtain funds from China. China's international economic frontier could subsequently expand, but the same may not be true when it comes to critical political, military, and international decisions. The truth is that when the developed countries stand together politically, China would become the minority. The alliance between China and its friends in Africa and other developing countries, especially in noneconomic areas, is yet to be seen. Nonetheless, much of its future development will also depend on China's domestic development, since African countries will not develop much even with China's assistance. While the EU is absorbing the social cost of some weaker EU member countries and the refugees from Middle East states, China is prepared to absorb the social cost of development from African and other developing countries.

In its relationship with the European countries, China's low labor cost and large domestic market have attracted much trade and investment from European countries. Furthermore, the EU as a whole has experienced crises and decline, and as growth within the EU community will not be too favorable (Sandbu, 2015; Caporaso and Rhodes, 2016), the EU's economic relationship with China will become more important, as many EU businesses still naively think of the large Chinese market. The "kowtow" from EU countries would provide China with an inflow of reserves through trade, inward investment, and the possibility of securing advanced technology. If deployed appropriately, the long-term decline in the EU should improve China's competitiveness. Strategically, while individual EU countries are dealing separately with China, it will be to the advantage of China who can "play-off" one EU country with another, after all China has surpassed all EU economies.

The prowelfare attitude among EU countries is very different from the socialist attitude China holds. Many EU countries that have adopted prosocialist policies in the form of high taxes and welfare have drained away their economic competitiveness. The behavior of fraternity in "giving, sharing, and tolerating" has been expressed through economics, while the pursuit of "equality" has been given higher priority than productivity and business-friendliness. Contrarily, socialism in China's reform has been based on the lack of freedom and democracy, political high-handedness, state-ownership, and state-control. China is a "one voice" economy. The extent of inequality, poverty, and low ethical standards in China would probably be unacceptable in the European context. Thus, while the EU countries thought they gained by the ability to enter the Chinese market, their economic relationships helped China to preserve its inadequacies. Few would think forward to how an economically, politically, and militarily powerful China could behave in the international community. Indeed, the large extent of investment in China by EU countries has strengthened the Chinese economy considerably, but at the expense of the EU's competitiveness. The EU does not seem to have a sense of awareness of China's global ambition, and it would be naive should the EU consider China's rise as if it was another Japan.

The EU economy is really losing on various fronts. Their prolonged use of redistributive policies has made them uncompetitive. Some EU members have to shoulder huge debts from other weaker members. The influx of refugees drained their resources and added to instability. Although the EU gained in exporting and kowtowed to the Chinese market, the Chinese economy competed with all EU member countries, though some EU countries, such as Germany, can still depend on their high-technology. With the excessive application of prosocialist policies, the economy of the EU will keep declining unless there are drastic reversals in their economic policies (see, e.g., Caselli et al., 2016).

Fig. 10.2 conveniently shows four pictures of the trade and investment relationship between China and the largest five EU countries (United Kingdom, Germany, France, Italy, and the Netherlands). The data for the period 2000–15 can be found in the *Direction of Trade Statistics* from the IMF, and *China's Statistical Yearbook*. The upper figure shows China's exports to these five EU countries, and China's exports to Germany have been larger than the other four EU countries. In the sample period, China's exports to these five countries have increased a lot. But China also imported a lot from Germany, as shown in the second picture giving the trade balance between China and the five countries. Germany is the only country which gained a trade surplus with China. The third picture in Fig. 10.2 shows a comparison of the trade performance between China and the five countries in the 2 years of 2000 and 2015. The Netherlands trade deficit with China between the 2 years has deteriorated most.

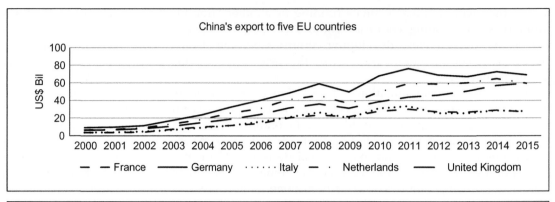

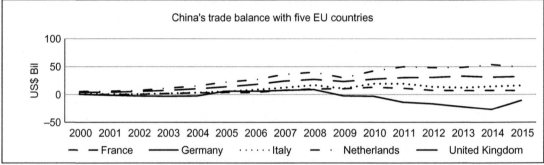

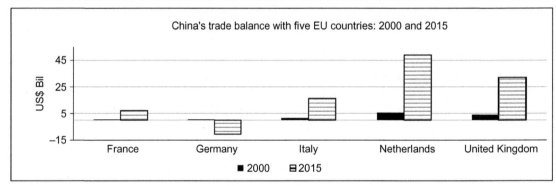

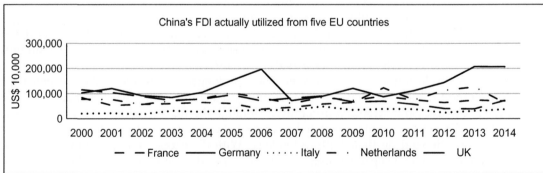

FIGURE 10.2 Trade and FDI: China and five EU countries.

The last picture shows the amount of foreign direct investment from the five EU countries actually utilized in China. Among the five EU countries, Germany has often been the biggest investor in China, while Italy has been the smallest investor among the five EU countries.

This section has made bold suggestions on economic alliances around the world. The strongest bond shall be between the three capitalist countries of Japan, the United Kingdom, and United States. While each of these three countries may have their own economic agenda and problems, their combined force could be formidable should the need arise. The next group of economic alliances relate to the European region between Russia and the EU. The ideological and military strength of Russia will soon be eroded by the economic rise of China. Although China has remained friendly to Russia, their inherent competition and rivalry could be complicated and subtle. On the contrary, Russia needs to modernize its approach to the EU, and military cooperation with the West would be needed in combating the conflicts arising from Middle East states. It is terrorism rather than ideology that has become the imminent problem between the EU and Russia. The EU also needs to reassess its "kowtow" relationship with China before it becomes peripheral to China. Given the various dimensions of economic weaknesses, a reversal of economic policies and political attitudes among EU countries is urgently needed. In particular, prowelfare policies that favored "demand-side" outcomes have to be replaced by business-friendly policies that aim at "supply-side" outcomes by stimulating output expansion and identifying new comparative advantages in investment and exports.

Though it may not be too significant, there is also another trend of global alliances between China and Africa and other developing countries. The relationship is probably built on the fact that China's excess liquidity would provide ample funds to the "fragile states" in Africa and elsewhere. China's approach in its outward investment is definitely different from that of Japan, as China surely would include an ideological tag in its foreign relationships. Given that many of these African, and also Latin American, states are still not making much progress, their relationship may not be too influential at the global level. The original intention of aiding China to become more developed was to use China's performance as a showcase to other developing countries. Ideology aside, and seen optimistically, China's economic involvement in African and other developing countries will hopefully help to remove poverty and promote development in these "fund-hungry" countries. But, seen pessimistically, these low-potential, fragile, and underdeveloped countries might just consider China as another "Santa Claus," where funds were made but not growth and development.

IV CANADA: A PROMISING ECONOMY

Economic development is relative, dynamic, and involves choice and forgone alternatives. Among the developed countries, Canada can be regarded as a representative country that exhibits steady progress and balanced growth that can nurture societal harmony. Recent studies have covered the various aspects of the Canadian economy (Kwan, 2002; Baldwin and Hanel, 2003; Baldwin and Gu, 2005; Leung et al., 2012). Canada has over the years adopted prowelfare policies, but given its short economic history and various potentials, the debate is whether the Canadian economy should opt to expand its potential more extensively, or have welfare policies dampened Canada's growth potential? For example, given its large land resources, should there be more "land-intensive" industries, despite Canada's cold weather that lasts for a few months over a year? Or, can there be more extensive use of technology that can compensate for the adverse weather?

Canada is considered as a "young" country. Historically, the settlement of Canada began with the arrival of the Paleo-Indians centuries ago, followed by the different groups of Aboriginal people before the British and French explored and settled along the Atlantic coast in the late 15th century. France ceded all colonies in North America to Britain in 1763 after the Seven Years' War. Canada was formed as a federal dominion on July 1, 1867, by the British colonies in North America. However, it was not until 1982 that the Federal Government of Canada successfully sought the passing of The Canada Act in the UK Parliament to end Canada's legal dependence on Great Britain. Canada is governed by a parliamentary democracy and a constitutional monarchy, with Queen Elizabeth II as its Head of State. Federal Canada consists of 10 provinces and 3 territories (Bryant and Clark, 2006; Morton, 2006).

As compared to other industrialized countries, and other than the separatist issue with the French-speaking province of Quebec, Canada is considered a "trouble-free" country, and does not have to shoulder many historic burdens, such as the slavery trade in the United States, a long historical past with the rise and fall of empires, wars, and conquerors like that of Italy, a colonial history and responsibility for the influx of immigrants from former colonies like that of the United Kingdom, France, and other former European colonial powers, or territorial, religious, and military disputes with countries in other parts of the world. Modern Canada is built upon a combination of Aboriginal, British, and French settlers, and immigrants from Asia and European countries. The historic case of Chinese immigrants to Canada can be used as an illustration. Chinese laborers, amounting to over 15,000, came to Canada in the mid-19th century and helped in the construction of the Canadian Pacific Railway. However, in the discriminatory, race-based Chinese Immigration

Act of 1885, a Head Tax of $50, which was eventually raised to $500 in 1903, was imposed on Chinese newcomers. The 1923 Chinese Immigration Act banned Chinese immigrants until 1947.

Although critics would argue that it was politically motivated, racial equality and mutual respect was eventually recognized on June 22, 2006, when the then Canadian Prime Minister Stephen Harper apologized in the House of Commons for the implementation of the Head Tax, as it was erroneous and inconsistent with the contemporary values that Canadians hold. It was announced that the Canadian government will offer a symbolic individual payment of $20,000 to living Chinese Head Tax payers, and living spouses of deceased payers. Along with the compensation was the establishment of a $24 million community historical recognition program (*Prime Minister Harper Offers Full Apology for the Chinese Head Tax*, Prime Minister's Office, Ottawa, June 22, 2006). As a country comprised of immigrants, the apology was seen as a gesture of harmony in a multiracial economy and the recognition of a fair contribution by all individual Canadians, regardless of their racial and ethnic background.

The Canadian economy is blessed with an abundance of land and natural resources, and coupled with the long tradition of British institutions, the Canadian economy has developed and become one of the advanced OECD countries in the world. Although the Canadian economy has largely been linked to the United States, Canada is increasingly building up its own image as an industrialized country (Burbridge and Harrison, 1985; Afxentiou and Serletis, 1992; Harris, 1993). In 2013, Canada ranked as the 11th largest economy measured in nominal GDP, with a real GDP increase of 118% between 1981 and 2013. In the Human Development Index (HDI), Canada ranked 8th out of a sample of 187 countries in 2013. Canada ranked 6th out of a total of 187 countries in the 2014 *Index of Economic Freedom* conducted by the Heritage Foundation in Washington DC, USA, and ranked 7th in the 2014 *Economic Freedom of the World* compiled by the Fraser Institute in Vancouver.

There are a few features of the Canadian economy that are worth mentioning. One is the balance among the three economic sectors of agriculture that consists of land farming and marine activities, industry that incorporates mining of minerals, and modern services. Data from *Statistics Canada* showed that in 1997, the percentages of GDP among the three sectors were 1.80% in agriculture, 32.64% in industry, and 65.51% in services. These have remained quite steady over the years. The percentages in 2014 were 1.61%, 28.71%, and 69.74%, respectively. The industrial share of GDP reached its peak of 33.22% in 2000. In the period 1997 − 2014, agriculture's share of GDP remained at or below 1.8%, and the share of industry in GDP showed an average of 30.5%.

Canada can claim to be an industrially based economy, with output of physical goods playing a key role in employment and export in the real sector of the economy. The five key industries are transportation equipment and manufacturing, food manufacturing, petroleum and coal product manufacturing, primary metal manufacturing, and wood product manufacturing. In minerals, data from the US Geological Survey and World Nuclear Association show that in 2012, Canada's output of potash ranked first in the world. In the production of uranium, Canada ranked second in the world after Kazakhstan. Canada ranked third in the production of aluminum, cobalt, titanium, and tungsten in the world. Canada's production of diamonds is fourth in the world rankings. The major mineable ores in Canada included gold, silver, zinc, lead, and copper. Energy production is another major industry in Canada, with the third largest reserves of oil in the world.

Canada is the recipient of "brain drain" from the rest of the world (Akbari and Devoretz, 1992; Alboim and Omidvar, 2002; Li, 2002, 2010). Based on the point system in the application process, and through its selective immigration policy, Canada ensures that immigrants will not impose a fiscal burden on tax payers. In other words, instead of relying on welfare provision, legal immigrants to Canada are expected to contribute to the output of the Canadian economy, thereby adding and improving the ethnic mix and proportions in the national economy. Fig. 10.3 shows four aspects of Canada's immigration statistics. Fig. 10.3A shows the trend and percentage growth rates for the period 1979–2012. Immigrant numbers increased rapidly in the mid-1980s. In 1980 (2012), the number of immigrants amounted to 143,137 (257,887), with a growth rate of 27.69% (3.67%), equivalent to 0.6% (0.7%) of the total population. Fig. 10.3B shows that Economic Immigrants are the largest category, followed by Family Class and Refugees. Fig. 10.3C gives the geographic origin of immigrants. Immigrants from Asia − Pacific countries formed the largest group, followed by Africa and the Middle East, while immigrants from Europe, the United Kingdom, and the United States are the third largest category. The remaining immigrants come from South and Central America. However, other than Asia − Pacific, the difference in the number of immigrants from all other regions is quite even, thereby providing a similar proportionate immigrant community in Canada. In 2012, the actual number of immigrants from Asia − Pacific was 129,593, followed by Africa and the Middle East with 56,061, and Europe, the United

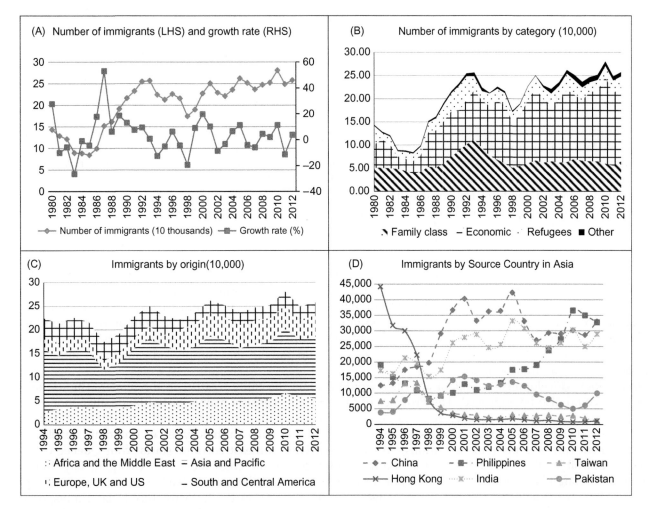

FIGURE 10.3 Canadian immigrants.

Kingdom, and the United States with 42,244, while South and Central America had the lowest number of immigrants, amounting to 26,865. Lastly, Fig. 10.3D shows that immigrants from China, India, and the Philippines are the largest group of immigrants from Asia.

Peaceful and harmonious coexistence among immigrant communities is important in an immigrant country. Indeed, although there are different origins among the immigrants, there exists in Canada a "microcommunity" in which immigrants communicate and mingle with people of the same origin in their leisure or private life, but there is also the "macrocommunity" in which all immigrants, like any other citizens, can seek employment and contribute to the development and progress of the Canadian economy.

Legal immigrants are the more enterprising group of individuals, as the major reasons for immigration would be to seek a better environment for individual progress (Borjas, 1994; Simon, 1999; O'Shea, 2009). The enterprising mentality and attitude of immigrants automatically promotes and fosters an effective and progressive economic environment, and the conflicts they experienced in their countries of origin will not be duplicated. This is particularly so, since Canada has never been an imperial power and new immigrants consider the possibility of a new and better life in promoting their own welfare and contributing to the peaceful development of the Canadian economy.

While education is still seen as the key to poverty reduction and opportunity enhancement, and given that Canada is still considered as "under-populated" when all the remote regions are taken into account, the application of technology is considered to be the answer in a large number of industrial and economic activities. The Canadian government spent a lot in clearing icy roads in winter once the snow forecast was announced. Could there be a technological device that helped to melt the ice on the roads? Much fiscal spending could be saved if there was an "ice-melting" mechanism that could be attached, e.g., to street lighting lamp-posts, so that ice could be melted without affecting traffic or human health. Given that there are numerous street and highway lamp-posts, a technological innovation could best be devised so that snow would automatically be dissolved in a timely manner, thereby saving the labor-intensive work of snow-clearing on all highways and roads. One should not worry about the loss of employment as jobs on snow-clearing would be reduced. Even if such device had been developed, it would take years before all production and installation work could be completed across Canada. The number of workers saved could then be deployed to other more productive and high value-added activities.

Other growth enhancing activities could include the development of a stronger transport infrastructure. Given that Canada is a geographically huge country, and the population is steadily growing, a modern transport infrastructure can promote and facilitate long-term growth tremendously. The development of a bullet train, e.g., that runs between the eastern and western coasts of Canada would definitely encourage the establishment of new population centers. Long-term rail construction can be developed at multiple points across Canada. While train development from Vancouver will be eastward, the five major population centers of Edmonton and Calgary in Alberta, Saskatoon and Regina in Saskatchewan, and Winnipeg in Manitoba form the core cities in the middle regions of Canada. The provinces of Ontario and Quebec form the eastern core of development in high speed rail transportation.

Infrastructure development can either be "demand-led" or "supply-led." The "demand-led" model will be a situation in which the population has grown and the development of rail transport will ease road congestion. The "supply-led" model will be a situation where the development of such infrastructure will facilitate various forms of economic development, including growth in population and structured urbanization. As transport infrastructure has been improved, it will become attractive for more economic and business activities. Given the vast amount of land and the growing population, Canada could pursue the "supply-led" model of infrastructure development in rail transportation.

In addition, development in indoor activities would contain the chilly weather in the winter. The use of land resources could also be improved. The Province of Ontario, e.g., consists mainly of flat land, surrounded by the four lakes of Lake Ontario, Lake Huron and Georgian Bay and Lake Erie in the south, and Hudson Bay in the north. Indeed, land close to lakes tends to be more fertile and suits various types of economic development. Development can take place along various city corridors. The southeast corridor starts from Quebec City and runs to Detroit in the United States. The south corridor covers the coast along the Georgian Bay and Lake Superior running from Toronto to Thunder Bay, or even extends to Winnipeg. Indeed, given its vast land supply, it would be most suitable to develop "land-intensive" industries in Canada. Infrastructure in land transportation would facilitate a number of "land-intensive" industries and technologies. Economic policies should therefore be geared to expand manufacturing industries that can promote output for growth. Business-friendly policies should be deployed to promote industries, especially in remote regions in order to develop more population centers. With the close proximity to the US market and good connections with both the Asia − Pacific region and the European countries on the Atlantic side, Canada has potential opportunity to become a strong industrial and manufacturing economy.

Although Canada is not so much a debt-prone economy, tax rates have remained on the high side when it comes to the promotion of a market-friendly economy. Indeed, more market-friendly policies should be adopted so as to promote a better business environment, especially among the immigrants who have an enterprising mentality and entrepreneurial attitude. One acceptable reason for the high taxation in Canada is the required redistribution and maintenance of public services, such as road clearance during the snowy season, and the welfare required, especially when the population is dispersed in remote regions. However, policy makers should be aware of the disincentive effect generated by the high tax system and generous welfare policy. Indeed, the Canadian economy is also faced with a considerable amount of prowelfare economic policies. The key argument is income inequality. For a progressive economy like that of Canada, the creation and availability of economic opportunity should be considered as a virtue in social value, as working individuals would be keen to gain better achievements and a rise in job security, especially employment expansion concentrating on the provision of professional jobs. Given the youthful nature of the Canadian economy with a high supply of resources, it would be more suitable for economic policies to aim at promoting economic opportunities than to engage in redistribution.

It is also important to have a proper "supply-side" mindset that encourages competition and facilitates productivity. In the case of medical services, e.g., there has to be a distinction between medical services and personal health. It is true that medical services should be made available to all economic classes, regardless of income status. But personal health is a private affair, and individuals should be given a choice in the provision of medical services. There is nothing wrong with individuals seeking improvements in their health on a private basis, such as obtaining a second opinion or having medical treatment in a private hospital. The Canadian authority should open up the medical sector to private practices, so that individuals can have a choice in treatments for their health, and such a choice should not be determined or influenced by ideology. At the same time, the private supply of medical services should ease the pressure on the public supply. Indeed, competition between the two forms of supply could benefit both the patients and the quality of service.

Despite its high tax and prowelfare policies, the Canadian economy should adhere more to a "supply-driven" than a "demand-led" strategy. With the balance between sectors and a steady increase in human capital, the Canadian economy will progress. With a steady growth in population and macroeconomic stability in a "young" country, it would be proper to nurture a stronger business mentality and an entrepreneurial spirit among the young and in various professions. Once economic opportunities can be created, the more relevant attitude and superior mindset is "equality in opportunity." While the democratic political system in Canada could generate governments with different political orientations, one thing to avoid is policy oscillations that would create instability, discontinuity, and ineffectiveness. With a progressive economy where there are still potential and opportunities, it is important for Canada to have output-generating policies, and not extreme dichotomy in the execution of policies along political and ideological lines.

In short, Canada differs from other advanced countries. Given its peaceful and highly civic environment, the Canadian economy can serve as a "show case" to other "younger" countries that would consider peaceful coexistence and growth as an alternative to religious, ethnic, ideological, and territorial conflicts. In the pursuit of international relations, the Canadian government can put more emphasis on the civic aspect of development, on the balance between industry (real economy) and service (nominal economy), on the need to nurture a "supply-side" economy so as to enhance job opportunities, business expansion, and upward social mobility, and on the way different ethnic communities can live in peaceful acceptability and mutual respect. In other words, the high degree of civic development in Canada can be "exported" as lessons or "good practices" to other emerging countries.

V EASTERN EUROPE: GREATER MARKETIZATION

Despite all the worldly problems, the direction of the world economy is still strongly under the influence and direction of the industrialized world. It is true that the end of the Cold War could have brought about the collapse of the Soviet Union, and the war on ideology has quietened down. But, the world has been nurturing another large country which is ideologically competing with the industrialized world — China. One can compare the post–Second World War economic aid to Japan and foreign investment to other smaller East Asian economies, and foreign investment to China since the early 1990s. The economic rise between the smaller East Asian economies and the huge Chinese economy showed very different political consequences. Development in East Asia tended to have integrated with the global economy, while ideological differences in China had already shown signs of displeasure and lack of willingness to cooperate with other international powers. By comparison, it would have been more effective and less risky for the global economy to aid a cluster of smaller emerging economies than to aid another huge country.

To aid the development of lower tier, smaller, emerging countries could create a cluster effect to complement the growth and development in the region, rather than the development of a single large country that would challenge the region and the global economy. There are two possible groups of medium-sized countries in the emerging world, namely the Southeast Asian group (to be discussed in Chapter 13) and the Eastern European group of countries. Most Eastern European countries regained independence after the collapse of the Soviet Union. This cluster of Eastern European countries comprises, from the Baltic Sea in the north to the Black Sea in the south, Estonia, Latvia, Lithuania, Poland, Belarus, Slovakia, Ukraine, Hungary, Moldova, Romania, Serbia, and Bulgaria. The cluster can extend southward to include the smaller countries of Croatia, Bosnia and Herzegovina, Montenegro, Albania, and Macedonia, and eastward to include Georgia, Armenia, and Azerbaijan. Since this list of countries is large, subregional bodies could initially be formed to promote intraregional activities, such as the development of transport infrastructure that could bring benefits to the region. There is a high degree of economic complementarity, because these countries can offer a good source of labor force and land. The level of human capital would be quite high, and should be ready for industrial take-off. Their manufacturers would reach and serve the Western European market easily.

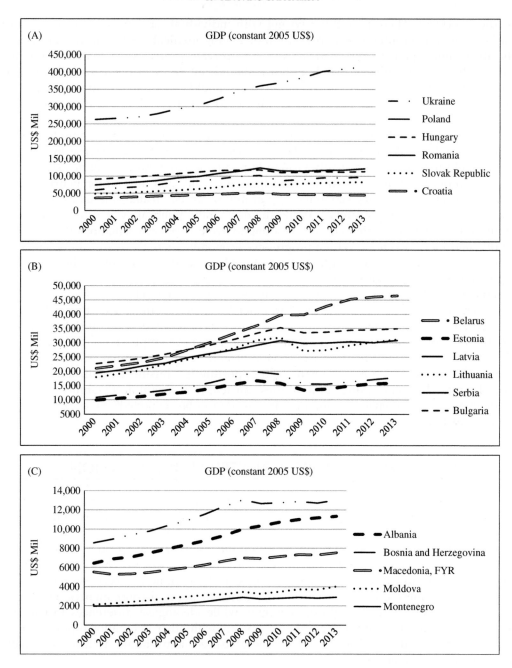

FIGURE 10.4   Eastern Europe: GDP (2000–13).

There are several constraints facing these East European countries. One would be the sustainability of stability, and the influence of any remaining socialist regime and mentality. Indeed, there was a need for these countries to reestablish their own governments and reconstruct basic institutions. Economic policies have to be market-friendly, and there should be built-in fiscal instruments to encourage business and investment. The promotion of an entrepreneurial spirit would be appropriate in enhancing businesses. The government should be involved more in infrastructure building and civic development, so as to enrich social capital. As some of the Eastern European countries have been incorporated into the EU, these countries may suffer from the "brain drain" problem, as the educated would migrate to Western Europe for better employment opportunities. Hence, there should be a policy to promote and maintain human capital. Despite the differences in geographical size, regional development and integration should be considered on an equitable basis. The idea is to create a regional cluster in order to permit mutual growth.

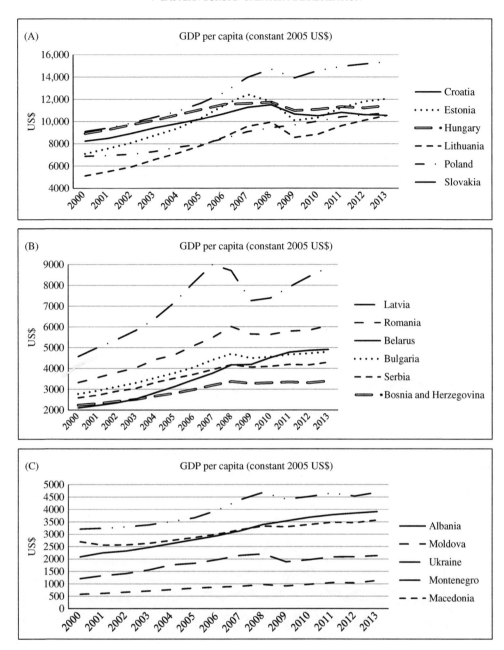

FIGURE 10.5   Eastern Europe: GDP per capita (2000–13). *Source: Data for Montenegro and Macedonia began in 2008 and 2003, respectively.*

Many Eastern European countries have to face influences from Russia, especially those immediately sharing a border with Russia. The answer would be to promote economic activity, as that would produce "relative" outcomes to benefit all parties. Eastern European countries would have two large neighbors, with Western Europe on their western front and Russia on their eastern front. The building up of a reliable relationship between Western Europe and Russia should provide good market access for industrial outputs. The answer would be to establish cross-border rules and practices that provide clear guidelines.

The data from the World Bank can be used to examine six sets of macroeconomic variables for the 17 countries in Eastern Europe. Fig. 10.4 shows the level of real GDP. The traditionally larger countries in Eastern Europe performed better at the level of GDP. Countries such as Ukraine and Poland in Fig. 10.4A show a higher level of real GDP, while the smaller countries of Moldova and Montenegro are weaker, as shown in Fig. 10.4C. Most Eastern European countries have experienced a rise in real GDP since 2000, but the 2008 crisis has led to a slow down. On the GDP per capita basis shown in Fig. 10.5, the better performers include Poland, Estonia, and Hungary in

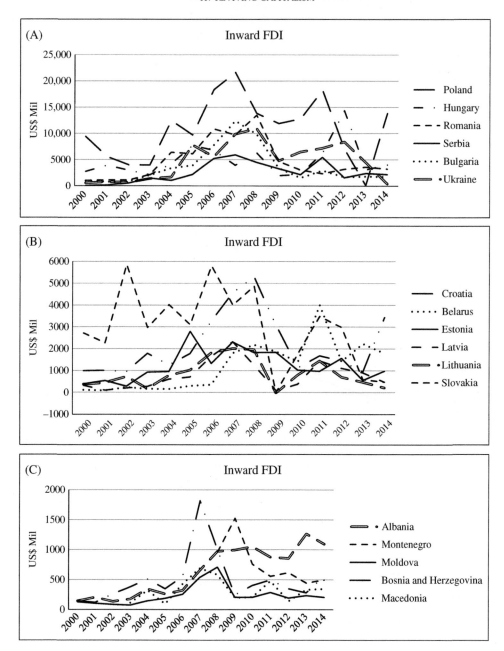

FIGURE 10.6   Eastern Europe: inward foreign direct investment (2000–14). *Source: Data for both Serbia and Montenegro has been available since 2008.*

Fig. 10.5A, while the worst performers shown in Fig. 10.5C include Moldova and Ukraine. While GDP per capita has been increasing since 2000, some Eastern European countries suffered a fall after 2008, the clearest example is Latvia in Fig. 10.5B. Nonetheless, the real GDP and GDP per capita of many Eastern European countries experienced a revival after the setback in 2008.

Fig. 10.6 shows the level of inward foreign direct investment to the 17 East European countries. Although the level has been rising, there have been fluctuations over the years, and a sharp drop after 2008. Poland and Hungary, shown in Fig. 10.6A, are still the better performers, while Macedonia and Moldova are least attractive to foreign direct investment, as shown in Fig. 10.6C. Similar to the GDP performance, there is a variation in the performance of inward investment among the 17 Eastern European countries. In export performance, as shown in Fig. 10.7, again Poland, Hungary, and Slovakia are the stronger performers, in contrast to Montenegro and Moldova in Fig. 10.7C. Despite the setback in 2008, exports have been rising in all Eastern European countries.

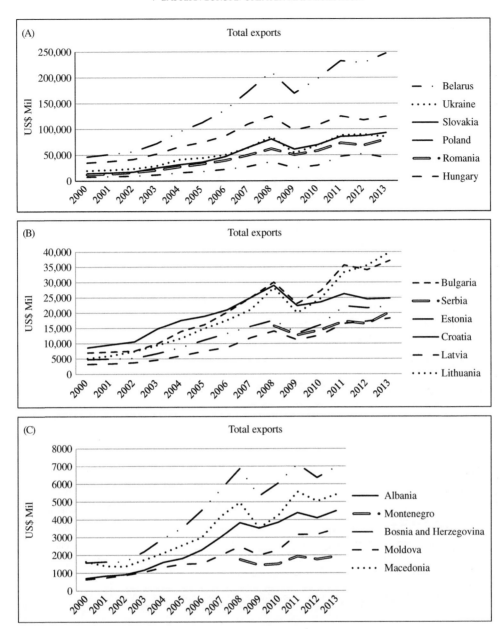

FIGURE 10.7   Eastern Europe: export performance (2000–13). *Source: Data for Bulgaria began in 2002.*

Debt as a percentage of GDP and fiscal deficit, shown in Figs. 10.8 and 10.9, respectively, examines the weak side of the Eastern European countries. As far as debt is concerned, most Eastern European countries are doing well, as all their debt as a percentage of GDP remained low, with Hungary being the worst performer at 79.2%, and Estonia with only 9.7% in 2012. However, while many Eastern European countries showed a decline in their debt before 2008, there are also countries which showed a rapid rise in the debt ratio after 2008, including Croatia and Slovakia in Fig. 10.8B, and others in Fig. 10.8C.

In the case of fiscal deficit, Fig. 10.9A shows the six Eastern European countries which experienced fiscal deficit in the whole sample period, with Poland being the worst performer. Those countries in Fig. 10.9B and C show a different performance. Either some have shown fiscal surplus (Belarus, Bulgaria, and Estonia) or others have a small deficit (Moldova and Montenegro). The deterioration in debt and fiscal deficit, however, could be due more to the fall in GDP than to the rise in debt and deficit.

One can conclude that the economic situations in some Eastern European countries are favorable, especially if these economies choose to include more business-friendly policies. This is particularly true in the geographically

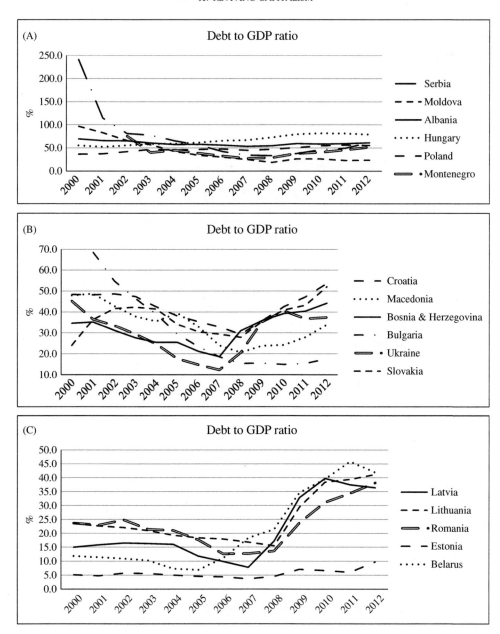

FIGURE 10.8   Eastern Europe: Debt-to-GDP ratios (2000–12). *Source: Data for Montenegro began in 2002.*

larger and traditionally stronger economies of Poland, Hungary, Romania, and Bulgaria, which are not directly neighboring Russia. On the contrary, smaller countries can form a subregional group in order to achieve economies of scale in their development. For example, the three countries of Latvia, Estonia, and Lithuania, who are sharing a border with Russia, can form a closer group. Or the Southern European countries of Croatia, Montenegro, Serbia, Macedonia, and Albania can be another example. Other than a need for a paradigm shift, the need to cooperate and the search for commonality should be a high priority in these subregional groups.

Nonetheless, the economic capability of these Eastern European countries does form a formidable group that can make a difference to the global economy. Given their drive to stability and a decent population size, these clusters of countries can show stronger performance if proper policies are instituted to promote growth and prosperity. In short, an economically stronger Eastern Europe could make a difference in the global world. A key political consideration is the mentality and broadmindedness of the leaders in these Eastern European countries. Mentality considerations include whether the country should return to the socialist style of administration, whether regional development could be more prosperous, or whether each of these countries should look after their own interests. There should be a number of "intraregional" considerations and advantages.

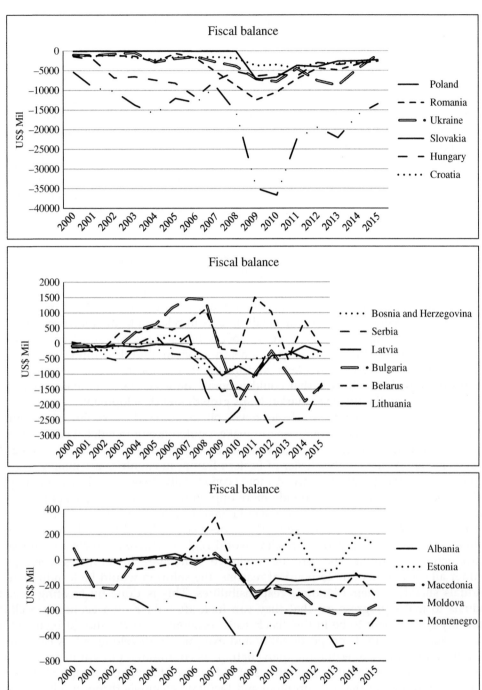

FIGURE 10.9   Eastern Europe: fiscal balances (2000–15).

VI CONCLUSION

One feature in the contemporary world economy is that much of the oil supply comes from the Middle East, but unfortunately, the huge oil revenues these exporting countries amassed have not been used constructively for their economic development. Instead, many Middle East countries are engaged in various regional conflicts that burden the peaceful world. There is a desperate need to start peace negotiations. While there can be multiple dimensions in the peace talks, the ultimate solution rests in the ability to introduce capitalist market activities, so that individuals are allowed to perform their best. The creation of economic opportunities should divert their energy away from war-oriented activities. The concept is to replace activities with "absolute" outcomes by activities with "relative" outcomes.

Peace among the oil exporting countries will also reduce insecurity in other peaceful regions of the world. Another possibility of introducing peace in the Middle East region would be a new international alignment between Western European countries and Russia, as the "third world war" would not be based on ideology differences. Their cooperation and integration should produce positive radiations in handling the various Middle East conflicts. In the reduction on the dependence on oil production, a steady solution would still be the possibility of technological innovation that provides alternative energy sources. Further development in technological commercialization would reduce the use of petroleum.

The humanitarian factor has been used as a reason to accommodate refugees from the Middle East and North African states. The basic feature of humanitarian aid is that people should help each other in difficult times. Humanitarian aid must be effective and could improve the overall situation, but the social cost burden of the refugee influx will have to be shouldered by the citizens of the host countries for a long period of time. There is no "win − win" outcome.

The aspect of economic rebalancing relates to the need to understand the economic proportionality between the financial sector and the real sector. Economic policies should not be carried away only by activities in the financial sector, even though it attracts much attention. It is the activities in the real sector, such as manufacturing, human capital, export and import trade, and infrastructure development that can truly reflect the long-term capability of the economy. Given the volatility and the amount of attention in the financial market, it will be appropriate to reexamine the economics of the financial markets in relation to the macroeconomy in terms of: (1) its short-term versus long-term impact; (2) the effect of speculation in investment activities; (3) the relationship and alignment between the financial market and the monetary economy; (4) the number of financial instruments that are created and used in the financial markets; and (5) the distinction between the private activities in the financial market and the possible spillovers that could generate undesirable social consequences. The ultimate economic intention is to see how the financial market helps growth and development.

The economy of Canada and the potential of cluster development among Eastern European countries have been discussed, as further development in these countries can make a difference in the global economy, serving as a balance with other rapidly growing countries. While Canada is a developed country and its large geographical size provides greater diversity and potential, the cluster of Eastern European countries are mainly medium-sized countries that can flexibly adapt to the global economy. A more economically diverse world would aid peace and stability, as the larger world economic pie would provide more opportunities and economies of scale in global growth and development, as the development of one country would have a multiplying effect on others.

There is no perfection in economics, but these world issues need to be addressed, and their solution should bring the world to a new stage of civilization. In some world regions where conflicts are rampant, the solution would be the introduction of activities that produce "relative" outcomes. In countries where governments are prepared to shoulder all social costs due to political reasons, the solution would be to minimize the possibility of private individuals shedding their economic responsibilities. This is done by creating economic opportunities for individuals to make progress, so that they can look after their own economic welfare. While it is more desirable for any government to be in the "back-seat," economic growth should be made more balanced between economic sectors, to avoid disproportionality and extremes in development. A capitalist market economy is destined to have the ability of economic rejuvenation, as continuous pursuit of individual freedom and economic openness allows new waves and generations of individuals to engage in replenishing activities. What the world needs is an environment that can promote and facilitate channels through which economically rejuvenating activities can take place.

CAPITALIST DEVELOPMENT: ASIA LESSONS

The Economics of "Push and Pull"

When one talks about the successful capitalist development of Asian economies, one relates mainly to economies along the Pacific Rim. The discussion on the rise of Asia − Pacific economies could probably begin from the early 1950s, after the end of the Second World War. Typically, the sequence of Asian economies that achieved growth began with Japan in the 1960s and early 1970s, followed by the four "dragon" economies of Hong Kong, Singapore, Taiwan (Chinese Taipei), and South Korea in the 1970s and 1980s. By the 1980s, the rise of the remaining four economies from the Association of Southeast Asian Nations (ASEAN) included Malaysia, Thailand, the Philippines, and Indonesia who were soon caught up by the rapid economic reform in China. After the 1990s, China became the "latecomer" that absorbed many foreign resources, especially in the first decade in the new century after China joined the World Trade Organization in 2001. However, the difference between China and other Asian economies is one of political ideology, though China also practiced a "market economy."

The sequence of development among Asian countries can be formalized into different tiers of economies in Asia. With Japan being the most developed economy in Asia, Japan is considered as the first tier of economy along with the United States and Canada on the other side of the Pacific. The first-tier economies are industrialized and serve as suppliers of capital and foreign direct investment to other less developed countries. The first-tier countries are prime export markets for other developing countries. The four "dragon" economies are considered as the second-tier economies in the Asia − Pacific region. Other than the rise of income through industrialization, these economies serve as headquarters to numerous corporations in the region. In the process of growth and development, these four economies also became suppliers of capital, and provided outward investment to nearby economies.

The four economies from ASEAN are considered as the third-tier economies. They are mainly manufacturing-based economies, and intend to catch up with the "dragon 4" economies. By the mid-1990s, however, these "ASEAN 4" economies were faced with competition from China. Among the three socialist Asian countries of China, Vietnam, and North Korea as the fourth-tier of economies in Asia, China has expanded rapidly and is ambitious to become the "number two" largest (or even the largest) economy in the world. The scale of the Vietnam economy is much smaller than that of China, but it is catching up by adopting market-friendly policies in order to attract foreign investment and promote industrial growth and exports. North Korea remains as a poor, least developed dynastic economy. All other remaining countries in Asia, e.g., Myanmar, Cambodia, Lao PDR, Brunei Darussalam, and Timor-Leste, can be grouped as the fifth-tier of Asian economies, as they are still in a much earlier stage of development, with primary industry as their main source of income, though they have potential to become more industrialized and serve as manufacturing centers for the export market. In addition, there are a number of smaller and island economies in the Pacific, such as Fiji and Samoa, that concentrate mainly on tourism and marine activities.

There is no shortage of analysis and studies that explain the successful development of the key economies in East Asia. The neoclassical school would have discussed the economic contribution from production factors, including domestic investment and saving, foreign investment and favorable exporting ability, while the endogenous growth advocates considered the importance of education and human capital. Studies by political economists concentrated on the role of the government, especially in relation to the doctrine of *laissez-faire* and economic freedom, and fiscal and monetary policies that are favorable to economic growth. In particular, discussion is related to drawing the distinction between equity and efficiency, between growth and redistribution, and between income equality and opportunity equality. Rightists would advocate the relevance of building up a bigger "economic pie," as there is more to share. Leftists would advocate for more equality at the expense of business efficiency and productivity, even to the extent that growth is restricted due to economic disincentives.

Development economists would attribute the successful economic development in many East Asia economies to the establishment of appropriate institutions, such as anticorruption and anti-discrimination divisions. The development of economic clusters in the "flying geese" model (Kojima, 2000) argued that the rise of the first East Asian economy, namely Japan, would give rise to other nearby economies, culminating in the rise of lower tier economies in the Asian region. The "flying geese" argument has been extended to the rise of specific industries among the East Asian region, as the rise of one industry, typically electronics, led to rise in other related industries for the export market.

Social science advocates would consider the various favorable social attributes, such as proximity in culture, use of chopsticks, and the influence of Confucian principles of individuality, self-reliance, hardwork, filial piety, and obedience, which have often been regarded as the ingredients of capitalism. Political scientists attribute the success of East Asian economies to the adoption of capitalism and market principles. Because of political uncertainty, the threat of communism from North Korea and the preparation for "war," historians would argue that such East Asian economies as South Korea and Taiwan (Chinese Taipei) should hold a "prepare for the rainy days" attitude, which in turn serves as a drive to economic growth and stability.

International studies would consider the geo-political principle of "encirclement," in that East Asian economies situated at the doorstep of communist China, namely Japan, South Korea, Taiwan, Hong Kong, Singapore, and other Southeast Asian nations, were assisted economically so that these countries would form a geo-political frontier against the spread of Chinese communism. Li (2002) reported the importance of postwar assistance given to these economies. Typically, postwar reconstruction assistance was provided by the United States to Japan, South Korea, and also Taiwan, while foreign direct investment from United Kingdom and other European countries poured into Hong Kong and Singapore, which were then the remaining two British colonies in Asia. Li (2002) pointed out that few noticed the importance of these injections of foreign investment at the time when investment resources, like "rain in the desert," were badly needed in these economies in Asia. It was important in that the new resources enabled economic redevelopment that provided employment and absorbed the "surplus labor." Foreign investment also gave rise to numerous small businesses locally. In short, economic stability was reinforced soon after the end of the Second World War, which in turn further attracted more foreign investment to the region.

The provision of economic stability in the five East Asian economies was a major attribute in their success. However, there are few studies that look at the intraregional development between Asia, Europe and North America. In the first instance, there was much postwar development and reconstruction in much of Western Europe and North America. The subsequent rise in income in these world regions led to an increase in demand for consumables that were not met by domestic production. At that time, when the European currencies were highly valued, cheap imports from East Asian manufacturers were welcomed. Since much of the manufacturing was labor-intensive industries and required the provision of a disciplined labor force, the low labor and production costs served as the "pull" factor in attracting investment and trade to the Asian region.

The rise in income in Europe and North America over the decades was accompanied by some elected governments that adopted welfare and redistributive policies which gave rise to high tax rates, rising welfare expenditures, and growing strength among labor unions. The pursuit of redistribution in the form of "income equality" would mean wages were linked more to political ideology than to productivity. The rise in wages, together with strong unions, would mean a rise in total costs of production. Economic competitiveness and business-friendliness were being eroded and weakened. But, investors can always have a choice of investing, not investing, or moving their investment to foreign destinations. This served as the "push" effect among European and American investors, who redirected their investment and relocated their production plants to the more stable, business-friendly East Asian countries.

Economic competitiveness is relative, as the rise of one would mean the fall of another. The rise of competitiveness (stability, low production costs, economic openness, etc.) in East Asia could be due squarely to the fall of competitiveness (high taxes, rising production costs, strong labor union bargaining, etc.) among countries in Europe and America. The loss in economic competitiveness would mean the loss of jobs and a rise in imports. In turn, additional welfare would be needed to cater to the unemployed, and labor unions would become more self-centered and seek higher wages to protect their members. To fund these rising payments, a higher tax system would be needed, and the rise in fiscal deficits would mean a growing national debt. The weakening of economic competitiveness would give rise to a "vicious circle" (outflow of investment, loss in jobs, more needed welfare, higher tax, fiscal deficits, and so on). In short, the rise of a number of East Asian economies could be the result of the economic weakness and loss in competitiveness in many western countries.

Among the three production factors of land, labor, and capital, capital is the most mobile, and modern communication ensures that capital can travel to other countries in a matter of hours. Hence, the consequence of any change in the conditions of economic competitiveness would be seen in the movement of capital. The rising costs of production and decrease in market-friendliness among industrialized countries would invite investment resources to travel to more business-friendly destinations. Hence, political leaders need a more comprehensive view, and should calculate the "deadweight loss" that the economy would suffer when adopting prowelfare redistributive policies.

Nonetheless, it may not be entirely true to argue that the economics of "push and pull" provides the complete cause of success among East Asian economies. However, both the exogenous and indigenous causes should serve as complements to each other. The neoclassical theories applied to East Asian development provide useful analysis, as East Asian economies put much emphasis on improvement in indigenous factors. Foreign investment also went to other developing countries, but the economic development experience of other developing countries is nowhere parallel to that of development among the East Asian economies. Hence, it is exactly this difference that makes East Asia special and worth analyzing, so that the East Asian experience can serves as a lesson or reference point to other "latecomers" in capitalist development.

Equally, one should not idolize the success of East Asia, as some of these economies are faced with new problems after their decades of economic growth and development. The emergence and interaction of international, regional, and domestic factors have led to new situations among East Asian economies that may not provide a rosy picture for their future development. Japan has been faced with decades of slow down since the early 1990s. The Asian financial crisis in 1997 – 98 imposed new hardships on a number of Asian countries. Having been excluded from the United Nations since the early 1970s, and owing to the pressure from China, the economy of Taiwan has increasingly been isolated. Since 1997, the sovereignty of Hong Kong has been reverted back to China, which ended the century-long period as a British colony. The decades of economic success among these East Asian countries are also faced with new uncertainties and challenges. The policy of economic reform in China since 1978 has provided both opportunities and challenges to Asian economies.

There is no perfection in economic development. There is no perfection in any ideology, but one is looking for an effective ideology that can maximize the outcomes and achieve the "Pareto optimum." In other words, the cumulative nature of economic progress will eventually bring some improvement that can benefit all, though the extent of benefit differs among individuals, corporations, and institutions. This section will provide new insights as to the causes of the success that occurred in the second half of the 20th century, but will also boldly assess their situation in the new century, as well as the future economic paths the East Asian countries should follow. Like the "flying geese" model or the "latecomer" argument, the analysis begins with Japan, the first economic power in Asia, and then the East Asian economies, followed by the four ASEAN economies and China.

There are similarities and differences between the past development and future potential among the Asian economies. In the past, the goody was the foreign investment from the west, and the baddy was the threat of communism from China, North Korea, and Vietnam. For the future, the goody will be the internal economic strength these Asian economies have achieved, but the baddy is the complications and uncertainties arising from religious faiths among many Asian countries, and the challenges from China. The rise of China offers both optimism and pessimism. Similar to Japan in the 1970s, China's outward investment should benefit many Asian countries. What differs is that China has a different ideology than that of Japan, and the nature of China's outward investment will produce different impacts in the Asian region. In addition, after about four decades of economic reform in China, will China's domestic economy be able to keep up, or will there be crises and more political uncertainty in the region?

The three chapters in this section first examine the economic success of Japan, followed by the experiences of East Asian development. Chapter 13, The Late Comers: Opportunities, Challenges and Comparisons, examines the regional aspects of development, the development of the smaller economies in Southeast Asia, and the regional implications arising from the role that China plays in the region. Indeed, the regions of Europe and Asia would certainly provide an interesting comparative discussion.

The Japanese Economy:
Successes and Challenges

I INTRODUCTION

Since the 1950s, one can argue that Japan has shown a complete cycle of development with rapid rises in 3—4 decades, followed by severe capacity constraints and prolonged challenges. While there are numerous studies on the economic rise of Japan as the world's economic superpower, the Japanese economy since the beginning of the 1990s has gone into "hibernation" for more than a decade. In the literature on Japan's "lost decade," stagnation and recession were the two common economic features, and there are as many causes to explain Japan's success as are used to explain the "lost decade" (Allen, 1981; Balassa and Noland, 1988; Tachi, 1993; Smith, 1995; Katz, 1998; Umematsu, 1999; Beasley, 2000; Weinert, 2001; Kobayashi and Inaba, 2002; Fukao, 2003; Macintyre and Naughton, 2005; Braun and Waki, 2006; Yoshikawa, 2007; Hamada and Okada, 2009; Leigh, 2010; Ichimura and Klein, 2010; Ichimura, 2015).

In the economic development of any single country, what Japan has shown in the 50 years from 1950 to 1999 or so was a case of rapid expansion when there was excess economic and industrial capacity, to a case of maturity and full capacity with bottlenecks emerging when the economy reached a high level. The period of expansion could have created complacency and a "comfort zone," where people would think that the good times would not end. There was definitely a lack of "prepare for the rainy days" attitude, and when the economy did approach full capacity, businesses and industries were not prepared to accept, or ready to make, structural changes. For example, it has been argued that Japan's industries excelled in their mechanical applications and electronics, but research into digital applications has been caught up by Korean and American competitors (Iwatani et al., 2011; EU-Japan Center, 2015). In other words, there are always other "latecomers" who will catch up with the Japanese products.

To use economic jargon, the economic lesson from Japan would be the concept of "comparative advantage," but the "comparative advantage" of yesterday may not be the "comparative advantage" of tomorrow. Indeed, forward looking economies should begin to develop future "comparative advantages" in order to stay competitive. In other words, "comparative advantage" is a dynamic concept, and economies have to develop new "comparative advantages" over time.

© 2017 Elsevier Inc. All rights reserved.

However, given the changing situation both in Asia and internationally, such as the rise of China and the terrorist attacks, the question is whether there could be a revival of the Japanese economy. The major attributes Japan possesses include high technology, especially in the consumer goods industry, good will in overseas countries as Japanese outward investment has been employment- and output-generating in the host countries, and Japan is not seen as a threat to any foreign country. The high ethical standards and quality of exports have made Japanese products highly acceptable in the world market. On the other hand, the economic downsides include the aging population, reflected in the shortage of labor, the high fiscal expenses, the lack of land for new industrial development, the occurrence of natural disasters in the form of earthquakes, and the reluctance to allow immigration that could dilute the homogeneity of the indigenous population.

The post-Second World War economic development of Japan provided a number of lessons. It served as a mirror-image for Japan's future development. How can the decades of economic success reflect on the future path of development? Japan's rise in industrial revolution provided useful lessons for both developing and industrialized countries in relation to the appropriate application of economic policies, including industrial research and development, and fiscal policy. One crucial factor that appeared in the decades of Japanese growth was the business – government – academics connection (Jorgenson et al., 1987; Jorgenson, 1988; Jorgenson and Kuroda, 1992; Jorgenson and Nomura, 2005). Looking at Japan's development, one can also make conjectures on China's postreform development since 1978. It would be interesting to compare and map, on a parallel time-line basis, the rise of Japan and China, and whether China would follow Japan's development footprints, bearing in mind their ideological differences. In the eyes of many Asian countries, Japanese investments are still very much welcomed, and a revival of the Japanese economy could bring another round of economic development and industrial growth.

Arguments proposed by scholars in economic geography (Gallup et al., 1999; Sachs and Warner, 1999, 2001) argued that both landlocked countries and countries exposed to extreme weather tend to produce lower growth rates, while countries with long ocean fronts or island economies tend to excel in economic development. In addition, the industrialization experiences of both Great Britain and Japan showed that countries with a lack of natural resources tended to be more successful than countries with an abundance of natural resources. The combined criteria of low resource availability and island nature of the economy could produce suitable chemistry for advances in development.

This chapter will provide new dimensions and coverage on both the rise and the "lost decade" of the Japanese economy, and propose a development strategy that will revive Japan's industrial economy.

II DRIVE TO ECONOMIC SUPERPOWER

It is generally agreed that the modernization of Japan dates back to the Meiji period between 1868 and 1912 (Morishima, 1982; Gluck, 1985). In particular, the import of foreign technology and machinery has formed the foundation of Japan's industrialization in that, as a "latecomer" in the industrial world, Japan not only imported and learned from foreign technology but also made improvements and alterations to suit the Japanese and Asian markets (Shinohara, 1982). As such, foreign technology was indigenized to become Japan's "home-grown" technology, which eventually competed successfully with foreign suppliers.

In the post-Second World War period, the reconstruction assistance provided by the United States in much of the 1950s was important, as it injected new capital into the economy. Despite the fighting between the United States and Japan in the Second World War, but given the similarity in ideology, the United States accepted Japan as a partner for development, geopolitically, in East Asia in order to balance the spread of communism from China. Japan turned out to be the first largest Asian economy. Several socioeconomic factors can be used in combination to explain Japan's success.

Japan's domestic economy is rather small, and industrialists would have to target the export market from the very beginning. The export drive attitude in Japan and other East Asia economies can contrast sharply to that of US producers, who would regard the US market as so large that supplying the US market would already produce handsome business profits. As such, foreign markets might not look as attractive to US manufacturers. Thus, household appliances produced in North America would be too big to suit the export market in Asia. A major economic attribute Japan holds is the attention to detail, especially in industrial goods. Other than indigenizing foreign technologies, Japanese producers did study in detail the features and possibilities of various consumer markets.

In household appliances, e.g., air conditioners, washing machines, hi-fi instruments, and refrigerators have also been redesigned to suit Japanese homes and other markets in Asia. In contrast to similar household appliances produced in the United States, the smaller sizes of Japanese appliances are designed specifically for smaller homes, so as to limit the use of space. Such attention to detail led to various product designs that enabled Japan to produce a large number of small but useful household appliances and products that facilitate work in homes, offices, and personal safety. The intention to study consumer needs and markets can also be found in the production of motor vehicles. The design of smaller and lighter cars and the provision of air conditioning in all Japanese cars proved to be a pioneer in the 1960s.

Commercialization of products using existing technology is another pioneer in modern industries. Based on the existing tape-recording technology which existed probably since the First World War, the redesigned production of the Walkman in the 1960s aimed especially at individual consumers, so that every individual consumer could carry a Walkman in their pocket. While each household will purchase a washing machine or refrigerator at home, the sale of the Walkman was aimed at individuals. The flourishing of the electronics industry led to further commercialization of technology, and a new generation of personal hi-fi products, such as the CD player and the iPod, were subsequently developed. A related example is the mobile phone industry that has passed through several generations in production.

Another factor which has not been discussed extensively is the loyalty of Japanese consumers. Japanese consumers are proud of their country's production and manufacturers, though this may be eroding slightly among the younger generation. During the expansion stage, the loyalty of the consumer was important, not only because they consumed local production, but Japanese manufacturers were also using the domestic market to test their products in order to improve quality. In that sense, Japanese producers have been "protected" by the loyalty of indigenous consumers. Hence, after several generations of improved production and testing of products, Japanese products eventually exhibited excellent, "second-to-none" quality, and together with a more affordable price, exports of Japanese products conquered the world market, and soon Japanese brand names become popular among foreign consumers.

As compared to the expensive high-tech products manufactured in America and Europe, the Japanese producers tend to cater for the more affordable market rather than the luxury market. The economic theory is that Japanese producers assumed elastic demand, that a lower price would encourage demand, and the rise in sales should eventually produce handsome revenues. The resulting high sales and business revenues would provide a stable source of support, reflecting at the same time the rising consumer loyalty to Japanese brands. The assumption of elastic demand is a good pricing strategy when commercializing technological products.

The strong discipline of Japanese workers showed high efficiency and productivity, though it has been said that jobs in Japan were too demanding, to the extent of sacrificing workers' family life. Along with the good work discipline were strong business and individual ethics. Japanese products and exports ensured quality and reliability. Japanese consumers' loyalty was gradually transformed to foster overseas consumers' confidence, which subsequently has become the world's new standard or reference point for other internationalized products. Good ethics in Japan can easily be seen at the individual level. Mutual respect, not only between persons and in business, but in daily behavior, quality of life, and people's interactions in public places have been kept to a high ethical standard. Possibly due to its highly homogenous population and the people's loyalty to their country, politeness, courtesy, and honesty are exhibited in daily interactions among Japanese.

There is also an institutional dimension in the successful growth and expansion of the Japanese economy. While there is much discussion on the role of government and the extent of government intervention, a major institutional quality in Japan is the cordial tripartite relationship between government officials, businesses, and academics, especially in industrial design, production, and marketing. The chemistry in the tripartite relationship worked in such a way that while the academics conducted the research, the business worked on the production and marketing, and the government worked on the policies in order to bring success to the industry. The former Ministry of International Trade and Investment (MITI) conducted and nurtured the interactions among the three parties; hence, the decisions on "policy – research – production" were simplified and facilitated, thereby promoting production efficiency and industrial effectiveness. Such a tripartite relationship has since been followed and duplicated by other Asian countries, though less successfully.

In short, other than the conventional causes of growth in Japan, the additional causes discussed included the learning and adoption of foreign technology, the protected domestic market where industrialists can test and improve their products before venturing into the world market, careful analysis of individual products and markets to ensure the manufactured products are favored by consumers, domestic consumer loyalty gradually turned to foster foreign consumer confidence, and the effective institutional connection between the academics, businesses, and officials are the socioeconomic features that contributed crucially to the fundamentals of Japan's path to an economic superpower.

III RESPONSE TO THE INTERNATIONAL COMMUNITY

Japan's role in the international community can also provide lessons for other "latecomers" in the chain of economic development. Partly because of consumer loyalty, partly because the lack of knowledge about foreign goods or the unsuitability of foreign appliances, and partly because of the good reliability and quality of Japanese products, traditional Japanese consumers do not favor foreign brands and products. As such, when Japanese exports increased rapidly in the 1960s, coupled with the lack of demand for imported goods on the part of Japanese consumers, a massive trade surplus resulted. Hence, while Japan became the world's number one exporter of products in the 1970s, there was mounting pressure for the Japanese currency to appreciate. However, knowing that a rapid appreciation would reduce considerably Japan's manufacturing exports, Japan choose to invest abroad as a way to address the trade surplus. In other words, the surplus in the trade account would be balanced with a deficit in the capital account, so as to ease the appreciation pressure on the overall balance of payment account (see, e.g., Inoguchi, 1988).

With huge reserves and large trade surpluses, Japan had a lot of potential in deploying their foreign investments. There are three types of Japanese outward investments. In industrial investment, Japanese industrialists practiced a strategy of "horizontal" investment overseas, implying that the same industrial plants in Japan were exported to North America, Europe, and some Asian countries. Thus, a number of Japanese brand names in motor vehicles and household appliances are now produced in North America, Europe, and Asia. The second type of Japanese outward investment involved in a number of business projects in retail, construction, and so on. Portfolio investment is another major form of Japanese investment. Since the 1970s, Japan has invested massively in treasury bonds in foreign countries, and has become the largest holder of US treasury bonds in the following decades.

Each of these three forms of Japanese investment has led to different results. The most visible type of "horizontal" industrial investment has been well received by host countries, as these investments have been employment-preserving, output-generating, and import-reducing. Models innovated and designed in Japan have been exported to the host countries, and the same Japanese model is produced overseas. There are two drawbacks to the Japan economy. One would be the reduction in Japan's exports and decline in trade surplus, though the pressure on currency appreciation was eased. There was also pressure on employment, as the reduction in exports also reduced domestic jobs in Japan. The other drawback could rest on the design, e.g., of Japanese motor vehicles. Due to the large US market, it was not surprising that the design of Japanese vehicles increasingly catered to US consumers. The drawback could be loss of the original Japanese style. And when the Japanese models were becoming similar to US designs, US consumers would not differentiate Japanese models from US models, thereby reducing the Japanese advantage. A solution would be to ensure that Japanese designs are stylistically different from US designs. The basic assumption of "elastic demand" with contemporary design, good quality, and economically priced products, are the Japanese advantage. In other words, aiming at the average consumer is still the best strategy.

Investment in foreign projects has not been discussed extensively. Numerous Japanese businesses and companies ventured into foreign countries in project investments, in retail stores, in construction projects, and so on. Japanese subsidies were set up in numerous foreign countries, and funds were used to bid for projects. In retail stores, e.g., the few largest Japanese retail stores have set up branches elsewhere, especially in Asian economies. In construction projects, such as building of roads, bridges, and infrastructure, Japanese companies were keen to bid on these projects. In Hong Kong, e.g., construction projects in the 1970s have successfully been bid on openly by Japanese firms, offering lower costs than local firms. Of course, the success in bidding for construction projects depended a lot on the Japanese subsidiaries in the host economies. Given that Japan was eager to invest, and the large pool of foreign reserves Japan had, the productivity and cost efficiency of these project investments might not have been properly estimated and communicated appropriately back to the headquarters in Tokyo. The Japanese representatives in their foreign subsidiaries would equally be prepared and happy to successfully bid for the projects. Typically, one argument was the belief that, in the long run, many investment projects would become profitable. Thus, it was feasible that underpriced bidding for investment projects occurred. The short run "loss" was tolerated, and it was probably thought that in the long run the "loss" would be covered or recovered, e.g., in retail stores. In a time frame of 20 years it was commonly argued that the Japanese retail and construction projects could turn profitable.

However, many of these projects were funded by Japanese banks and financial companies. Consider the situation and sequence of events more carefully in the conjecture. This was the 1970s, when Japan's economic peak began. It was probable that some Japanese project investments in foreign countries were not profit making, but funding by Japanese banks proceeded so long as the sentiment was that profit would be generated in the long run. As time passed, it was possible that different incidents occurred, such as the emergence of economic crises, inflation, and business cycles, and the "long run" did not look that promising. Hence, when many Japanese banks were faced with debts, beginning from the early 1990s, many of these projects and loans remained unprofitable, or might have difficulty in repaying the principals. In other words, the conjecture was that many Japanese subsidiaries were surviving on "debts," the funding agents, namely the banks in Japan, would sooner or later have evolved into trouble as the debt cumulated and snowballed (see, e.g., Ogawa et al., 2012).

The lesson from this conjecture was that Japan's banking crisis in the 1990s could be due to the accumulated debts used to fund project investments in overseas economies. In other words, the "short run loss" over time gradually became the "long run loss" if there were no improvements made to the invested projects, and the economic situation did not improve or even deteriorated. Thus, the belief in the "long run profit" turned out to be a myth, and contributed to the banking crisis in the 1990s and the difficulties in the "lost decade." It probably was true that risk had not been carefully measured and weighted when funds were abundant. The situation could be worse if the funds were state-owned. Many Japanese retail stops flourished in Asian cities in the 1960s and 1970s, but beginning from mid-1990s, many faced closure.

In the case of Japanese outward portfolio investment, over the years, Japan has become the largest holder of US treasury bonds. Portfolio investment affected only the financial market, but it could have led to the Asian financial crisis in 1997, when the Japanese economy was faced with difficulties in the "lost decade" of the 1990s. By 1997, when both the Thai baht and South Korean won were attacked in July and September, respectively, the Asian market remained sensitive (Li, 2002, 2006; Li and Kwok, 2009). When the Japanese prime minister visited the United States in November 1997, investors in other international stock markets became suspicious that Japan would come and inform the US president that Japan would withdraw funds from the United States and other world markets. It was reported that the US president made the remark after meeting the Japanese prime minister that Japan should "look for solutions within Japan." The stock market in the United States and elsewhere overreacted, and fund managers began to withdraw from other world markets in advance and in anticipation, in order to ensure sufficient funds to recover in case Japan withdrew funds from the United States. Such a sudden and massive withdrawal of funds deepened the Asian financial crisis in early 1998. Fortunately, Japan responsibly did not withdraw funds from the United States, and by 1999, the funds withdrawn from Asia by the financial companies in the United States were returned to the Asian market.

The different types of Japanese investment have particular features, and could provide lessons to other foreign investors. Indeed, with the rise of the Chinese economy since the turn of the century, Japan's experience can be used to compare directly with China's experience. Similarities include the massive trade surplus and huge international reserves both Japan and China have accumulated from the prolonged trade surplus. Both Japan, and now China, have acquired a lot of US treasury bonds. In overseas investment, Japan favored "horizontal" investments in industrial manufacturing, but China's outward investment has mostly been "vertical," and was largely geared to securing imports of oil and other natural resources that China lacked. Japan's foreign investment has never been accused of being "imperialistic." On the contrary, China's outward investments have largely been conducted by state-owned or state-controlled enterprises, which could also lack a good sense of risk measurement.

In relation to developing countries, especially those in Asia, Japan established in 1966 the Asian Development Bank (ADB) with headquarters in Manila, the Philippines. In 2013, the Chinese leaders reiterated the centuries-old silk-trade route and suggested the "one belt, one road" concept that links economic cooperation from China westwards all the way to Western Europe. In January 15, 2016, the China-initiated Asian Infrastructure Investment Bank (AIIB) was established in Beijing, with China contributing over 30% of its assets with the intention of helping countries along the "one belt, one road" route to build up their infrastructure for trade and regional transport (*South China Morning Post*, January, 16, 2016). The ultimate intention would be to expand China's exports to "one belt, one road" countries and secure raw materials imports from these resource-rich countries. Although some advanced European countries also agreed to become members of AIIB, one political argument is that many less developed countries along the route would serve as peripheries to China.

In other words, Japan's overseas investments tended to produce a complementary effect in the increase in employment, output, and exports in the host countries. China's outward investments tended to ensure a steady supply of resources and raw materials for China. The crucial difference is that industrial products could be replenished, but raw material and natural resources often could not be replenished. The more natural resources were being extracted, produced, and consumed, the lower the supply of such resources would become.

IV THE TURNING POINT

Various studies on the decline of the Japanese economy since the early 1990s tend to focus on the causes of rising debt, large welfare, decline in business-friendliness, and inability to catch up with the market trends in product design and research and development, crisis and collapse in the property sector, prolonged period of ultra-low interest rates, and the continuous use of the quantitative easing (QE) strategy that crippled the monetary economy, aging population and rigid immigration policy, lack of new land supply, and exposure to natural disasters (see, e.g., Fujiki et al., 2001; Shirakawa, 2002; Kimura and Small, 2004). The feeling of complacency could be the psychological cause, while economic and industrial restructuring would require time. Nonetheless, the academic discussion of the delay in economic revival in Japan has somewhat extended from the "lost decade" to the "loss of decades." Given its technological potential, investors and consumers are keen to see a revival, recovery, and restructuring of the Japanese industrial economy.

It would not be possible to isolate a single cause as the "turning point," as causes of decline were cumulative. However, the discussion can be separated into the "internal circuit" and the "external circuit" of decline. As Japan's industrial economy peaked in the late-1980s, the full capacity and possibly the complacent attitude acted as "counter forces" in further advances in industries. The "internal circuit" could begin with "demand-driven" policies of income redistribution through increasing welfare spending and rises in tax, which were thought to be acceptable when the economy was at its peak. Unfortunately, the overheated economy at the peak was accompanied by exorbitant property prices, speculation eventually led to a property bubble, and the subsequent collapse in property prices led to drastic asset depreciation. The economic collapse would, in turn, have hastened more "demand-driven" policies through the need to rescue the economy. The fall in the property economy obviously had spillover to the monetary economy, and subsequently generated a banking crisis as banks were faced with more debts.

The downfall of the economy produced various unfavorable expectations. Typically, business contraction would reduce employment, and the aging population hastened retirement. The working relationship among workers in various businesses that had existed in the period of economic expansion would have changed. To cut costs, the experienced would be replaced by the inexperienced, or by recruitment of young and unseasoned personnel. Such kinds of personality replacement could be obvious in difficult times, but could be critical if it eventually led to shrinkage in industrial leadership and in such pioneering activities as industrial design, and industrial research and development. In other words, the economic decline produced negative spillovers to the "supply-side" of the industrial economy.

The business sector could have become less optimistic in a period of economic downfall, and that would lead to a more conservative attitude to investment. The accumulated debts and banking crisis would also restrict activities in the loan market. Similarly, the attitude on long-term investment could have evaporated, and in its place was the drive to look for short-term investment, especially when Japan's interest rate was kept so low for so long. The low interest rate may have increased investment, but there are various unfavorable consequences. A low interest rate would mean a fall in the value of money, and that could have invited speculation and not investment. Since speculative activities are mostly short-term, the use of financial resources would have been diverted away from industrial investment and would take a longer gestation time for investment return.

In short, the economic crisis, coupled with business decline, prolonged distortion in the monetary economy, a rise in welfare and redistributive polices in the fiscal economy, and an aging population that reduced the size of the work force altogether created an "industrial vacuum" or "economic trap" in Japan, whereby the pace of industrial development slowed down and industrial progress lagged behind. This structural shock and rigidity created turmoil that dismantled the well-established and successful approach to industrial advancement. In other words, Japan's "industrial vacuum" in the "internal circuit" was the result of combined forces in the rise in "demand-driven" policies (rising tax and welfare, property crisis) on the one hand, and the fall in "supply-driven" strategies (distortion in investment, aging population, and shortage of replenishing human capital) on the other hand. Thus, Japan experienced the worst of two worlds in the "lost decade."

In the "external circuit," the popularity of Japanese products somewhat subsided by the 1990s, as there was a lack of new and innovative developments. Although overseas consumer confidence was still high, consumers got used to Japanese products. The delay in making creative innovations in industrial products in Japan was matched by foreign competitors, typically from South Korea, Sweden, Germany, and the United States, in the production of electronic appliances and motor vehicles. The domestic crisis in Japan also affected Japan's outward investment, which has not been that forthcoming compared to the 1970s and 1980s. At the same time, other Asian and foreign countries have been more aggressive in outward investment, and have captured much of the foreign market. Similarly, new international brand names in electronic appliances and motor vehicles have emerged that compete with Japanese manufacturers.

While as a "latecomer" to the industrial world since the 1960s, Japanese manufacturers have competed successfully with United States and European brand names in the 1970s and 1980s, it was the turn of other "latecomers" that emerged and competed with Japanese manufacturers since the 1990s. Once Japan lost its momentum in the race for industrial supremacy, other competitors were ready to capture Japan's market share. This applied not only in terms of actual amount of exports, but in terms of design and new product development, and the switch of consumer confidence and loyalty. Indeed, with the rising magnitude of other Asian and world economies, Japan's industrial manufacturing will face more challenges. Other than the BRICS countries (Brazil, Russia, India, China, and South Africa), there are other sizable emerging "latecomers" from Latin America, such as Mexico, Peru, and Chile, which are also entering the world export market at a rapid pace, though Japan's technological products and electronic appliances are more advanced and sophisticated than exports from emerging countries.

The industrial world is becoming more diverse, and "latecomers" emerge as industrial production has become standardized. And instead of the manufactured products that are traded among countries, the entire production process can also be exported. In other words, it is not only the products that are being exported from various parts of the world, but the process of manufacturing is also traveling around the world. Such a dynamic feature of production and manufacturing suggests that, in addition to the presence of "product life-cycle" (Vernon, 1979), there emerges also the "manufacturing life-cycle" and similar industries are being established in different world economies.

Another factor in the "external circuit" is the role of the exchange rate of the Japanese yen. Despite Japan's massive outward investment, the Japanese currency did appreciate, due either to its export strength or in period of a weak US currency that indirectly strengthened the Japanese yen. The Japanese yen has a peculiar position among the various world currencies that may not be due entirely to Japan's export strengths. Normally, when the United States and European currencies are strong, the Japanese yen would naturally become weak, regardless of Japan's export position. On the contrary, when other world currencies are weak, currency investors would look to the Japanese yen as a "shelter currency," and the yen became strong, regardless again of its trading position.

If the argument of a "shelter currency" is correct, then the strength of the Japanese yen would probably be influenced more by the movement of other world currencies, typically the US dollar, than by the strength of the Japanese economy itself. Hence, it is likely that in the past, when Japanese products were popular and foreign consumer confidence was high, demand for Japanese exports remained high, but demand was affected more by similar export suppliers from South Korea, Sweden, Germany, and the United States when new brand names from these countries appeared and competed with Japanese brands. For export promotion, Japan should keep a low exchange rate as much as possible, but it would also lead to high import prices that might hurt Japanese consumers or industries that use imported materials, such as petroleum.

Japan does have more room to maneuver in the "external circuit." For example, despite Japan's large debt, Japan has amassed large international reserves. Hence the "large debt, large reserve" scenario would mean that, at the national level, Japan "borrows and saves" at the same time. There are many countries with huge national debts, but few debt-prone countries have large reserves like that of Japan. By comparison, the large reserves will ease the economic burden from the large debt. Of course, Japan has to reduce its debt and/or improve its reserves.

Between the "internal circuit" and the "external circuit," it would be the former that hurt Japan's industrial economy more, because the "internal circuit" probably had crippled the supply-side of the industrial economy, and the "external circuit" just reflected the unfavorable consequences of the "internal circuit." Hence, it would be the endogenous factors that Japan's industrial economy has to look into. Beginning from the probability of a "full capacity" economy, Japan needs to improve and expand the "supply-side" factors, including further advances in technology, the possibility of technological commercialization, long-term investment geared to the industrial sector, fiscal friendliness, a rebalance of the education system to enhance human capital, and infrastructure development to prevent natural disasters. There are, of course, factors which have changed since the 1980s. For example, workers' discipline and working hours may not be as high as previously, the younger generation may look to other aspects of life, and their behavior may reflect more on individual personality than on collective corporate image and value.

Along with improvements in "supply-side" factors would be the need for a new market strategy and market image, so that consumer confidence can be reestablished in a new generation. The focus is to identify a workable strategy that revives Japan's competitive and comparative advantages in industry, technology, and exports. One optimistic argument is that the "manufacturing life-cycle" will also appear in other competitors too. When Japan can manage to create and establish another "manufacturing life-cycle," the reemergence of Japan's industrial power could allow Japan's industrial output to expand in the world market once again.

V PATHS FOR REVIVAL

The United States has been the economic, political, regional, and international partner of Japan. This will not change, and Japanese investors feel comfortable investing in the US market. What concerns one is the consolidation, deepening, and expansion of the North American market, as well as venturing into the South American market. One advantage is the market position Japan has nurtured in previous decades. Japan's industrial exports concentrate on capital- and technologically-intensive production, and commercialization of technology into household appliances. The high quality production has earned a high degree of consumer confidence for Japanese products.

The advantages Japan has include the high technology, strong capital support, high ethical standards and quality production, educated work force, mature infrastructure, and reliable institutions. The disadvantages Japan faces include lack of land and labor force resulting from the aging population, and the risk of such natural disasters as earthquakes. The industrial revival strategy will have to make use of the advantages, and look for ways to minimize the destructive impact from the disadvantages. The usual formula for improvement in technology is to nurture the culture of creativity and innovation at the personal and educational level, while effective expenditure on research and development will be the long-term answer. Given that Japan has achieved a high technological level, the concern is how to make progress and advances in order to lift Japan's current technology to a higher level.

Although the "borrow and save" strategy works well for Japan, for improvement in capital supply, the usual answer is the reduction in fiscal, government, and national debt on the one hand, and increase in international reserves on the other hand. In addition, the stock market can also help to generate capital from private sources, but stock development can also be restricted by the size of national debt and business potential. At the macro-level, Japan needs to identify a more business-friendly policy. Ethics and infrastructure are fixed factors that can only be improved gradually.

Labor and land are the only crucial constraint. An "inward brain drain" strategy can be useful in enriching Japan's human capital and aging population. While Japan has a strict immigration policy, importation of contract-term skilled labor to increase its work force can be an alternative. Import of short-term skilled labor allows the workers to seek industrial employment in Japan, but they cannot take up Japanese residence or citizenship. With imported workers, there will be a greater need for the use of English in communication. This requires the Japanese to have a greater skill in the English language over time. The land on the eastern coast of Japan is often at risk of earthquakes, storms, and other forms of disasters, the western coast is more reliable, and is sheltered from natural disasters. Industrial plants can be concentrated on the western side of Japan. There are other alternatives. One possibility is to avoid land-intensive industries, and concentrate on development that can make use of the sea and ocean, as that is a natural resource that Japan has.

By combining the use of land and labor importation, one possibility is for Japan to locate a remote but disaster-free region as an "industrial export zone" (IEZ) that works similar to Silicon Valley in California, where high technology is combined with industrial production, and recruitment of overseas scientists and professionals will help to solve the problem of human capital. The IEZ can be the "stone that kills two (or more) birds," because it allows technology to advance, manufacture to expand, and skilled labor to fill up the population gap. With the strong and mature financial structure that will provide capital when needed, new designs for existing brands, and new brand names that aim at the mass market will easily revive Japan's exports.

A further alternative would be to look for overseas partners for a steady supply of land and labor. Japan has invested massively in the United States previously, but to capture the market in both North and South America, the economy of Canada could be a good choice for industrial partnership. Canada has plenty of land and no restrictions on establishing land-intensive industries, such as the establishment of motor vehicle plants. Institutions in Canada follow closely the British style, and Canada's immigration policy is selective in the supply of skilled labor and professionals. A bilateral agreement with Canada in establishing a "Canada – Japan industrial region" (CJIR), e.g., would permit Japan's industries to have a permanent position in both North and South America.

Within Asia, the economy of Taiwan would also be a good alternative. Although Taiwan is geographically smaller than Japan, Taiwan has the locational advantage. The growth of the Taiwanese economy has been slow since the 1990s, the cost of production has remained low, and the education system in Taiwan does generate a steady flow of human capital. Hence, Japan's investment in Taiwan could just be right timing, as Taiwan needs new development in investment, industries, jobs, and exports. Taiwan also has a history of relationship with Japan.

In other words, domestic resource inadequacy can be overcome by conducting bilateral relationships with nearby friendly economies whose resources can complement that of the domestic economy. Thus, either Japan locating an effective "industrial export zone" domestically, or making joint agreements with Canada and/or Taiwan could be similar to that of Silicon Valley. Thinking along the reasoning on the "supply-side," the Japanese economy could have every prerequisite to revive its economic strength to bring a renewed round of industrialization in Japan.

VI CONCLUSION

Other than its war experience with some Asian neighbors, Japan's economic and industrial rise has been accepted by both the Asian and international community as more of a contributor than as a competitor in enhancing international harmony and world development. In particular, Japan's industrial manufacturers that concentrated on personal consumables, household appliances, and motor vehicles that aimed at the mass market have been well received, and Japanese exports have set new standards to other "latecomers" in the industrialization process. Indeed, as a medium-sized country, Japan is considered a success and will serve as a showcase in its growth and development to other emerging world economies. Within half a century, Japan has achieved a high stage of development domestically, and at the same time, maintained effective and friendly relationships with countries in the world community. Indeed, Japanese investments have never been criticized in any foreign country as imperialistic or hegemony, and other industrial manufacturers look to Japanese products as references and targets to compete with. The world economy can definitely reach a higher stage of development, economic advancement, and civilization if there were more countries that followed Japan's experience and pattern of industrial and economic development.

It is natural that other industrial manufacturers will compete with Japanese products. It is equally true that countries could reach their maximum capacity, and further growth would be restricted unless restructuring and technological advancement can enrich the country's capability, or in economic jargon, expand the production frontier. It is easier said in theory than in conducting policies and directing resources that can practically expand the production frontier. It would be worse if, in the meantime while restructuring was delayed, short-sighted economic policies were adopted that switched policy focus from "supply-side" factors to "demand-side" outcomes. Politically oriented policies, such as a drive to income equality, large and unjustified expenses on welfare and subsidies, increases in government intervention at the expense of market friendliness, mounting fiscal and national debt that paralyzed borrowing as an instrument of capital accumulation, would not be appropriate, even though the economy had reached its full capacity. In other words, it could be done easily for a country that has reached full capacity to divert away from focusing on "supply-side" economics to engaging increasingly on "demand-side" economics.

While there is a need for greater national security as situations require, Japan has rightly positioned itself as an economic giant with its industrial might that related largely to consumer goods in the international community. Such an approach to development can be an "evergreen" strategy, though the prerequisite is continued efforts in improving the "supply-side" factors. Seen in this light, the "lost decade" can be considered as a period prior to further restructuring. But if lessons are learnt and redirection of economic policies can timely be made, the swift revival to "supply-side" factors will enable Japan to reemerge in the world's industrial arena.

Indeed, Japan's experience has been noted by a large number of countries, especially its Asian neighbors. Those Asian neighbors who have formerly benefitted from Japanese investments are eager to see industrial revival in Japan, as that will lead to deepened growth and development in their industrial and manufacturing sectors, followed by increases in income and exports. Hence, Japan's pivotal role in the Asian region suggests that Japan's next phase of industrial development is a welcoming concern to a number of Asian and world economies.

12

East Asia: Flying Geese Against Wind Currents

I INTRODUCTION

The success of all East Asian economies can best be explained by neoclassical economic analysis, the application of market economy and capitalism. Having been considered as the "newly industrializing economies" since the early 1970s, the growth of the East Asian economies, typically South Korea, Taiwan, Singapore, and Hong Kong, have gone through a process of industrialization, though the type of export-oriented industries differed among these economies. Beginning from light manufacturing and labor-intensive industries, South Korea and Taiwan have ventured into heavy industries, such as shipping. The strong exports of the four East Asian economies have earned them a new status since 1979, namely graduation from the Generalized System of Preference (GSP) which specified that exports from developing countries were allowed to enter the United States and European markets without import tariffs (Kwok and Li, 1992). Effectively, this graduation changed the status of the four East Asian economies to "developed economies," and their exports would no longer be tariff-free.

The development experience of East Asia has shown distinct transition stages. The early stage of industrialization was financed mainly from foreign direct investment dominated by labor-intensive manufacturing. Industrial flexibility is another advantage. Other than the light manufacturing in the early stages of industrialization in the 1960s, industries that have flourished since late 1970s were electronics. Electronics should not be regarded as a land-intensive industry, and its development would best be in small and effective economies. However, their concentration on electronics became a constraint when new competitors emerged.

Due to their small market size, much of the industrial output from East Asia was exported, supplementing the supply bottleneck in consumer goods in the western economies. As income grew and economies became more mature in the 1980s, these economies were transformed to become suppliers of capital to neighboring economies

© 2017 Elsevier Inc. All rights reserved.

by investing in industrial plants in other Southeast Asian countries, typically, Indonesia, Malaysia, Thailand, and the Philippines, and later Vietnam and southern China. Singapore soon served as the regional headquarters among the countries in the Association of Southeast Asian Nations (ASEAN), while Hong Kong served as headquarters to foreign investors to China. Singapore tends to have a slight advantage over Hong Kong in Southeast Asia, since Singapore is a leading member in ASEAN, while Hong Kong has a slight advantage over Singapore in the economic relationship with China, due to geographical proximity. Nonetheless, their economic compositions are close to each other.

There has been a lack of regional protection among Asian economies. The establishment of the ASEAN in 1967 with the five initial members (Singapore, Malaysia, Thailand, Indonesia, and the Philippines) was more a political cooperation against the spread of communism from Vietnam than an economic cooperation body. Unlike the European Union, all Asian economies compete among themselves, especially given the similarities in their economic background. Hence, maintaining competitiveness meant economies would do their best to remain stable. Indeed, if any Asian economy falls, the economic benefits, such as outflow of capital and loss of foreign investment, would go immediately to neighboring economies. For example, when there was trouble in Indonesia or the Philippines, Singapore and Hong Kong would become the natural "shelter" of capital. Asian economies do not enjoy the kind of rescue from neighboring economies as in the European Union where stronger members could come to the rescue. This cannot be true among Asian countries. Hence, the "look after oneself" mentality in the "intraregional" competition became a force of growth in itself.

However, by the 1990s, rising domestic costs in the four East Asian countries have eroded their competitive advantage considerably. The emergence of China has diverted much foreign investments away from all East Asian economies, and at the same time, East Asian economies also increased their investment in China. In the "push and pull" analysis, the Chinese economy since the 1990s produced a combination of both complement and substitution effects on the East Asia economies. The low cost of production in China worked as a complement, as China "pulled" investment from East Asia. However, foreign investments that could have come to East Asia would have diverted to China, and such a loss of foreign investment, and exports subsequently, produced the substitution effect that constrained growth among East Asia economies.

Another major event was the Asian financial crisis in 1997 − 98, though it was short-lived, the crisis reflected the economic and industrial narrowness among key East Asian economies. Political realities in some East Asian economies have somewhat derailed their growth path, as political uncertainties generated risk and disincentives, thereby hastening their fall in economic competitiveness. While industrial diversity and economic restructuring takes time, there is a need to explore new "comparative advantage" for future development.

The human behavior of "give and take" is elaborated in the next section to enlighten the economic performance of successful East Asian economies, especially when compared to those "fragile states" with extremely low levels of development, or countries that have always remained in an unstable situation, with no potential to grow and survival based on a daily basis. East Asian economies have "taken" a lot from the international community over the years, but their development has been complemented by domestic improvements that enabled these economies to also "give" and develop neighboring economies. This chapter summarizes, renews, and extends the neoclassical debate on the causes of growth among East Asian economies. Discussions will be made in relation to their development in the period after the Asian financial crisis, as each of the East Asian economies are faced with new challenges and situations and their next stage of growth can provide useful lessons for other emerging countries.

II "TAKE AND GIVE" IN DEVELOPMENT

There are various economic jargons in development economics, the neoclassical advocates for domestic improvement, while the radical or Marxian school complains about the historical factors of imperialism and external exploitation. The "demand-driven" school advocates for the welfare or the spending side of the fiscal equation, while the "supply-driven" school advocates for the importance of supply factors in promoting growth. The conventional factors of production include land, labor, and capital, while the business sector considers the role of entrepreneurship. The availability and creation of economic opportunity has recently been argued as another scare factor of production (Li, 2014b). The various economic indicators, such as GDP, industrial output, consumption, and exports are ex post measures. The discussion on economic opportunity examines the ex-ante factors in the development process.

There is also a discussion on "economism" (Li, 2002) that distinguishes economics from other social disciplines, as the former produces "relative" outcomes and connects to a number of preconditions based on the development experience of East Asia, while other social science disciplines such as politics generates "absolute" dichotomous outcomes. The "purity" of economics has been affected when economics is used as a political instrument, and at the same time economic outcomes have been used as scapegoats when the outcomes were not politically acceptable. The short-term desires in politics would affect economic outcomes that would require a longer nurturing time.

The use of dichotomy is common in social science disciplines. While there are numerous theories and schools of thought in development, one can use the analogy of "give and take" in human behavior. The analogy in the use of the term "give and take" has been applied to governance and transaction cost analysis (see, e.g., Williamson, 2000, 2005). Through receiving education, the young generation obtains knowledge and becomes productive. Successful individuals become philanthropists, make donations, and give to charities to help others. Businesses make profits through the market, but also create employment. Governments take from society revenues through tax, but spend and give back to society through provision of education, infrastructure, security, and welfare to ensure survival. The act to "take" is the desire to obtain needed materials in order to enable individuals, business enterprises, or governments to become able and productive with the ultimate goal to "give" through generating employment. The act of "take and give" can become a chained relationship or a circuit in economic performance. The intuition is that while there are times when developing economies tended to be on the "take" side of the economic equation, the more important concern is what has been done after a developing economy has "taken" from the rest of the world through such inputs as foreign investment and assistance. To businesses and individuals in developing countries, the concern is what has been achieved after they have "taken" from the community such materials as education, business-friendly environments, and the market.

Simply put, the concerns are whether individuals, businesses, and governments have made achievements, progress, and growth after having "taken" materials and benefits from the domestic or international community. The East Asian growth and development experience seemed to have suggested a "take → progress → growth → give" circuit. After having "taken" materials and resources from the international community, there has been domestic improvement. The injection of external resources has been accompanied with indigenous progress that led to economic growth. Indigenous progress can include the rule of law and ethics. With continuous and prolonged growth, the East Asian economies in turn are able to "give" to nearby economies, providing others with lessons of success and funding resources.

The "take and give" mentality can provide useful intuition to other developing countries, in that the act of "taking" alone may not lead to growth and development if there is no contemporaneous improvement in the indigenous economy. This can easily be reflected from experience in some countries with extremely low levels of development. Poverty could have been accompanied by ineffective political leadership, and instabilities emerge one after another. Many "fragile" states are involved with multiple levels of conflict with "absolute" outcomes: ethical, territorial, military, social, religious, political, racial, and regional. By using data from the world economy, Li et al. (2016) show that without macroeconomic stability, countries faced with extremely low levels of development will not be able to experience income convergence with the rest of the world. Improvements in domestic conditions have to take place before a developing country can grow (Li and Zhou, 2010; Liu and Li, 2015). Merely "taking" from the international community in the form of aid, loans, and assistance from foreign governments and international institutions is at best the "necessary" condition. The "sufficient" condition is the improvement in various domestic shortcomings that serve as a complement to resource inputs. The worst is that the "taking" of resources from the international community is used to protect an unstable, unpopular, or ineffective regime. The resources are then squandered, or siphoned into the hands of corrupt officials, and the consequence would be a larger national debt, but conditions in these countries remain unchanged or even deteriorate as there is no effective system or government that could provide a minimum level of public trust.

III EXPORT-LED VERSUS IMPORT SUBSTITUTION

One debate on growth and development is the alternative strategies of export-led versus import substitution industrialization (Kruger, 1985, 1990b; Krugman, 1984). Latin American countries in their industrialization process adopted import substitution, while East Asian economies followed an export-led strategy in most cases. Among the four East Asian economies, the South Korean and Taiwan economies are bigger than the economies of Singapore and Hong Kong. However, in terms of GDP per capita, Singapore and Hong Kong have a higher GDP per capita than both South Korea and Taiwan. Hong Kong and Singapore have taken up economic openness and an export-led strategy has been adopted. For a short while in the early 1950s, South Korea and Taiwan did follow the import substitution strategy. But soon, both realized that their economies were not growing as rapidly as Singapore and Hong Kong. Hence, beginning from early 1960s, South Korea and Taiwan changed and adopted the export-led approach. The Asian experience shows that economies adopting an export-led strategy had been more successful than countries adopting the import substitution strategy.

Import substitution is popular in economies with a large domestic market. For large economies, promoting local industries provided several advantages: employment creation, import reduction, and saving in foreign currency that reduced the pressure on foreign reserves. Furthermore, if the locally produced domestic goods are successful, the economy could even increase its exports. Hence, it can produce a "virtuous economic cycle" of increase in employment, output, income, exports, and foreign reserve, and a decrease in imports, giving an overall improvement in the economy's balance of trade and payments. Why did economies adopting import substitution not succeed in growth and development? The answer lies in the initial stage of the strategy. To promote local industries, capital and investment was needed. In economies with a shortage of foreign reserves and unattractive to foreign investment, the alternative would be government subsidies. The problem started from the fact that large government subsidies were given to establish the "infant industries," hoping that once the industries have "matured" government subsidies would no longer be needed. Hence, the initial phase of government subsidy was meant to provide an initial injection of capital.

When any development involves government subsidy, it would mean government intervention and interference, especially if officials were involved in the management. And since government subsidy was provided free, the manufacturing plant could experience loss, which would persist or even expand. Furthermore, the "loss-making" enterprise might not be market-oriented and with weak management, inefficiency, and ineffectiveness, the goods so produced might not be of good quality, or even might not inspire local confidence. Hence, even if the goods were manufactured locally, sales would be low and the protected firm would face losses. There could be more unfavorable consequences. Firstly, the government subsidies might end up causing fiscal deficit and national debt if the economy had not been growing, or a heavy welfare burden might erode the economy's fiscal ability. Secondly, in the process of producing locally, imports of raw materials and machinery would be needed. Hence, total imports might not fall, as import of the final goods was replaced by imports of intermediate goods. Thirdly, if local consumers did not have confidence in locally made manufactured goods, imports of the final goods would continue. In aggregate, the economy could even face an increase in imports in both final and intermediate goods. The increase in total imports could end up with a fall in foreign reserves, thereby adding pressure on the exchange rate to depreciate.

The "vicious cycle" began with government intervention in the form of subsidy. The problem with "infant industry" was firms were protected and losses were accepted. Relying on subsidies, the management may not be cost-minimizing, and "profit" would reduce the provision of free subsidy. In other words, once subsidy is provided, the "infant" firm may prefer to remain in the "comfort zone" so as to escape from competition. The worst would be that the uncompetitive firm might not be allowed to close, as that could have other undesirable consequences, such as rise in unemployment, political spillover, and so on. Eventually, these uncompetitive enterprises were maintained and subsidies continued. The economy was trapped in the weak side of the strategy.

Economies that take up the export-led strategy are usually small, knowing that the domestic market cannot support large industrial production, and export is the only alternative. Similarly, given that a small economy might not have sufficient funding in its initial development, to attract foreign capital, the economy would pursue business-friendly policies. Hence, from the start, the economy is prepared to provide a competitive environment, including a healthy fiscal framework, and allow maximum potential for investors. The advantage is that foreign investments often lead to exports. Thus, the export market would automatically be taken care of. And since foreign investors know what is demanded in their home country, exports from host countries would have no problem in locating foreign markets. Over the years, as income in host economies rose, local industrialists could also be nurtured. The more established pool of local industrialists would in turn venture into the foreign market by gradually building up brand names, lifting industrial production to a higher technological scale. In short, an export-led strategy produces a "virtuous cycle" that begins with the attraction of foreign investment, promotion of domestic industries, rise in employment, outcome, and exports. Trade surplus improves the exchange rate and international reserves. There can also be drawbacks in the export-led strategy. Firstly, the economy could become dependent on foreign investment and markets. Although exports are "guaranteed," economic recessions in foreign market could create economic volatility. Secondly, development of local industries may be discouraged, especially in the area of research and development (R&D). Hence, the economy may lag behind technologically, as the economy depends on imported technology.

Nonetheless, the export-led strategy of industrialization explains the success of the East Asian economies. Industrialization, however, has produced different results among the four economies. South Korea is probably the most successful in manufacturing industries, and development has passed the stages from light manufacturing to technologically intensive, to capital-intensive industries. For example, the production of such heavy industries as shipping and motor vehicles, and the use of technology in such manufacturing as mobile phones and household appliances has caught up considerably. South Korea has followed Japan's style of establishing brand names and design in technological products. Indeed, after the 1990s, when Japan experienced the "lost decade," some South Korean brand names have rapidly achieved a global status and competed with Japanese products.

Textiles and clothing are the traditional light manufacturing in all East Asian economies, but production has spread to other light manufacturing, such as toys, wigs, watches and clocks, and plastic flowers. One feature among these light industries is that they are not land-intensive industries, and production is possible in small factories. By the 1980s, electronics has increasingly become the dominant industry in the four East Asian economies. Similar to South Korea, Taiwan has also established brand names in computer production. However, small- and medium-sized enterprises constitute the largest group of enterprises in Taiwan, Singapore, and Hong Kong. Both Singapore and Hong Kong concentrated mostly in the production of electronics components and subcontracting. The flourishing electronics industry among East Asia economies has made the Asian region a primer in the market for electronics products.

IV PROGROWTH REGIMES

Western economies looked to the ideal of income equality, at the same time not admitting the fact that through education and training opportunities, society creates "inequality" as jobs require different skills and expertise, and receive different rewards. Hence, it is a social dilemma as the result of societal needs that produces income inequality. There is, however, a difference between economic inequality and social inequality. While income inequality arises due to individual endowments, social inequality could be artificial due to cultural beliefs, social norms, behavior and practice, historical and geographical constraints, and political orientations. Hence, it is the inequality of opportunity that is more restrictive and detrimental than income inequality. Another difference is that income inequality can be changed and improved if proper policies are instituted, but noneconomic inequality can be life-long and cross-generational, because the institutional settings are biased in the first instance.

The pursuit of income equality has not been a top priority in the development experience among East Asian economies. Instead, a progrowth attitude has been held with the sequential intentions of: (1) reduce poverty through self-motivation; (2) create employment through investment; (3) a "trickle down" effect over time so that the "have" pool expands; (4) improve appropriate infrastructure and social capital so that opportunities can be openly made available to all, thereby minimizing discrimination and bias; (5) establish macroeconomic stability to promote economic security; (6) economic security will eventually take care of social security; and (7) inequality is restricted only to income inequality that can be improved, while social inequality is eradicated. One is not arguing that such a "virtuous cycle" is leading to perfection. Indeed, there can always be economic mishaps and misfortunes, as unexpected situations arise or cases of problematic individuals are exposed, but with an improving and transparent system, things can only get better.

Although the role of government has varied among the four East Asian economies, a business-friendly government seems to have worked successfully. As compared to western economies, East Asian countries tended to have exhibited the following features: (1) a lower corporate and income tax to avoid disincentives; (2) minimize the need for welfare, putting more efforts into improving individual ability and endowment; (3) avoid large and prolonged fiscal deficits and government debts and a low public spending to GDP ratio; (4) liberalize markets and encourage foreign businesses and competition; (5) government expenditures focus on "supply-side" factors; (6) promote fairness, economic openness, and equality of opportunity; (7) identify and develop potential comparative or competitive advantages; and (8) provide macroeconomic stability, avoid crises, but assist the needy when necessary.

In a nutshell, it is important to have an effective and progressive government that puts priority on economic outcomes so that a bigger "economic pie" will have more to share, and avoid extreme political dichotomy. Government power should be dispersed, as Friedman (1993) pointed out, because that allows a greater degree of checks and balances, and participation in various government bodies by people from different walks of life will hasten civic development. The development of strong, effective, professional, and reliable civic institutions will serve as another useful social infrastructure in contemporary economies, as they practically provide another layer of protection between the government and the governed. Measured on a scale between most and least interventionist, Li (2002, p. 82) observed from the three situations in industrial development, fiscal and budgetary policy, and public utilities and infrastructure of the four East Asian economies, that during their period of industrialization and development Hong Kong was least interventionist, followed by Singapore, Taiwan, and South Korea. One feature in the industrialization of South Korea was the establishment of large corporations, known as "chaebol," and national resources were artificially geared to nurture success. Consequently, small- and medium-sized enterprises and small-scale industries in South Korea were not much favored in receiving bank loans in the 1960s and 1970s (Van Wijnbergen, 1985). On the contrary, small- and medium-sized enterprises are the more popular form of industrial organization in the other three economies.

Since the late 1970s when electronics was the major trend of industrial development in East Asia, one debate had been the need for government assistance in the form of R&D support. While Japan's model of a "business − academics − government" relationship was seen as helpful, there was a clear difference between Singapore, Taiwan, and South Korea on the one hand, and Hong Kong on the other hand. When judged by the amount of R&D expenditure as a percentage of GDP, Hong Kong is lowest with no more than 1% of GDP. The Hong Kong argument was reliance on the private market. R&D spending was highest in South Korea, followed by Taiwan and Singapore. It is true that the electronics industry in Hong Kong is weaker than the other three economies. But, because Hong Kong has diversified into other advantages, Hong Kong's GDP per capita has remained higher than both Taiwan and South Korea, though after 1997, Singapore has surpassed Hong Kong. Some industrialists have advocated for the "Silicon sea belt" in the development of the electronics industry that spreads from Japan, South Korea, Eastern China, Taiwan and Hong Kong to Singapore. One possible problem could be overconcentration on the electronics industry in these small East Asian economies, and the desire to restructure would be delayed should competition emerge from neighboring "latecomer" economies.

V SIEGE MENTALITY

While there was the issue of geopolitics in the economic success of East Asia, as they are all located at the doorstep of communist China, there is an inverse discussion on the encirclement thesis. Each of the four East Asian economies was faced with a certain degree of political uncertainty. Political uncertainty itself could be an instrument of success, as domestic stability was seen as necessary. "Prepare for the rainy days" could be the pushing force, as individuals and businesses would make use of the "remaining time" to do their best so that their returns, rewards, and assets would provide them with sufficient protection should "uncertainty" come eventually. To maintain stability, it would mean that the government would ensure law and order, businesses would make use of the situation for their advantage, while individuals would earn as much as possible. Consequently, unneeded disruptions were minimized, as the society had only one goal of "making the best possible."

The siege mentality is most visible in South Korea, as the threat of war from North Korea is constant and continuous. The "preparation for war" attitude has produced social cohesion, while industries are performing their best so as to build up the country's economic strength and political credibility. War preparation can also be seen from town planning. For example, in downtown Seoul, most streets contain a mixture of office buildings, retail shops and business outlets, and residential homes. The idea is that casualties would be minimized at different times of the day should a bomb be dropped. Typically, people work in the offices in the day time, but residents remain in their homes in the evening. As compared to downtown Tokyo or Hong Kong where neon lights flourish, neon lights in downtown Seoul, especially on the two sides of the river, are fewer and scattered, intended to avoid bombing targets in the night time.

In the early days after its independence, Singapore was faced with potential threats from neighboring economies with racial and political intentions. However, the Singapore economy progressed and soon served as headquarters to neighboring countries. Together with its multilingual government and multiracial society, modern Singapore is prepared to maintain economic competitiveness, becoming the most racially diverse economy in East Asia, with four official languages (English, Chinese, Indian, and Malay).

Since 1949, the Nationalist Government retreated to Taiwan, and in much of the 1950s and 1960s, the Nationalist Government had prepared to retake mainland China. The situation changed when the US President Nixon replaced Taiwan by China in the United Nations. Since then, there have been cautious but unfruitful talks on the "cross-strait" issues between Taipei and Beijing. Beijing considered Taiwan as a province, while the Taipei regime considered itself as a parallel to Beijing. Ultimately, the political divide could be restricted to the battle between the two parties (Nationalist Party and Communist Party), or even between two leaders (Mao Zedong and Chiang Kai-shek). Integration would have to imply that both sides would be prepared to accept each other politically, but it has been ruled out by the one-party system in China.

Prior to 1997, Hong Kong was a British colony, and there was clear political divide since 1949. However, the British government, especially the successive Hong Kong governors who were Sinologists, were willing to hand over Hong Kong back to China. As the Qing Dynasty ended in 1912, one could question the legitimacy communist China has on the deeds conducted by the Qing government. When China was admitted to the United Nations in the early 1970s, China declared its intention to recover all former colonized territories, but no Chinese territories were colonialized since 1949. In the Sino − British negotiation over the future of Hong Kong in 1982−84, China intended to take back sovereignty of the entire Hong Kong island when the lease of New Territories expired on June 30, 1997. As a parallel, however, China made no attempt to recover Vladivostok (Hǎishēnwǎi), acquired from the Qing Dynasty by Russia in 1860. China used the historic factor selectively, and ignored the legitimacy question.

Other than South Korea, the siege mentality in the other three East Asian economies has changed. A new Hong Kong Special Administrative Region (SAR) government was instituted in 1997, while a new political party in Taiwan has taken over the government in elections. The economic rise of China does not accompany political acceptability among the East Asian economies. Indeed, it was Mr. Lee Kuan Yew, the first prime minister of Singapore, who in a meeting with US President Obama in 2009 asked the United States "to strike a balance," as Mr. Lee said that "the size of China makes it impossible for the rest of Asia, including Japan and India, to match it in weight and capacity in about 20 to 30 years" (*Channel News Asia*, March 23, 2015). Effectively, Mr. Lee was asking the United States to "return to Asia," and that inspired President Obama to seek renewed access to Asia in the depths of the growing strength of China.

VI PROTECTED BY PROTECTIONISM

Textile and clothing has been the industry which production has "traveled" around different parts of the world. It was the "industrial revolution" in Great Britain in the 1800s that turned textile and clothing production into a modern manufacturing process. Subsequently, British textiles, especially production of woolen products from Lancashire in the north of England, had prospered and remained a major export. Due to specialization of industry and production, many cities in the United Kingdom concentrated on one or two industries, such as coal production in coal mining cities, and textiles in wool production regions. These "mono-industry" cities in Britain, however, became problematic once their industries suffered competition from other sources of supply. Hence, the rise of the industry benefitted the city, but the decline of the industry led to an economic slump in the city, as there was no alternative industry to absorb the labor force.

The rising cost of production and increasing role of the labor unions that bargained for more workers' benefits led to a loss of competitiveness to the cheaper Asian imports. After the Second World War, when the rise in the demand for textiles and clothing in the British market was faced with the growing welfare and trade union power, textile and clothing investors migrated to other parts of the world for production destinations. As the "pull and push" thesis argued, Asian economies became attractive, due to the lower cost and availability of a disciplined labor force. The textile and clothing products were exported back to the British market.

The low cost imports from East Asia gained competitiveness, but the slow pace of industrial restructuring in European cities resulted in a reduction in production, employment, and market shares. The loss of income, employment, and markets in Britain and Europe led to the need for trade protectionism that aimed to restrict Asian exports. The first protection legislation against exports of textiles from Hong Kong was the Lancashire Pack imposed by Great Britain in 1959 (Li, 1991). The Multifiber Agreement (MFA) launched in the early 1970s by Europe inserted a more comprehensive protectionist trade policy. The three phases of the MFA negotiation that spread across the entire 1970s into the early 1980s involved talks on import restrictions on East Asia. The protectionist instruments employed in the different phases of the MFA included the imposition of import tariffs, export dumping, quota restriction, and "voluntary restraint." Both import tariffs and export dumping involved price controls. The import tariffs raised the import price, thereby making imports less competitive to domestic production. Export dumping occurred when the domestic price in the exporting country was higher than its export price. Hence, the imposed import tariff was set equal to the difference between the home economy's domestic price and its export price, so that producers would have no advantage for their exports. Export dumping arises when domestic producers do not face much competition at home, and their "monopolistic" position enables them to charge a higher price. At the same time, the secured home market might provide the producers with a handsome return already, and the low export price could simply boost sales.

The cases of quota restriction and "voluntary restraint" worked on quantity restrictions. "Voluntary restraint" was based on the voluntary behavior of individual Asian economies in reducing their exports. In the case of quota control, each Asian economy was given a quota of exports, and a certain percentage of increase was added to the export quota in the following year. Li (1991) showed from the Hong Kong experience that the quota practically reflected the export capacity of the producers, and it was rare for Hong Kong exporters to achieve 100% of the quota. Export quotas were allocated to prospective producers, but in the case of Hong Kong, it was unfortunate that many large producers turned to become speculators, and "farmed out" their quota to smaller producers. It turned out that the quota actually reflected the capacity of the export producers. Hence, the East Asian manufacturers did not suffer much from the export quotas. On the contrary, when "newcomers" joined the competition, typically the Southeast Asian countries, China and India, the original exporters from East Asia were "protected by protectionism" because their export was "guaranteed" by the importers in Europe. Thus, the "newcomers" could not compete with the export quotas from the East Asian economies.

By the early 1980s, a new round of protectionism, known as "country of origin" (COO) was imposed, initially by the United States, and soon by European countries. The COO differed from the MFA in that producers could not have their exports produced in another low cost neighbor. Exports under the COO specified that exporters have to prove that a large percentage of their production was actually carried out in the home economy. It turned out that many producers upgraded their production by using new machinery and technology, such as computer-aided design, while the assembly work was minimized to satisfy the COO conditions. However, the COO and production across the border, in the case of Hong Kong, has led to a process of "deindustrialization" as exports from China became cheaper than similar production in Hong Kong, though Hong Kong producers have upgraded their markets to luxury and brand name items.

The COO was replaced by the conditions specified by the World Trade Organization (WTO) that from 1995, no restrictions would be imposed on production and exports of textile and clothing. That ended the decades of trade protection in textile and clothing production. Given that the technology of textile and clothing is labor-intensive, production has largely been taken up by newly emerging low cost countries, such as Vietnam and India in Asia. Thus, the production of textiles and clothing has been internationalized, and that it has traveled through various countries as the cost of production changes. Nonetheless, textile and clothing manufacture has always served as the initial stage of industrialization in developing countries.

VII LESSONS OF ASIAN FINANCIAL CRISIS

Since the early 1970s, East Asia and Southeast Asia had enjoyed a period of stability, as their export demand was growing constantly, and despite periodic occurrences of crises and recessions around the world, Asian economies were simply responding to the events in the world market. The World Bank (1993) and Woronoff (1986) have summarized Asia's economic performance as a "miracle." Few would surmise that a financial crisis would erupt in Asia, as their exports were doing well. Starting from the mid-1980s, two trends could have disrupted their exports: the emergence of China since the 1980s as an export center, because foreign investors utilized its low labor cost of production; the Chinese currency, the Renminbi, had devalued by 30% in January 1994, thereby making investment in China attractive. This is the "substitution effect." Given that the volume of world exports and foreign investment was fixed in the short-term, the foreign investment that had gone to China would mean less was invested in other Asian economies. Similarly, what China exported would mean less was exported from other Asian economies. There could be some truth in this argument, as China's light manufacturing export production competed directly with other Southeast Asian economies.

The other trend shown in the export statistics among Asian countries related to the export of electronics, typically computers. By the mid-1990s, a number of East and Southeast Asian economies were manufacturing computers and semiconductors. In particular, there were different versions of Microsoft Windows, such as "Windows 1995" and "Windows 1997." Each version of "Windows" contained additional technological gimmicks that attracted consumers. However, exports were fine when "Windows 1995" was released, but when consumers expected the next version to emerge, demand for export would probably have slackened, and that could contribute to export volatility. This was exactly what happened to South Korea, Thailand, and Indonesia, whose exports fell drastically in 1996. Unfortunately, the export shock coexisted with a low level of international reserves in these three economies. Their currencies also remained strong in the early 1990s, due to their buoyant exports.

Numerous studies have documented the sequence, events, and explanations of the Asian financial crisis (Stiglitz, 1996; Eichengreen et al., 1998; Krugman, 1998; Radelet and Sachs, 1998a, 1998b; Corsetti et al., 1999). Li (2002) detailed the unfolding of the Asian financial crisis that began on July 2, 1997, with speculation on the Thai baht. The situation spread to Indonesia and South Korea, who had low international reserves. A number of key financial institutions collapsed in Seoul. Similar currency speculations appeared in Malaysia, thereby raising pressure on other economies, typically Singapore. A number of stock markets in Asia slumped, generating shocks in the financial and currency markets. The Hong Kong currency was being pursued by speculators in the first quarter of 1998. When the Hong Kong currency was attacked and the stock market tumbled in the first quarter of 1998, Hong Kong's financial economy was at the brink of collapse until the government, in May 1998, deployed a massive amount of reserve funds to buy up a large chunk of shares in the Hong Kong stock market. It was then currency and stock speculators were deterred, as they suffered huge losses. Hong Kong was rescued from the Asian financial crisis, but the failing industrial structure and shrinking real economy could not provide sustainability when the financial economy collapsed (Li, 2006, 2012a).

The Japanese economy had been in recession since the early 1990s, but held a large amount of US bonds. The stagnation of the Japanese economy since the early 1990s also slowed down growth in other Asian economies. Prior to November 1997, a few key Japanese banks and financial institutions suffered huge debts and closed down eventually. It was believed that these large institutions would be "too large to fail," but their large debt burden ultimately brought them down. Li (2002) also pointed to the relevance of the meeting in November 1997 between Japanese Prime Minister Ryutaro Hashimoto and US President Bill Clinton. When President Clinton remarked that Japan should look for solutions "domestically," investors and speculators in the financial market panicked, thinking that Japan would withdraw funds from US financial institutions. To prepare for Japan's withdrawal, US financial institutions began in advance to withdraw funds from the rest of the world, and the freer financial markets in the Asian region ended up like "automatic telling machines." As statistics showed, Japan did not withdraw funds from the United States, and by 1999, US financial institutions reinvested their funds back into the Asian markets, generating a V-shape movement in the stock market and GDP in most Asian economies between 1997 and 1999.

There are two schools of thought in the theoretical explanations to the Asian financial crisis (Li, 2002). The "fundamental-based" hypothesis argued that there was "bad equilibrium" in many Asian economies, and their drop in exports was not dealt with in an appropriate manner. These loopholes resulted in a "hard landing," when speculators took advantage of these weaknesses. There were "unnoticed changes," involving deterioration in macroeconomic fundamentals. The structural imbalances triggered currency speculation and crisis. Once started, the financial market overreacted, and the subsequent herding behavior caused exchange rate and asset prices to plunge severely. Consequently, there was the "beggar-thy-neighbor" competitive devaluation among the Asian currencies. Other "unnoticed" changes included excessive investment in risky and unprofitable projects that had arisen due to political pressure to growth. There could be the problem of moral hazard among financial institutions and loan officers. In addition, there was accumulation of short-term foreign-currency denominated debt, and there was a mismatch between short-term and long-term loans, resulting in cash-flow problems.

The "financial panic" hypothesis argued that financial overshoots created panic in one market, and the subsequent contagion spread to neighboring markets. It was a "panic" because the crisis was not predicted. Although there were warnings arising from Thailand and South Korea, exports from Indonesia, Malaysia, and the Philippines were fine. Indonesia was hardest hit, but its current account deficit was not the worst. Yet the meltdown of Indonesia was far more severe than expected, due probably to the multiple dimensions of religious, ethnic, territorial, and political problems. The other causes of the "panic" came from the increasing size of nonperforming loans, and lending not protected by state guarantees. The sudden withdrawal of funds from the region served as the "last straw."

These two hypotheses are related to each other, as poor economic fundamentals that produced a "bad equilibrium" would soon lead to market overreaction that generated financial panic, which in turn took its own course to generate a crisis. In a sense, the two hypotheses explained the different stages of the financial crisis, though it probably was the poor economic fundamentals that caused the market overshoot, followed subsequently by panic and contagion. In addition, the herd behavior played a role, as the interdependence among currencies and financial markets in the region resulted in instant transmissions.

The International Monetary Fund (IMF) has outlined a number of indicators as a safeguard against future financial crises (Kaminsky et al., 1998). The economic indicators included the level of international reserves, real exchange rate, domestic credit, inflation, trade balance, money growth rates, fiscal deficits, and national debts. Identifying certain thresholds in these indicators should signal to economies in advance. In the case of Indonesia and South Korea, the IMF encouraged these two economies to pursue sound economic policies and liberalize their trade and investment. The IMF recommendations to Indonesia, South Korea, and Thailand included a substantial rise in interest rates to stop the downward spiral of currency depreciation, closure of nonviable financial institutions, and restructuring according to internationally accepted accounting practice. Changes were required in business practice, corporate culture, and governance behavior. To maintain a sustainable balance of payment, the IMF's usual recipe was fiscal reduction in public expenditure and unprofitable investment projects.

The Asian financial crisis reflected that, other than the IMF, all the affected Asian economies had to find their own solutions. South Korea suffered most as its currency devaluated. However, as South Korea has a strong industrial base, many industries were sold to foreign corporations in the few years after 1997. Since the Asian financial crisis, South Korea has learned the importance of a large reserve, industrial upgrading in terms of product design, and international markets. A few South Korean brands are now capturing the world market with designs competitive to other world brands. The case of South Korea showed the importance of the real sector, which could rescue the economy in times of financial crisis. With the strong real economy, employment could be maintained, and the industries could invite foreign investment.

Other Asian economies have also recovered and their exports picked up. The Asian financial crisis produced a short-term shock, but the long-term economic wound could be seen from the need for economic and industrial restructuring in order to widen their economic base. Although electronics has been a success in many Asian economies, their concentration on the electronics industry produced narrowness once a new competitor emerged. In other words, the economics of "push and pull" also applied to the more advanced Asian economies. The drive to industrial restructuring took time to realize, as it requires new investment and the creation of new comparative advantages.

VIII SINGAPORE: A "SUPPLY-DRIVEN" ECONOMY

The economy of Singapore will always be associated with Mr. Lee Kuan Yew, the leader that led Singapore to gain political and sovereign independence from Malaysia in August 1965, even though both Malaysia and Singapore were British colonies. Although Lee Kuan Yew maintained that ethnic Chinese be the majority race in Singapore, Singapore has fostered the development of neighboring economies in Southeast Asia. Due to historical, cultural, and political reasons, ethnic Chinese who migrated to various Southeast Asia economies in past centuries settled and focused on trading and businesses, hence making them the more prosperous group of people in these countries. Unfortunately, instead of embracing the ethnic Chinese businesses and integrating them into the indigenous economy, ethnic Chinese had at times been the scape-goat for problems, typically in issues such as ethnic inequality and business achievement. For example, ethnic clashes occurred on different occasions in Malaysia and Indonesia (*The Washington Post*, August 18, 2012; *The Malay Mail Online*, September 17, 2015; and *The Wall Street Journal*, September 30, 2015).

As a result of the relative instability in other Southeast Asian countries, the stability of Singapore became the magnet that pulled both physical and human capital from other Southeast Asian countries. Hence, Singapore's stability turned out to be an asset for development. The inflow of free capital and people from the neighboring region aided Singapore's growth. Certainly, the economic policies that Lee Kuan Yew had adopted were most crucial, as discussed and reported in numerous studies, including his own publications (Lee, 2012; Barr, 2000; Lim, 2016). Being a small but flexible and dynamic economy, it was wise to adopt an open economic policy that allowed the economy to move along with the international economy, and strengthen domestic infrastructure through investment in human capital, public housing, and health, so as to reduce poverty and promote opportunities. Singapore cannot be regarded as a welfare economy, but the government has helped to reduce people's "survival costs" by the provision of government-aided housing, as that reduced the burden of the single most expensive household item.

By the 1980s, the growing importance of electronics, together with oil refinery, meant exports kept rising (Rao and Lee, 1995). The Singapore government intervened in industrial development through the provision of industrial land, and expenditure on R&D (Grice and Drakakis-Smith, 1985). The small nature of the Singapore economy means that the domestic market is small, and it would be difficult to promote domestic corporates. As a result, the Singapore economy became dependent on foreign investment, which proved to be problematic when world recession hurt the Singapore economy, such as the situation in 1985 when the international oil crisis that resulted in world economic recession led to a severe fall in foreign investment to Singapore (Chee, 1986; Rigg, 1988).

Since 1985, the Singapore government realized its economic weakness. The government promoted "government-linked corporations" (GLCs) in businesses by establishing large corporations to promote development and banking stability. The intention was to provide an alternative to foreign investment as a reliable and sustainable source of domestic investment (Low, 2002). Over the years, oil refinery and electronics comprised no less than 60% of Singapore's exports. In order to expand its economic capacity, economic widening and industrial promotion are needed. Since the 1990s, the new roles Singapore has developed include financial services and serving as the business headquarters for foreign corporations investing in Southeast Asia and West Asia. Its multilingual nature has made Singapore a metropolitan city. Racial equality and eradication of discrimination has added another asset to the Singapore economy. Singapore's movement from "the third to the first world" has served as a blueprint to neighboring economies. Indeed, with the restoration of macroeconomic stability in other Southeast Asian countries and the expected rise of such countries as India and Cambodia, Singapore is ready to serve and benefit from the development of neighboring countries.

Singapore's success counts a lot on its pursuit of "supply-driven" economic policies. To its neighbors and the international community, Singapore is always there to serve and to promote, rather than to threaten, conquer, and exploit. Hence, "supply-driven" policies have strengthened Singapore's domestic economy and produced "positive-sum" outcomes for countries that utilize Singapore both as a destination of investment and as an intermediary in conducting business in the Southeast and West Asia. As Singapore is a small country and does not pose any political, territorial, or religious threats to its neighbors, the "supply-driven" economic policies produce the most effective, workable, and long-lasting economic strategy for Singapore. Indeed, while Singapore's success serves as a reference to neighboring economies, the "supply-driven" economic policies have in turn served as reference to Singapore's own future development.

The "Lee Kuan Yew legacy" has probably become the only suitable and optimal ideology that Singapore can pursue. Indeed, it is only the deepening of these "supply-driven" policies that can keep Singapore competitive, though there is always the need to promote new comparative advantages. For example, focusing on industrial development and the real economy would be more preferable than promotion of such "demand-driven" services as tourism and retail outlets. Similarly, focusing on job creation is more preferable than welfare provision. Promotion of business-friendliness is more important than redistribution through a high tax regime. In a nutshell, a small and effective government is all that Singapore needs.

Like any other economy, Singapore is also faced with a number of challenges. One is the usual problem of full capacity and the direction of economic restructuring. Electronics, oil refinery, and financial services are the key "comparative advantages" Singapore has possessed for decades. A number of East Asian economies have become educational and medical service hubs, in addition to tourism and the development of theme parks. With its ethnic diversity, Singapore can easily become an educational and training hub for its Southeast and West Asia neighbors. This requires an increase in cooperation with all neighboring economies, and regional integration can go beyond industry and services, but include development in infrastructures.

Geopolitics can be another challenge to the Singapore economy. While Singapore leads in Southeast Asia, the challenge posed by the rise of China's economic and ideological differences is increasing. For example, should China be involved in the construction of the shipping canal through the Kra Isthmus in southern Thailand, Singapore would lose out, as ocean liners would no longer need to pass through the Straits of Malacca (*The Diplomat* , December 1, 2013; and *Channel News Asia*, May 19, 2015). The growing political and military pressure in the South China Sea between China and the three ASEAN countries of Indonesia, Vietnam, and the Philippines could spark off into a regional military conflict, and the stability and geopolitical position of Singapore could be disrupted. Indeed, Singapore was warned not to interfere in the disputes in the South China Sea (*South China Morning Post*, August 16, 2016). With China's growing military might and deployment of "cheque book diplomacy," different ASEAN members may hold different attitudes to China. Singapore should have an "early bird" attitude and policy in handling the geopolitical issue and its relationship with China along with other ASEAN members.

IX SOUTH KOREA: STAYING COMPETITIVE

Since the end of the Korean War in 1952 that ideologically divided Korea into the capitalist South Korea and the communist North Korea, South Korea has constantly remained alert to potential wars and conflicts with North Korea. Nonetheless, the economic modernization in South Korea dates back to the early 1950s when President Park Chung-hee insisted on turning South Korea into an export giant, by promoting and concentrating resources in establishing large corporations (Clifford, 1998; Kim, 2004, 2011). The "big is beautiful" attitude led to the concentration of bank loans geared to the development and expansion of the "chaebols" in ship building, motor vehicles, household appliances, and electronics (Amsden, 1989). South Korean exports all through the 1960s–80s were not popular, as consumers regarded the designs and quality as not comparable to Japanese products. Nonetheless, the domestic market was sufficiently large to absorb domestic production.

The leverage of the industrial "chaebols" would mean that small- and medium-sized enterprises (SMEs) would not have the same access to bank resources, resulting in the gradual development of the informal financial market in which SMEs would borrow at a much higher interest rate. Furthermore, the large corporations also gave rise to strong labor unions, and labor militancy tended to be strong. By the 1990s, there emerged clearly a few "chaebols" that captured world attention, especially when the decline in Japanese exports coincided with the rise of South Korean designs. South Korean brands eventually earned a place in the world market.

However, as the debts of "chaebols" grew over the years, the "big is beautiful" attitude soon replaced by the "too big to fail" thinking that South Korean corporations would be bailed out by the government. Failure of "chaebols" was thought not to be an option until the Asian financial crisis in 1997, as the closure of a few key financial institutions ended up in a debt crisis. The South Korean economy does not provide strong welfare support, as resources have been geared to military expenditure, the strong Confucian culture holds that aging parents would be taken care of by their offspring, and a good education for the young generation would ensure economic security. The South Korean economy was severely hurt during the Asian financial crisis. Rescue came when foreign investment poured into South Korea buying up industrial plants and brand names.

The economic lessons of the Asian financial crisis exposed the South Korean economy in a number of directions. While the government has favored the "chaebols" for decades, the concern was the extent of government intervention in the economy. The "chaebols" are effectively huge monopolies that dominated industrial progress, R&D spending, and human capital absorption (Lim, 1998). The South Korean economy depended on the survival of the "chaebols," but the economy might not be sustainable should crisis erupt if the difficulty faced by the "chaebols" could not be alleviated by other forms of enterprise. In other words, the over-concentration of resources in large corporates implied economic narrowness. As the South Korean currency depreciated after the Asian financial crisis, foreign investments were attracted by the competitive nature of many South Korean industries, and a number of South Korean brand names came under foreign ownership. With the revival of exports from South Korea since the turn of the 21st century, industries in the South Korean economy have caught up considerably. The Asian financial crisis did produce incentives that led to new designs and R&D development in South Korean industries. The increase in export sales and expansion in foreign markets have boosted production in South Korea, helping the economy to revive speedily. South Korea has indeed become a medium-sized industrialized giant that has diversified into various forms of capital-intensive and technology-intensive manufacturing.

The two issues that South Korea faces are how to stay competitive, and finding a political solution with North Korea. Although South Korea has achieved a sizable world market, exports are concentrated in a few brand names, typically in electronics and in motor vehicles. These are volatile markets, as consumers' taste and designs can change, and emergence of new products may compete with South Korean products. How to stay competitive among Japanese, German, and American products should be the biggest concern. In the short run, a good marketing strategy could be an answer. In the long run, new designs and further commercialization of technology could maintain the market gimmick. The more challenging question would be the lack of South Korean brand names. Although it would take years, if not decades, to build up a brand name, it could be a long-term comparative advantage building strategy for South Korea to expand into new products and new brand names, bearing in mind that there are other emerging new brand names.

The political relationship with North Korea has been sensitive. Although South Korea, especially since the 1980s, has developed into a fully democratic political system, and domestic conflicts could largely be contained through elections, the relationship with North Korea is multifaceted, as it involves ideological, military, technological, and territorial conflicts, as well as regional and international relations. At the international level, the issue is not only between South Korea and North Korea, but between China on the one hand, and Japan and the United States on the other. The North Korean economy is not only communistic, but is also dynastic and unpredictable. While the South Korean economy is industrialized, advanced, and democratic, and has been accepted by the international community, North Korea is primitive, underdeveloped, patriarchical, and facing material shortages. The economic gap between South Korea and North Korea would only expand as the South Korean economy advanced. The remaining instrument North Korea had was the exercise of military and nuclear threats. Indeed, military engagement in traditional warfare may not be enough when North Korea remains aggressive in imposing threats to South Korea and other regions. The experience of past communist countries, such as the Soviet Union, East Germany, and Cuba, showed that political and economic backwardness and material shortage, coupled with excessive military engagement, would in a matter of time, led to collapse of the regime. Nonetheless, the positive side of the siege mentality in South Korea is to maintain the status quo, but at the same time promote and strengthen the economy as much as possible so as to create stability within South Korea.

X TAIWAN: A NEW CHAPTER IN DEVELOPMENT

The modern Taiwanese economy dates back to 1949, when the Nationalist regime retreated from mainland China to the island. Other than postwar aid from the United States, the notable economic policy introduced by the Nationalist government was land reform in the 1950s and 1960s (Koo, 1968; Cheung, 1969; Yang, 1970). The previous land system created conflict between the landlords who owned the agricultural land, and the peasants who worked for the landlords. The agricultural land reform involved the tripartite relationship between the government, landlords, and peasants. The landlords were encouraged to give up their land, but in turn become industrialists. The peasants took over the land from the landlords, and became farmers of their own. Those peasants who did not prefer to remain in the rural areas could migrate to the urban areas to become industrial workers. The threefold outcome was that firstly the "landlord – peasant" conflict was removed, and secondly the peasants were content to have their own land, while the landlords became industrialists who invested their assets in manufacturing. This land reform process introduced industrialization into the Taiwanese economy.

There were other economic modernization milestones in Taiwan, including the "Ten Major Construction Projects" and "Twelve New Development Projects" in the 1970s involving development in highways, electrification, railways, airports, container ports, shipyards, steel factories, oil refinery and nuclear plants, and industrial parks. These economic accelerations led to double digit growth rates in Taiwan, and expansion to foreign exchange reserves ranked high internationally. By the 1970s, the Taiwanese economy, along with the other three East Asian economies, became a "newly industrializing economy" (NIEs), as industrialization and exports led to a rise in income and output. Taiwan's traditional comparative advantage was light manufacturing exports in the 1960s and 1970s, but the rise of the electronics industry in the 1980s led to expansion in Taiwan's industries, especially in computing. Given that Taiwan is not a large economy geographically, development in technology-intensive or skill-intensive industries is more preferred to land-intensive industries.

The 1980s and 1990s were the golden era of the Taiwanese economy, as its growing exports led to accumulation of large international reserves, and a New Taiwan Dollar currency was introduced in 2000. Taiwanese industrialists began to invest first in other parts of Southeast Asia, but by the turn of the century, mainland China has become the prime destination for Taiwan's outward investment, though it was argued that Taiwan's investment in mainland China would ease the resources for new domestic investment in Taiwan (Chen and Kan, 1997). Small- and medium-sized enterprises formed the majority of Taiwanese businesses. The Taiwan government does commit fiscal expenditures on industrial R&D, but the scale is much lower than that of Japan and South Korea.

The lack of foreign investment has to do partly with the declining international role that Taiwan faces, as Taiwan lost its seat to mainland China in the United Nations. Since then, Taiwan has been faced with a "two-front" political pressure from mainland China across the strait, and from within Taiwan. Packaged in the "Nixon – Kissinger initiative" (see Section III in Chapter 15), the complicated diplomatic relationship between the United States, China, and Taiwan led to the US pledging for a "one China policy" in 1972, which, according to the US State Department, states that "Chinese on both sides of the Taiwan Strait maintain that there is only one China and that Taiwan is a part of China." Beijing acknowledges that "the American people will continue to carry on commercial, cultural, and other unofficial contacts with the people of Taiwan." Implicitly, the United States acknowledges that the territories are governed by two separate and legitimate governments. Such a diplomatic outcome enabled Taiwan to maintain its status quo.

Over the years, the United States has stood firm on the grounds for "peaceful integration" between Beijing and Taipei, but the ideological difference is huge, as neither side is prepared to give in. Beijing claims that Taiwan is only one province of China, while Taipei sees the two governments as parallel and equal. To Beijing, the "one China policy" effectively meant that countries seeking diplomatic relations with mainland China must break official relations with Taiwan. Thus, countries that recognized Taiwan could only see Taiwan as the sole legitimate representative of all of China, and not just the island of Taiwan. On the contrary, countries that recognized China would see China as the legitimate representative of Taiwan, or acknowledge China's view on the policy ("One-China Policy," *Wikipedia*). Such a diplomatic practice by Beijing has limited Taiwan's external relationships considerably. This has economic repercussions, as foreign investment to Taiwan may not be that forthcoming, while Taiwan exports may not be that favorable. The economic rise of China certainly has caused substitution effects in the Taiwanese economy. In the 1992 Consensus between Beijing and Taipei, the "one China policy" was modified to become "one China principle" which insisted that both mainland China and Taiwan are "inalienable parts of a single China." Under the 1992 Consensus, both governments agreed that there was only one sovereign state, but disagreed about which of the two governments was the legitimate government of the Chinese state. However, the 1992 Consensus has been criticized and opposed by some sections of the Taiwanese people, who saw Taiwan as a different entity ("One-China Policy," *Wikipedia*).

Domestically, although Chiang Kai-Shek was succeeded by his son Chiang Ching-kuo, who served as the Premier of the Republic of China between 1972 and 1978, and was the president of the Republic of China from 1978 until his death in 1988, China Ching-kuo followed authoritarian rule ("Chiang Ching-kuo," *Wikipedia*). However, before passing the power to his successor, Lee Teng-hui, Chiang Ching-kuo became more open and tolerant of political dissent, and actually relaxed state controls on the media and allowed native Taiwanese to enter the government. On July 15, 1987, Chiang Ching-kuo finally ended martial law and allowed cross-strait visits. This was followed by the gradual loosening of political control, and opponents were no longer forbidden to hold meetings. The opposition Democratic Progressive Party (DPP), which was supposed to represent indigenous interests, was formally established on September 28, 1986, thereby ending the one-party authoritarian regime in Taiwan. Political freedom in Taiwan soon turned into democracy, and the popularity of the DPP exerted pressure on the Nationalist party. Over the years, the political trends between the two parties in Taiwan were such that, on the one hand, as Beijing worried that the DPP who represented Taiwan's younger generation might not choose to integrate with mainland China, but on the other hand, the Nationalist's loss of political influence in Taiwan began to soften and narrowed their stand with Beijing. Hence, while the Nationalist party had been anti-Beijing since 1949, the emergence and growing influence of DPP since the 1990s has turned the Nationalist party to become pro-Beijing. Indeed, Beijing definitely saw its difference with DPP was bigger than with the Nationalist.

The DPP first experienced political power when Chen Shui-bian, a native-born lawyer, was elected to be the president of the Republic of China for two terms from 2000 to 2008, thereby ending the 50 years of political control by the Nationalist party ("Chen Shui-bian," *Wikipedia*). However, the Taiwanese economy under Chen turned from bad to worse. Firstly, Beijing's diplomatic "isolation" of Taiwan continued, and while most world economies kowtowed to Beijing, external economic relations between Taiwan and the international community narrowed further. Secondly, the Chen government was found to be corrupt and manipulative. Distrust of Chen's government grew, and in the meantime, Taiwan's domestic economy suffered.

The Nationalist Party returned to govern Taiwan under the presidency of Ma Ying-jeou for the period 2008—16. Although President Ma did reassert and claim that the Nationalist government is the legitimate government of all of China in October 2008, President Ma's economic policy proved to have favored the Taiwanese businesses who invested in mainland China at the expense of domestic jobs and economic opportunities in Taiwan. His "one-sided" economic policy upset the Taiwanese people, especially the young generation who saw that the Nationalist government was becoming outdated as it was controlled mainly by the party elders. Effectively, the Taiwan economy was marginalized and people's livelihoods suffered. It was reported in 2012 that the popularity of President Ma, according to the TVBS Poll Center, had plummeted to a record low of 13%. *The Economist* commented that "a former heartthrob losses his shine" and that "Mr. Ma is an ineffective bumbler" (*The Economist*, November 17, 2012).

Instead of looking for more decisive actions to rescue the economy, various domestic economic issues have not been able to lift Taiwan from its economic sluggishness. Getting close to the mainland economy would not only be "one-way traffic," where Taiwanese industrial investment went to mainland China, the over-concentration in the mainland economy could mean economic narrowness and lack of diversity. President Ma's unpopularity led to disappointment within the party. In the meantime, Beijing provided a helping hand to President Ma by exercising the typical "people's strategy" of sending large numbers of tourists to Taiwan, hoping that will boost Taiwan's tourism. On the verge of losing the election to the DPP in January 2016, Taiwan's Ma Ying-jeou managed to arrange a historic meeting with Beijing's Xi Jingping in Singapore on November 7, 2015 ("2015 Ma — Xi Meeting," *Wikipedia*.). Although the Ma — Xi meeting was the first between the two leaders of the two sides of the Taiwan Strait since 1949, Taiwan voters were not impressed, as they saw the Nationalist party getting too close to Beijing. Eventually, the DPP's lady candidate, Tsai Ing-wen, won the election on January 16, 2016.

There are both political and economic challenges facing President Tsai. Politically, given Beijing's international influence, and the growing uncertainties in the South China Sea with some Southeast Asian countries, how Tsai can cultivate her policy with Beijing would be given high priority politically. Domestically, although the DPP has the majority, it still has to work with the Nationalist party. Economically, Taiwan needed a new injection of capital to revive the economy with new opportunities, jobs, and vitality. A tripartite relationship involving the "private sector—government—foreign investors" strategy would produce feasible results. The domestic private sector should be encouraged to conduct indigenous investments to boost employment and output, especially since small- and medium-sized enterprises are the largest group of businesses in Taiwan. Secondly, the government could engage more in infrastructure and civic development, including the establishment of an anticorruption body to ensure a clean government and systemic transparency. Infrastructure investment should include updating and upgrading of various construction projects, such as designs in earthquake-resistant buildings or typhoon-protected coastlines, to improve people's livelihood and security. The third dimension is to encourage foreign investments to Taiwan, especially investments from Japan and the United States. Given its advances in some aspects of technology, and because production costs in Taiwan have remained relatively low compared to neighboring economies, Taiwan can regain its industrial strength and its export industry can be revitalized without much difficulty.

In short, improvements in business-friendliness, a sound fiscal framework supplemented by various "supply-side" instruments, and focus on the real economy would be the "sure-win" policy to reenergize the Taiwanese economy. The decade of relying on the mainland economy should not be seen as the only choice. With the new government, the minimum would be to avoid the mistakes of former regimes, while the maximum would be to steer the Taiwanese economy to new development heights. The Taiwanese economy has been left in recession for some years, but it is also the golden opportunity for the new government to introduce effective policies. The "bad" time can become the "good" time when "supply-side" economic policies are successfully introduced and executed.

XI CONCLUSION

The doctrine of "economism" is used by Li (2002) in analyzing the economic success of the East Asian economies in the decades since the Second World War. The features in the doctrine include progrowth, openness, laissez-faire, dynamic comparative advantage, and a "back-seat" government. However, most East Asian economies were faced with changes and challenges since the late 1990s. There was the Asian financial crisis that was short-lived, but a number of East Asian economies were exposed to structural weakness. Japan's "lost decade" as the 1990s economic recession was extended to the first decade of the new century was significant. The South Korean economy was hit hard, but foreign investment came to its rescue. Both Hong Kong and Taiwan are faced with the challenge from mainland China.

The rapid emergence of China as a regional economy has led to new calculations among Asian economies, especially whether China would serve as an "economic complement" or a "competitive substitute" in the development of other Asian economies. The good news is that virtually all East Asian economies have come to an advanced stage of development, suggesting that they have their own system and infrastructure that can battle the ups and downs in the economic swing. However, East Asian economies would not be immune to economic recession, and long-term structural change would be required in order to develop new comparative advantages. The "prepare for the rainy days" mentality is still relevant in ensuring the next phase of development among Asian economies. Complacency does not have a place in market economies in Asia.

The neoclassical school of economic thought, in which economic development relies firstly on appropriate domestic provisions, has to be fully adopted and implemented by successful market economies in East Asia. The more "homework" an economy has done in terms of promoting effective "supply-side" policies, the more likely the economy can attract foreign investment and trade that eventually results in establishing a "virtuous cycle" in development. Such an approach generates a number of positive outcomes. Most Asian economies prefer not to accumulate large fiscal debts, to avoid imposing unnecessary burdens on their future generation. A balanced budget would provide the signal of a healthy government and a sound fiscal policy. All these are pivotal in pulling external resources into the domestic economy, and at the same time not encourage local resources to depart.

Prior to the Asian financial crisis, there was the discussion of the "Pacific Century" where the capitalist market economies on both sides of the Pacific Ocean would, in the 21st century, be the focus of world development, as economic success among capitalist economies in the Pacific region emerges in different waves with one after another. Capitalism has shown its best in the Pacific region. In turn, the successful market economies have been serving as lessons for others. Economic development is both dynamic and relative. It is dynamic because there is no such thing as perfection, but only improvement and progress. It is relative because economic activities always produce nonequal outcomes, with one activity producing a better outcome than another. Economic progress is often made on an unequal basis, but is acceptable provided outcomes allow upward movements. Different economic outcomes in Asia would not be considered as a source of conflict, so long as there is enlargement in the economic pie.

The Latecomers: Opportunities, Challenges, and Comparisons

I INTRODUCTION

As argued in the "flying geese" model, the economic rise of Japan provided resources to neighboring economies to also rise. The first group of "geese" that lifted off economically consisted of the East Asian economies of South Korea, Taiwan, Singapore, and Hong Kong after the 1970s. The war between North and South Vietnam in much of the 1960s led to the worry that communism would spread to other countries in Southeast Asia, typically Singapore, Thailand, Malaysia, Indonesia, and the Philippines. At the height of the Vietnam War in 1967, these five countries then established the Association of Southeast Asian Nations (ASEAN) that was meant to provide political affiliations.

Economically, with the exception of Singapore, these Southeast Asian countries did not have much to offer, because their level of development remained low in the 1960s. With similarities in their economic structures, the other four Southeast Asian countries could not exercise economic complementarity. With the end of the Vietnam War in April 1975, Vietnam's socialist economy suffered as it was "isolated" by the international community. Although Sweden was the first western country to establish a diplomatic relationship with Vietnam and exchanged embassies in June 1970, it was only in 1986 with the policy of "Doi Moi" (renovation) that a market economy was adopted gradually. With stability restored, and at the same time the economic rise of East Asian "geese," a "showcase" and references for the ASEAN countries was developed. With the rapid growth in Singapore, the other ASEAN countries determined to be the next group of "geese" that would join the growth ladder.

At the beginning, ASEAN was not that much of an economic association, but its bonds actually expanded to incorporate other new members within Southeast Asia, such as Brunei Darussalam, Cambodia, Laos PDR, Myanmar, and Vietnam. Hence, although ASEAN is not that strong, ASEAN does comprise a sizable region in Southeast Asia on both the supply and demand sides of the economic equation. On the supply side, ASEAN

© 2017 Elsevier Inc. All rights reserved.

provides a good source of labor and can become the destination for production of light manufacturing. On the demand side, the rise in income and the sizable population provide a good market for consumer goods.

While ASEAN was getting ready to welcome the third batch of Asian "geese," the situation changed rapidly when China's low production costs posed direct competition to ASEAN countries. By the 1990s, growth and exports among ASEAN countries had been maintained, but the Asian financial crisis in 1997 – 98 shocked ASEAN as the crisis came suddenly and unexpectedly. Although the IMF and international institutions provided rescue and recommendations, ASEAN member countries managed to tread through the Asian financial crisis and revitalize their economies through further industrial and export expansion. However, some ASEAN members engaged in economic restructuring, but others have been challenged by noneconomic problems, such as frequent changes of government and calls for elections in Thailand, continuous ethnic problems in Malaysia, and religious and ethnic disputes in Indonesia. The high energy price has weakened the exports of ASEAN members, such as Vietnam, as their exchange rates have been constrained by oil imports.

The Southeast Asian countries have to perform and position themselves differently from such emerging countries as India, Brazil, Mexico, and South Africa. Other than the environmental and geographical advantages, such as the close geographical proximity to China, conventional investment from Japan, and traditional relationship with the United States, the Southeast Asian countries are comparatively "better off" than other emerging countries. For example, religious problems in Southeast Asia are milder than similar problems in the Middle East countries. The overall education level is higher than other "fragile states" in Africa, and the wider use of English makes it easier to connect with the international community (Lim, 2009; Plummer, 2009; Rosefielde et al., 2011; Whally, 2016). However, while there are favorable "take-off" conditions, their success will depend on the exercise of indigenous factors, such as stability, human capital, business-friendliness, infrastructure, and other social fabrics that make them attractive to foreign investment and able to compete with other emerging countries. In other words, it will be the need to adopt the neoclassical growth model that will improve their domestic economic health, and the appropriate pursuit of "supply-side" economic policies.

The ASEAN countries do hold the key to the success of the "Pacific Century" as they form a formidable group of countries, if their political and economic stability can be sustained. The group would become even larger, especially when other emerging countries in the region, typically Myanmar, Laos, and Cambodia, open up and become the next "flying geese." The economic resources, typically in the form of land and labor, that are released once these countries adopt an industrialization process could have a lasting impact on the region and in the world economy.

II EUROPE VERSUS ASIA

By 1973, the European Economic Community consisted mainly of the western European countries that were the prosperous and powerful countries of Western Europe. In the Treaty of Maastricht that formed the European Union (EU), the supranational body expanded to a total of 28 member states, with a number of new members from former Eastern Europe countries. The large EU is meant to promote a single market without national barriers. Because many of the new members are economically weaker and less industrialized, it would be appropriate for the stronger EU members to aid and promote development of the weaker members. Indeed, there seemed to be a good complement between the provision of capital from the stronger members, and the provision of land and labor from the newer members. Indeed, the establishment of the EU has posed challenges to other world regions. There was the argument of "fortress" Europe in the 1980s that could generate "trade protectionism" against other world regions. Following the EU, other trade and economic blocks have been established, notably the establishment in 1994 of the North American Free Trade Agreement (NAFTA) that consists of the United States, Canada, and Mexico. In 1989, the Asia – Pacific Economic Cooperation (APEC) was established among a number of Asia – Pacific economies. However, when compared to the EU, both NAFTA and APEC deal more with economic cooperation rather than economic integration.

However, while the world was watching, the extent of economic integration among EU members did not seem to show strong results. Indeed, instead of the stronger EU members raising the economic strength of the weaker members, it looked more likely that the weaker members were pulling the stronger EU members down through lack of development in business-friendliness and the need for economic rescue due to huge debts. The weaker EU states were taking advantage of the stronger EU states as a source of "bail out," and that economic ills of the weaker states would have to be contained, rescued, and shared by the stronger states within the enlarged EU.

The weakness in the euro currency could only benefit such strong export EU members as Germany, but most EU members were becoming less competitive economically. There are other aspects that were eroding economic competitiveness in Europe. The high cost of production, high welfare expenses, high taxes, and large national debts all work against economic competitiveness. For example, the economic situation was worsened by the large influx of refugees from the Middle East and North African countries in 2015 − 16. The generosity and sympathy that German Chancellor Angela Merkel offered was criticized, as other EU members were reluctant and unable to absorb millions of refugees, as that would exert an excessive burden on their economic welfare, and the short-term shock could impose long-term pressure on economic competitiveness and growth (*Independent*, September 4, 2015; *American Thinker*, November 24, 2015; *Trend News Agency*, March 2, 2016; and *Mail Online News*, March 7, 2016).

However, the Asian countries certainly do not have the same degree of protection, bail out, rescue, or assistance from neighboring countries should problems and crises arise. Unlike EU members which are connected by land, many Asian countries are divided by sea. Indeed, Asian countries are very much diversified in economics (stage of development, income per capita, industrialization, etc.), politics (democratic vs undemocratic regimes), race, religion, language, land size, and so on. Each of the Asian economies are effectively "competing" among themselves in the neoclassical sense in that: (1) they have to maintain stability, as instability could result in capital flight that benefitted neighboring economies; (2) they need to show improvement in the domestic economy in terms of infrastructure and business-friendliness, so as to attract foreign investment and trade; and (3) as a region, Asia aims to compete successfully with Europe and other emerging world regions.

In other words, there is tight "intraregional" competition within Asia, as catching up becomes a survival strategy. To strive for economic progress is the means to avoid decline. It could be such fear of falling behind and the need to catch up that drives Asia economies forward, and to do the best would mean the need to remove problems and reduce instabilities. One can identify some common economic features. Most Asian economies do not have large national debts, and do promote business-friendliness in the form of lower tax rates and lower welfare expenditure when compared to European countries. The need to compete and the lack of support by neighboring economies has become the Asian legacy in growth and development. In the end, growth can proceed and be sustained in all Asian economies. Such "progrowth" behavior is where most Asian market economies differ from European countries.

III ECONOMIC COOPERATION

Echoing the establishment of the EU and the NAFTA, there was the call for more regional economic cooperation within the Asian economies to promote trade and growth. The response came in early 1989 when the Australian prime minister, Mr. Bob Hawke, called for the first meeting of the APEC forum attended by ministers from 12 countries. Due to the June 4th, 1989, political turmoil in Tiananmen Square in Beijing, the three Chinese economies of the People's Republic of China, Hong Kong, and Chinese Taipei (Taiwan) were excluded until 1991. In the 1990s, the member economies increased to 21. Since 1993, sovereign state members would take turns to host the APEC head of state meeting in November. The annual host of APEC has so far been based in the sovereign states, as both Hong Kong and Taiwan have not hosted APEC.

Trade promotion has been the single most important issue. For example, it was intended in 1993 that the leaders' meeting would help bring the stalled Uruguay Round of trade talks back on track, and leaders called for continued reduction of trade barriers. The Bogor Goals established in 1993 aimed for free and open trade, investment by 2010 for industrialized economies, and by 2020 for developing countries in the Asia − Pacific region. Subsequently, the APEC Business Advisory Council (ABAC) was established in 1995. The call for open trade among APEC economies continued, even after the failure of the 2002 Doha Round of trade liberalization talks conducted by the World Trade Organization (WTO). While the Doha Round concerned trade in services, agriculture, and market access, the disputed areas that emerged in 2003 related to the extent of agricultural subsidies and "Singapore issues" that included rules on competition, transparency in public procurement, and investment and trade facilitation.

The APEC forum adopted two approaches to economic cooperation. The sector approach allowed exchanges of views, knowledge, and cooperation in such economic sectors as tourism and information technology. The macroeconomic approach involved cooperation in trade and finance, especially after the Asian financial crisis in 1997, when members saw the need to have better exchange of financial information to avoid currency attacks.

Between 1989 and 1996, the establishment of APEC passed through three stages. The "setting the scene" stage in 1989 − 91 saw the expansion of member economies to include the three Chinese economies. The second stage of 1992 − 95 involved the structural setup. Since 1996, member economies can propose two types of action plans in the cooperation agenda. Individual Action Plans are proposed by individual economies, while Collective Action Plans involve actions applicable to a number of member economies. Over the years, APEC has looked into a large number of issues (Yamazawa, 2012).

APEC members do produce a complementary effect, as some members are suppliers of capital while others are suppliers of labor. But, there is also an element of competition, as the rise in exports of one member economy could mean a reduction of exports in a neighboring member. The major criticism is the nonbinding or nonmandatory nature of the agreements, implying that members can discuss and agree, but individual member economies have the choice of not implementing the policy. As compared to the EU, APEC does not have any supranational power over other members. Indeed, it is very often reduced to a "talk shop," though various "good practices" have been discussed and disseminated in meetings, and member economies have fruitfully learned from each other's experiences. Another criticism is the geographical diversity among member economies. While the Asian economies are traditionally closer to each other, the incorporation of far economies in South America may be thought to cover too wide a region. Nonetheless, one can only argue that APEC is still in its early stages as a regional body, and is far from being a body that aims at regional integration.

Although APEC has developed a high profile internationally since it has been established, there are other regional bodies that serve to promote economic cooperation. Other than the ASEAN countries, there is also the Pacific Economic Cooperation Council (PECC) which is a voluntary organization comprising representatives from businesses, governments, and academies involving research and regular meetings. There are also the international groups of institutions, such as the United Nations representative bodies, namely the Economic and Social Commission for Asia and Pacific (ESCAP), and the United Nations Development Program (UNDP). Both the IMF and the Bank of International Settlement (BIS) have offices in many Asian economies, though their role is more for monitoring than promoting cooperation.

Another active body that was initiated mainly by Japan and contributed to economic development among poorer Asian economies is the Asian Development Bank (ADB), established in 1966 with the aim of providing assistance on food production and rural development. By 2014, the ADB had 67 shareholding members, including 48 from the Asia − Pacific region and 19 from outside the Asian region. Unlike APEC, the 48 Asia − Pacific ADB members consist of a number of small island economies in the Pacific Ocean, such as Samoa, the Solomon Islands, and Tonga, as well as such western Asian countries as Georgia, Nepal, Sri Lanka, Tajikistan, and Uzbekistan. The 19 non-Asian members are mainly developed countries in Europe and North America. The funding of the ADB includes bond issues from world capital markets, as well as contributions from members, retained earnings, and repayment of loans.

The discussion on bilateralism versus multilateralism in world trade also affected Asian economies (Bhagwati et al., 1999; Woolcock and Sampson, 2003; Aggarwal and Urata, 2006; Heydon and Woolcock, 2009). The debate dates back to the establishment of the General Agreement on Trade and Tariff (GATT) in 1947, where multilateral trade was discussed between the developed countries and developing countries. The spirit of multilateralism is that once one developed country allowed exports from one developing country, the same developed country would have to open its market to other developing countries. Typically, developing countries wanted to export as much as possible to the developed countries, but developed countries experienced trade deficits with the exporting countries.

Before 1994, when the WTO was established to replace GATT, multilateral trade negotiations took place through seven "rounds" of negotiations: Annecy Round (1949), Torquay Round (1951), Geneva Round (1955 − 59), Dillion Round (1960 − 62), Kennedy Round (1962 − 67), Tokyo Round (1973 − 79), and Uruguay Round (1986 − 94). A major conflict in multilateral trade negotiation is that developed countries have different agendas from developing countries, as the concern was the mounting trade deficit of developed countries. Export advantage was also used to politically favor some developing countries. However, accession to the WTO was based on bilateral negotiations. The advantage of bilateral negotiation is that the developed countries can control where imported goods come from. The emphasis has changed from a situation of export promotion or trade expansion to a situation of trade equalization between trade partners (Tait and Li, 1997). All Free Trade Agreements (FTAs) contained an element of trade restriction (Levy, 1997; Baier and Bergstrand, 2007). Over the decades, bilateral trade negotiations have led to the conclusion of a large number of FTAs. A major problem in FTAs is the high administrative cost in the execution of bilateral trade agreements, as there could be similarities and overlap among the FTAs.

IV REGIONAL MULTILATERALISM

After the Asian financial crisis, ASEAN considered the need for the closer formation of an economic community, partly due to the need for greater exchange of information related to potential crises, and the need to face up to competition from the Chinese economy (Sharma and Chua, 2000; Saw, 2007; Severino, 2010). The position and role of ASEAN changed as China emerged as a regional power. Since the turn of the 21st century, and for political, regional, and trade purposes, China, Japan, and South Korea have attempted to develop a closer relationship with ASEAN. While Japan and South Korea are traditional economic partners, the novelty lay in the China − ASEAN relationship. Economically, competition exists between China and ASEAN in foreign direct investment and exports, but China in turn can contribute to ASEAN through outward investment and trade, as China needs a steady supply of raw materials. Politically, ASEAN countries would have to strike a balance between the capitalist Japan and the United States, on the one hand, and communist China on the other hand.

Each of the ASEAN members has a different relationship with the United States. For example, Vietnam had a war with the United States, but since the turn of the 21st century, the United States has started investing in and trading with Vietnam, as their foreign relationship returned to normal. During the 1990s, Malaysian Prime Minister Mahathir has been critical of the foreign policy of the United States. The Philippines hosted the largest US overseas naval base at Subic Bay, though it was closed in 1992. Indonesia has a long and cordial relationship with the United States, and Indonesia is the only ASEAN member in the G20 group of major world economies. Singapore was the first ASEAN country to sign with the United States the US − Singapore Free Trade Agreement (USSFTA) in May 2003, which helped Singapore's exporters to "benefit from tariff concessions, increase competitiveness and attract investors" (Singapore Government website on FTAs). The highlight of the Singapore − US relationship emerged in the visit to the United States by Singapore's founding father, Lee Kuan Yew, in November 2009. In the meeting, Mr. Lee remarked that: "the 21st century will be a contest for supremacy in the Pacific because that's where the growth will be …. If you (the United States) do not hold your ground in the Pacific you cannot be a world leader" (*Shanghaiist.com*, November 4, 2009). He basically asked the United States to play a vigorous economic role in the Asia − Pacific region.

At the 2005 APEC meeting, Brunei, Chile, Singapore, and New Zealand established the Trans-Pacific Strategic Economic Partnership Agreement (TPSEP) that called for greater freedom in trade in goods and services, rules of origin, intellectual property, government procurement, and competition policy, a reduction by 90% of all tariffs between member countries by January 2006, and a zero trade tariff by 2015 ("Trans − Pacific Partnership," *Wikipedia*). The TPSEP was not an APEC initiative, but the original agreement contained an accession clause that encourages other economies to join. By 2008, TPSEP included Australia, Canada, Japan, Malaysia, Mexico, Peru, the United States, and Vietnam, making a total of 12 member countries. The content of the other agreed FTAs would be adjusted to avoid conflicts with the TPSEP. The Obama administration saw the enlarged membership of the TPSEP as a new way to establish a regional multilateral trading body. From January 2008, the United States agreed to enter into talks with the original four TPSEP member countries regarding trade liberalization. After a total of 19 negotiation rounds and a series of meetings, the Trans-Pacific Partnership (TPP) agreement was announced on October 5, 2015. The TPP trade agreement among the 12 Pacific Rim countries was signed on February 4, 2016. As of 2015, other countries interested in TPP membership included South Korea, Colombia, Philippines, Taiwan, Thailand, Laos, Indonesia, Cambodia, Bangladesh, and India. The negotiation to become members of TPP would require dismantling of protectionist policies.

The TPP agreement covered comprehensive market access, a regional approach, addressed new trade challenges, and inclusive trade and platforms for regional integration. The agreement concerned public policy matters, as the stated goals were to "promote economic growth, support creation and retention of jobs, enhance innovation, productivity and competitiveness, raise living standards and reduce poverty, promote good governance and transparency and enhance environmental protection." The lowering of trade barriers and tariffs was supplemented also by the "investor-state dispute settlement" mechanism.

There are several arguments that led to the establishment of the TPP. Despite the presence of the WTO that incorporates world trade, some WTO members did not follow the "rule-base" negotiations, violated their own commitments, and did not adopt the WTO policies effectively. Examples included the lack of adherence to intellectual property rights and market openness. The relevant argument is that the TPP is meant to ensure that agreements are kept, and trade activities are conducted fairly and transparently. The TPP was seen politically as the return of the United States into the Asian region to balance the influence of China. The TPP also echoed the concern of Mr. Lee Kuan Yew when he met President Obama in 2009. To check the ideological expansion of China, the "encirclement" theory had reiterated that the United States formed close alliances with a number of East,

Southeast, and South Asian countries in order to counterbalance China's political and military influence in the region. Nonetheless, the door for China to seek accession to the TPP is open, as the TPP does welcome new members to join provided members follow, implement, and adhere to the "rule-based" agreements.

In short, the TPP is meant to be a regional multilateral trading body that serves not only the interests of the members, but members also practice and commit to the agreements effectively. The Obama administration considered the TPP as a parallel to the similar trade agreement with the EU in the Trans-Atlantic Trade and Investment Partnership (TTIP) agreement. The TPP could be seen as an alternative to the Cancun failure in 2003, when WTO trade talks broke down. As a subset of WTO membership, the TPP shows the possibility of a regional multilateral body in trade negotiation that improves bilateral trade agreements but avoids the complexity of diversity in multilateral trade agreements. The TPP was also seen as an improvement to bilateralism, as it would replace many of the FTAs among members.

V THE ASEAN COUNTRIES

The economic success of East Asian economies has prompted the ASEAN countries to follow and become the "latecomer" in the 1980s. However, the "latecomer" advantage was short-lived, as China rose to compete with ASEAN. As compared to ASEAN, China did have a bigger consumer market and an equally low, if not lower, cost of production in the decades before the new 21st century. China has the "absolute advantage" over ASEAN countries when compared to the factors of production of land, labor, and capital.

However, the strategy ASEAN can adopt depends on how ASEAN countries sharpen their "comparative advantage" over China. For example, it has been argued that China's "software" is not keeping up with its "hardware." Most ASEAN countries are market economies, and even Vietnam has been keen to make economic progress to avoid missing opportunities. Improvement in infrastructure and business efficiency should enrich the competitiveness of ASEAN countries. A successful factor of the East Asian economies has been improvement in indigenous factors as a complement to external factors. Indigenous factors are variables that the domestic economy can improve itself through the adoption of effective policies and implementation of economic openness. Within ASEAN, there can be more "interregional" cross-border development in infrastructure, such as land transport, educational and health facilities, and development in agriculture and industries. Improvements in regional "supply-side" factors can help to raise ASEAN's overall competitiveness. Eradication of corruption, e.g., should be a great plus to promote business transparency and economic openness. Another advantage ASEAN possesses is its multiracial nature and use of different languages.

Individual ASEAN countries should also work to improve their competitiveness by either adopting policies that can raise their "comparative advantages" or strengthen their social and physical infrastructure, so as to minimize their "comparative disadvantages." For example, Vietnam has a long sea coast on the east, and its economic advantage can be huge, as marine-related activities can be expanded along the long eastern seafront. Trade with China can be expanded in the northern region, while activities in southern Vietnam should relate to other ASEAN neighbors. Vietnam has the advantage of providing land transport and aiding the development of its western landlocked neighbors of Laos and Cambodia, as their exports may have to pass through Vietnam to the east coast. The middle region of Vietnam is rich in agriculture.

Thailand has been successful in light manufacturing industries and agriculture, such as rice plantation, and tourism. However, Thailand needs to stabilize its democratic political system to make it more mature and fully functional. Thailand's political structure comprises four elements that contain the two political factions, the Monarch and the military. In a civically elected democratic regime, the elected government is the ultimate power and rules until the next election. To avoid mutiny, the military is subordinate to the civically elected government. The high ranking military officials in Thailand make known their own political views, which could put pressure on the elected government. In Thailand, and for a number of years since 2009, regular and persistent political demonstrations by opposing political factions reflected political instability, as the sudden removal of a democratically elected government through military intervention dented Thailand's reliability and hurt economic competitiveness. For example, the series of political protests between March and May 2010 against the government led by the Democratic Party was organized by the National United Front of Democracy Against Dictatorship (UDD), popularly known as "Red Shirts." The UDD called for the premier to hold elections before the end of the elected term scheduled in 2012. The protests escalated into prolonged confrontations between the protesters and the military. Constitutionally, Thailand's next scheduled election should have been held in 2012, and that was when the people had the lawful right to elect a party to power. Corrupt leaders would have to be dealt with by anticorruption laws, independent from the political system, and not through the sudden removal of a government, which would lead to immediate and costly instability. A "system-led" institution would be more reliable than a "personality-driven" policy. A fully functioning political democracy requires a number of supporting institutions that provide a "check and balance" on government policies and the activities of officials and leaders. Thailand needs to introduce more civic institutions that can provide stability to the democratic system.

In other ASEAN economies, such as Indonesia, Malaysia, and Brunei, there is the presence of a Muslim population. There is an urgent need to modernize the Muslim faith to avoid unwanted disturbances and violence. For example, education and connectivity through land transport and opening up of remote villages should form the first stage in modernization, and religious diversity should be considered as an aspect of personal choice, freedom, and pursuits. It is only through the understanding and interaction of different religious faiths that modernization can be promoted. Indeed, these Muslim-populated ASEAN countries could serve as an "early bird" to set up examples of religious modernization for the promotion of peaceful coexistence.

Over the centuries, ethnic Chinese had been either brought or immigrated to various Southeast Asian countries. Generations of ethnic Chinese have considered these Southeast Asian countries as their home. Ethnic Chinese have been keen to conduct businesses in export trades, or establish small- and medium-sized industrial enterprises. In Thailand, e.g., ethnic Chinese have been integrated into the Thai economy through the change of names. In the Philippines, partly because of its long exposure to foreign relations and the Catholic faith, ethnic Chinese are not considered as a different ethnicity. However, the same is not true in Malaysia and Indonesia. Despite the rapid economic growth in Malaysia, there are still clear laws that discriminate against ethnic Chinese. For example, businesses owned by ethnic Chinese need to have a Malayan partner, and study of the Chinese language is prohibited in schools. In Indonesia, ethnic Chinese have been used as scapegoats in economic downfalls and recessions, and violent "antiethnic Chinese" clashes have broken out, though these are rare. The political reasons for these "apartheid-like" policies is to promote opportunities for the nonethnic Chinese population, but it is probable that such policies could be costly in terms of job creation and economic competitiveness. When troubles occurred, "brain-drains" and "capital flight" could easily occur in Malaysia and Indonesia. The divisive policy on ethnic Chinese in both Malaysia and Indonesia definitely posed higher economic costs than political benefits. Discriminatory laws and practices should be repealed. On the contrary, huge potential will be realized once the discriminatory policy is removed. The Chinese language will become useful for cross-border businesses with China, and the additional investment will open up more job opportunities for people with different ethnic backgrounds. The provision of equality of opportunity is the best way to eradicate discrimination. Both Malaysia and Indonesia do not need to look far, as good lessons can already be seen from the development experience of Singapore. Individuals with different racial backgrounds are employed in the government. Singapore's ethnic diversity has become a "comparative advantage." To remove discrimination is to promote opportunity and enhance competitiveness.

The Philippine economy was regarded as the second largest economy after Japan at the end of the Second World War, but the various forms of political high-handedness, including the declaration of Martial Law for the decade 1972 – 81 had eroded Philippine's economic competitiveness as an investment destination, especially with the concurrent rise of other East Asian economies in the same period. The Philippines' geographical features comprise a large number of islands where typhoons and hurricanes are common, resulting in natural destruction and loss of human lives. The solution can only be a long-term policy on the strengthening of infrastructure so as to avoid the loss of lives and minimize destruction. The building of stronger residences away from the oceanfront, and provision of stronger embankments can protect properties and reduce the rescue cost. These infrastructures may be costly, but the reduction in loss of lives and the minimization of destruction will produce a long-term positive impact on the Philippine economy. In short, the two aspects for the Philippine economy to maintain sustainable growth are development in infrastructure and further industrialization.

The success of Singapore's "supply-side" economics can provide good lessons for other ASEAN member countries. As compared to China and other emerging countries, ASEAN members will be strong if the economic foundations and fundamentals are improved and strengthened; ASEAN does have good potential in global development, especially as it also provides a sizeable consumption market in the region. In a nutshell, while it has been argued that China is the "latecomer" that has competed away the advantages of ASEAN, an improved ASEAN would in turn pose a challenge to China. Indeed, ASEAN can actually be the next "newcomer" to China as China matures and faces rising costs and weak fundamentals.

The economic strength of Southeast Asia can be seen from the World Bank data. Other than the performance of GDP and GDP per capita, as shown in Fig. 13.1, the other domestic economic aspects include fiscal balance

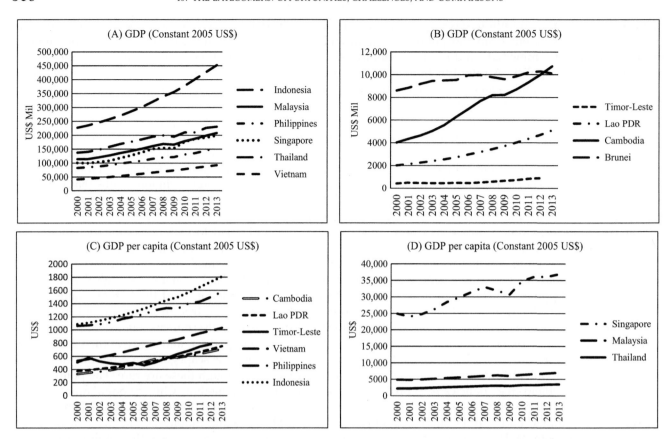

FIGURE 13.1   GDP and GDP per capita of ASEAN countries.

(Fig. 13.2), and debt-to-GDP ratio (Fig. 13.3). The two external economic performers include total export performance (Fig. 13.4) and inward foreign direct investment (Fig. 13.4). As far as GDP is concerned, the original five ASEAN members of Indonesia, Singapore, Malaysia, the Philippines, and Thailand are the better performers, followed by Vietnam as shown in Fig. 13.1A, while the remaining four, shown in Fig. 13.1B, are the weaker ones. However, on the basis of GDP per capita, most Southeast Asian economies are below US$1800, as shown in Fig. 13.1C. Singapore is the most developed country in the group, with GDP per capita exceeding US$35,000, as shown in Fig. 13.1D.

However, the fiscal performances of most Southeast Asian countries are weak, with more deficits than surpluses. As shown in Fig. 13.2, most economies suffered a big drop after the 2008 world financial crisis. The three better performers include Malaysia, Brunei, and the Philippines. There was much fiscal volatility after 2009, with a few deteriorating performers, including Vietnam and Indonesia. Due obviously to political changes, Myanmar (shown in Fig. 13.2B with the scale on the right hand side) is an exception, as it deteriorated sharply after 2009, but recovered dramatically with a small surplus after 2102. However, many countries have improved their debt-to-GDP ratio to below 50%. Only Singapore and Malaysia are faced with a high debt ratio. Between these two domestic economic indicators, the debt-to-GDP ratio can be the stronger indicator, as it reflects determination to lower debts. Indeed, the domestic economic performance will be stronger should these economies work to improve their fiscal deficits.

On the external economic front, the Southeast Asian countries are doing fine in both total exports and inward foreign direct investment. Despite the setback in 2008 − 09, exports have been increasing, with a few countries rising rapidly, as Fig. 13.4 shows. The three weaker economies include Myanmar, Laos, and Cambodia, as one can see from Fig. 13.4B. The performance in inward foreign direct investment has not been too favorable, as most are near or below US$10,000 million. Similar to total exports, there has been an increase since 2009, though Myanmar experienced high volatility, as shown in Fig. 13.5B. However, the low level of inward foreign direct investment should not be seen as a weakness, but rather as a potential yet to be discovered by international investors.

By examining these few economic indicators, one can conclude that this cluster of Southeast Asian economies can become the new "latecomers" in promoting industrialization and growth, similar to that of the East

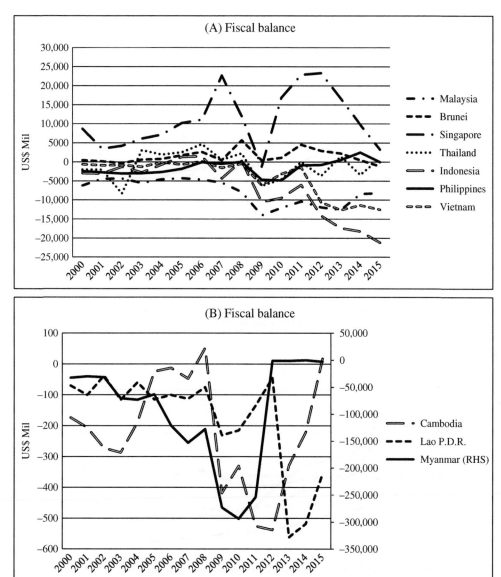

FIGURE 13.2   Fiscal balance of ASEAN countries.

European countries. Indeed, by comparing the rise of East Asia in the 1960s and 1970s, and the rise of China since the 1990s, the world economy should realize that aiding a group of small- to medium-sized economies that generate a cluster effect would be better than aiding another large country whose rise would challenge the world economically, ideologically, and militarily. With the development of a cluster of economies, there will be the dual advantage of intraregional competition among this cluster of economies, and interregional competition with similar economies in different world regions. The intention is not for the larger countries to "divide and rule" the smaller countries, but smaller countries can give a wider dispersal in world development, as smaller economies tend to be more pragmatic, and adhere more to the international economic community.

VI   CHINA IN ASIA

Chinese leaders since 1978 have repeatedly pointed out that China would not be a hegemony in establishing relationships with the rest of the world. Similarly, Chinese leaders have vowed that economic growth would be the prime target in development, and while a reduction in the number of military personnel has been announced, large expenditure has been made in modernizing military technology. Indeed, China's economic rise has led to

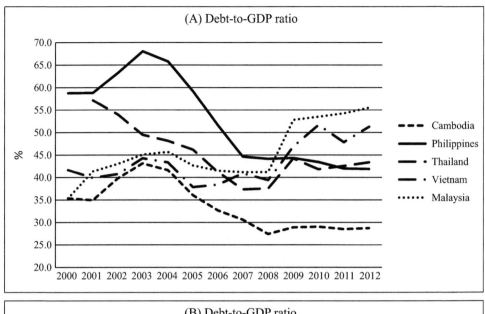

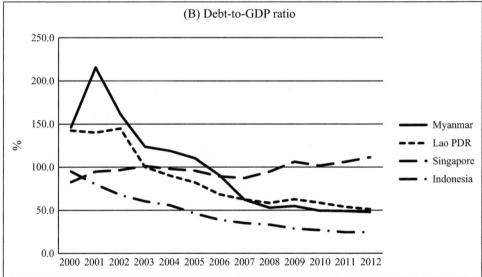

FIGURE 13.3   Debt-to-GDP ratio: ASEAN countries.

numerous studies debating whether China can be number one to rule the world. In favor of China's growing power, e.g., Jacques (2009) used economic data to show China's potential, especially after the financial crisis in 2008. Similarly, Chow (2002) argued that China's successful economic reform has been based on improvements in human capital and hard work, and predicted that with an assumed exponential growth rate of 0.06 for China and 0.0288 for the United States, their GDP would be equalized in 2020, based on the purchasing power parity estimation of 1998.

However, there are contrary arguments that China lacks superpower qualities, nearly two-thirds of China's population can be classified as peasants, foreign companies are responsible for 85% of all high-tech exports, China's key numbers are regularly omitted, and there are tens of thousands of "mass incidents" each year, rising from 74,000 in 2004 to 87,000 in 2005 (*CNBC*, August 23, 2011). China's high growth rates have been due more to the low economic base, the income per capita is still pretty low, and the gap between the "ultra-rich and dirt-poor" is accelerating (*Huffpost Business*, January 14, 2015). Parfitt (2011) argued that China could not rule the world because China's interest is in "the appearance of success rather than the substance," and the lack of innovation can be seen from the fact that the majority of goods produced come from non-Chinese companies.

There was a clear strategic difference between Mao and Deng in catching up with the world economy. Mao followed the Soviet Union's pursuit of economic centralization and propagandized that China would catch up

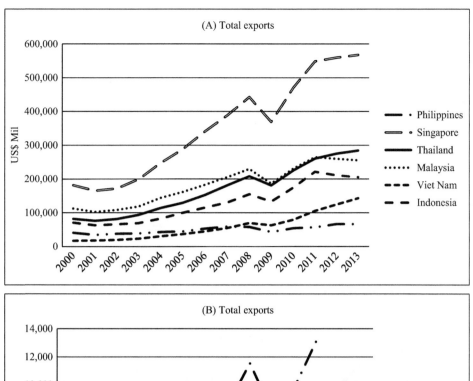

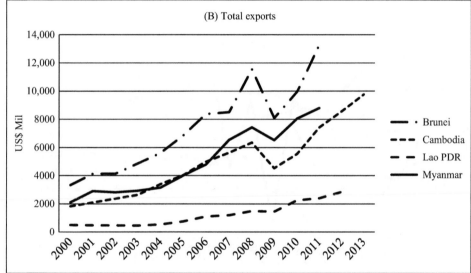

FIGURE 13.4 Total exports of ASEAN countries.

with the economies of Great Britain and the United States within a decade. Deng pleaded China's low economic development and poverty, and caught the world's sympathy. However, one feature in China's communist regime has been the difference between words and acts. For example, the repeated verbal intention that China would not become a hegemony has been met with large increases in military expenditures and modernization. China does have a long-term and ambitious view of international dominance. China has initiated regional multilateral organization in the Asian region. As early as 1996, China formed the Shanghai Five (China, Kazakhstan, Kyrgyzstan, Russia, and Tajikistan), but this was renamed the Shanghai Cooperation Organization (SCO) in 2001. The SCO expanded to include both India and Pakistan in 2015. There are four observer states (Afghanistan, Belarus, Iran, and Mongolia), and six dialogue partners (Armenia, Azerbaijan, Cambodia, Nepal, Sri Lanka, and Turkey). This Eurasian body touches on political, economic, and military matters ("Shanghai Cooperation Organization," *Wikipedia*). Politically, China is challenging Russia to show its leadership in the socialist world. With Russia and China, the region will have a closer military relationship, but it is questionable whether the military strength of the SCO could balance that of the North Atlantic Treaty Organization (NATO), because other than Russia, the other members are much weaker in military terms. Economic cooperation would probably be the continuous norm among the members, especially in raw materials and minerals. It is obvious that China would support the SCO with funds and assistance through its "cheque book diplomacy." In June 2009, at the SCO summit, e.g., China announced the provision of a US$10 billion loan to SCO member states to "shore up the

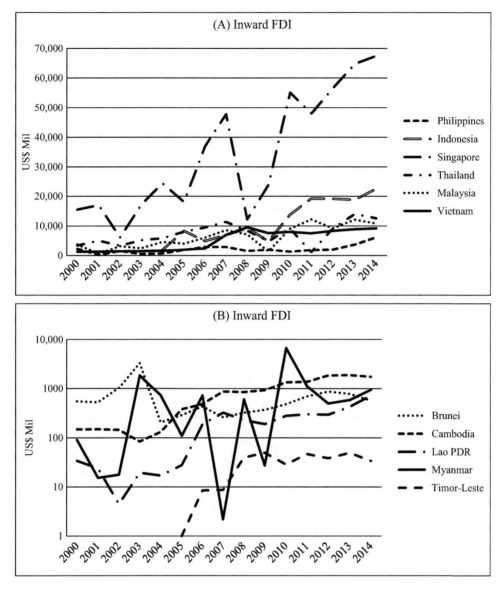

FIGURE 13.5   Inward foreign direct investments of ASEAN countries.

struggling economies of its members amid the global financial crisis" ("Shanghai Cooperation Organization," *Wikipedia*).

Similarly, in the "one belt, one road" initiative unveiled in October 2013, China will provide economic and financial assistance through trade and infrastructure development to friendly countries (See discussion in Section V in the Chapter 9). To support the "one belt, one road" the Asian Infrastructure Investment Bank (AIIB) was established in 2015 to finance the infrastructure investment activities. Although the AIIB has attracted a total of 57 founding members, it is meant to conduct development in infrastructure, and it would duplicate the governance of other international development institutions, such as the World Bank and the Asian Development Bank. Nonetheless, the "one belt, one road, one bank" initiative allows China to establish a regional multilateral body that extends westwards from China to Europe. Among the 57 founding members, Brazil is the only country from South America. Countries on the two sides of the Pacific may not be relevant geographically or geo-politically.

China's "belt, road, bank" (BRB) initiative has received world attention. Comments from some "China-watchers" hold the view that the global power is shifting to Asia, and to China in particular (See, e.g., *The Globe and Mail*, April 1, 2015). Others would argue that China is handing out "free cash" to countries which are prepared to kowtow to China. Building roads and railways across Central Asia and West Asia and so on would involve not only funds, but also time, political considerations, material supplies, and geological estimations, in addition to technology, human capital, and management. Infrastructure constructions will take years, if not decades, to complete, and may not show short-term results. The work of the AIIB is yet to be tested over time, as one possibility is that the AIIB could merely serve as another financial institution in China that engages in financial and speculative dealings that boosts the financial sector, similar to the establishment of other "shadow banks" in China. There can be constraints in the supply of materials for land and ocean projects. For example, although steel production may be exported from China, the funds for purchasing imports may have to come from the host country, which would face reserve constraints. If China was to provide the funding for the purchase of imported materials, the question then would be whether other conditions, such as the use of land rights around railway lines, would be attached. Similarly, there could be diplomatic friction in the negotiations for the projects about to what extent China would "interfere" in the internal affairs and resource deployment of the host country. Experience in China's Railway Group in Thailand and in Indonesia, e.g., has shown the difficulty in the negotiation and usage rights in the funding of China's railway projects (*South China Morning Post*, April 7, and 10, 2016).

In China's reform, the strategy of "bringing in" is meant to import resources, human capital, knowledge, institutions and practices, technology, and management that serve the economic reform process. For example, the organization of the Olympics and the World Expo provided China with an opportunity to learn how the outside world conducted international events. By joining the WTO, China needs to adhere to international guidelines in trade, and that in turn imposes the way external trade and economic openness has to be conducted domestically in China. The "going out" strategy implies, e.g., the use of Chinese outward investment and funds in other developing countries. There is, however, debate as to the essence of the strategy, if funds used were to secure other materials in short supply in China, especially when the outward investments were from state-owned or state-controlled funds.

While the BRB initiative requires blocks of funds, material inputs, time, and structural changes in the affected countries, the TPP trade agreement on the other hand provides opportunities in trade and investment that would benefit the member countries directly as their exports expand. As the TPP agreement would not be involved with infrastructure development, which should actually be left to the decision of indigenous governments, the advantage of the TPP agreement could easily be materialized once member countries increased their industrial and manufacturing outputs. The TPP does provide security in market access among members, its participation in investment and export is voluntarily and depends on the economic strength of member countries. In turn, TPP members could easily expand their exports and attract inward investment.

On noneconomic fronts, a number of conflicts with other smaller Asian neighbors in territorial and ocean disputes are involved. China's ideological difference is certainly the cause of not making compromises with Asian neighbors. While it has abundant arable land for development, China probably followed the expansionist policy of the Soviet Union in annexing territories. It is clear that no Asian neighbors, including Japan and the United States, would engage in war with China. But, to provide a reason for military expenditure and modernization, there could be the need for a "war preparation" mentality. One propaganda reason that China held on to claim islands in the East China Sea and South China Sea was China's possession in "historical" times. It is also true that other Asian countries and territories were once China's territories in history. For example, China had dominated Vietnam over four historic periods of 111 BC to 30 AD, $43-544$, $602-938$, and $1407-27$ ("History of Vietnam," *Wikipedia*). China's Han emperor conquered the northern part of the Korean peninsula in 108 BC, and administered the area around modern Pyongyang for nearly 400 years (*The Economist*, April 12, 2013). Mongolia (which used to be called Outer Mongolia) was ruled under the Qing dynasty ($1635-1912$) ("Mongolia under Qing Rule," *Wikipedia*). Vladivostok (known as Haishenwai in Chinese), now the home port of Russia's Pacific fleet and the largest Russian port on the Pacific Ocean, was acquired by Russia in the Treaty of Beijing in 1860 as the Qing dynasty failed to defend the region after being defeated in the Second Opium War by Great Britain in the same year ("Vladivostok," and "Opium Wars," *Wikipedia*). Indeed, many Chinese artifacts and historic treasures of previous dynasties are found in European museums.

The use of "history" has politically been exploited by China in an attempt to convince the international community in order to claim territories. The history of the People's Republic of China dates back only to 1949, when the revolutionary communist regime took over from the Nationalist government (Kuomingtang) which fled to Taiwan. The Qing dynasty was overthrown by Sun Yat-sen, who founded the Republic of China in 1912. The revolutionary communist regime in China was not a continuation of a former regime. How far in history that post-1949 China counted on could be an international law and legitimacy debate. Should today's China legitimately be accountable for all the deeds that the former, already extinguished, Chinese rulers, emperors, and dynasties had committed? What legality does China hold in dealings with the deeds conducted by previous rulers before 1949? The communist regime was not part of the signatories in the various treaties conducted in the Qing

Dynasty. With the communist revolution taking power in 1949, the territory of China could only contain the land and ocean rights that existed in 1949. Would it be more civilized for post-1949 China to move forward and make the best of peaceful coexistence and cooperation with other Asian neighbors, or dig up all pre-1949 wounds and establish conflicts with other neighbors, or whoever had done wrong to rulers and emperors in previous Chinese dynasties? Or are these simply instruments and scapegoats that are used by today's China for political manipulation to gain international recognition and ambition so as to compete with other world powers, to bully other smaller countries in the region, or to extend its aggressive communist ideology?

The difference between conflict and peace is that conflicts produce "absolute" outcomes, while peace allows cooperation for mutual benefits. The strategy should be mutual recognition and respect in international relations. Cooperation that yields "relative" outcomes is preferred to confrontation that yields "absolute" outcomes. If the question relates to the hidden and potential resources of the territories, can the resources be developed and explored to mutual advantage, so that all countries concerned could cooperate and share the advantages? After all, China is already the largest country in the Asian region.

One territorial dispute with Japan and Taiwan (Chinese Taipei) involves a group of five uninhabited islands in the East China Sea located east of China, northeast of Taiwan, but west of Okinawa Island and southwest of the Ryukyu Islands. These islands have been called differently: Diaoyutai Islands in China, Senkaku Islands in Japan, but are otherwise known as the Pinnacle Islands. China has claimed both the discovery and ownership of the islands as early as the 14th century. China and Taiwan regarded the islands as part of the Yilan County of Taiwan. Japan claimed its ownership of the islands from 1895 until the end of World War II, when the US administered the islands from 1945 to 1972. Under the Okinawa Reversion Agreement between the United States and Japan, the islands were returned to Japan. Japan regarded the islands as part of the Okinawa Prefecture. Prior to the transfer of administrative control from the United States to Japan in 1971, there was a report in 1968 of the discovery of potential undersea oil reserves.

China, in November 2015, declared unilaterally that the East China Sea Air Defense Identification Zone (ADIZ) extended air space to include the Diaoyu Islands or the Senkaku Islands, escalating the dispute between China and Japan and the United States (*The Diplomat*, October 13, 2015). By distance, these islands are closest to Taiwan. While it may not worth fighting for a few lone islands that are uninhabitable, and probably not sufficiently large for military purposes, the focus of attention could be the large undersea oil reserves. Since the conflict concerned a valuable economic resource, the problem should be dealt with using economic tools, but ideological and political differences could prolong the conflict. Although the exploration involves a huge amount of capital and technology, the long-term lower cost oil supply would benefit all partners in the joint exploration. Peaceful collaboration in resource exploration is definitely more preferable than regional conflicts.

China has been making unfriendly moves in the South China Sea, involving territorial disputes with the Philippines, Indonesia, Vietnam, Brunei, and Malaysia. Located south of the Hainan Island of China, southwest of Taiwan, east of Vietnam, west of the Philippines, east of the Malay Peninsula, and north of Borneo, the economic asset is that one-third of the world's shipping sails through the South China Sea, and it is believed to have huge oil and gas reserves hidden beneath its seabed. The conflicts in the South China Sea involve several groups of islands that are nearer to the Philippines, Indonesia, and Vietnam than to the southern coast of China (Storey, 2015). The South China Sea, which has been labeled differently by surrounding countries in different historical time periods, contains over 250 small islands, shoals, and reefs that form into archipelagos which have no indigenous people.

The Pratas Islands are closest to China, as these islands are located southwest of Taiwan and east of Hainan Island. The Scarborough Shoal is right outside the west coast of the Philippines. The largest group of the Spratly Islands are located southwest of the Philippines but north of Brunei, Malaysia, and Indonesia. The Paracels Islands are also located nearer to Vietnam than to China. The Subi Reef, Spratlys, and Fiery Cross Reefs are islands lying between Indonesia, Vietnam, and the Philippines. The most southern group of islands include Natuna and Anambas Islands that are located south of Vietnam, but between the water of east and west Malaysia. Hence, the multiple territorial claims that involve China and other ASEAN nations include the Paracel Islands between China, Taiwan, and Vietnam. The claims for the Spratly Islands involve China, Taiwan, Brunei, Vietnam, Malaysia, and the Philippines. The Scarborough Shoal has been in dispute between China, Taiwan, and the Philippines. The dispute on the southernmost Natuna Islands involves China, Taiwan, and Indonesia. Naval clashes were reported in the Paracel Islands in 1974, and in the Spratly Islands in 1988, between China and Vietnam. China claimed "historically" that all these islands were in Chinese territorial waters. Distance-wise, these islands are basically located on the doorsteps of the three Southeast Asia countries. Another economic issue is fishing rights in the South China Sea, as Chinese fishing vessels have been confronted about illegal fishing in the South China Sea, as well as in the territories of other countries, such as South Korea and Argentina. Strategically, it could have military value as it stretches from the Malacca Straits in the southwest to the Strait of Taiwan in the northeast. While ASEAN member countries have been keen to take up a multilateral approach to resolve the disputes and overlapping claims to avoid conflicts, China preferred to take a bilateral approach. ASEAN members feel disadvantaged in bilateral negotiations with the much larger China, and bilateral talks may not be effective when it comes to competing claims (*The Diplomat*, March 7, 2014; *AFP*, October 9, 2014; *The Independent*, March, 16, 2016; and *South China Morning Post*, May 28, 2014, March 20, and 25, 2016).

The ASEAN member countries surely are aware of China's assertive behavior in the South China Sea, which caught world attention when, in July 2010, the United States called for China to resolve the territorial dispute, but China warned the United States to "keep out of the issue." As the "police of the world," the United States has regularly engaged in naval exercises in the area, and on August 18, 2010, released a statement opposing the use of force in resolving the dispute. The issue of militarizing the South China Sea has been raised since 2012 as the US Navy has reportedly disclosed land reclamation conducted by China in a chain of islands and reefs. Within a short time, China has built airbases and installed powerful radar and missile launches. These aggressive attempts to control the South China Sea have raised tensions with Asian neighbors (*New York Times*, February 29, 2016; *The Washington Post*, March 16, 2016; *BBC News*, March 18, 2016; and *Reuters*, March 19, 2016). In mid-2015, the United States spotted through satellite images that China was conducting land reclamation on Fiery Cross Reef. Tensions grew in the region, especially between the United States and China. The artificial islands were thought to have been built for military purposes, though when pressured, China said that the purpose was aimed at "better weather forecasts" (Osawa, 2013) (*South China Morning Post*, April 17, April 21, May 30, and June 21, 2015).

With the typical communist ideological attitude, the Chinese leaders retorted that "the US not China is the nation militarizing the South China Sea ... it was the US sending the most advanced aircraft and military vessels to the South China Sea" (*South China Morning Post*, March 4, 2016; and *US News*; March 11, 2016). There is surely a difference between sending vessels to the region and building up airbases. In an interview during the National People's Congress (NPC) meeting in March 2016, Chinese Foreign Minister Wang Yi disclosed that "China will build essential infrastructure to better protect its growing offshore interests." Wang stressed that "China's build-up of defense facilities on its own islands and reefs is fully within its international rights and that the country is not militarizing the sea." The build-up in the Scarborough Shoal is seen as a Chinese plan to construct more supply bases around the world after setting up the first naval supply depot in Dijbouti (*China Daily Hong Kong Edition*; March 9, 2016; and *South China Morning Post*, March 9, 2016).

According to published materials, the origin of the conflict in the South China Sea dates back to 1947, when the Nationalist government (KMT) of the Republic of China drew the "eleven-dash lines" after taking control of some islands in the South China Sea that had been occupied by Japan during the Second World War. After the KMT fled to Taiwan in 1949, the communist regime in Beijing declared itself to be the sole legitimate representative of the maritime claims in the South China Sea. To make a gesture of friendship to North Vietnam, two "dash lines" that bypassed the Gulf of Tonkin were removed in early 1950. The consequent "nine-dash lines" encircle about 90% of the contested waters, as the lines run as far out as 2000 km from mainland China to about a few hundred kilometers away from the Philippines, Malaysia, and Vietnam. By using the "history" argument, Beijing maintained the area covered in the "dash lines" as "historical maritime rights" (*South China Morning Post*, May 25, July 10, and July 12, 2016).

In January 2013, the Philippines government took the maritime claim dispute to the Permanent Court of Arbitration (PCA) in The Hague, Netherlands ("The Republic of Philippines vs The People's Republic of China," Permanent Court of Arbitration, Netherlands, http://www.pcacases.com/web/view/7; and "South China Sea," *Wikipedia*.). The PCA is under the aegis of the United Nations Convention on the law of the Sea (UNCLOS). The Philippines argued that the lines exceeded the limits of the maritime entitlements permitted under UNCLOS, and at the same time sought clarification on the definition of the disputed areas as to whether they are islands, low-tide coral outcrops, or submerged banks, in order to determine the entitlement to the territorial waters in question. However, UNCLOS does not deal with sovereignty questions that the Philippines authority did not raise.

Although communist China is also a signatory to UNCLOS, Beijing's strategy, as reported, was to remain ambiguous and intentionally not define the legality of the "nine-dash lines," as that could blur the maritime boundary. Without a clear boundary, Beijing can take various advantages, including demanding economic rights, and control the island and waters, without making obligations to international law. The PCA eventually delivered its verdict on the friction in the South China Sea on July 12, 2016 ("The South China Sea Arbitration (The Republic of the Philippines vs The People's Republic of China)," Press Release, Permanent Court of Arbitration, The Hague, the Netherlands, July 12, 2016). The verdict was divided into five decision items. It began with the concern on the "Historic Rights and the 'Nine-Dash Line'" and concluded that "... to the extent China had historic rights to resources in the waters of the South China Sea, such rights were extinguished to the extent that they were incompatible with the exclusive economic zones provided for in the Convention..., there was no evidence that China had historically exercised exclusive control over the waters or their resources...."

In the concern on "Status of Features," the Tribunal concluded that "... none of the features claimed by China was capable of generating an exclusive economic zone, ... it could declare that certain sea areas are within the exclusive economic zone of the Philippines, because those areas are not overlapped by any possible entitlement of China." On the "Lawfulness of Chinese Actions," the Tribunal held that "Chinese law enforcement vessels had unlawfully created a serious risk of collision when they physically obstructed Philippines vessels." On the concern over "Harm to Marine Environment," the Tribunal found that "Chinese authorities were aware that Chinese fishermen have harvested endangered sea turtles, coral, and giant clams on a substantial scale in the South China Sea ..., and had not fulfilled their obligations to stop such activities." Lastly, the Tribunal concluded on the "Aggravation of Dispute" that "China's recent large-scale land reclamation and construction of artificial islands was incompatible with the obligations on a State during dispute resolution proceedings, insofar as China has inflicted irreparable harm to the marine environment, built large artificial islands in the Philippines' exclusive economic zone, and destroyed evidence of the natural condition of features in the South China Sea that formed part of the parties' dispute."

While the international community and neighboring ASEAN countries were showing support to the decisions of the Tribunal, and looking for a more compromising and self-restraining solution to avoid direct friction with China (Nguyen, 2016), China unilaterally defied the PCA's decisions and recommendations, arguing that China would not accept or accommodate the decisions of the Tribunal. Instead, China already pointed out that the United States cannot uproot China, ignored the international community, and went further by building aircraft hangers on disputed islands in South China Sea, as reported by a US think tank in August 2016 (*South China Morning Post*, April 7, July 12, and 25, and August 9, 2016). With growing military spending, it would be China's intention to militarize the South China Sea for its strategic ambition.

With a weaker US position in the Asia − Pacific region on the one hand, divided ASEAN members, and a change of leadership in the Philippines in 2016, China is asserting its gigantic size and may not respect its Southeast Asian neighbors and obligation to international law. ASEAN members have no match to China's growing military power. Other United States − China analysts would argue that the United States may have to balance the concerns of the ASEAN members with the bilateral interest between China and the United States. However, a closer US − ASEAN relationship would definitely be rewarding in maintaining peace in the region. The South China Sea incident should reflect back to the original intention of the "Nixon − Kissinger initiative" in the early 1970s by incorporating China into the United Nations, the conclusion could be that communist China would unilaterally defy international law and obligations.

With the rise of China, Southeast Asia in principle should be the first region to benefit. However, China's unilateral action in the South China Sea has brought political and military imbalances in the region, threatening regional stability considerably. Indeed, China's unsteady policy in Southeast Asia has resulted in differences in the approach to China by the ASEAN members, with Indonesia and Vietnam having disputes with China, while others may prefer to kowtow to China for potential economic advantages. The test will be whether the ASEAN members will stand as one single market with one voice and a united regional body, or become fragmented and fall into China's hands. If stability among the countries in the ASEAN region cannot be maintained, the economic cost could be high and development may be delayed.

When compared to the influence between Japan and China in the Asia region, one can immediately see that Japan has been aiding the economic development of other Asian countries. Economies in East Asia and Southeast Asia have benefitted through growth and increase in trade with Japan. China's rise provided selective assistance to its Asian neighbors, but it also brought with it military expansion and threats, as the international community has clearly observed with China's action in the South China Sea incident. There is, thus, a vast difference in the economic influence between Japan and China in the Asian region.

VII CONCLUSION

The progress in economic development can be "relative" within economies and across borders. Whether a country endowed with natural resources can be developed or not depends on the execution of appropriate policies and ideologies. Indeed, experience shows that countries endowed with natural resources can remain underdeveloped if ineffective policies are adopted. Similarly, the adoption of suitable economic policies can aid economic progress, even if a country lacks natural resources. The appropriateness of economic policies can be seen from an economy's overall competitiveness. An economy can become competitive, but can also become uncompetitive when compared to neighboring and other economies. This is due to the fact that economic resources, especially financial capital, are mobile across countries, territories, and regions. The competitive advantage that helps an economy to progress today may change tomorrow, as there are others making improvements in their competitiveness. Developing countries that can improve their domestic factors also perform better in external factors. The lesson is that foreign capital is always mobile, and often ends up in countries that perform strongly in domestic conditions. Similarly, an economy faced with deterioration in domestic conditions will likely experience an outflow of its capital resources to more attractive destinations. Thus, inappropriate domestic policies could end up driving away capital.

The Chinese economy has been made successful mainly by the expectation from the rest of the world that reduction in poverty in China would help to improve people's livelihood, that a peaceful rise in the Chinese economy would be used as a showcase to other developing countries, and that a more developed China economy would contribute to the development of the world economy. Deng Xiaoping's economic reform in 1978 that denounced poverty in China did encourage investment to China. Foreign investments made no secret about the benefit of a wealthier China as it became the world's next biggest consumer market. Few would have estimated the cost of a powerful Chinese economy to the international community. With roughly a fifth of the world's population, advances in the Chinese economy would not only provide a huge consumer market and a production site, but also consume much of the world's resources. A powerful but politically uncooperative China could pose challenges, at least to the Asian region, as the other smaller Asian countries could not have a military force parallel to that of China.

In economic jargon, the Chinese economy has "absolute advantage" over a number of neighboring Asian countries. Armed with large amounts of production factors, most Asian economies were in the position of "absolute disadvantage." Armed with political and ideological differences with all major Asian economies, China posed a bigger "threat" than Japan or the United States. Alternatively put, while Japan's involvement in Asia was in the economics arena of investment, production, and industrialization, China's involvement in Asia would include political, ideological, and military considerations.

Asian countries would have to stay alert in their economic development. Avoiding instability within and among ASEAN countries had become a prerequisite in ensuring that there would not be any "capital flight." Facing up to challenges from China required speedy improvements in "supply-side" factors, including improvements in infrastructure, business-friendly policies and ethical behavior, eradication of corruption and cronyism, nurturing human capital, and establishing a "system-driven" socioeconomic framework. In other words, Asian economies had to nurture new "comparative advantages." By improving their domestic factors and conditions, Asian countries could stay competitive "intraregionally" so that they could be more attractive to China, Japan, and other investors in the region, and "interregionally" so as to attract investments from Europe, North America, and other capital-rich regions. Further economic integration and policy cooperation within ASEAN countries would help to strengthen their "intraregional" power. By posting itself as a cohesive region, ASEAN countries could present and project a large consumer market for other investors, and resource diversity within ASEAN member countries should ensure diversity in production and industrial development. Balancing its Asian relationship with China, Japan, South Korea, and Australia, and international relationships with North America and Europe, ASEAN could find their own competitive advantages.

Due to the economic similarities among ASEAN countries, economic integration could extend to "supply-side" factors, including the exchange of "good practice" in development. The economic development of the ASEAN region has its own special features and when developed properly, ASEAN can be the "latecomer" to China in world development. Between the external factors and indigenous factors, ASEAN countries will have to compete with China in the external factors, while improvements in indigenous factors should be in the hands of the ASEAN countries themselves. Hence, it would be fruitful to make indigenous improvements so as to transform and strengthen their economies. The improvement in their domestic factors will in turn aid them in improving their external factors. This should be ASEAN's eventual outcome in the race to improve their competitiveness "intraregionally and interregionally."

While ASEAN member countries should integrate further, it would be interesting to observe the development of the China – ASEAN relationship. Due to ideological differences and the expanding Chinese power in the region, it is likely that China and ASEAN will have different development strategies. For example, will China prefer to see an integrated ASEAN? Or would it be to China's advantage to "divide and rule" the ASEAN members. ASEAN members would be in a "prisoner's dilemma" situation of choosing between further cooperating and integrating within ASEAN, or taking advantage from the economic gains by getting closer to China. The decision on the choice, however, should be in the hands of ASEAN members, as they need to be more open to ASEAN activities and at the same time avoid the economic temptation from China, bearing in mind that China's provision of economic resources and gains would carry a political cost.

A balancing strategy would be to weight the influence of China against the need to get close to an external power, typically the United States and Japan. Like Japan in the 1970s, when Japan invested massively in other East and Southeast Asian economies, China is likely to duplicate by investing in Southeast Asian countries, typically through the BRB initiative. ASEAN members will have to steer between economic gains and political influences. If carefully and strategically placed between BRB and TPP, ASEAN members could be in an excellent position to "make the best of both worlds."

THE FRONTIER OF CAPITALISM: CHINA VERSUS HONG KONG

Why China and Hong Kong?

The Chinese race probably provides one of the longest world civilizations in human history. As early as the Qing Dynasty (221 − 206 BC), the Chinese history documented through various dynasties had experienced wars, conflicts, successions, and natural disasters. The teaching of Confucius (551−479 BC) on, e.g., self-reliance, hard work, filial piety, and individual responsibility had been the dominant socioeconomic ideology that culminated in a culture, belief, behavior, and manner in which things were conducted. In olden times, China had primarily been an agricultural-based country with fertile land and supplies of natural resources, especially in southern regions. The centuries-long science of herbal drug and medicine development had supported the fact that Chinese territories were rich in agriculture and forestry. Economic self-sufficiency could have delayed the need for technological advances. For example, in his historic study of Admiral Zheng He, who could have been the first person to discover the world in 1421, Menzies (2002) concluded that the emperor in the Ming Dynasty (1368−1644) that improved and advanced seafaring techniques at the time could have developed new economic epochs and charted new history in globalization. Instead, the Ming Emperor narrow-mindedly adopted an inward-looking, isolationist policy, and destroyed all seafaring records and related technology. A major consequence would be the lack of attention and resources given to technological development and advance, including the building of an effective navy for defense.

The Ming Dynasty was succeeded by the Qing Dynasty (1644−1911). The early Qing administration took up institutions and customs left from the Ming Dynasty. The Qing Dynasty was largely feudalistic, self-centered, and superstitious, as emperors were surrounded by science-lacking, technology-lacking, and probably knowledge-lacking, concubines and eunuchs, while administrative decisions were mainly "top-down." For example, Empress Dowager Cixi (1835−1908) was a concubine herself in her adolescence ("Empress Dowager Cixi," *Wikipedia*). Dreyer (1995) has rightly pointed out that a major weakness in the 19th century Qing administration was the lack of awareness of sea power, and a weak navy. Instead, the approach to the western world was one of isolation, ignorance, insensitivity, and lack of engagement in international affairs. The introverted attitude and nature of governance in the Qing Dynasty eventually had to confront the challenge from European imperialism in the 18th century. The economic self-sufficiency under the Qing government meant it was not keen on international trade, but such products as silk, ceramics, and tea were in high demand in Europe. Instead of formulating a proper open trading system, the "single port commerce system" (known as the Canton system) instituted in 1757 granted trading monopolies to some private merchants, mostly in the Guangdong (Kwangtung) province ("Canton System," *Wikipedia*). However, despite the trade surplus from exports to European countries, China's growing demand for opium imported from India through the monopolized British East India Company raised concerns, as its damage to society was immense. In 1839, the Qing government seized and confiscated opium without compensation. This incident eventually led the British government to declare war on China in the following year.

The British government had, for some time, been looking for a territory in Asia to serve as a trading post. Armed with a strong navy, the British had already surveyed the water in Southern China for a "deep water" harbor, and Hong Kong Island's "lip-shaped" harbor and its adjacent Kowloon peninsula was favored, as it could be defended easily. The Qing navy that was comprised entirely of wooden sailing junks was no parallel to the superior British Royal Navy. The Qing government surrendered to Great Britain at the end of the First Opium War in 1842. The Treaty of Nanking included payment of war reparations, five ports (Canton, Amoy, Fuchow, Ningpo, and Shanghai) were to open for western trade and missionaries, and Hong Kong Island was ceded to Great Britain in perpetuity.

Despite its loss, the Qing government failed to realize its growing weakness, and widespread rebellions against the unpopular Qing government were further exploited by foreign states. At the end of the Second Opium War (1856–58), one of the conditions in the Treaty of Tientsin was that the British navy could access all navigable Chinese rivers. The Qing emperor was further humiliated in 1860, when Anglo — French forces looted and burned the Summer Palace (Imperial Gardens) in Beijing. European powers, including Russia, took advantage of the weak Qing government and demanded various territorial rights (Sun, 1927). The historical highlight of foreign aggression came in 1900 under the Eight — Nation Alliance (Japan, Russia, Great Britain, France, United States, Germany, Italy, and Austria — Hungary) when Peking was invaded, looted, and occupied, forcing the Qing government to sign the Boxer Protocol in 1901 ("Eight — Nation Alliance," *Wikipedia*).

The perpetual secession of Hong Kong Island to Great Britain after the end of the First Opium War in 1842 was followed by the secession of Kowloon Peninsula under the Convention of Peking in 1860. The New Territories (north of Boundary Street in Kowloon) were subsequently leased by the British for 99 years under the Second Convention of Peking in 1898 ("Hong Kong," and "Kowloon," *Wikipedia*). The colony of Hong Kong was open for trade as soon as it came under British rule. Nonetheless, the island of Hong Kong was described as a "barren rock," and the British government had to start building the colony from scratch, from the basic need for water collection during the rainy season, to physical and social infrastructure (*The Nation*, June 29, 1997). Although there were incidents of racial conflicts, clashes, and disputes between the British rulers and the local citizens, the colony of Hong Kong was basically used as a trading port, and the British colonial government maintained a high degree of stability and openness.

Subsequently, Hong Kong colony often served as a refuge for Chinese immigrants running away from mainland China for reasons of either natural or man-made disasters, crises and chaos. Entry and exit to Hong Kong was unrestricted until the early 1970s, when the growing population of Hong Kong led to housing shortages. Private businesses were unrestricted and government intervention was minimal, and the provision of welfare was largely absent. New immigrants were often supported by various charitable organizations, neighborhood, and village-related associations. Consequently, the Chinese immigrants provided not only a reliable source of labor supply, but also their ingenuity and entrepreneurial characters ensured a continued supply of enterprising individuals ready to take risks and conduct business with their own efforts and a minimum amount of capital. Economic freedom with minimum government intervention formed the foundation of capitalism in Hong Kong (Li, 2006, 2012a).

Meanwhile, while Hong Kong under the British government became a stable and growing economy, achieving the status of an industrialized and free world economy, mainland China followed a different ideological path. The Qing Dynasty ended in 1911 in the Xinhai Revolution organized by Sun Yat-sen, who founded the Nationalist Party (Kuomintang) (KMT). Unfortunately, although the Republic of China was formed in 1911, Sun did not have military power and ceded the first presidency to the military leader, Yuan Shikai. China was divided and controlled by warlords upon Yuan's death in 1916. The Kuomintang controlled only part of southern China. It was not until 1928 after the formation of the National Revolutionary Army by Chiang Kai-shek that northern China was unified. The Kuomintang was soon faced with two battle fronts, Japanese invasion, and the emerging Chinese Communist Party that created political unrest. Military resources often had to be deployed in separate battle fronts, thereby weakening the Nationalist Party's military ability. After defeat by the Communist Party in 1949, the KMT retreated to Taiwan ("Kuomintang," *Wikipedia*).

The Communist Party formed the People's Republic of China in 1949, and pursued communist ideological and socialist practices. China followed the Soviet Union's path of economic centralization, and production units were organized into communes. All resources became state-owned, and private properties were stripped. Thus, the agricultural-rich, resource-abundant China economy was reorganized into public ownership and heavy industries, resulting in extreme shortages of materials and consumables. The country was in a state of "equality in poverty." The situation turned from bad to worse upon the Soviet Union's withdrawal in the late 1950s Extreme economic hardship coexisted with political divides between the hardliners and reformists, and the power struggle eventually resulted in Mao's Cultural Revolution in the mid-1960s, at the expense of economic development.

History will provide a judgment as to the political, economic, and international costs and benefits of the "Nixon – Kissinger initiative," when US President Nixon at the height of the Cold War with the Soviet Union allowed communist China to replace Taiwan in the United Nations in 1972, thereby lifting China's communist state from one of an isolated, trade-embargoed country to the frontier of the international arena. Upon the death of Mao in 1976 and the subsequent arrest of the ultra-leftist Gang of Four in the power struggle, the reformist Deng Xiaoping eventually emerged in 1978, and a series of economic reforms were subsequently introduced. By 1979, Deng had made known his intention to take back Hong Kong from Britain in 1997 when the 99-year lease of the New Territories expired. The Sino – British Negotiation over post-1997 Hong Kong took place in 1982–84.

In 1842 when Qing China ceded Hong Kong to Britain at the end of the Opium War, it was meant to be perpetual. Since then, the Qing Dynasty was overthrown, and the People's Republic of China was established in 1949, and took over administrative and political power from the KMT government. Indeed, given its weakness, the Qing government had lost or ceded various territories to foreign governments, e.g., Vladivostok (Haishenwai in Chinese) was ceded to Russia in the Treaty of Beijing in 1860. In his various lectures in 1924, Sun Yat-sen (1927, p. 12) also documented that Chinese territories had either lost or ceded to such European powers as Great Britain, France, and Russia. While communist China often uses its "history" as the instrument in territorial disputes, the question of legitimacy should have focused on the fact that the contemporary regime in China began in 1949 when the communist regime established the People's Republic of China. Indeed, how could authoritative, lawful, and legitimate China take over the commitments and treaties made by foregone dynasties and emperors? The people of Hong Kong were not consulted when Qing China ceded Hong Kong to Britain. Similarly, Hong Kong people did not have a say and were not part of the negotiating team in the 1982 – 84 Sino – British Negotiation over post-1997 Hong Kong.

The legality of the perpetual secession of a territory would be permanent and not reversible. One simplistic argument in the sovereignty reversion has been the "survivability" of Hong Kong, as water and food supplies have to come from mainland China. Such an observation is practically true, but could be mistaken intuitively because the strength of the Hong Kong economy could "trade" with mainland China and the outside world for daily and basic supplies. Indeed, it is the Hong Kong economy that has served as a reference point and provided rescue to the mainland economy at different historical times. The shallow view rested on the misunderstanding that the mainland economy could exercise "absolute advantage" over the Hong Kong economy, but it would equally be important to know that the Hong Kong economy could exercise "comparative advantage" over the mainland economy. Indeed, there are numerous "tiny" economies in the world that have flourished and survived through trade and conducting proper business activities without relying on others.

The issue boils down to the difference in ideological and political systems. While communism developed in China after 1949, capitalism has become rooted in Hong Kong. Thus, it was dramatic for the freest capitalist economy to come under the rule of a communist country after 1997. Similar to the "Nixon – Kissinger initiative" that lifted China to the international arena, history would be written if the United Kingdom had rightly entrusted communist China to govern Hong Kong, the freest world economy. Or would it be a strategy to use Hong Kong's development as a mirror image to introduce further changes in China's ideology? Like the Qing government which was so reluctant to introduce changes to align with the contemporary world, the communist regime in China has also been reluctant to introduce changes indigenously, fearing that changes could weaken communist power.

Despite the reversion of sovereignty, the "China—Hong Kong" relationship in itself could be living history in the ideological battle. While the Basic Law was the outcome of the Sino — British Negotiation that guaranteed Hong Kong's capitalist way of life, Deng granted a period of 50 years (until 2047) to Hong Kong's capitalism under the "one country, two systems" framework, which was a novelty but has never been written or specified properly. Indeed, the "one country, two systems" has never been tested or implemented anywhere in the world; it is just an idea or even a convenience that could be subject to different interpretations. Thus, 1997 was merely a case of sovereignty reversion, but the test of the capitalist system will come in 2047.

Although China insists that the issue of Hong Kong after 1997 is an internal affair, the post-1997 development of the Hong Kong Special Administrative Region has multiple implications. The British colonial government has left behind a system that should be functional, regardless of the person in power. Hong Kong is an international city and has served as a pivot or reference point to the mainland economy in various ways. The post-1997 development of Hong Kong is not only a local issue, but also a Chinese issue, as China has to demonstrate to the international community how it runs and keeps Hong Kong "stable and prosperous." Hong Kong is also an international issue, as many foreign investors are conducting their businesses in Hong Kong, or in mainland China through Hong Kong. Finally, Hong Kong symbolizes the success of the capitalist system, with property rights, private ownership, effective governance, and business-friendly policies.

By using a political economic framework, the section will examine the development of capitalism through the interaction between China and Hong Kong. Beginning with some consolidated historical arguments, the analysis will discuss China since 1911, the political and economic orientation of China as a country, the economic role of Hong Kong in China's economic development, the Sino — British Negotiation leading to the development of post-1997 Hong Kong, and the challenges and implications to Hong Kong, China, the United Kingdom, and the international community at large in their expectations of the future development of both China and Hong Kong.

CHAPTER

14

China's 1911 Revolution and Sun's Legacy

I INTRODUCTION

The economics discipline concerns long-term analyses of productivity, growth, and development at the individual, corporate, industrial, and economic levels. Due to natural differences in the endowments of individuals and economies, economics by definition generates differences in outcomes. At the individual level, the economic solution to "inequality" is to promote ability and expand opportunity, so that individuals have the ability to look after their own economic welfare. At the level of the entire economy, the economic solution to "inequality" is to promote competitiveness and discover new comparative advantages. On the contrary, the political solution to "inequality" is through redistribution, as that can produce a short-term, popular political outcome. It is unfortunate that political decisions and outcomes are often seen through the use, inclusion, or exploitation of economic instruments. The economics purpose has often been manipulated for political and ideological ends through the implementation and execution of policies.

Market capitalism concentrates on production, profit, competition, and rewards the ingenuity of individual entrepreneurs and enterprises. "Unequal" economic outcomes generating social differences give rise to political opportunists in distinguishing between the "have" and the "don't have." Although capitalism in its early stages served as an engine to growth, a number of social inadequacies appeared, such as lacking provisions in education and public health, social protection for people with problems in economic survival, levels of infrastructure and social fabric that allowed upward social mobility in an open and transparent society. The existence of a class society had led to unfairness that on the one hand restricted economic opportunity to be shared, and on the other hand created social conflicts and distrust.

The preaching of Marxism gave rise to discussions on an alternative mode of production, which allowed concentration of resource ownership in the hands of the state or the communist regime. By taking away private ownership and giving it to the state, it was thought ideally that economic inequality would be eliminated, as the state would allocate economic materials "equally" to all citizens. Economic inequality could thus be eliminated as all individuals would be treated "equally," and as such, economic "exploitation" of one economic class over another would entirely be eliminated, as resource owners, typically landlords and capitalists, would be stripped of their "economic power." That sounds ideal and projects a "conflict-free" society. While there were criticisms about capitalism, the much discussed alternative mode of communism had never been

© 2017 Elsevier Inc. All rights reserved.

implemented until the Bolshevik Revolution in 1917 when the Soviet Union was established under a one-party state governed by the Communist Party. What the ruling regimes in Soviet Union had subsequently demonstrated was periods of political high-handedness and an absence of democracy with concentration of power, centralization of economic resources, and deprivation of freedom in all dimensions. Indeed, the Soviet Union demonstrated the most extreme form of inequality—political inequality.

When compared to economic inequality, political inequality could be more extreme because it took away all forms of individual freedom, incentives, and opportunities. While power was concentrated in the hands of the party and state officials, the "ruled" became the "subject" in a one-party political system. While imperialism was criticized when European countries colonized territories in other parts of the world, the Soviet Union annihilated much of Eastern Europe and other neighboring territories. Given the lack of natural resources, the threat of war and economic resources were all concentrated on the production of heavy industries, and economic equality could have been said to have been "achieved," but in the form of "poverty," as there was lack of consumable materials and supplies. The experience of the Soviet Union as the first and biggest communist country showed that human life was worse under communism because human affairs were conducted in activities with "absolute" outcomes characterized by extremes, dichotomies and opposites, concentration of power, and use of economic plans and directives. Politically, communist revolution was merely an alternative means for seeking power by another group of "power-hungry" dictators who were equally unwilling to share power and allow freedom to spread across different social sectors. There were no bourgeoisies, no aristocrats, no capitalists, and no investors, but political dictators who were interested in amassing power and centralizing authority, violating and disrespecting human rights. While successful revolutionaries took over power from previous regimes, these revolutionaries turned out to be equally undemocratic and not prepared to share power, and tried by all means to restrict new revolutionaries emerging.

This chapter summarizes China's development since the 1911 revolution that ended the Qing Dynasty, and the establishment of the Nationalist government, which also faced various inadequacies or missed opportunities, with a lack of economic development and its choice of leaning toward the Soviet Union which could have been a mistake. The conjecture was that had Sun, leader of the Nationalist government, chose the capitalist mode of production and followed that of the United States, the development in China since 1911 could have been very different, possibly the Japanese invasion would not have taken place, and a capitalist market economy would have associated more appropriately with the resource-rich Chinese economy, thereby producing a much stronger economy with agricultural and industrial production.

II THREE PRINCIPLES: REALITIES AND IMPLICATIONS

The Qing Dynasty was overthrown in 1911 in the Xinhai Revolution pioneered by Sun Yat-sen (1866—1925). The revolution was a succession of numerous failed uprisings in different parts of China, but the uprising that eventually toppled the Qing Dynasty was the military uprising at Wuchang in the Hubei Province on October 10, 1911, led by Sun's second in command, Huang Xing ("Huang Xing," *Wikipedia*). At the time of the Wuchang uprising, Sun was in exile in the United States, but became the first president and the founding father of the Republic of China (ROC) and the Nationalist Party (Kuomintang) in 1912.

As a southerner from Guangdong and through his family connections, Sun traveled extensively during his youth and exile years, received his education in Hawaii, and trained as a medical doctor in Hong Kong. However, his influence and support came mainly from southern China, but Sun lacked military support and control in the north. When the last Qing Emperor Puyi eventually abdicated in early 1912, Sun bowed to his military weakness and allowed Yuan Shikai, who controlled the military in northern China, to become the new provisional president in Peking. However, as Yuan proclaimed himself in 1915 as the Emperor of China (1915 – 16), China was effectively divided among different regional military warlords. After 1917, Sun advocated for reunification from his base in southern China.

Despite his various travels, exile in the capitalist economies of the United States, United Kingdom, and Japan, and living in Hong Kong, it was argued that Sun was influenced more by socialist ideals and Utopian ideas. It was reported that Sun, in the midst of ideological discussions in 1915, wrote to a socialist organization in Paris for a team of specialists to "help China set up the world's first socialist republic." Fearing his lack of military control in the north, Sun cooperated with the Communist Party of China (CPC), and sought help from the Soviet Union in 1923 after signing a manifesto with the Soviet Union. With military help from the Soviet Union, Sun established the Whampoa Military Academy near Guangzhou to develop the required military power, with the intention of hastening the unification of China. Chiang Kai-shek was made the commandant of the National Revolutionary Army. Historically, the cooperation with the CPC and the Soviet Union was known as the First United Front ("Sun Yat-sen," *Wikipedia*.).

Despite his role as a revolutionary, Sun was unable to bring stability to China as the newly formed ROC under the Nationalist (Kuomintang) government. In addition to the regional warlords who added difficulty to unification, the ROC soon faced new challenges. The external challenge was the Japanese invasion, while the internal challenge was the growing influence of the Communist Party. Sun's legacy probably rested in his doctrine of nation-building, commonly known as the Three Principles of the People: Nationalism, Democracy, and Livelihood (Sun, 1927; Leng and Palmer, 1960; Bedeski, 1977; Gregor, 1981; Gregor and Chang, 1982; Bergère, 1998). The doctrine of the Three Principles of the People, also known as the San-min Doctrine or Tridemism, is the philosophy developed by Sun with the intention of making the ROC a "free, prosperous, and powerful nation" ("Three Principles of the People," *Wikipedia*.).

The first doctrine of nationalism aimed to unite China as a nation rather than "ethnic-nationalism," independent from imperial domination and territorial aggression. In his own speech delivered on January 27, 1924, Sun (1927, p. 5) noted that "The development of Chinese nationalism will give our people a permanent place in the civilized world; so it is our duty to make effective the doctrine of nationalism." In his various lectures in 1924, Sun acknowledged the five ethnic groups that existed in China (Han, Mongols, Tibetans, Manchus, and Muslims), and that the spirit of Chinese nationalism had not been strong. Sun preferred peaceful integration and believed in "self-determination of nationalities."

The doctrine of democracy in "the People's power" and "government by the people" followed the Western spirit of constitutional government. Sun considered two sets of powers: the power of politics, and the power of governance. The political power related to powers of the people in their civic rights to express their political wishes through the exercise of power in the Right to Vote, Right to Recall, Initiative, and Referendum. The power of governance involved administration in different branches of the governmental system. Sun specified the "Five-Power Constitution" that consisted of administrative power in Judicial, Legislative, Executive, Supervisory, and Examining. Sun believed that the four elements in political power and the five administrative powers in governance should serve as checks and balances on each other.

However, there could be queries as to Sun's interpretation of democracy. A lack of clarity between democracy and liberty could have risen when reading Sun's speech on democracy and liberty delivered on March 16, 1924. For example, Sun (1927, pp. 64–68) noted the importance of liberty in the West, and that "the people of China have suffered very little tyranny from bad government... To be kind to the people was traditionally the golden rule for all emperors...." On the question of liberty, Sun remarked that "since the Chinese people have had the greatest possible freedom for thousands of years, it has not been necessary to pay much attention to the theory of liberty" ... "The Chinese people do not realize the importance of liberty, because in China it is as abundant as air." In a later speech, Sun (1927, pp. 93 and 101) differentiated between power and ability in government, noted the importance of an efficient government, and commented that "in the opinion of the mass of the Chinese people, only the very able should be their rulers." Sun's lecture, delivered on April 26, 1924, pointed to the relevance of "scientific government as the solution to democracy" (Sun, 1927, p. 104).

The more controversial aspect was the doctrine of livelihood, as analysts argued that it reflected Sun's support of communism. The doctrine advocated "government for the people," and Sun divided livelihood into four areas of clothing, food, housing, and transportation ("Three Principles of the People," *Wikipedia*.). In his speech on August 3, 1924, Sun (1927, p. 115) referred the doctrine of livelihood as including "social existence, national economy, and group life," and distinguished it from the ideology of socialism from Europe. In summarizing the experience from the West, Sun (1927, pp. 121 – 122) pointed out the four features of economic progress in modern states: (1) provision of schools, working conditions, and health laws for the working class, as that could increase work efficiency; (2) provision of public goods, such as street cars, railroads, postal and telegraphic services; (3) the need for effective and direct taxation to pay for government expenditures; and (4) the establishment of workers' cooperatives could eliminate the "middlemen" in commercial activities. Sun concluded that "modern economic progress is caused by the harmony, not the conflict, of the economic interests of society" ... "Because all men must live and must face the everlasting problem of livelihood, they either perish through conflict or live through cooperation. Class struggle, therefore, is not the cause of social progress, but a kind of social disease, which develops when a social group lacks the means of livelihood and resolves as the last resort to use abnormal means of obtaining its livelihood." By using medical terminologies, Sun criticized Marx that: "Marx's trouble was that he mistook a social pathological condition for the cause of social progress; so rightly he should be called a 'social pathologist not a social physiologist.'"

As was pointed out by a number of Kuomintang members, Sun (1927, p. 133) was aware of the lack of distinction in the Three Principles, especially between the doctrine of livelihood and communism. Sun reiterated that "livelihood is the determinant of all social activities and that lack of normal development in the livelihood of the people not only checks the progress of social culture and the reform of economic organization, but also causes moral degeneration, social inequality, oppression of labor, and class struggle; and that livelihood is the cause, and social changes are the effects," but concluded that "our doctrine of livelihood includes communism and socialism, and that communism is not an enemy of the doctrine of livelihood, but its good friend. For this reason adherents to the doctrine of livelihood should study carefully the theories of communism." Sun (1927, pp. 70 – 71) concluded that "our doctrine of nationalism corresponds with the French revolutionists' idea of liberty. To practice the doctrine of nationalism is to fight for the liberty of the nation. . . . If China were free, China would have been powerful and prosperous . . . we should sacrifice individual liberty for the liberty of the nation." "Our doctrine of democracy corresponds with the French doctrine of equality, for democracy designates the political equality of all persons. The term 'fraternity' corresponds with the Chinese expression 'tung pao' or brethren. In fact, our doctrine of livelihood is founded on the idea of fraternity; its thesis is to promote a good life for all fellow-nationals by means of economic wellbeing."

Sun definitely was a revolutionary, but it is debatable whether Sun performed strategically and appropriately as a revolutionary leader in nation-building in the postrevolutionary periods. Of course, there could be various reasons, including the lack of choice of leaders, available resources that could be mobilized, and assistance from the international community. The discussion of Sun's three doctrines revealed some degree of confusion, lack of clarity, and duality in political and ideological intuition. On nationalism, it was clear that Sun wanted to unite the north and south of China. Despite Sun's extensive travel to overseas countries, and experience and understanding of international affairs, Sun did not gain much support from northern China, and indeed had to share his authority with military warlords.

On the doctrine of democracy, Sun equally did not show a clear approach to the choice of ideologies. While he traveled extensively to nonsocialist countries and had seen the political, ideological, and economic advances in these foreign countries, Sun leaned toward the socialist movement in France, and sought help from Russia, which also was one of the European imperialist powers that took advantage of China's territory along with other imperialist countries, and made agreements with the CPC. Sun probably failed to see the ideological differences between the lack of political openness in nonsocialist countries and the Utopian ideals in socialism/communism. For example, what would be the practical and functional difference between communist Soviet Union and the Qing Emperor? In democracy, people are provided with the choice of the right to decide on political leaders through a rule-based, systematic, and transparent set of election criteria.

On the doctrine of livelihood, Sun was unclear between political ideology and provision of social capital. Sun was effectively advocating for a state where there would be more provision of public goods and infrastructure, so that all individuals could have a greater chance and choice. Social capital is often shown by the provision of common or social goods, such as the provision of education, health, and infrastructure that facilitate individuals' livelihoods in the four basic human necessities of food, housing, clothing, and transportation. Food and clothing could be secured when individuals could secure jobs and income. Housing could be costly, as it would involve the largest saving of an individual, but when housing is seen as a necessity and not a luxury, provision of government-supported low cost public housing would minimize the economic survival cost of individuals and families. To facilitate the work of individuals, it is true that provision of low cost public transport would promote efficiency in one's work. The issue of the doctrine of livelihood required a clearer policy on fiscal spending, and clarity in the role of government in the building and construction of social capital.

One can conclude that the Sun's Three Principles projected a grand outcome for China. It was more advanced than the conditions in China at the time. However, the ideological and territorial divide, and the economic backwardness in post-Qing China were the major issues bothering Sun. The unification of China then could have followed a federal system, where individual provinces in China would have their own laws and administration.

III MISSED OPPORTUNITIES

Sun lived in a historically turbulent time. While the Qing Emperor was incompetent, feudalistic, and outdated, the Qing government was hopeless when facing growing imperial powers in the world. After losing many battles and wars to foreign countries, and signing a number of "unequal" treaties, the Qing government either ceded or lost large amounts of territory to foreign countries. Sun was Cantonese, born in the province of Guangdong

(Kwangtung or Canton), he lived in Hong Kong which was a British colony, and was exposed to foreigners at a young age, either by living overseas or traveling extensively to foreign countries. Sun trained as a medical doctor and learned his political theory through experience and observation. Ideologically, Sun leaned more to France's socialist movement and Russia's revolution, even though both France and Russia were foreign imperialists.

In spite of his multiple contacts with foreigners and governments, it was unfortunate that Sun did not appreciate the advantages of the capitalist ideology practiced in the United States, Britain, and Japan. History could not be rewritten, but China's post-1911 history would be very different had Sun leaned more to the United States and other capitalist countries. One could make a historical conjecture that, e.g., had Sun been more pro-US, would there have been a Japanese invasion of China? Could there have been the rise of the Communist Party in China? Would the United States have come to aid Sun should China have been faced with a crisis?

As a Cantonese, Sun lived in Hong Kong, which had already become a British colony. It probably was true that indigenous people in Hong Kong in the early years of British colonialism could have suffered racial differences and conflicts, but Sun would have realized and sensed the kind of stability, order, and discipline that Hong Kong enjoyed under the British rule in terms of freedom of entry and exit, freedom of business, freedom of expression, and freedom of individuals in making economic progress. Sun could have pragmatically, not ideally in the Utopian sense, compared developments in the West, in Japan, and in Russia in order to consider what ideology would be suitable for China. In other words, the historic outcome would surely have been different if Sun, instead of writing to the socialists in France and seeking help from Russia, approached Great Britain or the United States and other capitalist countries for nation-building in terms of political ideology and economic strategy and freedom. It was true that European imperialist powers had hurt China during the Qing Dynasty, but instead of holding an attitude of remorse, a more positive attitude would be to study how and why these imperialist countries were so powerful, and why China was losing and lagging behind. Was the conflict with the imperialists due more to the power of the imperialists, or to the weakness of the Qing government? In other words, the activities of the imperialist countries could be used as lessons and references for development in post-1911 China. In economic development, Sun could have made simple comparisons between China, which was agriculturally-abandoned, and the Soviet Union which was resource-lacking.

It is interesting to point out the need to distinguish between behavior and ideology. It should be human behavior to show sympathy or fraternity to people with difficulties, to the sick, old, and poor. The psychological impact when people show sympathy would be to provide needed assistance. This is purely human behavior, but whether it should be raised or lifted to an ideological level is another question. When people who face difficulties needed help and assistance, it would not automatically nor necessarily mean that the government needs to spend more, that those not in difficulty should give more, or that society should opt for greater degree of income equality through redistribution and higher taxation. In other words, the economic difficulties of some individuals would not necessarily mean unfairness at the society level. It could be socially suicidal and economically detrimental when difficulties and problems faced by some individuals or sectors lead to some sort of "penalties" that the rest of the society and economy has to suffer. Microissues could remain and be dealt with at microlevels, and not magnified to become macroissues. It is thus normal for people to show sympathy toward human suffering, but society should not necessarily be responsible for every single individual problem. Otherwise, society would have to embrace all private costs. Sympathy is a social and psychological issue, and should not spill over to economics.

Sun probably held a sympathetic attitude toward the ideology of socialism and communism. His absence in making contact with the West and seeking assistance from capitalist countries should have exposed Sun's innate belief and choice of ideology, and that was not capitalism. The first missed opportunity, or even mistake, made by Sun was his absence of ever considering seeking assistance from the West, and learning how capitalist development in the West could have been applicable to post-Qing China. This could have vast implications politically and economically. Being a Cantonese himself, Sun should have realized that people from southern China were more enterprising and entrepreneurial. Indeed, in one of his lectures, Sun (1927, pp. 64 – 66) noted that "for 2,000 years, the emperors followed a *laissez-faire* policy, and never interfered with the private affairs of the people so long as they remained loyal to the throne." The British colony of Hong Kong was also pursuing *laissez-faire* principles. Sun made a mistake by not choosing and drawing references from the West as the suitable "mentor" in China's post-1911 development.

Associated with the lack of reference to the West in nation-building was the lack of economic development. Despite his lack of support from northern China, and his background as a medical doctor, Sun could have allowed post-1911 China to engage more actively in economic activities, through businesses, industrial expansion, and foreign trade. With his cordial and close contact with countries in Europe and North America, Sun could

IV. THE FRONTIER OF CAPITALISM: CHINA VERSUS HONG KONG

have easily attracted foreign investment to China, and made reference to the role and function of fiscal and monetary policies practiced in the West. The progressive Hong Kong economy then could be a useful reference for Sun to realize the importance of economic freedom as an instrument in building up a strong and free post-1911 China. Other than appointing his brother-in-law, T.V. Soong, to set up the Canton Central Bank to mobilize financial resources, and appointing Chiang Kai-Shek in establishing the Whampoa Military Academy in Guangzhou in 1924, Sun failed to pursue a more vigorous, functional, and pragmatic economic policy that would not only serve to promote the post-1911 economy, but could also utilize foreign knowledge and experience in nation-building. This could be due to his lack of economic knowledge, or lack of other reliable persons who could help to draft an economic path for post-Qing China.

On the contrary, should there have been more focus on economic development, Sun's military weakness and lack of support from the north could have been improved or strengthened. With the increase in economic activities, such as foreign investment from the United States, the increase in economic opportunities would have opened up other aspects and the economic "multiplier," engaged more people in economic activities, and economic outcomes would have spread to other activities. In relation to his doctrine on livelihood, Sun could have led his government to engage more in the construction of social capital and the establishment of a civic society, where people's "livelihood" would improve along with economic development and growth.

At the turn of the 20th century, the economies of Japan and the United States were the rising economies at the time. Sun could easily have learnt from these economies, their economic success, and the institution of suitable policies for development. Therefore, the second missed opportunity was the absence in the pursuit of an effective economic policy in the post-1911 government, despite the richness of China's resources, and the availability of references, experience and lessons from Hong Kong, Japan, the West, and other growing and stable capitalist economies. Indeed, should Sun's China have joined the league of capitalist market economies, the outcome of China's development would have been very different. Again, some conjecture would lend some support. For example, increase in foreign investment and export of goods would have expanded, and the rise in income would have had a number of favorable impacts on China's development. Learning the extent of economic openness in Hong Kong could have led to greater utilization of economic resources. Since Qing China was occupied mostly by family businesses and small- and medium-sized industries, Sun could have further boosted the entrepreneurial spirit of the people by encouraging more business establishments and the institution of a reliable and appropriate fiscal regime, so that a transparent and systemic fiscal policy would have produced positive signals to foreign investors.

In other words, Sun's China would have developed along with neighboring economies, and the economic, technological, and industrial simultaneous rise would have developed connections and contacts between Sun's China and Japan, e.g., could have produced a very different path of economic, and accordingly political, development after 1911, because economic successes could in turn have aided the political environment in the Kuomintang government. Similarly, development along with the West would have involved the United States, who could have checked Japan's territorial aggression. In short, by concentrating merely on military activities, Sun and the Kuomintang had strategically missed and wasted a lot of economic opportunities, which could have rescued the weakness of the Kuomintang regime, and as well strengthened the Chinese economy as an industrial, export, and technological center in line with the development of other industrialized countries.

Sun was definitely not a strategist, nor had Sun received useful suggestions on the strategy of nation-building, including political tactics. Since Sun traveled widely among different world powers, and had good knowledge on the outcomes of imperialism and socialism, he should have realized the importance of language as a political instrument. In his time, Sun should have noticed that Great Britain was a stronger imperialist country than France, as the United States and other British colonies, notably Canada, Australia, and India, were using English as the practical language. Sun should have noted the political significance and importance of language usage in China.

There are numerous Chinese dialects, but the larger two dialects were the Cantonese spoken in most southern regions while Mandarin or Putonghua was mainly used by people from the north. While the writing of Chinese in Cantonese and Mandarin dialects is the same, Sun could have been more forceful and officially pushed Cantonese and other dialects as a parallel to that of Mandarin used in northern regions in China, particularly as Sun himself was from the Guangdong region. It was reported that shortly after the fall of the Qing Dynasty, the founding fathers of the republic met in 1912 to decide which language should be spoken in the new China. Although there is still a need of historical authenticity, it was rumored in legend that in the formal voting, Cantonese lost by one vote. It has been argued that Cantonese "bears more resemblance to classical Chinese than Mandarin," but others argued that it was "groundless" to think of using Cantonese in parallel with Mandarin

(*South China Morning Post*, October 6, 2009; "Did Cantonese Almost Replace Mandarin as the Standard Spoken Version of Chinese?," *Quora*). There was another rumor that Sun, aware that he was a southerner, displayed statesmanship by allowing Mandarin to continue as the official Chinese dialect. Replacement would have been difficult, but elevating Cantonese and other major dialects as a parallel to Mandarin in official business could have been a possibility, after all the writing of Chinese was similar among dialects. Thus, "one language, few dialects" could be a linguistic instrument that could have helped to unify China. The inclusion of other dialects in the official language would present a sense of linguistic equality between the north and south of China. Dialect diversity elevated to the official level would have produced a greater sense of stability, equality, and openness (Erbaugh, 1995). Of course, history could not be rewritten, but was it a lack of foresight, a missed opportunity, or simply a mistake on the part of Sun by not being forceful enough in his leadership to stabilize linguistic diversity in China?

While Sun was preoccupied with issues that needed to be settled in the postrevolution years, history would decide if Sun had taken the right path for China, or whether Sun should have done much better and made choices that could have been beneficial to different ethnic origins. The missing link in many of the studies on Sun, on the ROC, or on the Kuomintang, was the lack of economic development. Post-1911 China was very much occupied by territorial conflicts, militarism, political and ideological differences, remains of the feudalistic Qing Empire, imperialism, and foreign occupation. The outcomes would have been more favorable should more attention, energy, and resources have been geared to economic development through Chinese virtues, competitive advantage, and economic features.

Another missing link Sun should have learned when contacting with the more advanced countries in the West would be the relevance and importance of instituting systems. Sun spoke about a civilized society, but a civilized society would only be governed by the establishment of transparent, reliable and fair systems, and not personality influences. The various conflicts Sun and the Kuomintang faced could have delayed the institution of a civilized society. But then, the longer the decision delay in instituting a civilized society, the longer the ideological and military conflicts would have lasted. It might not be a "chicken and egg" issue, but instability or conflicts and peace are substitutes: the greater the degree of peace that could be achieved through civic establishments, the sooner conflicts or instability would subside, because people could devote their energies to alternative activities. In general, human beings are "risk-averse," and certainty is preferred to uncertainty. Hence, if given a choice, activities that were peaceful in nature were always preferred to activities that were not peaceful. In the final analysis, one can conclude that Sun was a revolutionary, but did not perform well as a strategist in the postrevolution years. Planning a revolution was difficult, but it would be equally challenging to work on an effective development strategy for the postrevolution era.

IV THE SUITABLE ECONOMIC IDEOLOGY

It is true to argue that the long history of premodern China was filled by emperors and dynasties which were undemocratic and lacked political openness and participation. However, economic self-sufficiency in many of the historical periods would mean that individual entrepreneurial activities, family and small-scale businesses, creativity in the form of cultural artifacts, and retail trading were the economic foundations of China. Together with the Confucian teaching of self-reliance and hard-work, the economic history of premodern China would show that the economic ideology that adhered to private economic activities would be more suitable than for individuals and businesses to seek help or rely on government in different dynasties (Twitchett et al., 1978; Elvin, 1984; Eastman, 1989; Howell, 2012).

In short, capitalism should be the more appropriate ideology for China. Much of China, especially the coastal regions, was resource rich, and agriculture and other light manufacturing were the major economic activities. The modern form of social welfare and economic redistribution was absent, and there were not many systemic arrangements of state assistance through the dynasties. Rather, the payment of tax to the emperors and the state was the more important and dominant fiscal issue. Although there were a few worldly inventions, the lack of scientific creation in general made premodern China an uncompetitive country in the global context. Although there was an absence of massive industrial production in various undemocratic dynasties, primitive capitalism was dominated by the private sector and nonstate activities in historic China. One could argue that under the conditions of richness of resources and self-sufficiency, it was possible that scientific creations were delayed, as there was less urgent need for technological progress when life was mostly self-sufficient. Nonetheless, premodern China over the centuries did develop many of its own solutions, e.g., in medical science with herbal medicines and acupuncture treatments, and in the lunar calendar based on agricultural cycles.

In addition, the missing conditions in premodern China had more to do with the shortage of complements in the pursuit of a capitalist economic ideology. China was a vast country, but the lack of development, building and supply of social and public infrastructure, a reliable and sustainable monetary economy, and independent civic establishments reinforced the lack of industrial development and scientific innovation. It is also true that historic China had made connections with its neighboring territories, mainly through land connections, typically in trade in the form of barter exchanges, but delay in contacts with foreign countries through ocean transport could be due to ignorance and superstition. Although in recent centuries Chinese people in the coastal regions had migrated to foreign countries serving as laborers, the people in China were blessed with agricultural products and development. Hence, historic China was "civic" in terms of self-sufficiency, conducting economic exchanges through the private market mechanism. The capitalist mode of economic ideology in historic China found its roots in the teaching of Confucius, who preaches individualism rather than collectivism in social and economic activities, self-reliance rather than assistance-seeking, caring of others rather than burden shifting, and individuals adhering to the macroeconomy rather than using the macroeconomy to rescue individual difficulties, and so on (Wisman, 1988; Waley, 2005; Herrmann-Pillath, 2011).

With its economic and geographical vastness, and the availability of abundant resources, development in China could not be in the hands of the government alone. China's economic vastness would mean that the same region could be successful in a number of business activities, and the same economic activity could also be successful across regions. The economic multiplier could function to its fullest possible extent. Economic dispersal should maximize business development, and market competition would impose natural boundaries in economic activities. Indeed, market competition would encourage newcomers and bring creativity and novelty to economic activities. The "relative" outcomes should provide ample grounds for development, growth, and progress. In other words, capitalism would be more suitable to China, because the ideology allows individuals to explore new market opportunities that in turn would and could strengthen the macroeconomy. Given its vastness and differences in regional endowments, one should not expect perfect equality in development, but growth in the economic welfare of individuals would permit asset and wealth accumulation, social mobility, and eventually removal of poverty.

However, economic progress does not occur in a vacuum. Decisions on economic development should be dispersed in the hands of private individuals and corporations, but there should be an effective "check and balance" system that protects market players and consumers, and ensures there are no market abuses through insider-information, poor practice in ethics and morals, market manipulation, corruption, presence of vested interests, rent-seeking, and cronyism. Market capitalism governs the economic side of the society, but the presence of law and civic establishments are needed institutions that serve as "checks and balances" in economic activities to ensure legality, equity, and transparency. The successful functioning of capitalism requires a strong, progressive, and continuously-improving system. Other than the military that protects the country's borders, and the police force to eradicate crimes, individuals and businesses are protected by both government and civic institutions and establishments. Individuals in difficulties could be aided by government organizations and nongovernment bodies.

On the contrary, socialism or communism adheres to collectivization, where all individuals would be treated "equally," and the society would become "classless," as things would be arranged by the state and all individuals would be assigned their duties. Hence, instead of business leaders and individual entrepreneurs, party leaders would become the decision-makers. Effectively, party leaders are the "elite" class, and political inequality exists between party leaders and the people. Given the dominance of power in the communist party, it would not be foreseeable to institute other civic, nonparty institutions so as to perform effective "checks and balances" on the party-led political system. Once instituted, the one-party political system could become permanent, and political abuse and mistakes might not be uncovered.

Economically, different businesses, different industries and resources in different regions in China would require different production methods, exhibit different talents and skills, and local knowledge would be needed for development. This requires economic diversity and freedom, so that interested individuals would exercise their skills and build up their expertise to engage in production activities. A "one-formula" political structure would only limit possibilities and opportunities. Differences in economic endowments naturally create "unequal outcomes," but this should be seen positively and optimistically as an incentive and encouragement for individuals to progress, rather than negatively and pessimistically as an instrument for power-hungry politicians to amass and accumulate political power for their own benefit and advantage. It is true that there is no perfection in any system, but it is more important to adapt an effective system that is functional and improvable. Given China's vast economic opportunities and diversity, a diverse system with a high degree of freedom, discipline, morality, ethics, transparency, legality, and the ability to perform "checks and balances" should be more preferable than a system that concentrates power into one institution that could not be challenged or monitored.

The system in mature capitalism would allow freedom in private hands, but the government would exercise effective instruments to ensure equity, and avoid and eradicate misdeeds and wrongdoing. With the possibility of "checks and balances" in the political system, individual property rights and opportunities would be assured by the presence of an effective legal system. In addition, the building of social capital and infrastructure would be developed through the fiscal framework. In turn, instead of pursuing income equality, it would be social inequality and poverty that would be addressed. The ultimate intention would be to look for channels that promote "able people," so that they would be self-sufficient and rely less on government assistance, which in turn would allow more fiscal resources for long-term development and enhanced competitiveness. Hence, an equitable and opportunity-building *laissez-faire* system should be the more appropriate economic and political framework for China. It is the degree of economic diversity and the living standard of the people that serves as the judgment on the political leaders, not the amount of wealth and power leaders amassed during their term of office.

In a nutshell, in a mature democratic capitalist regime, there are two types of leaders. The business leaders are not meant to exploit the market, but to perform their best in production maximization with a strong sense of ethics, commitment, and discipline. The political leaders are not meant to abuse their power and authority in amassing wealth, but to serve the people selflessly, and show strong performance in ensuring improvements in people's welfare, civic advancement, and development. On the contrary, while the communist ideology advocates a Utopian nation, socialism exhibits the accumulation and concentration of power and authority in the hands of the party leaders and officials. Political inequality is extreme in a communist regimes. People under communism are suppressed and adopt passive behavior, and individuals' creative performance is restricted. On the contrary, the dispersed economic power in capitalism can serve as a check and balance to the power and authority of the government. The existence of relative economic inequality could be improved through policies and individual efforts. A capitalist market economy encourages the rise of more "able" individuals.

V CONCLUSION

The Qing Dynasty was controlled by knowledge-lacking emperors. Despite invasion by foreign imperialists, the stubborn nature of the Qing government knew little about the international community. Losses in wars, secession of land to foreign imperialists, and signing of treatments and agreements had shown the growing weakness of the Qing regime. The various uprisings were regarded more as disturbances and revolutions than as the urgent concerns and patriotic calls for modernization and restructuring. Opportunities were missed, as resources were misplaced in the outdated Qing regime.

Sun, who saw and experienced the declining Qing China, and the aggression from foreign imperialists, traveled extensively to Europe and had first-hand experience and information on the communist movement in Europe, especially in France and Russia. His path in the overthrow of the Qing Dynasty lasts a long time, as numerous uprisings ended in failure. Although Sun succeeded in the 1911 revolution that ended the Qing Dynasty, he was faced with pressure from the north as he did not gain support from the military. Internal conflicts erupted in different dimensions. One was the emergence of warlords in northern China. The Japanese invasion and the emergence of Chinese communism had exhausted the military strength in Sun's Kuomintang government. Sun reviewed his own ideology when he sought help from Russia, without considering the positive side of capitalism from his experience in Hong Kong and other western countries. Sun was weak in strategies and nation-building, and failed to lift China to a higher stage of economic development. In the end, the rise of the Chinese Communist Party expelled Sun's Kuomintang government to Taiwan. The new China was established in 1949 as a one-party communist state.

The spread of communism after the establishment of the Soviet Union in 1917 was seen as a "new world" in which people were treated "equally." In reality, leaders in the Soviet Union practiced political extremism, as power and authority were concentrated. Central planning was introduced, as there was insufficient food and materials. However, ideological popularity would not be the answer without studying the fundamental resources of the country. Sun and other Chinese leaders were preoccupied with political popularity and ideals and their ambition to gain power, and not functionality in the economic context. The economic geography of China is very different from that of the Soviet Union. In geographical terms, China spreads over different tropical zones, with areas of warm regions in the south and east, and cold regions in the north and west. Such geographical diversity permits agricultural growth and ample food supply that could multiply into a number of economic activities. China's large population is enterprising, and prefers to conduct private businesses. Although China has gone through various stages of difficulties in various dynasties, the economic, geographic, and human contours of China demonstrate that diversity and dispersal of activities should be most appropriate for China's development. The pursuit of a capitalist market economy should be the closest complement to China's resource contours. What would be needed is the establishment of a civic society that provides a legal framework, professionalism, and independent institutions to protect the citizenry, ensure quality, strong ethics, and discipline in the behavior of all citizens.

IV. THE FRONTIER OF CAPITALISM: CHINA VERSUS HONG KONG

CHAPTER

15

China's Economic Reform Path

I INTRODUCTION

There is a difference between revolution and evolution in politics. Evolution implies a situation of indigenous change, without the need to have a new political regime. The existing regime would introduce changes that would bring new political and economic dimensions or restructuring of policies. Political upheaval could be avoided in an evolutionary situation, though there could be political forces pressurizing the regime to make changes. Depending on the broad-mindedness of the leadership, the advantages of evolution include certainty and avoidance of potential violence. With evolution, people know what the problems are and can see or expect the outcome after the changes. There will be a certain degree of continuity and certainty. On the contrary, revolution could end up in a replacement of the government by the revolutionaries. Normally, revolutionaries are supposed to have their own ideals and ambitions, and intend to introduce policies, ideologies, and practices to improve society under the new regime, and do not mean just to forcefully obtain power. On the optimistic side, the success of a revolutionary regime could give new hope to the people, as the country would come under the control of a new political regime. There would be new opportunities, and regime change should give rise to a new group of leaders who would form new power centers. A major problem with revolution is that the power would be amassed in the hands of the revolutionaries and may not be democratically shared, the regime could

© 2017 Elsevier Inc. All rights reserved.

even be very forceful in ensuring their grip on power if challenged by another generation of revolutionaries and opposition. Once power was secured, revolutionaries could become equally reluctant to accept challenges.

However, new political regimes could produce a certain degree of uncertainty. Questions one could ask, e.g., would be whether the new regime would introduce everything new, or would it be just the same "old wine in new bottles?" How far and different would the new regime be, or were they just another group of political opportunists? Could the new regime have effective control and governance within a short time, or would they just practice favoritism among their cronies? The question in a revolution is not so much the cause of the revolution, but the organization of a new and effective government after the revolution. This is true in a number of "fragile" and communist states who gained political independence through decolonialization or an act of revolution, but the postrevolution regime was not effective or functional, with the end result that the situation after independence or revolution was no better, or even worse, than the preindependence or prerevolutionary period. The saying that "it is easier to criticize than to construct" is the most appropriate reminder to revolutionaries who are "hungry for power" and use revolution as their means to gain political power. At worst, a revolutionary government in turn would stop others from making progress, or would exercise its utmost power in restricting others making changes.

Prior to the fall of the Qing Dynasty in 1911, Sun Yat-sen and other revolutionaries organized a number of uprisings, but there was no visible plan for a post-Qing government should revolution end the Qing Dynasty. Thus, to many people in China, the post-Qing years were no better than the Qing years as the 1911 revolution ended up with political fragmentation and control by territorial warlords. The newly established Kuomintang government was busy engaged in dealing with conflicts rather than nation-building. Indeed, it was unfortunate that political troubles and conflicts spread and deepened as the economy remained stagnant for decades after Sun's 1911 revolution that toppled the Qing Dynasty.

The popular rise of the Soviet Union in 1917 could have inspired large number of pursuers and followers from China that communism would replace capitalism as the ideal world. Communist ideals had been discussed and written about, but never put into practice. The Soviet Union introduced communism, but its various practices were far different from those ideals. The principle adopted by Vladimir Lenin (1870–1924) was "democratic centralism," implying "democratic and open discussion on policy on the condition of unity in upholding the agreed upon policies" ("The Communist Party of China," *Wikipedia*). In reality, people in the Soviet Union were economically poor and materially starved. Political power was concentrated in the hands of the party officials. The young communists from China looked to the change of regime in Russia and intended to introduce communism in China. The Communist Party of China (CPC) was founded, along with eight other legal parties that comprised the United Front, in 1921. The size and followers of the CPC grew on the mainland and engaged in a decade-long civil war with the Kuomintang government, thereby weakening the Kuomintang considerably as the communist movement coexisted with the Japanese invasion (Chang, 1997). Eventually, the CPC established the People's Republic of China (PRC) in 1949, driving the Kuomintang to retreat to Taiwan (Fenby, 2003).

Having led the CPC and established the PRC in 1949, Mao Zedong (1893–1976) copied the principles of democratic centralism from the Soviet Union, and established various levels of state organizations. As a one-party state, the highest body in the PRC is the National Congress that convened every fifth year, but the Central Committee meets once a year, while most duties and responsibilities are vested in the Politburos and their Standing Committees. The party leader holds the offices of General Secretary, Chairman of the Central Military Commission, and serves as the State President.

Following the early 1950s, communist China introduced centralization and removed private property and ownership, organized communes as the basis of production and control, and conducted heavy industry through state-owned enterprises. The elimination of private property and organization of communes immediately eliminated "income inequality," as daily material needs of individual households were rationed. The removal of income inequality was replaced by political extremism as controls were in the hands of party officials. But China's economic fundamentals were far richer and very different from the Soviet Union. Although Soviet aid provided to China was in the form of military and industrial assistance, the Soviet leaders would have realized the economic potential of China, which could easily overtake that of the Soviet Union. History documented that the Sino–Soviet split (1960–89) was due to the ideological differences between China's Mao and the Soviet's Khrushchev ("Sino–Soviet Split," *Wikipedia*). The Soviet aid withdrawal from China in 1958 could have a hidden economic reason, in that a potentially strong Chinese economy could challenge the Soviet economy. The situation deteriorated in 1958 when Mao introduced "grassroots socialism" in the Great Leap Forward that aimed to accelerate China's industrial capability, especially in the production of steel. Communes were established and collectives were formed to mobilize workers, but unskilled workers could only use backyard furnaces for steel production in order to meet targets. Much of the steel output was of low quality ("Great Leap Forward," *Wikipedia*). The Soviet withdrawal in 1958 coexisted with the "Great Chinese Famine" in 1959. China faced the worst of two worlds, as both industrial and agricultural outputs plummeted. Statistics reported that deaths in the "Great Chinese Famine" amounted to 15 million ("Great Chinese Famine," *Wikipedia*).

Mao's ideology led also to an ideological split between Mao and his "hardline" followers who put politics, class-struggle, and mass public campaigns as the supreme consideration, and the "reformists" who advocated for some form of economic development through market mechanisms in order to facilitate economic growth and improve people's livelihood. The ideological divide led to the emergence of "one party, two divisions" within China. Mao's ideological struggle in the Cultural Revolution began in 1966 and ended in 1969. People's livelihood turned from bad to worse, and political victimization became the order of the time. Intellectuals and professionals were sent to do hard labor in remote regions, while the young generation constituted the "Red Guards" and were told to "love the country and ignore their parents." There were calls for social destruction of the "Four Olds," namely custom, culture, habits, and ideas, including the Temple of Confucius ("Cultural Revolution," *Wikipedia*). People with "foreign" connections were openly mocked and humiliated. Supporters and students holding the "Little Red Book" could travel free, attendance at political gatherings was compulsory, and ideological "wrong doers" were identified, caught, and punished. Reasoning and accusations were based purely on political and ideological lines. It was reported that some 1.5 million were killed, and millions of others were imprisoned, tortured, and humiliated ("Cultural Revolution," www.history.com/topics/cultural-revolution). Mao's Cultural Revolution was a showcase of communist extremism, and the extent of atrocities demonstrated clearly that communism in practice was not what people believed. Political inequality was extreme, irreversible, harmful, and detrimental when compared to income inequality in capitalism.

The turning point came in 1971 when US President Nixon visited China with the intention of luring China to the side of the United States in the Cold War with the Soviet Union. The "Nixon–Kissinger initiative" (NKI) summarized the political and economic intentions of pulling and lifting the PRC into the world arena. While the admission of China into the United Nations formed the first political phase in the NKI, the second phase that dealt with economics appeared in the subsequent rise of Deng Xiaoping (1904–97) as a reformist in 1978.

This chapter will document the major events and discuss the consequences and implications, focusing on the domestic, regional, and international aspects of economic reform. Each of the following sections identifies an important issue in the postreform years. Beginning with the legacy of the Cultural Revolution that completely distorted all economic issues, China was brought back to "normal" as a result of the external forces from the United States in the visit by President Nixon. The "NKI" did raise China up diplomatically, politically, and economically, but after China's nearly four decades of economic reform and performance, it would be interesting to debate using simple cost and benefit analysis whether the NKI was the right move on the part of the United States, because both Russia and China could exert pressure on the United States and the international community. One can also summarize the pace and path of economic reform in each of the decades since 1978, highlighting the key issues and their impact. The later sections consider the various impacts and consequences after nearly four decades of China's economic reform, discussing the successes and inadequacies.

II CULTURAL REVOLUTION: ECONOMIC LEGACIES

The Japanese invasion of China caused economic losses to China. However, Japan suffered defeat in the Second World War, and it would be more constructive to look forward instead of lamenting historical wounds. Chiang Kai-shek waived reparation claims for the war when Taiwan concluded the Treaty of Taipei with Japan in 1952. In 1970, Communist Party leader Mao remarked to Edgar Snow, an American journalist, that "Those Japanese were real good. Without Japanese's help, China's (Communist) revolution would not have succeeded." Similarly, during a visit to Nanjing by Japanese Prime Minister Takuei Tanaka in 1972, and responding to the Japanese Prime Minister's apology for what Japan had done during the war, Mao remarked that "(Japan) does not have to say sorry; you had contributed towards China, why? Because had Imperial Japan not start the war of invasion, how could we communists become mighty powerful? How could we stage the coup d'état? How could we defeat Chiang Kai-Shek? How are we going to pay back you guys? No, we do not want your war reparations!" ("Did Mao thank Japan for invading China?, *Quora*; "Talk Mao Zedong," *Wikiquote*; "China–Japan Relations," *Wikipedia*; and *The Washington Post*, May 13, 2013; see Article 5 of the 1972 Joint Communiqué of the Government of Japan and the Government of the PRC). One thing needs to be clarified. It was the Nationalist

Government that was at war with Imperial Japan from 1937 to 1945. The number of Chinese casualties (dead and wounded) in the Japanese invasion was estimated at between 20 and 35 million (Zachary Keck, "The CCP Didn't Fight Imperial Japan; the KMT Did," *The Diplomat*, September 4, 2014; and "Second Sino–Japanese War," *Wikipedia*).

According to the *Statistical Portal*, there were 82.6 million members of the Chinese Communist Party in 2011, increasing by 6.28% to 87.79 million in 2014. Although it was the largest communist party in the world, it represented only 6.31% of the Chinese population in 2011. The Chinese Communist Party recruited 3.18 million members in 2011, out of a total application of 21.6 million. In 2012, the number of members in the eight noncommunist political parties in China (China Democratic League, China National Democratic Construction Association, Jiusan Society, China Association for the Promotion of Democracy, Chinese Peasants and Workers' Democratic Party, China Revolutionary Committee of the Kuomintang, China Zhi Gong Dang, and Taiwan Democratic Self-government League) amounted to 873,565, equivalent to 1.03% of Chinese Communist Party members. However, the *Statistical Portal* also shows the (reported) corruption cases from party officials. Between 2009 and 2014, the number of registered cases increased from 115,420 to 226,000, while the number of closed corruption cases increased from 101,893 to 218,000, giving in 2014 a total number of party official corruption cases of 444,000, equivalent to about 5.06% of party members (*The Statistical Portal*, Statista, www.statista.com).

During the communist movement of 1934–35, Mao exploited the rural people in remote regions in China to gain support in what was known as the "Long March" ("Long March," *Wikipedia*). In the Cultural Revolution, Mao mobilized the nation's youth as "Red Guards" to purge the "impure" elements (notably the reformists). Supported and surrounded by a group of radicals, including his wife Jiang Qing, Mao attacked his "opponents" and reasserted his authority. However, prolonged violence occurred in different phases of the Cultural Revolution, which was considered as one of the worst genocides of the 20th century in the world. It was reported that the Cultural Revolution caused the deaths of 30 million people, but that might have excluded those who died of hunger. By comparison, the scale of atrocity in the Cultural Revolution was not that different from that of the Japanese invasion (*The Worst Genocides of the 20th and 21st Century*, www.scaruffi.com/politics/dictat.html; and "Cultural Revolution," *Wikipedia*). The Cultural Revolution led by Mao was utterly a case of a power struggle through mass mobilization of human resources, but it turned out to be totalitarian and authoritarian. It was concluded that "Mao's large-scale attack on the party and system he had created would eventually produce a result opposite to what he intended, leading many Chinese to lose faith in their government altogether" ("Cultural Revolution," www.history.com/topics/cultural-revolution).

Since the Cultural Revolution was a political and ideological battle, supporters and critics would probably either hold a supporting or an opposing view (Chang, 1973; Bettleheim, 1974; MacFarquhar, 1974; Dittmer, 1974; Clark, 2008; Su, 2011; Wu, 2014). Supporters argued that the Cultural Revolution opened up a new chapter in China, set the country on a new development path by eradicating all kinds of "foreign" influences, and made sure development would be "home-grown" with Chinese characteristics. By eliminating all elements of capitalism, communist China could start their own way of development and growth. This obviously served to "window dress" the atrocities. On the contrary, critics pointed to the detrimental nature of the Cultural Revolution, as it provided a negative precedence in nation-building, and questioned whether it would be realistic for a communist country to survive on an isolation basis without making contact with or references to the international community.

Mao's extremist ideological approach would produce a sense of political rigidity for future development in China, and such rigidity could even be worse than the situation in previous Chinese dynasties. The ideology-led China would mean, e.g., that economic activities would be secondary to ideology, while ideas and behavior would become unilateral or one-way. The lack of diversity and openness would limit opportunities.

Consumption Deprivation

There are a number of unfavorable and distorting economic consequences as a result of the Cultural Revolution. One could be "consumption deprivation," where the pursuit of heavy industries following the Soviet style and rationing of daily materials through the communes would mean people were "deprived" of the right and freedom to consume and spend on their favored goods. Such a distortion and restriction in consumption showed a huge contrast with the situation before communism, where people were free to shop for consumables and durables. Such deprivation and frustration was buried in all the prereform years, as living materials were rationed and private choice was regarded as "bourgeoisie." In clothing, e.g., the "Mao suit" in the three colors of black, gray, and dark blue was the only set of clothing people wore.

Although the choice of consumption was not imposed after reform, it was not until around 2005 when mainland people had sufficient financial resources, and traveled to foreign countries to shop and consume massively virtually all luxury foreign goods and brands. The manner in which mainland Chinese shopped in foreign cities for all sorts of luxury brands and necessities reflected their instinct for private consumption based on their choice and preferences, and not rationed by party officials. The extent of Chinese consumption and their ability to shop alarmed foreigners as unseasoned Chinese travelers at times exhibited unethical manners and uncivilized behavior, poor discipline, and lack of consideration and respect. Travel agents in China had to organize pretrip meetings on etiquette to intended travelers to avoid embarrassment and potential disputes.

In addition, since 1949, when the Chinese communist regime was faced with trade embargoes from the advanced countries, China could not engage in trade with foreign countries despite its import needs. Consequently, informal or underground economic activities developed along the southern Chinese borders. A clear example was the various informal activities through the border of Hong Kong. Since the 1950s, pro-Beijing businessmen in Hong Kong conducted trafficking of goods and arms (see, e.g., the Hong Kong businessman, "Mr. Henry Fok Ying Tung (1923–2006)," *Wikipedia*). At the personal level, as many Hong Kong citizens had family connections in southern China, and since there was no restriction from the Hong Kong side, families visiting China carried food and durable goods back to their own villages. In the 1950s and 1960s when life was difficult, such basic goods as cooking oil and clothing materials were brought across the border. In the 1970s and 1980s, consumable goods and electronic appliances became more popular, and entire sets of color televisions, air conditioners, and refrigerators were "hand carried" across the border.

However, the situation was reversed and instead of Hong Kong people carrying goods to the mainland, it was the turn of mainland travelers coming to Hong Kong to shop. Since 2003 when visa-free travel permits were increasingly given to mainland visitors, many mainland visitors came to Hong Kong for "daily shopping" as the various goods they brought back to Shenzhen, the city on the other side of the Hong Kong border, could immediately be sold to informal traders. Other than luxurious brands and expensive items, the informal or underground economy expanded to include such basic necessities and normal items as baby formulae, festive and seasonal items, cosmetics and drugs, infant wear and supplements, cell phones and tablet computers, and so on. The underground economy could have expanded to include the smuggling of Chinese currency. For example, a 20 m-long tunnel equipped with rail tracks and wagons built by smugglers between the borders of Hong Kong and Shenzhen was discovered in 2013 (*South China Morning Post*, December 25, 2013; and *The Wall Street Journal*, December 26, 2013). The two reasons that mainland visitors engage in informal economic activities were because the consumer tax in China is high, but there is no consumption tax in Hong Kong. The second reason was the unreliability of home-made products in China, as fake, toxic, and contaminated products had been found in large number of daily necessities, including eggs, baby formulae, soya source, toys, candies, jewelry, medicines, and so on. Parallel trade shoppers came with large suitcases and stuffed them with goodies from special retail shops, especially shops near the border town of Sheng Shui on the Hong Kong side, thereby creating inconvenience and nuisance to local residents with occasional crushes and demonstrations.

The unreliability of home-made products in China could be another unfavorable economic consequence. Lacking the establishment of a functional and transparent system, abuse of power had been common and continuous, though there were numerous reports on corruption. Corruption, cronyism, and promotion of princelings among the inner circle of top officials have been extensive and visible (*The Guardian*, October 24, 2001; *China Daily*, June 16, 2004; *Jiangmen News*, April 3, 2006; and *New York Times*, April 12, 2008) (Wederman, 2009; Guo, 2008; Quah, 2009; Feng and Johansson, 2016). Indeed, the Cultural Revolution had also resulted in distortion in a number of areas. For example, education had been used as a party instrument to control, and the young generation did not need to obey and respect their parents as the party and country took precedence over parents and family. The media reports were monitored and served as propaganda machinery.

Absolute political inequality became extreme, and individuals would have no chance to move up or secure better personal welfare without going through the political ladder. The fall in educational standards and the destruction of social ethics and discipline, coupled with the instinct for self-reliance, and a strong innate sense of business and entrepreneurship, would drive individuals through whatever means to "make money" by engaging in underground economic activities, such as production of fake products that violated intellectual property rights, or production of toxic products that could harm the life of innocent consumers (see, e.g., "2008 Chinese Milk Scandal," *Wikipedia*). Unsurprisingly, some of these producers had close relationships to the party, and they often could bribe their way out when caught. The lesson would be that if the entrepreneurial ability of Chinese was to be given proper treatment and a role in the economy supported by a strong rule of law, a reliable system and effective implementation of regulations, business opportunities in China should flourish, as ordinary Chinese people would prefer to engage in their own private businesses.

Centralization

As party politics and communist ideology had become the prime and dominant consideration in various activities, the party in the state would become the most powerful machinery in decision-making, though administratively many decisions were taken at the "local" level but with directives from the central authority. Over time, power, authority, and decision centralization had crippled individual incentives, creativity, and self-reliance. Lower level decisions would follow what the central authority had suggested or directed. It was true that there were rules and laws, but they were selectively applied and "double standards" appeared in the implementation of orders. The general public would be alienated from administrators and officials, thereby creating a dichotomy between the party and the people.

Since it was the state that organized all economic activities, the economy would become "dependent" on official assistance. A typical way of displaying disincentive, disapproval, and disenchantment would be to seek and wait for official subsidies by making losses in enterprises, while households would wait and seek for subsidies. Production would be based more on politics than on economic conditions, and losses and accumulation of debts would eventually be taken care of by the state. Such a "ready to bail out" mentality could have long-term implications, as state-related investments would be based more on political favor than cost-effectiveness. The centralization approach and attitude could impact on officials and individuals, as centralization would become the obvious approach to be applied once people were placed in a decision-making position. This could also be seen, e.g., even in nongovernment institutions, such as educational institutions. Indeed, the attitude to adopt a central approach could be used as a symbol of socialism or loyalty to the party.

Indeed, centralization would mean that enterprises and individuals could just wait for rescue from the central government for solutions, bailouts, and subsidies. After the 2008 global financial crisis, Premier Wan provided massive subsidies to households in cash and in kind, though many free provisions of household appliances were of those that could not be exported. In the stock market crash in mid-2015, Premier Li again came up with massive subsidies and compensation to rescue portfolio investors. Centralization simply promotes the "take" attitude whenever enterprises and individuals suffer hardship and loss.

III THE NIXON–KISSINGER INITIATIVE

"Nixon going to China" was the metaphor used to dramatize the visit to China by US President Richard Nixon in February 1972 after a number of missions by the US National Security Advisor, Henry Kissinger, thereby ending 25 years of separation between the United States and the PRC ("1972 Nixon Visit to China," *Wikipedia*). While the first phase of the "NKI" concentrated on the political and diplomatic sides of the Sino–US relationship, the second phase of the NKI was extended to the economy after the restoration of the reformists in 1978. The political/diplomatic phase in 1972 served as a prelude to the international reception given to Deng's economic reform in 1978.

One can theorize the NKI in a number of political-economics dimensions:

1. internationally and diplomatically, it was hoped that China would be a friendly ally to the United States and the West;
2. by replacing Taiwan as a member of the United Nations, China would play a high sounding role in the international community, despite its decades-long closed door policy;
3. despite ideological differences and through the process of international integration, China would become more open, especially in political and economic values, practices, and judgment;
4. economically, other world economies could connect with China, thereby allowing China to receive foreign investment;
5. economic improvement in China through trade and inward investment would lead to economic development, and together with funding assistance from other countries and international institutions, development and growth in China would reduce poverty substantially;
6. China's development and poverty reduction would serve as a "showcase" to other developing countries;
7. with economic growth and development, China would soon have to introduce other aspects of noneconomic changes, such as civic development, political participation, and peace keeping in the world community;
8. economic maturity in China would in turn play a positive world role in aiding other developing countries in their economic advancement; and
9. development in China could offer a large pool of cheap labor for foreign investment, while the large Chinese market could be the new market for industrialized products.

In short, the NKI optimistically predicted that a full-grown China could participate positively in international affairs and economic issues, and would not pose a threat to other countries or serve as an unwelcome force in the world community.

The Cold War (1947–91) symbolized the ideological conflict between the Western Bloc led by the United States and NATO allies, and the Eastern Bloc led by the Soviet Union and the Warsaw Pact countries. The Cold War was effectively the ideological and military battle between the United States and the Soviet Union. In the Sino–Soviet split (1960–89), the Soviet Union withdrew all its assistance to China in 1957–58 ("Sino–Soviet Split," *Wikipedia*). In his "détente" (relaxation of tension) strategy, Nixon was trying to gain geo-political supremacy over the Soviet Union by pulling China to the US side, thereby isolating the Soviet Union further ("Détente," *Wikipedia*). By the late 1960s, the peak of the Cultural Revolution had subsided, though Mao still had the grip of political power in China, it was considered as the right time to extend and reestablish China's international relationships, and the Nixon visit became symbolic. President Richard Nixon's détente strategy in much of the 1970s could be compared with President Ronald Reagan's "star wars" strategy in the 1980s that aimed at exposing the Soviet Union's economic weakness, which eventually led to its collapse and disintegration. History will judge whether the NKI had given in too much to China without examining comprehensively the risk and cost involved. Though it was a welcome act to integrate China into the world economy, replacing Taiwan in the United Nations membership would mean another communist member, in addition to the Soviet Union, in the United Nations Security Council.

In the meantime, communist China had nurtured cordial bilateral relationships with a number of United Nations members, especially among the developing countries. The political side of the NKI was that the PRC would replace the Nationalist Government in Taiwan as the member in the United Nations, and as one of the five members on the Security Council of the United Nations ("China and the United Nations," *Wikipedia*). At the conclusion of the Nixon visit, the Shanghai Communiqué was drafted and defined Sino–US bilateral relations. However, the Shanghai Communiqué mainly specified the peaceful settlement of the Taiwan question and the war in Vietnam, but did not specify the need for China to introduce any political changes or improvements. In the Taiwan question, e.g., neither the Taiwanese authority nor its people had any say in the Sino–US relationship. By unilaterally removing Taiwan from the United Nations, the NKI had effectively lifted communist China to an influential party in the United Nations, but China's ideology was different from the rest of the open world. The uncertainty could be that while China could side with the United States in the Cold War, a strong and powerful China with no change in its ideology could also turn against and compete with the United States in future. Hence, the geo-political situation could be worse if the United States were faced with both Russia and China. Even though the Shanghai Communiqué established the bilateral Sino–US relationship, situations could change, and those changes could pose new challenges to the United States and other countries. The NKI made no inroads in ensuring and securing any form of political and ideological change in China. President Nixon was known for his anticommunist stance, but whether his terms with China were too lenient, over-expecting, and gave away too much remained to be debated.

One has to note legitimately that the PRC was established in 1949, and its history can only begin in 1949. The newly established communist regime in China was not a continuation of the governing regimes of the Qing Dynasty or the Nationalist Government. Hence, the governance of communist China should not, would not, and could not be held retrospectively accountable to events that occurred before 1949. As such, it would remain a question of law whether the communist regime in post-1949 China could capitalize on the various deeds conducted in the previous regimes before 1949, as it did not legally represent either the government of the Qing dynasty or the Nationalist government which retreated to Taiwan.

Members of the United Nations had been receptive to the admission of PRC in the United Nations General Assembly Resolution in 1971. However, soon after its admission in March 1972, the Chinese UN Representative wrote to the United Nations Decolonization Committee stating the position of the Chinese government on the sovereignty issue of Hong Kong and Macau, which respectively were a British colony and a Portugese colony. The then Chinese UN Ambassador stated that "…The settlement of the questions of Hong Kong and Macau is entirely within China's sovereign right and do not at all fall under the ordinary category of colonial territories…. With regard to the questions of Hong Kong and Macau, the Chinese government has consistently held that they should be settled in an appropriate way when conditions are ripe." The United Nations General Assembly subsequently on November 8, 1972, passed without opposition the resolution on removing Hong Kong and Macau from the official list of colonies ("Transfer of Sovereignty over Hong Kong," *Wikipedia*.) (Chan and Postiglione, 1996; Liu, 2009; Li, 2012a).

However, the fact is that the PRC since 1949 had not suffered any territorial lost due to colonialism. In effect, the communist revolution by the PRC had overthrown all previous Chinese regimes. In 2009,

IV. THE FRONTIER OF CAPITALISM: CHINA VERSUS HONG KONG

e.g., the PRC celebrated the 60th anniversary of the founding of the PRC ("60th Anniversary of the People's Republic of China," *Wikipedia*). The PRC was not a signatory on any treaties concluded before 1949. The United Nations should have considered whether it was legitimate and lawful for post-1949 China to deal with colonial or territorial issues that were settled by governments in previous centuries, even before the United Nations existed.

On the contrary, Hong Kong was ceded to Great Britain in 1842, when Qing dynasty China lost to Great Britain in the Opium War. In the case of Macau, although Portuguese settlement began as early as 1513, it was in 1887, when the Qing and Portuguese government signed the Sino–Portuguese Treaty of Peking, that Qing China ceded the right of "perpetual occupation and government of Macau" to Portugal. In 1928, the Kuomintang signed a new Sino–Portuguese Friendship and Trade Treaty that kept the sovereignty of Macau in the hands of the Portuguese government ("Macau," *Wikipedia*). The sovereignty of both Hong Kong and Macau subsequently reverted to China in 1997 and 1999, respectively. One could possibly argue that Taiwan, Hong Kong, and Macau were the sacrifice in the NKI for admitting the PRC into the United Nations. Indeed, the economic rise of China could carry political and ideological influences, and some people have questioned whether China is the world's new imperialist in the 21st century (Toh, 2016).

The economic phase of the NKI came after Deng Xiaoping declared economic reform in 1978 by the Four Modernization framework in agriculture, industry, national defense, and science and technology, though it was argued that these goals were set forth by Premier Zhou Enlai in 1963. While the Four Modernization came down to the need to speed up technological development, which would be applied to national defense, industries, and agriculture, there was no emphasis on the modernization of education, ethics, customs, and culture which were destroyed during the Cultural Revolution. After touring Japan and the United States in 1978, Deng realized how backward communist China was and that the political reality in Mao's China was not suitable for modernization. A strategy was needed to pull resources together to reform the Chinese economy. It has been debated as to whether Deng was a socialist, capitalist, or nationalist. Deng should be a socialist or communist as he was involved in the communist movement in China and followed Mao in his centralization policy. Deng was a reformist as he sided with Zhou Enlai in China's economic policy. However, to move China which was so rooted in Mao's communism to a market-style economy was a rebuttal to communism. Other China watchers (e.g., Baum, 1996; Vogel, 2011) argued that Deng was not really a communist, but a revolutionary nationalist who would like to see China advance so that China could stand on equal terms with other great powers. Gao (2008) noted that there were others like Deng in the communist party who participated in the communist movement because there was the chance for them to be involved in Chinese nationalism. Deng was a political opportunist.

To introduce market reform in the post-Cultural Revolution era was an uphill battle, as Deng had to pacify the power and interests of the hardliners, who believed that any type of market reform would carry an element of capitalism. Hence, ideologically, Deng had to find a place for Mao so that the Maoists would not feel they were being purged, and had to look for new and acceptable market instruments that could institute economic reform. Indeed, there was some skepticism at the beginning of the reform, as it was opposed by the hardliners while the reformists were suspicious about Deng's intentions.

By declaring that China was a developing country with mass poverty, Deng's economic reform received goodwill. Firstly, it would be in line with the intentions of the NKI and that as a member of the United Nations, members would like to see a more participative China. Funds from foreign governments and international institutions had been targeted to aid China with the intention of removing poverty in China to serve as a showcase to other developing countries. Secondly, China held two economic advantages. One advantage was the large labor supply, which would provide cheap labor for the industrial world. With one fifth of the world population, a stable China would provide a large market for the manufacturers from the industrialized world, though there would be economic spillovers as additional supply and demand would constrain resources in energy and food supplies.

The two phases of the NKI brought the PRC to the world arena, but did not make a dent in China's political/ideological performance. With the accumulation of international reserves, China's communist party had become the richest communist institution in the world. It would be the work of historians and political scientists to judge if the NKI was correct in not limiting Chinese communism in principle and ending up with the emergence of two large socialist countries of Russia and China that competed with the United States. Within the economic discipline, studies often pointed to the success of China's economic reform, and not to the various inadequacies and dualities that China faced (Dreyer, 2008; Li, 2008; Hung, 2015).

IV ECONOMIC REFORM: FIRST DECADE, FIRST CRISIS

As Wu (2005) pointed out, the two problems in central planning were information cost, where the state would not be able to gain complete knowledge about all economic activities, and incentive cost, where the state could not integrate the interests of the whole society and did not allow for differences in value judgments. After decades of Soviet-style policies, China in 1978 was faced with four major imbalances. One was the imbalance between accumulation and consumption, where the state had engaged in accumulation of savings and heavy industries, but consumption needs were ignored as materials were rationed. Another area of imbalance was between industry and agriculture, as the focus was on industry in order to raise China's capability. Even within industry, imbalance existed between heavy industry and light manufacturing. The lack of infrastructure was another imbalance, as both physical and social infrastructures were far from adequate.

Incremental or Experimental

One key debate in China's economic reform has been the difference between incremental and experimental (A shorter discussion can be found in Section V in Chapter 9.) (Wong, 2009). The incremental argument was that the reform had been gradual and sequential over the years. On the other hand, a major criterion in China's economic reform was the possibility to exit should the policy prove to be faulty. Ultimately, the adoption of any reform policy was political. Such a criterion suggested that reform policies were experimental, and that the central authority could always have the choice to withdraw the policy if it proved to be politically undesirable. An early experiment on economic openness was the adoption of the special economic zones (SEZs) along the coastal areas adjacent to either Hong Kong or Taiwan to attract overseas Chinese investment in light manufacturing for exports (After 1980, there were five SEZs, namely the province of Hainan, the cities of Shenzhen, Zhuhai and Shantou in Guangdong province, and Xiamen in Fujian province. Subsequently, a total of 14 cities (Dalian, Qinhuangdao, Tianjin, Yantai, Qingdao, Lianyungang, Nantong, Shanghai, Ningbo, Wenzhou, Fuzhou, Guangzhou, Zhanjiang, and Beihai) were opened to overseas investments in 1984). It was experimental because, should the performance of overseas Chinese capital in these open cities became harmful to the mainland economy, the SEZs would be scrapped. It was only the successful operation of these open regions that other new areas and regions were opened further. By success, it probably would mean there was no political spillover (Nishitateno, 1983; Jao et al., 1986; Ge, 1999).

Other examples that exhibited the experimental criterion included the introduction of foreign exchange certificates (FECs) in 1979. To avoid spillovers to China's domestic economy as economic reform could generate uncertainty, a dual exchange rate policy was a form of foreign exchange control. Local residents had to obtain FECs in order to purchase imported goods. Export firms would have to obtain FECs in order to import goods. However, the popularity of the FECs grew at the expense of the official currency, the Renminbi, which was traded on the black market. The FECs became popular and were in high demand, and black markets for Renminbi developed (Wong and Lo, 1997; Lin and Schramm, 2003; Huang and Wang, 2004). In January 1994 Premier Zhu Rongji devalued the Renminbi by 30% and stopped the use of FECs so that the Renminbi stabilized.

Another example was the A-shares and B-shares in the two stock markets in Shenzhen and Shanghai. The A-share was meant for the local investors and was traded in Renminbi, while the B-share was traded in either Hong Kong dollars or US dollars by nonlocal investors. The original intention was to ensure the demarcation between local and nonlocal investors, but as the stock market grew and trading expanded, the division could become a nuisance, because it could not align with the practice in international stock markets. Merging the two shares should have occurred as local investors already had the financial and economic ability to invest in the stock market. Nonetheless, the division was maintained for the purpose of control should it be needed in times of financial crisis.

Contract Responsibility System

The "family responsibility system," also known as the "household responsibility system" or the "contract responsibility system" was introduced in the rural economy in 1979 (a shorter discussion can be found in Section V in Chapter 9). In the pre-1979 system, rural farmers had to fulfill their agricultural quota to the state, and the agricultural produce could only be sold in state-owned retail shops. Under the new contract responsibility system, however, rural households still had to fulfill the state quota, but were free to sell their surplus produce in the market. This provided incentives to rural farmers and "million Renminbi households" soon emerged. It was reported that by 1983, 93% of all production teams had adopted the system ("1983: Household Responsibility System," www.china.org.cn, September 16, 2009; "Household-Responsibility System," *Wikipedia*).

As rural households were allowed to sell their produce privately, what likely happened was that the good quality agricultural produce was kept, while the low quality produce was submitted to satisfy the state quota. This led to a number of possible economic consequences. Firstly, consumers had a choice and would be more willing to buy from the private market for the "high quality" produce, even though it was cheaper in state retail shops. The difference between the state price and the private price formed a "dual" price system in much of the 1980s. Thus, the dual price system worked in favor of the private market, and the state retail shops became unpopular. Eventually, the state retail shops closed down as the demand for retail shop space increased, especially in good locations. However, the rise in rural income led to excess demand. The rise in imports and black market activities, and the lack of progress in other areas of economic reform, could have caused other hidden turbulence in the Chinese economy toward the late 1980s. For example, the hoarding of goods and crucial industrial materials emerged in 1987. Hoarding of consumer goods led to higher prices, while hoarding of industrial materials led to speculation and a shortage in industrial output (Li, 1994). The contract responsibility system hastened the structural change of communes to become township and village enterprises.

Soft Budget Constraint

In a functional market economy, a balanced budget would bring a balance between government revenue and expenditure, thereby avoiding unnecessary inflation and market disruption. A prolonged budget deficit would distort resource allocation, weaken macroeconomic control, and disturb economic relationships. It has been argued that a budget deficit would have a push effect, as it could accelerate economic development and achieve economic results in the short run, but a prolonged budget deficit would have a burden effect as the enlarged purchasing power could lead to excess demand, inflation, and debt. The Chinese fiscal policy showed the coexistence of budgetary and extra-budgetary expenditures and revenues. While the budgetary estimates were done at the beginning of the year, the various outside government items from localities for different purposes constituted the extra-budgetary figures at the end of the year. China has experienced increasing budget deficits, due to large subsidies to agriculture, state-owned enterprises, and households (Lardy, 1998). In addition, there was also the paradox of fiscal decentralization, where localities had a greater say in their revenues, but the central authority ended up in fiscal decline. In the typical "central—local" conflict, the richer provinces were reluctant to submit more to the central area, as they would prefer to keep the revenue for their own development. The central government, on the other hand, would like to receive more from the richer provinces. On the contrary, the poorer provinces would prefer to receive more from the central government, but the central government would be reluctant to give more to poorer provinces (Wong, 2011).

China typically faced a "soft budget constraint" (SBC), where the government bailed out loss-making state-owned enterprises and undermined ex ante incentives (Kornai, 1986; Qian and Roland, 1996). The SBC emerged due to various reasons. The cost of liquidation was high, as strong interdependent relationships existed. There was also the incentive to remain passive so as to hide bad loans. The softness of the government budget could also be exploited by state-owned enterprises through rent-seeking activities. Since unemployment was not supposed to exist among state-owned enterprises, the ex post benefits of bailing out loss-making enterprises were higher than the benefit of liquidation. The initial investment was considered as a sunk cost, and the government exhibited paternalism.

The First Crisis

From 1980 to 1987, Premier Zhou Ziyang introduced various reforms, including the revitalization of the four state-owned banks and the "dual" price system. Premier Zhou also realized the industrial mismatch existed. While the state was still engaged in heavy industry, there was growing demand for light manufacturing household products. In the call for industrial reform in 1985, Premier Zhou attempted to redirect state-owned resources from production of heavy industry to light manufacturing. This proved problematic, as the industrial structure in the 1980s was still based on the heavy industrial mode inherited from the Soviet Union. State-owned enterprises used to produce heavy industries might not be prepared to restructure to produce light manufacturing goods. It was argued that Zhou went far to advocate for the separation between party and management in industrial enterprises, but such innovative suggestions proved to be unpopular among the hardliners in the party, as that would mean a loss of party control and political influence.

The first decade of reform was basically a period when economics was being reinstated in the Chinese economy. However, there were growing economic ills. There was, in general, a lack of systemic or structural reform, especially within the government circle, in terms of governance and administrative transparency. By the mid-1980s, it was clear that the rise in income due to the growing private sector activities in the rural economy had led to rising demand for household items. Excess demand soon emerged, and rapid inflation appeared. In a centrally planned economy where materials were rationed, inflation was not supposed to appear as prices and wages were set by the state. Inflation after the mid-1980s was a novelty, as there was a lack of policy to deal with inflation. On the contrary, there was still the provision of subsidies to households and state-owned enterprises. Hence, the money supply through large bank loan provisions and soft budget spending kept rising by two digits every year (Li, 1997). Inflation in consumer products soon spread to inflation in production materials, and by 1987 speculation appeared as suppliers hoarded production materials in anticipation of a high price, thereby adding pressure to the supply of industrial output. The official exchange rate was under pressure as the black market became rampant, while the other currency, the FECs, gained popularity and was in high demand.

In noneconomic areas, corruption among state and party officials mounted and public grievances grew, but there was a lack of action on the part of the government in dealing with corruption which cancer-spread to different levels of the government. The political inequality, unfairness, and abuse of power were becoming visible and obvious. The economic problem of excess demand and inflation coexisted with the noneconomic problem of corruption, and the lack of policy response formed the root of the first crisis in 1989 when these issues turned political as the party hardliners exploited these events for political capital to attack the reformists (Benewick, 1995; Fewsmith, 2001). The political turmoil in Tiananmen Square on June 4, 1989, highlighted the ideological battle between the hardliners and the reformists. The hardliners would prefer to bring an end to economic reform and a return to Maoist communism, as economic reform brought new problems. The reformists advocated that these problems were inevitable, and more reform would be needed. While the international community was shocked by the June 4, 1989, turmoil and bloodshed in Tiananmen Square, the political upheaval did contain the first economic crisis in China's reform.

V REFORM OF THE 1990s: BANKING AND STATE ENTERPRISES

There was a period of inactivity after the political turmoil in 1989, as there was a need for the dust of the ideological battle to settle. It was in the spring of 1992 that Deng made a personal tour to Shenzhen during the lunar New Year and expressed determination that economic reform was the only choice for China (Zhao, 1993). The pace of economic reform was then put back on track when foreign governments, beginning with Japan, and international institutions again endorsed China's economic reform. Economic reform in China in the 1990s was largely managed by Zhu Rongji, who served as the Vice Premier from 1993 to 1998, and as Premier from 1998 to 2003 (Wong, 2016).

There were three major reforms in the 1990s. Firstly, the Chinese currency was devalued in January 1994, and the other trading currency, the FECs, was removed. Thus, the Renminbi became the only currency in China, and the large devaluation by 30% changed China's trading position from one of constant trade deficit before 1994 to continuous growth in trade surplus. In addition, the devaluation improved China's competitiveness and foreign direct investment continued to grow, though the industrial economy was geared to the export market.

Banking Reform

The monetary policy in postreform China oscillated around a "stop–go" cycle (Tang and Li, 1997). Typically, a credit squeeze with a "stop" policy when the economy was overheated, cycled with a reverse "go" policy once economic overheating had passed. Money supply growth had been high as the percentage increase had been in double digits for many years, and in the initial reform years, the money supply growth rate could be as high as 50% (Li, 1994). The banking reform in 1995 was related to a number of concerns (Li, 1999). Despite the revitalization of the four state-owned banks in the mid-1980s, these banks were faced with large debts. The four banks were the Bank of China (BOC), Construction Bank of China (CBC), Industrial and Commercial Bank of China

(ICBC), and Agricultural Bank of China (ABC). Banks in socialist countries behaved more like "accounting houses," as financial activities were state-directed. Money merely served as a medium of exchange and a unit of account, as banks had to provide liquidity to state-owned enterprises. These banks were nonprofit making and "sector-oriented," as they served only their specific sector. The BOC would deal with foreign trade, while the CBC dealt with construction. The ICBC naturally served the production and service sector, while agriculture was handled by the ABC. Naturally, some sectors performed stronger than others. The BOC performed best, while the weakest bank was the ABC.

Also, China was in the process of accession to the World Trade Organization (WTO), and that accession required the opening up of the domestic banking sector to foreign banks. Hence, an unattractive and uncompetitive domestic banking sector would lose out to foreign banks should the sector open to foreign competition, as this would have political implications on the currency and the control of the economy. Thus, making domestic banks competitive became an urgent matter.

In the banking reform of 1995, the People's Bank of China (PBC) became the central bank. The number of PBC branches were restricted to only a few regions. One other intention of the 1995 banking reform was the need to separate the two issues of profit-making and provision of state loans. The three newly established "policy banks" would take over the state activities originally conducted by the four state-owned banks. The State Development Bank (SDB) would work on development matters, the China Import and Export Bank (CIEB) would be involved with external trade, while the Agriculture Development Bank (ADB) would engage in agricultural subsidies. With the "nonprofit making" or "loss-making" activities removed, the four state-owned banks, now "state-owned commercial banks," could engage in profit-making businesses and compete with each other in different economic sectors for loans and deposits.

The banking reform of 1995 also created a number of provincial, local government, city and corporate commercial banks, nonbank financial institutions including insurance companies, trust and investment companies, and credit cooperatives. The Minsheng Bank became the first private bank in China. Theoretically, restructuring the banking and financial sector provided new channels for financial development, and allowed competition between state and nonstate ownership in financial institutions. Indeed, nonstate financial and banking institutions could complement the development of state-owned banks. However, many newly established institutions were "window companies" of state and local government organs. One of their functions was to hide debts between state organizations, and the old form of management style was used, as the same officials moved from one institution to another (Wu, 2005). Indeed, the situation deteriorated as nonperforming loans (NPLs) increased, leading to the closure of a number of nonviable financial companies, banks, and institutions in the second half of the 1990s. Premier Zhu even warned foreign banks and investors of the possible problems in China's financial sector (Li, 1999).

Chinese banks used different indicators and measurements, e.g., in the definition of bad debts, risk, and NPLs, when compared to other international banks under the criteria specified by the Bank of International Settlement (BIS). To clean up the debts and NPLs of the four state-owned commercial banks, the trick was for the Ministry of Finance to set up four "asset management companies" (AMCs) in 1999. Thus, the AMCs of Xinda, Great Wall, Dongfang, and China Huarong were established, respectively, for the CBC, ABC, BOC, and ICBC. These AMCs used government funded bonds to purchase the NPLs from the four banks. In return, the AMCs performed to maximize asset recovery, sale of loans, swap between debt and equity, securitizing and auctioning NPLs, and restructuring debts in order to sell to domestic and foreign investors (Li, 1999). Within a short time, the debt-to-equity swap helped to lower the NPLs, leaving the four banks clear of debts. By then, these banks could show impressive accounting statements. One would wonder how the debts could be repackaged, and who would be interested in purchasing "debts." While many domestic investors were local governments and other quasi-official organizations and corporations, foreign investors would come mainly from Hong Kong. China's favorable economic expansion could be the attraction to foreign investors, believing that "debts" today could become "equities" tomorrow once the economy prospered. China's economic optimism in 1999 could have blinded the eyes of many Hong Kong and foreign investors. Nonetheless, the establishment of the AMCs had cleaned up the NPLs of the four state-owned commercial banks. With a new record, these four banks had, during the first decade of the 21st century, expanded through the issue of new shares in Shanghai and in Hong Kong. By 2016, these four banks ranked within the top six largest banks by market capitalization in the world (According to Top Banks by Market Capitalization 2016, ICBC ranked second, followed by CBC in fourth, ABC in fifth, and BOC in sixth. According to Banks by Assets 2015, the top four world rankings are ICBC, CBC, ABC, and BOC, *Banks Around the World*, www.relbanks.com).

The "debt-to-equity" swap strategy could have various loopholes. For example, banks' NPLs could have switched to become provincial or local government debt, as statistics showed increasingly that the burden of

China's debt rested on the size of the provincial and local government debts. This strategy could also be abused and used indiscriminately, and some AMCs still held part of the original debts. For example, the China Huarong Asset Management Company warned about the need to revive the strategy, as creditors did not have guarantees on the return of equity (*South China Morning Post*, April 6, 2016). When debts were being swap around, they would have to reappear somewhere in the system. This might reduce the debt level in the short term, but it would reappear in another account statement ("Chinese Banks: Quo Vadis?," China Hot Topics Economic Research, *Natixis*, April 22, 2016). This generated optimism on the part of the debtors, thinking that debts could be restructured to become equities. As such, debt accumulation should not have been a burden. In the long run, China would have accumulated larger debts. Ultimately, it would be the state which would shoulder the debt burden.

Foreign countries also requested the use of the same strategy when they could not repay debts to China. For example, during his visit to China in 2016, the Sri Lankan Prime Minister asked "China to accept equity in infrastructure projects in return for canceling some of the US$8 billion Sri Lanka owes to Beijing" (*South China Morning Post*, April 11, 2016). Indeed, while China was providing loans and funds to numerous developing countries which would not have the ability to repay, China would face a larger debt should these debtor countries request a swap between debt and equity. For example, during his 2016 visit to China, the Nigerian president was offered a US$6 billion infrastructure loan, which was considered as a currency swap to shore up the Nigerian currency ("Nigeria Offered $6 Billion Chinese Loan, Agrees Currency Swap to Shore Up Naira," www.thisdaylive.com, April 13, 2016; and *Punch Newspapers*, April 13, 2016).

State Enterprise Reform

The 1997 state-owned enterprises (SOEs) reform was another major task by Zhu Rongji. The role of SOEs was to accomplish the production plan and serve as grass root organizations in the party system with various social functions (Wu, 2005). Fig. 15.1 shows the "mini-society" nature of SOEs. The production unit had to take care of all other welfare units. The "iron rice bowl" concept was that individuals' employment and life-time welfare would be taken care of by the SOEs. Thus, the SOEs would be responsible for the various welfare provisions of the workers and their families, including housing, education, retirement, medical, transportation, and daily necessities. Since there was only one production unit that generated revenue, all other welfare units involved spending. As a result, it was common to find loss-making SOEs in China.

There are two theories explaining the SOEs in China. The "multitask theory" argued simply that the SOEs took on both production and nonproduction tasks, including the social task of ensuring employment and the political task of adhering to party doctrines (Bai et al., 2000; Huang et al., 2010). Another theory argued that Chinese SOEs were faced with "too many mothers-in-law," because there were many government bodies siphoning profits from the same SOEs. A government body obtained its "mother-in-law" status by investing in the fixed capital of the SOE (Saich, 2000; Scott, 2002). The decision-making power of SOEs was concentrated in the central government. Managers and workers in SOEs normally were not encouraged to show incentive. There could be redundant workers or "surplus labor," as the SOEs served as "employment agents." Appointments would be politically oriented and inappropriate persons could also be chosen. The SOEs debts were known as "triangular

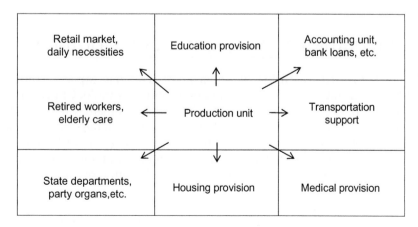

FIGURE 15.1 The SOEs as a mini-society.

debt," as one SOE owed another and a "debt chain" appeared among the SOEs, and it became impossible to identify which SOE would be the eventual debtor.

The discussion on the "low wage" of workers in China has been a misunderstanding. Workers and their families in a Chinese SOE received free welfare assistances from the production unit. Hence, housing needs, medical support, and retirement were arranged. The workers received the "net wage" or the "take-home wage," as income tax was not imposed. Such a "net wage" was surely considered to be low. But when workers' welfare assistance was included, the "gross wage" could be much higher. In market economies where the workers normally receive a "gross wage," that would have to be high because the workers would have to spend on their welfare needs. To the SOE, the wage of the workers was divided into "net wage" and "welfare provisions." The total wage might not necessarily be low.

The incorporation of SOEs began in October 1993, when about 100 of the largest SOEs were used in a pilot study involving separation of administrative and enterprise functions, reorganization of monopolistic enterprises into competitive enterprises, and asset restructuring. However, by 1996, the pilot study showed that most sample enterprises did not achieve the minimum standard of a modern corporation. The 1997 reform of SOEs adopted the "grasping the big, enlivening the small" policy. A total of about 1000 strategic and key SOEs were kept by the state, while other SOEs were either closed down, sold, or formed joint ventures with Hong Kong or foreign corporations. At the same time, the state wrote off a bad debt amounting to Rmb 30 billion in 1997. A 3-year grace period was given to dispose of all SOEs.

A number of economic consequences appeared from the SOEs reform. Those marketable SOEs were able to survive, as they were favored by investors. The various welfare units within the SOEs could join with their corresponding divisions in other SOEs to become new enterprises in such areas as medical, housing, and so on. The worse performers would be those uncompetitive SOEs, and their closure would immediately lead to a rise in unemployment. With the closure and removal of SOEs, many workers lost their welfare protection, while state support in similar utilities and welfare was not forthcoming as rapidly as the closure of SOEs. As a result, many workers had nowhere to turn as state welfare support did not come quickly enough, thereby adding to their social insecurity, and grievances accumulated. It had also been observed that it was the officials in the former SOEs or the "insiders" who started their own enterprises, leading to similar possible corruption and rent-seeking activities. At the microeconomic level, there could be problems of agency cost, moral hazard, and property rights issues (Wu, 2005).

A major advantage resulting from the SOEs reform was the growth of industrial small- and medium-sized enterprises (SMEs), as many able and skilled workers formed their own industrial enterprises and competed in the private market. The study of China's industrial SMEs (Li, 2016) showed that the size of industrial SMEs had been growing, but they were not that competitive compared to the large state-controlled industrial enterprises, and performed much weaker after the 2008 financial crisis. China's SMEs occupied the largest share in the number of industrial enterprises, but their percentage share in employment was lower.

One can conclude that China's reform in the 1990s aimed more at the pragmatic level by improving the efficient functioning of economic institutions. Macroeconomic stability was put in place, and economic reform aligned with industrial expansion and income growth. By and large, the 1990s were a successful decade in China's economic reform, though there was still no emphasis on systemic reform.

VI TRADE, FINANCE, AND EXCESS LIQUIDITY

While reform in the 1990s focused expansion of China's real economic capacity, reform was dominated by expansion in trade and finance in the first decade of the 21st century. In trade, China's accession to the WTO in 2001 had set the scene for trade expansion and a rise in inward investment. Subsequent to the 1995 banking reform and the need to improve the competitiveness of domestic banks, Chinese banks in the first decades of the new century had aggressively expanded their assets by massively raising capital through the Hong Kong stock market (Li, 2012a). These two aspects boosted the Chinese economy, but there were also unfavorable consequences that the Chinese economy had to face, including possibly the situation of full capacity in industrial production, and the ability to maintain high performance.

The WTO accession after 2001 provided a golden opportunity for China to expand. At the international level, China became the largest exporter, most attractive to foreign direct investment, and managed eventually to amass the largest international reserves. The favorable external economic conditions helped to promote the domestic economy in various dimensions. In banking, the four Chinese state-owned commercial banks had become the largest international banks. Economic expansion led to financial expansion, as the wealthy people engaged more and more in speculation in the stock market and in real estate development.

As China insisted on a high GDP growth rate over the years, loan provisions would have to take place so that the size of the investment would be sufficiently large to accomplish the high GDP growth rates "predicted" in the meetings of the National People's Congress every March. After the international financial crisis in 2008, China still engaged extensively in financial development and expansion, including the establishment of "shadow banking," so that institutions could maximize their financial expansion. Through the use of financial derivatives, there was rapid expansion and appreciation in assets and wealth. As a result of the rise in income and wealth, coupled with the appreciation of the Chinese currency, Chinese people became "big spenders" everywhere they traveled. China was no longer considered to be a "developing country," as its income caught up with and exceeded many advanced industrialized countries.

The rapid rise in consumption and currency appreciation, coupled with corruption at home, led to many individuals migrating to foreign countries taking with them cash to "invest" in foreign countries. For example, the term "naked officials" represented those officials who had sent their children to study abroad and transmitted their assets so that their families could migrate overseas. There were cases where corrupt officials stashed their cash at home. Many people in China have become so cash rich that they have to find a means to transmit their cash out of China. Indeed, "money" inside China remains as "cash," but once deposited in foreign currency outside China it becomes "assets" or "wealth." Indeed, the large amount of cash held could weaken China's monetary policy, as the cash may have been circulated outside the banking system, implying that the central bank may not have reliable information on the amount of cash circulating inside the economy.

Since the turn of the new century, financial expansion has been the economic target. Consider the various sources of financial expansion: (1) a prolonged period of high GDP growth; (2) largest recipient of foreign direct investment; (3) received aid and assistance from international institutions and governments; (4) largest trade surplus for a prolonged period of time; (5) banks have been making an increasing number of loans; (6) increasing amount of fiscal deficit; (7) fixed asset investment has been increasing rapidly over the years; (8) shadow banking and derivatives provided extra channels for financial expansion; and (9) banks and corporations have also raised large amounts of capital from Hong Kong and New York stock markets (*The Diplomat*, May 13, 2013).

For a number of years since 2005, most of the initial public offerings (IPOs) on the Hong Kong Stock Exchange were administered by Chinese enterprises. Given the fact that all major activities were under the control or influence of the state, China seems to have no difficulty in raising capital through financial markets. It is true that financial expansion in China has been rising uncontrollably, while the industrial and real economy has leveled off, especially after 2008 when both foreign direct investment and exports experienced a fall, implying that the industrial economy was faced with rigidity. The deviation between the real economy and nominal economy could lead to future financial crises, though most analysts after 2012 agreed that "soft landing" could be the worst China would experience. However, given the extent of state control and influence, and the huge amount of resources the central authority commanded, one can argue that China would not experience economic recession, as the state could always rescue and bailout economic difficulties, crises, and natural disasters.

Financial expansion can enlarge the economy in numbers and in magnitude, thereby projecting high performances and showing China's growing world power and strength. China has definitely capitalized on the economic and political optimism the international community has provided. Economically, the international community has looked up to China, as the advanced and industrialized countries fueled China with foreign direct investment and trade, even though China surpassed a number of industrialized countries. Few countries would dare to challenge China politically and ideologically. Other less developed countries look to China as an alternative for economic strength. Indeed, China's optimism has led many to conclude that China's ideology could provide a "way out" for developing countries. In short, foreigners have continuously been kowtowing to China for exports and markets in the case of industrialized countries, and for free assistance and aid in the case of developing countries. While China can deploy its domestic resources for political purposes at home, China's rise in competitiveness has provided China with ammunition to deal with others on China's terms (e.g., Taiwanese officials in an OECD meeting in Belgium were ordered to leave due to pressure from China. See, *Taipei Times*, April 20, 2016; *Focus Taiwan News Channel*, April 19, 2016; and *Associated Press*, April 19, 2016).

The extent of China's "cash rich" or "excess liquidity" can be seen from statistics showing both the international and domestic sources of funds injected into the Chinese economy (the discussion and data shown here lend further support to the discussion in Section V in Chapter 9). The data related to the domestic and external economy are obtained, respectively, from the official *China Statistical Yearbook* and World Bank sources. Many analysts would

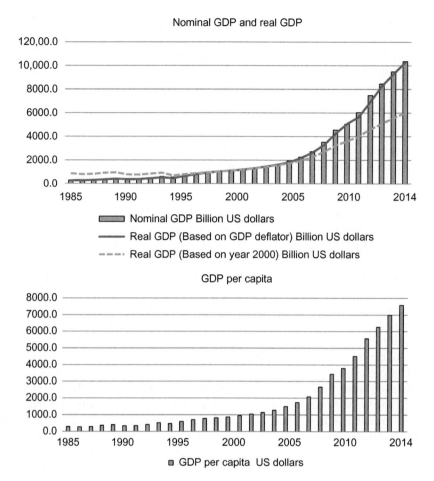

FIGURE 15.2   China's GDP.

also consider the annual real growth rates of GDP and other key economic variables. An alternative to examine China's excess liquidity can be seen from a trend analysis and their percentage performances in annual GDP.

To begin with, Fig. 15.2 shows the trend of nominal GDP, while the real GDP figures are measured by the GDP deflator, as well as using 2000 as the base year. The lower section of Fig. 15.2 shows the GDP per capita. On the whole, the pace of GDP increase was steadier in the two decades prior to the turn of the 21st century. Since China entered the WTO in 2001, the pace of economic rise really began in around 2003 or 2004, when China was preparing for the Olympics in 2008 and the Shanghai expo in 2010. The speed of increase in GDP accelerated after 2008, reflecting the impact of the 2008 world financial crisis and the Chinese government's rescue package. According to some analysts, such a rapid increase could have produced a bubble, as the performance of other variables had not been that rosy after 2008.

The external sources of funds injected into China are shown in two figures. Fig. 15.3 shows the ever rising level of foreign direct investment (FDI), though there were a couple of "level offs" in 1999, 2009, and 2011. In the case of the trade balance, other than some years of trade deficits before the devaluation of the Renminbi in 1994, China's trade balance shot up after 2005, but fell in 2009, and bottomed in 2011 before it shot up again, reflecting the unsteady exports after the 2008 crisis. Nonetheless, the foreign reserve has been rising since 2001, and its pace of increase speeded up after 2005. Fig. 15.4 shows the sources of funds from international institutions. Loans from the International Bank of Reconstruction and Development (IBRD), and credits from the International Development Agency (IDA) increased until 2010, though the size of the loans and credits were not that large. Loans from foreign governments and international institutions have been increasing steadily, while the use of credits from the IMF jumped massively from US$3.65 (100 million) in 2008 to US$109.58 (100 million) in 2009, reflecting obviously the sudden economic drop after the 2008 crisis.

The international community has been generous to the Chinese economy by providing ample funds, despite the fact that there are more urgent needs for assistance to other developing countries elsewhere. Such goodwill

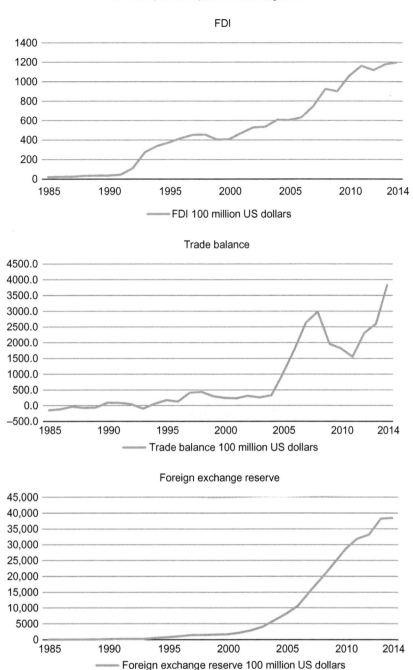

FIGURE 15.3   China's external sources of funds.

can be regarded as a "scarcity" in the international community. However, with China's economic rise and the communist party's total control of the massive international reserves, one really wondered how China would use its resources wisely in aiding others in the global community, or would it just deploy its resources in furthering its global ideological ambitions. China's unwise moves in the East and South China Sea by defying the decision of the international law court in The Hague would send different signals to the international community. China's rising economic might and its ambitious "one belt, one road" initiative would be another eye-catching project that the world economy would observe. Without changes in its ideology, China would be seen as the "economic Soviet Union": an economically strong but undemocratic and ideologically high-handed communist country.

On the domestic front, Fig. 15.5 shows the three sources of bank loans, fixed asset investment, and IPOs from the domestic market with A-shares, and the foreign market in Hong Kong (H-shares) and in New York (N-shares).

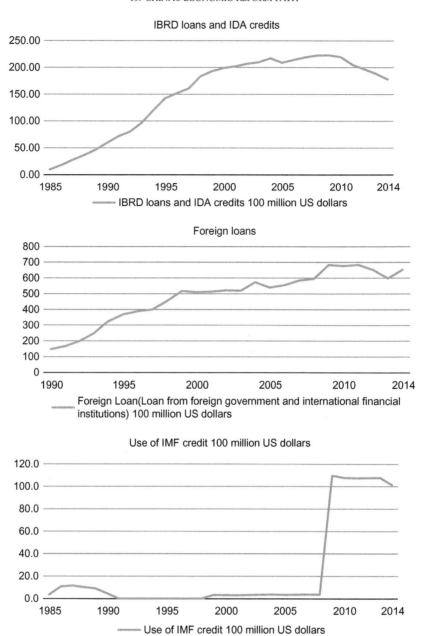

FIGURE 15.4   China's sources of funds from international institutions.

Although there could be overlap between bank loans and fixed asset investments, bank loans are much larger in quantity but they have both increased ultra-rapidly since around 2005. The IPO has been large, especially in the domestic stock market (A-shares), but the level of IPO has been unsteady. The inflation picture shown in Fig. 15.5 suggests that inflation has largely been contained since the turn of the 21st century. However, given the extent of state control in China, inflation would have been restricted and the statistics could be questionable. For example, knowing that inflation would not be welcomed by the authorities, one would set the price very high when the product was first put on the market, but the price would be unchanged for years as that would keep inflation low. As such, prices can remain high, especially prices on luxury items, but inflation is minimal.

Fig. 15.6 shows that fiscal deficit has become a regular occurrence, except in the 2 years of 1985 (surplus of US $0.02 billion) and 2007 (surplus of US$20.26 billion), though the surplus in 2007 could have been due to the appreciation of the Renminbi. Nonetheless, the fiscal deficit has risen massively since 2011. The money supply shows a similar performance, especially in M2, which has increased rapidly since 2008, reflecting the massive amount of economic rescue by the government. The performance of government gross debt conveyed the same

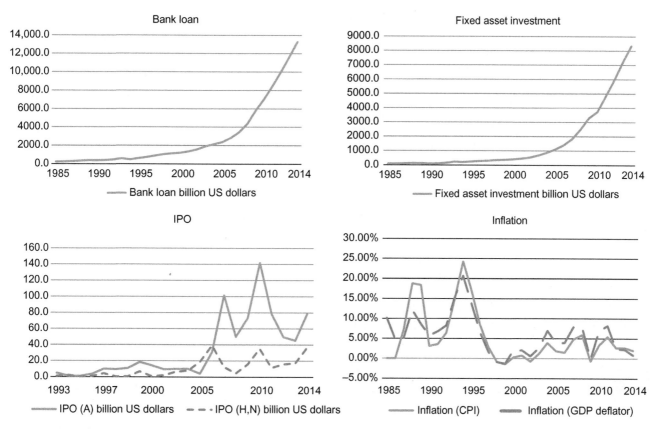

FIGURE 15.5   China's domestic sources of funds.

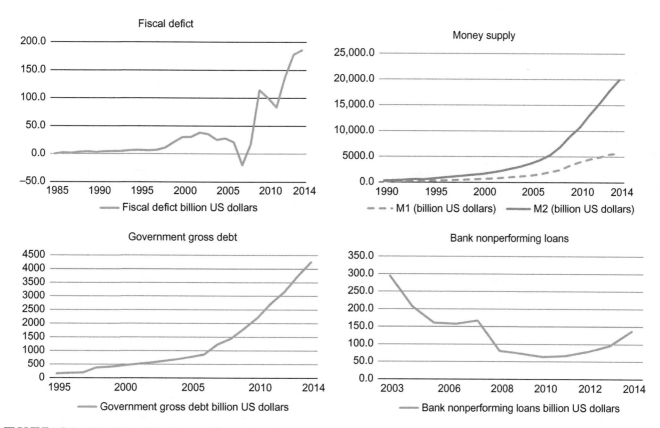

FIGURE 15.6   China's fiscal, banking and financial performance.

picture, but the total national debt could be higher. Bank's nonperforming loans have been declining, but were revised upwards since 2010.

While the analysis based on the percentage of shares in GDP could have magnified the situation, the alternative would be for the annual growth rates of economic variables to reflect the situation of excess liquidity in China, as the annual increase could be high in some variables and in different years. Nonetheless, one can conclude that funds still came mainly from domestic sources through the various state financial organs. Of course, there can be a multiplier effect between the domestic and foreign source of funds.

Table 15.1 and 15.2 show the external and domestic sources of funds expressed as a percentage of nominal GDP. The size of China's nominal GDP, exchange rate with the US$, and the domestic real interest rates, are also shown

TABLE 15.1 Percentage of Shares of Foreign Funds in China's GDP (%)

	GDP	FDI	Trade Bal.	Reserve	IBRD/IDA	IMF	Foreign Loans	Rmb/US	Real Interest Rate
1985	307.83	0.64	4.84	0.86	0.30	0.11		2.9367	−2.04
1986	298.56	0.75	4.01	0.69	0.58	0.36		3.4528	3.08
1987	325.14	0.71	1.16	0.90	0.85	0.36		3.7221	2.70
1988	405.71	0.79	1.91	0.83	0.90	0.25		3.7221	−2.77
1989	453.91	0.75	1.45	1.22	1.02	0.20		3.7651	2.53
1990	392.51	0.89	2.23	2.83	1.50	0.12	3.74	4.7832	3.47
1991	411.31	1.06	1.97	5.28	1.74	0.00	4.03	5.3233	1.79
1992	490.85	2.24	0.89	3.96	1.64	0.00	4.06	5.5146	0.42
1993	616.53	4.46	1.66	3.44	1.57	0.00	4.02	5.7620	−3.65
1994	562.26	6.01	0.96	9.18	2.14	0.00	5.79	8.6187	−8.00
1995	732.01	5.13	2.28	10.05	1.95	0.00	5.04	8.3510	−1.40
1996	860.84	4.85	1.42	12.20	1.77	0.00	4.52	8.3142	3.35
1997	958.16	4.72	4.22	14.60	1.68	0.00	4.17	8.2898	6.93
1998	1025.28	4.43	4.24	14.14	1.79	0.00	4.42	8.2791	7.37
1999	1089.45	3.70	2.68	14.20	1.77	0.03	4.75	8.2783	7.21
2000	1205.26	3.38	2.00	13.74	1.65	0.03	4.23	8.2784	3.74
2001	1332.25	3.52	1.69	15.93	1.52	0.02	3.85	8.2770	3.72
2002	1461.91	3.61	2.08	19.59	1.41	0.02	3.57	8.2770	4.69
2003	1649.93	3.24	1.54	24.44	1.27	0.02	3.14	8.2770	2.66
2004	1941.75	3.12	1.65	31.41	1.12	0.02	2.95	8.2768	−1.25
2005	2269.32	2.66	4.49	36.08	0.92	0.01	2.38	8.1917	1.64
2006	2730.33	2.31	6.50	39.06	0.78	0.01	2.03	7.9718	2.13
2007	3524.72	2.12	7.50	43.36	0.62	0.01	1.66	7.6040	−0.34
2008	4560.79	2.03	6.54	42.67	0.49	0.01	1.31	6.9451	−2.32
2009	5059.72	1.78	3.87	47.42	0.44	0.22	1.35	6.8310	5.42
2010	6040.37	1.75	3.00	47.14	0.36	0.18	1.12	6.7695	−1.05
2011	7495.56	1.55	2.07	42.44	0.27	0.14	0.91	6.4588	−1.46
2012	8461.36	1.32	2.72	39.14	0.23	0.13	0.77	6.3125	3.52
2013	9494.59	1.24	2.73	40.25	0.20	0.11	0.63	6.1932	3.68
2014	10,355.84	1.15	3.70	37.11	0.17	0.10	0.63	6.1428	4.71

GDP, nominal GDP in Billion US$.

TABLE 15.2 Percentage Shares of Domestic Funds in China's GDP (%)

	Bank Loan	FAI	Fiscal Def.	IPO(A)	IPO(H,N)	M1	M2	GN Debt	NPL
1985	68.57	28.13	0.01						
1986	78.99	30.27	0.80						
1987	81.09	31.33	0.52						
1988	79.23	31.48	0.89						
1989	83.37	25.81	0.93						
1990	93.27	24.06	0.78			37.02	81.46		
1991	96.44	25.55	1.08			39.43	88.37		
1992	95.10	29.85	0.96			43.34	93.84		
1993	92.77	36.80	0.83	0.78	0.17	45.83	98.19		
1994	82.49	35.17	1.19	0.21	0.39	42.39	96.83		
1995	82.68	32.75	0.95	0.14	0.05	39.24	99.38	20.88	
1996	85.45	32.01	0.74	0.41	0.12	39.84	106.32	20.67	
1997	94.32	31.40	0.73	1.04	0.45	43.85	114.56	19.99	
1998	101.93	33.46	1.09	0.92	0.04	45.89	123.11	36.41	
1999	103.93	33.10	1.93	0.99	0.05	50.82	132.94	37.00	28.50
2000	99.59	32.99	2.50	1.53	0.56	53.27	134.91	37.44	22.40
2001	101.85	33.75	2.28	1.07	0.06	54.30	143.56	37.75	29.80
2002	108.51	35.95	2.60	0.64	0.15	58.58	152.90	37.74	26.00
2003	116.43	40.69	2.15	0.60	0.39	61.60	161.99	37.16	20.40
2004	110.36	43.85	1.30	0.52	0.40	59.71	158.11	35.16	13.20
2005	104.73	47.75	1.23	0.18	0.83	57.71	160.71	33.81	8.60
2006	103.50	50.54	0.76	1.13	1.44	57.90	158.77	31.49	7.10
2007	97.64	51.24	0.57	2.88	0.36	56.92	150.53	34.83	6.20
2008	95.78	54.56	0.40	1.09	0.10	52.48	150.01	31.67	2.40
2009	115.64	64.98	2.25	1.45	0.31	64.07	176.55	35.79	1.60
2010	117.19	61.55	1.66	2.35	0.58	65.20	177.51	36.56	1.13
2011	113.18	64.34	1.11	1.05	0.15	59.87	175.90	36.47	0.96
2012	117.93	70.15	1.63	0.59	0.19	57.79	182.38	37.30	0.95
2013	122.27	75.90	1.87	0.48	0.18	57.36	188.18	39.38	1.00
2014	128.39	80.49	1.79	0.76	0.35	54.71	193.10	41.06	1.25

FAI, fixed asset investment; *GN Debt*, gross national debt; *NPL*, nonperforming loans.

in Tables 15.1. Although there could be some overlapping between foreign direct investment, trade balance, and international reserves, the percentage shares of the six external sources are low in general (Due to the use of different data sources and the specific definitions, the Chinese data here may differ slightly from those shown in other chapters). International reserves occupied the largest percentage share of GDP. For simplicity, the aggregate of all the percentage shares in 2014 amounted to 42.86% of GDP. Table 15.2 shows that the percentage shares in GDP for the nine domestic sources of funds in 2014 amounted to 501.9%, though again there could be overlapping between, e.g., bank loans and M2. The percentage shares of bank loans and M2 exceeded 100% in 2014.

However, the situations regarding the level of national debt and nonperforming loans (NPLS) have been debated, partly because their definitions are looser when compared to other economies. The reliability of accurate data has also been challenged. While the maturity dates may differ, and there would not be any urgency on debt repayment in China, the somewhat low level of government debt would increase once corporate debts and other borrowings were included in the calculation. For example, Wu (2016) noted that local debts that have increased rapidly since 2008 amounted to 40% of GDP, with an equivalent of US$3.8 trillion in 2014. A different report by the IMF and the Federal Reserve Bank of St. Louis showed similarly that China's national debt at the end of 2014 amounted to 41.54% of GDP, equivalent to around US$4.3 trillion, while the foreign debt by June 2015 stood at around US$1.68 trillion ("National Debt of China," *Wikipedia*). While some argued that the debt issue in China has not reached a threshold when compared to other OCED countries, others have been worried about China's ability to finance the debts (Wu, 2014; Clarke and Lu, 2016).

However, it has been reported that China's bad debts are at least nine times larger than the official figures, due to economic slowdown and the excessive use of stimulus packages. One estimate showed that the China banks' NPL ratio ranged between 15% and 19%, while the official ratio was given at only 1.6%, and about 10%−15% of GDP (about US$1.04 trillion to US$1.62 trillion) would be needed to cover the bad loans. The news report concluded that China's bad debt-to-GDP ratio would exceed 300% by 2020, up from 200% in 2016. The explanation for the low NPL ratio was the implicit guarantee provided to SOEs and the continuous rollover of bad debts, and that stimulus would not be effective as the funding measures could simply provide liquidity to infrastructural projects rather than to strengthen manufacturing activities. To reduce default risk as a result of the mounting debt, the government implemented a number of schemes, including debt-to-bond swap schemes, debt-to-equity swap schemes, NPL securitization, and the sale of NPLs to AMCs. However, analysts pointed out that as an instrument of public policy, the four AMCs established to bail out loss-making banks in the 1995 banking reform have since become profit-seeking corporations, and may not want to take over new bad assets. Although the size of shadow financing remained small compared to similar institutions elsewhere, the bad debt of shadow financing amounted to about 4% of GDP, equivalent to US$4 trillion. One other feature in Chinese banking is the rapid expansion in online banking that eliminated the need for a physical presence, resulting in the closure of foreign bank branches (*The Diplomat*, May 21, 2013; and *South China Morning Post*, February 16, April 15, May 4, and 6, 2016).

By examining macroeconomic variables and sources of funds, one can see that the bulk of the rise in the Chinese economy appeared around 2005, partly because of flourishing trade and inward investment after WTO accession in 2001, and partly because of the need for preparation for the 2008 Olympics, the sequences of rescues and stimuli due to the 2008 crisis, the earthquakes since 2008, and the 2010 Shanghai Expo. The trend analysis obviously showed rapid increases, but the question is how far such a rapid pace of growth could last. Indeed, the nominal economy has surpassed the real economy. Given the continuous large increase in money supply, the excess liquidity situation would only get worse, as holders of cash would look for channels to secure their assets. By acquiring foreign assets, cash from China can be exported. Any form of monetary policy or instruments could be ineffective when large amounts of cash were circulating outside the banking system.

VII DICHOTOMIES AND DUALITIES

Foreigners tend to look at the successful side of the Chinese economy, partly due to the lack of understanding, and partly because foreigners were still attracted to the Chinese market and the "lower" cost of labor, while socialist "sympathizers" were keen to kowtow to China's economic success, thinking that could constitute a new model of development without realizing that it was foreign resources that China exploited to its own advantage. Deng basically played the "sympathy" card, and lured the international community to come to the aid of China, while the political scene was left unchanged. Deng's strategy of declaring China's poverty proven to be more successful than Mao's hardline approach.

What many foreigners failed to see were the various dichotomies in China's domestic economy. China since the early 1980s accumulated a large number of distortions and conflicts, thereby generating a snowball effect both in width and in depth. On the hardware side and through the "bringing in" policy, China has gained foreign resources and imitated foreign technologies through trade and Chinese nationals obtaining qualifications overseas. In exports, China has become the largest world exporter. In industries and technological advancement, China has been a "copycat." Although domestic businesses expanded and foreign multinational enterprises made direct contact with the central government, key corporations and markets were still under state control and influence. The state has a firm grip on the entire economy as the extent of state control and influence has extensively and intensively infiltrated into the business community. Through the attainment of the largest international reserves, the Chinese currency has been used for trade settlement, and as another international currency in the IMF starting from late 2016. One should not be surprised if other countries ignorant of China's internal issues would see China's performance has produced an excellent "report card" (Some of these dualities have been discussed in Chapter 9: Cases of Economic Vulnerabilities).

Fiscal Deficits and Inflation

China has been running fiscal deficits for decades, and it had become a "take it for granted" attitude that subsidy provisions would become part of China's policy. In the 4 years from 2012 to 2015, e.g., the inflation rates measured by the Consumer Price Index (CP) in China were 2.71% in 2012, 2.62% in 2013, 2.0% in 2014, and 1.44% in 2015 (CEIC Data). The answer is simply that when state instructions on price changes were given, inflation could be controlled. One way for businesses to "bypass" state directives on inflation was to set a high price at the beginning, so that there would not be any price "increase" in subsequent years. Thus, prices could remain "stable" for years. The people's desire to travel to shop in Hong Kong and overseas could avoid the high price, and consumption tax, and expect higher product reliability and variety.

Unreliable Products

The production of fake, toxic, and health-hazardous products in the consumer market has effectively eroded consumer confidence in China. Many of the producers were fearless, as they were related to the party or high level officials, implying the highly privileged nature of party and government officials. Consequently, there was a lack of loyalty to Chinese home-made products. In the long run, if consumer confidence was not restored, China would likely face trade imbalance as imports could soon exceed exports.

One could argue that individuals were eager to "get rich." Since officials could enrich themselves with corrupt and rent-seeking practices, individuals who engaged in production of "bad" goods would consider such practices as alternative market opportunities, especially when the implementation of laws and orders was loose, and standards and quality were not strongly adhered to. On the positive side, one could argue that individuals in China were just entrepreneurial and wished to start their own business. Ultimately, it is an issue of business ethics, discipline and responsibility that needs to be improved. Simply put, if individuals saw officials were abusing their power, the production of "bad" would just be the "mirror image" to the unjust practices.

Land Acquisition

Although land is officially state-owned, there have been numerous cases where old residential and rural lands have been confiscated for industrial or infrastructural development without proper compensation (Chan, 2003; Ding, 2007). Social grievances simply grew and spread (*The Economic Times*, November 1, 2014). China should not be faced with a shortage of land, as it is the third biggest country in the world geographically, but the model of urban development could lead to problems as the usage of land become concentrated. There are at least two theories of urbanization. In land-intensive countries, urbanization should be spread out so as to avoid congestion and over-concentration. When developments were spread out land-wise, individuals would have more space as buildings would not be constructed too close to each other. As such, the price of properties would not rise too rapidly, and individuals would have time and a chance to prepare for residential settlement. On the contrary, when economies are faced with a limited supply of land, construction would be concentrated and close together. The social cost would not only increase congestion, but also the price of properties would be high. Individuals would have fewer chances of property acquisition when property prices increased disproportionately faster than the increase in wages and income.

There could be a number of policy considerations. Would the authority regard housing as a necessity or a luxury? As a necessity, the authority would have to ensure that housing could be made affordable. Property prices would have to be relatively low and stable, so as to leave the affordability ratio high. As a luxury, the price of property could be high, fluctuating, and speculative. Developers would use the market supply to their advantage. The rapid rise in property prices would become destabilizing, and the rising prices would produce lower purchasing power and therefore lower overall economic welfare.

Household Registration

The household registration (*hukou*) system was carried over from 1958, when Mao decided to restrict mobility by not allowing citizens to move around different parts of China (Cheng and Selden, 1994). In the postreform years, workers were allowed to seek employment in the coastal regions, but their *hukou* remained in their place of birth. Thus, workers who migrated would not have the same entitlement compared to indigenous workers in all welfare aspects. Instead, they would have to pay for welfare services in the private market. In kindergartens, e.g., parents who migrated would have to pay a much higher fee, or even a large stipend or donation to a privately run kindergarten, before their children could be accepted. Effectively, such sources of discrepancies between indigenous and migrated workers would constitute another source of cronyism through the "*guanxi*" system of relationships.

The *hukou* system has other implications ("Hukou System," *Wikipedia*; *The Guardian* July 31, 2014; and *The Diplomat*, February 3, 2016). As workers who migrated from rural areas were typically working in the coastal cities, there would be a potential loss in agricultural output once the "surplus labor" was exhausted. Over time, China would produce less agricultural output if rural workers were not replenished, and there would probably be a rise in agricultural imports. Workers who had migrated tended to remit their income and earnings back to families in their home villages. But these remittances were considered as transfer earning, and were not counted as output from the villages. Hence, the income of rural villages typically declined in statistical terms, and the "poverty" in rural areas would actually have been supported by the remittance of the migrated workers from urban cities.

One-Child Policy

The quality of the population should be more important than its size when it comes to development. China, between 1978 and 1980, introduced the "one-child" policy as an instrument of demographic control, though there could be exemptions for ethnic minorities (Conly, 2016; Fong, 2016). As traditional Chinese families preferred male to female infants, various unintended and inhuman consequences appeared. However, a parent who chose to have a second child would have to pay a tax to the local officials (*BBC News*, October 29, 2015; and *CNN*, January 1, 2016). This effectively worked like a "population tax" or privilege for the "rich and powerful," and another source for officials to siphon off the "population tax" that varied between regions. Dependent on locality, the tax on the second child could range between 0.2 million and 0.5 million yuan.

The discrepancy in the preference between the two sexes has over the decades resulted in imbalance in the sex ratio and fertility, with more males than females in China's demography. The sex imbalances raised other social concerns, such as the family as a social unit and the choice of marriage, as married couples might have to take care of multiple parents and grandparents. There had been calls to remove the "one-child" policy, it was finally in the March 2015 meeting of National People's Congress that, effective from January 2016, the policy was replaced by a "two children" policy. Young parents, however, agreed that this came too late as it has become very costly and expensive to raise another child, given the rising economic cost of living and quality of life, and that both parents would usually seek full-time employment.

Welfare and Public Goods

It was the SOEs that used to serve as "mini-societies." State provision of welfare support proved to be inadequate after the 1997 SOEs reform, as laid-off workers did not receive the same amount of welfare provisions from the state, though there had been gradual improvements in government provisions. With the loss of the "iron rice bowl," the demand for social welfare and public goods has risen, but it would take years if not decades for the government to increase its supply of public goods, public utilities, and social welfare (Davis, 1989; Wong, 1998). In the meantime, excess demand drove up the price of supply by nonstate organizations (*The Guardian*, April 23, 2013; and *CNN*, March 5, 2013). The situation was crucial in remote regions, as basic needs were inadequate.

Income and Political Inequality

The ideology of communism projected equality, as the state-owned everything and rationed materials. Economically, this sounded egalitarian, as everyone would be treated equally. The question then was who would consider what to distribute and what kind of rations would be provided to individuals. As the process of becoming a party member was already selective, the "power" to decide what and how much to ration was in the hands of the party officials. Protection of vested interests, collusion, cronyism, and corruption among party officials was hidden and invisible. In China, power and authority were concentrated among the party officials, and their princelings were provided with various privileges. Armed with state control and influence in various big businesses, cronyism would appear among high officials, and the benefits and gains derived from businesses were allotted according to the "*guanxi*" within the close circle. The irrevocable form of political inequality gave rise to economic and income inequality.

The coexistence of political and economic inequalities could become extreme in remote regions. Concentration of political power itself would be the source of inequality, and the abuse of political authority could be seen in the unfair allocation of economic gains, especially in key sectors conducted by multinational and state corporations. In addition, regional imbalances gave rise to regional inequality between the rich coastal provinces and the poor remote inner provinces. It was reported in early 2016 that income inequality in China was the world's worst, as the richest 1% of households owned one third of wealth in China, while the poorest 25% owned just 1% of the country's total wealth. Between 1980 and 2012, China's Gini coefficient had deteriorated by 25 index points, from 0.3 to 0.55 ("Income Inequality in China," *Wikipedia*; *BBC News*, June 29, 2011; *The Wall Street Journal*, March 26, 2015; and *Financial Times*, January 14, 2016).

System

The root of inequalities in "one country, no system" China came from the lack of a transparent and equitable system of conducting affairs. Instead, personality influences remained dominant in decision-making. There existed also the possibility of a "vicious cycle," as the greater the extent of personal influence, the lower the chance of ever allowing a sustainable and reliable system to function. During the period 2014–16, President Xi Jinping purged a number of corrupt officials, but many argued that the "anticorruption" campaign was directed more to potential political opponents than to the intention of establishing an anticorruption body. The lack of a reliable and open system could have political consequences when it came to succession (Zheng, 2000). Deng was succeeded by Jiang Zemin, and Hu Jintao in turn succeeded Jiang, but both Jiang and Hu were "finger-pointed" by Deng before he died in 1997. However, Xi Jinping, who succeeded from Hu in 2012, was not "appointed" by Deng, and could face challenges within the party. And whoever will succeed Xi could certainly invite more ideological and political debates. Since 2015, it has become clearer that Xi has taken shelter from Mao by reiterating Maoism and the Cultural Revolution.

Data Reliability

In the 1980s and 1990s, both real and nominal GDP growth rates were close to two digits. The same has been true since the turn of the 21st century. It was only after the 2008 crisis that GDP growth rates edged downwards. Such performances raised eyebrows among analysts and governments. Statistically, the economic base should be larger, since the China economy has expanded. It would only be natural for a rising GDP economy to experience a lower GDP growth rate. Such should be true, in that while the absolute level was still rising, the relative level would drop as growth proceeded. China cannot be an exception. The reliability of China's economic data has been questioned by academics, the media, and professional analysts (Koch–Weser, 2013) (*The Economist*, July 15, 2015; *South China Morning Post*, January 20, 2016; and *The New York Times*, January 26, 2016). One possibility would be to consider the data trend over the decades, rather than the absolute level in a particular year. The pragmatic question is whether China could maintain high growth for so long, and for how long? While there was much optimism in the 1980s and 1990s, could the same degree of optimism be expected in post-2008 China?

Other than examining the GDP, one could also examine the sectors and different resources. The financial sector was booming, but could that be viable when individual economic sectors or the performance of a particular resource was considered. For example, would the agricultural supply be sustainable given the rising income of the households? The same concern could be raised in energy resources, and so on. In other words, how competitive could the Chinese economy be today, versus three decades ago, and three decades in the future. As a reliable economy in the international community, a lack of honest and transparent economic data would make analysis difficult and unreliable, and therefore also the predictions.

Environment

In the early 1980s when bicycles were the major form of land transport, visitors to China would see much more greenery and few high rise buildings. Overall transportation could be less effective, but the air was fresh and clear blue skies were common. Rapid modernization and urbanization promoted wealth at the expense of environment protection, though the environment has been on the official agenda for a number of years.

Industrialization was one aspect of economic reform. Previously, light manufacturing outputs were geared to the export market, but the success of "industrialization" was measured by a number of indicators. Unscrupulous consumption behavior among the Chinese elite turned them into "market bourgeoisies." China's consumption pattern has caught up with the advanced countries, and so has the number of vehicles on the roads and the levels of urban congestion and pollution. Hence, in large cities, clear blue skies have become a rarity, while wearing face masks has become common. Instead of rows of bicycles on the streets, the major roads are congested with luxury cars. And yet, China is thinking of exporting cars and other high-tech products to boost China's exports in the "going out" strategy.

Pollution has long-term implications in the food chain, in medical expenses, in fiscal financing, and in mortality rates. These will have further economic repercussions, such as tourism and related businesses.

Capital Flight

The rise in the value of the Chinese currency permitted individuals to transfer assets overseas, despite the lack of full convertibility in the currency. So long as the economy was growing, the outflow of currency could be tolerated, as that could be supported by international reserves. However, domestic citizens would consider "stability" and "uncertainty" differently, as money in China is cash, but money in foreign countries becomes assets and wealth. It would be possible for domestic citizens to transfer their money out when the economy was considered as "stable." Clear examples of currency outflow include large purchases of property, resources, and industrial plants in foreign countries. If China could maintain the "sunny days," coupled with the extent of economic intervention, monetary outflows could continue and control could still be managed. However, once the situation reversed, such as a gradual reduction in international reserves, prolonged trade weakness, political upheaval, currency depreciation or financial attack, and revision in world interest rates, the erosion of confidence on the Chinese currency could lead to massive capital flight through formal and underground channels.

Noneconomic Issues

A host of noneconomic issues have caused China not to be accepted by the international community. In many ways, China still pursues protectionist and selective policies. Protectionism still exists, in the sense that official consents and permissions are needed, while connections, contacts, and relationships are chosen selectively. Common examples include restriction of a number of freedoms, such as the control of media, religion, NGOs, democracy, publications, and so on (*South China Morning Post*, April 29, 2016). While there are laws in China, respect of the rule of law could also be abused by officials. Extreme incidents include the lawyer who had his clothes ripped off in court when his request to file a case in the district court of Nanning was rejected (*BBC News*, June 7, 2016).

These restrictions reflect the absolute nature of state power, and that authority is not only not shared, but the channel of communication is "top-down," "one-way" and nonnegotiable. The totalitarian nature of the state means other instruments are deployed when needed, such as the police, intelligence gathering, and restrictions on the internet. The lack of freedom gives rise to a variety of social behaviors, such as selfishness, low ethics, and "do not care" attitudes, while social displeasure can only be expressed in thought but not in act. Thus, stability did not convey security. Economic expansion has provided the state with more resources and more power, while a number of noneconomic areas remain restricted and undeveloped, and shielded from advancement. The power controlled by a few has become the deprivation sacrificed by the majority.

These are some of the noneconomic issues that have been reported in the media, with some were more severe than others. The Chinese economy is still in its development stage, and one should not expect perfection but would like to see constant improvements. On balance, there are also incidences of good behavior and human virtues reported in the media. For example, it was reported in 2016 that through the DNA database, a man abducted almost two decades ago was reunited with his biological parents (*China Daily*, April 13, 2016).

The centralization advocates argued that China needed to be ruled and governed because it is a large country and things could get out of hand if not supervised closely. The dominance of a personality-driven society could provide a "speedier" way of solving things, especially in difficult times and crises. On the contrary, the system-driven advocates provide the opposite argument, that due exactly to the fact that China is a large country, and to avoid abuse of authority, it would be better to decentralize authority through an effective and transparent system so that influence through personality or cronyism could be minimized. Thus, to establish a reliable and sustainable system should be a great task not to be delayed, as the leaders need to have broad-mindedness, charisma, vision, and selflessness.

There is a major difference between business leaders and political leaders. Business leaders may need to involve their own wealth and assets. Business is risky, and profit may not be forthcoming. On the contrary, a true and unbiased political leader is supposed to serve the people. Political leaders often rely on popularity, but once in office, they have power in directing resources to their own advantage, especially in poor countries. Hence, the attainment of power was not to serve but to amass wealth and assets through exploiting power. Thus, it would be unlikely for political leaders in developing countries to establish a reliable system, as that would work against their private interests. Indeed, in "fragile" states, a situation of "no system" could in itself be a "system" already, as that work to the best interests of the leaders, unfortunately.

Hence, a way of dealing with the economic and noneconomic dichotomies and dualities would be the development of a fair and open system where all participants would know the rules and practices. In contemporary advanced countries, it is the establishment of a civic system that stands between the state and the individuals. "No one is above the rule of law" would be the ultimate spirit of a functioning system.

VIII CONCLUSION

An opposite thought would be interesting. Should the industrialized countries be more competitive in terms of lower tax rates, lower costs of production, and less government welfare, would investors from industrialized countries still rush to investment in China? Would China's gain in competitiveness be due to falling competitiveness in many of the advanced industrialized countries?

A major, but probably hidden, economic reason in the "NKI" was the intention to free China's massive labor force for low cost production, and China's huge potential domestic market for consumption of industrial goods. China had been growing and had, in the first three decades of economic reform since 1978, provided the world with a large supply of low cost labor and in turn had consumed much industrial manufacturing from other advanced countries. These economic relationships also had implications for the industrialized countries. The imports from China could be cheaper, thereby providing both a bigger profit margin to the businesses, and lower inflationary pressure as retail prices would become lower. The exports from industrialized countries to China would benefit from their high-tech manufacturing and brand-name consumer products. In the process, China would have gained access to a large amount of technological knowledge, and that could speed up China's technological development. There are other aspects of achievement in China's economic reform. Economic growth in China had removed poverty starting from the coastal provinces, and spreading gradually to the inner provinces.

The more controversial areas in the NKI would certainly be the political and international aspects of development in China. If the political intentions in the NKI were to pull China to the US side in the Cold War, the historical evidence would probably be negative. The Cold War had ended largely through the economic supremacy of the United States and European Union countries in the Reagan—Thatcher era of the 1980s. Although China had been raised to the global arena through its membership of the United Nations, China made no political and ideological compromise. Indeed, with a growing Chinese economy, the ideological bond between Russia and China could be even more formidable and a bigger headache to the Western world. It was also true that the Sino—US bilateral relationship had developed, but one could also conclude which country gained more in the bilateral relationship.

While the rapid economic growth was fueled by the injection of foreign resources, coupled with the utmost reluctance to make changes in political and ideological terms, China's economic reform generated a number of controversies, dichotomies, and distortions. For example, income expansion did result in uneven growth between provinces and households, and the degree of inequality had risen. Political high-handedness would lead to poor ethics and irresponsibility at different levels. The era of the Cultural Revolution that destroyed much of the classical side of Chinese culture, custom, and discipline has come back to haunt its people and neighboring regions.

Income grew rapidly in the decades of economic reform, but attention seemed to have concentrated on the gross speed of growth, rather than the substance of growth.

One positive argument would be that China's development was still young, and in its infant stage and it would naturally meet various obstacles. On the contrary, others argued that the expansion in the hardware had not been complemented by improvements in the software. It could become a vicious circle, because the growing gap between the hardware and software could mistakenly be translated to mean the need to expand the hardware further, and the need to improve China's software would further be ignored. It would not be a surprise for some to argue that the lack of progress in software would be covered by the achievements in hardware, because improvements in software boiled down to the elements of political and ideological change.

Between the "bringing in" and "going out" strategy, changes in China could take place through various conditions, forces, or requirements that were attached or adhered to the "bringing in" policy. China's WTO accession, e.g., has "brought in" conditions that required China to change along with market practices. To liberalize the Chinese currency, China has to "bring in" trade and financial requirements. One can identify other examples where changes would have to be introduced in the "bringing in" strategy. One can conclude that China would not introduce change by itself, probably due to the static nature of its political system and ideological thoughts. Changes would have to come from external forces that China would have to adhere to.

16

Frontier of Capitalism:
The Sino—British Negotiation

I INTRODUCTION

China's Qing Dynasty (1644—1912) was feudalistic and inward-looking, with weak technological advances and it was unprepared to establish connections with the outside world. Richness in agricultural and natural resources fueled China's inward-oriented behavior, and the teaching of Confucian principles made the Chinese race depend more on self-reliance. China's self-imposed isolation from the rest of the world proved to be costly. In the 19th and 20th centuries, the world was undergoing epochs of western imperialism. The unpreparedness of the Qing government reflected more on its shear incompetence than the incidences of foreign aggression. With little focus on modern technology, armory, and navy, the Qing government was fighting a losing battle in virtually all incidents of foreign aggression, throughout the two centuries. It would be alarming or totally unacceptable in modern times if such a government were so incapable of defending the land and so eager to cede land to foreign countries. Surely, the indigenous residents were not "consulted" when land was ceded. Land cession was meant to be permanent and not recoverable.

At the end of the First Opium War (1839—42) between the Great Britain and Qing China, the 1842 Nanking Treaty concluded with the perpetual cession of Hong Kong Island to the British, followed by a similar cession of the Kowloon Peninsula in 1860 after the Second Opium War. As a result of the need for more land for the purposes of defense, and to ensure the steady supply of daily materials, the New Territories was leased by the Qing government to the British government for 99 years in 1898. The lease was negotiated between the United Kingdom and the Guangxu Emperor of China.

The Qing government was overthrown in 1911, and the succeeding Nationalist government was replaced in 1949 by the People's Republic of China. Despite China's statement of anticolonialism and the intention to recover former colonies in the United Nations in 1972, there was no land under the rule of the People's Republic of China that was being colonized. Western imperialism, as well as Japanese occupation and invasion, all took place before the birth of the People's Republic of China. The loophole in international law was the 99-year lease of the

© 2017 Elsevier Inc. All rights reserved.

New Territories that expired in 1997, but the lease was made between the Qing government and Great Britain. For the last century, the New Territories had been developed by the British colonial government, and urbanization resulted in a growing number of residents. Thus, the so-called "indigenous" people had been diluted, and most local villages had been left destroyed along with rapid urbanization. The legitimate question was whether the land in the New Territories should be returned to the People Republic of China at all, since the People's Republic of China was not a signatory in the lease agreement. Strictly speaking, given that the Qing government no longer existed, the expiry of the lease would not exist and the New Territories should be considered as part of Hong Kong along with the two land cessions in 1842 and 1860.

Hong Kong is a small place on the world map, and may not catch the attention of members of the United Nations. As a new member in the United Nations, China had received goodwill from other countries. Since the end of the Second World War, the United Kingdom was faced with domestic problems. The United Kingdom since the 1950s had granted political independence to a number of former colonies. The colonial British government held the view that Hong Kong was geographically and territorially too tiny, and could not survive without various daily supplements from mainland China. The UK government had expressed their "willingness" to return Hong Kong to China on at least two occasions: at the end of the Second World War and the withdrawal of Japanese occupation in 1945; and at the peak of the Cultural Revolution and the political riots in Hong Kong in 1967. By not standing firm on the validity and legitimacy of the two land cessions in 1842 and 1860, and the insistence that the People's Republic of China was not a signatory of the cession treaties and lease agreement, the British government had already given an advantage to the Chinese authorities.

In the incidents in 1945 and 1967, Premier Zhou En-lai replied that China would take back Hong Kong at an "appropriate time." One of the first things that Deng Xiaoping did after ensuring his power in 1978 was that 1997 was considered as the "right time" to take back not only the New Territories, but the entire Hong Kong Island. After China's statement in the United Nations in 1972, the British government had quietly been working on an "exit" strategy. The ignition point in the Hong Kong issue came to light in the late 1970s, when business people in Hong Kong asked what would happen to Hong Kong when the New Territories lease expired. There were a number of "testing the water" trips, visits, and exchanges by Hong Kong officials, Legislative Council members, and key businesses from Hong Kong, as well as Chinese officials and "Hong Kong watchers" from Beijing. Despite Deng's promise of "capitalistic life as usual" in his famous idiom of "keep betting in horse racing, keep taking steps in dancing," business confidence was shaken as the business community did not rely on words.

Many analysts considered that the Hong Kong handover was not just a reversion of Hong Kong's sovereignty to China, it was the clash of two polarized systems of capitalism and communism. Since its heydays as a British colony, Hong Kong was based on the ideology of market capitalism, *laissez-faire* principles of economic freedom, and nonintervention by the government (Dean, 1974; Tsang, 1995). A strong rule of common law and the presence of professional institutions had gradually been instituted. Local power rested independently in the three divisions of the Executive, the Judiciary, and the Legislature. Over the decades, such a system had basically taken root in Hong Kong. On the contrary, China since 1949 had chosen communism as its own ideology, and experienced periods of violence and crises, and maintained a closed door policy. Given the regime's low international credibility, it was unimaginable or even absurd for Great Britain to handover the most capitalistic and freest economy to the control and rule of the largest communist country. There were vast differences between China and Hong Kong in almost every aspect of life.

There has been a debate when looking at the performance of other former British colonies that, other than Canada, Australia, and New Zealand, many former British colonies were not growing and their economic performance was often worse than before independence, due probably to fragmentation, undemocratic and ineffective regimes, absence of reliable systems, unattractiveness to foreign investment, and lack of economic competitiveness. By looking at the experience of former British colonies, some conspiracy advocates argued that before their departure in 1997, the colonial government would "plant" policies that could weaken Hong Kong's future development. Although Hong Kong was not given independence but a reversion of sovereignty, the arguments for postcolonial Hong Kong remained cautious.

The concerns about post-1997 Hong Kong erupted as business confidence remained low. Leaders in London and Beijing finally agreed to have a Sino–British Negotiation on the future of Hong Kong in 1982. While the Hong Kong economy experienced a period of uncertainty, the Joint Declaration was reached in 1984 between London and Beijing. The two governments agreed to return Hong Kong to China in 1997, and Beijing agreed to maintain Hong Kong's capitalistic system for 50 years under the "one country, two systems" framework. Autonomy, self-rule, or "Hong Kong people ruling Hong Kong" was promised to post-1997 Hong Kong. A Basic

Law that represented the post-1997 constitution was drafted between London and Beijing. Under the "one country, two systems" framework, 1997 was a reversion of sovereignty, but the system remained unchanged. The 50 years until 2047 would be the "transition" as to whether the Hong Kong system would be removed, or Beijing would extend autonomy beyond 2047. Whether there would be a system change in 2047 would depend on how these 50 years would be governed, or how both Hong Kong and China would change in their own pace and directions within these 50 years. Thus, these 50 years would be a period full of unknown and uncertain interactions.

From a political economy point of view, the sovereignty change was not the only issue, it really would constitute a battle between the two ideologies, as each side has to accept, change, and live with each other. Could the two ideologies weld together into a more harmonious ideology, or would ideological divides lead to instability, antagonism, and bitterness? As a country, China should welcome Hong Kong, which has been used as a reference point. What Hong Kong people worried about would be the infiltration of communist ideology, especially in the extreme policies conducted during the Cultural Revolution. This is the essence of the ideological battle, in that while the two ideologies were bonded together, given time which would be the more influential ideology? Equally, would the intention of the United Kingdom to return Hong Kong to China be a possibility in allowing China to embrace capitalism through the Hong Kong connection? Would taking over Hong Kong be another "bringing in" policy in China, as Hong Kong would provide lessons of economic openness, property rights, and market economy to China? This ideological battle presents living history in a contemporary world political economy, as both economic and political activities between the two economies unfold on a daily basis from July 1997 to June 2047.

II THE BASIC LAW

The formal Sino—British Negotiation over post-1997 Hong Kong in the 2 years from 1982 to 1984 was international, and studies covered a number of analytical dimensions, especially in politics and economics. While some hailed the Sino—British Negotiation as a landmark in international relations, others were more critical on the future survival of Hong Kong (Dunn, 1985; Jao et al., 1985; Hicks, 1988; Yahuda, 1993; Lo, 1994; Ma, 1997). The negotiation took a total of 12 rounds before the Sino—British Joint Declaration on Hong Kong was concluded and signed between British Prime Minister Margaret Thatcher and Chinese Premier Zhao Ziyang on December 19, 1984, in Beijing. The Joint Declaration was registered by both governments at the United Nations on June 12, 1985. Effectively, China would resume sovereignty of Hong Kong Island, Kowloon, and the New Territories on July 1, 1997, from Great Britain. Hong Kong would become a Special Administrative Region (HKSAR) of China, but in accordance with the "one country, two systems" and autonomy principles, China's socialist system would not be practiced in the HKSAR. Hong Kong will maintain the capitalist way of life for a period of 50 years until 2047, as stipulated in Hong Kong Basic Law.

The Joint Declaration basically incorporated all the existing economic, legal, and administrative aspects of Hong Kong. The HKSAR will be under the authority of the central government in Beijing, but will enjoy a high degree of autonomy, except in foreign and defense affairs. The Chief Executive will be appointed by the central government based on election results or consultations to be held locally. Principal officials will be nominated by the Chief Executive for appointment by the central government. The various policies will be stipulated in the Basic Law of the HKSAR by the National People's Congress, and will remain unchanged for 50 years ("Basic Law," *Wikipedia*).

While Chapter I of the Basic Law specified the general principles in Articles 1–11, Articles 12–23 in Chapter II showed the relationship between the central authority and the HKSAR. Chapter III that covered Articles 24–42, illustrated the fundamental rights and duties of residents. The articles provided support to various aspects of individual freedom in post-1997 HKSAR. Chapter IV on political structure that related to post-1997 elections at different levels would be controversial. Article 45 and Annex I showed the method for selecting the Chief Executive. The wordings were general, if not vague, as can be seen from the following italic words in Article 45. Article 45 says "The method for selecting the Chief Executive shall be specified in the light of *actual situation* in the HKSAR and in accordance with the principle of *gradual and orderly* progress. The *ultimate* aim is the selection of the Chief Executive by *universal suffrage* upon nomination by a *broadly representative nominating committee* in accordance with democratic procedures." The choice of words looked general, but could have deliverable consequences. For example, what would constitute "actual situations?" What would constitute the principle of "gradual and orderly" progress? Could "gradual and orderly" be regarded as a principle? How should "gradual and orderly" be interpreted? And "progress" in what areas and directions? Would it take 10 or 50 years to be regarded as "gradual?" What would be the end point in the "gradual process?" Would "orderly" be meant to exclude violence, demonstration, and riots? How should "ultimate" be considered in actuality? What would have to occur before "ultimate?" How long would it take before the arrival of "ultimate?" Finally, "universal suffrage" should mean equal participation for all in open elections, and not by establishing a "broadly representative nominating committee," as the nomination of such a committee would naturally mean the inclusion of the minority and exclusion of the majority. This in itself contradicted the spirit of "universal suffrage." Such a lack of clarity also applied to Article 68 that specified the method for electing Legislative Council members. Annex I referred to the representation in the Election Committee, but not an elaboration on universal suffrage. The last statement in Annex I should be taken to mean that amendments could only take place after 2007 under the various specified conditions.

Chapter V (Articles 105–135) of the Basic Law looked into the economy. Article 106 stated that the HKSAR shall have independent finances, use its financial revenues exclusively for its own purposes, and these should not be handed over to central government. The central government should not levy taxes in the HKSAR. Article 107 specified the fiscal condition in the HKSAR, and expenditures must be kept within the limits of revenues. Article 111 stated that the Hong Kong dollar should continue to circulate. While other articles concerned the various aspects that existed in Hong Kong at the time of the handover, such as education, science, and cultural issues, one other concern was the ability of the HKSAR to introduce amendments to the Basic Law. Article 159 provided the procedure to amend the Basic Law, and the procedure seemed to be that even if amendment bills from the HKSAR had secured a two-thirds majority in the Legislative Council and consent from the Chief Executive, the amendment would have to be submitted to the Standing Committee of the National People's Congress for its views and approval. This would have imposed limits on the "high degree of autonomy" stipulated in Article 12.

While the Basic Law tried to incorporate the situation before 1997, a number of issues originated in the Basic Law had appeared to be problematic, controversial, and divisive. For example, Article 23 related to national security proved to be sensitive when attempts were made to draft it into a law in 2003, as many suspected that Article 23 could be used against the people of Hong Kong, while others argued that such aspects as "treason and subversion" would have already been dealt with in other aspects of the common law in the HKSAR, and enacting a national security law was unnecessary. In in the final analysis, it was a matter of distrust.

The issue of the 99 years lease of the New Territories did not seem to have been solved in the Basic Law. Because the New Territories was leased to Britain, some indigenous villagers went as far back to the 1898 lease and argued that land would have to return to them after the land lease expired in 1997. Over the years, and due to the need to expand residential demands, the British Hong Kong government in December 1972 established the Small House Policy in which "any male indigenous villager who is descended through the male line from someone who was a resident in 1898 of a recognized village in the New Territories may apply to build a small house (a maximum of three storeys in height and 700 ft^2 in each floor) on their own land at zero premium, or on public land through a private treaty grant, once during his lifetime" (*Hong Kong Free Press*, January 21, 2016).

In the People's Republic of China, all land belonged to the state. Land occupants would only have the "use right." Indigenous villagers in the New Territories claimed that their right was constitutionally protected, as Article 40 of the Basic Law recognized the lawful traditional rights of the indigenous inhabitants of the New Territories. Article 122 provided further protection to old land lots and village lots. This argument used by the village descendants was ill-intended. If land in the New Territories were to return to indigenous village descendants, the same should apply to those village descendants who settled in the Hong Kong Island and Kowloon areas before 1842 and 1860, respectively. Indeed, the 1972 policy on the entitlement of land by the villagers in Hong Kong should be outdated in a number of ways. It violated the law on equal opportunity between the two sexes, as land titles were given only to male descendants. The policy discriminated against urban residents and created a privileged class, as urban residents would never receive a piece of "free" land. Thus, there appeared a clear bias in resource and land distribution. The government would have to calculate the amount of land needed to be reserved for village descendants. It would be true that in "n" years, land in the New Territories would have to be totally occupied by these village descendants. And when the aging descendant passed away, the young descendant would then inherit another small house. As such, one descendant could end up with the ownership of more than one "small house" for sale and transaction.

Other problems include the abuse of the policy, as many male "descendants" were not born nor lived in Hong Kong. Villagers owned agricultural land, but the work on agricultural farming had long been abandoned as young villagers migrated overseas or earned their living in urban areas. Villagers could have sold their rural land to developers and other buyers for different purposes in the property market, and these "descendants" in turn could approach the government for their own land entitlement. In short, these descendants could have received double benefits. Criticisms should also be made on the part of the relevant government department, because of their inefficiency in the implementation of policy. Since 1997, there have been clashes and debates between village descendants, nonindigenous residents, and developers. Ultimately, it would be a simple case of vested interest on the part of the village descendants in amassing land and wealth. It is clear that the "small house policy" would evolve into a problem in the Basic Law.

The Basic Law was an "untested" constitution, as it had not been implemented before 1997. The remote possibility of making amendments to the Basic Law would mean that problems might not be dealt with effectively. Identified problems in the Basic Law could accumulate and eventually snowball into bigger issues that would exert political pressure on the government.

III THE BRITISH STRATEGY

The British Prime Minister Margaret Thatcher led the Sino–British Negotiation in 1982 – 84. She was assisted by Sir Geoffrey Howe, the British Secretary of State for Foreign and Commonwealth Affairs, and three sinologists, Sir Percy Cradock, the British Ambassador to the People's Republic of China, and the two successive Hong Kong Governors, Sir Edward Youde and Sir David Wilson, together with a number of bureaucrats and administrators. The official encounter on the future of Hong Kong began in 1979 with the visit by Hong Kong Governor Sir Murray MacLehose to meet Premier Deng Xiaoping in Beijing.

The British had been making preparation for an "exit" strategy. There were a number of considerations. High priority was given to the economy, as investments in Hong Kong came from Britain and overseas countries, and the geographical size of Hong Kong was too small for any sustainable development. Given there were vast differences between Hong Kong and mainland China, one workable approach was to develop and expand the Hong Kong economy to an advanced and modern stage, so that the Hong Kong economy would be ahead of the mainland economy. A vibrant Hong Kong economy would serve as a reference point to the development in the mainland economy. The "economic card" was thought to be the right strategy for Hong Kong, as this would be acceptable to Beijing politically.

Hong Kong should maintain market capitalism, so that private ownership and the market could function and perform to their utmost. Economic policies would gear to the functioning of a *laissez-faire* economy, with low tax rates, low welfare spending, and a reliable currency, so as to build up strong business confidence. After the early 1970s, the Hong Kong government started to improve the infrastructure by building the cross-harbor tunnels and the underground railway system in the urban areas. In the 1980s, more traffic infrastructure had been under construction, including bridges, tunnels, light-rail trains, and highways, culminating in the building of the new airport, completed in 1998. The business community had gradually been transformed to become more international, and was supported by greater use of English, and establishment and expansion of new tertiary and vocational educational institutions.

Assistance was provided to civil servants to have their children study in Britain and gain international qualifications. Professional associations were allowed to set local standards, so that they could play a part in the overall requirements of their professions. International standards were applied in businesses and professions so that Hong Kong could develop in parallel with the international community. Welfare spending was kept low, and "supply-side" economics were pursued. The policies on public housing and medical needs were adequate. As early in 1954, public housing provisions protected the needs of low income households, while the Home Ownership Scheme (HOS) instituted in late 1970s assisted "sandwich" income earners in a subsidized-sale program of housing ownership. Medical provisions were supplied through both public and private channels, so that all medically-needy individuals would be attended to (Li, 2006, 2012a).

The political dimension was the establishment of the "special administration district" suggested by Governor Murray MacLehose in 1971. It would serve three primary functions: (1) preserve for China some of the economic and political benefits of the present status of Hong Kong; (2) save China from having to absorb a population with different standard of living and attitude of mind; and (3) preserve for foreigners a tolerable trading base while concentrating them in a single area where they did not affect life in the rest of China (Li, 2012a, p. 36). The fundamental difference between Hong Kong and mainland China was that the British had constructed a reliable and sustainable capitalist system in Hong Kong, and whoever came to rule Hong Kong would have to adhere to the system.

In the actual Sino–British Negotiation, there were discrepancies within the British team, especially between Prime Minister Thatcher and the sinologists. Prime Minister Thatcher put forward two related proposals. One was that the land cessions in the two treaties were legitimate in the eyes of international laws, and should be permanent and nonnegotiable. The negotiation should only be confined to the 99-year lease that expired in 1997. However, the unfounded fear of a geographically small Hong Kong which would need supplies across the border weakened the insistence on the two treaties. The alternative was to allow the sovereignty to return to China, but the British government would remain the governing body. This would allow the greatest degree of stability and certainty in the transition. Prime Minister Thatcher was firm in her proposal, and even suggested the possibility of independence for Hong Kong after the June 1989 political turmoil in Beijing, thinking that the capitalistic way of life in Hong Kong would not be kept under China's rule (Li, 2012a, p. 37). However, Prime Minister Thatcher could have extended her secession argument to the fact that the other signatory in the 99-year lease no longer existed.

Thatcher's proposals could have unfortunately been "hi-jacked" by other sinologist members in her team. The sinologists, led by Sir Percy Cradock (1994), took a different approach. While he was the *charge d'affaires* in Peking, Sir Percy Cradock was "manhandled by the Red Guards and the mobs" when his office was set on fire in 1967 at the peak of the Cultural Revolution. Nonetheless, the sinologists were sympathetic to socialist China, eager to turn Hong Kong back to China, and prepared to accept China's terms, but they were unprepared to introduce political changes to Hong Kong. Their ready to "kowtow" attitude would have weakened the proposals by Prime Minister Thatcher. The sinologists were fighting a "losing" battle in the negotiation, as their strategy could not pierce through the negotiation for the benefit of Britain and Hong Kong, especially in the political area.

The views of Hong Kong were supposedly to be represented by the sinologists in the Sino–British negotiation, as no Hong Kong citizens were included. On the contrary, democrats in Hong Kong, led by Mr. Martin Lee who was the founding chairman of the Democratic Party in Hong Kong, warned that China could exercise political high-handedness in Hong Kong after 1997, and a more democratic Hong Kong would serve as another "cushion" for the stability and sustainability of Hong Kong. The Hong Kong Governor, Sir David Wilson, showed no support to suggestions from Martin Lee. Thus, Sir David Wilson produced minor changes and largely maintained the status-quo of the existing political structure, which was more of representation than free election or universal suffrage. The outcome of the negotiation by sinologists was the Sino–British Joint Declaration that basically prescribed all the economic, political, administrative, and social aspects existing in Hong Kong, and all these aspects were to be preserved and guaranteed by the Basic Law for 50 years until 2047.

While the outcome of the Sino–British Negotiation had been made known, one could surmise the ideas in the British side of the negotiation. There could be several arguments. One argument was that many former British colonies performed poorly. British imperialists would depart with a legacy that would result in a lack of sustainability in the postcolonial period. Policies could be instituted to allow divisive political factions, lead to a fall in education standards and decline in both physical and public infrastructure, and so on. As such, a post-1997 Hong Kong would perform weaker than pre-1997 Hong Kong. Secondly, the sinologists probably believed that the economic "cushion" would be enough for Hong Kong to maintain its "stability and prosperity." Thus, by not introducing deep political change before 1997, the sinologists should have been aware that it would be an "uphill" battle for Hong Kong people to fight on their own for political changes and freedom from Beijing in the post-1997 years. As such, the sinologists would have shed their responsibility, as the 50 years would become the "transition" years, while the outcome of that "transition" was unknown and uncertain, and would not be the responsibility of the sinologists in the negotiation team. Or, was it the "bitter pill" argument and the purpose of allowing China to take over Hong Kong was to impose changes in China along with the capitalist experience of Hong Kong? If so, Hong Kong served as the "bait" in modernizing China, bringing it closer to the international community. Indeed, it is yet to be seen who would influence who in the 50 years.

However, the successor to Margaret Thatcher, British Prime Minister John Major in 1990, did not pursue the sinologists' line of negotiation, though the Sino–British Negotiation was already concluded and the Basic Law had been drafted. Prime Minister John Major replaced Sir David Wilson, and brought Mr. Christopher Patten to become the 28th and last Governor of Hong Kong for the remaining years of 1992 – 97. Similar to Margaret Thatcher's line of strategic thinking, Governor Patten agreed to the need to establish a political "cushion" for Hong Kong. Governor Patten attempted to introduce political reform permissible within the Basic Law and the various agreements in the negotiation. His most controversial actions were the 1994 electoral reform. The original format was that those Legislative Council members who served the 1995 term would serve beyond the handover until 1999. This was known as the "through train," as it should provide continuity. However, Governor Patten redefined the use of functional constituencies to ensure that Hong Kong residents were able to vote for the so-called indirectly elected members of the Legislative Council, thereby widening the voters and taking a step closer to free elections.

The institutional reform proposed by Governor Patten proved to be popular, and unprecedented support was shown not only by the democrats, but he was seen as a leader who would stand up for the rights of the Hong Kong people. His British eloquence was shown to its best and was admired even by his critics. However, his measures were strongly criticized by the pro-China camp, who argued that Hong Kong would suffer as a result of his measures. In the end, there was no "through train," as members of the Legislative Council elected in 1995 were dissolved in July 1997, and replaced by a Provisional Legislative Council until elections in 1998. The attack on Governor Patten from the pro-Beijing camp was severe and vicious. In different media exposures provided by Chinese officials, Chris Patten was denounced the "whore of the East" and "a wrong doer who would be condemned for a thousand generations." The accusations on Chris Patten served another political purpose. They showed vividly to the people of Hong Kong the communist way and manner of conducting things in mainland China. It was political "capping" that aimed to identify Chris Patten as someone not acceptable. The use of a propaganda war and rhetoric went beyond the integrity of a leader, and it was unethical for leaders in an international negotiation to make personal attacks on others.

The key difference between Chris Patten and the sinologists was that Chris Patten was a professional politician who would look for political solutions and maximize gains. On the contrary, the sinologists' attitude remained soft and were ready to give in. Although their expert knowledge on China was thought to be useful in the negotiations, it turned out that might not have acted for the benefit of Hong Kong. Thus, should Margaret Thatcher have picked and trusted professional politicians rather than sinologists from the very beginning, the outcome of the Sino—British Negotiation and post-1997 Hong Kong would have been very different.

Since 1997, declassified files had revealed some details of the Sino—British Negotiation (*South China Morning Post*, August 18, 2013). It was revealed in the early stage of the negotiation that in September 1982 Prime Minister Thatcher believed that continued British administration of Hong Kong was feasible after 1997. Thatcher argued that "China's proposal for Hong Kong to become a largely self-governing special administrative zone ... would be 'disastrous' for investor confidence and lead to its collapse as a financial center," and "there would certainly be a wholesale flight of capital from Hong Kong and that this money having left Hong Kong would not return." To retain confidence in Hong Kong, Thatcher concluded that "Britain wanted to continue administering Hong Kong after 1997 under Chinese sovereignty ... Confidence in Hong Kong, and thus its continued prosperity, depends on British administration." Thatcher rightly pointed out that under the 19th century treaties between Britain and Qing China, both Hong Kong Island and Kowloon would remain British. Thatcher went as far as making an assessment of the military capability to defend Hong Kong, but China had larger armed forces and the Hong Kong garrison would be too weak for any large-scale attack.

Although Ambassador Percy Cradock was a sinologist and was ready to give in to Beijing, he also remarked on Chinese leaders as "an 'incorrigible and ineducable' group, otherwise they would not be where they are.... They are elderly men with rigid views, blinkered by dogma and national pride and deeply ignorant of how a place like Hong Kong works." It was recorded in the British minutes that China did not recognize the two treaties. Zhao Ziyang rejected Thatcher's proposal and that "China would not let others administer Hong Kong on its behalf nor place Hong Kong under the trusteeship of others." The Chinese negotiators considered that "their British counterparts had a colonialist and imperialist attitude which was outmoded, lacking in reality and would get nowhere." Unfortunately, the sinologists in the British team were concerned that the outlook of the talks was "bleak," and a confidence breakdown would occur should the talks breakdown. It was only by December 1982 that Thatcher softened her position, and Geoffrey Howe wrote in the minutes that the negotiation would have to be "on the basis of the Chinese proposal." The British feared that Deng might decide upon an early takeover of Hong Kong should agreements not be reached. Britain was on the defensive side of the negotiation until December 1984 with the signing of the Joint Declaration.

There were still policy areas where one could criticize the British Hong Kong government. Governor Chris Patten was a member of the Conservative Party in the United Kingdom, and one would expect his contribution would concentrate on the business community. Beginning from April 1995, the social welfare network in Hong Kong was widened, and the Comprehensive Social Security Assistance (CSSA) scheme replaced the simple Public Assistance Scheme introduced in 1971. Li (2012a, pp. 522 – 534) documented that since 1995 welfare expenditure had kept expanding at a disproportionate rate. Furthermore, there was no economic recession in the 1990s as the Hong Kong economy boomed and overheated, before it collapsed after the Asian financial crisis in

IV. THE FRONTIER OF CAPITALISM: CHINA VERSUS HONG KONG

1998. The issue was why a prowelfare policy was introduced and large welfare provisions were made prior to a time of economic boom. The political interpretation could be the planting of a fiscal bomb and increase of the fiscal burden in Hong Kong, meant that fiscal policy would become more politicized. Spending more at a time of economic boom would fuel inflation and overheating. Given economic openness in Hong Kong, a prowelfare and heavy fiscal burden regime should best be avoided. It should be best to remain flexible, for the Hong Kong economy to move along with the international community.

Another concern would be the United Kingdom's unwillingness to allow Hong Kong's seven million residents to come to Britain. Many Hong Kong residents held British nationality. Instead, the British National (Overseas) status was "tailor-made" in the Hong Kong Act 1985. British National (Overseas) are British nationals and Commonwealth citizens, but not British citizens, they do not have the right of abode in the United Kingdom and do not have consular protection in mainland China. The British National (Overseas) merely allowed the people of Hong Kong to retain a relationship with the United Kingdom after 1997, and enjoy consular protection when traveling outside Hong Kong and mainland China. At the peak of the political uncertainty in the 1980s, other English-speaking Commonwealth countries, typically Australia, Canada, and Singapore, were willing to take on financially able and professional migrants from Hong Kong.

The Sino–British Negotiation could produce an excellent case study on strategy and negotiation. For example, should Britain have made it clear about the meaning of the two treaties when China made the remark on colonialism in 1972? Or, was it a wrong move on the part of Britain to allow Governor Sir Murray MacLehose to visit Beijing in 1979? Would the sinologists' approach have already been predicted by the Chinese side? The year 1979 was the time when Deng was rising as the reformist leader who needed to accumulate more political capital and charisma. As such, the British move fitted squarely into Deng's "trap" in building up his personality strength in China. Would it be strategically stronger if Britain had waited until nearer to the end of the lease of the New Territories? Would the use of the "economic card" strategy be unsuitable, as China then was so poor and would not appreciate economic success in a capitalist Hong Kong? There was a total of 18 years between 1979 and 1997. Britain could have gained more time for strategic preparation, and waited for such better timing as 1989. These can only serve as the academic food for thought, as history cannot be rewritten.

In any case, the territories of Hong Kong and Kowloon that were ceded to Great Britain and the 99-year lease of the New Territories occurred in the Qing Dynasty, while the People's Republic of China came into existence in 1949 and was not a signatory to these territorial cessions and lease. The legal logic could be simple, and analogy would be that if the father of person A owed money to the father of person B and the two fathers have passed away, could person A claim the money back from person B?

IV THE CHINESE STRATEGY

To China, the Sino–British Negotiation came at the right time, as both the charisma of Deng and the goodwill shown on China's economic reform by the international community provided a good political mood. Deng was assertive and insisted on a few political criteria in recovering Hong Kong. From the very beginning, Deng made it clear that the return of the whole of Hong Kong was not negotiable. Hong Kong's successful economic performance would not be taken into account, as Hong Kong was built mostly from foreign and local capital. China would have nothing to lose even if the Hong Kong economy collapsed. The first bargaining point Deng held was that an economically recessed Hong Kong would hurt Britain and Hong Kong investors more, as there was little investment from China. Thus, while the British strategy was using the "economic card," China ignored the "economic card" and considered it as a "sunk cost" from the very beginning.

Secondly, while Prime Minister Margaret Thatcher insisted on the legitimacy of the two treaties that ceded Hong Kong and Kowloon to Great Britain in 1842 and 1860, respectively, Deng ignored that fact completely and emphasis was put on the "unequal" nature of the two treaties made by the Qing government. China's decision to take over Hong Kong's sovereignty was surely selective, even though other imperial powers had taken over land from the Qing government before 1911. The logic was what would be the legitimate argument for the post-1949 China regime to undo what had been done before 1949. Deng's move could have targeted the weakness of the United Kingdom, as it would probably not send military support to Hong Kong. As Hong Kong had been an international economy, China's decision to take back Hong Kong would have a high degree of political and ideological significance and recognition in the international community. Furthermore, the United Kingdom had previously made it known to China on two occasions that Britain would be prepared to return Hong Kong to China.

The end of the 99-year lease of the New Territories in 1997 was just the "appropriate time." It was thought that the return of Hong Kong would serve as a blueprint to the unification of Macau and Taiwan.

There were various observable features of Chinese communism that had troubled the people in Hong Kong. For example, words and actions could be very different. The "goal switching" attitude in policy implementation produced a low degree of trust of the Chinese government. Confidence in the future of Hong Kong under communist rule was low. Despite Deng's attempt to pacify the people of Hong Kong and the business community, the reality was that the Hong Kong economy was extremely vulnerable within a short time when foreign investment withdrew, people were emigrating, capital switched to foreign currencies, and the downfall of the Hong Kong currency occurred. The potential collapse of the Hong Kong economy would be a loss on all three sides, though Deng insisted that China would take back Hong Kong regardless of its economic outcome, as politics was the ultimate goal of the takeover.

Deng's dilemma was that China's strategy had to be pragmatic, and the capitalist aspects of life and ways of conducting affairs had to be kept, including a market system, existence of a separate currency, rule of law, monetary and press freedom, and so on. The former Hong Kong Governor Sir Murray MacLehose in 1971 raised the idea of turning Hong Kong into a "special administrative district," Deng came up with a similar idea of "one country, two systems," but such provision of autonomy would last only for 50 years until 2047. Hong Kong would become the "special administrative region" of China after 1997, and the "two systems" were meant to preserve the capitalist way of life and autonomy for 50 years. Deng's bottom line was that Hong Kong could only retain whatever the British government had given or provided to the people of Hong Kong, and nothing else.

There were numerous observed differences in the various rounds of negotiation. For example, the British team preferred to be more precise, exact, and detailed, so that there would be no room for manipulation and abuse in future. On the contrary, the Chinese side preferred broad principles only, with a loose choice of words and vagueness in the interpretation of terms, as that would allow variations and differences in future implementation of the terms in the agreement. While the reversion of sovereignty would take place in 1997, the change in system, if at all, would take place in 2047. The 50 years became the transition period, and the entire 1997 issue actually turned into a "two-stage" tactic. The uncertainty then would be the situation in post-2047 Hong Kong. If post-2047 Hong Kong were to be ruled by a communist regime, there would no longer be "two systems." The uncertainty over 1997 was effectively extended to 2047, and such an extension would generate various turbulences which had spillover effects to other aspects of life in Hong Kong.

The Chinese involvement in Hong Kong took place through various channels of infiltration since 1949 with the activities of the "united front," which is in charge of communist propaganda work. Hong Kong had been a place where mainland China could take advantage, and at the same time exercise its influence. Before 1978, the official institution that represented the mainland regime was the New China News Agency, and probably the Bank of China, the few leftwing newspapers, and the various retail outlets for Chinese consumer goods. Much work, however, had been conducted below the surface through infiltration, connections, persuasion, and provision of monetary gains. Youth associations, schools, local organizations, welfare units, and labor unions were the targets where leftwing propaganda materials were disseminated. There were also channels through which intelligence and information were gathered. There was the underground operation of the Communist Party in Hong Kong, and Leung (2012) documented in detail the various channels and activities of how the communist regime established their influence. Leung (2012) went further to point out the communist party members in Hong Kong, including many in the leadership echelon.

With geographical proximity, China could easily indoctrinate people from Hong Kong on their visits and travels to China. The entire state machinery and financial resources were mobilized to support the indoctrination activities. Basically, China needed support from Hong Kong, and by nurturing a group of Hong Kong people with a "communist mindset, capitalist living" mentality, China could hold an invisible but tangible key in the control of Hong Kong, including the need to select future leaders from this "reliable" group of businesses, professionals, individuals, and grassroots organizations. Other than the use of the monetary instrument, the psychological front included the use of political patriotic jargon. In other words, the ideological battle in Hong Kong started after 1949, and political infiltration had been conducted continuously through various invisible channels.

At a deeper, more subtle and intuitive level, one should not consider the issue of Hong Kong as only a Hong Kong issue. The Hong Kong issue can very much be considered as a China issue when the two factions of hardliners and reformists are taken into account within the one-party state. The discussion on the return to Hong Kong had indeed become a new political instrument in the ideological battle between the two factions. Typically, the reformists would prefer to take back Hong Kong so that the market economy of Hong Kong could be used as a reference point for further reform in the Chinese economy. Hence, the attitude of the reformists had been one of complement between the mainland and Hong Kong, and development could produce "positive-sum" outcomes of mutual benefit. On the other side of the ideological battle, the hardliners looked to the return of Hong Kong as an extension of communism, that post-1997 Hong Kong would have to be "decolonized," Hong Kong would have to return to become a city similar to other cities in China, and Hong Kong would probably come under the jurisdiction of Shenzhen after 2047. The idea was to erase the colonial history of Hong Kong through political absolutism. Hong Kong had to start with a brand new chapter of development in Chinese communism.

The sovereignty reversion of Hong Kong had become an added topic in China's political and economic circles where party leaders, party potentials, ambitious officials, and scholars could show their loyalty to their preferred party leaders by involving, engaging, and commenting on Hong Kong affairs. The ideological battle could occur both in action and in words, especially in relation to the discussion and interpretation of "one country, two systems." Typically, the hardliners would insist on the importance and priority of "one country," and that the "two systems" was provided by the "country." The reformists, on the contrary, would allow the "two systems" to function pragmatically more to the advantage of Hong Kong. Hence, when speeches or remarks were made by the hardline officials, one observed that other reformist officials would make a more accommodating remark after a few days. One wondered if this type of "negative, positive" approach in their remarks was a play of "cat and mouse" with the Hong Kong people, or whether it reflected factional conflict within the party.

The ideological divide on Hong Kong affairs could subtly be observed through the speeches made by leaders in both pre- and post-1997 years. For example, there were politically sensitive times in China every year, such as June 4, July 1, and October 1. And there had always been peaceful demonstrations in Hong Kong around these days for various reasons. However, reformist leaders in Beijing would make some politically repressive remarks on Hong Kong's political activities in the days before, say June 4. These remarks would then resonate into the political nerves of Hong Kong people, resulting in more people turning out on demonstrations. (Readers can easily examine statements made by Chinese leaders on Hong Kong SAR in the days before the politically sensitive days.) The question was whether these remarks made by Beijing leaders were just untimely, or were made in order to use Hong Kong's demonstrations as a political tool. The hardliners, on the contrary, would not allow political changes or democratic movements in Hong Kong, because they believed that would radiate back to the mainland and might lead to more political demands in mainland China that could eventually challenge their political power and authority.

There were various social and economic unpleasant incidents in mainland China, such as manufacture of fake products, use of toxic chemicals and environmental decay, and cases of social discontent and unethical behavior. These incidents could have been covered up in the mainland's media, but when they were leaked to the media in Hong Kong, the news in Hong Kong would again radiate back to the mainland and government action would then be taken.

Hence, one would need to have a "clear head" in reading remarks and speeches by mainland officials and scholars on Hong Kong affairs, whether they were made in Beijing or in Hong Kong, because one would never know if these remarks on Hong Kong were made as a show of their loyalty, an intention to seek for higher posts, or a reflection of their political stand. The same could be true for those "Beijing-loyal" Hong Kong people when they remarked on the political situation in Hong Kong. Again, one would never know if their remarks were addressed to people in Hong Kong, or served as a "kowtow" to leaders in Beijing.

In other words, there could be a lot of "noise" in the affairs of Hong Kong, as the politics of Hong Kong sovereignty reversion were intertwined with the political complexity in mainland China. Indeed, there would be various problems. One could be the problem of "revealed preference," as people remarking on Hong Kong affairs could have different and hidden intentions. The other could be the "agency" problem, where officials dealing with Hong Kong affairs could have other interests in mind. For example, the children, or the "princelings" (fuerdai, wealthy children and offspring of officials and party members) and relatives of many Beijing leaders had business connections and activities in Hong Kong, and their business behavior and activities were no different from other capitalists in advanced countries. Thus, while they were insisting on the "one country," their princelings were exploiting the "two systems" to their own advantages. Again, political inconsistency was found between deeds and words.

The Chinese strategy can be summarized into a few features. Firstly, the Sino–British Negotiation was dominated largely by Deng. As a reformist, Deng's approach was socialist and looked to the realities and reactions from the international community. However, Deng's solution would last only for 50 years till 2047. The "two stage" decisions in the 1997 sovereignty reversion and the 2047 system change could produce new uncertainties within the 50 years. With the passing of Deng, there would not be any guarantee whether the incumbent leaders would interpret the Hong Kong situation differently from that of Deng. The possibility of personality change in leadership would add uncertain scenarios in Hong Kong affairs, thereby raising and extending the risk factor in the transition years to 2047.

V INTERPRETING "ONE COUNTRY, TWO SYSTEMS"

The Basic Law of the Hong Kong SAR states that "... upon China's resumption of the exercise of sovereignty over Hong Kong, a Hong Kong Special Administrative Region will be established ... and that under the principles of 'one country, two systems,' the socialist system and policies will not be practiced in Hong Kong ...." Article 2 of the Basic Law states "The National People's Congress authorizes the Hong Kong Special Administrative Region to exercise a high degree of autonomy and enjoy executive, legislative and independent judicial power ... in accordance with the provisions of this Law." Article 5 of the Basic Law says "The socialist system and policies shall not be practiced in the Hong Kong Special Administrative Region, and the previous capitalist system and way of life shall remain unchanged for 50 years." Deng's original idea on unification would allow Hong Kong to retain its own established capitalist economic, legal, and political systems.

However, Deng's "principle" of "one country, two systems" can raise a number of conceptual arguments. There has been a lack of clarity in stating the exact details in terms of coverage, depth, and implementation of the "one country, two systems." For example, was it meant to be temporary and would it last only for 50 years? The "principle" involved two aspects: country and system. If it was implemented as a whole or in its entirety, it would mean both "country and system" would last for 50 years. Would the "country" and "system" be considered on a parallel and equal basis? What if there were conflicts between the two systems? Or to be exact, the two "what" systems: political system, education system, medical system, cultural system, traffic system, immigration system, fiscal and monetary system? Indeed, would the "two systems" be confined narrowly to the difference in "political system" only?

Similarly, the "autonomy" in Article 2 could be subject to various magnitudes. Article 2 stated that autonomy would have to be "authorized" by the National People's Congress, which could mean that it could also be "deauthorized." The "high degree" of autonomy would be enjoyed by the executive, legislative, and judiciary power. Conceptually, how extensive and intensive would be given by the "high degree?" Similarly, if autonomy were to be granted only to these three aspects of the government, did that mean that other aspects of autonomy might not be covered? Autonomy is an "absolute" term in that there is either autonomy or no autonomy. Autonomy could not be measured in proportions, say 51% or 99%.

Indeed, it would be difficult to argue whether the "one country, two systems" could be regarded as a "principle"; it could only be considered as a framework through which Beijing would rule Hong Kong after 1997. "One country, two systems" has never been adopted, imposed, used, or implemented anywhere in the world. Such a lack of reference would further impose vagueness in the term. Such terms as autonomy and system could be qualified either in time, in coverage, in magnitude, and probably in implementation. The result was that there could be a large margin for interpretation, depending on the particular incident, personality, and time that might not work favorably to Hong Kong.

Since 1997, incidents that appeared and emerged in Hong Kong had challenged the different ways of interpreting the "one country, two (what) systems." Other interpretations would include that the "one country" would have to come before the "two systems," insisting that people in Hong Kong would have to consider the "country" first. A considerable amount of political discussions that were somewhat nonsensical had been made. For example, on the issue of patriotism, propaganda-like discussions included "should one love one's country also love the party?" Could one just love Hong Kong and not the country? Or would loving Hong Kong naturally mean loving the country? There were variations in the "two systems." Strictly speaking, if Article 5 was interpreted literally, it would only be that the "socialist system" would not be practiced in Hong Kong, what about other systems? In language, e.g., what about insisting people in Hong Kong use simplified Chinese, or reduce the use of Cantonese, or incorporate socialist studies in history classes in schools? In the category of immigration on "family reunion," it would be the mainland authority that would decide and screen the incoming immigrants from the mainland. Over the years, "goal shifting" seemed to have intervened in the various interpretations of the "two systems."

Equally, how would one define the "socialist system" and "socialist practices," other than the obvious political aspects? Other Beijing officials argued that the "principle" was provided to Hong Kong by the central government in Beijing, and as such, the central government could also take it back and Hong Kong would have no say. And the ultimate authority was vested in the central government, implying anything Hong Kong suggested would need to have consent from Beijing. That effectively meant that the provision of the "two systems" would be phenomenal, depending on the issue, timing, and personality, but could be taken away at any time. Intuitively, what would Hong Kong have if "one country, two systems" were taken away? Would Hong Kong be returned to Britain or have its own system?

In a way, the "one country, two systems" framework was not meant to allow Hong Kong to move forward, but was an instrument that would "freeze" Hong Kong at the time of the handover. Namely, whatever Hong Kong enjoyed before 1997 would be guaranteed, but anything else, especially sensitive issues, would have to seek permission and consent. Indeed, from day one in the Sino–British Negotiation, both countries knew that Hong Kong was way ahead of mainland China, and the systemic differences were too vast. But Hong Kong people were not represented in the negotiation. To return Hong Kong to China without the participation of the Hong Kong people was really a "sell out."

Although the British colonial government did not allow full political democracy in Hong Kong, political parties have been active. While political parties are meant to promote political freedom, Hong Kong has gained a high degree of freedom in very many areas. The alternative to full political democracy was the establishment of a civic model, in that political parties as well as other institutions have been established to serve Hong Kong people. The successful implementation of a civic model provides a large "security belt" between the individuals and the government, as various civic institutions set their standards and practices that would gain the trustworthiness of people in Hong Kong. Li (2012a) illustrated the Hong Kong civic system, as shown in Fig. 16.1, where what stands between the government and the people included a large number of established institutions. The government consisted of all government departments, law enforcement bodies, and related organizations, and the people represent the general public. In Hong Kong, although there is no full political democracy, a large number of civic institutions have been established so as to protect the various aspects of life in Hong Kong. Individuals are protected through the activities and presence of civic institutions.

In the civic model, political parties can influence and monitor the government and participate in political elections. But, the general public does not need to rely solely on political parties for their survival. Different types of institutions would serve the same purpose of ensuring equity and transparency, thereby eradicating victimization, discrimination, and cronyism. Choice is what the civic model provides, as individuals can rely on multiple channels and means of protection. Similarly, the government can dispense its influence through multiple channels. This ensures balance in the society.

One can contrast the Hong Kong system with the socialist system in China. Fig. 16.2 shows two similar and simplified pictures of the Chinese system. The party in a one-party state is the ultimate power and authority, and control would be absolute. In reality, the party and government are closely related and connected, while the people would be positioned within the authority of the party and the government. The left hand side of Fig. 16.2 reflects the ultimate authority of the party, which would then send instructions to the government, and the government would exercise control over the people. The right hand side of Fig. 16.2 reflects the top down nature of authority and power from the party to the government, and to the people.

The "one country, two systems" is neither a principle nor a theory, but a framework that enabled the reversion of Hong Kong's sovereignty to China, bearing in mind the vast systemic differences between the two economies. Within the framework, however, detailed elaborations had not been given, and the vagueness of the framework did lead to contrasting interpretations that worked in favor of mainland China. However, since the "one country, two systems" were applied to Hong Kong and Macau, and not elsewhere on the Chinese mainland, the framework must be intended to work in favor of Hong Kong. What should be the true spirit in the "one country' two systems" and "high degree of autonomy?" Given in the Basic Law that China would be responsible for Hong Kong's military defense and foreign diplomatic affairs, anything and everything that were related to the internal matters in Hong Kong should be seen within the "autonomy" and the "two systems" framework. Whether the issues were educational, cultural, media and publication, immigration and rule of law, or political elections, Hong Kong would have autonomy in executing and deciding on these domestic and internal issues. The "one country, two systems" framework would have given the consent to post-1997 Hong Kong for 50 years that these systemic issues would be dealt with internally within the autonomous authority of the Hong Kong SAR.

It is certainly true that the "one country, two systems" was a novelty in politics. The irony would be that China was still largely ruled by the party and the personality of the leaders, and was still in the process of developing a well-defined, transparent, open, and equitable system. It is still the control of the majority by a minority. Indeed, the 50 years from 1997 to 2047 would see the grinding of the two political systems. It would be a battle between the "growing economic strength and politics-oriented" China versus the "economically free and civic-oriented" Hong Kong. On the contrary, if the "one country, two systems" were given unequal weight between "country and system," the "two systems" would be redundant and become a fallacy, because the "country" would be interpreted to take precedence. If so, it will effectively be reduced to "one country, one system."

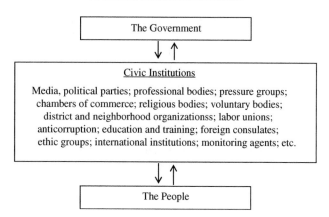

FIGURE 16.1 The Hong Kong civic system.

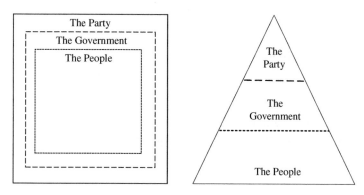

FIGURE 16.2 The China system.

VI INTERNATIONAL IMPLICATIONS

With the Joint Declaration signed between the United Kingdom and the People's Republic of China having been deposited in the United Nations, and even though Hong Kong's sovereignty had reverted to China without the participation of the Hong Kong people, the United Kingdom as well as the international community at large have the responsibility to see to the development as agreed in the Joint Declaration. On numerous occasions and incidents, China insisted that Hong Kong belonged to its internal affairs, and foreign countries should not have any say in the Hong Kong affairs. However, this could not deter foreign governments and international institutions from observing developments in Hong Kong in such areas as human rights and media freedom. Indeed, the fact that China agreed to the registration of the Joint Declaration with the United Nations already meant that post-1997 Hong Kong would be scrutinized by members in the United Nations.

Hong Kong's economic advancement has been made possible because of its economic openness and extensive foreign involvement in investment and connectivity. However, the economy of Hong Kong could be vulnerable to shocks and crises originating from foreign markets. Finance could be a shaky sector, as capital resources could come and go within a short time if foreign investors lost confidence in Hong Kong. Although the economy of China would be "rich" enough to "rescue" Hong Kong, foreign investors would think otherwise. Leaning more toward the Chinese market without making efforts to attract foreign investors might not be a good alternative.

The more worrying problem would be the spillover from political incidents and shocks to economic performance in Hong Kong. Although the Basic Law specified that Hong Kong would have its own currency, the Hong Kong currency is linked to the US dollar. Every Hong Kong dollar is backed by an equivalent value in the US dollar. Indeed, the Hong Kong currency is actually the US currency in disguise. However, there have been calls for the Hong Kong currency to delink, especially because of the appreciating Chinese currency, and part of the discussion has been politically oriented. However, instability and shocks could be generated should the Hong Kong currency become unstable. Indeed, as the 50 years period approaches 2047, there will be pressure on the Hong Kong currency, if there is no solution well in advance.

Hence, because of its extensive openness and the established connectivity with the international community and engagement by both foreign and mainland investors, the different economic aspects in Hong Kong could become political instruments in one form or another. As ideology is often of prime importance in China, economic performance would possibly have to be sacrificed. In the past, foreign investments tended to become rooted in Hong Kong. However, the international community has become more globalized and open, and there is severe competition for foreign investments and capital resources, there are plenty of new investment destinations in other parts of the world, if foreign investment departed from Hong Kong it would be unlikely to come back. Similarly, as foreign investments departed, it would be an "uphill battle" for Hong Kong to attract new investors. At the worst, foreign investors would consider Hong Kong as a sacrifice should the political situation between China and Hong Kong became unsteady, as there are always alternative investment destinations in Asia and other world regions. Hong Kong's economic performance would become the "thermometer" for China's political performance in Hong Kong, and possibly China's behavior in the international arena.

Since the turn of the century as Chinese individuals and enterprises are gaining economic strength, a major source of investment would come from mainland China. Increasingly, mainland individuals are buying properties, while mainland businesses are establishing their business empire in Hong Kong. For example, mainland businesses have bought up news media and television stations in Hong Kong, and local businesses have been keen to sell to mainland buyers as they can afford to pay a high price. For example, even The Center, the 73-storey landmark office building in Central Hong Kong owned by Cheung Kong has been put up for sale (*South China Morning Post*, August 23, 2016). Would one foresee that by 2047, mainland investors could be the majority of property owners and business corporations in Hong Kong? Deng was prepared to take back Hong Kong during the Sino–British Negotiation without regard to the economy as foreign and local investors were the majority. However, as 2047 approaches, could Beijing disregard the economic situation in Hong Kong if the bulk of business capital in Hong Kong was owned by mainland investors? Or, would mainland investors sell off the assets in Hong Kong before 2047, and the 50 years was basically a period for speculation?

VII CONCLUSION

Despite the fact that China has been rising and showing various nominal strengths, such as a prolonged rise in growth rate, the number one in such and such, the most of this and that, and so on, increasingly the hardware and the various numbers do not seem to match with the software and substance. Can China's quantitative picture stand up to its qualitative performance? China's rise has been due to the great leniency the international community has shown to China, especially after 1978. The "Nixon – Kissinger initiative" in the early 1970s had lifted China to the international community within a short time. The economic reform in the 1980s attracted loads of foreign investment to boost up the Chinese economy. The accession to the World Trade Organization resulted in rapid expansion of exports and trade. One should ask if the world has given too much resources and attention to the Chinese economy, especially when one considers that the same socialistic and communistic approach remained. Or it was too much resource for China to absorb within such a short time, and the country is suffering from "indigestion," suggesting that the quantity increased but the ingredients remain weak. China probably needed the "bringing in" policy as domestic improvements could only be brought about by pressures, rules, conditions and requirements imposed by or derived from the world community. While China was ready to show off its economic muscles, it still tried to seek and learn from foreign practices. For example, China had been aiming to make the Shanghai stock market bigger than the Hong Kong stock market, but after China's stock market crashed in summer 2015, China sought advice from London on how to establish a sound financial regulator (*Reuters*, May 14, 2016).

China would have thought that recovering Hong Kong was a symbol of unification, but Hong Kong was an extraordinary economy. It was small, but had strong exposure to the international community, and the capitalist system and ideology had become rooted in Hong Kong. For the largest socialist country to swallow the freest capitalist economy would not be a "piece of cake." The Joint Declaration and the Basic Law effectively divided the Hong Kong issue into two issues of sovereignty change in 1997 and the systemic change, if any, in 2047. The 50 years of 1997 – 2047 became the transition years in which mainland China and Hong Kong had to find a way out. While Hong Kong was the weaker side, Hong Kong's advantage rested with the maintenance of a reliable system and infrastructure that could stand against turbulence from personality changes, though there was still the need for perfecting various systemic elements.

On the contrary, ruling Hong Kong would not be a smooth task. To the ruler, having the right mentality to rule Hong Kong would be the first task. To govern Hong Kong with high-handed policies could be costly and ineffective. In many ways, the ball would be in China's court. Hong Kong could not, should not, and would not be treated similar to another city in China. Indeed, China's increasing involvement in Hong Kong affairs could backfire, as other China regions would start to make comparisons. To leave Hong Kong to handle its domestic affairs should be the true spirit in the "one country, two systems" framework. But party opportunists in China would not lose the chance, as becoming involved in Hong Kong affairs could be a strong ticket in the party hierarchy. Hong Kong did not have full political democracy, but the degree of freedom far exceeded that existing in China. Thus, the vast difference between mainland China and Hong Kong would lead to an administrative dilemma when freedom-lacking officials engaged in the affairs of the freest economy. To exercise control of Hong Kong would arouse uproar in Hong Kong and the international community, even though Beijing would like to see less of it. To relax control on Hong Kong would invite similar requests from other regions in China. Thus, Beijing faces a bigger dilemma among the different provinces and localities than the dilemma between Hong Kong and the central government.

The history of the Sino–British Negotiation will unfold in 50 years (1997 – 2047), and the outcome cannot be easily and precisely predicted, as there could be several scenarios. There will be multiple factors that could influence the outcome. Officials in Beijing obviously thought they were on the leading side of the relationship, and as such, unilateral decisions would adhere to the "one country" goal, but unstructured and one-sided responses to changes in the Hong Kong situation would fail, as one would feel confused in the "cause – consequence" relationship. Holding a communist mentality to govern the freest economy would simply result in more friction.

17

Hong Kong: Pathway to the Freest Economy

I INTRODUCTION

It has been observed that many former British colonies performed poorly after gaining independence. Whether the Hong Kong economy would be an exception to other former British colonies was yet to be seen, as Hong Kong was not given independence but sovereignty reversion to China in 1997. There were several differences between Hong Kong and other former British colonies. Hong Kong comprised mainly people from Southern China, and ethnic Cantonese are usually entrepreneurial and keen to start businesses rather than seek assistance from the government. The preference on self-reliance and enterprising behavior among traditional Chinese had further implications for economic activity. Economic difficulties tended to be localized, and obtaining assistance from family or relatives in difficult times was a more common practice than seeking welfare assistance in the early colonial days in Hong Kong.

During the 155 years of British colonialism, Hong Kong was transformed from a "barren rock" to a flamboyant immigration center, industrial and export center, international banking and financial center. The extent of economic openness, together with the well-established and rooted British institutions, made the Hong Kong economy acceptable to the international community. The "business as usual" nature meant that the economy was influenced by the economic scene of the world, taking advantage of economic booms, but also suffering from economic crises. While other former British colonies gained political independence, in Hong Kong the case was a reversion of sovereignty to communist China, which had a different and opposing political and ideological system to that of capitalist Hong Kong.

There are numerous recent studies on the Hong Kong economy, covering different economic areas and the Sino − British Negotiations (Haddon-Cave, 1980; Jao, 1988; Rabushka, 1989; Huang, 2003; Latter, 2007; Mushkat and Mushkat, 2009; Goodstadt, 2013; Ip, 2015). This chapter summarizes the discussion on the Hong Kong economy based on the ideas in Li (2006, 2012a). While the pre-1997 performance was a world record of economic freedom and *laissez-faire* practices, the focus is on whether the post-1997 period would suffer a similar fate of economic decline as in other former British colonies, or stand up to confront the ideological battle with mainland China. Hong Kong's post-1997 development would be a unique case in world economic development.

II LAISSEZ-FAIRE POLICIES

The economics adopted by the British colonial government were to keep things simple, meaning that Hong Kong citizens were allowed to conduct their own businesses and the government was "hands-off" in business activities, involved only when necessary. Hong Kong began as a "free port" between mainland China and overseas countries. Immigrants were free to enter, while British types of institutions were gradually introduced, including the rule of law and a business-friendly fiscal policy. The big British businesses were dominant, but local businesses also flourished. The enterprising immigrants formed a key component in the development of Hong Kong. Appropriate infrastructure and public utilities had been developed as the pace of urbanization and population expanded.

The role of the *laissez-faire* government was to monitor and ensure efficiency. Fiscal consistency and certainty had over the years become an advantage. The growth-led nature of economic development would focus on "supply-side" economics. The high degree of domestic "preparedness" was important in the political economy in Hong Kong. Other *laissez-faire* practices included the duality in the supply of such public goods as schools, hospitals, and medical centers, housing provision, media, and transportation. The combined economic forces of "supply-side" economics and "duality in supply" produced promising scenarios for foreign investment. Economic opportunities expanded exponentially, and mutual positive-sum outcomes were realized, as both foreign and local businesses benefitted from their activities in Hong Kong.

The high degree of stability in Hong Kong contrasted with the periodic instability in mainland China, resulting in a continuous inflow of enterprising immigrants who came to look for opportunities and alternatives. It was only after the 1960s that border control was instituted as the population in Hong Kong expanded, but there were still periodic floods of immigrants from mainland China. In many ways, the stability and "supply-driven" nature of economic development in Hong Kong was shown to be a better alternative to development in mainland China at various historical periods. Thus, Hong Kong had been serving as a shelter for mainland refugees whenever mainland China was faced with crises and difficulties. This, in itself, would make the enterprising immigrants to act, behave, and conduct activities differently from people in mainland China. The opportunities and alternatives that Hong Kong offered eventually created differences between Hong Kong and mainland China.

The only period when the British colonial government lost control of Hong Kong was the "3 years and 8 months" during the Japanese occupation from December 25, 1941, to the end of the Second World War. The establishment of the communist regime in China in 1949, and the subsequent trade embargo by the western world, had put an end to the reexport trade of Hong Kong. Instead, the migration of Chinese capital to Hong Kong paved the way for industrialization, with labor-intensive manufacturing from the 1950s. Hong Kong also attracted much foreign investment after the end of the Second World War, as world demand for light manufacturing increased. Thus, Hong Kong's exports increased gradually and labor-intensive manufacturing included wigs, toys, transistor radio, textiles and clothing, plastic flowers, and related products. Electronics production became popular after the 1980s.

In much of the 1950s and 1960s, the colonial government was reluctant to introduce welfare-related policies, arguing that improvements in "supply-side" factors should be the more appropriate prerequisites for development in Hong Kong. Other than the rule of law, the colonial government also introduced professional institutions from Britain so that local students could follow the practice and standards that existed in the United Kingdom. The establishment of the Independent Commission Against Corruption (ICAC) on February 15, 1974, was a milestone in lifting Hong Kong to a fully fledged civic society where privileges, vested interests, cronyism, and "backdoor" activities were replaced by transparency, fairness, and equity before the law. Beginning from the mid-1960s, the Hong Kong colonial government began to modernize Hong Kong. Massive "supply-side" developments turned Hong Kong into a modern metropolitan economy. Examples included the construction of industrial towns for low-cost labor supply for industrial plants, urbanization and creation of new towns in the New Territories to cater for the growing population, provision of public housing for low income families and the "sandwich" class, construction of cross-harbor tunnels and underground railways, reclamation of land for residential purposes, and expansion of public health provisions and postsecondary educational institutions.

Laissez-faire noninterventionism based on capitalist market principles, popularly known as "positive noninterventionism," was the approach adopted by the colonial government in the 1970s, although the provision of water, land use, and road and park construction were entirely controlled by the government. The Hong Kong experience showed that there were numerous advantages in *laissez-faire* economic principles, typically in the form of a private-led economy, macroeconomic stability and fiscal certainty, indirect support through "supply-side" channels, coupled with a hard-working, enterprising, and disciplined labor force; opportunities and chances of upward mobility were the major outcome of these advantages.

However, there were inadequacies. For example, technological advancement had not been a major concern. Government spending on research and development activities was minimal. Foreign investment related to industrial production either concentrated in labor-intensive manufacturing, or brought along with their own technology. The local businesses comprised mainly small- and medium-sized enterprises (SMEs) which did not promote technology. Nonetheless, the *laissez-faire* nature permitted Hong Kong to achieve a high level of development, and the flexibility and ability to move along with the international economic community remained the cutting-edge of the Hong Kong economy. Nonetheless, Hong Kong over the decades had developed brand names in several lines of consumer products, especially in clothing, food processing, and beverage industries. Despite the lack in technological advancement, growth in Hong Kong proceeded favorably, diversifying into such areas as finance and business services.

As the British sinologists' strategy was to ensure Hong Kong's economic supremacy over the socialist economy in mainland China, the advance economy would serve as a "cushion" for Hong Kong in its post-1997 years. As Hong Kong people were keen on making "money" and economic progress, rising incomes and growth would serve to pacify the political demand for democratic changes. This could be a misunderstanding on the part of the sinologists. Hong Kong had all along been an immigrant city, and many held a "siege mentality" as certainty and stability was not guaranteed. As such, amassing wealth and assets were seen as an "insurance" policy and a source of security and reliance. Should they eventually have to emigrate to another destination as a result of political uncertainty, their economic survival would be assured.

III PERFORMANCE PRIOR TO 1997

The rise in incomes and growth in the two decades of the 1960s and 1970s in Hong Kong also led to a rise in the costs of production, thereby eroding Hong Kong's competitiveness, as discussed in the "pull and push" argument. The opening-up of China in 1978 had profusely influenced the Hong Kong economy. China's low costs of production attracted investment from Hong Kong. Hence, there emerged a process of "industrial-hollowing" in much of the 1980s and 1990s. Unfortunately, the departed industries were not replenished by new and different kinds of industrial investment to Hong Kong. The "industrial vacuum," however, was made up for by the rapid expansion in the service sector. Instead of exports of local manufacturing, e.g., reexport business flourished as exports from China used Hong Kong's port facilities. The "front office, back factory" concept gained popularity as Hong Kong's rise in producer services (front office) would complement the industrial production (back factory) in mainland China.

Political uncertainty during the Sino—British Negotiation (1982—84) in Hong Kong led to professionals and businesses migrating to other English-speaking Commonwealth countries and the United States. The United Kingdom government was not prepared to allow large numbers of Hong Kong citizens to migrate to Britain. Thus, the colonial government had to deliver policies that would maintain economic vitality in Hong Kong. "Stability and prosperity" had been promoted to maintain the confidence of the Hong Kong people. While there was continuous construction in large infrastructure projects, such as the new international airport and all the related railway constructions, there were various expansions and upgrading of institutions, such as the establishment of the Hospital Authority and additional universities that involved large fiscal capital commitments. There were handsome pay rises and wage increases in all these years, in some years reaching double digit growth rates (Li, 2006, 2012a). Large increments in salary boosted the employees in the short-term, but the gap in the salary range had increased over time.

The fast increase in salaries and the persistent low interest rates should have promoted inflationary pressures. Indeed, after the late-1980s, high inflation, large salary increases, and low interest rates coexisted and encouraged bank lending. Together with the trend in "industrial-hollowing," industrialists looked to "investment" that produced higher returns by turning to invest or speculate in stocks and properties, causing a continuous rise in the stock price and property prices. The resulting economic boom produced short-term "stability and prosperity," but it had long-term unintended consequences. The rising property prices further eroded Hong Kong's cost competitiveness. Li (2006, 2012a) talked about "short-term investment behavior," as investors and speculators considered July 1997 as the terminal date when profits and gains would have to be maximized. As investment and speculation in stocks and properties became the most effective route to maximize gains and profits, few investors would consider long-term investment in industries. Such behavior did not help to rescue the process of "industrial-hollowing" in Hong Kong, as people got used to speculation.

Beginning from 1994, a new welfare scheme known as Comprehensive Social Security Assistance (CSSA) was introduced that substantially enlarged social welfare. While it was fiscally manageable at that time, the widening of the welfare spending took place over two dimensions by enlarging the number of welfare-related items, and spending more on each welfare item. At the same time, the rapid increase in salary tax exemption had effectively narrowed the salary tax base from a V-shape to a T-shape, where different income groups would have to pay salary tax creating a situation where the salary tax burden was shouldered only by the high income earners. Government statistics show that in the fiscal year of 2011—12 the taxpaying population was 1,634,000, while the nontax paying population amounted to 1,971,000. In the case of the salaries tax, the top highest 100,000 tax payers paid 65.9% of the salaries tax, and the cumulated 0.5 million of salary tax payers paid 97.1% of the salaries tax (Treasury Branch, Hong Kong SAR Government). Effectively, the 0.5 million salary tax payers supported the entire population of about 7 million people in Hong Kong. The salary tax burden could further deteriorate when income had fallen and the government would be faced with an I-shape, where little tax could be collected. The change in the welfare policy came in at the wrong time, when Hong Kong experienced an economic boom in the early 1990s. Indeed, fiscal theory argues the contrary, that government spending should contract and shrink at times of economic boom so as to avoid overheating. The colonial government kept increasing its fiscal spending on welfare at times of economic boom, to make the economy look "prosperous."

One can conclude that the colonial government in the years before 1997, other than the construction of large scale infrastructure projects, basically changed their economic policies from "supply-side" to "demand-side" policies that involved high spending and subsidies. The prolonged low interest rates further discouraged saving on the one hand, and encouraged borrowing to hedge against inflation on the other. The rise in income was based purely on expansion in the nominal economy, while such real activities as industrial production and export of manufactures were shrinking. The coexistence of expansion in nominal economic activities and contraction in real economic activities provided the best combination for the formation of a financial bubble.

The massive shift in the orientation of economic policies was overshadowed as income kept rising literally in a "one-way" direction, but these policies would have numerous drawbacks over time in terms of competitiveness and sustainability. The erosion of economic competitiveness over time could endanger economic sustainability, thereby challenging the Hong Kong economy in regaining its vitality, strength, and diversity. In focusing on "demand-side" factors, industrial output gave way to services. Among the three economic sectors in Hong Kong, services occupied over 90% of Gross Domestic Product (GDP), while industry occupied less than two digits in GDP, and agriculture's share in GDP was minimal. While industrial outputs were regarded as tradable goods, many services were regarded as nontradable, thereby reducing the amount of exports from Hong Kong. Many services did not require much skill, and salaries in unskilled service jobs tended to be low, thereby limiting the chances of upward mobility. Indeed, many service jobs had a rather short employment life, as they did not favor aging workers. A shorter employment life would mean a greater chance of seeking welfare and unemployment assistance, should unskilled service workers become unemployed. A generous welfare package would mean more fiscal spending that would work against the long-term sustainability of the Hong Kong economy.

Typical businesses in a "demand-driven" economy include tourism, retail, restaurants, and personal services. However, many of these services are regarded as "derived," meaning that their survival depends a lot on income trends and business cycles. Once there is a drop in income and growth, the demand for these services immediately falls. In other words, a heavy service-oriented economy tends to be more vulnerable to shocks and crises, especially in a small and open economy with little natural resources. In "supply-driven" economies, economic policies aim to promote employment, job expansion, and upward mobility, and individuals become more progressive economically. On the other hand, economies that pursue "demand-driven" policies concentrate on fiscal spending on welfare and subsidy provisions that ensure a certain level of living standards, but the recipients might not be provided with employment and job possibilities. As such, growth would be unlikely, as welfare spending is merely a transfer payment that is not output-promoting. It is easier to promote "demand-driven" policies than "supply-driven" policies at the individual level, but will not help the economy at the macrolevel. Indeed, once an economy switched from "supply-driven" to "demand-driven" economic policies, it would be difficult for the economy to switch back, because subsidies, once given, cannot possibly be cut.

The reorientation of economic policies in pre-1997 Hong Kong also meant that the Hong Kong economy was geared more to "internal" than "external" issues. The dominance of domestic features and issues meant that the economy might not align closely with the international community. With the high cost of production and low competitiveness, the Hong Kong economy could price itself out of the market. In short, appropriate policies would have to be introduced so that continued economic expansion would be possible.

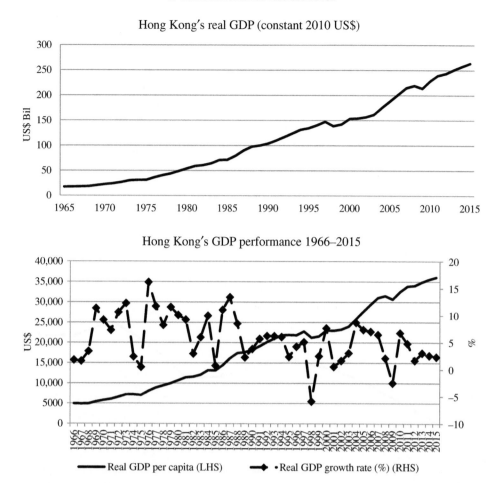

FIGURE 17.1 GDP performance of Hong Kong.

IV MACROECONOMIC PERFORMANCE

The data on the Hong Kong macroeconomy can be obtained from various established sources, including the Census and Statistics Department, Hong Kong SAR Government, the World Bank, the International Monetary Fund, and UNCTAD. The *China Statistical Yearbook* annually provides China's economic data with Hong Kong, e.g., in the amount of utilized outward foreign investment from Hong Kong to China. In the statistics, utilized foreign direct investment in China refers to the actual amount, while the contractual amount will be bigger. Fig. 17.1 shows the GDP trend, its growth rates, and GDP per capita. In the case of the GDP trend, the "dips" Hong Kong experienced included the oil crisis in 1975, the Sino—British Negotiation 1982—84, the Asian financial crisis after 1997, the severe acute respiratory syndrome (SARS) outbreak in 2003, and the global financial crisis of 2008. The Asian financial crisis in 1998 was the hardest hit, with a negative growth rate of 5%.

Fig. 17.2 reports the healthy fiscal performance. Other than the few years after the Asian financial crisis, it has become normal for Hong Kong to have a fiscal surplus, though in all cases, the size of the fiscal surplus has never exceeded 10% of GDP. Nonetheless, Hong Kong also enjoyed a healthy public debt-to-GDP ratio, which has never exceeded 36% of GDP. Without the need to spend on the military, the healthy fiscal policy owes more to Hong Kong's economic openness and adherence to "supply-side" economic policies.

As shown in Fig. 17.3, the level of market capitalization in the Hong Kong stock exchange increased drastically around 2005 when many mainland enterprises, especially the state-owned commercial banks, came to raise capital in Hong Kong. The trends of inward and outward foreign direct investment are similar, implying that much foreign direct investment may have passed through Hong Kong. By 2014, close to 70% of China's utilized foreign direct investment came from Hong Kong. It is possible that inward foreign direct investment from mainland

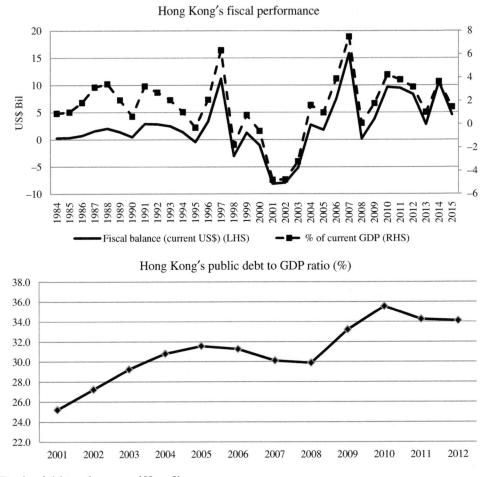

FIGURE 17.2   Fiscal and debt performance of Hong Kong.

China to Hong Kong would become outward foreign direct investment from Hong Kong to China, as that would be regarded as foreign investment in China and would enjoy some advantages.

Since Hong Kong has served as a trading post between China and foreign countries, reexport business has flourished. The export of domestic manufacturing has risen since the industrialization process in Hong Kong in the 1960s. By the 1980s, after China opened up, the reexport business returned. However, with the new establishment of port facilities in southern China, Hong Kong is faced with a decline in the export of manufactured goods as the level of industrial activities declined, and there are challenges from mainland ports for the reexport business. Fig. 17.4 shows that Hong Kong has enjoyed trade surpluses, but the level of exports has slackened since 2010. However, export as a percentage of GDP has been very high, exceeding 200% of GDP, reflecting very much the open nature of the Hong Kong economy. Since the turn of the 21st century, Hong Kong's exports to mainland China have surpassed that of the United States. Nonetheless, both mainland China and the United States are the two largest export destinations. However, one can see from Fig. 17.5 that reexport has become the dominant export in Hong Kong, as reexport as a percentage of total exports is close to 100%. But the total value of reexport has declined since 2013, suggesting that either Hong Kong's reexport business is losing it competitiveness, or that there is a fall in Chinese exports, resulting in a lower level of reexports. China is Hong Kong's largest reexport destination, while other reexport destinations include the United States, Japan, South Korea, and Taiwan.

Hong Kong still shows a healthy economy statistically, especially in the fiscal aspect. Hong Kong's economic openness has been its greatest asset for all activities. It is probably true that the financial sector is increasingly becoming more important, while the trade sector may face severe challenges. To improve the trade sector, there is a need to revitalize the industrial sector so that more manufactured goods can boost the level of domestic exports.

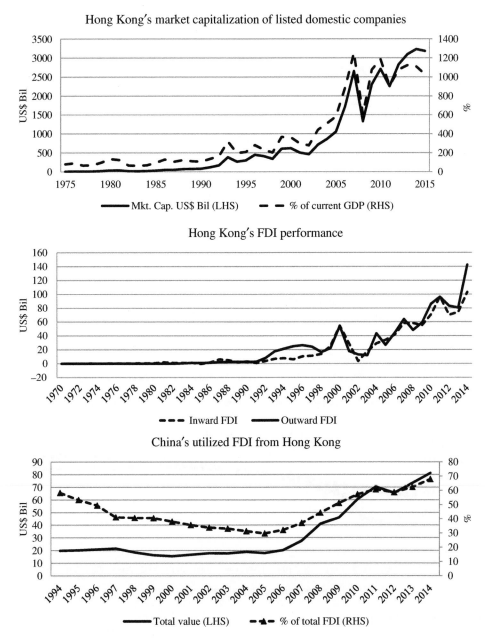

FIGURE 17.3 Market capitalization and foreign direct investment of Hong Kong.

V ABILITY TO RESTRUCTURE POST-1997

The economic prosperity based on various short-term policies prior to 1997 provided channels for Hong Kong's people to gain wealth as the value of their assets expanded until the outbreak of crises. One was the "chicken-flu" crisis in late 1997, and more devastatingly the Asian financial crisis in mid-1998, with the deployment of large reserve funds to rescue the stock market. The "stability and prosperity" image was soon shattered as the crisis deepened into a prolonged period of economic recession. When the economic bubble burst, the hardest hit areas were those speculative activities in the stock market and the property market. While the Hong Kong SAR government attempted to rescue the stock market from falling, ad hoc policies on restricting housing supply were instituted so as to rescue the property market, especially when pressed by the developers. Business and investment confidence remained weak as the number of bankruptcy cases rocketed. Fiscal surplus turned to face deficit, and large tax exemptions granted previously would now expose the government to fiscal narrowness.

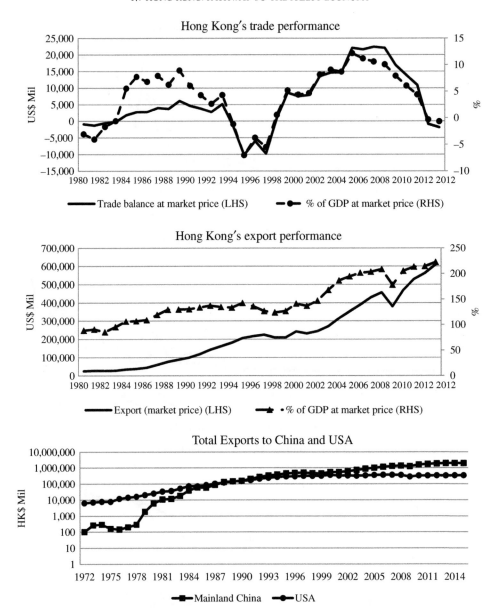

FIGURE 17.4   Trade performance of Hong Kong.

The government did marginally rewind the salary exemption down, but preferred to bite the bullet by running down the fiscal reserve and raising the salary tax rate. The fiscal deficit was spent largely on welfare provisions, as unemployment reached a record high level.

The first decade after the turn of the 21st century experienced more crises and shocks, some originating from foreign countries, such as the September 11, 2001, terrorist attack in the United States, and the world financial crisis in 2008, but the 2003 severe acute respiratory syndrome (SARS) health hazard was originated from Guangdong across the border. However, economic recovery started around 2005, and it was only after a government decision to issue short-term bonds that fiscal performance returned to normal. As fiscal surplus reappeared, salary tax exemptions expanded again to return to the T-shape nature. Despite fiscal recovery, the Hong Kong economy in the first decade of the new century was faced with a number of rigidities. The "demand-driven" policies introduced in the 1990s expanded further when the second Chief Executive, Mr. Donald Tsang, introduced the Community Care Fund (CCF) in 2011 to provide another layer of welfare subsidy on top of the existing social security net.

The numerous economic and financial crises had resulted in a "crisis mentality," meaning that fiscal spending and investment activities were conducted as if the economy was in a crisis situation. This implied that fiscal spending concentrated mainly on solving short-term ills, rather than creating and building long-term potential

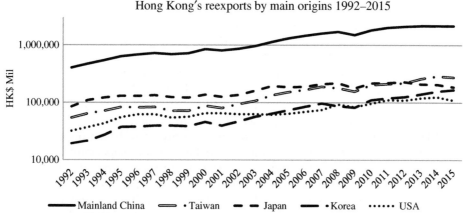

FIGURE 17.5   Reexport performance of Hong Kong.

and capacity. At the same time, the focus on immediate problems would reduce short-term pains, but the delay in constructing long-term potential would result in further delays in economic progress. And in turn, the lack of progress would produce more short-term problems as the economy could not see any light at the end of the tunnel. A "vicious circle" could have developed, which would further be reinforced by "short-term investment behavior" as investment returned mainly to speculative activities.

The "demand-driven" policies persisted when mainland China provided a number of rescue packages to Hong Kong after the SARS epidemic in 2003. By using the "people's strategy," the "visa free" travel policy allowed a large number of mainland travelers into Hong Kong. The influx led to rapid increases in retail rentals that benefitted property owners, especially in those popular locations. Many retail shops opened, but their business concentrated on foreign luxurious brand products catering solely for the mainland tourist market. Due to the unreliability of many consumer products and the high consumption tax in mainland China, large numbers of mainland "shoppers" made multiple trips as an informal market had developed across the border in Shenzhen, where popular consumer items could easily be sold to agents on the "black market."

Hong Kong was designated as the offshore center for the Chinese currency, the Renminbi. As it was Beijing's ambition to internationalize the Renminbi, Hong Kong could be a good "collection center" for the Renminbi which had been taken out of China through various channels. At the beginning when Hong Kong gained the offshore center in 2005, commercial banks in Hong Kong were not too enthusiastic, as loans could not be made in Renminbi. However, trading of Renminbi increased rapidly after 2009 when Beijing required Hong Kong's trade with mainland China to use the Renminbi as the trading currency (Hong Kong Monetary Authority, 2016). Effectively, the Renminbi would just be another currency traded in the commercial banks. The greater connectivity between the Hong Kong currency and the Renminbi could have other advantages to the mainland economy, including the ability for mainland corporations and state-commercial banks to raise capital in the Hong Kong stock market after 2005. This, in turn, has made Hong Kong the largest world financial center in market capitalization. The Shanghai–Hong Kong Stock Connect begun in November 2014 widened the possibility for both mainland and Hong Kong investors to invest in each other's stock market. The Shenzhen–Hong Kong Stock Connect was eventually approved on August 16, 2016 ("Hong Kong becomes world's largest exchange operator," *Developing Markets and Asia*, April 13, 2015; "Hong Kong Stock Exchange," "List of Public Corporations by Market Capitalization," "Shanghai–Hong Kong Stock Connect," *Wikipedia*; *South China Morning Post*, August 17, 2016; and "Shenzhen–Shanghai–Hong Kong Stock Connect," Hong Kong Stock Exchange Limited, August 17, 2016).

The various phases of the Closer Economic Partnership Agreement (CEPA) after 2005 allowed tariff-free exports of Hong Kong manufactured goods to mainland China (Trade Department, Hong Kong SAR Government website). The agreement covered three areas: export of manufactured goods, services trade, and government-to-government facilitation. Tariff-free exports covered over 1700 export goods, but many items included in the list had not been produced in Hong Kong. Industrialists have not been taking advantage of the CEPA in conducting industrial production in Hong Kong for export. In the case of professional services, some professions that would benefit mainland China, typically medical, construction, and hospitality professions, were highly welcomed, but some sensitive professions, such as legal and accounting professions, would have to seek mainland qualifications. Facilitation involved information exchanges between the two governments in such issues as medical incidents, immigration matters, cross-border issues, and custom regulations.

Although there was economic recovery after 2005, the Hong Kong economy was still based on "investments" in the stock and property markets. Property prices had skyrocketed and earned the status of the highest property prices in the world ("Hong Kong tops global cities list as most valuable residential location in 2015," *World Property Journal*, October 23, 2015; and *South China Morning Post*, January 25, 2016). Although the economy was hurt in the 2008 crisis, the fiscal situation improved as surpluses returned. Nonetheless, opportunities for economic restructuring did not come forward as time passed. There are numerous explanations for the slow pace of economic restructuring. The achievements of the Hong Kong economy were based on the dominance of the private sector, but calls for an increased role of government had been made, especially after the 1998 crisis. One should note that government officials would not be a suitable group of people for developing business. Unfortunately, due to the sequence of crises after 1997, the Hong Kong SAR government was equipped with a "crisis mentality," even when the crisis was over. To keep a crisis mentality in a noncrisis situation means that policies would focus more on short-term results than on promoting long-term potential.

Another political argument for the lack of action could be the psychological need to wait for "orders, approvals, and/or instructions" from Beijing. Instead of making initiatives and drafting investment plans, local business people and government officials could have kowtowed to the "new boss" on what to do. On the contrary, Beijing officials, at least nominally, had been urging Hong Kong to work on its economic affairs. It was a mistake on the part of Hong Kong businesses and officials to seek "directives" from Beijing. Or indeed, Beijing did give "instructions" on what and what not to do in Hong Kong. After all, the economic fate of Hong Kong would have a direct impact on the mainland economy. For example, an economically weaker Hong Kong could suit the political outcome in Beijing as the mainland economy rises, or could demonstrate the relevance and importance of the "one country." Such a scenario would not be infeasible, as one could indeed judge from the lack of investment action and low degree of economic advances in Hong Kong SAR since 1997, especially from the business sector.

The various domestic developments could have produced obstacles in economic restructuring. The emphasis on "demand-driven" policies, coupled with the rising welfare spending, has reduced business incentives. Although the minimum wage was introduced in 2010, the long-term impact to business may not be favorable, as there are alternative investment destinations nearby (*Bloomberg*, November 10, 2010). The economy had increasingly become "domestic-led." The existence of strong pressure groups, especially the green groups which preferred to see less development, would have taken up protectionist policies unfavorable to economic growth. Hence, a dilemma was created: social groups complained about the lack of job opportunities and social upward mobility, the green groups insisted on nondevelopment.

There were other mistaken attitudes that investors in Hong Kong held. They had been led to believe that industrial development in the form of light manufacturing was no longer appropriate, because of a lack of industrial land, high costs, and the development in mainland China. Investors' mindsets were still related to the former "glories" when Hong Kong excelled in labor-intensive manufacturing. Few thought how and what kind of industrial production would suit Hong Kong most. For example, through the CEPA, Hong Kong could be the first supplier and manufacturer to capture the mainland market, as the huge market potential in the mainland could easily cover the "high costs" in Hong Kong. Hong Kong could concentrate on nonland intensive production, such as testing and quality control activities, and medical related supplies. With rising incomes in the large main-land population, Hong Kong manufacturers needed to identify the market inadequacies on the mainland, and venture into the large potential market. More creativity would be needed on the part of the business sector. What Hong Kong has most is the sea. Different types of yacht and boat racing in the warm seasons would generate not only tourism, but also marine-related industries in the islands.

There were also complaints on the "one-sided" bias in development in infrastructure and tourism in favor of mainland visitors. The two typical examples were the Guangzhou–Kowloon rail link and the Hong Kong–Zhuhai Bridge, where massive over-budget spending was needed. The terminal of the Guangzhou–Kowloon rail link would have to be in the heart of Kowloon, but another express train service already existed there, in addition to the numerous ferries that provided daily multiple services to ports in Guangdong, and bus or cross-border bus services that provided efficient land transport. The Hong Kong–Zhuhai Bridge was meant to link Hong Kong to the western side of Guangdong and western provinces in mainland China. Other than the high cost, other practical concerns included traffic safety, as Hong Kong adopted right-hand drive while China adopted left-hand drive.

Indeed, there is no shortage of possibilities, but there is a shortage of initiative. High costs and lack of land were excuses rather than reasons for not engaging in new investment ventures in Hong Kong. Another possible explanation could be the aging business sector. Many successful business people in the 1970–80s had reached retirement age and would not be aggressive enough in creating new investment ventures, and their children stayed in their "comfort zone" and lacked foresight in creative business ventures. A new generation of young entrepreneurs would be needed. Young people with enterprising minds would have to come forward to take risks and venture into new businesses.

On the whole, economic restructuring in post-1997 Hong Kong was slow to come. Initiatives and opportunities had to be weighed against risk and cost. Returns and profits had to be weighed against time and alternatives. Would speculation in stocks and property be a better choice than investment in industries? Would securing paid employment be a better alternative to setting up a business? Would relying on welfare be a more secure outcome than remaining in employment? Would severe competition erode profits? Would the dynamic and ever changing nature of business favor only brand name products and not starters? Would the political situation erode business confidence?

The post-1997 government began to operate in July 1997, but the economy was much more mature. Since the Chief Executive was not freely elected, the government might become cautious in introducing policies. As a result of the "demand-driven" policies introduced in the years before 1997, welfare expenses became dominant and occupied a large percentage of the fiscal budget. Consequently, government intervention increased in various directions, such as assistance to small- and medium-sized enterprises, and subsidies to the movie industry. In the case of SMEs, government assistance did not meet with much success, as applications required financial and accounting disclosure by SMEs. In the case of movie production, one wondered why celebrities in Hong Kong had to be assisted by the tax payers. Once started, the network of government intervention could only expand, and more and more businesses and industries would in turn seek similar assistance.

There was a lack of distinction between welfare assistance and government intervention. Welfare assistance should be given to the needy on a "blanket" or "lump sum" basis when faced with difficulties. Intervention occurred when welfare spending was geared to a particular aspect of one's private life, or a particular business activity. In some years, welfare spending was geared to the payment of after-school tutorial classes and piano les-sons for children in welfare recipient families. This raised concerns as to why and how the government would know that children from welfare-receiving families needed after-school tutorial assistance. The irony was whether the education system was not being provided adequately. In short, the government was increasing the size of "social cost." Yet, the tax players who financed the welfare spending did not have a say.

The severe consequences resulting from the various crises had led Hong Kong to a weaker or even a depleting private sector, and people began to seek answers from the government, which was not supposed to provide solu-tions for private sector activities. A "chicken and egg" situation developed when crises struck, the weakened pri-vate sector complained about the lack of government directives, initiatives, and assistance. Yet, the government excelled more in administrative implementation than in business initiation. As such, except in the provision of welfare, the Hong Kong SAR government was unable to lead the economy away from the crises and promote a new stage of development by reorienting the utilization of resources.

The ultimate prerequisite for economic restructuring, widening, and deepening would be the development of an enterprising attitude and behavior. While creative individuals look for and create opportunities, the govern-ment should facilitate through indirect means and by promoting a business-friendly infrastructure. Intervention is cancerous, as more will always be required as it spreads. Intervention and entrepreneurship are inversely related to each other, the rise of one will mean the fall of the other, and vice versa. With a population of over seven million, there would still be the need to restructure the economy by creating and diversifying industries and businesses. There needs to be a change of attitude from one of reliance on government to one of pursuit of private initiatives, from one of speculative investment to physical investment, from one of servicing the mainland economy to one of becoming the recipient of physical investment from the mainland, from one of integrating with the mainland economy to one of enlarged business corporations to capture the world market, from one of low cost service provisions to application of technology-related manufacturing, from one of a high cost mentality to one of a large market size mentality, from one of politicization with unwanted, unpleasant, or unintended "absolute" outcomes to one of profit-maximization with different magnitudes in "relative" outcomes, from one of a welfare recipient to one of a tax contributor, and finally from being the follower to becoming the creator.

VI ABSOLUTE VERSUS COMPARATIVE ADVANTAGE

In many ways, the Hong Kong economy survives on the various inadequacies of the mainland economy. One could just apolitically consider the facts. From day one as a British colony, Hong Kong served as an entrépot between Qing China and the outside world. The high degree of global insensitivity in the Qing government can be blamed on no one but itself. Hong Kong had been the popular destination for immigrants whenever there were crises and hardships in mainland China. During the trade embargo imposed on communist China after 1949, it was the pro-Beijing business people in Hong Kong that helped to smuggle needed materials to mainland China. Private individuals used to bring consumables back to their villages. In the 1950s and 1960s, clothing materials, cooking oil, and processed food were high on the agenda. In the 1970s and 1980s, household appliances, such as refrigerators, televisions, and air conditioners were carried across the border.

Since China's economic reform in 1978, provisions of formal economic activities from Hong Kong included outward investment, knowledge, management and technology transfer by businesses and institutions, financial and banking facilities provided by the financial sector, and international connectivity through Hong Kong. As the mainland economy expanded, and despite the development of various markets on the mainland, state and other large corporations came to Hong Kong to raise capital through the Hong Kong stock market. After the Asian financial crisis in 1998 when recession occurred in Hong Kong, there was a period when people in Hong Kong went shopping across the border for low-cost materials, such as curtains, massages, and restaurants. Such trends, however, ended gradually as recession gave way to recovery in Hong Kong, and the lack of improvement on the mainland discouraged cross-border spenders. However, after the "visa free" travel policy was issued to mainland citizens in 2005, Hong Kong became a shopping paradise for mainlanders for numerous consumer items. Parallel trade, informal economic activities, and "black markets" flourished on the other side of the border. Li (2006, 2012a) used the "complement—competition" model to describe the dynamic relationship between the two economies. As mainland businesses and institutions looked to Hong Kong for references and lessons, Hong Kong served as a complement to the development of these mainland institutions. While the "complement" relationship is on the "need" of Hong Kong, the "competition" relationship is about the "use" of Hong Kong by mainland enterprises. As businesses, industries, and institutions on the mainland developed and progressed, there was every possibility that they would overtake and compete with similar activities in Hong Kong. Hong Kong would lose out, unless mainland businesses also used Hong Kong for other services. The Hong Kong economy would survive so long as there were new developments in the mainland economy.

Indeed, the economic relationship between mainland China and Hong Kong has also been propagandized. Leftists have been raising the flag that the rapid economic progress in Shanghai would overtake Hong Kong, and the Hong Kong economy would be marginalized. Politics aside, the economic analysis in the relationship between the two economies is an understanding between "absolute advantage" and "comparative advantage." Given that the three economic factors of production are land, labor, and capital, one can observe that the mainland economy has much more of these three factors than the Hong Kong economy. As such, the mainland economy is said to have "absolute advantage" over the Hong Kong economy. The Hong Kong economy loses out completely when one employs the "absolute advantage" concept. The more appropriate and realistic way to consider the relationship between the two economies is to use the "comparative advantage" concept, as the Hong Kong economy does have various advantages that perform comparatively better than the mainland economy. The economic strategy for Hong Kong should be to maintain, extend, expand, and deepen the various "comparative advantages," rather than making absolute comparisons. Therefore, one has to look for economic substance, rather than just quantified factors. Between Hong Kong and Shanghai, e.g., one has developed using free market instruments, while the other has developed from a process of deliberate designations from the state.

In many ways, one should examine the extent of cooperation rather than integration between the two economies. Economic cooperation should be mutual and show "positive-sum" outcomes, so that both economies will gain, though the magnitude of the gain can differ. The rise of the mainland economy does not mean diminishing of the Hong Kong economy. Indeed, the mainland economy should develop more modern metropolitan cities similar to that of Shanghai. It would be naive and propaganda-prone to think that the development of more urban cities and financial centers on the mainland would mean the fall of Hong Kong.

Hong Kong excels in the reliability and sustainability of the capitalist market and civic system. Businesses, investors, and leaders come and go, but the system remains to serve existing participants and new players. The economic success of Hong Kong will not rely on personalities or words from some leaders or government officials. It is the system that people trust. What will be needed is to ensure the functionality of the system, that it will be improved and can be defended. There is no perfection in the Hong Kong system, but the relevance is in perfecting the Hong Kong system.

Other than the "visa free" travel policy, the offshore Renminbi center, and the CEPA trade agreement, there are other channels of cooperation between the two economies. One has to bear in mind that Hong Kong is an open economy, and "business is always as usual" for investors and businesses. Over the years, a large number of mainland businesses have established their posts in Hong Kong, and mainland funds that came to Hong Kong were invested back to the mainland. One medium of economic cooperation established around 2008 was the Pan–Pearl River Delta Regional Cooperation (Pan–PRD) that linked Hong Kong SAR, Macau SAR, and nine southern provinces (Sichuan, Yunnan, Guizhou, Hunan, Guangxi, Jiangxi, Fujian, Hainan, and Guangdong) in mainland China. The economic zone is popularly known as the $9 + 2$ project, and is meant to become a parallel development to that of the Yangtze River Delta Economic Zone, the Bohai Economic Rim, and the Western Triangle Economic Zone in different parts of China. The Pan–PRD consists of a sizable region as it has a population of 453 million, equivalent to 35% of the total population of China. In 2003, the collective GDP of the region amounted to US$652 billion, amounting to 40% of total economic output of mainland China (Pan–Pearl River Delta Regional Cooperation). There are annual meetings among the leaders in the $9 + 2$, but various regional differences exist. Hong Kong could indeed be easily accessible distance-wise from western provinces in China. Hong Kong can also serve China's growing relationship with Southeast Asian economies.

The "one belt, one road" initiative, and the subsequent development of the Asian Infrastructure Investment Bank (AIIB), had led to extensive talks as if Hong Kong would definitely benefit from the project. The benefits Hong Kong could have can be summarized in the acronym "BLITT" that involved businesses in Banking, Logistics, Industry, Technology, and Trade. Commercial banks in Hong Kong will start developing trading of currencies among the countries on the "one belt, one road" route. Logistics involve various forms of logistic businesses, ranging from transportation, education, and training, to management and professional activities. Investment in industries could take place along the "belt and road" route. Hong Kong excels in applied technology and commercialization that can be used in manufacturing of consumer goods. The activities in banks, logistics, investment, and technology would add up to an increase in trade. These five areas should widen the base of the Hong Kong economy. Businesses in these areas should think forward and be the "early bird" in capturing the various opportunities. Similarly, the Hong Kong SAR can start establishing connections and facilitations with cities along the "belt and road" route. However, the "one belt, one road" proposal is still in its constructive stage, it may take years, if not decades, for projects to materialize, and may involve various types of risks: political, currency, territorial, diplomatic, security, material supplies, and financing (Szczudlik-Tatar, 2013; Rolland, 2015; Summers, 2015). Nonetheless, getting prepared will be the most appropriate action for Hong Kong. Once again, Hong Kong is exercising its comparative advantage, which should be conducted and expanded in both directions. The "extensive" direction involves the exploration of more areas of comparative advantage, while the "intensive" direction involves doing a better job in each area of comparative advantage.

VII THE "ECONOMIC CUSHION"

Despite its success and the reliability of the capitalist market and civic system, the Hong Kong economy is vulnerable to shocks and decline. Yet, economic advancement is a long-term process, is apolitical, and requires the development of a "virtuous cycle" and positive participation. Hong Kong's economic advance is the responsibility of all and every individual, business, official, and institution. The post-1997 Hong Kong economy is faced with a number of unfavorable trends that will generate more of a turning point from a rising trend to a falling trend, rather than a crossroad where the direction of the development remains unclear.

The adoption of "demand-driven" policies had unfortunately reorientated Hong Kong's economic path negatively. And the various crises in post-1997 prolonged and deepened the effect and impact of these policies. Hong Kong is increasingly becoming a welfare state, where demand for more welfare and assistance to low income groups is rising more rapidly than the ability to generate a rise in income and output. At the same time, economic narrowness is appearing, as investment activities concentrate on speculative activities in stocks and properties. Indeed, speculation has become the only channel through which a handsome return can be obtained. Thus, despite its periodic fiscal surplus, the SAR government has not been able to widen the economy and provide visions of growth, which should be obvious as government officials are not meant to excel in business ventures. Nonetheless, policies tend to be monolithic, and not integrative and comprehensive enough to produce a convincing picture of development. For example, the land redeployment policy met with opposition from various pressure groups. Officials holding a "crisis mentality" to manage a "noncrisis" economy can only engage in policies that produce short-term results. Meanwhile, time and opportunities are wasted as restructuring is best introduced in noncrisis situations. Given the appalling property prices and the lack of opportunities, the younger generation would more likely face "downward" than "upward" social mobility.

Hong Kong cannot hold on to its "economic cushion" for too long. The dominance in the domestic nature of the Hong Kong economy cannot be sustained if only "demand-side" policies are practiced. Greater spending with delays and prolongation of new development and restructuring would generate a "vicious circle" on its own. While there is sympathy for low income earners, it is output and productivity that count. For economic sustainability, the increase in output has to be higher than the increase in welfare assistance and government spending. A growth- or productivity-related welfare system has to be instituted to ensure a balance between growth and spending. There is also a need to clarify and study what constitutes the needy group of individuals. Is aging equivalent to poverty? Is sympathy an ideology, or a propaganda instrument that imposes economic constraints?

To build up Hong Kong's "economic cushion," efforts are needed to redirect resources and policies to favor "supply-side" factors that promote Hong Kong's competitiveness. Hong Kong excelled in the ability to serve others, and gained in the process of facilitating the business of others. Flexibility that allow economic factors to move with the world economy is the prerequisite condition, not rigidity that imposes economic burdens on competitiveness. Hong Kong provides an economic platform for all to work and perform, not for parasites that do not contribute but live on others. It is the multiplication of opportunities that lubricates the Hong Kong economic engine.

VIII CONCLUSION

The 50 years from 1997 to 2047 are a testing ground for the Hong Kong economy. Economic development and progress will have to be compromised with political development and demands, domestic issues that could erode economic competitiveness, effectiveness of governance in directing the economy into new directions, high levels of economic capability that require further restructuring, short-term investment behavior that provides a "comfort zone" for speculation, aging businesses that need "new blood" in promoting enterprising behavior, and the various distortions in resource deployment.

The ultimate cushion Hong Kong has is its capitalist principles and the free and transparent market system that provide a base for possible revitalization, rejuvenation, recovery, and restructuring. While Hong Kong is faced with transition in the period leading to 2047, many hold a "wait and see" attitude as transition produces challenges to the local economy. On the contrary, this transition period could be Hong Kong's opportunity to show to the world economy how Hong Kong could proceed and excel to a stage of development higher and better than that before 1997. Hong Kong does not have any "comfort zone" from being a British colony, nor should it expect to have mass subsidy from the mainland without political cost. Holding a "siege mentality" will still be needed for the Hong Kong people.

Other systemic improvements include effective governance, equality of opportunity, eradication of discrimination, ethical standards and practices, elimination of malpractice, and so on. Hong Kong will serve as a showcase to other countries that economic growth within a civic model of development will produce an optimal society.

As such, Hong Kong should take the initiative and be creative instead of waiting for blessings, orders, and permissions. Hong Kong is a mature economy and should not exhibit any fear, but should be courageous to venture out into new areas of development, using opportunities to bury conflicts, using results to destroy abuse, using intellect and wisdom to overcome selfishness and bias, and using systemic effectiveness to eradicate cronyism and personality influences.

In humanity, virtues are goals that are always easier said than done. Developmental goals are often agreed in the discussion stage, but divergent views always arise in the implementation stage. Time is costly, and the longer the delay, the poorer the result could be. Leaders need to be courageous in taking bold steps, while businesses should show long-term perspectives and be forward looking in their investments. Individuals should find a way to show their best, rather than to complain about various inadequacies and wait for assistance. Hong Kong is a land of opportunities, but nothing comes free. Progress in the Hong Kong economy should not be thwarted and disillusioned by crises, but should overcome crises in the shortest possible time and reorientate its energy and resources for a faster pace in restructuring and redevelopment activities.

Hong Kong does not have a "fall back" sector, like a large agriculture sector which could absorb people's livelihood at times of crisis and difficulty. Hence, moving forward is the only answer for the survival of the Hong Kong economy. For example, Hong Kong in 2016 has been ranked the most competitive economy based on the annual survey of 61 jurisdictions around the world conducted by the IMD World Competitiveness Center in Switzerland. Business-friendliness in the form of simple taxation and unrestricted movement of capital are the key factors in the high ranking (IMD Competitiveness Center, May 30, 2016). The economy has to proceed at the fastest possible pace through policies that foster and fortify "supply-side" factors in both extensive and intensive dimensions.

It is equally true that politicization in post-1997 Hong Kong would hurt Hong Kong, because the nature of "absolute" outcomes in politics would be divisive, fragmented, rivalrous, and antagonistic. Political problems tended to show a cumulative momentum. Between the leaders and the people, it involved compromise when the people demanded political changes, and how the leaders responded requires the art of diplomacy. The political situation would deteriorate should demands be suppressed. In a politically sensitive economy, fragmentation would occur among different groups that considered only their own narrow interests. As such, compromise and consensus would even be more difficult to achieve. Hence, the more important key in the solution to political conflict will first rest with the leaders as to whether they are prepared to respond positively or adopt a "divide and rule" strategy, thinking that would amass support by marginalizing the opponents.

18

Hong Kong 1997−2047: The Political Scene

I INTRODUCTION

While the sinologists in the Sino−British Negotiation concentrated on making Hong Kong economically superior to the mainland, they were reluctant to introduce further political changes in pre-1997 Hong Kong. Hong Kong, therefore, is destined in the 50 years leading to 2047 to voice political demands by exercising the "high degree" of autonomy in the "two systems," which is in itself the root cause of political differences exhibited in the form of fear, discomfort, distrust, and uncertainty expressed by the Hong Kong people. There was the need for a "political cushion" in the form of an open and transparent political framework and government, to fend off political infiltration and control from the mainland. It has been argued that people in Hong Kong have a high degree of political apathy as "money and wealth" is all that they were interested in. That was probably true in the colonial days when political security was guaranteed. The people of Hong Kong would have to react differently in situations where capitalist Hong Kong was faced with socialist China.

The 1997 solution only dealt with sovereignty reversion, the issue of "system" was left to be sorted out by the people of Hong Kong themselves. As such, it would be natural for Hong Kong to become more politically-oriented in electing the city's leaders. The first debate would surely be the "format" through which democratic change could take place, as interpretations of democracy differed considerably. Typically, people in Hong Kong expected universal suffrage in the form of a "one person, one vote" free election without prior selection or screening. Beijing would have thought that Hong Kong people would be left on their own without the British after 1997. In some ways, allowing political changes to be instituted in post-1997 Hong Kong would be more challenging to Beijing than in the pre-1997 period. This is because political changes in post-1997 Hong Kong could radiate back to situations in mainland China, while political changes in pre-1997 Hong Kong were a British affair that would not impact on mainland China.

However, the kind of political forces in Hong Kong differed considerably from those in the mainland. For example, Hong Kong has the presence of foreign consulates, though Beijing argued repeatedly at sensitive times that the Hong Kong issue belonged to the internal affairs of China after 1997, and foreigners should be hands off.

© 2017 Elsevier Inc. All rights reserved.

The media in Hong Kong comprises local, Chinese, and foreign media, which would observe and report all political movements in Hong Kong. Very often, mainland issues and affairs were leaked to the Hong Kong media before the mainland authorities reacted. Connectivity in Hong Kong is international and efficient.

Hence, it was not an easy task to regain Hong Kong's sovereignty, as systemic change in the 50 years (1997–2047) could have a mutual effect on each other's ideology. Indeed, one could even argue, using the reformists' concept of "bringing in," that Hong Kong was used as a reference to introduce changes, including political changes, in China. Hong Kong, thus, would serve as the ammunition in the "battle" between the two factions in China. The systemic and ideological differences between mainland and Hong Kong, the time period of 50 years, and the presence of factional and provincial rivalries on the mainland would all have added to the complications in the political scene. Perhaps it would be the "economic cushion" that would count more than the "political cushion," and political changes would not go too far. There are numerous studies on the politics of Hong Kong. Debates include the political apathy of the Hong Kong people, the colonial heritage and sequence of political changes, the drive for democracy in pre-1997 years, the post-1997 administrations, the Beijing attitude and policy on Hong Kong, and the 2014 Umbrella Movement (So and Kwitko, 1990; Kuan and Lau, 1995; Ngai, 1995; Degolyer and Scott, 1996; Roberti, 1996; Willnat, 1996; Yahuda, 1996; Liu, 1997; Li, 2000; Kwok and Chan, 2001; Lam, 2004; Lee, 2005; Ma, 2007; Lee and Chan, 2008; Lo, 2010; Sing, 2010; Oksenen, 2011; Chan, 2014; Kurata, 2015; Lam, 2015; Ortmann, 2015).

There are also complications in Hong Kong's internal political scene. The communist mainland has infiltrated many aspects in Hong Kong, and there are political parties and factions that exhibit loyalty to Beijing. Hence, in addition to the traditional divide between capitalist and socialist ideologies in the form of right and left, and the employers and workers divide, there is the division between pro-Beijing, commonly known as proestablishment, and those who prefer not to affiliate with the mainland. Since the Umbrella Movement, or Occupy Central Movement in 2014, there emerged a new force composed mainly of the young generation in their teens, 20s, and early 30s who went further to seek independence, and do not regard themselves as Chinese in the political sense. Thus, there are at least three dichotomies in the political scene in Hong Kong: capitalist versus working class, proestablishment versus democrats, and Hong Kong remains in China versus separating from mainland China. One thing is sure, the longer the delay in allowing Hong Kong to have political freedom, the more complicated the situation would become, because while Beijing insisted on predetermined elections and worried about the consequent spillover to other regions and provinces on the mainland, Hong Kong people preferred to draft their own path. On the contrary, should Beijing have permitted political freedom in Hong Kong in the early stages, things could have remained simpler and the political cost could have been lower. So, who was fighting an uphill battle or a losing battle is yet to be decided. Whether the mainland can crush democratic movements in Hong Kong, or whether movements in Hong Kong can change the political imbalance on the mainland will depend on how events unfold in the years leading up to 2047.

This chapter examines some fundamental issues in Hong Kong's political scene. The political system in Hong King has made little change or progress toward full democracy since 1997, other than the increase in a few freely elected seats in the Legislative Council. There have been occasions when Beijing suggested counter-proposals, but the distrust of Beijing was strong enough to vote down these proposals. In other words, the only acceptable condition would be that democratic changes have to come within the context of Hong Kong, and should therefore be in Hong Kong's favor.

II THE POLITICAL TREND

Table 18.1 shows a summary of political highlights in Hong Kong from the beginning of the Sino–British Negotiation in 1982 until the end of August 2016. The source of all the events listed in Table 18.1 can be located in major newspaper reports, or from government websites on the specific date. Many of the events listed are related to the exercise of authority from Beijing, thereby sending chills to many about the original intention of giving "autonomy" to the people of Hong Kong. The two events that occurred between 1999 and 2002 were the right of abode issue, when mainland families were allowed to reside in Hong Kong and the Court of Appeal applied to seek interpretation from the National Peoples' Congress, which was seen to be unnecessary and produced a poor precedent, as the common law system in Hong Kong could have solved the problem. Eventually, Beijing allowed children born to Hong Kong parent/s the right of abode in Hong Kong, giving a daily quota of 150 families, but it would be up to Beijing to screen and decide on the applications. Hong Kong lost its right to decide on its immigrants.

TABLE 18.1 Key Political Events in Hong Kong: 1982–2016

Year	Month	Day	Event
1982	9	22	Sino–British Negotiation began with Margaret Thatcher visiting China
1984	12	19	The Sino–British Joint Declaration signed in Beijing
1990	4	4	The National People's Congress passed the Basic Law
1992	10	7	Governor Chris Patten announced the reform of the 1994—95 electoral arrangements
1994	6	30	The electoral arrangements reform proposals contained in The Legislative Council (Electoral Provisions) (Amendment) Bill 1994 were passed in the Legislative Council
1995	9	17	Election for Hong Kong's first fully elected Legislative Council held
	12	28	China named the 150 members of the Special Administrative Region Preparatory Committee responsible for preparing the establishment of the Hong Kong SAR; prescribing the specific method for forming the first Government and the first Legislative Council; and preparing the establishment of the Selection Committee for the first government of the Hong Kong SAR
1997	7	1	Hong Kong returned to China
1998	5	24	The first posthandover election for the legislature held
1999	1	29	Landmark ruling by the Court of Final Appeal on the right of abode
	5	20	Government invited the National People's Congress to interpret the Basic Law related to the right of abode
	6	26	The interpretation by the Standing Committee, National People's Congress was contrary to the Court of Final Appeal's judgment on the right of abode
2000	9	6	Two top officials at Hong Kong University resigned due to their exerting pressure not to publish a prominent pollster survey critical of the Chief Executive, Mr. Tung Chee-hwa
2001	9	17	China's accession to the WTO
2002	7	1	Introduction of the Accountability System of the Principal Officials
2003	2	21	Outbreak of SARS
	6	29	Hong Kong and China signed the CEPA
	7	1	1st July rally on the controversial legislation of Basic Law Article 23
2004	4	26	The Standing Committee of the National People's Congress ruled out universal suffrage for the election of Hong Kong's chief executive in 2007 and the Legislative Council in 2008
	7	1	1st July protest march, demands for universal suffrage
2005	9	25	The landmark visit by the Democratic Party to the mainland, the trip included many democrats who were permitted to cross the border for the first time since 1989
	10	20	Hong Kong government unveils contentious election reform plan
	12	21	The Legislative Council voted down the government proposal on election reform
2007	7	11	The government released its official Green Paper on political reform
	12	29	The Standing Committee of the National People's Congress made a decision that the election of the HKSAR Chief Executive in 2017 may be by universal suffrage
2009	11	18	The government announced the constitutional development consultation paper for 2012
2010	1	26	Five elected pan-democrat legislators officially resigned, forced by-elections, and let the citizens vote for real universal suffrage and the abolition of functional constituencies
	4	14	The government released new proposal on 2012 Constitutional Reform
	5	16	Five resigned pan-democrat legislators returned to the Council in by-elections with a low election turnout
	6	17	TV debate between Chief Executive Donald Tsang and Legislator Andrey Eu on 2012 constitutional reform package
	6	25	The Legislative Council approved Beijing-backed constitutional reform package with a three-quarters majority
2011	10	23	Protest against pregnant mainland Chinese women coming to Hong Kong to give birth

(Continued)

TABLE 18.1   *(Continued)*

Year	Month	Day	Event
2012	7	29	Protest on moral and national education
	9	8	Hong Kong government backed down on a plan to introduce moral and national education
2013	3	24	National People's Congress Law Committee chairman said that no one opposed to the central government is allowed to serve as Hong Kong's Chief Executive
	6	9	Occupy Central's first deliberation day
	12	4	Public consultation on constitutional reforms began
2014	6	10	The Central Government published a White Paper on "The Practice of the 'One Country, Two Systems' Policy in the Hong Kong Special Administrative Region"
	6	20	Unofficial civil referendum on three proposals for election reforms
	7	1	Democracy March
	8	31	The Decision of the National People's Congress Standing Committee on Issues Relating to the Selection of the Chief Executive of the Hong Kong Special Administrative Region by Universal Suffrage and on the Method for Forming the Legislative Council of the Hong Kong Special Administrative Region in the Year 2016
	9	22	Students boycott classes in support of universal suffrage in constitutional reform
	9	28	Occupy Central, also known as the Umbrella Movement, began
	12	15	Umbrella Movement ended
2015	4	22	The Government released the Consultation Report and Proposals on the Method for Selecting the Chief Executive by Universal Suffrage based on the Basic Law and relevant decisions of the National People's Congress Standing Committee regarding the method for selecting the Chief Executive by universal suffrage in 2017
	6	18	Legislative Council rejected the Proposals
2016	7	30	A proindependence Legislative Council election (in September, 2016) candidate was invalidated by the Electoral Affairs Commission
	8	2	Proindependence candidates are banned from running in Legislative Council election
	8	16	The Chief Executive said that talk of independence in local schools is "not a matter of freedom of speech"
	9	4	Election of the Legislative Council

The Chief Executive in 2002 introduced the accountability system for principal officials. These were seen as political appointments and eroded the political neutrality of government officials. Pro-Beijing officials were subsequently recruited. The attempt to pass the legislation of Article 23 on national security in early 2003 was a turning point, as a large turnout in the demonstration on July 1, 2003, forced the resignation of two top officials, as well as the subsequent early step down of the Chief Executive in 2005 before the end of his second term.

The political debate since 2004 centered on three issues. One related to the removal of functional constituencies elected from professions and economic sectors which were seen as undemocratic and unfair. The original intention was to allow fair representation from various walks of life in the legislature, as that should provide political balance to the elected members. Indeed, both proestablishment and prodemocracy candidates have been occupying these seats. The other two issues related to universal suffrage on the election of all members of the legislature and the election of the Chief Executive. The dates to be implemented after 2007 and the method of election have been debated. Prescreening of candidates, including the election of the Chief Executive, was considered to be necessary by Beijing, but that would mean the election of only pro-Beijing candidates. Such would and should not be considered as universal suffrage.

The events since 2004 have shown the high degree of restriction and reluctance on the part of Beijing in allowing Hong Kong to achieve political freedom, as that obviously would radiate back to the political scene on the mainland. Equally, suppressing democracy in Hong Kong could also serve as yardstick to similar demands for political freedom on the mainland. Thus, it may not entirely be the desire for not granting democracy in Hong Kong, but also the need to maintain political control on the mainland. This proves that the Hong Kong issue is more of a Chinese issue than a Hong Kong issue. The list of reasons used by Beijing to exercise political control included: (1) prescreening; (2) one needs to love Hong Kong, love country, and presumably, love party; (3) one country comes before two systems; (4) a high degree of autonomy is not the same as full autonomy; (5) the "two systems" have been granted by the central government, and are not an automatic entitlement; and (6) Hong Kong should thank the motherland for various privileges.

Whenever there were instructions to Hong Kong, such as the decision delivered to Hong Kong on August 31, 2014, that candidates for the Chief Executive election in 2017 would have to be screened and restricted to only two to three candidates, because that would rule out the democrats, new waves of protest and demonstrations followed. Many people fell so choked and upset that this eventually led to the outbreak of the "Occupy Central" or "Umbrella" movement that lasted for 79 days between September 28 and December 15, 2014 (Lim and Ping, 2015). While teargas was used and there were clashes between the demonstrators and the police, the entire movement was peaceful and involved no deaths, reflecting the high degree of good civic behavior in Hong Kong.

The "one-way traffic," high-handedness, and top down attitude of Beijing officials left no room for divergent views from Hong Kong. By 2017, Hong Kong has been under Chinese rule for two decades, yet the people of Hong Kong, through the various elected members and functional constituent members in the legislature, voted against any proposals from Beijing, believing that any move not in Hong Kong's political favor may as well be rejected in favor of the original position, fearing that any move could eventually reduce Hong Kong's autonomy and chance of universal suffrage. Many people in Hong Kong considered that what has been written in the Basic Law has not been followed, reflecting the difference between what was said and what was done by the Beijing authority. The "shifting goal" behavior by Beijing officials has led to distrust among the Hong Kong people.

III "SHADE HUNTING": COMMUNIST MIND, CAPITALIST LIFE

In all political regime change, there are always some people who are ready to side with the new regime so as to gain some advantages. Before the Sino–British Negotiation (1982–84), many business personalities and professionals in Hong Kong who were appointed by the colonial government to different positions, were probably approached through the "united front," and turned gradually to side with and show loyalty to Beijing. While Beijing needed their support and knowledge about the colony, they knew that their loyalty would be paid back by being appointed to a high and important position post-1997.

These Beijing-loyalists in Hong Kong were "shade hunters" as they would be "trusted, favored, and secured" in the post-1997 regime. Before 1997, many were appointed as "consultants" on Hong Kong affairs. Some were given key official positions in the post-1997 government, or assisted to take important positions, such as Legislative Council members, Executive Council members, and high ranking positions in institutions with government-subvention or quasi-government institutions, and so on. A number of pro-Beijing political parties, groups, and associations were set up by these "shade hunters," and some even claimed they were politically impartial. Together, they formed a privileged network to gain mutual advantage with the central government.

The loyalty shown by these "shade hunters" could be more for convenience, political survival, and advantage than ideology. After all, the combination of a "communist mind, capitalist life" could be the best form of survival in Hong Kong, with political protection and a privileged life. Connecting to mainland officials and influential individuals would prove to be advantageous. However, the laws of Hong Kong could not apply to their activities conducted in mainland China. Hence, cross-border "corruption" and "relationships" would be unrestricted, and could not be checked by Hong Kong authorities. In attending national meetings in Beijing, e.g., these "shade hunters" could give views different from those they gave in Hong Kong. It would be possible for activities to be conducted or agreement to be made on the mainland, but the outcomes were to be realized in Hong Kong.

One thing for sure is that none of these "shade hunters" would move back or migrate to live on the mainland, and their children always study in foreign countries. The more pragmatic question in their loyalty to Beijing is whether they would tell Beijing their own views on Hong Kong, or what Beijing wanted to hear from them. Given the different leadership factions in Beijing, and since each leadership faction would have their own "power centers," these "shade hunters" from Hong Kong would need to side with different political factions in Beijing. There would be divisions among these Hong Kong "shade hunters," as some would be closer, more loyal, more trusted, more listened to, and had a louder voice than others. There was indeed severe competition among these "shade hunters" in getting closer to the leadership echelon in Beijing.

One source of shade hunting activities would come from the business sector in Hong Kong. Both large corporations and small businesses in Hong Kong tended to be supportive of the regime in Beijing. Other than being drafted into the "united front" or as "Hong Kong consultants" over the years, Hong Kong businesses had been making investments in China since 1978. In much of the 1980s and 1990s, Hong Kong investors, mostly in light-manufacturing and services, received a lot of advantages from local governments in China, when capital from Hong Kong was badly needed. Similarly, Hong Kong investors thought they could make handsome profits as the cost of production across the border was low, while others believed that their output could sell well in the huge Chinese market. The "economic bait" had been used as a political instrument in ensuring loyalty from Hong Kong investors. In the process, many Hong Kong investors learned the need to get "close" to important people in China, in order to ensure their business contacts. The success of Hong Kong businesses in mainland China varied considerably, with many making handsome profits, while others suffered losses and quietly retreated.

However, after four decades of economic reform, the Chinese economy has become "cash rich." Industries were not only focused on the light-manufacturing sector, and more development had focused on high-tech and capital-intensive manufacturing, which had gone beyond the source of investment from Hong Kong. Consequently, the influence of Hong Kong investment definitely had proportionately declined, partly because China had become capital-abundant, light-manufacturing had been taken up considerably by indigenous firms, and industrial focus had changed to promote high-tech industries. Furthermore, the Hong Kong investors of the 1980s would already be aging, marginalized by the new entry of indigenous enterprises, and could not keep pace with the rapid development in China. Other than the large corporations, Hong Kong investors would no longer be the dominant force of investment in China. As such, their political "value" also declined. For example, even the Hong Kong tycoon, Mr. Li Ka-Shing, who had invested massively in China, was considered as "disloyal" when investment from his corporation pulled out of China during the stock market crash in mid-2015. Thus, investment returns in China would not simply be based purely on business calculations, but also on political orientation. This incident should serve as a reflection on all other Hong Kong businesses investing in China.

Hence, while businesses from Hong Kong were attempting to take advantage of the Chinese market, the economic gain would carry a political cost. Indeed, as the Chinese economy grew, the need to rely on Hong Kong investment would decline, and the importance of Hong Kong businesses would diminish. The cash-rich mainland businesses would easily have taken over the same kind of businesses from Hong Kong investors. Furthermore, it would even be possible that mainland capital would flood Hong Kong by buying up Hong Kong businesses through mergers and acquisition. It is thus probable that mainland capital could come to Hong Kong to buy up local companies, especially strategic businesses. For example, the media had been a sensitive business to communist China. Mainland capital had bought up a local television station, as well as the most popular English newspaper in Hong Kong (*China Daily Asia*, September 10, 2015; and *South China Morning Post*, November 28, 2014, December 11, 2015, and March 14, 2016). Indeed, it would be a wholly different political game when mainland capital became the dominant investment force in Hong Kong, because by then China would hold Hong Kong's economic key. In short, the "shade hunters" from the business sector would have to work out both the economic and political "cost and benefit" in their own area of survival.

Nonetheless, a positive note would be that these "shade hunters" provided a voice to leaders in Beijing regarding the situation in Hong Kong. There could be several considerations, including their professional ethics, level of education, "communist mindedness," and advantage from Beijing. On the contrary, these "shade hunters" were considered as "betrayers" in the eyes of many Hong Kong people. The worst positions included the sacrifice of Hong Kong's overall interest for their own private gains, as their views would not be disclosed or accountable to the people of Hong Kong.

China's political machinery contained levels of administration in central, provincial, and city governments. Different "shade hunters" had often been rewarded by having been appointed to positions in different levels of administration in the mainland's political machinery. The politically more loyal "shade hunters" would be given central appointments, while others were given position at the provincial and city levels. Many of these positions were often in the form of consultants and advisors, and were "window dressing" positions. These were known as "hand-raising" appointments when they appeared in political meetings. Indeed, one wondered how much these "shade hunters" knew about the affairs and issues at the central, provincial, and city levels. Equally, it would be questionable the impact their engagement and involvement could have on various mainland affairs. Nonetheless, these appointments did provide a sense of "VIP-treatment" to these "shade hunters."

IV PROESTABLISHMENT: INFILTRATION, CAPPING, AND FREE LUNCHES

The Hong Kong branch of the New China News Agency, which was the main representative of the mainland authority in Hong Kong, was replaced after 1997 by the Liaison Office of the Central People's Government in the

Hong Kong SAR. The highly influential nature of the Liaison Office had been considered as a "shadow" government in Hong Kong. As early as the 1950s, a key instrument in extending Chinese communism was the underground activities conducted by the "united front" through a network of organizations in Hong Kong. Communist potentials were identified through infiltration into various bodies, targeting youth associations, labor unions, local organizations, women's groups, and cultural associations. Some could have been recruited as party members (*Reuters*, July 1, 2014). The Hok Yau Club, e.g., was a nongovernment organization in Hong Kong which was regarded as a peripheral organization of the Chinese Communist Party (Leung, 2012). In communism, political judgment, possible biased, would be made once the "appropriate authority" had gathered sufficient information on a person. As a communist sympathizer, the person would be "protected," but would have an obligation to assist in various activities. On the contrary, "capping" or "tagging" was common in identifying "political enemies," and acts of victimization, marginalization, and elimination would be conducted against the capped individual.

Since 1997, the kind of influence and infiltration from mainland China had explicitly been changed to cater to the various interest groups in Hong Kong. Typically, sympathizers would be captured through provision of various advantages in organized activities, especially on festive occasions. Individuals affiliated to associations and groups which nominally appeared nonpolitical would provide "low cost" or "subsidized" travel and holiday tours to places in mainland China for weekends and various short trips. In particular, there were popular talks on the free provision of "snake soup, vegetarian meals, moon cakes, and seasonal dumplings" for various festivals. Snake soup was popular in cold seasons, while vegetarian meals were popular among the elderly, and mooncakes and dumplings were offered in the Mid-Autumn Festival in September, and the Tuen Ng Festival in June, respectively.

In addition, there would be various offers and assistance that local and neighborhood groups and associations would provide freely or at low cost. These activities were meant to reach out to the general public on a friendly basis, especially households and nonprofessionals who were registered voters in district and general elections. On Election Day, e.g., free transport was provided to the elderly with walking difficulties. The main intention obviously was to influence the votes in an election in favor of pro-Beijing candidates. Since these activities were conducted by local associations and neighborhood groups over the years and at different times consistently and continuously, it was not possible to relate the expenses of their activities directly to elections. The source of funding for these activities could be large, but did not need to be accountable to election budgets, as they were absorbed or hidden in the form of neighborhood activities. One would easily surmise which institution would have such a rich source of funding to support these pro-Beijing activities in Hong Kong. However, there was no guarantee of the result of this support, and it would be difficult to access the political outcomes of these social activities, as participants could regard them as "free lunch" provisions.

There were also "payments" in the organizations and participation in politics-related activities, such as demonstrations organized in parallel against other political groups. As the periodic political elections increased after 1997 and there were increased clashes between pro-Beijing and prodemocracy groups, it was reported that individuals who participated in pro-Beijing demonstrations were paid on an ad hoc basis to hold banners and chant in demonstrations. Cash payments made to the participants before they dispersed after the demonstrations were caught on camera by the media. Pro-Beijing demonstrations would be organized by various proestablishment groups when needed on such occasions as support of police action, against the activities of a certain newspaper, or providing parallel demonstrations against prodemocracy groups, and so on. These proestablishment demonstrations were usually organized by various neighborhood activists, housewives, and individuals from the grassroots community who would use these occasions to show their "loyalty and love of country." Leaders in the proestablishment camp were educated in communist-led schools in Hong Kong in the 1960s, but they suffered from a lack of high quality members (*South China Morning Post*, February 3, 2015).

V THE THREE WAVES OF DEMOCRATIC MOVEMENTS

It was true that during the decades of British colonial rule, there was no urgent need for political change. There could be several reasons for this. There was a high degree of economic freedom and business-friendliness, and the entrepreneurial and enterprising nature of Chinese immigrants produced good chemistry for progress, development, and upward mobility. The gradual improvement of required infrastructure provisions did minimize social discontent and grievances. As compared to mainland China, the colony of Hong Kong for decades had been the more stable and prosperous place, and economic progress was the "cushion" good enough for the enterprising people in Hong Kong. Most important of all, capitalism was introduced into Hong Kong, and the United Kingdom was not a communist country.

The biggest worry Hong Kong people had was the fact that post-1997 sovereignty was reverting to a communist regime, and how much trust one would have in the communist regime could hopefully be balanced by the introduction of an open and democratic government, as a democratic governing regime would be seen as a "political insurance policy." On the contrary, not having much experience of democracy in communist China, democratic changes in Hong Kong would radiate back to the mainland. Thus, the more difficult issue was not to allow Hong Kong to have democracy, but how to contain regions in various parts of China from seeking open democracy and universal suffrage.

Indeed, should a more democratic regime have been instituted in pre-1997 Hong Kong during the Sino–British Negotiation, the political change would have been simpler because time was constrained before 1997 as the negotiation needed to be concluded within a reasonable period of time. On the contrary, while there was not much political change before 1997, Hong Kong would have the entire 50 years (1997–2047) to seek political change, though China would obviously exercise a high hand in limiting political change in Hong Kong. In other words, the resulting uncertainty and risk could be higher and worse than simply having an agreement on political change during the Sino–British Negotiation in the years prior to 1997. There were only 15 years between 1982 and 1997. Hence, by comparison, it would be easier to sort out a problem within 15 years than to allow the problem to last for 50 years.

However, one also would have to agree that the British government could have produced a better package on political change should the sinologists in the Sino–British Negotiation have been willing to do so, as the Great Britain government had a much richer experience of democracy than the colony of Hong Kong. Indeed, the people of Hong Kong and the Hong Kong SAR Government after 1997 would have to negotiate with Beijing on its own on the issue of political change. Hong Kong was inexperienced in the development of political democracy, and one would have to ask how the people of Hong Kong could battle with Beijing in the post-1997 years. However, the Hong Kong situation could be more dynamic than Beijing would have imagined. Indeed, one could observe that the demand for democracy had progressively changed in Hong Kong through the different generations of prodemocracy advocates as events unfolded. In the two decades after 1997, Hong Kong has experienced three generations of prodemocracy advocates. Indeed, the situation has become more complicated and difficult for Beijing to handle. Indeed, the static attitude Beijing took could face an uphill battle when faced with a dynamic situation in Hong Kong's political scene. While Beijing posed a harsh and one-sided attitude toward democracy demands from Hong Kong, the response from Hong Kong was continuous extension and expansion in the interpretation and demand for democracy.

The first generation of democracy advocates started with a number of democracy-seeking groups and associations that have existed since the early 1980s, but merged to form the Democratic Party of Hong Kong in 1994 and regarded itself as holding a "center to center-left" political position, and a "social liberal" ideology. The founding chairman of the Democratic Party in Hong Kong is Mr. Martin C. M. Lee, who as a barrister-at-law was a directly elected Member of the Legislative Council and earned himself the title "Father of Democracy" in Hong Kong. Even though he had been a member of the Hong Kong Basic Law Drafting Committee since 1985, Mr. Lee was forced to leave the committee after his remarks on the 1989 Tiananmen Square student protest. His famous remark on the mainland–Hong Kong relationship was the analogy between "river water and well water," as a burst of the former would overthrow the latter, but not the reverse. Mr. Lee summarized his viewpoints on the political problems facing Hong Kong: (1) political intervention by Beijing and communist party members in Hong Kong, and the erosion of the "one country, two systems" framework; (2) erosion of fundamental values, such as press freedom, and selective practices in the rule of law; (3) introduction of universal suffrage in the election of the Chief Executive and Legislative Council members, and the "prescreening" of candidates by Beijing should be removed; (4) changes should be made to the election system; and (5) excessive protection and power granted to the indigenous people in the New Territories (*Mingpao*, October 10, 2011, p. A6 (in Chinese)).

Over the years, the Democratic Party has effected various achievements. In 1994, the United Democrats of Hong Kong won a landslide victory in the first ever Legislative Council election in 1990 and another one in 1994, thereby becoming the largest party in the legislature. Due to opposition from Beijing, there was no "through train," and the 1994 Legislative Council elected members could only become the "Provisional Legislative Council" after 1997. However, the Democratic Party regained the largest party status in the 1998 Legislative Council election, but there were intraparty divisions, and the emergence of prodemocracy independents and the newly formed middle-class, professionally led Civic Party provided fresh interpretations of the democracy movement in post-1997 Hong Kong.

There were a number of incidents that showed other prodemocracy allies did not seem to agree with the Democratic Party. For example, the 2010 breakthrough agreement with Beijing over the constitutional reform proposal was seen as a weakness on the part of the Democratic Party. In the 2012 Chief Executive election, party chairman, Albert Ho Chun-yan, ran against two other pro-Beijing candidates, Henry Tang Ying-yen and Leung Chun-ying, but was severely defeated in the 1200-member Election Committee. The question raised was why the Democratic Party would join the race when many democrats did not agree to the method of electing the Chief Executive. Subsequently, the party suffered its largest defeat in the 2012 Legislative Council election, losing to other pan-democrat members.

Established in 2006, the Civic Party is a prodemocracy, social liberal political party oriented mainly to the middle-class. The Civic Party basically was a follow-up to the Basic Law Article 45 Concern Group in 2006. The Civic Party was against the legislation of Article 23 related to "national security and antisubversion." Following the political crisis resulting from the unpopularity in legislating Article 23, together with the economic recession, there was a mass protest on July 1, 2003, leading to the removal of two key government officials. The main objective of the Civic Party was aimed at promoting a democratic political system built upon universal suffrage, the rule of law, civil liberties, constitutionalism, and equality of opportunities. Mr. Alan Leong was nominated by the Civic Party in the 2007 Chief Executive election against Mr. Donald Y. K. Tsang.

Together with the Democratic Party and other smaller prodemocracy and left-wing factions and parties, such as the Labor Party, People Power, Professional Commons, and League of Social Democrats, the pan-democracy camp supported an increase in democracy in Hong Kong. Despite their differences, the pan-democrats would work together in areas of common interest, but the camp has also been labeled as the opposition camp "due to its noncooperative stance against the Chinese central government." Although many of the prodemocracy parties and factions held a "center-left" political attitude, they probably adhered to welfare principles.

While the leadership by the Democratic Party formed the first wave of democratic movement in Hong Kong in much of the 1990s, the pan-democratic camp formed the second wave of prodemocracy movements in Hong Kong as the camp gained popularity after the mass demonstration on July 1, 2003, against the legislation of Article 23 in Hong Kong. As the opposition, the pan-democrats were critical of the post-1997 Hong Kong SAR government, as well as central government. While the pan-democrats considered democracy as an important value in Hong Kong, they did provide a certain force of "checks and balances" when it came to deal with the two governments. By adhering to the "one country, two systems" framework, the pan-democrats advocated a faster and more extensive pace in the implementation of universal suffrage in post-1997 Hong Kong.

However, the way the pan-democrats expressed their displeasure or criticism about the lack of democratic changes in Hong Kong was conducted through street demonstrations, use of banners and loud speakers on specific and sensitive days, typically the days nearer to or on June 4, July 1, and October 1, though there were other occasions that called for demonstrations. These activities remained peaceful, but the effects were minimal, as both the Hong Kong SAR government and the central government in Beijing did not respond to calls for democratic changes. Throughout the years, there have been numerous occasions when Beijing officials talked about the success and interpretation of the "one country, two systems" with the intention of pacifying the Hong Kong people. Over the years, calls by the pan-democrats for universal suffrage and removal of functional constituencies were in vain. For example, although the second Chief Executive Mr. Donald Tsang (2005–12) promised to resolve universal suffrage during his term of office, the constitutional package he proposed in 2009 was criticized for a lack of genuine progress by the pan-democrats.

The turning point came after the 2012 Chief Executive election, which was based on the Election Committee that comprised 1,200 individuals elected from different sectors in Hong Kong. However, the majority of the Election Committee members belonged to the pro-Beijing camp. The situation turned from bad to worse when Mr. Leung Chun-ying who rejected the rumor that he was a communist party member himself, was elected as the third Chief Executive in Hong Kong (Leung, 2012) (*South China Morning Post*, March 19, 2012; and *Sentinel*, July 9, 2012). However, others questioned his personal integrity and some ministers he brought to his government were seen as biased. With years of experience in dealing with the central government, he tended to adhere to divisiveness, but became unpopular to the extent of losing support from some pro-Beijing followers. The antagonistic nature of his governance led to growing discontent and grievances in policies on education, housing, and universal suffrage in the 2017 Chief Executive election.

Some background knowledge is needed to understand the 2017 election of the Chief Executive. Clause 7 of Annex I in the Basic Law stipulated that the method for selecting the Chief Executive subsequent to the year

2007 could be made "with the endorsement of a two-thirds majority of all the members of the Legislative Council and . . .." In December 2007, the National People's Congress Law Committee ruled on the issue of universal suffrage in Hong Kong that "the election . . . in the year 2017 may be implemented by the method of universal suffrage. . .." However, new qualifications in the form of "shifting goals" were added by Beijing leaders in manipulating the interpretation of the "one country, two systems" and "universal suffrage" to their advantage, resulting in further disappointment in Hong Kong.

While the Chief Executive was supposed to submit the views of the Hong Kong SAR government to Beijing on how to proceed with universal suffrage in 2017, leaders in Beijing insisted that the Chief Executive so elected in 2017 must "conform to the standard of loving the country and loving Hong Kong," implying that the Chief Executive would have to "love the party" as well. The Hong Kong SAR government, with support from Beijing, reiterated that the Chief Executive nominees must first be screened and there would be no provision for civic nominations. Beijing's position was reaffirmed in the State Council White paper issued in June 2014, which reasserted its "comprehensive jurisdiction" over Hong Kong SAR. The wordings in the State Council White Papers were extremely harsh, and in many ways defied the spirit of the "two systems." It said that "the high degree of autonomy . . . is not full autonomy, nor a decentralized power. . . . It is the power to run local affairs as authorized by the central leadership. . . and loving the country is the basic principle for Hong Kong's administrators. . . to safeguard the country's sovereignty, security and development interests . . . and to stay alert to the attempt by outside forces to use Hong Kong to interfere in China's internal affairs, and prevent and repel the attempt made by a small number of people who act in collusion with outside forces to interfere with the implementation of 'one country, two systems' in Hong Kong" (*The Practice of the "One Country, Two Systems" Policy in the Hong Kong SAR*, June 10, 2014, Information Office of the State Council, People's Republic of China; *BBC News*, June 11, 2014; *CNN*, June 13, 2014; and *South China Morning Post*, July 5, 2014). The content basically suggested that Beijing would not trust any nomination without prior screening by the pro-Beijing camp in Hong Kong, implying that any pan-democrat candidate would not be accepted as a chief executive nominee.

In July 2014, the Chief Executive did produce a report to the Standing Committee of the National People's Congress (*Report by the Chief Executive of the Hong Kong SAR to the Standing Committee of the National People's Congress on Whether There is a Need to Amend the Methods for Selecting the Chief Executive of the Hong Kong SAR in 2017 and for Forming the Legislative Council of the Hong Kong SAR in 2016*, Hong Kong SAR Government, July 15, 2014). The report was criticized for not reflecting the true picture from Hong Kong, and new conditions and requirements were inserted. For example, in Clause 8 (i) in the report, and in addition to the Basic Law, the proposal would need to meet the "relevant interpretation and decisions of the National People's Congress Standing Committee (NPCSC)." However, similar harsh wordings and terms were reiterated in the National People's Congress Standing Committee decision on Hong Kong's 2017 elections in a meeting on August 31, 2014. It concluded that, in conducting the method of universal suffrage, a "broadly representative nominating committee shall be formed. . ., the nominating committee shall nominate two to three candidates for the office of the Chief Executive. . . The Chief Executive-elect . . . will have to be appointed by the Central People's Government." However, the Standing Committee also stressed that "if the specific method of universal suffrage for selecting the Chief Executive is not adopted in accordance with legal procedures, the method used for selecting the Chief Executive for the preceding term shall continue to apply" (*South China Morning Post*, August 31, and September 1, 2014). It was widely believed that Beijing leaders had dictated their terms on the method of universal suffrage.

The political displeasure in Hong Kong culminated in the Occupy Central, popularly known as the Umbrella Movement or Revolution, that started on September 28 and ended on December 15, 2014. Umbrellas were used as shields from the teargas. Occupy Central was initiated by scholars, Benny Y. T. Tai, Chan Kin-man, and Reverend Chu Yiu-ming. It was meant to be a "civil disobedience" campaign that aimed at pressurizing for equal suffrage. However, as soon as Occupied Central was declared, crowds gathered in Admiralty near the government headquarters clashed with the police. The police deployed 87 rounds of teargas in dispersing the crowds. Demonstrations and occupation immediately spread to Causeway Bay on Hong Kong Island and Mongkok in Kowloon, both of which are major commercial districts (*South China Morning Post*, October 28, 2014).

The Umbrella Revolution ended peacefully with 247 arrests, but it had already attracted attention from the international community, especially the United States, United Kingdom, and Canada who had urged Beijing to open up elections in Hong Kong. By contrast, Beijing responded by asking foreign governments not to interfere with China's internal affairs, including the situation in Hong Kong. Prodemocracy members from the British Parliament were banned from visiting China (*New York Times*, October 20, and 21, 2014; *CNN*, October 20, 2014; *Asia Pacific Foundation of China*, September 22, 2015; *South China Morning Post*, September 2, and 5, October 16, and 29, November 5, 21, 25, and 28, December 3, 8, and 11, 2014, and October 23, 2015). During the period of protests, there were also contrary voices, and parallel demonstrations and movements by the pro-Beijing camp, though some were paid or manipulated.

However, the ugliest outcome appeared in June 2015, when the reform package was rejected in the Legislative Council as pro-Beijing legislators walked out of the council chamber supposedly to give time for another Beijing-loyalist to arrive, thinking that the ballot would be adjourned due to the low turnout. However, the walkout was poorly communicated to all proestablishment lawmakers, eight Beijing-loyalists remained in the chamber, and that, together with the pan-democrats, produced a sufficient quorum for the ballot. The Beijing-loyal Chairman proceeded to allow the ballot to take place, yielding within minutes a clear majority against the political reform package. The walkout fiasco was seen surely as a careless and embarrassing mistake on the part of the proestablishment legislators.

Even though the pan-democrats engaged in the Occupy Central protests, the unexpected outcome was the extensive involvement by students and the younger generation who are either in their teens or in their early 20s. There were several groups of students and a new generation of young prodemocracy activists. A book entitled "Hong Kong Nationalism" was published by *Undergrad*, the official magazine of the Hong Kong University Students' Union advocating for self-reliance and self-determination. Another similar article entitled "Hong Kong Youth's Declaration" appeared in the February 2014 issue of *Undergrad*, calling for Hong Kong to "break away from mainland and become a sovereign state recognized by the United Nations when the Sino−British Joint Declaration expires in 2047." Nobody would have noticed these publications until the Chief Executive, C. Y. Leung, probably intentionally singled out the content of these publications in paragraph 10 of his 2015 Policy Address delivered in January 2015. Obviously, the Chief Executive had dismissed the ideas in the students' publication, but one wondered why one student's publication would have received so much attention in the Policy Address. Conspiracy advocates jumped to the conclusion that it was C. Y. Leung who stirred up the ideas on self-determination and aroused the debate on separation (*South China Morning Post*, January 14, 2015, and March 15, 2016). Others argued that this was a typical instrument of antagonism in the communist movement. By highlighting, establishing, and arousing a clear political monolith, full political vigor and attention would then be devoted to hit the target hard in order to beat the opponent. That could form part of his strategy in preparation for the next election in April 2017 for his second term as Chief Executive.

Meanwhile, discussions ranging from self-reliance, self-determination, and separation from the mainland to independence have since been raised. The more vocal group was Scholarism, which was a local prodemocracy student activist group involved in Hong Kong's education policy, political reform, and youth policy. Founded by a number of secondary school students in May 2011, Scholarism was first known for its defense of Hong Kong's educational autonomy from Beijing's influence on "moral and national education" in 2012. However, it turned out to be a leading organization during the Umbrella Revolution in 2014. At the peak of the Umbrella Revolution, one of the core members of Scholarism, Joshua Wong, who was only 19 years of age, was named one of TIME's Persons of the Year 2014, and was listed by Fortune as one of the world's greatest leaders in 2015. The Hong Kong Federation of Students, led by Nathan K. C. Law, the secretary general, also played an active and crucial role in the Umbrella Revolution.

The third wave of democracy movements in Hong Kong began after the Umbrella Revolution, with the involvement of students and young people in their 20s establishing different political parties and groups that went beyond the traditional approach and advocacy adopted by the pan-democracy camp. Joshua Wong, together with Nathan Law and Oscar Lai, established the Demosistō Party in April 2016, pledging to be a center-left prodemocracy party in Hong Kong. The Demosistō Party advocates for a referendum to determine Hong Kong's sovereignty after 2047, with the four missions of self-initiation, self-standing, autonomy, and self-determination (*South China Morning Post*, April 6, 2016). Subsequently, Mr. Nathan K. C. Law was popularly elected to the Legislative Council in the Legislative Council on September 4, 2016.

While the Demosistō Party accepts the "one country, two systems" framework but looks to changes in post-2047, the Hong Kong National Party, founded in March 2016 by Mr. Jason H. F. Chow, who is also a young pro-democracy activist, is a political party advocating for localism and the building of a Hong Kong nation state. The Hong Kong National Party advocates for independence and would not recognize the Basic Law, and together with other student, localism advocates intend to seek support and field candidates in future Legislative Council elections (*South China Morning Post*, March 28, and 31, and April 11, 2016). A group of independent activists has set up another political party campaigning for Hong Kong's independence, as well as a resumption of British rule in Hong Kong. This group that advocates for Hong Kong's independence is called the Alliance to Resume British Sovereignty over Hong Kong and Independence. By not recognizing the Sino−British Joint Declaration, this group advocates for the return of British rule, but aims ultimately at going independent (*South China*

Morning Post, June 22, 2016). These various forms of independence advocates basically have not been satisfied with the way Hong Kong has been controlled by Beijing since 1997, as Hong Kong did not take part in the entire Sino–British Negotiation and the outcome of the Sino–British Joint Declaration.

The ideas of the young prodemocracy activists differ from the pan-democrats, as the latter adhere to the "one country, two systems" and seek democratic changes in mainland China. For example, the Hong Kong Alliance in Support of Patriotic Democratic Movements of China that organized annual vigil events in memory of the Tiananmen Square student massacre on June 4, 1989, argued for more democracy and free political elections in mainland China. The localism groups, on the contrary, argue that Hong Kong should not bother about mainland issues, but should focus on Hong Kong as a place different and separate from mainland China. Indeed, the extent of Beijing's intervention in Hong Kong, the lack of political advances in China, and the "goal shifting" nature in the manipulation of the "one country, two systems" have imposed greater uncertainty and reduced the trust Hong Kong people have in the central government. For example, people of Hong Kong donated billions after the Sichuan earthquake in May 2008, but after knowing the extent of corruption in the use of donations and the poor supervision by the government officials, Hong Kong people refused to donate any more to another Sichuan earthquake in 2012. In early 2016, the disappearance of three booksellers in Hong Kong who later appeared in mainland media had alarmed not only Hong Kong, but the international community. Since early 2016, China under Xi Jinping had reiterated the doctrine of Marxism and exercised tighter control on the media in China (*South China Morning Post*, April 30, 2013, May 18, June 2, and 9, 2016). The argument put forward by the localism advocates is that it would be more realistic to ensure a higher level of protection for Hong Kong, both before and after 2047.

However, in July 2016, the SAR government, probably instructed by communist central government, reacted by barring Mr. Chan Ho-tin of the National Party and five other proindependence nominations from entering the election race in the Legislative Council election, arguing that the proindependence advocates do not uphold the Basic Law. Indeed, C. Y. Leung went far in August 2016, warning local schools that talking about Hong Kong independence to pupils could be "poisonous" and was "not a matter of freedom of speech" (*Financial Times*, July 31, 2016; *The New York Times*, August 31, 2016; and *South China Morning* Post, August 16, 2016). It is becoming clear that C. Y. Leung is raising the "independence" issue as an attack target for his own election for the second term in April 2017, thinking that Beijing's worry about the "independence" issue would mean they would prefer to let him stay.

The emergence of the third wave of prodemocracy activists received criticism from leaders in Beijing and the pro-Beijing camp in Hong Kong. Their arguments included that independence is illegal, not feasible as tiny Hong Kong relies on supplies from mainland China, against the Basic Law, and that Hong Kong geographically belongs to mainland China. Indeed, since the end of the Umbrella Revolution, leaders from the central government and pro-Beijing loyalists have tried to reassert the power of the central government. For example, it has been stated the "one country, two systems" must comply with the Chinese constitution, supporting the Chief Executive would mean supporting the country, Beijing would be willing to hold out an "olive branch", develop a new understanding on the "one country, two systems," the transcendent position of the Chief Executive, and the establishment of a new think tank by the former Chief Executive, Tung Chee-hwa, that comprised all of his former cronies to propose new strategies for Hong Kong (*South China Morning Post*, November 14, and 17, 2014, January 17, March 3, and 5, August 31, September 15, 2015, and March 16, 2016).

Many argued that the political scene in Hong Kong has deteriorated since 1997, for a number of reasons. One obviously has been the antagonistic manner of the Chief Executive since 2012. The hardline approach adopted by the central government in Beijing has resulted in more confusion and distrust over the "one country, two systems" framework, as new but inconsistent interpretations have regularly been adopted in the "goal shifting" behavior of central officials. Direct intervention by Beijing has increased. Indeed, Occupy Central reflected the problems in Beijing, typically in the fight between the hardliner and reformist factions. One observation was that previously, when some probably hardliner officials made harsh remarks about Hong Kong, they would be followed by other more moderate remarks made by reformist officials so as to calm the unpleasant feelings of the Hong Kong people. This was considered as a "negative, positive" approach in monitoring Hong Kong.

However, one could equally observe a change in the tone of remarks by Beijing officials, probably since China President Xi Jinping and/or Hong Kong Chief Executive C. Y. Leung had been in office. When one Beijing official made a harsh and negative remark about Hong Kong, it was followed by an even harsher remark by another official. Such a "negative, negative" approach could have reflected more on the conflict between the two ideological factions in mainland China. One interpretation of the "negative, negative" approach was that officials from the reformist camp would not bother to make moderate remarks on Hong Kong and were prepared to let the situation in Hong Kong "deteriorate" so as to gain more attention from the international community. Another possibility was that the "second negative" remark indicated the way the reformists were not in alignment with the hardliners and intended to fight back within the ideological circle in Beijing. In other words, instead of trying to rescue Hong Kong from the communist hardliners, the reformists would use the Hong Kong issue to go further to make a harsher and even more negative remark about Hong Kong, thereby fueling a more intense situation and escalating the Hong Kong issue so that the hardliner camp in Beijing would face more difficulty in handling Hong Kong. The two kinds of negative remarks would lead to a rebound in the feelings of the Hong Kong people, disappointed about the way Beijing handled the affairs in Hong Kong, as a more turbulent Hong Kong would embarrass the leaders and expose their inadequacies in their policy on Hong Kong.

The political situation in Hong Kong would be seen as an important instrument in Beijing. Superficially, the political scene in Hong Kong would look more like a deteriorating situation, but the waves of prodemocracy and self-determination movements in Hong Kong could become another bargaining chip for Hong Kong and the reformist camp in mainland China. In short, Hong Kong is involved in two levels of battle, with one level where Hong Kong is used as an instrument between the reformists and hardliners in mainland China, and the another level in Hong Kong between the "shade hunters" and the prodemocrats. In the meantime, there would certainly be more political noise and voices from the different factions in Hong Kong, and the outcome will depend on the growing political maturity of the Hong Kong people.

VI EFFECTIVE GOVERNANCE: THE "HALF-CUP" ARGUMENT

During the century-long period of colonial rule, the various Hong Kong governors were sent from London, but upon their retirement from the post of governorship in Hong Kong, they would not be given any position in the political hierarchy back in the United Kingdom. In other words, the position of being Hong Kong governor was prestigious, an obligation, and an honor, but also was a "terminal" post. This might have sounded unfortunate, but there could be ethical implications. These governors would have to devote their energy to working for the good of Hong Kong, and should not have had any ambition of eyeing up another position in London. Thus, their entire work, effort, and contribution in Hong Kong could not be used as a "report card" in ascending to another political position in London. At most, they could affiliate to some universities as scholars. Such a practice added to the prestige of the Hong Kong governor with a sense of nobility and respect. The civility of such a practice was that while the governor was in position, the governor would perform his best, but would not get involved once he had departed from the governorship post.

In the first two decades after 1997, the Hong Kong SAR experienced three chief executives: Mr. Tung Chee-hwa (July 1, 1997—March 12, 2005), Sir Donald Y. K. Tsang (June 21, 2005—June 30, 2012), and Mr. C. Y. Leung (July 1, 2012—June 30, 2017). The first Chief Executive, Mr. Tung, was originally favored by the Hong Kong public, but his popularity declined after taking office, due probably to the poor handling of policies and the emergence of crises and recession. Although his father, Mr. Tung Chao-yung, was an influential shipping magnate in Hong Kong, Mr. Tung Chee-hwa was on the edge of bankruptcy four years after the death of his father in 1985, but his business was saved by the Beijing government. Tung had been loyal to the mainland government. It could politically be argued that Tung used Hong Kong to show his "gratitude" to the Beijing government for rescuing his family business.

Although the various crises, such as the Asian financial crisis and the two health crises of avian flu and severe acute respiratory (SAR) syndrome, had caused much difficulty to his administration, Mr. Tung's government had to rescue the economy. For example, his government proposed a number of controversial infrastructure and development projects, such as the technology and science park, Chinese medicine center, the Disney theme park, and the Cyberport project. Some of these projects were heavily criticized subsequently, but it was understandable as the economy then was in a crisis period and some answers, however short-term, were urgently needed in order to rescue the economy. Surely, in a noncrisis time, one could have given more thought to these projects. In any case, these projects did help, and did not hurt the economy then.

Other than the lack of political change, the introduction of the Right of Abode (ROA) issue in January 1999 was criticized, when his government sought clarification from the Standing Committee of the National People's Congress in Beijing for the interpretation of the ROA issue, which resulted in a potential large influx of mainland children with Hong Kong parents migrating to Hong Kong. Critics argued that such an act defied judicial independence and destroyed Hong Kong's autonomy. The other two highly critical acts included the introduction of principal officials into the administration in the promotion of "accountability" in 2002, meaning that heads of government bureaux would no longer be political neutral career civil servants, they would all be political appointees chosen by the Chief Executive. This was heavily criticized, as the removal of administrative-neutrality would lead to bias. The then Chief Secretary of Administration, Mrs. Anson Chan, disagreed with the new political accountability system and resigned.

The last straw for Mr. Tung's government was the forceful push in September 2002 to legislate Article 23 of the Basic Law, which required Hong Kong SAR to "enact laws on its own to prohibit any act of treason, secession, sedition, subversion against the Central People's Government, or theft of state secrets, to prohibit foreign political organization of bodies from conducting political activities in the Region…." Critics believed that could be seen as a limitation to Hong Kong's rule of law, and freedom, and the unfavorable interpretation of various terms. Public displeasure culminated in a large protest on July 1, 2003, the subsequent resignation of two officials, and Mr. Tung eventually resigned in 2005 without finishing his second term. However, Mr. Tung was elevated to become the Vice-Chairman of the National Committee of the Chinese People's Political Consultative Conference, thereby setting a precedent that an ex-Chief Executive could be rewarded with a high position in the central government. Hence, unlike the Hong Kong governors, the office of Chief Executive could just be a stepping stone to a higher position in the central government.

Even though Mr. Donald Tsang was given the Knight Commander of the Most Excellent Order of the British Empire in June 1997 hours before the handover, Mr. Tsang was trusted by the Beijing authority to be the second Chief Executive. Mr. Donald Tsang had joined the Hong Kong civil service in 1970, served in 1993 as Secretary for the Treasury, was Financial Secretary in 1995, and Chief Secretary for Administration in 2001. Being labeled as "bow tie Tsang," his pledge in 2005 was "do my job well." Mr. Tsang became prominent in tackling the Asian financial crisis in 1998. During his term as Chief Executive, however, Hong Kong was in a noncrisis time until 2008. Instead of engaging more in long-term development, Mr. Tsang favored welfare policies that yielded short-term results, including the establishment of the Community Care Fund that provided a second layer of welfare protection, and the introduction of a minimum wage.

Although Mr. Tsang did introduce 10 major infrastructure projects in his second term, he defied the "positive noninterventionism" approach used in colonial Hong Kong since the 1970s, and attempted to incorporate Hong Kong's development into China's 5-year plan, thereby making Hong Kong more dependent on the mainland economy than enabling Hong Kong to seek new comparative advantages. On the political front, Mr. Tsang did produce results for the 2012 elections. Changes included the increase in the number of seats in the Legislative Council from 60 to 70, an increase in the number of Election Committee members who elect the Chief Executive from 800 to 1200, but the package was rejected as the pan-democrats thought that the proposals did not go far enough. Given the degree of distrust on mainland China, stay-put was thought to be the better strategy. Before his departure, Mr. Tsang was charged with two counts of misconduct in public office on October 5, 2015, by the Independent Commission Against Corruption (ICAC).

In the 2012 Chief Executive election, Mr. Henry Tang, the Chief Secretary of Administration, was considered as Beijing's favorite. The other two candidates were Mr. C. Y. Leung, the Convener of the Executive Council who was regarded as a Beijing-loyal, and Mr. Albert Ho from the Democratic Party who had least support in the Election Committee. Among the three, Mr. C. Y. Leung had done most "preparation," including exposing the faults and weaknesses of other candidates. Due probably to Mr. Tang's over-confidence and lack of political sensitivity, the media exposed the illegal basement in Mr. Tang's residence weeks before the election. Instead of taking appropriate action while there was time to restore the basement back to its original form, he passed the responsibility to his wife and blamed the politically fierce, wolf-like attacks from his opponents and the media. In the end, Mr. Leung was elected as the third Chief Executive in July 2012 with 689 votes from the 1200 members.

Many would agree that Mr. C. Y. Leung has an antagonistic character, and divisiveness was chosen over compromise. Mr. Leung, in addition to his business in surveying, had held various political posts in Beijing in relation to Hong Kong during the Sino–British Negotiation and drafting of the Basic Law. However, his personal integrity had been questioned soon after he took up the office of Chief Executive. For example, he was found to have illegal and unauthorized structures in his own house, and accepted large compensation from his overseas business. His loyalty to Beijing brought worries to the people of Hong Kong. For example, it was reported that the online version of the People's Daily addressed Leung as "Comrade Leung Chun Ying" when he was selected. Upon victory in his election, the first visit Leung made was to the central government's liaison office in Hong Kong (*South China Morning Post*, March 27, 2012). There were numerous incidents where his antagonistic character led to controversy in Hong Kong, e.g., in education and housing policies, granting of new television licenses, and instigating conflicts among different factions. Although he was proud to have stopped mothers from mainland coming to give birth illegally in Hong Kong hospitals, it was generally believed that the unpopularity of the Chief Executive resulted in the high sentiments of the people in Hong Kong, leading eventually to the outbreak of the Umbrella Revolution in 2014. Although by 2016 there had been debates as to whether Beijing would let Leung to stay for his second term in the 2017 Chief Executive election, one wondered if leaders in Beijing would provide Leung with another high ranking position in the political echelon in Beijing as a "save face" for Leung. Despite the great displeasure the people of Hong Kong have shown, his strategy would probably be to stir up new troubles or weaken the proestablishment camp, so that Beijing would need him as a guard against the opposition in Hong Kong SAR.

One debate in the post-1997 Hong Kong has been on the extent of "top down" and "intervention" by Beijing leaders. The discussion should relate to the institution of "autonomy" in Hong Kong. Many have complained about the lack of economic progress and political changes in the post-1997 years. Indeed, looking at Hong Kong's previous experience as an enterprising economy that provided progress and upward social mobility, one would have to wonder why Hong Kong had not been able to make progress. The situation could have been trapped in the "half cup" argument, which hypothesized that things had been working but not progressing, business as usual but not expanding, employment as normal but no upward mobility, economic growth secured but missing long-term potential, peace but no harmony, and diversity coexisting with conflict. In short, although things in Hong Kong appeared to be normal, the "half-cup" and complacency attitude, especially on the part of government administrators, could easily explode into a crisis that would lead to losses for all sides.

The severity of the political divide in post-1997 Hong Kong would not be a blessing. Consider the case of human capital. With a population exceeding seven million, the number of highly trained and educated people would be a minority, as seen from the number of salaried tax payers. Hence, if political orientation was exercised in the recruitment of top civil servants, the pool of educated people from which the government leaders could choose would be even smaller. Hong Kong would face a situation of "brain deprivation" in human capital, as people whose political orientation differed from that of the leaders would not be used to serve Hong Kong. On the contrary, the smaller pool of educated human capital could mean the employment of "lower-educated but politically correct" individuals into the government administration. Hence, the ball should be in the court of the government leaders. To maintain stability or prosperity, or stir up antagonistic feelings and behavior would be the choice made by the leaders. After all, it is true in all legitimate states that the government has the power to command all its institutions and departments, including the police force. The Hong Kong SAR government needs to get away from the "half cup" argument, and needs to do more to earn the trust of the Hong Kong people. The difference between business leaders and political leaders is that business leaders should show their ability in making profits and business deals, but political leaders should show their best in public performance and in gaining trust and earning popularity with the people. Politics is not a way for leaders to get rich, but exercising effective governance in the administration should be the long-term infrastructure that all political leaders should build.

The Hong Kong SAR Government was politically standing between the leaders in Beijing and the people of Hong Kong, but it needs to build up a strong team of administrators who will see to the effectiveness and efficiency of various policies. In other words, good governance will be needed at least in maintaining, but preferably also in deepening and expanding, the internal system in Hong Kong. In other words, the government policies should help to "fill up" the cup, rather than leaving it half full. To do a good governing job should be the first and top priority. Hong Kong has to perform to prove that Hong Kong can still be useful to the mainland. On the contrary, Hong Kong would lose its color and be ignored should Hong Kong's performance be no different from other cities in mainland China. Hence, assimilating Hong Kong to become a mainland city would be a poor strategy.

VII CONCLUSION

The reversion of Hong Kong's sovereignty was definitely not a "piece of cake" for China, as there were vast systemic differences. As the largest socialist but "cash rich" economy, China would have to handle the freest capitalist economy of Hong Kong. The existence of various dualities and dichotomies within China, and the difference between Hong Kong and China, made the post-1997 relationship like a game of chess, with each side having strong ammunition that could be used against the other side. The issue of 1997 Hong Kong and the subsequent period of 50 years (1997—2047) was not only a Hong Kong issue, but would have an equal, if not bigger, impact on China, as all provinces, regions, and ethnic groups in China and the world community were watching how Beijing handled Hong Kong. The local population in Hong Kong would have their own preferences and choices, and the outcome of their decisions might be controversial for Beijing to accept.

History would come to a better conclusion about a number of questions. Should the Hong Kong issue be legitimately dealt with by the contemporary Chinese regime that came into existence only after 1949, while the colony of Hong Kong ceded by the Qing government had existed since 1842? Was 1997 the right time for China to take back Hong Kong? Great Britain did not colonize Hong Kong from the communist regime in China after 1949. Was Deng Xiaoping trying to use the Hong Kong issue to build up his personal charisma? Would the British Prime Minister's suggestion of the "sovereignty reversion but British governance" model be more suitable and pragmatic? Did the British team led by the sinologists not try hard enough to bargain for Hong Kong? Would it be easier to have the systemic issue sorted out before 1997 so that the 50 years of 1997–2047 would be free from political disturbance? Was it the intention of the British negotiation team to delay Hong Kong's political change to post-1997 so that instability in Hong Kong would introduce a political cost to China? Would the majority of the people in Hong Kong be willing to accept the communist system?

The 1997 sovereignty reversion took 15 years to be sorted out, but the solution, if any, to systemic differences will take the subsequent 50 years. To the international community, one could compare the significance of the people in Hong Kong becoming communists to the need for political reorientation in communist China. The answer will not be known until 2047, or earlier, say 2030. The outcome depends on a number of dynamic factors. One could examine the various political costs and benefits. Given its huge power, China could easily swamp Hong Kong, but would the resulting instability in Hong Kong not hurt China? While China did not have much investment in Hong Kong before 1982, corporations from China have since used Hong Kong as a financial center, and mainland citizens and "princelings," have acquired large numbers of properties in Hong Kong. The economic table may turn, and it may be costly to China should the Hong Kong economic system collapse as 2047 draws closer.

The political cost to China resulting from a "communist Hong Kong" could be enormous. Firstly, foreign investors would withdraw their capital, not only from Hong Kong but also from China. One could easily guestimate the amount of capital funds leaving China, and the resulting impact on its currency. Would the international community sit back and take action on China's rule over Hong Kong? What would be the behavior of regional neighbors, and would they still trust China in international affairs? China has grown and amassed huge international reserves, but the international community does not yet consider China as the pivot of the world.

On the contrary, what would be the "gain" China could amass by democratizing Hong Kong? It would show that China's rule of Hong Kong was better than that experienced under colonial rule. China's response to popular and open political calls would elevate its civic status in the world community, which in turn would radiate back to China similar behavior, changes and respect, where repression would be substituted by civic behavior, power would be replaced by participation, social discontent would be rescued by neighborhood support, and so on. Hong Kong's systemic strength is what China needs to develop, acquire, and maintain, while political democracy would simply serve as the vehicle. Hence, it should be the resulting outcome that counts, not the conveying vehicle.

WHY HAS CAPITALISM SUCCEEDED?

Centuries of Theories, Decades of Practice

There is still no solution to the ideological debate. Or there are solutions, but there is no consensus on any single solution, because the political outcome would dictate the ideological choice. Despite the existence of extremes between capitalism and communism, and decades of practice of both ideologies in the world economy, there are still endless debates on the virtues and drawbacks of the two ideologies (Schram, 2015; Watson, 2015; Shikh, 2016). Confusion arose as capitalist economies took up welfare-oriented policies, while socialist economies followed market-capitalist policies. There are also economies that are not driven by ideology, but became rich just because of the availability of resources. There are also rich countries that exhibited a high degree of instability.

Despite progress in human civilization, religion and ideology are the two origins of contemporary world conflicts. The issue of human faith has existed for thousands of years, and the world comprises a few key religious faiths. Over the centuries, instead of allowing humans to choose their religious faith freely, it is surprising to see that there are still so many conflicts and monopolies in religious faiths. Similarly, ideological differences have been discussed, debated, and practiced for centuries. While much of the world has adopted a system closer to capitalism than to socialism, as that permitted individual freedom protected by a civic system, there are still socialist/communist countries whose power and authority is concentrated in a minority coercively controlling the majority in the name of equality. The minority worked like a political club that recruited members who were given "legitimate" authority to control and abuse. Ideology has often been associated with personalities, while capitalism often relates to the practices within a system. A broad-minded, charismatic leader that wanted to bring wealth, peace, and freedom to the people would always end up with a system closer to capitalism. A power-hungry leader with vested interests, political ambitions, and intentions to control and amass authority would wrongly regard personal freedom and availability of choice as roots of instability, without knowing to the contrary that the source of instability and discontent would come from rule by an undemocratic minority government.

Capitalism is definitely preferred to socialism, for various reasons. Capitalism cherishes individual endowments, as it enables the individual to gain and contribute to the economy, while externalities are dealt with through the rule of law and established regulations. Abuse by the minority is minimized, though checks and balances need to be enforced to ensure transparency and equality. In short, the capitalist engine would have to run on its own, but continuous monitoring would be needed to avoid breakdown, malfunctioning, or control by ill-intentioned leaders. The discussions so far have touched on analyses in four related areas of the political economy: (1) intuitive discussion on the behavior of individual persons and conceptual differences between social disciplines; (2) features of the five groups of the world economies; (3) capitalist development among Asian economies; and (4) systemic differences between mainland China and Hong Kong amidst much political and ideological controversy. The two chapters in this summary section are intended to make an intuitive attempt to distinguish the pros and cons of the two ideologies, comparing and contrasting their strengths and how the human race should embrace capitalism when it is redefined and reinterpreted in a more contemporary framework, focusing on substances and ingredients.

Why Has Socialism Failed?

I INTRODUCTION

If a person were to take a birds-eye view of the world economy since the end of the Second World War, one could summarize a few crucial trends in the political economy of the world. Foremost was the ideological divide between the West and the Soviet Union, followed by the Cold War that lasted for four decades. The Cold War was tense at various times, but it was due eventually to the economic weakness of the communist Soviet Union that could not compete with the West over the political bond between US President Ronald Reagan and British Prime Minister Margaret Thatcher. After the disintegration of the Soviet Union, many former Soviet states gained independence, but subsequent Russian leaders did not change their ideological views.

Secondly, the United Nations, together with a number of international institutions, was established supposedly to bring lasting peace and aid to poor countries. At the same time, a number of former colonies were given independence, and were expected to grow. The industrialized countries contributed to the funding of the international institutions. However, many poor countries did not make much progress, and their economic situation remained largely weak. There were indeed many types of conflict in poor countries that made stability a remote possibility. One really should wonder what had been going on for so long between the funding institutions and the recipient countries. There are studies that have questioned the role and effectiveness of international institutions in world development. For example, international economic institutions concentrated mainly on examining short- to medium-term forecasts of individual economies without making changes to the fundamental issues.

Since the late 1970s, many world leaders and economies believe that aiding communist China could be an acceptable strategy in world development. While many western economies were attracted to China's potential market and the low costs of production, aid from foreign governments, international institutions, and foreign direct investment to China became "one-way traffic." It was true that the world economy benefitted from low cost production in China, and world inflation could have been lowered, China did experience unprecedented rapid growth, and by the turn of the 21st century, China's growth escalated to have the largest trade surplus and international reserves in the world, raising China to the second largest economy in the world. China's growth would surely be seen quantitatively, but China's rise has also brought unwanted problems. Domestically, China focused on quantifiable factors and performance, but lacked improvement in behavior and practices. China's rise has alarmed the world with various types of behavior, including corruption, production of fake products, and

© 2017 Elsevier Inc. All rights reserved.

violation of intellectual property rights. Regionally, China is building up its military strength in the East China Sea and South China Sea. In short, while the world economy since 1978 had aided China to grow, the economic rise of China has instead imposed uncertainty on its neighbors in the region.

The oil exporting countries held the key to the world supply of energy, and amassed large reserves, but there are still numerous conflicts, instability, and uncertainty in many oil exporting countries. Much of the oil revenue could have been channeled to activities conducted by extremist groups, thereby threatening the international community with different forms of terrorist attacks. Around 2014, the instability in the Middle East and North African countries had caused a massive outflow of refugees across the Mediterranean to reach southern European countries. The show of "sympathy" caused controversy among member countries in the European Union (EU), as millions of refugees fled to the more advanced countries. While there was international rescue, few asked why these fragile states were exporting refugees, and how the advanced countries could economically absorb the large numbers of refugees with welfare provision and servicing the resulting social burden.

Looking at these various world features and phenomena, one could ask if the world economy has progressed or deteriorated since the end of the Second World War. Has the developed world spent too much on aid, or has aid gone to the wrong hands? Would the developed countries do a better job by providing bilateral aid to individual developing countries, instead of giving multilateral aid through international institutions? Have the officials in international institutions done their part in ensuring that assistance did lead to development? Or there is a need for more concentration on improving the domestic issues in each country in the first instance? A number of humanitarian issues have been the focus of international institutions for decades. For example, the issues of income equality and reduction in poverty have been tackled for decades and numerous resources had been committed, yet there is still inequality and poverty in the world. Should the focus be changed from poverty reduction to productivity promotion? When individuals' productivity improves, these individuals naturally depart from the poverty pool. Similarly, should income equality be replaced by a focus on job opportunities? With more job opportunities, difference in pay and earnings would still be unequal, but individuals would have the economic ability to fulfill their own welfare needs.

Has the world economy been plagued by policy decisions that imposed excessive "social costs" on industrialized countries? In short, there was an excessive amount of socialist policies in the world economy that immensely expanded the provision of "free lunches" and allowed individuals to unrestrictedly "take," but at the same time there was no improvement or sufficient replenishment on the productivity side of the equation. As the overall "social cost" increased, there would be less and less people willing to take up their "private cost" or people are more prepared to pass their "private cost" to the society, as the rapid rise in "social cost" was so alarming that individuals might as well decide to jump on the "bandwagon." The ultimate question is how much of their resources economies would have to mobilize to pay for the rising "social cost."

There are two groups of left-wing economies. The communist groups consist mainly of Russia and China along with a few dynastic communists states, such as North Korea and Cuba. Political ideology takes prime consideration in this group of communist countries. Claimed to have "freed" their people from imperialism and capitalism, the communist countries are the least free countries, as power is concentrated and decisions are often personality-driven. The second group of "soft socialist" countries consists of a number of world economies that have either elected socialist leaders or adopted socialist policies that have weakened their economic competitiveness considerably. Political considerations have often eaten into economic performance, and economic tools are used to satisfy political goals and ambitions. Hence, the politically distorted economy would be bogged down by the political decisions. Genuine economic goals could not be achieved, and the low performance in economic activities would further spill over to the need for more political decisions.

The next two sections will discuss the drawbacks of the two types of socialist countries. Before concluding, the section on Brexit will relate the discussion to the implications and lessons for European and other world economies. With the exercise and deployment of socialist policies in numerous countries, Brexit basically conveys the message that "enough is enough," and there will be a return to rightist economic policies and principles to rebuild and restrengthen countries' competitiveness and capability.

II COMMUNISM: POWER CONCENTRATION

The ideology of Marxism and communism provides a vivid discussion on the difference between theory and practice, between concepts and realities, and between what is said and what is done. The advocacy in communism is that a state without capitalists should be best, as there would be no "exploitation" of people by people, as they would become their own masters. But it turned out that a communist country would be a much stronger, more powerful, and undemocratic state that exercised close control of individuals. Visible control would be administered by the military and police, while invisible control would be undertaken by the "united front," propaganda and media, and threats. In a communist state, different opinions could be voiced but not broadcast, while acts of opposition would be suppressed. Instead of being one's own master, a communist state was usually ruled by a minority of party members in association with government officials, supported by a vast network of intelligence-gathering to pin down all forms of opposition that could lead to potential threats.

As the Marxists argued that capitalism exploited people by people, there would not be any private business in a communist state. Hence, state provision of economic materials would be most "equal," as no one would have any privilege, nor could employers "exploit" the workers. There would not be any employers, workers would be assigned to jobs by the state, and there would be no unemployed resources. Human beings would live with dignity, as the state would look after every individual. However, it turned out that economic materials would be allocated sufficiently to all individuals, but insufficiency would appear if there was a shortage of materials. The allocation of materials would be managed by officials, who would accept bribes if any individual wanted to be treated differently. Hence, instead of "exploitation" by employers, it would become "exploitation" by empowered officials.

Workers would be provided with a job, but job satisfaction, promotion, and incentives could be considered along political lines, and did not depend on the workers' initiative and productivity. The top down approach in job assignment and industrial production would mean workers might not have the freedom or right to change jobs. It would likely be life-time secured employment, but choice and job preference would not be guaranteed. Since workers would be paid a similarly low wage, other welfare supplies, such as housing, children's education, and medical attention would also be provided, but might not be adequate or the provisions would be based on political hierarchies.

To adhere to the principle of equality, individuals would not be allowed to hold wealth and assets. Private savings would not be required, and consumer choice would not be given. As enterprises were part of the state organ, enterprises would have to submit their surplus to the state, which would have full authority to distribute or redistribute surpluses, probably along ideological preferences. The "wealth" would be amassed at the state level, as economic power would simply be concentrated in the hands of the state and the top officials. One could ask if workers were being protected by the state, or being "exploited" by the state. The so-called "surplus" was no longer held by individuals and businesses, but would be massed in the hands of the state leaders and officials.

The intellectuals and the media would be the most vulnerable people in a communist state, as the former would provide thoughts, while the latter would report things that might not align with the ideas of the state. Under a communist state, people should have a "simple" mind and just listen and trust what was told and given. Suggestions, proposals, ideas, disagreements, innovations, and initiatives might not be entertained as they could pose potential challenges to the absolute power and authority of the state. Indeed, the absence of nonstate activities would produce a "stable" society, as government officials would be the only agents that would conduct activities. Hence, to assume a stateless society in communism would be naive, as the policy decisions would all be concentrated in the hands of party members and government officials.

Communism in practice produced extreme forms of inequality, with power concentration solely vested in one minority group. When compared to a capitalist market economy, the production relationship between employers and employees in a communist country would be transformed into the state-owned enterprises and workers relationship. The market wage payment and differences in earnings in businesses would be transformed into the provision of a net wage and welfare support. Consumer choice would be transformed into material rationing by the state. Personal initiatives in production and intellectual freedom would be transformed into state control and monitoring of individual deeds. Instead of freedom of expression, ownership, and adherence to intellectual property rights, communist countries would prefer not to have a reliable rule of law, as that could provide the officials with "flexibility" to deal with individual legal cases. Civic development that relied on systems would be transformed into control through the personality of the leader. There would not be any nonpolitical institutions, but party members were all-powerful while the mass was powerless. Control was achieved through personal dictatorship, rather than the establishment of a reliable system. With a lack of individualistic behavior and freedom of thought that used to propel society to move forward, people in communist countries would just have to wait to be given, and take whatever was given. The extent of immobility would effectively freeze a country in time, as people just lived to survive on state provisions.

In a nutshell, the drawback in the communist ideology is that it transformed all sorts of human activities into activities with "absolute" outcomes of different extremes, making one-sided decisions, amassing of power, topdown control, and absence of choice and alternatives. In actuality, communism produces extremes of political

V. WHY HAS CAPITALISM SUCCEEDED?

inequality, erosion of individual freedom, privilege of the powerful with corrupt practices, personality-led policies with no support from a well-established and reliable system, and political victimization on opposing views. These extremes largely reflected communism in the Soviet Union. Given that the Soviet Union was not blessed with many economic resources on the one hand, and the drive for ideological and military supremacy in the Cold War on the other, resource constraint meant that shortages of materials were common. The situation in pre-1978 China was similar, as China adopted the Soviet model inappropriately after the early 1950s. The commune system stripped all aspects of individualism and introduced collectivism. Economic equality was synonymous with poverty, while party members were privileged. Power absolutism and ideological high-handedness was practiced in all communist countries.

In the case of the Soviet Union, it was President Mikhail Gorbachev, whose attitude on openness had hastened the end of the Cold War, and it was argued that his decision to remove the constitutional role of the Communist Party in governing the state had led to the dissolution of the Soviet Union. While President Gorbachev was more receptive to the West, he criticized his followers in post-Soviet Russia. For example, he criticized President Vladimir Putin for "backsliding on democracy, corruption, and the dominance of security officers." Thus, instead of moving away from communism, power in post-Gorbachev Russia was concentrated in the executive branch, and limited the rights and freedom of individuals and the establishment of civic organizations. Gorbachev commented that such was a "destructive path with no future" (Mikhail Gorbachev, *Wikipedia*).

In the case of China, despite the rise in economic growth since the early 1980s, inequality emerged in various dimensions. Politically, power was vested firmly in the hands of the communist party, and would even be reinforced by the rising economy because the party had become the "wealthiest" institution in the world. The country was still ruled by a minority government, divided into at least two major factions. Corruption and abuse of power could commonly be found, and despite the effort to hunt down corrupt "tigers and flies" in government circles, the effort was seen more as a case of political struggle than the introduction of a reliable anticorruption system. Economic growth was transformed into a "cash rich" situation, with many ultra-wealthy individuals related to high level officials. After nearly four decades of growth, industrial production probably would have reached a bottleneck unless there was industrial restructuring. The unstructured financial development had led to rapid growth in the financial economy, which had grown disproportionately to the real economy. State-owned enterprises were replaced by state-controlled enterprises. Production of fake goods remained common, as one popular Chinese business person openly stated that "fake products were better than the real products both in quality and in price" (*Financial Times*, June 14, 2016; and *The Wall Street Journal*, June 15, 2016).

The economic rise of China had led to an imbalance in regional harmony, especially in the East China Sea and the South China Sea. With China flexing its economic muscles, and together with the weaker world economy after 2008, the world economy would begin to give new consideration to their economic relationship with China. China's economic attraction in the form of low labor costs and a large domestic market for imports would have to be reassessed, though some were still eager to kowtow to China for the export market. Given the rise in the Chinese currency, the world economy would have a choice of either investing in China or investing elsewhere and trading with China. The lesson is that given the world's generous economic attention to China over the last four decades or so, China's economic rise might not be considered as a good "showcase" to other developing countries, due probably to China's ideological rigidity, and lack of political advance and alignment with the major world economies.

III SOCIALISM: AMASSING SOCIAL COST

In the second group of "soft" socialist countries, proleftist policies had been instituted through the political process, such as the election of socialist leaders and/or pursuit of strong welfare and redistribution policies. Political diversity in free economies allowed differences in political views, but elections could produce leaders that looked to political goals. Such humanitarian pursuits as income equality and assistance to the minority were politically translated into economic policies. Given that, in all world economies, the number of low-endowment individuals would be larger than the quantity of high-endowment individuals, there would be a need to provide assistance to those who were faced with difficulty in economic survival, but politically oriented "redistributive" policies would have different impacts on different economies. Thus, politicians interested in achieving political goals might not be concerned with the economic cost involved, because they would not be responsible for footing the economic bills during their term of office. While political goals are usually short-term, consequences on the economy could be long-term. Given periodical elections, political leaders would have departed before the economic consequences of their political decisions surfaced. Hence, there is surely an agency problem between political decisions and economic consequences.

A prosocialist regime in a free economy usually took a "two legs" strategy. On the one hand, there would be political pressure to reduce income inequality and poverty. This could be a political ideal, but strategy could differ. A "supply-side" policy would employ indirect means that would promote investment, improve education and training, and speed up infrastructure development with the intention of creating more job opportunities. Supply-side results could only materialize after a period of time. A left-wing leader may not welcome more investment, as that would allow businesses to make profits. Thus, a socialist leader would choose a "demand-side" policy on welfare provision. Taxing the rich seemed to produce political capital to the socialist leaders, as capitalists were often made synonymous to "villains." With high taxes, a socialist leader would think that higher revenue would be forthcoming. The demand-side policy fitted short-term political goals, as that could produce results within a short time, as taxes were raised, fiscal spending was undertaken, subsidies were given, and redistribution was achieved, thereby accomplishing the political goal.

But, a few periods of short-term policies would produce long-term outcomes. Consider how demand-side policies would produce unfavorable economic results in the long-term on the part of investors, businesses, tax payers, and subsidy recipients. Of course, there could be instances where capital inflow coexisted with a high tax regime, depending on the nature of the business and the size of the market. In businesses where machines are needed more than workers, e.g., the small number of workers required could mean a saving on labor costs. In exceptional cases, investment could still be viable if the market was sufficiently large.

Capital is mobile and flows to business-friendly markets. An investor always has the choice to invest or not to invest. Investors will probably gain by investing, but will not lose by not investing. Outflow of capital would mean a reduction in jobs at home. Capital mobility allows investors to have a greater choice of investments across time, markets, and countries. On the contrary, when investors found that an economy became unattractive, capital could flow out. Departed capital would be unlikely to return, but would promote the economy of the host country. In turn, the "capital-losing" economy would become less competitive, while the "capital-gaining" economy would become more competitive. Hence, there is a transfer of economic competitiveness. To the home country, that will be translated in terms of losses in jobs, output, exports, income, and growth. In a worse scenario, the capital that has gone to the host country could produce goods that would be imported back to the home country, which would suffer losses not only in investment, but also in foreign exchange and reserves, as the rise in imports will then be translated into a decline in the value of the currency.

On the part of the government, the departed capital would mean lower production at home, a fall in output, jobs, and employment, and the fall in profits would lower government tax revenue. Government revenues could fluctuate, but committed fiscal subsidies and welfare spending could not be reduced. The loss of jobs and rise in unemployment would require more fiscal welfare spending. Thus, the government would be faced with the two sides of the sword: the loss of capital and jobs would result in loss of competitiveness, a rise in unemployment would require greater expenditure on welfare, and the shrinkage in business would mean less revenue will be forthcoming. On balance, the government would end up with fiscal deficits. How would a prosocialist government deal with a fiscal deficit? A demand-side policy should imply that even higher taxes would be needed, as it would be the able individuals who were "punished," and higher taxes would be thought to bring higher revenue. This would hasten the departure of capital to business-friendly markets, resulting in a further shrinkage of the business sector, and subsequently even lower fiscal revenues.

The alternative would be to issue government bonds, a decision to issue bonds usually would not receive much criticism, because the monetary authority would have the power to do so, and no one from the current generation would get hurt. It would be the future generation that would have to repay the debt. However, government bonds issued to cover fiscal deficits would not generate productivity that could provide the ability to repay, and the unpaid bonds would accumulate to become national debts. Consequently, the outcome would be a situation where "deficits-breed-deficits" and "debts-breed-debts" emerged. A prosocialist elected leader would probably have finished his or her term of office by the time these unfavorable results occurred.

What about the welfare recipients? Would the provision of "free lunches" make them better off? The short-term answer should be positive, but the dynamic nature of economics could produce other consequences. If welfare subsidies were provided on a permanent basis, the recipients would surely have lower incentives to look for productive jobs, and would become dependent on subsidy. Even if the number of welfare-dependent workers involved was small, their exclusion from the labor market would mean a fall in overall economic productivity. Incentives could include making efforts to look for jobs, learning a skill, or moving to a more job-favorable geographical location. The welfare subsidy could only cover their survival cost, but employment should provide the

V. WHY HAS CAPITALISM SUCCEEDED?

worker with a higher or rising wage, as experience gained could enable the worker to save or have more to spend. In other words, employed workers could accumulate their own assets over time. But when workers depend on welfare subsidies and do not equip themselves with higher individual endowments or human capital, their chance of seeking employment will be lower. Thus, the consequence would be a static labor force, high reluctance on the part of workers to seek employment, and the persistence of low wages. With welfare subsidies, workers who would be assisted permanently would not have any chance of gaining any upward mobility. In aggregate, welfare expenditures would not reduce poverty and would even restrict upward mobility. In effect, welfare spending effectively freezes society in its current status, as employment, earnings, and upward mobility would all be maintained at the current level.

It looks as if the welfare recipients gained, but they could be instruments used by the politicians. Given that the quantity of low-endowment individuals would always be higher than the quantity of high-endowment individuals, prosocialist politicians could easily secure their popularity by siding with the low-endowment individuals, but whether prosocialist economic policies would be a viable policy would not be a political concern. Indeed, many low-endowment individuals would politically not object to become dependent on welfare, as "free lunches" could be preferred to employed work. In fact, welfare recipients would also face losses, as the welfare subsidy they receive takes away their chance of getting a better job in the market. The welfare subsidy would become static, but the dynamics should be that an individual working in the market could earn more with experience, or by moving up to a higher paid job, and so on. Hence, economic opportunities and the chance of upward mobility would be lost. The welfare recipient would remain "poor."

Then, who gained? The prosocialist politicians, as they would obtain power and authority through elections, have the desire to spend public funds which come from the tax payers, and behave like a "Santa Claus" when deciding on welfare policies. Demand-side policies are not only unsustainable, but also weaken the economy permanently. Capital and funds depart, jobs are lost, welfare spending is higher, higher taxes and more redistribution are required, there is loss of upward mobility and economic competitiveness, and low domestic production would mean more imports are needed for local consumption, and a weakened currency with trade imbalances results. Prosocialist politicians gain, but the entire economy suffers for the loss.

Supply-side policies that involved fiscal spending on education, housing, health, social goods, and infrastructure provision should be regarded as supplementary factors to all businesses and individuals. On the contrary, fiscal spending on demand-side policies requires an understanding on the notion of social cost. The size of the "social cost" and the extent and amount of welfare provisions often become a political decision. Redistributive policies basically imply that the "private cost" of those low-endowment individuals would have to be passed on to become a "social cost" of the high-endowment individuals through the fiscal authority of the government. Likewise, by introducing more redistributive policies, the government effectively increases its size, authority, influence, and position through the need to manage the larger "social cost" burden. As more welfare spending is needed, there would be more administrative work on the part of the government, the number of government officials would have to expand, and a "big government" would emerge. By taking up all these "social costs," the government would have stronger justification to raise taxes and engage in redistribution activities. The rise in "social costs" and the need for more redistributive policies would reinforce itself in a prosocialist government.

It could even be possible that the movement between "private cost" and "social cost" is inversely correlated, as the rise of one would lead to a fall in the other. Indeed, as more welfare was given, people would be more prepared to pass their "private cost" to be shouldered by the government, and the "social cost" would rise. The shrinkage of "private cost" on the one hand, would immediately expand the size of the "social cost" on the other hand. On the contrary, when welfare spending was cut, the lower fiscal burden of the government would reduce the size of the "social cost." In turn, with lower welfare provision, welfare recipients would have to look for alternatives, implying that they would have to take back their own "private cost." In other words, deficit-prone or debt-prone countries would mean that their level of "social cost" had exceeded their ability to finance, and the government would have to shed their "social cost" burden by reducing welfare, so as to encourage individuals to take back their "private cost."

Socialism in many market economies failed because they had amassed excessive amounts of "social cost" that went beyond the economy's ability to fund or finance the prolonged debts and deficits. Countries that pursued extensive prosocialist policies suffered the worst of both worlds. On the one hand, the policy of redistribution with high taxation produced unfriendly markets, and capital departure would reduce the economy's competitiveness. On the other hand, the demand-side policies that promoted fiscal spending would result in various drawbacks: fiscal and trade deficits, a weak currency, and national debt. The disincentive on the part of individuals and businesses in taking up their "private costs," and the generous welfare policy that encouraged individuals to give up their "private costs" would result in the huge accumulation of "social cost." The final outcome would be the emergence of a vicious economic circle that restricted growth and promoted decline.

IV THE BREXIT LESSONS

Many British and European citizens, international leaders, economists, and analysts were caught by surprise when the British referendum on June 23, 2016, voted that Great Britain would exit from membership of the EU, with the leave vote winning by 52%–48% (*BBC News*, June 24, 2016). The superficial evidence against Brexit included the loss of the bigger EU market, and such economic advantages as investment and employment for British nationals in the EU. The question, then, was if there were truly that many economic advantages, why would the majority of voters chose to leave the EU?

Consider a few analytical observations. Firstly, economic activities between United Kingdom and the EU are mutual, and there is no change in their economic fundamentals. The vote was a political move, though it would create a temporary shock in stock markets. It is true that the EU is a much larger market than the United Kingdom, but the UK itself is not that a small market on its own. The United Kingdom also can reach out to the international market like any major EU country. Being a member of the EU, the United Kingdom also made financial submissions to the EU headquarters. Exiting from the EU, the UK economy could save all those official submissions. In 2015, it was reported that the UK government contributed £13 billion to the EU budget, and the EU spending on the United Kingdom was £4.5 billion, making a net contribution of £8.5 billion to the EU (*The UK's Independent Factchecking Charity*, May 27, 2016; and *The Telegraph*, February 29, 2016). Thus, even if there was a reduction of economic activities between the United Kingdom and EU countries after Brexit, the simple calculation is whether the loss to the United Kingdom would have to exceed £8.5 billion annually.

Originally, the European market comprised of a few strong industrialized countries that were backed up high technology industries with exports. Over the years, many industrialized European countries have adopted prosocialist economic policies, which often involved heavy redistribution and demand-side policies that eventually weakened their economies considerably. Furthermore, as the EU community expanded, weaker European countries were incorporated and imposed new economic burdens on the few industrialized EU members. Hence, the entire EU community was bogged down by various economic problems of the weaker EU members.

The political turning point was the huge influx of refugees from the Middle Eastern, West Asian, and North African countries between 2014 and 2016. Instead of stopping the flow of refugees at their origins, German Chancellor Angela Merkel adopted an "open door" policy by openly accepting one million refugees in 2015 alone (*The Guardian*, December 8, 2015). The United Nations Higher Commission for Refugees (UNHCR) pledged the international community to accept refugees, but few efforts were made to stop the flow. However, it was later found that there was a security problem, as the refugee flows included a "Trojan horse," with terrorists camouflaged among the refugees (*CNN Politics*, November 16, 2015).

Should sympathy and fraternity be incorporated into an ideology? It is a human virtue when a person expresses sympathy for another person suffering from unfortunate circumstances. Sympathetic offerings can be in the form of personal services, and offerings in pecuniary terms are often limited to the financial ability of the giving individual. The economics of sympathy at the individual level involve only pecuniary transactions, and the receiver of the offering will not impose additional economic burdens on the giving individual. At the country level, disaster relief is provided when crises and disasters strike in certain affected areas. This could be a lump sum from government funds, depending on the extent of destruction. But, the amount would still be restricted, and there would be no extra burden on the relief providers. At the international level, when one country is faced with natural disasters or crises, international aid could come to the rescue as a humanitarian gesture and goodwill from a foreign country or the international community. Again, the relief would usually be a limited amount, and there would be no additional burden on the relief-providing country.

Sympathy and fraternity should not carry any political message or implications, as it is meant to be a reflection of humanity and goodwill. However, it would be a different ballgame if sympathy and fraternity was politicized or capitalized for political purposes. Sympathy and fraternity could also be mobilized by free-ride politicians to become an instrument in reflecting a social phenomenon. It would indeed be easy to express one's sympathy, but similar to the provision of welfare, the politician would not be responsible for the relief provision, but would pass it on to someone else, namely the tax payers. It could be worse if the amount of relief burden was not a one-time payment, but required post-event expenses. Sympathy expressed at the personal level could be escalated to an ideological level, requiring prolonged fiscal commitment that would simply impose extra burdens on the size of the "social cost."

The problem of the refugees was that even though it was Germany which was keen to open its doors to the refugees, once they obtained EU status they would travel to the English speaking United Kingdom for jobs and welfare. Hence, it was Germany who was keen to express sympathy and get the political capital from shouldering the burden of the refugees, but the burden of the high "social cost" would fall onto UK tax payers. On the other hand, low-skilled British workers would face strong competition from incoming refugees as the supply of workers increased. Hence, other than the British tax payers who would see that their interests were hurt by the influx of refugees, ordinary workers, including earlier immigrants who had managed to find employment in Britain, would definitely feel threatened by the incoming refugees as competition in the labor market could reduce their chance of employment. Thus, the preference to leave the EU came from tax payers and salaried workers.

There is also the social dimension in receiving illegal refugees. In addition to welfare expenses, how easily and quickly would these refugees integrate into the local economy, or would they form small ethnic colonies inside the host country? Hence, welfare assistance may not just include the amount of entitlement, but also the impact on schools, hospitals, and housing would add to the required resources. In some cases, these refugees would send the welfare back to their home country for families in need. In addition, there is also the cultural, ethical, racial, religious, and language divide, especially when crimes, violence, and acts of terrorism are committed by these refugees. Hence, one can imagine the risk involved in the security of the host country and its people.

There was also the political side in the lessons of Brexit, when British politicians looked forward to the next general election. While the Conservative Party, led by Prime Minister David Cameron, who advocated for "remain," the Labor Party in Britain also chose to support the "remain" ticket. What the British Labor Party failed to see was the sentiment of the workers who were uncomfortable with the influx of refugees competing for jobs. Hence, the Conservative Party would likely win the next British election, whatever the outcome of the referendum would be. Should the referendum have voted to "remain," the Conservative Party would have benefitted from the political capital from the referendum, as both the Conservative Party and Labor Party advocated for "remain." With the referendum result of "leave," and subsequent resignation by Prime Minister David Cameron, the new Conservative Prime Minister Teresa May would have to steer the "exit" policy, and that would provide credibility for the Conservative Party to win the next election. Thus, the Brexit referendum was an excellent political strategy on the part of the Conservative Party in improving their chance to win the next general election in the United Kingdom.

Although the stock market all over the world experienced some shocks and the British pound depreciated, the shocks soon settled as the value of the British pound revived, and the international stock markets returned to normal. Investors and speculators usually look for events like Brexit to give them an opportunity to trade and gain in the stock markets. Hence, it would not have any long-term impact after some initial shocks in the international stock markets. It would indeed be simple-minded to think that the British economy would suffer from leaving the EU. Politically, as Boris Johnson, the former London Mayor, advocated repeatedly, the United Kingdom could regain its own autonomy in dealing with various issues without interference or concern with the EU community (*RealClear Politics*, June 21, 2016). In many ways, it would be easier to revise the economic competitiveness in the single UK economy than the collective EU member countries. The strategy would have to come from the supply-side factors, such as tax reduction that boosted business confidence and attracted investment from the EU (*Mail Online*, July 3, 2016). Should the post-Brexit British government decide to adopt more business-friendly policies, such as a lowering of profit tax, investment could even leave the EU and come to the United Kingdom. Thus, with Brexit, the chance of regaining its economic competitiveness will be high for the UK economy.

The first lesson of Brexit is that the British voters were not prepared to shoulder the economic "social cost" of refugees, as the UK government might not have control over the influx once these refugees entered from other EU countries. By departing from the EU which has taken up numerous prosocialist policies, the UK economy could look for fresh policies that could lead to new economic directions and pathways. The favorable outcomes of Brexit should be seen in 3–5 years' time, when the new policies in the UK lead to a recovery of economic competitiveness, while countries in the EU probably will remain stagnant and stay unchanged. The end result should be a stronger UK economy, partly because the United Kingdom will be able to get away from the "social cost" burden of the EU, and partly because it will give the United Kingdom new opportunities to plan its own economic path. It is even possible that the UK economy will lead the economies of other EU members.

Would Brexit lead to more "Eurexit"? As the size of the EU's "social cost" was jumping, other EU members could see the advantage of, or the need for exiting, especially those EU countries which were not keen to adopt prosocialist policies. The implications of Brexit should relate more to other EU members than to the United Kingdom. Indeed, the EU should rethink its strategies in relation to its refugee policy, and question whether extensive demand-side policies are appropriate and sustainable. The refugee issue and Brexit could serve as a "wake up" call to the EU. If there was the desire to reduce its "social cost" burden, the EU would have to revise its policy orientations. Instead of "demand-side" policies, the EU would have to adopt "supply-side" policies, in order to revitalize and reenergize its economic competitiveness by restricting further decline and encouraging growth.

Indeed, there are a number of EU countries that could be revitalized easily if prosocialist and prowelfare "demand-side" economic policies were replaced by "supply-side" policies promoting business-friendliness. Such medium-sized EU countries as Spain and Portugal could gradually replace their redistributive policy by promoting more entrepreneurship and reintroducing a low tax environment, in order to attract business and investment. Indeed, the ultimate objective is to regain economic vigor in these countries through market-friendliness, and individuality through creativity and innovation. The prolonged adoption of prosocialist policies in many EU countries has limited regional growth considerably, the lack of growth in turn has contributed to economic decline. And the economic decline in the EU would comparatively culminate in the economic rise of other countries through "push" and "pull" effects in investment and other economic activities. The implication of Brexit would be the extent of accumulated economic weakness brought about by prosocialist economic policies, and the desire to regain a country's economic strength through cutting the excessive "social cost" burden and reinstituting the role of individuals being responsible for their "private cost." The lesson of Brexit is that the EU has taken up too many socialist policies, and it is time to look for answers elsewhere, probably from the "rightist" ideology and from "supply-side" economics.

V CONCLUSION

Have world leaders mixed up personal sympathy and fraternity with political ideology? It is necessary to provide economic assistance to people with low endowments in all economies, but assistance should be structured in such a way that it will stimulate the recipients, and not make the recipients dependent on the assistance. Assistance should only be given within the economic ability of the giver. An agency problem exists in the provision of economic assistance, as the policy decision-makers are not the actual funders of the assistance, as the spending decisions made by officials are separated from the financiers who are the tax payers. Socialists tend to complain about the extent of economic exploitation by capitalists. This assumes the dichotomous nature between employers and workers. The logic is that employers create jobs, and workers should be free to move between jobs. Hence, employers need workers, and vice versa. Thus, their relationship should be complementary. Economic activity produces "relative" outcomes, whereas political activity generates "absolute" outcomes or extremes. Political inequality is worse than economic inequality, because political relationships are often "one-way," while choices and alternatives are often available in economic relationships.

Communism failed because it generated extreme and absolute political inequality and a privileged minority, and individual freedom was severely restricted and suppressed. Socialism failed because the large government reinforced itself by amassing the increasing "social cost" that demoted growth and promoted decline. The economic spillovers from socialist economic policies included the possible departure of capital funds and loss of domestic jobs, and the loss in output led to economic shrinkage. The fall in economic competitiveness would not only contain a loss that would spread across the entire economy, but the economic opportunity of the future generation would also be restricted as national debts hurt the economic potential of the younger generation.

Consider the analysis of some humanitarian issues, such as poverty reduction and attainment of equality. Numerous studies (e.g., Huidrom et al., 2016) by the United Nations and other international institutions have for decades called for poverty reduction and elimination of inequality. If there were effective policies to deal with poverty and inequality, how come these issues are still vividly alive in many developing countries today? How would all these international institutions explain such an outcome after spending so much on their studies, research, and consultancies? The emphasis could depend on how policies have been recommended and executed. Demand-side policies would encourage more spending to aid the poor. Supply-side policies would improve productivity through education and the creation of job opportunities. Productivity improvement would reduce poverty, but inequality could remain.

However, which world economy has ever achieved economic equality? Differences in endowments, differences in education provision, differences in earnings and rewards, and differences in many other input factors suggest economic outcomes are diverse. Economists would use the term "difference," while politicians would use the term "inequality" to indicate the extent of diversity among economic activities. Given that economic activities produce "relative" outcomes, it would be natural for the emergence of diversity, differences, or inequality. Political inequality is more damaging and "absolute," while economic inequality can be improved. Economic differences should not be politicized. Economic growth and development through supply-side policies are the effective answers to poverty reduction. Politics often turn out to be the obstacle to genuine economic progress.

Brexit should not be considered as a protectionist policy, but an attempt to reduce the country's vast "social cost" imposed by other EU members and refugees from fragile states. Economic vitality has been given a higher priority than fraternity. Indeed, it is the promotion of productivity and growth that allows an economy to have the resources to help others. On the contrary, it would not be viable for a country to accept an economic burden that was not generated by its own people. Fraternity does not mean that one economy's ability is constrained by the problems originated in another country.

Brexit symbolized the failure and unsustainability of prosocialist economic policies. The weakness in economic competitiveness in many European and world economies has to come to an end, and political efforts have to concentrate on revitalizing the country's economic strength. The UK referendum has shown that there is no change in the economic fundamentals between the United Kingdom and EU, but the UK economy would be brought down by the burden of the "social cost." Hence, instead of spending the UK's resources shouldering the "social cost," the same amount of resources could be productively used to expand the UK economy, making it more competitive and regaining its vitality through a different set of principles and policies. Given that there is no change in economic fundamentals, the political argument of Brexit was only superficial.

Brexit serves as the precedent to show that socialist economic policies are not sustainable, and other European and world economies should start to think about the undesirability of socialist economic policies, and make comparisons with capitalist economies. The voters in democratic countries should start making political assessments when looking at the numerous problems arising from the adoption of socialist economic policies, such as rising national debt, falling economic competitiveness, loss of individual economic control but increase in the size of the government, losing export markets and falling investment attractiveness resulting from redistribution policies, and growing economic dependence with lack of opportunities. Politically, there is every possibility that "right wing" parties will be elected in democratic countries in the post-Brexit years, as voters in democratic countries would like to regain their economic vitality, recover their competitiveness, and expand their economic capability.

20

How Capitalism Works

I INTRODUCTION

To understand how capitalism can serve the global economy, it is necessary to pull all the relevant areas of discussion under one roof in order to see how each area of discussion is connected to the others. In other words, one needs to consider both the intra- and interrelationships between and among the discussion areas. While it would be natural to cherish the success of an economy, analysis on complacency would not get far. In most cases, progress can be made by examining the various inadequacies, which could positively be regarded as advice and suggestions, but could negatively be regarded as criticisms. Economic activities are all connected with each other, and some have opposing impacts on others. The chain-like or globe-like relationships in economic decisions could make life difficult, as a decision aimed at the solution of one problem could create another problem, and in turn new solutions might then result in new problems, and so on. Environmental protection could be considered as the classic example. All human beings have to survive, but the process of survival imposes costs on the environment, such as overpopulation, constraints on agricultural output, creation of garbage, and requirement for new habitable land for human development, and so on. Human activities are full of externalities, but it will only be the intelligence of the human race that can protect the environment.

Since politics has no physical form, economic activities have been used as political instruments for political purposes. But, since economic decisions can be politically motivated and are not necessarily made for economic ends, the results may earn political capital, but could produce economic distortions of one type or another. Consequently, economic distortions could be cumulative, but may not be attended to if these distortions do not fall into the decision sphere of political leaders. On the contrary, politicians holding different ideologies would equally use economic activities as a means to gain their political goals. Hence, political and ideological fights between parties and factions would only mean that economic activities would be massaged for political ends, but unfavorable economic consequences would either be ignored or dealt with by the need for other political decisions. Thus, different types of political decisions would influence economic policies, and the outcomes of these

© 2017 Elsevier Inc. All rights reserved.

economic policies could produce economic inconsistencies, distortions, and knots. And when people complain about these economic outcomes, further action would be called for.

The creation, possession, availability, and deployment of economic resources are the central issues in all economic activities and policy decisions. Globally, the political decision of one country that involved some sort of economic activity would also produce economic outcomes in another economy. The pace and magnitude of global economic connectivity would generate different economic results. Within a single economy, the "intraconsequence" would be that some economic sectors would benefit more than others, or at the expense of others. Within the global economy, the "interconsequence" would also be that some countries would benefit more than others, or at the expense of others. The difference in personal endowment applies to differences in country endowments across the world economy.

This concluding chapter aims to serve a number of purposes. One purpose will be to consolidate some of the findings, observations, and arguments about the global economy, focusing on the major economic knots accumulated over the years as a result of differences in countries' endowments, and consequent political and economic policies. The second purpose will concentrate on the importance and relevance of the role played by the industrialized countries on the global scene. Despite the group of emerging economies, the world economy will still be led by the industrialized countries, as shown by the advantages their ideologies have. It will be their responsibility and role to promote and police the next stage of the world economy.

What remains will be to elaborate on the virtues of capitalism and how it promotes civilization, permits freedom of individuals, productivity and economic revival after crises, and progress based on maximization of economic "relativity." There is no perfection in any ideology, but the best is to identify, adopt, and practice a most suitable, appropriate, effective, and functional ideology that benefits all individuals. And although benefits differ among individuals, it is important that there are chances open to all. The dynamism of the capitalist economy does produce sustainability, revitalization, and recovery, and crises also produce new market opportunities. This final chapter summarizes the various ingredients in a capitalist economy, arguing that proper coordination of the ingredients can generate a more progressive and civilized economy.

II UNTYING GLOBAL ECONOMIC KNOTS

Studies have shown that globalization is a multifaceted issue intermingled with multilevels of economic, political, and policy decisions. Indeed, while most studies on globalization have tended to examine the consequences of globalized activities, few could identify the causes. Or there is a lack of distinction between causes and consequences. Indeed, when economic decisions would impact on other world economies, were those economic decisions made as a means to lead and drive the world economy to new heights, or as a response to activities in other parts of the world? One can start by asking the question as to why resource-rich countries, even including some oil exporting countries, tend to be poor and under-developed countries, but resource-poor countries tend to be the richer and more industrialized countries in the world economy. Is the availability of resources an obstacle to growth? Or does the problem lie with the domestic policies applied to the use of resources? There are other global economic phenomena too. Industrialized countries are faced with both trade deficits and fiscal deficits, but they are still the main suppliers of world capital and foreign direct investment. But then, there are also exporting countries with trade surpluses, and huge national debts. Are there not enough applicable economic standards that countries can look to, or are countries not keen to adhere to economic standards?

In many ways, the world economy has been "trapped" as the result of the coexistence of economic causes and consequences in that no single policy could be used effectively, nor can the policy decisions of any single world economy offer impactful solutions. Or in the extreme, is economics the pivot or the victim of many world problems? Very often, complaints from politicians and environmentalists were expressed in resulting ex post economic terms, but the origins of the complaints were often noneconomic. The situation among countries cannot be clear-cut in the dichotomy of developed and developing, industrialized and agricultural, first world and third world, capitalist market and socialist economies, and so on. The use of economic variables, such as Gross Domestic Product, foreign investment, taxation, and level of international reserves may not be factors in measuring the world economy. The world economy has been highlighted more by religious fanatics and terrorism, rather than pure economic and ideological grounds. While on the one hand there are the civilized forces that advocate for freedom, human rights, and equality, there are on the other hand uncivilized groups and extremists that practice the opposite by encouraging terrorist activities, coercive behavior, inequality, and discrimination.

Fragile States

A summary of economic knots can be observed from the five groups of world economies. Many fragile states are rich in natural resources, including oil, but these fragile states are always on the edge of economic collapse, even though they have been the recipients of foreign economic aid. Ideologies could be the obstacle to growth and development in fragile states, as many remain poor after taking up a socialist path of development, while the other so-called market economies were often riddled with corruption and abuse, which resulted in them being trapped in poverty and underdevelopment. The extent of malfunctioning in fragile states could have its origin probably not in the economic arena of development, but in the ideological, religious, political, governance, and other policies inappropriately and mistakenly adopted by their leaders.

Given the extent of economic mess and fragmentation in the fragile states, the only way to untie their knots would be to locate, identify, and deliver more effective domestic policies that would build up a reliable system and minimize the influence of personality and connections. Unless and until the fragile states conduct "their homework" in restoring stability, the chances for growth and advancement will be minimal, even if economic assistance is made available from foreign governments and organizations. In situations when economic crises appeared in other parts of the world economy, these fragile states would simply be marginalized, as resources could not come to their rescue. A minimal amount of activity would still take place, such as exporting and receiving aid from international organizations and/or foreign assistance from friendly countries that would have other intentions, such as ideological or geo-political ambitions. Fragile states have to learn not just to "take" from the rest of the world, but to build up their own economic strength and foundations.

Hence, the key to untie the knots in fragile states would depend largely on their own internal strength and policy directions, especially on the part of the leaders who are either freely elected or come about through political or military coercion. The worst scenario would be the formation of a group of crony leaders who just take advantage of their power to amass wealth and assets. It would indeed be difficult for selfless leaders to emerge, due largely to the "chicken and egg" problem between political power and economic gains. The economy may possess natural resources, but a full market system may not have been developed to coordinate the production and deployment of natural resources. There may be a lack of an effective group of businesses. On the contrary, politics has entered into the economic scene, as leaders and government officials abuse authority to their own advantage, especially if they are allied with businesses and the military. In other words, it is not underdevelopment that is restricting progress in fragile states, but it is the deliberate policy of underdevelopment that preserves the power of the leaders at the expense of economic development and progress.

Emerging Economies

When compared to the fragile states, the emerging states seem to show a higher degree of stability, which is the prerequisite condition for growth and development. The next condition after stability is opportunity. Economic opportunity relates to an ex ante situation or environment through which jobs and mobility can be created. Li (2014b) argued that economic opportunity is an issue involving both "width and depth" in development factors. "Width" concerns the variety of quantifiable factors that can be used for growth and development. Typical factors include foreign direct investment, trade, and bank borrowing. "Depth" concerns how far these development factors can be reflected qualitatively through noneconomic factors, including religion, ideology, governance, and geographical factors.

Stability shown in emerging countries would probably serve as an important "depth" factor. Leaders in the emerging economies would have to explore and improve both the "width and depth" factors in order to raise their economic competitiveness and increase their comparative advantage. When compared with the "depth" factors, the quantifiable "width" factors should be easier to obtain and understand. Low costs of production, e.g., could already be an attractive factor to foreign direct investment. It would be more difficult to improve the "depth" factors. Many "depth" factors would require nonpolitical, but cultural and value judgments. To the emerging countries, their economic knots relate mostly to "depth" factors, and how prepared they are to improve the "depth" factors so that they can complement productivity with the available "width" factors.

Oil and Petroleum Exporting Countries and the Middle East

The issue in Oil and Petroleum Exporting Countries (OPEC) and the oil exporting countries is more complicated. Over the decades, many oil exporting countries have been enriched by oil revenues, but there is huge diversity in the economic performance in oil exporting countries. For example, one would wonder why such an oil exporting country as Venezuela is on the brink of poverty and shortages of food (*Time*, June 16, 2016.). Some OPEC countries in the Middle East have built up new megacities, with super building structures that raised the standard of living immensely for a few, but could have trickled down to others over the decades. The most destructive aspect of oil revenue was the fueling and funding of terrorist activities conducted by religious extremists who have haunted the world with organized terrorist attacks on innocent civilians. Indeed, terrorist groups were offering loans in order to attract innocent people to join, reflecting how "rich" they were, and raising questions as to where their funds have come from (*CNN*, April 21, 2016.). These extremists have effectively declared a world war on civilization.

The knot can be seen from the intuition that funds from oil revenues geared to terrorism on the input side of the equation have led to loss of innocent life and stability and security threats on the output side of the equation. Such an "input − output" equation produced the worst combination, as the world economy had no choice but to keep pumping oil revenues into these unstable regions. In one sense, these oil exporting countries should be blessed with the monopoly they had over the natural resources, but the domestic situations in these countries had channeled the oil revenues to dishonorable uses. Indeed, if the oil revenue was to be excluded, many of these developing countries would have little to offer. Yet, the large oil revenues could have been used for development and construction. Consider the vast amount of land in the Middle East countries, e.g., human settlements could have been promoted immensely. Unfortunately, many of these countries were faced with numerous internal, regional, religious, racial, and military conflicts, with the outcome of instability, war, and extremism. The situation was worsened as the world community became involved in these conflicts, and extremists then pointed their weapons towards the international community, rather than seeking viable solutions amongst themselves.

How can these knots be untied? These multiple levels of conflict will not change unless and until these countries choose peace over war, development over destruction, cooperation over antagonism, and civilization over violence. Intuitively, the requirement is to introduce activities with "relative" outcomes. The first noneconomic requirement would be a change of attitude from one of exclusion to mutual acceptability and trust. The installation of stability would have to be the prerequisite to unwind the entire trend of conflict and extremism. An entirely different approach will be needed if conflicts in the Middle East are to come to an end. In short, the solution must be initiated from the member countries within the region.

The international community has been placed in a more passive role. Considerable resources would have to be used in eradicating terrorism, and the indirect economic effect could be enormous. In addition to the need to minimize military involvement against the various extremist groups, the international community could help to hasten the civil side of development in the conflicted countries. Modernization in the interpretation of religious faith, advantages arising from peaceful coexistence and development, and the ability to engage in business activities could be examples of civil activities. One advantage many Middle East countries have is the ample supply of oil revenues that can be used for progressive development.

Russia and China

In the case of Russia, it would be unwise to dwell on its old days of hardcore communism, as the world since the end of the Cold War has changed significantly. By the turn of the 21st century, Russia has ideologically lost to the western world, and economically lost to China. Russia has to reposition itself in order to maintain its influence in the international community. Its military strength has not been deployed appropriately, and indeed has upset a number of former allies in the region. Even though Russia can control its domestic propaganda in promoting the charisma of certain leaders, Russia has to be careful of trapping itself in the worst of "three worlds": ideologically weak, economically uncompetitive, and militarily untrustworthy. In addition, Russia has to maintain its domestic stability, so that economic progress can proceed.

In short, Russia should avoid engaging in ideological and military conflict with the west, while at the same time losing its economic competitiveness to China. Russia could untie its knots by merging closer with Western Europe or by revitalizing economic development among former Eastern and Southern European neighbors. Russia's former ideological and military strategy would have to change to become economic partners in development, exploring mutual advantages both interregionally and intraregionally. Indeed, as Russia will no longer be dominant in the socialist ideological world, and since not all contemporary global conflicts are ideological in nature, Russia's economic development and long-term success will depend on the choice Russia makes between integrating with Western Europe and competing with China. The choice will depend on where Russia can gain most in economic and other activities. If ideology is no longer Russia's trump card, it will have removed a major obstacle with Western Europe, or the West in general. On the other hand, conflicts in other parts of the world, typically prolonged instability in various parts of the Middle East, are not all ideology-related. If Russia's military ability was to aid the Western world in peace and conflict reduction, Russia's relationship with the West should improve. Economically, Russia needs the Western market. Should Russia's political relationship improve with the West, new economic activities would follow, including trading with the Western world, foreign direct investment, and Russia's export of oil. There is a high degree of economic complementarity between Russia and Western Europe. As Russia's ideological differences with the West subside, the military conflict with the West would be reduced. In turn, more resources would be geared to economic development.

Russia loses to China miserably when it comes to comparative advantage in the economic domain. With China's rise in economic ability, it would soon overtake and marginalize Russia, both economically and ideologically. Russia might have some comparative advantage over China in military terms, but this could be eroded when China builds up its military capability. Russia could easily lose to China on all three fronts: ideological, military, and economic. Russia's economy would become a periphery to China's economy if Russia did not have other economic alternatives. Hence, in comparison, Russia would be better off by improving its relationship with Western Europe.

As compared to Russia, socialist China has been given much better treatment by the western world since 1978. By exploiting its mass poverty, China attracted much foreign assistance, which boosted its economic strength while maintaining its political power and ideological grip. Many Western industrialized countries had been eyeing the Chinese market for their industrial products, but missed the long-term impact that China would "indigenize" their technology, and similar products over time would be produced and even exported back to Western countries. With the low costs of production in China, China's export of light manufacturing could have helped to lower the inflationary pressure in the importing countries. Thus, the need to reduce poverty, low labor costs, and the potential large market lured Western investors, governments, and international institutions to China.

However, with its rise in economic status, analysts have been asking whether China could play a pivotal role in the world economy, helping others as the industrialized world had unconditionally aided China since 1978. Although foreign leaders have warned about the rigidity of the communist ideology, China remains immobile in its political stance (*South China Morning Post*, March 23, 2016.). China has been flexing its economic muscles through massive accumulation in its international reserves. After four decades of growth, China since 2008 has been facing more of a "turning point" than a "crossroads," as a number of domestic and international dichotomies have emerged or not been solved.

Domestically, the political divide between the various factions led to numerous distortions. First and foremost, corruption had been rampant. In the military, e.g., every military rank would have a price, and promotion was based on the ability to pay (bribe) (*South China Morning Post*, March 28, and April 4, 2016.). Land policy remained controversial, as rural land could be taken away for development without adequate compensation (*South China Morning Post*, June 20, 2016.). While the economy stayed "cash rich," debts had been accumulating. Despite Shanghai's claim on the large financial market, Morgan Stanley Capital International (MSCI) rejected China's A-share application for inclusion in the MSCI Index in 2016, claiming that the A-share market had not been functioning efficiently like other world financial markets (*South China Morning Post*, February 16, May 4, and 6, June 11, 15, and 16, 2016.). After 2008, China suffered fluctuations in exports and foreign direct investment, together with the rising labor costs at home, China was faced with a loss of competitiveness, and domestic policy was geared more to boost domestic consumption and demand by providing subsidies. Despite the call for solutions by Xi Jinping in May, 2016, economic restructuring was slow to come (*South China Morning Post*, May 16, and June 15, 2016.).

Externally, through its "poverty" strategy, China had been building up mutual alliances with almost all countries the Chinese leader visited. For example, while China was seeking to "create greater trust" with the United States, China had ambitious plans that would exclude the United States. With its "cheque book diplomacy" of providing assistance, investment and aid to both developed and developing countries, China has been buying foreign portfolios and physical assets. Some had also expressed concern about China's diplomatic arrogance (*China Daily*, April 13, 2016; and *South China Morning Post*, June 2, and 6, 2016.).

China's growing economy has not been able to bring peace and mutual development in the Asian region, as its military expansion and territorial disputes with Japan in East Asia and Southeast Asian countries of the Philippines, Indonesia, Malaysia, and Vietnam threaten regional stability. China has been building military facilities in the South China Sea, and blamed the United States for unfair surveillance in the region (*South China Morning Post*, February 23, May 7, 13, and 31, June 1, 2016; *CNN*, May 15, 2016.). While the South China Sea would not have much to do with non-Asian countries, China's claim could have shown a "mirror image" in the annihilation of Eastern European countries by the Soviet Union after the Second World War. It would be possible that, with its gradually growing military strength in the region, it would not be simply the sea routes that China was protecting, but turning the Southeast Asian countries into China's peripheries could be the more ambitious and hidden goal. Since 2014, through the ambitious "one belt, one road" proposal and the Asian Infrastructure Investment Bank (AIIB), China has been prepared to export its railway and shipping technology. By extending its influence westwards, China will encircle Russia's entire southern and western border. The economic equation might have favored China more than the recipient countries. For example, in railway construction, China would have provided the technology, but what about the material imports and the land usage involved? Other concerns would be the distribution of future revenues, reliability of technology, accountability, and management.

China is faced with unprecedented problems from domestic forces and external pressures. Chinese leaders often made the remark when visiting foreign countries that China would never practice hegemony, but analysts often noticed the difference between China's deeds and words. Ideological factional conflicts in China deter any systemic improvements, as it is difficult for leaders in a personality-driven system to give way to the establishment of a reliable, equitable, and transparent civic system. At most, China will use its huge international reserves to influence the world. World economies can exploit China's "cheque book diplomacy," but China's influence and world acceptability will be constrained by its own systemic inadequacies and inconsistencies.

Each of these four groups of world economies are faced with problems which are often man-made or even "leader-made," because while solutions are clearly available, the question is how willing the leaders are prepared to change their policies in bringing their economies to a more functional footing, or will they put their vested interests as their prime goals. With the absence of a reliable system, the choice of policies usually rests in the hands of the leaders. Despite the debate on ideology, the decision for leaders to change from a personality-driven to a system-driven economy could already be a big jump to stability and the establishment of a modern civic economy.

III LEADERSHIP OF INDUSTRIALIZED COUNTRIES

Despite the various world problems, whether man-made or natural disasters, the world economy is still policed largely by the key industrialized countries. Other than the possession of clear economic indicators, such as capital, technology, productivity, and markets, the G7 (United States, United Kingdom, Germany, France, Japan, Italy, and Canada) still collectively play the world leadership role. The United States obviously plays the largest international role. In addition to its economic and military capabilities, the United States has to face both the eastern and western sides of its coastal borders. In policing the world, the G7 cooperates among them and looks to cooperation with other regional allies. Thus, there is an international network of cooperation and peacekeeping, in conjunction with the United Nations.

It would be true to argue that many world problems turned out to produce "absolute" outcomes, and the process of policing in various world regions could confront countries with challenges and difficulties in the planning, implementation, and execution stages. For example, opposition from local and indigenous populations could be high, foreign contact could be thwarted, and mistakes made by some agents during the execution stage would certainly add to the complexity of the policing job. Hence, mistakes would be unavoidable, but it is important that the overall principles and the ultimate targets were made clear.

The values that the industrialized world stands for include not only economic and technological achievement, but also such human qualities as individual freedom, ownership rights, civic development and reliance on trusted institutions, transparency in governance, peace, nondiscrimination and fairness, democracy, and equality of opportunity. The objective of policing the world is to introduce these values to other world economies, and to see other countries taking up these human values and behaviors, so as to bring the world to a higher level of civilization. But then, one should not assume that the G7 countries speak with the same voice or share the same thoughts in all international cases and incidents. There could certainly be rivalries among the G7 countries. Diversity and democracy would mean that opposing voices and views would have to be taken into account, and socialist-oriented leaders could be elected in political elections, resulting in the introduction of "market-unfriendly" policies that lower economic performance. While most G7 countries hold similar world views, individual G7 countries can also show different attitudes and policies towards other countries. There are worldly issues on which the G7 countries hold similar views, including Russia's military and territorial expansion, the fight against religious extremism and terrorism, and peace in the Middle East. For example, all G7 countries considered the lack of human rights in China, but each G7 country works with China differently in the economic arena. For example, Germany had been keen to invest and export technological goods to China, aiming at low production costs, as well as the large Chinese market. It was true that German industrial enterprises gained, but their Chinese counterparts quickly "copycatted" the technology.

Another example happened in the third quarter of 2015, when the US Federal Reserve was expected to raise the interest rate, but the decision was delayed because the Federal Open Market Committee (FOMC) did not want to exert an unnecessary interest rate burden on the Chinese economy (*The New York Times*, September 17, 2015.). Given the ideological differences between China and the United States, one would wonder why the FOMC would need to worry about the Chinese economy and not the US economy, especially when the Chinese economy had already been rising over the last four decades. It was possible that individual G7 countries would look more to their economic than noneconomic relationship with China. In the end, China could play off one G7 country against another, and was able eventually to acquire foreign investment and technology, while the situation over other noneconomic issues was practically left untouched in China. Because of the economic advantages, some G7 countries only took a "skin deep" look at China's political inadequacies. In the legal arena, e.g., there are indeed a large number of laws in China, but whether the laws are properly implemented or the law-breakers charged could turn out to be a personality decision. The "soft" attitude exhibited by individual G7 countries would be strategically exploited by communist China.

Nonetheless, there would supposedly be a bottom line below which the industrialized countries would react. Indeed, armed with the experience of handling the Soviet Union, the industrialized countries would be aware that time and events would be needed in dealing with another large communist country. While the Soviet Union had military strength but was economically-weak, China had economic strength and could ultimately expand its military ability. Compared to Russia, China has emerged to become a bigger challenge to the G7. Even though the close relationship between Russia and China could be temporary, the G7 countries need to develop more strategic efforts to tackle the Russia – China coalition.

It has also been argued that the industrialized countries were on the losing end as they were becoming weaker economically, especially with their welfare-prone domestic policies that were not growth-promoting. Full industrial capability, an aging economy, high energy prices, and declining competitiveness were the reasons used to explain the economic weakness of the G7 countries. This was true, but not the whole truth. In aggregate, the G7 countries are still strong economically, and their collective decisions influence the world considerably. Although many world economies looked to China as a new source of economic aid, that would be limited only to economic assistance in most cases. Much of the world economy would still look to the industrialized world over international issues. One would have to judge if a rising communist China could economically overpower the combined strength of the industrialized countries. The original intention of the industrialized countries to aid and develop China after the late 1970s was to promote an economically successful China, in order to reduce world poverty and serve as a precedent for the development of other emerging countries.

IV THE BEST AMONG ALL EVILS?

Individual freedom is an essential ingredient in capitalism. Every society is built on individuals. The productivity of every individual in aggregate produces growth in the economy. Hence, at the macrolevel, economics growth should contain "bottom up" activities that sum up the contribution from each individual at different levels of production, depending on each individual's ability, ingenuity, creativity, and effort. Economic growth is a complementary activity, as no single economic unit can accomplish everything on its own. It has to be true that the contribution of different individuals in an economic activity differs, and each individual's contribution has therefore to be rewarded with different gains and returns. In economics, because there is a difference at the input end of the production process, there will be differences in the rewards at the output end. Unfortunately, the difference in economic rewards is unsoundly regarded as "inequality" in political jargon, and this has been termed politically as a social evil.

In market capitalism, such "unequal outcomes" are the driving force of economic progress. Activities with high rewards become popular, and resources will be attracted to high earning activities. The market produces forces of supply and demand that dynamically and automatically shift resources from one kind of production to another. With freedom and mobility, individuals will maximize their own benefits and no resources will be wasted. Similarly, in the process of resource utilization, the market also generates new demands and requires new supplies. There is thus a multiplying effect as the generation of one activity gives rise to another. As more is employed, the administrative hierarchy of business organizations requires more senior positions, and that promotes upward mobility.

The rise in economic welfare of individuals will stimulate others to follow, and one layer of upward mobility will give rise to another. In the process, there will be competition among individuals, but the multiplying effect of economic activities and upward mobility will produce social stability that effectively serves as a social fabric that enhances other activities, such as an increase in business attractiveness, and improvement in economic security. Given that economics is an activity that generates "relative" outcomes, the economic activities of all individuals generate waves of outcomes in economic performance. And since economic activities are measured in pecuniary terms, the difference in rewards can change over time. Indeed, actual rewards can change in different activities in a particular time, or in the same activity at different times. The beauty about economic activities is that there can be a high degree of flexibility and multiplicity in both the level and dimension. Hence, economic activities can improve individuals' welfare at the microlevel, promote growth at the macrolevel, attain stability at the societal-level, achieve economic security at the household-level, and enhance peace and civic harmony at the administrative and political level.

An important element in the free market is competition that appears in different forms and kinds of economic activities. An intuitive concept about competition is that "less is better than more," and there are business strategies to avoid competition. Mergers and acquisitions, increases in market size, advertising, and the creation of brand names are different strategies to conquer competition. Over time, it is true that market leaders are created, and these market leaders could have a bigger "comfort zone." However, given that market entry is open and there are laws to protect newcomers, there is still a possibility for other contenders to enter the market. Laws on competition are instituted to protect both businesses and consumers, to ensure fair deals and open competition. But competition exists in different stages of the market and nature of the goods and services. In a more mature market, it is possible that market leaders exist and new businesses may find it difficult to compete. Similarly, there are markets that have little competition. All these should add to the flexibility and potential of economic activities. This leads to the importance of market-friendliness, as it provides the maximum potential of economic opportunity. Monitoring the economic process is the task of the government, including the institution of appropriate factors that promote market-friendliness. While business leaders aim to achieve profits and gain, political and government leaders should ensure adequate "supply-side" factors. Hence, there are different orientations between business leaders and government officials.

Contemporary economies are faced with periodic crises. Individual economic behavior is based on market information and expectation, but when the expectation of individual decision-makers differs from each other, their effect may cancel out each other. When the expectation of individual decision-makers is similar to each other, economic waves will be generated. In the extreme, economic waves can be transformed into crises, especially in the financial world, where speculative transactions are based on short-term phenomena. Economic and financial crises do result in severe economic recessions, as assets are depreciated and evaporate within a short time. In the financial world, decision-makers who are either investors or speculators actually do look for shocks, as these will give them opportunities to trade. And the activities of some traders will generate sequences of waves that stimulate other traders. Thus, fluctuations in the financial markets should be taken for granted, as that is the nature of financial business. The financial market is always fluctuating, though in the process some gain and others face losses. It would indeed be inappropriate for government leaders, such as those in charge of the monetary policy of the economy, to view the policy impact on the financial market as too important. This is because whatever the monetary authority decides, there will always be fluctuations in the financial markets. The policy decisions of the monetary authority should therefore look more into the real economy that produces long-term results, rather than the financial fluctuations that show short-term results.

Economic and financial crises could be the result of "collective expectation and behavior," and the result will be various losses that businesses and individuals suffer. It is true that crises will lead to economic decline, but the flexibility in economics permits revitalization, recovery, and rejuvenation of other economic activities that will produce positive expectations through information about supply and demand. Crises do occur, but so do economic recovery and expansion. Other than the achievement of expectations, government policies could instigate expectations which would translate into activities, and the outcomes may or may not be favorable. The orientation of economic policies could play a crucial role in the direction of the business cycles. Should the policy be procyclical or anticyclical, or cycle-leading or cycle-responding would have great impact on the business and economic cycles. While either procyclical or anticyclical policies will produce short-term impacts, cycle-leading policies play a more dominate and pioneering position in the direction of economic growth. On the contrary, cycle-responding policies are usually passive and involve time-lags that could eventually destabilize rather than stabilize the business cycle. For example, if interest rate policies are geared towards the performance of the stock market, it may produce distorting implications for other economic aspects.

Crises can be chaotic in a short time, but usually are unsustainable through time because the market mechanism permits free movement of resources. Hence, crises promote opportunities for newcomers to enter the market. The element of revitalization and rejuvenation becomes a "built-in" factor in market economies. The forces of supply and demand provide excellent market indicators for investors and individuals to shift to areas where there is potential. As such, economic dynamism means an everlasting chain of economic activity. Other than the family as a social unit, human beings are connected through various relationships: racial, religious, territorial, sexual, hierarchical, anthropological, and organizational. Unfortunately, most of these relationships tend to be divisive among human beings. One race may look to the drawback of another race, while one religion may argue in favor of a certain spiritual faith, and so on. Political relationships are surely divisive, as different supporters would oppose one another.

Economics is harmonious, because its function is to pull people together complementarily to complete certain activities that benefit all participants, though not all participants can have equal rewards. Economics is probably the only discipline that advocates for rewards and produces "relative" outcomes. And capitalism is probably the only ideological vehicle through which economic activities can best be conducted openly and freely, supported by a strong rule of law and market-friendly government machinery. It is the best ideological vehicle, because economic activity permits opportunity to increase, and participants can have the chance of obtaining gains from market opportunities. Gains will then depend on one's efforts, and not through some form of arbitrary allocation. Freedom and power will rest in the hands of every individual. Evolution in economic activities gives rise to new dimensions, as creative ideas can be materialized into innovations, and the accumulation of capital funds enables huge infrastructure projects to be built and technology to advance.

There is no perfection in any ideology, but one is searching for one that serves to benefit all, and not the vested interests of a few. It is true that in a mature capitalist market, enterprises expand to become giants, and individual assets expand to become wealth holders, but so long as there is market freedom and no entry restrictions, the fluidity of the market exists to serve and not to limit. Indeed, there are cases where large enterprises collapse as losses mount, and equally there are cases where small enterprises vanish in the process of competition. Looking at all kinds of human relationships, the economic dynamism in capitalism ultimately provides the most flexible and suitable ex ante condition for economies to progress.

V CAN CAPITALISM SAVE THE WORLD?

The contemporary world economy has been polarized. The monopolistic nature of the oil exporting countries has amassed huge amounts of wealth from consumers, but many of these countries are either unstable states or engage in terrorist activities. In either case, many oil exporting countries effectively are taxing the world economy, and not engaging mutually and productively with the world economy. It is likely that the conflicts within these terrorist-pone countries cannot be solved intraregionally, and may even spread to other world regions as if the conflicts originated elsewhere and these countries are suffering from unwanted intervention from outside their region. Thus, instead of admitting that their instability is the "cause," they wrongly take it for granted that they were a "consequence" of outside intervention. The intuition is that these terrorist-prone states actually "exported" their conflicts to the rest of the world, and yet mistakenly and ironically believed that their conflicts were "imported" from the outside world when the outside world interfered in solving their conflicts. There is confusion in the "cause and consequence" in their conflicts. So long as they hold a monopolistic position in the supply of oil, and so long as they are not prepared to face and deal with their own conflicts, they will put the blame on the world community.

The coalition between the two communist countries of Russia and China has equally imposed instability on their neighboring regions. China's economy has been built up by amassing huge international reserves through its exports and inward investment, but instead of aligning ideologically with the world economy, the signs of an ambitious China were clearly that it aimed to "conquer" the world economy. While its external impact has been growing with exaggeration, the internal imbalance in China reflects not only the reluctance to establish a reliable and sustainable system, but also the factional conflicts continue, in addition to the growing discontent in various social dimensions. Economically, China could be vulnerable in a number of aspects.

An excessive amount of prosocialist economic policies have been adopted by many economies in the industrialized world, especially in Europe and North America. Over the years, the interference of politics in economics in the form of redistribution, pursuit of "equality" through large and prolonged welfare spending on the one hand, and the rise in wages and cost of production through collective bargaining on the other hand, have come to a clear economic conclusion: decline in competitiveness and output. The "spending" side has far exceeded the "production" side of the economic equation in many countries, and although they realize their growing debts, few attempts have been made to reduce the mounting levels of debt. Yet, for reasons of sympathy, fraternity, and humanity, some European countries were prepared to embrace refugees from neighboring regions in an "open door" policy. The large extent of political interference in economics has become intolerable. It was highlighted in the Brexit vote as the British people decided to exit from the European Union in view of the potential large influx of refugees that would eat into their fiscal resources and compete for jobs.

Each of these three world economic issues has imposed great economic burdens on many industrialized countries. The worst was that their decline resulting from prosocialist policies had in fact aided other economies that followed different ideologies, and these countries returned to challenge the industrialized economies. In many ways, the world has turned around, with the communist countries gaining wealth, while many freer countries were weakened after prolonged use of prosocialist policies. A strategy of economic consolidation and self-strengthening is needed to regain much of the economic vitality in many western countries, which over the last decades have excessively adopted prosocialist policies to the extent of damaging their competitiveness and pushing their resources away. The primary intuition is to regain economic strength and leadership, implying that there will be a set of appropriate domestic and external policies leading to self-strengthening, without imposing unfavorable impacts on other world economies.

Domestic Strategy

Domestically, the strategy should aim to boost the economy's competitiveness and capacity-building through instituting and applying "supply-side" policies. On the issue of capacity-building, the policies could aim to promote applied technology in consumer products. Promoting new areas of comparative advantage could in turn enrich competitiveness. Resources should be geared more to industries that are employment-promoting than to financial businesses and activities that often involve speculation. In conjunction with industrial expansion there needs to be infrastructure promotion and expansion. For example, transport infrastructure with high-speed trains should be energy-saving and reduce road traffic. Investment in the environment could minimize waste and maximize the redeployment of materials. These examples of infrastructure development would require large funds, but their favorable prospects in the future should be able to repay the borrowed loans. Thus, one possibility is to issue treasury bonds that are geared specifically to funding long-term infrastructure projects. This would be a more useful and productive alternative than to issue bonds to cover debts.

Another area of improvement in many industrialized countries could be the revitalization and rejuvenation of run-down cities and regions. Previous industrial development was often based on the development and success of a single industry, such as the motor car industry in one city and coal mining in another. The decline of these "mono-industry" cities and regions provide good potential for economic capacity expansion, as the cost of redevelopment should be low, and new industries could be set up depending on market forces and supply of inputs. Consortiums could be established so that new investments could create jobs, industries, and output.

At the macroeconomic level, weak deflation may be a good policy choice as that should attract investment. To boost investment, both fiscal and monetary policies could be more effective. A cut in tax, combined with a rise in interest rates, could work effectively, as one produces investment incentive, while the other encourages high productivity projects to emerge. A cut in profit tax and salary tax does not mean lower government revenue. It could be the reverse if the tax cut led to an increase in businesses and employment, leading to higher government revenues in the next round. The revised interest rate policy should be used to steer long-term growth in the real economy, rather than to cater for such short-term goals as inflation and speculation. A stable and high interest rate policy does not mean to hurt investment, but to ensure that funds are geared to high-return investments. The combination of these domestic policies can produce multiple results. The combination of a tax cut and issue of treasury bonds to boost infrastructure development would definitely stimulate investment in the private sector and increase overall employment. A high interest rate may not hurt the issue of bonds if the future returns of the project are economically viable and could generate the ability to repay. Infrastructure projects normally are expensive to build, but will become more expensive as time passes. The important consideration is whether the infrastructure project will generate long-term gains for the community.

There is a need to get away from political considerations as much as possible when it comes to economic policy decisions. Instead of aiming at "equality," the policy should aim at job opportunities and output creation.

Instead of aiming at taxing the very few rich, the policy shall encourage the rich to invest more at home, so that more jobs can be created. Economic self-strengthening means policy reorientation to boost "supply-side" factors, and separate unnecessary politics from pure economic decisions. Most industrialized countries have reached a mature stage of political democracy, but it is the economy that should be given a chance to improve and grow. The battle of equality should be based on productivity and opportunity, and not simply on pecuniary differences. Wage improvement should be based on economic sustainability and potential for capacity expansion. Although labor unions and wage bargaining were politically oriented in the early stage of capitalism, contemporary developments in labor relationships in industrialized countries has gone much further.

In addition to government agencies, nongovernment organizations have provided services to alleviate people's hardship through professional and voluntary works that attend to needs which are not politically oriented. Civic society is playing an increasing role in closing various social and economic gaps. The outdated "dichotomy" between employers and laborers should be reconsidered economically from the point of mutual need and interests, rather than the power of one over the other politically. The ultimate goal in any economy is to build a bigger economic pie so that there is more to share, rather than to argue over how the pie will be shared. With improvements in the civic economy, there are new criteria for deciding how the pie should be shared. Although wage is a direct criterion, the quality of labor and work environment should be considered as alternative criteria. Intrapersonal development in income and output should be more relevant than interpersonal differences.

In a nutshell, there should be efforts to reenergize the domestic economy by reducing the size and volume of redistribution, while at the same time promoting real economic activities through fiscal and monetary policies. Capacity and capability building policies could be enhanced through technology and rejuvenating run-down cities. Allowing the economic game that generates "relative" outcome to have a bigger role, and creating jobs and employment will promote individuals' economic welfare, and when individuals are occupied "economically," they will be interested more in attaining upward mobility than concentrating on the extent of inequality interpersonally. Industrialized countries should engage in policies that will look into the potential of their own economies, rather than "punish" the minority of "able individuals." The intention is to enable society to have more "able individuals" than to encourage more "dependent individuals" that rely on assistance. The prosocialist policies in many industrialized countries have gone too far, both in coverage and in substance, to the extent of crippling competitiveness, dismantling capacity, and promoting dependence.

External Strategy

Internal restructuring and capability building among the industrialized countries does not mean there is less to contribute to the international community. Once the capitalist economies have been revitalized and rejuvenated, they can redirect resources through trade, foreign direct investment, and regional policies. In restructuring the world economy, the industrialized countries can help to promote other growth regions among the emerging countries. With the rise of China, the industrialized world could trade with China, but redirect their foreign investment to other medium-sized emerging countries that adhere to capitalist ideology and cherish economic and political freedom. Given the experience of China, it is unlikely that the advanced countries will aid and promote another large country with clear differences in ideology. With the rise of more emerging countries, the world economy should grow, and the larger world "economic pie" should have more to share. The traditional formula of foreign investment that promoted light manufacturing, and labor-intensive production in emerging countries could still apply, but attention should be given to environmental friendliness and technological applications. Trade promotion bodies would help to promote trade among ideology-friendly countries. Another possibility is to create new financial markets among the "newcomers" to facilitate currency trading, portfolio investment, and international banking activities.

While ideological differences could be handled politically, the tougher issue is the various conflicted regions in the Middle East and the performance of the fragile states. The easy answer would be a rapid reduction in the consumption of oil, but this would require the cooperation of manufacturers and industrialists. Frankly, other than the need for oil, the world economy would not have much to do with these conflict-prone countries. The speedy development of energy-saving cars with elastic pricing should help to reduce oil consumption considerably. One strategy for the industrialized world would be to maintain their monitoring task, but minimize interference and allow time for these conflicted countries to settle down. Letting these countries solve their own conflicts may be a viable alternative that would minimize the spread of conflicts to other parts of the world.

Indeed, the vulnerability of many fragile states may invite the spread of communism, as both key communist countries would feed them with cheap loans and assistance. A major issue among the fragile states is that funds provided to these states would probably not bear many positive economic results, as they would be channeled to various types of corruption and mismanagement. These countries would just "take" whatever and whenever was given to them from the world community. The worse should not be the amount of funds provided, but all kinds of fund assistance would vanish as the state of the economy remained the same.

One strategy would be to provide direct assistance through the various international organizations and institutions, ensuring that the funding must be geared to productivity and be output enhancing. The monitoring process must be conducted efficiently to ensure funds are used effectively and productivity. A problem could be that those personnel in charge of fund allocation and dispersion must have the right ideological and ethical mindset. Economic logic, reasoning, and results must precede sympathy, fraternity, and corruption. This could be difficult, as it would involve the "principle – agent" problem. Assistance and funding support to fragile states can also come from individual industrialized countries. For example, the building up of economic capacity through infrastructure development can enhance stability in some infant states. Assistance to the fragile states should focus on "supply-side" factors. Indeed, many former colonies and fragile states adopted socialism after colonialism without knowing and experiencing the strength and successes that a capitalist market economic ideology could bring.

One alternative would be to nurture capitalist development in the emerging and fragile states, and let domestic business establishments mobilize resources and the market sort out supply and demand. The nurturing of individualism could be a force for change in economies with "primitive" development. Development through individual efforts could be easier and flexible, as the individual entrepreneur would have better local knowledge. Another advantage would be the low cost of development, as small-scale industries and businesses would stimulate the market to function. Indeed, it would not be appropriate to insist on a large role for the government in many emerging and fragile states, as the task of governmental organization could be bureaucratic and huge given the resources, and ineffective given the extent of knowledge and technology. It would be inappropriate to complain about capitalism when many of these emerging and fragile countries had never introduced capitalism. One effective strategy would be to allow the economy to grow using market instruments, but avoid the drawbacks of capitalism along the path of development. In a nutshell, the promotion of "supply-side" economics should be seen as appropriate in the emerging and fragile states, as it should introduce economic formalism gradually, and the economic multiplier could be set to function productively.

The international strategy will have to take into account the divergence of world regions and differences in ideological paths and resource availability. First and foremost, the industrialized countries should adopt policies that will strengthen their own domestic economy in order to expand their industrial capacity and economic capability. The regeneration of economic strength in the industrialized world would send signals to other world regions, and at the same time, serve as a reference to noncapitalist countries. The industrialized countries should form regional and international partnerships and consortia with others that adhere to a similar ideology of freedom and democracy. Resources and assistance should withdraw from countries that hold different ideologies or are conflict-prone, as that would impose unnecessary burdens on the industrialized countries. Hence, the strategy is to promote development among friendly countries that share similar values, and cooperation would produce mutual advancement in various dimensions. By aiding weaker countries which share similar values, there would be improvement, cooperation, and connection among countries in the freer parts of the world, and that should send clear messages and simultaneously serve as showcases of revitalized growth and development in the international community.

Both domestic and external policies should complement each other to increase the impact of the economic multiplier. An economic virtuous cycle can be created first by making adjustments in domestic policies. A reduction in business tax, combined with a moderate rise in real interest rates, e.g., should attract investment back to the real sector of the economy with reduction in speculative activities. This should create employment subsequently, even if there is no increase in wages. The economic multiplier effect gives rise to numerous possibilities. A prosperous economic scene so created would send positive messages to other investors, and a rise in employment would allow upward mobility, and so on. A strong domestic economy would then provide opportunities for trade that benefit other exporting countries. An "elastic" tax structure could eventually produce more government revenue. The possible rise in government revenue should lift the economy from fiscal deficit, or the government would have more to spend on improving "supply-side" factors. A healthier fiscal performance would reduce deficits and national debts. A healthier currency would invite foreign investment, and that should lengthen and expand the economy's multiplier effects further.

Economics is a dynamic subject, and economic achievements take time and need a stable and market-friendly environment. Unfortunately, economic performance has often been interfered with by political decisions and ideologies that result in distortions. The economic situation worsens as different economic instruments are used to correct different noneconomic situations. The economic mess created is due more to the misuse and abuse of economic instruments than the lack of deployable economic instruments. For example, every economy agrees to the need to have a more highly educated work force. Fiscal funding is therefore spent on education. Yet, the more educated should surely receive earnings higher than the less educated. Hence, there is definitely the emergence of "inequality," as productivity between the two groups differs. Political activists would then come to capitalize on the income differences. Elected politicians with socialist orientations would seek higher taxes to redistribute. There is the "principle – agent" problem as the initiators of income redistribution pass the payment burden to another group who might not agree to the high taxes. There are numerous examples of contradictions between economic values and political ideals.

Economic distortions are often the result of political decisions. In economics, there can always be alternatives for improvement, but economic opportunities could be sacrificed due to unfavorable political decisions. Thus, the lack of economic development and growth may not entirely be due to the shortage of economic resources. On the contrary, it would be possible to identify potential growth regions, where conditions could be ripe for development and growth. By using simple criteria, the region of Southeast Asia and Eastern European countries would qualify to be the next "latecomer" countries where economic growth could proceed at a faster pace. However, if other world regions could reorientate their economic policies and political scenarios, there is every possibility that growth could be regenerated in other world regions. For example, as it will be argued, smaller western European countries could catch up on the growth ladder if appropriate economic and political policies were to be reinstituted so as to revitalize their economic competitiveness. In the final analysis, the institution of trustworthy leadership and governance would improve stability considerably.

The world economy would still have to be led by key industrialized countries along with their regional allies. Given the kind of civic values built up over the centuries by the industrialized countries, they should serve as the monitor of the world economy in ensuring peace and progress for the rest of the world. Clearly, it would be the G7 countries whose resources would be sufficiently strong to battle against worldly problems. Although the industrialized countries may differ when it comes to individual issues from other world economies, they would form a strong bond when it comes to international issues of security and ideology. Indeed, the G7 countries would exercise different strategies, either by individual country or regionally, with a few countries, or collectively as a whole. Strategies could cover instruments in economics, military, diplomatic, political and ideological, geographical, technological, and social and cultural. To ensure progress in civilization, peace, and security, there is still the need for international order to be maintained by the industrialized countries.

VI CONCLUSION

A number of dichotomous terms have been discussed. Other than capitalism and socialism or communism, others include relative versus absolute when it comes to the outcome between economic and political activities, supply-side versus demand-side when it comes to the choice in government spending, *laissez-faire* versus government intervention when it comes to government policy, comparative advantage versus absolute advantage when comparing the resources of one economy to another, push versus pull when it comes to industrial policies, give versus take when it comes to discussion on fragile countries, inequality versus poverty when it relates to economic outcomes, ex ante versus ex post when it comes to relevant development factors, turning point versus crossroads when such an economy as China was faced with economic saturation, private cost versus social cost when discussion concerns the spillover from the burden of individual's welfare, and peace and war when it relates to regions in conflict.

What would be the best possible combinations among these dichotomies? Economic activities always produce relative outcomes, and the emphasis on supply-side factors enhances economic capacity. Capitalist institutions do strengthen the ex ante economic situation, though the results are often known ex post. *Laissez-faire* economic policies provide the greatest freedom to the private sector, though government policies should aim to alleviate hardship. A large private sector means that individuals are responsible for their private costs, and minimizes the amount of social costs society has to tolerate. An economy should strive for comparative advantage in its industrial and business development. A prospective economy should be able to pull resources from the international community. Fragile states should not simply take from the world community, but have to develop their own competitive advantages. Of course, a peaceful and stable environment is always the prerequisite to growth and development. Furthermore, economic saturation occurs, and to avoid turning points, new capacities and new comparative advantages have to be developed. A lasting peace agreement would involve alternative deployment of resources from war-related activities that produce absolute outcomes, to economic activities that generate relative outcomes.

On the contrary, an unviable and unsustainable combination would consist of countries engaging excessively in political activities that generate absolute outcomes and antagonize the different factions. Government intervention usually applies demand-side policies that involve the spending side of the fiscal equation. A greater use of redistributive policies would reduce comparative advantage, and may even push resources out of the country. A loss of resources would mean a greater chance of increasing the poverty pool, which would end up with an increase in social costs, as more individuals are faced with economic survival problems. A weak economy would have to take from the international community when, e.g., the national debt is mounting. Economic stagnation would lead to economic downfall and disrupt stability.

One should not be looking for an ideal situation, but a functional and progressive situation that allows individuals to maximize their welfare, minimizes social cost so that the government can help to nurture future possibilities and not be burdened by debts, and enable the economy to reach its highest possible potential. If every individual contains his or her own private costs, and shows the best possible performance, and if every economy deals with its problems and imposes no spillover to burden other economies, the relative nature of economics should reach its optimum. There is no guarantee of perfection, but the institution of capitalist economic policies will enable individuals and societies to produce the greatest possible potential.

The discussion on the various dichotomies should enable one to make effective choices and combinations for a progressive economy. Diversity allows alternatives and choices, but some alternatives are superior to others, and the right choices should be made to benefit all. Individuals in every economy are often at the mercy of the leaders, who have the authority to make policy decisions. The ingenuity and smartness of the leaders are important, so is the right for people to choose their leaders, and the right to monitor the activities of political leaders and government officials. The ultimate intention is to avoid the mistakes of the leaders in politicizing the relative nature of economics. Activities with relative outcomes are more acceptable than activities with absolute outcomes.

The ideology of capitalism still provides a solution to numerous human and world problems, because it begins with the work of an individual, and when equipped with freedom, choices, and alternatives, progress can be made. Variations exist, but checks and balances can be instituted to ensure equity, continuity, and sustainability. Crises and recessions occur, but the market mechanisms allow economic revitalization. Economic waves can be seen as dynamic forces that perpetually generate economic relativity movements.

By examining the contemporary world economy that consists of different groups, capitalism does offer a number of suggestions and solutions. To begin with, the industrialized countries can start by improving their own domestic economic strength. Typically, policies can be instituted such that individuals and businesses could have ample economic maneuverability, so that a greater number of productive activities can be conducted by the private sector. Ultimately, it is the increase in domestic output, especially in the real economy, that can open up new opportunities either in terms of expanding some economic sectors or reducing loss in other economic sectors. The economic strength of industrialized countries should guide the pace and direction of world development. Should the industrialized countries regain their economic vitality, it is likely that investment resources will go to other "newcomers" that have potential.

International economic promotion should start to look at countries that have economic potential, and that would not pose ideological challenges to the advanced capitalist free world. There should be a redirection of movement in world resources away from terrorism-prone countries. Countries or regions that are in constant conflict can only be monitored, but solutions must be initiated from within the regions. International institutions can do more, but are often constrained by their own approach to world issues. To the recipients of economic aid and assistance, funding must have to be productivity-related. The two communist giants of Russia and China have more or less reached economic saturation, at least in the short-term, and it will take time, resource-wise and ideology-wise, for them to reach the next stage of development and world acceptability. Nonetheless, the political influence of Russia and the economic influence of China will lead to new problems between these countries, especially when economically-strong China announces itself as the new world power.

What remains are the weaker states in South America and Africa. There are several possibilities. One would be to ensure stability in the first instance, and the leaders of these countries would have to perform so as to show a functioning government. Functioning in the sense that issues and problems would be dealt with appropriately and properly, and results could be seen and quantified. A distinction would have to be made between business leaders who make profits, while political and government leaders have to get things done. Political leaders are not meant to make "profits" through the administrative machinery of the government. Another possibility would be for the few smaller but stable countries to work together by forming some kind of regional body, so that "good practices" can be shared and positive results can be generated to achieve a multiplier effect. For the few large countries, such as Brazil and Mexico, improvements have to be home-grown, as their economies should produce sufficient strength for sustainable growth. Establishment of proper institutions to promote civic society should enhance stability, growth, and investment attraction.

One should not be arguing for protectionism, but globalization does not mean one can pass on its "dirty linen" to neighbors or other countries. Self-strengthening is the best strategy all capitalist market economies could choose. It is only through a stronger domestic economy that a country can participate more in the globalization process. Whether countries are blessed with natural resources may not be the key concern, as many advanced countries do not have many natural resources, but the establishment of institutions that provide civic security counts a lot in the process of self-strengthening. With stability ensured, the instruments of growth and development rely on the way individuals are connected through the market. Globalization just provides a platform for individuals and countries to engage and react with each other. It follows that the stronger countries can participate in the global economy. In turn, it is each and every individual who should take the least from, and contribute the most to, society.

The pursuit of capitalism and the adoption of "supply-side" economic policies will be the answer to the world economy, as these serve as the ex ante factors in economic development, maximize the potentials of every individual, improve the economy's capability and capacity, bring prosperity to communities, and bring peace and freedom to the world economy. Capitalism is the best vehicle that allows "economic relativity" to perform its utmost for the world economy and, ultimately, for humanity.

V. WHY HAS CAPITALISM SUCCEEDED?

References

Abeysinghe, T., 2001. Estimation of direct and indirect impact of oil price on growth. Econ. Lett. 73 (2), 147–153.

Acemoglu, D., 2005. Politics and economics in weak and strong states. J. Monet. Econ. 52, 1199–1226.

Acemoglu, D., Robinson, J.A., 2012. Why Nations Fail? Profile Books, London.

Ackerman, F., 2005. The Shrinking Gains from Trade: A Critical Assessment of Doha Round Projections. Working Paper No. 05-01, Global Development and Environment Institute, Tufts University, October.

Afxentiou, P.C., Serletis, A., 1992. Openness in the Canadian economy: 1870–1988. Appl. Econ. 24 (11), 1191–1198.

Agell, J., Persson, M., 2001. On the analytics of the dynamic Laffer curve. J. Monet. Econ. 48 (2), 397–414.

Agénor, P.-R., Montiel, P.J., 1999. Macroeconomic Development, second ed. Princeton University Press, Princeton.

Aggarwal, V.K., Urata, S. (Eds.), 2006. Bilateral Trade Agreements in the Asia-Pacific: Origins, Evolution and Implications. Routledge, London.

Aghion, P., Howitt, P., 1998. Endogenous Growth Theory. The MIT Press, Cambridge, MA.

Aghion, P., Caroli, E., Garcia-Penalosa, C., 1999. Inequality and economic growth: the perspective of new growth theories. J. Econ. Literat. 37, 1615–1660.

Ahluwalia, M.S., 1976. Inequality, poverty and development. J. Dev. Econ. 3 (4), 307–342.

Aisbett, E., 2005. Why Are the Critics so Convinced that Globalization is Bad for the Poor? Working Paper 11066. National Bureau of Economic Research, Cambridge, MA.

Akbari, A.H., Devoretz, D.J., 1992. The substitutability of foreign-born labour in Canadian-production: circa 1980. Can. J. Econ. 25 (3), 604–614.

Akerlof, G., 1970. The market for 'lemons': quality and the market mechanism. Quart. J. Econ. 84, 488–500.

Akerlof, G., Shiller, R.J., 2015. Phishing for Phools: The Economics of Manipulation and Deception. Princeton University Press, Princeton.

Al Faris, A., Soto, R., 2016. The Economy of Dubai. Oxford University Press, Oxford.

Alboim, N., Omidvar, R., 2002. Fulfilling the Promise: Integrating Immigrant Skills into the Canadian Economy. Caledon Institute of Social Policy, Queen's University, Ottawa.

Alesina, A., Dollar, D., 2000. Who gives foreign aid to whom and why? J. Econ. Growth 5 (1), 33–63.

Alesina, A., Spolaore, E., 2005. War, peace, and the size of countries. J. Public Econ. 89 (7), 1333–1354.

Alesina, A., Wacziarg, R., 1998. Openness, country size and government. J. Public Econ. 69 (3), 305–321.

Alesina, A., Devleeschauwer, A., Easterly, W., Kurlat, S., Wacziarg, R., 2003. Fractionalization. J. Econ. Growth 8, 155–194.

Allen, G.C., 1981. The Japanese Economy. Weidenfeld and Nicolson, London.

Alogoskoufis, G., 2013. Macroeconomics and Politics in the Accumulation of Greece's Debt: An Econometric Investigation, 1975-2009. GreeSE Paper No. 68, Hellenic Observatory Papers on Greece and Southeast Europe, Hellenic Observatory European Institute, March.

Alquist, R., Kilian, L., 2010. What do we learn from the price of crude oil futures? J. Appl. Econ. 25, 539–573.

Amin, S., 1976. Unequal Development. Monthly Review Press, New York.

Amsden, A., 1989. Asia's Next Giant: South Korea and Late Industrialization. Oxford University Press, New York.

Anand, S., 1993. The Kuznets process and the inequality-development relationship. J. Dev. Econ. 40 (1), 25–52.

Andrès, J., Domènech, R., Fatás, A., 2008. The stabilizing role of government size. J. Econ. Dynam. Control 32 (2), 571–593.

Apergis, N., Cooray, A., 2013. New Evidence on the Remedies of the Greek Sovereign Debt Problem. GreeSE Paper No. 79, Hellenic Observatory Papers on Greece and Southeast Europe, Hellenic Observatory European Institute, November.

Ardagna, S., Caselli, F., Lane, T., 2007. Fiscal discipline and the cost of public debt service: some estimates for OECD countries. BE J. Macroecon. 7 (1), 1935–1960.

Arestis, P., Sawyer, M., 2003. Reinventing fiscal policy. J. Post-Keynesian Econ. 26 (1), 3–25.

Arneson, R.J., 1989. Equality and equal opportunity for welfare. Philosop. Stud. 56, 77–93.

Ashton, T.S., 1948. The Industrial Revolution (1760-1830). Oxford University Press, Oxford.

Asian Development Bank, 2014. Redefining Poverty in Asia and the Pacific: ADB's Take. Asian Development Bank, Manila.

Aspers, P., 2001. Crossing the boundary of economics and sociology: the case of Vilfredo Pareto. Am. J. Econ. Sociol. 60 (2), 519–545.

Atkinson, A.B., 1983. The Economics of Inequality. Clarendon Press, Oxford.

Atkinson, A.B., 1987. On the measurement of poverty. Econometrica 55 (4), 749–764.

Auerbach, A., Gale, W.G., 2009. The Economic Crisis and the Fiscal Crisis: 2009 and Beyond. Working Paper, Berkeley Economics, University of California Berkeley.

Awartani, H., Kleiman, E., 1997. Economic interactions among participants in the middle east peace process. Middle East J. 51 (2), 215–229.

Bai, C.-E., David, D.L., Tao, Z., Wang, Y., 2000. A multitask theory of state enterprise reform. J. Comparat. Econ. 28 (4), 716–738.

Baier, S.L., Bergstrand, J.H., 2007. Do free trade agreements actually increase members' international trade? J. Int. Econ. 71 (1), 72–95.

Balakrishnan, S., Koza, M.P., 1993. Information asymmetry, adverse selection and joint-ventures: theory and evidence. J. Econ. Behav. Org. 20 (1), 99–117.

Balassa, B., 1962. The Theory of Economic Integration. Routledge, London.

Balassa, B., 1981. The Newly Industrializing Countries in the World Economy. Pergamon Press, New York.

Balassa, B., Noland, M., 1988. Japan in the World Economy. Institute of International Economics, Washington, DC.

Baldwin, J.R., Gu, W., 2005. Global Links: Multinationals, Foreign Ownership and Productivity Growth in Canadian Manufacturing. Microeconomic Analysis Division, Statistics Canada, Ottawa.

Baldwin, J.R., Hanel, P., 2003. Innovation and Knowledge Creation in an Open Economy: Canadian Industry and International Implications. Cambridge University Press, New York.

Baran, P.A., 1952. On the political economy of backwardness. Manch. Sch. 20 (1), 68–84.

Baran, P.A., Hobsbawm, E.J., 1961. The stages of economic growth. KYKLOS 14 (2), 234–242.

Baranovsky, V., 2000. Russia: a part of Europe or apart from Europe? Int. Aff. 76 (3), 443–458.

Barling, J., Fullagag, C., Kelloway, K.E., 1992. The Union and Its Members: A Psychological Approach. Oxford University Press, New York.

Barr, M.D., 2000. Lee Kuan Yew: The Beliefs Behind the Man. Curzon Press, Richmond, Surrey.

Barro, R.J., 1976. Rational expectations and the role of monetary policy. J. Monet. Econ. 2, 1–32.

Barro, R.J., 1979. On the determination of the public debt. J. Polit. Econ. 87 (5), 940–971.

Barro, R.J., 1991. Economic growth in cross section of countries. Quart. J. Econ. 106 (5), 407–443.

Barro, R.J., 1999. Determinants of democracy. J. Polit. Econ. 107 (S6), S158–S183.

Barro, R.J., 2000. Inequality and growth in a panel of countries. J. Econ. Growth 5, 5–32.

Barro, R.J., Gordon, D.B., 1983. Rules, discretion and reputation in a model of monetary policy. J. Monet. Econ. 12, 101–122.

Barro, R.J., Sala-i-Martin, X., 1995. Capital mobility in neoclassical models of growth. Am. Econ. Rev. 85 (1), 103–115.

Baum, R., 1980. China's Four Modernizations: The New Technological Revolution. Westview Press, Boulder.

Baum, R., 1996. Burying Mao: Chinese Politics in the Age of Deng Xiaoping. Princeton University Press, Princeton, NJ.

Baumol, W.J., 1982. Contestable markets: an uprising in the theory of industry structure. Am. Econ. Rev. 72 (1), 1–15.

Beasley, W.G., 2000. The Rise of Modern Japan: Political, Economic and Social Change Since 1950. MacMillan, New York.

Becker, G., 2012. Is Capitalism in Crisis? E-axes. www.e-axes.com.

Bedeski, R.E., 1977. The concept of the state: Sun Yat-sen and Mao tse-tung. China Quart. 70, 338–354.

Beine, M., Docquier, F., Rapoport, H., 2001. Brain drain and economic growth: theory and evidence. J. Dev. Econ. 64 (1), 275–289.

Bell, D.A., 2015. The China Model: Political Meritocracy and the Limits of Democracy. Princeton University Press, Princeton.

Bell, M.W., Khor, H.E., Kochhar, K., 1993. China at the Threshold of a Market Economy, Occasional Paper 107. International Monetary Fund, Washington, DC.

Bénabou, R., 1996. Inequality and Growth, Discussion Paper No. 1460. Center for Economic Policy Research, London.

Ben-David, D., 1996. Trade and convergence among countries. J. Int. Econ. 40 (3-4), 279–298.

Bender, B., 1984. An analysis of the Laffer curve. Econ. Enq. 22 (3), 414–420.

Benewick, R., 1995. The Tiananmen crackdown and its legacy. In: Benewick, R., Wingrove, P. (Eds.), China in the 1990s. Macmillan Education, London.

Berger, S., 2015. Making in America: From Innovation to Market. The MIT Press, Cambridge, MA.

Bergère, M.-C., 1998. Sun Yat-sen. Stanford University Press, Stanford.

Beresford, M., 2008. Doi Moi in review: the challenges of building market socialism in Vietnam. J. Contemp. Asia 38 (2), 221–243.

Bernanke, B.S., 2015. The Federal Reserve and the Financial Crisis. Princeton University Press, Princeton.

Bernanke, B.S., Mishkin, F.S., 1997. Inflation targeting: a new framework for monetary policy? J. Econ. Perspect. 11, 97–116.

Bettleheim, C., 1974. Cultural Revolution and Industrial Organization in China: Changes in Management and the Division of Labor. Monthly Review Press, New York.

Bettleheim, C., 1988. Economic reform in China. J. Dev. Stud. 24 (4), 15–49.

Bhagwati, J., 2004. In Defense of Globalization. Oxford University Press, New York.

Bhagwati, J., Hamada, K., 1974. The brain drain, international integration of markets for professionals and unemployment. J. Dev. Econ. 1, 19–42.

Bhagwati, J., Krishna, P., Panagariya, A. (Eds.), 1999. Trading Blocs: Alternative Approaches to Analyzing Preferential Trade Agreements. The MIT Press, Cambridge, MA.

Birdsall, N., Ross, D., Sabot, R., 1995. Inequality and growth reconsidered: lessons from East Asia. World Bank Econ. Rev. 9 (3), 477–508.

Bitros, G., 2012. From Riches to Rugs or What Went Wrong in Greece. Research on the Greek Debt Crisis, E-axes, July.

Blackcorby, C., Donaldson, D., 1978. Measures of relative equality and their meaning in terms of social welfare. J. Econ. Theory 18, 59–80.

Blanchard, O.J., 1984. Debt, Deficits and Finite Horizons, NBER Working Paper No. 1389. National Bureau of Economic Research, Cambridge, MA.

Blanchard, O.J., Shleifer, A., 2000. Federalism With and Without Political Centralization: China Versus Russia, NBER Working Paper No. 7616. National Bureau of Economic Research, Cambridge, MA.

Blejer, M., Burton, D., Dunaway, S., Szapary, G., 1991. China: Economic Reform and Macroeconomic Management, Occasional Paper 76. International Monetary Fund, Washington, DC.

Blinder, A.S., Reis, R., 2005. Understanding the Greenspan Standard. Economic Symposium on "The Greenspan Era: Lessons for the Future", Federal Reserve Bank of Kansas City, Jackson Hole, WY.

Block, F., 1981. The fiscal crisis of the capitalist state. Ann. Rev. Sociol. 7, 1–7.

Blomberg, S.B., Hess, G.D., 2003. Is the political business cycle for real? J. Public Econ. 87 (5–6), 1091–1121.

Boettke, P.J., 1998. Rational choice and human agency in economics and sociology: explaining the Weber-Austrian connections. In: Giersch, H. (Ed.), Merits and Limits of Markets. Springer-Verlag, Berlin, pp. 53–81.

Bohn, H., 1998. The behavior of U.S. public debt and deficits. Quart. J. Econ. 113 (3), 949–963.

Boone, P., 1996. Politics and the effectiveness of foreign aid. Eur. Econ. Rev. 40 (2), 289–329.

Borensztein, E., De Greforio, J., Lee, J.-W., 1998. How does foreign direct investment affect economic growth? J. Int. Econ. 45 (1), 115–135.

Borich, J.J., 1999. Zhu Rongji's US Visit and the World Trade Organization. Washington State China Relations Council, Washington, April 30.

Borjas, G.J., 1994. The Economic Benefits from Immigration, NBER Working Paper No. 4955. National Bureau of Economic Research, December.

Bourguignon, F., 1979. Decomposable income inequality measures. Econometrica 47 (4), 901–920.

Braguinsky, S., Yavlinsky, G., 2000. Incentives and Institutions: The Transition to a Market Economy in Russia. Princeton University Press, Princeton.

Brandt, W., 1980. North-South: A Program of Survival: Report of the Independent Commission on International Development Issues. MIT Press, Cambridge, MA.

Braun, R.A., Waki, Y., 2006. Monetary policy during Japan's lost decade. Jpn. Econ. Rev. 57 (2), 324–344.

Brautigam, D., 2011. The Dragon's Gift: The Real Story of China in Africa. Oxford University Press, Oxford.

Brautigam, D., 2016. Will Africa Feed China? Oxford University Press, Oxford.

Brenton, P., Di Mauro, F., Lúcke, M., 1999. Economic integration and FDI: an empirical analysis of foreign investment in the EU and in Central and Eastern Europe. Empirica 26, 95–121.

Bronfenbrenner, M., 1971. Income Distribution Theory. Aldine Publishing Company, New York.

Brown, D.K., Deardorff, A.V., Stern, R.M., 2003. Multilateral, regional and bilateral trade-policy options for the United States and Japan. The World Economy 26 (6), 803–828.

Brown, M.B., 1974. Economics of Imperialism. Penguin Books, London.

Bryant, D., Clark, P., 2006. History empathy and "Canada: a people's history". Can. J. Edu. 29 (4), 1039–1063.

Buchanan, J.M., 1959. Positive economics, welfare economics and political economy. J. Law Econ. 2 (October), 124–138.

Buchanan, J.M., Lee, D.R., 1982. Politics, time, and the Laffer curve. J. Polit. Econ 90 (4), 816–819.

Buchanan, J.M., Stubblebine, W.C., 1962. Externality. Economica 29 (116), 371–384.

Bulíř, A., 2001. Income inequality: does inflation matter? IMF Staff Papers 48, 139–159.

Bullard, J., Mitra, K., 2006. Determinacy, learnability and monetary policy inertia. J. Money, Cred. Bank. 39 (5), 1177–1212.

Burbridge, J., Harrison, A., 1985. (Innovation) accounting for the impact of fluctuation in U.S. variables on the Canadian economy. Can. J. Econ. 18 (4), 784–798.

Bussiere, M., Fratzscher, M., 2006. Towards a new early warning system of financial crises. J. Int. Money Finance 25 (6), 953–973.

Butler, E., 2007. Adam Smith – A Primer, Occasional Paper No. 141. Institute of Economic Affairs, London.

Cahuc, P., Michel, P., 1996. Minimum wage unemployment and growth. Eur. Econ. Rev. 40 (7), 1463–1482.

Calvo, G.A., Mendoza, E.G., 1996. Mexico's balance-of-payments crisis: a chronicle of a death foretold. J. Int. Econ 41 (3–4), 235–264.

Canto, V.A., Joines, D.H., Laffer, A.B. (Eds.), 1983. Foundations of Supply-Side Economics: Theory and Evidence. Academic Press, New York.

Caplin, A., Leahy, J., 1996. Monetary policy as a process of search. Am. Econ. Rev. 86 (4), 689–702.

Caporaso, J.A., Rhodes, M., 2016. The Political and Economic Dynamics of the Eurozone Crisis. Oxford University Press, Oxford.

Card, D., Krueger, A.B., 1995. Myth and Measurement: The New Economics of the Minimum Wage. Princeton University Press, New Jersey.

Carnoy, M., 1984. The State and Political Theory. Princeton University Press, New Jersey.

Carr, E.H., 1985. The Bolshevik Revolution, 1917-1923. WW Norton & Company, New York.

Caselli, F., Centeno, M., Tavares, J. (Eds.), 2016. After the Crisis: Reform, Recovery and Growth in Europe. Oxford University Press, Oxford.

Cass, D., 1965. Optimum growth in an aggregative model of capital accumulation. Rev. Econ. Stud. 32 (3), 233–240.

del Castillo, G., 2008. Rebuilding War-torn States: The Challenge of Post-Conflict Economic Reconstruction. Oxford University Press, Oxford.

Cavanugh, F.X., 1996. The Truth About the National Debt: Five Myths and One Reality. Harvard Business School Press, Boston, MA.

Cecchetti, S., 1996. Practical issues in monetary policy targeting. Feder. Res. Bank Cleveland Econ. Rev. 32 (1), 2–15.

Cecchetti, S., K. Schoenholtz, 2015, "What Should Greece Do?", Commentary on the Greek Debt Crisis, E-axes, August.

Chan, J., 2014. Hong Kong's umbrella movement. Commonwealth J. Int. Aff. 103 (6), 571–580.

Chan, M.K., Postiglione, G.A., 1996. The Hong Kong Reader: Passage to Chinese Sovereignty. M. E. Sharpe, New York.

Chan, N., 2003. Land acquisition compensation in China – problems and answers. Int. Real Estate Rev. 6 (1), 136–152.

Chanda, N., 2015. The silk road: old and new. Global Asia 10 (3), 13–15.

Chang, I., 1997. The Rape of Nanking: The Forgotten Holocaust of World War II. Basic Books, New York.

Chang, J., Jon, H., 2005. Mao: The Unknown Story. Globalflair Ltd, London.

Chang, P.H., 1973. Radicals and Radical Ideology in China's Cultural Revolution. School of International Affairs, Columbia University, New York.

Charlton, A.H., Stiglitz, J.E., 2005. A development-friendly prioritisation of doha round proposals. World Econ. 28 (3), 293–312.

Chee, C.H., 1986. Singapore in 1985: managing political transition and economic recession. Asian Survey 26 (2), 158–167.

Chen, B.-L., 2003. An inverted-U relationship between inequality and long-run growth. Econ. Lett. 78, 205–212.

Chen, J., 2001. Mao's China and the Cold War. University of North Carolina Press, North Carolina.

Chen, P., Kan, C.-Y., 1997. Taiwan's trade and investment in China. In: Li, K.-W. (Ed.), Financing China Trade and Investment. Praeger Publisher, Connecticut, pp. 121–138.

Cheng, H., Ma, L., 2009. White collar crime and the criminal justice system: government response to bank fraud and corruption in China. J. Financial Crime 16 (2), 166–179.

Cheng, T., Selden, M., 1994. The origins and social consequences of China's Hukou System. China Quart. 139, 644–668.

Cheung, S.N.S., 1969. The Theory of Share Tenancy, With Special Application to Asian Agriculture and the First Phase of Taiwan Land Reform. University of Chicago Press, Chicago.

Cheung, Y.W., Qian, X., 2009. Empirics of China's outward direct investment. Pacif. Econ. Rev. 14, 312–341.

Chow, G.C., 1985. A model of Chinese national income determination. J. Polit. Econ. 93 (4), 782–792.

Chow, G.C., 2002. China's Economic Transformation. Blackwell, Oxford.

Chow, G.C., Li, K.-W., 2002. China's economic growth: 1952–2010. Econ. Dev. Cult. Change 51 (1), 247–256.

Chu, W.-W., 2010. Market socialism, Chinese style: bringing development back into economic theory. China Econ. J. 3 (3), 307–312.

Chung, J.H., 2015. View from Northeast Asia: a Chinese-style pivot or a mega-opportunity. Global Asia 10 (3), 22–26.

Claessens, S., 1990. The debt Laffer curve: some estimates. World Dev. 18 (12), 1671–1677.

Clark, P., 2008. The Chinese Cultural Revolution: A History. Cambridge University Press, New York.

Clarke, D., Lu, F., 2016. The Law of China's Local Government Debt Crisis: Local Government Financing Vehicles and Their Bonds. GWU Legal Studies Research Paper No. 2016-31, George Washington University Law School, June.

Cleveland, W.L., 1994. A History of the Modern Middle East. Westview Press, Boulder.

Clifford, M.L., 1998. Troubled Tiger: Businessmen, Bureaucrats, and Generals in South Korea, revised ed. M. E. Sharpe, New York.

Cohen, S.F., 1980. Bukharin and the Bolshevik Revolution: A Political Biography, 1888–1938. Oxford University Press, Oxford.

Cole, H.L., Kehoe, T.J., 1996. A self-fulfilling model of Mexico's 1994-1995 debt crisis. J. Int. Econ. 41 (304), 309–330.

Coleman, J.S., 1983. Equality of opportunity and equality of results. In: Letwin, W. (Ed.), Against Equality. MacMillan, London.

Committeri, M., Spadafora, F., 2013. You Never Give Me Your Money? Sovereign Debt Crisis, Collective Action Problems, and IMF Lending, IMF Working Paper No. 13/20. IMF, Washington, DC.

Conly, S., 2016. One Child: Do We have a Right to More? Oxford University Press, New York.

Conti-Brown, P., 2016. The Power and Independence of the Federal Reserve. Princeton University Press, Princeton.

Cooper, A.F., 2016. The BRICS: A Very Short Introduction. Oxford University Press, Oxford.

Corsetti, G., Pesenti, P., Roubini, N., 1999. Paper tigers? A model of the Asian crisis. Eur. Econ. Rev. 43, 1211–1236.

Cowell, F.A., 2000. Measurement of inequality. In: Atkinson, A.B., Bourguignon, François (Eds.), Handbook of Income Distribution, 1. North Holland, Amsterdam, pp. 87–166.

Cradock, P., 1994. Experiences of China. John Murray Publishers Ltd, London.

Crafts, N.F.R., 1985. British Economic Growth During the Industrial Revolution. Oxford University Press, New York.

Crețu, C., 2015. Investing in Greece: More than 35 Million Euro from EU Funds for Jobs and Growth. Blog Post, European Commission, July 16.

Crichton, K., 2006. Party games. China Rises (video recording). Morningstar Entertainment Inc, Toronto.

Cruces, J.J., Trebesch, C., 2012. Sovereign Defaults: The Price of Haircuts. CESifo Area Conference on Macro, Money and International Finance, Munich, March.

Cunningham, F., 2002. Theories of Democracy: A Critical Introduction. Routledge, New York.

Cutter, W.B., Spero, J., D'Andrea Tyson, L., 2000. New world, new deal: a democratic approach to globalization. Foreign Aff. 79 (2), 80–98.

Dahl, R.A., 1957. The concept of power. Behav. Sci. 2 (3), 201–215.

Dahl, R.A., 1991. Democracy and Its Critics. Yale University Press, New Haven.

Dahl, R.A., 1992. Why free markets are not enough. J. Democr. 3 (1), 82–89.

Dahl, R.A., 1996. Equality versus inequality. Polit. Sci. Polit. 29 (4), 639–648.

Dahl, R.A., 2000. On Democracy. Yale University Press, New Haven.

Dahl, R.A., 2006a. On Political Equality. Yale University Press, New Haven.

Dahl, R.A., 2006b. A Preface to Democratic Theory, expanded ed. University of Chicago Press, Chicago.

Dahlman, C.J., 1979. The problem of externality. J. Law Econ. 22 (1), 141–162.

Dalgaard, C.-J., Hansen, H., Tarp, F., 2004. On the empirics of foreign aid and growth. Econ. J. 114 (496), F-191–F216.

Dalziel, P., Higgins, J., 2006. Pareto, parsons and the boundary between economics and sociology. Am. J. Econ. Sociol. 65 (1), 109–126.

Daunton, M.J., 1995. Progress and Poverty: An Economic and Social History of Britain, 1700–1850. Oxford University Press, Oxford.

Davis, D., 1989. Chinese social welfare: policies and outcomes. China Quart. 119, 577–597.

De Meza, D., Webb, D.C., 1987. Too much investment: a problem of asymmetric information. Quart. J. Econ. 102 (2), 281–292.

De Morais, R.M., 2011. The new imperialism: China in Angola. World Affairs, March/April.

De Soto, H., 2000. The Mystery of Capital: Why Capitalism Triumphs in the West and Fails Everywhere Else. Basic Books, New York.

Dean, B., 1974. China and Great Britain: The Diplomacy of Commercial Relations, 1860–1864. Harvard University Press, Cambridge, MA.

Deardorff, A.V., 2006. Terms of Trade. World Scientific Publishers, Singapore.

Debreu, G., 1954. Valuation equilibrium and pareto optimum. Proc. Natl. Acad. Sci. U.S.A. pp. 588–592.

DeGarmo, D., Wrobbel, E.D., 2015. Thinking About War and Peace. Routledge, London.

Degolyer, M.E., Scott, J.L., 1996. The myth of political apathy in Hong Kong. Ann. Am. Acad. Polit. Soc. Sci. 547, 68–78, September.

Deininger, K., Squire, L., 1996. A new data set measuring income inequality. World Bank Econ. Rev. 10 (3), 565–592.

Deininger, K., Squire, L., 1997. Economic growth and income inequality: reexamining the links. Finance and Development, March.

Demsetz, H., 1967. Toward a theory of property rights. Am. Econ. Rev. 57 (2), 347–359.

Desai, M., 1974. Marxian Economic Theory. Gray-Mills Publishing Limited, London.

Devlin, J.C., 2016. Economics of the Middle East: Development Challenges. World Scientific Publishers, Singapore.

Diamond, P.A., 1965. National debt in a neoclassical growth model. Am. Econ. Rev. 55 (5), 1126–1150.

Dimoulas, C., 2014. Exploring the impact of employment policy measures in the context of crisis: the case of Greece. Int. Soc. Sec. Rev. 67 (2), 49–65.

Ding, C., 2007. Policy and praxis of land acquisition in China. Land Use Policy 24, 1–13.

Dittmer, L., 1974. Liu Shao-chi and the Chinese Cultural Revolution: The Politics of Mass Criticism. University of California Press, Berkeley.

Dobb, M., 1969. Welfare Economics and the Economics of Socialism. Cambridge University Press, Cambridge.

Dong, Y., Li, K.-W., Zhang, D., 2011. Comparing the determinants of outward investment from China and the United States. Chinese Econ. 44 (2), 58–77.

Dornbusch, R., 1987. Dollars, Debts, and Deficits. MIT Press, Cambridge, MA.

Dornbusch, R., 1993. Stabilization, Debt, and Reform. Harvester Wheatsheaf, Hemel Hempstead.

Dornbusch, R., Fischer, S., Samuelson, P.A., 1977. Comparative advantage, trade, and payments in a Ricardian model with a continuum of goods. Am. Econ. Rev. 67 (5), 823–839.

Dore, R., 2000. Stock Market Capitalism: Welfare Capitalism: Japan and Germany Versus the Anglo-Saxons. Oxford University Press, Oxford.

Dorsey, J.M., 2015. Anti-Chinese Protests in Turkey: Relations with China Under Test, RSIS Commentary No. 153. Nanyang Technological University, Singapore, July 15.

Doyle, M., 2006. On the Optimality of Delay in Monetary Policy as a Process of Search. Working Paper No. 06006. Department of Economics, Iowa State University.

Drazen, A., 2001. The political business cycle after 25 years. In: Bernanke, B.S., Rogoff, K. (Eds.), NBER Macroeconomics Annual 2000, Volume 15. MIT Press, Cambridge, MA, pp. 75–138.

Dreher, A., 2004. A public choice perspective of IMF and World Bank lending and conditionality. Public Choice 119 (3–4), 445–464.

Dreyer, E.L., 1995. China at War 1901-1949. Taylor & Francis, London.

Dreyer, E.L., 2008. The myth of "One China". In: Chow, P.C.Y. (Ed.), The "One China" Dilemma. Palgrave Macmillan, New York, pp. 18–36.

Dunn, L., 1985. Hong Kong after the Sino-British declaration. Int. Aff. 61 (2), 197–204.

Durlauf, S.N., Quah, D.T., 1999. The new empirics of economic growth. In: Taylor, J.B., Woodford, M. (Eds.), Handbook of Macroeconomics, Volume 1. North-Holland, The Netherlands, pp. 235–308. Part A, Chapter 4.

Durlauf, S.N., Johnson, P.A., Temple, J.R.W., 2005. Growth econometrics. In: Aghion, P., Durlauf, S.N. (Eds.), Handbook of Economic Growth, Volume 1. North Holland, The Netherlands, pp. 555–677. Part A, Chapter Eight.

Durlauf, S.N., Kourtellos, A., Tan, C.M., 2012. Is god in the details? A reexamination of the role of religion in economic growth. J. Appl. Econ. 27 (7), 1059–1075.

Dworkin, R., 1981. What is equality? Part I: equality of welfare and part II: equality of resources. Philos. Public Aff. 10 (3), 185–246, and 10 (4) Fall: 283–345.

Dyker, D.A., 1992. Restructuring the Soviet Economy. Routledge, London.

Eagleton, T., 2006. Criticism and Ideology: A Study in Marxist Literary Theory. Verso, London.

Easterly, W., 2003a. Can foreign aid buy growth? J. Econ. Perspect. 17 (3), 23–48.

Easterly, W., 2003b. The IMF and World Bank structural adjustment programs and poverty. In: Dooley, M., Frankel, J.A. (Eds.), Managing Currency Crises in Emerging Markets. University of Chicago Press, Chicago, pp. 361–391.

Easterly, W., Levine, R., 1997. Africa's growth tragedy: policies and ethnic divisions. Quart. J. Econ. 111 (4), 1203–1250.

Eastman, L.E., 1989. Family, Fields, and Ancestors: Constancy and Change in China's Social and Economic History, 1550–1949. Oxford University Press, Oxford.

Eaton, J., 1987. Public debt guarantees and private capital flight. World Bank Econ. Rev. 1 (3), 377–395.

Eckstein, A., 1975. China's Economic Development: The Interplay of Scarcity and Ideology. University of Michigan Press, Michigan.

The Economist Intelligence Unit, 2015. Prospects and Challenges on China's 'One Belt, One Road': A Risk Assessment Report. The Economists EIU, London.

Edison, H.J., 2003. Do indicators of financial crises work? An evaluation of an early warning system. Int. J. Finance Econ. 8 (1), 11–53.

Eichengreen, B., Tong, H., 2006. How China is reorganizing the world economy. Asian Econ. Policy Rev. 1, 73–97.

Eichengreen, B., Rose, A.K., Wyplosz, C., 1998. Contagious currency tests: first tests. Scandin. J. Econ. 4, 463–484.

El-Agraa, A.M., 2011. The European Union: Economics and Policies. Cambridge University Press, Cambridge.

Elvin, M., 1984. Why China failed to create an endogenous industrial capitalism: a critique of max weber's explanation. Theory Soc. 13 (3), 379–391.

Enderlin, C., 2002. Shattered Dreams: The Failure of the Peace Process in the Middle East, 1995-2002. Other Press, New York.

Energy Information Administration, 2015. OPEC Revenues Fact Sheet. U.S. Energy Information Administration, Washington, DC.

Epstein, T.S., 1968. Capitalism, Primitive and Modern. Australian National University Press, Canberra.

Erbaugh, M.S., 1995. Southern Chinese dialects as a medium for reconciliation within greater China. Lang. Soc. 24 (1), 79–94.

Etzkowitz, N., 2003. Innovations in innovation: the Triple Helix of University-Industry-Government Relations. Soc. Sci. Inf. 42 (3), 293–337.

EU-Japan Center for Industrial Cooperation, 2015. Digital Economy in Japan and the EU: An Assessment of the Common Challenges and the Collaboration Potential. Tokyo, March.

European Commission, 2015. Euro 54 Million for Improved Cross Border Cooperation between Greece and Cyprus. European Commission, July 28.

Exadaktylos, T., Zahariadis, N., 2012. Policy Implementation and Political Trust: Greece in the Age of Austerity. GreeSE Paper No. 65, Hellenic Observatory Papers on Greece and Southeast Europe, Hellenic Observatory European Institute, December.

Fahrholz, C., Wójcik, C., 2010. The Bail-Out! Positive Political Economics of Greek-type Crisis in the EMU. CESifo Working Paper No. 3178, September.

Fanon, F., 1967. The Wretched of the Earth. Penguin Books, London.

Fatás, A., Mihov, I., 2001. Government size and automatic stabilizers: international and intra-national evidence. J. Int. Econ. 55 (1), 3–28.

Fawcett, L., 2013. International Relations of the Middle East, third ed. Oxford University Press, Oxford.

Feldman, A.M., 1989. Welfare Economics and Social Choice Theory. Martinus Nijhoff Publishing, Amsterdam.

Feldstein, M., 1986. Supply-side economics: old truths and new claims. Am. Econ. Rev. 76 (2), 26–30.

Feldstein, M., 2002. Economic and Financial Crises in Emerging Market Economies: Overview of Prevention and Management, NBER Working Paper No. 8837. National Bureau of Economic Research, Cambridge, MA.

Fenby, J., 2003. Generalissimo Chiang Kai-Shek and the China He Lost. The Free Press, London.

Feng, H., 2006. The Politics of China's Accession to the World Trade Organization. Routledge, London.

Feng, X., Johansson, A.C., 2016. Underpaid and corrupt executives in China's State sector. Journal of Business Ethics, Published online, May.

Fewsmith, J., 2001. China Since Tiananmen: The Politics of Transition. Cambridge University Press, Cambridge.

Financial Services Authority, 2009. The Turner Review: A Regulatory Response to the Global Banking Crisis. London, March.

Fine, B., 1975. Marx's Capital. MacMillan Press, London.

Fischer, B.A., 1997. The Reagan Reversal: Foreign Policy and the End of the Cold War. University of Missouri Press, Columbia.

Fischer, M.M., Stirböck, C., 2004. Regional Income Convergence in the Enlarged Europe, 1995-2000: A Spatial Econometric Perspective. ZEW - Centre for European Economic Research Discussion Paper No. 04-042.

Fischer, S., 1990. Rules versus discretion. In: Friedman, B.M., Hahn, F.H. (Eds.), Handbook of Monetary Economics. North-Holland, Amsterdam, pp. 1155–1184.

Fischer, S., 2003. Globalization and Its Challenges. In: Ely Lecture, American Economic Association Meeting, Washington, DC, January.

Floyd, D., 1964. Mao Against Khrushchev: A Short History of the Sino-Soviet Conflict. Praeger Publishers, Connecticut.

Fong, M., 2016. One Child: The Story of China's Most Radical Experiment. Houghton Mifflin Harcourt, Boston.

Foster, J., Greer, J., Thorbecke, E., 1984. A class of decomposable poverty measures. Econometrica 52 (3), 761–766.

Frank, A.G., 1981. Crisis: In the Third World. Heinemann, London.

Frankel, C., 1983. Equality of opportunity. In: Letwin, W. (Ed.), Against Equality. MacMillan, London.

Frankfurt, H.G., 1987. Equality as a moral ideal. Ethics 98, 21–43.

Freeman, D.B., 1996. Doi Moi policy and the small-enterprise boom in Ho Chi Minh City, Vietnam. Geograph. Rev. 86 (2), 178–197.

Freeman, R.B., 1996. The minimum wage as a redistribution tool. Econ. J. 106 (436), 639–649.

French, K.R., Baily, M.N., Campbell, J.Y., Cochrane, J.H., Diamond, D.W., Duffie, D., et al., 2010. The Squam Lake Report: Fixing the Financial System. Princeton University Press, Princeton.

Friedman, M., 1962. Capitalism and Freedom. University of Chicago Press, Chicago.

Friedman, M., 1981. Free to Choose. Pelican, London.

Friedman, M., 1991. Monetary Economics. Blackwell Publisher, Oxford.

Friedman, M., 1993. Why Government Is the Problem? Hoover Institution, Stanford University, Stanford, CA.

Fund for Peace, 2015. Fragile State Index. Washington, DC.

Fujiki, H., Okina, K., Shiratsuka, S., 2001. Monetary policy under zero interest rate: viewpoints of central bank economists. Monet. Econ. Stud.89–130, February.

Fukao, M., 2003. Japan's Lost Decade and Its Financial System. World Economy 26 (3), 365–384.

Gaddis, J.L., 1992. The United States and the End of the Cold War: Implications, Reconsiderations, Provocations. Oxford University Press, New York.

Gaddis, J.L., 2005. The Cold War: A New History. Penguin Press, London.

Gaddy, C.G., Ickes, B.W., 1998. Russia's virtual economy. Foreign Affairs 77 (5), 53–67.

Gaidar, Y., 2014. Russia: A Long View. The MIT Press, Cambridge, MA.

Galenianos, M., 2014. The Greek Crisis: Origins and Implications. Research Papers on the Greek Debt Crisis, E-axes, March.

Gali, J., 2015. Monetary Policy, Inflation, and the Business Cycle, second ed. Princeton University Press, Princeton.

Gallagher, K.P., 2007. Understanding developing country resistance to the doha round. Rev. Int. Polit. Econ. 15 (91), 62–85.

Gallup, J.L., Sacks, J.D., Mellinger, A.D., 1999. Geography and economic development. Int. Reg. Sci. Rev. 22 (2), 179–232.

Gang, F., 1994. Incremental changes and dual-track transition: understanding the case of China. Econ. Policy 9 (19), 99–122.

Gao, M., 2008. The Battle for China's Past: Mao and the Cultural Revolution. Pluto Press, London.

Garen, J., Trask, K., 2005. Do more open economies have bigger governments: another look. J. Dev. Econ. 77 (2), 533–551.

Garthoff, R.L., 1982. Détente and Confrontation: American-Soviet Relations from Nixon to Reagan, National Council for Soviet and East European Research, December.

Ge, W., 1999. Special economic zones and the opening of the Chinese economy: some lessons for economic liberalization. World Dev. 27 (7), 1267–1285.

Gechert, S., Rannenberg, A., 2015. The Costs of Greece's Fiscal Consolidation. Policy Brief, Macroeconomic Policy Institute, Düsseldorf, Germany, March.

Gelb, A., Jefferson, G., Singh, I., 1993. Can communist economies transform incrementally? The experience of China. Econ. Transit. 1 (4), 401–435.

Gerrard, B., 1989. Theory of the Capitalist Economy. Basil Blackwell, Oxford.

Ghosh, P.K., 2015. Daunting realities: territorial disputes and shipping challenges to China's maritime silk road. Global Asia 10 (3), 48–52.

Giannitsis, T., Zografakis, S., 2015. Greece: Solidarity and Adjustment in Times of Crisis. Macroeconomic Policy Institute, Düsseldorf, March.

Gibbons, W.C., 1995. The U.S. Government and the Vietnam War. Princeton University Press, New Jersey.

Giese, K., 2015. Chinese Traders in Africa – Trapped in Liminality. CEFC Seminar, University Center for China Studies, Chinese University of Hong Kong, Hong Kong.

Gillis, M., Perkins, D.H., Roemer, M., Snodgrass, D.R., 1983. Economics of Development. W. W. Norton, New York.

Gini, C., 1912. Variability and Mutability. C. Cuppini, Bologna.

Ginty, R.M., Richmond, O., 2007. Myth or reality: opposing views on the liberal peace and post-war reconstruction. Global Soc. 21 (4), 491–497.

Gluck, C., 1985. Japan's Modern Myths: Ideology in the Late Meiji Period. Princeton University Press, Princeton.

Godement, F., 2015. Europe scrambles to benefit from China's 21st-century silk road. Global Asia 10 (3), 34–38.

Gokhale, J., Van Doren, P., 2009. Would stricter Fed policy and financial regulation have averted the financial crisis? Cato Instit. Policy Anal. 648, October.

Golden, D.G., Poterba, J.M., 1980. The price of popularity: the political business cycle reexamined. Am. J. Polit. Sci. 24 (4), 696–714.

Goldstein, S.M., 1995. China in transition: the political foundation of incremental reform. China Quart. 144 (December), 1105–1131.

Goodfriend, M., 2005. Inflation targeting for the United States? In: Bernanke, B.S., Woodford, M. (Eds.), The Inflation Targeting Debate. National Bureau of Economic Research, Cambridge, MA, pp. 311–337.

Goodstadt, L.F., 2013. Poverty in the Midst of Affluence: How Hong Kong Mismanaged Its Prosperity. Hong Kong University Press, Hong Kong.

Gopin, M., 2002. Holy War, Holy Peace: How Religion Can Bring Peace to the Middle East. Oxford University Press, New York.

Gottschalk, P., Smeeding, T.M., 1997. Cross-national comparisons of earnings and income inequality. J. Econ. Literat. 35 (2), 633–687.

Gough, I., 1979. The Political Economy of the Welfare State. Palgrave Macmillan, London.

Graaff, J. de V., 1957. Theoretical Welfare Economics. Cambridge University Press, Cambridge.

Greenspan, A., 2004. Risk and uncertainty in monetary policy. Am. Econ. Rev. 94 (2), 33–40, Papers and Proceedings.

Gregor, A.J., 1981. Confucianism and the political thought of Sun Yat-sen. Philos. East West 31 (1), 55–70.

Gregor, A.J., and M.H. Chang, 1982, "Marxism, Sun Yat-sen, and the concept of "imperialism"", Pac. Aff., 55 (1) Spring: 54–79.

Grice, K., Drakakis-Smith, D., 1985. The role of the state in shaping development: two decades of growth in Singapore. Trans. Instit. Br. Geograph. 10 (3), 347–359.

Griffin, E., 2010. Short History of the British Industrial Revolution. Palgrave, London.

Grossman, G.M., Helpman, E., 1990. Comparative advantage and long-run growth. Am. Econ. Rev. 80 (4), 796–815.

Guidetti, A., 2015. Confront and accommodate? The maritime silk road will test U.S.-China rivalries. Global Asia 10 (3), 42–47.

Guo, Y., 2008. The intensification of corruption in transitional China: an empirical analysis of corruption in China. China Quart. 194, 349–364.

Gwartney, J.D., Lawson, R.A., 2003. The concept and measurement of economic freedom. Eur. J. Polit. Econ. 19 (3), 405–430.

Gwartney, J.D., Lawson, R.A., Holcombe, R.G., 1999. Economic freedom and the environment for economic growth. J. Instit. Theoret. Econ. 155 (4), 643–653.

de Haan, J., Sturm, J.-E., 2003. Does more democracy lead to greater economic freedom? New evidence from developing countries. Eur. J. Polit. Econ. 19 (3), 547–563.

Haddon-Cave, P., 1980. Introduction: the making of some aspects of public policy in Hong Kong. In: Lethbridge, D. (Ed.), The Business Environment in Hong Kong. Oxford University Press, Hong Kong.

Haggard, S., 1990. Pathways from the Periphery: The Politics of Growth in the Newly Industrializing Countries. Cornell University Press, New York.

Haggard, S., 2000. The Political Economy of the Asian Financial Crisis. Institute of International Economics, Washington, DC.

Haggard, S., 2016. Reflections on inequality in Asia. Global Asia 11 (2), 8–13.

Haggard, S., Kaufman, R.R., 1995. The Political Economy of Democratic Transitions. Princeton University Press, New Jersey.

Haley, U.C.V., Haley, G.T., 2008. Subsidies and the China Price. Harvard Business Review, June.

Haley, U.C.V., Haley, G.T., 2014. The hidden advantage of Chinese subsidies. World Financial Rev. September 26.

Hallak, J.C., Levinsohn, J., 2004. Fooling Ourselves: Evaluating the Globalization and Growth Debate, Working Paper 10244. National Bureau of Economic Research, Cambridge, MA, January.

Hamada, K., Okada, Y., 2009. Monetary and international factors behind Japan's lost decade. J. Jap. Int. Econ. 23 (2), 200−219.

Hamre, J.J., Sullivan, G.R., 2002. Towards post-conflict reconstruction. Washington Quart. 25 (4), 83−96.

Haque, S.M., 1998. The paradox of bureaucratic accountability in developing nations under a premarket state. Int. Polit. Sci. Rev. 19 (4), 357−372.

Harbom, L., Högbladh, S., Wallensteen, P., 2006. Armed conflict and peace agreements. J. Peace Res. 43 (5), 617−631.

Harris, R.G., 1993. Trade, Money and Wealth in the Canadian Economy. C. D. Howe Institute, Toronto, September.

Hartung, W.D., 1998. Reagan redux: the enduring myth of star wars. World Policy J. 15 (3), 17−24.

Harvey, D., 1982. The Limits to Capital. University of Chicago Press, Chicago.

Harvey, D.I., Kellard, N.M., Madsen, J.B., Wohar, M.E., 2010. The Presbisch-Singer hypothesis: four centuries of evidence. Rev. Econ. Statis. 92 (1), 367−377.

Hausman, D.M., McPherson, M.S., 1993. Taking ethics seriously: economics and contemporary moral philosophy. J. Econ. Literat. 31 (June), 671−731.

Hausmann, R., Hwang, J., Rodrik, D., 2005. What You Export Matters, NBER Working Paper No. 11905. National Bureau of Economic Research, Cambridge, MA, December.

Hayek, F.A., 1944. The Road to Serfdom. George Routledge and Sons, London.

Held, D., 1989. Political Theory and the Modern State. Polity Press, Cambridge.

Helleiner, G.K., 1980. International Economic Disorder: Essays in North-South Relations. Macmillan, London.

Helliwell, J.F., 1986. Supply-side macroeconomics. Can. J. Econ. 19 (4), 597−625.

Hemming, R., Kay, J.A., 1980. The Laffer curve. Fiscal Stud. 1 (2), 83−90.

Hemming, R., Kell, M., Mahfouz, S., 2002. The Effectiveness of Fiscal Policy in Stimulating Economic Activities: A Review of the Literature. IMF Working Paper No. 02/208, December.

Herrmann-Pillath, C., 2011. A 'Third Culture' in Economics? An Essay on Smith, Confucius and the Rise of China, Working Paper Series 159. Frankfurt School of Finance and Management.

Hertel, T.W., Winters, A.L., 2006. Poverty and the WTO: Impacts of the Doha Development Agenda. World Bank, Washington, DC.

Heydon, K., Woolcock, S., 2009. The Rise of Bilateralism: Comparing American, European and Asian Approach to Preferential Trade Agreements. United Nations University Press, Tokyo.

Hicks, G., 1988. Hong Kong after the Sino-British agreement: the illusion of stability. In: Domes, J., Shaw, Y.-M. (Eds.), Hong Kong: A Chinese and International Concern. Westview Press, Boulder, pp. 231−245.

Hicks, J.R., 1939. The foundations of welfare economics. Econ. J. 49 (196), 696−712.

Hoekman, B., Nicita, A., 2010. Assessing the Doha round: market access, transaction costs and aid for trade facilitation. J. Int. Trade Econ. Dev. 19 (1), 65−79.

Hoeller, P., Joumard, I., Koske, I., 2014. Reducing income inequality while boosting economic growth: can it be done? Evidence from OECD countries. Singapore Econ. Rev. 59 (1), 4−26.

Hoff, T.J.B., 1981. Economic Calculation in the Socialist Society. Liberty Press, Indianapolis.

Hofstede, G., Bond, M.H., 1988. The Confucius connection: from cultural roots and economic growth. Org. Dynam. 16 (4), 5−21.

Holbig, H., Ash, R. (Eds.), 2003. China's Accession to the World Trade Organization: National and International Perspectives. RourtledgeCurzon, London.

Hölmstrom, B., 1979. Moral hazard and observability. Bell J. Econ. 10 (1), 74−91.

Hong Kong Monetary Authority, 2016. Hong Kong: The Global Offshore Renminbi Business Hub. Hong Kong, January.

Howard, M.C., King, J.E. (Eds.), 1976. The Economics of Marx. Penguin Books, New York.

Howe, C., 1978. China's Economy: A Basic Guide. Paul Elek, London.

Howell, J., 2012. Civil society, corporatism and capitalism in China. J. Comp. Asian Dev. 11 (2), 271−297.

Howitt, P., Aghion, P., 1998. Capital accumulation and innovation as complementary factors in long-run growth. J. Econ. Growth 3 (2), 111−130.

Huang, H., Wang, S., 2004. Exchange rate regimes: China's experience and choices. China Econ. Rev. 15 (3), 336−342.

Huang, H.-C.R., 2004. A flexible nonlinear inference to the Kuznets hypothesis. Econ. Lett. 84, 289−296.

Huang, N.C., 1958. China Will Overtake Britain. Foreign Language Press, Peking.

Huang, X., Li, P., Lotspeich, R., 2010. Economic growth and multitasking by state-owned enterprises: an analytical framework and empirical study based on Chinese provincial data. Econ. Syst. 34 (2), 160−177.

Huang, Y., 2003. The economic and political integration of Hong Kong: implications for government-business relations. In: Sing, M. (Ed.), Hong Kong Government and Politics. Oxford University Press, Hong Kong.

Huidrom, R., Kose, A.A., Ohnsorge, F.L., 2016. Challenges of Fiscal Policy in Emerging and Developing Economics, Policy Research Working Paper, WP7725. The World Bank, Washington, DC, June.

Hung, H.-F., 2015. The China Boom: Why China Will Not Rule the World. Columbia University Press, New York.

Hunt, M.H., 2015. The World Transformed: 1945 to the Present. Oxford University Press, Oxford.

Ichimura, S., Klein, L.R. (Eds.), 2010. Macroeconomic Models of Japan. World Scientific Publisher, Singapore.

Ichimura, S., 2015. World Scientific Publisher, Japan and Asia, Singapore.

Ihori, T., 1978. The golden rule and the role of government in a life cycle growth model. Am. Econ. Rev. 68 (3), 389−396.

Inoguchi, T., 1988. The Political Economy of Japan: The Changing International Context. Stanford University Press, Stanford.

International Monetary Fund, 2009. Global Financial Stability Report: Responding to the Financial Crisis and Measuring Systemic Risk. International Monetary Fund, Washington, DC.

International Monetary Fund, 2012. Historical Public Debt Database. Fiscal Affairs Department, Washington, DC, September.

International Monetary Fund, 2013. Greece: Ex-post Evaluation of Exceptional Access under the 2010 Stand-By Arrangement. IMF Country Report No. 13/156. IMF, Washington DC, June.

International Monetary Fund, 2015a. Greece: Preliminary Draft Debt Sustainability Analysis. IMF Country Report No. 15/165. IMF, Washington, DC, June.

International Monetary Fund, 2015b. Greece: An Update of IMF Staff's Preliminary Public Debt Sustainability Analysis. IMF Country Report No. 15/186. IMF, Washington, DC, July.

International Monetary Fund, 2015c. Nine Key Questions on Greece, Greece and the IMF: Materials about Greece and Its Activities with the IMF. IMF, Washington, DC, July.

Ioannides, Y.M., Pissarides, C.A., 2015. Is the Greek Debt Crisis One of Supply and Demand? Brookings Papers on Economic Activity, September.

Ip, E.C., 2015. The constitution of economic liberty in Hong Kong. Constitut. Polit. Econ. 26 (3), 307−327.

Iradian, G., 2005. Inequality, Poverty, and Growth: Cross-country Evidence. Working Paper No. 05/28, International Monetary Fund. IMF, Washington, DC.

Irvin, G., 1994. Vietnam: assessing the achievements of Doi Moi. J. Dev. Stud. 31 (5), 725–750.

Ismail, S., 2006. Rethinking Islamist Politics: Culture, the State and Islamism. I. B. Tauris & Co Ltd, London.

Iwatani, N., Orr, G., Salsberg, B., 2011. Japan's Globalization Imperative. McKinsey Quarterly1–7.

Jackson, J.H., 1997. The WTO dispute settlement understanding-misunderstandings on the nature of legal obligation. Am. J. Int. Law 91 (1), 60–64.

Jacobs, L., King, D., 2016. Fed Power: How Finance Wins. Oxford University Press, Oxford.

Jacoby, T., 2007. Hegemony, modernisation and post-war reconstruction. Global Soc. 21 (4), 521–537.

Jacques, M., 2009. When China Rules the World: The End of the Western World and the Birth of a New Global Order. Penguin Books, London.

Jao, Y.C., 1988. Hong Kong's future as a free market economy. In: Domes, J., Shaw, Y. (Eds.), Hong Kong: A Chinese and International Concern. Westview Press, Boulder, CO.

Jao, Y.C., Leung, C.K., Wesley-Smith, P., Wong, S.-L. (Eds.), 1985. Hong Kong and 1997 Strategies for the Future. University of Hong Kong, Hong Kong.

Jao, Y.C., Leung, C.K., Chai, C.H., 1986. China's Special Economic Zones: Policies, Problems and Prospects. Oxford University Press, Oxford.

Jenkins, R., 1970. Exploitation. Paladin, London.

Johnson, H., 1973. The Theory of Income Distribution. Gray-Mills Publishing Ltd, London.

Johnson, C., 1982. MITI and the Japanese Miracle: The Growth of Industrial Policy, 1925-1975. Stanford University Press, Stanford, CA.

Joreskog, K.G., Goldberger, A.S., 1975. Estimation of a model with multiple indicators and multiple causes of a single latent variable. J. Am. Statist. Assoc. 70 (351), 631–639.

Jorgenson, D.W., Kuroda, M., Nishimzu, M., 1987. Japan-U.S. industry-level productivity comparisons, 1960–1979. J. Jpn. Int. Econ. 1 (1), 1–30.

Jorgenson, D.W., 1988. Productivity and economic growth in Japan and the United States. Am. Econ. Rev. 78 (2), 217–222.

Jorgenson, D.W., Kuroda, M., 1992. Productivity and international competitiveness in Japan and the United States, 1960–1985. Econ. Stud. Quart 42 (4), 313–325.

Jorgenson, D.W., Nomura, K., 2005. The industry origins of Japanese economic growth. J. Jpn. Int. Econ. 19 (4), 482–542.

Josten, van S.D., 2002. National debt in an endogenous growth model. Rev. Econ. 53 (1), 107–123.

Ju, H., 2015. China's Maritime Power and Strategy. World Scientific Publishers, Singapore.

Joyce, J.P., 2015, Greece's Missing Drivers of Growth. Commentary on the Greek Debt Crisis, *E-axes*, August.

Judd, J.P., Rudebusch, G.D., 1998. Taylor's rule and the fed: 1970–1997. Fed. Res. Bank San Francisco Econ. Rev. 3, 3–16.

Juvenal, L., Petrella, I., 2015. Speculation in the oil market. J. Appl. Econ. 30 (4), 621–649.

Kaletsky, A., 2015. Why the Greek Deal Will Work. Commentary on the Greek Debt Crisis, E-axes, July.

Kaminsky, G.L., Reinhart, C.M., 1998. Financial crises in Asia and Latin America: then and now. Am. Econ. Rev. 88 (2), 444–448, Papers and Proceedings.

Kaminsky, G.L., Lizondo, S., Reinhart, C.M., Di Tata, J.C., Hernández-Catá, E., 1998. Leading indicators of currency crisis. IMF Staff Papers 45 (1), 1–48.

Kanbur, R., 2000. Income distribution and development. In: Atkinson, A.B., Bourguignon, F. (Eds.), Handbook of Income Distribution. Elsevier, Amsterdam, pp. 791–841.

Karatnycky, A., 2002. Muslim countries and the democracy gap. J. Dem. 13 (1), 99–112, January.

Kartasasmita, G., Stern, J., 2015. Reinvesting Indonesia. World Scientific Publisher, Singapore.

Katz, R., 1998. Japan: The System that Soured, The Rise and Fall of the Japanese Economic Miracle. M. E. Sharpe, New York.

Kennedy, S., Parker, D.A., 2015. Building China's "One Belt, One Road". Center for Strategic and International Studies, Washington, DC, April 3.

Keohane, R.O., 1984. After Hegemony: Cooperation and Discord in the World Political Economy. Princeton University Press, New Jersey.

Keynes, J.M., 1926. The End of Laissez-Faire. Hogarth, London.

Keynes, J.M., 1937. The General Theory of Employment, Interest and Money. Harcourt, Brace and World, New York.

Kilian, L., 2006. Not All Oil Price Shocks are Alike: Disentangling Demand and Supply Shocks in the Crude Oil Market. CEPR Discussion Paper No. 5994. Centre for Economic Policy Research, London, December.

Kim, D.H., 2012. What is an oil shock? Panel data evidence. Emp. Econ. 43, 121–143.

Kim, H.-A., 2004. Korea's Development Under Park Chung Hee: Rapid Industrialization, 1961-1979. RoutledgeCurzon, London.

Kim, J., 2011. Foreign aid and economic development: the success story of South Korea. Pacific Focus 28 (2), 260–286.

Kimura, T., Small, D., 2004. Quantitative Monetary Easing and Risk and Financial Asset Market. Finance and Economics Discussion Series, Federal Reserve Board, Washington, DC, September.

Kindleberger, C.P., 1993. A Financial History of Western Europe. Oxford University Press, New York.

Kindleberger, C.P., Aliber, R.Z., 2011. Manias, Panics and Crashes: A History of Financial Crises, sixth ed. Palgrave Macmillan, Basingstoke.

King, R.G., Plosser, C.I., Rebelo, S.T., 1988. Production, growth and business cycles: the basic neoclassical model. J. Monet. Econ. 21 (2-3), 195–232.

Kobayashi, K., Inaba, M., 2002. Japan's Lost Decade and the Complexity Externality. RIETI Discussion Paper Series 02-E-004. The Research Institute of Economy, Trade and Industry, Tokyo, March.

Koch-Weser, J., 2013. The Reliability of China's Economic Data: An Analysis of National Output. U.S.-China Economic and Security Review Commission Staff Research Project, Washington, DC, January.

Kocka, J., 2016. Capitalism: A Short History. Princeton University Press, New Jersey.

Kokko, A., 1998. Vietnam: ready for Doi Moi II? ASEAN Econ. Bulletin 15 (3), 319–327.

Kojima, K., 2000. The "flying geese" model of Asian economic development: origin, theoretical extensions and regional policy implications. J. Asian Econ. 11 (4), 375–401.

Koo, A.Y.C., 1968. The Role of Land Reform in Economic Development: A Case Study of Taiwan. Praeger Publisher, New York.

Kornai, J., 1986. The soft budget constraint. KYKLOS 39 (1), 3–30.

Kroeber, A.R., 2016. China's Economy. Oxford University Press, Oxford.

Kruger, A.O., 1974. The political economy of the rent-seeking society. Am. Econ. Rev. 64 (3), 291–303.

Kruger, A.O., 1985. The experience and lessons of Asia's super exporters. In: Corbo, V., Kruger, A.O., Ossa, F. (Eds.), Export-Oriented Development Strategies. Westview Press, Boulder, CO, pp. 187–212.

Kruger, A.O., 1990a. Government Failure in Development. NBER Working Paper No. 3340. National Bureau of Economic Research, Cambridge MA, April.

Kruger, A.O., 1990b. Perspectives on Trade and Development. Harvester Wheatsheaf, Hemel Hempstead.

Kruger, A.O., 1997. Whither the World Bank and the IMF? NBER Working Paper No. 6327. National Bureau of Economic Research, Cambridge MA, December.

Kruger, A.O., 2012. Struggling With Success: Challenges Facing the International Economy. World Scientific, Singapore.

Krugman, P., 1984. Import protection as export promotion. In: Kierskowski, H. (Ed.), Monopolistic Competition and International Trade. Clarendon Press, Oxford.

Krugman, P., 1994. Peddling Prosperity. W. W. Norton & Company, New York.

Krugman, P., 1998. What Happened to Asia? Massachusetts Institute of Technology, Cambridge, MA.

Kuan, H.-C., Lau, S.-K., 1995. The partial vision of democracy in Hong Kong: a survey of popular opinion. China J. 34, 239–264, July.

Kumar, M., Woo, J., 2010. Public Debt and Growth. IMF Working Paper No. 10/174. International Monetary Fund, Washington, DC.

Kurata, T., 2015. Support for and opposition to democratization in Hong Kong. Asia-Pacific Rev. 22 (1), 16–33.

Kurlantzick, J., 2016. State Capitalism: How the Return of Statism is Transforming the World. Oxford University Press, New York.

Kuznets, S., 1955. Economic growth and income inequality. Am. Econ. Rev. 45, 1–28.

Kvint, V., 2010. The Global Emerging Market: Strategic Management and Economics. Routledge, New York, London.

Kwan, C.C., 2002. Restructuring in the Canadian Economy: A Survey of Firms. Bank of Canada Working Paper 2002-8, Ottawa, April.

Kwok, R.H.F., Li, K.-W., 1992. Generalized system of preference graduation and Hong Kong's export performance. Seoul J. Econ. 4 (2), 173–187.

Kwok, R.Y.F., Chan, E.Y.M., 2001. Functional representation in Hong Kong: problems and possibilities. Int. J. Public Admin. 24 (9), 869–885.

Kydland, F., Prescott, E.C., 1977. Rules rather than discretion: the inconsistency of optimal plans. J. Polit. Econ. 85 (3), 473–491.

Laffer, A.B., 2004. The Laffer curve: past, present, and future. Backgrounder 1756 (June), 1–16.

Lam, J.T.M., 2015. Political decay in Hong Kong after the occupy central movement. Asian Aff. Am. Rev. 42 (2), 99–121.

Lam, W.-M., 2004. Understanding the Political Culture of Hong Kong: The Paradox of Activism and Depolitization. M. E. Sharpe, New York.

Lambsdorff, J.G., 2007. The Institutional Economics of Corruption and Reform: Theory, Evidence and Policy. Cambridge University Press, Cambridge.

Lange, O., 1942. The foundations of welfare economics. Econometrica 19 (3/4), 215–228.

Lapidus, I.M., 1997. Islamic revival and modernity: the contemporary movements and the historical paradigms. J. Econ. Soc. History Orient 40 (4), 444–460.

Lardy, N., 1998. China's Unfinished Economic Revolution. Brookings Institution Press, Washington, DC.

Lardy, N.R., 1978. Economic Growth and Distribution in China. Cambridge University Press, Cambridge.

Larkin, S., 2015. China's "Great Leap Outward": The AIIB in Context. ISEAS Perspectives, No, 27. ISEAS, Singapore, June 9.

Larrain, J., 1983. Marxism and Ideology. Macmillan Press Ltd, London.

Latter, T., 2007. Hands On or Hands Off? The Nature and Process of Economic Policy in Hong Kong. Hong Kong University Press, Hong Kong.

Lebow, R.N., Stein, J.G., 1994. Reagan and the Russians. The Atlantic Monthly, February.

Lee, F.L.F., 2005. Collective efficacy, support for democratization, and political participation in Hong Kong. Int. J. Public Opin. Res. 18 (3), 297–317.

Lee, F.L.F., Chan, J.M., 2008. Making sense of participation: the political cultural of pro-democracy demonstration in Hong Kong. China Quart. 193 (March), 84–101.

Lee, J.-W., 2015. Asia's View of the Greek Crisis. Project Syndicate: The World's Opinion Page, July 16.

Lee, J.-W., 2016. Crisis and Recovery: Learning from the Asian Experience. World Scientific Publisher, Singapore.

Lee, K.Y., 2012. From Third World to First: The Singapore Story, 1965-2000. Marshall Cavendish International, Singapore.

Lee, S.-H., Lee, C.-Y., 2015. The TPP and WTO: A Win-win or Zero-sum Situation? RSIS Commentary No. 222, Singapore, October 21.

Leigh, D., 2010. Monetary policy and the lost decade: lessons from Japan. J. Money, Credit Banking 42 (5), 833–857.

Leng, S.C., Palmer, N.D., 1960. Sun Yat-sen and Communism. Praeger, New York.

Lenin, V.I., 1976. The State and Revolution. Foreign Language Press, Beijing.

Letwin, W., 1983. The case against equality. In: Letwin, W. (Ed.), Against Equality. MacMillan, London.

Leung, D., Rispoli, L., Chan, R., 2012. Small, Medium-Sized, and Large Businesses in the Canadian Economy: Measuring Their Contribution to Gross Domestic Product from 2001–2008. Economic Analysis Research Paper Series, Economic Analysis Division, Ottawa: Statistics Canada.

Leung, F.M.H., 2012. My Time in Hong Kong's Underground Communist Party. Open Book, Hong Kong (in Chinese).

Levine, R., Renelt, D., 1992. A sensitivity analysis of cross-country growth regressions. Am. Econ. Rev. 82 (4), 942–963.

Levy, P.I., 1997. A political-economic analysis of free-trade agreements. Am. Econ. Rev. 87 (4), 506–519.

Lewis, W.A., 1954. Economic development with unlimited supplies of labour. Manchester School 22 (2), 139–191.

Leydesdorff, L., 2000. The Triple Helix: an evolutionary model of innovations. Res. Policy 29 (2), 243–255.

Leydesdorff, L., Etzkowitz, H., 1996. Emergence of a Triple Helix of University-Industry-Government Relations. Sci. Public Policy 23 (5), 279–286.

Li, H., Squire, L., Zou, H.-F., 1998. Explaining international and intertemporal variations in income inequality. Econ. J. 108 (446), 26–43.

Li, K.-W., 1991. Positive adjustment against protectionism: the case of Textile and Clothing Industry in Hong Kong. Dev. Econ. 29 (September), 197–209.

Li, K.-W., 1994. Financial Repression and Economic Reform in China. Praeger Publishers, Westport.

Li, K.-W., 1997. Money and monetization in China's economic reform. Appl. Econ. 29, 1139–1145.

Li, K.-W., 1999. China. In: East Asia Analytical Unit (Ed.), Asia's Financial Markets: Capitalising on Reform. Department of Foreign Affairs and Trade, Australia, pp. 285–318.

Li, K.-W., 2000. The changing economic environment in the people's Republic of China. In: Yau, O.H.M., Steele, H.C. (Eds.), China Business: Challenges in the 21st Century. Chinese University Press, Hong Kong, pp. 29–68.

Li, K.-W., 2001. The two decades of China's economic reform compared. World Econ. China 9 (2), 55–60.

Li, K.-W., 2002. Capitalist Development and Economism in East Asia: The Rise of Hong Kong, Singapore, Taiwan and South Korea. Routledge, London.

Li, K.-W., 2006. The Hong Kong Economy: Recovery and Restructuring. McGraw Hill Educational, Singapore.

Li, K.-W., 2009. China's total factor productivity estimates by region, investment sources and ownership. Econ. Syst. 33 (3), 213–230.

Li, K.-W., 2012a. Economic Freedom: Lessons of Hong Kong. World Scientific, Singapore.

Li, K.-W., 2012b. Is there a "low interest rate trap"? Ekonomika 91 (1), 7–23.

Li, K.-W., 2013. The U.S. monetary performance prior to the 2008 crisis. Appl. Econ. 45 (24), 3450–3461.

Li, K.-W., 2014a. The China Economy: at the Crossroad or at the Turning Point? E-axes, Commentary on China, New York, April.

Li, K.-W., 2014b. An analysis on economic opportunity. Appl. Econ. 46 (33), 4060–4074.

Li, K.-W., 2014c. Could there be a "Sub-market Interest Rate" in the IS-LM Framework? E-axes, Research Paper on Monetary Policy and Banking, New York, May.

Li, K.-W., 2017. Analyzing the TFP performance of Chinese industrial enterprises. Singapore Econ. Rev., forthcoming.

Li, K.-W., 2017. Is there an "interest rate – speculation" relationship? Evidence from G7 in the pre- and post-2008 crisis. Appl. Econ. 49 (21), 2041–2059.

Li, K.-W., Bender, S., 2007. Productivity and manufacture export causality among world regions: 1989–1999. Int. Trade J. 21 (2), 121–159.

Li, K.-W., Hazari, B.R., 2015. The Possible Tragedy of Quantitative Easing: An IS-LM Approach. E-axes, Research on Monetary Policy and Central Banking, New York, May.

Li, K.-W., Kwok, M.-L., 2009. Output volatility of five crisis-affected East Asia economies. Jpn. World Econ. 21 (2), 172–182.

Li, K.-W., Liu, T., 2001. Financial liberalization and growth in China's economic reform. World Econ. 24 (5), 673–687.

Li, K.-W., Liu, T., 2004. Performance of financial resources in China's provinces. J. Asia Pacific Econ. 9 (1), 32–48.

Li, K.-W., Liu, T., 2006. Disparity in factor contributions between coastal and inner provinces in post-reform China. China Econ. Rev. 17 (4), 449–470.

Li, K.-W., Ma, J., 2004. The economic intricacies of banking reform in China. Chinese Econ. 37 (4), 50–77.

Li, K.-W., Wong, K.F., 1997. The stock markets in China. In: Li, Kui-Wai (Ed.), Financing China Trade and Investment. Praeger Publisher, Connecticut, pp. 215–238.

Li, K.-W., Zhou, X., 2010. Openness, domestic performance and growth. Econ. Lett. 107 (January), 13–16.

Li, K.-W., Zhou, X., 2013. A nonparametric and semiparametric analysis on inequality and development: evidence from OECD and non-OECD countries. Econ. Polit. Stud. 1 (2), 55–79.

Li, K.-W., Zhou, X., Pan, Z., 2016. Cross-country output convergence and growth: evidence from varying coefficient nonparametric method. Econ. Model. 55, 32–41.

Li, M., 2008. The Rise of China and the Demise of the Capitalist World Economy. Pluto Press, London.

Li, P.K., 2000. Hong Kong from Britain to China: Political Cleavages, Electoral Dynamics and Institutional Changes. Ashgate Publishing Ltd, Aldershot.

Li, P.S., 2002. Destination Canada: Immigration Debates and Issues. Oxford University Press, Oxford.

Li, P.S., 2010. Immigrants from China to Canada: Issues of Supply and Demand of Human Capital. China Paper No. 2. Canadian International Council, January.

Liargovas, P., 2015, The Economic Adjustment Program of Greece (2010–15): Why Failure?, Insider's View on the Greek Debt Crisis, E-axes, May.

Lichtheim, G., 1971. Imperialism. Penguin Books, London.

Lim, C.Y., 2009. Southeast Asia: The Long Road Ahead, third ed. World Scientific Publishers, Singapore.

Lim, L.Y.C. (Ed.), 2016. Singapore's Economic Development: Retrospection and Reflections. World Scientific Publishers, Singapore.

Lim, T.C., 1998. Power, capitalism, and the authoritarian state in South Korea. J. Contemp. Asia 28 (4), 457–483.

Lim, T.W., Ping, X., 2015. Contextualizing Occupy Central in Contemporary Hong Kong. World Scientific Publisher, Singapore.

Lin, G., Schramm, R.M., 2003. China's foreign exchange policies since 1979: a review of developments and an assessment. China Econ. Rev. 14 (3), 246–280.

Lin, S.-C., Huang, H.-C., Weng, H.-W., 2006. A semiparametric partially linear investigation of the Kuznets' hypothesis. J. Comparat. Econ. 34, 634–647.

Lindert, P.H., Williamson, J.G., 1983. English workers' living standards during the industrial revolution: a new look. Econ. History Rev. 36 (1), 1–25.

Lindert, P.H., Williamson, J.G., 2001. Does Globalization Make the World More Unequal?, Working Paper 8228. National Bureau of Economic Research, Cambridge, MA, April.

Litwak, R.S., 1984. Détente and the Nixon Doctrine. Cambridge University Press, New York.

Liu, S.-Y., 2009. A Brief History of Hong Kong. Joint Publishing Co. Ltd., Hong Kong (in Chinese).

Liu, T., Li, K.-W., 2015. The Empirics of Economic Growth and Industrialization Using Growth Identity Equation, Working Paper. Department of Economics, Ball State University, Indiana, USA, November.

Liu, Z., 1997. Hongkongese or Chinese: The Problem of Identity on the Eve of Resumption of Chinese Sovereignty over Hong Kong, No. 65. Hong Kong Institute of Asia-Pacific Studies, Chinese University of Hong Kong, Hong Kong.

Ljungqvist, L., Uhlig, H., 2000. Tax policy and aggregate demand management under catching up with the Joneses. Am. Econ. Rev. 90 (3), 356–366.

Lo, S.H., 1994. An analysis of Sino-British negotiations over Hong Kong's political reform. Contemp. Southeast Asia 16 (2), 178–209.

Lo, S.H., 2010. Competing Chinese Political Visions: Hong Kong vs. Beijing on Democracy. Praeger Security International, New York.

Loehlin, J.C., 1998. Latent Variable Models: An Introduction to Factor, Path and Structural Analysis. Lawrence Erlbaum Associates Publishers, New Jersey.

Lorenz, M.O., 1905. "Method of Measuring the Concentration of Wealth". Quart. Publ. Am. Stat. Assoc 9 (70), 209–219.

Low, L., 2002. Rethinking Singapore Inc. and GLCs. Southeast Asia Affairs. 282–302.

Lowe, P., Ellis, L., 1997. The smoothing of official interest rates. In: Lowe, P. (Ed.), Monetary Policy and Inflation Targeting. Reserve Bank of Australia.

Lowenthal, R., 1971. Russia and China: controlled conflict. Foreign Aff. 49 (3), 507–518.

Lucas, J.R., 1983. Against equality again. In: Letwin, W. (Ed.), Against Equality. MacMillan, London.

Lucas Jr., R.E., 1977. Understanding business cycles. Carnegie-Rochester Conf. Series Public Policy 5, 7–29.

Lucas Jr., R.E., 1981. Studies in Business-Cycle Theory. MIT Press, Cambridge, MA.

Lucas Jr., R.E., 1988. On the mechanics of economics development. J. Monet. Econ. 22, 3–42.

Lucas Jr., R.E., 1990. Supply-side economics: an analytical review. Oxford Econ. Papers 42 (2), 293–316.

Lucas, R.E. Jr., 2004. The Industrial Revolution: Past and Future, 2003 Annual Report Essay, Federal Reserve Bank of Minneapolis, May.

Luthi, L.M., 2008. The Sino-Soviet Split: Cold War in the Communist World. Princeton University Press, Princeton.

Luttwak, E., 2003. Strategy: The Logic of War and Peace, second ed. President and Fellows of Harvard College, Cambridge, MA.

Ma, N., 1997. The Sino-British dispute over Hong Kong: a game theory interpretation. Asian Survey 37 (8), 738–751.

Ma, N., 2007. Political Development in Hong Kong: State, Political Society and Civic Society. Hong Kong University Press, Hong Kong.

MacFarquhar, R., 1974. The Origins of the Cultural Revolution. Columbia University Press, New York.

Macintyre, A., Naughton, B., 2005. The decline of a Japan-led model of the East Asian economy. In: Pempel, T.J. (Ed.), Remapping East Asia: The Construction of a Region. Cornell University Press, Ithaca, pp. 77–100.

Mahmoud, A. El-Gamal, Jeffe, A.M., 2010. Oil, Dollars, Debt and Crises: The Global Curse of Black Gold. Cambridge University Press, Cambridge.

Malcomson, J.M., 1986. Some analytics of the Laffer curve. J. Public Econ. 29 (3), 263–279.

Mankiw, G.N., 2002. U.S. monetary policy during the 1990s. In: Frankel, F., Orszag, P. (Eds.), American Economic Policy in the 1990s. MIT Press, Cambridge, MA.

Marshall, M.G., Arestis, P., 1989. Reaganomics' and supply-side economics: a British view. J. Econ. Issues 23 (4), 965–975.

Marx, K., 1867. Capital: Critique of Political Economy. Verlag von Otto Meisner, Germany.

Matsushita, M., 2015. The World Trade Organization: Law, Practice, and Policy. Oxford University Press, Oxford.

McAuley, A., 1991. The economic consequences of soviet disintegration. Soviet Econ. 7 (3), 189–214.

McCallum, B., 1988. Robustness properties of a rule for monetary policy. Carnegie Rochester Conf. Series Public Policy 29, 173–203.

McCallum, B.T., 1978. The political business cycle: an empirical test. Southern Econ. J. 44 (3), 504–515.

McKinsey & Company, 2012. Greece 10 Years Ahead: Defining Greece's New Growth Model and Strategy. Athens Office, June.

McMahon, R., 2003. The Cold War: A Very Short Introduction. Oxford University Press, Oxford.

Meade, J.E., 1976. The Just Economy. George Allen Unwin Publishers, London.

Mehra, Y.P., Minton, B.D., 2007. A Taylor rule and the Greenspan Era. Econ. Quart. 93 (3), 229–250.

Meltzer, A.H., 2009. Reflections on the financial crisis. Cato J. 29 (1), 25–30.

Menzies, G., 2002. 1421 The Year China Discovered the World. Bantam Books, London.

de Mesquita, B.B., 2006. Game theory, political economy, and the evolving study of war and peace. Am. Polit. Sci. Rev. 100 (4), 637–642.

Michas, T., 2011. Putting Politics above Markets: Historical Background to the Greek Deb Crisis, Working Paper. CATO Institute, August.

Milanovic, B., 2005. Worlds Apart: Measuring International and Global Inequality. Princeton University Press, Princeton.

Miller, M.H., Rock, K., 1985. Dividend policy under asymmetric information. J. Finance 40 (4), 1031–1051.

Miller, M., Weller, P., Zhang, L., 2002. Moral hazard and the US stock market: analysing the 'Greenspan Put'. Econ. J. 112 (478), C171–186.

Mishkin, F.S., 1990. Asymmetric Information and Financial Crises: A Historical Perspective, NBER Working Paper No. 3400. National Bureau of Economic Research, Cambridge, MA, July.

Mishra, D.P., Heide, J.B., Cort, S.G., 1998. Information asymmetry and levels of agency relationships. J. Marketing Res. 35 (3), 277–295.

Modigliani, F., 1961. Long-run implications of alternative fiscal policies and the Burden of the National Debt. Econ. J. 71 (284), 730–755.

Modigliani, F., 1977. The monetarist controversy or should we forsake stabilization policies? Am. Econ. Rev. 67 (March), 1–19.

Momani, B., 2007. A middle east free trade area: economic interdependence and peace considered. World Econ. 30 (11), 1682–1700.

Monokroussos, P., Thomakos, D.D., 2012. Can Greece be Saved? Current Account, Fiscal Imbalances and Competitiveness, GreeSE Paper No. 59. Hellenic Observatory Papers on Greece and Southeast Europe, Hellenic Observatory European Institute, June.

Moran, T.H., 2012. Foreign Direct Investment. John Wiley and Sons, Ltd, New York.

More, C., 2000. Understanding the Industrial Revolution. Routledge, London.

Morishima, M., 1973. Marx's Economics: A Dual Theory of Value and Growth. Cambridge University Press, Cambridge.

Morishima, M., 1982. Why has Japan Succeeded?: Western Technology and the Japanese Ethos. Cambridge University Press, Cambridge.

Morton, D., 2006. A Short History of Canada, sixth ed. McClelland and Stewart, Toronto.

Moscovici, P., 2015. A Way Forward for Greece. Blog Post, European Commission, July 14.

Mosley, P., 2015. The Politics of Poverty Reduction. Oxford University Press, Oxford.

Mundell, R.A., 1961. A theory of optimum currency areas. Am. Econ. Rev. 51 (4), 657–665.

Murphy, K.M., Shleifer, A., Vishny, R.W., 1993. Why is rent-seeking so costly to growth. Am. Econ. Rev. 83 (2), 409–414.

Mushinski, D.W., 2001. Using non-parametric to inform parametric tests of Kuznets' hypothesis. Appl. Econ. Lett. 8, 77–79.

Mushkat, M., Mushkat, R., 2009. The economic dimension of Hong Kong's basic law: an analytical overview. NZ J. Public Int. Law 7, 273–316.

Mussa, M., Savastano, M., 2000. The IMF approach to economic stabilization. In: Bernanke, B., Rotemberg, J.J. (Eds.), NBER Macroeconomics Annual 1999, Volume 14. National Bureau of Economic Research, Cambridge, MA, pp. 79–128. January.

Muth, J.F., 1961. Rational expectation and the theory of price movements. Econometrica 29 (2), 315–335.

Myrdal, G., 1968. Asia Drama: An Inquiry into the Poverty of Nations. The Penguin Press, London.

Myrdal, G., 1989. The equality issue in world development. Am. Econ. Rev. 79 (6), 8–17.

Nafziger, E.W., 1997. The Economics of Developing Countries, third ed. Prentice Hall International, London.

Naughton, B., 2009. Understanding the Chinese Stimulus Package. China Leadership Monitor, No, 28, Hoover Institution, May 8.

Ngai, L.S., 1995. More than a 'war of words': identity, politics and struggle of dominance during the recent 'political reform' period in Hong Kong. Econ. Soc. 24 (1), 67–100.

Nghiep, L.T., Quy, L.H., 2000. Measuring the impact of Doi Moi on Vietnam's gross domestic product. Asian Econ. J. 14 (3), 317–332.

Nguyen, H.T., 2016. How to Make China Comply with the Tribunal Award, Analysis from the Maritime Awareness Project. The National Bureau of Asian Research, Seattle.

Nikiforce, M., Papadimitrou, D.B., Zezza, G., 2015. The Greek Public Debt Problem. Research on the Greek Debt Crisis, E-axes, February.

Nishitateno, S., 1983. China's special economic zones: experimental units for economic reform. Int. Comp. Law Quart. 32 (1), 175–185.

Niskanen Jr., W.A., 2007. Bureaucracy and Representative Government. Aldine Transaction, New Jersey.

Nkrumah, K., 1963. Africa Must Unite. Panaf Books, London.

Nordhaus, W.D., 1975. The political business cycle. Rev. Econ. Stud. 42 (2), 169–190.

Noreen, E., 1988. The economics of ethics: a new perspective on agency theory. Account. Org. Soc. 13 (4), 359–369.

Norris, P., Inglehart, R., 2002. Islamic culture and democracy: testing the 'clash of civilization' thesis. Comp. Sociol. 1 (3), 235–263.

North, D.C., 1992. Institutions, ideology, and economic performance. Cato J. 11 (3), 477–488.

Nove, A., 1961. The Soviet Economy: An Introduction. George Allen and Unwin Ltd, London.

O'Connor, J.R., 1973. The Fiscal Crisis of the State. St. Martin's Press, New York.

Ogawa, K., Sterken, E., Tokutsu, I., 2012. Financial distress and industry structure: an inter-industry approach to the lost decade in Japan. Econ. Syst. Res. 24 (3), 229–249.

Okeowo, A., 2013. China in Africa: the new imperialists? The New Yorkers, June 12.

Oksenen, K., 2011. Framing the democracy debate in Hong Kong. J. Contemp. China 20 (70), 479–497.

O'Neill, J., 2001. Building Better Global Economic BRICs. Global Economics Paper No: 66, Goldman Sachs, November.

Organization for Economic Cooperation and Development (OECD), 2013. Greece: Reform of Social Welfare Programmes. OECD Public Governance Reviews, Paris, July.

Organization of the Petroleum Exporting Countries (OPEC), 2014. OPEC Annual Statistical Bulletin. OPEC, Vienna.

Ortmann, S., 2015. The umbrella movement and Hong Kong's protracted democratization process. Asian Aff. 46 (1), 32–50.

Osawa, J., 2013. China's ADIZ Over the East China Sea: A "Great Wall in the Sky"? Brookings Research, December 17.

O'Shea, E., 2009. Missing the Point(s): The Declining Fortunes of Canada's Economic Immigration Program. Transatlantic Academy Paper Series, April.

Ostry, J.D., Ghosh, A.R., Espinoza, R., 2015. When Should Public Debt be Reduced?, IMF Staff Discussion Note. International Monetary Fund, Washington, DC, June.

Ostry, S., 1990. Governments and Corporations in a Shrinking World: Trade and Innovation Policies in the United States, Europe and Japan. Council on Foreign Relations Press, New York.

Overholt, W.H., 1993. The Rise of China: How Economic Reform is Creating a Superpower. W. W. Norton & Company, New York.

Overholt, W.H., 2015. Posture problems undermining one belt, one road and the US pivot. Global Asia 10 (3), 16–21, Fall.

Parfitt, T., 2011. Why China Will Never Rule the World: Travels in the Two Chinas. Western Hemisphere Press, New York.

Parijs, P.V., 1997. Real Freedom for All: What (if Anything) Can Justify Capitalism? Oxford University Press, Oxford.

Paris, R., Sisk, T.D. (Eds.), 2009. The Dilemmas of Statebuilding: Confronting the Contradictions of Postwar Peace Operations. Routledge, Abingdon.

Parkin, F., 1981. Marxism and class theory: a bourgeois critique. Philosop. Rev. 90 (4), 619–621.

Pattanaik, P.K., Suzumura, K., 1994. Rights, welfarism, and social choice. Am. Econ. Rev. 84 (2), 435–439.

Pei, M., 1994. From Reform to Revolution: The Demise of Communism in China and the Soviet Union. Harvard University Press, Cambridge, MA.

Perelman, M., 2000. The Invention of Capitalism: Classical Political Economy and the Secret History of Primitive Accumulation. Duke University Press, New York.

Perkins, D.H., 1988. Reforming China's economic system. J. Econ. Literat. 26 (June), 601–645.

Perkins, D.H., 2015. The Economic Transformation of China. World Scientific, Singapore, August.

Perry, J.C., 2016. Singapore: Unlikely Power. Oxford University Press, Oxford.

Petralias, A., Petros, S., Prodromídis, P., 2013. Greece in Recession: Economic Predictions, Mispredictions and Policy Implications, GreeSE paper No. 75. Hellenic Observatory Papers on Greece and Southeast Europe, Hellenic Observatory European Institute, September.

Pew Research Center, 2015. How Asia-Pacific publics see each other and their national leaders. Global Attitude Survey. Pew Research Center, Washington, DC, Spring.

Phelps, E., 2015. The Foundations of Greece's Failed Economy. Commentary on the Greek Debt Crisis, E-axes, September.

Philippopoulos, A. (Ed.), 2016. Public Sector Economics and the Need for Reform. The MIT Press, Cambridge, MA.

Piazolo, D., 1996. Trade Integration between Eastern and Western Europe: Politics Follows the Market. Kiel Working Paper No. 745, May.

Picot, A., Florio, M., Grave, N., Kranz, J. (Eds.), 2015. The Economics of Infrastructure Provisioning. The MIT Press, Cambridge, MA.

Pigou, A.C., 1920. The Economics of Welfare. Macmillan, London.

Piketty, T., 2014. Capital in the Twenty-First Century. Harvard University Press, Cambridge, MA.

Piore, M., 2002. Economics and sociology. Rev. Écon. 53 (2), 291–300.

Plummer, M.G., 2009. ASEAN Economic Integration: Trade, Foreign Direct Investment, and Finance. World Scientific Publisher, Singapore.

Poterba, J.M., 1993. State Responses to Fiscal Crisis: The Effects of Budgetary Institutions and Politics, NBER Working Paper No. 4375. National Bureau of Economic Research, Cambridge, MA, May.

Price, G., 2015. India's talk on China's silk road: ambivalence with lurking worries. Global Asia 10 (3), 30–33, Fall.

Przeworski, A., 1985. Capitalism and Social Democracy. Cambridge University Press, Cambridge.

Qian, Y., Roland, G., 1996. The soft budget constraint in China. Jpn World Econ. 8, 207–223.

Quah, D.T., 1996. Empirics for economic growth and convergence. Eur. Econ. Rev. 40 (6), 1353–1375.

Quah, J.S.T., 2009. Curbing Corruption in a One-Party Dominant System. Routledge, New York.

Rabushka, A., 1989. A free-market constitution for Hong Kong: a blueprint for China. Cato J. 8, 641–652.

Radelet, S., Sachs, J., 1998. The East Asian Financial Crisis: Diagnosis, Remedies, Prospects. Harvard Institute for International Development, Cambridge, MA.

Radelet, S., and J. Sachs, 1998a, The Onset of the East Asian Financial Crisis, NBER Working Paper Np. 6680, Cambridge MA: National Bureau of Economic Research, August.

Radelet, S., Sachs, J., 1998b. The East Asian Financial Crisis: Diagnosis, Remedies, Prospects. Harvard Institute for International Development, Cambridge MA.

Ram, R., 1991. Kuznets' inverted-U hypothesis: evidence from a highly developed country. Southern Econ. J. 57, 1112–1123.

Ranis, G., 2004. Labor Surplus Economies. Discussion Paper No. 900. Economic Growth Center, Yale University, December.

Ranis, G., Fei, J.C.H., 1961. A theory of economic development. Am. Econ. Rev. 51 (4), 533–565.

Rao, B.V.V., Lee, C., 1995. Sources of growth in the Singapore economy and its manufacturing and service sectors. Singapore Econ. Rev. 40 (1), 83–115.

Rao, B.V.V., Ramakrishnan, M.K., 1980. Income Inequality in Singapore. Singapore University Press, Singapore.

Ravallion, M., 1997. Can high-inequality developing countries escape absolute poverty. Econ. Lett. 56 (1), 51–57.

Ravallion, M., 2016. The Economics of Poverty. Oxford University Press, Oxford.

Rawls, J., 1971. A Theory of Justice. Oxford University Press, Oxford.

Rawski, T.G., 2001. What is happening to China's GDP statistics? China Econ. Rev. 12 (4), 347–354.

Razin, A., 2015. Understanding Global Crisis: An Emerging Paradigm. The MIT Press, Cambridge, MA.

Read, J., 2002. Primitive accumulation: the aleatory foundation of capitalism. Rethinking Marxism J. Econ. Cult. Soc. 14 (2), 24–49.

Reagan, M.D., Sanzone, J.G., 1981. The New Federalism, second ed. Oxford University Press, New York.

Reinhart, C.M., Rogoff, K.S., 2009. The Aftermath of Financial Crises, NBER Working Paper No. 14654. National Bureau of Economic Research, Cambridge, MA, January.

Reno, W., 1997. African weak states and commercial alliances. African Aff. 96 (383), 165–186.

Rigg, J., 1988. Singapore and the recession of 1985. Asian Survey 28 (3), 340–352.

Roberti, M., 1996. The Fall of Hong Kong: China's Triumph and Britain's Betrayal. Wiley, London.

Robinson, J., 1933. The Economics of Imperfect Competition. Macmillan, London.

Robinson, W., 2004. A Theory of Global Capitalism: Production, Class, and State in a Transnational World. John Hopkins University Press, Baltimore.

Rogoff, K., 2011. Is Modern Capitalism Sustainable? E-axes, www.e-axes.com.

Rolland, N., 2015. China's New Silk Road, Commentary,. The National Bureau of Asian Research, February, Seattle.

Romer, P.M., 1986. Increasing returns and long run growth. J. Polit. Econ. 94, 1002–1037.

Romer, P.M., 1993. Idea gaps and objective gaps in economic development. J. Monet. Econ. 32, 543–573.

Rose, A.K., 2004. Do WTO members have more liberal trade policy? J. Int. Econ. 63 (2), 209–235.

Rose-Ackerman, S., 1975. The economics of corruption. J. Public Econ. 4 (2), 187–203.

Rose-Ackerman, S., 1999. Corruption and Government. Cambridge University Press, New York.

Rosefielde, S., Kuboniwa, M., Mizobata, S. (Eds.), 2011. Two Asias: The Emerging Postcrisis Divide. World Scientific Publisher, Singapore.

Ross, D., 2004. The Missing Peace: The Inside Story of the Fight for Middle East Peace. Farrar, Straus and Giroux, New York.

Ross, S.A., 1973. The economic theory of agency: the principal's problem. Am. Econ. Rev. 63 (2), 134–139, Papers and Proceedings.

Rostow, W.W., 1960. The Stages of Economic Growth: A Non-Communist Manifesto. Cambridge University Press, Cambridge.

Roy, D., 1998. China's Foreign Relations. Rowman & Littlefield Publishers., Maryland.

Sachs, J.D., Warner, A.M., 2001. Natural resources and economic development: the curse of natural resources. Eur. Econ. Rev. 45, 827–838.

Saggi, K., Yildiz, H.M., 2010. Bilateralism, multilateralism, and the quest for global free trade. J. Int. Econ. 81 (1), 26–37.

Saich, T., 2000. Negotiating the state: the developmental of social organizations in China. China Quart. 161 (March), 124–141.

Said, E.W., 1996. Peace and Its Discontent: Essays on Palestine in the Middle East Peace Progress. Vintage Books, New York.

Sala-i-Martin, X., 2002. The Disturbing "Rise" of Global Income Inequality, NBER Working Paper No. 8904, April. National Bureau of Economic Research, Cambridge, MA.

Sala-i-Martin, X., Doppelhofer, G., Miller, R.I., 2004. Determinants of long- term growth: A Bayesian averaging of classical estimates (BACE) approach. Am. Econ. Rev. 94 (4), 813–835.

Salverda, W., Nolan, B., Smeeding, T.M. (Eds.), 2009. The Oxford Handbook of Economic Inequality. Oxford University Press, Oxford.

Salt, J., 2008. The Unmaking of the Middle East: A History of Western Disorder in Arab Lands. University of California Press, California.

Samuelson, P.A., 1947. Foundation of Economic Analysis. Harvard University Press, Cambridge MA.

Samwick, A.A., 2009. Moral hazard in the policy response to the 2008 financial market meltdown. Cato J. 29 (1), 131–139.

Sandbu, M., 2015. Europe's Orphan: The Future of the Euro and the Politics of Debt. Princeton University Press, Princeton.

Sargent, T.J., Wallace, N., 1975. 'Rational' expectations, the optimal monetary instrument, and the optimal money supply rule. J. Polit. Econ.241–254, April.

Sargent, T.J., Wallace, N., 1976. Rational expectations and the theory of economic policy. J. Monet. Econ. 2 (2), 169–183.

Saw, S.-H. (Ed.), 2007. ASEAN-China Economic Relations. Institute of Southeast Asian Studies, Singapore.

Schram, S.F., 2015. The Return of Ordinary Capitalism: Neoliberalism, Precarity, Occupy. Oxford University Press, New York.

Schroeder, G.E., 1985. The slowdown in soviet industry, 1976-1982. Soviet Econ. 1 (1), 42–74.

Schumpeter, J.A., 1942. Capitalism, Socialism and Democracy (reprinted in 1976). London: Routledge.

Schwartz, A.J., 2009. Origins of the financial market crisis of 2008. Cato J. 29 (1), 19–23.

Scott, W.R., 2002. The changing world of Chinese enterprises: an institutional perspective. In: Tsui, A.S., Lau, C.-M. (Eds.), The Management of Enterprises in the People's Republic of China. Springer, New York.

Self, P., 2010. Political Theories of Modern Government. Routledge, New York.

Sen, A.K., 1973. On Economic Inequality. Oxford University Press, New Delhi.

Sen, A.K., 1976. Poverty: an ordinal approach to measurement. Econometrica 44 (2), 219–231.

Sen, A.K., 1979. Utilitarianism and welfarism. J. Philos. 76 (9), 463–489.

Sen, A.K., 1987. On Ethics and Economics. Blackwell, Oxford.

Sen, A.K., 1991. The nature of inequality. In: Arrow, K. (Ed.), Issues in Contemporary Economics: Markets and Welfare, Volume 1. MacMillan Academic and Professional Ltd, London, pp. 3–21.

Sen, A.K., 1992. Inequality Reexamined. Harvard University Press, Cambridge, MA.

Sen, A.K., 1993. Capability and well-being. In: Nussbaum, M., Sen, A.K. (Eds.), The Quality of Life. Clarendon Press, London, pp. 30–53.

Sen, A.K., 1997. From income inequality to economic inequality. Southern Econ. J. 64 (2), 384–401.

Severino, R.C., 2010. ASEAN and the South China Sea. Secur. Challenges 6 (2), 37–47.

Shadlen, K.C., 2005. Exchanging development for market access? Deep integration and industrial policy under multilateral and regional-bilateral trade agreements. Rev. Int. Polit. Econ. 12 (5), 750–775.

Shapiro, S.P., 2005. Agency theory. Ann. Rev. Sociol. 31, 263–284.

Sharansky, N., 2009. The Case for Democracy: The Power of Freedom to Overcome Tyranny and Terror. Public Affairs, New York.

Sharma, S., Chua, S.Y., 2000. ASEAN: economic integration and intra-regional trade. Appl. Econ. Lett. 7 (3), 165–169.

Sheikh, N.S., 2003. The New Politics of Islam: Pan-Islamic Foreign Policy in a World of States. Routledge, London.

Shen, Z., 2000. Sino-Soviet relations and the origins of the Korean war: Stalin's strategic goals in the far east. J. Cold War Stud. 2 (2), 44–68.

Shikh, A., 2016. Capitalism: Competition, Conflict Crises. Oxford University Press, New York.

Shiller, R.J., 2008. The Subprime Solution: How Today's Global Financial Crisis Happened and What to Do about It. Princeton University Press, Princeton.

Shiller, R.J., 2015. Irrational Exuberance, revised and expanded third ed. Princeton University Press, Princeton.

Shinohara, M., 1982. Industrial Growth, Trade and Dynamic Patterns in the Japanese Economy. University of Tokyo Press, Tokyo.

Shirakawa, M., 2002, One Year Under "Quantitative Easing", IMES Discussion Paper No.2002-E-3, Bank of Japan, Tokyo.

Shmelev, N., Popov, V., 1990. The Turning Point: Revitalizing the Soviet Economy. I. B. Tauris & Co. Ltd., London.

Silber, J. (Ed.), 1999. Handbook of Income Inequality Measurement. Kluwer Academic, Boston.

Simon, J.L., 1999. The Economic Consequences of Immigration, second ed. The University of Michigan Press, Ann Arbor.

Sing, M., 2010. Explaining mass support for democracy in Hong Kong. Democratization 17 (1), 175–205.

Singh, A., 1994. Openness and the market friendly approach to development: learning the right lessons from development experience. World Dev. 22 (12), 1811–1923.

Sklair, L., 2002. Globalization: Capitalism and Its Alternatives. Oxford University Press, Oxford.

Slaughter, M.J., 2001. Trade liberalization and per capita income convergence: a difference-in-difference analysis. J. Int. Econ. 55 (1), 203–228.

Smallbone, D., Welter, F., 2001. The role of government in SME development in transition economies. Int. Small Business J. 19 (4), 63–77.

Smarzynska Javorcik, B., 2004. Does foreign direct investment increase the productivity of domestic firms? In search of spillovers through backward linkages. Am. Econ. Rev. 94 (1), 605–627.

Smil, V., 2015. Made in the USA: The Rise and Retreat of American Manufacturing. The MIT Press, Cambridge, MA.

Smith, A., 1776. An Inquiry into the Nature and Causes of the Wealth of Nations. Reprinted in March 2003, New York: Bantam Dell.

Smith, D.B., 1995. Japan Since 1945: The Rise of an Economic Superpower. MacMillan, London.

Smolny, W., 2000. Post-war growth, productivity convergence and reconstruction. Oxford Bullet. Econ. Statist. 62 (5), 589–606.

So, A.Y., Kwitko, L., 1990. The new middle class and the democratic movement in Hong Kong. J. Contemp. Asia 20 (3), 384–398.

Solow, R.M., 1957. Technical change and the aggregate production function. Rev. Econ. Statist. 39 (3), 312–320.

Sowell, T., 1972. Say's Law: An Historical Analysis. Princeton University Press, Princeton.

Sowell, T., 1974. Classical Economics Reconsidered. Princeton University Press, New Jersey.

Spero, J.E., Hart, J.A., 2010. The Politics of International Economic Relations, seventh ed. Wadsworth Cengage Learning, Boston.

Steil, B., 2014. The Battle of Bretton Woods. Princeton University Press, Princeton.

Stigler, G.J., 1946. The economics of minimum wage legislation. Am. Econ. Rev. 36 (3), 358–365.

Stiglitz, J., 1996. Some lessons from the East Asia Miracle. World Bank Rese. Obs. 11 (2), 151–178.

Stiglitz, J., 1998. The private uses of public interests: incentives and institutions. J. Econ. Perspect. 12 (2), 3–22.

Stiglitz, J., 2002. Globalization and Its Discontent. Allen Lane, London.

Stokes, J., 2015. China's road rules: Beijing looks west toward Eurasian integration. Foreign Aff. April 19.

Storey, I., 2015. China's Terraforming in the Spratlys: A Game Changer in the South China Sea? ISEAS Perspectives, No 29, Singapore, June 23.

Stroup, M.D., 2007. Economic freedom, democracy, and the quality of life. World Dev. 35 (1), 52–66.

Su, Y., 2011. Collective Killings in Rural China during the Cultural Revolution. Cambridge University Press, New York.

Subramanian, A., Wei, S.-J., 2007. The WTO promotes trade, strongly but unevenly. J. Int. Econ. 72 (1), 151–175.

Summer, A., 2016. Global Poverty. Oxford University Press, Oxford.

Summers, T., 2015. What Exactly is 'One Belt, One Road'? The World Today, Chatham House, The Royal Institute of International Affairs, 71 (5) September.

Sun, Y.-S., 1927. San Min Chu I: The Three Principles of the People. Larouchejapan.com.

Sung, Y.-W., 1991. The China-Hong Kong Connection: The Key to China's Open Door Policy. Cambridge University Press, Cambridge.

Sutela, P., 2000. The financial crisis in Russia. In: Bisignano, J.R., Hunter, W.C., Kaufman, G.G. (Eds.), Global Financial Crises: Lessons from Recent Events. Springer, New York, pp. 63–73.

Sutherland, A., 1997. Fiscal crises and aggregate demand: can high public debt reverse the effects of fiscal policy? J. Public Econ. 65 (2), 147–162.

Svensson, J., 2000. Foreign aid and rent-seeking. J. Int. Econ. 51 (2), 437–461.

Swan, T.W., 1956. Economic growth and capital accumulation. Econ. Rec. 32 (2), 334–361.

Swedberg, R., 1990. Economics and Sociology: Redefining Their Boundaries. Princeton University Press, New Jersey.

Szczudlik-Tatar, J., 2013. China's New Silk Road Diplomacy. Policy Paper, The Polish Institute of International Affairs, 34 (82) December.

Tachi, R., 1993. The Contemporary Japanese Economy: An Overview. University of Tokyo Press, Tokyo.

Tait, A.N., Li, K.-W., 1997. Trade regimes and China's accession to world trade organization. J. World Trade 31, 93–112.

Tamura, R., 1991. Income convergence in an endogenous growth model. J. Polit. Econ. 99 (3), 522–540.

Tan, T.L., 1985. Economic Debates in Vietnam: Issues and Problems in Reconstruction and Development (1975–1984). Institute of Southeast Asian Studies, Singapore.

Tang, X., Li, K.-W., 1997. Money and banking in China. In: Li, K.-W. (Ed.), Financing China Trade and Investment. Praeger Publisher, Westport.

Tanzi, V., 1995. Government Role and the Efficiency of Policy Instruments. IMF Working Paper No. 95/100, October.

Tanzi, V., Schuknecht, L., 1997. Reconsidering the fiscal role of government: the international perspective. Am. Econ. Rev. 87 (2), 164–168.

Taylor, B., 2015. Australia's crumbling China consensus. Global Asia 10 (3), 39–41.

Taylor, J.B., 1992. New Directions in Monetary Policy Research: Comments on the Federal Reserve System's Special Meeting on Operating Procedures. Federal Reserve System Committee on Financial Analysis, Federal Reserve Bank of St. Louis, June: 18-19.

Taylor, J.B., 1993. Discretion versus policy rules in practice. Carnegie-Rochester Conf. Series Public Policy 39, 195–214.

Taylor, L., 1983. Structuralist Macroeconomics: Applicable Models for the Third World. Basic Books, New York.

Thirlwall, A.P., 2006. Growth and Development, eighth ed. Palgrave Macmillan, London.

Thompson, V.B., 1969. Africa and Unity: The Evolution of Pan-Africanism. Longman Group, London.

Thurow, L.C., 1980. Zero-Sum Society: Distribution and the Possibilities for Economic Change. Basic Books, New York.

Thurow, L.C., 1996. The Future of Capitalism: How Today's Economic Forces Shape Tomorrow's World. W. Morrow and Company, New York.

Tian, G., 2015. Caution against Corruption: Cases of the High-ranking Corrupt Officials. Central Party School Publisher, Beijing, July (in Chinese).

Tirole, J., 2002. Financial Crises, Liquidity, and the International Monetary System. Princeton University Press, Princeton.

Toh, H.S., 2016. Is China a 21st Century Imperialist? World Scientific Publisher, Singapore.

Torrance, J., 1995. Studies in Marxism and Social Theory. Cambridge University Press, Cambridge.

Toye, J., 2000. Fiscal crisis and fiscal reform in developing countries. Cambridge J. Econ. 24 (1), 21−44.

Trenery Dolbear Jr., F., 1967. On the theory of optimum externality. Am. Econ. Rev. 57 (1), 90−103.

Trenin, D., 2015. The new silk road and Russia's Pivot to China. Global Asia 10 (3), 27−29.

Trotsky, L., 2008. History of the Russian Revolution. Haymarket Books, Chicago.

Tsang, S., 1995. A Documentary History of Hong Kong: Government and Politics. Hong Kong University Press, Hong Kong.

Tsoucalas, C., 1978. On the problem of political clientelism in Greece in the nineteenth century. J. Hellenic Diaspora, Part I, 1 (1) Spring: 5-15, and Part II, 1 (2) Summer: 5017.

Turner, S., Nguyen, P.A., 2005. Young entrepreneurs, social capital and Doi Moi in Hanoi, Vietnam. Urban Stud. 42 (10), 1693−1710.

Twitchett, D.C., Fairbank, J.K., Loewe, M., Franke, H., 1978. The Cambridge History of China. Cambridge University Press, Cambridge.

Umematsu, T., 1999. Japan's Decade-Long Recession. Kobe University Economic Review 45, 19−29.

United Nations, 1992. GSP Graduation, International Trade and Investment in the Asia and Pacific Region. Economic and Social Commission for Asia and the Pacific, ST/ESCAP/1146.

United Nations, 2000. The Millennium Development Goals. United Nations, New York.

United Nations Conference on Trade and Development, 2005. Evolution of the term of trade and its impact on developing countries. Trade Dev Rep. UNCTAD, New York, Chapter Three.

Urata, S., 2002. Globalization and the growth in free trade agreements. Asia-Pacific Rev. 9 (2), 20−32.

U.S. International Trade Commission, 1999. Assessment of the Economic Effects on the United States of China's Accession to the WTO, Publication 3228. U.S. International Trade Commission, Washington, DC, August.

Van de Berg, H., 2016. Economic Growth and Development, third ed. World Scientific Publishers, Singapore.

Van Wijnbergen, S., 1982. Stagflationary effects of monetary stabilization policies − a quantitative analysis of South Korea. J. Dev. Econ. 10 (2), 133−169.

Van Wijnbergen, S., 1985. Macroeconomic effects on change in bank interest rate: simulation results for South Korea. J. Dev. Econ. 18 (2-3), 541−554.

Vanhanen, T., 2000. A new dataset for measuring democracy, 1810-1998. J. Peace Res. 37 (2), 251−265.

Velasco, A., 2000. Debts and deficits with fragmented fiscal policymaking. J. Public Econ. 76 (1), 105−125.

Vercueil, J., 2012. Emerging Countries. Brazil - Russia - India - China. Economic Change and New Challenges, third ed. Bréal, Paris (in French).

Vernon, R., 1979. The product cycle hypothesis in a new international environment. Oxford Bulletin Econ. Statist.(4), 255−267.

Vogel, E.F., 2011. Deng Xiaoping and the Transformation of China. Belknap Press of Harvard University Press, Cambridge, MA.

Von Tunzelmann, G.N., 1978. State Power and British Industrialization to 1860. Oxford University Press, Oxford.

Vonyó, T., 2008. Post-war reconstruction and the golden age of economic growth. Eur. Rev. Econ. History 12 (2), 221−241.

Voskressenski, A.D., 2003. Russia and China: A Theory of Inter-State Relations. Routledge, London.

Wade, R.A., 2005. The Russia Revolution, 1917. Cambridge University Press, Cambridge.

Wade, R., 1990. Governing the Market: Economic Theory and the Role of Government in East Asia Industrialization. Princeton University Press, New Jersey.

Waley, A., 2005. The Analects of Confucius. Routledge, London.

Walker, A., 1978. Marx: His Theory and Its Context. Longman Group Limited, London.

Wallach, L., Woodall, P., 2004. Whose Trade Organization. The New Press, New York.

Wallensteen, P., 1997. Armed conflicts, conflict termination and peace agreements, 1989-1996. J. Peace Res. 34 (3), 339−358.

Wan, G.H., 2002. Income Inequality and Growth in Transition Economies: Are Nonlinear Models Needed?, Discussion Paper No. 2002/104. World Institute for Development Research, United Nations University.

Wang, P., Yu, Z., 2014. China's outward foreign direct investment: the role of natural resources and technology. Econ. Polit. Stud. 2 (2), 89−120.

Wang, Y., 2013. Demystifying the Chinese Miracle: The Rise and Future of Relational Capitalism. Routledge, London.

Wärneryd, K., 2014. The Economics of Conflicts: Theory and Empirical Evidence. The MIT Press, Cambridge, MA.

Watson, S., 2015. The Left Divided: The Development and Transformation of Advanced Welfare States. Oxford University Press, New York.

Wedeman, A., 2004. The intensification of corruption in China. China Quart. 180, 895−921.

Wederman, A., 2009. China's War on Corruption. Routledge, New York.

Weinert, G., 2001. What went wrong in Japan: a decade-long slump. Vierteljahrshefte zur Wirtschaftsforschung 70 (4), 460−475.

Weichenrider, A.J., 2015, Greece: Threatening Recovery, SAFE Policy Letter, No. 37, Goethe University Frankfurt, February.

Weingast, B.R., Shepsle, K.A., Johnsen, C., 1981. The political economy of benefits and costs: a neoclassical approach to distributive politics. J. Polit. Econ. 89 (4), 642−664.

Westad, O.A. (Ed.), 1998. Brothers in Arms: The Rise and Fall of the Sino-Soviet Alliance 1945−1963. The Woodrow Wilson Center Press, Washington, DC.

Western, B., 1997. Between Class and Market: Postwar Unionization in the Capitalist Democracies. Princeton University Press, Princeton.

Whally, J. (Ed.), 2016. Asia and the World Economy, Volume 1. World Scientific Publisher, Singapore.

Wilczynski, J., 1970. The Economics of Socialism. George Allen and Unwin Ltd, London.

Williamson, J., Milner, C., 1991. The World Economy: A Textbook in International Economics. Harvester Wheatsheaf, Hemel Hempstead.

Williamson, O.E., 1985. The Economic Institutions of Capitalism. The Free Press, New York.

Williamson, O.E., 2000. The new institutional economics: taking stock, looking ahead. J. Econ. Literat. 38 (3), 595−613.

Williamson, O.E., 2005. Transaction cost economics and business administration. Scandin. J. Manag. 21 (1), 19−40.

Willnat, L., 1996. Mass media and political outspokenness in Hong Kong: linking the third-person effect and the spiral of silence. Int. J. Public Opin. Res. 8 (2), 187−212.

Wintrobe, R., 1998. The Political Economy of Dictatorship. Cambridge University Press, New York.

Wisman, J.D., 1988. The dominance of consensual over technical rationality in Confucius' socio-economic thought. Int. J. Soc. Econ. 15 (1), 58−67.

Wong, C., 2009. Rebuilding government for the 21st century: can China incrementally reform the public sector? China Quart. 200 (December), 929−952.

Wong, C., 2011. The Fiscal Stimulus Program and Problems of Macroeconomic Management in China. Public Governance Committee, OECD Senior Budget Officials, Luxembourg, June 6-7.

Wong, C.Y.-P., Lo, K.W. K., 1997. Foreign exchange markets in China: evolution and performance. In: Li, K.-W. (Ed.), Financing China Trade and Investment. Praeger Publisher, Connecticut, pp. 139−162.

Wong, J., 2016. Zhu Rongji and China's Economic Take-Off. World Scientific, Singapore, May.

Wong, L., 1998. Marginalization and Social Welfare in China. Routledge, London.

Woodford, M., 1990. Public debt as private equity. Am. Econ. Rev. 80 (2), 382−388.

Woodford, M., 2001. The Taylor rule and optimal monetary policy. Am. Econ. Rev. 91 (2), 232−237.

Woods, N., 2002. Making the IMF and the world bank more accountable. Int. Aff. 77 (10), 83−100.

Woods, N., 2006. The Globalizers: The IMF, the World Bank and Their Borrowers. Cornell University Press, Ithaca.

Woolcock, S., Sampson, G., 2003. Regionalism, Multilateralism and Economic Integration: The Recent Experience. United Nations University Press, Tokyo.

World Bank, 1983. China: Socialist Economic Development, Volume 1, 2 and 3. The World Bank, Washington, DC, August.

World Bank, 1988a. China: Finance and Investment. The World Bank, Washington, DC.

World Bank, 1988b. China: External Trade and Capital. The World Bank, Washington, DC.

World Bank, 1993. The East Asia Miracle: Economic Growth and Public Policy. Oxford University Press, New York.

World Bank, 2013. Ending Extreme Poverty and Promoting Shared Prosperity. The World Bank, Washington, DC, April.

Woronoff, J., 1986. Asia's Miracle Economies. M. E. Sharpe, New York.

Wu, G., 2015. Paradox of China's Prosperity. World Scientific Publishers, Singapore.

Wu, J., 2005. Understanding and Interpreting Chinese Economic Reform. Thompson Publishing, Ohio.

Wu, J., Ma, G., 2016. Whither China? Restarting the Reform Agenda. Oxford University Press, Oxford.

Wu, X., 2016. China's Growing Local Government Debt Levels. Policy Brief, MIT Center for Finance and Policy, Massachusetts Institute of Technology, January.

Wu, Y., 2014. Local Government Debt and Economic Growth in China. Conference on Industrial Upgrading and Urbanization, Stockholm China Economic Research Institute, Stockholm School of Economics, August.

Wu, Y., 2014. The Cultural Revolution at the Margin: Chinese Socialism in Crisis. Harvard University Press, Cambridge, MA.

Wyplosz, C. (Ed.), 2015. Thirty Years of Economic Policy: Inspiration for Debate. Oxford University Press, Oxford.

Yahuda, M., 1993. Hong Kong's future: Sino-British negotiations, perceptions, organization and political culture. Int. Aff. 69 (2), 245−266.

Yahuda, M., 1996. Hong Kong: China's Challenge. Routledge, London.

Yamazawa, I., 2012. APEC: New Agenda in Its Third Decade. Institute of Southeast Asian Studies, Singapore.

Yang, M.M.C., 1970. Socio Economic Results of Land Reform in Taiwan. East-West Center Press, Hawaii.

Yao, S., Wang, P., 2014. China's Outward Foreign Direct Investments and Impact on the World Economy. Palgrave Macmillan, Basingstoke.

Yellen, J., 2004. Innovations and issues in monetary policy. Am. Econ. Rev. Paper Proc. 94, 45−47.

Yoshikawa, H., 2007. Japan's lost decade: what have we learned and where are we heading? Asian Econ. Policy Rev. 2 (2), 186−203.

Young, A., 2000. The Razor's edge: distortions and incremental reform in the people's Republic of China. Quart. J. Econ. 115 (4), 1091−1135.

Young, H.P., 1994. Equity in Theory and Practice. Princeton University Press, New Jersey.

Young, G., 1978. Justice and capitalist production: marx and bourgeois ideology. Can. J. Philos. 8 (3), 421−455.

Zagoria, D.S., 1974. Mao's role in the Sino-Soviet conflict. Pacific Aff. 47 (2), 139−153.

Zhang, W.-B., 1999. Confucianism and Modernization. St. Martin's Press, New York.

Zhang, W.-B., 2000. On Adam Smith and Confucius: The Theory of Moral Sentiments and the Analects. Nova Science Publishers, Commack, NY.

Zhang, X., Tan, K.-Y., 2007. Incremental reform and distortions in China's product and factor markets. World Bank Econ. Rev. 21 (2), 279−299.

Zhang, Y., 2015. One belt, one road: a Chinese view. Global Asia 10 (3), 8−12.

Zhao, S., 1993. Deng Xiaoping's southern tour: elite politics in post-Tiananmen China. Asian Survey 33 (8), 739−756.

Zheng, Y., 2000. The politics of power succession in post-deng China. Asian J. Polit. Sci. 8 (1), 13−32.

Zhou, X., Li, K.-W., 2011. Inequality and development: evidence from semiparametric estimation with panel data. Econ. Lett. 113 (3), 203−207.

Zivot, E., Andrews, D.W.K., 2002. Further evidence on the great crash, the oil- price shock, and the unit root hypothesis. J. Business Econ. Stat. 20 (1), 25−44.

Index

Note: Page numbers followed by "*f*" and "*t*" refer to figures and tables, respectively.

Printed and bound by CPI Group (UK) Ltd, Croydon, CR0 4YY

08/05/2025

01864796-0001